Global Marketing

THIRD EDITION

Warren J. Keegan

Lubin Graduate School of Business
Pace University—New York City and Westchester, New York

Mark C. Green

Department of Management, Accounting and Economics
Simpson College—Indianola, Iowa

Prentice
Hall

Upper Saddle River, New Jersey 07458

Library of Congress Catalogue-in-Publication
Keegan, Warren J.
    Global marketing/Warren J. Keegan, Mark C. Green.—3rd ed.
      p. cm.
    Includes bibliographical references and index.
    ISBN 0-13-066998-9 (pbk.)
    1. Export marketing. I. Green, Mark C. II. Title.

HF1416.K443 2002
658.8'48—dc21   2002190399

Senior Editor: Wendy Craven
Editor-in-Chief: Jeff Shelstad
Assistant Editor: Melissa Pellerano
Editorial Assistant: Danielle Serra
Media Project Manager: Michele Faranda
Marketing Manager: Michelle O'Brien
Marketing Assistant: Amanda Fisher
Managing Editor (Production): John Roberts
Production Editor: Maureen Wilson
Permissions Coordinator: Suzanne Grappi
Associate Director, Manufacturing: Vincent Scelta
Production Manager: Arnold Vila
Manufacturing Buyer: Michelle Klein
Cover Design: Bruce Kenselaar
Cover Illustration/Photo: Lorraine Silvestri/Stock Illustration Source, Inc.
Full-Service Project Management and Composition: Carlisle Communications, Ltd.
Project Manager: Lynn Steines
Printer/Binder: Courier-Westford

Credits and acknowledgments borrowed from other sources and reproduced, with permission, in this textbook appear on appropriate page within text.

Pearson Education LTD.
Pearson Education Australia PTY, Limited
Pearson Education Singapore, Pte. Ltd.
Pearson Education North Asia Ltd.
Pearson Education, Canada, Ltd.
Pearson Educación de Mexico, S.A. de C.V.
Pearson Education–Japan
Pearson Education Malaysia, Pte. Ltd

10 9 8 7 6 5 4 3 2
ISBN 0-13-066998-9

To Lisa and Tracy
WJK

To John W. Green, Jr. and Virginia G. Green
MCG

BRIEF CONTENTS

CONTENTS

Contents

Contents

PREFACE

Global Marketing, Third Edition, builds on the worldwide success of *Principles of Global Marketing* and *Global Marketing*, Second Edition. The first two editions utilized an environmental and strategic approach by outlining the major dimensions of the global business environment and by providing a set of conceptual and analytical tools designed to prepare students to successfully apply the 4Ps to global marketing. Additionally, the first two editions were designed to be compact but comprehensive, authoritative but engaging, and highly readable. Comments from satisfied students attest that we accomplished our goal: "the textbook is very clear and easy to understand"; "an excellent textbook with many real-life examples"; "the authors use simple language and clearly state the important points"; "this is the best textbook that I am using this term"; "the authors have done an excellent job of writing a text that can be read easily." *Principles of Global Marketing* was the first textbook on the subject to be published in a full four-color format. In addition, when it appeared in fall 1996, the first edition invited students to "look ahead" and stay abreast of such developments as the ending of America's trade embargo with Vietnam, Europe's new currency, Daimler-Benz's Smart car project, and the controversy concerning Benetton's advertising. Those topics represented "big stories" in the global marketing arena and they continue to receive press coverage on a regular basis.

As was the case with the first two editions, we approached *Global Marketing*, Third Edition, with today's students and instructors in mind. Guided by our experience using the text in undergraduate and graduate classrooms and in corporate training seminars, we have revised, updated, and expanded *Global Marketing*, Third Edition, while retaining the best features of the first two editions. We have benefited tremendously from adopter feedback and input; we also continue to draw on our direct experience in the Americas, Asia, Europe, Africa, and the Middle East. The result is a text that addresses the needs of students and instructors in every part of the world. The English-language editions of *Principles of Global Marketing* and *Global Marketing*, Second Edition, have been used in many countries, including Australia, Canada, China, Ireland, Japan, Malaysia, and Sri Lanka; the texts are also available in Spanish, Portuguese, and Japanese editions.

The third edition includes new material on newsworthy and relevant topics such as the price of AIDS drugs in developing countries and the impact of electronic music file swapping on the global music industry. Current research findings have been incorporated into each of the chapters. For example, Dana L. Alden, Jan-Benedict Steenkamp, and Rajeev Batra's work on global consumer culture positioning (from *Journal of Marketing*, January 1999) is an important addition to Chapter 7 "Segmentation, Targeting, and Positioning," and Alan M. Rugman and Joseph R. D'Cruz's five partners model (discussed in their 2000 book *Multinationals as Flagship Firms*) is included in Chapter 10 "Strategic Elements of Competitive Advantage." We have added scores of up-to-date examples of global marketing practice as well as quotations from global marketing practitioners and industry experts. Throughout the text, organizational Web sites are referenced not as ornamental adornment but as essential pedagogical tools for further student study and exploration. A Companion Website (www.prenhall.com/keegan) is integrated with the text as well.

Each chapter contains several illustrations that bring global marketing to life. Chapter-opening vignettes introduce a company, country, product, or global marketing issue that directly relates to chapter themes and content. Many of the opening vignettes in the third edition are new, including those in Chapter 2, Chapter 5, Chapter 11, and Chapter 15. In addition, every chapter contains one or more sidebars with information on various themes including global marketing in action, risks and gambles, a look behind the scenes of global marketing, issues that are "open to discussion," and the cultural differences that challenge the global marketer.

The case set in *Global Marketing*, Third Edition, includes updates and revisions of earlier cases (e.g., Case 1-1 "McDonald's Expands Globally While Adjusting Its Local Recipe"); entirely new cases (e.g., Case 12-1 "Pricing AIDS Drugs in Emerging Markets," Case 13-1 "Wal-Mart's Global Expansion," and Case 15-1 "Napster and the Global Music Industry"); as well as holdovers of "oldies but goodies" (e.g., Case 9-2 "Airlines Take to the Skies in Global Strategic Alliances"). The cases vary in length from a few hundred words to more than 2600 words, yet they are all short enough to be covered in an efficient manner. The new and revised cases were written with the same objectives in mind: to raise issues that will stimulate student interest and learning, to provoke class discussion, and to enhance the classroom experience for students and instructors alike. Every chapter and case has been classroom tested. Supplements to the text include an instructor's resource manual with a complete test item file and a Web site (www. prenhall.com/keegan). The Web site also includes downloadable PowerPoint files. Special consideration was given to the test bank, with considerable effort devoted to minimizing the number of simplistic and superficial multiple-choice questions with "all of the above" type answers and replacing them with more challenging, thought-provoking questions.

One of the constant challenges authors of books about global marketing face is the rate of change in the global business environment. Yesterday's impossibility becomes today's reality. Books are quickly outdated by events. Even so, we believe that adopters will find *Global Marketing* Third Edition, to be as up-to-date, relevant, and useful to today's students of global marketing as any comparable text on the market, perhaps even more so.

ACKNOWLEDGMENTS

This book reflects the contributions, labor, and insights of many persons.

I would like to thank my students, colleagues, associates, and clients, for their many insights and contributions. It is impossible to single out all of the people who have contributed to this edition, but I would especially like to thank:

Peter Allen, Stephen Blank, Jean Boddewyn, Lawrence G. Bridwell, Steve Burgess, Arthur Centonze, Marcos Cobra, Fernando de Campos, Bertrand de Frondeville, John Dory, Bob Fulmer, Pradeep Gopalakrisna, Doug Jebb, Steve Kobrin, Jean-Marc de Leersnyder, Susan Douglas, Donald Gibson, Jim Gould, Tayfur Gullulu, Salah Hassan, David Heenan, Peter Hoefer, Robert Isaak, Hermawan Kartajaya, Suren Kaushik, Mark Keegan, Hermann Kopp, Jem Li, Raymond Lopez, Malcolm McDonald, Dorothy Minkus-McKenna, Jan Morgan, Stan Paliwoda, Howard Perlmutter, Robert Radway, Alan Rugman, John Ryans, Bodo B. Schlegelmilch, Donald Sexton, Barbara Stöttinger, Francoise Simon, Oleg Smirnoff, Ralph Z. Sorenson, Earl Spencer, Moshe Speter, William Stolze, John Stopford, Jim Stoner, Martin Topol, Robert Vambery, Terry Vavra, Len Vickers, Dianna Powell Ward, Colin Watson, Kathy Winsted, Dominique Xardel, George Yip, Philip Young, and Alan Zimmerman.

I would especially like to acknowledge the many contributions of the students in my doctoral seminar on global strategic marketing. My research assistants, Tayfur Gullulu and Thomas Sillery, provided invaluable research assistance in many areas, including the very difficult task of creating the Global Income and Population data that appears in this edition. My office managers, Gail Pietrangolare Weldon and Lisa DeFonce and my secretaries Mary O'Connor, Vicki Underwood and Marie Loprieno have provided outstanding and creative support above and beyond the call of duty, and always with a cheerful attitude.

Special thanks are due the superb librarians at Pace University: Michelle Lang, Head, Graduate Center Library, Anne B. Campbell, Reference Librarian, and Christa Burns, Head Of Research & Information Services have a remarkable ability to find anything. Like the Canadian Mounties who always get their man, Michelle, Anne, and Christa always get the document. My admiration for their talent and appreciation for their effort is unbounded.

Whitney Blake, our editor at Prentice Hall, was quick to endorse and support this great third edition as was Wendy Craven, our new acquisitions editor. We are grateful for the continuity of the support at Prentice Hall.

Warren J. Keegan

I am indebted to the many colleagues and friends who carefully read and critiqued individual manuscript sections and chapters. Their comments improved the clarity and readability of the text. In particular, I would like to thank Hunter Clark, Frank Colella, Dave Collins, Wendy Foughty, Mark Freyberg, Alexandre Gilfanov, Carl Halgren, Kathy Hill, Mark Juffernbruch, Peter Kvetko, Keith Miller, Gayle Moberg, Marilyn Mueller, James Palmieri, Alexandre Plokhov, and Thomas Schmidt.

I would also like to thank the many present and former Simpson College students who offered feedback on the second edition of *Global Marketing* and suggested improvements to the manuscript of "version 3.0" as it evolved over many months in 2001-2002. Special thanks go to my departmental assistants, Michelle Archibald and Sara Bieker, for their help with fact checking and creating data tables and charts. Beth Dorrell graciously contributed her story for this edition's "A Day in the Life" sidebar. Thanks also to Roslyn Haskins for suggesting the Celtic Tiger vignette that opens Chapter 2. I also benefited greatly from weekly conversations with Yoshimi Mochizuki about consumer behavior in Japan.

It was a great pleasure working with the Prentice Hall team that supervised production of this edition. My heartfelt thanks to Wendy Craven, Melissa Pellerano, Danielle Serra, and Maureen Wilson. Kudos also to our photo researcher, Teri Stratford, for demonstrating once again that "every picture tells a story." Thanks also to Michelle O'Brien for her great work on marketing support materials, and to the entire PH sales team for helping promote the book in the field. I also want to acknowledge the contributions of Susan Leshnower at Midlands College, Midlands, Texas, for her fine work on the Instructor's Manual, and Tracy Tuten Ryan of Virginia Commonwealth University for preparing a new set of PowerPoint slides. As was the case with the first two editions, several friends and colleagues at Simpson College were very supportive of my research and writing endeavors. Once again, Kristi Ellingson at Dunn Library cheerfully and tirelessly processed my many interlibrary loan requests, and Robyn Copeland extended special consideration regarding "due dates" of books and periodicals that I checked out.

Mark C. Green

Dr. Warren J. Keegan

Dr. Keegan is Professor of International Business and Marketing and Director of the Center for Global Business Strategy at the Lubin School of Business of Pace University—New York, and is Visiting Professor, Cranfield University School of Management (UK), CEIBS (China European International Business School)—Shanghai, Wharton Executive Programs, University of Pennsylvania, and ESSEC, Cergy-Pontoise—France. He is the founder of Warren Keegan Associates, Inc., a consulting consortium of experts in global strategy formulation and implementation. The firm is affiliated with Marketing Strategy & Planning, Inc.—New York, and MarkPlus, Indonesia's leading marketing consulting firm. Dr. Keegan is Chairman of the MarkPlus Global Institute—Singapore.

He wrote the first multinational marketing textbook and is one of the world's leading experts on marketing and global business. He holds B.S. and M.S. degrees in economics from Kansas State University and an MBA and doctorate in marketing and international business from the Harvard Business School. He has held faculty positions at a number of business schools including Columbia, George Washington University, New York University, INSEAD, IMD, and the Stockholm School of Economics.

His experience includes consulting with Boston Consulting Group and Arthur D. Little, marketing planning with the Pontiac Division of General Motors, and Chairman of Douglas A. Edwards, Inc., a New York commercial real estate firm. He is a consultant to a number of global firms. Current or former clients include AT&T, Bertelsmann, Bell Atlantic, General Electric, J. Walter Thompson, PurduePharma, Philips, Reckitt & Colman, Singapore International Airlines, and the Singapore Trade Development Board.

Dr. Keegan is the author or co-author of many books, including *Global Marketing Management* (7th ed., Prentice Hall, 2002), *Global Marketing Management: A European Perspective* (Financial Times/Prentice Hall, 2001), *Marketing Plans That Work: Targeting Growth and Profitability* (Butterworth Heinemann, 1997), *Marketing* (2nd ed., Prentice Hall, 1996), *Marketing Sans Frontiers* (InterEditions, 1994), *Advertising Worldwide* (Prentice Hall, 1991), and *Judgments, Choices, and Decisions: Effective Management Through Self-Knowledge* (John Wiley & Sons). He has published numerous articles in leading journals including *Harvard Business Review, Administrative Science Quarterly, Journal of Marketing, Journal of International Business Studies,* and *The Columbia Journal of World Business.*

Dr. Keegan is a former MIT Fellow in Africa, Assistant Secretary, Ministry of Development Planning and Secretary of the Economic Development Commission, Government of Tanzania, consultant with Boston Consulting Group and Arthur D. Little, and Chairman of Douglas A. Edwards, a New York corporate real estate firm.

He is a Lifetime Fellow of the Academy of International Business; Individual Eminent Person (IEP) appointed by Asian Global Business Leaders Society (other awardees include Noel Tichy, Rosabeth Moss Kanter, and Gary Wendt); listed in Marquis Who's Who in America, 55th and earlier editions; member of the International Advisory Board of École des Hautes Études Commerciales (HEC)—Montreal; Member, Editorial Advisory Board, Cranfield School of Management and Financial Times/Prentice Hall Management Monograph Series, *The International Journal of Medical Marketing;* and is a commissioner of PT Indofood Sukses Makmur (Jakarta). He is a former director of The S.M. Stoller Company, Inc., The Cooper

Companies, Inc. (NYSE), Inter-Ad, Inc., American Thermal Corporation, Inc., Halfway Houses of Westchester, Inc., Wainwright House, and The Rye Arts Center.

Dr. Mark C. Green

Dr. Green is Professor of Management and Marketing at Simpson College in Indianola, Iowa, where he teaches courses in management, marketing, advertising, international marketing, innovation, and Russian language. He earned his B.A. degree in Russian literature from Lawrence University, M.A. and Ph.D. degrees in Russian linguistics from Cornell University, and an M.B.A. degree in marketing management from Syracuse University.

In addition to co-authoring *Global Marketing* Third Edition with Warren Keegan, Dr. Green has also contributed case studies and chapter materials to several other textbooks published by Prentice Hall. These include: *Advertising Principles and Practices*, 4th ed., by William Wells, John Burnett, and Sandra Moriarty (1997); *Behavior in Organizations*, 6th ed., by Jerald Greenberg and Robert Baron (1996); *Business*, 4th ed., by Ricky Griffin and Ronald Ebert (1995); and *Principles of Marketing*, by Warren Keegan, Sandra Moriarty, and Thomas Duncan (1992). Dr. Green has also written essays on technology and global business that have appeared in *The Des Moines Register* and other newspapers.

Dr. Green has traveled to the former Soviet Union on numerous occasions. In 1995 and 1996, he participated in a grant project funded by the U.S. Agency for International Development and presented marketing seminars to audiences in Nizhny Novgorod. In addition, Dr. Green has served as a consultant to several Iowa organizations that have business and cultural ties with Russia and other former Soviet republics. Dr. Green has lectured in Russia and Ukraine on topics relating to emerging market economies. His 1992 monograph, "Developing the Russian Market in the 1990s," received an award from the Iowa-based International Network on Trade.

In 1997, Dr. Green was recipient of Simpson College's Distinguished Research and Writing Award. Dr. Green also received the 1995 Distinguished Teaching Award for senior faculty. In 1990, he was the recipient of Simpson's Excellence in Teaching Award for junior faculty. He also received the 1988 Outstanding Faculty of the Year awarded by the Alpha Sigma Lambda adult student honorary at Simpson College.

Chapter 1

Introduction to Global Marketing

We live in a global marketplace. McDonald's sandwiches, Sony consumer electronics, Nokia cellular phones, and Caterpillar earthmoving equipment are available for sale around the globe. But ask the average consumer where this global "horn of plenty" comes from, and you'll likely hear a variety of answers that reflect widely differing perceptions. It's certainly true that some brands—McDonald's, Corona Extra, Swatch, Waterford, Benetton, and Dr. Martens, for instance—are strongly identified with a particular country. In much of the world, McDonald's is the quintessential American fast-food restaurant, just as Dr. Martens are synonymous with British youth culture. But, for many other products, brands, and companies, the sense of identity with a particular country is becoming blurred. Which brands are Japanese, or American, or German? Does a Big Mac taste the same everywhere in the world?

The global marketplace finds expression in subtler ways as well. While shopping, you may have noticed more multi-language labeling on your favorite products and brands. If you had an Amoco or Standard Oil credit card, it was recently replaced by a card for BP. When you shop at your local gourmet coffee store, you may have noticed that some beans are labeled "Free Trade Certified." You have probably heard or read news accounts of anti-globalization protesters disrupting meetings of the World Trade Organization in various cities around the globe.

The preceding paragraphs provide some clues to the sweeping transformation that has profoundly affected the people and industries of many nations during the past 150 years. Prior to 1840, students sitting at their desks would not have had any item in their possession that was manufactured more than a few miles from where they lived—with the possible exception of the books they were reading. International trade has existed since the beginning of civilization. However, since

Dr. Martens have long been popular with rock stars and club kids. Recently, people from all walks of life—including the pope—have taken to wearing the rugged shoes with the distinctive yellow "Z Welt" stitching. The brand's owner, R. Griggs Group, is headquartered in Northamptonshire, but 85 percent of the company's footwear sales are generated outside of the United Kingdom.

World War II there has been an unparalleled expansion into global markets by companies that previously served only customers located in their home country. Two decades ago, the phrase *global marketing* did not even exist. Today, savvy business people utilize global marketing for the realization of their companies' full commercial potential. That is why you may be familiar with the brands mentioned in the preceding paragraph whether you live in Asia, Europe, or North or South America. But there is another even more critical reason why companies need to take global marketing seriously—survival. A company that fails to become global in outlook risks losing its domestic business to competitors with lower costs, more experience, and better products.

But what is global marketing? How does it differ from "regular" marketing? *Marketing* is the process of planning and executing the conception, pricing, promotion, and distribution of ideas, goods, and services to create exchanges that satisfy individual and organization goals.[1] Marketing activities center on an organization's efforts to satisfy customer wants and needs with products and services that offer competitive value. The marketing mix (product, price, place, and promotion) comprises a contemporary marketer's primary tools.[2] Marketing is a universal discipline, as applicable in Argentina as it is in Zimbabwe.

This book is about *global marketing.* An organization that engages in **global marketing** focuses its resources on global market opportunities and threats. One difference between "regular" marketing and "global" marketing is the scope of activities. A company that engages in global marketing conducts important business activities outside the home-country market. Another difference is that global marketing involves an understanding of specific concepts, considerations, and strategies that must be skillfully applied in conjunction with universal marketing fundamentals to ensure success in global markets. This book concentrates on the major dimensions of global marketing. A brief overview of marketing is presented next, although the authors assume that the reader has completed an introductory marketing course or has equivalent experience.

OVERVIEW OF MARKETING

Marketing can be described as one of the functional areas of a business, distinct from finance and operations. Marketing can also be thought of as one of the activities that, along with product design, manufacturing, and transportation logistics, comprise a firm's **value chain.** Decisions at every stage, from idea conception to support after the sale, should be assessed in terms of their ability to create value for customers. Historically, marketing was considered just another link in the chain. Today, however, many organizations are emphasizing the effective coordination of marketing with other functional areas. Competitive pressures have prompted many firms to involve marketers in design, manufacturing, and other value-related decisions from the start. This approach is known in some circles as *boundaryless marketing.* Rather than linking marketing sequentially with other activities, the goal is to eliminate the communication barriers between marketing and other functional areas. Properly implemented, boundaryless marketing ensures that a marketing orientation permeates *all* value-creating activities in a company. This change in emphasis is reflected in Figure 1-1. GE and other companies that subscribe to the "boundaryless" concept give employees at all levels and in all departments the opportunity to be involved in marketing.

---

[1]   Peter D. Bennett, ed., *Dictionary of Marketing Terms,* 2d ed. (Chicago: NTC Business Books, 1995), p. 166.
[2]   For a recent review of the strengths and limitations of the 4P classification, see Walter van Waterschoot and Christophe Van den Bulte, "The 4P Classification of the Marketing Mix Revisited," *Journal of Marketing* 56, no. 4 (October 1992), pp. 83–93.

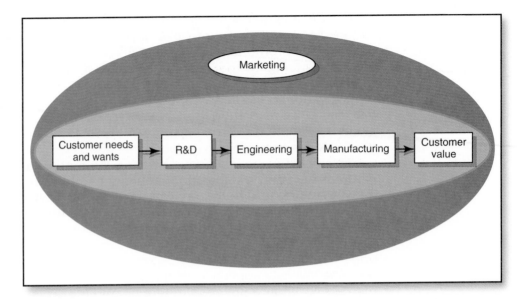

Figure 1-1
The Value Chain and Boundaryless Marketing

CUSTOMER VALUE AND THE VALUE EQUATION

For any organization operating anywhere in the world, the essence of marketing is to surpass the competition at the task of creating perceived value for customers. The **value equation** is a guide to this task:

Value = Benefits/Price (money, time, effort, etc.)

The marketing mix is integral to the equation because benefits are a combination of the product, promotion, and distribution. As a general rule, value as perceived by the customer can be increased in two basic ways. Markets can offer customers an improved bundle of benefits or lower prices (or both!). Marketers may strive to improve the product itself, to design new channels of distribution, to create better communications strategies, or a combination of all three. Marketers may also seek to increase value by finding ways to cut costs and prices. Nonmonetary costs are also a factor, and marketers may be able to decrease the time and effort that customers must expend to learn about or seek out the product.[3] Companies that use price as a competitive weapon may enjoy an ample supply of low-wage labor or access to cheap raw materials. Companies can also reduce prices if costs are low because of process efficiencies in manufacturing. If a company is able to offer a combination of superior product, distribution, or promotion benefits *and* lower prices than the competition, it enjoys an extremely advantageous position. This is precisely how Toyota, Nissan, and other Japanese automakers made significant gains in the American market in the 1980s. They offered cars with higher quality and lower prices than those made by Chrysler, Ford, and General Motors. Needless to say, to become a market success a product must measure up to a threshold of acceptable quality. Some of Japan's initial auto exports were market failures. In the late 1960s, for example,

---

[3] With certain categories of differentiated goods, including designer clothing and other luxury products, higher price is often associated with increased value.

Subaru of America began importing the Subaru 360 automobile and offering it for sale with a sticker price of $1,297. After *Consumer Reports* judged the 360 "not acceptable," however, sales ground to a halt. Similarly, the Yugo automobile achieved a modest level of U.S. sales in the 1980s (despite a "don't buy" rating from a consumer magazine) because its sticker price of $3,999 made it the cheapest new car available. Low quality was the primary reason for the market failure of both the Subaru 360 and the Yugo.[4]

Competitive Advantage, Globalization, and Global Industries

When a company succeeds in creating more value for customers than its competitors, that company is said to enjoy **competitive advantage** in an industry. Competitive advantage is measured relative to rivals in a given industry. For example, your local laundromat is in a local industry; its competitors are local. In a national industry, competitors are national. In a global industry—automobiles, consumer electronics, athletic shoes, watches, pharmaceuticals, steel, furniture, and a host of other sectors—the competition is, likewise, global. Global marketing is essential if a company competes in a global industry or one that is globalizing. The transformation of formerly local or national industries into global ones is part of a broader process of *globalization*, which Thomas L. Friedman defines as follows:

> Globalization is the inexorable integration of markets, nation-states and technologies to a degree never witnessed before—in a way that is enabling individuals, corporations and nation-states to reach around the world farther, faster, deeper and cheaper than ever before, and in a way that is enabling the world to reach into individuals, corporations and nation-states farther, faster, deeper, and cheaper than ever before.[5]

From a marketing point of view, globalization presents companies with tantalizing opportunities—and challenges—as executives decide whether or not to offer their products and services everywhere. At the same time, globalization presents companies with unprecedented opportunities to reconfigure themselves; as John Micklethwait and Adrian Wooldridge put it, "the same global bazaar that allows consumers to buy the best that the world can offer also allows producers to find the best partners."[6]

What, then, is a global industry? As management guru Michael Porter has noted, a **global industry** is one in which competitive advantage can be achieved by integrating and leveraging operations on a worldwide scale. Put another way, an industry is global to the extent that a company's industry position in one country is interdependent with its industry position in other countries. Indicators of globalization include the ratio of cross-border trade to total worldwide production, the ratio of cross-border investment to total capital investment, and the proportion of industry revenue generated by companies that compete in all key world regions.[7]

Achieving competitive advantage in a global industry requires executives and managers to maintain a well-defined strategic focus. **Focus** is simply the concentration of attention on a core business or competence. The importance of focus for a

---

4   The history of the Subaru 360 is documented in Randall Rothman, *Where the Suckers Moon: The Life and Death of an Advertising Campaign* (New York: Vintage Books, 1994), pp. 47–56.
5   Thomas L. Friedman, *The Lexus and the Olive Tree* (New York: Anchor Books, 2000), p. 9.
6   John Micklethwait and Adrian Wooldridge, *A Future Perfect: The Challenge and Hidden Promise of Globalization* (New York: Crown Publishers, 2000), p. xxvii.
7   Vijay Govindarajan and Anil Gupta, "Setting a Course for the New Global Landscape," *Financial Times—Mastering Global Business*, part I (1998), p. 3.

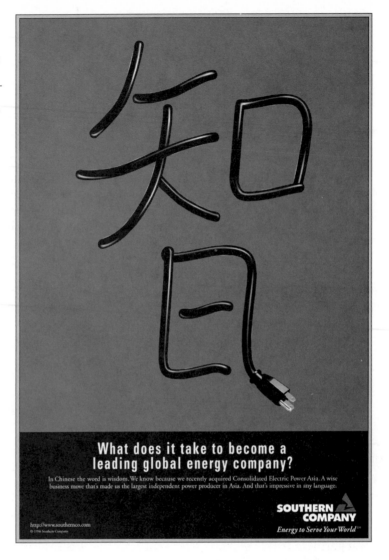

global company is evident in the following comment by Helmut Maucher, former chairman of Nestlé SA:

> Nestlé is focused: We are food and beverages. We are not running bicycle shops. Even in food we are not in all fields. There are certain areas we do not touch. For the time being we have no biscuits [cookies] in Europe and the United States for competitive reasons, and no margarine. We have no soft drinks because I have said we either buy Coca-Cola or we leave it alone. This is focus.[8]

However, company management may choose to initiate a change in focus as part of an overall strategy shift. Even Coca-Cola has been forced to sharpen its focus on its core beverage brands. Following sluggish sales in 2000–2001, chief executive

---

[8] Elizabeth Ashcroft, "Nestlé and the Twenty-First Century," Harvard Business School Case 9-595-074, 1995. See also Ernest Beck, "Nestlé Feels Little Pressure to Make Big Acquisitions," *The Wall Street Journal* (June 22, 2000), p. B4.

Douglas Daft announced a new alliance with Nestlé that will jointly develop and market coffees and teas. Daft also outlined plans for transforming Coca-Cola's Minute Maid unit into a global division that will market juice brands worldwide. As Daft explained:

> We're a network of brands and businesses. You don't just want to be a total beverage company. Each brand has a different return on investment, is sold differently, drunk for different reasons, and has different managing structures. If you mix them all together, you lose the focus.[9]

There are many similar examples of corporate executives addressing the issue of focus, often in response to changes in the global business environment. In recent years Fiat, Volvo, Electrolux, Toshiba, Colgate and many other companies have stepped up efforts to sharpen their strategic focus on core businesses. Specific actions can take a number of different forms besides alliances, including mergers, acquisitions, divestitures, and folding some businesses into other company divisions.[10] In 1998, Edgar Bronfman, Jr., the CEO of Montreal-based Seagram Company, paid $1 billion for music giant PolyGram NV and sold the company's Tropicana orange juice unit to PepsiCo. Bronfman then sold Chivas Regal and several other major spirits brands plus Seagram's wine business to Diageo PLC and Pernod-Ricard SA. Collectively, these transactions shifted Seagram's focus from beverages to entertainment; the combination of PolyGram with Seagram's MCA record unit created a global music powerhouse. In 2000, Bronfman agreed to a $32 billion takeover by France's Vivendi. The resulting company, Vivendi Universal, is tightly focused in two industry sectors: environmental services and communications. The strategic plan for the communications businesses calls for distributing Universal's entertainment content via an Internet portal that can be accessed by PCs, wireless phones, and other electronic devices.[11]

IBM originally succeeded in the data processing industry by focusing on customer needs and wants better than Univac. After decades of success, however, IBM remained focused on mainframe computers, despite customers who were increasingly turning to PCs. IBM was a key player in the early days of the PC revolution, but its corporate culture was still oriented toward mainframes. "Big Blue" faltered in the early 1990s—it lost more than $8 billion in 1993—in part because competitors specializing in PCs had become even *more* clearly focused on what PC customers needed and wanted—namely, low prices and increased speed. Within a few years, however, new CEO Lou Gerstner succeeded in refocusing the company's PC business and broadening its scope to higher-margin products such as servers for electronic commerce and the Thinkpad laptop. Gerstner and e-business marketing chief Abby Kohnstamm also leveraged IBM's reputation for providing expertise-based solutions for its customers; IBM enjoyed record revenues in 2000 with global services accounting for a full 50 percent of profits.[12]

Value, competitive advantage, and the focus required to achieve them are universal in their relevance. They should guide marketing efforts in any part of the world. Global marketing requires attention to these issues on a worldwide basis and utilization of an information system capable of monitoring the globe for opportunities

---

[9] Betsey McKay, "Coke's 'Think Local' Strategy has Yet to Prove Itself," *The Wall Street Journal* (March 1, 2001), p. B6.

[10] Robert A. Guth, "How Japan's Toshiba Got Its Focus Back," *The Wall Street Journal* (December 12, 2000), p. A6.

[11] Bruce Orwall, "Universal Script: Vivendi-Seagram Deal has the Former MCA Playing Familiar Role," *The Wall Street Journal* (June 20, 2000), pp. A1, A8.

[12] Scott M. Davis, "Great Brands Continue to Find Relevance," *Brandweek* (April 16, 2001), p. 16.

Assessment of an industry's actual or potential degree of globalization may vary among companies. Recalling Whirlpool's assessment of the changing business environment, CEO David Whitwam noted, "The closer we looked, the more we said to ourselves, 'This is becoming a global industry. One of these days someone is going to figure that out and build lots of competitive advantage. That someone should be us.'" Today, Whirlpool produces white goods (as major appliances are known in the industry) in 11 countries and is the only appliance manufacturer with strategic positions in North America, Latin America, Europe, and Asia. To date, however, the European strategy has not paid off as expected, as large competitors such as Bosch-Siemens and Electrolux invested heavily in product and efficiency improvements. Meanwhile, Whirlpool made marketing and management mistakes. Executives were forced to scale back the objective of capturing 20 percent of the European appliance market by 2000. Despite its disappointments, Whirlpool is proceeding with plans to globalize the development of new products by creating "platforms" (core design elements) that can be used throughout the world. It is noteworthy that appliance makers in Japan have not targeted the United States, in part because they do not share the view that the appliance industry is global.

SOURCES: William C. Taylor and Alan M. Webber, *Going Global: Four Entrepreneurs Map the New World Marketplace* (New York: Penguin Books USA, 1996), p. 7; Greg Steinmetz and Carl Quintanilla, "Tough Target: Whirlpool Expected Easy Going in Europe, and It Got a Big Shock," *The Wall Street Journal* (April 10, 1998), pp. A1, A6. See also Peter Marsh and Nikki Tait, "Whirlpool's Platform for Growth," *Financial Times* (March 26, 1998), p. 8.

and threats. A fundamental premise of this book can be stated as follows: Companies that understand and engage in global marketing can offer more overall value to customers than companies that do not have that understanding. There are many who share this conviction. For example, C. Samuel Craig and Susan P. Douglas recently noted:

> Globalization is no longer an abstraction but a stark reality. . . . Choosing not to participate in global markets is no longer an option. All firms, regardless of their size, have to craft strategies in the broader context of world markets to anticipate, respond, and adapt to the changing configuration of these markets.[13]

GLOBAL MARKETING: WHAT IT IS AND WHAT IT ISN'T

The discipline of marketing is universal. It is natural, however, that marketing practices will vary from country to country, for the simple reason that the countries and peoples of the world are different. These differences mean that a marketing approach that has proven successful in one country will not *necessarily* succeed in another country. Customer preferences, competitors, channels of distribution, and communication media may differ. An important task in global marketing is learning to recognize the extent to which marketing plans and programs can be extended worldwide, as well as the extent to which they must be adapted.

A second important task in global marketing is sorting through controversies among both academicians and business practitioners about the nature of the field

---

[13] C. Samuel Craig and Susan P. Douglas, "Responding to the Challenges of Global Markets: Change, Complexity, Competition, and Conscience," *Columbia Journal of World Business* 31, no. 4 (Winter 1996), pp. 6–18.

itself. Much of the controversy dates back to Professor Theodore Levitt's 1983 article in the *Harvard Business Review*, "The Globalization of Markets." Levitt argued that marketers were confronted with a "homogeneous global village." He advised organizations to develop standardized, high-quality world products and market them around the globe by using standardized advertising, pricing, and distribution. Some well-publicized failures by Parker Pen and other companies that tried to follow Levitt's advice brought his proposals into question. The business press frequently quoted industry observers who disputed Levitt's views. For example, Carl Spielvogel, chairman and CEO of the Backer Spielvogel Bates Worldwide advertising agency, told *The Wall Street Journal*, "Theodore Levitt's comment about the world becoming homogenized is bunk. There are about two products that lend themselves to global marketing—and one of them is Coca-Cola."[14]

Indeed, global marketing made Coke a worldwide success. However, that success was *not* based on a total standardization of marketing mix elements. For example, Coca-Cola achieved success in Japan by spending a great deal of time and money to become an insider; that is, the company built a complete local infrastructure with its sales force and vending machine operations. Coke's success in Japan is a function of its ability to achieve "global localization," being as much of an insider as a local company but still reaping the benefits that result from world-scale operations.[15] Similarly, in India, the company's local Thums Up cola brand competes with—and even outsells—the flagship cola.[16]

What does the phrase *global localization* really mean? In a nutshell, it means that a successful global marketer must have the ability to "think globally and act locally." As we will see many times in this book, "global" marketing may include a combination of standard (e.g., the actual product itself) and nonstandard (e.g., distribution or packaging) approaches. A global product may be the same product everywhere and yet different. Global marketing requires marketers to behave in a way that is global *and* local at the same time by responding to similarities and differences in world markets. Kenichi Ohmae recently summed up this paradox as follows:

> The essence of being a global company is to maintain a kind of tension within the organization without being undone by it. Some companies say the new world requires homogeneous products—"one size fits all"—everywhere. Others say the world requires endless customization—special products for every region. The best global companies understand it's neither and it's both. They keep the two perspectives in mind simultaneously.[17]

As the Coca-Cola Company has demonstrated, the ability to think globally and act locally can be a source of competitive advantage. By adapting sales promotion, distribution, and customer service efforts to local needs, Coke established such strong brand preference that the company claims a 70 percent share of the soft drink market in Japan. At first, Coca-Cola managers did not understand the Japanese distribution system. However, with considerable investment of time and money, they succeeded in establishing a sales force that was as effective in Japan as it was in the United States. Today, Coca-Cola Japan generates higher profits than the U.S. operation.

---

[14] Joanne Lipman, "Ad Fad: Marketers Turn Sour on Global Sales Pitch Harvard Guru Makes," *The Wall Street Journal* (May 12, 1988), p. 1.

[15] Kenichi Ohmae, *The Borderless World: Power and Strategy* (New York: Harper Perennial, 1991), p. 26.

[16] Nikhil Deogun and Jonathan Karp, "For Coke in India, Thums Up is the Real Thing," *The Wall Street Journal* (April 29, 1998), pp. B1, B2.

[17] William C. Taylor and Alan M. Webber, *Going Global: Four Entrepreneurs Map the New World Marketplace* (New York: Penguin Books USA, 1996), pp. 48–49.

Some of Coke's many faces around the world. Although the basic design of the label is the same (white letters against a red background), the Coca-Cola name is frequently transliterated into local languages. In the left-hand column, the Arabic label (second from top) is read from right to left; the Chinese label (fourth from the top) translates "delicious/happiness."

To complement cola sales, the Japanese unit has created new products such as Georgia-brand canned coffee expressly for the Japanese market.[18]

Coke is a product supported by marketing mix elements that are both global and local. In this book, we do *not* propose that global marketing is a knee-jerk attempt to impose a totally standardized approach to marketing around the world. A central issue in global marketing is how to tailor the global marketing concept to fit particular products, businesses, and markets.[19]

Finally, global marketing does *not* mean entering every country in the world. Global marketing *does* mean widening business horizons to encompass the world in scanning for opportunity and threat. The decision to enter markets outside the home country depends on a company's resources, its managerial mind-set, and the nature of opportunity and threat. The Coca-Cola Company's drink products are distributed in some 200 countries; in fact, the theme of a recent annual report was "A Global Business System Dedicated to Customer Service." Coke is the best-known, strongest brand in the world; its enviable global position has resulted in part from the Coca-Cola Company's willingness and ability to back its flagship product with a network of local bottlers and a strong local marketing effort.

---

18 David McHardy Reid, "Perspectives for International Marketers on the Japanese Market," *Journal of International Marketing* 3, no. 1 (1995), p. 74.
19 John A. Quelch and Edward J. Hoff, "Customizing Global Marketing," *Harvard Business Review* 64, no. 3 (May-June 1986), p. 59.

A number of other companies have successfully pursued global marketing by creating strong global brands. The Altria Group (formerly Philip Morris), for example, has made Marlboro the number one cigarette brand in the world. In automobiles, DaimlerChrysler enjoys global recognition for its Mercedes nameplate. However, as shown in Table 1-1, effective global marketing strategies can also be based on product or system design, product positioning, packaging, distribution, customer service, and sourcing considerations. For example, McDonald's has designed a restaurant system that can be set up virtually anywhere in the world. Like Coca-Cola, McDonald's also customizes its menu offerings in accordance with local eating customs. Cisco Systems, which makes local area network routers that allow computers to communicate with each other, designs new products that can be programmed to operate under virtually any conditions in the world.[20] Unilever uses a teddy bear to communicate the benefits of the company's fabric softener. Harley-Davidson's motorcycles are perceived around the world as *the* all-American bike. Gillette uses the same packaging for its flagship Mach3 razor everywhere in the world. Italy's Benetton utilizes a sophisticated distribution system to quickly deliver the latest fashions to its worldwide network of stores. The backbone of Caterpillar's global success is a network of dealers who support a promise of "24-hour parts and service" anywhere in the world. About 85 percent of Gap's 3,000 stores are located in the United States, and its design group is based in New York. However, the company relies on apparel factories in Honduras, the Philippines, India, and other low-wage countries to supply most of its clothing. The success of Honda and Toyota in world markets was initially based on exporting cars from factories in Japan. Now, both companies have invested in manufacturing and assembly facilities in the Americas, Asia, and Europe. From these sites, the automakers supply customers in the local market and also export to the rest of the world. For example, each year Honda exports tens of thousands of Accords and Civics from U.S. plants to Japan and dozens of other countries.

The particular approach to global marketing that a company adopts will depend on industry conditions and its source or sources of competitive advantage. Should Harley-Davidson start manufacturing motorcycles in a low-wage country such as Mexico? Will American consumers continue to snap up American-built Toyotas? Should Gap open more stores in Japan? The answer to these questions is: "It all depends." Because Harley's competitive advantage is based in part on its "Made in

Table 1-1
Examples of Effective Global Marketing

GLOBAL MARKETING STRATEGY	COMPANY/HOME COUNTRY
Brand name	Coca-Cola (USA); Altria Group (Marlboro, USA); Daimler-Chrysler (Mercedes, Germany); Virgin (Great Britain)
Product/System design	McDonald's (USA); Toyota (Japan); Ford (USA); Cisco Systems (USA)
Product positioning	Unilever (UK/Netherlands); Harley-Davidson (USA); Gillette (USA); LVMH (France)
Advertising	Philips (Netherlands); Citibank (USA)
Packaging	Gillette (USA)
Distribution	Benetton (Italy)
Customer service	Caterpillar (USA); IBM (USA)
Sourcing	Toyota (Japan); Honda (Japan); Gap (USA)

---

[20] Gregory L. Miles, "Tailoring a Global Product," *International Business* (March 1995), p. 50.

the USA" positioning, shifting production outside the United States is not advisable. The company has opened a new production facility in Kansas and taken a majority stake in Buell Motorcycle, a manufacturer of "American street bikes." Toyota's success in the United States is partly attributable to its ability to transfer world-class manufacturing skills to America while using advertising to stress that its Camry is built by Americans with many components purchased from American suppliers. Gap has more than 500 stores outside the United States, including units in Canada, the United Kingdom, Japan, France, and Germany. Japan may present an opportunity for Gap to increase revenues and profits in a major non-U.S. market. A recent annual report noted that, in terms of sales revenues, the apparel market outside the United States is twice as large as that within the United States. Also, "American style" is in high demand in Japan and other parts of the world. Gap's management team has responded to this situation by selectively targeting key country markets—especially areas with high population densities—while continuing to concentrate on trends in the U.S. fashion marketplace. However, recent operating difficulties in the core U.S. market led to the departure of several executives, suggesting management's top priority at this time should be the domestic market.[21]

THE IMPORTANCE OF GLOBAL MARKETING

The largest single market in the world in terms of national income, the United States represents roughly 25 percent of the total world market for all products and services. Thus, U.S. companies that wish to achieve maximum growth potential must "go global" because 75 percent of world market potential is outside their home country. Management at Coca-Cola clearly understands this; about 90 percent of the company's operating income and two-thirds of revenues are generated by its soft drink business outside the United States. Non-U.S. companies have an even greater motivation to seek market opportunities beyond their own borders; their opportunities include the 270 million people in the United States. For example, even though the dollar value of the home market for Japanese companies is the second largest in the world (after the United States), the market *outside* Japan is 85 percent of the world potential for Japanese companies. For European countries, the picture is even more dramatic. Even though Germany is the largest single country market in Europe, 94 percent of the world market potential for German companies is outside Germany.

Many companies have recognized the importance of conducting business activities outside the home country. Industries that were essentially national in scope only a few years ago are dominated today by a handful of global companies. The rise of the global corporation closely parallels the rise of the national corporation, which emerged from the local and regional corporation in the 1880s and 1890s in the United States. The auto industry provides a dramatic example: In the early twentieth century, there were thousands of auto companies scattered around the globe. The United States alone was home to more than 500 automakers. Today, fewer than 20 major companies remain worldwide. A dramatic illustration of the ongoing consolidation in the auto industry is Daimler-Benz's $36 billion takeover of Chrysler in 1998. In most industries, the companies that will survive and prosper in the twenty-first century will be global enterprises. Some companies that fail to formulate adequate responses to the challenges and opportunities of globalization will be absorbed by

---

[21] Gap's transformation into a global brand is chronicled in Nina Munk, "Gap Gets It," *Fortune* (August 3, 1998), pp. 68–74+; see also Calmetta Coleman, "Gap is Making Management Changes to Fight Sales Slump," *The Wall Street Journal* (November 7, 2000), p. B4.

William Greider believes that the globalization of industries and markets will have some unintended, possibly dire, consequences in the coming years. In his book *One World, Ready or Not,* Greider describes how the logic of commerce and capital in the closing years of the twentieth century has created an economic revolution and launched great social transformations. As Greider sees it, the message of globalization contains good news and bad news. The good news is that modern technology and global marketing are enabling people and nations throughout the world to leap into the modern era. The bad news, Greider warns, is that modern technology tends to be more individualistic and anti-egalitarian than the mass assembly technology that revolutionized production in the first part of the twentieth century. As a result, disregard for basic human rights and the exploitation of the weak in developing nations may result in great social upheavals and, eventually, a breakdown in the global system.

One issue that concerns Greider is the fact that productivity and revenues at many global corporations have risen dramatically, while overall worldwide employment has not. Meanwhile, a dispersal of productive wealth is underway as global corporations establish operations in key developing countries like Brazil and China. Many economists agree that this dispersal will narrow the gap between poor and rich nations. Back in the industrialized nations, however, there is an increasing sense of social distress as workers see their plants close and jobs shipped out of the country. One byproduct of globalization, Greider observes, is that it pits the interests of the older, more prosperous workers against the interests of newly recruited, lower-paid workers. Greider warns that deeper political instability lies ahead for the United States, Germany, France, and Britain as workers take up the fight to save their jobs.

In addition, the globalization of industries such as steel, automobiles, and consumer electronics has created surplus production capacity on a massive scale. Greider notes that the U.S. economy serves as a sort of safety valve for the global system. Because the U.S. market places relatively few restrictions on imports, this "benevolent openness" means that America serves as a "buyer of last resort" by absorbing much of the world's excess production. As a result of the chronic imbalance in the trading system, the United States continues to post massive trade deficits that defy conventional economic analysis.

What can, or should, be done? Greider argues that U.S.-based global companies that create jobs overseas at the expense of domestic jobs should not be permitted to finance export deals by borrowing from tax-supported agencies such as the Export-Import Bank. At the same time, Greider says that American public interest would be better served if government policy shifted away from supporting and underwriting the interests of global companies and focused instead on jobs and wages. Finally, Greider advocates the use of emergency tariffs to reduce the trade deficit if American policymakers are unable to gain more access in foreign markets to U.S. export.

SOURCES: William Greider, *One World, Ready or Not: The Manic Logic of Global Capitalism* (Upper Saddle River, NJ: Simon & Schuster, 1997); Greider, "Who Governs Globalism?" *The American Prospect,* no. 30 (January-February 1997), pp. 73–80.

---

more dynamic, visionary enterprises; others will simply disappear. Table 1-2 shows 25 of *The Wall Street Journal*'s top 100 companies in terms of market capitalization—that is, the market value of all shares of stock outstanding. Table 1-3 provides a different perspective—the top 25 of *Fortune* magazine's 2000 ranking of the 500 largest service and manufacturing companies by revenues.

Comparing the two tables, one is struck by GE's strong showing: It is first in market capitalization, ninth in revenues, but first in profits. Much credit for this outstanding performance goes to former CEO Jack Welch, who set out in the mid-1980s to globalize his company. Not every company in the tables is truly global, however; Nippon Telegraph and Telephone (NTT), for example, ranks 20th in market capitalization, 13th in revenues, but 483rd in profit! A downturn in the telecommunications sector and Japan's ongoing economic woes help explain the poor profit performance.

Table 1-2

The Largest Corporations by Market Value (US$ millions)

COMPANY	MARKET VALUE*
1. General Electric (USA)	$562,937
2. Intel (USA)	453,541
3. Cisco Systems (USA)	432,357
4. Microsoft (USA)	372,798
5. Exxon Mobil (USA)	281,469
6. Pfizer (USA)	265,664
7. Vodafone Group (USA)	259,218
8. Citigroup (USA)	249,292
9. NTT DoCoMo (Japan)	242,430
10. Nortel Networks (USA)	233,625
11. Wal-Mart Stores (USA)	230,481
12. Oracle (USA)	229,249
13. International Business Machines (USA)	219,918
14. Royal Dutch/Shell Group (UK/Nether.)	215,164
15. BP Amoco (UK)	204,797
16. American International Group (USA)	201,320
17. Nokia (Finland)	191,041
18. Sun Microsystems (USA)	186,205
19. EMC (USA)	182,560
20. Nippon Telegraph & Telephone (Japan)	181,883
21. Merck (USA)	171,216
22. Toyota Motor (USA)	161,642
23. Coca-Cola (USA)	152,830
24. SBC Communications (USA)	143,491
25. Ericsson (UK)	137,446

*Data reflect market value on August 15, 2000.

Source: "The World's 100 Largest Public Companies," *The Wall Street Journal* (September 25, 2000), p. R24.

Until recently, Japanese regulations severely limited NTT's reach outside of Japan. After regulations were relaxed in 1999, NTT embarked on a global shopping spree. Acquisitions include Verio Inc., a U.S.-based Internet company; NTT also bought a stake in the mobile phone unit of a Dutch company, KPN NV. The company's strategic goal is to become a global company with a strong base in Asia.[22] Wal-Mart, the world's number-one retailer, currently generates only about 5 percent of revenues outside the United States. However, global expansion is the key to the company's growth strategy over the next few years.

Examining the size of individual product markets, measured in terms of annual sales, provides another perspective on global marketing's importance. Not surprisingly, many of the companies identified in Tables 1-2 and 1-3 are key players in the global marketplace. Selected markets are shown in Table 1-4.

---

[22] Robert Guth, "Japan's NTT Steps Up Its Push Into U.S. and Europe," *The Wall Street Journal* (May 26, 2000), pp. A16, A19.

Table 1-3
The Fortune Global
500: Largest
Corporations by
Revenues (US$
millions)

COMPANY	REVENUES	PROFITS	PROFITS RANK
1. General Motors (USA)	$176,558	6,002.0	14
2. Wal-Mart Stores (USA)	166,809	5,377.0	19
3. Exxon Mobil (USA)	163,881	7,910.0	5
4. Ford Motor (USA)	162,558	7,237.0	12
5. DaimlerChrysler (Germany)	159,985	6,129.1	13
6. Mitsui (Japan)	118,555	320.5	330
7. Mitsubishi (Japan)	117,765	233.7	367
8. Toyota Motor (Japan)	115,670	3,653.4	39
9. General Electric (USA)	111,630	10,717.0	1
10. Itochu (Japan)	109,068	(792.8)	484
11. Royal Dutch/Shell Group (UK/Nether.)	105,366	8,584.0	3
12. Sumimoto (Japan)	95,701	314.9	331
13. Nippon Telegraph & Telephone (Japan)	93,591	(609.0)	483
14. Marubeni (Japan)	91,807	18.5	444
15. AXA (France)	87,645	2,155.8	86
16. International Business Machines (USA)	87,548	7,712.0	8
17. BP Amoco (UK)	83,566	5,008.0	23
18. Citigroup (USA)	82,005	9,067.0	2
19. Volkswagen (Germany)	80,072	874.7	199
20. Nippon Life Insurance (Japan)	78,515	3,405.4	45
21. Siemens (Germany)	75,337	1,773.7	104
22. Allianz (Germany)	74,178	2,382.1	77
23. Hitachi (Japan)	71,858	152.0	396
24. Matsushita Electrical Industrial (Japan)	65,555	895.5	195
25. Nissho Iwai (Japan)	65,393	91.8	416

Source: "The *Fortune* Global 500," *Fortune* (July 24, 2000), p. F1. Figures cited from most recent fiscal year.

MANAGEMENT ORIENTATIONS

The form and substance of a company's response to global market opportunities depend greatly on management's assumptions or beliefs—both conscious and unconscious—about the nature of the world. The world view of a company's personnel can be described as ethnocentric, polycentric, regiocentric, and geocentric.[23] Management at a company with a prevailing ethnocentric orientation may consciously make a decision to move in the direction of geocentricism. The orientations—collectively known as the EPRG framework—are summarized in Figure 1-2.

Ethnocentric Orientation

A person who assumes that his or her home country is superior to the rest of the world is said to have an **ethnocentric orientation.** Ethnocentrism is sometimes associated with attitudes of national arrogance or assumptions of national superiority.

---

[23] Adapted from Howard Perlmutter, "The Tortuous Evolution of the Multinational Corporation," *Columbia Journal of World Business* (January-February 1969).

Table 1-4
How Big Is the Market?

PRODUCT OR SERVICE	SIZE OF MARKET	KEY PLAYERS/BRANDS
Auto parts	$720 billion	Delphi Automotive Systems (USA); Ford Automotive Products Operations (USA); Robert Bosch GmbH (Germany); Denso Corp. (Japan); Aisin Seiki (Japan)
Computers	$650 billion	IBM (USA); Compaq (USA); Hewlett-Packard (USA); Dell (USA)
Telecommunications	$600 billion	AT&T (USA); Global One (USA, Germany, France)
Internetworking products and services	$470 billion	IBM (USA); Microsoft (USA); Oracle (USA); Computer Associates (USA); SAP (Germany)
Packaging	$400 billion	Sealed Air (USA); Crown Cork and Seal (USA)
Personal financial services	$300 billion	Citigroup (USA)
Cigarettes	$295 billion	Altria Group (USA); B.A.T Industries (UK); Japan Tobacco (Japan); Gallaher Group (UK)
Computer software	$95 billion	IBM (USA); Microsoft (USA); Oracle (USA); SAP (Germany)
White goods (major appliances)	$85 billion	Whirlpool (USA); Electrolux (Sweden); Bosch-Siemens (Germany)
Construction equipment	$70 billion	Caterpillar (USA); Komatsu (Japan); Volvo (Sweden)
Luxury goods	$39 billion	LVMH Group (France); Giorgio Armani (Italy)
Recorded music	$40 billion	PolyGram (Netherlands); Sony (Japan); Warner (USA); Bertelsmann (Germany); EMI (UK); Vivendi-Universal (France)
Pet food	$30 billion	Iams (Procter & Gamble USA); Ralston Purina (Nestlé Switzerland); Pedigree (Mars USA)
Farm equipment (tractors, combines, bailers)	$20 billion	John Deere (USA); Case (USA); New Holland NV (Netherlands)

Source: Compiled by the authors.

The Global Marketplace
The Rest of the Story

Now that we've got you thinking about global marketing, it's time to test your knowledge of global current events. Some well-known companies and brands are listed in the left-hand column below. The question is, in what country is the parent corporation located? Possible answers are shown in the right-hand column. Write the letter corresponding to the country of your choice in the space provided; each country can be used more than once. Answers are provided below.

_____ 1. Firestone Tire & Rubber

_____ 2. Burger King

_____ 3. Rolls-Royce

_____ 4. RCA Electronics

_____ 5. Dr Pepper

_____ 6. Jaguar

_____ 7. Gerber

_____ 8. Baskin Robbins

_____ 9. Rollerblade

_____ 10. Dunkin' Donuts

a. Germany

b. France

c. Japan

d. Great Britain

e. United States

f. Switzerland

g. Italy

Answers: 1. Japan (Bridgestone), 2. Great Britain (Diageo), 3. Germany (Volkswagen), 4. France (Thomson SA), 5. Great Britain (Cadbury Schweppes), 6. United States (Ford), 7. Switzerland (Novartis), 8. Great Britain (Allied Domecq), 9. Italy (Benetton), 10. Great Britain (Allied Domecq)

**Figure 1-2
Management
Orientations**

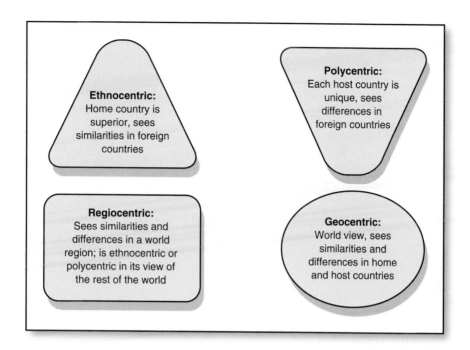

Company personnel with an ethnocentric orientation see only similarities in markets, and *assume* that products and practices that succeed in the home country will be successful anywhere. At some companies, the ethnocentric orientation means that opportunities outside the home country are largely ignored. Such companies are sometimes called *domestic companies.* Ethnocentric companies that do conduct business outside the home country can be described as *international companies;* they adhere to the notion that the products that succeed in the home country are superior. This point of view leads to a **standardized** or **extension approach** to marketing based on the premise that products can be sold everywhere without adaptation.

In the ethnocentric international company, foreign operations or markets are typically viewed as being secondary or subordinate to domestic ones. (We are using the term "domestic" to mean the country in which a company is headquartered.) An ethnocentric company operates under the assumption that "tried and true" headquarters knowledge and organizational capabilities can be applied in other parts of the world. While this can sometimes work to a company's advantage, valuable managerial knowledge and experience in local markets may go unnoticed. For a manufacturing firm, ethnocentrism may mean foreign markets are viewed as a dumping ground for surplus domestic production. Plans for overseas markets are developed utilizing policies and procedures modeled on those employed at home. Little or no systematic marketing research is conducted outside the home country, and no major modifications are made to products. Even if customer needs or wants differ from those in the home country, such differences are ignored at headquarters.

Nissan's ethnocentric orientation was quite apparent during its first few years of exporting cars and trucks to America. Designed for mild Japanese winters, the vehicles were difficult to start in many parts of the United States during the cold winter months. In northern Japan, many car owners would put blankets over the hoods of their cars. Nissan's assumption—which turned out to be false—was that Americans would do the same thing. As a Nissan spokesman said recently, "We tried for a long time to design cars in Japan and shove them down the American consumer's throat.

That didn't work very well."[24] Until the 1980s, Eli Lilly and Company operated as an ethnocentric company: Activity outside the United States was tightly controlled by headquarters and the focus was on selling products originally developed for the U.S. market.[25] Similarly, executives at California's Robert Mondavi Corporation operated the company for many years as an ethnocentric international entity. As CEO Michael Mondavi explains:

> Robert Mondavi was a local winery that thought locally, grew locally, produced locally, and sold globally . . . To be a truly global company, I believe it's imperative to grow and produce great wines in the world in the best wine-growing regions of the world, regardless of the country or the borders.[26]

Fifty years ago, most business enterprises—and especially those located in a large country like the United States—could operate quite successfully with an ethnocentric orientation. Today, however, as CEO Mondavi's words make clear, ethnocentrism is one of the major internal weaknesses that must be overcome if a company is to transform itself into an effective global competitor.

Polycentric Orientation

Polycentric orientation is the opposite of ethnocentrism. The term polycentric describes management's belief or assumption that each country in which a company does business is unique. This assumption lays the groundwork for each subsidiary to develop its own unique business and marketing strategies in order to succeed; the term *multinational company* is often used to describe such a structure. This point of view leads to a **localized** or **adaptation approach** that assumes products must be adapted in response to different market conditions. Until the mid-1990s, Citicorp's financial services around the world operated on a polycentric basis. James Bailey, a Citicorp executive, offered this description of the company: "We were like a medieval state. There was the king and his court and they were in charge, right? No. It was the land barons who were in charge. The king and his court might declare this or that, but the land barons went and did their thing."[27] Realizing that the financial services industry was globalizing, then-CEO John Reed attempted to achieve a higher degree of integration between Citicorp's operating units. Like Jack Welch at GE, Reed sought to instill a geocentric orientation throughout his company.

Prior to 1994, Ford Motor Company was also organized as a multinational corporation. Each of the company's four geographical regions operated autonomously. That meant four separate development centers, each designing vehicles to be marketed in their respective regions. In January 1994, CEO Alex Trotman launched Ford 2000, an ambitious reorganization designed to transform Ford into a global company as opposed to a multinational one. A key element in the plan was the centralization of worldwide product development. In November 1999, Trotman's successor announced plans to reintroduce some of the regional focus. Jacques Nasser's reversal was viewed as an effort to ensure that Ford products and the Ford brand are responsive to local preferences, especially in Europe.

---

[24] Norihiko Shirouzu, "Tailoring World's Cars to U.S. Tastes," *The Wall Street Journal* (January 1, 2001), pp. B1, B6.

[25] T. W. Malnight, "Globalization of an Ethnocentric Firm: An Evolutionary Perspective," *Strategic Management Journal* 16, no. 2 (February 1995), p. 125.

[26] Robert Mondavi, *Harvests of Joy: My Passion for Excellence* (New York: Harcourt Brace & Company, 1998), p. 333.

[27] Saul Hansell, "Uniting the Feudal Lords at Citicorp," *The New York Times* (January 16, 1994), Sec. 3, p. 1.

Regiocentric and Geocentric Orientations

In a company with a **regiocentric orientation,** a region becomes the relevant geographic unit; management's goal is to develop an integrated regional strategy. For example, a U.S. company that focuses on the countries included in the North American Free Trade Agreement (NAFTA)—the United States, Canada, and Mexico—has a regiocentric orientation. Similarly, a European company that focuses its attention on Europe is regiocentric. A company with a **geocentric orientation** views the entire world as a potential market and strives to develop integrated world market strategies. A company whose management has a regiocentric or geocentric orientation is sometimes known as a *global* or *transnational company.*[28] A global company can be further described as one that pursues either a strategy of serving world markets from a single country, or that sources globally for the purposes of focusing on select country markets. In addition, global companies tend to retain their association with a particular headquarters country. Harley-Davidson and Waterford serve world markets from the United States and Ireland, respectively; Gap sources its apparel from low-wage countries in all parts of the world and focuses primarily on the key U.S. market. All three may be thought of as global companies. Transnational companies both serve global markets and source globally; in addition, there is often a blurring of national identity. A true transnational would be characterized as "stateless." Toyota is a good example of a company that is coming close to fulfilling the criteria of transnationality. At global and transnational companies, management uses a combination of standardized (extension) and localized (adaptation) elements in the marketing program. A key factor that distinguishes global and transnational companies from international or multinational companies is *mindset:* at global and transnational companies, decisions regarding extension and adaptation are not based on assumptions. Rather, such decisions are made on the basis of ongoing research into market needs and wants.

Table 1-5 shows a ranking of companies according to an "index of transnationality," which is an average of three figures: sales outside the home country to total sales; assets outside the home country to total assets; and employees outside the home country to total employees. One characteristic that the companies all have in common is that relatively small home country markets have compelled management to adopt regiocentric or geocentric orientations to achieve revenue and profit growth.

The geocentric orientation represents a synthesis of ethnocentrism and polycentrism; it is a "world view" that sees similarities and differences in markets and countries, and seeks to create a global strategy that is fully responsive to local needs and wants. A regiocentric manager might be said to have a world view on a regional scale; the world outside the region of interest will be viewed with an ethnocentric or a polycentric orientation, or a combination of the two. However, recent research suggests that many companies are seeking to strengthen their regional competitiveness rather than moving directly to develop global responses to changes in the competitive environment.[29]

---

[28] Although the definitions provided here are important, to avoid confusion we will use the term *global marketing* when describing the general activities of global companies. Another note of caution is in order: Usage of the terms *international, multinational,* and *global* varies widely. Alert readers of the business press are likely to recognize inconsistencies; usage does not always reflect the definitions provided here. In particular, companies that are (in the view of the authors as well as numerous other academics) global, are often described as *multinational enterprises* (abbreviated MNE) or *multinational corporations* (abbreviated MNC). The United Nations prefers the term *transnational company* rather than *global company.* When we refer to an "international company" or a "multinational," we will do so in a way that maintains the distinctions described in the text.

[29] Allan J. Morrison, David A. Ricks, and Kendall Roth, "Globalization Versus Regionalization: Which Way for the Multinational?" *Organizational Dynamics* (Winter 1991), p. 18.

Table 1-5

Companies Ranked by "Transnationality"

1. Nestlé (Switzerland)	11. SCA (Sweden)
2. Thomson Corporation (Canada)	12. Northern Telecom (Canada)
3. Holderbank Financiére (Switzerland)	13. GlaxoSmithKline (UK)
4. Seagram Company (Canada)	14. Cable & Wireless (UK)
5. Solvay (Belgium)	15. Volvo (Sweden)
6. ABB (Switzerland)	16. News Corporation (Australia)
7. Electrolux (Sweden)	17. Royal Dutch/Shell (UK/Netherlands)
8. Unilever (UK/Netherlands)	18. Diageo (UK)
9. Royal Philips Electronics (Netherlands)	19. Petrofina (Belgium)
10. Roche Holdings (Switzerland)	20. Saint-Gobain (France)

Source: Alan Rugman, "Multinationals as Regional Flagships," *Financial Times—Mastering Global Business,* Part I (January 30, 1998), p. 8.

The ethnocentric company is centralized in its marketing management, the polycentric company is decentralized, and the regiocentric and geocentric companies are integrated on a regional and global scale, respectively. A crucial difference between the orientations is the underlying assumption for each. The ethnocentric orientation is based on a belief in home-country superiority. The underlying assumption of the polycentric approach is that there are so many differences in cultural, economic, and marketing conditions in the world that it is futile to attempt to transfer experience across national boundaries. A key challenge facing organizational leaders today is managing a company's evolution beyond an ethnocentric or polycentric orientation toward a regiocentric or geocentric one. As noted in one recent book on global business, "The multinational solution encounters problems by ignoring a number of organizational impediments to the implementation of a global strategy and underestimating the impact of global competition."[30] At many companies, management realizes the need to change. For example, Louis R. Hughes, a General Motors executive, said recently, "We are on our way to becoming a transnational corporation." His view was echoed by Basil Drossos, president of GM de Argentina, who noted, "We are talking about becoming a global corporation as opposed to a multinational company; that implies that the centers of expertise may reside anywhere they best reside."[31]

> "There are no German and American companies. There are only successful and unsuccessful ones."
> —Thomas Middelhoff, Chairman, Bertelsmann AG[32]

FORCES AFFECTING GLOBAL INTEGRATION AND GLOBAL MARKETING

The remarkable growth of the global economy over the past 50 years has been shaped by the dynamic interplay of various driving and restraining forces. During most of those decades, companies from different parts of the world in different

---

[30] Michael A. Yoshino and U. Srinivasa Rangan, *Strategic Alliances: An Entrepreneurial Approach to Globalization* (Boston: Harvard Business School Press, 1995), p. 64.

[31] Rebecca Blumenstein, "Global Strategy: GM is Building Plants in Developing Nations to Woo New Markets," *The Wall Street Journal* (August 4, 1997), p. A4.

[32] Joseph B. White, "Global Mall: 'There are No German and American Companies. Only Successful Ones'," *The Wall Street Journal* (May 7, 1998), p. A1.

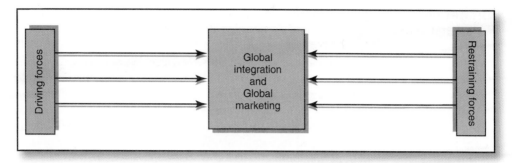

Figure 1-3
Driving and Restraining Forces Affecting Global Integration

industries achieved great success by pursuing international, multinational, or global strategies. During the 1990s, changes in the business environment have presented a number of challenges to established ways of doing business. Today, the growing importance of global marketing stems from the fact that driving forces have more momentum than the restraining forces. The forces affecting global integration are shown in Figure 1-3.

Regional economic agreements, converging market needs and wants, technology advances, pressure to cut costs, pressure to improve quality, improvements in communication and transportation technology, global economic growth, and opportunities for leverage all represent important driving forces; any industry subject to these forces is a candidate for globalization.

Regional Economic Agreements

A number of multilateral trade agreements have accelerated the pace of global integration. NAFTA is already expanding trade among the United States, Canada, and Mexico. The General Agreement on Tariffs and Trade (GATT), which was ratified by more than 120 nations in 1994, has created the World Trade Organization to promote and protect free trade. In Europe, the expanding membership of the European Union is lowering boundaries to trade within the region. The creation of a single currency zone and the introduction of the euro are also expected to dramatically expand European trade in the 21st century.

Market Needs and Wants

A person studying markets around the world will discover cultural universals as well as differences. The common elements in human nature provide an underlying basis for the opportunity to create and serve global markets. The word *create* is deliberate. Most global markets do not exist in nature; they must be created by marketing effort. For example, no one *needs* soft drinks, and yet today in some countries per capita soft drink consumption *exceeds* the consumption of water. Marketing has driven this change in behavior, and today, the soft drink industry is a truly global one. Evidence is mounting that consumer needs and wants around the world are converging today as never before. This creates an opportunity for global marketing. Multinational companies pursuing strategies of product adaptation run the risk of falling victim to global competitors that have recognized opportunities to serve global customers.

Until recently, Royal Philips Electronics, headquartered in Eindhoven, Netherlands, was a classic example of a company with a polycentric orientation. Philips relied upon relatively autonomous national organizations (called "NOs" in company parlance) in each country. Each NO developed its own strategy. This approach worked quite well until Philips faced competition from Matsushita and other Japanese consumer electronics companies in which management's orientation was geocentric. The difference in competitive advantage between Philips and its Japanese competition was dramatic.

For example, Matsushita adopted a global strategy that focused its resources on serving a world market for home entertainment products. In television receivers, Matsushita offered European customers two basic models based on a single chassis. In contrast, Philips's European NOs offered customers seven different models based on four different chassis. If customers had demanded this variety, Philips would have been the stronger competitor. Unfortunately, the product designs created by the NOs were not based upon customer preferences. Customers wanted value in the form of quality, features, design—and price. Philips's decision to offer greater design variety was based not upon what customers were asking for but, rather, on Philips's structure and strategy. Each major country organization had its own engineering and manufacturing group. Each country unit had its own design and manufacturing operations. This polycentric, multinational approach was part of Philips's heritage, and was attractive to NOs that had grown accustomed to functioning independently. However, the polycentric orientation was irrelevant to consumers, who were looking for value. They were getting more value from Matsushita's global strategy than from Philips's multinational strategy. Why? Matsushita's global strategy created value for consumers by lowering costs, and, in turn, prices.

As a multinational company, Philips squandered resources in a duplication of effort that led to greater product variety. Variety entailed higher costs which were passed on to consumers with no offsetting increase in consumer benefit. It is easy to understand how the right strategy resulted in Matsushita's success in the global consumer electronics industry. Since the Matsushita strategy offered greater customer value, Philips lost market share. Clearly, Philips needed a new company strategy. To meet the Japanese challenge, Philips executives consciously abandoned the polycentric, multinational approach and adopted a more geocentric orientation. A first step in this direction was to create industry groups in the Netherlands responsible for developing global strategies for R&D, marketing, and manufacturing.

Marlboro is an example of an enormously successful global brand. Targeted at urban smokers around the world, the brand appeals to the spirit of freedom, independence, and open space symbolized by the image of the cowboy in beautiful, open American western settings. Notwithstanding the tobacco industry's recent legal battle in the United States and the worldwide threat of increased regulation of tobacco advertising, Marlboro remains popular throughout the world. The need addressed by Marlboro is universal, and therefore the basic appeal and execution of its advertising and positioning are global. Altria (formerly Philip Morris), which markets Marlboro, is a global company that discovered years ago how the same basic market need can be met with a global approach.

Technology

Technology is a universal factor that crosses national and cultural boundaries. Technology is truly "stateless"; there are no cultural boundaries limiting its application. Once a technology is developed, it soon becomes available virtually everywhere in the world. This phenomenon supports Professor Levitt's prediction concerning the emergence of global markets for standardized products. In his *Harvard Business Review* article, Levitt anticipated the communication revolution that has, in fact, become a driving force behind global marketing.[33] Satellite dishes and globe-spanning TV networks such as CNN and MTV are just a few of the technology-related factors underlying the emergence of a true global village. In regional markets such as Europe, the increasing overlap of advertising across national boundaries and the mobility of consumers have created opportunities for marketers to pursue pan-European product positionings. The Internet and World Wide Web are also driving forces. As John Quelch and Lisa Klein have noted, when a company establishes a site on the Internet, it automatically becomes global, at least in terms of its potential to reach global customers with information.[34] At present, Internet usage is heaviest in the United States. Even as that situation changes, however, many constraints must still be overcome before Internet merchandise purchase transactions can become borderless.

Transportation and Communication Improvements

The time and cost barriers associated with distance have fallen tremendously over the past 100 years. The jet airplane revolutionized communication by making it possible for people to travel around the world in less than 48 hours. Tourism enables people from many countries to see and experience the newest products being sold abroad. International air travel has grown from 75 million passengers annually in 1970 to more than 400 million in 1996. One essential characteristic of the effective global business is face-to-face communication among employees and between the company and its customers. Without modern jet travel, such communication would be difficult to accomplish. Today's information technology allows airline alliance partners to sell seats on each other's flights, thereby helping travelers get from point to point more easily while boosting revenues for companies such as United Airlines and Lufthansa. Meanwhile, the cost of international telephone calls has fallen dramatically over the past several decades. That fact, plus the advent of new communication technologies such as e-mail, fax, and video teleconferencing, means that managers, executives, and customers can link up electronically from virtually any part of the world without traveling at all.

A similar revolution has occurred in transportation technology. The costs associated with physical distribution—both in terms of money and time—have been greatly reduced as well. The per-unit cost of shipping automobiles from Japan and Korea to the United States by specially designed auto-transport ships is less than the cost of overland shipping from Detroit to either U.S. coast. Another key innovation has been increased utilization of 20- and 40-foot metal containers that can be transferred from trucks to railroad cars to ships.

Product Development Costs

The pressure for globalization is intense when new products require major investments and long periods of development time. The pharmaceuticals industry provides a striking illustration of this driving force. According to the Pharmaceutical Manufacturers Association, the cost of developing a new drug in 1976 was $54 million; by 1982, the cost had increased to $87 million. By 1993, the cost of developing a new drug had reached $359 million. Such costs must be recovered in the global marketplace,

---

[33] Theodore Levitt, "The Globalization of Markets," *Harvard Business Review* (May-June, 1983), p. 92.
[34] John A. Quelch and Lisa R. Klein, "The Internet and International Marketing," *Sloan Management Review* 37, no. 3 (Spring 1996).

because no single national market is likely to be large enough to support investments of this size. Thus Merck, GlaxoSmithKline, Novartis, Bristol-Myers Squibb, Aventis, and other leading pharmaceutical companies have little choice but to engage in global marketing. As noted earlier, however, global marketing does not necessarily mean operating everywhere; in the $200 billion pharmaceutical industry, for example, seven countries account for 75 percent of sales. Similarly, in the $40 billion market for recorded music, 12 countries account for 70 percent of sales.

Quality

Global marketing strategies can generate greater revenue and greater operating margins which, in turn, support design and manufacturing quality. A global and a domestic company may each spend 5 percent of sales on research and development, but the global company may have many times the total revenue of the domestic because it serves the world market. It is easy to understand how Nissan, Matsushita, Caterpillar, and other global companies can achieve world-class quality. Global companies "raise the bar" for all competitors in an industry. When a global company establishes a benchmark in quality, competitors must quickly make their own improvements and come up to par. Global competition has forced many U.S. manufacturers to improve quality; in a 1994 survey conducted by the International Mass Retail Association, 85 percent of respondents indicated they believed that U.S.-made goods had improved in recent years. That is a significant change from 1990, when only 67 percent of those surveyed thought the quality of U.S.-made goods had improved. For truly global products, uniformity can drive down research, engineering, design, and production costs across business functions. Quality, uniformity, and cost reduction were all driving forces behind Ford's $6 billion investment in a "World Car," which is sold in the United States as the Ford Contour and Mercury Mystique and in Europe as the Mondeo. The same imperatives drove the 1998 launch of the Ford Focus in Europe; company plans call for offering the Focus in a total of 60 countries.

World Economic Trends

Economic growth has been a driving force in the expansion of the international economy and the growth of global marketing for three reasons. First, economic growth in key developing countries has created market opportunities that provide a major incentive for companies to expand globally. At the same time, slow growth in industrialized countries has compelled management to look abroad for opportunities in nations or regions with high rates of growth.

Second, economic growth has reduced resistance that might otherwise have developed in response to the entry of foreign firms into domestic economies. When a country such as China is experiencing rapid economic growth, policymakers are likely to look more favorably on outsiders. A growing country means growing markets; there is often plenty of opportunity for everyone. It is possible for a "foreign" company to enter a domestic economy and establish itself without threatening the existence of local firms. Indeed, the latter can ultimately be strengthened by the new competitive environment. Without economic growth, however, global enterprises may take business away from domestic ones. Domestic businesses are more likely to seek governmental intervention to protect their local position if markets are not growing. Predictably, the worldwide recession of the early 1990s created pressure in most countries to limit foreign access to domestic markets.

The worldwide movement toward free markets, deregulation, and privatization is a third driving force. The trend toward privatization is opening up formerly closed markets; tremendous opportunities are being created as a result. In a recent book, Daniel Yergin and Joseph Stanislaw described these trends as follows:

> It is the greatest sale in the history of the world. Governments are getting out of businesses by disposing of what amounts to trillions of dollars of assets. Everything is going—from steel plants and phone companies and electric utilities to airlines and railroads to hotels, restaurants, and nightclubs. It is happening not only in the former Soviet Union, Eastern Europe, and China but also in Western Europe, Asia, Latin America, and Africa— and in the United States.[35]

For example, when a nation's telephone company is a state monopoly, it is much easier to require it to buy only from national companies. An independent, private company will be more inclined to look for the best offer, regardless of the nationality of the supplier. Privatization of telephone systems around the world is creating huge opportunities for companies such as Lucent Technologies and Northern Telcom.

Leverage

A global company possesses the unique opportunity to develop leverage. In the context of global marketing, **leverage** means some type of advantage that a company enjoys by virtue of the fact that it has experience in more than one country. Leverage allows a company to conserve resources when pursuing opportunities in new geographical markets. In other words, leverage enables a company to expend less time, less effort, or less money. Four important types of leverage are experience transfers, scale economies, resource utilization, and global strategy.

Experience Transfers. A global company can leverage its experience in any market in the world. It can draw upon management practices, strategies, products, advertising appeals, or sales or promotional ideas that have been market-tested in one country or region and apply them in other comparable markets.

For example, ABB Inc., a giant industrial organization with 1,300 companies in 120 countries, has considerable experience with a well-tested management "model" that it transfers across national boundaries. The Zurich-based company knows that a company's headquarters can be run with a lean staff. When ABB acquired a Finnish company, it reduced the headquarters staff from 880 to 25 between 1986 to 1989. Headquarters staff at a German unit was reduced from 1,600 to 100 between 1988 to 1989. After acquiring Combustion Engineering (CE) (an American company producing powerplant boilers), ABB *knew* from experience that the headquarters staff of 800 could be drastically reduced, in spite of the fact that CE had a justification for every one of the headquarters staff positions. Similarly, Whirlpool has considerable experience in the United States dealing with powerful retail buyers such as Sears and Circuit City. The majority of European appliance retailers have plans to establish their own cross-border "power" retailing systems; as Whirlpool CEO

---

[35] Daniel Yergin and Joseph Stanislaw, *The Commanding Heights* (New York: Simon & Schuster, 1998), p. 13.

*A farm would never become a reality
for this family without the irrigation system;*

*the irrigation system would never become a reality
without electricity;*

*electricity might never become a reality
if not for the engineers of ABB.*

INGENUITY AT WORK **ABB**

David Whitwam explains, "When power retailers take hold in Europe, we will be ready for it. The skills we've developed here are directly transferable."[36]

A company in which a polycentric orientation predominates cannot take advantage of experience transfers if each national unit is run like a fiefdom and expertise does not diffuse throughout the company. This was the situation at Paris-based Cap Gemini Sogeti SA, the largest computer-services company in Europe and, along with IBM and EDS, among the top five worldwide. Although the United States accounts for two-thirds of the world market in computer services, Cap Gemini has not been among the key players. Realizing that a change was necessary, management began to transform Cap Gemini into an integrated global company capable of developing sophisticated new computer systems for customers or managing computer systems as an outside contractor. Company officials in Paris considered the ability to leverage experience critical to transforming the company.[37]

Scale Economies.   The global company can take advantage of its greater manufacturing volume to obtain traditional scale advantages within a single factory. Also, finished products can be manufactured by combining components manufactured in scale-efficient plants in different countries. Japan's giant Matsushita Electric Company is a classic example of global marketing in action; it achieved scale economies by exporting VCRs, televisions, and other consumer electronics products throughout the world from world-scale factories in Japan. The importance of manufacturing scale has diminished somewhat as companies implement flexible manufacturing techniques and invest in factories outside the home country. However, scale economies were a cornerstone of Japanese success in the 1970s and 1980s.

Leverage from scale economies is not limited to manufacturing. Just as a domestic company can achieve economies in staffing by eliminating duplicate positions

---

36   William C. Taylor and Alan M. Webber, *Going Global: Four Entrepreneurs Map the New World Marketplace* (New York: Penguin USA, 1996), p. 18.
37   E. S. Browning, "Cap Gemini Makes Another Run at the U.S. Market," *The Wall Street Journal* (October 25, 1994), p. B4.

after an acquisition, a global company can achieve the same economies on a global scale by centralizing functional activities. The larger scale of the global company also creates opportunities to improve corporate staff competence and quality.

Resource Utilization. A major strength of the global company is its ability to scan the entire world to identify people, money, and raw materials that will enable it to compete most effectively in world markets. For a global company, it is not problematic if the value of the "home" currency rises or falls dramatically, because for this company there really is no such thing as a home currency. The world is full of currencies, and a global company seeks financial resources on the best available terms. In turn, it uses them where there is the greatest opportunity to serve a need at a profit.

Global Strategy. The global company's greatest single advantage can be its global strategy. A global strategy is built on an information system that scans the world business environment to identify opportunities, trends, threats, and resources. When opportunities are identified, the global company adheres to the three principles identified earlier: It leverages its skills and focuses its resources to create superior perceived value for customers and achieve competitive advantage. *The global strategy is a design to create a winning offering on a global scale.* This takes great discipline, much creativity, and constant effort. The reward is not just success—it's survival. For years, French automaker Renault operated as a regional company. However, in an industry dominated by global competitors, chairman Louis Schweitzer had no choice but to devise a global strategy. Recent initiatives include acquiring majority stakes in Nissan Motor and Romania's Dacia; Schweitzer has also invested $1 billion in a plant in Brazil.[38] Companies that cannot formulate or successfully implement a coherent global strategy may lose their independence, as evidenced by the fortunes of Chrysler, Gerber, Helene Curtis, and others.

Restraining Forces

Despite the impact of the driving forces identified previously, several restraining forces may slow a company's efforts to engage in global marketing. In addition to the market differences discussed earlier, three important restraining forces are management myopia, organizational culture, and national controls. As we have noted, however, in today's world the driving forces predominate over the restraining forces. That is why the importance of global marketing is steadily growing.

Management Myopia and Organizational Culture

In many cases, management simply ignores opportunities to pursue global marketing. A company that is "nearsighted" and ethnocentric will not expand geographically. Myopia is also a recipe for market disaster if headquarters attempts to dictate when it should listen. Global marketing does not work without a strong local team that can provide information about local market conditions. Executives at Parker Pen once attempted to implement a top-down marketing strategy that ignored experience gained by local market representatives. Costly market failures resulted in

---

[38] John Tagliabue, "Renault Pins Its Survival on a Global Gamble," *The New York Times* (July 2, 2000), sec. 3, pp. 1, 6.

Parker's buyout by managers of the former U.K. subsidiary. Eventually, the Gillette Company acquired Parker.

In companies where subsidiary management "knows it all," there is no room for vision from the top. In companies where headquarters management is all-knowing, there is no room for local initiative or an in-depth knowledge of local needs and conditions. Executives and managers at successful global companies have learned how to integrate global vision and perspective with local market initiative and input. A striking theme emerged during interviews conducted by one of the authors with executives of successful global companies. That theme was the respect for local initiative and input by headquarters executives, and the corresponding respect for headquarters' vision by local executives.

National Controls

Every country protects the commercial interests of local enterprises by maintaining control over market access and entry in both low- and high-tech industries. Such control ranges from a monopoly controlling access to tobacco markets to national government control of broadcast, equipment, and data transmission markets. Today, tariff barriers have been largely removed in the high-income countries, thanks to the World Trade Organization (WTO), GATT, NAFTA, and other economic agreements. However, **non-tariff barriers** (NTBs) such as "Buy Local" campaigns, food safety rules, and other bureaucratic obstacles still make it difficult for companies to gain access to some individual country and regional markets.

OUTLINE OF THIS BOOK

This book has been written for students and businesspersons interested in global marketing. Throughout the book, we present and discuss important concepts and tools specifically applicable to global marketing.

The book is divided into five parts. Part I consists of Chapter 1, an overview of global marketing and the basic theory of global marketing. Chapters 2 through 6 comprise Part II, in which we cover the environments of global marketing. Chapters 2 and 3 cover economic and regional market characteristics, including the location of income and population, patterns of trade and investment, and stages of market development. In Chapter 4, social and cultural elements are examined; the legal, political, and regulatory dimensions are presented in Chapter 5. We discuss marketing information systems and research in Chapter 6.

Part III is devoted to global strategy. Chapter 7 discusses market segmentation, targeting, and positioning. Chapter 8 covers the basics of importing, exporting, and sourcing. Chapters 9 and 10 are devoted to various aspects of global strategy, including strategy alternatives for market entry and expansion, global strategic partnerships, and competitive advantage.

Part IV is devoted to global considerations pertaining to the marketing mix. The application of product, price, channel, and marketing communications decisions in response to global market opportunity and threat is covered in detail in Chapters 11 through 15.

Part V consists of one final chapter. Chapter 16 describes the organization and control of global marketing programs and examines the integrating and managerial dimensions of global marketing: planning, organization, control and the marketing audit, and strategy implementation. In the final chapter we also offer some thoughts on the future of global marketing.

SUMMARY

A company that engages in **global marketing** focuses its resources on global market opportunities and threats. Successful global marketers such as Nestlé, Coca-Cola, and Honda use familiar **marketing mix** elements—the four Ps—to create global marketing programs. Marketing, R&D, manufacturing, and other activities comprise a firm's **value chain;** firms configure these activities to create superior customer **value** on a global basis. Global companies also maintain strategic **focus** while relentlessly pursuing **competitive advantage.** The marketing mix, value chain, competitive advantage, and focus are universal in their applicability, irrespective of whether a company does business only in the home country or has a presence in many markets around the world. However, in a **global industry,** companies that fail to pursue global opportunities risk being pushed aside by stronger global competitors.

Global marketing does not necessarily mean offering identical products to consumers and organizations in all parts of the world; this issue has been widely debated during the two decades that have passed since the publication of Theodore Levitt's groundbreaking article "The Globalization of Markets." The essence of global marketing is finding the balance between a **standardized (extension) approach** to the marketing mix and a **localized (adaptation) approach** that is responsive to country or regional differences. Global marketing strategies can be based on a number of different elements, including brand names, product design, product positioning, advertising, packaging, distribution, customer service, and sourcing.

The importance of global marketing today can be seen in the company rankings compiled by *The Wall Street Journal, Fortune* magazine, *Financial Times,* and other publications. Whether ranked by revenues, market capitalization, or some other measure, most of the world's major corporations are active regionally or globally. The size of global markets for individual industries or product categories helps explain why companies "go global." Global markets for some product categories represent hundreds of billions of dollars in annual sales; other markets are much smaller. Whatever the size of the opportunity, successful industry competitors find that increasing revenues and profits means seeking markets outside the home country.

Company management can be classified in terms of its orientation toward the world: **ethnocentric, polycentric, regiocentric,** or **geocentric.** An ethnocentric orientation characterizes *domestic* and *international companies;* international companies pursue marketing opportunities outside the home market by extending various elements of the marketing mix. A polycentric world view predominates at a *multinational company,* where the marketing mix is adapted by country managers operating autonomously. Managers at *global* and *transnational companies* are regiocentric or geocentric in their orientation and pursue both extension and adaptation strategies in global markets.

Global marketing's importance today is shaped by the dynamic interplay of several driving and restraining forces. The former include market needs and wants, technology, transportation and communication improvements, product costs, quality, world economic trends, and a recognition of opportunities to develop **leverage** by operating globally. Restraining forces include market differences, management myopia, organizational culture, and national controls such as **nontariff barriers.**

DISCUSSION QUESTIONS

1. What are the basic goals of marketing? Are these goals relevant to global marketing?
2. What is meant by "global localization"? Is Coca-Cola a global product? Explain.
3. Describe some of the global marketing strategies available to companies. Give examples of companies that use the different strategies.
4. How do the global marketing strategies of Harley-Davidson and Toyota differ?
5. Describe the difference between ethnocentric, polycentric, regiocentric, and geocentric management orientations.
6. Identify and briefly describe some of the forces that have resulted in increased global integration and the growing importance of global marketing.
7. Define *leverage* and explain the different types of leverage utilized by companies with global operations.

Virtually every company mentioned in this chapter is using the Internet as a communications tool. You can learn a great deal about a company's geographic scope and marketing activities by visiting its Web site. Many companies also post their annual reports online; you can read and print them if your computer is equipped with Adobe's Acrobat software. A company's universal resource locator (URL) is often based on its name (e.g., *www.caterpillar.com*) or ini-tials (e.g., www.ibm.com). If, after a couple of tries, you are unable to locate a company's homepage, consult Hoover's (*www.hoovers.com*). You may already be familiar with the company's printed reference book, *Hoover's Handbook.* Hoover's Web site offers free Company Capsules that contain basic information including names of top executives, headquarters address, annual sales, and links to other corporate Web sites.

BUILD YOUR GLOBAL MARKETING SKILLS

Each August, *Fortune* magazine publishes its survey of the Global 500. The top-ranked companies for 2000 are shown in Table 1-3. Browse through the list and choose any company that interests you. Compare its 2000 ranking with the most recent ranking (which you can find either by referring to the print version of *Fortune* or by visiting *www.fortune.com*). How has the company's ranking changed? Consult additional sources (e.g., magazine articles, annual reports, the company's Web site) to enhance your understanding of the factors and forces that contributed to the company's move up or down in the rankings.

SUGGESTED READING

Books

Barnet, Richard J., and John Cavanaugh. *Global Dreams: Imperial Corporations and the New World Order.* New York: Simon & Schuster, 1994.

Bryan, Lowell. *Race for the World: Strategies to Build a Great Global Firm.* Boston: Harvard Business School Press, 1999.

Burtless, Gary. *Globaphobia: Confronting Fears About Global Trade.* Washington, D.C.: Brookings Institute Press, 1998.

Doremus, Paul. *The Myth of the Global Corporation.* Princeton, NJ: Princeton University Press, 1998.

Friedman, Thomas L. *The Lexus and the Olive Tree.* New York: Anchor Books, 2000.

Garten, Jeffrey. *World View: Global Strategies for the New Economy.* Cambridge, MA: Harvard University Press.

Greider, William. *One World, Ready or Not: The Manic Logic of Global Capitalism.* New York: Simon & Schuster, 1997.

Kets de Vries, Manfred F. R., and Ellizabeth Florent-Treacy. *The New Global Leaders: Richard Branson, Percy Barnevik, David Simon and the Remaking of International Business.* San Francisco: Jossey-Bass, 1999.

Micklethwait, John, and Adrian Wooldridge. *A Future Perfect: The Challenge and Hidden Promise of Globalization.* New York: Crown Publishers, 2000.

Ohmae, Kenichi. *The End of the Nation State: The Rise of Regional Economies.* New York: Free Press, 1995.

Ries, Al. *Focus: The Future of Your Company Depends on It.* New York: Harper Business, 1997.

Taylor, William C., and Alan M. Webber. *Going Global: Four Entrepreneurs Map the New World Marketplace.* New York: Penguin Books USA, 1996.

Watson, James L., ed., *Golden Arches East: McDonald's in East Asia.* Stanford, CA: Stanford University Press, 1997.

Wendt, Henry. *Global Embrace: Corporate Challenges in a Transnational World.* New York: HarperBusiness, 1993.

Yergin, Daniel, and Joseph Stanislaw. *The Commanding Heights.* New York: Simon & Schuster, 1998.

Articles

Bartlett, Christopher A., and Sumantra Ghoshal. "Going Global: Lessons from Late Movers." *Harvard Business Review* 78, no. 2 (March-April 2000), pp. 132–142.

Bassiry, G. R., and R. Hrair Dekmejian. "America's Global Companies: A Leadership Profile." *Business Horizons* 36, no. 1 (January-February 1993), pp. 47–53.

Collins, Robert S., and William A. Fischer. "American Manufacturing Competitiveness: The View from Europe." *Business Horizons* 35, no. 4 (July-August 1992), pp. 15–23.

Craig, C. Samuel, and Susan P. Douglas. "Responding to the Challenges of Global Markets: Change, Complexity, Competition, and Conscience." *Columbia Journal of World Business* 31, no. 4 (Winter 1996), pp. 6–18.

Franko, Lawrence G. "Global Corporate Competition II: Is the Large American Firm an Endangered Species?" *Business Horizons* 34, no. 6 (November-December 1991), pp. 14–22.

Halal, William E. "Global Strategic Management in a New World Order." *Business Horizons* 36, no. 6 (November-December 1993), pp. 5–10.

Hu, Tao-Su. "Global or Stateless Corporations are National Firms with International Operations." *California Management Review* 34, no. 2 (Winter 1992), pp. 107–126.

Kogut, Bruce, and Udo Zander. "Knowledge of the Firm and the Evolutionary Theory of the Multinational Corporation." *Journal of International Business Studies* 24, no. 4 (Fourth Quarter 1993), pp. 625–646.

Li, Jiatao, and Stephen Guisinger. "How Well Do Foreign Firms Compete in the United States?" *Business Horizons* 34, no. 6 (November-December 1991), pp. 49–53.

Malnight, T.W. "Globalization of an Ethnocentric Firm: An Evolutionary Perspective." *Strategic Management Journal* 16, no. 2 (February 1995), pp. 119–141.

Morrison, Allen J., David A. Ricks, and Kendall Roth. "Globalization Versus Regionalization: Which Way for the Multinational?" *Organizational Dynamics* (Winter 1991), pp. 17–29.

Prahalad, C. K., and Kenneth Lieberthal. "The End of Corporate Imperialism." *Harvard Business Review* 76, no. 4 (July-August 1998), pp. 68–79.

Rao, T. R., and G. M. Naidu. "Are the Stages of Internationalization Empirically Supportable?" *Journal of Global Marketing* 1, no. 2 (1992), pp. 147–170.

Reid, David McHardy. "Perspectives for International Marketers on the Japanese Market." *Journal of International Marketing* 3, no. 1 (1995), pp. 63–84.

Smith, Paul M., and Cynthia D. West. "The Globalization of Furniture Industries/Markets," *Journal of Global Marketing* 7, no. 3 (1994), pp. 103–132.

CASES

Case 1-1 McDonald's Expands Globally While Adjusting Its Local Recipe

McDonald's, a fast-food legend known for quality and service, is pursuing a global expansion strategy that has brought the famous golden arches to more than 120 different countries. Why go abroad when the company already has more than 13,000 restaurants in the United States and serves up 40 percent of the hamburgers that Americans consume? Indeed, in a recent issue devoted to twentieth century advertising milestones, *Advertising Age* magazine ranked McDonald's "You Deserve A Break Today" ad campaign as the fifth most popular in the last 100 years. Ronald McDonald ranked number two on *Ad Age*'s list of Top Ten Icons. However, despite such achievements in advertising and promotion, per-store operating profits in the United States have fallen in recent years, as have the percentage of U.S fast-food dollars spent at McDonald's.

Outside the United States, the picture appears brighter. While overall U.S. sales only increased by 3 percent from 1999 to 2000, sales in the Asia/Pacific region increased 10 percent. Latin American sales grew 7 percent. From 1999 to 2000, Europe posted a 3 percent decline in sales, due in large part to consumer concerns about mad cow disease. The higher overall growth outside the United States reflects, in part, changing lifestyles around the globe in which fast food plays an increasingly important role. Also, the competitive picture is different in other countries. The United States boasts 25 hamburger restaurants for every 100,000 people, but the figure is much lower elsewhere. In Japan, for example, there are only five hamburger restaurants per 100,000 people; in many European countries, the ratio is two for every 100,000 people.

McDonald's has responded by stepping up its rate of new unit openings. In 1991, the company had 3,355 units in 53 countries; by the end of 2000, more than 17,200 non-U.S. restaurants were in operation. These comprise about 57 percent of the total number of restaurants (in all, there were 30,200 units worldwide in 2000) and account for about 45 percent of sales. In dollar terms, $18.1 billion of McDonald's $40 billion in 2000 systemwide sales came from outside the United States. Over the 10-year period from 1987 to 1997, operating profits from outside the United States grew at a compound annual rate of 23.3 percent, compared with 3.5 percent in the United States (see Table 1).

ASIA-PACIFIC

McDonald's opened its first Japanese location in 1972; by 1998, the company's 2,500 locations accounted for about 50 percent of the fast-food hamburger market in Japan. Approximately 80 percent of the restaurants are company owned, with about 20 percent operated by franchisees (the ratios are reversed in the United States). Skyrocketing real estate and construction costs during the so-called bubble years of the late 1980s translated into a slow rate of new store openings. As Japan's economy cooled off in the late 1990s, McDonald's took advantage of lower costs and stepped up the pace of store openings. The company is also experimenting with new locations such as gas stations.

Among the menu items tailored to local palates are the soy-flavored Teriyaki McBurger and Chicken Tatsuta.

Table 1
McDonald's Operating Income 1993–2000 (millions)

	2000	1999	1998	1997	1996	1995	1994	1993
U.S. Operating Income	$1,773	$1,653	$1,202	$1,211	$1,144[a]	$1,252	$1,217	$1,156
Operating Income Outside the U.S.[*]	$1,725	$1,832	$1,716	$1,659	$1,541[b]	$1,397	$1,072	$ 865

[*]Excludes Canada, Africa, and the Middle East.

[a]Includes $72 million special charge.

[b]Includes $16 million asset impairment charge.

Source: Adapted from McDonald's Corporation *Annual Report*, 2000.

McDonald's marketing strategy for Japan also contains some global elements. For example, TV ads feature idealized images of family men sharing quality time with the kids while enjoying McDonald's french fries. Such scenes of family interaction are part of a global campaign that features consistent images. Even so, they have struck a responsive chord in Japan where the balance between work life and family life has become a hotly debated topic.

Despite an ongoing price war and so-so results for Wendy's, in 1997 Burger King announced plans to open 200 restaurants in Japan over a five-year period. Management acknowledged that the company has low brand recognition but hoped to use this fact as an opportunity to position itself as an upscale alternative to the golden arches. The president of Burger King Japan intends to bring the company's flame broilers out of the kitchen and put them up front where customers can see them.

In fall 1996, McDonald's opened its first restaurants in New Delhi and Mumbai. (PepsiCo beat McDonald's into India with the June 1995 opening of a Kentucky Fried Chicken restaurant in Bangalore.) The golden arches will be competing with Nirula's, a local restaurant chain with 26 outlets. Because the Hindu religion prohibits eating beef, McDonald's developed the lamb-based Maharaja Mac. To accommodate vegetarians, each restaurant has two separate food preparation areas. The "green" kitchen is devoted to vegetarian fare such as the McAloo Tikka potato burger. The meat items are prepared on the red side. Despite the company's pronouncements that as much as 98 percent of the food ingredients would be produced locally, several Hindu nationalist groups protested the first restaurant's opening. India is plagued by power shortages, and companies face restrictions to ensure that farmers, hospitals, and other institutions have enough to sustain their operations. At one point shortly after the New Delhi restaurant opened, officials at the city's power company accused McDonald's of using nearly three times more electricity than it was allotted.

China is currently home to the world's largest McDonald's. The first Chinese location opened in mid-1992 in central Beijing, a few blocks from the infamous Tiananmen Square. By mid-1995, McDonald's had 12 restaurants in the Chinese capital and 40 throughout the rest of the country. The restaurants get 95 percent of their supplies—including lettuce—from within China. Despite McDonald's 20-year lease for its central Beijing location, the company found itself in the middle of a dispute between the central government and Beijing's city government. City officials decided to build a new $1.2 billion commercial complex in the city center and demanded that McDonald's vacate the site. However, central government officials had not approved the city's plans.

McDonald's has felt the effects of the currency crisis in Asia that started in July 1997. In Indonesia, for example, where the rupiah's value fell 80 percent, the company was forced to close 14 of its 101 restaurants as a result of slow sales. An additional six restaurants were destroyed in May 1998 in rioting that led to the ouster of President Suharto. Then again, it now costs about 80 percent less to build a new restaurant, thanks to lower labor and real estate costs. McDonald's also protects itself from currency fluctuations by purchasing as much as possible from local suppliers. For example, the company's Singapore locations now buy chicken patties from Thailand rather than from the United States. However, french fries must still be imported from Australia or the United States. To help offset higher costs to consumers, McDonald's offers customers the choice of rice as a side dish at a lower price.

WESTERN EUROPE

The golden arches are a familiar sight in Europe, particularly in England, France, and Germany. The company has suffered some setbacks, however, particularly in Britain. In 1996, a public health scare linked to "mad cow disease" resulted in bans on British beef exports to continental Europe. Responding to public concerns, McDonald's immediately substituted imported beef at its British restaurants. By mid-1997, convinced that British beef was safe, McDonald's put it back on the menu. The move was applauded by Britain's beef producers, because McDonald's local meat purchases represent $50 million in annual revenues. Ironically, no sooner had the beef furor subsided than Burger King brought its aptly named Big King sandwich ("20 percent more beef than a Big Mac") to England. In 2000 and 2001, concerns over the safety of the meat supply surfaced again amid an outbreak of hoof and mouth disease and ongoing media reports about mad cow disease. The public's reduced appetite for beef was reflected in decreases in systemwide sales, revenues, and operating income for McDonald's European division in 2000.

Meanwhile, another controversy kept McDonald's in the public eye in Britain during the 1990s. The company became embroiled in a highly publicized lawsuit that eventually earned the dubious distinction as the longest-running trial in British legal history. McDonald's sued several environmental activists for defamation after they distributed pamphlets that criticized the company's food and environmental policies. The lawsuit quickly took on David and Goliath overtones. The defendants, unable to obtain legal aid, represented themselves. McDonald's, by contrast, established a legal fund of more than $16 million.

McDonald's ultimately won the battle; the judge ruled that the defendants were guilty of defamation and ordered them to pay $96,000 in damages.

CENTRAL AND EASTERN EUROPE

On January 31, 1990, after 14 years of negotiation and preparation, the first Bolshoi Mac went on sale in what was then the Soviet Union. The Moscow McDonald's is located on Pushkin Square, just a few blocks from the Kremlin. It has 700 indoor seats and another 200 outside. It boasts 800 employees and features a 70-foot counter with 27 cash registers—equivalent to 20 ordinary McDonald's rolled into one. The restaurant serves up 18,000 orders of fries, 12,000 Big Macs, and 11,000 apple pies every day. To ensure a steady supply of raw materials, the company built a huge processing facility on the outskirts of Moscow and worked closely with local farmers. Despite the turmoil stemming from the dissolution of the Soviet Union and the political upheaval in the fall of 1993, to date more than 50 million sandwiches have been sold at the Pushkin Square location. Meanwhile, two more McDonald's restaurants were opened in Moscow in 1993. By 1995, the three stores were serving a total of 70,000 customers each day. Ukraine and Belarus are among the other members of the Commonwealth of Independent States with newly opened restaurants. McDonald's has also set its sights on Central Europe, where 350 new restaurants will be opened in Croatia, Slovakia, Romania, and other countries.

"ACTING LOCAL" WITH McMENU

The menu in Moscow—where "meat and potatoes" are staples—has the same basic offerings as in the United States. In other countries, however, McDonald's has adapted its fare in response to local tastes. Fried chicken is on the menu in many Asian countries. Other offerings include banana fruit pies in Latin America, Kiwiburger (served with beet root sauce) in New Zealand, beer in Germany, McSpaghetti noodles and a sweeter Burger McDo in the Philippines, and chili sauce to go with fries in Singapore. In some countries, McDonald's changes its food preparation methods to comply with religious customs; in Singapore and Malaysia, for example, the beef that goes into Halal burgers must be slaughtered according to Muslim law.

McDonald's has occasionally stumbled in its efforts to promote fast food around the world. A poster that was displayed in dozens of Dutch restaurants in October 1991 caused a furor in France, where McDonald's first opened its doors in 1979. The poster featured a photo of five chefs examining a batch of dressed chickens; the caption indicated that the chefs were actually dreaming of Big Mac sandwiches. The poster caused an uproar for two reasons. One of the people in the photo was Paul Bocuse, a legendary three-star French chef. Also, the chickens were identified as being from a French region renowned for its poultry. All in all, the posters were not well received in the land of *haut cuisine*. In a letter of apology to Bocuse, McDonald's inadvertently made a diplomatic blunder by attributing its error in part to the fact that Bocuse is not well known in the Netherlands.

McDonald's continues to move forward with its expansion plans. McDonald's International is organized into four geographic regions: Europe, which currently accounts for about 45 percent of international sales; Asia/Pacific, with 34 percent; Latin America, with 9 percent; and Canada, Africa, and the Middle East, with 11 percent. McDonald's recent strategy included a unified global advertising campaign—a first for the company—used during the 1994 World Cup soccer playoffs. In the words of one market analyst, "McDonald's is similar to Coca-Cola ten years ago. It's on the verge of becoming an international giant, with the United States as a major market, but overseas as the driving force."

REFOCUSING ON THE U.S. MARKET

In January 1996, against this backdrop of international expansion, company executives surprised industry observers by announcing an aggressive new goal of 3,200 new restaurant openings during the year—a rate of nine per day. Despite its emphasis on opening new restaurants—or perhaps because of it—McDonald's has posted disappointing results in the key U.S. market. There have been bright spots, such as the company's wildly successful promotions featuring Teenie Beanie Babies and toys based on characters from Disney movies such as *101 Dalmatians*. For all its popularity with youngsters, however, McDonald's is struggling to increase its appeal to grown-ups. The Arch Deluxe sandwich, introduced with a $200 million promotion budget in 1996 and targeted at adults, failed to ring up big sales. The following year, a Campaign 55 promotion angered and confused some consumers who did not understand that they had to buy a drink and french fries to get a Big Mac for 55 cents. Meanwhile, "arch"-competitors Burger King and Wendy's continued to win customers in search of tastier, hotter, made-to-order fast food.

By early 1998, McDonald's ongoing woes led to a management shakeup: Chairman and CEO Michael R. Quinlan relinquished the chief executive position to

Maharaja Mac™

Entdecken Sie die köstliche Spezialität aus der Tiefsee:
McDonald's
FISCHMAC

Jack M. Greenberg, who had headed McDonald's USA. Greenberg immediately launched a new food preparation initiative called Made For You. The goal was to improve customer perceptions of the taste and freshness of menu items. The quest for new ideas to fuel growth also prompted executives to make their first forays outside the core business. In February 1998, McDonald's acquired a majority stake in the Chipotle Mexican Grill chain. The move signaled McDonald's recognition both of the increasing popularity of ethnic foods and of heightened interest among consumers in healthy eating. In 1998, McDonald's also acquired Aroma, a coffeehouse chain in London. The acquisition trend continued over the next two years as McDonald's snapped up Donatos Pizza and Boston Market, a floundering chain featuring home-style cooking. As CEO Greenberg conceded, "There are pieces of the business we can't do under the arches. When you're out with friends on a Saturday night for pizza and wine, you don't go to McDonald's." Patrons of Donatos and the other partner brands are offered no hint of the McDonald's connection. Greenberg envisions these partner brands adding at least 2 percent to McDonald's growth rate within a few years.

As Adrian J. Slywotzky, author of *Value Migration*, has noted, "McDonald's needs to move the question from 'How can we sell more hamburgers?' to 'What does our brand allow us to consider selling to our customers?'" McDonald's is addressing this key question in several different ways. It has opened a gourmet coffee shop called McCafé in downtown Chicago. It is also testing a diner concept with scores of new menu items such as meat loaf. A McTreat Spot ice cream parlor was recently opened in Houston. The biggest stretch to date, however, is the four star Golden Arch hotel that McDonald's has opened in Zurich.

The new millennium brought additional challenges that had a direct impact on McDonald's core business. As noted, continuing concern about mad cow disease in Europe has dampened diners' appetite for hamburgers and other beef items. In spring 2001, McDonald's was faced with a consumer lawsuit from diners who charged the company with "fraudulently concealing the existence of beef in their french fries." Since 1990, the company had touted its fries as being cooked in 100% vegetable oil. In response to the lawsuit, McDonald's conceded that a small amount of beef extract was added to the potatoes as they were being processed. ∎

DISCUSSION QUESTIONS

1. Does McDonald's success outside the United States provide support for Levitt's views about the global marketplace?
2. Do you think government officials in developing countries such as Russia, China, and India welcome McDonald's? Do consumers in these countries welcome McDonald's? Why or why not?
3. Assess McDonald's prospects for success beyond the burger-and-fries model. Do customers care who owns a company such as Donato's Pizza?

4. Is it realistic to expect that McDonald's—or any well-known company—can expand globally without occasionally making mistakes or generating controversy?

SOURCES: Bruce Horovitz, "McDonald's Tries a New Recipe to Revive Sales," *USA Today* (July 10, 2001), pp. 1A, 2A; Geoff Winestock and Yaroslav Trofimov, "McDonald's Reassures Italians About Beef," *The Wall Street Journal* (January 16, 2001), pp. A3, A6; Kevin Helliker and Richard Gibson, "The New Chief is Ordering Up Changes at McDonald's," *The Wall Street Journal* (August 24, 1998), pp. B1, B4; Bethan Hutton, "Fast-food Group Blows a McBubble in Slow Economy," *Financial Times* (May 8, 1998), p. 24; Bruce Horovitz, " 'My Job is Always on the Line,' " *USA Today* (March 16, 1998), p. 8B; David Leonhardt, "McDonald's: Can It Regain Its Golden Touch?" *Business Week* (March 9, 1998),

pp. 70–74+; Richard Tomkins, "When the Chips are Down," *Financial Times* (August 16, 1997), p. 13; Yumiko Ono, "Japan Warms to McDonald's Doting Dad Ads," *The Wall Street Journal* (May 8, 1997), pp. B1, B12; Norihiko Shirouzu, "Whoppers Face Entrenched Foes in Japan: Big Macs," *The Wall Street Journal* (February 4, 1997), pp. B1, B5.
The following trademarks used herein are the property of McDonald's Corporation and affiliates: Maharaja Mac, Fischmac, McDonald's, McMenu, Kiwiburger, McSpaghetti, McDo, Big Mac, Arch Deluxe, Chipotle Mexican Grill, Donatos, Boston Market, McCafe, McTreat Spot, Golden Arch Hotel, www.mcdonalds.com

Case 1-2   Acer Inc.

Despite McDonald's recent problems (see Case 1-1), the company's business model has served as a source of inspiration for Taiwan businessman Stan Shih. However, Mr. Shih is not in the fast-food business; his company, Acer Inc., manufactures and markets personal computers for the consumer and home office markets as well as chips, monitors, keyboards, CD-ROM drives, and other hardware. Just as hungry consumers will shun a restaurant that serves warmed-over food, most computer buyers want the absolute latest technology. For more than 15 years, Acer manufactured computers in Taiwan and shipped them to dealers throughout the world. By building and marketing computers under its own brand name as well as supplying Hitachi, Siemens, and other companies on an "original equipment manufacturer" (OEM) basis, Acer became Taiwan's number-one exporter. Acer's success also helped change the public's perception that "Made in Taiwan" was synonymous with cheap, low-tech products.

However, because of the fast pace of technological change in the computer industry, Acer's PCs sometimes became obsolete by the time they were shipped to their destinations. Shih realized that one of the keys to McDonald's success was the company's system of delivering beef patties, buns, and other ingredients to local restaurants, where they are assembled into sandwiches as needed. He decided to decentralize computer assembly in nearly three dozen locations around the globe and use a combination of locally purchased components plus components shipped in from Taiwan. As Shih explains, "We are providing the customer with the freshest technology at the most reasonable price."

McDonald's hasn't been Shih's only source of inspiration. When Shih first founded his company in the 1970s, it was called Multitech International Corporation. After a decade, Shih decided a name change was in order. For one thing, the original name was too long. Another problem: It didn't convey the image of technical innovation the way names like Sony, BMW, and Honda do. Shih spent two years searching for a new name; a consulting firm helped generate some 20,000 possible alternatives. From the short list of finalists, Acer was the top choice for several reasons—it means "sharp" in Latin and implies "energetic" and "capable." It also sounds like *ace*, which has a positive connotation for many people.

Once the name change had been implemented, Shih made a number of deeper changes. He developed a policy of "global brand, local touch," a break from the traditional Asian preference for hierarchical, top-down corporate structures and corporate cultures that stress deference to authority. Shih realized that hierarchies couldn't act quickly enough in the fast-moving computer industry. Now Acer is organized into strategic business units for manufacturing and regional business units for marketing. Acer's local management teams in individual country or regional markets are empowered to make decisions on a wide range of marketing mix elements. Acer America, for example, is a wholly owned subsidiary, but Marketing Vice President Marlene Williamson was afforded free rein to target the home-user market segment by distributing Acer's sleek and stylish Aspire line through the Best Buy chain.

"Local touch" also has financial ramifications: Because joint venture partners have their own investments at stake, Shih believes he can trust them to make prudent decisions. This trust has paid off handsomely. In South Africa, for example, Acer became the number-two brand by expanding during the shift from apartheid to majority rule; some competitors marked time out of fear of market volatility. In Mexico, the government's devaluation of the peso in December 1994 prompted several computer companies to cut back on marketing. Managers at Acer Computec Latinoamerica adjusted to the new financial circumstances and, within a year, Acer commanded a 30 percent share of the market.

Back in Taiwan, Shih also made fundamental changes in how his company is run. Acer's executive teams encouraged employees to speak up and share ideas without bowing their heads in deference to higher-ranking personnel. Simon Lin, the chief executive of the information products unit, explained, "Sometimes I have to keep my opinions to myself so that others will speak. You need to have different voices speak up—that's how innovation comes about. I tell our people, 'You can bring up anything that you want to discuss.'" To encourage a free exchange of ideas, Shih, Lin, and their colleagues practice "management by wandering around"; that is, they drop in on employees to exchange ideas and glean bits of information that may not be available through more formal channels. Lin says, "We come in to communicate with each other, to create a spirit of teamwork. This is part of our new way of thinking."

Shih has used a number of different approaches to build his company. A joint venture with Texas Instruments produces dynamic random-access memory chips (DRAMs) in Hsinchu, Taiwan. Acer acquired Counterpoint Computers in the United States and bought a stake in Germany's Cetec Data Technology. Acer also has built assembly plants in Australia, Britain, Germany, Japan, the Netherlands, New Zealand, the Philippines, South Korea, and the United States.

Of the regional and global issues that will have an impact on the company, perhaps the most significant is the economic crisis in Asia that began in 1997. Acer's sales in the region are likely to suffer as consumer spending falls. Then there are broader geopolitical issues involving Taiwan's relationship with China, which has long claimed sovereignty over its smaller neighbor. Taiwan lobbied to join 18 other nations in the Asia-Pacific Economic Cooperation forum. However, thanks to maneuvering by Beijing, Taiwan was allowed to join only as "Chinese Taipei." Similarly, Taiwan's hopes to join the World Trade Organization have been stymied by Beijing's insistence that mainland China become a member first. For now, Taiwan is shut out of the world's most important organization for resolving trade disputes.

Meanwhile, in the United States, Acer's market share fell from nearly 15 percent in 1995 to only 5 percent by the end of 1997. The Aspire line of home PCs failed to achieve profitability in the face of aggressive price cutting by Compaq and other competitors. Despite a $20 million advertising budget in 1996, the Acer brand name is still not nearly as well known as Compaq, Dell, Gateway, IBM, or Sony. In 1997, Acer America shifted its communication emphasis from brand image advertising to product-oriented advertising. Also, more money will be allocated to retail promotions, trade shows, and public relations communications efforts. In terms of products, Shih and marketing VP Williamson hope to achieve more success by targeting small- and medium-size businesses with a new modular desktop PC called AcerPower. Shih also acquired Texas Instrument's global computer notebook business; the deal brought an 80-person sales force on board.

Despite these setbacks and challenges, Shih continues to set ambitious goals for his company. One goal was to be the fifth-largest computer company by the turn of the century; by mid-1998, Acer already ranked number eight. To position Acer for the next century, Shih envisions a corporate structure that he calls "21 in 21." Shih intends to break up Acer into a borderless network of 21 independent companies that maintain close ties with Taipei. *Fortune* magazine described Shih's vision as "a global federation of highly autonomous Acer companies." "Eventually," Shih said in 1995, "Acer will have a majority of local ownership in each country, and no one will be able to say that we are a Taiwanese company."

The problems in the U.S. market, however, may make it more difficult to reach $15 billion in sales by 2010. Shih still aspires to challenge Japan's dominance in the consumer electronics industry. To achieve these goals, Shih hopes to move beyond PCs and attain leadership in next-generation low-priced "information appliances." One new product is the AcerBasic, a computer that provides Internet access when hooked up to a television set. By competing in this segment, Acer will come face-to-face with a new set of competitors, such as marketing heavyweight Sony. Some industry observers believe that Shih should concentrate on supplying PCs to other companies. Shih maintains, "Brand is critical to our long-term success." Some industry observers disagree; as one analyst noted, "Brand name doesn't bring investors any benefit." He advises Stan Shih to give up his dream of becoming a global brand. To be blunt, the analyst said, "I'd pull the plug." ∎

DISCUSSION QUESTIONS

1. How would you classify Acer in terms of the stages of development described in Chapter 1?
2. Assess the market potential for Acer's new lines, including children's computers, "information appliances," and video game players.
3. Can you think of any risks associated with Shih's vision of "21 in 21"?
4. Advise Shih on global marketing strategy. Should Acer continue its quest to establish Acer as a global consumer brand, or pull the plug and focus on being a top-tier supplier to global brand marketers?

Visit the Web site
www.acer.com

SOURCES: Jonathan Moore and Peter Burrows, "A New Attack Plan for Acer America," *Business Week* (December 8, 1997), pp. 82–83; Bradley Johnson, "Struggling Acer Exits Branding," *Advertising Age* (April 7, 1997), p. 19; Richard Halloran, "Parallel Lives," *World Business* (November-December 1996), pp. 24–29; Emily Thornton, "The Reckoning," *Far Eastern Economic Review* (July 25, 1996), pp. 74–76; Pete Engardio and Peter Burrows, "Acer: A Global Powerhouse," *Business Week* (July 1, 1996), pp. 94–96; Dan Shapiro, "Ronald McDonald, Meet Stan Shih," *Sales & Marketing Management* (November 1995), pp. 85–86+; Louis Kraar, "Acer's Edge: PCs to Go," *Fortune* (October 30, 1995), pp. 187–188+.

The 18 Guiding Principles of the Marketing Company

INTRODUCTION
The Marketing Company

Welcome to the global marketplace! Regardless of size, profit, and market strength, every company on the earth has entered a new era of competition.

The change drivers such as technology, economy, and market conditions have increasingly redefined almost every sector of industries, and the way we do business. The advance of information technology has transformed the marketplace; it has provided industry players a vast array of alternatives to compete more strategically and forcefully.

The dynamic change of economic and social conditions have revolutionized consumer behavior and attitudes. With a dizzying array of product choices in the marketplace, consumers, to the highest degree, have more demanding expectations than ever before. They do not just expect a high-quality product; product quality has become a norm and requirement. This new breed of consumers wants high product quality with an affordable price within their convenient reach.

The traditional strategy that brought companies successes will lose applicability in this new marketplace. The conventional disciplines that guaranteed market leadership during the past years will lose their adaptability. In order to survive in this new marketplace, companies need a new set of strategies and tools. They need a set of guiding principles that will create a sustainable competitive advantage. They need to become a new breed of company: the Marketing Company!

What is the Marketing Company? As you will soon explore the characters of the company in the following pages, it is not just a marketing-oriented company. The Marketing Company is not just a market-driven company. The Marketing Company is an organization that adopts the 18 Guiding Principles of the Marketing Company as its credo—as its guiding values, its principles to compete in the new marketplace. It endures **external and internal change drivers, more demanding customers, and even fiercer competitors.** After all, a new competition needs a different kind of rules and principles to survive and win the race. *Be ready to rewrite your credo or your company will die!*

Principle #1—The Principle of the Company: Marketing Is a Strategic Business Concept

This principle is the first foundation of the Marketing Company. In the chaotic marketplace in the global economy era, the traditional concept of marketing has lost its adaptability in market competition. As companies are squeezed by external change drivers such as technology, economy, and market—and as they face internal organizational changes within themselves (shareholders, people, and organization culture)—marketing is no longer about selling, advertising, or even the 4Ps introduced by Jerome McCarthy.

Marketing should become the *strategic business concept* within corporations. It is no longer functional tasks and responsibilities carried by a department. Marketing is strategic because it should be *formulated by top-level management, long-term oriented, navigate a company's direction,* and *hold the responsibilities of creating loyal business customers* (*internal, external, and investor customers*).

Al Ries, in his book, *Focus,* says that, "A good Chief Executive Officer should also be a Chief Marketing Officer." David Packard, a cofounder of Hewlett-Packard, once said that "Marketing is too important for a marketing department." Peter Drucker long ago envisioned that: "Business has only two basic functions: marketing and innovation. Marketing and innovation produce results; the rest are cost!"

Admittedly, their statements are definitely true. In other words, they agree with this first principle: *Marketing is a strategic business concept.*

Principle #2—The Principle of the Community: Marketing Is Everyone's Business

This principle is the second foundation of the Marketing Company. Within a Marketing Company, marketing should be adopted as a strategic business concept. In the company, ideally, the organization structure is almost flat and layerless. There is even no marketing department and function in the Marketing Company because marketing is not a department, and marketing as a department is becoming weaker. *Therefore, all departments are marketing departments, and all functions are marketing functions.*

All people within the Marketing Company form a community, called a *marketing community.* So in the community *everyone is a marketer,* meaning that the responsibilities and tasks of acquiring, satisfying, and retaining customers lie on the shoulders of everyone. Regardless of what level and department a person works in, he/she should be involved in the process of retaining customers.

New roles such as Accounting–Marketer, Operations–Marketer, R&D–Marketer, Janitor–Marketer, Maintenance–Marketer, and the like will be emerging as this principle is instilled in the Marketing Company. While their jobs will not be exactly similar, the responsibility to create customer loyalty becomes the central theme of their work.

Thus, everyone led by the Chief Executive Officer (acting as Chief Marketing Officer) of the company, should march in the same direction. They should carry a similar mission: It is the responsibility of everyone to attract, satisfy, and retain customers. *Everyone is a marketer, whatever his/her job description is.*

Principle #3—The Principle of Competition: Marketing War Is About Value War

This principle is the third foundation of the Marketing Company. The Marketing Company does not pursue short-term profits; it creates customer value for long-term relationships. Unfortunately, the company's principle does not parallel with stockholders' short-term orientation in stock exchange institutions. While they rely upon companies' quarterly financial reports to buy and sell stocks, the Marketing Company looks beyond this short-term time frame for result.

The company regards profit as short term and value creation as long term. By continuously and consistently creating customer value, the Marketing Company will generate profits. Hence, profit follows value. This is because marketing war is not merely marketing war. Marketing war is value war.

While value is defined as total get (customer benefits) divided by total give (customer expenses), there are five value-creating formula alternatives to win competition. First, increase benefits and lower expenses. Second, increase benefits and hold expenses constant. Third, hold benefits constant and lower expenses. Fourth, increase benefits significantly and increase expenses. Fifth, lower benefits and significantly lower expenses.

Though the value impact among the formula alternatives varies significantly, the core idea behind the principle remains unchanged: Value is the key to winning and keeping customers. *Therefore, improve customer value to win the marketing war.*

Principle #4—The Principle of Retention: Concentrate on Loyalty, Not Just on Satisfaction

In addition to the three previous founding principles, the Marketing Company concentrates on loyalty, not just on satisfaction.

As marketing war becomes value war and as industry competition becomes value competition, it is inadequate for the Marketing Company to concentrate merely on customer satisfaction. The ultimate objective of the Marketing Company should be customer loyalty.

As we enter the *era of choices,* there is no guarantee that satisfied customers will become loyal customers. Satisfaction has increasingly become a commodity. It is only the process, not the end result. The final goal of the Marketing Company is customer loyalty. *Customer loyalty has become the moving target* every Marketing Company must pursue to remain competitive. What matters most to the Marketing Company is now the *quality of profit, not just the quantity of profit.* It is already evident that customer attraction activities cost a company much more than a customer retention program; the cost to acquire a new customer will cost more than retaining one good customer. Profits, therefore, should come more from old, existing customers than from new, first-time buyers.

A company's profit record, accordingly, provides an insight on the level of customer loyalty. As customer attraction, customer satisfaction, and customer retention will become an endless process of company survival, the ultimate effort of the Marketing Company should remain clear: *Concentrate on loyalty, not just on satisfaction.*

Principle #5—The Principle of Integration: Concentrate on Differences, Not Just on Averages

The Marketing Company concentrates on differences, not just averages.

In order for the Marketing Company to create the loyal customer base mentioned in the first topping principle, it has to concentrate on customers individually. The principle commands the company to build intimate relationships with customers—intimate enough to learn about customers' needs and wants; close enough to understand customers' expectations. In the chaotic competitive setting, every customer will become unique.

Underlying this principle is a profound fact that *all customers are not created equal.* Many companies are tempted to think that their customers have roughly similar needs and wants. This dangerous assumption, however, will lead them to create mediocre and average offers for their diversified customers.

The principle emphasizes that by no means are customers equal. *They are uniquely different and their needs are distinctively diversified.* In other words, *there are no average customers.* The Marketing Company, as a result, has to integrate itself with customers to create a bonding that produces a vivid picture about customers' needs, wants, and expectations.

There are no average customers. *In order to build customer loyalty, a company has to concentrate on differences, not just on averages.*

Principle #6—The Principle of Anticipation: Concentrate on Proactivity, Not Just on Reactivity

The Marketing Company concentrates on proactivity, not just reactivity.

To fully integrate with customers, as described in the second topping principle, the Marketing Company should be ready for change. It has to be adaptive to the current state of industry. It even should anticipate any change and be proactive in coping with the change.

Stephen Covey, in his landmark book, *The Seven Habits of Highly Effective People,* defines *proactivity* as *responsibility.* In this context, responsibility means the ability of an organization to choose responses within a given circumstance and environment. Between a stimulus and a response, there is a gap. It is the gap of freedom to react, freedom to choose a response.

Thus, to be competitive, a company has to be ready for change in its environment. It has to be able to anticipate change of technology, economy, and markets. It has to be proactive to operate in an uncertain and unpredictable environment. To be fluid and dynamic operationally, the Marketing Company concentrates on proactivity, not just reactivity. Be a *change agent, change driver,* or even *change surpriser* to your competitors.

Principle #7—The Principle of Brand: Avoid the Commodity-Like Trap

This is the first value-creating principle of the Marketing Company. To the company, brand is not just a name, nor is it a logo and symbols. Brand is the *value indicator* of the Marketing Company. It is the umbrella that represents the product or service, companies, persons, or even countries. It is determined by the company's new product development, customer satisfaction and retention, and value-chain management.

It is the equity of the firm that adds value to products and services it offers. It is an asset that creates value

to consumers by enhancing satisfaction and recognition of quality. With brand, the company is able to liberate itself from the supply–demand curve.

When the firm successfully liberates itself from the supply–demand curve, the price of the firm's offers will not be dependent on the price equilibrium point. The firm, as a result, is able to be the *price maker, not price taker.*

Unfortunately, macroeconomists, to a certain extent, do not realize the power of brand. They view economy from a global perspective and derive numbers from a macro point of view. This ignores the most crucial element of a price driver: brand.

It is brand that determines a price. It is brand that liberates the company to create values for internal customers, external customers, and investor customers. It is brand that indicates a value of the firm's products and services. Therefore, use, build, and protect your brand. *It is the brand that will enable the company to avoid the commodity-like trap.*

Principle #8—The Principle of Service: Avoid the Business-Category Trap

This is the second value-creating principle of the Marketing Company. To the company, service is not just after-sales service, before-sales service, or even during-sales service. Service is not customer toll-free numbers, maintenance service, or customer service. Service is a *value enhancer* of the Marketing Company. It is the paradigm of the company to create a lasting value to customers through products (small "p") and services (small "s"). Service in this principle refers to service with a big "S," not a small "s." It is the answer to Peter Drucker's question: "What business are you in?" The only answer to the question is: "We are in the service business!" There is only one business category: service. Why? It is because *service means solution.* Companies must give the true solution to customers.

Whether the company's business is a restaurant, hotel, or shoe manufacturing, the only category for all businesses must become a service business. To become a real service company, a firm has to continuously enhance the small "p" and the small "s." To create a long-lasting value and build relationships with customers, the firm's offers should provide constant value to customers. Therefore, a CEO acting as CMO has the key role between *corporate governance* and *corporate management* to create, maintain, and even develop this sense of service throughout the whole organization.

In this sense, service is a paradigm. It is the spirit of the company. It is the attitude to sustain and win tomorrow's competition. *It is the strategy to avoid the business-category trap.*

Principle #9—The Principle of Process: Avoid the Function-Orientation Trap

This is the third value-creating principle of the Marketing Company. It refers to the process of creating value to customers. It reflects the product quality, cost, and delivery of a company to customers. It is the *value enabler* of a company.

The principle commands the company to be the captain of supply-chain process. It should manage the supply-chain process, from raw materials to finished products, in a way that would enhance value-creating activities and reduce and eliminate value-eroding activities within the company.

In addition, it requires a firm to be *the hub of network organizations* where it could establish relationships with organizations that have the potential to add value. The renowned term for this is *strategic alliance*. These partnering organizations may be the company's suppliers, customers, or even competitors. Benchmarking, reengineering, outsourcing, merger, and acquisition are examples of strategic actions to improve process.

The value-creating drivers such as brand, service, and process (as the value enabler) should not only create value to external customers and investor customers, but also become the credo of internal customers, who are people. People within the organization should be marketers. They should avoid functional arrogance within the company because everyone holds a similar belief: Customer value is the end result, not titles and job positions in the company. *Brand, service, and process as three value-creating principles are drivers to win the heart share of customers.*

Principle #10—The Principle of Segmentation: View Your Market Creatively

Another crucial part of a company: marketing strategy. The strategy comprises three elements, namely segmentation, targeting, and positioning. Together they are *drivers to win shares of customers.*

The first element of marketing strategy is Segmentation. A typical definition of segmentation is the process of segmenting or partitioning the market into several segments. However, segmentation to us is about *viewing a market creatively*. It is about mapping a market into several categories by gathering similar behavior of consumers into a segment. It is the *mapping strategy* of a company.

Segmentation is an art to identify and pinpoint opportunity emerging in the markets. At the same time, it is a science to view the market based on *geographic,* *demographic, psychographic,* and *behavior* variables or even a *segment of one*. Whatever segmentation variables are used, please make sure that each person in a segment has similar behavior, especially in purchasing, using, or servicing the products.

The Marketing Company should be creative enough to view a market from a unique angle. It also has to clearly identify the market from an advanced perspective, using segmentation variables. Segmentation is the first marketing strategy element. It is the initial step that determines the life of the company. *Market opportunities are in the eyes of the beholder. In order to exploit the opportunity arising in the market, that beholder must first view the market creatively.*

Principle #11—The Principle of Targeting: Allocate Your Resources Effectively

The second element of marketing strategy is *targeting*. By the traditional definition, targeting is the process of selecting the right target market for a company's products and services. We, however, define targeting as the strategy to *allocate the company's resources effectively*. Why? Because resources are always limited. It is about how to fit the company within a selected target market segment. Hence, we call it the *fitting strategy of a company*.

There are several criteria used to select an appropriate market segment for the company's resources. The first criterion is market size. The company has to select the market segment that has "good" size to generate expected financial returns. The bigger the market size, the more lucrative the segment is to the company.

The second criterion used to choose market segment is growth. The potential growth of a market segment is a crucial attribute for the company. The better and higher the growth is, the more promising the market segment to the company.

The third criterion is competitive advantage. Competitive advantage is a way to measure whether the company has such strength and expertise to dominate the chosen market segment.

The fourth criterion is competitive situation. The company has to consider the competition intensity within the industry including the number of players, suppliers, and entry barriers. Using these main criteria, the company has to find its "fit" with the right market segment.

Principle #12—The Principle of Positioning: Lead Your Customers Credibly

The third element of marketing strategy is *positioning*. By the traditional definition, positioning is the strategy to occupy the consumers' minds with our company's offerings. In this principle, however, we define positioning as the strategy to *lead the company's customers credibly*. It is about how to establish trustworthiness, confidence, and competence for customers. If the company has those elements, customers will then have the "being" of the company or product within their minds. Therefore, positioning is about the *being strategy* of the company or product in the customers' minds. It is about earning customers' trust to make them willingly follow the company.

Yoram Wind, a marketing strategy professor, defines positioning as *the reason for being*. He advocates that positioning is about defining the company's identity and personality in the customers' minds. As we move toward the era of choices, the company can no longer force customers to buy their products; they no longer can manage the customers. In this era, the company should have credibility in the minds of customers. Because customers cannot be managed, they have to be led. In order to successfully lead customers, companies have to have credibility. So positioning is not just about persuading and creating image in the consumers' minds, it is about earning consumers' trust. It is about *the quest of trustworthiness. It is about creating a being in the consumers' minds and leading them credibly.*

Principle #13—The Principle of Differentiation: Integrate Your Content, Context, and Infrastructure

The first element of marketing tactics is *differentiation*. Traditionally, differentiation is the act of designing a set of meaningful differences in the company's offers. To us, this definition by Philip Kotler is still valid. We define differentiation as "integrating the content, context, and infrastructure of our offers to customers." Different products are the core tactic of the company to support its positioning. Differentiation, therefore, is the *core tactic* of the Marketing Company.

As the first marketing tactic element, differentiation should create a truly different and unique product for customers. The product not only has to be perceived differently by customers (positioning), it has to be really different in content, context, and infrastructure (differentiation).

A company can ideally create a unique offer by concentrating on three aspects of differentiation: *content, context,* and *infrastructure*. Content (what to offer) is the core benefit of the product itself. Context (how to offer), in addition, refers to the way the company offers the product. Infrastructure (enabler) is the technology, facilities, and people used to create the content and context.

When positioning strategy is not supported by differentiation, the company may overpromise and underdeliver to customers, which could ruin the company's

brand and reputation. On the other hand, if the positioning is supported by differentiation, the company will establish *strong brand integrity*. It means the brand image in the consumers' minds is similar to brand identity communicated by companies.

Principle #14—The Principle of Marketing Mix: Integrate Your Offer, Logistics, and Communications

The second element of marketing tactics is *marketing mix*. To many practitioners, this is considered as the whole marketing concept. The 4Ps (product, price, place, promotion), initially introduced by Jerome McCarthy, is often thought of as the complete marketing principle. To us, marketing mix is only an element of marketing tactic. It is also the tip of an iceberg—the most visible part of the company in the market.

The marketing mix, to us, is about *integrating the company's offers, logistics, and communications*. The company's offers, consisting of products and prices, should well be integrated with logistics (including channel distribution) and communications to create a powerful marketing force in the marketplace. Therefore, we call it the *creation tactic* of the company. Why? Because marketing mix has to be the creation of content–context–infrastructure differentiation. There are three types of marketing mix in the market. First is *destructive marketing mix*. It is marketing mix that does not add customer value and does not build company's brand. Second is *me-too marketing mix*. It is marketing mix that often imitates other existing marketing mix from other players in an industry. Third is *creative marketing mix*. It is the marketing mix that supports the marketing strategy (segmentation–targeting–positioning) and other marketing tactic principles (differentiation–selling) of the company and builds marketing value (brand–service–process).

Principle #15—The Principle of Selling: Integrate Your Company, Customers, and Relationships

The last element of marketing tactics is *selling*. The principle of selling does not refer to personal selling at all, nor is it related to the activities of selling products to customers. What we mean by selling is "the tactic to create long-term relationship with customers through company's products." It is the tactic to *integrate company, customers, and relationships.*

After developing marketing strategy and creating marketing mix, the company should be able to generate financial returns through selling. Thus, it is the *capture tactic* of the company. There are three main levels of selling: feature selling, benefit selling, and solution selling. As the choice of products in the marketplace overwhelm customers, companies have to sell solutions to customers, not just features and benefits. There is a relevant framework called *customer bonding* that emphasizes the importance of this principle. In the concept, customers have to go through five steps, from consumers to loyalists, as follows: awareness–identity–relationship–community–advocacy.

Hence, consumers should be made aware of our products and drive them to become advocacies. The principle of differentiation, marketing mix, and selling are *drivers to win the market share*.

Principle #16—The Principle of Totality: Balance Your Strategy, Tactics, and Value

After focusing on the nine core elements of marketing (segmentation, targeting, positioning, differentiation, marketing mix, selling, brand, service, and process) individually, in the implementation, the Marketing Company should be able to balance those elements operationally as well as strategically. The Marketing Company should be able to balance the strategy, tactic, and value in the implementation. Marketing strategy is about how to win *the mind share*. Marketing tactic is about how to win *the market share*. Marketing value is about how to win *the heart share*. Together, they will win the mind, heart, and market shares.

As the business environment changes dynamically, the strategy, tactic, and value of the company may not be as precise as when it was developed. The maneuvers of competitors, the revolution of technology, and the changes in consumer behavior will require the company to adjust and readjust the strategy, tactic, and value. It demands the company to align strategy, tactic, and value to adapt to the most current business environment. The dynamic business environment will necessitate the company to constantly monitor or review the balance of strategy, tactic, and value; to build the totality of the business. The Marketing Company should also *balance the time allocation* in strategy, tactic, and value activities.

Principle #17—The Principle of Agility: Integrate Your What, Why, and How

To operate in a competitive, dynamic environment, where technology, consumer behavior, and competitor movement change in a chaotic pattern, a company has to be agile to survive. The question, then, is, *"What does it take to be agile?"*

In this principle, an agile company continually engages in three main activities: First, it constantly monitors the competitors' movement and consumer behavior (what). It has marketing intelligence and information systems to take a picture of the business environment. Second, it continuously uses and analyzes the information gathered from the first activity to get a useful insight about the environment (why). Third, the gathered and analyzed information is incorporated in its strategy and tactic development process (how).

To put it simply, an agile company monitors, scans, and reviews the business environment continually. It analyzes the information and uses it to respond and pre-empt the competitor movement.

This principle will allow the company to be informed about the changes in the marketplace. This principle will allow the company to be not just a change agent and a change driver, but also a *change surpriser*. A change surpriser is a company who is agile. It is the organization that can balance what, why, and how. Balance your time allocation on what–why–how activities in the implementation.

Principle #18—The Principle of Utility: Integrate Your Present, Future, and Gap

The Marketing Company does not just create profit for today and lose tomorrow. It does not just think about tomorrow and forget about today. The Marketing Company knows exactly the utility to integrate the present, future, and gap.

Together with the principles of totality and agility, utility is *the driver to win the activity share*, which is important, as mentioned by Michael Porter in one of his writings in *Harvard Business Review*. In the implementation, finally, the Marketing Company can successfully balance present activities, future activities, and gap activities.

Present activities are about today's products, which create profit by servicing today's customers. Future activities, meanwhile, are about developing tomorrow's products, which create sustainable growth by servicing tomorrow's different customers.

Gap activities are about enhancing capabilities of the technology and people, internally and externally, or by creating a strategic alliance or merger and acquisition in order to create future's activities.

Living by this principle, the company can maintain its competitiveness today and tomorrow and pursue whatever it lacks (the gap) to stay competitive in the present and future.

FINAL THOUGHT
The Company Making

Throughout this writing, we have learned about the new principles of marketing. It is not just a set of static principles. It is a set of dynamic, guiding principles of the Marketing Company.

The 18 principles are organized around six dimensions—Foundation, Topping, Strategy, Tactic, Value, and

Figure 1A.1
Strategy, Tactic,
and Value Model

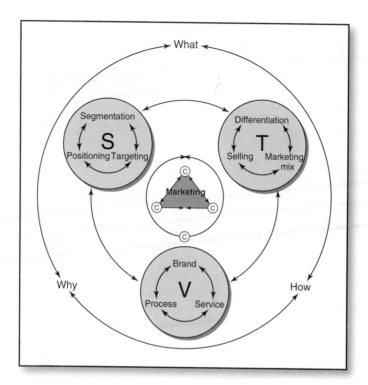

Implementation—in which each dimension contains three principles.

Using these principles, a company's transformation from production oriented, selling oriented, marketing oriented, and market driven to a customer-driven company should be clearly guided along the way to become the Marketing Company.

The making of the Marketing Company involves strategic processes and steps as follows: The company should conduct an internal and external marketing audit. The results of the audit will produce what we call CAP (company alignment profile) and CSP (competitive setting profile). The gap between CAP and CSP portrays what the company should do.

In addition, the Marketing Company should adopt the 18 Guiding Principles as the corporate guiding credo and value that determine how it should act and react in the marketplace. The set of principles should become the guidance, culture, and foundation to live by.

Furthermore, the Marketing Company should be navigated by top management or a CEO (Chief Executive Officer) who acts as a CMO (Chief Marketing Officer). How the company behaves in the marketplace—and which direction it should take—must be decided by the top management based on the gap.

One final word: *The Marketing Company is not a destination.* It is not a goal or objective. Becoming the Marketing Company is a *process.* It is the never-ending pursuit of excellence. It is a *moving target* every company should pursue if it wants to survive and become competitive.

The Anatomy of Marketing

Many people who come to the subject of marketing with little or no business experiences think of it as a study of selling. Those who already have extensive professional experience or have undergone intensive academic training regard marketing as marketing mix. We at MarkPlus define marketing with three strategic dimensions: marketing strategy, marketing tactic, and marketing value (STV). The integrated concept of marketing is illustrated in Figure 1A.1.

In the global marketplace of the new millennium, marketing should be redefined to reflect the increasingly intensified competition in almost every sector of industries.

Marketing Strategy: How to Win the Mind Share

Marketing strategy is the first dimension in the marketing concept. Its role is to *win the mind share* of consumers. Because of its strategic importance, it is in the Strategic Business Unit (SBU) level of a company.

The first element of marketing strategy is segmentation. Segmentation is defined as a way to view a market creatively. We call it the *mapping strategy* of a company.

After the market is mapped and segmented into groups of potential customers with similar characteristics and behavior, the company needs to select which segments to enter. This act is called *targeting*, which is the second element of the marketing strategy. Targeting is defined as a way to allocate company's resources effectively—by selecting the right target market. We also define it as a company's *fitting strategy*.

The 18 Guiding Principles of the Marketing Company
Rewrite your credo or your company will die.

1. **The Principle of the Company** Marketing Is a Strategic Business Concept
2. **The Principle of the Community** Marketing Is Everyone's Business
3. **The Principle of Competition** Marketing War Is about Value War
4. **The Principle of Retention** Concentrate on Loyalty, Not Just on Satisfaction
5. **The Principle of Integration** Concentrate on Differences, Not Just on Averages
6. **The Principle of Anticipation** Concentrate on Proactivity, Not Just on Reactivity
7. **The Principle of Brand** Avoid the Commodity-like Trap
8. **The Principle of Service** Avoid the Business-Category Trap
9. **The Principle of Process** Avoid the Function-Orientation Trap
10. **The Principle of Segmentation** View Your Market Creatively
11. **The Principle of Targeting** Allocate Your Resources Effectively
12. **The Principle of Positioning** Lead Your Customers Credibly
13. **The Principle of Differentiation** Integrate Your Content, Context, and Infrastructure
14. **The Principle of the Marketing Mix** Integrate Your Offer, Logistics, and Communications
15. **The Principle of Selling** Integrate Your Company, Customers, and Relationships
16. **The Principle of Totality** Balance Your Strategy, Tactic, and Value
17. **The Principle of Agility** Balance Your What, Why, and How
18. **The Principle of Utility** Balance Your Present, Future, and Gap

The last element of strategy is *positioning*. Positioning is defined as a way to lead customers credibly. We call it the *being strategy* of a company. After mapping the market and fitting the company's resources into its selected market segment, a company has to define its *being* in the mind of the target market—in order to have a credible position in their minds.

Marketing Tactic: How to Win the Market Share

The second dimension of *The STV Model* is marketing tactic. Marketing tactic, because of its role, is regarded as elements to *win the market share*. Whereas marketing strategy is in the SBU level, marketing tactics occur in the operational level.

The first element of marketing tactic is differentiation. Differentiation is the *core tactic* to differentiate the content, context, and infrastructure of a company's offers to the target markets. Meanwhile, we call marketing mix a *creation tactic*, which integrates a company's offer, logistics, and communications. Selling, furthermore, is the third element of marketing tactic, which we define as the *capture tactic* to generate cash inflows for the company and to integrate the customer and company in a long-term, satisfying relationship.

Marketing Value: How to Win the Heart Share

Marketing value is the last dimension of *The STV Model*. It is the corporate-level responsibility and is intended to *win the heart share* of target markets.

The first element of marketing value is brand. Brand is the *value indicator* of a company, which enables the company to avoid the commodity trap. Service is the second element of marketing. It is the paradigm of a company to always meet or exceed the customers' needs, wants, and expectations. We define it as the *value enhancer* of a company.

The last element of marketing value is process. It is the *value enabler* of a company that enables it to deliver value to customers through the process within and without the firm.

DISCUSSION QUESTIONS

1. What do you think of The 18 Guiding Principles of the Marketing Company? How do these principles compare to the marketing concepts and principles that you learned in your basic marketing course or that you have acquired through your experience as a marketer?
2. Hermawan Kartajaya is an Asian marketer. Do his 18 Guiding Principles apply in your country? Is marketing a universal discipline? Do the marketing concepts, tools, and methods that are used in a home country need to be modified or changed when used in other countries? Explain your answer.
3. What, in your view, are the key principles of marketing? List your principles (no more than six), and explain their importance to marketing success.

Chapter 2

The Global Economic Environment

The term "tiger" has frequently been used to describe fast-growing economies in Asia. For years, Hong Kong, Singapore, Taiwan, and South Korea were considered tigers because they posted double-digit rates of economic growth. As the decade of the 1990s came to an end, however, the Asian "economic miracle" had given way to hard times. Concurrently, some observers began calling Ireland the "Celtic Tiger." Riding the wave of the technology boom of the late 1990s, Ireland's economy grew at an annual rate of 9.6 percent. Lured by low corporate tax rates and a skilled work force, companies from the United States, the United Kingdom, Germany, and Japan established subsidiaries in Ireland. The country best known for exports such as Waterford crystal, Guinness stout, Riverdance, and U2 had been transformed into a preferred location for high-tech manufacturing. More than 500 U.S. companies created tens of thousands of jobs as Intel, Motorola, and Gateway built factories to keep pace with burgeoning global demand for personal computers and other high-tech products. Before long, however, there were signs that Ireland's economic bubble might burst. The country's infrastructure was showing signs of stress, labor was in short supply, and inflation soared. By mid-2000, the pot of gold at the end of the rainbow gave way to gray and gloom. As the global economy slowed down and the technology sector slumped, the impact on Ireland was immediate. Exports fell as foreign companies severely curtailed operations in Ireland or even closed down altogether.

The rise of Ireland's economy in the 1990s and its subsequent leveling off in the first years of the new millennium vividly illustrate globalization's impact around the world. Recall the basic definition of a **market**: people or organizations with needs and wants and both the willingness and ability to buy or sell. As noted in Chapter 1, many companies engage in global marketing in an effort to reach new customers

47

When he's not fronting the world's greatest rock band, U2's Bono promotes debt cancellation for developing countries as a means of fostering sound economic policies. Noting that Africa owes about $227 billion to Western creditors, Bono has urged politicians in wealthy countries to recognize that "the money lenders have gone too far." Bono has also taken up the cause of alleviating the AIDS epidemic in Africa.

outside the home country and thereby increase sales, profits, and market share. This chapter will identify the most salient characteristics of the world economic environment, starting with an overview of the world economy, a survey of economic system types, a discussion of stages of market development, and balance of payments. Foreign exchange is discussed in the appendix at the end of the chapter.

THE WORLD ECONOMY—AN OVERVIEW

The world economy has changed profoundly since World War II.[1] Perhaps the most fundamental change is the emergence of global markets; responding to new opportunities, global competitors have steadily displaced or absorbed local ones.

---

1   See Peter F. Drucker's excellent article "The Changed World Economy," *Foreign Affairs* (Spring 1986), and various issues of *Economist*. For example, "The European Community—Survey," *The Economist* (July 11, 1992). See also Lowell Bryan et. al., *Race for the World: Strategies to Build a Great Global Firm* (Boston: Harvard Business School Press, 1999).

Concurrently, the integration of the world economy has increased significantly. Economic integration stood at 10 percent at the beginning of the twentieth century; today, it is approximately 50 percent. Integration is particularly striking in two regions, the European Union (EU) and the North American Free Trade Area.

Just 30 years ago, the world was far less integrated than it is today.[2] As evidence of the changes that have taken place, consider the automobile. Cars with European nameplates such as Renault, Citroen, Peugeot, Morris, Volvo, and others were radically different from the American Chevrolet, Ford, or Plymouth, or Japanese models from Toyota or Nissan. These were local cars built by local companies, mostly destined for local or regional markets. Even today, global and regional auto companies make cars for their home markets that would not be marketable in North America, and vice versa, but it is also true that the world car is a reality for Toyota, Nissan, Honda, and Ford. Product changes reflect organizational changes as well: The world's largest automakers have, for the most part, evolved into global companies. At Ford Motor Company, for example, change is reflected in the Ford 2000 restructuring plan announced in the mid-1990s. Ford 2000 represented a dramatic rethinking in the way the company designs and manufactures cars; the fact that former CEO Jacques Nasser altered some key elements of the program during his tenure illustrates that globalization is a process to which companies must continually adapt.

Within the past decade, there have been several remarkable changes in the world economy. Organizations stand a better chance of achieving success when plans and strategies are based on the new realities of the changed world economy:[3]

- Capital movements have replaced trade as the driving force of the world economy.
- Production has become "uncoupled" from employment.
- The world economy dominates the scene; individual country economies play a subordinate role.
- The 75-year struggle between capitalism and socialism is largely over.
- The growth of e-commerce diminishes the importance of national barriers and forces companies to re-evaluate their business models.

The first change is the increased volume of capital movements. The dollar value of world trade in merchandise is running at roughly $5.5 trillion per year. But the London Eurodollar market turns over $400 billion each working day; overall, foreign exchange transactions are running at approximately $1.5 trillion per day worldwide—40 times the volume of world trade in goods and services.[4] There is an inescapable conclusion in these data: Global capital movements far exceed the dollar volume of global trade. This explains the paradoxical combination of U.S. trade deficits and a strong dollar during the first half of the 1980s and again in the early twenty-first century. According to orthodox economic theory, when a country runs a deficit on its trade accounts, its

---

2 As economist Paul Krugman and others have pointed out, the trend toward global integration that began in the 1970s is actually the second of the century; the first ended with the outbreak of World War I. Krugman has written extensively expressing a contrarian view of the extent of global integration. See, for example, "A Global Economy is Not the Wave of the Future," *Financial Executive* (March-April 1992), pp. 10–13.

3 William Greider offers a thought-provoking analysis of these new realities in *One World, Ready or Not: The Manic Logic of Global Capitalism* (New York: Simon & Schuster, 1997).

4 Alan C. Shapiro, *Multinational Financial Management*, 5th ed. (Upper Saddle River, NJ: Prentice Hall, 1995), p. 137. A Eurodollar is a U.S. dollar held outside the United States. U.S. dollars are subject to U.S. banking regulations; Eurodollars are not.

currency should depreciate in value. Today, it is capital movements and trade that determine currency value.

The second change concerns the relationship between productivity and employment. Although employment in manufacturing remains steady or has declined, productivity continues to grow. The pattern is especially clear in American agriculture, where fewer farm employees produce more output. In the United States, manufacturing's share of gross domestic product (GDP) has declined from 19.2 percent in 1989 to 16.1 percent in 1999.[5] Similar trends can be found in many other major industrial economies as well. Manufacturing is not in decline—it is *employment* in manufacturing that is in decline.[6] Countries like the United Kingdom, which have tried to maintain blue-collar employment in manufacturing, have lost both production and jobs for their efforts.

The third major change is the emergence of the world economy as the dominant economic unit. Company executives and national leaders who recognize this have the greatest chance of success. Those who do not recognize this fact will likely suffer decline and bankruptcy (in business) or overthrow (in politics). The real secret of the economic success of Germany and Japan is the fact that business leaders and policy makers focus on the world economy and world markets; a top priority for government and business in both Japan and Germany has been their respective competitive positions in the world. In contrast, many other countries, including the United States, have focused upon domestic objectives and priorities to the exclusion of their global competitive position.

The fourth change is the end of the Cold War. The demise of communism as an economic and political system can be explained in a straightforward manner: Communism is not an effective economic system. The overwhelmingly superior performance of the world's market economies has given leaders in socialist countries little choice but to renounce their ideology. A key policy change in such countries has been the abandonment of futile attempts to manage national economies with a single central plan. This policy change frequently goes hand in hand with governmental efforts to foster increased public participation in matters of state by introducing democratic reforms.[7]

Finally, the personal computer revolution and the advent of the Internet era have in some ways diminished the importance of national boundaries. Two-thirds of American households have PCs; worldwide, an estimated 500 million personal computers are installed in homes and businesses. In the so-called Information Age, barriers of time and place have been subverted by a transnational cyberworld that functions "24/7." Napster, America Online, and eBay are just a few of the companies that are pushing the envelope in this brave new world.

---

[5] Gross national product (GNP) is a numerical representation of the economic activity in a country for a given time period. It is calculated as the sum of the value of *finished* goods and services produced in a country by its citizens and domestic business enterprises, plus the value of output produced by citizens working outside their home country. Gross domestic product (GDP) also measures economic activity; however, GDP includes *all* income produced within a country's borders by its citizens and domestic enterprises as well as foreign-owned enterprises. Income earned by citizens working abroad is *not* included. As noted, Ireland has attracted a great deal of foreign investment by companies that generate a significant amount of economic output within the country's borders. Thus, Ireland's GDP figures have been running 10 to 12 percent ahead of those for GNP. However, as a practical matter, GNP and GDP figures for many countries will be roughly the same.

[6] Some companies have cut employment by outsourcing or subcontracting nonmanufacturing activities such as data processing, housekeeping, and food service.

[7] Marcus W. Brauchli, "Poll Vaults: More Nations Embrace Democracy—and Find It Can Often Be Messy," *The Wall Street Journal* (June 25, 1996), pp. A1, A6.

A potential bright spot for Ireland is the Media Lab Europe, which opened in July 2000 in Dublin in a building that once was the site of a Guinness brewery. Media Lab Europe is an offshoot of the original Media Lab that was established at the Massachusetts Institute of Technology (MIT) more than 20 years ago. The Media Lab is a research facility; in exchange for sponsorship contributions of $5 million or more, global companies such as BT, Intel, the Lego Group, and Swatch AG get a first look at the Lab's innovations in such areas as robotic design, speech synthesis, and holographic imaging. Total corporate funding for the original Lab has passed the $500 million mark, and 50 new companies have been spun off after being incubated at the Lab.

The Irish government allocated nearly $50 million in funding to establish the Media Lab Europe, including a $10 million payment to MIT for the right to use the Media Lab name. Government officials believe the investment will pay off by strengthening the country's position in advanced information-technology research. By the end of 2001, several organizational sponsors had signed on and pledged an additional $7.5 million in support. However, there were problems. For one thing, some researchers at MIT have been reluctant to move their work to Ireland. By mid-2001, only six researchers and about two dozen research associates, assistants, and graduate students were working in a facility designed to accommodate 250 people. Some Irish academics were offended by the notion that Ireland needs outside help; critics also question whether the Lab will contribute to economic growth to the extent envisioned by the government. To placate such critics, the government has increased funding for local research efforts. With new Media Labs on the drawing board for India, South Korea, and Latin America, the Celtic version may be the harbinger of things to come.

Visit the Web site
www.medialabeurope.org

SOURCES: David Armstrong, "Many Irish Eyes Aren't Smiling on MIT Import," *The Wall Street Journal* (July 5, 2001), pp. B1, B4; Jeffrey R. Young, "MIT's Media Lab, a Media Darling, Seeks Global Role and New Missions," *The Chronicle of Higher Education* (October 12, 2001), pp. A41–A43; Christopher Rhoads, "U.S. Slowdown Muffles the Volume of Ireland's Boom," *The Wall Street Journal* (March 6, 2001), p. A18; Mike Burns, "High-tech Shudders for the Celtic Tiger," *Europe* 14–15, no. 406 (May 2001), pp. 14–15; Stewart Brand, *The Media Lab: Inventing the Future at M.I.T.* (New York: Viking Penguin, 1988).

ECONOMIC SYSTEMS

There are four main types of economic systems: market capitalism, centrally-planned socialism, centrally-planned capitalism, and market socialism (see Figure 2-1). This classification is based on the dominant method of resource allocation (market versus command) and the dominant form of resource ownership (private versus state).

Market Capitalism

Market capitalism is an economic system in which individuals and firms allocate resources and production resources are privately owned. Simply put, consumers decide what goods they desire and firms determine what and how much to produce; the role of the state in market capitalism is to promote competition among firms and ensure consumer protection. Today, market capitalism is widely practiced around the world, most notably in North America and Western Europe.

It would be a gross oversimplification, however, to assume that all market-oriented economies function in an identical manner. Economist Paul Krugman has remarked that the United States is distinguished by its competitive, "wild free-for-all" and decentralized initiative. By contrast, outsiders sometimes refer to Japan as

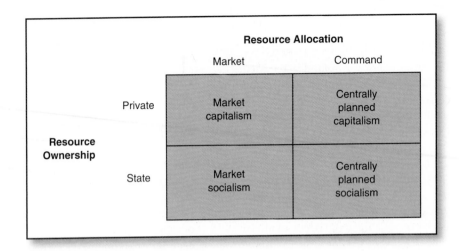

Figure 2-1
Economic Systems

"Japan Inc." The label can be interpreted in different ways, but it basically refers to a tightly run, highly regulated economic system that is also market oriented.

Centrally-Planned Socialism

At the opposite end of the spectrum from market capitalism is *centrally-planned socialism*. In this type of economic system, the state has broad powers to serve the public interest as it sees fit. State planners make "top-down" decisions about what goods and services are produced and in what quantities; consumers can spend their money on what is available. Government ownership of entire industries as well as individual enterprises is characteristic of centrally-planned socialism. Because demand typically exceeds supply, the elements of the marketing mix are not used as strategic variables.[8] There is little reliance on product differentiation, advertising, or promotion; to eliminate "exploitation" by intermediaries, the government also controls distribution.

The clear superiority of market capitalism in delivering the goods and services that people need and want has led to its adoption in many formerly socialist countries. An ideology developed in the nineteenth century by Marx and perpetuated in the twentieth century by Lenin and others has been resoundingly refuted. As William Greider writes:

> Marxism is utterly vanquished, if not yet entirely extinct, as an alternative economic system. Capitalism is triumphant. The ideological conflict first joined in the mid-nineteenth century in response to the rise of industrial capitalism, the deep argument that has preoccupied political imagination for 150 years, is ended.[9]

---

8   Peggy A. Golden, Patricia M. Doney, Denise M. Johnson, and Jerald R. Smith, "The Dynamics of a Marketing Orientation in Transition Economies: A Study of Russian Firms," *Journal of International Marketing* 3, no. 2 (1995), pp. 29–49.
9   William Greider, *One World, Ready or Not: The Manic Logic of Global Capitalism* (New York: Simon & Schuster, 1997), p. 37.

For decades, the economies of China, the former Soviet Union, and India functioned according to the tenets of centrally-planned socialism. All three countries are now engaged in economic reforms characterized, in varying proportions, by increased reliance on market allocation and private ownership. Even as China's leaders attempt to maintain control over society, they acknowledge the importance of economic reform. At a recent plenum, the Communist Party said that reform "is an inevitable road for invigorating the country's economy and promoting social progress, and a great pioneering undertaking without parallel in history."

Centrally-Planned Capitalism and Market Socialism

In reality, market capitalism and centrally-planned socialism do not exist in "pure" form. In most countries, to a greater or lesser degree, command and market resource allocation are practiced simultaneously, as are private and state resource ownership. The role of government in modern market economies varies widely. An economic system in which command resource allocation is utilized extensively in an environment of private resource ownership can be called *centrally-planned capitalism*. In Sweden, for example, where two-thirds of all expenditures are controlled by the government, resource allocation is more "command"-oriented than "market"-oriented. To a certain extent, the same is true in Japan. This type of system is represented by the upper-right quadrant in Figure 2-1.

A fourth variant, *market socialism*, is also possible. In such a system, market allocation policies are permitted within an overall environment of state ownership. For example, China has given considerable freedom to businesses and individuals in the

Author Thomas L. Friedman compares and contrasts various types of economic systems by drawing an analogy with the main elements of a computer system. First is the "hardware," the basic shell around a country's economy. In the Cold War era, there were three basic types of hardware: free-market capitalism, communism, and hybrid. Second is the "operating system," which Friedman compares to a country's broad economic policies. He categorizes these operating systems in a continuum ranging from DOScapital 0.0 through DOScapital 6.0. The basic "economic operating system" in communist countries, as noted previously, was central planning, which is version 0.0. The liberalized economies of the United States, Hong Kong, Taiwan, and the United Kingdom appear at the other end of the continuum. The hybrid states are characterized by various combinations of socialism, free markets, and crony capitalism. For example, Friedman classifies Hungary as DOScapital 1.0, China is 1.0 in rural provinces but 4.0 in Shanghai, Thailand and Indonesia are both DOScapital 3.0, and Korea is 4.0. To get the most out of its hardware and operating system, or course, a computer needs software. In Friedman's analysis, country "software" is comprised of "all the things that fall broadly in the category of the rule of law." It is a measure of the country's legal and regulatory systems and the degree to which laws are understood, embraced, and made workable. As Friedman asserts, with the end of the Cold War, virtually every country in the world is using the same basic hardware: free-market capitalism.

SOURCE: Thomas L. Friedman, *The Lexus and the Olive Tree* (New York: Anchor Books, 2000), pp. 151–152.

Guangdon Providence to operate within a market system. Today, China's private sector accounts for more than 75 percent of national output. Even so, state enterprises still receive more than two thirds of the credit available from the country's banks. In the late 1980s and early 1990s, Mikhail Gorbachev tried to preserve socialist principles in the USSR while pursuing a policy of gradual economic reform known as perestroika. Ultimately, however, Gorbachev was unable to reconcile the conflicting demands of Communist hard-liners with those of an increasingly discontented, democracy-minded population. His failure to establish a system of "capitalism with a human face" contributed to the dissolution of the Soviet Union.

Market reforms and nascent capitalism in many parts of the world are creating opportunities for large-scale investments by global companies. Indeed, Coca-Cola returned to India in 1994, two decades after being forced out by the government. A new law allowing 100 percent foreign ownership of enterprises helped pave the way. By contrast, Cuba stands as one of the last bastions of the command allocation approach. Daniel Yergin and Joseph Stanislaw sum up the situation in the following way:

> Socialists are embracing capitalism, governments are selling off companies they had nationalized, and countries are seeking to entice multinational corporations expelled just two decades earlier. Today, politicians on the left admit that their governments can no longer afford the expansive welfare state . . . The decamping of the state from the "commanding heights" marks a great divide between the 20th and 21st centuries. It is opening the doors of many formerly closed countries to trade and investment, and vastly increasing the global market.[10]

The Washington, D.C.-based Heritage Foundation, a conservative think-tank, takes a more conventional approach classifying economies: It compiles a survey of

---

[10] Daniel Yergin and Joseph Stanislaw, "Sale of the Century," *Financial Times Weekend* (January 24–25, 1998), p. I.

Vladimir Ilyich Lenin was the Bolshevik revolutionary who brought communism to Russia and laid the groundwork for the modern Soviet state. A crowd in the Latvian capital of Riga pulls down a statue of Lenin in August 1991 after Latvia's break with the Soviet Union. Similar actions were repeated many times in Eastern Europe in the early 1990s. In Vilnius, Lithuania, a statue of Frank Zappa was erected on a plinth where Lenin's statue had once stood; nonconformity and free expression were hallmarks of the late musician's career.

more than 150 countries ranked by degree of economic freedom (Table 2-1). A number of key economic variables are considered: trade policy, taxation policy, government consumption of economic output, monetary policy, capital flows and foreign investment, banking policy, wage and price controls, property rights, regulations, and the black market. The rankings form a continuum from "free" to "repressed," with "mostly free" and "mostly unfree" in between. Hong Kong and Singapore are ranked first and second in terms of economic freedom; Sierra Leone, Somalia, and Sudan are ranked lowest.

Visit the Web site
www.heritage.org

There is a high correlation between the degree of economic freedom and the extent to which a nation's mixed economy is heavily market oriented. However, the validity of the ranking has been subject to some debate. For example, author William Greider has observed that the authoritarian state capitalism practiced in Singapore deprives the nation's citizens of free speech, a free press, and free assembly. Greider writes, "Singaporeans are comfortably provided for by a harshly autocratic government that administers paranoid control over press and politics and an effective welfare state that keeps everyone well housed and fed, but not free."[11] As Greider's observation makes clear, some aspects of "free economies" bear more than a passing resemblance to command-style economic systems.

STAGES OF MARKET DEVELOPMENT

At any point in time, individual country markets are at different stages of economic development. The World Bank has developed a four-category system of classification that uses per capita gross national product (GNP) as a base. Although the

---

[11] William Greider, *One World, Ready or Not: The Manic Logic of Global Capitalism* (New York: Simon & Schuster, 1997), pp. 36–37. See also Steve Glain, "Political Grudges? For South Korean Firms, Speaking Too Freely May Carry Steep Price," *The Wall Street Journal* (August 18, 1995), pp. A1, A10.

Table 2-1

Index of Economic Freedom

Free	Trinidad & Tobago	81. Philippines	Moldova
1. Hong Kong	Hungary	Senegal	Rwanda
2. Singapore	42. Kuwait	South Africa	124. Ethiopia
3. Ireland	Lithuania	84. Ghana	Kyrgz Rep.
4. New Zealand	Panama	Guinea	Romania
5. Luxembourg	Costa Rica	Madagascar	127. Congo (Rep.)
United States	46. Latvia	87. Kenya	Mauritania
7. United Kingdom	Belize	Qatar	Russia
8. Netherlands	48. Greece	Zambia	130. Kazakhstan
9. Australia	Guatemala	90. Algeria	Togo
Bahrain	Morocco	Cameroon	132. Bangladesh
Switzerland	Oman	Paraguay	133. India
12. El Salvador	Sri Lanka	93. Brazil	Suriname
Mostly Free	Israel	Gabon	Ukraine
13. Chile	54. Poland	95. Bulgaria	Yemen
14. Austria	Jamaica	Burkina Faso	137. Equatorial Guinea
Canada	56. Malta	97. Cape Verde	Haiti
Denmark	Samoa	Djibouti	139. Azerbaijan
Estonia	Cambodia	Gambia	Tajikistan
Japan	59. Dom. Rep.	Guyana	**Repressed**
U.A.E.	Lebanon	Honduras	141. Bosnia
20. Belgium	Slovak Rep.	Mozambique	Guinea-Bissau
Germany	Benin	Nigeria	Syria
Taiwan	63. Jordan	104. Fiji	144. Vietnam
23. Bahamas	68. Slovenia	Lesotho	145. Burma
Cyprus	Tunisia	106. Croatia	146. Belarus
Finland	Turkey	Ecuador	Zimbabwe
Iceland	Armenia	Nicaragua	148. Turkmenistan
27. Czech Republic	Botswana	Pakistan	149. Uzbekistan
Thailand	Colombia	110. Albania	150. Laos
29. Argentina	Mali	Nepal	151. Iran
South Korea	75. Mauritius	Niger	152. Cuba
Sweden	Mexico	Tanzania	153. Iraq
32. Italy	Namibia	114. China	Libya
Portugal	**Mostly Unfree**	Georgia	155. North Korea
34. Uruguay	Ivory Coast	Indonesia	Angola
35. Barbados	Malaysia	Malawi	Burundi
Bolivia	Mongolia	Papua New Guinea	Congo (Dem. Rep.)
Spain	Saudi Arabia	Venezuela	Sierra Leone
38. Norway	Swaziland	120. Chad	Somalia
39. France	Uganda	Egypt	Sudan
Peru			

Source: Gerald P. O'Driscoll, Jr., Kim R. Holmes, and Melanie Kirkpatrick, "Who's Free, Who's Not," *The Wall Street Journal* (November 1, 2000), p. A26.

On July 2, 1997, Thailand's minister of finance cut his country's currency from its peg to the U.S. dollar. Because the dollar had strengthened over the course of previous months, exports from Thailand and other Asian countries were gradually becoming uncompetitive in world markets. But a bigger problem for Thailand was the fact that financial institutions such as Finance One were overextended with questionable loans. The Thai government itself had seen its financial reserves dwindle to dangerously low levels. By allowing the baht to fluctuate in value, or "float," government officials ensured that Thailand would not default on its debts to international lenders. The action also signaled the onset of a crisis that has been called the "Asian flu." Words like "contagion" and "domino effect" were used to describe what happened next. On July 14, Malaysia's central bank stopped supporting its national currency, the ringgit; on July 17, Singapore's central bank allowed the Singapore dollar to depreciate. In August, finance officials in Indonesia followed suit and allowed the rupiah to float. Even South Korea fell into line with the others; despite the country's tightly-closed economy, officials took action on November 17 when they floated the won. Taken together, these actions signaled to the world that the phenomenal "bubble" of growth enjoyed by the tiger economies had occurred despite fundamental structural problems in the countries' economic and financial systems. In the future, policies such as "crony capitalism" whereby bank loans were freely given to the well connected, would be replaced by more rigorous, Western-style approaches.

By October, Hong Kong's currency was put to the test as currency speculators sold Hong Kong dollars and bought U.S. dollars. Fortunately, the Hong Kong Monetary Authority had US$90 billion in foreign exchange reserves that were sufficient to maintain the peg. Even so, investor concern around the world was reflected in falling stock prices on the world's major exchanges. On Wall Street, the Dow Jones Industrial Average plummeted more than 500 points, the biggest one-day loss ever. To help rebuild the shell-shocked Asian economies, the International Monetary Fund extended loans to bail out the worst-hit victims: $17 billion to Thailand, $40 billion to Indonesia, and a record $58 billion to South Korea.

During the first year after the crisis began, capital took flight as some $200 billion was transferred out of the region. Meanwhile, Western investors were quick to snap up companies, factories, and other assets in Asia at fire-sale prices. Some observers warned that foreign businesses could face a backlash if investors were perceived as exploiting the situation. However, the impact of the Asian crisis in the West spread beyond the financial and investment communities. Global marketers were affected in several ways.

First, with Asia's tiger economies in recession, exports to the region fell sharply. Rising unemployment and a decline in real income prevented many consumers from making purchases, and credit-strapped Asian importers were unable to obtain the letters of credit needed to pay for imports. Earnings at French luxury goods marketer LVMH were negatively impacted since Asia accounts for 40 percent of annual sales. Nike reported a loss for the quarter ended May 31, 1998; Hewlett-Packard saw earnings drop 13 percent in the second quarter. Tourist and airline revenues in important travel destinations such as Australia also dropped. Industrial companies, including those in construction and power generation, were hurt as important infrastructure projects such as dams, bridges, and highways were canceled.

Second, because of the devalued currencies, exports from Asia soared as Asian companies slashed prices. American bike-maker Huffy, hit hard by price cuts on the part of Asian manufacturers, was forced to cut 25 percent of its workforce. A third issue concerns pricing of products produced locally by global corporations. Toyota produces Soluna sedans in Thailand; production costs since the crisis began rose 30 to 40 percent in baht terms. Rather than raise prices to compensate the weaker baht, Toyota managers hoped to retain market share. Toyota raised prices by a modest 6 percent, with another 15 percent increase scheduled later. Mazda slashed the U.S. price of its 1999 Millenia model by $5,000.

Some companies hoped to use the short-term situation as an opportunity for brand building and increasing market share. Early in 1998, for example, Coca-Cola's regional manager for Southeast and west Asia said, "Our attitude to the economic blip in Thailand is to go ahead and aggressively build our brand. There will be a substantial increase in our investment in advertising and marketing this year."

SOURCES: John Ridding, Ted Bardacke and Sander Thoenes, "Tough Message for Regional Advertisers," *Financial Times* (February 19, 1998), p. 20; Paul M. Sherer, "Thai Baht Devaluations Fails to Trigger Classic Inflation," *The Wall Street Journal* (February 3, 1998), p. A17.

Table 2-2

Stages of Market Development

Income Group By Per Capita GNP	2000 GNP ($ MILLIONS)	2000 GNP PER CAPITA ($)	% OF WORLD GNP	2000 POPULATION (MILLIONS)
High-income countries GNP per Capita >$9,656	24,280,533	24,693	80	983
Upper-middle-income countries GNP per Capita ≥$3,126 but ≤$9,656	2,010,621	4,476	7	449
Lower-middle-income countries GNP per Capita ≥$786 but ≤$3,125	3,150,490	1,303	10	2,418
Low-income countries GNP per Capita ≤$785	809,846	355	3	2,283

income definition for each of the stages is arbitrary, countries within a given category generally have a number of characteristics in common. Thus, the stages provide a useful basis for global market segmentation and target marketing. The categories are shown in Table 2-2.

A handful of countries in Central Europe, Latin America, and Asia have experienced rapid economic growth throughout most of the past decade. Because this fast growth presents significant marketing opportunities, the countries are known as **big emerging markets** (BEMs). Ten countries generally recognized as BEMs are China, India, Indonesia, South Korea, Brazil, Mexico, Argentina, South Africa, Poland, and Turkey.[12] These BEMs cut across the four stages of economic development; per capita income ranges from $10,992 in South Korea to $424 in India. China is the largest, with a population of 1.268 billion people; Argentina is the smallest, with a population of 37 million people. Despite these contrasts, experts predict that the BEMs will be key players in global trade even as their track records on human rights, environmental protection, and other issues come under closer scrutiny by their trading partners. The BEM government leaders will also come under pressure at home as their developing market economies create greater income disparity. For each of the stages of economic development discussed here, special attention is given to the BEMs.

Low-Income Countries

Low-income countries have a GNP per capita of $785 or less. The characteristics shared by countries at this income level are:

1. Limited industrialization and a high percentage of the population engaged in agriculture and subsistence farming
2. High birth rates
3. Low literacy rates
4. Heavy reliance on foreign aid
5. Political instability and unrest
6. Concentration in Africa south of the Sahara

Although more than one-third of the world's population is included in this economic category, many low-income countries represent limited markets for products.

---

[12] For an excellent discussion of BEMs, see Jeffrey E. Garten, *The Big Ten: The Big Emerging Markets and How They Will Change Our Lives* (New York: Basic Books, 1997).

The rural family in this photo lives in a world that is deeply rooted in tradition but that has also been touched by Western civilization. As is often the case in low-income countries, self-sufficiency is a way of life in Ethiopia. The farm animals are sources of both food and labor. The mortar in the left foreground is an important traditional cooking utensil in Africa. This family produces food for its own needs and sells the excess in the market, thereby earning money to purchase a few goods and to pay for the children's schooling. The family members are wearing both traditional and Western-style clothes, including plastic shoes that will survive wet weather.

Still, there are exceptions; for example, in Bangladesh, where per capita GNP is approximately $366, the garment industry has enjoyed burgeoning exports. The annual value of finished clothing exports exceeds $1 billion, surpassing that of jute, tea, and other agricultural exports. Although Bengalis have endured a succession of military coups and political killings, in recent years the government has managed to make progress in its economic reform program. Perhaps the reforms will enable Bangladesh to capitalize on its reputation for intellectual accomplishment and its track record for producing distinguished scholars, scientists, and doctors.[13]

Many low-income countries have such serious economic, social, and political problems that they represent very limited opportunities for investment and operations. Some are low-income, no-growth countries such as Burundi and Rwanda that are beset by one disaster after another. Others were once growing, relatively stable countries that have become divided by political struggles. The result is a tinderbox or flash point environment characterized by civil strife, declining income, and, often, considerable danger to residents. Yugoslavia is a case in point. Countries embroiled in civil wars are dangerous areas; most companies find it prudent to avoid them.

The newly independent countries of the former Soviet Union present an interesting situation: Income is declining, and there is considerable economic hardship. The potential for disruption is certainly high. Are they problem cases, or are they attractive opportunities with good potential for moving out of the low-income category? These countries present an interesting risk-reward trade-off; many companies have

---

[13] John F. Burns, "A Legal Case to Show the World Bangladesh Is Not a 'Basket Case,' " *The New York Times* (May 4, 1997), pp. 1, 8.

taken the plunge, but many others are still assessing whether to take the risk. Table 2-1 rates Kyrgyzstan, Turkmenistan, and other former Soviet republics as "repressed" in terms of economic freedom. This is one indication of a risky business environment. Russia itself is near the middle of the ranking; however, as the events of 1998 made clear, economic and political instability are present here as well. Indeed, one of the authors invested $1,000 in a Russian mutual fund in April 1997; by April 2001, the investment was worth only $350.

Of all the countries in the low-income category, only China and India are considered BEMs. China represents the largest single destination for foreign investment in the developing world. Attracted by the country's vast size and market potential, companies in Japan, Europe, and the United States are making China a key country in their global strategies. President Clinton visited in June 1998. Despite ongoing market reforms, Chinese society does not have democratic foundations. Although China has joined the World Trade Organization, trading partners are still concerned about human rights, protection of intellectual property rights, and other issues. Premier Zhu Rongji came to power in 1998; he must deal with China's sprawling bureaucracy while reforming the banking system and the state enterprise sector. General Motors, Ford, Honda, Volkswagen, Motorola, Procter & Gamble, Avon, Siemens AG, and McDonald's are actively pursuing opportunities in China.

In 1997, India commemorated the 50th anniversary of its independence from Great Britain. During that half century, economic growth was weak. As the decade of the 1990s began, India was in the throes of economic crisis: Inflation was high, and foreign exchange reserves were low. Country leaders opened India's economy to trade and investment during the 1990s and dramatically improved market opportunities. Following the assassination of Rajiv Gandhi and the election of P. V. Narasimha Rao to the office of prime minister in 1991, Monmohan Singh was placed in charge of India's economy. Singh, former governor of the Indian central bank and finance minister, noted, "For years, India has been taking the wrong road." Accordingly, he set about dismantling the planned economy by eliminating import licensing requirements for many products, reducing tariffs, easing restrictions on foreign investment, and liberalizing the rupee. The results were impressive: Foreign exchange reserves jumped to $13 billion in 1993 from $1 billion in 1991. Yashwant Sinha, the country's current finance minister, has declared that the twenty-first century will be "the century of India." Although India's economy has faltered in recent years and the pace of economic reform has slowed, Sinha has outlined steps for achieving annual economic growth of nine percent over the next decade.

Lower-Middle-Income Countries

Sometimes, countries that can be assigned to the lower-income and lower-middle income categories are known collectively as **less-developed countries** (LDCs); the term is meant to indicate a contrast with **developing** (upper-middle-income) **countries** and **developed** (high-income) **countries.** Lower-middle-income countries are those with a GNP per capita between $786 and $3,125. These countries are typically at the early stages of industrialization. Factories supply a growing domestic market with such items as clothing, batteries, tires, building materials, and packaged foods. Consumer markets in these countries are expanding. Countries such as Belarus, Indonesia, and Turkey represent an increasing competitive threat as they mobilize their relatively cheap—and often highly motivated—labor forces to serve target markets in the rest of the world. The LDCs in the lower-middle-income category have a major competitive advantage in mature, standardized, labor-intensive industries such as making toys and textiles. Indonesia, the largest noncommunist country in Southeast Asia, is a good example of an

A portable cassette player, looms and tools, dolls for the kids, and religious objects figure prominently in the lives of this family in Guatemala. Guatemala is a lower-middle-income country where per capita income is $1,619. Elsewhere in Central America, El Salvador, and Costa Rica are also lower-middle-income countries; Honduras and Nicaragua are in the low-income category.

LDC on the move: Per capita GNP has risen from $250 in 1985 to $1,176 in 2000. Several factories there produce athletic shoes under contract for Nike.

There are three BEMs in this category: Poland, Turkey, and Indonesia. In the post-Soviet era, Poland established a democratic government and has moved quickly to privatize banking, the state telephone monopoly, and other enterprises. Two-thirds of both export and import trade is conducted with the European Union, which Poland hopes to join by 2003; Germany is Poland's single most important trading partner. Poland, Hungary, and the Czech Republic will join NATO as well, pending votes of approval by all 16 current NATO members.

Strategically located at the intersection of Asia and Europe, Turkey is a member of NATO. An industrialized country with a strong economy, Turkey has suffered from high inflation (more than 80 percent in 1997); in 2000, a three-year plan was launched to bring inflation down to single digits. Germany is Turkey's top trading partner, receiving about 24 percent of exports and providing about 19 percent of imports. Children in the labor force and human rights issues concern trading partners. An Islamic opposition party is active, but radicalism is not spreading. A major issue is the EU's refusal to extend to Turkey an offer of membership. Global companies in Turkey include American Express, Citibank, Coca-Cola, Kodak, Procter & Gamble, and Siemens.

Prior to the onset of the Asian flu, Indonesia's fast-growing economy attracted billions of dollars in foreign investment. The world's fourth most populous nation, Indonesia plays a key economic role in Southeast Asia. Following student protests in 1998, President Suharto was forced to resign. Indonesia's economy was severely affected by the Asian currency crisis of 1997; the 1998 GNP declined an estimated 15 percent.

Upper-Middle-Income Countries

Upper-middle-income countries, also known as industrializing or developing countries, are those with GNP per capita ranging from $3,126 to $9,655. In these countries, the percentage of population engaged in agriculture drops sharply as people move to the industrial sector and the degree of urbanization increases. Malaysia, Brazil, Chile, Hungary, and many other countries in this stage are rapidly industrializing. They have rising wages and high rates of literacy and advanced education but significantly lower wage costs than the advanced countries. Innovative local companies can become formidable competitors and help contribute to their nations' rapid, export-driven economic growth.

Visit the Web site

Economist magazine's Web site offers briefings on more than 60 countries representing all stages of development at: www.economist. com/countries

Upper-middle-income countries that achieve the highest rates of economic growth are sometimes referred to collectively as **newly industrializing economies** (NIEs). In Hungary and other upper-middle-income countries, scores of manufacturing companies have received ISO-9000 certification for documenting compliance with recognized quality standards. The influx of technology, particularly the computer revolution, creates startling juxtapositions of the old and the new in these countries. In Brazil, for example, grocery distribution firms use sophisticated logistics software to route their trucks; meanwhile, horse-drawn carts are still a common sight on many roads. Despite Brazil's unreliable telephone system, Uniao de Bancos offers customers a sophisticated home banking system and sells IBM and Compaq PCs in its lobbies.[14]

Three BEMs in the upper-middle-income category are located in Latin America. In Argentina, the runaway inflation of the 1980s has been brought under control. A massive privatization effort has transferred ownership of many enterprises from the government into the hands of private investors. Key export markets include the United States, Brazil, and Germany. The peso has been pegged to the U.S. dollar since April 1991. Patent protection is a key issue, especially in the pharmaceuticals industry. Brazil is the largest country in South America in terms of the size of its economy, population, and geographic territory. Brazil also boasts the richest reserves of natural resources in the hemisphere. Like Argentina, Brazil has tamed hyperinflation. Liberalized trade is replacing tariff protection and an import quota system as Brazil joins Argentina in the Mercosur customs union. Global companies doing business in Brazil include Whirlpool, Electrolux, Raytheon, Fiat, and Ford. French president Chirac underscored Brazil's importance on the world trade scene when he noted, "Geographically, Brazil is part of America. But it's European because of its culture and global because of its interests."[15]

Mexico is the second-largest country in Latin America after Brazil. It is a key trading partner of the United States, thanks to a thousand-mile shared border and the NAFTA. Companies that want to manufacture in Mexico can set up a wholly-owned subsidiary, a joint venture or a maquiladora program. The **maquiladora** allows manufacturing, assembly, or processing plants to import materials, components, and equipment duty-free; in return, they use Mexican labor. When the completed product is exported to the United States, the manufacturer pays duty only on the value added in Mexico.

The fourth BEM among the upper-middle-income nations is South Africa. It boasts the largest economy in Africa south of the Sahara, with a GDP that represents 45 percent of the Continent's output of goods and services. South Africa has a modern infrastructure and several well-developed industry sectors including finance, communications, and energy. The best-known South African company is the De Beers diamond cooperative.

---

14 Scott McCartney and Jonathan Friedland, "Catching Up: Computer Sales Sizzle as Developing Nations Try to Shrink the PC Gap," *The Wall Street Journal* (June 29, 1995), pp. A1, A4.
15 Matt Moffett and Helene Cooper, "Silent Invasion: In Backyard of the U.S., Europe Gains Ground in Trade, Diplomacy," *The Wall Street Journal* (September 18, 1997), pp. A1, A8.

The relative affluence of this Brazilian family can be judged by the fact the stucco covering on their brick dwelling has been painted. Brazil's per capita income of $4,986 qualifies it as an upper-middle-income country. The open air design and lack of window screens is typical of Brazilian residences; armoires are necessary because few homes have closets. Like most Brazilians, this family owns a TV and a large stereo but has no washer or dryer.

Marketing Opportunities in LDCs and Developing Countries

The shortage of goods and services is the central problem in LDCs and developing countries, and the most pressing need is to expand production. Long-term opportunities can be nurtured in these countries. Today, Nike produces and sells only a small portion of its output in China, but when the firm refers to China as a "two-billion-foot market," it clearly has the future in mind. Greater competitive pressures will force firms to reevaluate their strategies and look for new markets in the developing world. Some fast-growing LDCs are even initiating business in countries that lag behind them. Market opportunities in emerging economies can be lost through indifference and preemptive foreign competition. In deciding whether to enter a developing country market, one study suggested the following:[16]

- Look beyond per capita GNP. The per capita figures may hide the existence of a sizable middle class in that market. India, for example, has a huge middle class market whose existence is masked by the country's average statistics.
- Consider LDCs and developing countries collectively rather than singly. One market may not provide sufficient opportunity; however, there may be broader possibilities in conjunction with neighboring countries.
- Weigh the benefits and costs of being the first firm to offer a product or service in a developing country. Governments often bestow tax subsidies or other special treatment on companies that set up operations. The term *first-mover advantage*

---

[16] Donald G. Halper and H. Chang Moon, "Striving for First-Rate Markets in Third-World Nations," *Management Review* (May 1990), pp. 20–21.

applies to the company that gets in on the ground floor of a significant market opportunity in a fast-growing LDC or developing country.

• Set realistic deadlines for results. Legal, political, or social forces events may make events move slowly.

Despite the difficult economic conditions in parts of Southeast Asia, Latin America, Africa, and Eastern Europe, many nations in these regions will evolve into attractive markets. One of marketing's roles in developing countries is to focus resources on the task of creating and delivering products that are best suited to local needs and incomes. Appropriate marketing communications techniques can also be applied to accelerate acceptance of these products. Marketing can be the link that relates resources to opportunity and facilitates need satisfaction on the consumer's terms.

An interesting debate in marketing is whether it has any relevance to the process of economic development. Some people believe that marketing is relevant only in affluent, industrialized countries, where the major problem is directing society's resources into ever-changing output or production to satisfy a dynamic marketplace. In the less-developed country, the argument goes, the major problem is the allocation of scarce resources toward obvious production needs. Efforts should focus on production and how to increase output, not on customer needs and wants.

Conversely, it can be argued that the marketing process of focusing an organization's resources on environmental opportunities is a process of universal relevance. The role of marketing—to identify people's needs and wants, and to focus individual and organizational efforts to respond to these needs and wants—is the same in all countries, irrespective of level of economic development. For example, pursuing alternative sources of energy such as wind and solar power is important for two reasons: the lack of coal reserves in many countries and concerns that heavy reliance on fossil fuels contributes to global warming. There is also an opportunity to help developing countries join the Information Age. Hewlett-Packard CEO Carly Fiorina recently unveiled an ambitious program to market communication products in LDCs. Dubbed World e-Inclusion, HP will sell, lease, or donate products and services valued at $1 billion to governments and nonprofit groups in Bangladesh and other low-income countries. Fiorina has directed the company's engineers to develop solar-powered communication devices that can link remote areas to the Internet.[17]

Global companies can also contribute to economic development by finding creative ways to preserve old-growth forests and other resources while creating economic opportunities for local inhabitants. In Brazil, for example, DaimlerChrysler works with a cooperative of farmers who transform coconut husks into natural rubber to be used in auto seats, headrests, and sun visors. French luxury-goods marketer Hermes has created a line of handbags called "Amazonia" made of latex extracted by traditional rubber tappers. Both DaimlerChrysler and Hermes are responding to the opportunity to promote themselves as environmentally conscious while appealing to "green"-oriented consumers. As Isabela Fortes, director of a company in Rio de Janeiro that retrains forest workers, notes, "You can only prevent forest people from destroying the jungle by giving them viable economic alternatives."[18]

[17] David Kirkpatrick, "Looking for Profits in Poverty," *Fortune* (February 5, 2001), pp. 174–176

[18] Miriam Jordan, "From the Amazon to Your Armrest," *The Wall Street Journal* (May 1, 2001), pp. B1, B4.

The Fabric of a Nation

CONTINUING A PROUD CANADIAN HERITAGE...

Did you know that 80,000 Canadians work in the fur trade today?

The fur trade contributes **$800 million to the Canadian economy** – including more than **$300 million in exports.** Exports of Canadian fur apparel to fashion centers in the USA, Europe and Asia increased by 25 per cent last year.

But business is only part of this Canadian heritage industry. The fur trade is also a remarkable environmental success story.

Respect for wildlife.

After 400 years of commercial trading, there are as many beavers in Canada now as when Europeans first arrived. Thanks to excellent conservation policies, Canadian furs are abundant and absolutely no endangered species are used. That is assured by provincial and national regulations and by provisions of the Convention on International Trade in Endangered Species (CITES).

In fact, the fur trade uses only a small part of the surplus nature produces each year. This is what biologists call "sustainable use of renewable resources", a principle promoted by the United Nations Environment Program (UNEP) and every major world conservation organization.

Canadians are also world leaders in promoting high standards of animal-welfare on fur farms and in the wild. Research directed by the Fur Institute of Canada provided a scientific basis for the Agreement on International Humane Trapping Standards that has now been adopted by the European Union, Russia and Canada.

Respect for the diversity of people and cultures.

Many Canadian families rely on beaver, muskrat and other fur animals for food as well as income. Animals not used for food are returned to the woods to feed other wildlife through the winter. Farmed mink and foxes provide organic fertilizers, fine oils and other useful products in addition to fur. **Nothing is wasted!**

Respect for the land.

When you buy and wear fur you are supporting aboriginal and other Canadians who live in some of the most remote regions of our country – people who have a direct personal interest in protecting vital wildlife habitat. Trappers are our "eyes and ears" on the land. They are the first to sound the alarm when wildlife is threatened by disease, pollution or poorly planned development projects.

We are the people of the Canadian fur trade – continuing a proud tradition of craftsmanship and responsible use of Canada's precious natural resources.

The Fur Council of Canada is a national non-profit association representing all sectors of the Canadian fur trade. For more information about our trade, please visit our website...

CanadaFur.com

CONSEIL CANADIEN DE LA FOURRURE
FUR COUNCIL OF CANADA

The Fur Council of Canada recently took out full-page newspaper ads promoting the fur industry. The ads were designed to inform consumers of the fur trade's role in Canada's heritage and its importance to indigenous people living in remote regions.

High-Income Countries

High-income countries, also known as advanced, developed, industrialized, or postindustrial countries, are those with GNP per capita above $9,656. With the exception of a few oil-rich nations, the countries in this category reached their present income level through a process of sustained economic growth.

The phrase "postindustrial countries" was first used by Daniel Bell of Harvard to describe the United States, Sweden, Japan, and other advanced, high-income societies. Bell suggests that there is a difference between the industrial and the postindustrial societies that goes beyond mere measures of income. Bell's thesis is that the sources of innovation in postindustrial societies are derived increasingly from the codification of theoretical knowledge rather than from "random" inventions. Other characteristics are the importance of the service sector (more than 50 percent of GNP); the crucial importance of information processing and exchange; and the ascendancy of knowledge over capital as the key strategic resource, of intellectual technology over machine technology, and of scientists and professionals over engineers and semiskilled workers. Other aspects of the postindustrial society are an orientation toward the future and the importance of interpersonal relationships in the functioning of society.

Product and market opportunities in a postindustrial society are more heavily dependent upon new products and innovations than in industrial societies. Ownership levels for basic products are extremely high in most households. Organizations seeking to grow often face a difficult task if they attempt to expand their share of existing markets. Alternatively, they can endeavor to create new markets. For example, in the 1990s, global companies in a range of communication-related industries are seeking to create new markets for multimedia, interactive forms of electronic communication.

South Korea occupies a unique position among the BEMs in that it is the only one of the 10 to have achieved the status of a high-income country. The most industrialized BEM nation, South Korea is home to Samsung Electronics, LG Electronics, Goldstar, Daewoo Corporation, Hyundai Corporation, and other well-known global enterprises. Per capita income doubled in the decade from 1985 to 1995. In place of substantial barriers to free trade, South Korea has initiated major reforms in its political and economic system in response to the "Asian flu."

Among the high-income countries, the United States, Japan, Germany, France, Britain, Canada, and Italy are known as the **Group of Seven** (G-7). Finance ministers, central bankers, and heads of state from the seven nations have worked together for a quarter of a century in an effort to steer the global economy in the direction of prosperity and to ensure monetary stability. Whenever a global crisis looms—be it the Latin American debt crisis of the 1980s, or Russia's struggle to transform its economy in the 1990s—representatives from the G-7 nations gather and try to coordinate policy. An advantage of the G-7 is "strength in numbers"; however, talk is one thing and action is another. As a former official at the U.S. Federal Reserve Bank observed, "Governments rarely want to do what outsiders want them to do."[19] In 1998, as Japan's recession deepened and the value of the yen plummeted, the G-7 leaders devoted a great deal of attention to the economic crisis in Asia. Other items on the agenda at the group's 1998 annual meeting included India's nuclear tests and the debt crisis in Africa's poorest nations. With regard to Africa, British Prime Minister Tony Blair said in an interview, "There's an increasing recognition in our countries that—providing we're not just throwing money at the problem, but geared to real

---

[19] David Wessel, "Dollar Days: Can Wealthy Nations Save Japan from Itself? They're Going to Try," *The Wall Street Journal* (June 18, 1998), pp. A1, A9.

This middle class family has a typical Japanese lifestyle. The head of the household is a "salaryman" who works 50 hour weeks and is expected to go drinking after work to talk business with his boss and coworkers. The children in the family have many toys and personal possessions; most Japanese insist that children attend after-school classes for extra tutoring in mathematics, English, or Japanese. Because houses lack central heat, the dining table in the foreground has a heater under it; in the wintertime, family members might sit at the table to stay warm while they watch TV. Because space is at a premium in Japan, the dining room also serves as the living room. The combination washer-dryer unit takes less space than separate units; however, most families do not use the dryer, preferring instead to hang clothes to conserve energy.

economic reform and progress—it's in our interest, too, that countries in Africa can exploit the huge potential they have there without being submerged in this burden of debt from which they can't escape."[20]

Another institution comprised of high-income countries is the **Organization for Economic Cooperation and Development** (OECD). The 29 nations that belong to the OECD believe in market-allocation economic systems and pluralistic democracy. The organization has been variously described as an "economic think-tank" and a "rich-man's club"; in any event, the OECD's fundamental task is to "enable its members to achieve the highest sustainable economic growth and improve the economic and social well-being of their populations." Today's organization is based in Paris and evolved from a group of European nations that worked together after World War II to rebuild the region's economy. Canada and the United States have been members since 1961; Japan joined in 1964. Evidence of the increasing importance of the BEMs is the fact that China, India, Indonesia, Brazil, and Russia have all formally announced their intention to join the OECD. Applicants must demonstrate progress towards economic reform.[21]

---

[20] "Talks of the Rich Focus on Debt of the Poor," *The New York Times* (May 17, 1998), p. 11.
[21] Wolfgang Münchau, "Think-Tank Has Clearer Goals," *Financial Times—World Economy and Finance* (September 19, 1997), p. xv.

Representatives from OECD member nations work together in committees to review economic and social policies that affect world trade. The Secretary-General presides over a Council that meets regularly and has decision-making power. Committees comprised of specialists from member countries provide a forum for discussion of trade and other issues. Consultation, peer pressure, and diplomacy are the keys to helping member nations candidly assess their own economic policies and actions. The OECD publishes country surveys and an annual Economic Outlook. Recently, the OECD has become more focused on global issues, social policy, and labor market deregulation. For example, the OECD tackled the vexing problem of bribery; the goal is to establish a treaty aimed at outlawing bribery of foreign officials.[22]

Visit the Web site
www.oecd.org

The Triad

The ascendancy of the global economy has been noted by many observers in recent years. One of the most astute is Kenichi Ohmae, former chairman of McKinsey & Company Japan. His 1985 book *Triad Power* represented one of the first attempts to develop a coherent conceptualization of the new emerging order. Ohmae argued that successful global companies had to be equally strong in Japan, Western Europe, and the United States. These three regions, which Ohmae collectively called the **Triad,** represented the dominant economic centers of the world. Today, fully 75 percent of world income as measured by GNP is located in the Triad. Ohmae has recently revised his view of the world; in the **expanded Triad,** the Japanese leg encompasses the entire Pacific region; the American leg includes Canada and Mexico; and the boundary in Europe is moving eastward. Acer Inc. provides a perfect illustration of a company with a well-balanced revenue stream; one-third of the company's sales of computers and related equipment are in Asia, one-third in North America, and another 20 percent are in Europe (see Case 1-2).

Marketing Implications of the Stages of Development

The stages of economic development described previously can serve as a guide to marketers in evaluating **product saturation levels,** or the percentage of potential buyers or households who own a particular product. In countries with low per capita income, product saturation levels for many products are low. In India, for example, ownership of private telephones is limited to about 1 percent of the population (see Figure 2-2). In China, saturation levels of private cars and personal computers are similarly low; there is only one car for every 20,000 Chinese, and only one PC for every 6,000 people. Management at Unilever NV considers the company's strength in emerging countries to be a source of competitive advantage. Unilever has operations in 90 countries, sells its products in 70 more countries, and gets 30 percent of sales from developing markets. Unilever's strategic goal over the next decade is to focus on southern South America, Central and Eastern Europe, and the Asia-Pacific region in an effort to raise emerging markets' share of revenue to 50 percent.[23]

BALANCE OF PAYMENTS

The **balance of payments** is a record of all economic transactions between the residents of a country and the rest of the world. The United States and Japanese balance

---

[22] Michael Hershman, "A Blow Against Bribery," *Financial Times* (February 28, 1998), p. 14.
[23] Tara Parker-Pope, "Unilever Plans a Long-Overdue Pruning," *The Wall Street Journal* (September 3, 1996), p. A11.

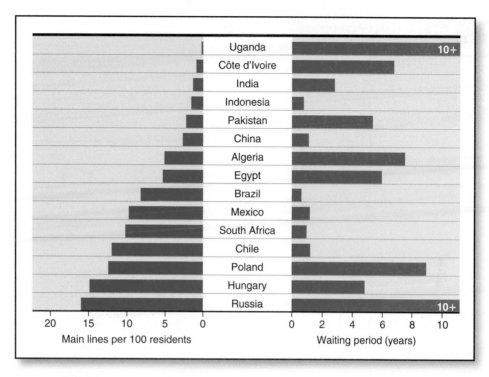

Figure 2-2
Telephone Coverage in Developing Countries

of payments statistics for the period 1995 to 1999 are shown in Tables 2-3 and 2-4. The data in the tables is drawn from the International Monetary Fund's *Balance of Payments Statistics Yearbook,* which summarizes economic activity for all the countries of the world.[24]

The balance of payments is divided into the current and capital accounts. The **current account** is a record of all recurring trade in merchandise and services, private gifts, and public aid transactions between countries. A country with a negative current account balance has a **trade deficit;** that is, the outflow of money to pay for imports exceeds the inflow of money for sales of exports. Conversely, a country with a positive current account balance has a **trade surplus.** The **capital account** is a record of all long-term direct investment, portfolio investment, and other short- and long-term capital flows. The minus signs signify outflows of cash; for example, in Table 2-3, line 2 shows an outflow of $1 trillion in 1999 that represents payment for U.S. merchandise imports. Other entries included in the *Yearbook,* but not shown in Tables 2-3 and 2-4, represent changes in net errors and omissions, foreign liabilities, and reserves. These are the entries that make the balance of payments balance. In general, a country accumulates reserves when the net of its current and capital account transactions shows a surplus; it gives up reserves when the net shows a deficit. The important fact to recognize about the overall balance of payments is that it is always in balance. Imbalances occur in subsets of the overall balance. For example, a commonly reported balance is the trade balance on goods (line 3 in both tables).

Table 2-4 shows that, between 1995 and 1999, Japan enjoyed a surplus in both its current account and its trade balance in goods. Japan's current account balance grew

---

[24] Balance of payments data are available from a number of different sources, each of which may show slightly different figures for a given line item.

Table 2-3
U.S. Balance of Payments, 1995–1999 (US$ billions)

	1995	1996	1997	1998	1999
A. Current Account	**−109.45**	**−123.31**	**−140.54**	**−217.48**	**−331.48**
1. Goods: Exports FOB	577.69	613.96	681.65	672.29	686.66
2. Goods: Imports FOB	−749.57	−803.33	−876.37	−917.19	−1,029.92
3. Balance on Goods	*−171.88*	*−189.37*	*−194.72*	*−244.90*	*−343.26*
4. Services: Credit	217.39	238.12	255.29	260.69	269.58
5. Services: Debit	−141.45	−150.85	−166.51	−182.68	−191.30
6. Balance on goods and services	*−95.94*	*−102.10*	*−105.93*	*−166.89*	*−264.97*
B. Capital Account	**.37**	**.69**	**.35**	**.64**	**−3.50**
Total A+B	−109.08	−122.62	−140.19	−216.50	−334.98

Source: Reprinted by permission of the International Monetary Fund.

Table 2-4
Japan Balance of Payments, 1995–1999 (US$ billions)

	1995	1996	1997	1998	1999
A. Current Account	**111.04**	**65.88**	**94.35**	**120.70**	**106.87**
1. Goods: Exports FOB	428.72	400.28	409.24	374.04	403.69
2. Goods: Imports FOB	−296.93	−316.72	−307.64	−251.66	280.37
3. Balance on Goods	*131.79*	*83.56*	*101.60*	*122.39*	*123.32*
4. Services: Credit	65.27	67.72	69.30	62.41	61.00
5. Services: Debit	−122.63	−129.96	−123.45	−111.83	−115.16
6. Balance on goods and services	*74.43*	*21.32*	*47.45*	*72.97*	*69.16*
B. Capital Account	**−2.23**	**−3.29**	**−4.05**	**−14.45**	**−16.47**
Total A + B	108.82	62.59	90.30	106.24	90.40

Source: Reprinted by permission of the International Monetary Fund.

each year from 1990 to 1993; however, the data for the period 1996 to 1999 reflect the downturn in Japan's economy. An examination of Table 2-3 also reveals that, for several years, the United States has posted deficits in both the current account and the trade balance in goods. The United States' growing trade deficit reflects a number of factors, including the economic turmoil in Asia, a strong dollar which raises the cost of American exports to Asia, and a strong economy that supports demand for imported goods. A comparison of lines 4 and 5 in the two tables shows a bright spot from the U.S. perspective: The United States has maintained a surplus in services trade while Japan runs a deficit. The tables show that, overall, the United States posts balance of payments deficits while Japan has surpluses. Since the mid-1990s, the U.S. merchandise trade deficit with Japan has grown by about $10 billion per year; in 2000, the deficit reached $81 billion. Japan offsets its trade surplus with an outflow of capital, while the United States offsets its trade deficit with an inflow of capital. As trading partners, U.S. consumers and businesses own an increasing quantity of Japanese products, while the Japanese own more U.S. land, real estate, and government securities.

In today's Russia, average citizens aren't the only ones struggling to keep pace with rapid and revolutionary economic change; government statisticians can't even keep up. The result is that economic information and statistics coming from Russia are inaccurate, inadequate, distorted, and biased.

Russia's main source of economic statistics is an agency called "Goskomstat," or the Russian State Statistical Committee. The inherent problem with the statistics generated by Goskomstat is one of original intent: Historically, Goskomstat measured the state economy of the Soviet Union; the purpose of the statistics that are still used for economic measurement today doesn't exist anymore because of the change from a planned economy to a market economy.

Goskomstat continues to collect data and measure production in the least productive sectors, such as industries that have not been privatized and farms still owned by the state. If those statistics were somewhat balanced by equivalent numbers from the private sector, Russian GNP might not be so severely underestimated. However, Goskomstat is not at all aggressive about counting the growing private sector in the Russian economy. The growth in Russian joint ventures, retail and service trade, and private banking has been well documented in the press, but not by Goskomstat. The official estimate of Russia's 1994 gross domestic product was $277 billion—smaller than the Netherlands.

The problem of gathering data from start-up businesses in the emerging private sector is compounded by the fact that those enterprises are reluctant to be included because of potential tax implications. Also, because of inadequate survey techniques, thousands of sole proprietorships, entrepreneurial and barter trade enterprises, as well as informal, black and gray markets are all outside the reach of Goskomstat's reckoning.

Even the data generated from the fading state sector is inadequate because organizations on the government dole are not motivated to report any increased production. Those enterprises could stand to lose government subsidies if production is up. Ironically, in the Soviet era, managers of state-owned businesses were inclined to inflate production numbers in order to reach goals set by state planners.

So what is the impact of the skewed numbers put forth by Goskomstat? The faulty numbers create a ripple effect worldwide. Other agencies that rely on this imperfect source for economic data include the World Bank, International Monetary Fund, U.S. Department of Commerce, the CIA, plus countless banks, and industrial and investment analysts. At the very least, statistics severely understate production, especially in the growing private economy. The estimated amount of underreported production ranges from 25 percent to 60 percent, with most experts estimating a 45 percent undercount to be closest to reality. One consequence for the Russian economy is slowed growth, because unsophisticated marketers may be reluctant to enter a market depicted by such bleak numbers.

SOURCES: John Thornhill, "Russians Grow Rich in the Shadows," *Financial Times* (January 16, 1998), p. 2; Avi Shama, "Notes from the Underground: Russia's Economy Booms," *The Wall Street Journal* (December 12, 1997), p. A10; Thornhill, "Russia's Statistics Fail to Add Up," *Financial Times* (November 4, 1996), p. 8; S. Frederick Starr, "The 'Glass Is Half Full' Case For Russia," *The International Economy* (March-April 1995), pp. 46+; Judy Shelton, *The Coming Soviet Crash: Gorbachev's Desperate Pursuit of Credit in Western Financial Markets* (New York: Free Press, 1989).

TRADE PATTERNS

Thanks in part to the achievements of GATT, world merchandise trade has grown at a faster rate than world production since the end of World War II. Put differently, import and export growth has outpaced the rate of increase in GNP. Moreover, since 1983, foreign direct investment has grown five times faster than world trade and 10 times faster than GNP. The structure of world trade is summarized in Figure 2-3. The importance of the Triad countries is quite pronounced: North America, the EU, and Japan accounted for two-thirds of world exports and imports. Industrialized nations

On December 20, 1994, the Bank of Mexico embarked on a course of action that sent shock waves around the world. A combination of circumstances, including a $28 billion current-account deficit, dwindling reserves, the murder of presidential candidate Donaldo Colosio, and eroding investor confidence, forced the Bank of Mexico to devalue the peso. The Clinton administration quickly arranged $20 billion in loans and loan guarantees, secured in part by some of Mexico's $7 billion in annual oil export revenues. Opponents of NAFTA—notably Ross Perot—seized the opportunity to denounce both the loans and the trade agreement itself. The devalued peso, critics predicted, would make U.S. exports to Mexico more expensive and reduce the $2 billion trade surplus that the U.S. enjoys with Mexico. NAFTA opponents also noted that increased imports of Mexican goods into the United States would constitute a new threat to U.S. jobs.

The Bank of Mexico's decision to devalue the peso meant that the Mexican currency declined nearly 40 percent relative to key currencies such as the dollar, the mark, and the yen. One immediate effect of the devaluation was a sharp decline in Mexican purchases of U.S. imports. For example, Westinghouse and Lennox had been aggressively selling air conditioners after NAFTA reduced tariffs; sales quickly slowed down after the devaluation. McDonald's, Kentucky Fried Chicken, Dunkin' Donuts, and other U.S. restaurant chains were also hard hit as they were forced to raise prices. Many franchisors had contracted to pay rent for their facilities in dollars; after the devaluation, franchisors who couldn't pay the rent were forced to shut down. Simply put, the purchasing power of Mexican consumers was cut nearly in half. To reduce the risk of inflation, the Mexican government pledged

to cut spending and allow interest rates to rise. Meanwhile, investors who had poured money into Mexico since the late 1980s—lured by the promise of low inflation and a stable currency—faced huge declines in the value of their holdings.

For many manufacturing companies, the weaker peso wreaked havoc with 1995 sales forecasts. GM, for example, had hoped to export 15,000 vehicles to Mexico in 1995, a goal rendered unattainable by the financial crisis. Ford raised vehicle prices in Mexico; the increases applied to vehicles built in Mexico as well as those imported from Canada and the United States. Shares of Avon Products, whose Mexican sales comprise 11 percent of the company's $4 billion in annual revenue, declined sharply on Wall Street. Hoping to calm investors' fears, company executives predicted that a decline in Mexican sales would be offset in 1995 by gains in Brazil and other countries.

Supporters and opponents of NAFTA debated the long-term effects of the devaluation. Harley Shaiken, a labor professor at the University of California and NAFTA critic, noted, "It will have a dual impact: It will diminish the market for U.S. goods in Mexico, but the more sizable impact will be the transfer of production to Mexico. It's going to make Mexico less desirable as a place to sell things and far more desirable as a place to make things." Persons holding opposing views acknowledged that the devaluation cut Mexican wages in dollar terms. However, NAFTA supporters have pointed out that labor's percentage of total cost in autos and auto parts—which constitute Mexico's largest export sector—is relatively low. Thus, despite the devaluation, NAFTA supporters deny that there will be a "giant sucking sound" caused by an exodus of U.S. jobs south of the border.

SOURCES: Craig Torres, "Headed South: Mexico's Devaluation Stuns Latin America—and U.S. Investors," *The Wall Street Journal* (December 22, 1994), pp. A1, A12; "Ford Lifts Prices, Avon Tries To Calm Holders, Dina Estimates Loss as Peso Fallout Continues," *The Wall Street Journal* (January 13, 1995); Michael Clements and Bill Montague, "Will Peso's Fall Prove Perot Right?" *USA Today* (January 17, 1995), pp. B1, B2.

have increased their share of world trade by trading more among themselves and less with the rest of the world.

Merchandise Trade

Table 2-5 shows trade patterns for the world. In 1999, the dollar value of world trade exceeded $5.9 trillion. Trade growth outside industrialized countries has been accelerating. In 1997, two-thirds of world exports were generated by industrialized countries

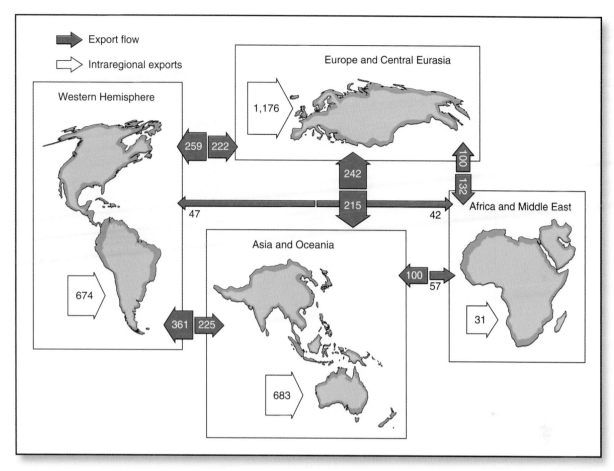

Figure 2-3
World Trade Flows, 1998 ($ billions)

Legend:
- Export flow
- Intraregional exports

Western Hemisphere — 674 (intraregional)
Europe and Central Eurasia — 1,176 (intraregional)
Asia and Oceania — 683 (intraregional)
Africa and Middle East — 31 (intraregional)

Western Hemisphere ↔ Europe and Central Eurasia: 259 / 222
Western Hemisphere ↔ Asia and Oceania: 361 / 225
Western Hemisphere ↔ Africa and Middle East: 47 / 42
Europe and Central Eurasia ↔ Asia and Oceania: 242 / 215
Europe and Central Eurasia ↔ Africa and Middle East: 100 / 132
Asia and Oceania ↔ Africa and Middle East: 100 / 57

Table 2-5
World Merchandise Exports and Imports, 1999 (millions except as noted)

Areas	Exports to 1999	Imports from 1999
DOT World Total	$5,643.8*	$5,793.6*
Industrial Countries	3,835.7*	3,755.8*
Developing Countries	1,744.7*	1,979.4*
Africa	97,542	108,842
Asia	905,262	1,056,930
Europe	276,866	270,280
Middle East	160,406	177,540
Western Hemisphere	304,655	316,786

* billions

Source: Reprinted by permission of the International Monetary Fund.

Table 2-6
Twenty Leading
Exporters and
Importers in World
Merchandise Trade,
1999 (US$ billions)

LEADING EXPORTERS	1999	LEADING IMPORTERS	1999
1. United States	765.3	1. United States	1,013.3
2. Germany	517.8	2. Germany	465.9
3. Japan	448.6	3. United Kingdom	319.2
4. China, P.R.	323.5	4. France	298.0
5. France	295.7	5. Japan	278.2
6. United Kingdom	262.1	6. Netherlands	212.4
7. Canada	243.3	7. Canada	211.6
8. Italy	217.0	8. Italy	204.7
9. Netherlands	182.3	9. China, P.R.	163.3
10. South Korea	146.5	10. Hong Kong	154.7
11. Belgium	142.7	11. Belgium	152.8
12. Taiwan	138.5	12. Spain	143.8
13. Mexico	132.2	13. Mexico	114.4
14. Spain	105.1	14. South Korea	109.3
15. Malaysia	97.2	15. Singapore	106.1
16. Switzerland	93.8	16. Taiwan	105.5
17. Singapore	90.8	17. Switzerland	92.1
18. Sweden	83.7	18. Malaysia	66.0
19. Russia	77.3	19. Brazil	49.8
20. Thailand	64.4	20. Thailand	46.7

Source: Reprinted by permission of the International Monetary Fund.

and one-third by developing countries. By comparison, in 1994, 75 percent of exports originated in industrialized countries and 25 percent came from developing nations. The European Union accounted for 35 percent of 1997 exports, the United States and Canada for 20 percent, and Japan for about 5 percent. Sixty percent of the European Union's total trade is with other member countries.

The top 20 exporting and importing countries of the world (based on data compiled by the International Monetary Fund) are shown in Table 2-6. China's fourth place in the export rankings underscores its role as an export powerhouse. Even in the face of Asia's economic downturn in the late 1990s, China demonstrated continued economic strength by achieving double-digit export growth. Chinese exports to the United States are expected to surge now that China has joined the World Trade Organization. In the Western Hemisphere, Mexico's robust export growth since the mid-1990s shows the continuing impact of NAFTA. For the past several years, Mexico has been running a trade surplus with the United States. Much of the surplus can be attributed to American firms that assemble products at factories in Mexico for the American market. By comparison, Mexico's exports grew only 9 percent from 1992 to 1993.

Services Trade

Probably the fastest-growing sector of world trade is trade in services. Services include travel and entertainment; education; business services such as engineering, accounting, and legal services; and payments of royalties and license fees. One of the

Visit the Web site
The United States Bureau of Economic Analysis posts a great deal of information about the U.S. economy. You can access the database at:
www.bea.doc.gov

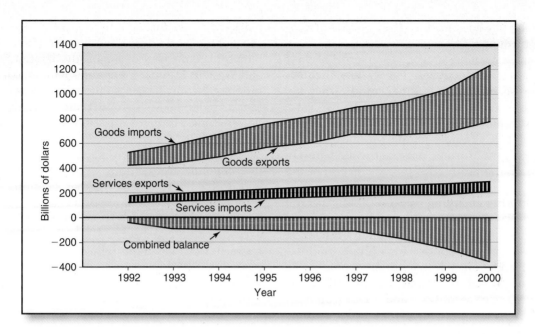

Figure 2-4
U.S. Trade Balance on Services and on Merchandise Trade (US$ billions)
Source: U.S. Census Bureau

Visit the Web Site
The U.S. Census Bureau compiles data on U.S. trade and makes it available on the Web. You can find this data under the headings "FT900" and "Supplement" at: www.census.gov/ foreign-trade/www

major issues in trade relations between the high- and lower-income countries is trade in services. As a group, low-, lower-middle, and even upper-middle-income countries are lax in enforcing international copyrights and protecting intellectual property and patent laws. As a result, countries that export service products such as computer software, music, and video entertainment suffer a loss of income. According to the Software Publishers Association, annual worldwide losses due to software piracy amount to $8 billion. In China and the countries of the former Soviet Union, it is estimated that more than 95 percent of the personal computer software in use is pirated.

The United States is a major service trader. As shown in Figure 2-4, U.S. services exports in 2000 totaled $295 billion. This represented slightly more than one-quarter of all U.S. exports. The U.S. services surplus—service exports minus imports—stood at $80 billion. This surplus partially offset the U.S. merchandise trade deficit, which reached a record $450 billion in 2000. American Express, Walt Disney, IBM, and Microsoft are a few of the U.S. companies currently enjoying rapid growth in demand for their services around the world.

SUMMARY

The economic environment is a major determinant of global market potential and opportunity. In today's global economy, capital movements are the key driving force, production has become uncoupled from employment, and capitalism has vanquished communism. Based on patterns of resource allocation and ownership, the world's

national economies can be categorized as **market capitalism, centrally-planned capitalism, centrally-planned socialism,** and **market socialism.** The final years of the twentieth century have been marked by a transition toward market capitalism in many countries that had been centrally controlled. However, there still exists a great disparity among the nations of the world in terms of **economic freedom.**

Countries can be categorized in terms of their stage of economic development: **low-income, lower-middle-income, upper-middle-income,** and **high-income.** Countries in the first two categories are sometimes known as **less-developed countries** (LDCs). Upper-middle-income countries with high growth rates are often called **newly industrializing economies** (NIEs). Several of the world's economies are notable for their fast growth; the **big emerging markets** (BEMs) include China and India (low-income), Poland, Turkey, and Indonesia (lower-middle-income), Argentina, Brazil, Mexico, and South Africa (upper-middle-income), and South Korea (high-income). The **Group of Seven** (G7) and **Organization for Economic Cooperation and Development** (OECD) represent two initiatives by high-income nations to promote democratic ideals and free-market policies throughout the rest of the world. Most of the world's income is located in the **Triad,** which is comprised of Japan, the United States, and Western Europe. Companies with global aspirations generally have operations in all three areas. Market potential for a product can be evaluated by determining **product saturation levels** in light of income levels.

A country's **balance of payments** is a record of its economic transactions with the rest of the world; this record shows whether a country has a **trade surplus** (value of exports exceeds value of imports) or a **trade deficit** (value of imports exceeds value of exports). The U.S. **merchandise trade deficit** was $450 billion in 2000 and has passed the $100 billion mark several times in recent years. However, the U.S. enjoys an annual **service trade surplus.** Overall, however, the United States is a debtor; Japan enjoys an overall trade surplus and serves as a creditor nation.

DISCUSSION QUESTIONS

1. Explain the difference between **market capitalism, centrally-planned capitalism, centrally-planned socialism,** and **market socialism.** Give an example of a country that illustrates each type of system.
2. What is a big emerging market (BEM)? Identify the BEMs according to their respective stages of economic development.
3. Turn to the Index of Economic Freedom (Table 2-1) and identify where the BEMs are ranked. What does the result tell you in terms of the relevance of the index to global marketers?

4. A manufacturer of satellite dishes is assessing the world market potential for his products. He asks you if he should consider developing countries as potential markets. How would you advise him?
5. A friend is distressed to learn that America's merchandise trade deficit hit a record $450 billion in 2000. You want to cheer your friend up by demonstrating that the trade picture is not as bleak as it sounds. What do you say?

RESEARCH EXERCISE

1. The big emerging markets (BEMs) discussed in this chapter are frequently in the news. Choose one of the countries to follow during the semester; keep a journal with notes or pasted-up articles from the press. What issues identified in the chapter continue to affect trade prospects in your country? What new issues, if any, have developed?

SUGGESTED READINGS

Books

Enghold, Christopher. *Doing Business in Asia's Booming China Triangle.* Upper Saddle River, NJ: Prentice Hall, 1994.

Garten, Jeffrey E. *The Big Ten: The Big Emerging Markets and How They Will Change Our Lives.* New York: BasicBooks, 1997.

Gilder, George F. *Microcosm: The Quantum Revolution in Economics and Technology.* New York: Simon and Schuster, 1989.

Isaak, Robert A. *Managing World Economic Change.* Upper Saddle River, NJ: Prentice Hall, Inc., 1995.

Kennedy, Paul. *The Rise and Fall of Great Powers.* New York: Random House, 1987.

Porter, Michael E. *The Competitive Advantage of Nations.* New York: The Free Press, 1990.

Roberts, Paul C., and Karen Le Follette Araujo. *The Capitalist Revolution in Latin America.* Oxford: Oxford University Press, 1997.

Shapiro, Alan C. *Multinational Financial Management,* 5th ed. Upper Saddle River, NJ: Prentice Hall, Inc., 1995.

Thurow, Lester. *Head to Head: The Coming Economic Battle Among Japan, Europe, and America.* New York: William Morrow and Company, Inc., 1992.

Articles

Ardrey, William J., Anthony Pecotich, and Clifford J. Schultz, "American Involvement in Vietnam, Part II: Prospects for U.S. Business in a New Era." *Business Horizons,* 38 (March-April 1995), pp. 21–27.

Cavusgil, S. Tamer. "Measuring the Potential of Emerging Markets: An Indexing Approach." *Business Horizons* 40, no. 1 (January-February 1997), pp. 87–91.

Dowlah, C. A. F. "The Future of the Readymade Clothing Industry in the Post-Uruguay Round World." *World Economy* 22, no. 7 (September 1999), pp. 933–953.

Golden, Peggy A., Patricia M. Doney, Denise M. Johnson, and Jerald R. Smith, "The Dynamics of a Marketing Orientation in Transition Economies: A Study of Russian Firms." *Journal of International Marketing* 3, no. 2 (1995), pp. 29–49.

Prowse, Michael. "Is America in Decline?" *Harvard Business Review* 70, no. 4 (July-August 1992), pp. 36–37.

Quddus, Munir. "Apparel Exports from Bangladesh: Brilliant Entrepreneurship or Spurious Success?" *Journal of Asian Business* 12, no. 4 (1996), pp. 51–70.

Yan, Rick. "To Reach China's Consumers, Adapt to Guo Qing." *Harvard Business Review* 72, no. 5 (September-October 1994), pp. 66–74.

CASES

Case 2-1   *Vietnam's Market Potential*

In July 2000, U.S. President Bill Clinton signed a trade pact with Vietnam that promised a new era in two-way trade between the former adversaries. If ratified by Congress, the pact would establish normal trading relations (NTR) between the two countries. In particular, Vietnam would benefit from an immediate lowering of duties on a number of goods produced by its light industry sector (see Figure 1). The World Bank estimated that the trade pact could lead to $800 million in new exports from Vietnam. Vietnamese tariffs and quotas on imports from the United States would be lowered more gradually. The trade pact was the latest in a series of initiatives intended to bolster two-way trade between the United States and Vietnam. A few years earlier, in February 1994, President Clinton had ended America's 19-year economic embargo of Vietnam and opened the door for U.S. companies to target one of the world's most populous countries. A number of U.S. companies immediately seized the opportunity. As Brian Watson, a Hong Kong-based deputy regional director for the McCann-Erickson

advertising agency, said, "Vietnam is the next great frontier. There is an enormous amount of interest among clients. Every meeting starts with a question about going into Vietnam."

On July 11, 1995, President Clinton provided a further boost to business by reestablishing diplomatic relations with Vietnam. In the absence of diplomatic relations, many Vietnamese-manufactured exports to the United States faced prohibitive tariffs. In 1998, the White House announced that it would exempt Vietnam from the Jackson-Vanik amendment. The exemption meant that, pending Congressional approval, American companies investing in Vietnam could apply for financial assistance from the Overseas Private Investment Corporation (OPIC) and the Export-Import Bank.

While the U.S. business community hailed the initiatives, many firms were playing catch up; by the early 1990s, many non-U.S. global companies had preceded the Americans into Vietnam. South Korean industrial giant Daewoo was a key investor; other companies with major commitments included Sony, Toshiba, Honda, Peugeot, and British Petroleum. Carrier was among the first U.S. companies to legally market in Vietnam in 1994; the company's window air conditioners appeared in stores in Hanoi and Ho Chi Minh City. Gillette began shipping razor blades and disposable razors, and AT&T began selling home and office telephone products through a distributor in Taiwan. Mobil began exploring for oil, Caterpillar set up equipment-leasing operations, and the Otis Elevator division of United Technologies joined in the construction boom. J. Walter Thompson, Ogilvy & Mather, and Backer Spielvogel Bates Worldwide became the first Western ad agencies to open liaison offices in Vietnam.

Since 60 percent of Vietnam's population is under the age of 25, it is no surprise that PepsiCo and the Coca-Cola Company were also quick to make moves in Vietnam. In fact, at the time of the official announcement about ending the embargo, McCann-Erickson had already produced a TV commercial for Coca-Cola that included the global slogan "Always"; Ogilvy & Mather had a Pepsi ad ready for TV. Coca-Cola is building a $20 million bottling plant outside of Hanoi, but was denied permission to build in Ho Chi Minh City (formerly Saigon). Pepsi's joint venture with a Vietnamese firm in Ho Chi Minh City is bottling Pepsi; local production began within hours of President Clinton's announce-

Figure 1
Duty Rates on Vietnamese Exports to U.S. with and without NTR

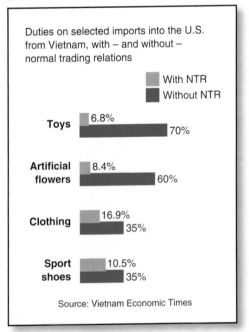

Duties on selected imports into the U.S. from Vietnam, with – and without – normal trading relations

- With NTR
- Without NTR

	With NTR	Without NTR
Toys	6.8%	70%
Artificial flowers	8.4%	60%
Clothing	16.9%	35%
Sport shoes	10.5%	35%

Source: Vietnam Economic Times

Figure 2
Foreign Direct Investment in Vietnam, 1992–1999

in 1998. U.S. investment in Vietnam has lagged well behind that of other countries.

There are many challenges for companies seeking to invest in Vietnam. The population is very poor, with 2000 annual per capita income of only about $350. However, urbanites with savings estimated at $1 to $2 billion comprise one-quarter of the population. The infrastructure is undeveloped: Only 10 percent of roads are paved, electricity sources are unreliable, there is less than one telephone per 100 people, and the banking system is undeveloped. The Communist Party of Vietnam (CPV) is struggling to adapt to the principles of a market economy, and the layers of bureaucracy built up over decades of communist rule slow the pace of change. A key agency is the State Committee for Cooperation and Investment; as Vu Tien Phuc, a deputy director of the agency, explained, "Every authority would like to have the last say. We have to improve the investment climate." William Ratliff, an analyst with the Hoover Institute, points out that the question for Vietnam is "whether it's possible to carry on free-market reforms and maintain absolute political power."

Yvonne Gupwell, a business consultant who was born in Vietnam, believes that "The biggest mistake companies make is they think because the Vietnamese are so polite, they're a little bit dim. The Vietnamese are poor, but they are not mentally poor at all." Statistics support this view; for example, adult literacy is nearly 90 percent. In fact, an emerging entrepreneurial class has developed a taste for expensive products such as Nikon cameras and Ray Ban sunglasses—both of which are available in stores. Notes Do Duc Dinh of the Institute on the World Economy, "There is a huge unofficial economy. For most people, we can live only five days or 10 days a month on our salary. But people build houses. Where does the money come from? Even in government ministries, there are two sets of books—one for the official money and one for unofficial."

Meanwhile, Eugene Matthews is proceeding with plans to establish Vietnam's biggest dairy by importing Holstein cattle from the United States. After working for many years as a consultant to companies doing business in Vietnam, Matthews has a feel for the place. "I don't want to look at anything the government doesn't regard as a priority. In this case dairy is a priority, so people are nice to you. They want to get this done." However, he notes, "It's still Vietnam. It's still a complicated place. It's still bureaucratic. But there is a system, and it does work."

Despite such optimism, euphoria over Vietnam's potential showed signs of waning at the end of the 1990s. Part of the problem was the "currency contagion" that had gripped Asia since mid-1997. Asian countries that

ment. To supply the market in the south, Coca-Cola must import canned soda from Singapore. As a result, a can of Coke costs twice as much as a bottle of Pepsi.

Experts agree that the Vietnamese market holds tremendous potential over the long term. It may be two decades before Vietnam reaches the level of economic development found in Thailand today. Meanwhile, the country's location in the heart of Asia and the presence of an ample, low-wage workforce are powerful magnets for foreign companies. By the end of 1999, France ranked first in foreign investment while Japan was the top trading partner. Overall foreign direct investment peaked at about $3.1 billion in 1997 after rising steadily since the early 1990s (see Figure 2). Investment pledges totaled $1.48 billion in 1999, down dramatically from $4 billion

Doonesbury

had been major investors were scaling back their activities in Vietnam. More generally, many companies were finding it difficult to make a profit. Cross-border smuggling from Thailand depressed legitimate sales of products produced locally by Procter & Gamble, Unilever, American Standard, and other companies. Although still strongly influenced by Communist hard-liners, the Hanoi bureaucracy is showing an increased willingness to adopt much-need reforms that will make investment more attractive. In January 2000, for example, the regulatory environment improved with the enactment of an enterprise law that streamlined the process of setting up a business; a stock market was also opened. Noted one local businessman approvingly, "In the past, it was absolutely horrendous to set up a private company. Now 99 percent of the difficulties are gone." ∎

DISCUSSION QUESTIONS

1. Assess the market opportunities in Vietnam for both consumer-products companies and industrial-products companies. How well will goods "Made in Vietnam" fare in the United States?
2. Conduct library research to determine which nation currently leads in foreign direct investment in Vietnam. What is the explanation for the ranking?
3. Some critics have argued that Cuba is more deserving of diplomatic and trade relations with the United States than Vietnam. What are some of the factors behind this argument?

SOURCES: Frederik Balfour, "Back on the Radar Screen," *Business Week* (November 20, 2000), pp. 56–57; Wayne Arnold, "Clearing the Decks for a Trade Pact's Riches," *The New York Times* (August 27, 2000), sec. 3, pp. 1, 12; Samantha Marshall, "Vietnam Pullout: This Time, Investors Pack Up Gear, Stymied by Bureaucracy, Lack of Reforms," *The Wall Street Journal* (June 30, 1998), p. A15; Marshall, "P&G Squabbles with Vietnamese Partner," *The Wall Street Journal* (February 27, 1998), p. A10; Reginald Chua, "Vietnam Frustrate Foreign Investors as Leaders Waffle on Market Economy," *The Wall Street Journal* (November 25, 1996), p. A10; "Vietnam," *The Economist* (July 8, 1995), pp. 1–18 (Survey); William J. Ardrey, Anthony Pecotich, and Clifford J. Schultz, "American Involvement in Vietnam, Part II: Prospects for U.S. Business in a New Era," *Business Horizons* 38 (March-April 1995), pp. 21–27; Edward A. Gargan, "For U.S. Business, a Hard Road to Vietnam," *The New York Times* (July 14, 1995), p. C1; Marilyn Greene, " 'Very Soon, Vietnam Will Be Very Good,' " *USA Today* (April 1, 1994), p. 8A; Robert Keatley, "Vietnam, Despite Promise, Faces Climb," *The Wall Street Journal* (August 18, 1994), p. A8; Philip Shenon, "Vietnam: Behind a Red-Tape Curtain," *The New York Times* (November 13, 1994), Sec. 3, p. 6; James Cox, "Vietnamese Look Forward to Trade, Jobs," *USA Today* (July 12, 1995), pp. 1A, 2A; Kevin Goldman, "Agencies Get Ready for Vietnam Business," *The Wall Street Journal* (February 7, 1994), p. B10.

Case 2-2   *The Road to European Monetary Union*

When leaders of the European Union member nations met in the Netherlands in 1991, they drafted a Maastricht Treaty on European Union to create, among other things, an "economic and monetary union" (EMU). Creating the EMU would require member nations to put control of monetary policy in the hands of a European central bank. Implementation of the EMU would also create a single European currency called the euro, thus eliminating costs associated with currency conversion and exchange rate uncertainty. In addition, an EU study noted that the single Eurocurrency would "permit a genuine comparison of the prices of goods and services across frontiers." The EU also hoped that the new currency would be a strong head-to-head contender with the dollar in international finance. Governments inside the single-currency zone would no longer be able to use currency devaluations or revaluations as economic adjustment mechanisms.

Meeting in Madrid in December 1995, EU representatives hoped to finalize details of the plan for a new European economic order. It was agreed that the EMU would be implemented in two stages. Starting January 1, 1999, governments and the European central bank would begin using the new currency whose exchange rate value would be fixed as of that date. Other financial institutions and private companies would be allowed nearly four years to convert to the new currency. Thus, each participating country could have two parallel currencies in circulation during the transition period. Individual shop owners might be required to re-program their cash registers, accept cash and make change in two currencies, and maintain a separate bank account for each currency. The open-ended nature of the two-stage schedule has prompted criticism; for example, Graham Bishop of the Salomon Brothers investment firm warned, "The longer the changeover, the greater the risk of some shock." Some observers predicted that, during a year-long Intergovernmental Conference (IGC) of EU nations scheduled to run from March 1996 to March 1997, the final implementation date would be pushed back.

Representatives of the European Commission insisted that it was important to adhere to the original timetable even if only two countries met the stringent economic criteria. To qualify for inclusion in the EMU, the Maastricht Treaty specified that a country's leaders must maintain stable exchange rates for two years, keep budget deficits at or below three percent of GDP, and reduce public debt to less than 60 percent of GDP. Germany, France, the Netherlands, Belgium, Luxembourg, and Austria were expected to qualify. Many obstacles remained, however. The United Kingdom and Denmark retained the right to exclude themselves from the EMU if concerns about national independence were not resolved. Several other countries—in particular, Italy, Greece, Portugal and Spain—were unlikely to qualify because of high national debt levels and other economic difficulties.

Many of the Continent's heads of state hoped that EMU would provide the means by which important and much-needed economic reforms could be achieved. In France and other countries, public spending to reduce unemployment and provide a social safety net had contributed to huge budget deficits. Many companies were already merging to take advantage of industry deregulation in Europe. The euro will accelerate efforts to streamline operations, contributing to unemployment in the process. High-cost countries such as France and Germany will undoubtedly lose jobs, while countries such as Spain with low taxes and wages will gain them. According to one estimate, 20 percent of employees in the euro zone would be affected by mergers and downsizing. The banking industry was expected to be especially hard hit as tens of thousands of bank branches were closed. Fortunately, the job cuts would be phased in over a long period of time during which thousands of new jobs would be created. Overall, some experts believed the coming of the euro would allow Europe to achieve sustained economic growth rates of 3 or 4 percent.

In the United Kingdom, business leaders were deeply divided on whether their country should be part of EMU. Sir Clive Thompson, CEO of the environmental services company Rentokil Initial, dismissed the notion that the UK should retain its own currency so that the government could resort to devaluation to stimulate the economy. "We cannot avoid the issue of improving our competitiveness. We need better products and more innovation, not a cheaper currency," Sir Clive told the *Financial Times.* Executives at many manufacturing and utility companies in the UK adopted a more cautious tone; noting the strength of the pound and low inflation, these executives suggested a go-slow approach for the immediate future. A third group was more blunt in its opposition. For example, Chris Miller, CEO of a UK-based industrial firm, was concerned that harmonization of exchange rates would lead to other types of integration, including labor laws. He explained, "I'm not surprised that German companies want Britain in a single currency. They'd like us to have their high wage and social costs, so that everyone's on the same playing field."

For their part, many Germans feared that a common European currency would be less stable than the strong Deutsche mark, the bedrock of Germany's economic success. A poll published in Germany's *DM* business magazine in mid-1995 indicated that nearly two-thirds of the country's population opposed the EMU currency plan. (In a separate poll published by the EU, only 51 percent of EU citizens showed support for the single currency.) Many Germans still fear that the value of their savings will be cut when the new currency is introduced. Finance minister Theo Waigel caused an uproar in 1997 when he proposed to restate the value of the country's gold reserves from $92 an ounce to the current market rate of $344 per ounce. He intended to use the paper gains to reduce Germany's budget deficit by about $7 billion without instituting spending cuts. Meanwhile, German investors helped drive up the Swiss franc more than 12 percent as they shifted holdings to the Swiss currency and purchased Swiss bonds rather than German ones. The Swiss franc's appreciation, in turn, drove up prices of Swiss exports of industrial products such as precision machine tools and consumer products such as popular Swatch watches.

Most observers agreed that Italy was unlikely to meet the EMU criteria. Government debt stood at 122 percent of GDP, twice as high as the Maastricht limit; annual inflation exceeded 5 percent. The situation in Italy presented a dilemma for the EU. If Italy were excluded from the EMU, some observers feared that it would have an advantage over the rest of Europe because its government would not have to adhere to stringent monetary rules. Then again, there was the danger that Italy's inclusion would make the single euro currency rather weak. The situation with Italy, Britain, and Denmark prompted some observers to question whether the EMU could function properly if some major countries were not included.

The prospects for French participation in EMU were clouded after the Socialist Party won a legislative victory in the 1997 elections. With unemployment in France exceeding 12 percent, French voters stunned President Jacques Chirac by electing nearly 300 Socialists to the National Assembly. Lionel Jospin, France's new prime minister, favored a flexible interpretation of Maastricht criteria that would preserve public sector jobs and limit the need for austerity measures in France. Jospin also favored allowing Italy and other southern European countries to join EMU if their governments could come close to meeting the criteria.

On a more personal level, the EMU means eliminating currencies that are closely associated with individual countries, such as the German mark, the French franc, and the Italian lira. This pending loss has sparked emotional concern in individual countries even among people who acknowledge that a single currency could be the cornerstone of a united Europe. As one retired French businesswoman said, "I am for the French franc, for the national money. I am not for the European money. The franc is part of the spirit of the country, its vigor, its weaknesses. It seems France will lose a bit of its personality. The money of a country is something personal. It is more than a tool of a market."

Despite such misgivings, confidence grew throughout 1996 and 1997 that EMU was, in fact, on track. After a recession in the early 1990s, economic growth in Europe picked up once again. This enabled more countries to meet the Maastricht criteria than had been expected. Companies in all parts of the world began to assess the potential threats and opportunities from the new order. IBM expected to reap billions in sales of new software necessary to convert accounting, payroll, and other systems to the euro. European companies with extensive operations across Europe such as BMW, British Petroleum, and Unilever were expected to benefit from lower transaction costs. However, local companies whose operations were concentrated in a single domestic market would face a one-two punch; they would not reap significant economies from the euro, but they would nonetheless be faced with the high costs associated with computer system conversions.

On May 2, 1998, the heads of government from the EU nations selected 11 countries as founding members of EMU. Defying expectations, Italy, Spain, and Portugal all qualified, thanks to near-miraculous transformations of their respective economies. Great Britain, Denmark, and Sweden, despite qualifying, chose not to join immediately. Greece did not qualify.

Much work remains to be done. Although the euro era started on January 1, 1999, the actual currency did not go into circulation until 2002. The European Central Bank has been established; between 1999 and 2002, member nations faced up to the challenges of maintaining budgetary discipline. Writing in *The Wall Street Journal*, Columbia University economist Robert Mundell noted, "The introduction of the euro will represent the most dramatic change in the international monetary system since President Nixon took the dollar off gold in 1971." ■

DISCUSSION QUESTIONS

1. How will Europe benefit from a single currency? Will some countries benefit more than others? Why?

2. What, if any, pricing adjustments will companies marketing in all EU countries have to make when EMU is implemented?

3. Will the EMU work? Why? What are the chances that it will fail? Why?

4. What do you think will be the biggest impediments to successful implementation of the EMU? What will be the major forces behind successful implementation?

SOURCES: Robert Mundell, "The Case for the Euro—II," *The Wall Street Journal* (March 25, 1998), p. A22; Thomas Kamm and Greg Steinmetz, "Twin Piques: Europeans See March to One Currency Hit New Stumbling Blocks," *The Wall Street Journal* (June 2, 1997), pp. A1, A12; Stefan Wagstyl and Peter Marshall, Two Sides of the Coin, *Financial Times* (November 11, 1996), p. 17; "Worries about Identity, Values," *Associated Press* (November 18, 1995), Jay Branegan, "With E.U. Countries Struggling to Qualify on Time, Economic and Monetary Union May be Delayed," *Time International* (December 1995); Peter Gumbel, "Germans Fret About Currency Union," *The Wall Street Journal* (July 25, 1995), p. A11; Christopher Taylor, "EMU: The State of Play," *The World Today* (April 1995), pp. 75–78; Kevin Dowd, "European Monetary Reform: Pitfalls of Central Planning," *USA Today* (March 1995), pp. 70–73; "A Funny New EMU," *The Economist* (March 4, 1995), pp. 49–50.

APPENDIX

Foreign Exchange

The Asian crisis described earlier in the chapter highlights the importance of one specific aspect of the economic environment: foreign exchange rates. Foreign exchange makes it possible to do business across the boundary of a national currency. However, foreign exchange is an aspect of global marketing that involves certain financial risks, decisions, and activities that are completely different than those facing a domestic marketer. Moreover, those risks can be even higher in developing markets such as Thailand, Malaysia, and South Korea. When a company conducts business within a single country, with domestic customers and suppliers paying in the domestic currency, there is no exchange risk. All prices, payments, receipts, assets, and liabilities are in the national currency. However, when a company conducts business across boundaries it is thrust into the turbulent world of exchange risk.

The foreign exchange market consists literally of a buyer's and a seller's market where currencies are traded for both spot and future delivery on a continuous basis. The *spot* market is for immediate delivery; the market for future delivery is called the *forward* market. This is a true market where prices are based on the combined forces of supply and demand that come into play at the moment of any transaction. A currency in this market is worth what people are willing to pay for it; put another way, it is worth what people are prepared to sell it for. It is a commodity. The principal players in the foreign exchange market are major banks such as Citicorp, Bankers Trust, and J.P. Morgan whose trading activities comprise nearly 80 percent of foreign exchange transactions. Other players include: the International Monetary Market (IMM) of the Chicago Mercantile Exchange, which trades currency futures; the London International Financial Futures Exchange (LIFFE); and the Philadelphia Stock Exchange (PSE), which specializes in currency options.

The volume of trading in the foreign exchange market is enormous. The Bank for International Settlements estimates that daily turnover exceeds $1.5 trillion, making foreign exchange the world's largest financial market. This figure is so huge it is hard to get a handle on; $1.5 trillion represents one-fifth of U.S. GNP, one-third of Japan's GNP, and two-thirds of Germany's GNP. In any two weeks, foreign exchange traders do as much business as importers and exporters of goods and services do in a year. Put differently, it takes the New York Stock Exchange two months to ring up a dollar volume equivalent to the value of foreign exchange transactions recorded in a single day. The dollar is the most heavily traded currency, accounting for 80 percent of transactions. London is the world's leading foreign exchange market. In 1997, London's daily turnover totaled $637 billion, which represents about 40 percent of the average daily foreign exchange turnover (see Table 1). Each market has its own focus: London is dollars per pound sterling (£), New York is dollars per euro (€), and Tokyo is dollars per yen (¥).

Visit the Web site
www.xe.com/ucc
This site offers a foreign exchange calculator that allows easy comparison of currency exchange rates.

Managed Dirty Float with SDRs

Today's global financial system can be described as a "managed dirty float with SDRs." What does this mean? *Float* refers to the system of fluctuating exchange rates. As currency trader Andrew Krieger has described this system, currencies are "up for auction," with rates "floating" or adjusting in the foreign exchange market subject to all the forces of supply and demand. In other words, the

Table 1
Leading Foreign Exchange Markets by Percent of Average Daily Turnover

CITY	PERCENT
London	40
New York	23
Tokyo	10
Singapore	10
Hong Kong	6
Zurich	5
Frankfurt	5
Paris	4

Source: Bank for International Settlements.

buying and selling activities of currency traders partially determine a specific currency's value on a given day. *Managed* refers to the specific use of fiscal and monetary policy by governments to influence exchange rates.

Devaluation can result from government action that decrees a reduction in the value of the local currency against other currencies. In 1994, for example, the Chinese devalued the yuan (also known as *renminbhi* or "people's money"). The immediate result was to ensure the low-cost position of Chinese exporters. However, the action also set the stage for the 1997 devaluations of the Thai baht, Malaysian ringgit, and Indonesian rupiah; the expression "beggar-thy-neighbor" is sometimes used to describe devaluations designed to increase export competitiveness.

The effect of devaluation on BEM economies was also demonstrated on December 20, 1994, when the Bank of Mexico was forced to devalue the peso. A combination of circumstances led to the action, including a $28 billion current-account deficit, dwindling reserves, the murder of presidential candidate Donaldo Colosio, and eroding investor confidence. One immediate effect of the devaluation was a sharp decline in Mexican purchases of products from the United States. For example, Westinghouse and Lennox had been aggressively selling air conditioners in Mexico; sales quickly slowed to a trickle immediately after the devaluation. McDonald's, KFC, Dunkin' Donuts, and other U.S. restaurant chains were also hard hit as they were forced to raise prices. Mexico has since recovered from the shock of the devaluation, and the country remains an important destination for foreign investment.

Market forces can also trigger devaluation; once the governments of Thailand, Malaysia, and Indonesia allowed their respective currencies to float, market forces led to the subsequent depreciation in value. *Dirty* refers to the fact that, besides currency traders, central banks buy and sell currencies in the foreign exchange market in an effort to influence exchange rates. Such interventions may be intended to dampen fluctuations in foreign exchange rates. A good illustration occurred in October 1997, when currency speculators mounted an attack on the Hong Kong dollar, which was still pegged to the U.S. dollar. The head of the Hong Kong Monetary Authority defended the peg by using his country's ample reserves to buy, and therefore support the value of the Hong Kong dollar. Central bank intervention can also represent government attempts to change the relative values of currencies over the short and medium term. An example of the latter occurred on Wednesday, June 17, 1998, when the central banks of Japan and the United States intervened in currency markets by selling dollars and buying $4 billion worth of yen. By the end of the trading day in New York, the yen had gained 5 percent, from $1/¥143.47 to $1/¥136.37.

Foreign Exchange Market Dynamics

Some of the trading in the foreign exchange market represents the forces of supply and demand driven by the need to settle accounts for the global trade in goods and services. To the extent that a country sells more goods and services abroad than it buys, there will be a greater demand for its currency and a tendency for it to *appreciate* in value. The strength of the Japanese yen in the mid-1990s was a case in point. High demand for Japanese goods resulted in high demand for yen; the strong demand for yen caused its value to increase. If the foreign exchange market were influenced only by purchases and sales to settle accounts for merchandise and services trade, it would be a fairly simple matter to forecast foreign exchange rates. However, short- and long-term capital flows and speculative purchases and sales are a major source of supply and demand for foreign exchange. Short-term capital is sensitive to interest rates, long-term capital to return expectations, and both are sensitive to perceptions of risk. Today, currency speculators appear to have more power to move currency markets than government central bankers (see Millman 1995).[25]

Table 2 shows how fluctuating currency values can affect financial risk, depending on the terms of payment specified in the contract. Suppose, at the time a deal is made, the exchange rate is €1.10=$1. What happens to a U.S. exporter if the dollar strengthens against the euro—trades at, say, €1.25=$1—and the contract specifies payment in dollars? What happens if the dollar weakens (e.g., €0.85=$1)? Conversely, what if the European buyer contracts to pay in euros rather than dollars?

Purchasing Power Parity

Given that currencies fluctuate in value, a reasonable question to ask is whether, due either to market forces or government intervention, a given currency is over- or undervalued compared with another. One way to answer the question is to compare world prices for a single well-known product: McDonald's Big Mac hamburger. The so-called Big Mac Index is a "quick and dirty" way of determining which of the world's currencies are too weak or strong. The underlying assumption is that the price of a Big Mac in any world currency should, after being converted to dollars, equal the price of a Big Mac in the United States. A country's currency would be over-valued if the Big Mac price (converted to dollars) is

---

25 This issue has also been widely covered in the business press. For example, see Randall Smith, "The Big Casino: How Currency Traders Play for High Stakes against Central Banks," *The Wall Street Journal* (September 18, 1992), pp. A1, A5.

Table 2
Exchange Risks and Gains in Foreign Transactions

Foreign Exchange Rates	$1,000,000 Contract		€ 1,100,000 Contract	
	U.S. Seller Receives	European Buyer Pays	U.S. Seller Receives	European Buyer Pays
€1.25=$1	$1,000,000	€1,250,000	$880,000	€1,100,000
€1.10=$1	$1,000,000	€1,100,000	$1,000,000	€1,100,000
€1.00=$1	$1,000,000	€1,000,000	$1,100,000	€1,100,000
€0.85=$1	$1,000,000	€850,000	$1,294,118	€1,100,000

Table 3
The Big Mac Index

Country	Big Mac Price in Local Currency	Exchange Rate Implied by PPP	Actual Official Exchange Rate	Over- or Undervaluation of Local Currency
France	FFr18.50	7.28FFr/$1	7.44/$1	−2
Euro zone	2.57	.99	.88/$1	−11
Switzerland	SwFr6.30	2.48/$1	1.73/$1	+44
Canada	C $3.33	1.31/$1	1.56/$1	−16
Japan	¥294	116/$1	124/$1	−7
Russia	Ruble 35.00	13.8/$1	28.9/$1	−52
U.S.	$2.54	—	—	—

Source: Adapted from "Big Mac Currencies," *The Economist* (April 21, 2001), p. 74.

higher than the U.S. price. Conversely, a country's currency would be undervalued if the converted Big Mac price was lower than the U.S. price. Economists use the concept of **purchasing power parity** (PPP) when adjusting national income data to improve comparability.

Table 3 shows the Big Mac index for selected countries in 2001. The first column of figures shows the price of a Big Mac in the local currency. The second column shows the implied PPP of the dollar, obtained by dividing the local currency price by the dollar price. Thus, for example, in Japan a Big Mac costs ¥294 yielding a Big Mac PPP of 116 (294÷2.54). Note that the yen/dollar exchange rate at the time was only 124 to 1, meaning that $2.54 would be the equivalent of ¥314.9—more than enough to buy a Big Mac in Tokyo! Thus, we can see that the yen is undervalued against the dollar by about 7 percent. In other words, based on the U.S price for a Big Mac, the yen/dollar exchange rate ought to be 116 to 1, not 124 to 1.

In its annual survey of earnings around the world, Union Bank of Zurich also uses the Big Mac as a reference point. The survey assesses purchasing power around the world in terms of how long the average wage earner must work to earn enough money to pay for a Big Mac. According to the most recent survey, employees in Zurich, Geneva, Tokyo, Luxembourg, and New York have the highest take-home pay. Workers in Nairobi, Bombay, Shanghai, Budapest, Moscow, and Manila rank at the bottom in terms of take-home pay. Table 4 shows the longest and shortest average times required to earn enough for a Big Mac.

ECONOMIC EXPOSURE

The degree to which exchange rates affect a company's market value as measured by its stock price is known as economic exposure. **Economic exposure** refers to the impact of currency fluctuations on the present value of a company's expected future cash flows. For example,

Table 4
Time Worked to Pay for a Big Mac

LONGEST TIME		SHORTEST TIME	
CITY	MINUTES	CITY	MINUTES
Nairobi	193	Chicago, Houston, Tokyo	9
Caracas	117	Los Angeles	10
Moscow	104	Hong Kong	11
Jakarta	103	Toronto, New York	12
Budapest	91	Luxembourg	13
Bombay	85	Montreal, Sydney, Zurich	14
Manila	77	Athens, Geneva	15
Shanghai	75	Frankfurt	16
Mexico City	71	Vienna	17
Prague	56	Berlin	18

Source: Union Bank of Switzerland.

Mexican sales account for 11 percent of Avon Products' annual sales; thus, Avon had a great deal of economic exposure to the peso's devaluation in 1994. The extent of the exposure prompted many investors to sell Avon stock.

Economic exposure can be further divided into two categories: transaction exposure and real operating exposure. *Transaction exposure* arises when the company's activities result in sales or purchases denominated in foreign currencies. Guinness, for example faces transaction exposure to the extent that it agrees to accept payment for exports of scotch at one exchange rate but actually settles its accounts at a different rate of exchange.[26] Similarly, in the mid-1980s, a third of Eastman Kodak's revenues were generated from non-U.S. sales; according to company estimates, the strength of the dollar in the early 1980s resulted in lost profits totaling $500 million over a four-year period. This loss occurred despite the fact that Kodak's foreign exchange trading team bought and sold $10 billion worth of currencies on foreign exchange markets every year to protect the company's $1.5 billion transaction exposure.[27] The importance of transaction exposure is directly proportional to the amount of business a company conducts outside the home market. Obviously, currency exposure is a critical issue for Nestlé, with 98 percent of annual sales taking place outside Switzerland. By contrast, GE generated about 70 percent of its 2001 revenues in the United States, so the relative extent of GE's exposure is less than that of Nestlé.

Transaction exposure may vary among a company's business units. Consider, for example, DaimlerChrysler's aircraft group, DaimlerChrysler Aerospace Airbus (Dasa). World prices for aircraft are denominated in dollars, and 75 percent of Dasa's revenues are in dollars. In the early 1990s, this had serious implications in view of the mark's strength. Compounding the problem was the fact that most of Dasa's employees were paid in marks. Dasa's net losses for 1992 to 1994 totaled nearly 1.5 billion marks. Company executives simply misforecast how far the dollar would fall against the mark. Budgets for 1995 were based on an exchange rate of 1.6 marks to the dollar, but by mid-1995 the actual rate was 1.38 to 1.[28]

Real operating exposure arises when currency fluctuations, together with price changes, alter a company's future revenues and costs. According to this definition, the firms that face operating exposure include not only those that have overseas operations but also those whose manufacturing plan calls for sourcing goods abroad. Economic exposure arises whenever companies commit to setting up new product development centers and distribution systems, getting foreign supply, or investing in foreign production facilities.

In dealing with the economic exposure introduced by currency fluctuations, a key issue is whether the company can use price as a strategic tool for maintaining its profit margins. Can the company adjust prices in response to a rise or fall of foreign exchange rates in various markets? That depends on the price elasticity of demand. The less

[26] John Willman, "Currency Squeeze on Guinness," *Financial Times—Weekend Money* (September 27–28, 1997), p. 5.
[27] Michael Sesit, "Avoiding Losses: By Trading Currencies, Kodak's Eric R. Nelson Saves the Firm Millions," *The Wall Street Journal* (March 5, 1985), p. 1.
[28] Brian Coleman, "Daimler Aerospace Comes Down to Earth," *The Wall Street Journal* (July 27, 1995), p. A7.

price-sensitive the demand, the greater the flexibility a company has in responding to exchange rate changes. Price elasticity, in turn, depends on the degree of competition and the location of the competitors. Ford managers believed a 10 percent price increase following the peso devaluation in Mexico was feasible. In the case of DaimlerChrysler's Dasa unit, the presence of numerous regional competitors constrained the company's ability to push through price increases. In 1995, Dasa executives launched a Competition Initiative to examine various measures, such as cutting jobs and rethinking supplier agreements. Dasa purchased only 25 percent of its parts outside Germany, so one option was to switch to suppliers in the United States or other countries with relatively weak currencies. Another option was to persuade German suppliers to "share the pain" by accepting payment in dollars. Ultimately, Dasa may be forced to exit some segments of the industry.

MANAGING EXCHANGE RATE EXPOSURE

As the Dasa example illustrates, it is very difficult to accurately forecast the movement of exchange rates. Over the years, the search for other ways of managing cash flows to eliminate or reduce exchange rate risks has resulted in the development of numerous techniques and financial strategies. For example, it may be desirable to sell products in the company's home country currency. When this is not possible, techniques are available to reduce both transaction and operating exposure.

Hedging

Hedging exchange rate exposure involves establishing an offsetting currency position such that the loss or gain of one currency position is offset by a corresponding gain or loss in some other currency. The practice is common among global companies that sell products and maintain operations in different countries. For example, DaimlerChrysler spends tens of millions of dollars each year on foreign currency and hedging transactions. A basic rule of thumb is this: If company forecasts indicate that the value of the foreign currency will weaken against the home currency, a hedge to protect against potential transaction losses is a prudent course of action. Conversely, for predictions that the foreign currency will appreciate (strengthen) against the home currency, then a gain, rather than a loss, can be expected on foreign transactions when revenues are converted into the home currency. Given this expectation, the best decision may be not to hedge at all.

External hedging methods for managing both transaction and translation exposure call for participating in the foreign currency market. Specific hedging tools include for-

ward contracts and currency options. Internal hedging methods include price adjustment clauses and intracorporate borrowing or lending in foreign currencies. For example, when Robert J. Prantis joined Sun Microsystems in Silicon Valley, more than 50 percent of Sun's sales were overseas; sales transactions involved 20 different currencies. Mr. Prantis's first task was to identify Sun's exposure to foreign exchange risk. This task was complicated by the slow pace of information flow due to the company's decentralized structure. Thomas J. Meredith, treasurer at Sun, noted, "In a place like the United States that is tied to the quarterly earnings report, foreign exchange is more and more a driving force. Sun has to be vigilant month to month and has to identify all the exposures." Prantis and Meredith discovered that Sun's Japanese subsidiary was buying computer work stations from headquarters for dollars and selling them back in Japan for yen even as headquarters was buying yen for dollars to pay for work station components that it sourced in Japan. Thus, the company was experiencing transaction exposure from both the yen/dollar and the dollar/yen sides. To insulate the company from this exposure, headquarters instituted a policy whereby its Japanese subsidiary would pay for work stations with yen; the same yen would be used by headquarters to pay Japanese component suppliers. Meredith estimated that natural hedging saved Sun about $1 million in its first year. The losers were the Japanese banks that lost Sun's foreign currency business.

Forward Contracts

The **forward market** is a mechanism for buying and selling currencies at a preset price for future delivery. If it is known that a certain amount of foreign currency is going to be paid out or received at some future date, a company can insure itself against exchange loss by buying or selling forward. With a forward contract, the company can lock in a specific fixed exchange rate for a future date and thus immunize itself from the loss (or gain) caused by the exchange rate fluctuation. By consulting any published source (*The Wall Street Journal*'s foreign exchange page is in its Section 3), it is possible to determine exchange rates on any given day. In addition to spot prices, 30-, 60-, and 180-day forward prices are quoted for dozens of world currencies.

In the first half of the 1980s, the dollar rose in value against the world's currencies. Consider, for example, the case of an American exporter selling in West Germany. At the beginning of 1984, the Deutsche mark/dollar exchange rate was 2.7458 to $1. If the U.S. exporter anticipated receiving DM100 million by the end of 1984, the dollar value of the deal would have been $36.4 million (see Table 5). However, by the end of 1984 the dollar had strengthened against the mark to DM3.1570/$1. Thus, those DM100 million were only worth $31.7 million, and the exporter would

Table 5
Dollar Value of DM Denominated Contract for Delivery of Goods

	EXCHANGE RATE	VALUE OF DM 100M CONTRACT
January 1984—Actual	DM2.7458=$1	$36.4 million
December 1984—Actual	DM3.1570=$1	$31.7 million
December 1984—Future	DM2.6450=$1	$37.8 million

have faced a $4.7 million transaction loss. Ideally, the exporter would have turned to the forward market at the beginning of 1984 to hedge the dollar value of the German receivables due at year's end. He or she could have locked in a rate of DM2.6450/$1, a rate which reflected the predictions of many forecasters that the dollar would fall in 1984 (which, in fact, it did not do). Note that at the prevailing forward rate in January 1984, our exporter would have done better than simply covering potential losses from a weaker mark. The exporter would have received $37.8 million for the DM100 million, a price that was actually $1.4 million *more* than the dollar amount originally expected.[29]

Options

Companies use the forward market when the currency exposure is known in advance (e.g., when a firm contract of sale exists). In some situations, however, companies are not certain about the future foreign currency cash inflow or outflow. Consider the risk exposure of a U.S. company that bids for a foreign project but won't know if the project will be granted until sometime later. The company needs to protect the dollar value of the contract by hedging the *potential* foreign currency cash inflow that will be generated if the company turns out to be the winning bidder. In such an instance, forward contracts are not the appropriate hedging tool.

A foreign currency **option** is best for such situations. A **put option** gives the buyer the right, not the obligation, to sell a specified number of foreign currency units at a fixed price, up to the option's expiration date. (Conversely, a **call option** is the right, but not the obligation, to buy the foreign currency.) In the example of bidding the foreign project, the company can take out a put option to sell the foreign currency for dollars at a set price in the future. In other words, the U.S. company locks in the value of the contract in dollars. Thus, if the project is granted, the future foreign currency cash inflow has been hedged by means of the put option. If the project is *not* granted, the company can trade the put option in the options market without exercising it; remember, options are rights, not obligations. The only money the company stands to lose is the difference between what it paid for the option and what it receives upon selling it.

Avon Products' attitude that "turmoil presents opportunities" served it well in the wake of the Asian currency crisis. In 1996, Asian sales accounted for $751 million of Avon's $4.8 billion in worldwide revenues. Avon purchases most raw materials locally, and has factories in China, Indonesia, the Philippines, and Japan. Rather than borrow in dollars, country managers who need capital for operations arrange for loans denominated in local currencies. When the crisis unfolded in Thailand in the summer of 1997, Joe Ferreira, Jr., head of Avon's Asia-Pacific region, and treasurer Dennis Ling stipulated that the 10 country units in Asia remit earnings on a weekly, rather than monthly basis. This allowed for quicker conversion of local currencies into dollars. As of August, 1997, however, the company had not hedged in Asia; Ferreira and Ling agreed to spend about $3 million to protect $50 million in Asian currency exposure. The two Avon executives also took other steps that reflected the changes in the financial environment: Avon's Latin American managers were invited to Asia to share their experiences of the peso devaluation with the Asian managers; a European lace vendor was replaced by a Thai company; and a contract was renegotiated with a South Korean supplier of jewelry for the United States. As Ling said, "Part of my job is to help our managers understand and take advantage of the impact of currencies on their business."[30]

Financial officers of global firms can avoid transaction exposure altogether by demanding a particular currency as the payment for its foreign sales. As noted, a U.S-based company might demand U.S. dollars as the payment currency for its foreign sales. This, however, does not eliminate currency risk; it simply shifts that risk to the customers. In common practice, companies typically attempt to invoice exports (receivables) in strong currencies and imports (payables) in weak currencies. However, in today's highly competitive world market, such practice may reduce a company's competitive edge.

---

[29] Sesit, p. 1.

[30] Fred R. Bleakley, "How U.S. Firm Copes with Asia Crisis," *The Wall Street Journal* (December 26, 1997), pp. A2, A4.

Chapter 3

The Global Trade Environment: Regional Market Characteristics and Preferential Trade Agreements

*I*n the spring of 2001, leaders from 34 North and South American nations convened the third Summit of the Americas in Quebec City, Canada, to discuss plans for a proposed Free Trade Area of the Americas (FTAA). As thousands of labor and environmental activists gathered behind barricades, Mexican president Vicente Fox, Brazilian president Henrique Cardoso, and their colleagues hoped for a clear signal from president George W. Bush that the United States was serious about free trade. If negotiations are successfully completed by January 2005, the FTAA will stretch from Alaska to Tierra del Fuego, Argentina; the area would account for $11 trillion in annual economic output (approximately one-third of the world total) and encompass 800 million people. Back home, however, Bush and trade representative Robert Zoellick were under pressure from a variety of constituents. For example, farmers wanted assurances that subsidy programs would not be cut back. America's steel producers wanted the government to maintain anti-dumping duties to curtail the influx of low-priced steel imports. Another problem was the refusal of the U.S. Congress to grant the president trade promotion authority. TPA would enable the president to negotiate trade agreements, which Congress would then have to vote on without making any changes or amendments.

Since World War II there has been a tremendous interest among nations in economic cooperation. This interest has been stimulated by the success of the European Community (now the European Union), which was itself inspired by the U.S. economy. Although the Free Trade Area of the Americas represents a very ambitious multilateral effort, there are varying degrees of economic cooperation and several different types of preferential trade agreements in existence today. These range from agreement among two or more nations to reductions of barriers to trade, to the full-scale economic integration of two or more national

The Canadian government went to unprecedented lengths to ensure security during the Summit of the Americas meeting in 2001, spending about $100 million on the effort. The meeting venue was enclosed by a 2.3 mile concrete and chain-link fence that demonstrators called the "Wall of Shame." Around the world, antiglobalization activists are demanding that global companies show more concern for the physical environment, exert pressure on suppliers to improve factory working conditions in developing countries, and support human rights initiatives. The signs read, "Tomorrow, It's Death."

economies. The best-known preferential arrangement of the twentieth century was the British Commonwealth preference system. This system provided a foundation for trade between the United Kingdom, Canada, Australia, New Zealand, India, and other former British colonies in Africa, Asia, and the Middle East. The decision by the United Kingdom to join the European Economic Community resulted in the demise of this system and illustrates the constantly evolving nature of international economic cooperation.

Our survey of the world trade environment begins with the World Trade Organization and its predecessor, the GATT, and then general trade patterns are discussed. Next, the four main types of preferential trade agreements are identified and described. An introduction to individual countries in the world's major market regions follows; each section also includes detailed discussion of the specific preferential trade agreements in which those countries participate. Important marketing issues in each region are also discussed. Several important emerging country markets were described in Chapter 2; in this chapter, special attention will be given to individual country markets that were not previously discussed.

THE WORLD TRADE ORGANIZATION AND GATT

The year 1997 marked the fiftieth anniversary of the General Agreement on Tariffs and Trade (GATT), a treaty among nations whose governments agree, at least in principle, to promote trade among members. GATT was intended to be a multilateral, global initiative, and GATT negotiators did indeed succeed in liberalizing world merchandise trade. GATT was also an organization that handled 300 trade disputes—many involving food—during its half century of existence. GATT itself had no enforcement power (the losing party in a dispute was entitled to ignore the ruling), and the process of dealing with disputes sometimes stretched on for years. Little wonder, then, that some critics referred to GATT as the "General Agreement to Talk and Talk."

The successor to GATT, the World Trade Organization (WTO), came into existence on January 1, 1995. From its base in Geneva, the WTO provides a forum for trade-related negotiations among its 141 members. The WTO's staff of neutral trade experts will also serve as mediators in global trade disputes. The WTO has a Dispute Settlement Body (DSB) that mediates complaints concerning unfair trade barriers and other issues between the WTO's member countries. During a 60-day consultation period, parties to a complaint are expected to engage in good-faith negotiations and reach an amicable resolution. Failing that, the complainant can ask the DSB to appoint a three-member panel of trade experts to hear the case behind closed doors. After convening, the panel has nine months within which to issue its ruling. The DSB is empowered to act on the panel's recommendations. The losing party has the option of turning to a seven-member appellate body. If, after due process, a country's trade policies are found to violate WTO rules, it is expected to change those policies. If changes are not forthcoming, the WTO can authorize trade sanctions against the loser.

One of the WTO's first major tasks was hosting negotiations on the General Agreement on Trade in Services, in which 76 signatories made binding market access commitments in banking, securities, and insurance. The WTO faced its first real test when representatives from the United States and Japan met to try and resolve a dispute over Washington's claims that the Japanese engaged in unfair trade practices that limited imports of U.S. car parts. The Clinton administration was responding to the fact that, between 1990 to 1994, the annual U.S. merchandise trade deficit with Japan averaged $51 billion—about one-third of the total U.S. deficit. Moreover, cars and auto parts consistently accounted for approximately two-thirds of the deficit with Japan. In the spring of 1995, the United States threatened to slap 100 percent tariffs on 13 models of Japanese imported cars. Japan formally filed a complaint with the WTO objecting to the tariffs. Although a trade war was narrowly averted at the last moment, trade-related tensions between the two countries continue to simmer. Trade tensions flared up again in 1998 as the United States announced plans to impose 100 percent tariffs on select European imports such as Italian hams and bed linens. Washington was acting in response to Europe's banana import quota system (see Case 3-2). Even before that situation was resolved, the EU asked the WTO to impose a record $4 billion in trade sanctions on the United States in retaliation for alleged unfair tax breaks available to U.S. companies that export.

Trade ministers representing the WTO member nations meet annually to work on improving world trade. At the 1996 meeting in Singapore, agreement was reached concerning tariffs on information technology. Zero tariffs are now slated for 500 products, ranging from calculators, fax machines, and CD-ROM drives to computer keyboards and ATM machines. The United States, Canada, and several Asian countries will benefit the most, because they are home to companies that command 80 percent of world trade in high-tech products, compared with a 15 percent share held by Western European companies. The agreement could result in lower prices for businesses and consumers, especially in Asia and Europe where tariffs had been relatively high.[1] Still, it remains to be seen whether the WTO will live up to expectations

---

[1]   Helene Cooper and Bhushan Bahree, "Nations Agree to Drop Computer Tariffs," *The Wall Street Journal* (December 13, 1996), pp. A2, A6.

Visit the Web site
The World Trade
Organization maintains
a very informative
Web site at:
www.wto.org

when it comes to additional major policy initiatives on such issues as competition of foreign investment. One problem is that politicians in many countries are resisting the WTO's plans to move swiftly in removing trade barriers. A Norwegian trade group told reporters that the WTO's motto should be, "If you can decide it tomorrow, why decide it today?" Still, as Renato Ruggiero, former Director General of the WTO, said recently, "Free trade is a process that cannot be stopped."[2]

PREFERENTIAL TRADE AGREEMENTS

In addition to the multilateral initiative of GATT, countries in each of the world's regions are seeking to lower barriers to trade within their regions. Historically, when countries entered into preference agreements, they notified GATT. Between 1947 and 1992, 85 agreements were notified; 77 new agreements have been added since 1992. Strictly speaking, few of the trade agreements fully conform with GATT requirements; none, however, have been disallowed. Of all WTO members, only Japan, South Korea, and Hong Kong have not signed preferential trade agreements.[3]

Free Trade Area

A **free trade area** (FTA) is formed when two or more countries agree to abolish all internal barriers to trade among themselves. Countries that belong to a free trade area can and do maintain independent trade policies with respect to third countries. A system of certificates of origin is used to avoid trade diversion in favor of low-tariff members. The system discourages importing goods into the member country with the lowest tariff for transshipment to countries within the area with higher external tariffs; customs inspectors police the borders between members. The European Economic Area is an example of a free trade area and includes the 15-nation European Union, plus Norway, Liechtenstein, and Iceland.

Customs Union

A **customs union** represents the logical evolution of a free trade area. In addition to eliminating internal barriers to trade, members of a customs union agree to the establishment of common external barriers. On January 1, 1996, the European Union and Turkey initiated a customs union in an effort to boost two-way trade above the average annual level of $20 billion. The arrangement called for elimination of tariffs averaging 14 percent that added $1.5 billion each year to the cost of European goods imported by Turkey.

Common Market

A **common market** is the next level of economic integration. In addition to the removal of internal barriers to trade and the establishment of common external barriers, the common market allows for free movement of factors of production, including labor, capital, and information. The Central American Integration System (SICA) and the Andean Community may ultimately evolve into true common markets.

---

2   Helene Cooper and Bhushan Bahree, "No 'Gattzilla': World's Best Hope for Global Trade Topples Few Barriers," *The Wall Street Journal* (December 3, 1996), p. A8.
3   Martin Wolf, "An Unhealthy Trade-off," *Financial Times* (October 29, 1996), p. 14.

Former U.S. President Bill Clinton first formally proposed the idea for a hemispheric free trade area in 1994 during a summit of heads of state in Miami. Meeting in Brazil in May 1997, trade ministers from the 34 participating countries agreed to create "preparatory committees" in anticipation of formal talks that would begin in 1998. The Clinton administration was keen to open the region's fast growing, big emerging markets to U.S. companies. In particular, the president wanted talks to focus immediately on tariffs and "early harvest" agreements on individual industry sectors such as information technology. The FTAA was formally launched in April 1998 during the second Summit of the Americas in Santiago, Chile.

After President Bush took office, he viewed FTAA as one aspect of a multi-level approach to trade issues. Bush also hoped to pursue bilateral agreements between the United States and individual nations as well as global negotiations within the framework of the World Trade Organization. Prospects for the latter had been dimmed somewhat by the disastrous global trade talks in Seattle in the fall of 1999; protesters succeeded in disrupting the event. However, the prospect of improved access to one of the world's most attractive consumer market holds considerable allure for many Latin American nations.

However, for policy makers in Brazil, the potential benefits are not so clear-cut. The textile industry stands to benefit greatly if U.S. import quotas are lifted. As Brazilian Foreign Minister Celso Lafer said, "This negotiation is not a tariff negotiation. This is a negotiation of market access." However, Brazil's paper and chemical industries could be severely hurt by strong American competitors. Executives in these and other industries have pleaded with the government for more time to improve productivity and marketing. Brazil has responded by refusing to yield to U.S. pressure to move up the implementation date to December 2003. In some circles, a preference has been expressed for a trade pact with the European Union.

Visit the Web site

There has been considerable grassroots opposition to the FTAA. For a sampling, visit:
wtoaction.org/ftaa
www.corpwatch.org/globalization/treaties

SOURCES: "All in the Familia," *Economist* (April 21, 2001), pp. 19–21; "Breaking Barriers in the Americas," *Economist* (April 21, 2001); p. 14; Jonathan Karp, "Brazil to Be Vocal in Americas Trade Talks," *The Wall Street Journal* (April 19, 2001), p. A13; Helene Cooper, "New Trade Representative Faces an Old Obstacle: Fast-Track Fight," *The Wall Street Journal* (April 6, 2001), p. A16; Kenneth Maxwell, "Brazil's Free Traders Are in Dire Need of a U.S. Boost," *The Wall Street Journal* (April 6, 2001), p. A15.

Economic Union

An **economic union** builds upon the elimination of the internal tariff barriers, the establishment of common external barriers, and the free flow of factors. It seeks to coordinate and harmonize economic and social policy within the union to facilitate the free flow of capital, labor, and goods and services from country to country. An economic union is a common marketplace not only for goods but also for services and capital. For example, if professionals are going to be able to work anywhere in the EU, the members must harmonize their practice licensing so that a doctor or lawyer qualified in one country may practice in any other. The full evolution of an economic union would involve the creation of a unified central bank, the use of a single currency, and common policies on agriculture, social services and welfare, regional development, transport, taxation, competition, and mergers. A fully developed economic union requires extensive political unity, which makes it similar to a nation. The further integration of nations that were members of fully developed economic unions would be the formation of a central government that would bring together independent

Behind the Scenes
A Half Century of Trade Negotiation

Between 1947 and 1994, the member countries of GATT completed eight rounds of multilateral trade negotiations. Tariffs have been reduced from an average of 40 percent in 1945 to 5 percent today. The result has been a tremendous growth in trade: In the three decades from 1945 and 1975, the volume of world trade expanded by roughly 500 percent. The seventh round of negotiations was launched in Tokyo and ran from 1973 to 1979. These talks succeeded in cutting duties on industrial products valued at $150 billion by another 30 percent so that the remaining tariffs averaged about 6 percent. In terms of agricultural trade, there was a major clash between the U.S. and protectionist European and Japanese markets. The clash pitted the American farmer—the world's most efficient producer—against the high-cost, but politically powerful, farmers of Europe and Japan. These deep-rooted differences resulted in little change in the agricultural area during the Tokyo Round. The most notable feature of the Tokyo Round was not the duty cuts, but rather a series of nine new agreements on nontariff trade barriers.

GATT officials also devoted considerable attention to the services industry, addressing market-entry barriers in banking, insurance, telecommunications, and other sectors. The services issue was so volatile that the opening of the Uruguay Round was delayed from 1982 until 1986. In addition to trade in services, these negotiations focused on the fore-mentioned nontariff measures that restrict or distort trade, including agricultural trade policy, intellectual property protection, and restrictions on foreign investment.

Agricultural subsidies and quotas that developed outside the multilateral framework have also been a divisive issue. Affluent countries protect and subsidize farm production. While home-market consumers pay higher prices, surplus output is sold abroad at artificially low prices. Sugar subsidies in the European Union cost European shoppers an estimated $7.5 billion extra because high sugar prices result in higher prices for ice cream, soft drinks, and candy bars. In France, government expenditures for agricultural subsidies in 1992 amounted to $44 billion; French consumers paid an additional $85 billion for higher-priced food products. According to the OECD, the total cost of these subsidies to rich-country taxpayers and consumers is more than $200 billion a year. Poor countries (including those in Eastern Europe) are denied their natural path out of poverty, namely food exports. The Uruguay negotiations were suspended in December 1990 after 30,000 French farmers took to the streets of Brussels to protest a proposed 30 percent cut in agricultural export subsidies. Negotiations resumed a few months later against the background of the united Western war effort in the Persian Gulf war. Negotiators finally succeeded in reaching agreement by the December 15, 1993 deadline. A stalemate over agricultural subsidies was broken, with France and the EU nations agreeing to reductions. The U.S. Congress voted in favor of GATT at the end of 1994.

Competitive companies will benefit as tariffs are cut or eliminated entirely. The Triad nations agreed to end tariffs in pharmaceuticals, construction and agricultural equipment, Scotch whiskey, furniture, paper, steel, and medical equipment. Also, U.S. restrictions on textile and apparel imports from Third World countries will be phased out over a 10-year period. Another breakthrough was the Chemical Tariff Harmonization Agreement (CTHA), whose signatories agreed to reduce tariffs on chemicals to a maximum of 6.5 percent. Major issues remain unresolved in the entertainment industry; France has insisted on preferences and subsidies for French producers of television programming and motion pictures in order to limit what they feel is "cultural imperialism." Efforts to reduce European broadcast restrictions on U.S.-produced movies and television programming were unsuccessful.

SOURCES: Shailagh Murray, "Subsidies Shackle EU Competitiveness," *The Wall Street Journal* (October 28, 1996), p. A13; "GATT's Last Gasp," *The Economist* (December 1, 1990), p. 16; Joseph A. McKinney, "How Multilateral Trade Talks Affect the U.S.," *Baylor Business Review* (Fall 1991), pp. 24–25; Bob Davis, "Squeaky Wheels: GATT Talks Resume, with France and India Calling Many of the Shots," *The Wall Street Journal* (January 31, 1992), pp. A1, A13; "Free Trade's Fading Champion," *The Economist* (April 11, 1992), p. 65; Bob Davis and Lawrence Ingrassia, "Trade Acceptance: After Years of Talks, GATT Is at Last Ready to Sign Off On a Pact," *The Wall Street Journal* (December 15, 1993), pp. A1, A7.

Table 3-1
Forms of Regional Economic Integration

Stage of Integration	Elimination of Tariffs and Quotas Among Members	Common Tariff and Quota System	Elimination of Restrictions on Factor Movements	Harmonization and Unification of Economic and Social Policies and Institutions
Free Trade Area	Yes	No	No	No
Customs Union	Yes	Yes	No	No
Common Market	Yes	Yes	Yes	No
Economic Union	Yes	Yes	Yes	Yes

political states into a single political framework. The European Union is approaching its target of completing most of the steps required to become a full economic union. The various forms of economic integration are compared in Table 3-1.

NORTH AMERICA

North America, which includes Canada, the United States, and Mexico, comprises a distinctive regional market. The United States combines great wealth, a large population, vast space, and plentiful natural resources in a single national economic and political environment and thus presents unique marketing characteristics. High product ownership levels are associated with high income and relatively high receptivity to innovations and new ideas both in consumer and industrial products. The United States is home to more global industry leaders—a total of 162 companies according to *Fortune* magazine's Global 500 ranking—than any other nation in the world. For example, U.S. companies are the dominant producers in the computer, software, aerospace, entertainment, medical equipment, and jet engine industry sectors.

In 1988, the United States and Canada signed a free trade agreement (U.S.-Canada Free Trade Agreement, or CFTA); the Canada-U.S. Free Trade Area formally came into existence in 1989. This helps explain the fact that more than $400 billion per year in goods and services flows between Canada and the United States—the biggest trading relationship between any two nations. Canada takes 20 percent of U.S. exports and the United States buys approximately 85 percent of Canada's exports. Figure 3-1 illustrates the economic integration of North America: Canada is the number one trading partner of the United States; Mexico is second, and Japan ranks third as a market for U.S. exports in spite of the fact that Mexico's GNP is only 9 percent of Japan's. American companies have more invested in Canada than any other country. Many U.S. manufacturers, including GE and IBM, use their Canadian operations as major global suppliers for some product lines. By participating in the Canadian auto market, U.S. automakers gain greater economies of scale. The U.S.-Canadian Free Trade Agreement, which was fully implemented in January 1998, is creating a continental market for most other products.

On August 12, 1992, representatives from the United States, Canada, and Mexico concluded negotiations for the **North American Free Trade Agreement** (NAFTA). The agreement was approved by both houses of the U.S. Congress and became effective

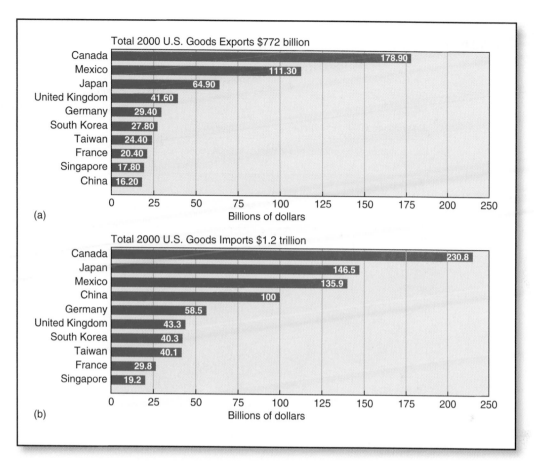

Total 2000 U.S. Goods Exports $772 billion

Country	Billions of dollars
Canada	178.90
Mexico	111.30
Japan	64.90
United Kingdom	41.60
Germany	29.40
South Korea	27.80
Taiwan	24.40
France	20.40
Singapore	17.80
China	16.20

(a)

Total 2000 U.S. Goods Imports $1.2 trillion

Country	Billions of dollars
Canada	230.8
Japan	146.5
Mexico	135.9
China	100
Germany	58.5
United Kingdom	43.3
South Korea	40.3
Taiwan	40.1
France	29.8
Singapore	19.2

(b)

Figure 3-1
U.S. Trade Partners (a) Top Ten Purchasers of U. S. Exports; (b) Top Ten Sources
of U. S. Imports
Source: U.S. Bureau of the Census

on January 1, 1994. The result is a free trade area with a combined population of more than 400 million and a total GNP of $9.2 trillion (see Table 3-2 and Figure 3-2).

Why does NAFTA create a free trade area as opposed to a customs union or a common market? The governments of all three nations pledge to promote economic growth through tariff reductions and expanded trade and investment. At present, however, there are no common external tariffs, nor have restrictions on labor and other factor movements been eliminated. The issue of illegal immigration from Mexico into the United States remains a contentious one. The benefits of continental free trade will enable all three countries to meet the economic challenges of the decades to come. The gradual elimination of barriers to the flow of goods, services, and investment, coupled with strong protection of intellectual property rights (patents, trademarks, and copyrights), will further benefit businesses, workers, farmers, and consumers.

The agreement does leave the door open for discretionary protectionism, however. For example, California avocado growers won government protection for a market worth $250 million; Mexican avocado growers can only ship their fruit to the United States during the winter months, and only to states in the northeast. Moreover, Mexican avocados are subject to quotas, so only $30 million worth of avocados reach the United States each year. Mexican farmer Ricardo Salgado complained, "The

Table 3-2
NAFTA Income and
Population—2000

	2000 GNP (IN MILLIONS)	2000 POPULATION (IN THOUSANDS)	2000 GNP PER CAPITA
United States	$8,259,358	275,746	29,953
Canada	602,158	31,390	19,183
Mexico	392,513	99,536	3,943
*Total/Mean GNP per capita**	*$9,254,029*	*406,672*	*$22,756**

Source: Reprinted by permission of Warren Keegan Associates, Inc.

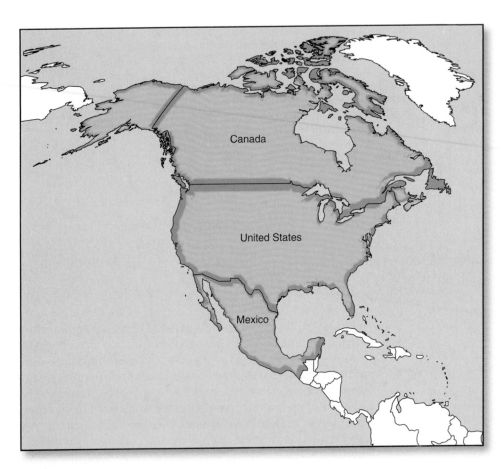

Figure 3-2
NAFTA Countries

California growers want to control all of the supply—that way they get the best prices. We'd love to have a bigger selling season, but right now we have to wait for the U.S. Congress to give us permission."[4]

---

[4] Joel Millman, "Bitter Fruit: Spats Persist Despite Nafta," *The Wall Street Journal* (June 19, 2000), p. A23.

LATIN AMERICA: SICA, ANDEAN COMMUNITY, MERCOSUR

Latin America includes the Caribbean and Central and South America (because of NAFTA, Mexico is grouped with North America). Total population in the region is 480 million people—greater than Western Europe or the combined regions of Central and Eastern Europe. The allure of the Latin American market has been its considerable size and huge resource base. After a decade of no growth, crippling inflation, increasing foreign debt, protectionism, and bloated government payrolls, the countries of Latin America have begun the process of economic transformation. Balanced budgets are a priority and privatization is underway. Free markets, open economies, and deregulation have begun to replace the policies of the past. With the exception of Cuba, democratically elected governments are found throughout Latin America. Policy makers have recognized the benefits of free-market forces and the advantages of participating fully in the global economy. In many countries, tariffs that sometimes reached as much as 100 percent or more have been lowered to 10 to 20 percent. Global corporations are watching developments closely. They are encouraged by import liberalization, the prospects for lower tariffs within sub-regional trading groups, and the potential for establishing more efficient regional production. Many observers envision a free trade area throughout the hemisphere. The four most important preferential trading arrangements in Latin America are the Central American Integration System (SICA), the Andean Community, the Common Market of the South (Mercosur), and the Caribbean Community and Common Market (CARICOM).

Central American Integration System

Central America is trying to revive its common market, which was set up in the 1960s. It collapsed in 1969 when war broke out between Honduras and El Salvador after a riot at a soccer match between teams from the two countries. The five original members, El Salvador, Honduras, Guatemala, Nicaragua, and Costa Rica, decided in July 1991 to reestablish the Central American Common Market (CACM) by 1994. Efforts to improve regional integration gained momentum with the granting of observer status to Panama. Between 1994 and 1996, the volume of intra-regional trade grew from $1.1 billion to $1.6 billion. In 1997, with Panama as a member, the group's name was changed to the Central American Integration System (*Sistema de la Integracion Centroamericana,* or SICA).

The Secretariat for Central American Economic Integration, headquartered in Guatemala City, is charged with helping to coordinate the movement toward a Central American common market. It provided oversight to a group of customs experts who revised the Central American Customs Duty. Effective April 1, 1993, all CACM countries conformed to a common external tariff (CET) of 5 to 20 percent for most goods; many tariffs had previously exceeded 100 percent. There was some resistance to this change; for example, the Costa Rican government had previously benefited from the revenues generated by triple-digit tariffs on automobiles imported from Japan and elsewhere. Lower tariffs are expected to result in improved export prospects for U.S. companies. Common rules of origin were also adopted, allowing for freer movement of goods among current SICA countries. Still, the region's attempts to achieve integration have been described as uncoordinated, inefficient, and costly. Powerful lobbies protect local sugar, coffee, and alcoholic beverages markets. As one Guatemalan analyst remarked, "Only when I see Salvadorean

Figure 3-3
SICA Countries

Table 3-3
SICA Income and
Population

	2000 GNP (IN MILLIONS)	2000 POPULATION (IN THOUSANDS)	2000 GNP PER CAPITA
Costa Rica	$ 9,978	3,654	$2,730
El Salvador	12,391	6,309	1,964
Guatemala	18,397	11,361	1,619
Honduras	4,707	6,522	722
Nicaragua	1,949	5,096	382
Panama	9,180	2,868	3,200
*Total/Mean GNP per capita**	*$56,602*	*35,810*	*$1,580**

Source: Reprinted by permission of Warren Keegan Associates, Inc.

beer on sale in Guatemala and Guatemalan beer on sale in El Salvador will I believe that trade liberalization and integration is a reality."[5] The SICA group is shown in Figure 3-3; income and population data are in Table 3-3.

Andean Community

The Andean Community (formerly the Andean Pact; see Figure 3-4 and Table 3-4) was formed in 1969 to accelerate development of member states Bolivia, Colombia, Ecuador, Peru, and Venezuela through economic and social integration. Members agreed to lower tariffs on intra-group trade and work together to decide what prod-

---

[5] Johanna Tuckman, "Central Americans Start to Act Together," *Financial Times* (July 9, 1997), p. 4.

Figure 3-4
The Andean
Community and
Mercosur

Table 3-4
Andean
Community Income
and Population

	2000 GNP (IN MILLIONS)	2000 POPULATION (IN THOUSANDS)	2000 GNP PER CAPITA
Bolivia	$ 8,241	8,340	$ 988
Colombia	99,763	42,368	2,355
Ecuador	19,301	12,742	1,515
Peru	71,495	25,635	2,789
Venezuela	84,969	24,314	3,495
*Total/Mean GNP per Capita**	*$283,769*	*113,399*	*$2,502**

Source: Reprinted by permission of Warren Keegan Associates, Inc.

ucts each country should produce. At the same time, foreign goods and companies were kept out as much as possible. One Bolivian described the unfortunate result of this lack of competition in the following way: "We had agreed, 'You buy our over-priced goods and we'll buy yours.' "[6]

---

[6] "NAFTA Is Not Alone," *The Economist* (June 18, 1994), pp. 47–48.

In 1988, the group members decided to get a fresh start. Beginning in 1992, the Andean Pact signatories agreed to form Latin America's first operating sub-regional free trade zone. More than 100 million consumers would be affected by the pact, which abolished all foreign exchange, financial and fiscal incentives, and export subsidies at the end of 1992. Common external tariffs were established, marking the transition to a true customs union. A high-level commission will look into any alleged unfair trade practices among countries. The new approach seems to be working; for example, Peru now boasts one of the fastest-growing economies in the region. However, nationalism could still threaten free trade in the region, as evidenced by a recent flare-up of a decades-old dispute between Peru and Ecuador over a small stretch of border.

Common Market of the South (Mercosur)

March 2001 marked the tenth anniversary of the signing of the Asunción Treaty. With this action, the governments of Argentina, Brazil, Paraguay, and Uruguay agreed to form the Common Market of the South (in Spanish, *Mercado Comun del Sur*, or Mercosur; see Figure 3-4 and Table 3-5). The presidents of the four countries had agreed to begin phasing in tariff reform on January 1, 1995. Internal tariffs were eliminated, and common external tariffs of up to 20 percent were established. Ultimately, goods, services, and factors of production will move freely throughout the member countries; until this goal is achieved, however, Mercosur will actually operate as a customs union rather than a true common market. About 15 percent of trade, including advanced electronics and capital goods, is not covered by the agreement. In particular, separate tariff barriers were maintained for cars and trucks.

Much depends on the successful outcome of this experiment in regional cooperation. The early signs were positive, as trade between the four full member nations grew from $4.2 billion in 1990 and peaked at $20 billion in 1998. Brazil and Argentina must work well together if increased integration is to take place in the region. By mid-1996, more than 150 joint ventures had been formed between companies in Argentina and Brazil. A major impediment to further integration is the lack of economic and political discipline and responsibility, a situation reflected in the volatility of currencies in the Mercosur countries. For example, Brazil devalued its currency in early 1995, much to the dismay of the other three Mercosur members; the *real* was

Table 3-5
Mercosur Income and Population, 2000

	2000 GNP (IN MILLIONS)	2000 POPULATION (IN THOUSANDS)	2000 GNP PER CAPITA
Argentina	$360,472	37,087	$9,720
Bolivia*	8,241	8,340	988
Brazil	850,852	170,661	4,986
Chile*	89,280	15,335	5,822
Paraguay	9,877	5,508	1,793
Uruguay	21,924	3,335	6,574
*Total/Mean GNP per capita**	$1,340,646	240,266	$5,579*

*Associate members that participate in free trade area only.

Source: Reprinted by permission of Warren Keegan Associates, Inc.

Part II   The Global Marketing Environment

Chile's winemakers are gaining international acclaim; quality has increased dramatically as wines that were once produced for local consumption only are crafted to appeal to discerning palates around the globe. ProChile, an agency of the Ministry of Foreign Affairs, spends about $3 million annually on print advertising in export markets. Because Chile's climate is ideally suited for grape growing, the country has attracted a great deal of foreign investment. For example, Robert Mondavi recently established a 50/50 partnership with Vina Errazuriz.

devalued again in 1999. In the 1990s, Argentina's currency was pegged to the U.S. dollar. However, by the end of the decade Argentina's economy had become mired in recession, and concern mounted that the country might default on $130 billion in foreign debt. In January 2002, economy minister Jorge Remes Lenicov announced emergency measures that included a 29 percent currency devaluation for exports and capital transactions.

In 1996, Chile became an associate member of Mercosur. Policy makers opted against full membership because Chile already had lower external tariffs than the rest of Mercosur; ironically, full membership would have required raising them. (In other words, Chile participates in the free-trade-area aspect of Mercosur, not the customs union.) Chile had been negotiating for inclusion in NAFTA; when Mexico's trade deficit with the United States turned into a trade surplus following the peso crisis, Washington's interest in expanding NAFTA cooled. Chile's export-driven success makes it a role model for the rest of Latin America as well as Central and Eastern Europe. Chile's booming economy and access to other Mercosur markets has had a direct impact on global company strategy. By investing in Chile or other Mercosur countries, companies that meet the general rule of origin are not treated as foreign. Caterpillar, for example, manufactures bulldozers, excavators, and other earth-moving equipment in Brazil for export to Chile. Tariffs on Brazilian exports to Chile are being phased out, while American exports to Chile face tariffs averaging 11 percent.[7]

---

[7] Robert Mosbacher, "U.S. Exporters to Latin America Need Fast Track," *The Wall Street Journal* (September 12, 1997), p. A23.

Despite the increasing willingness of many nations to enter into trade agreements, some observers are disturbed by the trend. For example, Columbia University professor Jagdish Bhagwati calls NAFTA, Mercosur, and similar agreements a "spaghetti bowl" that represents "a pox on the world trading system." Professor Bhagwati's concern is that regional trade preferences are discriminatory. They can result in diversion of imports away from cheaper country sources towards more expensive country sources that are signatories to a given agreement. For example, one researcher has concluded that the added cost to Mexico of buying goods and services from its NAFTA partners amounts to more than $3 billion annually.

Professor Bhagwati is not the only critic of trade agreements. As an executive at the World Bank noted, "Our view is it's easy to get overly enthusiastic about preferential trade agreements. They might confer significant benefits, but there are also very significant dangers." In a 1996 report, World Bank economist Alexander Yeats acknowledged that Mercosur has generated a great deal of trade and investment; the problem is that much intra-Mercosur trade is in cars, agricultural machinery, and other industry sectors for which the four full trading partners are inefficient producers. Efficient foreign producers that would like to export to Mercosur are deterred because of tariffs and quotas. Meanwhile, Mercosur partners buy goods from each other at prices that do not reflect global competition. In particular, because Mercosur's auto producers are uncompetitive, exports to countries outside of the customs union have suffered. Yeats' conclusion: Mercosur distorts international trade.

According to an opposing viewpoint, Mercosur has not become a fortress. Edward Hudgins of the Cato Institute attributes Mercosur's reduced exports to Western Europe to the fall of communism. Western European countries have stepped up trade with their neighbors to the east, partly at the expense of Mercosur.

SOURCES: Jagdish Bhagwati, "Short on Trade Vision," *Financial Times* (June 3, 1997), p. 12; Edward L. Hudgins, "Mercosur Gets a 'Not Guilty' on Trade Diversion," *The Wall Street Journal* (March 21, 1997), p. A19; Martin Wolf, "Fast Track to Nowhere," *Financial Times* (November 11, 1997), p. 19; Wolf, "An Unhealthy Trade-off," *Financial Times* (October 29, 1996), p. 14; Michael M. Phillips, "South American Trade Pact is Under Fire," *The Wall Street Journal* (October 23, 1996), pp. A2, A4.

Visit the Web site
For more information on Mercosur, log on to:
www.mercosur.org
www.falkland-malvinas.com

Like Chile, Bolivia is an associate member of Mercosur. Some observers expect Mercosur and the Andean Community to merge. The EU is Mercosur's number-one trading partner, with exports to Europe totaling about $19 billion in 1999. Mercosur has also signed an agreement with the European Union to establish a free trade area by the year 2005; Germany and France are opposed to such an agreement on the grounds that low-cost agricultural exports would harm farmers in Europe.

Caribbean Community and Common Market (CARICOM)

CARICOM was formed in 1973 as a movement toward unity in the Caribbean. It replaced the Caribbean Free Trade Association (CARIFTA) founded in 1965. The members are Antigua and Barbuda, Bahamas, Barbados, Belize, Dominica, Grenada, Guyana, Haiti, Jamaica, Montserrat, St. Kitts and Nevis, St. Lucia, St. Vincent and the Grenadines, and Trinidad and Tobago. The population of the entire 15-member CARICOM is 13.9 million; disparate levels of economic development can be seen by comparing GNP per capita in Antigua and Barbuda with that of Haiti (see Table 3-6).

To date, CARICOM's main objective has been to achieve a deepening of economic integration by means of a Caribbean common market. During the 1980s, the economic difficulties of member states hindered the development of interregional trade. Another problem concerned applying rules of origin to verify that imported goods genuinely come from within the community. As a result, CARICOM was

Table 3-6

Caricom Income and Population, 2000

	2000 GNP (IN MILLIONS)	2000 POPULATION (IN THOUSANDS)	2000 GNP PER CAPITA
Antigua and Barbuda	515	67	7,685
Bahamas	na	304	na
Barbados	na	268	na
Belize	622	250	2488
Dominica	231	75	3,091
Grenada	314	97	3,241
Guyana	981	871	1,127
Haiti	2,451	7,974	307
Jamaica	4,104	2,624	1,564
Montserrat	na	12	na
St. Kitts and Nevis	287	41	7,081
St. Lucia	641	163	3,924
St. Vincent & Grenadines	287	114	2,509
Suriname	666	416	1,602
Trinidad and Tobago	5,655	1,339	4,224
Total		*14,615*	

Source: Reprinted by permission of Warren Keegan Associates, Inc.

largely stagnant during its first two decades of existence. At its annual meeting in July 1991, member countries agreed to speed integration; a customs union was established with common external tariffs. At the 1998 summit meeting, leaders from the 15 countries agreed to move quickly to establish an economic union with a common currency. A recent study of the issue has suggested, however, that the low volume of intra-regional trade will limit the potential gains from lower transaction costs.[8]

If achieved, such actions would qualify CARICOM for membership in the proposed Free Trade Area of the Americas (FTAA) in 2005. CARICOM nations could join if the original 1973 treaty were revised. As Owen Arthur, prime minister of Barbados explained, "The old treaty limited the movement of capital, skills, and business in the region. The treaty has to be changed so that regional trade policy can be widened to deal with the FTAA and the EU, and such matters as bilateral investments treaties, intellectual property rights, and trade in services."[9]

The English-speaking CARICOM members in the eastern Caribbean are also concerned with defending their privileged trading position with the United States. That status dates to the Caribbean Basin Initiative (CBI) of 1984, which promoted export production of certain products by providing duty-free U.S. market access to 20 countries, including members of CARICOM. Guatemala quickly attracted manufacturers based in Taiwan and South Korea and subsequently became the region's

---

[8] Myrvin L. Anthony and Andrew Hughes Hallett, "Is the Case for Economic and Monetary Union in the Caribbean Realistic?" *World Economy* 23, no. 1 (January 2000), pp. 119–144.

[9] Canute James, "Caribbean Community Grapples with Challenge of Creating a Single Market," *Financial Times* (July 10, 1998), p. 7.

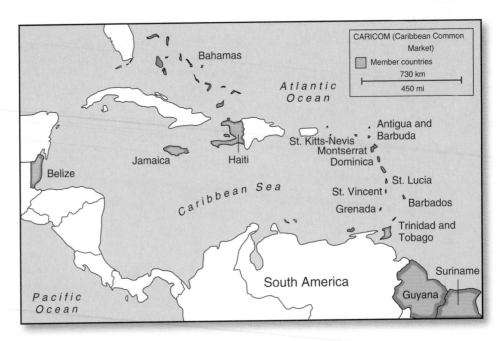

Figure 3-5
CARICOM

leading exporter of apparel to the United States.[10] Unfortunately for CARICOM, the Enterprise for the Americas Initiative—with the Mexican free trade agreement as its centerpiece—has overtaken the CBI as the flagship U.S. trade policy in the area. In response to the situation, the CBI members requested that the CBI be expanded and its members granted the same trade privileges that are available to Mexico. The Caribbean Basin Trade Partnership Act, which went into effect on October 1, 2000, exempts textile and apparel exports from the Caribbean to the United States from duties and tariffs. (Students studying in America take note: Check the labels on your school's sports apparel. Chances are they read "Made in Guatemala," "Assembled in El Salvador," etc.). CARICOM is shown in Figure 3-5.

Current Trade-Related Issues

One of the biggest issues pertaining to trade in the Western Hemisphere is the Free Trade Area of the Americas. As noted earlier, leaders in many Latin American countries—Brazil in particular—are frustrated by what they perceive as America's failure to follow through on its promises in the region. As a result, Brazil and its Mercosur partners are advocating a slower, three-stage approach to negotiations. The first stage would include discussions on business facilitation issues such as standardized customs forms and industry deregulation; the second would focus on dispute settlement and rules of origin; and the third would focus on tariffs. However, it was also clear that the U.S. Congress must grant trade promotion authority (TPA; formerly known as fast track authority) to the president if he is to successfully conclude the negotiations. Meanwhile, Mercosur, CARICOM, SICA, and the Andean Community intend to pursue further integration among themselves as well as with Europe.

10 Lucy Martinez-Mont, "Sweatshops Are Better Than No Shops," *The Wall Street Journal* (June 25, 1996), p. A14.

Visit the Web site
The Secretariat of CARICOM maintains a Web site offering information, publications, and membership information.
www.caricom.org

Visit the Web site
The American Enterprise Institute, the Institute of International Economics, the Council on Hemispheric Affairs, the Cato Institute, and a number of other think-tanks offer analysis and position papers on the FTAA and other trade-related topics.
www.iie.org
www.aei.org
www.coha.org
www.cato.org

With 56 percent of the world's population, the 23-country Pacific Rim region merits discussion in its own right. The region accounted for approximately one-third of global income in 1997. Japan's presence looms large in the Asia-Pacific region. Population density and geographic isolation are the two crucial factors that cannot be overstated when discussing Japan. Most of Japan's land area is mountainous; and therefore, the residential area represents only 3 percent, and the industrial area is only 1.4 percent. However, Japan still generates an astounding 14 percent of the world's GNP!

South Korea, Taiwan, Singapore, and Hong Kong are sometimes collectively referred to as "tigers" or **newly industrializing economies** (**NIEs**). Fueled by foreign investment and export-driven industrial development, these four countries achieved stunning rates of economic growth in the 1980s and early 1990s. Another four countries—Thailand, Malaysia, Indonesia, and China—were getting close to the point of industrial take-off prior to the onset of the "Asian flu" in July 1997. Economic growth in Thailand, Malaysia, and Indonesia screeched to a halt; China appeared to be relatively unscathed by the crisis. Table 3-7 contains statistics on Asia/Pacific countries with the largest economies; note in particular the GNP growth rates of the tigers during the decade preceding the economic crisis.

The Association of Southeast Asian Nations

The Association of Southeast Asian Nations (ASEAN) is the flagship preferential trade agreement in the Asia-Pacific area, although Japan is not a member. ASEAN was established in 1967 as an organization for economic, political, social, and cultural cooperation among its member countries. The United States, which at the time was embroiled in the Vietnam War, played a role in establishing ASEAN with the signing of the Bangkok Declaration. Brunei, Indonesia, Malaysia, the Philippines, Singapore,

Table 3-7
Asia/Pacific Comparison, 2000 Data

COUNTRY	GNP (IN MILLIONS)	POPULATION (IN THOUSANDS)	GNP PER CAPITA	GNP GROWTH RATE 1985–1995
Singapore	$ 120,177	3,294	$36,484	8.0%
Japan	4,427,104	127,229	34,796	3.3%
Hong Kong	188,936	6,880	27,463	6.1%
Australia	407,949	19,207	21,239	2.8%
Taiwan	362,000	22,113	16,370	6.0%
New Zealand	60,649	3,944	15,376	1.6%
South Korea	520,855	47,385	10,992	8.5%
Malaysia	110,739	23,333	4,746	8.2%
Thailand	177,265	62,810	2,822	9.7%
Indonesia	247,846	210,785	1,176	7.7%
China	1,179,345	1,268,121	930	9.3%
India	430,096	1,015,287	424	5.0%

Source: Reprinted by permission of Warren Keegan Associates, Inc.

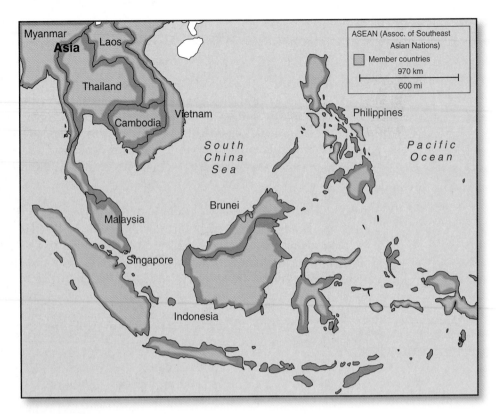

Figure 3-6
ASEAN

and Thailand were the original six members. Vietnam became the first Communist nation in the group when it was admitted to ASEAN in July 1995. Cambodia and Laos were admitted to ASEAN at the organization's 30th anniversary meeting in July 1997 (see Figure 3-6 and Table 3-8). Burma (known as Myanmar by the ruling military junta) joined in 1998, following delays related to the country's internal politics and human rights record.

Individually and collectively, ASEAN countries are active in regional and global trade. For example, 20.7 percent of Malaysia's 1995 exports went to the United States, while 20.3 percent went to Singapore. Imports from Japan accounted for 27.3 percent of total imports; the United States provided 16.3 percent of total imports. Two-way trade between the United States and ASEAN totaled $83.8 billion in 1994. There is a growing realization among ASEAN officials that broad common goals and perceptions are not enough to keep the association alive. A constant problem is the strict need for consensus among all members before proceeding with any form of cooperative effort. Although the ASEAN member countries are geographically close, they have historically been divided in many respects. One of the reasons the association remained in existence is because it accomplished almost nothing. The situation is changing today, however; in 1994, economic ministers from the member nations agreed to implement an ASEAN Free Trade Area (AFTA) by 2003, five years earlier than previously discussed. Under the agreement, tariffs of 20 percent or more will be reduced to 0 to 5 percent.[11] In 1996, intra-ASEAN trade surpassed $70 billion.

---

[11] "ASEAN Economic Ministers Agree to Accelerate AFTA," *ASEAN Business Report* 5, no. 9 (September 1994), pp. 1, 6.

Table 3-8
ASEAN Income and
Population, 2000

	GNP 2000 (IN MILLIONS)	POPULATION 2000 (IN THOUSANDS)	GNP PER CAPITA 2000
Brunei	na	333	na
Cambodia	$ 3,297	11,352	$ 290
Indonesia	247,846	210,785	1,176
Laos		5,237	375
Malaysia	110,739	23,333	4,746
Myanmar	na	45,357	na
Philippines	89,835	78,718	1,141
Singapore	120,177	3,294	36,484
Thailand	177,265	62,810	2,822
Vietnam	28,896	81,646	354
*Total/Mean GNP per capita**	$780,021	522,865	$1,491[a]

[a]Excluding Brunei and Myanmar

Source: Reprinted by permission of Warren Keegan Associates, Inc.

Singapore represents a special case among the ASEAN nations. In fewer than three decades, Singapore has transformed itself from a British colony to a vibrant, 240-square-mile industrial power. Singapore has an extremely efficient infrastructure—the Port of Singapore is the world's second-largest container port (Hong Kong's ranks first)—and a standard of living second only to Japan's in the region. Singapore's three million citizens have played a critical role in the country's economic achievements by readily accepting the notion that "the country with the most knowledge will win" in global competition. Excellent training programs and a 97 percent literacy rate help explain why Singapore has more engineers per capita than the United States. Singapore's Economic Development Board has also actively recruited business interest in the nation. The manufacturing companies that have been attracted to Singapore read like a "who's who" of global marketing and include Hewlett-Packard, IBM, Philips, and Apple Computer; in all, more than 3,000 companies have operations or investments in Singapore.

Singapore alone accounts for more than one-third of U.S. trading activities with ASEAN countries; U.S. exports to Singapore in 2000 totaled $17.8 billion, while imports totaled $19.2 billion. Singapore is closely tied with its neighbors; more than 32 percent of imports are re-exported to other Asian countries. Singapore's efforts to fashion a civil society have gained the country some notoriety; crime is nearly nonexistent, thanks to the government's severe treatment of criminals. Some people in the United States objected after an American youth living in Singapore was sentenced to a caning after being arrested and convicted of vandalism. Singaporeans believe the United States has given individuals too many liberties while imprisoning American society.

Marketing Issues in the Asia-Pacific Region

Mastering the Japanese market takes flexibility, ambition, and a long-term commitment. Japan has changed from being a closed market to one that's just tough. There are barriers in Japan in terms of attitudes as well as laws. Any organization wishing

Anyone examining Table 3-11 is sure to be impressed by the growth rates achieved by Japan, Hong Kong, Indonesia, Thailand, Malaysia, Taiwan, South Korea, and Singapore. These countries have garnered a great deal of attention from the press and policy makers; in 1994, the World Bank published a report titled "The East Asian Miracle," in which it chronicled the "high performing Asian economies" (HPAEs). In particular, the report applauded these countries for their superior accumulation of physical and human capital, their ability to allocate resources to highly productive investments, and their ability to acquire and master technology.

Even before the onset of the Asian flu in July 1997, could anything be wrong with this picture? "Plenty," according to MIT economist Paul Krugman. In a 1994 *Foreign Affairs* article titled "The Myth of Asia's Miracle," Krugman pointed out a weakness in the *"how"* of these gains. He argued that the stunning economic growth achieved by Singapore and other HPAEs was based on increases in labor and capital alone. However, to be sustainable, economic growth must include "total factor productivity," or TFP. TFP is basically a measure of how efficiently a country uses its labor and capital and includes technology improvements and innovation. Using a sophisticated quantitative tool known as growth accounting, Krugman determined that the HPAEs had achieved virtually no growth in TFP. His conclusion: growth had been achieved by "perspiration, not inspiration." He compared the mobilization of resources in HPAEs to Stalin's industrialization initiatives in the Soviet Union during the 1930s. The problem, as Krugman sees it, is that the HPAEs can't continue to grow by simply adding workers or building better highways.

Krugman's views on Asia represented quite a departure from conventional wisdom; his methodology and conclusions were hotly debated by fellow economists and by policy makers in some of the HPAEs that he described. However, Yeo Cheow Tong, Singapore's minister of trade and industry, took Krugman's message to heart. Within months after Krugman's article appeared in *Foreign Affairs*, the nation embarked upon a massive campaign to raise productivity. Policy makers placed a new emphasis on targeting higher added-value industry sectors, de-emphasize low-skill jobs, and train workers for high-tech manufacturing. New initiatives include programs to solicit suggestions from workers on ways to cut costs. The government is also putting pressure on companies to move low-skill manual and clerical operations offshore. In the schools, a new emphasis is being placed on critical analysis and creative thinking as opposed to memorization and regurgitation. The head of the new Productivity and Standards Board noted, "We want to change the very way people think."

SOURCES: Darren McDermott, "Singapore Swing: Krugman Was Right," *The Wall Street Journal* (October 23, 1996), p. A15; Urban C. Lehner, "Is the Vaunted 'Asian Miracle' Really Just an Illusion?" *The Wall Street Journal* (October 23, 1996), p. A15; James Kynge, "Efficiency, Hard Work . . . Now For a Spot of Creativity," *Financial Times* (October 26–27, 1996), p. 3.

to compete in Japan must be committed to providing top-quality products and services. In many cases, products and marketing must be tailored to local tastes. Countless visits and socializing with distributors are necessary to build trust. Marketers must also master the *keiretsu* system of tightly knit corporate alliances. All of these factors served as a backdrop to the trade dispute between Japan and the United States that escalated in mid-1995. In an effort to pry open Japan's market for auto parts, the United States government threatened to impose stiff tariffs on Japanese luxury car imports.

India's huge population base also presents attractive opportunities. GE has established a joint venture with Wipro, Ltd., to make medical devices such as CAT scanners and ultrasound equipment. Some products are being designed especially for the local market. For example, GE has developed a portable ultrasound machine that squeezes 75 percent of the functions of a conventional design into a 20-pound unit that will allow doctors to provide prenatal care in rural areas. Several automakers—

including Mitsubishi, Honda, and Ford—are studying the market. Other companies currently investing in India are BMW, DuPont, General Motors, Fujitsu, IBM, and Coca-Cola. During 1995, there were several ominous reminders that the political environment is still unstable and hostile to foreigners. The government of the Indian state of Maharashtra abruptly canceled a $2.9 billion power project with the Houston-based Enron Corporation. It was the single largest private investment deal in India since 1991, and the cancellation prompted Enron to sue for $300 million in compensation. In 1999, the new Dabhol Power Company began producing electricity. By 2001, however, the project was still mired in conflict; the Maharashtra government quit buying electricity on the grounds that the rates were too high.[12] The nationalistic Bharatiya Janata Party (BJP) remains a vocal and powerful opponent of reform; in New Delhi, pressure from the BJP led to the temporary closing of one of India's first Kentucky Fried Chicken restaurants.

WESTERN, CENTRAL, AND EASTERN EUROPE

The countries of Western Europe are among the most prosperous in the world. Despite the fact that there are significant differences in income between the north and the south and obvious differences in language and culture, the once-varied societies of Western Europe have grown remarkably alike. Still, enough differences remain that many observers view Western Europe in terms of three tiers. Many Britons view themselves as somewhat apart from the rest of the continent; Euro-skepticism is widespread, and the country still has problems seeing eye-to-eye with historic rivals Germany and France. Meanwhile, across the English Channel, Portugal, Italy, Greece, and Spain have struggled mightily to overcome the stigma of being called "Club Med" nations and other derogatory nicknames by their northern neighbors.[13] Still, as they enter the first decade of the twenty-first century, the governments of Western Europe are on the threshold of achieving hitherto unheard of levels of economic integration.

The European Union (EU)

The origins of the European Union (EU) can be traced back to the 1958 Treaty of Rome. The six original members of the European Community (EC), as the group was called then, were Belgium, France, Holland, Italy, Luxembourg, and West Germany. In 1973, Great Britain, Denmark, and Ireland were admitted, followed by Greece in 1981, and Spain and Portugal in 1986. Beginning in 1987, the 12 countries that were EC members set about the difficult task of creating a genuine single market in goods, services, and capital. Adopting the Single European Act by the end of 1992 was a major EC achievement; the Council of Ministers adopted 282 pieces of legislation and regulations to make the single market a reality.

The objective of the EU member countries is to harmonize national laws and regulations so that goods, services, people, and eventually money can flow freely across

---

[12] Daniel Pearl, "In India, Other Firms Feel Enron's Pain," *The Wall Street Journal* (July 5, 2001), A8; see also Jonathan Karp and Kathryn Kranhold, "Power Politics: Enron's Plant in India Was Dead; This Month, It Will Go On Stream," *The Wall Street Journal* (February 5, 1999), pp. A1, A6.

[13] Thomas Kamm, "Snobbery: The Latest Hitch in Unifying Europe," *The Wall Street Journal* (November 6, 1996), p. A17; Kyle Pope, "More Than Water Divides U.K., Europe," *The Wall Street Journal* (June 30, 1995), p. A12.

Table 3-9
EU Income and
Population, 2000

	2000 (IN MILLIONS)	2000 POPULATION (IN THOUSANDS)	2000 GNP PER CAPITA
Austria	$ 212,469	8,218	$25,854
Belgium	255,828	10,282	24,881
Denmark	181,253	5,348	33,894
Finland	120,100	5,202	23,088
France	1,446,515	59,491	24,315
Germany	2,127,086	83,308	25,533
Greece	123,350	10,681	11,549
Ireland	74,331	3,727	19,942
Italy	1,168,771	57,869	20,197
Luxembourg	16,977	440	38,587
Netherlands	384,534	15,890	24,200
Portugal	107,701	9,975	10,797
Spain	544,944	39,559	13,775
Sweden	219,950	8,982	24,487
United Kingdom	1,359,764	59,720	22,769
*Total/Mean GNP per capita**	$8,343,573	378,692	$22,032*

Source: Reprinted by permission of Warren Keegan Associates, Inc.

national boundaries. December 31, 1992, marked the dawn of the new economic era in Europe. Evidence that this is more than a free trade area, customs union, or common market is the fact that citizens of the 15 member countries are now able to freely cross borders within the union. The EU is encouraging the development of a community-wide labor pool; it is also attempting to shake up Europe's cartel mentality by handing down rules of competition patterned after the U.S. antitrust law. Improvements to highway and rail networks are now being coordinated as well.

Further EU enlargement has become a major issue. In December 1991, Czechoslovakia, Hungary, and Poland became associate members through the so-called "European Agreements." By 2002, the Czech Republic, Hungary, Poland, Estonia, and Slovenia are expected to become full members of the EU. Latvia, Lithuania, Bulgaria, Romania, and Slovakia may join sometime later. Finland, Sweden, and Austria officially joined on January 1, 1995. (In November 1994, voters in Norway rejected a membership proposal.) Today, the 15 nations of the EU represent 378 million people, a combined GNP of $8.3 trillion, and a 39 percent share of world exports (see Table 3-9). The map in Figure 3-7 shows the EU membership.

During the two decades between 1979 and 1999, the European Monetary System (EMS) was an important foundation of Western European commerce. The EMS was based on the European Currency Unit (ECU), a unit of account comprised of a hypothetical basket of "weighted" currencies. The ECU did not take the form of an actual currency; it existed physically in the form of checks and electronically in computers. Some companies priced their raw materials and products in ECU, thereby saving the time and cost of exchange transactions. The 1991 **Maastricht Treaty** set the stage for the transition from the EMS to an economic and monetary union (EMU) that includes a European central bank and a single European currency known as the **euro.** In May 1998, Austria, Belgium, Finland, Ireland, the Netherlands, France, Germany,

Figure 3-7
The EU

Italy, Luxembourg, Portugal, and Spain were chosen as the 11 charter members of the **euro zone.** Greece became the 12th member in January 2001. The single currency era, which officially began on January 1, 1999, is expected to bring many benefits to companies in the euro zone such as eliminating costs associated with currency conversion and exchange rate uncertainty. The euro existed as a unit of account until 2002, when actual coins and paper money were issued and national currencies such as the French franc were withdrawn from circulation.

The European Free Trade Area (EFTA) and European Economic Area (EEA)

Since 1990, the EU has concluded more than 20 trade pacts with other nations. For example, in October 1991, the then-EC and the seven-nation European Free Trade Association (EFTA) reached agreement on the creation of the European Economic Area (EEA) beginning January 1993. The ultimate goal is to achieve the free movement of goods, services, capital, and labor between the two groups, but the EEA is a free trade area, not a customs union with common external tariffs. With Austria, Finland, and Sweden now members of the EU, Norway, Iceland, and Liechtenstein are the only remaining EFTA countries that are not EU members (Switzerland voted not to be part of the EEA). The EEA is the world's largest trading bloc, with 384 million consumers, $8.5 trillion combined GNP, and nearly 50 percent of world trade. The three non-EU members of the new EEA are expected to adopt all the EU's single-market legislation. Meanwhile, the four members of EFTA (Norway, Iceland, Liechtenstein, and Switzerland) maintain free trade agreements with Israel and Turkey as well as nations in Central and Eastern Europe. EFTA also has cooperation agreements with Morocco, Tunisia, and Egypt.

Marketing Issues in the European Union

The European Commission establishes directives and sets deadlines for their implementation by legislation in individual nations. The business environment in Europe has undergone considerable transformation since 1992, with significant implications for all elements of the marketing mix. Table 3-10 summarizes some of the marketing mix issues that must be addressed in Europe's single market. For example, content and other product standards that varied among nations have been harmonized. As a result, companies may have an opportunity to reap economies by cutting back on the number of variations. Case Europe, for example, manufactures and markets farm machinery. When it introduced the Magnum tractor in Europe in 1988, it offered 17 different versions because of country regulations regarding placement of lights and brakes. Thanks to harmonization, Case offers the current model, the Magnum MX, in one version. However, because different types of implements and trailers are used in different countries, the MX is available with different kinds of hitches.[14] The advent of the euro on January 1, 1999, brought about more changes. Direct comparability of prices in the euro zone will force companies to review pricing policies. The marketing challenge is to develop strategies to take advantage of opportunities in one of the largest, wealthiest, most stable markets in the world. Corporations must assess the extent to which they can treat the region as one entity and how to change organizational policies and structures to adapt to and take advantage of a unified Europe.

The music industry is a case in point; long before online music distribution and MP3 file swapping had become issues, the major record companies faced a number of challenges. The single market meant that, for the first time, music retailers in Europe were allowed to buy CDs and tapes from distributors throughout the EU. This practice, known as transshipment, had not been permitted prior to the single market. Now, for example, a music retailer in Germany is no longer tied to a local supplier in Germany if better prices are available elsewhere. The change means that Sony, Warner, Bertelsmann, EMI, and the other major record companies have been forced to adopt more uniform pricing policies across Europe. This, in turn, has required them to find ways to cut costs without compromising the need to respond quickly to consumer demand. One solution has been to realign distribution via joint ventures or other arrangements; previously, each company had maintained its own distribution system. In 1998, however, Warner and Sony merged their distribution facilities in the United Kingdom.[15]

---

[14] George Russel, "Marketing in the 'Old Country': The Diversity of Europe Presents Unique Challenges," *Agri Marketing* 37, no. 1 (January 1999), p. 38.

[15] Jeff Clark-Meads, "The Year in Europe: Union Members Confront Parallel Imports and Universes," *Billboard* 107 (December 23, 1995), p. YE14; Alice Rawsthorn, "Music's 'Big Five' Dip Toes in Common Distribution Pool," *Financial Times* (August 14, 1998), p. 60.

Table 3-10
Marketing Strategies in the European Union

	CHANGES AFFECTING STRATEGIES	THREATS TO MARKETERS' PLANNING	MANAGEMENT'S STRATEGIC OPTIONS
Product Strategies	Harmonization in product standards, testing, and certification process Common patenting and branding Harmonization in packaging, labeling, and processing requirements	Incorporating changes mandated by EC directives Complying with rules of origin Local content rules Differences in marketing research	Consolidate production Seek marketing economies Shift from brand to benefit segmentation Standardize packaging and labeling where possible
Pricing Strategies	More competitive environment Lifting of restrictions on foreign products Anti-monopoly measures Opening up of the public procurement market	Parallel importing Different taxation of goods Less freedom in setting transfer prices	Exploit different excise and value-added taxes Understand price elasticity of consumer demand Emphasize high-margin products Introduce low-cost brands
Promotion Strategies	Common guidelines on TV broadcasting Deregulation of national broadcasting monopolies Uniform standards for TV commercials	Restrictions on alcohol and tobacco advertising Limits on foreign TV production Differences in permissible promotional techniques	Coordinate components of promotional mix via IMC Exploit advantage of pan-European media Position products according to local market preferences
Distribution Strategies	Simplification of transit documents and procedures Elimination of customs formalities	Increase in distributors' margins Lack of direct marketing infrastructure Restrictions in the use of computer databases	Consolidate manufacturing facilities Centralize distribution Develop nontraditional channels (direct marketing, telemarketing)

Source: Reprinted from *Long Range Planning,* 4, no. 5, G. Guide, Implementing a Pan-European Strategy, p. 32, Copyright © 1991, with permission of Elsevir Science.

The Lomé Convention

The EU maintains an accord with 71 countries in Africa, the Caribbean, and the Pacific (ACP). The Lomé Convention was designed to promote trade and provide poor countries with financial assistance from a European Development Fund. The ACP signatories generally consider the treaty to be a success, as it allows for preferential access to the EU for such commodities as sugar, bananas, rum, and rice. However, the World Trade Organization has ruled that some of the banana preferences are unfair. Recently, budget pressures at home have prompted some EU nations to push for cuts in Lomé aid. The Convention took effect in 1975 and expired in 2000. The ACP nations are currently meeting to work out details of a successor agreement, with negotiations scheduled to conclude in 2003. The European Commission has proposed that the 40 least-developed ACP countries choose between Lomé-type provisions or membership in regional free trade areas. The remaining 30 ACP countries must choose between either WTO-compatible FTAs, agreements with a limited but increasing degree of reciprocity, or preferences under the Generalized System of Preferences. As a whole, leaders of the ACP nations have expressed a preference for a renewal of Lomé. Government officials in Cuba have expressed a desire to become part of a post-Lomé arrangement; Cuba is also interested in joining CARICOM.

Central European Free Trade Association (CEFTA)

In the early 1990s, the extraordinary political and economic reforms that swept through Central and Eastern Europe focused attention on a new 430-million-person market. The transition in the region from command to market economies—a process which is ongoing today—has toppled a number of entrenched institutions, including the Council for Mutual Economic Assistance. COMECON (or CMEA, as it was also known) was a group of Communist bloc countries allied with the Soviet Union. In the years since COMECON's demise in 1992, a number of proposals for multilateral cooperation have been advanced. In December 1992, Hungary, Poland, the Czech Republic, and Slovakia signed an agreement creating the Central European Free Trade Association (CEFTA). Slovenia, which declared its autonomy from the Yugoslav federation in 1992, is also a member. The signatories pledged cooperation in a number of areas, including infrastructure and telecommunications; an overriding common goal is to join the EU as a group. Meanwhile, within the Commonwealth of Independent States, formal economic integration between the former Soviet republics is proceeding slowly. In May 1995, the governments of Russia and Belarus agreed to form a customs union and remove border posts between their two countries. Hoping to capitalize on the opportunity to export to Russia without incurring prohibitive tariffs, Ford opened a $10 million vehicle assembly plant outside Minsk.

Because they are in transition, the markets of Central and Eastern Europe present interesting opportunities and challenges. Global companies view the region as an important new source of growth, and the first company to penetrate a country market often emerges as the industry leader. Exporting has been favored as a market entry mode, but direct investment in the region is on the rise; with wage rates much lower than those in Spain, Portugal, and Greece, the region offers attractive locations for low-cost manufacturing. For consumer products, distribution is a critical marketing mix element because availability is the key to sales.

A recent study examined the approaches utilized by 3M International, McDonald's, Philips Electronics, Henkel, Südzucker AG, and several other companies operating in Central Europe. Consumers in the region are eagerly embracing well-known global brands that were once available only to government elites and others in privileged positions. The study found a high degree of standardization of marketing program elements; in particular, core product and brand elements are largely unchanged from those used in Western Europe. Consumer companies generally target high-end segments of the market and focus on brand image and product quality; industrial marketers concentrate on opportunities to do business with the largest firms in a given country.[16]

---

[16] Arnold Shuh, "Global Standardization as a Success Formula for Marketing in Central Eastern Europe," *Journal of World Business* 35, no. 2 (Summer 2000), pp. 133–148.

The Middle East includes 16 countries: Afghanistan, Cyprus, Bahrain, Egypt, Iran, Iraq, Israel, Jordan, Kuwait, Lebanon, Oman, Qatar, Saudi Arabia, Syria, the United Arab Emirates, and the reunited Yemen. The majority of the population is Arab, a large percentage are Persian, and a small percentage are Jews. Persians and most Arabs share the same religion, beliefs, and Islamic traditions, making the population 95 percent Muslim and 5 percent Christian and Jewish.

Despite this apparent homogeneity, diversity exists within each country and within religious groups. The Middle East does not have a single societal type with a typical belief, behavior, and tradition. Each capital and major city in the Middle East has a variety of social groups that can be differentiated on the basis of religion, social class, education, and degree of wealth. In general, Middle Easterners are warm, friendly, and clannish. Tribal pride and generosity toward guests are basic beliefs. Decisions are arrived at by consensus, and seniority has more weight than educational expertise. The life centers on the family. Authority comes with age, and power is related to family size and seniority. In business relations, Middle Easterners prefer to act through trusted third parties, and they also prefer oral communications.

Business in the Middle East is driven by the price of oil. Seven of the countries have high oil revenues: Bahrain, Iraq, Iran, Kuwait, Oman, Qatar, and Saudi Arabia hold significant world oil reserves. Oil revenues have widened the gap between poor and rich nations in the Middle East, and the disparities contribute to political and social instability in the area. Saudi Arabia, a monarchy with 16 million people and 25 percent of the world's known oil reserves, remains the most important market in this region.

In the past, the region was characterized by pan-Arabism, a form of nationalism and loyalty that transcended borders and amounted to anti-Western dogma. During the Persian Gulf War, this pan-Arabism weakened somewhat. To defeat Iraq, the Gulf Arabs and their allies broke many of their unwritten rules including accepting help from the United States, a traditional ally of Israel. Some observers interpret this change as a harbinger of new market opportunities in the region. Another positive sign was the July 1994 peace declaration by Israel and Jordan, which may pave the way for a free trade area in the Middle East. Currently, intraregional trade amounts to less than 10 percent of total trade; bilateral trade by both the Israelis and Arabs is conducted primarily with Triad countries.

Cooperation Council for the Arab States of the Gulf

The key regional organization is the Gulf Cooperation Council (GCC), which was established in 1981 by Bahrain, Kuwait, Oman, Qatar, Saudi Arabia, and the United Arab Emirates (Table 3-11 and Figure 3-8). These six countries hold more than one-third of the world's known oil reserves, but production is only about 18 percent of world oil output. Ironically, Saudi Arabia and several other Middle Eastern countries post current account deficits, largely because they must import most of the goods and services that their citizens consume. The countries are heavily dependent on oil revenues to pay for their imports. The combined effect of low world prices for crude oil, the Asian economic crisis, and surging domestic demand for goods and services has forced leaders to liberalize their economies and adopt a range of administrative reforms.[17]

---

[17] Jon Marks, "Gulf of Expectations: Momentum for Economic and Political Reform," *World Link* 12, no. 1 (January-February 1999), pp. 130–133.

Table 3-11
GCC Income and
Population, 2000

	2000 GNP (IN MILLIONS)	2000 POPULATION (IN THOUSANDS)	2000 GNP PER CAPITA
Bahrain	$ 5,580	677	$ 8,236
Kuwait	59,455	1,687	35,242
Oman	na	2,589	na
Qatar	na	849	na
Saudi Arabia	135,453	22,183	6,106
United Arab Emirates	na	2,970	na
Total		*28,784*	

Source: Reprinted by permission of Warren Keegan Associates, Inc.

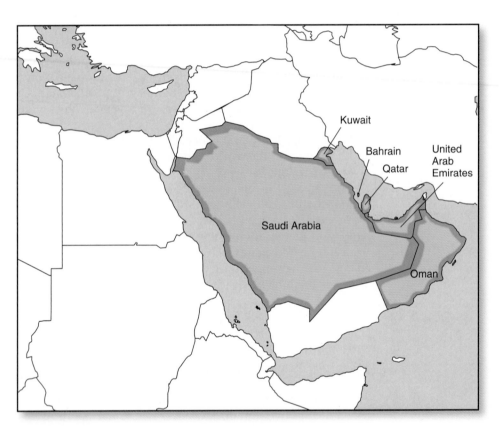

Figure 3-8
The GCC Countries

The organization provides a means of realizing coordination, integration, and cooperation in all economic, social, and cultural affairs. Gulf finance ministers drew up an economic cooperation agreement covering investment, petroleum, the abolition of customs duties, harmonization of banking regulations, and financial and monetary coordination. GCC committees coordinate trade development in the region, industrial strategy, agricultural policy, and uniform petroleum policies and prices. Current goals include establishing an Arab Common Market and increasing trade ties with Asia.

The GCC is one of three newer regional organizations. In 1989, two other organizations were established. Morocco, Algeria, Mauritania, Tunisia, and Libya banded together in the Arab Maghreb Union (AMU); Egypt, Iraq, Jordan, and North Yemen created the Arab Cooperation Council (ACC). Many Arabs see their new regional groups—the GCC, ACC, and AMU—as embryonic economic communities that will foster the development of inter-Arab trade and investment. The newer organizations are more promising than the Arab League, which consists of 21 member states and has a constitution that requires unanimous decisions.

Marketing Issues in the Middle East

Connection is a key word in conducting business in the Middle East. Those who take the time to develop relationships with key business and government figures are more likely to cut through red tape than those who do not. A predilection for bargaining is culturally ingrained, and the visiting businessperson must be prepared for some old-fashioned haggling. Establishing personal rapport, mutual trust, and respect are essentially the most important factors leading to a successful business relationship. Decisions are usually not made by correspondence or telephone. The Arab businessperson does business with the individual, not with the company. Most social customs are based on the Arab male-dominated society. Women are usually not part of the business or entertainment scene for traditional Muslim Arabs.

Some conversation subjects should be avoided, as they are considered an invasion of privacy. For example:

1. Avoid bringing up subjects of business before getting to know your Arab host. This is considered rude.
2. It is taboo to ask questions or make comments concerning a man's wife or female children.
3. Avoid pursuing the subjects of politics or religion.
4. Avoid any discussion of Israel.[18]

AFRICA

The African continent is an enormous landmass with a territory of 11.7 million square miles; the United States would fit into Africa about three and a half times. It is not really possible to treat Africa as a single economic unit. The 53 nations on the continent can be divided into three distinct areas: the Republic of South Africa, North Africa, and sub-Saharan or Black Africa, located between the Sahara in the north and the Zambezi River in the south. With 1.4 percent of the world's wealth and 11.3 percent of its population, Africa is a developing region with an average per capita income of $700. Many African nations are former colonies of Europe, and the EU remains the continent's most important trading partner.

The 78 million Arabs living in North Africa are differentiated politically and economically. The northern nations are richer and more developed, and many of the states benefit from large oil resources. The Arab states have been independent for a longer period than have the black African nations. The Middle East and North Africa are sometimes viewed as a regional entity known as "Mena"; since oil prices slumped in the 1980s, the region has been marked by slow economic growth. Most governments are working to reduce their reliance on oil revenues and their public aid levels. The

---

18 Philip R. Harris and Robert T. Moran, *Managing Cultural Differences*, 3d ed. (Houston: Gulf Publishing Co., 1991), p. 506.

In March 1998, U.S. President Bill Clinton toured six African nations in an effort to promote the region's political and economic accomplishments to the American people. The tour came just days after the U.S. House of Representatives passed the African Growth and Opportunities Act. Keyed to a theme of "Trade, not Aid," the bill's sponsors intended to support nations that had made significant progress toward economic liberalization. The bill would make it easier for African nations to gain access to financing from the U.S. Export-Import Bank; it also represents a formal step toward a U.S.-Africa free trade area. One of the bill's key provisions grants textile and apparel manufacturers in Kenya and Mauritius free access to the American market on up to $3.5 billion in exports each year. As Benjamin Kipkorir, Kenya's ambassador to the United States, observed, "Every country that has industrialized, starting from England in the eighteenth century, began with textiles. We'd like to do the same thing."

Under the Agreement on Textiles and Clothing negotiated during the Uruguay Round of GATT negotiations, global textile quotas will be eliminated in 2005. Nevertheless, the textile provision in the new bill is proving to be controversial. The United States imports about $50 billion in textiles and apparel each year, much of it from Asia, Latin America, and Africa. Wary legislators from textile-producing states fear job losses among their constituents if the bill becomes law. The bill's opponents point out that, by the mid-1990s, dozens of Asian companies had established operations in Kenya to take advantage of quota-free exports to the United States. Kenya's flourishing textile export industry eventually caught the attention of U.S. officials, who imposed import restrictions. As a result, dozens of companies shut down and 10,000 Kenyans lost their jobs.

More generally, there is concern that the Act will not, in fact, "create a transition path from development assistance to economic self-reliance." One especially harsh critic is representative Jesse Jackson Jr., who voted against the Act. In a letter to *The Wall Street Journal*, he wrote:

> In my view, this bill will not benefit the common people of Africa or America, black or white. It will benefit multinational corporations operating in the global economy, but not African-American or American workers. Protection of African workers' rights, assurance of safe working conditions, prohibition of child labor or sweatshop conditions, and protection of the African environment are markedly absent. . . The bill will force 48 sub-Saharan African nations into a straitjacket of economic austerity and deepening poverty in order to benefit transnational financial institutions, wealthy investors, and large corporations.

Beyond the ethical concerns expressed by Representative Jackson, other questions have been raised about general prospects for improved trade with Africa. Communications are unreliable, the overall infrastructure remains underdeveloped, and basic legal protections for businesses are lacking. Exporters and importers quickly learn that the cost of moving freight, including port charges and air transport rates, are much higher than in Asia. Import barriers remain high in many nations. While some observers believe that Africa is poised for an era of growth similar to that in Asia, others feel that such comparisons are not justified.

SOURCES: Robert Block and Michael K. Frisby, "Clinton Tour Aims to Sell New Image of Africa," *The Wall Street Journal* (March 20, 1998), p. A13; Tony Hawkins and Michael Holman, "Clinton Talks Up Africa's Prospects for Investment," *Financial Times* (March 31, 1998), p. A10; Michael M. Phillips, "Some Blacks are Torn by Africa Trade Bill," *The Wall Street Journal* (March 11, 1998), pp. A2, A8; Nicholas D. Kristof, "Why Africa Can Thrive Like Asia," *The New York Times* (May 25, 1997), sec. 4, pp. 1, 4; Phillips, "U.S. is Seeking to Build Its Trade with Africa," *The Wall Street Journal* (June 2, 1996), p. A1; Phillips, "U.S. Rethinks Trade Policy with Africa," *The Wall Street Journal* (July 15, 1996), p. A2.

---

economies of non-oil, "emerging Mena" countries, which include Egypt, Jordan, Lebanon, Morocco, and Tunisia, have performed best in recent years.[19]

Economic Community of West African States (ECOWAS)

The Treaty of Lagos establishing the Economic Community of West African States (ECOWAS) was signed in May 1975 by 16 states with the object of promoting trade,

---

[19] Roula Khalaf, "World's Slowest Growing Developing Region," *Financial Times,* Survey—World Economy and Finance (September 19, 1997), p. 28.

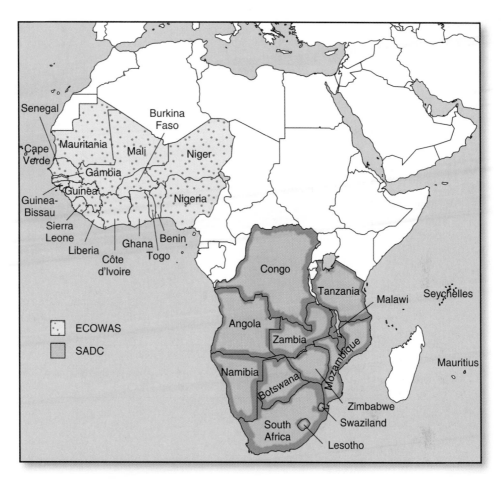

Figure 3-9
ECOWAS and SADC Countries

cooperation, and self-reliance in West Africa. The members are Benin, Burkina Faso, Cape Verde, The Gambia, Ghana, Guinea, Guinea-Bissau, Côte d'Ivoire, Liberia, Mali, Mauritania, Niger, Nigeria, Senegal, Sierra Leone, and Togo (see Figure 3-9 and Table 3-12). In 1980, the member countries agreed to establish a free trade area for unprocessed agricultural products and handicrafts. Tariffs on industrial goods were also to be abolished; however, there were implementation delays. By January 1990, tariffs on 25 items manufactured in ECOWAS member states had been eliminated. The organization installed a computer system to process customs and trade statistics and to calculate the loss of revenue resulting from the liberalization of inter-community trade. In June 1990, ECOWAS adopted measures that would create a single monetary zone in the region by 1994. Despite such achievements, economic development has occurred unevenly in the region. In recent years, the economies of Benin, the Côte d'Ivoire, and Ghana have performed impressively, while Liberia and Sierra Leone are still experiencing political conflict and economic decline.

East African Cooperation

In 1996, the presidents of Kenya, Uganda, and Tanzania established a formal mechanism to promote free trade and economic integration. Tariff issues will be resolved and prospects for a customs union are being explored. Efforts are also underway to

Table 3-12
ECOWAS Income
and Population,
2000

	2000 GNP (IN MILLIONS)	2000 POPULATION (IN THOUSANDS)	2000 GNP PER CAPITA
Benin	$ 2,221	6,315	$ 352
Burkina Faso	2,447	11,246	218
Cape Verde	432	429	1,006
Côte d'Ivoire	9,698	15,484	626
The Gambia	393	1,313	299
Ghana	7,042	19,481	361
Guinea	4,000	7,474	535
Guinea-Bissau	259	1,214	213
Liberia	na	3,099	na
Mali	2,492	11,179	223
Mauritania	1,093	2,674	409
Niger	1,729	10,833	160
Nigeria	38,416	128,454	299
Senegal	4,427	9,494	466
Sierra Leone	681	5,113	133
Togo	1,395	4,748	294
*Total/Mean GNP per capita**	$76,725[a]	238,550	$ 321[*,a]

[a]Excludes Liberia

Source: Reprinted by permission of Warren Keegan Associates, Inc.

develop regional ties in tourism and coordinate energy projects. Although Kenya is the most developed of the three nations, Francis Muthaura, the executive secretary of the secretariat of the Commission of East African Cooperation, expressed optimism that all three will benefit: "A free market is going to generate competition and already we are seeing a lot of cross-border investment. If you have free movement of capital and goods and labor, imbalances will be sorted out in the long term."[20]

South African Development Community (SADC)

In 1992, the SADC superseded the South African Development Coordination Council as a mechanism by which the region's black-ruled states could promote trade, cooperation, and economic integration. The members are Angola, Botswana, Democratic Republic of Congo (formerly Zaire), Lesotho, Malawi, Mauritius, Mozambique, Namibia, South Africa, Seychelles, Swaziland, Tanzania, Zambia, and Zimbabwe (see Figure 3-9). The ultimate goal is a fully developed customs union; however, real progress toward integration has been slow in coming. South Africa joined the community in 1994; it represents about 75 percent of the income in the region and 86 percent of intraregional exports (Table 3-13). South Africa has been in discussions with the European Union about the formation of a free trade area; other SADC members are concerned that such an arrangement would provide European global companies with a base from which to dominate the continent. South Africa, Botswana, Lesotho,

---

[20] Michael Holman, "Learning from the Past," *Financial Times Survey* (November 5, 1996), p. 1.

Table 3-13
SADC Income and
Population, 2000

	2000 GNP (IN MILLIONS)	2000 POPULATION (IN THOUSANDS)	2000 GNP PER CAPITA
Angola	$ 3,196	12,852	$ 249
Botswana	5,085	1,656	3,071
DR of Congo	4775	58,856	81
Lesotho	1,370	2,150	637
Malawi	2,538	11,131	228
Mauritius	4,864	1,190	4,088
Mozambique	2,779	17,804	156
Namibia	3,445	1,753	1,965
Seychelles	556	82	6,822
South Africa	125,054	43,089	2,902
Swaziland	1,421	1,050	1,354
Tanzania	7,583	34,220	222
Zambia	3,563	10,259	347
Zimbabwe	8,311	12,278	677
*Total/Mean GNP per capita**	*174,540*	*208,370*	*837*

Source: Reprinted by permission of Warren Keegan Associates, Inc.

Namibia, and Swaziland also belong to the Southern African Customs Union (SACU). Another concern is war in the Congo, which threatens a severe impact on economic growth in the region.[21]

SUMMARY

This chapter examines the environment for world trade, focusing on the institutions and regional cooperation agreements that affect trade patterns. The multilateral **World Trade Organization,** created in 1995 as the successor to the General Agreement on Tariffs and Trade, provides a forum for settling disputes among member nations and tries to set policy for world trade. The world trading environment is also characterized by **preferential trading agreements** among smaller numbers of countries on a regional and subregional basis. These agreements can be conceptualized on a continuum of increasing economic integration. **Free trade areas** such as the one created by the North American Free Trade Agreement (NAFTA) represent the lowest level of economic integration. The purpose of a free trade area is to eliminate tariffs and quotas. A **customs union** (e.g. Mercosur) represents a further degree of integration in the form of common external tariffs. In a **common market,** such as the Central American Integration System (SICA), restrictions on the movement of labor and capital are eased in an effort to further increase integration. In an **economic union** such as the European Union (EU), the highest level of economic integration is achieved by unification of economic policies and institutions. Other important cooperation arrangements include the Association of Southeast Asian Nations (ASEAN) and the Cooperation Council for the Arab States of the Gulf (GCC). In Africa, the two main cooperation agreements are the Economic Community of West African States (ECOWAS) and the South African Development Community (SADC).

---

21 Tony Hawkins and Michael Holman, "Trade Tensions Send Southern Africa Regional Link-Up Reeling," *Financial Times* (September 2, 1998), p. 4.

DISCUSSION QUESTIONS

1. Explain the role of the World Trade Organization.
2. Describe the similarities and differences between a free trade area, a customs union, a common market, and an economic union. Give an example of each.
3. Identify a regional economic organization or agreement in each of the following areas: Latin America, Asia/Pacific, Western Europe, Central Europe, the Middle East, and Africa.

GLOBAL MARKETING PRACTICUM

The Inter-American Development Bank (IADB) is the oldest regional development institution for the Western Hemisphere. To learn more about the functions of the IADB and the services it provides, visit the Web site at www.iadb.org.

TEST YOUR SKILLS

Several key dates mentioned in the chapter are listed here. Can you identify the event associated with each? (Answers are following.)

December 31, 1992
January 1, 1994
January 1, 1995
January 1, 1999
January 1, 2002

Answers: December 31, 1992—Single Market Act goes into effect; January 1, 1994—NAFTA becomes effective; January 1, 1995—GATT is renamed the WTO; January 1, 1999—introduction of the euro as unit of account; January 1, 2002—euro currency goes into circulation.

SUGGESTED READINGS

Books

Abengunrin, Olayiwola. *Economic Dependence and Regional Cooperation in Southern Africa: SADCC and South Africa in Confrontation.* Lewiston, N.Y.: The Edwin Mellen Press, 1990.

Anderson, Kym, and Richard Blackhurst, eds. *Regional Integration and the Global Trading System.* New York: Harvester/Wheatsheaf, 1993.

Axline, W. Andrew. *The Political Economy of Regional Cooperation.* London: Pinter, 1994.

De Melo, Jaime, and Arvind Panagariya. *New Dimensions in Regional Integration.* Oxford: Oxford University Press, 1993.

Fallows, James M. *Looking at the Sun: The Rise of the New East Asian Economic and Political System.* New York: Vintage Books, 1995.

Ohmae, Kenichi. *The End of the Nation State: The Rise of Regional Economies.* New York: Free Press, 1995.

Shaw, Timothy M., and Julius Emeka Okolo, eds. *The Political Economy of Foreign Policy in ECOWAS.* London: Macmillan-St. Martin's Press, 1994.

Articles

Aho, C. Michael. " 'Fortress Europe': Will the EU Isolate Itself from North America and Asia?" *The Columbia Journal of World Business* 29, no. 3 (Fall 1994), pp. 32–39.

Atkinson, Glenn, and Ted Oleson. "Europe 1992: From Customs Union to Economic Community." *Journal of Economic Issues* 28, no. 4 (December 1994), pp. 977–995.

Bakos, Gabor. "After COMECON: A Free Trade Area in Central Europe?" *Europe-Asia Studies* 45, no. 6 (1993), pp. 1025–1044.

Banks, Philip. "India: The New Asian Tiger?" *Business Horizons* 38, no. 3 (May 1995), pp. 47–50.

Bernal, Richard L. "From NAFTA to Hemispheric Free Trade." *The Columbia Journal of World Business* 29, no. 3 (Fall 1994), pp. 22–31.

Cosgrove, Carol. "Has the Lome Convention Failed ACP Trade?" *Journal of International Affairs* 48, no. 1 (Summer 1994), pp. 223–249.

Curry, Robert L., Jr. "A Case for Further Collaboration between the EU and ASEAN." *ASEAN Economic Bulletin* 11, no. 2 (November 1994), pp. 150–157.

Czinkota, Michael R. "The World Trade Organization—Perspectives and Prospects." *Journal of International Marketing* 3, no. 1 (1995), pp. 85–91.

Granell, Francisco. "The European Union's Enlargement Negotiations with Austria, Finland, Norway and Sweden." *Journal of Common Market Studies* 33, no. 1 (March 1995), pp. 117–141.

Healey, Nigel M. "The Transition Economies of Central and Eastern Europe: A Political, Economic, Social and Technological Analysis." *The Columbia Journal of World Business* 29, no. 1 (Spring 1994), pp. 62–70.

Hooley, Graham, Tony Cox, and John Fahy. "Market Orientation in the Transition Economies of Central Europe: Tests of the Narver and Slater Market Orientation Scales." *Journal of Business Research* 50, no. 3 (December 2000), pp. 273–285.

Jessop, Bob. "Regional Economic Blocs, Cross-Border Cooperation, and Local Economic Strategies in Postsocialism." *American Behavioral Scientist* 38, no. 5 (March 1995), pp. 764–775.

Koch-Weser, Caio. "Economic Reform and Regional Cooperation: A Development Agenda for the Middle East and North Africa." *Middle East Policy* 2, no. 2 (1993), pp. 28–36.

Krum, James R., and Pradeep A. Rau. "Organizational Responses of U.S. Multinationals to EC-1992: An Empirical Study." *Journal of International Marketing* 1, no. 2 (1993), pp. 49–70.

Kurus, Bilson. "The ASEAN Triad: National Interest, Consensus-Seeking, and Economic Cooperation." *Contemporary Southeast Asia* 16, no. 4 (March 1995), pp. 404–420.

Lee, Helen D. "CACM: Reforms and Integration Spur Growth of Market." *Business America* 114, no. 8 (April 19, 1993), pp. 10–11.

Mejias, Roberto J., and Jose G. Vargohernandez. "Emerging Mexican and Canadian Strategic Trade Alliances under NAFTA." *Journal of Global Marketing* 14, no. 4 (2001), pp. 89–116.

Miyoshi, Masao. "A Borderless World? From Colonialism to Transnationalism and the Decline of the Nation-State." *Critical Inquiry* 19, no. 4 (Summer 1993), pp. 726–751.

Paine, George, and Raphael Craig. "ASEAN Nations Look to Trade and Technology to Maintain High Growth." *Business America* 115, no. 11 (November 1994), pp. 14–17.

Paribatra, Sukhumbhand. "From ASEAN Six to ASEAN Ten: Issues and Prospects." *Contemporary Southeast Asia* 16, no. 3 (December 1994), pp. 243–258.

Quelch, John A., and James E. Austin. "Should Multinationals Invest in Africa?" *Sloan Management Review* 4, no. 3 (Spring 1993), pp. 107–119.

Robson, Peter, and Ian Wooton. "The Transnational Enterprise and Regional Economic Integration." *Journal of Common Market Studies* 31, no. 1 (March 1993), pp. 71–90.

Shuh, Arnold. "Global Standardization as a Success Formula for Marketing in Central Eastern Europe." *Journal of World Business* 35, no. 2 (Summer 2000), pp. 133–148.

Tuan, Hoang Anh. "Vietnam's Membership in ASEAN: Economic, Political, and Security Implications." *Contemporary Southeast Asia* 16, no. 3 (December 1994), pp. 243–258.

Tyler, Gus. "The Nation-State vs. the Global Economy." *Challenge* 36, no. 2 (March 1993), pp. 26–32.

Wu, Friedrich. "The ASEAN Economies in the 1990s and Singapore's Regional Role." *California Management Review* 34, no. 1 (Fall 1991), pp. 103–114.

CASES

Case 3-1   Asia-Pacific Economic Cooperation

Each November, representatives of 18 countries that border on the Pacific Ocean meet formally to discuss prospects for liberalizing trade. Collectively, the countries that make up the Asia-Pacific Economic Cooperation (APEC) forum account for about 46 percent of world trade, 38 percent of world population, and 55 percent of world GNP (see map that follows). In some trade sectors, including consumer electronics, trucks, and bicycles, APEC members account for 70 percent or more of global trade. APEC provides a chance for annual discussions by people at various levels: academics and business executives, ministers, and heads of state. Some small Asian countries view APEC as a wel-

come means of using the United States to counterbalance the dominance of Japan and China in the region. And, as noted in *The Economist*, "Not so long ago, the thought of South Korea or Indonesia, let alone China, having anything to do with even a 'vision' of free trade would have been fantastic."

U.S. President Bill Clinton put APEC at the center of his administration's Asian trade strategy. In 1993, when Clinton convened the fifth APEC forum in Seattle, Washington, the United States hoped to boost trade with fast-growing Asian Pacific Rim nations by cutting tariffs, reaching agreement on competition policies, and eliminating subsidies. In fact, after the heads of government

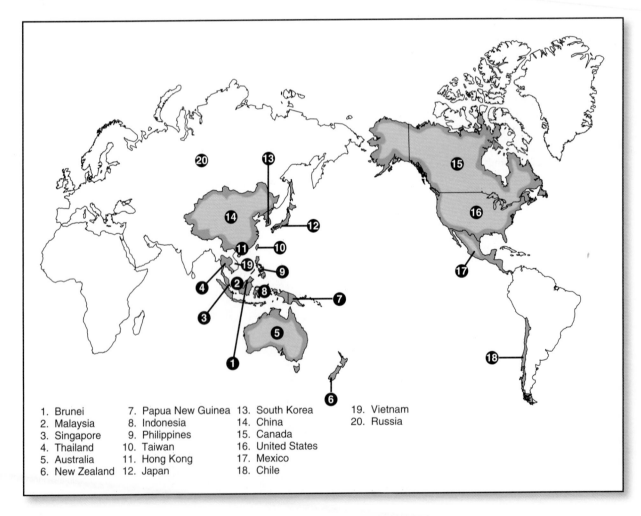

1. Brunei	7. Papua New Guinea	13. South Korea	19. Vietnam
2. Malaysia	8. Indonesia	14. China	20. Russia
3. Singapore	9. Philippines	15. Canada	
4. Thailand	10. Taiwan	16. United States	
5. Australia	11. Hong Kong	17. Mexico	
6. New Zealand	12. Japan	18. Chile	

met in a special leadership summit convened by President Clinton, an announcement was made regarding commitment to a "vision" of free trade. Washington's efforts came at a time when the Asian nations had increased the share of overall trade that stays within Asia to about 65 percent, up from 58 percent in 1980. Meanwhile, Asian imports from the United States had fallen from 41 percent of overall trade in 1980 to 34 percent of overall trade in 1992. During the decade of the 1980s, the economies of Southeast Asian countries grew twice as fast as the rest of the world; international trade in the region grew at twice the rate experienced in Europe and North America. Observers noted that the U.S. role in the 1993 forum provided political momentum in Washington that helped convince the U.S. Congress to approve NAFTA and GATT despite growing protectionist sentiment in some circles.

At APEC's 1994 meeting in Bogor, Indonesia, 10 separate working groups began preparing plans to transform the vision into practice by reducing country differences in such areas as customs, product quality standards, and telecommunications. Cabinet ministers arrived at a set of non-binding principles regarding foreign investment. Included were proposals to minimize performance requirements such as local content laws and export quotas, guidelines pertaining to equal treatment for foreign and domestic investors, and improved clarity in laws. Some of these policy issues had not been sufficiently addressed by the Uruguay Round of GATT negotiations. For example, APEC members hoped to address investment rules for service providers (GATT dealt with investments by manufacturers); moreover, GATT left opportunities open for countries to insist that local managers be hired and technology be transferred by any company wishing to invest.

Much debate among APEC members has centered on whether all trade barriers in Asia can be eliminated among industrialized member nations by 2010 and by the year 2020 for developing members. It has become apparent that policy makers and farmers in South Korea, China, and Japan still support agricultural subsidies. Agricultural producers in the United States, Canada, and Australia want to sell more food products in Asia. Although the Japanese government took action in 1993 to end an outright ban on imports of foreign rice, market access is still restricted to outsiders. Australian farmers have worked particularly hard to develop varieties of rice that will appeal to finicky Japanese consumers. Notes a member of an Australian rice growers' cooperative, "Japanese are connoisseurs of rice. If we can sell our product in Japan, we can sell it anywhere. All we need is the market to open up."

Besides agriculture, other divisive issues are Washington's annual review of China's most-favored-nation trading status and the Clinton administration's firm stand on human rights. Some in attendance at the 1995 APEC meeting in Osaka, Japan, worried that special interest groups lobbying for "sensitive sectors" in individual countries could derail the agreement. Japan's rice farmers, for example, wield a great deal of political clout. Warned one U.S. trade official, "Australia will pull motor vehicles off the list, and we'll pull textiles. The only thing left to talk about will be widgets." President Clinton was unable to attend the Osaka meeting because of a budget battle in Washington; some observers took his non-appearance as a sign that U.S. commitment to Asia was diminishing.

One lesson from the 1995 APEC meeting was that compromise seemed to be inevitable; for example, countries might be allowed to reduce agricultural subsidies gradually. Some trade ministers showed a propensity for using vague phrases such as "economic cooperation" instead of talking about "opening trade." Despite concerns that compromise would slow the pace of trade liberalization, some countries in the region have already made progress toward freer trade. At the Osaka meeting, Chinese President Jiang Zemin announced that China would lower tariffs by 30 percent overall beginning in 1996. Indonesia recently announced tariff reductions of up to 35 percent on 6,000 manufactured and agricultural products. In addition, some telecommunications monopolies are being opened to foreign investment. South Korea's president pledged to open 200 types of businesses to foreign investment and simplify customs procedures for imports and exports. As a result of these and other successes, expectations were running high as the 1996 APEC meeting in the Philippines approached.

At the 1996 summit in Manila, members issued a statement calling for the World Trade Organization to move ahead with a global Information Technology Agreement that would eliminate tariffs in the electronics and computer market sectors by the year 2000. However, some leaders present at the meeting indicated that they did not consider the statement to be binding. For example, Singapore's prime minister said the statement "Can be interpreted by members as anything they want it to be." The group also began considering expansion of APEC membership to as many as 10 additional countries, including Vietnam, Russia, and India. Discussion of an APEC-wide business visa got bogged down in disagreement on what mechanism would be used. Member nations also submitted Individual Action Plans (IAPs) representing measures for liberalizing trade and investment. Some observers noted, however, that many of the proposals contained little of substance beyond what some members had agreed to as members of the WTO. Some observers dismissed the 1996 forum as a failure, suggesting that "APEC" had come to stand for "A Perfect Excuse to Chat."

Not surprisingly, when APEC convened for its 1997 meeting in Vancouver, the economic crisis in Asia was high on the agenda. Some delegates were anxious to create a fund for regional finance stabilization; such hopes were dimmed after the U.S. Congress withheld approval of an additional $3.5 billion allocation for the International Monetary Fund. Another sign of Washington's mood was its refusal to grant the president fast-track approval in trade negotiations. This move was widely viewed as a sign of Clinton's weakened authority in the international trade arena. Washington was determined, however, to secure Asian commitment to a WTO agreement that would open the banking and insurance sectors to competition.

The path to Asian recovery represents a double-edged sword for the United States. On the one hand, increased exports are acknowledged to be a key component of the recovery. On the other hand, increased exports to the United States by China, Japan, and other Asian nations will undoubtedly worsen the U.S. trade deficit unless those country markets become more open to U.S. exports.

Despite APEC's preoccupation with financial issues, trade matters were also considered. An initiative called Early Voluntary Sectoral Liberalization targeted 15 industry sectors for trade liberalization by the year 2005. The sectors included chemicals, energy, medical equipment, forestry products, and fish.

The problematic regional situation prompted many observers to ask whether APEC was up to the task of making contributions leading to a solution. Edward Graham of the Washington, D.C. Institute for International Economics said, "Rather than long-term and idealistic goals, this requires an immediate commitment." Charles Morrison of the East-West Center echoed that view. He asked, "This year is much more a test for APEC. The question is: Can this institution be relevant given what the region is going through?"

Expert opinion is divided on whether the course APEC is pursuing is the right one. Some observers believe that APEC lacks procedures for the type of serious bargaining and negotiation that can lead to compromise and agreements. The operative phrase is "open regionalism," which can be interpreted in various ways but basically means that APEC members can lower trade barriers to non-APEC countries if they wish to. Thus, non-member countries have an opportunity to become "free riders" by benefiting from APEC's trade gains without lowering their own trade barriers. Other experts, including Columbia University's Jagdish Bhagwati, believe that a policy of open regionalism represents one of APEC's chief successes.

A second APEC principle is "concerted unilateralism," which means that IAPs brought to the summit by various member nations are not subject to negotiation. Further, these IAPs are not subject to bargaining, nor are they conditional on liberalization offers by other nations. It was suggested that IAPs represented an Asian tendency to avoid formal negotiation on trade matters, thereby sidestepping serious disagreements or debate. However, some observers believe that a consequence of this approach is that APEC members have an incentive to offer little while hoping for a lot in the way of trade concessions. One recommendation called for APEC to abandon concerted unilateralism in favor of a policy of "open reciprocal regionalism." This, it was suggested, would entail real negotiation rather than the IAP approach and would lead to regional agreements that bind member nations willing to make specific commitments to liberalized trade. Instead of being "free riders," non-APEC nations wishing to participate in the regional agreements would be free to do so as long as they offered reciprocal trade-liberalizing measures. ■

Visit the Web site
You can access APEC on the Internet at:
www.apecsec.org.sg

DISCUSSION QUESTIONS

1. What are the implications of APEC for global companies?
2. What are the biggest barriers to achieving improved trade conditions under the APEC framework?
3. The Japanese government uses tariffs to protect rice farmers from imports. Why?
4. The most recent APEC meetings have convened in the following locations:

Kuala Lumpur, Malaysia (1998)
Auckland, New Zealand (1999)
Brunei (2000)
Shanghai, China (2001)
Using your choice of reference resources, find information about one of these APEC meetings. Have any of the issues identified in this case been resolved? What new issues have emerged?

SOURCES: Kenneth Flam and Edward Lincoln, "Reinvigorating APEC," *The International Economy* (January-February 1998), pp. 54–58; Matt Miller, "Which Way Ahead?" *Far Eastern Economic Review* (November 27, 1997), pp. 79–80; Guy de Jonquiéres and Gerard Baker, "Apec Grapples with Market Turmoil," *Financial Times* (November 11, 1997), p. A4; Guy de Jonquiéres and Edward Luce, "Apec Opts for Slow and Steady Jog," *Financial Times* (November 25, 1996), p. 4; Jonathan Clark, "APEC as a Semi-Solution," *Orbis* 39, no. 1 (Winter 1995), pp. 81–95; Martin Rudner, "APEC: The Challenges of Asia Pacific Economic Cooperation," *Modern Asian Studies,* 29, no. 2 (1995), pp. 403–437; Peter Engardio, "Free-Trade Showdown," *Business Week* (November 20, 1995), pp. 60–61; "Australian, Japanese Ways Differ," *Associated Press* (November 12, 1995); Helene Cooper and Michael Williams, "U.S. Limits APEC-Summit Expectations," *The Wall Street Journal* (November 16, 1995), p. A12; Douglas Harbrecht and Amy Borus, "Marching Toward Free Trade in Asia?" *Business Week* (November 14, 1994), pp. 52–53; "The Opening of Asia," *The Economist* (November 13, 1995), pp. 23–24+; Robert S. Greenberger and Marcus W. Brauchli, "U.S. Has Lost Some of Its Clout in Asia," *The Wall Street Journal* (November 14, 1994), p. A10; Dan Biers and Craig Forman, "Asia-Pacific Forum Finds Focus: Trade," *The Wall Street Journal* (November 14, 1994), p. A8.

Case 3-2   *Europe Goes Bananas for . . .*

The European Union represents the world's second largest market for bananas; Europeans consume about 4 million tons of the tropical fruit each year. Prior to July 1993, European imports of bananas followed a number of different patterns. Several countries offered preferential access and high prices to banana-producing countries in the Africa, Caribbean, and Pacific (ACP) regions where trading relationships dated to the colonial era. For example, Dominica, Grenada, St Lucia, and St Vincent supply two-thirds of the bananas imported by the UK and depend on bananas for 60 percent of their export earnings. Market access by non-preferred producers to the UK, France, Italy, and several other countries was blocked by import restrictions. Elsewhere in Europe, countries imported bananas on either a free trade basis or with minimal tariff barriers. Responding to a complaint by Colombia, Costa Rica, Guatemala, Nicaragua, and Venezuela, a GATT panel ruled in May 1993 that the existing regimes violated Articles I and IX of the GATT treaty.

The panel's ruling was essentially rendered moot when, on July 1, 1993, as part of the Single European Market initiative, a uniform market regime concerning EU banana imports was implemented. The action promised to be challenging, since the new regime had to protect the interests of banana producers in the EU, which included the Canary Islands and a handful of other territories. Second, the action had to fulfill the EU's commitment under the Lomé convention to give preference to small-scale, relatively inefficient ACP banana producers whose production costs run as high as $515 per ton. Finally, it was necessary for the regime to honor the GATT framework for liberalized trade.

The new regulation, known as 404/93, allowed for tariff-free annual banana imports from EU producers and ACP producers amounting to 854,000 tons and 857,700 tons, respectively. Shares of the quota were allocated to individual nations. Up to two additional tons per year could be imported from so-called third countries—mostly in Latin America—with a duty of 100 ECUs per ton. Once the two-ton quota had been met, tariffs on "dollar bananas," as the Latin American fruit was known, rose to a prohibitive 850 ECUs per ton. Importers of "dollar bananas" were also required to apply for import licenses on a quarterly basis. One controversial aspect of the regime was that it reserved one-third of the dollar banana import licenses for established European marketers of ACP bananas. In principle, this encouraged importers with ACP experience to maintain those trading links while improving market integration by importing the cheaper Latin American fruit as well. Instead of using the dollar banana license, however, an ACP importer could sell it to another party and pass along the profit from the sale to ACP producers. One stipulation was that any ACP importer that sold the dollar banana license was obligated to continue buying the more expensive ACP bananas. In essence, then, the cheaper bananas provided a cross subsidy to the less-efficient ACP producers. At the same time, industry observers estimated, the artificially high banana prices created by the regime cost EU consumers $2 billion each year.

A second GATT panel ruled that the new regime also violated several GATT articles. Eventually, Colombia, Costa Rica, Nicaragua, and Venezuela came to an agreement with the EU. Under the Framework Agreement, the four nations agreed to disregard the GATT panel's finding and file no more complaints. In return, the EU agreed to modify the import licensing system, increase the third-country quotas to 2.2 tons, and lower the tariff to 75 ECU/ton.

By no means did this action settle the matter, however. Spurred by intense lobbying from Carl Lindner, chairman and chief executive of Chiquita Brands International, the

U.S. government complained that 404/93 discriminated against its marketers and distributors. The governments of Honduras, Guatemala, and Mexico were also party to the complaint. In 1995, the four countries formally requested that the World Trade Organization initiate the dispute settlement process. In 1996, much to the annoyance of the European Commission, Ecuador joined forces with the complainants. Ecuador had previously signed an agreement with the EU that called for bilateral negotiations prior to involving the WTO. The Central American country is the world's number one banana producer as well as the low-cost producer thanks to large-scale plantations and production costs of $162 per ton.

In March 1997, the WTO ruled that 404/93 and the Framework Agreement did, in fact, violate more than a dozen trade rules. In particular, the ruling was the first case won under the General Agreement on Trade in Services. The WTO noted that the system of distributing import licenses for Latin American bananas to French and British companies discriminated against marketing companies in the United States. However, the report did not address the preferences afforded ACP producers by 404/93. The response to the ruling was varied. While the Caribbean countries insisted that their economies would be damaged if 404/93 were dismantled, Ecuador's ambassador to the EU insisted that his country's economy had been badly hurt by the framework. For his part, the EU agriculture minister reiterated to the European Parliament that the EU believed the regime was non-discriminatory. In the United States, the decision was hailed as "an important precedent for all U.S. exporters of services and agricultural goods."

The European Union appealed the ruling, as permitted under WTO rules. However, in September 1998 the appeals body upheld the complaint, leaving the EU with the task of modifying the regime by the beginning of 1999. However, when the European Commission met later in September to discuss its response, it became clear that opinions among the 15 EU member nations were divided. Nine were willing to change the trade rules, while six, including the UK, France, and Spain, were not. The Caribbean Banana Exporters Association warned that, if the regime were dismantled, farmers might be compelled to grow illegal crops such as cocaine. The association also urged the EU to honor its Lomé commitment to the ACP, and compensate the complainants if necessary. In an editorial in the *Financial Times*, Sir Leon Brittan, vice president of the European Commission, called for cooler heads to prevail in the face of the first-ever WTO ruling against the EU:

It is tempting to conclude that the machinery of world trade suits the powerful at the expense of the vulnerable, and that it may be time to reassess the merits of the WTO. . . Europe's consumers, producers, and traders must not hasten to the conclusion that the WTO is turning the global economy into a wild west of untrammeled capitalism, impervious to the environment, social rights, food safety, and other issues. If used properly, the WTO could turn out to be the ideal tool to tame globalization, enabling such causes to sit comfortably alongside the pursuit of free trade.

One proposal developed by the European Commission would retain the third-country quota at 2.2 tons with a tariff of ECU75 (about $83) per ton. However, an additional "autonomous" quota of 353,000 tons would be allowed into the EU at a tariff of ECU300 per ton. The European Commission also anticipating extending aid totaling $450 million ECUs to ACP countries whose economies would be harmed if import quotas for Latin American bananas were increased. Meeting in Geneva at the WTO in January 1998, the United States and other complainants rejected the Commission's initial proposals. Some observers not involved in the case suggested that the Commission's response demonstrated disregard to the WTO's ruling. EU diplomats remained convinced that the amended proposal was neither arbitrary nor discriminatory and complied with the rulings of the WTO panel and the appeals body. The United States was pushing for a system with a single import quota for all exporters with one tariff rate for ACP bananas and a second rate for bananas from non-ACP producers. The real issue, some said, was obstinate American trade officials. Said one diplomat, "The American threat of 'See You in Geneva' applies, whatever happens. It would be very difficult to see a majority for any proposals which will not leave the United States questioning their WTO validity."

"Bananas are to us what cars are to Detroit."
—Mr. Percival Patterson, prime minister,
Jamaica, and chairman, CARICOM

By mid-1998, a new EU proposal seemed to satisfy most parties. ACP producers would compete with each other to supply the 857,700 tons annual EU banana quota. An aid package of $390 million would also be distributed among ACP nations over a ten-year period. Dollar banana quotas would be expanded, and the system for allocating export licenses would be modified. The proposal provided some breathing room among Caribbean banana producers and a chance to prepare for the future. The prime minister of Grenada said, "We thought we would have been cut off from our market right away, so this is a hopeful sign for us. But the message is clear—we cannot sit and wait because the preferences we have now will not be there for long. We now have some time, but we must recognize the reality of the situation and deal with it." Still, some officials wondered whether local farmers could adjust to the new global realities. An official in St. Lucia commented, "Genera-

tions of farmers and entire families in these islands have been weaned on bananas and they know nothing else. They do not and could not understand how to produce anything else. And we would not know where to start with marketing anything else." ■

DISCUSSION QUESTIONS

1. Neither the United States nor Europe grows bananas. Why, then, did the two sides square off against each other?
2. In March 1999, the United States was prepared to impose 100 percent tariffs on 16 categories of goods imported from Europe worth $520 million. Many were luxury items such as Pecorino cheese from Italy, cashmere sweaters, and plastic-lined leather handbags. Model trains, wine from Portugal, fruit

juices, and wooden toys were originally targeted but were ultimately spared. On what basis do you think that the office of the U.S. trade representative made its choices as to which goods to target for tariffs?
3. Do you agree with those who warn that Caribbean democracies will be destabilized if the United States prevails in its bid to reduce those countries' share of banana exports to Europe?

SOURCES: James Cox, "Fruit War May Hike Price of European Luxuries," *USA Today* (January 25, 1999), pp. B1, B2; Canute James, "Producers Welcome Planned New Rules on Market Access," *Financial Times* (July 8, 1998), p. 3; Michael Smith, "Brussels Farm Ministers Push On with Search for Banana Import Deal," *Financial Times* (June 21, 1998), p. 5; Doniel Dombey, "EU Finds Bananas a Slippery Case," *Financial Times* (January 16, 1998), p. 5; Rikke Thagesen and Alan Matthews, "The EU's Common Banana Regime: An Initial Evaluation," *Journal of Common Market Studies* 35, no. 4 (December 1997), pp. 615–627; Sir Leon Brittan, "The Rough with the Smooth," *Financial Times* (September 10, 1997), p. 16; Neil Buckley, Canute James, and Nancy Dunne, "EU Split on Response to WTO Banana Ruling," *Financial Times* (September 10, 1997), p. 4; Buckley, "WTO Attacks EU Banana Licensing Arrangements," *Financial Times* (May 24–25, 1997), p. 4; James, "Clinton in Pledge on Caribbean Exports," *Financial Times* (May 13, 1997), p. 8; Laurence S. Grossman, *The Political Ecology of Bananas* (Chapel Hill: University of North Carolina Press, 1998).

Chapter 4

Social and Cultural Environments

*T*he world of ice cream marketing pits two global giants against each other. Unilever, the Anglo-Dutch consumer products company, commands 16 percent of the global market with annual sales of $4 billion. Nestlé is the number two player, with 9 percent global share and $2.3 billion in sales. The ice cream wars are heating up, so to speak, as both companies seek to capture larger shares of a growing global market. In 2000, Unilever added Vermont-based Ben & Jerry's Homemade to a portfolio of brands that includes Breyer's, Good Humor, and Wall's in Britain. In 1999, Nestlé capped an acquisition-filled decade by forming Ice Cream Partners with Diageo PLC's Pillsbury unit; the venture markets Häagen-Dazs throughout North America. Prospects for the industry are excellent; in Europe alone, analysts forecast about 8 percent growth by 2005. However, the market is crowded with competitors, including McDonald's, Mars, and thousands of small independent operators. The competitive climate has gotten chilly at times; for example, Mars argued successfully to the European Commission that Unilever was unfairly monopolizing the Irish ice cream market. One thing is for sure: While food preferences are deeply embedded in culture and often vary from country to country, everybody, everywhere loves ice cream.

The warm reception that ice-cold treats enjoy around the world is but one example of the range of global marketing opportunities that exist in different cultural environments. This chapter focuses on the social and cultural forces that shape and affect individual and corporate behavior in the marketplace. Because the world's cultures are characterized by both differences and similarities, the task of the global marketer is twofold. First, marketers must study and understand the country cultures in which they will be doing business. Second, this understanding must be incorporated into the marketing planning process. In some instances, strategies and marketing programs will have to be adapted; however, marketers should also take advantage of

Ben & Jerry's launched supermarket distribution in France in 1996; the company opened three scoop shops Paris in 1998, including the one pictured here. Despite high transportation costs, the ice cream is produced in Vermont and shipped to France. The managing director for France predicted that sales would reach 150 million francs ($25 million) by 2001; that number turned out to be overly optimistic. Some observers assert that the brand's close association with American culture has hindered the company's efforts to win over the French consumers; indeed, food is a serious matter to the French while Ben & Jerry's is a distinctly "fun" brand. Another problem: The French don't typically buy ice cream in grocery stores to consume at home.

shared cultural characteristics and avoid unneeded and costly adaptations of the marketing mix. Deep cultural understanding can actually be a source of competitive advantage for global companies. The aggressive expansion of Spain's Telefónica in Latin America provides a case in point. Chairman Juan Villalonga notes, "It is not just speaking a common language. It is sharing a culture and understanding friendships in the same way."[1]

Any systematic study of a new geographic market requires a combination of tough-mindedness and generosity. While marketers should be secure in their own convictions and traditions, generosity is required to appreciate the integrity and value of other ways of life and points of view. People must, in other words, overcome the prejudices that are a natural result of the human tendency toward ethnocentricity. Although "culture shock" is a normal human reaction to the new and unknown, successful global marketers strive to comprehend human experience from the local point of view. One reason cultural factors challenge global marketers is that many of them are hidden from view. Because culture is learned behavior passed on from generation to generation, it can be difficult for the inexperienced or untrained outsider to fathom. As they endeavor to understand cultural factors, outsiders gradually

[1] Tom Burns, "Spanish Telecoms Visionary Beholds a Brave New World," *Financial Times* (May 2, 1998), p. 24.

become insiders and develop cultural empathy. There are many different paths to the same goals in life. The global marketer understands this and rejoices in life's rich diversity.

This chapter begins with a general discussion of the basic aspects of culture and society and the emergence of a twenty-first century global consumer culture. To help marketers better understand social and cultural dynamics in the global marketplace, this chapter discusses several useful conceptual frameworks for understanding culture: Hall's notion of high- and low-context cultures, Maslow's hierarchy, Hofstede's cultural typology, the self-reference criterion, and diffusion theory. Next is a discussion of specific examples of the impact of culture and society on the marketing of both consumer and industrial products. The chapter ends with suggested solutions to cross-cultural challenges and a review of global companies' cross-cultural training procedures.

SOCIETY, CULTURE, AND GLOBAL CONSUMER CULTURE

Anthropologists and sociologists have offered scores of different definitions of culture. As a starting point, **culture** can be defined as "ways of living, built up by a group of human beings, that are transmitted from one generation to another." A culture acts out its ways of living in the context of *social institutions,* including family, educational, religious, governmental, and business institutions. Those institutions, in turn, function to reinforce cultural norms. Culture includes both conscious and unconscious values, ideas, attitudes, and symbols that shape human behavior *and that are transmitted from one generation to the next.* Organizational anthropologist Geert Hofstede defines *culture* as "the collective programming of the mind that distinguishes the members of one category of people from those of another."[2] A particular "category of people" may constitute a nation, an ethnic group, a gender group, an organization, a family, or some other unit.

Some anthropologists and sociologists divide cultural elements into two broad categories: material culture and nonmaterial culture. The former is sometimes referred to as the *physical component* or *physical culture* and includes physical objects and artifacts created by humans such as clothing and tools. Nonmaterial culture (also known as *subjective* or *abstract culture*) includes intangibles such as religion, perceptions, attitudes, beliefs, and values. There is general agreement that the material and non-material elements of culture are interrelated and interactive. Cultural anthropologist George P. Murdock studied material and nonmaterial culture and identified dozens of "cultural universals," including athletic sports, body adornment, cooking, courtship, dancing, decorative art, education, ethics, etiquette, family feasting, food taboos, language, marriage, mealtime, medicine, mourning, music, property rights, religious rituals, residence rules, status differentiation, and trade.[3]

---

[2] Geert Hofstede and Michael Harris Bond, "The Confucius Connection: From Cultural Roots to Economic Growth," *Organizational Dynamics* (Spring 1988), p. 5.
[3] George P. Murdock, "The Common Denominator of Culture," in *The Science of Man in the World Crisis,* Ralph Linton, ed. (New York: Columbia University Press, 1945), p. 145.

It is against this background of traditional definitions that global marketers should understand a worldwide sociocultural phenomenon of the late twentieth and early twenty-first centuries.[4] It has been argued that consumption has become the hallmark of postmodern society. As cultural information and imagery flow ever more freely via satellite TV, the Internet, and similar communication channels, new global consumer cultures are emerging. Persons who identify with these cultures share meaningful sets of consumption-related symbols. Some of these cultures are associated with specific product categories; marketers speak of "fast-food culture," "credit card culture," "pub culture," "coffee culture," and so on. This cosmopolitan culture, which is comprised of various segments, owes its existence in large part to a wired world in which there is increasing interconnectedness of various local cultures. It can be exploited by **global consumer culture positioning** (GCCP), a marketing tool that will be explained in more detail in Chapter 7. In particular, marketers can use advertising to communicate the notion that people everywhere consume a particular brand or to appeal to human universals.

Attitudes, Beliefs, and Values

If we accept Hofstede's notion of culture as "the collective programming of the mind," then it makes sense to learn about culture by studying the attitudes, beliefs, and values shared by a specific group of people. An **attitude** is a learned tendency to respond in a consistent way to a given object or entity. Attitudes are clusters of interrelated beliefs. A **belief** is an organized pattern of knowledge that an individual holds to be true about the world. Attitudes and beliefs, in turn, are closely related to values. A **value** can be defined as an enduring belief or feeling that a specific mode of conduct is personally or socially preferable to another mode of conduct.[5] In the view of Hofstede and others, values represent the deepest level of a culture and are present in the majority of the members of a particular culture.

Some specific examples will allow us to illustrate these definitions by comparing and contrasting attitudes, beliefs, and values. The Japanese, for example, strive to achieve cooperation, consensus, self-denial, and harmony. Because these all represent feelings about modes of conduct, they are *values.* Japan's monocultural society reflects the *belief* among the Japanese that they are unique in the world. Many Japanese, especially young people, also believe that the West is the source of important fashion trends. As a result, many Japanese share a favorable *attitude* toward American brands. Within any large, dominant cultural group, there are likely to be **subcultures,** that is, smaller groups of people with their own shared subset of attitudes, beliefs, and values. Values, attitudes, and beliefs can also be surveyed at the level of any "category of people" that is embedded within a broad culture. For example, if you are a vegetarian, then eating meat represents a mode of conduct that you and others who share your views avoid. Subcultures often represent attractive niche marketing opportunities.

Globalization can result in situations that challenge beliefs, attitudes, and values. A case in point is the 1998 merger of Germany's Daimler-Benz and the American Chrysler Corporation. Many American Jews shun products from German companies in an effort to honor the memory of Holocaust victims. It's no secret, for example, that *Volkswagen,* the "people's car," was designed on Hitler's orders. Some Jewish

---

4   The following discussion is adapted from Dana L. Alden, Jan-Benedict Steenkamp, and Rajeev Batra, "Brand Positioning through Advertising in Asia, North America, and Europe: The Role of Global Consumer Culture," *Journal of Marketing* 63, no. 1 (January 1999), pp. 75–87.
5   Milton Rokeach, *Beliefs, Attitudes, and Values* (San Francisco: Jossey-Bass, 1968), p. 160.

consumers have also made a conscious decision not to buy Bayer brand aspirin or Braun shavers. Those who are too young to have experienced the horrors of World War II directly were taught by their parents not to buy German products. There is a sense of betrayal among this group that Chrysler joined forces with a German company; Daimler made engines for the German air force and used prisoners of war as factory laborers. Now, some of those who have boycotted German products have indicated that they will not buy a Chrysler automobile because of the company's ties to Daimler. Chrysler dealers have offered differing opinions on whether the merger will have a negative effect on sales.[6]

Aesthetics

Within every culture, there is a shared sense of what is beautiful as opposed to ugly and what represents good taste as opposed to tastelessness or even obscenity. Such considerations are matters of **aesthetics.** Global marketers must understand the importance of *visual aesthetics* embodied in the color or shape of a product, label, or package. Likewise, *aesthetic styles*—various degrees of complexity, for example—are perceived differently in different parts of the world. Aesthetic elements that are deemed attractive, appealing, and in good taste in one country may be perceived differently in another. In some cases, a standardized color can be used in all countries; examples include the distinctive yellow color on Caterpillar's earth-moving equipment and its licensed outdoor gear and the red Marlboro chevron. U.S. companies seem to be experiencing a case of the "blues," as evidenced by a rash of new companies with names such as Bluetooth, Blue Moon, and JetBlue Airways.[7] However, because color perceptions can vary among cultures, adaptation to local preferences may be required. Such perceptions should be taken into account when making decisions about product packaging and other brand-related communications. In highly competitive markets, inappropriate or unattractive product packaging may put a company or brand at a disadvantage. New color schemes may also be mandated by a changing competitive environment. For example, in the wake of Wal-Mart's expansion into Germany in the 1990s, retailer Metro AG added blue, white, and yellow to the logo of its Real hypermarket stores.

There is nothing inherently "good" or "bad" about any color of the spectrum; all associations and perceptions regarding color arise from culture. Red is a popular color in most parts of the world; besides being the color of blood, in many countries red also is tied to centuries-old traditions of viticulture and winemaking. Blue, because of its associations with sky and water, has an elemental connotation with undertones of dependability, constancy, and eternity. One recent study of perceptions in eight countries found that red is associated with "active," "hot," and "vibrant"; in most countries studied, it also conveys meanings such as "emotional" and "sharp."[8] As such, red has positive connotations in many societies. However, red is poorly received in some African countries. White connotes purity and cleanliness in the West, but it is associated with death in parts of Asia. Another research team

---

6   Lisa Miller, "For Some Jews, Chrysler Opens Up a Delicate Debate," *The Wall Street Journal* (May 13, 1998), pp. B1, B18. See also Arch G. Woodside and Jean-Charles Chebat, "Updating Heider's Balance Theory in Consumer Behavior: A Jewish Couple Buys a German Car and Additional Buying-Consuming Transformation Stories," *Psychology & Marketing* 18, no. 5 (May 2001), pp. 475–495.

7   Susan Carey, "More U.S. Companies are Blue, and It's Not Just the Stock Market," *The Wall Street Journal* (August 30, 2001), pp. A1, A2.

8   Thomas J. Madden, Kelly Hewett, and Martin S. Roth, "Managing Images in Different Cultures: A Cross-National Study of Color Meanings and Preferences," *Journal of International Marketing* 8, no. 4 (2000), p. 98.

In the mid-1990s, PepsiCo unleashed a $500 million marketing blitz code named "Project Blue." The PR tools included a leased Concorde supersonic jet painted in the new Pepsi colors. As chief marketing officer Brian Swette noted recently, "The first thing people associate with blue is cold and refreshment. The second thing is blue jeans or their favorite piece of clothing. So the color hits on two dimensions: It supports the product quality—refreshment— and it reinforces consumers' affection for their favorite things."

concluded that gray connotes inexpensive in China and Japan, while it is associated with high quality and expensive in the United States. The researchers also found that the Chinese associated brown with soft drink labels and associated the color with good tasting; South Korean and Japanese consumers associated yellow with soft drinks and good tasting. For Americans, the color red has those associations.[9]

Sensitivity and a willingness to accommodate such perceptions can help generate rapport and build goodwill. For example, when GM was vying for the right to build a sedan in China, company executives gave Chinese officials gifts from upscale Tiffany & Company in the jeweler's signature blue box. (It has been said that Tiffany & Company is in the "blue box business" rather than the jewelry business.) However, the Americans replaced Tiffany & Company's white ribbons with red ones, since red is considered a lucky color in China and white has negative connotations. GM ultimately won government approval of its proposal.[10]

Music is an aesthetic component of all cultures, accepted as a form of artistic expression and source of entertainment. In one sense, music represents a "transculture" that is not identified with any particular nation. For example, rhythm, or movement through time, is a universal aspect of music. However, music is also characterized by considerable stylistic variation with regional or country specific associations. For example, bossa nova rhythms are associated with Argentina, samba with Brazil, salsa with Cuba, reggae with Jamaica, merengue with the Dominican Republic, and blues, driving rock rhythms, hip hop, and rap with America. Sociologists have noted that national identity derives in part from a country's indigenous or popular music; a unique music style can "represent the uniqueness of the cultural entity and of the community."[11] In fact, music provides an interesting example of the "think global, act local" theme of this book. Musicians in different countries draw from, absorb,

9   Laurence E. Jacobs, Charles Keown, Reginald Worthley, and Kyung-I Ghymn, "Cross-Cultural Colour Comparisons: Global Marketers Beware!" *International Marketing Review* 8, no. 3 (1991), pp. 21–30.
10 Craig S. Smith and Rebecca Blumenstein, "Uncertain Terrain: In China, GM Bets Billions on a Market Strewn with Casualties," *The Wall Street Journal* (February 11, 1998), p. A11.
11 Martin Stokes, *Ethnicity, Identity, and Music: The Musical Construction of Place* (Oxford: Berg, 1994).

adapt, and synthesize transcultural music influences as well as country-specific ones, as they create hybrid styles such as Polish reggae or Italian hip hop. Motti Regev describes this paradox as follows:

> Producers of and listeners to these types of music feel, at one and the same time, participants in a specific contemporary, global-universal form of expression *and* innovators of local, national, ethnic, and other identities. A cultural form associated with American culture and with the powerful commercial interests of the international music industry is being used in order to construct a sense of local difference and authenticity.[12]

Because music plays an important role in advertising, marketers must understand what style is appropriate in a given national market. Although background music can be used effectively in broadcast commercials, the type of music appropriate for a commercial in one part of the world may not be acceptable or effective in another part. For example, when Nissan Motor Company challenged its U.S. advertising agency to create unconventional TV spots, the agency's creative team chose a popular Van Halen recording to communicate hipness and vitality. Nissan's Japanese agency, however, created quieter, more philosophical TV ads. Needless to say, Van Halen's music was not used. The different ads reflect Nissan's corporate philosophy that consumer tastes and values vary from country to country. Advertising at Nissan is decentralized, and local country managers have considerable autonomy.[13] Similarly, to promote movies in Hong Kong, Taiwan, and other Asian countries, Hollywood studios often enlist the services of local artists. For example, Warner Brothers commissioned a theme song and music video by Beyond, a hugely popular Hong Kong heavy metal band, to promote *Lethal Weapon 4* in Asia.[14]

Across Asia, the under-16 segment totals 500 million people; this group is particularly receptive to the idea of joining the "credit card culture." To ensure that the message gets across, the credit card companies are carefully tailoring communications for individual country markets. In Indonesia and Thailand, for example, MasterCard presents itself as hip and cutting edge with ads featuring the classic tune "Money (That's What I Want)." In Singapore and Hong Kong, the pitch is smoother. Ads have featured tag lines such as "Don't let possessions possess you" and music from British pop singer Des'ree. Visa International also believes in a local touch; as Suresh Nanoo, Visa's director of marketing for Asia-Pacific, noted, "With the diversity of Asia, we have to address local needs before getting wrapped up in the global campaign."[15]

Dietary Preferences

Cultural influences are also quite apparent in food preparation and consumption patterns and habits. Russians eat caviar from sturgeon harvested in the Caspian Sea. In Finland, reindeer meat is on the menu; the French consider rabbit to be a delicacy.

---

[12] Motti Regev, "Rock Aesthetics and Musics of the World," *Theory, Culture & Society* 14, no. 3 (August 1997), pp. 125–142.

[13] Yumiko Ono, "McCann Finds Global a Tough Sell in Japan," *The Wall Street Journal* (June 19, 1997), p. B12.

[14] Louise Lee, "To Sell Movies in Asia, Sing a Local Tune," *The Wall Street Journal* (September 22, 1998), pp. B1, B4.

[15] Steven Lipin, "Pick a Card: Visa, American Express and MasterCard Vie in Overseas Strategies," *The Wall Street Journal* (February 5, 1994), p. A1; Fara Warner, "Booming Asia Lures Credit-Card Firms," *The Wall Street Journal* (November 24, 1995), p. B10.

Americans have the biggest appetite for ice cream on the planet, with per capita consumption totaling 46 pints per year. Japan is home to the world's second largest market; in Europe, Italy and Germany rank first and second, respectively. The rationale behind Unilever's $326 million acquisition of Ben & Jerry's sheds light on some of the opportunities and challenges in the market. Ben & Jerry's focuses on the super-premium segment, offering a product with a rich taste from a high butterfat content, premium ingredients, and offbeat flavor names. The company's main competitor is Häagen-Dazs. Faced with a stagnant growth in the key U.S. market, which accounted for approximately 85 percent of revenues, executives at Ben & Jerry's had made limited and uncoordinated forays into select international markets. By contrast, Häagen-Dazs was available in some 30 countries and was sold by the scoop in more than 800 ice cream parlors in various parts of the world.

In the late 1980s, a friend of Ben's began selling Ben & Jerry's in Israel after negotiating a licensing agreement. In the early 1990s, Ben & Jerry's established one of the first manufacturing agreements between the United States and Russia. These were ad hoc rather than strategic moves, but by the mid-1990s the company made its first deliberate efforts to export ice cream from the United States. As Jerry noted, "We picked England because we thought the language and cultural differences would be less of a problem." Häagen-Dazs had preceded them with a strong public relations program and an advertising campaign that compared eating the ice cream with another sensual indulgence—sex. Ben & Jerry's market entrance was well received. The BBC Greater London radio said, "If Häagen-Dazs is the ice cream you have after sex, Ben & Jerry's is the ice cream you have instead of sex." Subsequently, Ben & Jerry's was introduced in France and the Benelux countries.

As Cohen and Greenberg contemplated entering Japan, they were facing stronger competition in the United States from the Edy's Dreamery brand marketed by Dreyer's Grand Ice Cream. By the end of 1999, it was clear than Ben & Jerry's needed help. Unilever has the resources to build Ben & Jerry's into a strong global brand alongside other company mainstays such as Lipton Tea and Knorr soups. Needless to say, however, founders Ben Cohen and Jerry Greenfield had strong reservations about "selling out" to a global corporation. Ben & Jerry's had become an American business icon by seamlessly blending a values-driven mission of social responsibility and corporate citizenship with the spirit of pure fun. Ben expressed fears that his company would become "just another brand like any other soulless, heartless, spiritless brand out there." He was mollified somewhat by Unilever's pledge to create a venture capital fund for start-up companies in low-income countries. As a Unilever spokesman put it, "Ben was doing what he should be doing, challenging us to respect our commitments."

> "The best way to integrate social values into international expansion is to choose those countries where we can find a social-mission-driven organization to partner with . . . I wouldn't enter a country if it's not going to be profitable. But I wouldn't choose based solely on which would be most profitable."
> —Ben Cohen

SOURCES: John Tagliabue, "In a Global Fight, Sprinkles Are Extra," *The New York Times* (August 19, 2001), sec. 3, p. 6; Shelly Branch and Ernest Beck, "For Unilever, It's Sweetness and Light," *The Wall Street Journal* (April 13, 2000), pp. B1, B4; John Hechinger and Joseph Pereira, "White Knight Swirl: Sympathizers Scramble to Rid Ben & Jerry's of 2 Unwanted Suitors," *The Wall Street Journal* (February 4, 2000), pp. A1, A20; James M. Hagen, "Ben & Jerry's—Japan: Strategic Decision by an Emergent Global Marketer," *Journal of International Marketing* 8, no. 2 (2000), pp. 98–110; Shelly Branch, "Double Dip: Merger Creates a New Emperor of Ice Cream," *The Wall Street Journal* (August 20, 1999), p. B1; Constance L. Hays, "Ben & Jerry's Ponders the Meaning of Selling Its Ice Cream Business," *The New York Times* (December 3, 1999), p. C7; Ben Cohen and Jerry Greenfield, "International Growth," chap. 8 in *Ben & Jerry's Double-Dip* (New York: Simon & Schuster, 1997).

Rice and grilled fish are regularly eaten for breakfast in Japan. When eating, Hindus in India serve themselves with the right hand rather than use utensils; they prepare food with spices that create a level of hotness that many Westerners would find unpalatable. Hindus enculturate their children to hot food at a very early age by starting with small quantities and gradually increasing the amount.

I scream, you scream ...

Americans ate far more ice cream last year than the global average of about a half-gallon per person. Top nations in 1997 for ice cream eating, in gallons eaten per person:

USA	5.4
Australia	4.9
Sweden	4.2
Canada	2.4
Italy	2.4
Netherlands	2.3
Israel	2.3
Belgium	2.2
Britain	2.2
France	1.9

Source: Euromonitor

By Anne R. Carey and Genevieve Lynn, USA TODAY

A solid understanding of food-related cultural preferences is important for any company that markets food or beverage products globally. Titoo Ahluwalia, chairman of a market research firm in Bombay, points out that local companies can also leverage superior cultural understanding to compete effectively with large foreign firms. He says, "Indian companies have an advantage when they are drawing from tradition. When it comes to food, drink, and medicine, you have to be culturally sensitive."[16] Companies that lack such sensitivity are bound to make marketing mistakes. For example, U.S. companies once introduced mixes for fluffy frosted cakes to the United Kingdom, where cake is eaten at tea time with the fingers rather than as a dessert with a fork. Green Giant Foods attempted to market corn in Europe where the prevailing attitude is that corn is a grain fed to hogs, not to people. In both instances, cultural differences resulted in market failures.

These blunders notwithstanding, there is plenty of evidence that global dietary preferences are converging. For example, "fast food" is gaining increased acceptance around the world. There are several explanations. Heads of families in many countries are pressed for time and are disinclined to prepare home-cooked meals. Also, young people are experimenting with different foods, and the global tourism boom has exposed travelers to pizza, pasta, and other ethnic foods. Shorter lunch hours and tighter budgets are forcing workers to find a place to grab a quick, cheap bite before returning to work.[17] As cultural differences become less relevant, such convenience products will be purchased in any country when consumer disposable income is high enough.

As we have seen, such processes can provoke a nationalist backlash. To counteract the exposure of its young citizens to *le Big Mac* and other American-style fast foods, the French National Council of Culinary Arts designed a course on French cuisine and "good taste" for elementary school students. The director of the council,

---

[16]   Fara Warner, "Savvy Indian Marketers Hold Their Ground," *The Wall Street Journal Asia* (December 1, 1997), p. 8.
[17]   John Willman, "'Fast Food' Spreads as Lifestyles Change," *Financial Times* (March 27, 1998), p. 7.

Quick! What's the most popular fast-food restaurant in the Philippines? If you answered "McDonald's," then you're probably not familiar with Jollibee. With 225 restaurants, Jollibee has twice as many outlets in the Philippines as McDonald's. In the late 1970s, company president Tony Tan decided against acquiring the local McDonald's franchise. Instead, he studied the American fast-food icon, then built a regional empire from the ground up by tailoring menus, advertising, and store atmospherics to the preferences of the 70 million people who live in the Philippines. Even Jollibee's marketing vice president concedes that McDonald's provided the basic blueprint. "They have playlands, we have playgrounds. They have a mascot, we have a mascot. In terms of service and execution, we are all the same." However, at Jollibee, sweet and spicy flavors predominate in the burgers and chicken dishes, and Jollibee's menu offerings are much more varied than competitors'. Advertising stresses interaction among closely-knit family members and national pride; a 1998 ad campaign theme was the 100th anniversary of the nation's independence from Spain. Restaurant interiors are kid-friendly, with play areas and decorations reflecting a cheerful, carnival theme.

In 1989, Jollibee got an unexpected boost when the threat of a military coup prompted McDonald's to temporarily suspend operations. Jollibee has even managed to ride out the Asian currency crisis. Manolo Tingzon, the general manager for the international division explained, "People will cut back on everything except food. And even when they do cut back on food spending, they usually will skip fancy and expensive restaurants in times of crisis. We therefore expect fast-food sales to go up." Tan's formula has been so well received that Jollibee commands 56 percent of the fast-food market, compared with McDonald's 19 percent. Sales in 1997 totaled $140 million.

Since 1994, the company has been gradually pursuing international expansion. There are dozens of Jollibee restaurants in Hong Kong, China, Guam, Indonesia, and other Asian countries, plus ten in the Middle East and twenty in the United States. Noting that international sales are currently at the $10 million mark, Mr. Tingzon noted, "It took McDonald's 30 years before its foreign outlets accounted for 40 percent of total sales. So we're not worried."

SOURCES: Gertrude Chavez, "The Buzz: Jollibee Hungers to Export Filipino Tastes, Dominate Asian Fast Food," *Advertising Age* (March 9, 1998), p. 14; William McGurn, "Home Advantage: Local Chain Upstages McDonald's in the Philippines," *Far Eastern Economic Review* (November 20, 1997), p. 70; Andrew Tanzer, "Bee Bites Clown," *Forbes* (October 20, 1997), pp. 182–183; Hugh Filman, "Happy Meals for a McDonald's Rival," *Business Week* (July 29, 1996), p. 77.

Alexandre Lazareff, recently published *The French Culinary Exception*. Lazareff warns that France's vaunted *haute cuisine* is under attack by the globalization of taste. More generally, Lazareff is speaking out against perceived challenges to France's culinary identity and way of life. His concerns are real enough; while McDonald's continues to open new restaurants in France (there were 600 by the end of 1997), the number of traditional bistros has declined from 55,000 to 25,000 over the past decade.[18] Meanwhile, the French have coined a new buzzword, *le fooding*, to express the notion that the nation's passion for food goes beyond mere gastronomy:

> To eat with feeling in France is to eat with your head and your spirit, with your nose, your eyes, and your ears, not simply your palate. *Le fooding* seeks to give witness to the modernity and new reality of drinking and eating in the 21st century . . . Everything is *fooding* so long as audacity, sense, and the senses mix.[19]

[18] Marlow Hood, "The Holy Terroir," *Financial Times Weekend* (July 4–5, 1998), p. I.
[19] Jacqueline Friedrich, "All the Rage in Paris? Le Fooding," *The Wall Street Journal* (February 9, 2001), p. W11.

LINGUISTIC CATEGORY	LANGUAGE EXAMPLE
Syntax	English has relatively fixed word order; Russian has relatively free word order.
Semantics	Japanese words convey nuances of feeling for which other languages lack exact correlations; "yes" and "no" can be interpreted differently than in other languages.
Phonology	Japanese does not distinguish between the sounds "l" and "r"; English and Russian both have "l" and "r" sounds.
Morphology	Russian is a highly inflected language, with six different case endings for nouns and adjectives; English has fewer inflections.

Language and Communication

The diversity of cultures around the world is also reflected in language. A person can learn a great deal about another culture without leaving home by studying its language and literature; such study is the next best thing to actually living in another country. Linguists have divided the study of *spoken* or *verbal* language into four main areas: syntax (rules of sentence formation), semantics (system of meaning), phonology (system of sound patterns), and morphology (word formation). *Unspoken* or *nonverbal* communication includes gestures, touching, and other forms of body language that supplement spoken communication. (Nonverbal communication is sometimes called the silent language.) Both the spoken and unspoken aspects of language are included in the broader linguistic field of *semiotics*, which is the study of signs and their meanings. Several examples of linguistic differences are shown in Table 4-1.

In global marketing, of course, language is a crucial tool for communicating with customers, channel intermediaries, and others. The marketing literature is full of anecdotal references to costly blunders caused by incorrect or inept translations of product names and advertising copy. In some countries, marketers must be aware of subcultures created by intranational language or dialect differences. In Switzerland, for example, in addition to Swiss German dialects, there are communities of French, Italian, and Romansch speakers. In addition, of course, Swiss German and standard German differ in significant ways. American English and British English provide another illustration of how the same language in different countries can be characterized by linguistic differences.

Semantic issues frequently arise in global marketing. For example, when British retail-development firm BAA McArthurGlen set up a U.S.-style factory outlet mall in Austria, local officials wanted to know, "Where's the factory?" To win approval for the project, McArthurGlen was forced to call its development a "designer outlet center."[20] Before Hearst Corporation launched *Good Housekeeping* magazine in Japan, managers experimented with Japanese translations. The closest word in Japanese, *kaji*, means "domestic duties." However, that word can be interpreted as tasks performed by servants. In the end, the American title was retained, with the word "Good" in much larger type on the front cover than the word "Housekeeping." Inside the magazine, some of the editorial content has also been adapted to appeal to

---

[20] Ernest Beck, "American-Style Outlet Malls in Europe Make Headway Despite Local Resistance," *The Wall Street Journal* (September 17, 1998), p. A17.

Japanese women; the famous Seal of Approval was eliminated because the concept confused readers. Editor-in-chief Ellen Levine said, "We have no interest in trying to export our product exactly as it is. That would be cultural suicide."[21]

Phonology can also come into play; Colgate discovered that, in Spanish, *colgate* is a command that means "go hang yourself." Whirlpool spent considerable sums of money on brand advertising in Europe only to discover that consumers in Italy, France, and Germany had trouble pronouncing the company's name.[22] Conversely, Renzo Rosso deliberately chose "Diesel" for a new jeans brand because, as he notes, "It's one of the few words pronounced the same in every language." Rosso has built Diesel into a successful global youth brand distributed in more than 80 countries with annual sales of more than $300 million.[23] Technology is providing interesting new opportunities for exploiting linguistics in the name of marketing. For example, young people throughout the world are using mobile phones to send text messages; it turns out that certain number combinations have meaning in particular languages. For example, in Korean, the phonetic pronunciation of the numerical sequence 8282 means "hurry up" and 7170 sounds like "close friend"; also, on most keypads, 4 5683 968 can be interpreted as "I love you."[24] Korean marketers are using these and other numerical sequences in their advertising.

One impact of globalization on culture is the diffusion of the English language around the globe. Today there are more people who speak English as a foreign language than there are people whose native language is English. Nearly 85 percent of the teenagers in the European Union are studying English. Despite the fact that Sony Corp. is headquartered in Japan, the company makes it clear to job applicants in any part of the world that it does not consider English to be a "foreign language." The same is true for Finland's Nokia. Throughout the world, non-native English speakers are freely adapting the language to suit particular needs in particular places. At the Daihatsu Auto dealership in Prague, for example, English is the only language the Czech and Korean employees have in common. However, an American eavesdropping on a conversation might find it hard to comprehend. Then again, CNN's English-language satellite broadcasts may not be comprehensible to all viewers.[25]

It goes without saying that people interested in international business and global marketing will benefit many times over from the time they invest in learning one or more new languages. The difficult part is convincing people to invest the time and effort in the first place! Foreign language study imparts many benefits. For Americans in particular, language study can help individuals develop rapport with persons who speak English as a second language. Rather than belittling or mocking persons who mispronounce English words, those who have studied another language have insights into the underlying linguistic sources of those mistakes. While acquiring language performance skills, students also gain important cross-cultural insights. Such knowledge can be crucial during negotiations. Negotiations put global marketers

21 Yumiko Ono, "Will Good Housekeeping Translate into Japanese?" *The Wall Street Journal* (December 30, 1997), p. B1.
22 Greg Steinmetz and Carl Quintanilla, "Tough Target: Whirlpool Expected Easy Going in Europe, and It Got a Big Shock," *The Wall Street Journal* (April 10, 1998), pp. A1, A6.
23 Alice Rawsthorn, "A Hipster on Jean Therapy," *Financial Times* (August 20, 1998), p. 8.
24 Meeyoung Song, "How to Sell in Korea? Marketers Count the Ways," *The Wall Street Journal* (August 24, 2001), p. A6.
25 Barry Newman, "Global Chatter: World Speaks English, Often None Too Well; Results are Tragicomic," *The Wall Street Journal* (March 22, 1995), pp. A1, A15. See also Christian Tyler, "The Mother of All Tongues," *Financial Times Weekend* (April 4–5, 1998), p. I.

A Matter of Culture
Using English as a Marketing Tool in Japan

In Japan, many consumer packaged goods—including some that are not imported—have English, French, or German on the labels to suggest a stylish image and Western look. A Westerner may wonder, however, what point the copywriters are actually trying to get across. For example, English on the label of City Original Coffee proclaims "Ease Your Bosoms. This coffee has carefully selected high quality beans and roasted by our all the experience." The intended message: Drinking the coffee provides a relaxing break and "takes a load off your chest." Other products, such as casual wear and sports apparel, are also emblazoned with fractured messages. These words appeared on the back of a jacket: "Vigorous throw up. Go on a journey." A sports bag bore the message, "A drop of sweat is the precious gift for your guts."

Finally, consider the message printed on the cover of a notebook: "Be a man I recommend it with confidence as like a most intelligent stationary of basic design." One expert on "Japanese English" believes messages like these highlight basic differences between Japanese and other languages. Many Western languages lack exact equivalents for the rich variety of Japanese words that convey feelings. This presents difficulties for copywriters trying to render feelings in a language other than Japanese. The message on the black notebook was supposed to convey manliness. As the English-speaking Japanese copywriter explained, "I wanted to say I'm proud to present the product to the consumer because it's got a simple, masculine image." While a Westerner might wonder whether the copywriter succeeded, the fact is that some people actually *do* read the labels and like the sayings. Sometimes the intended message *does* get interpreted correctly in the Japanese consumer's mind. Japanese retailers do not seem at all concerned that the messages are syntactically suspect. As one retailer explained, the point is that a message in English, French, or German can convey hipness and help sell a product. "I don't expect people to *read* it," she said.

SOURCES: Nicholas D. Kristof, "Japan's Favorite Import from America: English," *The New York Times* (February 21, 1995), p. A3; Yumiko Ono, "A Little Bad English Goes a Long Way in Japan's Boutiques," *The Wall Street Journal* (May 20, 1992), pp. A1, A6; Charles Goldsmith, "Look See! Anyone Do Read This And It Will Make You Laughable," *The Wall Street Journal* (November 19, 1992), p. B1.

"Global business makes sense, but it's much more difficult to do it than to talk about it. The American manager prides himself or herself on directness, frankness, being in-your-face, being accountable. But that's almost unique in the world."
—A. Paul Flask, managing partner, Korn/Ferry International[27]

face-to-face with counterparts from diverse cultural backgrounds, challenging both sides to surmount verbal and nonverbal communications barriers. Training and a heightened sense of the host country cultural context are necessary to counteract the tendency to bring one's cultural ethnocentrism to the negotiating table.

The challenges presented by nonverbal communication are perhaps even more formidable. For example, Westerners doing business in the Middle East must be careful not to reveal the soles of their shoes to hosts or pass documents with the left hand. In Japan, bowing is an important form of nonverbal communication that has many nuances. People who grow up in the West tend to be verbal; those from Asia exhibit behavior that places more weight on nonverbal aspects of interpersonal communication. Not surprisingly, there is a greater expectation in the East that people will pick up nonverbal cues and understand intuitively without being told.[26] Westerners must pay close attention not only to what they hear but also to what they see when conducting business in such cultures.

26 See Anthony C. diBenedetto, Miriko Tamate, and Rajan Chandran, "Developing Strategy for the Japanese Marketplace," *Journal of Advertising Research* (January/February 1992), pp. 39–48.
27 Robert Frank and Thomas M. Burton, "Side Effects: Cross-Border Merger Results in Headaches for a Drug Company," *The Wall Street Journal* (February 4, 1997), p. A1.

Several important communication issues may emerge. One is *sequencing,* which concerns whether the discussion goes directly from point A to point B or seems to go off on tangents. Another is *phasing,* which pertains to whether certain important agenda items are discussed immediately or after the parties have taken some time to establish rapport. According to two experts on international negotiations, there are ten distinctly American tactics that frequently emerge during negotiations. These tactics are often effective with other Americans, but may require modification for people from other cultural backgrounds. In any communication situation, speakers offer a variety of verbal cues that can help astute observers understand the speaker's mind-set and mental programming. Table 4-2 summarizes some typical American English cues, the underlying culture-influenced attitudes and behaviors they signify, and suggested adaptations.

Marketing's Impact on Culture

Universal aspects of the cultural environment represent opportunities for global marketers to standardize some or all elements of a marketing program. The astute global marketer often discovers that much of the apparent cultural diversity in the world turns out to be different ways of accomplishing the same thing. Widespread shared preference for convenience foods, disposable products, popular music, and movies in the United States, Europe, and Asia suggests that many consumer products have broad, even universal, appeal. Increasing travel and improving communications have contributed to a convergence of tastes and preferences in a number of product categories. The cultural change and the globalization of culture have been capitalized upon, and even significantly accelerated, by companies that have seized opportunities to find customers around the world. However, as noted at the beginning of this chapter, the impact of marketing and, more generally, of global capitalism on culture can be controversial. For example, sociologist George Ritzer and others lament the so-called "McDonaldization of culture" that, they say, occurs when global companies break down cultural barriers while expanding into new markets with their products. As Ritzer noted in a recent book:

> Eating is at the heart of most cultures and for many it is something on which much time, attention and money are lavished. In attempting to alter the way people eat, McDonaldization poses a profound threat to the entire cultural complex of many societies.[28]

Fabien Ouaki is living proof that persons outside of academe and government have also joined the battle against McDonaldization. Ouaki is the managing director of Tati, a discount retailer based in France. Ouaki is opening new stores in select countries, including the United States. Ouaki claims that "personal revenge" is one motivation for entering the U.S. market. "As a Frenchman, it makes me sick to see kids crying to go see 'Titanic,' eat at McDonald's, or drink Coke. I want to see New Yorkers crying to have a Tati wedding dress," he said recently.[29] Similarly, the international Slow Food movement boasts 70,000 members in 35 countries. Slow Food grew out of a 1986 protest over the opening of a

---

[28] George Ritzer, *The McDonaldization Thesis* (London: Sage Publications, 1998), p. 8.
[29] Amy Barrett, "French Discounter Takes Cheap Chic World-Wide," *The Wall Street Journal* (May 27, 1998), p. B8.

Table 4-2

American Communication Styles: Verbal Cues, Underlying Realities, and Suggested Adaptations

VERBAL CUES	UNDERLYING REALITY	ADAPTATION REQUIRED
1. "I can go it alone."	Americans are typically outnumbered in negotiations. Reflects culture of individualism.	Greater reliance on teamwork and division of negotiating labor, especially in collectivist culture.
2. "Just call me 'John'."	Americans place a high value on informality and equality of participants in negotiations. This may conflict with the customs and class structures of foreign cultures.	Respect the customs, hierarchies, and class structure of other cultures. Learn more via self study; ask country nationals to explain local attitudes and values.
3. "Pardon my French."	Americans are culturally monolingual. (Old joke: Q: What do you call someone who speaks two languages? A: Bilingual. Q: What do you call someone who speaks one language? A: American!)	Ignore the conventional wisdom about how difficult it is to learn a foreign language; if you have ongoing business in a country, make the effort to study the language. At a minimum, develop a good working relationship with a skilled interpreter.
4. "Get to the point."	Americans' short term orientation manifests itself as a tendency to be blunt and impatient.	Understand that people from other cultures need to develop a sense of connection and personal trust in order to feel comfortable about doing business. This takes time.
5. "Lay your cards on the table."	Americans like to state the case up front, and are not accustomed to "feeling out" prospective partners.	Slow down, and recognize the need to rephrase the question, several times if necessary. Prepare to spend double the time you think is needed to get the information you seek.
6. "Why doesn't somebody say something?"	Americans are uncomfortable with silence during negotiations and often deal with their discomfort by continuing to speak.	Recognize that silence is golden in many cultures. It can be detrimental—to keep a constant stream of chatter. If there is silence, let it be. Reflect. Take in nonverbal information. *Value* the silence. Take advantage of it.
7. "Don't take 'no' for an answer."	Tenacity and the hard sell are highly valued in the United States.	If the answer is "no," stop selling and find out why. Respond to the reasons for the answer "no."
8. "One thing at a time."	Many Americans favor a linear, organized, "left brain" negotiation style. "Point One, Point Two"-style sequencing is not a universal approach.	Recognize your own right brain capability. Embrace a more holistic approach toward negotiations. Be patient if the discussion seems to proceed in loops and spirals.
9. "A deal is a deal."	Expectations and perceptions may not be shared by all parties. Have you agreed on all the points in the contract, or have you agreed to work together?	Accept a more gradual, supplemental view of negotiations and joint effort.
10. "I am what I am."	Americans have a tendency to see things in black-and-white terms.	Adopt a more flexible standpoint. Be willing to change your mind and manner and to adapt to your opposite.

Source: Adapted from John L. Graham and Roy A. Heberger Jr., "Negotiators Abroad—Don't Shoot from the Hip," *Harvard Business Review* 61, no. 4 (July-August 1983), pp. 160–168.

McDonald's on a popular plaza in Rome; every two years, Slow Food stages a Salone del Gusto in Italy that is designed to showcase traditional food preparation. As a spokesperson said, "Slow Food is about the idea that things should not taste the same everywhere."[30]

HIGH- AND LOW-CONTEXT CULTURES

Edward T. Hall has suggested the concept of high and low context as a way of understanding different cultural orientations.[31] In a **low-context culture,** messages are explicit and specific; words carry most of the communication power. In a **high-context culture,** less information is contained in the verbal part of a message. Much more information resides in the context of communication, including the background, associations, and basic values of the communicators. In general, high-context cultures function with much less legal paperwork than is deemed essential in low-context cultures. Japan, Saudi Arabia, and other high-context cultures place a great deal of emphasis on a person's values and position or place in society. In such cultures, a business loan is more likely to be based on "who you are" than on formal analysis of pro forma financial documents. In a low-context culture such as the United States, Switzerland, or Germany, deals are made with much less information about the character, background, and values of the participants. Much more reliance is placed upon the words and numbers in the loan application. Similarly, Japanese companies such as Sony traditionally paid a great deal of attention to the university background of a new hire; preference would be given to graduates of Tokyo University. Specific elements on a resume were less important.

In a high-context culture, a person's word is his or her bond. There is less need to anticipate contingencies and provide for external legal sanctions because the culture emphasizes obligations and trust as important values. In these cultures, shared feelings of obligation and honor take the place of impersonal legal sanctions. This helps explain the importance of long and protracted negotiations that never seem to get to the point. Part of the purpose of negotiating, for a person from a high-context culture, is to get to know the potential partner.

For example, insisting on competitive bidding can cause complications in low-context cultures. In a high-context culture, the job is given to the person who will do the best work and whom you can trust and control. In a low-context culture, one tries to make the specifications so precise that a builder is forced by the threat of legal sanction to do a good job. As Hall has noted, a builder in Japan is likely to say, "What has that piece of paper got to do with the situation? If we can't trust each other enough to go ahead without it, why bother?"

Although countries can be classified as high- or low-context in their overall tendency, there are exceptions to the general tendency. These exceptions are found in subcultures. The United States is a low-context culture with subcultures that operate in the high-context mode. The world of the central banker, for example, is a "gentleman's" world, that is, a high-context culture. Even during the most hectic day of trading in the foreign exchange markets, a central banker's word is sufficient

---

30 Jerry Shriver, "At Slow Food Fest, Taste Trumps Time," *USA Today* (November 9, 1998), p. 1D. See also Alexander Stille, "Slow Food's Pleasure Principles," *The Utne Reader* (May-June 2002), pp. 56–58.
31 Edward T. Hall, "How Cultures Collide," *Psychology Today* (July 1976), pp. 66–97.

When Madonna appeared onstage during the 1998 MTV Video Music Awards, she struck a pose intended to evoke a deep Indian spirituality. Wearing a bindhi on her forehead and draped in white linen cloth, she chanted, "Om shanti om," an ancient Hindu mantra. Abruptly, as Madonna tossed aside her faux-Indian costume to reveal tight leather pants, she began singing "And I feel like I just got home!" to the driving beat of her "Ray of Light" dance track. While Madonna has based her career on appropriating various cultural symbols (she has recently moved on to assume the role of a "cowgirl"), her MTV performance was interpreted by many in India as yet another neo-colonial act of cultural insensitivity.

Even as Channel V and MTV have attracted new viewers in India in the 1990s, middle- and upper-class youths in large cities such as New Delhi and Mumbai can purchase many of the same recordings that are popular in the West. Local music stores stock Madonna's compact disks as well as dance mix compilations featuring music from all over the world. Even cassettes by relatively new bands are available in the stores within months of their commercial breakthrough at home. This globalization of music is due primarily to the vast distribution networks established by global giants Sony, Bertelsmann, EMI, Warner, and Polygram. Despite the growing popularity of Western music, however, regional artists and Hindi film music continue to dominate India's music industry. American pop music accounts for less than 5 percent of total sales.

Lucky Ali, Silk Route, and other regional artists that incorporate Western instrumentation and music styles enjoy great popularity in India. By singing lyrics in Hindi or Urdu, these artists are perceived as having vocal styles that are "more Indian." In addition, their performances are felt to come from a South Asian perspective. Such artists avoid the risk of cultural *faux pas* such as Madonna's.

Looking at the Top 40 charts in India reveals one aspect of American pop music's global reach. However, a more compelling approach would be to look not at the *content* but rather at the *form* of popular music. This approach was first employed by Marshall McLuhan (the person who coined the term *global village*). In his 1967 book, *The Medium is the Message*, McLuhan argued that the form of a new technology and its impact on social organization is vastly more significant than the specific content the new technology delivers. For example, the observation that "Mad About You" is a popular TV show in Nigeria may disguise the fact that television as a media form has had a profound effect on the daily lives of many Nigerian households. In India, then, the wide availability of Madonna's recordings may be less notable than the growing significance of a Western-style music industry based on music television and massive advertising campaigns. The latter aspects point to a dramatic change for the place of music in Indian society.

Globalization has come to India's rural communities in other forms as well. Even in the smallest villages, one can see the occasional vendor's cart painted with the familiar blue Pepsi logo. Nevertheless, the uneven flow of global commerce is starkly evident, as many Western products and sensibilities have yet to penetrate the provincial areas to the extent that they have in the big cities. For reasons of language, aesthetics, and world view, consumption of Western pop music is mostly confined to the relatively wealthy inhabitants of India's largest cities. Responding to the influx of Western visitors, however, rural shopkeepers make an effort to cater primarily to the tastes of the tourists. At the local music shop, the recordings of Hindu devotional singers have been displaced by global pop stars such as Madonna, Celine Dion, Van Halen, and Jamirquoi.

SOURCE: Personal communication, Peter Kvetko.

Table 4-3
High- and Low-
Context Cultures

FACTORS/DIMENSIONS	HIGH-CONTEXT	LOW-CONTEXT
Lawyers	Less important	Very important
A person's word	Is his or her bond	Is not to be relied upon; "get it in writing"
Responsibility for organizational error	Taken by highest level	Pushed to lowest level
Space	People breathe on each other	People maintain a bubble of private space and resent intrusions
Time	Polychronic—everything in life must be dealt with in terms of its own time	Monochronic—time is money. Linear—one thing at a time
Negotiations	Are lengthy—a major purpose is to allow the parties to get to know each other	Proceed quickly
Competitive bidding	Infrequent	Common
Country/regional examples	Japan, Middle East	United States, Northern Europe

for him or her to borrow millions of dollars. In a high-context culture there is trust, a sense of fair play, and a widespread acceptance of the rules of the game as it is played. Table 4-3 summarizes some of the ways in which high- and low-context cultures differ.

HOFSTEDE'S CULTURAL TYPOLOGY

Organizational anthropologist Geert Hofstede was introduced earlier in this chapter in a discussion of his widely-quoted definition of culture. Hofstede is also well known for research studies suggesting that the cultures of different nations can be compared in terms of five dimensions.[32] Hofstede notes that three of the dimensions refer to expected social behavior, the fourth dimension is concerned with "man's search for Truth," and a fifth reflects the importance of time. A summary of Triad country rankings, plus Hong Kong and Taiwan, is shown in Table 4-4.

The first dimension, *power distance*, is the extent to which the less powerful members of a society accept—even expect—power to be distributed unequally. To paraphrase Orwell, all societies are unequal, but some are more unequal than others. Hong Kong and France are both high-power distance cultures; low-power distance characterizes Germany, Austria, the Netherlands, and Scandinavia.

The second dimension is a reflection of the degree to which individuals in a society are integrated into groups. In *individualist cultures*, each member of society is

---

[32] Geert Hofstede and Michael Harris Bond, "The Confucius Connection: From Cultural Roots to Economic Growth," *Organizational Dynamics* 16 (Spring 1988), p. 5.

Table 4-4
Hofstede's Cultural Dimension Rankings: Triad

COUNTRY	POWER DISTANCE (PDI)		INDIVIDUALISM		MASCULINITY		UNCERTAINTY AVOIDANCE		LONG TERM ORIENTATION (LTO)	
	Index	Rank	Index	Rank	Index	Rank	Index	Rank	Index	Rank
Austria	11	53	55	18	79	**2**	70	24–25	—	—
Belgium	65	20	75	8	54	22	94	5–6	—	—
Denmark	18	51	74	9	16	50	23	51	—	—
Finland	33	46	63	17	26	47	59	31–32	—	—
France	68	**15–16**	71	10–11	43	35–36	86	10–15	—	—
Germany	35	42–44	67	15	66	9–10	65	29	31	11–12
Greece	60	27–28	35	30	57	18–19	112	**1**	—	—
Ireland	28	49	70	12	68	7–8	35	47–48	—	—
Italy	50	34	76	7	70	4–5	75	23	—	—
Netherlands	38	40	80	4–5	14	51	53	35	—	—
Portugal	63	24–25	69	13	31	45	104	2	—	—
Spain	57	31	51	20	42	37–38	86	10–15	—	—
Sweden	31	47–48	71	10–11	5	52	29	49–50	33	10
UK	65	42–44	89	3	66	9–10	35	47–48	25	15–16
USA	40	38	91	**1**	62	15	41	43	29	15–16
Japan	54	33	46	22–23	95	**1**	92	7	80	3
Hong Kong	68	**15–16**	25	37	57	18–19	29	49–50	96	**1**
Taiwan	58	29–30	17	44	45	32–33	69	26	87	2

Source: Organizational Dynamics, 16, Spring, Geert Hoftstede & Michael Harris Bond, The Confuscious Connection, pp. 4–21, Copyright © 1998, with permission of Elsevir Science.

primarily concerned with his or her own interest and those of the immediate family. In *collectivist cultures,* all of society's members are integrated into cohesive in-groups. High individualism is a general aspect of culture in the United States and Europe; low individualism is characteristic of Japanese and other Asian culture patterns.

Masculinity, the third dimension, describes a society in which men are expected to be assertive, competitive, and concerned with material success, and women fulfill the role of nurturer and are concerned with issues such as the welfare of children. *Femininity,* by contrast, describes a society in which the social roles of men and women overlap, with neither gender exhibiting overly ambitious or competitive behavior. Japan and Austria ranked highest in masculinity; Spain, Taiwan, the Netherlands, and the Scandinavian countries were among the lowest.

Uncertainty avoidance is the extent to which the members of a society are uncomfortable with unclear, ambiguous, or unstructured situations. Members of some cultures express strong uncertainty avoidance by resorting to aggressive, emotional, intolerant behavior; they are characterized by a belief in absolute truth. Greece and Portugal outrank the others in Table 4-4 in uncertainty avoidance; other Mediterranean countries and much of Latin America ranks high in uncertainty avoidance as well. Acceptance of uncertainty generally manifests itself in behavior that is more contemplative, relativistic, and tolerant; these values are evident in Southeast Asia and India

Hofstede's research convinced him that, although these four dimensions yielded interesting and useful interpretations, they did not provide sufficient insight into possible cultural bases for economic growth. Hofstede was also disturbed by the fact that the surveys used in the research had been developed by Western social scientists. Because many economists had failed to predict the explosive economic development of Japan and the tigers (i.e., South Korea, Taiwan, Hong Kong, and Singapore), Hofstede surmised that some cultural dimensions in Asia were eluding the researchers. This methodological problem was remedied by a Chinese Value Survey (CVS) developed by Chinese social scientists in Hong Kong and Taiwan. The CVS data supported the first three "social behavior" dimensions of culture: power distance, individualism/collectivism, and masculinity/femininity. Uncertainty avoidance, however, did not show up in the CVS. Instead, the CVS revealed a dimension, *long-term orientation* (LTO) versus *short-term orientation,* that had eluded Western researchers.[33] Hofstede interpreted this dimension as concerning "a society's search for virtue," rather than a search for truth. It assesses the sense of immediacy within a culture, whether gratification should be immediate or deferred.

Long-term values include *persistence* (perseverance), defined as a general tenacity in the pursuit of a goal. *Ordering relationships* by status reflects the presence of societal hierarchies, and *observing this order* indicates the acceptance of complementary relations. *Thrift* manifests itself in high savings rates. Finally, *a sense of shame* leads to sensitivity in social contacts. Hofstede notes that these values are widely held within high-performing Asian countries such as Hong Kong, Taiwan, and Japan, but that the presence of these values by themselves is not sufficient to lead to economic growth. Two other conditions are necessary: the existence of a market and a supportive political context. Thus, although Hofstede determined that India ranked quite high on the LTO dimension, market restrictions and political forces have, until recently, held back that nation's economic growth.

By studying Hofstede's work, marketers gain insights that can guide them in a range of activities, including product development, interacting with joint venture partners, and conducting sales meetings. For example, understanding the time orientation of one's native culture compared to others' is crucial. In Japan, Brazil, and India, building a relationship with a potential business partner takes precedence over transacting the deal. People from cultures that emphasize the short term must adapt to the slower pace of business in some countries. As noted earlier, language can offer some insights into cultural differences. For example, the phrase "in a New York minute" captures the urgent pace of American urban life.

Conversely, the Japanese notion of *gaman* (persistence) provides insight into the willingness of Japanese corporations to pursue research and development projects for which the odds of short-term success appear low. When Sony licensed the newly invented transistor from Bell Laboratories in the mid-1950s, for example, the limited high-frequency yield (sound output) of the device suggested to American engineers that the most appropriate application would be for a hearing aid. However, *gaman* meant that Sony engineers were not deterred by the slow progress of their efforts to increase the yield. As Sony cofounder Masaru Ibuka recalled, "To challenge the yield is a very interesting point for us. At that time no one recognized the importance of it." Sony's persistence was rewarded when company engineers eventually made the yield breakthrough that resulted in a wildly successful global product—the pocket-sized transistor radio.[34]

---

[33] In some articles, Hofstede refers to this dimension as "Confucian Dynamism" because it is highest in Japan, Hong Kong, and Taiwan.

[34] James Lardner, *Fast Forward: Hollywood, the Japanese, and the VCR Wars* (New York: NAL Penguin, 1987), p. 45.

By understanding the dimension of uncertainty avoidance, global marketers are better equipped to assess the amount of risk buyers are comfortable with. In Japan and other Asian cultures characterized by a low tolerance for ambiguity, buyers will be conscious of brand names and are likely to exhibit high brand loyalty. Advertising copy in countries with high levels of uncertainty avoidance should provide reassurance by stressing warranties, money-back guarantees, and other risk-reducing features. Interestingly, Hong Kong is characterized by an even higher tolerance for ambiguity than the United States; Japan, however, ranks quite high in uncertainty avoidance, as do France and Spain.

The power distance dimension reflects the degree of trust among members of society. The higher the power distance (PDI), the lower the level of trust. Organizationally, high PDI finds expression in tall, hierarchical designs, a preference for centralization, and relatively more supervisory personnel. The PDI dimension also provides insights into the dynamics between superiors and subordinates. In cultures where respect for hierarchy is high, subordinates may have to navigate through several layers of assistants to get to the boss. If so, the latter is likely to be isolated in an office with the door closed. In such cultures, lower-level employees may be easily intimidated by superiors. Recent research has suggested that, when evaluating alternatives for entering global markets, companies in high PDI cultures prefer sole ownership of subsidiaries because it provides them with more control. Conversely, companies in low PDI cultures are more apt to use joint ventures.[35] Of the Triad countries in Table 4-4, France has the highest PDI. Other countries with high PDI scores are Mexico, India, and Hong Kong.

The masculinity-femininity dimension is likely to manifest itself in the relative importance of achievement and possessions (masculine values) compared with a spirit of helpfulness and social support (feminine values). Overall, an aggressive, achievement-oriented salesperson is better matched to the culture of Austria, Japan, or Mexico than that of Denmark. (Of course, such a salesperson would also have to bear in mind that both Japan and Mexico rank high in LTO, a dimension that can be at odds with transaction-oriented assertiveness.) Similarly, a Western woman who is sent to make a presentation to a Japanese company will undoubtedly find that her audience consists of men. The Japanese managers may react negatively to a woman, especially if she is younger than they are.

The collective-individual orientation deserves special comment because there is wide agreement that it is an important component of culture. Knowing which cultures value the collective and which value the individual can help marketers in various ways. In Japan, for example, the team orientation and desire for *wa* (harmony) means that singling out one person for distinction and praise in front of peers can be awkward for those involved. Again, language provides important cues about these cultural dimensions; as the saying goes in Japan, "The nail that sticks up gets hammered down." Throughout much of Asia, the collectivist orientation is dominant. In the highly individualist U.S. culture, however, a person whose individual accomplishments are publicly acknowledged is likely to be pleased by the recognition.[36]

Several teams of researchers have attempted to determine whether cross-national collective/individual differences are reflected in print and television advertisements. In theory, a global company's communication efforts should be adapted in

[35] Scott A. Shane, "The Effect of Cultural Differences in Perceptions of Transactions Costs on National Differences in the Preference for International Joint Ventures," *Asia Pacific Journal of Management* 10, no. 1 (1993), pp. 57–69.

[36] Adapted from Anne Macquin and Dominique Rouziès, "Selling across the Culture Gap," *Financial Times—Mastering Global Business*, Part Seven, 1998, pp. 10–11.

accordance with a particular country's orientation. For example, in cultures where individualism is highly valued, ads would typically feature one person; in countries where individualism is less highly valued, ads would feature groups. Although one team[37] claimed to have found a strong correlation, the findings were not confirmed by a later study.[38] However, Cutler argues that print advertising is, by its very nature, designed to communicate to an individual reader. This suggests that the individualism-collectivism distinction may be a moot issue in print advertising.

In highly collectivist cultures, however, products or services that enjoy an early word-of-mouth buzz among influential consumer groups can quickly achieve phenomenon status that then spreads to other countries. The Tamagotchi craze of the late 1990s is a perfect example. The virtual pets were test marketed in central Tokyo in a shopping area frequented by teenage girls. *Kuchikomi* (word of mouth) was so strong among schoolgirls that toymaker Bandai was hard-pressed to keep up with demand. By the time Tamagotchis reached New York toy retailer FAO Schwartz, the prerelease buzz ensured that the initial 10,000-unit shipment sold out immediately. Although Japanese teens also pay attention to print and television advertising, it is clear that marketers can reach this segment by providing selected youngsters with product samples.[39]

Other recent research suggests that Hofstede's framework can provide useful insights for global marketers hoping to create culturally appropriate consumer brand images. For example, researcher Martin Ross described three types of brand images: functional, social, and sensory. A product with a *functional brand image* is oriented toward problem solving and problem prevention; products with a *social brand image* fulfill consumers' needs for group membership and affiliation; a product with *sensory appeal* provides novelty, variety, and sensory gratification. In the United States, for example, the Crest, Ultra Brite, and Aim toothpaste brands respectively embody these images. Ross surveyed marketing managers at U.S. companies that market blue jeans and athletic shoes. His research suggests that in countries where power distance is high, social brand images enhance brand performance. Conversely, by limiting the use of social and sensory images and emphasizing functional benefits, marketers can enhance brand performance in countries or regions with low power distance. Ross also found strong evidence that sensory brand images would perform well in countries where high individualism is a dominant cultural pattern and that social brand image strategies would be effective in countries characterized by low individualism.[40]

THE SELF-REFERENCE CRITERION AND PERCEPTION

As we have shown, a person's perception of market needs is framed by his or her own cultural experience. A framework for systematically reducing perceptual blockage and distortion was developed by James Lee and published in *Harvard Business*

---

[37] Katherine Toland Frith and Subir Sengupta, "Individualism: A Cross-Cultural Analysis of Print Advertisements from the U.S. and India," paper presented at 1991 Annual Conference of Advertising Division of Association for Education in Journalism and Mass Communication, Boston, MA.

[38] Bob D. Cutler, S. Altan Erdem, and Rajshekhar G. Javalgi, "Advertisers' Relative Reliance on Collectivism-Individualism Appeals," *Journal of International Consumer Marketing* 9, no. 3 (1997), pp. 43–55.

[39] Bethan Hutton, "Winning Word-of-Mouth Approval," *Financial Times* (September 8, 1997), p. 10.

[40] Martin S. Ross, "The Effects of Culture and Socioeconomics on the Performance of Global Brand Image Strategies," *Journal of Marketing Research* 32 (May 1995), pp. 163–175.

Review in 1966. Lee termed the unconscious reference to one's own cultural values the **self-reference criterion,** or **SRC.** To address this problem and eliminate or reduce cultural myopia, he proposed a systematic four-step framework.

1. Define the problem or goal in terms of home country cultural traits, habits, and norms.
2. Define the problem or goal in terms of host-country cultural traits, habits, and norms. Make no value judgments.
3. Isolate the SRC influence and examine it carefully to see how it complicates the problem.
4. Redefine the problem without the SRC influence and solve for the host-country market situation.[41]

The Euro Disney case at the end of this chapter provides an excellent vehicle for understanding SRC. As they planned their entry into the French market, how might Disney executives have done things differently had they used the steps of SRC?

Step 1. Disney executives believe there is virtually unlimited demand for American cultural exports around the world. Evidence includes the success of McDonald's, Coca-Cola, Hollywood movies, and American rock music. Disney has a stellar track record in exporting its American management system and business style. Tokyo Disneyland, a virtual carbon copy of the park in Anaheim, California, has been a runaway success. Disney policies prohibit sale or consumption of alcohol inside its theme parks.

Step 2. Europeans in general and the French in particular are sensitive about American cultural imperialism. Consuming wine with the midday meal is a long-established custom. Europeans have their own real castles, and many popular Disney characters come from European folk tales.

Step 3. The significant differences revealed by comparing the findings in steps 1 and 2 suggest strongly that the needs upon which the American and Japanese Disney theme parks were based did not exist in France. A modification of this design was needed for European success.

Step 4. This would require the design of a theme park that is more in keeping with French and European cultural norms. Allow the French to put their own identity on the park.

The lesson that the SRC teaches is that a vital, critical skill of the global marketer is unbiased perception, the ability to see what is so in a culture. Although this skill is as valuable at home as it is abroad, it is critical to the global marketer because of the widespread tendency toward ethnocentrism and use of the self-reference criterion. The SRC can be a powerful negative force in global business, and forgetting to check for it can lead to misunderstanding and failure. While planning Euro Disney, chairman Michael Eisner and other company executives were blinded by a potent combination of their own prior success and ethnocentrism. Avoiding the SRC requires a person to suspend assumptions based on prior experience and success and be prepared to acquire new knowledge about human behavior and motivation.

---

[41] James A. Lee, "Cultural Analysis in Overseas Operations," *Harvard Business Review* (March–April 1966), pp. 106–114.

The globalization of food tastes is one sign of broader cultural shifts that are taking place in many countries. Changes in eating habits are being driven by changing lifestyles as well as global retailing and food processing trends. Many Europeans, for example, are eating bigger breakfasts because lunch breaks have been shortened. Options for breakfast foods, in turn, have multiplied because supermarkets are popping up in neighborhoods in competition with small mom-and-pop stores. Supermarkets can stock a broader selection of food items and are more likely to offer new products to their customers. Global companies such as Kellogg and Cereal Partners Worldwide are engaged in fierce competition with each other and with smaller, local firms for a share of palates and pocketbooks.

Europeans are also developing a taste for salty snacks like tortilla chips. As with breakfast cereal, consumption of tortilla chips in Europe has historically been much lower than in the United States. However, the Tex-Mex concept is gaining momentum. Although Frito-Lay introduced its Doritos brand in Europe in 1994, Europeans viewed the chips as a snack for special occasions and sales were below expectations. In 1998, Frito-Lay relaunched Doritos in the UK, France, Spain, Portugal, Belgium, the Netherlands, and Luxembourg. A $20 million advertising campaign, identical across the seven countries except for the indi-

vidual languages, was intended to raise European consumption of the snack chips. Following the recommendations of a brand consultant, Frito-Lay made two significant changes to the packaging. First, it dropped the America-style "see through window" in favor of the type of sealed foil package that is used for potato chips in Europe. Second, the dominant color of the package was changed from white to black.

In another global food trend that some have likened to "taking coals to Newcastle," food items are being introduced in some countries from unlikely sources. American versions of cheddar cheese are being exported to southwest England, where cheddar was first produced. German imports of American wine increased sevenfold between 1991 and 1996. A Hong Kong noodle maker has achieved great success exporting to China. Grass-fed beef from Argentina is becoming popular in the United States.

Despite these trends, some local food preferences are likely to remain entrenched—at least for a while. For example, many Japanese prefer a traditional breakfast of *okayu* (rice porridge) with *umeboshi* (pickled plums). In Vietnam, street venders offer *pho* ('fuh') for breakfast, lunch, dinner, or as a snack. It consists of a broth made of oxtail, beef, and shrimp paste, seasoned with spices and served over rice noodles. One sign of the times: *pho* is now being sold from street carts in New York, Chicago, and Los Angeles.

SOURCES: Ernest Beck and Rekha Balu, "Europe Is Deaf to Snap! Crackle! Pop!" *The Wall Street Journal* (June 28, 1998), pp. B1, B8; Helene Cooper and Scott Kilman, "Exotic Tastes: Trade Wars Aside, U.S. and Europe Buy More of Each Other's Foods," *The Wall Street Journal* (June 28, 1998), pp. A1, A8; Anna Wilde Mathews, "Modern Menus Star Flown-in Fish, Game," *The Wall Street Journal* (July 7, 1998), pp. B1, B2; John Willman, "Salty Snack Attack on Europe," *Financial Times* (February 2, 1998), p. 11.

DIFFUSION THEORY[42]

Hundreds of studies have described the process by which an individual adopts a new idea. Sociologist Everett Rogers reviewed these studies and discovered a pattern of remarkably similar findings. In *Diffusion of Innovations*, Rogers distilled the research into three concepts that are extremely useful to global marketers: the adoption process, characteristics of innovations, and adopter categories.

An innovation is something new. When applied to a product, "new" can mean different things. In an absolute sense, once a product has been introduced anywhere in the world, it is no longer an innovation because it is no longer new to the world.

---

[42] This section draws from Everett M. Rogers, *Diffusion of Innovations* (New York: Free Press, 1962).

Relatively speaking, however, a product already introduced in one market may be an innovation elsewhere because it is new and different for the targeted market. Global marketing often entails just such product introductions. Managers find themselves marketing products that may be, simultaneously, innovations in some markets and mature or declining products in other markets.

The Adoption Process

One of the basic elements of Rogers's diffusion theory is the concept of an **adoption process**—the mental stages through which an individual passes from the time of his or her first knowledge of an innovation to the time of product adoption or purchase. Rogers suggests that an individual passes through five different stages in proceeding from first knowledge of a product to the final adoption or purchase of that product: awareness, interest, evaluation, trial, and adoption.

1. *Awareness.* In the first stage the customer becomes aware for the first time of the product or innovation. Studies have shown that at this stage impersonal sources of information such as mass media advertising are most important. An important early communication objective in global marketing is to create awareness of a new product through general exposure to advertising messages.
2. *Interest.* During this stage, the customer is interested enough to learn more. The customer has focused his or her attention on communications relating to the product and will engage in research activities and seek out additional information.
3. *Evaluation.* In this stage the individual mentally assesses the product's benefits in relation to present and anticipated future needs and, based on this judgment, decides whether or not to try it.
4. *Trial.* Most customers will not purchase expensive products without the "hands on" experience marketers call *trial*. A good example of a product trial that does not involve purchase is the automobile test drive. For healthcare products and other inexpensive consumer packaged goods, trial often involves actual purchase. Marketers frequently induce trial by distributing free samples. For inexpensive products, an initial single purchase is defined as trial.
5. *Adoption.* At this point, the individual either makes an initial purchase (in the case of the more expensive product) or continues to purchase—adopts and exhibits brand loyalty to—the less expensive product. Studies show that, as a person moves from the evaluation through trial to adoption, personal sources of information are more important than impersonal sources. It is during these stages that sales representatives and word of mouth become major persuasive forces affecting the decision to buy.

Characteristics of Innovations

In addition to describing the product adoption process, Rogers also identifies five major factors affecting the rate at which innovations are adopted: relative advantage, compatibility, complexity, divisibility, and communicability.

1. *Relative advantage.* How a new product compares with existing products or methods in the eyes of customers. The perceived relative advantage of a new product versus existing products is a major influence on the rate of adoption. If a product has a substantial relative advantage vis-à-vis the competition, it is likely to gain quick acceptance. When compact disc players were first introduced in the early 1980s, industry observers predicted that only audiophiles

would care enough about digital sound—and have the money—to purchase them. However, the convenience and sonic advantages of CDs compared to LPs were obvious to the mass market; as prices for CD players plummeted, the 12-inch black vinyl LP was rendered virtually extinct in less than a decade.

2. *Compatibility.* The extent to which a product is consistent with existing values and past experiences of adopters. The history of innovations in international marketing is replete with failures caused by the lack of compatibility of new products in the target market. For example, the first consumer VCR, the Sony Betamax, ultimately failed because it could only record for one hour. Most buyers wanted to record movies and sports events; they shunned the Betamax in favor of VHS-format VCRs that could record four hours of programming.

3. *Complexity.* The degree to which an innovation or new product is difficult to understand and use. Product complexity is a factor that can slow down the rate of adoption, particularly in developing country markets with low rates of literacy. In the 1990s, dozens of global companies were developing new interactive multimedia consumer electronics products. Complexity is a key design issue; it is a standing joke that, in most households, VCR clocks flash 12:00 because users don't know how to set them. To achieve mass success, new products will have to be as simple to use as slipping a prerecorded videocassette into a VCR.

4. *Divisibility.* The ability of a product to be tried and used on a limited basis without great expense. Wide discrepancies in income levels around the globe result in major differences in preferred purchase quantities, serving sizes, and product portions. CPC International's Hellmann's mayonnaise was simply not selling in U.S.-size jars in Latin America. Sales took off after the company placed the mayonnaise in small plastic packets. The plastic packets were within the food budgets of local consumers, and they required no refrigeration—another plus.

5. *Communicability.* The degree to which benefits of an innovation or the value of a product may be communicated to a potential market. A new digital cassette recorder from Philips was a market failure, in part because advertisements did not clearly communicate the fact that the product could make CD-quality recordings using new cassette technology while still playing older analog tapes.

Adopter Categories

Adopter categories are classifications of individuals within a market on the basis of their innovativeness. Hundreds of studies of the diffusion of innovation demonstrate that, at least in the West, adoption is a social phenomenon that is characterized by a normal distribution curve, as shown in Figure 4-1.

Five categories have been assigned to the segments of this normal distribution. The first 2.5 percent of people to purchase a product are defined as innovators. The next 13.5 percent are early adopters, the next 34 percent are the early majority, the next 34 percent are the late majority, and the final 16 percent are laggards. Studies show that innovators tend to be venturesome, more cosmopolitan in their social relationships, and wealthier than those who adopt later. Early adopters are the most influential people in their communities, even more than the innovators. Thus the early adopters are a critical group in the adoption process, and they have great influence on the early and late majority, who comprise the bulk of the adopters of any product. Several characteristics of early adopters stand out. First, they tend to be younger, with higher social status, and in a more favorable financial position than later adopters. They must be responsive to mass media information sources and must learn about innovations from these sources because they cannot simply copy the behavior of early adopters.

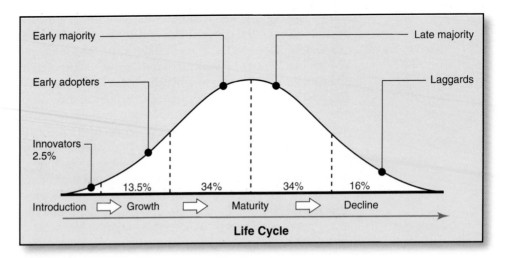

Figure 4-1
Adopter Categories

One of the major reasons for the normal distribution of adopter categories is the *interaction effect,* that is, the process through which individuals who have adopted an innovation influence others. Adoption of a new idea or product is the result of human interaction in a social system. If the first adopter of an innovation or new product discusses it with two other people, and each of these two adopters passes the new idea along to two other people, and so on, the resulting distribution yields a normal bell shape when plotted.

From the point of view of the marketing manager, steps taken to persuade innovators and early adopters to purchase a product are critical. These groups must make the first move and are the basis for the eventual penetration of a product into a new market because, over time, the majority copy their behavior.

Diffusion of Innovations in Pacific Rim Countries

In a recent cross-national comparison of the United States, Japan, South Korea, and Taiwan, Takada and Jain present evidence that different country characteristics—in particular, culture and communication patterns—affect diffusion processes for room air conditioners, washing machines, and calculators.[43] Proceeding from the observation that Japan, South Korea, and Taiwan are high-context cultures with relatively homogeneous populations and the United States is a low-context, heterogeneous culture, Takada and Jain surmised that Asia would show faster rates of diffusion than the United States. A second hypothesis supported by the research was that adoption would proceed more quickly in markets where innovations were introduced relatively late. Presumably, the lag time would give potential consumers more opportunity to assess the relative advantages, compatibility, and other product attributes. Takada and Jain's research has important marketing implications. They note:

> If a marketing manager plans to enter the newly industrializing countries (NICs) or other Asia markets with a product that has proved to be successful in the home market, the product's diffusion processes are likely to be much faster than in the home market.

[43] Hirokazu Takada and Dipak Jain, "Cross-National Analysis of Diffusion of Consumer Durable Goods in Pacific Rim Countries," *Journal of Marketing* 55 (April 1991), pp. 48–53.

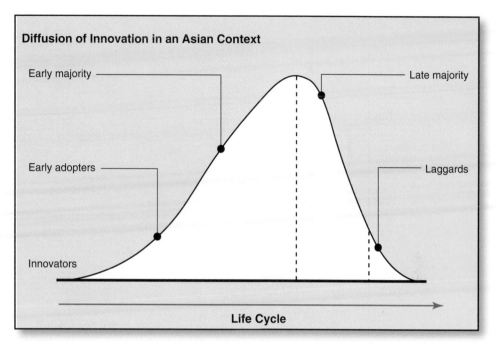

Figure 4-2
Adopter Categories in Asia

Source: Hellmut Schütte, "Asian Culture and the Global Consumer," *Financial Times—Mastering Marketing* (September 21, 1998), p. 2.

Figure 4-2 shows how the curve of Asian adopter categories would differ from the curve associated with Western consumer behavior. As noted before, there are likely to be fewer innovators in Japan and other Asian countries, where risk avoidance is high. However, as the Tamagotchi story illustrated, once consumers become aware that others have tried the product, they follow suit quickly so as not to be left behind. Hence the left tail in Figure 4-2 is longer, reflecting hesitancy to try a new product; moreover, the curve is steeper and less symmetrical, reflecting the speed with which early adopters and early majority try the product.[44]

MARKETING IMPLICATIONS OF SOCIAL AND CULTURAL ENVIRONMENTS

The various cultural factors described earlier can exert important influences on consumer and industrial products marketing around the globe. These factors must be recognized in formulating a global marketing plan. **Environmental sensitivity** reflects the extent to which products must be adapted to the culture-specific needs of different national markets. A useful approach is to view products on a continuum of environmental sensitivity. At one end of the continuum are environmentally insensitive products that do not require significant adaptation to the environments of various world markets. At the other end of the continuum are products that are highly sensitive to different environmental factors. A company with environmentally insensitive products

---

[44] Hellmut Schütte, "Asian Culture and the Global Consumer," *Financial Times—Mastering Marketing, Part Two* (September 21, 1998), p. 2.

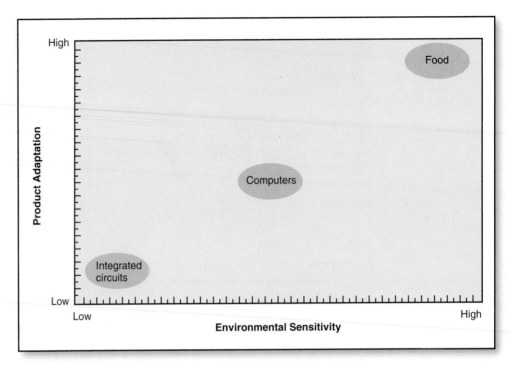

Figure 4-3
Environmental Sensitivity

will spend relatively less time determining the specific and unique conditions of local markets because the product is basically universal. The greater a product's environmental sensitivity, the greater the need for managers to address country-specific economic, regulatory, technological, social, and cultural environmental conditions.

The sensitivity of products can be represented on a two-dimensional scale as shown in Figure 4-3. The horizontal axis shows environmental sensitivity, the vertical axis the degree for product adaptation needed. Any product exhibiting low levels of environmental sensitivity—integrated circuits, for example—belongs in the lower left of the figure. Intel has sold more than 100 million microprocessors because a chip is a chip anywhere around the world. Moving to the right on the horizontal axis, the level of sensitivity increases, as does the amount of adaptation. Computers are characterized by moderate levels of environmental sensitivity; variations in country voltage requirements require some adaptation. In addition, the computer's software documentation should be in the local language. At the upper right of Figure 4-3 are products with high environmental sensitivity. Food sometimes falls into this category because it is sensitive to climate and culture. As we saw in the McDonald's case at the end of Chapter 1, the fast-food giant has achieved great success outside the United States by adapting its menu items to local tastes. GE's turbine-generating equipment may also appear on the high-sensitivity end of the continuum; in many countries, local equipment manufacturers receive preferential treatment when bidding on national projects.

Research studies show that, independent of social class and income, culture is a significant influence on consumption behavior and durable goods ownership.[45] Consumer products are probably more sensitive to cultural difference than are

---

[45] Charles M. Schaninger, Jacques C. Bourgeois, and Christian W. Buss, "French-English Canadian Subcultural Consumption Differences," *Journal of Marketing* 49 (Spring 1985), pp. 82–92.

industrial products. Hunger is a basic physiological need in Maslow's hierarchy; everyone needs to eat, but what we want to eat can be strongly influenced by culture. Evidence from the front lines of the marketing wars suggests that food is probably the most sensitive category of consumer products. CPC International failed to win popularity for Knorr dehydrated soups among Americans. The U.S. soup market was dominated by Campbell Soup Company; 90 percent of the soup consumed by households was canned. Knorr was a Swiss company acquired by CPC that had a major share of the European prepared food market, where bouillon and dehydrated soups account for 80 percent of consumer soup sales. Despite CPC's failure to change the soup-eating habits of Americans, the company (now called Bestfoods and a unit of Unilever) is a successful global marketer with operations in more than 60 countries and sales in 110 countries.

At Campbell, by contrast, the figures are reversed: 75 percent of 2001 revenues were generated in the United States, 25 percent from global markets. Despite the fact that Campbell is one of the world's best-known brand names, the company has discovered that the attitude of homemakers toward food preparation is a major cultural factor in marketing prepared foods. Recall that cooking was one of the cultural universals identified by Murdock. However, cooking habits and customs vary from country to country. Campbell's research revealed that Italian housewives devote approximately 4.5 hours per day to food preparation, versus 60 minutes a day spent by their U.S. counterparts. The difference reflects cultural norms regarding the kitchen as well as the fact that a higher percentage of American women work outside the home.

Campbell discovered a strong negative opinion toward convenience food in Italy. A panel of randomly selected Italian housewives was asked: "Would you want your son to marry a canned soup user?" The response to this question was sobering: All but a small fraction of a percent of the respondents answered, "No." Increased incomes as well as product innovations may have an impact on Italian attitudes toward time and convenience, with a corresponding positive effect on the market for convenience foods. Already, taste improvements in frozen pizza have boosted sales in Italy.

When David Johnson was Campbell's CEO in the mid-1990s, he acquired a majority stake in Arnotts, Australia's leading biscuit company. Johnson was setting his sights on the $1 billion Asian cracker market, which he expected to triple or quadruple in size in the coming years. Will consumers in Beijing and Bangkok clamor for Australian baked goods? Only time will tell, but Johnson—a native of Australia—was relying on sophisticated market research to guide the company's product adaptation effort.[46] Other Campbell executives share Johnson's global vision. As C. David Clark, former CEO of Campbell Canada, noted, "The strategy for North America is very simple. You market locally, manufacture regionally, and resource globally—with common technology, knowledge, and supplies."[47]

Thirst also shows how needs differ from wants. Liquid intake is a universal physiological need. As is the case with food and cooking, however, the particular beverages people *want* to drink can be strongly influenced by culture. Coffee is a beverage category that illustrates the point. On the European continent, coffee has been consumed for centuries. Britain has historically been a nation of tea drinkers, and the notion of afternoon tea is firmly entrenched in British culture. In the 1970s, tea outsold coffee by a ratio of 4-to-1. Brits who did drink coffee tended to buy it in instant form, since the preparation of instant is similar to that of tea. By the 1990s,

---

[46] Stephen W. Quickel, "Can Campbell Survive the Global Food Wars? M'm! M'm! Maybe!" *CFO* (February 1994), p. 26.
[47] Bill Saporito, "Campbell Soup Gets Piping Hot," *Fortune* (September 9, 1991), p. 143.

however, Britain was experiencing an economic boom and an explosion of new nightclubs and restaurants. Trendy Londoners looking for a change from the traditional pub found it in the form of Seattle Coffee Company shops. An instant success after the first store was opened by coffee-starved Americans in 1995, by 1998 Seattle Coffee had 55 locations around London. Starbucks bought the business from its founders for $84 million.[48]

CROSS-CULTURAL COMPLICATIONS AND SUGGESTED SOLUTIONS

As we have seen in this chapter and the last, global marketing activities are conducted in an ever-changing environment that blends economic, cultural, and social forces. Stepping out of the global perspective for a moment, we should acknowledge one thing: Even when the parties to a commercial transaction belong to the *same* low-context society and the terms of the deal are spelled out "in black and white," different understandings of the respective obligations of the parties will often occur.

Business relationships between parties of *different* cultures and/or nationalities are subject to additional challenges. Parties from different countries may have trouble coming to contract terms because of differences in the laws governing their respective activities and problems of enforcement across international boundaries. No matter what is stated in a contract, taking another party to court for breach of contract will probably require a suit in the defendant's home turf, which may be an insurmountable advantage for the home country participant.

When a party from a high-context culture engages in a business deal, the proceedings are likely to be even further complicated by very different beliefs about the significance of formal business understandings and the ongoing obligations of all parties. The business environment in many countries outside the Triad markets can be characterized by all manner of "hostile" elements: natural and human-induced catastrophes, political problems, foreign exchange inconvertibility, widely fluctuating exchange rates, depressions, and changes in national economic priorities and tariff schedules. One cannot predict precisely how the most carefully laid plans will go awry, only that they will. Marketing executives and managers with dealings outside the home market must build mutual trust, rapport, and empathy with business contacts; all are required to sustain enduring relationships. Appointing a host-country national to a position as sales representative will not automatically guarantee success. If a corporation constantly shuffles its international staff, it risks impeding the formation of what we might call "high-context subcultures" between home office personnel and host nationals. This diminishes the company's chances of effectively dealing with the business crises that will inevitably occur.

In 1986, Mexico's government imposed severe foreign exchange restrictions. Companies that had sold products or services to Mexican parties on terms other than "confirmed irrevocable international letter of credit" learned that they would have a lengthy wait before receiving payment in U.S. dollars or other "hard" currencies. Mexican companies dependent on essential ingredients, spare parts, and other critical foreign supplies had to deal with a rationed supply of foreign exchange to pay for new orders. In this situation, personal relationships superseded contractual obligations. In some instances, government officials needed to be convinced that a certain

---

[48] Marco R. della Cava, "Brewing a British Coup," *USA Today* (September 16, 1998), pp. D1, D2.

transaction deserved a priority allocation of foreign exchange. Some foreign sellers had to accept payment in Mexican products or in pesos that had to be invested in Mexico. Such contingencies arise routinely as companies conduct business around the globe. Solutions often result from individual initiative; personal ties create opportunities for both sides to keep a business relationship alive.

India is an important supplier of crude and processed agricultural and forest product raw materials to world markets. Small, family-owned enterprises collect, process, and sell these materials. Typically, months before the crop is in, sellers are required to contract with foreign buyers for later delivery of these products. The buyers, in turn, make long-term contractual commitments to their own customers. It is not possible for the Indian firms to hedge reliably by making forward crop purchases; there are no regulated commodity exchanges for these products. Nor do the farmers and forest product collectors have the resources to cover their sales if the crop fails. There are major problems during most growing seasons: Natural disaster or insufficient plantings result in short crops; strikes, protracted power shortages, or the lack of spare parts result in excessive shipment delays and reduced capacity. Business downturns or unexpected changes in required inventory levels may prompt buyers to request—or even insist—that shipments be held back or prices be reduced. Of course, such actions will cause the supplier severe financial hardship. Sometimes the supplier is unable to comply precisely with the terms of the contract and therefore provides a substitute order (usually without advance notice). The hope is that the buyer will inadvertently pay before discovering the switch and then reluctantly accept the merchandise with only minor adjustment.

Ongoing business between India and its global customers is, of course, perpetuated by mutual interest, but personal relationships are what make it possible. False rumors, supplier defaults, and customer cancellations are prevalent. Therefore, the greatest importance is assigned to contacts and business associates who can be fully trusted and whose culture-influenced perceptions are understood and predictable. Indian society is at least as ethnically and culturally diverse as that in Europe, and business practices are probably even more varied than in Europe.

TRAINING IN CROSS-CULTURAL COMPETENCY

Personal relationships are an essential ingredient for the international businessperson. Peace Corps volunteers devote one-third of their training to learning how things are done in the host country (particularly personal relationships). The international businessperson should have comparable preparation and a willingness to at least consider the merits of accommodating to the host culture's ways of doing business. The stakes are high: Experts estimate that billions of dollars worth of business is lost each year because of employee mistakes that occur in other cultures.

Samsung, GE, AT&T, and other large companies that are globalizing are taking steps to train managers and sensitize them to other ways of thinking, feeling, and acting. The goal is to improve their ability to deal effectively with customers, suppliers, bosses, and employees from other countries and regions. Managers must learn to question their own beliefs, to overcome the SRC, and to adapt the way they communicate, solve problems, and even make decisions. Multicultural managers must learn to question and to reevaluate their feelings concerning such rudimentary management issues as leadership, motivation, and teamwork; this means an examination of some extremely fundamental and personal systems of belief. Lastly, managers must learn to overcome stereotypes they hold regarding individuals of various races and religions from other countries; managers must also diplomatically deal with stereo-types others may have about them.

Samsung Group, South Korea's largest company, recently launched an internationalization campaign. Prior to departing for overseas assignments, managers attend a month-long "boot camp," where the topics range from Western table manners to sexual harassment. Hundreds of promising Samsung junior managers spend a year in Western countries pursuing an unusual assignment—goofing off. Notes one Korean management theorist, "International exposure is important, but you have to develop international taste. You have to do more than visit. You have to goof off at the mall, watch people and develop international tastes." Park Kwang Moo, an employee at Samsung's trading subsidiary, didn't get to spend time in malls: His assignment was to visit the former Soviet Union. He spent his first six months immersed in language study, then traveled to all 15 former Soviet republics. Park's superiors were delighted with the 80-page report he filed upon his return, despite the fact that there was very little in it about business issues per se. A director at the trading company noted that the report was mostly about Russians' drinking habits and idiosyncrasies. "But," he noted, "in 20 years, if this man is representing Samsung in Moscow, he will have friends and he will be able to communicate, and then we will get the payoff."[49]

Another widely used approach to accomplish sensitization is the use of workshops, incorporating case studies, role playing, and other exercises designed to permit participants to confront a relevant situation, contemplate what their own thoughts and actions would be in such a situation, and analyze and learn from the results. Participants must be able to understand and evaluate their motivations and approaches. Often, role-playing will bring out thoughts and feelings that otherwise might go unexamined or even unacknowledged. A variety of other techniques have been used for cross-cultural training; the common goal is to teach members of one culture ways of interacting effectively in another culture.

SUMMARY

Culture, a society's "programming of the mind," has both a pervasive and changing influence on each national market environment. Global marketers must recognize the influence of culture and be prepared to either respond to it or change it. Human behavior is a function of a person's own unique personality and that person's interaction with the collective forces of the particular society and culture in which he or she has lived. In particular, attitudes, values, and beliefs can vary significantly from country to country. Also, difference pertaining to aesthetics, dietary customs, and language and communication can affect local reaction to a company's brands or products as well as the ability of company personnel to function effectively in different cultures. A number of concepts and theoretical frameworks provide insights into these and other cultural issues.

Cultures can be classified as high- or low-context; communication and negotiation styles can differ from country to country. Hofstede's typology sheds important light on national cultures in terms of power distance, individualism, masculinity, uncertainty avoidance, and time orientation. By understanding the self-reference criterion, global marketers can overcome the unconscious tendency for perceptual blockage and distortion. Rogers' classic study on the diffusion of innovations helps

49 "Sensitivity Kick: Korea's Biggest Firm Teaches Junior Execs Strange Foreign Ways," *The Wall Street Journal* (December 30, 1992), p. A1.

explain how products are adopted over time by different **adopter categories.** Rogers' findings concerning the **characteristics of innovations** can also help marketers successfully launch new products in global markets. Recent research has suggested that Asian adopter categories differ from the Western model. An awareness of **environmental** **sensitivity** can help marketers determine whether consumer and industry products must be adapted to the needs of different markets. Any persons doing business in a new culture should avail themselves of training in **cross-cultural competency** to avoid complications that arise because of cultural differences.

DISCUSSION QUESTIONS

1. What are some of the elements that make up culture? How do these find expression in your native culture?
2. What is the difference between a low-context culture and a high-context culture? Give an example of a country that is an example of each type, and provide evidence for your answer.
3. How can Hofstede's cultural typologies help Western marketers better understand Asian culture?
4. Explain the self-reference criterion. Go to the library and find examples of product failures that might have been avoided through the application of the SRC.
5. Briefly explain the social research of Everett Rogers regarding diffusion of innovations, characteristics of innovations, and adopter categories. How does the adoption process in Asia differ from the traditional Western model?
6. Compare and contrast the United States and Japan in terms of traditions and organizational behavior and norms.

SUGGESTED READINGS

Books

Abegglen, James C., and George Stalk Jr. *Kaisha, The Japanese Corporation.* New York: Basic Books, 1985.

Alfino, Mark, John S. Caputo, and Robin Wynyard. *McDonaldization Revisited: Critical Essays on Consumer Culture.* Westport, CT: Praeger, 1998.

Benedict, Ruth. *Patterns of Culture.* Boston: Houghton Mifflin, 1959.

____. *The Chrysanthemum and the Sword.* Rutland, VT: Charles E. Tuttle, 1972.

Dale, Peter N. *The Myth of Japanese Uniqueness.* New York: St. Martin's Press, 1986.

Featherstone, Mike, ed. *Global Culture: Nationalism, Globalization and Modernity.* London: Sage Publications, 1990.

Fields, George. *From Bonsai to Levis.* New York: Mentor, New American Library, 1983.

____. *Gucci on the Ginza.* Tokyo and New York: Kodansha International, 1989.

Hall, Edward T. *Beyond Culture.* Garden City, N.Y.: Anchor, 1976.

____, and Mildred Reed Hall. *Hidden Differences: Doing Business with the Japanese.* New York: Doubleday, 1990.

Harris, Philip R., and Robert T. Moran. *Managing Cultural Differences: High Performance Strategies for a New World of Business,* 3d ed. Houston: Gulf Publishing Company, 1991.

Hofstede, Geert. *Cultures and Organizations: Software of the Mind.* New York: McGraw-Hill, 1991.

Kappel, G., R. Rathmayr, and N. Diehl-Zelonkina. *Verhandlen Mit Russen.* Vienna: Service Fachverlag, 1992.

Moran, R., and W. Stripp. *Dynamics of Successful International Business Negotiations.* Houston: Gulf Publishing Company, 1991.

Articles

Alden, Dana L., Jan-Benedict Steenkamp, and Rajeev Batra. "Brand Positioning through Advertising in Asia, North America, and Europe: The Role of Global Consumer Culture." *Journal of Marketing* 63, no. 1 (January 1999), pp. 75–87.

Bonvillian, Gary, and William A. Nowlin. "Cultural Awareness: An Essential Element of Doing Business Abroad." *Business Horizons* 37, no. 6 (November 1994), p. 44.

Cutler, Bob D., S. Altan Erdem, and Rajshekhar G. Javalgi. "Advertiser's Relative Reliance on

Collectivism-Individualism Appeals." *Journal of International Consumer Marketing* 9, no. 3 (1997), pp. 43–55.

Dulek, Ronald E., John S. Fielden, and John S. Hill. "International Communications: An Executive Primer." *Business Horizons* 34, no. 1 (January-February 1991), pp. 20–25.

Fedor, Kenneth J., and William B. Werther, Jr. "Making Sense of Cultural Factors in International Alliances." *Organizational Dynamics* 24, no. 4 (Spring 1995), pp. 33–48.

Ford, John B., and Earl D. Honeycutt, Jr. "Japanese National Culture as a Basis for Understanding Japanese Business Practices." *Business Horizons* 35, no. 6 (November-December 1992), pp. 27–34.

Guptara, Prabhu, "Multicultural Aspects of Managing Multinationals," *Management Japan* 26, no. 1 (Spring 1993), pp. 7–14.

Herbig, Paul A., and Hugh E. Kramer. "Do's and Don'ts of Cross-Cultural Negotiations." *Industrial Marketing Management* 21, no. 4 (November 1992), pp. 287–298.

Hofstede, Geert, and Michael Harris Bond. "The Confucius Connection: From Cultural Roots to Economic Growth." *Organizational Dynamics* (Spring 1988), pp. 5–21.

Jacobs, Laurence E., Charles Keown, Reginald Worthley, and Kyung-I Ghymn. "Cross-Cultural Colour Comparisons: Global Marketers Beware!" *International Marketing Review* 8, no. 3 (1991), pp. 21–30.

Kim, Donghoon, Yigang Pan, and Heung Soo Park. "High- Versus Low-Context Culture: A Comparison of Chinese, Korean, and American Cultures." *Psychology & Marketing* 15, no. 6 (September 1998), pp. 507–521.

Kvint, Vladimir. "Don't Give Up on Russia." *Harvard Business Review* 72, no. 2 (March-April 1994), pp. 62–74.

Lin, Carloyn A. "Cultural Values Reflected in Chinese and American Television Advertising." *Journal of Advertising* 30, no. 4 (Winter 2001), pp. 83–94.

Manrai, Lalita A., and Ajay K. Manrai. "Current Issues in the Cross-Cultural and Cross-National Consumer Research." *Journal of International Consumer Marketing* 8, no. 3–4 (1996), pp. 9–22.

Menger, Richard. "Japanese and American Negotiators: Overcoming Cultural Barriers to Understanding." *Academy of Management Executive* 13, no. 4 (November 1999), pp. 100–101.

Mintu, Alma T., and Roger J. Calantone. "A Comparative Approach to International Marketing Negotiation." *Journal of Applied Business Research* 7, no. 4 (Fall 1991), pp. 90–97.

Miracle, Gordon E., Kyu Yeol Chang, and Charles R. Taylor. "Culture and Advertising Executions: A Comparison of Selected Characteristics of Korean and U.S. Television Commercials." *International Marketing Review* 9, no. 4 (1992), pp. 5–17.

Money, R. Bruce, Mary C. Gilly, and John L. Graham. "Explorations of National Culture and Word-of-Mouth Referral Behavior in the Purchase of Industrial Services in the United States and Japan." *Journal of Marketing* 62, no. 4 (October 1998), pp. 76–87.

Reardon, Kathleen Kelley, and Robert E. Spekman. "Starting Out Right: Negotiating Lessons for Domestic and Cross-Cultural Business Alliances." *Business Horizons* 37, no. 1 (January-February 1994), pp. 71–79.

Robertson, Christopher. "The Global Dispersion of Chinese Values: A Three-Country Study of Confucian Dynamism. *Management International Review* 40, no. 3 (2000), pp. 253–268.

Ross, Martin S. "The Effects of Culture and Socioeconomics on the Performance of Global Brand Image Strategies." *Journal of Marketing Research* 32 (May 1995), pp. 163–175.

Schneider, Susan C., and Arnoud De Meyer. "Interpreting and Responding to Strategic Issues: The Impact of National Culture." *Strategic Management Journal* 12, no. 4 (May 1991), pp. 307–320.

Shane, Scott A. "The Effect of Cultural Differences in Perceptions of Transactions Costs on National Differences in the Preference for International Joint Ventures." *Asia Pacific Journal of Management* 10, no. 1 (1993), pp. 57–69.

Sivakumar, K., and Cheryl Nakata. "The Stampede toward Hofstede's Framework: Avoiding the Sample Design Pit in Cross-Cultural Research." *Journal of International Business Studies* 32, no. 3 (2001), pp. 555–574.

Stening, Bruce W., and Mitchell R. Hammer. "Cultural Baggage and the Adaption of Expatriate American and Japanese Managers." *Management International Review* 32, no. 1 (First Quarter 1992), pp. 77–89.

Sugiura, Hideo. "How Honda Localizes Its Global Strategy." *Sloan Management Review* 32, no. 1 (Fall 1990), pp. 77–82.

Tung, Rosalie L. "Handshakes Across the Sea: Cross-Cultural Negotiating for Business Success." *Organizational Dynamics* 19, no. 3 (Winter 1991), pp. 30–40.

Usunier, Jean-Claude G. "Business Time Perception and National Cultures: A Comparative Survey." *Management International Review* 31, no. 3 (Third Quarter 1991), pp. 197–217.

Yeh, Ryh-song, and John J. Lawrence. "Individualism and Confucian Dynamism: A Note on Hofstede's Cultural Root to Economic Growth." *Journal of International Business Studies* 26, no. 3 (1995), pp. 655–669.

CASES

Case 4-1   Disneyland Paris

Executives at Walt Disney Company found themselves working frantically to keep the new Euro Disney in Marne-la-Vallée, France, from drowning in a sea of red ink just two years after the theme park's April 1992 grand opening. Despite the fact that Euro Disney achieved target attendance objectives of 11 million guests in just over a year of operation, cumulative losses at the end of 1993 exceeded $1 billion, and the park was losing $1 million a day. The $4.4 billion, 5,000-acre park represented the second-largest construction project in Europe's history, after the building of the Chunnel, the tunnel beneath the English Channel connecting England and France. Unfortunately, a number of basic assumptions and forecasts made during the planning of Euro Disney turned out to be faulty or misguided.

For example, in their quest for European-style grandeur and perfection, Disney executives spared no expense in building the park and adjacent hotels. The plan called for some of the hotels to be sold at a handsome profit after the park was opened. Disney appointed Robert Fitzpatrick to be the head Euro Disney S.C.A; although American, he had traveled extensively in Europe, spoke French, and had a French wife. Disney anticipated that the French would, in fact, represent the park's core clientele. An effort was made to ensure that Euro Disney's cast members would be able to speak with guests in French. (Disney uses the words "cast member" and "guest" instead of "employee" and "visitor," respectively.) French food was widely available in restaurants, and characters such as Snow White and Pinocchio from European fairy tales were emphasized rather than Bambi or Dumbo.

Unfortunately, Disney planners failed to anticipate major changes in Europe's economy. The Paris real estate market slumped, making it impossible to sell any of the hotels. Moreover, Europe was heading into a recession at the time the park opened, and the adult admission to the park, the equivalent of about $43, was out of sync with the times. To make matters worse, currency devaluations in Great Britain and Italy reduced the purchasing power of guests from those countries.

Unanticipated cultural issues compounded the financial problems. Many in the French establishment were vocal critics of the park. For example, the literary critic for the newspaper *Le Figaro* wrote, "Euro Disney is the very symbol of the process by which people's cultural standards are lowered and money becomes all-conquering." When Disney chairman Michael Eisner dis-

missed such criticism, he and others in his management team were accused of arrogance. Despite negative publicity in the local press, most of the guests were, indeed, from France. However, their numbers were lower than expected; visitors from Great Britain and Germany, taken together, outnumbered the French. Thus, although the hosts of various attractions such as Buffalo Bill's Wild West Show were prepared to speak to guests in French, on any given night the audience could be predominantly from Germany or Spain.

Other embarrassing cross-cultural blunders occurred and were widely, even gleefully, reported in the press. For example, prior to opening the park, Disney insisted employees comply with a detailed written code regarding clothing, jewelry, and other aspects of personal appearance. Women were expected to wear "appropriate undergarments" and keep their fingernails short. Disney defended its move, noting that similar codes were used in its other parks. The goal was to ensure that guests receive the kind of experience associated with the Disney name. Despite such statements, the French considered the code to be an insult to French culture, individualism, and privacy.

There were other missteps as well. Disney had mistakenly assumed that European parents would readily take their kids out of school in midsemester for short family sojourns to a Disney theme park as Americans often do. Also, in designing hotel restaurants, Disney officials assumed that Europeans don't eat breakfast. The restaurants were scaled down as a result. In reality, most guests wanted to eat a morning meal of more than just a continental breakfast of coffee and pastry, resulting in long lines and disgruntled guests. A similar problem occurred inside the park at lunchtime. The United States is a nation of snackers, and the Disney team assumed that Europeans would be content to "graze" and then eat in shifts. It turned out that at 1 p.m. each day, the park's restaurants were inundated with hungry patrons. To make matters worse, the extension of Disney's standard "no alcohol" policy meant that wine was not available at Euro Disney. This, too, was deemed inappropriate in a country renowned for production and consumption of wine.

A number of changes were made to remedy some of these problems and revitalize Euro Disney. Fitzpatrick left his position as head of Euro Disney and was replaced by a French national, Philippe Bourguignon;

the theme park's official name was changed to Disneyland Paris; and a new program called Challenge 1994 was implemented, with efficiency and economy as its hallmarks. To reduce costs, nearly 2,000 full- and part-time employees were dismissed. The number of different souvenirs in the park's shops—30,000 at first—was cut in half. In the hotel restaurants, the selection of food items was reduced from 5,400 to 2,000. Reductions in admission prices after 5 p.m. were introduced to encourage people to visit the park in the evening. Training programs for Euro Disney's cast members used the Mary Poppins character to promote a better service attitude. In an attempt to increase revenue, new flexible job descriptions allowed employees to shift from selling tickets in the morning to selling souvenirs in the afternoon. On September 30, 1995, when Euro Disney closed the books on its fiscal year, the park had finally turned a profit. ∎

DISCUSSION QUESTIONS

1. What issues are at the heart of Euro Disney's problems? Why?
2. How could Disney have avoided some of the problems with the new theme park?
3. Do you predict Euro Disney will continue to be profitable? Why or why not?

SOURCES: "A Disney Dress Code Chafes in the Land of Haute Couture," *The New York Times* (December 25, 1991), pp. 1, 22; Martin Parker, "Selling Mickey by the Pound," *New Statement and Policy* (January 5, 1990), pp. 46–47; Peter Gumbel and David J. Jefferson, "Disney Continues Drive to Expand World-Wide," *The Wall Street Journal* (November 20, 1992), p. B5; Roger Cohen, "When You Wish Upon a Deficit," *The New York Times* (July 18, 1993), sec. 2, pp. 1, 18, 19; Peter Gumbel, "Euro Disney Calls in Mary Poppins to Tidy Up Mess at Resort in France," *The Wall Street Journal* (February 22, 1994), p. A13; Peter Gumbel and Richard Turner, "Mouse Trap: Fans Like Euro Disney but Its Parent's Goofs Weigh the Park Down," *The Wall Street Journal* (March 10, 1994), pp. A1, A12.

Case 4-2 *Canada versus the United States: The Culture Wars*

The United States and Canada are bound together by many things, including a trade agreement, a shared border, and a common language. Still, the two nations do not always see eye-to-eye, as evidenced by the trade-related issues that have arisen in recent years. Take, for example, U.S. exports of items related to popular culture. On one side is the American entertainment industry. Exports of music CDs and cassettes, print publications, television shows, and Hollywood movies all contribute to the U.S. trade surplus in services. In Canada, policymakers, arts organizations, and cultural activists point with concern to statistics indicating that 95 percent of the movies shown in theaters are not Canadian and that 84 percent of the recorded music that Canadians buy is foreign. Competition is one facet of the issue; Canadians fear that their own national industries will not be able to survive the global juggernaut originating south of the border. Canadians are also concerned about cultural preservation. In 1996, Arthur C. Eggleton, Canada's minister for international trade, said, "There is a very strong dominance in the cultural industries of the Canadian marketplace by the United States. We come at this from the point of preserving culture and identity, while the United States comes at it from the standpoint of wanting to do business in our country."

Since the 1960s, Canada has enacted various pieces of legislation that restrict foreign ownership in the book publishing, telecommunications, and broadcasting industries. There are also regulations governing the percentage of Canadian programming that is broadcast by radio and television stations. In the negotiations leading to NAFTA, Canada was successful in excluding culture industries from the liberalized trade and investment framework. The issue came to a head in 1995, when Canada's Parliament imposed an 80 percent excise tax on advertising in the Canadian edition of Time Warner's *Sport's Illustrated*. The dispute focused on split-run magazines, in which the U.S. and Canadian editions are virtually identical in terms of editorial content but carry different advertising. Canadian publishers complained that

Time Warner and other U.S. media companies possessed the resources to dominate Canadian culture. The United States took the matter to the World Trade Organization; a trade panel ruled that Canada's actions violated international trade agreements. After the initial ruling was issued, Canada filed an appeal but did not receive a favorable ruling. The U.S. trade representative Charlene Barshefsky hailed the decision, saying it "makes clear WTO rules prevent government from using 'culture' as a pretense for discriminating against imports."

Despite the WTO's ruling in this case, France and other nations share Canada's concerns. OECD member nations have conducted meetings to discuss a multilateral agreement on investment (MAI) that would eliminate barriers to foreign investment; France, Canada, and other nations are seeking to exclude cultural industries from the pact. In 1998, Canada convened a conference of 20 culture ministers in Ottawa in the hope of drafting a trade agreement that would ensure that culture industries received special treatment in trade rules. The agreement would be negotiated in Geneva at the World Trade Organization. Sheila Copps, Canadian heritage minister and host of the meeting, said attendees had agreed to establish a permanent network. In the future, she said, steps would be taken so that "culture is not treated simply like every other commodity." Copps also noted that the United States was not invited to take part in the conference because it does not have a culture minister. ■

DISCUSSION QUESTIONS

1. Why is Canada so concerned about cultural exports from the United States? Why aren't there similar concerns about Canadian cultural exports in America?
2. If you were a Canadian filmmaker or recording artist, what are some things that you might do to improve your chances of succeeding in a global industry that seems dominated by Hollywood films and American pop stars?
3. Do you agree with Sheila Copps that culture-related trade needs special treatment so that culture is not "commoditized"?

SOURCES: Roger Ricklefs, "Canada Fights to Fend Off American Tastes and Tunes," *The Wall Street Journal* (September 24, 1998), pp. B1, B8; Anthony DePalma, "Happy 4th of July, Canada!" *The New York Times* (July 5, 1998), p. 3; Rosanna Tamburri, "Canada to Promote Pact to Curb U.S.'s Cultural Exports," *The Wall Street Journal* (June 29, 1998), p. B5; Tamburri, "Canada Considers New Stand Against American Culture," *The Wall Street Journal* (February 4, 1998), p. A18; Bernard Simon, "Canada Scrambles to Protect Magazines," *Financial Times* (July 2, 1997), p. 6; John Urquhart, "Canada Appealing Panel Ruling Backing U.S. Complaints on Magazines," *The Wall Street Journal* (March 17, 1997), p. B8; Anthony DePalma, "Trade vs. Cultural Identity in Canada," *The New York Times* (October 7, 1996), p. D9.

Case 4-3 *Marketing an Industrial Product in Latin America*

The government of a Latin American republic had decided to modernize one of its communication networks at a cost of several million dollars. Because of its reputation for quality, the government approached American company "Y." Company management, having been sounded out informally, considered the size of the order and decided to bypass its regular Latin American representative and send its sales manager instead. The following describes what took place.

The sales manager arrived and checked into the leading hotel. He immediately had some difficulty pinning down just who was his business contact. After several days without results, he called at the American Embassy where he found the commercial attaché had the necessary up-to-the-minute information. The commercial attaché listened to his story. The attaché realized the sales manager had already made a number of mistakes but, figuring that the Latins were used to American blundering, he reasoned that all was not lost. The attaché informed the sales manager that the Minister of Communications was the key man and that whoever got the nod from him would get the contract. He also briefed the sales manager on methods of conducting business in Latin America and offered some pointers about dealing with the minister.

The attaché's advice ran somewhat as follows:

1. "You don't do business here the way you do in the States; it is necessary to spend much more time. You have to get to know your man and vice versa."

2. "You must meet with him several times before you talk business. I will tell you at what point you can bring up the subject. Take your cues from me." (At this point, our American sales manager made a few observations to himself about "cookie pushers" and wondered how many payrolls had been met by the commercial attaché.)

3. "Take that price list and put it in your pocket. Don't get it out until I tell you to. Down here price is only one of the many things taken into account before closing a deal. In the United States, your past experience will prompt you to act according to a certain set of principles, but many of these principles will not work here. Every time you feel the urge to act or to say something, look at me. Suppress the urge and take your cues from me. This is very important."

4. "Down here people like to do business with men who are somebody. 'Being somebody' means having written a book, lectured at a university, or developed your intellect in some way. The man you are going to see is a poet. He has published several volumes of poetry. Like many Latin Americans, he prizes poetry highly. You will find that he will spend a good deal of business time quoting his poetry to you, and he will take great pleasure in this."

5. "You will also note that the people here are very proud of their past and of their Spanish blood, but they are also exceedingly proud of their liberation from Spain and their independence. The fact that they are a democracy, that they are free, and also that they are no longer a colony is very, very important to them. They are warm and friendly and enthusiastic if they like you. If they don't, they are cold and withdrawn."

6. "And another thing, time down here means something different. It works in a different way. You know how it is back in the States when a certain type blurts out whatever is on his mind without waiting to see if the situation is right. He is considered an impatient bore and somewhat egocentric. Well, down here you have to wait much, much longer, and I really mean much, *much* longer, before you can begin to talk about the reason for your visit."

7. "There is another point I want to caution you about. At home, the man who sells takes the initiative. Here, *they* tell you when they are ready to do business. But most of all, don't discuss price until you are asked and don't rush things."

The Pitch

The next day the commercial attaché introduced the sales manager to the Minister of Communications. First, there was a long wait in the outer office while people went in and out. The sales manager looked at his watch, fidgeted, and finally asked whether the minister was really expecting him. The reply he received was scarcely reassuring, "Oh yes, he is expecting you but several things have come up that require his attention. Besides, one gets used to waiting down here." The sales manager irritably replied, "But doesn't he know I flew all the way down here from the United States to see him, and I have spent over a week already of my valuable time trying to find him?" "Yes, I know," was the answer, "but things just move much more slowly here."

At the end of about 30 minutes, the minister emerged from the office, greeted the commercial attaché with a double abrazo, throwing his arms around him and patting him on the back as though they were long-lost brothers. Now, turning and smiling, the minister extended his hand to the sales manager, who, by this time, was feeling rather miffed because he had been kept in the outer office so long.

After what seemed to be an all too short chat, the minister rose, suggesting a well-known cafe where they might meet for dinner the next evening. The sales manager expected, of course, that, considering the nature of their business and the size of the order, he might be taken to the minister's home, not realizing that the Latin home is reserved for family and very close friends.

Until now, nothing at all had been said about the reason for the sales manager's visit, a fact which bothered him somewhat. The whole setup seemed wrong; nor did he like the idea of wasting another day in town. He told the home office before he left that he would be gone for a week or ten days at most, and made a mental note that he would clean this order up in three days and enjoy a few days in Acapulco or Mexico City. Now the week had already gone and he would be lucky if he made it home in ten days.

Voicing his misgivings to the commercial attaché, he wanted to know if the minister really meant business, and if he did, why could they not get together and talk about it? The commercial attaché by now was beginning to show the strain of constantly having to reassure the sales manager. Nevertheless, he tried again: "What you don't realize is that part of the time we were waiting, the minister was rearranging a very tight schedule so that he could spend tomorrow night with you. You see, down here they don't delegate responsibility the way we do in the States. They exercise much tighter control than we do. As a consequence, this man spends up to 15 hours a day at his desk. It may not look like it to you, but I assure you he really means business. He wants to give your company the order; if you play your cards right, you will get it."

The next evening was more of the same. Much conversation about food and music, about many people the sales manager had never heard of. They went to a night club, where the sales manager brightened up and began to think that perhaps he and the minister might have something in common after all. It bothered him, however, that the principal reason for his visit was not even alluded to tangentially. Instead, every time he started to talk about electronics, the commercial attaché would nudge him and proceed to change the subject.

The next meeting was to be held over morning coffee at a café. By now the sales manager was having difficulty hiding his impatience. To make matters worse the minister had a mannerism that he did not like. When they talked he was likely to put his hand on him; he would take hold of his arm and get so close that he nearly spit in his face. Consequently, the sales manager kept trying to dodge and put more distance between himself and the minister.

Following coffee, they walked in a nearby park. The minister expounded on the shrubs, the birds, and the beauties of nature, and at one spot he stopped to point at a statue and said: "There is a statue of the world's greatest hero, the liberator of mankind!" At this point, the worst happened, for the sales manager asked who the statue was of and, when told the name of a famous Latin American patriot, said, "I never heard of him," and walked on. After this meeting, the American sales manager was never able to see the minister again. The order went to a Swedish concern. ■

DISCUSSION QUESTIONS

1. What impression do you think the sales manager made on the minister?
2. How would you critique the quality of the communication between all parties in this case?

3. Is a high-context culture or a low-context culture at work in this case? Explain your answer.

SOURCES: Edward T. Hall, "The Silent Language in Overseas Business," *Harvard Business Review* (May-June 1960), pp. 93–96; Philip R. Harris and Robert T. Moran, "Doing Business with Latin Americans—Mexico, Central & South America," chap. 14 in *Managing Cultural Differences:*

High Performance Strategies for a New World of Business, 3d ed. (Houston: Gulf Publishing Company, 1991); Paul Leppert, *Doing Business with Mexico* (Fremont, CA: Jain Publishing Company, 1995); Lawrence Tuller, *Doing Business in Latin America and the Caribbean* (Chicago: Amacom, 1993).

Chapter 5

The Political, Legal, and Regulatory Environments of Global Marketing

*I*n the late 1990s, a growing debate about genetically modified organisms (GMOs) pitted the biotechnology industry against a broad coalition of environmentalists and small-scale farmers. For a number of years, giant global companies such as Monsanto, DuPont, ConAgra, Novartis, and Zeneca PLC had reaped significant profits from sales of genetically modified seeds for soybeans, corn, cotton, tomatoes, and other crops. Farmers, in turn, generated higher yields by planting crops with an enhanced ability to withstand stressors such as insects, drought, and disease. In the United States alone, 50 percent of the yearly corn harvest is produced from genetically modified seed. As one industry executive enthusiastically noted, "The next Silicon Valley is plant biotechnology." GMOs were already present in a wide range of food products from well-known companies such as Coca-Cola, H.J. Heinz, Quaker Oats, and Nestlé. Future breakthroughs were expected to include healthier cooking oil and soybean protein that doesn't taste "beany." There was a problem, however: A growing number of consumers around the world were deeply concerned about food products that had not been produced naturally. As a result, the European Union began to require mandatory labeling for some foods containing GMOs, and regulators in Australia, New Zealand, Japan, and several other countries also began devising labeling strategies.

The GMO issue illustrates the impact that the political, legal, and regulatory environments can have on international trade and global marketing activities. Each of the world's national governments regulates trade and commerce with other countries and attempts to control the access of outside enterprises to national resources. Every country has its own unique legal and regulatory system that affects the operations and activities of the global enterprise, including the global marketer's ability to address market opportunities and threats. Laws and regulations constrain the cross-border movement of products, services, peo-

A protester dressed as a "killer tomato" marches through downtown San Diego in 2001 en route to the Convention Center where the Biotechnology Industry Organization was holding its annual conference. The demonstrators were expressing concern about the long-term effects of introducing food from genetically-modified crops into the food supply. The biotech industry contends that such products will be accepted by consumers as long as they are fully informed about the benefits and potential risks.

ple, money, and know-how. The global marketer must attempt to comply with each set of national—and, in some instances, regional—constraints. These efforts are hampered by the fact that laws and regulations are frequently ambiguous and continually changing.

In this chapter, we consider the basic elements of the political, legal, and regulatory environments of global marketing, including the most pressing current issues and some suggested approaches for dealing with those issues. Some specific topics, such as rules for exporting and importing industrial and consumer products, standards for health and safety, and regulations regarding packaging, labeling, advertising, and promotion, are covered in later chapters devoted to individual marketing mix elements.

THE POLITICAL ENVIRONMENT

Global marketing activities take place within the political environment of governmental institutions, political parties, and organizations through which a country's people and rulers exercise power. As we saw in Chapter 4, each nation has a unique culture that reflects its society. Each nation also has a *political culture,* which reflects the relative importance of the government and legal system and provides a context within which individuals and corporations understand their relationship to the political system. Any company doing business outside its home country should carefully study the political culture in the target country and analyze salient issues arising from the political environment. These include the governing party's attitude toward sovereignty, political risk, taxes, the threat of equity dilution, and expropriation.

Nation-States and Sovereignty

Sovereignty can be defined as supreme and independent political authority. A century ago, U.S. Supreme Court Chief Justice Fuller said, "Every sovereign state is bound to respect the independence of every other sovereign state, and the courts in one country will not sit in judgment on the acts of government of another done within its territory." More recently, Richard Stanley, president of the Stanley Foundation, offered the following concise description:

> A sovereign state was considered free and independent. It regulated trade, managed the flow of people into and out of its boundaries, and exercised undivided jurisdiction over all persons and property within its territory. It had the right, authority, and ability to conduct its domestic affairs without outside interference and to use its international power and influence with full discretion.[1]

Government actions taken in the name of sovereignty occur in the context of two important criteria: a country's stage of development and the political and economic system in place in the country.

As outlined in Chapter 2, the economies of individual nations may be classified as industrialized, newly industrializing, or developing. Many governments in developing countries exercise control over their nations' economic development by passing protectionist laws and regulations. Their objective is to encourage economic development by protecting emerging or strategic industries. Government leaders can also engage in cronyism and provide favors for family members or "good friends." For example, former Indonesian president Suharto established a national car program that granted tax breaks and tariff privileges to a company established in South Korea by his youngest son. The United States, EU, and Japan responded by taking the matter to the World Trade Organization. Conversely, when many nations reach advanced stages of economic development, their governments declare that (in theory, at least) any practice or policy that restrains free trade is illegal. Antitrust laws and regulations are established to promote fair competition. Advanced country laws often define and preserve a nation's social order; laws may extend to political, cultural, and even intellectual activities and social conduct. In France, for example, laws forbid the use of foreign words such as *le weekend* or *le marketing* in official documents. Also, a French law passed in 1996 requires that at least 40 percent of the songs played by popular radio stations must be French.

We also noted in Chapter 2 that most of the world's economies combine elements of market and nonmarket systems. The sovereign political power of a government in a predominantly nonmarket economy reaches quite far into the economic life of a country. By contrast, in a capitalist, market-oriented democracy, that power tends to be much more constrained. A current global phenomenon in both nonmarket and market structures is the trend toward privatization, which reduces direct governmental involvement as a supplier of goods and services in a given economy. In essence, each act of privatization moves a nation's economy further in the free-market direction. The trend is clearly evident in Mexico, where, at one time, the government controlled over 1,000 "parastatals." By the early 1990s, most had been sold, as President Carlos Salinas de Gortari presided over the sale of full or partial stakes in enterprises worth $23 billion, including the two Mexican airlines, mines, and banks.

---

[1] See *Changing Concepts of Sovereignty: Can the United Nations Keep Pace?* (Muscatine, IA: The Stanley Foundation, 1992), p. 7.

Privatization in Mexico and elsewhere is evidence that national governments are changing *how* they exercise sovereign power.

Some observers believe global market integration is eroding national economic sovereignty. Economic consultant Neal Soss notes, "The ultimate resource of a government is power, and we've seen repeatedly that the willpower of governments can be overcome by persistent attacks from the marketplace."[2] Is this a disturbing trend? If the issue is framed in terms of marketing, the concept of the exchange comes to the fore: Nations may be willing to give up sovereignty in return for something of value.

---

[2] Cited in Karen Pennar, "Is the Nation-State Obsolete in a Global Economy?" *Business Week* (July 17, 1995), p. 80.

If countries can increase their share of world trade and increase national income, perhaps they will be willing to cede some sovereignty. In Europe, the individual EU countries are giving up the right to have their own currencies, ceding the right to set their own product standards and making other sacrifices in exchange for improved market access.

Political Risk

Political risk is the risk of a change in political environment or government policy that would adversely affect a company's ability to operate effectively and profitably. It can deter a company from investing abroad. When the perceived level of political risk is high, a country will have greater difficulty in attracting foreign investment. Unfortunately, it is often the case that managers fail to include political risk assessment in the global strategic planning process because they think it is esoteric, too expensive, or unreliable. Political forces can drastically change the business environment with little advance notice. For example, businesspeople need to stay apprised of the formation and evolution of political parties. Valuable sources of information include *The Economist, Financial Times*, and other business periodicals. A number of organizations such as the Economist Intelligence Unit (EIU), the Geneva-based Business Environment Risk Intelligence (BERI), and the PRS Group specialize in providing up-to-date political risk reports on individual country markets. These commercial sources, however, vary somewhat in the criteria that constitute political risk. For example, BERI is concerned with societal and system attributes, whereas PRS Group focuses more directly on government actions and economic functions. The EIU analyzes political risk in terms of five subcategories of political stability, and five subcategories of political effectiveness. Political risk, in turn, is one of four components in an overall country risk rating. The BERI system examines six internal causes of political risk, two external causes, and two symptoms (see Table 5-1).

Visit the Web site
The Economist Intelligence Unit, BERI, and the PRS Group can be found online at:
www.eiu.com
www.beri.com
www.prsgroup.com

Causes of Political Risk

The fundamental cause of political risk is tension between the residents' aspirations and goals and the real conditions at a given time. Whenever the public perceives a wide gap between its aspirations and reality, there is political risk. The gap between aspirations and reality in high-income countries is seldom great enough to generate a significant level of political risk. When political risk is present in a high-income country, it can be traced to identifiable, long-standing issues in the country such as the conflict between the Protestants and Catholics in Northern Ireland.

In lower- and lower-middle-income countries, an economic crisis can trigger political risk. Indonesia is a prime example: After the rupiah plunged from 2,300 to 18,000 to the U.S. dollar and then settled at a rate of 10,000 rupiah to the dollar, Indonesia went into a free fall of economic decline. What had been the most stable country in Southeast Asia overnight became a country where all bets were off. The incompetence of the government and private sector in Indonesia provoked the expulsion of President Suharto and ushered in a period of significant risk to marketers and investors.

The political maneuverings of former president Boris Yeltsin's government in Russia similarly created a high level of political risk. Current president Vladimir Putin is implementing reforms in an effort to pave the way for Russia's membership in the WTO and to attract foreign investment. Thanks to high world oil prices, Russia's economy grew at an average rate of about 6.5 percent between 1998 and

Table 5-1
Categories of
Political Risk

EIU	BUSINESS ENVIRONMENT RISK INTELLIGENCE (BERI)	PRS GROUP WORLD POLITICAL RISK FORECASTS
War	Fractionalization of the political spectrum	Political Turmoil Probability
Social unrest	Fractionalization by language, ethnic, and/or religious groups	Equity Restrictions
Orderly political transfer	Restrictive/coercive measures required to retain power	Local Operations Restrictions
Politically motivated violence	Mentality (xenophobia, nationalism, corruption, nepotism)	Taxation Discrimination
International disputes	Social conditions (including population density and wealth distribution)	Repatriation Restrictions
Change in government/ pro-business orientation	Organization and strength of forces for a radical government	Exchange Controls
Institutional effectiveness	Dependence on and/or importance to a major hostile power	Tariff Barriers
Bureaucracy	Negative influences of regional political forces	Other Barriers
Transparency/fairness	Societal conflict involving demonstrations, strikes, and street violence	Payment Delays
Corruption	Instability as perceived by assassinations and guerilla war	Fiscal/Monetary Expansion
Crime		Labor Costs Foreign Debt

Source: Adapted from Llewellyn D. Howell, *The Handbook of Country and Political Risk Analysis,* 2d ed. (Syracuse, NY: PRS Group, 1998).

2001. The government has a number of bills pending that, if adopted, will strengthen intellectual property and contract law. Medium-term prospects for the transformation of the Russian market appear good. The current political climate in the rest of Central and Eastern Europe is still characterized by varying degrees of uncertainty. Hungary, Latvia, and Albania represent three different levels of risk. Hungary has already achieved upper-middle-income status. Latvia, a lower-middle-income country, is projected to grow slowly. Economic data for Albania are not even available. Diligent attention to risk assessment throughout the region should be ongoing to determine when the risk has decreased to levels acceptable to management.[3]

---

[3] A thoughtful, detailed discussion of potential political scenarios in Russia can be found in Daniel Yergin and Thane Gustafson, *Russia 2010 and What It Means for the World* (New York: Vintage Books, 1995).

Expressions and Symptoms of Political Risk

The level of political risk is inversely related to a country's stage of economic development: All other things being equal, the less developed a country, the greater the political risk (Figure 5-1). A number of symptoms can indicate possible increases in political risk. Currency depreciation is frequently accompanied by economic decline, which, in turn, churns up the political waters. In a country such as China with a nonconvertible currency, there is risk that the government will block repatriation of profit by foreign companies. The threat of civil disorder or ethnic conflict is also a symptom of political risk. Risk in the Triad and high-income countries, for example, is quite limited as compared with a country in low-middle-income and low-income categories.

Southeast Asia and Indonesia in particular illustrate how economic and political risk are intertwined. For the past 30 years, Southeast Asia was a paragon of political calm. Even the poorest countries in the region, like Indonesia, were stable because the Indonesians had accepted a single-party government and restrictions on freedom of expression and democracy in exchange for a government that promised economic growth. In Indonesia, everyone referred to President Suharto and his family as the Royal Family. Indonesians looked the other way at the clear evidence of cronyism and favoritism of the Suharto children. They remained silent about their lack of political freedom and choice. The reason is simple: They thought they were getting rich.

The economic collapse of Indonesia has changed all of that. Today, Indonesia is a country with a high degree of political risk. When Indonesians realized that they were not as rich as they thought, and that they were getting poorer under Suharto, they decided that they wanted more political expression. The old order (Suharto) was forced out of office, and a new era of political turmoil was launched. In the long term, the change is surely for the good; in the short term, where previously there had been calm and predictability, today there is great uncertainty.

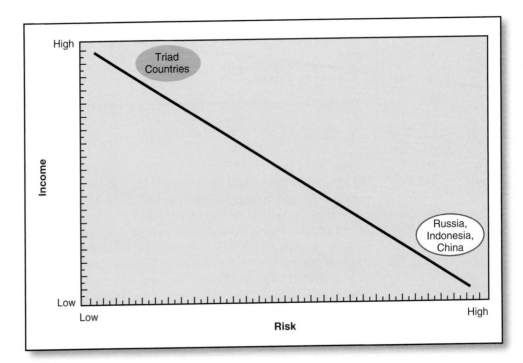

Figure 5-1
Income versus Political Risk

Part II   The Global Marketing Environment

Indonesian students sit with a defaced portrait of former Indonesian President Suharto in November 1998. Suharto was ousted in May 1998, following riots and protests, but many Indonesians still blame him for the country's ongoing troubles.

Because political risk cannot be accurately predicted, the corporate culture also must be considered when making a strategic decision. For the aggressive, entrepreneurial company wishing to make a minimum investment, a country with some political risk may have great market potential. For a conservative company or one considering a multimillion-dollar investment, the same country may have potential for a great market loss.

Companies can purchase insurance to offset potential risks arising from the political environment. In Japan, Germany, France, Britain, the United States, and other industrialized nations, various agencies offer investment insurance to corporations doing business abroad. The Overseas Private Investment Corporation (OPIC) provides various

Pepper . . . and Salt

THE WALL STREET JOURNAL

". . . it says, 'You will enjoy genetically modified rice.'"

Genetically Altered Crops
The Rest of the Story

In Europe, a number of activist groups, including Greenpeace and Friends of the Earth, have taken up the fight against GMOs. They claim that GMOs pose threats to both people and the environment; the general public, already cynical thanks to perceived governmental mishandling of the "mad cow" scare, has been receptive. As a result, a number of companies have changed their marketing strategies. In Great Britain, for example, Sainsbury and other grocery store chains responded to the labeling requirements by touting the fact that their "own-brand" (private label) products are GMO free. In an effort to avoid the possible stigma associated with GMO labeling, McDonald's, Pillsbury, and several other American companies doing business in Europe are eliminating altered ingredients from the processed food products they sell. By contrast, Swiss giant Nestlé is complying with the labeling law; a spokesperson noted that there has been "surprisingly little reaction to the labels in terms of sales figures." In the United States, Gerber and Heinz announced that they would strive to eliminate GMOs from their popular baby food products.

In the fall of 2000, StarLink, a brand of genetically-modified corn that was not approved for human consumption, was detected in taco shells sold at Taco Bell restaurants. The immediate concern was that StarLink might contain an allergen that would cause a reaction in some humans. Anticipating increasing awareness on the part of American consumers, Monsanto and other biotech companies have begun to work more closely with government regulators. The companies had already been supplying regulatory agencies with their research; now, the companies are advocating certain changes in the U.S. Food and Drug Administration's policies concerning GMOs. The FDA currently regards most modified crops as identical to conventional ones as long as there is no change in nutrient content or composition. The agribusiness companies are hoping that the FDA can help reassure consumers so that mandatory labeling along the lines of the European model won't be required. American companies are also frustrated by lengthy regulatory delays in Europe, where all 15 EU governments are involved in the process of approving new food products for sale to the public. A product is approved if a Qualified Majority is reached as a result of a weighted vote. At the European Commission itself, five separate directorates are involved in biotechnology issues, and two—DG Sanco and DG Environment—have responsibility for assessing the safety of the food supply.

Some biotech companies are presenting their case directly to consumers. Zeneca, a British chemical company, began distributing leaflets in supermarkets explaining the benefits of genetically altered crops. Meanwhile, in the summer of 1998, Monsanto launched an unusual advertising campaign in British and French newspapers. Featuring headlines such as "Qu'est-ce que la biotechnologie vegetale?", the ads encouraged consumers to directly contact advocacy groups such as Greenpeace. As Philip S. Angell, former director of corporate relations at Monsanto, said, "We believe the facts about biotechnology stand up under scrutiny. And we're ready to debate."

SOURCES: Scott Kilman, "Food Fright: Biotech Scare Sweeps Europe, and Companies Wonder if U.S. is Next," *The Wall Street Journal* (October 9, 1999), pp. A1, A15; Kilman, "Green Genes: If Fat-Free Pork is Your Idea of Savory, It's a Bright Future," *The Wall Street Journal* (January 29, 1998), pp. A1, A10; Clive Cookson, "Field of Genes," *Financial Times* (August 11, 1998), p. 10; Guy de Jonquieres, "One Man's Meat," *Financial Times* (April 15, 1998), p. 13.

types of political risk insurance to U.S. companies; in Canada, the Export Development Corporation performs a similar function. OPIC's activities came under scrutiny in 1997 when the Clinton administration proposed reauthorizing it, along with the Ex-Im Bank. Some legislators wanted to dismantle both agencies as part of an effort to reduce government involvement in business. These legislators criticized the agencies for providing unnecessary subsidies to large corporations.[4]

Visit the Web site
Learn more about OPIC
at: www.opic.gov

---

[4] Nancy Dunne, "Eximbank and Opic Face Survival Test in U.S." *Financial Times* (May 8, 1997), p. 8.

Taxes

Governments rely on tax revenues to generate funds necessary for social services, the military, and other expenditures. Unfortunately, government taxation policies on the sale of goods and services frequently motivate companies and individuals to profit by *not* paying taxes. In China, for example, most imports are subject to high duties, plus a 17 percent value-added tax. As a result, significant quantities of oil, cigarettes, photographic film, personal computers, and other products are smuggled into China. In some instances, customs documents are falsified to undercount goods in a shipment; the Chinese military has allegedly escorted goods into the country as well. Ironically, global companies can still profit from the practice; it has been estimated, for example, that 90 percent of the foreign cigarettes sold in China are smuggled in. For Philip Morris, this means annual sales of $100 million to distributors in Hong Kong, who then smuggle the smokes across the border.[5] High excise and VAT taxes can also encourage legal cross-border shopping as consumers go abroad in search of good values. In Great Britain, for example, the Wine and Spirit Association estimates that, on average, cars returning from France are loaded with 80 bottles of wine.

Corporate taxation is another issue. The high level of political risk currently evident in Russia can be attributed in part to excessively high taxes on business operations. High taxes encourage many enterprises to engage in cash or barter transactions that are off the books and sheltered from the eyes of tax authorities. This, in turn, has created a liquidity squeeze that prevents companies from paying wages to employees. Needless to say, unpaid, disgruntled workers can contribute to political instability. Meanwhile, the Putin government is pursuing a tough new tax policy in an effort to shrink Russia's budget deficit and qualify for IMF loans. However, such policies should not have the effect of deterring foreign investment. As Bruce Bean, head of the American Chamber of Commerce in Moscow, recently summed up the situation:

> Change the name of the country, change the flag, change the border. Yes, this was done overnight. But build a market economy, introduce a meaningful tax system, create new accounting rules, accept the concept that companies which cannot compete should go bankrupt and the workers there lose their jobs? These things take time.[6]

Meanwhile, global companies are being caught up in the chaos. In July 1998, tax collectors seized 89 automobiles belonging to Johnson & Johnson's Russian division and froze the group's assets. The authorities claimed J&J owed $19 million in back taxes.

The diverse geographical activity of the global corporation also requires special attention to tax laws. Many companies make efforts to minimize their tax liability by shifting the location of income. For example, it has been estimated that tax minimization by foreign companies doing business in the United States costs the U.S. government $3 billion each year in lost revenue. In one approach, called "earnings stripping," foreign companies reduce earnings by making loans to U.S. affiliates rather than using direct investment to finance U.S. activities. The U.S. subsidiary can deduct the interest it pays on such loans and thereby reduce its tax burden.

Seizure of Assets

The ultimate threat a government can pose toward a company is seizing assets. *Expropriation* refers to governmental action to dispossess a foreign company or investor. Compensation is generally provided, although not often in the "prompt, effective, and adequate" manner provided for by international standard. If no compensation is provided, the action is referred to as *confiscation*.[7] International law is generally interpreted as prohibiting any act by a government to take foreign property without compensation. *Nationalization* is generally broader in scope than expropriation; it occurs when the government takes control of some or all of the enterprises in a particular industry. International law recognizes nationalization as a

---

5   Craig S. Smith and Wayne Arnold, "China's Antismuggling Drive to Hurt U.S. Exporters that Support Crackdown," *The Wall Street Journal* (August 5, 1998), p. A12.

6   Andrew Higgins, "Go Figure: At Russian Companies, Hard Numbers Often Hard to Come By," *The Wall Street Journal* (August 20, 1998), p. A9.

7   Franklin R. Root, *Entry Strategies for International Markets* (New York: Lexington Books, 1994), p. 154.

legitimate exercise of government power, as long as the act satisfies a "public purpose" and is accompanied by "adequate payment" (i.e., one that reflects fair market value of the property). In 1959, for example, the newly-empowered Castro government nationalized property belonging to American sugar producers in retaliation for new American import quotas on sugar. Cuban-owned production sources were not nationalized. Castro offered compensation in the form of Cuban government bonds, which was adequate under Cuban law. The U.S. State Department viewed the particular act of nationalization as discriminatory and the compensation offered as inadequate.[8] More recently, South Korea nationalized Kia, the nation's number three automaker, in the wake of the Asian currency crisis. In 1998, the Japanese government was debating whether or not to nationalize the country's banking system.

Short of outright expropriation or nationalization, the phrase *creeping expropriation* has been applied to limitations on economic activities of foreign firms in particular countries. These have included limitations on repatriation of profits, dividends, royalties, and technical assistance fees from local investments or technology arrangements. Other issues are increased local content requirements, quotas for hiring local nationals, price controls, and other restrictions affecting return on investment. Global companies have also suffered discriminatory tariffs and nontariff barriers that limit market entry of certain industrial and consumer goods, as well as discriminatory laws on patents and trademarks. Intellectual property restrictions have had the practical effect of eliminating or drastically reducing protection of pharmaceutical products.

In April 1997, for example, the Canadian government banned a gasoline additive known as MMT. The U.S.-based Ethyl Corporation is the world's sole manufacturer of MMT. Ethyl sued the Canadian government for $231 million, citing the "expropriation and compensation" rule in the NAFTA agreement. In essence, Ethyl claimed that the Canadian government's ban had the effect of restricting Ethyl's ability to make a profit and thus constituted an expropriation of assets.

In the mid-1970s, Johnson & Johnson and other foreign investors in India had to submit to a host of government regulations to retain majority equity positions in companies already established. Many of these rules were later copied in whole or in part by Malaysia, Indonesia, the Philippines, Nigeria, and Brazil. By the late 1980s, after a "lost decade" in Latin America characterized by debt crises and low GNP growth, lawmakers reversed many of these restrictive and discriminatory laws. The goal was to again attract foreign direct investment and badly needed Western technology. The end of the Cold War and restructuring of political allegiances contributed significantly to these changes.

When governments expropriate foreign property, there are impediments to action to reclaim that property. For example, according to the U.S. Act of State Doctrine, if the government of a foreign state is involved in a specific act, the U.S. court will not get involved. Representatives of expropriated companies may seek recourse through arbitration at the World Bank Investment Dispute Settlement Center. It is also possible to buy expropriation insurance from either a private company or a government agency such as OPIC. The expropriation of copper companies operating in Chile in 1970 to 1971 shows the impact that companies can have on their own fate. Companies that strenuously resisted government efforts to introduce home-country nationals into the company management were expropriated outright;

---

8   William R. Slomanson, *Fundamental Perspectives on International Law* (St. Paul: West Publishing, 1990), p. 356.

Many countries attempt to exercise control over the transfer of goods, services, money, people, technology, and rights across their borders. Historically, an important control motive was economic: The goal was to generate revenue by levying tariffs and duties. Today, policymakers have additional motives for controlling cross-border flows, including protection of local industry and fostering the development of local enterprise. Such policies are known as protectionism, or economic nationalism.

Differing economic and political goals and different value systems are the primary reasons for protectionism. The barriers that exist between the United States and Cuba, for example, exist because of major differences between the values and objectives of the two countries. Many barriers based upon different political systems have come down with the end of the Cold War. However, barriers based upon different value systems continue. The world's farmers—be they Japanese, European, or American—are committed to getting as much protection as possible from their respective governments. Because of the political influence of the farm lobby in every country, and in spite of the efforts of trade negotiators to open up agricultural markets, controls on trade in agricultural products continue to distort economic efficiency. Such controls work against the driving forces of economic integration.

The price of protection can be very high, for two basic reasons. The first is the cost to consumers: When foreign producers are presented with barriers rather than free access to a market, the result is higher prices for domestic consumers and a reduction in their standard of living. The second cost is the impact on the competitiveness of domestic companies. Companies that are protected from competition may lack the motivation to create and sustain world-class competitive advantage. One of the greatest stimuli to competitiveness is the open market. When a company faces world competition it must figure out how to serve a niche market better than any company in the world, or it must figure out how to compete in face-to-face competition.

Located in The Hague, the International Court of Justice (ICJ) is the judicial arm of the United Nations. The court's 15 judges are elected to nine-year terms. The primary function of the ICJ is to settle disputes among different countries according to international law. The ICJ also offers advice on legal issues submitted by various international agencies.

other companies that made genuine efforts to follow Chilean guidelines were allowed to remain under joint Chilean-U.S. management.

International Law

International law may be defined as the rules and principles that nation-states consider binding upon themselves. International law pertains to property, trade, immigration, and other areas that have traditionally been under the jurisdiction of individual nations. International law applies only to the extent that countries are willing to assume all rights and obligations in these areas. The roots of modern international law can be traced back to the seventeenth-century Peace of Westphalia. Early international law was concerned with waging war, establishing peace, and other political issues such as diplomatic recognition of new national entities and governments. Although elaborate international rules gradually emerged—covering, for example, the status of neutral nations—the creation of laws governing commerce proceeded on a state-by-state basis in the nineteenth century. International law still has the function of upholding order, although in a broader sense than dealing with problems arising from war. At first, international law was essentially an amalgam of treaties, covenants, codes, and agreements. As trade grew among nations, order in commercial affairs assumed increasing importance. The law had originally dealt only with nations as entities, but a growing body of law rejected the idea that only nations can be subject to international law.

Paralleling the expanding body of international case law in the twentieth century, new international judiciary organizations have contributed to the creation of an established rule of international law: The Permanent Court of International Justice (1920–1945); the International Court of Justice (ICJ), the judicial arm of the United Nations, founded in 1946; and the International Law Commission, established by the United States in 1947. Disputes arising between nations are issues of *public international law,* and they may be taken before the World Court, located in the Hague, or the ICJ. As described in the supplemental documents to the United Nations Charter, article 38 of the ICJ Statute concerns international law:

> The Court, whose function is to decide in accordance with international law such disputes as are submitted to it, shall apply:
> a. international conventions, whether general or particular, establishing rules expressly recognized by the contesting states;
> b. international custom, as evidence of a general practice accepted as law;
> c. the general principles of law recognized by civilized nations;
> d. subject to the provisions of Article 59, judicial decisions and the teachings of the most highly qualified publicists of the various nations, as subsidiary means for the determination of rules of law.

Visit the Web site
The International Court of Justice can be accessed via the United Nations homepage, or directly at: www.icj-cij.org.

Other sources of modern international law include treaties, international custom, judicial case decisions in the courts of law of various nations, and scholarly writings. What happens if a nation has allowed a case against it to be brought before the International Court of Justice and then refuses to accept a judgment against it? The plaintiff nation can seek recourse through the United Nations Security Council, which can use its full range of powers to enforce the judgment.

Common Law versus Civil Law

Private international law is the body of law that applies to disputes arising from commercial transactions between companies of different nations. As noted, laws governing commerce emerged gradually, leading to a major split in legal systems between various countries.[9] The story of law in the Western world can be traced to two sources: Rome, from which the continental European civil law tradition originated, and English common law, from which the U.S. legal system originated.

A civil-law country is one in which the legal system reflects the structural concepts and principles of the Roman Empire in the sixth century.

> For complex historical reasons, Roman law was received differently and at vastly different times in various regions of Europe, and in the nineteenth century each European country made a new start and adopted its own set of national private-law codes, for which the *Code Napoleon* of 1804 was the prototype. But the new national codes drew largely on Roman law in conceptual structure and substantive content. In civil-law countries, the codes in which private law is cast are formulated in broad general terms and are thought of as completely comprehensive, that is, as the all-inclusive source of authority by reference to which every disputed case must be referred for decision.[10]

In common-law countries, many disputes are decided by reliance on the authority of past judicial decisions (cases). Although much of contemporary American and English law is legislative in origin, the law inferred from past judicial decisions is equal in importance to the law set down in codes. Common-law countries often rely on codification in certain areas—the U.S. Uniform Commercial Code is one example—but these codes are not the all-inclusive, systematic statements found in civil-law countries.

The Uniform Commercial Code, fully adopted by 49 U.S. states, codifies a body of specifically designed rules covering commercial conduct. (Louisiana has adopted parts of the UCC, but its laws are still heavily influenced by the French civil code.) The host country's legal system—that is, common or civil law—directly affects the form a legal business entity will take. In common-law countries, companies are legally incorporated by state authority. In civil-law countries, companies are formed by contract between two or more parties, who are fully liable for the actions of the company.

The United States, nine of Canada's ten provinces, and other former colonies with an Anglo-Saxon history, founded their systems on common law. Historically, much of continental Europe was influenced by Roman law and, later, the Napoleonic Code. Asian countries are split: India, Pakistan, Malaysia, Singapore, and Hong Kong are common-law jurisdictions. Japan, Korea, Thailand, Indochina, Taiwan, Indonesia, and China are civil-law jurisdictions. The legal systems in Scandinavia are mixed, displaying some civil-law attributes and some common-law attributes. Today, the majority of countries have legal systems based on civil-law traditions.

As various countries in Eastern and Central Europe wrestle with establishing legal systems in the post-Communist era, a struggle of sorts has broken out; consultants representing both common-law and civil-law countries are trying to influence the process. In much of Central Europe, including Poland, Hungary, and the Czech Republic, the German civil-law tradition prevails. As a result, banks not only take deposits and make loans but also engage in the buying and selling of securities. In Eastern Europe—particularly Russia—the United States has had greater influence. Germany has accused the United States of promoting a system so complex that it requires legions of lawyers. The U.S. response is that the German system is out-

---

[9] Much of the material in this section is adapted from Randall Kelso and Charles D. Kelso, *Studying Law: An Introduction* (St. Paul: West Publishing, 1984).

[10] Harry Jones, "Our Uncommon Common Law," *Tennessee Law Review* 30 (1975), p. 447.

Napoleon's code of 1804 was the prototype for the code-law system that predominates in Europe today.

dated.[11] In any event, the constant stream of laws and decrees issued by the Russian government creates an unpredictable, evolving legal environment. Specialized publications such as *The Russian and Commonwealth Business Law Report* are important resources for anyone doing business in Russia or the CIS.

Islamic Law

The legal system in many Middle Eastern countries is identified with the laws of Islam, which are associated with "the one and only one God, the Almighty."[12] In Islamic law, the *sharia* is a comprehensive code governing Muslim conduct in all areas of life, including business. The code is derived from two sources. First is the Koran, the Holy Book written in Arabic that is a record of the revelations made to the Prophet Mohammed by Allah. The second source is the Hadith, which is based on the life, sayings, and practices of Muhammad. In particular, the Hadith spells out the products and practices that are *haram* ("forbidden"). The orders and instructions found in the Koran are analogous to code laws; the guidelines of the Hadith correspond to common law. Any Westerner doing business in Malaysia in the Middle East should have, at minimum, a rudimentary understanding of Islamic law and its

---

[11] Mark M. Nelson, "Two Styles of Business Vie in East Europe," *The Wall Street Journal* (April 3, 1995), p. A14.

[12] This section is adapted from Mushtaq Luqmani, Ugur Yavas, and Zahir Quraeshi, "Advertising in Saudi Arabia: Content and Regulation," *International Marketing Review* 6, no. 1 (1989), pp. 61–63.

In 1995, the OECD began talks on a new initiative known as the Multilateral Agreement on Investment (MAI) that will set rules for foreign investment and provide a forum for dispute settlement. In some countries, so-called "performance requirements" favor local investors over foreigners. For example, foreign companies may be required to obtain some goods and services from local companies rather than the home office. Performance requirements can also take the form of stipulations that a certain number of senior managers must be local nationals or that the foreign company must export a set percentage of its production.

The existence of the MAI negotiations remained largely unknown to the general public until a Canadian consumer rights group obtained the text of MAI and posted it on the Internet. In fact, a large number of consumer and environmentalist action groups have joined in opposition to the agreement. As Mark A. Vallianatos, an international policy analyst at Friends of the Earth, explained:

> Our fear is that MAI will give multinational corporations the opportunity to treat the whole world as their raw pool of natural resources and labor and consumer markets. It may allow them to do everything based on profit motives without environmental considerations providing sensible limits on how they operate. MAI gives new rights to corporations without addressing their responsibilities to workers and the environment. . . An MAI that is worth

doing should deal with how investments will affect sustainable development, how they will affect workers' rights, and how they will affect excessive resource extraction—those kinds of issues.

Some industry experts downplay MAI's potential to contribute to environmental degradation. R. Garrity Baker, senior director at the Chemical Manufacturers Association, says, "When foreign companies that have better environmental performance come in and invest in a market bring that know-how with them, then over time that know-how kind of trickles down to other companies. Foreign companies set an example that others can learn from." MAI supporters also point out that the agreement allows countries to adopt any measure deemed appropriate to ensure investment is undertaken in a manner that reflects sensitivity to environmental issues. As of mid-1998, prospects for MAI approval in the United States were clouded by disagreements between key Washington agencies that might be affected by the agreement's provisions. The U.S. State Department and Commerce Department are generally supportive, but the Environmental Protection Agency, the U.S. Agency for International Development, and the Justice Department are concerned that MAI will lead to a rash of lawsuits against the United States. At the state level, a number of governors felt that MAI would impinge on state sovereignty.

SOURCES: Bette Hileman, "A Globalization Conundrum," *Chemical & Engineering News* (April 20, 1998), p. 45; "Bye-bye, MAI?" *Financial Times* (February 19, 1998), p. 13.

---

implications for commercial activities. Brewers, for example, must refrain from advertising beer on billboards or in local-language newspapers.

Sidestepping Legal Problems: Important Business Issues

Clearly, the global legal environment is very dynamic and complex. Therefore, the best course to follow is to get expert legal help. However, the astute, proactive marketer can do a great deal to prevent conflicts from arising in the first place, especially concerning issues such as establishment, jurisdiction, patents and trademarks, antitrust, licensing and trade secrets, bribery, and advertising and other promotion tools. Regulation of specific promotion activities is discussed in Chapters 14 and 15.

Jurisdiction
Company personnel working abroad should understand the extent to which they are subject to the jurisdiction of host-country courts. Employees of foreign companies

working in the United States must understand that courts have jurisdiction to the extent that the company can be demonstrated to be doing business in the state in which the court sits. The court may examine whether the foreign company maintains an office, solicits business, maintains bank accounts or other property, or has agents or other employees in the state in question. In a recent case, Revlon sued United Overseas Limited (UOL) in U.S. District Court for the Southern District of New York. Revlon charged the British company with breach of contract, contending that UOL had failed to purchase some specialty shampoos as agreed. Claiming lack of jurisdiction, UOL asked the court to dismiss the complaint. Revlon countered with the argument that UOL was, in fact, subject to the court's jurisdiction; Revlon cited the presence of a UOL sign above the entrance to the offices of a New York company in which UOL had a 50 percent ownership interest. The court denied UOL's motion to dismiss.[13]

Jurisdiction played an important role in two recent trade-related disputes. One pitted Volkswagen AG against General Motors. After GM's world-wide head of purchasing, José Ignacio López de Arriortúa, was hired by Volkswagen in 1992, his former employer accused him of taking trade secrets. Volkswagen accepted U.S. court jurisdiction in the dispute, although the company's lawyers requested that the U.S. District Court in Detroit transfer the case to Germany. Jurisdiction was also an issue in a trade dispute that pitted Eastman Kodak against Fuji Photo Film. Kodak alleged that the Japanese government helped Fuji in Japan by blocking the distribution of Kodak film. The U.S. government turned the case over to the World Trade Organization, despite the opinion expressed by many experts that the WTO lacks jurisdiction in complaints over trade and competition policy.

Intellectual Property: Patents, Trademarks, and Copyrights

Patents and trademarks that are protected in one country are not necessarily protected in another, so global marketers must ensure that patents and trademarks are registered in each country where business is conducted. A **patent** is a formal legal document that gives an inventor the exclusive right to make, use, and sell an invention for a specified period of time. Typically, the invention represents an "inventive leap" that is "novel" or "nonobvious." A **trademark** is defined as a distinctive mark, motto, device, or emblem that a manufacturer affixes to a particular product or package to distinguish it from goods produced by other manufacturers. A **copyright** establishes ownership of a written, recorded, performed, or filmed creative work.

Infringement of intellectual property can take a variety of forms. **Counterfeiting** is the unauthorized copying and production of a product. An *associative counterfeit*, or *imitation*, uses a product name that differs slightly from a well-known brand but is close enough that consumers will associate it with the genuine product. A third type of counterfeiting is *piracy*, the unauthorized publication or reproduction of copyrighted work. Counterfeiting and piracy are particularly important in industries such as motion pictures, recorded music, computer software, and textbook publishing. Companies in these industries produce products that can be easily duplicated and distributed on a mass basis. The United States in particular has a vested interest in intellectual property protection around the globe because it is home to many companies in the industries just mentioned. However, the United States faces significant challenges in countries such as China. As one expert has noted:

---

[13] Joseph Ortego and Josh Kardisch, "Foreign Companies Can Limit the Risk of Being Subject to U.S. Courts," *National Law Journal* 17, no. 3 (September 19, 1994), p. C2.

Current attempts to establish intellectual property law, particularly on the Chinese mainland, have been deeply flawed in their failure to address the difficulties of reconciling legal values, institutions, and forms generated in the West with the legacy of China's past and the constraints imposed by its present circumstances.[14]

Case 5-1 at the end of this chapter describes some of the problems companies encounter as they try to enforce trademarks around the world.

In the United States, where patents, trademarks, and copyrights are registered with the Federal Patent Office, the patent holder retains all rights for the life of the patent even if the product is not produced or sold. Patent and trademark protection in the United States is very good, and U.S. law relies on the precedent of previously decided court cases for guidance. To register a patent in Europe, a company has the option of filing on a country-by-country basis or applying to the European Patent Office in Munich for patent registration in a specific number of countries. A third option will soon be available: The Community Patent Convention will offer a single patent valid throughout the European Union. Patent procedures in Europe are quite expensive, in part because of the cost of translating technical documents into all the languages of the EU countries.[15] In July 1997, in response to complaints, the European Patent Office instituted a 19 percent reduction in the average cost of an eight-country patent registration. Trademarks in the United States are covered by the Trademark Act of 1946, also known as the Lanham Act. President Reagan signed the

In China, Russia, and many other countries, pirated CDs and video-cassettes are on open display in kiosks and street markets. Sometimes new movies become available mere weeks after their theatrical release in the West.

---

[14] William P. Alford, *To Steal a Book is an Elegant Offense: Intellectual Property Law in Chinese Civilization* (Stanford, California: Stanford University Press, 1995), p. 2.
[15] Frances Williams, "Call for Stronger EU Patent Laws," *Financial Times* (May 22, 1997).

This print advertisement from Germany serves as a humorous reminder that anyone who buys fake Levi's is unwittingly supporting the ill-gotten lifestyles of unsavory characters.

WARNUNG!

DIESE tYPEN WERDEN REICH MIT GEFÄLSCHTEN LEVI'S.

sagt nicht wiR hätten Euch nicht gewarnt.

echte Levi's gibt's in laden mit diesem zeichen.

Trademark Law Revision Act into law in November 1988. The law makes it easier for companies to register new trademarks.

Companies sometimes find ways to exploit loopholes or other unique opportunities offered by patent and trademark laws in individual nations. In France, designer Yves St. Laurent was barred from marketing a new luxury perfume called Champagne because French laws allow the name to be applied only to sparkling wines produced in the Champagne region. St. Laurent proceeded to launch Champagne in the United States, Great Britain, Germany, and Belgium where Champagne and other geographic names are not protected trademarks. In France, the perfume is sold without a name.[16] In 1992, Germany's Bayer AG received permission from Russia's patent office to register *aspirin* as a trademark in that country. Rival pharmaceutical companies, such as France's Laboratoire UPSA, were infuriated because the ruling meant that they would effectively be shut out of the Russian market of 150 million people. According to a spokesperson for the French company, "The word never should have been registered in the first place. It's a universally accepted generic name." In June 1994, the Russian patent office rescinded permission; Bayer immediately announced its intention to appeal.[17]

International concern about intellectual property issues in the nineteenth century resulted in two important agreements. The first is the International Convention for the Protection of Industrial Property. Also known as the Paris Union or Paris Convention, the convention dates to 1883 and is now honored by nearly 100 countries. This treaty facilitates multicountry patent registrations by ensuring that, once a company files in a signatory country, it will be afforded a "right of priority" in other countries for one year from the date of the original filing. A U.S. company wishing to obtain foreign patent rights must apply to the Paris Union within one year of filing in the United States or

---

[16] Karla Vermeulen, "Champagne Perfume Launched in United States but Barred in France," *Wine Spectator* (October 31, 1994), p. 9.

[17] Marya Fogel, "Bayer Trademarks the Word 'Aspirin' in Russia, Leaving Rivals Apoplectic," *The Wall Street Journal* (October 29, 1993), p. A13.

risk a permanent loss of patent rights abroad.[18] In 1886, the International Union for the Protection of Literary and Artistic Property was formed. Also known as the Berne Convention, this was a landmark agreement on copyright protection.

Two other treaties deserve mention. The Patent Cooperation Treaty (PCT) has 39 signatories, including Australia, Brazil, France, Germany, Japan, North Korea, South Korea, the Netherlands, Switzerland, the former Soviet Union, and the United States. The members constitute a union that provides certain technical services and cooperates in the filing, searching, and examination of patent applications in all member countries. The European Patent Office administers applications for the European Patent Convention, which is effective in the EU and Switzerland. An applicant can file a single patent application covering all of the convention states; the advantage is that the application will be subject to only one procedure of grant. Although national patent laws remain effective under this system, approved patents are effective in all member countries for a period of 20 years from the filing date.

In recent years, the U.S. government has devoted considerable diplomatic effort to improving the worldwide environment for intellectual property protection. For example, China agreed to accede to the Berne Convention in 1992; on January 1, 1994, China became an official signatory of the PCT. After years of discussion, the United States and Japan have agreed to make changes in their respective patent systems; Japan has promised to speed up patent examinations, eliminate challenges to patent submissions, and allow patent applications to be filed in English. Effective June 7, 1995, in accordance with GATT, new U.S. patents are granted for a period of 20 years from the filing date. Previously, patents had been valid for a 17-year term effective after being granted. Thus, U.S. patent laws now harmonize with those in the EU as well as Japan. Even with the changes, however, patents in Japan are narrower than those in the United States. As a result, companies such as Caterpillar have been unable to protect critical innovations in Japan because products very similar to those made by U.S. companies can be patented without fear of infringement.[19] Another key issue is global patent protection for software. Although copyright laws protect the computer code, it does not apply to the idea embodied in the software. The U.S. Patent and Trademark Office has extended patent protection to software since 1981; Microsoft has more than 500 software patents. In Europe, software patents were not allowed under the Munich Convention; in June 1997, however, the EU indicated it was ready to revise patent laws so they cover software.[20] Table 5-2 ranks the ten companies that received the most U.S. patents in 2000. Note that five of the ten are Japanese companies.

Antitrust

Antitrust laws in the United States and other countries are designed to combat restrictive business practices and to encourage competition. The laws are enforced by agencies such as the U.S. Federal Trade Commission, Japan's Fair Trade Commission, and the European Commission. Some legal experts believe that the pressures of global competition have resulted in an increased incidence of price-fixing and collusion among companies. As FTC chairman Robert Pitofsky said recently, "For years, tariffs and trade barriers blocked global trade. Now those are falling, and we are forced to confront the private anticompetitive behavior that often remains."[21]

---

[18] Franklin R. Root, *Entry Strategies for International Markets* (New York: Lexington Books, 1994), p. 113.

[19] John Carey, "Inching toward a Borderless Patent," *Business Week* (September 5, 1994), p. 35.

[20] Richard Pynder, "Intellectual Property in Need of Protection," *Financial Times* (July 7, 1998), p. 22.

[21] John R. Wilke, "Hunting Cartels: U.S. Trust-Busters Increasingly Target International Business," *The Wall Street Journal* (February 5, 1997), p. A10.

Table 5-2

Companies Receiving the Most U.S. Patents, 2000

COMPANY	NO. OF PATENTS
1. IBM	2,922
2. NEC	2,034
3. Canon	1,897
4. Samsung Electronics	1,442
5. Lucent Technologies	1,415
6. Sony	1,394
7. Micron Technology	1,306
8. Toshiba	1,264
9. Motorola	1,203
10. Fujitsu	1,169

Source: U.S. Department of Commerce and IFI Claims Patent Services.

A recent rash of antitrust actions brought in the United States against foreign companies has raised concerns that the United States is violating international law as well as the sovereignty of other nations. The U.S. antitrust laws are a legacy of the nineteenth-century trust-busting era and are intended to maintain free competition by limiting the concentration of economic power. The Sherman Act of 1890 prohibits certain restrictive business practices, including fixing prices, limiting production, allocating markets, or any other scheme designed to limit or avoid competition. The law applies to the activities of U.S. companies outside U.S. boundaries, as well as to foreign companies conducting business in the United States. In a recent precedent-setting case, Nippon Paper Industries was found guilty in a U.S. court of conspiring with other Japanese companies to raise fax paper prices in the United States. The Japanese government denounced the U.S. indictment of Nippon Paper in December 1995 as a violation of international law and Japan's sovereignty. The meetings at which pricing strategies were allegedly discussed took place outside the United States; a U.S. federal judge struck down the indictment, ruling that the Sherman Act does not apply to foreign conduct. However, a federal appeals court in Boston reversed the decision. In his opinion, U.S. Circuit Judge Bruce Selya wrote, "We live in an age of international commerce, where decisions reached in one corner of the world can reverberate around the globe."[22]

Although similar antitrust laws are on the books in many countries, they are often weak or loosely enforced. In the fall of 1996, the OECD began working on an agreement to coordinate antitrust laws. Meanwhile, antitrust is taking on increasing importance in emerging country markets. For example, Colgate-Palmolive's 1995 acquisition of Brazil's Kolynos oral care company for $1 billion was subject to review by that country's Administrative Council of Economic Defense (Cade). Rival Procter & Gamble instigated the review by complaining that the acquisition would give Colgate a 79 percent share of the market. Cade ruled that Colgate must either license the trademark to another company for 20 years or halt sales of Kolynos brand toothpaste in Brazil for four years; Colgate agreed to the latter. The Miller Brewing unit of

---

[22] John R. Wilke, "U.S. Court Rules Antitrust Laws Apply to Foreigners," *The Wall Street Journal* (March 19, 1997), p. B5.

Philip Morris also ran into antitrust problems in Brazil following its 1995 investment of $50 million in a 50/50 joint venture with Cia. Cervejaria Brahma Cade ruled that the venture, which produced and distributed Miller Genuine Draft beer, deprived consumers of head-to-head competition between the two brewing companies. Cade also criticized Miller for choosing a market entry strategy that required a relatively low level of investment. Nelio Weiss, a consultant at Coopers & Lybrand's Sao Paulo office, noted, "The message is that foreign companies shouldn't assume that antitrust authorities will be passive."[23]

For the past four decades, the competition authority of the European Commission has had the power to prohibit agreements and practices that prevent, restrict, and distort competition. The commission has jurisdiction over European-based companies as well as non-European ones such as Microsoft that generate significant revenues in Europe. For example, the commission can block a proposed merger or joint venture, approve it with only minor modifications, or demand substantial concessions before granting approval. The commission begins with a preliminary study of a proposed deal; serious concerns can lead to an in-depth investigation lasting several months. Since the mid-1990s, the commission has taken an increasingly activist approach. The current competition minister is Mario Monti, an Italian with an economics background. Nicknamed "Super Mario" by the European press, Monti blocked the proposed merger of WorldCom and Sprint in 2000. He also demanded major concessions before allowing America Online to acquire Time Warner.[24] There have been calls for the EU to revamp its approach to antitrust issues and reduce its caseload. Any proposed changes will pit modernists against traditionalists. As one European attorney complained, "The commission is putting resources into regulating cases that don't actually restrict competition, which means that the cases that do need to be looked at are not being resolved efficiently."[25] Table 5-3 summarizes some recent joint ventures, mergers, and other global business deals that have been subject to review by antitrust authorities on both sides of the Atlantic.

The interstate trade clause of the Treaty of Rome applies to trade with third countries, so that a company must be aware of the conduct of its affiliates. The commission also exempts certain cartels from Articles 85 and 86 of the treaty in an effort to encourage the growth of important businesses. The intent is to allow European companies to compete on an equal footing with Japan and the United States. In some instances, individual country laws in Europe apply to specific marketing mix elements. For example, some countries permit selective or exclusive product distribution. However, European Community law can take precedence.

In one case, Consten, a French company, had exclusive French rights to import and distribute consumer electronics products from the German Grundig company. Consten sued another French firm, charging the latter with bringing "parallel imports" into France illegally. That is, Consten charged that the competitor bought Grundig products from various foreign suppliers without Consten's knowledge and was selling them in France. Although Consten's complaint was upheld by two French courts, the Paris Court of Appeals suspended the judgment, pending a ruling by the European Commission on whether the Grundig-Consten arrangement violated Articles 85 and 86 of the Treaty of Rome. The commission ruled against Consten

---

23 Yumiko Ono, "Colgate Purchase Gets Brazil's Blessing But with Restrictions on Brand Name," *The Wall Street Journal* (September 20, 1996), p. A11; Matt Moffett, "Miller Brewing is Ordered to Sell Its Stake in Brazilian Joint Venture," *The Wall Street Journal* (June 13, 1997), p. A15.

24 Anita Raghavan and Brandon Mitchener, " 'Super Mario': EU's Antitrust Czar Isn't Afraid to Say No; Just Ask Time Warner," *The Wall Street Journal* (October 2, 2000), pp. A1, A10.

25 Emma Tucker, "Europe's Paper Mountain," *Financial Times* (February 11, 1998), p. 213.

Table 5-3
Antitrust
Investigations

COMPANIES INVOLVED	ANTITRUST REVIEW IN EU	ANTITRUST REVIEW IN USA
Acquisition of Honeywell (USA) by GE (USA), 2001, $40 billion	Deal was vetoed on grounds that merged firm would be stronger than competitors in aviation equipment	Deal was on track for approval, subject to conditions
Joint venture between music businesses of EMI Group PLC (Great Britain) and Time Warner (USA), 2000, $20 billion	Regulators expressed concern that the new EMI-Time Warner would dominate growing market for digital music distribution	Deal was scrapped in October 2000 before regulatory review began
Merger of WorldCom (USA) and MCI (USA), 1998, $37 billion	MCI ordered to divest all Internet-related assets	U.S. concerns were incorporated into review by EU, which occurred first; EU's terms were acceptable to Federal Communications Commission and Department of Justice
Strategic alliance between British Airways (UK) and American Airlines (USA), 1998	Commission required the two carriers to give up 267 weekly slot's at London's Heathrow Airport	Washington has demanded an "open skies" agreement with the UK allowing U.S. carriers other than United and American to fly into Heathrow
Acquisition of Random House Inc. (USA) by Bertelsmann AG (Germany); proposed 1997, approved 1998, $1.5 billion	Approved	Approved after delay by Federal Trade Commission
Merger of Boeing (USA) and McDonnell Douglas (USA), 1997, $14 billion	Contentious review process. EU required significant concessions, including non-enforcement of two-year "sole-supplier" contracts with three U.S. carriers	Approved merger without conditions, although FTC found the sole supplier contracts "potentially troubling"
Merger of Guinness (UK) and Grand Metropolitan PLC (UK), 1997, $19.3 billion	Partners required to divest several brands of spirits	Required sale of Dewars scotch whisky, Bombay Sapphire and Original gin brands
Merger of Sandoz (Switzerland) and Ciba-Geigy (Switzerland), 1996, $27 billion	Approved with little modification	FTC required new entity to freely license gene-therapy technology

Source: Compiled by the authors.

on the grounds that "territorial protection proved to be particularly damaging to the realization of the Common Market."[26]

A major antitrust case involving a U.S.-based global company pitted the European Community against IBM during the 1970s and 1980s. IBM was the European market leader in mainframe computers such as the powerful System 370 with 55 percent unit share in 1983. The company's operations were especially strong in Great Britain, France, and West Germany. IBM was charged with four specific violations of Article 86: failure to supply competitors with timely information about interfaces; selling computers without including memory capacity in the price; selling computers without software necessary to operate them; and refusing to supply IBM software to companies that used competing brands of computers. Coincidentally, the U.S. Justice Department had also filed an antitrust case against IBM in the United States with the aim of breaking up the company (the suit was dropped in 1982 after 14 years of litigation). The EC action, however, was an attempt to force IBM to disclose proprietary designs and other trade secrets of benefit to European companies that were IBM suppliers.[27] More recently, Microsoft was the object of antitrust investigations in both the United States and Europe.

In some instances, companies or entire industries have been able to secure exemption from antitrust rules. In the airline industry, for example, KLM and Northwestern won an exemption from the U.S. government and now share computer codes and set prices jointly. Similarly, the European Commission permitted United International Pictures (UIP), a joint venture between Paramount, Universal, and MGM/UA, to cut costs by collaborating on motion picture distribution in Europe. In 1998, the Commission reversed itself and notified the three studios that they must distribute their films independently in Europe.[28] A **cartel** is a group of separate companies that collectively set prices, control output, or take other actions to maximize profits. For example, the group of oil producing countries known as OPEC is a cartel. In the United States, most cartels are illegal. One notable exception, however, has a direct impact on global marketing. A number of the world's major shipping lines, including the U.S.-based Sea-Land Service and Denmark's A. P. Moller/Maersk line, have enjoyed exemption from antitrust laws since the passage of the Shipping Act of 1916. The law was originally enacted to ensure reliability; today, it has been estimated that the cartel results in shipping prices that are 18 percent higher than they would be if shippers set prices independently. Attempts in recent years to change the law have not been successful.[29]

Licensing and Trade Secrets

Licensing is a contractual agreement in which a licensor allows a licensee to use patents, trademarks, trade secrets, technology, or other intangible assets in return for royalty payments or other forms of compensation. U.S. laws do not regulate the licensing process per se as do technology transfer laws in the European Union, Australia, Japan, and many developing countries. The duration of the licensing agreement and the amount of royalties a company can receive are considered a matter of commercial negotiation between licensor and licensee, and there are no government

[26] Detlev Vagts, *Transnational Business Problems* (Mineola, New York: The Foundation Press, 1986), pp. 285–291.
[27] David Sanger, "I.B.M.'s European Accord: Concessions End a Decade of Debate," *The New York Times* (August 3, 1984), p. 38.
[28] Alice Rawsthorn and Emma Tucker, "Movie Studios May Have to Scrap Joint Distributor," *Financial Times* (February 6, 1998), p. 1.
[29] Anna Wilde Mathews, "Making Waves: As U.S. Trade Grows, Shipping Cartels Get a Bit More Scrutiny," *The Wall Street Journal* (October 7, 1997), pp. A1, A8.

restrictions on remittances of royalties abroad. Important considerations in licensing include analysis of what assets a firm may offer for license, how to price the assets, and whether to grant only the right to "make" the product or to grant the rights to "use" and to "sell" the product as well. The right to sublicense is another important issue. As with distribution agreements, decisions must also be made regarding exclusive or nonexclusive arrangements and the size of the licensee's territory.

To prevent the licensee from using the licensed technology to compete directly with the licensor, the latter may try to limit the licensee to selling only in its home country. The licensor may also seek to contractually bind the licensee to discontinue use of the technology after the contract has expired. In practice, host-government laws and even U.S. antitrust laws may make such agreements impossible to obtain. Licensing is a potentially dangerous action: It may be instrumental in creating a competitor. Therefore, licensors should be careful to ensure that their own competitive position remains advantageous. This requires constant innovation.

As noted, licensing agreements can come under antitrust scrutiny. In one recent case, Bayer AG granted an exclusive patent license for a new household insecticide to S. C. Johnson & Sons. The German firm's decision to license was based in part on the time required for EPA approval, which had stretched to three years. Bayer decided it made better business sense to let the U.S. firm deal with regulatory authorities in return for a 5 percent royalty on sales. However, a class action suit filed against the companies alleged that the licensing deal would allow Johnson to monopolize the $450 million home insecticide market. Then the U.S. Justice Department stepped in, calling the licensing agreement anticompetitive. In a statement, Anne Bingaman, then head of the Justice Department's antitrust unit, said, "The cozy arrangement that Bayer and Johnson maintained is unacceptable in a highly concentrated market." Bayer agreed to offer licenses to any interested company on better terms than the original contract with Johnson. Johnson agreed to notify the U.S. government of any future pending exclusive licensing agreements for household insecticides. If Bayer is party to any such agreements, the Justice Department has the right to veto them. Not surprisingly, the reaction from the legal community has been negative. One Washington lawyer who specializes in intellectual property law noted that the case "really attacks traditional licensing practices." As Melvin Jager, president of the Licensing Executives Society, explained, "An exclusive license is a very valuable tool to promote intellectual property and get it out into the marketplace."[30]

What happens if a licensee gains knowledge of the licensor's trade secrets? *Trade secrets* are confidential information or knowledge that has commercial value and is not in the public domain, and for which steps have been taken to keep it secret. Trade secrets include manufacturing processes, formulas, designs, and customer lists. To prevent disclosure, the licensing of unpatented trade secrets should be linked to confidentiality contracts with each employee who has access to the protected information. In the United States, trade secrets are protected by state law rather than federal statute; most states have adopted the Uniform Trade Secrets Act (UTSA). The U.S. law provides trade secret liability against third parties that obtain confidential information through an intermediary. Remedies include damages and other forms of relief.

The 1990s have seen widespread improvements in laws pertaining to trade secrets. Several countries have recently adopted trade secret statutes for the first time. Mexico's first statute protecting trade secrets became effective on June 28, 1991; China's first trade secret law took effect December 1, 1993. In both countries, the new laws were part of broader revisions of intellectual property laws. Japan and South

---

[30] Brigid McMenamin, "Eroding Patent Rights," *Forbes* (October 24, 1994), p. 92.

Korea have also recently amended their intellectual property laws to include trade secrets. Many countries in Central and Eastern Europe have also enacted laws to protect trade secrets. When NAFTA became effective on January 1, 1994, it marked the first international trade agreement with provisions for protecting trade secrets. This milestone was quickly followed by the Agreement on Trade-Related Aspects of Intellectual Property Rights (TRIPs) that resulted from the Uruguay Round of GATT negotiations. The TRIPs agreement requires signatory countries to protect against acquisition, disclosure, or use of trade secrets "in a manner contrary to honest commercial practices."[31] Despite these formal legal developments, in practice, enforcement is the key issue. Companies transferring trade secrets across borders should apprise themselves not only of the existence of legal protection but also of the risks associated with lax enforcement.

Bribery and Corruption: Legal and Ethical Issues

History does not record a burst of international outrage when Charles M. Schwab, head of Bethlehem Steel at the beginning of the twentieth century, presented a $200,000 diamond and pearl necklace to the mistress of Czar Alexander III's nephew.[32] In return for that consideration, Bethlehem Steel won the contract to supply the rails for the Trans-Siberian railroad. Today, in the post-Soviet era, Western companies are again being lured by emerging opportunities in Eastern Europe. Here, as in the Middle East and other parts of the world, they are finding that bribery is a way of life, and that corruption is widespread. U.S. companies in particular are constrained in their responses to such a situation by U.S. government policies of the post-Watergate age. Transparency International compiles an annual report ranking countries in terms of corruption. The 1996 ranking is shown in Table 5-4.

In the United States, the **Foreign Corrupt Practices Act** (FCPA) is a legacy of the Watergate scandal during Richard Nixon's presidency. In the course of his investigation, the Watergate special prosecutor discovered that more than 300 American companies had made undisclosed payments to foreign officials totaling hundreds of millions of dollars. The act was unanimously passed by Congress and signed into law by President Jimmy Carter on December 17, 1977. Administered by the Department of Justice and the Securities and Exchange Commission, the act was concerned with disclosure and prohibition. The disclosure part of the Act required publicly held companies to institute internal accounting controls that would record all transactions. The prohibition part made it a crime for U.S. corporations to bribe an official of a foreign government or political party to obtain or retain business. Payments to third parties were also prohibited when the company had reason to believe that part or all of the money would be channeled to foreign officials.

The U.S. business community immediately began lobbying for changes to the act, complaining that the statute was too vague and so broad in scope that it threatened to severely curtail U.S. business activities abroad. Amendments to the statutes were signed into law by President Ronald Reagan in 1988, as part of the Omnibus Trade and Competitiveness Act. Among the changes were exclusions for "grease" payments to low-level officials to cut red tape and expedite "routine governmental actions" such as clearing shipments through customs, securing permits, or getting airport passport clearance to leave a country.

---

31 Salem M. Katsh and Michael P. Dierks, "Globally, Trade Secrets Laws Are All Over the Map," *The National Law Journal* 17, no. 36 (May 8, 1995), p. C12.

32 Much of the material in this section is adapted from Daniel Pines, "Amending the Foreign Corrupt Practices Act to Include a Private Right of Action," *California Law Review* (January 1994), pp. 185–229.

Table 5-4
1996 Corruption Rankings

1. Nigeria	15. Brazil	29. Malaysia	42. Germany
2. Pakistan	16. Ecuador	30. Czech Rep.	43. Britain
3. Kenya	17. Mexico	31. Poland	44. Ireland
4. Bangladesh	18. Thailand	32. South Africa	45. Australia
5. China	19. Bolivia	33. Portugal	46. Netherlands
6. Cameroon	20. Argentina	34. Chile	47. Switzerland
7. Venezuela	21. Italy	35. Belgium	48. Singapore
8. Russia	22. Turkey	36. France	49. Norway
9. India	23. Spain	37. Hong Kong	50. Canada
10. Indonesia	24. Hungary	38. Japan	51. Finland
11. Philippines	25. Jordan	39. Austria	52. Sweden
12. Uganda	26. Taiwan	40. U.S.	53. Denmark
13. Colombia	27. Greece	41. Israel	54. New Zealand
14. Egypt	28. South Korea		

Source: Transparency International.

Although several well-known U.S. companies have pleaded guilty to violations of the antibribery provisions, enforcement of the act has generally been lax. A total of 23 cases were filed between 1977 and 1988. In a recent case, a business executive was convicted of giving money and honeymoon airplane tickets to a Nigerian government official in the hopes of securing a contract.[33] There are stiff penalties for violating the law: Convictions carry severe jail sentences (in excess of one to five years) and heavy fines (in excess of $1 million). Fines cannot be paid or reimbursed by the company, under the theory that individuals commit such crimes. It has also been made clear that the law will not let a person do indirectly (e.g., through an agent, joint venture partner, or other third party) what it prohibits directly.

Some critics of the FCPA decry it as a regrettable display of moral imperialism. At issue is the extraterritorial sovereignty of U.S. law. It is wrong, according to these critics, to impose U.S. laws, standards, values, and mores on American companies and citizens worldwide. As one legal expert points out, however, this criticism has one fundamental flaw: There is no nation in which the letter of the law condones bribery of government officials. Thus, the standard set by the FCPA is shared, in principle at least, by other nations.[34]

A second criticism of the FCPA is that it puts U.S. companies in a difficult position vis-à-vis foreign competitors, especially those in Japan and Europe. Several opinion polls and surveys of the business community have revealed the widespread perception that the act adversely affects U.S. businesses overseas. Some academic researchers have concluded that the FCPA has not negatively affected the export performance of U.S. industry. However, a Commerce Department report prepared with the help of U.S. intelligence services indicated that in 1994 alone, bribes offered by non-U.S. companies were a factor in 100 business deals valued at $45 billion. Foreign

---

[33] Katherine Albright and Grace Won, "Foreign Corrupt Practices Act," *American Criminal Law Review* (Spring 1993), p. 787.

[34] Pines, "Amending the Foreign Corrupt Practices Act to Include a Private Right of Action," p. 205.

Table 5-5
Countries Most
Likely to Bribe

HOME COUNTRY OF BRIBING COMPANY	COUNTRY IN WHICH BRIBES WERE ACCEPTED
1. Belgium/Luxembourg	Nigeria
2. France	Bolivia
3. Italy	Colombia
4. Netherlands	Russia
5. South Korea	Pakistan
6. UK	Mexico
7. Spain	Indonesia
8. China/Hong Kong	India
9. Germany	Venezuela
10. Singapore	Vietnam
11. Canada	Argentina
12. Japan	China
13. Switzerland	Philippines
14. USA	Thailand
15. Austria	Turkey

Source: Neil King, Jr., "Coming Clean: EU Firms Await Pact on Banning Bribery with Mixed Feelings," *The Wall Street Journal Europe* (September 23, 1997), p. 1.

companies prevailed in 80 percent of those deals.[35] Although accurate statistics are hard to come by, one recent ranking of bribery activity is shown in Table 5-5.

The existence of bribery as a fact of life in world markets will not change because it is condemned by the U.S. Congress. In fact, bribery payments are considered a deductible business expense in many European countries. According to one estimate, the annual price tag for illegal payments by German firms alone is more than $5 billion. Still, increasing numbers of global companies are adopting codes of conduct designed to reduce illegal activities. Moreover, in May 1997, the 29-member OECD adopted a formal standard against bribery by drafting a binding international convention that makes it a crime for a company bidding on a contract to bribe foreign officials. Representatives of OECD member nations put the legislation before their respective parliaments in 1998; the convention went into effect in February 1999. The OECD is also working on a smaller scale to create so-called islands of integrity. The goal is to achieve transparency at the level of an individual deal, with all the players pledging not to bribe. In one recent example, Cable & Wireless PLC from the UK was selected over GTE to acquire 49 percent of Panama's telephone company. The Panamanian government pledged to make all documents public after the bidding process was completed.[36]

Despite the progress made to date on the new agreement, industry observers have expressed several concerns about the proposed treaty. First, it is unclear whether the new law will be enforced with equal rigor everywhere, and, if not, what sanctions will be imposed. Second, the treaty contains legal loopholes, such as the provision that business contracts can be linked to public aid projects such as building

---

[35] Amy Borrus, "Inside the World of Greased Palms," *Business Week* (November 6, 1995), pp. 36–38.

[36] Neil King Jr., "Coming Clean: EU Firms Await Pact on Banning Bribery with Mixed Feelings," *The Wall Street Journal Europe* (September 23, 1997), pp. 1, 7.

Part II   The Global Marketing Environment

hospitals. Third, there is disagreement on what constitutes a "normal" versus an "abnormal" payment. Finally, it will be necessary to arrive at a workable definition of what constitutes a "public official."[37]

When companies operate abroad in the absence of home-country legal constraints, they face a continuum of choices concerning company ethics. At one extreme, they can maintain home-country ethics worldwide with absolutely no adjustment or adaptation to local practice. At the other extreme, they can abandon any attempt to maintain company ethics and adapt entirely to local conditions and circumstances as they are perceived by company managers in each local environment. Between these extremes, one approach that companies may select is to utilize varying degrees of extension of home-country ethics. Alternatively, they may adapt in varying degrees to local customs and practices.

What should a U.S. company do if competitors are willing to offer a bribe? Two alternative courses of action are possible. One is to ignore bribery and act as if it does not exist. The other is to recognize the existence of bribery and evaluate its effect on the customer's purchase decision as if it were just another element of the marketing mix. The overall value of a company's offer must be as good as, or better than, the competitor's overall offering, bribe included. It may be possible to offer a lower price, a better product, better distribution, or better advertising to offset the value added by the bribe. The best line of defense is to have a product that is clearly superior to that of the competition. In such a case, a bribe should not sway the purchase decision. Alternatively, clear superiority in service and in local representation may tip the scales.

Conflict Resolution, Dispute Settlement, and Litigation

The degree of legal cooperation and harmony in the EU is unique and stems in part from the existence of code law as a common bond. Other regional organizations have made far less progress toward harmonization. Countries vary in their approach toward conflict resolution. Table 5-6 shows the number of practicing lawyers per 100,000 in population in selected countries. The U.S. has more lawyers than any

Table 5-6
Lawyers: An International Comparison

Country	Lawyers per 100,000 People
USA	290
Australia	242
United Kingdom	141
France	80
Germany	79
Hungary	79
Japan	11
Korea	3

Source: Adapted from Frank B. Cross, "Lawyers, the Economy, and Society," American Business Law Journal (Summer 1998), pp. 477+.

---

[37] John Mason and Guy de Jonquières, "Goodbye Mr. 10%," Financial Times (July 22, 1997), p. 13.

other country in the world and is arguably the most litigious nation on earth. In part, this is a reflection of the low-context nature of American culture, a spirit of confrontational competitiveness, and the absence of one important principle of code law: The loser pays all court costs for all parties.

Conflicts inevitably arise in business anywhere, especially when different cultures come together to buy, sell, establish joint ventures, compete, and cooperate in global markets. For American companies, the dispute with a foreign party is frequently in the home country jurisdiction. The issue can be litigated in the United States, where the company and its attorneys might be said to enjoy "home court" advantage. Litigation in foreign courts, however, becomes vastly more complex, partly because of differences in language, legal systems, currencies, and traditional business customs and patterns. In addition, problems arise from differences in procedures relating to discovery. In essence, *discovery* is the process of obtaining evidence to prove claims and determining which evidence may be admissible in which countries under which conditions. A further complication is the fact that judgments handed down in courts in another country may not be enforceable in the home country. For all these reasons, many companies prefer to pursue arbitration before proceeding to litigate.

Alternatives to Litigation for Dispute Settlement[38]

In 1995, the Cuban government abruptly cancelled contracts with Endesa, a Spanish utility company. Rather than seek restitution in a Cuban court, Endesa turned to the International Arbitration Tribunal in Paris, seeking damages of $12 million. Endesa's actions illustrate how alternative dispute resolution (ADR) methods allow parties to resolve international commercial disputes without resorting to the court system. Formal arbitration is one means of settling international business disputes outside the courtroom. Arbitration is a negotiation process that the two parties have, by prior agreement, committed themselves to using. It is a fair process in the sense that the parties using it have created it themselves. Generally, arbitration involves a hearing of the parties before a three-member panel; each party selects one panel member, and those two panel members in turn select the third member. The panel renders a judgment that the parties agree to abide by in advance.

The most important treaty regarding international arbitration is the 1958 United Nations Convention on the Recognition and Enforcement of Foreign Arbitral Awards. Also known as the New York Convention, the treaty has 107 signatory countries, including China. Brazil is notable among the big emerging markets for not being a signatory. The framework created by the New York Convention is important for several reasons. First, when parties enter into agreements that provide for international arbitration, the signatory countries can hold the parties to their pledge to use arbitration. Second, after arbitration has taken place and the arbitrators have made an award, the signatories recognize and can enforce the judgment. Third, the signatories agree that there are limited grounds for challenging arbitration decisions. The grounds that are recognized are different than the typical appeals that are permitted in a court of law.

Visit the Web site
The International Chamber of Commerce can be found online at: www.iccwbo.org

Some firms and lawyers inexperienced in the practice of international commercial arbitration approach the arbitration clauses in a contract as "just another clause." In fact, the terms of every contract are different and therefore no two arbitration clauses should be the same. Consider, for example, the case of a contract between an American firm and a Japanese one. If the parties resort to arbitration, where will it

---

[38] The authors are indebted to Louis B. Kimmelman of O'Melveny & Meyers LLP, New York City, New York, for his contributions to this section.

take place? The American side will be reluctant to go to Japan; conversely, the Japanese side will not want to arbitrate in the United States. An alternative, "neutral" location—Singapore or London, for example—must be considered and specified in the arbitration clause. In what language will the proceedings be conducted? If no language is specified in the arbitration clause, the arbitrators themselves will choose.

In addition to location and language, other issues must be addressed as well. For example, if the parties to a patent-licensing arrangement agree in the arbitration clause that the validity of the patent cannot be contested, such a provision may not be enforceable in some countries. Which country's laws will be used as the standard for invalidity? Pursuing such an issue on a country-by-country basis would be inordinately time-consuming. In addition, there is the issue of acceptance: By law, U.S. courts must accept an arbitrator's decision in patent disputes; in other countries, however, there is no general rule of acceptance. To reduce delays relating to such issues, one expert suggests drafting arbitration clauses with as much specificity as possible. To the extent possible, for example, patent policies in various countries should be addressed; arbitration clauses may also include a provision that all foreign patent issues will be judged according to the standard of home-country law. Another provision could forbid the parties from commencing separate legal actions in other countries. The goal is to help the arbitration tribunal zero in on the express intentions of the parties.[39]

For decades, business arbitration has also been promoted through the International Court of Arbitration at the Paris-based International Chamber of Commerce (ICC). The ICC recently modernized some of its older rules. However, because it is such a well-known organization, it has an extensive backlog of cases. Overall, the ICC has gained a reputation for being slower, more expensive, and more cumbersome than some alternatives. As U.S. involvement in global commerce grew dramatically during the post-World War II period, the American Arbitration Association (AAA) also became recognized as an effective institution within which to resolve disputes. In 1992, the AAA signed a cooperation agreement with China's Beijing Conciliation Center. Each year, the AAA uses mediation to help resolve thousands of disputes. The AAA has entered into cooperation agreements with the ICC and other global organizations to promote the use of ADR methods; it serves as the agent to administer arbitrations in the United States under ICC auspices. In one recent case, Toys "R" Us was the losing party in a dispute brought to the AAA. The dispute's origins date back to a 1982 licensing agreement between the toy retailer and Alghanin & Sons regarding toy stores in the Middle East. The AAA ruled that Toys "R" Us was to pay a $55 million arbitration award.

Another agency for settling disputes is the Swedish Arbitration Institute of the Stockholm Chamber of Commerce. This agency frequently administered disputes between Western and Socialist countries and has gained credibility for its even-handed administration. Other alternatives have proliferated in recent years. In addition to those mentioned, active centers for arbitration exist in Vancouver, Hong Kong, Cairo, Kuala Lumpur, Singapore, Buenos Aires, Bogotá, and Mexico City. A World Arbitration Institute was established in New York; in the United Kingdom, Advisory, Conciliation, and Arbitration Service (ACAS) has achieved great success at handling industrial disputes. An International Council for Commercial Arbitration (ICCA) was established to coordinate the far-flung activities of arbitration organizations. The ICCA meets in different locations around the world every four years.

The United Nations Conference on International Trade Law (UNCITRAL) has also been a significant force in the area of arbitration. Its rules have become more or less standard, as many of the organizations just named have adopted them with some modifications. Many developing countries, for example, long held prejudices against the ICC, AAA, and other developed-country organizations. Representatives of developing nations assumed that such organizations would be biased in favor of multinational corporations. Developing nations insisted on settlement in national courts, which was unacceptable to the multinational firms. This was especially true in Latin America, where the Calvo Doctrine required disputes arising with foreign investors be resolved in national courts under national laws. The growing influence of the ICCA and UNCITRAL rules, coupled with the proliferation of regional arbitration centers, have contributed to changing attitudes in developing countries and resulted in the increased use of arbitration around the world.

Visit the Web site
The UNCITRAL homepage can be accessed at:
www.un.or.at/uncitral

---

[39] Bruce Londa, "An Agreement to Arbitrate Disputes Isn't the Same in Every Language," *Brandweek* (September 26, 1994), p. 18. See also John M. Allen, Jr., and Bruce G. Merritt, "Drafters of Arbitration Clauses Face a Variety of Unforeseen Perils," *National Law Journal* 17, no. 33 (April 17, 1995), pp. C6–C7.

The Regulatory Environment

The regulatory environment of global marketing consists of a variety of governmental and nongovernmental agencies that enforce laws or set guidelines for conducting business. These regulatory agencies address a wide range of marketing issues, including price control, valuation of imports and exports, trade practices, labeling, food and drug regulations, employment conditions, collective bargaining, advertising content, and competitive practices. As noted recently in *The Wall Street Journal*:

> Each nation's regulations reflect and reinforce its brand of capitalism—predatory in the U.S., paternal in Germany, and protected in Japan—and its social values. It's easier to open a business in the U.S. than in Germany because Germans value social consensus above risk-taking, but it's harder to hire people because Americans worry more about discrimination lawsuits. It's easier to import children's clothes in the U.S. than Japan because Japanese bureaucrats defend a jumble of import restrictions, but it's harder to open bank branches across the U.S. because Americans strongly defend state prerogatives.[40]

The influence of regulatory agencies is pervasive, and an understanding of how they operate is essential to protect business interests and advance new programs. For example, in the United States, the International Trade Commission administers the Tariff Act of 1930. Section 337 prohibits "unfair methods of competition" if the effect of this competition is to destroy or substantially injure an industry. To seek relief or defend access to the U.S. market if challenged under this act, a company should retain the services of specialized legal talent, supported by technical expertise in patents and in international marketing. It is useful to call on the assistance of home-country diplomatic staff to assist and support the effort to obtain a favorable ruling.

Regional Economic Organizations: The European Union Example

The overall importance of regional organizations such as the World Trade Organization and the European Union (EU) was discussed in Chapter 3. The legal dimensions are important, however, and will be briefly mentioned here. The Treaty of Rome established the European Community (EC), the precursor to the European Union. The Treaty created an institutional framework in which a council (the Council of Ministers) serves as the main decision-making body, with each country member having direct representation. The European Commission, the European Parliament, and the European Court of Justice were the other three main institutions of the community. The 1987 Single European Act amended the Treaty of Rome and provided strong impetus for the creation of a single market beginning January 1, 1993. Although technically the target was not completely met, approximately 85 percent of the new recommendations were implemented into national law by most member states by the target date, resulting in substantial harmonization. A relatively new body known as the European Council (a distinct entity from the Council of Ministers) was formally incorporated into the EC institutional structure by Article 2 of the 1987 act. Comprised of heads of member states plus the president of the commission, the European Council's role is to define general political guidelines for the

---

[40] Bob Davis, "Red-Tape Traumas, To All U.S. Managers Upset by Regulations: Try Germany or Japan," *The Wall Street Journal* (December 14, 1995), p. A1.

union and provide direction on integration-related issues such as monetary union.[41] Governments in Central and Eastern European countries that hope to join are currently getting their laws in line with those of the EU.

The Treaty of Rome contains hundreds of articles, several of which are directly applicable to global companies and global marketers. Articles 30 through 36 establish the general policy referred to as "Free Flow of Goods, People, Capital and Technology" among the member states. Articles 85 through 86 contain competition rules, as amended by various directives of the 20-member EU Commission. The Commission is the administrative arm of the EU; from its base in Brussels, the commission proposes laws and policies, monitors the observance of EU laws, administers and implements EU legislation, and represents the EU to international organizations.[42] Commission members represent the union rather than their respective nations. The laws, regulations, directives, and policies that originate in the Commission must be submitted to the parliament for an opinion and then passed along to the council for a final decision. Once the council approves a prospective law, it becomes union law, which is somewhat analogous to U.S. federal law. Regulations automatically become law throughout the union; directives include a time frame for implementation by legislation in each member state. For example, in 1994, the commission issued a directive regarding use of trademarks in comparative advertising. Individual member nations of the EU have been working to implement the directive; for example, in the UK, the 1994 Trade Marks Act gave companies the right to apply for trademark protection of smells, sounds, and images and also provides improved protection against trademark counterfeiting.

The Single Market era is one in which many industries face new regulatory environments. The European Court of Justice, based in Luxembourg, is responsible for ensuring that EU laws and treaties are upheld throughout the Union. For example, the Court can assess damages against countries that fail to introduce directives by the date set. The Court also hears disputes that arise among the 15 EU member nations on trade issues such as mergers, monopolies, trade barriers and regulations, and exports. The Court is also empowered to resolve conflicts between national law and EU law. In most cases, the latter supersedes national laws of individual European countries. Marketers must be aware, however, that national laws should always be consulted. National laws may be *stricter* than community law, especially in such areas as competition and antitrust. Community law is intended to harmonize, to the extent possible, national laws to promote the purposes defined in Articles 30 through 36. The goal is to bring the lax laws of some member states up to designated minimum standards. However, more restrictive positions may still exist in some national laws. Conversely, national laws may be *less* restrictive than community law. Germany, for example, had traditionally placed few restrictions on banana imports. When a German court decreed that German companies could import bananas without complying with the EU's 1993 banana regime regulations, the International Court of Justice ruled that national courts could not grant interim judicial relief.[43]

A case from Germany helps illustrate the point. A West German court ruled that Pronuptia, a French wedding dress manufacturer and retailer, couldn't require its German franchisees to buy all their goods from the parent company. Pronuptia took

41   Klaus-Dieter Borchardt, *European Integration: The Origins and Growth of the European Union.* (Luxembourg: Office for Official Publications of the European Communities, 1995), p. 30.
42   Klaus-Dieter Borchardt, *The ABC of Community Law* (Luxembourg: Office for Official Publications of the European Communities, 1994), p. 25.
43   Rikke Thagesen and Alan Matthews, "The EU's Common Banana Regime: An Initial Evaluation," *Journal of Common Market Studies* 35, no. 4 (December 1997), p. 623.

its case to the European Court of Appeals, the EU's main forum for arbitration that makes recommendations to the Court of Justice. Had the German court's ruling been upheld on antitrust grounds, *all* franchisors doing business in Europe—including such well-known companies as McDonald's, Midas Muffler, and PepsiCo's Kentucky Fried Chicken and Pizza Hut units—would have been stripped of their ability to operate U.S.-style franchises in Europe. Key policies, including the right to dictate corporate logos, store designs, and outside suppliers, would have been nullified. After intense lobbying by the International Franchising Association, the Court issued a ruling that was generally favorable to franchisors. Still, the new regulations prohibit franchisers from requiring franchisees to sell specific *branded* products from outside suppliers. Thus, while McDonald's retains the right to designate suppliers for commodities such as meat and potatoes, it can't force franchisees to conform to the U.S. policy that calls for selling only Coca-Cola beverages at its restaurants.[44]

SUMMARY

The **political environment** of global marketing is the set of governmental institutions, political parties, and organizations that are the expression of the people in the nations of the world. In particular, anyone engaged in global marketing should have an overall understanding of the importance of **sovereignty** to national governments. The political environment varies from country to country, and **political risk** assessment is crucial. It is also important to understand a particular government's actions with respect to taxes and seizure of assets. Historically, the latter have taken the form of **expropriation, confiscation,** and **nationalization.**

The **legal environment** consists of laws, courts, attorneys, legal customs, and practices. The countries of the world can be broadly categorized in terms of common-law system or civil-law system. The United States and Canada and many former British colonies are **common-law countries**; most other countries use **code law.** A third system,

Islamic law, predominates in the Middle East. Some of the most important legal issues pertain to **jurisdiction, intellectual property protection, antitrust, licensing,** and **bribery.** In particular, **counterfeiting** is a major problem for many global companies. When legal conflicts arise, companies can pursue the matter in court or use arbitration.

The **regulatory environment** consists of agencies, both governmental and non-governmental, that enforce laws or set guidelines for conducting business. Global marketing activities can be affected by a number of international or regional economic organizations; in Europe, for example, the European Union makes laws governing member states. The World Trade Organization will have a broad impact on global marketing activities in the years to come. Although all three environments are complex, astute marketers plan ahead to avoid situations that might result in conflict, misunderstanding, or outright violation of national laws.

DISCUSSION QUESTIONS

1. What is sovereignty? Why is it an important consideration in the political environment of global marketing?
2. Describe some of the sources of political risk. Specifically, what forms can political risk take?

3. Briefly describe some of the differences between the legal environment of a country that embraces common law and one that observes civil law.

---

[44] Philip Revzin, "European Bureaucrats are Writing the Rules Americans Will Live By," *The Wall Street Journal* (May 17, 1989), pp. A1, A12.

4. Global marketers can avoid legal conflicts by understanding the reasons conflicts arise in the first place. Identify and describe several legal issues that relate to global commerce.

5. You are an American traveling on business in the Middle East. As you are leaving country X, the passport control officer at the airport tells you there will be a passport "processing" delay of 12 hours. You explain that your plane leaves in 30 minutes, and the official suggests that a contribution of $50 would probably speed things up. If you comply with the suggestion, have you violated U.S. law? Explain.

6. "See you in court" is one way to respond when legal issues arise. What other approaches are possible?

SUGGESTED READINGS

Books

Alford, William P. *To Steal a Book is an Elegant Offense: Intellectual Property Law in Chinese Civilization.* Stanford, California: Stanford University Press, 1995.

Borchardt, Klaus-Dieter. *The ABC of Community Law.* Luxembourg: Office for Official Publications of the European Communities, 1994.

____. *European Integration: The Origins and Growth of the European Union.* Luxembourg: Office for Official Publications of the European Communities, 1995.

Chukwumerige, Okezie. *Choice of Law in International Commercial Arbitration.* Westport, CT: Quorum Books, 1994.

Fishbein, Bette K. *Germany, Garbage, and the Green Dot: Challenging the Throwaway Society.* New York: Inform, 1994.

Jacoby, Neil H., Peter Nehmenkis, and Richard Eells. *Bribery and Extortion in World Business.* New York: McMillan, 1977.

Kelso, R. Randall, and Charles D. Kelso. *Studying Law: An Introduction.* St. Paul, Minn.: West Publishing, 1984.

Ohmae, Kenichi. *The Borderless World.* New York: Harper Perennial, 1991.

Robock, Stephan H., and Kenneth Simmonds. *International Business and Multinational Enterprises.* Homewood, Ill.: Irwin, 1989.

Root, Franklin R. *Entry Strategies for International Markets.* New York: Lexington Books, 1994.

Samuels, Barbara C. *Managing Risk in Developing Countries: National Demands and Multinational Response.* New Jersey: Princeton University Press, 1990.

Slomanson, William R. *Fundamental Perspectives on International Law.* St. Paul: West Publishing, 1990.

Sohn, Louis B., ed. *Basic Documents of the United Nations.* Brooklyn: The Foundations Press, Inc., 1968.

Vagts, Detlev. *Transnational Business Problems.* Mineola, New York: The Foundation Press, 1986.

Articles

Akhter, Syed H., and Yusuf A. Choudhry. "Forced Withdrawal From a Country Market: Managing Political Risk." *Business Horizons* (May-June 1993), pp. 47–54.

Albright, Katherine, and Grace Won. "Foreign Corrupt Practices Act." *American Criminal Law Review* (Spring 1993), p. 787.

Bagley, Jennifer M., Stephanie S. Glickman, and Elizabeth B. Wyatt. "Intellectual Property." *American Criminal Law Review* 32, no. 2 (Winter 1995), pp. 457–479.

Bradley, David G. "Managing Against Expropriation." *Harvard Business Review* (July-August 1977).

Braithwaite, John. "Transnational Regulation of the Pharmaceutical Industry." *Annals of the American Academy of Political & Social Science* 525 (January 1993), pp. 12–30.

Carbone, June, and Margaret McClean. "Genetically Modified Foods: The Creation of Trust and Access to Global Markets." *Business & Professional Ethics Journal* 20, no. 3/4 (Fall/Winter 2001) pp. 79–104.

Cleveland, Harlon. "Rethinking International Governance." *The Futurist* (May 1991).

Gillespie, Kate. "Middle East Response to the U.S. Foreign Corrupt Practices Act." *California Management Review* 29 (1987).

Graham, John L. "The Foreign Corrupt Practice Act: A New Perspective." *Journal of International Business Studies* (Winter 1984), pp. 107–121.

Hawkins, Robert B., Norman Mintz, and Michael Provissoiero. "Government Takeovers of U.S. Foreign Affiliates." *Journal of International Business Studies* (Spring 1976).

Jain, Subhash C. "Problems in International Protection of Intellectual Property Rights." *Journal of International Marketing* 4, no. 1 (1996), pp. 9–32.

Kaikati, Jack, and Wayne A. Label, "The Foreign Antibribery Law: Friend or Foe?" *Columbia Journal of World Business* (Spring 1980), pp. 46–51.

Katsh, Salem M., and Michael P. Dierks. "Globally, Trade Secrets Laws Are All Over the Map." *The National Law Journal* 17, no. 36 (May 8, 1995), pp. C12–C14.

Nash, Marian Leich. "Contemporary Practice of the United States Relating to International Law."

American Journal of International Law 88, no. 4 (October 1994), pp. 719–765.

Ortego, Joseph, and Josh Kardisch. "Foreign Companies Can Limit the Risk of Being Subject to U.S. Courts." *National Law Journal* 17, no. 3 (September 19, 1994), pp. C2–C3+.

Pines, Daniel. "Amending the Foreign Corrupt Practices Act to Include a Private Right of Action." *California Law Review* (January 1994), pp. 185–229.

Rodgers, Frank A. "The War is Won, But Peace is Not." *Vital Speeches of the Day* (May 14, 1991), pp. 430–432.

Roessler, Frieder. "The Scope, Limits and Function of the GATT Legal System." *World Economy* (September-1985), pp. 287–298.

Spero, Donald M. "Patent Protection or Piracy: A CEO Views Japan." *Harvard Business Review* (September-October 1990), pp. 58–62.

Vernon, Raymond. "The World Trade Organization: A New Stage in International Trade and Development." *Harvard International Law Journal* 36, no. 2 (Spring 1995), pp. 329–340.

Vogel, David. "The Globalization of Business Ethics: Why America Remains Distinctive." *California Management Review* 35, no. 1 (Fall 1992), pp. 30–49.

Voitovich, Sergei A. "Normative Acts of International Economic Organizations in International Law Making." *Journal of World Trade* (August 4, 1990), pp. 21–38.

CASES

Case 5-1 *Trademark Infringement in World Markets*

In many parts of the world, particularly Southeast Asia, well-known global companies are frequently the victims of trademark violations and product counterfeiting. The scale of the problem is so vast that it costs companies billions of dollars in lost sales each year. In South Korea, for example, chewing gum called Juicy & Fresh has the same yellow wrapper, black lettering, and package shape as Wrigley's Juicy Fruit. Other imitations in South Korea include Tie detergent in orange boxes that resemble Procter & Gamble's Tide. Italy's Benetton S.p.A. has also been imitated: A Korean fashion retailer sells brightly colored casual clothes in a chain of stores called Paselton. The store's logo features the same typeface as Benetton's, including the distinctive design of the letter "t." Similar products abound in China, where consumers can pick up a tube of "Cologate" toothpaste in a bright red box and "Kongalu" Corn Strips whose box is emblazoned with the distinctive signature of Kellogg's cereals. The issue extends far beyond consumer packaged goods, however; Chrysler Corporation has even discovered sports utility vehicles on the streets of Beijing that are nearly identical to Jeep Cherokees.

The garment and fashion industries have also been hard hit. Levi Strauss has faced an uphill battle trying to stop counterfeit sales of its popular jeans in more than 30 countries. The problem is especially acute in Europe,

where Levis are a status symbol. The company can't keep up with demand, so counterfeiters take up the slack. The fake jeans are such close copies that, a Levi spokesperson says, "The typical consumer would not be able to detect that they are buying counterfeits." After a few washings, however, the bogus jeans deteriorate quickly; colors fade, seams come apart, and rivets begin to rust. Many of the counterfeits now come from China, where factories produce jeans for about $5 per pair and sell them to people who falsely claim to be legitimate Levi representatives. To disguise their Asian origins, the jeans may be shipped through the Panama Canal and then across the Mexican border; jeans bound for Europe are often shipped overland through the former Soviet bloc countries.

There are various explanations for why counterfeiting and piracy are so widespread. The reasons are partially cultural. One U.S. trade official noted that, in South Korea, there is the notion that "the thoughts of one man should benefit all." Another reason is the "hands off" policy of local law enforcement agencies. Even though the South Korean government passed trademark, patent, and copyright protection laws in the late 1980s, enforcement is lax. Steven M. Weinberg, an attorney who is also executive editor of a newsletter on trademarks, says, "It's one thing to have a law on the books. It's another thing to have cultural values and views change in order to accommodate, particularly, the interests of people who are from outside the country or region."

The issue of intellectual property rights is especially problematic in China. In 1994, the Clinton administration considered launching an investigation to determine whether U.S. companies had been hurt by piracy and trademark infringements. Under Section 301 of the U.S. trade act, findings of harm could lead to trade sanctions. To head off such confrontation, China has passed stringent laws on counterfeiting. According to lawyer David Buxbaum, "It's quite clear that in terms of a comprehensive legal framework, China has done an excellent job." However, he notes, "It's only beginning to dawn on people that copyrights and trademarks are property." A lot is at stake: The International Intellectual Property Alliance estimates that Chinese counterfeiting of copyrighted material alone costs U.S. companies $800 million annually; the figure would be much higher if trademark and patent infringement were added.

A steamroller crushes pirated CDs and videocassettes at Changping, near Beijing in March 1997. The action represented an attempt by the Chinese government to demonstrate to foreign journalists, businesspeople, and authorities that it was clamping down on violations of intellectual property rights.

In fall 1994, Universal Pictures, Twentieth Century Fox, and six other U.S. movie companies filed a joint suit against a Chinese video distributor. The filmmakers asked the Beijing Intermediate Peoples Court to stop distributors from selling illegal laser disc copies of "Rocky," "The Godfather," and other hit movies. Each of the eight studios joining in the suit asked for 50,000 yuan ($5,882) in damages as well as legal costs. The suit was filed in the midst of ongoing talks between U.S. and Chinese trade officials. The United States wanted the Chinese government to close the more than two dozen CD plants that produce pirated music and movie discs. The piracy issue threatened to diminish China's chances of joining the World Trade Organization.

There are other ways to deal with the video piracy problem. The Motion Picture Export Association of America hired Richard O'Neill, a Green Beret and Vietnam veteran. Using guerrilla tactics, O'Neill raided hundreds of South Korea's 30,000 video stores. His efforts have helped reduce the number of stores selling pirated videos from 85 percent to below 20 percent. ∎

DISCUSSION QUESTIONS

1. What legal woes might befall a businessperson from a common-law country hoping to protect intellectual property in a code-law country?

2. Identify the different types of trademark infringement described in the case.

3. What would you do in South Korea if you were Benetton?

4. If you were a studio executive responsible for protecting your company's intellectual property rights, what would you do to address the piracy problem in China? in Africa and the Middle East? in the CIS? in Southeast Asia?

SOURCES: Marcus W. Brauchli, "Chinese Blatantly Copy Trademarks of Foreigners," *The Wall Street Journal* (June 20, 1994), pp. B1, B5; Junda Woo and Richard Borsuk, "Asian Trademark Litigation Continues," *The Wall Street Journal* (February 16, 1994), p. B10; Marcus W. Brauchli, "Fake CDs Are a Growth Industry in China," *The Wall Street Journal* (February 11, 1994), pp. B1, B10; Damon Darlin, "Copycat Crime: Video Pirates Abroad Face a Swashbuckler Worthy of Hollywood," *The Wall Street Journal* (January 28, 1992), pp. A1, A8; Thomas C. O'Donnell and Elizabeth Weiner, "The Counterfeit Trade," *Business Week* (December 16, 1985), pp. 64+; Damon Darlin, "Where Trademarks Are Up for Grabs," *The Wall Street Journal* (December 5, 1989), pp. B1, B8; Carrie Dolan, "Levi Tries to Round Up Counterfeiters," *The Wall Street Journal* (February 19, 1992), p. B1; Joshua Levine and Nancy Rotenier, "Seller Beware," *Forbes* (October 25, 1993), pp. 170, 174.

Case 5-2   *Bud versus Bud*

What's in a name? In the case of Budweiser, the answer is, "Quite a bit." Budweiser, of course, is a registered trademark of St. Louis-based Anheuser-Busch, the world's largest brewing company. At the present time, however, Anheuser-Busch can't market beer using the Budweiser brand name in every country of the world. The reason is firmly rooted in history: The European brewing industry dates to the fourteenth century. During the days of the Austro-Hungarian Empire, Bohemia was famous for its beers; beers from the Bohemian town of Budweis were held in especially high esteem. A person from Budweis would be known as a Budweiser; the same would be true of the town's beer. While traveling in Europe in the mid-1800s, Adolphus Busch, the founder of Anheuser-Busch, became familiar with beers from Budweis—Budweisers, in other words. After emigrating to the United States, Busch married into the Anheuser brewing family; in the 1870s, he registered Budweiser as a trademark. Two decades later, in 1895, the Budejovicky Budvar brewery was established in Budweis, and its beer was officially named Budweiser, "the beer of kings." Adolphus Busch dubbed his company's Budweiser "the king of beers."

In 1911, representatives of Anheuser-Busch and Budvar signed an agreement that entitled the European company to market Budweiser beer in continental Europe. The American company would have rights to the name in the United States and Latin America. Later, the name of the town was changed from Budweis to Ceske Budejovice. In several European countries, including France, Italy, and Spain, Anheuser-Busch markets beer using the "Bud" brand name. The American company also won a court decision in Britain allowing it to sell Budweiser in Britain alongside the Czech brew with the same name.

Today, Anheuser-Busch's various brands command a 45 percent share of the U.S. beer market. Although it is the world's largest brewer, nearly 94 percent of its output is consumed in the United States. Faced with slackening demand at home, competition from microbreweries and imported brands, and increased scrutiny by regulators, executives at Anheuser-Busch are looking to international markets for growth in the twenty-first century. In Japan, Anheuser-Busch has established a joint venture with Kirin Brewery, the local market leader. Similarly, the company has acquired a 5 percent share in China's Tsingtao Brewery. After communist rule ended in Czechoslovakia in 1989, many breweries and other government-owned enterprises were privatized. For example, in 1992 the Czech government sold all but an 18 percent stake in Plzensky Prazdoj, maker of the Pilsner Urquell brand that competes directly with Budvar. Anheuser-Busch officials hoped to capitalize on the opportunity in 1993 by investing in Budejovicky Budvar and, at the same time, resolving the trademark issue. August Busch III, the chairman and president of Anheuser-Busch and the great-great-grandson of Adolphus Busch, wrote to Czech officials promising to invest capital in the brewery and share management and marketing expertise.

The Czech response to Anheuser-Busch's overtures was less than enthusiastic. For one thing, Czechs consider Budweiser to be more than a mere brand name; it is a geographic name that indicates a product's origin and is a source of Czech national pride. According to a 1958 agreement signed by the Czech government but not the United States, brand names that denote geographic origin are protected. Strictly speaking, therefore, only wine made from grapes grown in the Burgundy region of France can be called Burgundy, Champagne refers only to sparkling wine made from grapes grown in the Champagne region of France, and the Czechs firmly believe that their beer is the only one entitled to the name "Budweiser."

A second concern is related to the general issue of privatization. Germany's Volkswagen AG bought a stake in Skoda, the Czech automaker, and Air France invested in Czechoslovak Airlines. Many Czechs are uneasy about selling off these industrial crown jewels (or "family silver," as they are known in the Czech language) to Western companies, and there is concern about allowing Budvar to have a similar fate. In the case of Skoda, autoworkers were disappointed that wage levels after the deal were still far below those of workers in the company's plants in Germany. Also, Volkswagen offi-cials scaled back the amount of money that they had originally promised to invest for expansion of Skoda's facilities.

Third, there is the matter of taste. Simply put, the Czechs consider American beer to be markedly inferior to European brews in general and Budvar's in particular. Experts agree. Beer authority and master taster Michael Jackson says, "Budweiser Budvar is one of the world's truly great beers. It just has a wonderful creamy malt character and a very, very delicate, almost perfumy flowery hop aroma." As one middle-aged Czech put it, "I like Americans, their culture, their films. But I know American beer doesn't reach the quality of Czech beer. It's much poorer, much weaker."

To help win over the Czechs, Anheuser-Busch embarked upon an extensive public relations effort. It spent $1 million on a cultural center in Ceske Budejovice, started a baseball team and equipped it with red and white Cardinals uniforms, opened a café, and began offering English-language lessons—all, apparently, to no avail. The two sides continued to differ as to who would reap the most benefit from a new business arrangement. The sheer size of the American company made its intentions seem more imperialistic than honorable. Petr Jansky, finance director at Budvar, said, "Foreign partners need us as a strategic partner to help them. We don't need Anheuser-Busch, they need us." If Budvar began producing American-style Budweiser, Jansky added, "It could end up being the same as asking Rolls-Royce to produce mass cars." Not surprisingly, Anheuser-Busch representatives took a different view. John Koykka, chief financial officer for Anheuser-Busch International, believes that both companies could benefit. "The consumer base is quite different and the products quite different. We have a younger consumer base. We don't see a direct consumer competition."

Ultimately, the Czech government decided not to proceed with the privatization of the Budvar brewery planned for 1993. At a meeting in St. Louis in September 1996, the parties disagreed on how much Budvar was worth, and Anheuser-Busch broke off negotiations. In a prepared statement, Jack H. Purcell, chairman and chief executive of Anheuser-Busch International, said, "Due to our success in selling our Budweiser beer in disputed markets in Europe under the Bud brand name, coupled with recent litigation successes with both the Budweiser and Bud brand names, it is no longer necessary for us to have a trademark settlement to develop our Budweiser business in Europe." Purcell was referring to the company's new strategy of suing on a country-by-country basis to win the right to the Budweiser name. By the end of 1996, it had won cases in Ireland, Portugal, Sweden, and six other European countries and had another 27 cases pending worldwide. Anheuser-Busch even pulled out of a $145 million proposed joint venture in Vietnam because Budvar had registered the Budweiser name there in 1960. Anheuser-Busch officials believe they will prevail in Vietnamese courts and that country officials will award them the right to register the Budweiser name. In January 1997, the Czech government announced that Budvar's management would have the opportunity to purchase a 10 percent stake in Budvar. ∎

DISCUSSION QUESTIONS

1. Assess Anheuser-Busch's effort to reach an agreement with the Czechs to invest in Budvar. What, if anything, should the American company have done differently?
2. Do you agree with Anheuser-Busch's decision to break off negotiations and go to court on a country-by-country basis to assert its rights to the Budweiser name?
3. What are the prospects for Budejovicky Budvar in the future? Do you think the company should reach a settlement with Budweiser? If so, what should the terms be?

VIDEO SOURCE: "When You Say 'Bud'. . .The World of the Other Budweiser," *Nightline* (January 23, 1997).
ADDITIONAL SOURCES: Vincent Boland and Roderick Oram, "U.S. Brewer Leaves Budvar Fighting for Identity," *Financial Times* (November 1, 1996), p. 20; Boland, "Budvar Takes Lid off U.S. Rival's Offer," *Financial Times* (December 20, 1996), p. 22; Jane Perlez, "This Bud's Not for You," *The New York Times* (June 30, 1995), pp. D1, D4; Shaillagh Murray, "Prazdoj's Beer: Rich History, Poor Sales," *The Wall Street Journal Europe* (June 16–17, 1995), p. 4; Yumiko Ono, "'King of Beers' Want to Rule More of Japan," *The Wall Street Journal* (October 28, 1993), pp. B1, B8.

Case 5-3   *United States versus Cuba*

On March 12, 1996, President Clinton signed the Cuban Liberty and Democratic Solidarity Act, also known as the Helms-Burton Act. The president's actions came after Cuban MiGs shot down two U.S. civilian airplanes, killing the four Cuban-Americans who were on board. The act has two key provisions. First, it denied entry into the United States to corporate officers of companies from other countries doing business on U.S. property in Cuba that was confiscated by the Cuban government. Second, it allowed U.S. companies and citizens to sue foreign firms and investors doing business on U.S. property confiscated in Cuba. However, in July 1996, the president ordered a six-month moratorium on lawsuits. Washington pledged to keep the embargo in place until Cuban president Fidel Castro held free elections and released political prisoners.

CUBA-U.S. RELATIONS PRIOR TO 1996

Cuba is a communist outpost in the Caribbean where "socialism or death" is the national motto. After Fidel Castro came to power in 1959, his government took control of most private companies without providing compensation to the owners. American assets owned by both consumer and industrial companies worth approximately $1.8 billion were among those expropriated;

today, those assets are worth about $6 billion. President Kennedy responded by imposing a trade embargo on the island nation. Four decades later, Fidel Castro was still in power, despite the fact that his politics had fallen from fashion in many parts of the world. In 1990, Cuba opened its economy to foreign investment; by the mid-1990s, foreign commitments to invest in Cuba totaled more than half a billion dollars. Cuba desperately needs investment, in part to compensate for the end of subsidies following the demise of the Soviet Union. Oil companies from Europe and Canada were among the first to seek potential opportunities in Cuba. Many American executives are concerned that lucrative opportunities will be lost as Spain, Mexico, Italy, Canada, and other countries move aggressively into Cuba. Anticipating a softening in the U.S. government's stance, representatives from scores of U.S. companies visit Cuba regularly to meet with officials from state enterprises.

Those U.S. companies that are found guilty of violating trade embargoes, including the one on Cuba, are subject to fines of up to $1 million. Cuba remained officially off-limits to all but a handful of U.S. companies. Some telecommunications and financial services were allowed; AT&T, Sprint, and other companies have offered direct-dial service between the United States

Table 1

American Companies Seeking Restitution from Cuba

COMPANY	AMOUNT OF CLAIM (MILLIONS)
American Brands	$10.6
Coca-Cola	$27.5
General Dynamics	$10.4
ITT	$47.6
Lone Star Cement	$24.9
Standard Oil	$71.6
Texaco	$50.1

Source: U.S. Justice Department.

and Cuba since 1994. Also, a limited number of charter flights were available each day between Miami and Havana. Sale of medicines was also permitted under the embargo, and Cuban exiles living in the United States were allowed to send money to relatives still in Cuba. At a State Department briefing for business executives, Assistant Secretary of State for Inter-American Affairs Alexander Watson told his audience, "The Europeans and the Asians are knocking on the door in Latin America. The game is on and we can compete effectively, but it will be a big mistake if we leave the game to others." Secretary Watson was asked whether his comments on free trade applied to Cuba. "No, no. That simply can't be, not for now," Watson replied. "Cuba is a special case. This administration will maintain the embargo until major democratic changes take place in Cuba."

Within the United States, the government's stance toward Cuba had both supporters and opponents. Senator Jesse Helms pushed for a tougher embargo and sponsored a bill in Congress that would penalize foreign countries and companies for doing business with Cuba. The Cuban-American National Foundation actively engaged in anti-Cuba and anti-Castro lobbying. Companies that have openly spoken out against the embargo include Carlson Companies, owner of the Radisson Hotel chain, grain-processing giant Archer Daniels Midland, and the Otis Elevator division of United Technologies. A spokesperson for Carlson noted, "We see Cuba as an exciting new opportunity—the forbidden fruit of the Caribbean." A number of executives, including Ron Perelman, whose corporate holdings include Revlon and Consolidated Cigar Corporation, are optimistic that the embargo will be lifted within a few years.

Meanwhile, opinion was divided on the question of whether the embargo was costing U.S. companies once-in-a-lifetime opportunities. Some observers argued that many European and Latin American investments in Cuba were short-term, high-risk propositions that would not create barriers to U.S. companies. The opponents of the embargo, however, pointed to evidence that some investments were substantial. Three thousand new hotel rooms have been added by Spain's Grupo Sol Melia and Germany's LTI International Hotels. Both companies were taking advantage of the Cuban government's goal to increase tourism. Moreover, Italian and Mexican companies were snapping up contracts to overhaul the country's telecommunications infrastructure. Wayne Andreas, chairman of Archer Daniels Midland, summed up the views of many American executives when he said, "Our embargo has been a total failure for 30 years. We ought to have all the Americans in Cuba doing all the business they can. It's time for a change."

THE HELMS-BURTON ERA

The Helms-Burton Act brought change, but not the type advocated by ADM's Andreas. The toughened U.S. stance signaled by Helms-Burton greatly concerned key trading partners, even though Washington insisted that the act was consistent with international law. In particular, supporters noted, the "effects doctrine" of international law permits a nation to take "reasonable" measures to protect its interests when an act outside its boundaries produces a direct effect inside its boundaries. Unmoved by such rationalizations, the European Commission responded in mid-1996 by proposing legislation barring European companies from complying with Helms-Burton. Although such a "blocking statute" was permitted under Article 235 of the EU treaty, Denmark threatened to veto the action on the grounds that doing so exceeded the European Commission's authority; its concerns were accommodated, and the legislation was adopted. Similarly, the Canadian government enacted legislation that would allow Canadian companies to retaliate against U.S. court orders regarding sanctions. Also, Canadian companies that complied with the U.S. sanctions could be fined $1 million dollars for doing so.

Meanwhile, executives at Canada's Sherritt International Corp. and Mexico's Grupo Domos received letters from the U.S. government informing them that they would be barred from entering the United States because of their business ties with Cuba. Sherritt operated a Cuban nickel mine, and Grupo Domos owned a 37 percent stake in Cuba's national telephone company. Both assets had been confiscated from U.S. companies.

Canada and Mexico initiated arbitration proceedings as provided for under NAFTA. Meanwhile, in the fall of 1996, Canada registered its defiance of Helms-Burton by hosting Cuba's vice president for a four-day visit.

In August 1996, President Clinton signed another piece of legislation designed to put economic pressure on foreign governments. The Iran and Libya Sanctions Act stipulated that foreign governments and companies that invest $40 million or more in the oil or gas industry sectors in Iran or Libya would be subject to U.S. sanctions. Expert opinion was divided as to whether such sanctions would be effective.

In the fall of 1996, the World Trade Organization agreed to a request by the EU to convene a three-person trade panel that would determine whether Helms-Burton violated international trade rules. The official U.S. position was that Helms-Burton was a foreign policy measure designed to promote the transition to democracy in Cuba. The United States also hinted that, if necessary, it could legitimize Helms-Burton by invoking the WTO's national security exemption. That exemption, in turn, hinged on whether the United States faced "an emergency in international relations."

Meanwhile, efforts were underway to resolve the issue on a diplomatic basis. Sir Leon Brittan, trade commissioner for the EU, visited the United States in early November with an invitation for the United States and EU to put aside misunderstandings and join forces in promoting democracy and human rights in Cuba. He noted:

> By opposing Helms-Burton, Europe is challenging one country's presumed right to impose its foreign policy on others by using the threat of trade sanctions. This has nothing whatever to do with human rights. We are merely attacking a precedent which the U.S. would oppose in many other circumstances, with the full support of the EU.

In December, senior EU officials approved a resolution sponsored by Spain that formally clarified the EU's intention to step up pressure on Castro. The U.S. State Department hailed the move as "a breakthrough in U.S.-EU relations." The EU insisted that the policy statement did not represent a change in its position or a concession to the United States. Even so, Spain's move surprised Havana, because Spain is Cuba's biggest foreign investor. However, Spain's newly-elected conservative government was taking a harder line. Spain's prime minister and Castro even engaged in a bit of public name-calling.

In January 1997, President Clinton extended the moratorium on lawsuits against foreign investors in Cuba. In the months since the Helms-Burton Act had been in effect, a dozen companies had ceased operating on confiscated U.S. property in Cuba. Stet, the Italian telecommunications company, agreed to pay ITT for confiscated assets thereby exempting itself from possible sanctions. However, in some parts of the world, reaction to the president's action was lukewarm. The EU issued a statement noting that the action "falls short of the European Commission's hopes for a more comprehensive resolution of this difficult issue in trans-Atlantic relations." The EU also reiterated its intention of pursuing the case at the WTO. Art Eggleton, Canada's international trade minister responded with a less guarded tone. "It continues to be unacceptable behavior by the United States in foisting its foreign policy onto Canada, and other countries, and threatening Canadian business and anybody who wants to do business legally with Cuba."

Meanwhile, there was evidence that the U.S. sanctions, combined with other factors, were hurting Cuba. Sherritt and other foreign investors found the going slower than they expected. A number of legal reforms had still not been implemented. Also, the 1997 sugar crop, critical to Cuba's export earnings, was lower than anticipated. Another interesting twist occurred in Canada, where Wal-Mart temporarily removed Cuban-made pajamas from its 136 retail outlets. The issue was whether Wal-Mart was in violation of the Cuban Democracy Act, which makes U.S. global firms responsible for any boycott violations committed by foreign subsidiaries. After spending two weeks studying the matter and consulting with legal experts, Wal-Mart executives ordered the Cuban goods to be returned to the shelves.

In February, the WTO appointed the panel that would consider the dispute. However, Washington declared that it would boycott the panel proceedings on the grounds that the panel's members weren't competent to review U.S. foreign policy interests. Stuart Eizenstat, undersecretary for international trade at the U.S. Commerce Department, said, "The WTO was not created to decide foreign-policy and national-security issues." One expert on international trade law cautioned that the United States was jeopardizing the future of the WTO. Professor John Jackson of the University of Michigan School of Law said, "If the U.S. takes these kinds of unilateral stonewalling tactics, then it may find itself against other countries doing the same thing in the future."

The parties averted a confrontation at the WTO when the EU suspended its complaint in April, following President Clinton's pledge to seek congressional amendments to Helms-Burton. In particular, the president agreed to seek a waiver of the provision denying U.S. visas to employees of companies using expropriated property. A few days later, the EU and the United States announced plans to develop an agreement on property claims in Cuba with "common disciplines" designed to deter and inhibit investment in confiscated property. Washington hoped such a bilateral agreement could be introduced into the negotiations at the OECD pertaining to the Multilateral Agreement on Investment. However, the agreement spelled out the EU's right to resume the trade panel or launch new proceedings if the United States took action against any European companies. The EU had one year to reactivate its complaint; it chose not to, however, and the panel was allowed to lapse in April 1998.

The U.S. stance was seen in a new perspective following the Pope's visit to Cuba in January 1998. Many observers were heartened by Cuban authorities' decision to release nearly 300 political prisoners in February. Opinion within the Cuban-American community in Miami, which had historically supported the embargo, now appeared to be divided. In the fall of 1998, several former U.S. Secretaries of State called upon President Clinton to create a National Bipartisan Commission on Cuba to review U.S. policy. Still, the *Commandante* himself remained unrepentant and appeared determined to cling to his economic policies. In denouncing "neo-liberal globalization," Castro said, "The more contact we have with capitalism, the more repugnance I feel." ■

DISCUSSION QUESTIONS

1. What was the key issue that prompted the EU to take the Helms-Burton dispute to the WTO?
2. Who benefits the most from an embargo of this type? Who suffers?
3. Do you believe the United States should continue its embargo of Cuba, or should the embargo be lifted? Why?

SOURCES: Pascal Fletcher, "Cuba Sees Itself As Shining Example Amid Global Troubles," *Financial Times* (September 19–September 20, 1998), p. 3; Carl Gershman, "Thanks to the Pope, Civil Society Stirs in Cuba," *The Wall Street Journal* (September 18, 1998), p. A11; Stuart E. Eizenstat, "A Multilateral Approach to Property Rights," *The Wall Street Journal* (April 11, 1997), p. A18; Therese Raphael, "U.S. and Europe Clash over Cuba," *The Wall Street Journal* (March 31, 1997), p. A14; Robert Greenberger, "Washington Will Boycott WTO Panel," *The Wall Street Journal* (February 21, 1997), p. A2; Greenberger, "U.S. Holds Up Cuba Suits, Pleasing Few," *The Wall Street Journal* (January 6, 1997), p. A7, Brian Coleman, "EU to Push for Human Rights in Cuba," *The Wall Street Journal* (December 2, 1996), p. A12; Guy de Jonquières, "Brittan Calls for End to Cuba Row," *Financial Times* (November 7, 1996), p. 10; Julie Wolf and Brian Coleman, "EU Challenges U.S. Plan to Penalize Foreign Firms That Trade with Cuba," *The Wall Street Journal* (July 31, 1996), p. A1; Gail DeGeorge, "U.S. Business Isn't Afraid to Shout *Cuba Si!*" *Business Week* (November 6, 1995), p. 39; Jose De Cordoba, "Cuba's Business Law Puts Off Foreigners," *The Wall Street Journal* (October 10, 1995), p. A14; Sam Dillon, "Companies Press Clinton to Lift Embargo on Cuba," *The New York Times* (August 27, 1995), pp. 1, 4; Thomas T. Vogel, Jr., "Havana Headaches: Investors Find Cuba Tantalizing yet Murky In Financial Matters," *The Wall Street Journal* (August 7, 1995), pp. A1, A4.

Chapter 6

Global Information Systems and Market Research

K M. S. "Titoo" Ahuwalia is the president of ORG-MARG, the largest marketing research company in India. His client list reads like a who's who of global companies: Avon Products, Gillette, Coca-Cola, and Unilever. And, as Titoo is fond of telling them, they are finding that "India is different." India is the second most populous nation on earth, with a middle class of more than 200 million people. Despite increasing affluence, however, centuries-old cultural traditions and customs still prevail. As a result, consumer behavior sometimes confounds Western expectations. Despite summer temperatures that frequently reach triple digits, only 2 percent of urban dwellers use deodorant. Instead, Indians bathe twice daily. Only 1 percent of households own air conditioners, and a recent Gallup survey revealed that only 1 percent intended to buy an air conditioner in the near future. The virtues of frugality once preached by Gandhi remain uppermost in the minds of many; smokers refill disposable lighters, and women recycle old sheets instead of spending money on sanitary napkins. Likewise, in a country where food is believed to shape personality and mood and hot breakfasts are thought to be a source of energy, Kellogg has had little luck at winning converts to cold cereal.

For marketers who hope to achieve success in India and other emerging markets, information about buyer behavior and the overall business environment is vital to effective managerial decision making. When researching any market, marketers must know where to go to obtain information, what subject areas to investigate and information to look for, the different ways information can be acquired, and the various analysis approaches that will yield important insights and understanding. Obviously, India's 16 languages, 200 dialects, and low level of urbanization create special research challenges. However, similar challenges are likely to present themselves wherever the marketer goes. It is the marketer's good fortune that, since the mid-1990s, a veritable

As these billboards demonstrate, the Coke/Pepsi rivalry is as intense in India as it is in the rest of the world. For much of the 1990s, Coke was promoted in India as a global brand. By contrast, Pepsi achieved market dominance in the cola segment by pursuing a more local approach. Here, Pepsi appeals to national sentiments by appending the phrase "yeh hi hai" (literally "This only is") to the global "right choice Baby" tag line. Recently, Coke brought its strategy more in line with Pepsi's; now both companies use local film stars in their advertising and sponsor sports, music, and religious events.

cornucopia of market information has become available on the Internet. A few keystrokes can yield literally hundreds of articles, research findings, and Web sites that offer a wealth of information about particular country markets. Even so, marketers need to study several important topics to make the most of modern information technology. First, they need to understand the importance of information technology and marketing information systems as strategic assets. Second, they need a framework for information scanning and opportunity identification. Third, they should have a general understanding of the formal market research process. Finally, they should know how to manage the marketing information collection system and the marketing research effort. These topics are the focus of this chapter.

INFORMATION TECHNOLOGY FOR GLOBAL MARKETING

A **management information system (MIS)** provides managers and other decision makers with a continuous flow of information about company operations. A company's MIS should provide a means for gathering, analyzing, classifying, storing, retrieving, and reporting relevant data. The MIS should also cover important aspects of a company's external environment, including customers and competitors. Global competition intensifies the need for an effective MIS that is accessible throughout the company. As James Wogland, vice chairman at Caterpillar, noted recently, "To survive in this new globally-competitive world, we had to modernize. Information technology is the glue for everything we do." Caterpillar, GE, Boeing, Federal Express, Diageo, Ford, and Texas Instruments are a few of the companies with global operations that have made significant investments in information technology (IT) in recent years.

Such investment is typically directed at upgrading a company's computer hardware and software. One beneficiary is Microsoft, thanks to high global acceptance of its Windows NT operating system. An **intranet** allows authorized company personnel or outsiders to share information electronically in a secure fashion while reducing the amount of paper generated. Colgate-Palmolive recently succeeded in standardizing and integrating its disparate and frequently incompatible electronic mail systems at locations around the globe. The process was tedious, but Colgate executives realized that a global messaging system would increase employee productivity. As a result, employees in 165 countries can now easily exchange messages and files; electronic mail traffic almost doubled in a three-year period after the system was fully implemented. An undertaking of this magnitude required the full support of senior management inside and outside the marketing function and integration into the strategic planning process. Boeing used intranet technology to create an online database known as Boeing Online Data (BOLD). The system provides suppliers and airline customers with electronic access to engineering drawings, maintenance manuals, service bulletins, and other data. A typical airline requires a library of 40,000 information cards for each type of Boeing aircraft in its fleet plus 30,000 updates each year; BOLD cuts down on the amount of paper needed, with annual savings that can total $200,000 per aircraft.[1]

Visit the Web site
www.tpn.geis.com
The Trading Process Network, operated by GE Information Systems, enables GE and outside companies to conduct business on the Internet.

An **electronic data interchange** (EDI) system allows a company's business units to submit orders, issue invoices, and conduct business electronically with other company units as well as outside companies. One of the key features of EDI is that its transaction formats are universal. This allows computer systems at different companies to speak the same language. Wal-Mart is legendary for its sophisticated EDI system. GE Information Systems (GEIS) designed an EDI system that allows GE's various business units to make purchases worth $500 million from vendors. In 1997, GEIS went a step further by moving the system to the Web and making it available to other companies. Bruce Chovnick, vice president of global Internet solutions at GEIS, predicts that the value of transactions conducted on the trading process network will quickly reach $5 billion.[2]

Poor operating results can often be traced to insufficient data and information about events both inside and outside the company. For example, when a new management team was installed at the U.S. unit of Adidas AG, the German athletic shoe marketer, data were not even available on normal inventory turnover rates. A new reporting system revealed that arch-rivals Reebok and Nike turned inventories five times a year, compared with twice a year at Adidas. This information was used to tighten the marketing focus on the best-selling Adidas products. Benetton S.p.A.'s use of MIS as a strategic competitive tool is described later. In Japan, 7-Eleven's computerized distribution system also provides it with a competitive advantage in the convenience store industry. Every 7-Eleven store is linked with each other and with distribution centers. As one retail analyst noted:

---

[1]   Geoffrey Nairn, "Business Benefits Come First," *Financial Times-Information Technology Review* (March 4, 1998), p. 9.
[2]   Dana Blankenhorn, "GE's E-commerce Network Opens up to Other Marketers," *Business Marketing* (May 1997), p. M4.

"With the system they have established, whatever time you go, the shelves are never empty. If people come in at 4 am and the stores don't have what they want, that will have a big impact on what people think of the store."[3]

Globalization puts increased pressure on companies to achieve as many economies as possible. Information technology provides a number of helpful tools. For example, retailers are increasingly using a technique known as **efficient consumer response** (ECR) in an effort to work more closely with vendors on stock replenishment. ECR entails sharing **electronic point of sale** (EPOS) data in an effort to ensure that the retail supply chain functions as efficiently as possible. EPOS is purchase data gathered by checkout scanners that help retailers identify patterns about what products are selling and how consumer preferences vary with geography. In addition, EDI links with vendors enable them to improve inventory management and restock hot-selling products in a timely, cost-effective manner. Although currently most popular in the United States, ECR is also catching on in Canada as well as Germany, the UK, and other European countries. The Coopers & Lybrand consulting firm recently estimated that grocery companies with stores across Europe could realize $33 billion in annual savings by utilizing ECR.[4]

EPOS and other IT tools are also helping businesses improve their ability to target consumers and increase loyalty. The trend among retailers is from demand-led to customer-focused strategies that will personalize and differentiate the business. In addition to point-of-sale scanner data, loyalty programs that use electronic smart cards will provide retailers with important information about shopping habits. Companies are also creating databases called **data warehouses** to support management decision making. In particular, data warehouses can help retailers with multiple store locations fine-tune product assortments. Company personnel, including persons who are not computer specialists, can access data warehouses via standard Web browsers. Behind the familiar interfaces, however, is specialized software capable of performing multidimensional analysis by using sophisticated techniques such as linear programming and regression. This will enhance the ability of managers to respond to changing business conditions by adjusting marketing mix elements. Annual sales of data-warehousing software, hardware, and services are expected to grow from $2 billion in 1996 to $12 billion by 2000. MicroStrategy, an information services company in the UK, is one of several companies creating data warehouses for clients. As manager Stewart Holness explains, "Many corporations have a vast amount of information which they have spent money accumulating, but they have not been able to distribute it. The Web is the perfect vehicle for it."[5]

There is no question that the Internet is revolutionizing corporate information processing. Companies that are slow to recognize the revolution risk falling behind competitors. For example, Germany is home to the *Mittelstand*, a group of three million small and mid-size manufacturers that have traditionally been focused and successful global marketers. The *Mittelstand* are often cited as an illustration of how small companies can help propel economic growth and sustain prosperity. However, according to one 1997 estimate, only 4 percent of *Mittelstand* companies use the

3   Bethan Hutton, "Japan's 7-Eleven Sets Store by Computer Links," *Financial Times* (March 17, 1998), p. 26.
4   Geoffrey Nairn, "Potential for Big Savings in the Food Industry," *Financial Times Survey-Information Technology* (October 2, 1996), p. 6. See also James Pollack, "Faster, Cheaper, Better," *Marketing* (February 7, 1994), p. 11.
5   Vanessa Houlder, "Warehouse Parties," *Financial Times* (October 23, 1996), p. 8. See also John W. Verity, "Coaxing Meaning out of Raw Data," *Business Week* (February 3, 1997), pp. 134+.

Internet, while two-thirds of Germany's large companies do. Dietmar Hopp, chief executive of Germany's largest software firm, said recently:

> The *Mittelstand* is lagging behind. Opportunities to improve productivity are being missed. With globalization there is no difference now between the *Mittelstand* and big companies—the business processes are comparable. It is only a matter of time before foreign competitors use the Internet to strengthen their foothold in Germany. German companies should follow their example and build up their U.S. and Asian activities through electronic marketing and commerce.[6]

These examples show just some of the ways that information technology is affecting global marketing. However, EDI, ECR, EPOS, and other aspects of IT do not simply represent marketing issues; they are organizational imperatives. The tasks of designing, organizing, and implementing information systems must be coordinated in a coherent manner that contributes to the overall strategic direction of the organization. Modern information technology tools provide the means for a company's marketing information system and research functions to provide relevant information in a timely, cost-efficient, and actionable manner.

A more detailed discussion of the information technology issues is beyond the scope of this book. The discussion that follows in this section focuses on the subject agenda, scanning modes, and information sources characteristic of a global information system that is oriented toward the external environment.

Information Subject Agenda

A starting point for a global marketing information system is a list of subjects about which information is desired. The resulting "subject agenda" should be tailored to the specific needs and objectives of the company. The general framework suggested in Table 6-1 consists of six broad information areas. The framework satisfies two essential criteria. First, it is all the information subject areas relevant to a company with global operations. Second, the categories in the framework are mutually exclusive; any kind of information encompassed by the framework can be correctly placed in one and only one category. The basic elements of the external environment outlined in the last four chapters—economic, social and cultural, legal and regulatory, and financial factors—will undoubtedly be on the information agenda of most companies, as shown in the table.

Scanning Modes: Surveillance and Search

Once the subject agenda has been determined, the next step is the actual collection of information. This can be accomplished by using either surveillance or search.

In the *surveillance* mode, the marketer engages in informal information gathering. Globally oriented marketers are constantly on the lookout for information about potential opportunities and threats in various parts of the world. They want to know everything about the industry, the business, the marketplace, and consumers. This passion shows up in the way they keep their ears and eyes tuned for clues, rumors,

---

[6] Graham Bowley, "In the Information Technology Slow Lane," *Financial Times* (November 11, 1997), p. 14.

The Rest of the Story
Market Research in Developing Countries

Nestlé demonstrates how understanding the market can lead to success. It successfully positioned its Maggi brand noodles in India as a between-meal snack food rather than a pasta meal item. Nestlé also caters to the Indian preference for local brands; although Nescafe is the company's flagship global coffee brand in many countries, Nestlé created chicory-flavored Sunrise especially for the Indian market. Nestlé managers have also learned that the 20 million wealthy households in its core target market exhibit a value orientation traditionally associated with mass markets. Nestlé has responded by keeping prices down; more than half of the products it sells in India cost less than 25 rupees—about 70 cents.

The tobacco industry is also learning about India. Sixty percent of adult Indian males smoke, although many prefer the native *bidi*, which is hand-rolled with a leaf outer wrapper rather than paper. As Darryl Jayson, economist at the Tobacco Merchants Association (TMA), noted recently, "Many companies, local and international, are hoping that these bidi-smokers move up to cigarettes as India becomes more affluent." Although Western brands enjoy high levels of awareness, the government taxes make up 70 percent of the retail price of a single pack. As a result, premium European brands such as Dunhill cost $4 per pack, whereas Indian brands from Indian Tobacco Company and other local manufacturers sell for $.50 to $1.50. Taste is an issue facing American tobacco companies; Indian smokers prefer Virginia blend tobaccos, while the typical American smoke uses oriental and burley blends. The TMA's Jayson says, "Indian smokers perceive U.S. cigarettes as roasted and harsh. I think it is very difficult to change the smoking habits of the Indians. It may take up to 20 years to bring about the change."

SOURCES: Daniel Pearl, " The Rigors of Cracking India's Markets," *The Wall Street Journal* (November 27, 2000), pp. A25, A28; Miriam Jordan, "Marketing Gurus Say: In India, Think Cheap, Lose the Cold Cereal," *The Wall Street Journal* (October 11, 1996), p. A7; O. P. Malik, "The World's Tobacco Marketers Think 20 Million Indians Can't be Wrong," *Brandweek* (October 9, 1995), pp. 46, 48; Malik, "The Great Indian Brand Bazaar," *Brandweek* (June 5, 1995), pp. 31–32.

Table 6-1
Subject Agenda Categories for a Global Marketing Information System

CATEGORY	COVERAGE
1. Market potential	Demand estimates, consumer behavior, review of products, channels, communication media
2. Competitor information	Corporate, business, and functional strategies. Resources and intentions. Capabilities.
3. Foreign exchange	Balance of payments, interest rates, stability of country currency, expectations of analysts
4. Prescriptive information	Laws, regulations, rulings concerning taxes, earnings, dividends in both host and home countries
5. Resource information	Availability of human, financial, physical, and information resources
6. General conditions	Overall review of sociocultural, political, technological environments

nuggets of information, and insights. Browsing through newspapers and magazines is one way to ensure exposure to information on a regular basis. Global marketers may also develop a habit of watching news programs from around the world via satellite. This type of general exposure to information is known as *viewing*. If a particular news story has special relevance for a company—for example, renewal of China's most-favored-nation status or the currency crisis in Asia—the marketer will pay special attention, tracking the story as it develops. This is known as *monitoring*.

The *search* mode is characterized by more formal activity. Search involves the deliberate seeking out of specific information. Search often includes *investigation,* a relatively limited and informal type of search. Investigation often means seeking out books or articles in trade publications on a particular topic or issue. Search may also consist of *research,* a formally organized effort to acquire specific information for a specific purpose. This type of formal, organized research is described later in the chapter.

One study found that nearly 75 percent of the information acquired by headquarters executives at U.S. global companies comes from surveillance as opposed to search. However, the viewing mode generated only 13 percent of important external information, and monitoring generated 60 percent. Two factors contribute to the paucity of information generated by viewing. One is the limited extent to which executives are exposed to information that is not included in a clearly defined subject agenda. The other is the limited receptivity of the typical executive to information outside this agenda. Every executive limits his or her exposure to information that will not have a high probability of being relevant to the job or company. This is rational; a person can absorb only a minute fraction of the data available. Exposure to and retention of information stimuli must be selective.

Nevertheless, the organization as a whole must be receptive to information not explicitly recognized as important. To be effective, a scanning system must ensure that the organization is viewing areas where developments that could be important to the company might occur. Innovations in information technology have increased the speed with which information is transmitted and simultaneously shortened the life of its usefulness to the company. Advances in technology have also placed new demands on the global firm in terms of shrinking reaction times to information acquired. In some instances, the creation of a full-time scanning unit with explicit responsibility for acquiring and disseminating strategic information may be required.

Of all the changes in recent years that have affected the availability of information, perhaps none is more apparent than the explosion of documentary and electronic information. An overabundance of information has created a major problem for anyone attempting to stay abreast of key developments in multiple national markets. Today, **information overload** occurs when executives and other company personnel cannot effectively assimilate all the information available to them. Unfortunately, too few companies employ a formal system for coordinating scanning activities. This situation results in considerable duplication of effort. For example, it is not uncommon for members of an entire management group to read a single publication covering a particular subject area despite the fact that several other excellent publications covering the same area may be available.

The best way to identify unnecessary duplication is to carry out an audit of reading activity by asking each person involved to list the publications he or she reads regularly. A consolidation of the lists will reveal the surveillance coverage. Often, the scope of the group will be limited to a handful of publications to the exclusion of other worthwhile ones. A good remedy for this situation is consultation with outside experts regarding the availability and quality of publications in relevant fields or subject areas.

Information technology can also provide solutions to the problem of information overload. For example, Swiss Bank Corporation (SBC) determined that, in theory, staff members would have to spend several hours reading each day if they were to keep up with internal documents, let alone material from outside sources. SBC also estimated that 80 percent of the publications produced for in-house use were read either sporadically or not at all. SBC developed a "know-how pool project" utilizing an artificial intelligence technique known as case-based reasoning (CBR). The majority of SBC's documents are available in the company's database; a user can query the system with a request such as "I would like to have information about private banking." The computer then retrieves the necessary information. Users can also define their information needs so that "intelligent agent" software searches for new information that matches the user's profile.[7] Boeing, Andersen Consulting, and other companies are making similar progress in using information technology for knowledge management.

Overall, then, the global organization is faced with the following needs:

- An efficient, effective system that will scan and digest published sources and technical journals in the headquarters country as well as all countries in which the company has operations or customers.
- Daily scanning, translating, digesting, abstracting, and electronic input of information into a market intelligence system. Today, thanks to advances in IT, full-text versions of many sources are available online. Print documentary material can be easily scanned, digitized, and added to a company's information system.
- Expanding information coverage to other regions of the world.

Sources of Market Information

Human Sources. Although scanning is a vital source of information, research has shown that headquarters executives of global companies obtain as much as two-thirds of the information they need from personal sources. A great deal of external information comes from executives based abroad in company subsidiaries, affiliates, and branches. These executives are likely to have established communication with distributors, consumers, customers, suppliers, and government officials. Indeed, a striking feature of the global corporation—and a major source of competitive strength—is the role that executives abroad play in acquiring and disseminating information about the world environment. Headquarters executives generally acknowledge that company executives overseas are the people who know best what is going on in their areas. The following is a typical comment of headquarters executives:

> Our principal sources are internal. We have a very well-informed and able overseas establishment. The local people have a double advantage. They know the local scene and they know our business. Therefore, they are an excellent source. They know what we are interested in learning, and because of their local knowledge they are able to effectively cover available information from all sources.

The information issue exposes one of the key weaknesses of a domestic company: Although more attractive opportunities may be present outside existing areas of operation, they are likely to go unnoticed by inside sources in a domestic company because the scanning horizon tends to end at the home-country border. Similarly, a company with only limited geographical operations may be at risk because internal sources abroad tend to scan only information about their own countries or regions.

Other important information sources are friends, acquaintances, professional colleagues, consultants, and prospective new employees. The last are particularly important if they have worked for competitors. Sometimes information-related ethi-

---

[7] Vanessa Houlder, "Intelligent Reading," *Financial Times* (June 11, 1997), p. 8.

cal and legal issues arise when a person changes jobs. In 1993, J. Ignacio Lopéz de Arriortúa, head of purchasing at General Motors, accepted a job as production chief with Volkswagen. GM charged that he had taken important documents and computer files when he moved to VW. The resulting publicity was the source of considerable embarrassment to Volkswagen.

As noted in Chapter 4, it is hard to overstate the importance of travel and contact for building rapport and personal relationships. Moreover, one study found that three-quarters of the information acquired from human sources is gained in face-to-face conversation. Why? Some information is too sensitive to transmit in any other way. For example, highly placed government employees could find their careers compromised if they are identified as information sources. In such cases the most secure way of transmitting information is face to face rather than in writing. Information that includes estimates of future developments or even appraisals of the significance of current happenings is often considered too uncertain to commit to writing. Commenting upon this point, one executive said:

> People are reluctant to commit themselves in writing to highly "iffy" things. They are not cowards or overly cautious; they simply know that you are bound to be wrong in trying to predict the future, and they prefer to not have their names associated with documents that will someday look foolish.

The great importance of face-to-face communication lies also in the dynamics of personal interaction. Personal contact provides an occasion for executives to get together long enough to permit communication in some depth. Face-to-face discussion also exposes highly significant forms of nonverbal communication, as discussed in Chapter 4. One executive described the value of face-to-face contact in these terms:

> If you really want to find out about an area, you must see people personally. There is no comparison between written reports and actually sitting down with a man and talking. A personal meeting is worth 4,000 written reports.

Direct Perception. Direct sensory perception provides a vital background for the information that comes from human and documentary sources. Direct perception gets all the senses involved. It means seeing, feeling, hearing, smelling, or tasting for oneself to find out what is going on in a particular country, rather than getting secondhand information by hearing or reading about a particular issue. Some information is easily available from other sources but requires sensory experience to sink in. Often, the background information or context one gets from observing a situation can help fill in the big picture. For example, Wal-Mart's first stores in China stocked a number of products—extension ladders and giant bottles of soy sauce, for example—that were inappropriate for local customers. Joe Hatfield, Wal-Mart's top executive for Asia, began roaming the streets of Shenzhen in search of ideas. His observations paid off; when Wal-Mart's giant store in Dalian opened in April 2000, a million shoppers passed through its doors in the first week. They snapped up products ranging from lunch boxes to pizza topped with corn and pineapple.[8]

The chief executive of a small U.S. company that manufactures an electronic device for controlling corrosion had a similar experience. After spending much time in Japan, the executive managed to book several orders for the device. Following an

---

[8]   Peter Wonacott, "Wal-Mart Finds Market Footing in China," *The Wall Street Journal* (July 17, 2000), p. A31.

Behind the Scenes
Benetton's Information System

In the fashion business, the company that gets preferred styles and colors to market in the shortest length of time gains an edge over competitors. Luciano Benetton, founder of the Italian company that bears his name, notes that "Benetton's market is, for reasons of product and target, very dynamic, evolving rapidly." The company's information system includes relational databases and a network for electronic data interchange. Benetton managers rely heavily on inbound data generated at the point of purchase; data about each sales transaction are instantly transmitted via satellite to headquarters from cash registers at the company's 7,000 stores around the world. Analysts sift through the data to identify trends, which are conveyed to manufacturing.

Most of Benetton's knitwear is produced as undyed "gray goods"; garments are dyed in batches in accordance with the fashion trends identified by the MIS. Benetton's system helps to cut inventory carrying costs and reduce the number of slow-selling items that must be marked down. The company's staff of field agents uses a tracking system to follow the movement of outbound merchandise. The system shows whether a particular item is in production, in a warehouse, or in transit. In Benetton's state-of-the-art, $57 million distribution center, computer-controlled robots sort, store, and retrieve up to 12,000 bar-coded boxes of merchandise each day.

The MIS even helps the designer team work more efficiently. Before the MIS was installed, designers had to personally visit the warehouse to review samples of clothing from previous seasons. With the new system, all clothing items are photographed and the images digitized and stored on a laser disc connected to a personal computer. A designer sitting at the computer can request any item from seasonal collections dating back several years and it will be displayed on screen.

Taken as a whole, Benetton's MIS has slashed the amount of time required to design and ship knitwear from six months to a matter of weeks. Reorders from any Benetton store can be filled in 13 to 27 days. Still, Luciano Benetton is not satisfied. He hopes to go beyond data processing and use information technology as a tool for motivating employees. Explains MIS manager Bruno Zuccaro, "He says it's not enough to know what we sold, but we need to know what we should have sold and that we lost X dollars by not realizing our potential."

SOURCES: Michael M. Phillips, "Retailers Rely on High-Tech Distribution," *The Wall Street Journal* (December 12, 1996), p. A2; Janette Martin, "Benetton's IS Instinct," *Datamation* (July 1, 1989), pp. 68-15–68-16.

initial burst of success, Japanese orders dropped off; for one thing, the executive was told the packaging was too plain. "We couldn't understand why we needed a five-color label and a custom-made box for this device, which goes under the hood of a car or in the boiler room of a utility company," the executive said. While waiting for the bullet train in Japan one day, the executive's local distributor purchased a cheap watch at the station and had it elegantly wrapped. The distributor asked the American executive to guess the value of the watch based on the packaging. Despite everything he had heard and read about the Japanese obsession with quality, it was the first time the American understood that, in Japan, "a book is judged by its cover." As a result, the company revamped its packaging, seeing to such details as ensuring that strips of tape used to seal the boxes were cut to precisely the same length.[9]

As these examples show, cultural and language differences require first-hand visits to important markets to get the lay of the land. Travel should be seen not only as a tool for management control of existing operations but also as a vital and indispensable tool in information scanning.

---

[9] Nilly Landau, "Face to Face Marketing Is Best," *International Business* (June 1994), p. 64.

Information is a critical ingredient in formulating and implementing a successful marketing strategy. As described earlier, a marketing information system should produce a continuous flow of information. **Marketing research,** by contrast, is the project-specific, systematic gathering of data in the search scanning mode. The American Marketing Association defines *marketing research* as "the activity that links the consumer, customer and public to the marketer through information."[10] In **global marketing research,** this activity is carried out on a global scale. The challenge of global marketing research is to recognize and respond to the important national differences that influence the way information can be obtained. These include cultural, linguistic, economic, political, religious, historical, and market differences.

Michael Czinkota and Illka Ronkainen note that the objectives of international market research are the same as the objectives of domestic research. However, they have identified four specific environmental factors that may require international research efforts to be conducted differently than domestic research. First, researchers must be prepared for new parameters of doing business. Not only will there be different requirements, but the ways in which rules are applied may differ as well. Second, "cultural megashock" may occur as company personnel come to grips with a new set of culture-based assumptions about conducting business. Third, a company entering more than one new geographic market faces a burgeoning network of interacting factors; research may help prevent psychological overload. Fourth, company researchers may have to broaden the definition of competitors in international markets to include competitive pressures that would not be present in the domestic market.[11]

According to a recent survey, 21 percent of *Fortune* 2000 companies conducted market research outside the home country in 1995; 61 percent indicated that they intended to do more.[12] There are two basic ways to conduct marketing research. One is to design and implement a study with in-house staff. The other is to use an outside firm specializing in marketing research. In global marketing, a combination of in-house and outside research efforts is often advisable. Many large outside firms have considerable international expertise; some specialize in particular industry segments. For example, IMS Health focuses on the pharmaceuticals and health care industries, London-based Ovum Limited specializes in IT, telecommunications, and new media, and Canadean Limited limits itself to the global beverage industry. In some country markets, smaller local agencies such as ORG-MARG offer advantages such as valuable contacts and cultural insight.

The importance of the global marketplace to independent research firms has increased considerably in recent years. About two thirds of annual expenditures on marketing research are made outside the United States. For example, AC Nielsen's 1998 revenues from non-U.S. research totaled $1.4 billion, nearly three-fourths of total revenue. With offices in Poland, the Czech Republic, the Slovak Republic, and Hungary, Nielsen is spearheading the move into Central and Eastern Europe. (Market research companies are ranked in Table 6-2 according to revenues generated outside the United States.)

---

[10] Peter D. Bennett, ed., *Dictionary of Marketing Terms,* 2d ed. (Chicago: American Marketing Association, 1995), p. 169.

[11] Michael R. Czinkota and Ilkka A. Ronkainen, "Market Research for Your Export Operations: Part I—Using Secondary Sources of Research," *International Trade Forum* 30, no. 3 (1994), pp. 22–33.

[12] Jack Edmonston, "U.S., Overseas Differences Abound: Researchers, However, Find Similarities in Some Market Segments," *Business Marketing* (January 1998), p. 32.

Table 6-2

Research
Companies Ranked
by Non-U.S.
Revenue, 1998

COMPANY (HOME COUNTRY)	NON-U.S. RESEARCH REVENUES (MILLIONS)
1 AC Nielsen Corp. (USA/Switz)	$1,035.0
2 IMS Health (UK/USA)	671.7
3 Research International USA (Kantar Group-USA)	255.7
4 NFO Worldwide (USA)	270.0
5 Gartner Group (USA)	183.0
6 Millward Brown International (Kantar Group)	154.6
7 Video Research (Japan)	50.2
8 United Information Group (UK)	46.7
9 Information Resources (USA)	27.0
10 VNU Marketing Information Services (USA)	18.0

Source: Adapted from "100 Leading Research Companies," *Advertising Age* (May 24, 1999), p. s4.

Visit the Web site
Here are Web
addresses for several of
the market research
firms identified in
Table 6-2.
www.acnielsen.com
www.imshealth.com
www.sofresfsa.com
www.research-int.com
The Council of American
Survey Research
Organizations is a trade
association for America-
based research compa-
nies. Learn more about
the council at:
www.casro.org

The process of collecting data and converting it into useful information can be quite detailed, as shown in Figure 6-1. In the discussion that follows, we will focus on five basic steps: identifying the research problem, developing a research plan, collecting data, analyzing data, and presenting the research findings.

Step 1: Identifying the Research Problem

The following story illustrates the first step in the formal marketing research process:

> The vice presidents of finance and marketing of a shoe company were traveling around the world to estimate the market potential for their products. They arrived in a very poor country and both immediately noticed that none of the local citizens wore shoes. The vice president of finance said, "We might as well get back on the plane. There is no market for shoes in this country." The vice president of marketing replied, "What an opportunity! Everyone in this country is a potential customer!"

The potential market for shoes was enormous in the eyes of the marketing executive. To formally confirm his instinct, some research would be required. As this story shows, research is often undertaken after a problem or opportunity has presented itself. Perhaps a competitor is making inroads in one or more important markets around the world. Maybe research on local taste preferences is required to determine if a food recipe must be adapted. Or, like this story, a company may wish to determine whether a particular country or regional market provides good growth potential. It is a truism of market research that a problem well defined is a problem half solved. Thus, regardless of what situation sets the research effort in motion, the first two questions a marketer should ask are "What information do I need?" and "Why do I need this information?"

The research problem may be framed as the need to identify in what part(s) of the world the company should be doing business and finding out as much as possible about the business environment in the areas identified. These issues were reflected in the subject agenda categories in Table 6-1. The research problem may also be more narrowly focused on marketing issues, such as the need to adapt products and other mix elements to local tastes and assessing the demand and profit potential. Demand and profit potential, in turn, depend in part on whether the market that is the focus of the research effort can be classified as existing or potential.

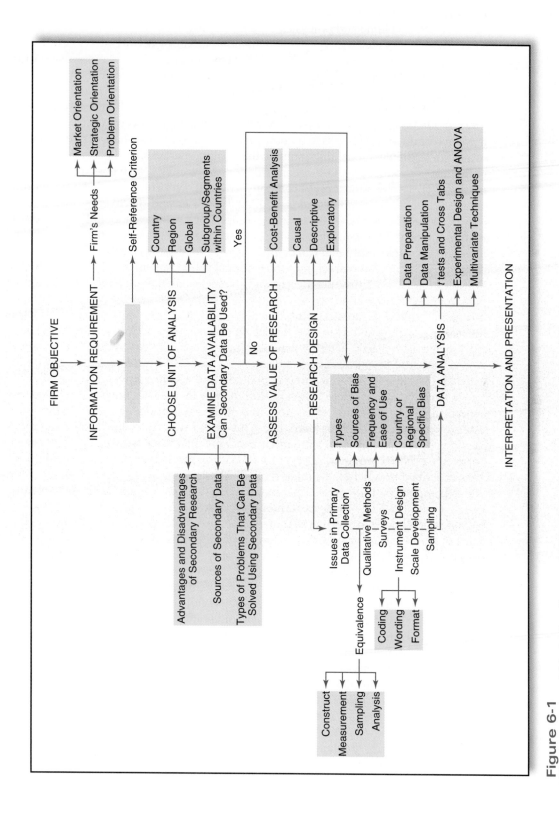

Figure 6-1
The International Marketing Research Process

Source: INTERNATIONAL MARKETING RESEARCH by Kumar, V., © Reprinted by permission of Pearson Education, Inc. Upper Saddle River, NJ

229

Existing markets are those in which customer needs are already being served by one or more companies. In many countries, data about the size of existing markets—in terms of dollar volume and unit sales—are readily available. In some countries, formal market research is a relatively new phenomenon. McKinsey & Co, Gartner Group Asia, and Grey China Advertising have been very active in China. For example, using focus groups and other techniques, Grey China gathers a wealth of information about attitudes and buying patterns that it publishes in its Grey ChinaBase Annual Consumer Study. Recent findings point to growing concerns about the future, Westernization of grocery purchases, growing market saturation, increasingly discerning customers, and a rise in consumer willingness to try new products. In countries where such data are not available, researchers must first estimate the existing market size, the level of demand, or the rate of product purchase or consumption. A second research objective in existing markets may be assessment of the company's overall competitiveness in terms of product appeal, price, distribution, and promotional coverage and effectiveness. Researchers may be able to pinpoint a weakness in the competitor's product or identify an unserved market segment. The minivan and sport utility vehicle segments of the auto industry illustrate the opportunity that can be presented by an existing market. Chrysler dominates the U.S. minivan market, for which annual sales total about 1.2 million vehicles. Ford and GM have introduced competing vehicles, as have Japanese automakers. Nissan joined forces with Ford to create the Nissan Quest and the Mercury Villager. Toyota introduced its Japanese-built Previa in the United States in 1991; critics mocked the teardrop styling and dismissed it as being underpowered. For the 1998 model year, the Previa was replaced with the American-built Sienna. To ensure that Sienna suited American tastes, Toyota designers and engineers studied Chrysler minivans and duplicated key features such as numerous cupholders and a sliding driver-side rear door.

In some instances, there is no existing market to research. Such *potential markets* can be further subdivided into latent and incipient markets. A *latent market* is, in essence, an undiscovered segment. It is a market in which demand would materialize *if* an appropriate product were made available. In a latent market, demand is zero before the product is offered. In the case of existing markets such as the one for minivans described previously, the main research challenge is to understand the extent to which competition fully meets customer needs. As J. Davis Illingworth, an executive at Toyota Motor Sales USA, explained, "I think the American public will look at Sienna as an American product that meets their needs."[13] With latent markets, initial success is not based on a company's competitiveness. Rather, it depends on the prime mover advantage—a company's ability to uncover the opportunity and launch a marketing program that taps the latent demand. This is precisely what Chrysler achieved by single-handedly creating the minivan market.

Sometimes, traditional marketing research is not an effective means for identifying latent markets. As Peter Drucker has pointed out, the failure of American companies to successfully commercialize fax machines—an American innovation—can be traced to research that indicated no potential demand for such a product. The problem, in Drucker's view, stems from the typical survey question for a product targeted at a latent market. Suppose a researcher asks, "Would you buy a telephone accessory that costs upwards of $1,500 and enables you to send, for $1 a page, the same letter the post office delivers for 25 cents?" On the basis of economics alone, the respondent most likely will answer, "No."

Drucker explains that Japanese companies are the leading sellers of fax machines today because their understanding of the market was not based on survey research. Instead, they reviewed the early days of mainframe computers, photocopy

---

13 Kathleen Kerwin, "Can This Minivan Dent Detroit?" *Business Week* (February 3, 1997), p. 37.

machines, cellular telephones, and other information and communications products. The Japanese realized that, judging only by the initial economics of buying and using these new products, the prospects of market acceptance were low. Yet, each of these products had become a huge success after people began to use them. This realization prompted the Japanese to focus on the market for the *benefits* provided by fax machines, rather than the market for the machines themselves. By looking at the success of courier services such as Federal Express, the Japanese realized that, in essence, the fax machine market already existed.[14]

An *incipient market* is a market that will emerge if a particular economic, demographic, political, or sociocultural trend continues. A company is not likely to achieve satisfactory results if it offers a product in an incipient market before the trends have taken root. After the trends have had a chance to unfold, the incipient market will become latent and, later, existing. For example, one-third of Indonesia's 200 million people are under the age of 15. This represents a huge incipient market for cigarette marketers: About 4.4 million teenagers will become old enough to smoke each year.[15] The concept of incipient markets can also be illustrated by the impact of rising income on demand for automobiles and other expensive consumer durables. As per capita income rises in a country, the demand for automobiles will also rise. Therefore, if a company can predict a country's future rate of income growth, it can also predict the growth rate of its automobile market. For example, to capitalize on China's rapid economic growth, Volkswagon, Peugeot, Chrysler, and other global automakers have established in-country manufacturing operations. There is even incipient demand in China for exotic cars; in early 1994, Ferrari opened its first showroom in Beijing. The company has sold several cars, including a Testarossa that cost $700,000 after the 150 percent import tax had been added. The first buyers were entrepreneurs who had profited from China's increasing openness to Western-style marketing and capitalism. By the end of the 1990s, demand for luxury cars had grown at a faster rate than anticipated. However, some companies have concluded that China has limited potential at present. For example, UK-based retailer Marks and Spencer recently closed its office in Shanghai and tabled plans to open a store in China. Commenting to the press, a company representative directly addressed the issue of whether or not China represents an incipient market:

> After three years of research, we have come to the conclusion that the timing is not right. The majority of our customers are from middle income groups. But, our interest is in Shanghai, and the size of the middle income group, although it is growing, is not yet at a level that would justify us opening a store there.[16]

Step 2: Developing a Methodology and Research Plan

After defining the problem to be studied or the question to be answered, the marketer must address a new set of questions. Should the research effort be geared toward quantitative, numerical data that can be subjected to statistical analysis or should qualitative techniques be used? In global marketing research, it is advisable for the plan to call for a mix of techniques. For consumer products, qualitative research is especially well suited to accomplish the following tasks:[17]

---

[14] Peter F. Drucker, "Marketing 101 for a Fast-Changing Decade," *The Wall Street Journal* (November 20, 1990), p. A17.

[15] Michael Shari, "Will Cloves Lite Set the World on Fire?" *Business Week* (April 28, 1997), p. 55.

[16] James Harding, "Foreign Investors Face New Curbs on Ownership of Stores," *Financial Times* (November 10, 1998), p. 7.

[17] John Pawle, "Mining the International Consumer," *Journal of the Market Research Society* 41, no. 1 (1999), p. 20.

- To provide consumer understanding, to "get close" to the consumer
- To describe the social and cultural context of consumer behavior, including cultural, religious, and political factors that impact decision making
- To identify core brand equity and "get under the skin" of brands
- To "mine" the consumer and identify what people really feel

However, collecting information costs money. Thus, the plan should also spell out what this information is worth to the company in dollars (or yen, etc.) compared with what it would cost to collect it. What will the company gain by collecting this data? What would be the cost of not getting the data that could be converted into useful information? Research requires investment of both money and managerial time, and it is necessary to perform a cost-benefit analysis before proceeding further.

In some instances, a company may pursue the same course of action no matter what the research reveals. Even when more information is needed to ensure a high-quality decision, a realistic estimate of a formal study may reveal that the cost to perform research is simply too high. As discussed in the next section, a great deal of potentially useful data may already exist; utilizing such data instead of commissioning a major study can result in significant savings. In any event, during the planning step, methodologies, budgets, and time parameters are all spelled out. Only when the plan is completed should the next step be undertaken.

Step 3: Collecting Data

Are data available in company files, a library, industry or trade journals, or online? When is the information needed? Marketers must address these issues as they proceed to the data collection step of the research. Using data that are readily available saves both money and time. A formal market study can cost hundreds of thousands of dollars and take many months to complete. However, as Czinkota and Ronkainen note,[18] secondary data may support the decision to pursue a market opportunity outside the home country, but it is unlikely to shed light on specific questions: What is the market potential for our furniture in Indonesia? How much does the typical Nigerian consumer spend on soft drinks? What effect will packaging changes that ensure compliance with Germany's Green Dot Ordinance have on consumer purchasing behavior?

Secondary Data. A low-cost approach to market research and data collection begins with desk research. In other words, "the key to creating a cost-effective way of surveying foreign markets is to climb on the shoulders of those who have gone before."[19] Suppose a marketer wants to assess the basic market potential for a particular product. To find the answer, secondary sources are a good place to start. Personal files, company or public libraries, online databases, government census records, and trade associations are just a few of the data sources that can be tapped with minimal effort and cost. Data from these sources already exist. Such data are known as *secondary* data because they were not gathered for the specific project at hand. *Statistical Abstract of the United States* is just one of the annual publications issued by the U.S. government that contain myriad facts about international markets. The U.S. government's most comprehensive source of world trade data is the National Trade Data Base (NTDB), a CD-ROM resource published by the U.S. Department of

[18] Michael R. Czinkota and Ilkka A. Ronkainen, "Market Research for Your Export Operations: Part II—Conducting Primary Marketing Research," *International Trade Forum* 31, no. 1 (1995), p. 16.
[19] Michael R. Czinkota and Ilkka A. Ronkainen, "Market Research for Your Export Operations: Part I—Using Secondary Sources of Research," *International Trade Forum*, no. 3 (1994), p. 22.

Commerce. Most countries compile national accounts estimates of gross national product (GNP), gross domestic product (GDP), consumption, investment, government expenditures, and price levels. Demographic data indicating the population size, distribution of population by age category, and rates of population growth are also available. Market information is also available from export census documents compiled by the Department of Commerce on the basis of shipper's export declarations (known as "ex-decs" or SEDs, these must be filled out for any export valued at $1,500 or more). Another important source of market data is the Foreign Commercial Service. Many countries have set up Web sites to help small firms find opportunities in world markets. For example, WIN (World Information Network) Export is a service of Canada's Department of Foreign Affairs and International Trade (DFAIT). The site is a computerized database containing the names of Canadian companies that export.

These do not exhaust the types of data available, however. A single source, *The Statistical Yearbook of the United Nations,* contains global data on agriculture, mining, manufacturing, construction, energy production and consumption, internal and external trade, railroad and air transport, wages and prices, health, housing, education, communication infrastructure, and availability of mass communications media. The U.S. Central Intelligence Agency publishes *World Factbook,* which is revised yearly. Other important sources are the World Bank, the International Monetary Fund, the U.S. Department of Commerce's National Trade Data Bank, and Japan's Ministry of International Trade and Industry (MITI). *The Economist* and *Financial Times* regularly compile comprehensive surveys of regional and country markets and include them in their publications. Data from these sources are generally available in both print and electronic form.

Visit the Web site
www.alberta-canada.
com/export
www.imf.org
www.jetro.org
www.unsystem.org
www.worldbank.org
www.odci.gov/cia/
publications/factbook
www.miti.go.jp
www.stern.nyu.edu~
nroubini/asia
web.mit.edu/
krugman/www
www.euromonitor.com
www.ft.com

Since the mid-1990s, there has been an explosion of economic data and information on the Internet. A perfect example is the site devoted to the Asian economic crisis that was established by a professor at New York University; during the height of the crisis, the site received 50,000 hits each month. Visitors include academics, journalists, and central bankers, as well as students.[20] Similarly, MIT economist Paul Krugman uses the Internet as a forum for sharing his self-avowed "extremely annoying" views on matters pertaining to international trade.

A word of caution is in order at this point: Remember that data are compiled from various sources, some of which may not be reliable. Even when the sources are reliable, there is likely to be some variability from source to source. Anyone using data should be clear on exactly what the data are measuring. For example, studying income data requires understanding whether one is working with gross national product or gross domestic product figures. Also, anyone using the Internet as an information source should evaluate the credibility of the person(s) responsible for the Web site.

Visit the Web site
Find out more about MarketResearch.com and Euromonitor or browse their online catalogs at:
www.MarketResearch.
com
www.euromonitor.com

Syndicated studies published by private research companies are another source of secondary data and information (the word "syndicated" is borrowed from the newspaper industry and refers to the practice of selling articles or features to a number of different organizations). For example, MarketResearch.com sells reports on a wide range of global business sectors; the company partners with 350 research firms to offer a comprehensive set of reports. A sampling of reports available from MarketResearch.com is shown in Table 6-3; the cost of a single report can run thousands of dollars.

---

[20] Bob Davis, "Internet Hot Spot Emerges from Asian Economic Crisis," *The Wall Street Journal* (June 23, 1998), p. B1.

Table 6-3

Global Market
Research
Reports from
MarketResearch.com

TITLE OF STUDY	LENGTH IN PAGES	PRICE
World Pharmaceutical Chemicals	438	$4,500
Internet Commerce in Canada 2000–2006	22	$4,500
World Alcohol—Strategic Review	900	$3,950
Global Airport Retailing	185	$1,115
The Market for Travel and Tourism in Russia	73	$1,000
Pet Food and Pet Products in India	36	$1,000
Online Music in Japan	12	$995
The 2000–2005 World Ice Cream Outlook	110	$795
Automobiles and Automotive Parts in Brazil	170	$136

Source: The Information Catalog, 2nd Quarter 2002, MarketResearch.com.

Primary Data and Survey Research. When data are not available through published statistics or studies, direct collection is necessary. *Primary data* are gathered through original research pertaining to the particular problem identified in step 1. Survey research, interviews, consumer panels, observation, and focus groups are some of the tools used to collect primary market data. These are the same tools used by marketers whose activities are not global; some adaptations and special considerations for global marketing may be required, however.

Survey research utilizes questionnaires designed to elicit either quantitative data ("How much would you buy?"), qualitative data ("Why would you buy?"), or both. Survey research often obtains data from customers or some other designated group by means of a questionnaire distributed through the mail, by telephone, or in person. Many good marketing research textbooks provide details on questionnaire design and administration.

A good questionnaire has three main characteristics:

1. It is simple.
2. It is easy for respondents to answer and for the interviewer to record.
3. It keeps the interview to the point and obtains desired information.

In global marketing research, a number of survey design and administration issues may arise. For example, telephone directories or lists may not be available; also, important differences may exist between urban dwellers and people in rural areas. Open-ended questions may help the researcher identify a respondent's frame of reference. In some cultures, respondents may be unwilling to answer certain questions, or they may intentionally give inaccurate answers. Another important survey issue in global marketing is potential SRC bias because of the cultural background of those designing the questionnaire. For example, a survey designed and administered in the United States may be inappropriate in non-Western cultures, even if it is carefully translated.[21] This is especially true if the person designing the questionnaire is not familiar with the self-reference criterion. A technique known as *back translation* can help increase comprehension and validity; the technique requires that, after a questionnaire or survey instrument is translated into a particular target language, it is translated once again into the original by a different translator. For even greater

---

[21] Geert Hofstede and Michael Harris Bond, "The Confucius Connection: From Cultural Roots to Economic Growth," *Organizational Dynamics* (Spring 1988), p. 15.

accuracy, *parallel translations*—that is, two versions by different translators—can be used as input to the back translation. The same techniques can be used to ensure that advertising copy is accurately translated into different languages.

Sometimes bias is introduced when a survey is sponsored by a company with a financial stake in the outcome plans to publicize the results. For example, American Express joined with the French tourist bureau in producing a study that, among other things, covered the personality of the French people. The report ostensibly showed that, contrary to a long-standing stereotype, the French are not "unfriendly" to foreigners. However, the survey respondents were people who already had traveled to France on pleasure trips in the previous two years—a fact that likely biased the result.[22]

Personal interviews allow researchers to ask why and then explore answers. Interviews may be conducted in person or by telephone. However, what is customary in one country may be impossible in others because of infrastructure differences, cultural barriers, or other reasons. For example, telephone interviewing is a popular mass market research tool in the United States and other countries where most households have at least one telephone. However, the technique is quite inappropriate as a research tool in emerging markets where only 1 or 2 percent of households have telephones. At a deeper level, culture shapes attitudes and values in a way that will directly affect people's willingness to respond to interviewer questions.

Consumer panels are often used by Nielsen Media Research and other organizations to track television viewership. Participating panelists maintain a diary in which they keep a written record of the shows they view. In the United States, Nielsen has enjoyed a virtual monopoly on viewership research for half a century. For years, however, the four major U.S. television networks have complained that they lose advertising revenues because Nielsen data collection undercounts viewership. In 1998, CBS and the other networks announced plans to invest in a new service that will compete with Nielsen. Nevertheless, the panel approach is being adopted outside the United States. For example, France's Sofres Group and China's Central Viewers Survey & Consulting Center have formed a joint venture that will gather data from the world's largest consumer panel.

A recent plan to conduct research on pan-Asian TV viewership got off to a slow start amid concerns that data gathered in Asia would not be comparable with worldwide TV viewing information. The goal was to provide uniform data on a regional basis to supplement existing data gathered on a country-by-country basis. One of the firms bidding for the project, New York-based Audits & Surveys (A&S), intended to use a model that it had developed for the Latin American model. However, executives at Asia's Star TV, a possible sponsor of the new study, balked at backing the project because Asia lacks the common language and cultural traditions found in Latin America. Consequently, the type of uniform questionnaires, surveys, and interviews developed by A&S for Latin America could not be used to good effect in Asia. A&S announced that it would find other sources of financial support for its research.[23]

When **observation** is used as a data collection method, one or more trained observers (or a mechanical device such as a video camera) watch and record the behavior of actual or prospective buyers. Observation can take the form of home visits. For example, Toyota used observation when redesigning its flagship luxury car, the Lexus LS 400, for the 1995 model year. The chief engineer of Lexus and a five-person

---

[22] Cynthia Crossen, "Margin of Error: Studies Galore Support Products and Positions, But Are They Reliable?" *The Wall Street Journal* (November 4, 1991), pp. A1, A7.
[23] Jeffery D. Zbar, "Asian Research Project Hits Wall in Development," *Ad Age International* (July 1997), p. i2.

team came to the United States in 1991. They stayed in luxury hotels to gain an understanding of the level of service Lexus customers demanded. Design team members visited customers' homes and took notes on preferences for such things as furniture, paintings—even briefcases. As Ron Brown, a U.S.-based product planning manager for Lexus, recalled, "It's like if you just bought a new washer-dryer, and the Kenmore people called and said they wanted to bring a bunch of people out to watch you wash your clothes." One thing the team discovered was that the coat hooks in the first-generation LS 400 were too small. The Japanese thought a coat hook was, literally, for hanging a coat. In reality, Lexus owners regularly hang their dry-cleaning in the car. The hook has been redesigned for 1995. "You can get five coat hangers on it. But now it's big enough that you wouldn't want it out all the time, so it retracts," says Brown.[24] The research effort paid off; by 2001, Lexus ranked in the top three of luxury car nameplates sold in the United States; Cadillac, meanwhile, had fallen from first place to sixth. How did Cadillac respond? The company sent *its* designers and engineers to Los Angeles and New York for "luxury immersions." Teams stayed in luxury hotels, drove BMWs and Mercedes, and shopped in upscale stores. As one designer noted, "You've got to live the lifestyle for a couple of days."[25]

A marketer of breakfast cereals might send researchers to preselected households at 6 a.m. to watch families go about their morning routines. The client could also assign a researcher to accompany family members to the grocery store to observe their behavior under actual shopping conditions. The client might wish to know about the shoppers' reactions to in-store promotions linked to an advertising campaign. The researcher could record comments using a microcassette recorder or discretely take photographs with a small camera. Companies using observation as a research methodology must be sensitive to public concerns about privacy issues. A second problem with observation is **reactivity,** which is the tendency of research subjects to behave differently for the simple reason that they know they are under study.

Procter & Gamble has recently undertaken an ambitious observation program that will send video crews into 80 households in the United Kingdom, Italy, Germany, and China. The filmmakers will arrive each day when the subject family rises and film until bedtime. Faced with sluggish annual sales growth, marketers at the packaged-goods giant are hoping to gain insights into consumer behavior that other forms of research might miss. Those insights could be translated directly into product and package design improvements that could provide a competitive advantage for P&G. P&G's ultimate goal is to amass an in-house video library that can be directly accessed by key word searches. Stan Joosten, an information-technology manager, noted "You could search for 'eating snacks' and find all clips from all over the world on that topic. Immediately, it gives you a global perspective on certain topics."[26]

In **focus group** research, a trained moderator facilitates discussion of a product concept, advertisement, social trend, or other topic with a group comprised of 6 to 10 people. A typical focus group meets at a facility equipped with recording equipment and a one-way mirror behind which representatives of the client company observe the proceedings. The moderator can utilize a number of approaches to elicit reactions and responses, including projective techniques, visualization, and role plays. For example, in a focus group convened to assess car-buying preferences among a

---

[24] James R. Healy, "Toyota Strives for New Look, Same Edge," *USA Today* (October 13, 1994), pp. 1B–2B.
[25] Gregory While, "GM Shifts Into Overdrive in Luxury Sport-Sedan Race," *The Wall Street Journal* (August 17, 2001), p. B4.
[26] Emily Nelson, "P&G Checks Out Real Life," *The Wall Street Journal* (May 17, 2001), pp. B1, B4.

Striver-type segment, the researcher might ask participants to describe a party where various automotive brands are present. What is Nissan wearing, eating, and drinking? What kind of sneakers does Honda have on? What are their personalities like? Who's shy? Who's loud? Who gets the girl (or guy)? Interaction among group members can result in synergies that yield important qualitative insights significantly different from those based on data gathered through more direct questioning. Focus group research is a technique that is growing in popularity; in the United States alone, companies spent an estimated $300 million on focus groups in 2000.

Focus group research yields qualitative data that does not lend itself to statistical projection. Such data suggests, rather than confirms hypotheses; also, qualitative data tends to be directional rather than conclusive. Such data is extremely valuable in the exploratory phase of a project and is typically used in conjunction with data gathered via observation and other methods. For example, the Coca-Cola Company convened focus groups in Japan, England, and the United States to explore potential consumer reaction to a prototype 12-ounce contoured aluminum soft drink can. Coca-Cola was searching for ways to counteract competition from private-label colas in key markets; in England, for example, Sainsbury's store brand cola has an 18 percent market share.[27] Similarly, focus groups have helped PepsiCo's Frito-Lay snack unit build its business in Asia. In Thailand, focus group research indicated that *tom yan* (prawn) was the favorite flavor; in China, focus groups prefer dog. But that did not automatically mean that Thai consumers would prefer prawn-flavored potato chips. The researchers discovered that a "good" snack is one with a Western flavor such as barbeque.[28]

Waterford/Wedgwood PLC also used focus groups to determine the best growth strategy in the crystal and fine china market. Focus groups were conducted in three countries; management then reviewed 30 hours of taped interviews. Analysis of the data pointed to several opportunities to segment the market. First, a new, lower-priced line of crystal called Marquis by Waterford was introduced. Wedgwood has also rolled out two new porcelain lines, "Embassy" and "Home." The new brands are less expensive than Waterford's traditional lines but benefit from association with the upscale Waterford/Wedgwood name.[29]

Technology and New Media. As noted earlier in the chapter, electronic scanning at the point of purchase is providing retailers with a great deal of data. The Internet is also an important source of customer information; visitors to a particular Web site are often invited to submit information about themselves when making purchases, joining clubs, or entering sweepstakes. Television viewership can be tracked electronically by "people meters." The first metered viewership data for Latin American homes with cable and satellite dishes became available from Audits & Surveys Worldwide in 1997. Several hundred homes in Buenos Aires and Mexico were wired with meters; plans to meter cable and satellite homes in Brazil, Chile, Colombia, Venezuela, and Peru were slated.[30]

In some instances, product characteristics dictate a particular country location for primary data collection. For example, Case Corporation recently needed input

Visit the Web site
Focus group moderators are also known as *qualitative researchers.* Many belong to the Qualitative Research Consultants Association. The QRCA Web site includes the Association's code of ethics and links to other research-oriented sites. The Web site for the UK-based Association of Qualitative Research Practitioners (AQRP) includes a concise history of qualitative research.
www.qrca.org
www.aqrp.co.uk

Visit the Web site
Find Audits & Surveys Worldwide at:
www.surveys.com

---

[27] Karen Benezra, "Coke Queries on Contour Can," *Brandweek* (November 7, 1994), p. 4.
[28] G. Pascal Zachary, "Strategic Shift: Major U.S. Companies Expand Efforts to Sell to Consumers Abroad," *The Wall Street Journal* (June 13, 1996), pp. A1, A6.
[29] Judith Valente, "A New Brand Restores Sparkle to Waterford," *The Wall Street Journal* (November 10, 1994), pp. B1, B4.
[30] Jeffery D. Zbar, "Panregional TV Begins Rolling Out First Hard Numbers," *Ad Age International* (September 1997), p. i26.

from farmers about cab design on a new generation of tractors. Case markets tractors in North America, Europe, and Australia, but the prototypes it had developed were too expensive and fragile to ship. Working in conjunction with Jefferson Davis Associates, an Iowa-based market research company, Case invited 40 farmers to an engineering facility near Chicago for interviews and reactions to instrument and control mock-ups. The visiting farmers were also asked to examine tractors made by Case's competitors and evaluate them on more than 100 different design elements. Case personnel from France and Germany were on hand to assist as interpreters.[31]

Sampling. When collecting data, researchers generally cannot administer a survey to every possible person in the designated group. A sample is a selected subset of a population that is representative of the entire population. The two best-known types of samples are probability samples and nonprobability samples. A probability sample is generated by following statistical rules that ensure that each member of the population under study has an equal chance—or probability—of being included in the sample. The results of a probability sample can be projected to the entire population with statistical reliability reflecting sampling error, degree of confidence, and standard deviation.

The results of a nonprobability sample cannot be projected with statistical reliability. One form of nonprobability sample is a *convenience sample.* As the name implies, researchers select people who are easy to reach. For example, in one study comparing consumer shopping attitudes in the United States, Jordan, Singapore, and Turkey, data for the latter three countries were gathered from convenience samples recruited by an acquaintance of the researcher. Although data gathered in this way are not subject to statistical inference, they may be adequate to address the problem defined in Step 1. In this study, for example, the researchers were able to identify a clear trend toward cultural convergence in shopping attitudes and customs that cut across modern industrial countries, emerging industrial countries, and developing countries.[32]

To obtain a *quota sample,* the researcher divides the population under study into categories; a sample is taken from each category. The term *quota* refers to the need to make sure that enough people are chosen in each category to reflect the overall makeup of the population. For example, assume a country's population may be divided into six categories according to monthly income as follows:

Percent of population	10%	15%	25%	25%	15%	10%
Earnings per month	0–9	10–19	20–39	40–59	60–69	70–100

If it is assumed that income is the characteristic that adequately differentiates the population for study purposes, then a quota sample would include respondents of different income levels in the same proportion as they occurred in the population, that is, 15 percent with monthly earnings from 10 to 19, and so on.

Step 4: Analyzing Data

Demand Pattern Analysis. Industrial growth patterns provide an insight into market demand. Because they generally reveal consumption patterns, production patterns are helpful in assessing market opportunities. Additionally, trends in

---

[31] Jonathan Reed, "Unique Approach to International Research," *Agri Marketing* (March 1995), pp. 10–13.

[32] Eugene H. Fram and Riad Ajami, "Globalization of Markets and Shopping Stress: Cross-Country Comparisons," *Business Horizons* (January-February 1994), pp. 17–23.

manufacturing production indicate potential markets for companies that supply manufacturing inputs. At the early stages of growth in a country, when per capita incomes are low, manufacturing centers on such necessities as food and beverages, textiles, and other forms of light industry. As incomes rise, the relative importance of these industries declines as heavy industry begins to develop.

Income Elasticity Measurements. Income elasticity describes the relationship between demand for a good and changes in income. Income elasticity studies of consumer products show that necessities such as food and clothing are characterized by inelastic demand. Stated differently, expenditures on products in these categories increase but at a slower percentage rate than do increases in income. This is the corollary of Engel's law, which states that as incomes rise, smaller proportions of total income are spent on food. Demand for durable consumer goods such as furniture and appliances tends to be income elastic, increasing relatively faster than increases in income.

Market Estimation by Analogy. Estimating market size with available data presents challenging analytical tasks. Global marketers often find that certain types of desired data are unavailable. If this is the case, it is sometimes possible to estimate market size by analogy. Drawing an analogy is simply stating a partial resemblance. For example, the advertising and computer industries in the United States both have geographic nicknames. The advertising industry is often referred to as "Madison Avenue," while the phrase "Silicon Valley" is synonymous with California's high-tech industry center. Thus, Silicon Valley is to the computer industry as Madison Avenue is to the advertising industry. Statements such as this are analogies.

Time-series displacement is an analogy technique based on the assumption that an analogy between markets exists in different time periods. Displacing time is a useful form of market analysis when data are available for two markets at different levels of development. The time displacement method requires a marketer to estimate when two markets are at similar stages of development. For example, the market for Polaroid instant cameras in Russia at present is comparable to the instant camera market in the United States in the mid-1960s. By obtaining data on the factors associated with demand for instant cameras in the United States in 1964 and in Russia today, as well as actual U.S. demand in 1964, one could estimate current potential in Russia.

Several issues should be kept in mind in using estimation by analogy:

1. Are the two countries for which the analogy is assumed really similar? To answer this question with regard to a consumer product, the analyst must understand the similarities and differences in the cultural systems in the two countries. If the market for an industrial product is under study, an understanding of the respective national technology bases is required.
2. Have technological and social developments resulted in a situation in which demand for a particular product or commodity will leapfrog previous patterns, skipping entire growth patterns that occurred in more-developed countries? For example, washing machine sales in Europe leapfrogged the pattern of sales in the United States. In the United States, washing evolved from hand-washing methods to nonautomatic washing machines and then, when reliable units were finally available, to semiautomatic and fully automatic machines. In Europe many consumers are skipping the nonautomatic and semiautomatic machines and are moving from hand washing to fully automatic equipment. A simple analogy between the growth in sales for manual, semiautomatic, and automatic machines does not exist between the United States and Europe. Nevertheless,

the market analyst might combine sales of nonautomatic and semiautomatic equipment in the U.S. market and use this growth pattern in an analogy-based estimation of potential demand in Europe.

3. If there are differences in the availability, price, quality, and other variables associated with the product in the two markets, potential demand in a target market will not develop into actual sales of a product because the market conditions are not comparable.

Comparative Analysis. One of the unique opportunities in global marketing analysis is to conduct comparisons of market potential and marketing performance in different country or regional markets at the same point in time. One form of comparative analysis is the intracompany cross-national comparison. For example, general market conditions in two or more countries (as measured by income, stage of industrialization, or some other measure) may be similar. If there is a significant discrepancy between per capita sales of a given product in the countries, the marketer might reasonably wonder about it and determine what actions need to be taken. Soon after George Fisher became CEO of Kodak, he asked for a review of market share in color film on a country-by-country basis. Fisher was shocked to learn that Kodak's market share in Japan was only 7 percent, compared with 40 percent in most other countries. The situation prompted Fisher to lodge a petition with the U.S. trade representative seeking removal of alleged anticompetitive barriers in Japan.[33] Similarly, Campbell's commands nearly 80 percent of the U.S. canned soup market. However, former CEO Dale Morrison set aggressive growth goals for Campbell's based on figures showing that Campbell's has just 10 percent market share throughout the rest of the world.[34] A third example of comparative analysis helps explain why U.S.-based catalog marketers are expanding in selected European markets. Catalog sales in the United States represent about 3 percent of overall retail sales. By comparison, catalog sales in Germany account for 5.8 percent of overall sales. This suggests that there is a catalog marketing opportunity in Germany.[35]

Cluster Analysis. The objective of cluster analysis is to group variables into clusters that maximize within-group similarities and between-group differences. Cluster analysis is well suited to global marketing research because similarities and differences can be established between local, national, and regional markets of the world. For example, Claritas/NPDC uses geodemographic data to cluster neighborhoods into types. Claritas has begun matching some U.S. cities to "twins" in Canada.[36]

Step 5: Presenting the Findings

The report based on the market research must be useful to managers as input to the decision-making process. Whether the report is presented in written form, orally, or electronically via videotape, it must relate clearly to the problem or opportunity identified in Step 1. Generally, it is advisable for major findings to be summarized concisely in a memo that indicates the answer or answers to the problem first proposed in Step 1. Many managers are uncomfortable with research jargon and com-

---

33 Wendy Bounds, "George Fisher Pushes Kodak into Digital Era," *The Wall Street Journal* (June 8, 1995), p. B1.
34 Amy Barrett, "Souping Up Campbell's," *Business Week* (November 3, 1997), p. 70.
35 Cacilie Rohwedder, "U.S. Mail-Order Firms Shake Up Europe," *The Wall Street Journal* (January 6, 1998), p. A15.
36 Claudi Montague, "Is Calgary Denver's Long-Lost Twin?" *American Demographics* (June 1993), pp. 12–13.

plex quantitative analysis. Results should be clearly stated and provide a basis for managerial action; judicious use of tables and graphs can improve the clarity of data presented. A poorly written report may end up unused on the shelf. As the data provided by a corporate information system and market research become increasingly available on a worldwide basis, it becomes possible to analyze marketing expenditure effectiveness across national boundaries. Managers can then decide where they are achieving the greatest marginal effectiveness for their marketing expenditures and can adjust expenditures accordingly.

Current Issues in Global Marketing Research

Marketers engaged in global research face special problems and conditions that differentiate their task from that of the domestic market researcher. First, instead of analyzing a single national market, the global market researcher must analyze many national markets, each of which has unique characteristics that must be recognized in an analysis. As noted earlier, for many countries, the availability of data is limited.

Second, the small markets around the world pose a special problem for the researcher. The relatively low profit potential in smaller markets justifies only a modest marketing research expenditure. Therefore, the global researcher must devise techniques and methods that keep expenditures in line with the market's profit potential. In smaller markets, there is pressure on the researcher to discover economic and demographic relationships that permit estimates of demand based on a minimum of information. It may also be necessary to use inexpensive survey research that sacrifices some elegance or statistical rigor to achieve results within the constraints of the smaller market research budget.

Another frequently encountered problem in developing countries is that data may be inflated or deflated, either inadvertently or for political expediency. For example, a Middle Eastern country deliberately revised its balance of trade in a chemical product by adding 1,000 tons to its consumption statistics in an attempt to encourage foreign investors to install domestic production facilities. In Russia, Goskomstat, the state agency that measures the economy, generates mountains of misleading statistics. Real economic output may be 40 percent higher than the official numbers because much of the economic activity in Russia's transitional economy is off the books because of high taxes and confusing laws.[37]

Another problem is that the comparability of international statistics varies greatly. An absence of standard data-gathering techniques contributes to the problem. In Germany, for example, consumer expenditures are estimated largely on the basis of turnover tax receipts, whereas in the United Kingdom data from tax receipts are used in conjunction with data from household surveys and production sources. Also, Germany classifies television set purchases as expenditures for "recreation and entertainment," whereas the same expenditure falls into the "furniture, furnishings, and household equipment" classification in the United States.

Even with standard data-gathering techniques, their application may differ around the world. Matthew Draper, vice president at New Jersey-based Total Research Corporation, cites "scalar bias" as a major problem: "There are substantial differences in the way people use scales, and research data based on scales such as rating product usefulness on a scale of 1 to 10 is therefore frequently cluttered with biases disguising the truth." For example, while the typical American scale would

---

[37] Claudia Rosett, "Figures Never Lie, but They Seldom Tell the Truth about the Russian Economy," *The Wall Street Journal* (July 1, 1994), p. A6.

equate a high number such as 10 with "most" or "best" and 1 with "least," Germans prefer scales in which 1 is "most/best." Also, while American survey items pertaining to spending provide a range of figures, Germans prefer the opportunity to provide an exact answer.[38]

When PepsiCo International, a typical user of global research, reviewed its data, it found a considerable lack of comparability in a number of major areas. Table 6-4 shows how age categories were developed in seven countries surveyed by PepsiCo. PepsiCo's headquarters marketing research group pointed out that findings in one country could be compared with those in another only if data were reported in standard five-year intervals. Without this standardization, comparability was not possible. The marketing research group recommended, therefore, that standard five-year intervals be required in all reporting to headquarters, but that any other intervals deemed useful for local purposes be allowed. Thus, for the purposes of local analysis, ages 14 to 19 might be a pertinent "youth" classification in one country, whereas ages 14 to 24 might be a more useful definition of the same segment in another country.

PepsiCo also found that local market definitions of consumption differed so greatly that it was unable to make intermarket comparisons of brand share figures. Representative definitions of consumption are shown in Table 6-5.

Finally, global consumer research is inhibited by people's reluctance to talk to strangers, greater difficulty in locating people, and fewer telephones. Both industrial and consumer research services are less developed, although the cost of these services is much lower than in a high-wage country.

Table 6-4
Age Classifications from Consumer Surveys, Major Markets

MEXICO	VENEZUELA	ARGENTINA	GERMANY	SPAIN	ITALY	PHILIPPINES
14–18	10–14	14–18	14–19	15–24	13–20	14–18
19–25	15–24	19–24	20–29	25–34	21–25	19–25
26–35	25–34	25–34	30–39	35–44	26–35	26–35
36–45	35–45	35–44	40–49	45–54	36–45	36–50
46+	45+	45–65	50+	55–64	46–60	
				65+		

Source: PepsiCo International.

Table 6-5
Definition of Consumption Used by Pepsico Market Researcher

Mexico	Count of number of occasions product was consumed on day prior to interview
Venezuela	Count of number of occasions product was consumed on day prior to interview
Argentina	Count of number of drinks consumed on day prior to interview
Germany	Count of number of respondents consuming "daily or almost daily"
Spain	Count of number of drinks consumed "at least once a week"
Italy	Count of number of respondents consuming product on day prior to interview
Philippines	Count of number of glasses of product consumed on day prior to interview

Source: PepsiCo International.

---

[38] Jack Edmonston, "U.S., Overseas Differences Abound," *Business Marketing* (January 1998), p. 32.

Headquarters Control of Global Marketing Research

An important issue for the global company is where to locate control of the organization's research capability. The difference between a multinational, polycentric company and a global, geocentric company on this issue is significant. In the multinational company, responsibility for research is delegated to the operating subsidiary. The global company delegates responsibility for research to operating subsidiaries but retains overall responsibility and control of research as a headquarters function. In practice, this means that the global company will, as in the PepsiCo example, ensure that research is designed and executed so as to yield comparable data.

A key difference between single country market research and global market research is the importance of comparability. Simply put, **comparability** means that the results can be used to make valid comparisons between the countries covered by the research.[39] To achieve this, the company must inject a level of control and review of marketing research at the global level. The director of worldwide marketing research must respond to local conditions as he or she develops a research program that can be implemented on a global basis. The research director must pay particular attention to whether data gathered is based on emic analysis or etic analysis. These terms, which come from anthropology, refer to the perspective taken in the study of another culture. **Emic analysis** is similar to ethnography in that it attempts to study a culture from within, using its own system of meanings and values. **Etic analysis** is "from the outside"; in other words, it is a more detached perspective that is often used in comparative or multicountry studies. In a particular research study, an etic scale would entail using the same set of items across all countries. This approach enhances comparability but some precision is lost. By contrast, an emic study would be tailored to fit a particular country; inferences about cross-cultural similarities based on emic research have to be made subjectively. A good compromise is to use a survey instrument that incorporates elements of both types of analysis. It is likely that the marketing director will end up with a number of marketing programs tailored to clusters of countries that exhibit within-group similarities. The agenda of a coordinated worldwide research program might look like the one in Table 6-6.

The director of worldwide research should not simply direct the efforts of country research managers. His or her job is to ensure that the corporation achieves maximum results worldwide from the total allocation of its research resources. Achieving this requires that personnel in each country are aware of research being carried out in the rest of the world and are involved in influencing the design of their own in-country research as well as the overall research program. Ultimately, the director of worldwide research must be responsible for the overall research design and program. It is

Table 6-6
Worldwide
Marketing
Research Plan

RESEARCH OBJECTIVE	COUNTRY CLUSTER A	COUNTRY CLUSTER B	COUNTRY CLUSTER C
Identify market potential			X
Appraise competitive intentions		X	X
Evaluate product appeal	X	X	X
Study market response to price	X		
Appraise distribution channels	X	X	X

---

[39] V. Kumar, *International Marketing Research* (Upper Saddle River, NJ: Prentice Hall, 1999), p. 15.

his or her job to take inputs from the entire world and produce a coordinated research strategy that generates the information needed to achieve global sales and profit objectives.

The Marketing Information System as a Strategic Asset

The advent of the transnational enterprise means that boundaries between the firm and the outside world are dissolving. Marketing has historically been responsible for managing many of the relationships across that boundary. The boundary between marketing and other functions is also dissolving, and the traditional notion of marketing as a distinct functional area within the firm may be giving way to a new model. The process of marketing decision making is also changing, largely because of the changing role of information from a support tool to a wealth-generating, strategic asset.

Some firms are experimenting with flattened organizations, with less hierarchical, less centralized decision-making structures. Such organizations facilitate the exchange and flow of information between otherwise noncommunicative departments. The more information intensive the firm, the greater the degree to which marketing is involved in activities traditionally associated with other functional areas. In such firms there is parallel processing of information.

Information intensity in the firm has an impact on perceptions of market attractiveness, competitive position, and organizational structure. The greater a company's information intensity, the more the traditional product and market boundaries shift. In essence, companies increasingly face new sources of competition from other firms in historically noncompetitive industries, particularly if those firms are also information intensive. The most obvious and dramatic example is the emergence of the "superindustry," combining telecommunications, computers, financial services, and retailing into what is essentially an information industry. Such diverse firms as AT&T, IBM, Merrill Lynch, Citicorp, and Sears now find themselves in direct competition with each other. They offer essentially the same products, although not as a result of diversification. Rather, the new competition reflects a natural extension and redefinition of traditional product lines and marketing activities. Today, when a company speaks of "value added," it is less likely to be referring to unique product features. Rather, the emphasis is on the information exchanged as part of customer transactions—much of which cuts across traditional product lines.

An Integrated Approach to Information Collection

Coordinated organization activity is required to maintain surveillance of those aspects of the environment about which the organization wishes to stay informed.[40] The goal of this activity, which may be termed *organized intelligence,* is to systematize the collecting and analysis of competitive intelligence to serve the needs of the organization as a whole. Organizing for intelligence requires more than gathering and disseminating good intelligence. Many companies that simply assign an analyst to the task of gathering, analyzing, and disseminating intelligence encounter problems in getting managers to use the output, in gaining credibility for the output and its function, and in establishing the relevance of the output for users.

---

[40] This section is adapted from Benjamin Gilad, "The Role of Organized Competitive Intelligence in Corporate Strategy," *Columbia Journal of World Business* 24 (Winter 1989), pp. 29–35.

The role of organized competitive intelligence in shaping strategy will depend on its ability to supplement, rather than replace, the informal activities of employees, especially top management. One obstacle to a fully integrated marketing information system that encompasses both formal and informal information-gathering techniques is that monitoring activities are not usually fully integrated with the decision-making process. If the information isn't used, the monitoring effort invariably fails to increase a company's competitiveness. Michael Porter's influential work on competitive strategy, together with increasing global competitive pressures and loss of market dominance by many U.S. companies, has helped bring environmental scanning into a new focus. The emphasis has been on competitive intelligence rather than on broader environmental scanning. When considering the possibility of establishing an organized intelligence system, a company may want to review the following questions:

1. Are top executives well informed about the competitive conditions in the market, or do they typically grumble about lack of sufficient knowledge?
2. Do proposals and presentations by middle management show an intimate knowledge of competitors and other industry players? Do these managers seem to know more than what has been published in trade literature?
3. Do managers in one department or division know of intelligence activities in other units? Do they share intelligence regularly?
4. How many times during the last six months was management surprised by developments in the marketplace? How many decisions yielded less than satisfactory results, and what percentage was caused by lack of accurate assessment of competitive response?
5. Has competitive pressure increased in the industry? Does management feel comfortable about its state of familiarity with foreign competitors?
6. How much does the company spend on online databases? How many users know about the availability of the system and how to access it?
7. Do information users suffer from an overload of data but an insufficiency of good analysis and estimates with clear implications to the company?

SUMMARY

Information is one of the most basic ingredients of a successful marketing strategy. A company's **management information system** provides decision makers with a continuous flow of information. Interactive technology is profoundly affecting global marketing activities by allowing managers to access and manipulate data to assist in decision making. **Electronic data interchange, efficient consumer response,** and **data warehouses** are some of the new tools and techniques available. The global marketer must scan the world for information about opportunities and threats and make information available via a management information system. **Scanning** can be accomplished by keeping in touch with an area of information via **surveillance** or by actively seeking out information via **search.** Information can be obtained from human and documentary sources or from **direct perception.**

Formal research is often required before specific marketing decisions can be made. The research process begins when marketers define the problem and set research objectives; this step may entail assessing whether a particular market should be classified as **latent** or **incipient.** A research plan specifies the relative amounts of **qualitative** and **quantitative** information desired. Information is collected by using either **primary** or **secondary data** sources. In today's wired world, the Internet has taken its place alongside more traditional channels as an important secondary information source. In some instances, the cost of collecting primary data may outweigh the potential benefits. Secondary sources are especially useful for researching a market that is too small to justify a large commitment of time and money. If collection of primary data can be justified on a cost-benefit basis, research can be conducted via **surveys, personal interviews, consumer panels, observation,** and **focus groups.** Before collecting data, researchers must determine whether a probability sample is required. In global marketing, careful attention must be paid to issues such as eliminating cultural bias in research, accurately translating surveys, and ensuring data comparability in different markets. A number of techniques are available for analyzing data, including demand pattern analysis, income elasticity measurements, estimation by analogy, comparative analysis, and cluster analysis. Research findings and recommendations must be presented clearly. A final issue is how much control headquarters will have over research and the overall management of the organization's information system. To ensure comparability of data, the researcher should utilize both **emic** and **etic** approaches.

DISCUSSION QUESTIONS

1. Explain how information technology puts powerful tools in the hands of global marketers.
2. What are the different modes of information acquisition? Which is the most important for gathering strategic information?
3. Assume that you have been asked by the president of your organization to devise a systematic approach to scanning. The president does not want to be surprised by major market or competitive developments. What would you recommend?
4. Outline the basic steps of the market research process.
5. What is the difference between existing, latent, and incipient demand? How might these differences affect the design of a marketing research project?
6. Describe some of the analytical techniques used by global marketers. When is it appropriate to use each technique?

PUTTING THEORY INTO PRACTICE

1. See for yourself how the Internet can help with marketing research needs. Suppose your boss asks you to find a market research firm that can help your company in India. Using Yahoo!, Google, or another search engine, type "India market research" and see what happens.

SUGGESTED READINGS

Books

Crossen, Cynthia. *Tainted Truth: The Manipulation of Fact in America.* Englewood Cliffs, New Jersey: Simon & Schuster, 1994.

Douglas, Susan P., and C. Samuel Craig. *International Marketing Research.* Englewood Cliffs, New Jersey: Prentice-Hall, 1983.

Keyes, Jessica. *Infotrends: The Competitive Use of Information.* New York: McGraw-Hill, 1993.

Krugman, Paul R. *The Age of Diminished Expectations: U.S. Economic Policy in the 1990s.* Cambridge, Mass: MIT Press, 1990.

Kumar, V. *International Marketing Research.* Upper Saddle River, New Jersey: Prentice Hall, 1999.

Articles

Cavusgil, S. Tamer. "Qualitative Insights into Company Experiences in International Marketing Research." *Journal of Business and Industrial Marketing* (Summer 1987), pp. 41–54.

Czinkota, Michael R., and Ilkka A. Ronkainen. "Market Research for Your Export Operations: Part I—Using Secondary Sources of Research." *International Trade Forum* 30, no. 3 (1994), pp. 22–33.

———. "Market Research for Your Export Operations: Part II—Conducting Primary Market Research." *International Trade Forum* 31, no. 1 (1995), pp. 16+.

Davenport, Thomas H., Michael Hammer, and Tauno J. Metsisto. "How Executives Can Shape Their

Company's Information Systems." *Harvard Business Review* 67, no. 2 (March-April 1989), pp. 130–134.

Douglas, Susan P., C. Samuel Craig, and Warren J. Keegan. "Approaches to Assessing International Marketing Opportunities for Small- and Medium-sized Companies." *Columbia Journal of World Business* 17, no. 3 (Fall 1982), pp. 2–30.

Ferley, Stephen, Tony Lea, and Barry Watson. "A Comparison of U.S. and Canadian Consumers." *Journal of Advertising Research* 39, no. 5 (September-October 1999), pp. 55–65.

Gilad, Benjamin. "The Role of Organized Competitive Intelligence in Corporate Strategy." *Columbia Journal of World Business* 24 (Winter 1989), pp. 29–35.

Glazer, Rashi. "Marketing in an Information-Intensive Environment: Strategic Implications of Knowledge as an Asset." *Journal of Marketing* 55 (October 1991), pp. 1–19.

Keegan, Warren J. "Scanning the International Business Environment: A Study of the Informational Acquisition Process." Ph.D. Diss., Harvard Business School, 1967.

King, W. R., and V. Sethi. "Developing Transnational Information Systems: A Case Study." *Omega* (January 1993), pp. 53–59.

Naumann, Earl, Donald W. Jackson Jr., and William G. Wolfe. "Comparing U.S. and Japanese Market Research Firms." *California Management Review* 36, no. 4, (Summer 1994), pp. 49–69.

Sethi, S. Prakash. "Comparative Cluster Analysis for World Markets." *Journal of Marketing Research* 8 (August 1971), p. 350.

Sharer, Kevin. "Top Management's Intelligence Needs: An Executive's View of Competitive Intelligence." *Competitive Intelligence Review* (Spring 1991), pp. 3–5.

Wasilewski, Nikolai. "Dimensions of Environmental Scanning Systems in Multinational Enterprises." Pace University, Working Papers, no. 3 (May 1993).

CASE

Case 6-1   *Research Points Whirlpool toward a Global Market*

At the beginning of 1993, David Whitwam, chairman and CEO of Whirlpool Corporation, told an interviewer, "Five years ago we were essentially a domestic company. Today about 40 percent of our revenues are overseas, and by the latter part of this decade, a majority will be." The CEO's comments came three years after he placed his first bet that the appliance industry is globalizing. By acquiring Philips Electronics' European appliance business for $1 billion, Whirlpool vaulted into the number three position in Europe. Whitwam pledged another $2 billion investment in Europe alone. As the decade of the 1990s drew to a close, however, Whitwam's ambitious plans for expanding beyond Europe into Japan and the developing nations in Asia hadn't yet achieved the desired results.

Whirlpool, headquartered in Benton Harbor, Michigan, is the number one appliance company in the United States. The company sells more than $8 billion worth of "white goods" each year; the category includes refrigerators, stoves, washing machines, and microwave ovens. Whirlpool's success has been achieved in part by offering products in three different price ranges: top-of-the-line Kitchen Aid appliances, the medium-priced Whirlpool and Sears Kenmore lines, and Roper and Estate at the low end. In part, the impetus for overseas expansion comes from a mature domestic market that is only growing 2 or 3 percent annually. However, Whirlpool is not new to foreign markets; the company has been in Latin America since 1957. Today, it is the market share leader in that region.

In Europe, the presence of more than 200 brands and 170 factories makes the appliance industry highly fragmented—and highly competitive. Electrolux, a Swedish company, ranks number one. In 1996, 95 of its 150 factories were in Europe; in the United States, where Electrolux owns Frigidaire, the company operates 33 factories. Germany's Bosch-Siemens Hausgerate GmbH is the number two company in Europe. For most of the 1990s, European appliance sales have essentially been flat, and industry overcapacity has become a major issue. However, analysts expect to see a surge in demand from Central and Eastern Europe within a few years. Meanwhile, because many of Whirlpool's European plants are located in Italy, margins have been squeezed in the mid-1990s as the lira strengthened against other European currencies. Because of the difficult business environment, operating margins in Europe fell well below the 1993 figure of 7 percent; in the United States, operating margins are 11 percent.

To cut costs and bring margins up, the company streamlined its European organization. Four regional sales offices have replaced sales organizations in 17 separate countries. Hank Bowman, president of Whirlpool Europe BV, has trimmed the number of warehouses from 30 to 16 and hopes eventually to have as few as five or six. A global parts-sourcing strategy has helped reduce the number of suppliers by 40 percent. Over the next sev-

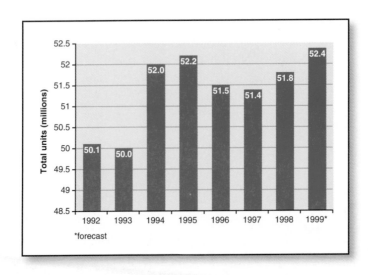

eral years, Whirlpool will invest hundreds of millions of dollars in new product development. It has already begun marketing a new clothes dryer designed to operate more efficiently and provide higher quality despite containing fewer parts.

Bowman seems convinced that a global market segmentation approach is the key to success in Europe. Whirlpool relies heavily on market research to maintain its leadership in the United States; listening to consumers is also important in Europe. "Research tells us that the trends, preferences and biases of consumers, country by country, are reducing as opposed to increasing," Bowman said recently. He believes that European homemakers fall into distinct "Euro-segments"—traditionalists and aspirers, for example—allowing Whirlpool to duplicate the three-tiered approach to brands that has worked so well in the United States. Thus, the Baukneckt brand is positioned at the high end of the market, with Whirlpool in the middle, and Ignis at the lower end. Whirlpool's research also indicated that Philips's strategy of using 10 different advertising agencies to create different ads for 14 countries was unnecessary. To the extent possible, the Whirlpool brand will be marketed on a pan-European basis. In 1990, Whirlpool became the first appliance manufacturer to launch a pan-European ad campaign.

Bowman's global approach does not ignore regional preferences. For example, research data showed that fewer than one-third of European households had microwave ovens; the research also indicated that more Europeans might buy microwave ovens that functioned more like conventional ovens. The findings were based in part on data gathered at the company's Usability Lab in Italy, where customers are paid to come in and experiment with various appliances. In response, Whirlpool introduced the VIP Crisp microwave with a broiler coil to brown meat on the top and an attachment that sizzles the bottom of food as it cooks. The new features ensure that microwaved bacon comes out crisp on top while pizza crust is crisp, not soggy, on the bottom. Today the VIP is the top-selling microwave in Europe and 40 percent of households in the region now have microwave ovens. The company is backing up its products with advertising expenditures of more than $100 million each year.

However, Whirlpool managers also acknowledge that cooking styles, customs, and preferences also vary on a country-by-country basis. When it comes to ovens, for example, the British want a handy grill pan for cooking bacon, Germans want to roast meat, and Swedish cooks want a unit that is well suited for baking cookies. Similarly, while U.S. consumers like large, frost-free refrigerators, Germans want plenty of space to store meat and Italians want special compartments for vegetables. To meet the challenge of economically producing localized versions of ovens, refrigerators, and other appliance lines, Whirlpool is beginning to emphasize product platforms. A platform is essentially a technological core underneath the metal casing of an appliance. The platform—for example, the compressor and sealant system in a refrigerator—can be the same throughout the world. Country or region-specific capabilities can be added late in the production cycle. Whirlpool management hopes to cut 10 percent from the $200 million annual production development budget and achieve a 30 percent productivity increase among the company's 2,000 employees who work in product development. The platform project team hopes to reduce the total number of platforms in the company from 135 to 65. Specific goals include reducing the number of dishwasher platforms from six to three, and refrigerator platforms from 48 to 25.

Whirlpool hopes that a global approach will work well in Asia. As Whitwam has stated, "Our success as a global company rests on our ability to position Whirlpool in Asia." The Whirlpool brand will be used throughout the region, with attention to local preferences. Thus, bright red refrigerators and green top-loading washers are available in several Asian countries. China symbolizes the market opportunity in the region: Only 10 percent of Chinese households currently have refrigerators, air conditioners, microwave ovens, or washers. Still, the Whirlpool name will not appear on appliances produced in China until significant product quality improvements have been made. To that end, Whirlpool's plans call for investing billions of dollars in engineering and testing facilities.

Whitwam also earmarked hundreds of millions of dollars to invest in Asian manufacturing facilities. In China, Whirlpool bought controlling interests in four local companies: Beijing Whirlpool Snowflake Electric Appliance Group, Whirlpool Narcissus in Shanghai, Szenzhen Whirlpool Raybo Air Conditioner Industrial, and Whirlpool SMC Microwave Products in Shunde. In India, Whirlpool is majority shareholder in Kelvinator of India in New Delhi and Whirlpool Washing Machines in Chennai. The Indian market is especially attractive, with refrigerator sales growing 30 percent annually and washing machine sales increasing 40 percent. Together, China and India account for 70 percent of Whirlpool's Asian sales.

After Whirlpool established Asian headquarters in Tokyo, a regional office in Hong Kong, and a design center in Singapore, many industry observers were singing the company's praises. As Jerry Herman, an analyst with Kemper Securities, noted in 1994, "Whirlpool gets very high marks in its global strategy. They are outpacing the industry dramatically." Despite such optimism, the company has encountered some serious challenges in the region. For one thing, Whirlpool faces stiff competition from the Japanese. Not surprisingly, Matsushita, Sharp, Toshiba, and other companies have a strong presence in the region; back home in the United States, the Japanese are not a factor in major appliances. Also, four companies—Whirlpool, GE, Frigidaire, and Maytag—control 93 percent of the U.S. market. In Asia, the situation is reversed: Asian companies have a 98 percent share. Whirlpool has stepped up its marketing efforts to import-hungry Japanese consumers; it will soon sell several appliance lines through the Daiichi discount retail chain.

Unfortunately, the economic crisis in Asia and ongoing difficulties in Europe have put a strain on Whirlpool's financial performance. In 1996, Whirlpool posted a $70 million loss in Asia; the European unit lost $13 million. In September 1997, the company announced that it would cut 4,700 jobs, many of them in Europe. Whirlpool also pulled out of two of its joint ventures in China. Other companies have also experienced difficulties in the region; in June 1997, Electrolux officials announced plans to cut 12,000 jobs representing 11 percent of its workforce and close 25 plants and 50 warehouses. Given the industry's ongoing problems, and the fact that Whirlpool stock has generally underperformed in the bull market of the 1990s, analysts have begun questioning whether Whitwam's global vision is on target. As one analyst put it, "The strategy has been a failure. Whirlpool went big into global markets and investors have paid for it." Others fault the company on execution. Another analyst said, "I respect Whirlpool's strategy. They just missed on the blocking and tackling." ∎

DISCUSSION QUESTIONS

1. Summarize the role of market research in Whirlpool's globalization effort.
2. Describe Whirlpool's global marketing strategy.
3. What do you think are the requirements for market success in Japan, which accounts for one-third of major appliance sales in Asia?

SOURCES: Peter Marsh and Nikki Tait, "Whirlpool's Platform for Growth," *Financial Times* (March 26, 1998), p. 8; Peter Marsh and Nikki Tait, "Whirlpool Sticks to Its Global Guns" (February 2, 1998), p. 4; Greg Steinmetz and Carl Quintanilla, "Tough Target: Whirlpool Expected Easy Going in Europe, and It Got a Big Shock," *The Wall Street Journal* (April 10, 1998), pp. A1, A6; Carl Quintanilla, "Despite Setbacks, Whirlpool Pursues Overseas Markets," *The Wall Street Journal* (December 9, 1997), p. B4; Peter Marsh, "Rough and Tumble Industry," *Financial Times* (July 2, 1997), p. 13; Bill Vlasic, "Did Whirlpool Spin Too Far Too Fast?" *Business Week* (June 24, 1996), pp. 134–136; Robert Rose, "For Whirlpool, Asia Is the New Frontier," *The Wall Street Journal* (April 25, 1996), pp. B1, B4; Patrick Oster, "Call It Worldpool," *Business Week* (November 28, 1994), pp. 98–99; Robert L. Rose, "Whirlpool Is Expanding in Europe Despite the Slump," *The Wall Street Journal* (January 27, 1994), p. B4; David Woodruff, "Whirlpool Goes Off on a World Tour," *Business Week* (June 3, 1991), pp. 99–100; Barry Rehfield, "Where Whirlpool Flies, and Maytag Sputters," *The New York Times* (January 3, 1993), sec. 3, p. 5; Sally Solo, "Whirlpool: How to Listen to Consumers," *Fortune* (January 11, 1993), pp. 77, 79; Gregory E. David, "Spin Dry: Asia Is the Last Phase in Whirlpool's Global Wash Cycle," *Financial World* (October 26, 1993), pp. 30–31.

Chapter 7

Segmentation, Targeting, and Positioning

$2$001 marked the twentieth anniversary of the U.S. broadcast debut of Music Television, the 24-hour channel better as known MTV. Worldwide, musical tastes and trends have changed significantly during the two decades since MTV first went on the air. Indeed, few current viewers are likely to remember the Buggles, the British duo whose song "Video Killed the Radio Star" was featured in the first clip aired. Yet, in some ways, MTV looks the same in the twenty-first century as it did in the 1980s. For example, Madonna, the self-proclaimed "Material Girl," hitched her star to that of the fledgling cable channel, and her dramatic rise to fame closely paralleled MTV's. In 2001, Madonna had proven her staying power with a best-selling album, a sold out world tour, and, of course, videos in regular rotation on MTV. Today, MTV's reach extends far beyond the United States; together with sister channels VH1 and Nickelodeon, it comprises the world's largest network with nearly 340 million viewing households around the globe. But MTV has not prospered by offering the same sights and sounds in every market. Rather, it has prospered by realizing that viewer sensibilities and tastes vary on a regional and country-by-country basis. MTV carefully researches those sensibilities and tastes, and then caters to them. MTV is especially popular with persons aged 15 to 34, with 15-to-24 year olds as the core audience. MTV executives are quick to point out that the channel's programming is very much audience driven; shows like "Total Request Live" (TRL) allow the channel to stay close to its viewing audience.

MTV's worldwide success is a convincing example of the power of superior global market segmentation and targeting. *Market segmentation* represents an effort to identify and categorize groups of customers and countries according to common characteristics. *Targeting* is the process of evaluating the segments and focusing marketing efforts on a country, region, or group of people that has significant potential to respond. Such targeting reflects the reality that a company

Def Jam recording artist Jay-Z performs at the MTV Europe Music Awards in Frankfurt, Germany, on November 8, 2001. Musicians and other celebrities offer an alternative for global companies exploring unconventional ways to connect with young people. For example, a Motorola pager is featured prominently in a recent Jay-Z music video. The rapper has also appeared on posters for Davidoff's Zino Platinum Series cigars.

should identify those consumers it can reach most effectively and efficiently. Finally, proper *positioning* is required to influence perceptions of target customers. Segmentation, targeting, and positioning are all examined in this chapter.

GLOBAL MARKET SEGMENTATION

Global market segmentation has been defined as the process of identifying specific segments—whether they be country groups or individual consumer groups—of potential customers with homogeneous attributes who are likely to exhibit similar responses to a company's marketing mix.[1] Interest in global market segmentation dates back several decades. In the late 1960s, one observer suggested that the European market could be divided into three broad categories—international sophisticate, semi-sophisticate, and provincial—solely on the basis of consumers' presumed receptivity to a common advertising approach.[2] Another writer suggested that some themes—for example, the desire to be beautiful, the desire to be healthy and free of pain, the love of mother and child—were universal and could be used in advertising around the globe.[3]

1   Salah S. Hassan and Lea Prevel Katsanis, "Identification of Global Consumer Segments: A Behavioral Framework," *Journal of International Consumer Marketing* 3, no. 2 (1991), p. 17.
2   John K. Ryans Jr., "Is It Too Soon to Put a Tiger in Every Tank?" *Columbia Journal of World Business* (March-April 1969), p. 73.
3   Arther C. Fatt, "The Danger of 'Local' International Advertising," *Journal of Marketing* 31, no. 1 (January 1967), pp. 60–62.

Table 7-1
Contrasting Views
of Global
Segmentation

CONVENTIONAL WISDOM	UNCONVENTIONAL WISDOM
1. Assumes heterogeneity between countries.	1. Assumes the emergence of segments that transcend national boundaries.
2. Assumes homogeneity within any given country.	2. Acknowledges the existence of within-country differences.
3. Focuses heavily on cultural differences at a macro level.	3. Emphasizes differences and commonalities in micro-level values, consumption patterns, etc.
4. Segmentation relies heavily on clustering of national markets.	4. Segmentation relies on grouping micro markets within a country or between countries.
5. Within-country micro segments are assigned secondary priority.	5. Micro segments based on consumer behavior are assigned high priority.

Source: Adapted from A. Coskun Samli, *International Consumer Behavior* (Westport, Connecticut: Quorum, 1995), p. 130.

As noted in earlier chapters, in the 1980s, Professor Theodore Levitt advanced the thesis that consumers in different countries increasingly seek variety, and that the same new segments are likely to show up in multiple national markets. Thus, ethnic or regional foods such as sushi, Greek salad, or pizza might be in demand anywhere in the world. Levitt suggested that this trend, known variously as the *pluralization of consumption* and *segment simultaneity*, provides an opportunity for marketers to pursue one or more segments on a global scale. Frank Brown, president of MTV Networks Asia, acknowledged this trend in explaining MTV's success in Asia despite the recent economic turmoil in the region. "When marketing budgets are tight, advertisers look for a more effective buy, and we can deliver a niche audience with truly panregional reach," he said.[4]

A. Coskun Samli has extended Levitt's analysis by contrasting "conventional" versus "unconventional" wisdom regarding global market segmentation (see Table 7-1). For example, conventional wisdom might assume that consumers in Europe and Latin America are interested in World Cup soccer while those in America are not. Unconventional wisdom would note that the "global jock" segment exists in many countries, including the United States.[5] Similarly, conventional wisdom might assume that, because per capita income in India is $424, all Indians have low-income levels. Unconventional wisdom would note the presence of a higher-income, middle-class segment.

Today, global companies (and the research and advertising agencies that serve them) use market segmentation to identify, define, understand, and respond to customer wants and needs on a worldwide, rather than strictly local, basis. As we have noted many times in this book, global marketers must determine whether a standardized or adapted marketing mix is required to best serve those wants and needs. The process of market segmentation can provide marketers with the insights needed

---

4   Magz Osborne, "Second Chance in Japan," *Ad Age Global* 1, no. 9 (May 2001), p. 28.
5   Robert Frank, "When World Cup Soccer Starts, World-Wide Productivity Stalls," *The Wall Street Journal* (June 12, 1998), pp. B1, B2; Daniela Deane, "Their Cup Runneth Over: Ethnic Americans Going Soccer Crazy," *USA Today* (July 2, 1998), p. 13A.

Within six years of its launch, MTV had penetrated some 50 million U.S. households—virtually the entire domestic cable audience at the time. Having conquered America, and with support from youth-oriented advertisers such as Coca-Cola, Levi's, and Nike, MTV Europe was launched in Rotterdam in 1987. Today, MTV has 16 local feeds in Europe with coverage stretching from Ireland to Russia. The local feeds are important, because as much as 70 percent of revenues come from advertisers in local markets. One driver of local ad revenues is MTV's commitment to introducing its viewers to local music groups. Despite its sensitivity to local preferences, however, executives and producers still seek economies. As Bill Roedy, president of MTV Networks International, told *Billboard* magazine, "MTV looks for format opportunities to make content from one area travel to another with a local look and feel."

The blend of global and local elements in proportions that reflect local preferences is especially clear in Asia. When MTV first entered Japan in 1992, it met with limited success because a licensing agreement with several electronics manufacturers restricted the control that channel executives had over content; the result was an overemphasis on international pop music that was out of sync with viewers. MTV Japan was relaunched with an emphasis on extensive audience research and a new focus on local music and artists.

Today, MTV Asia reaches 125 million households and is comprised of seven channels: Japan, Taiwan, Hong Kong, China, Korea, MTV India, and MTV Southeast Asia (with English-language local feeds for Singapore, Indonesia, Malaysia, Thailand, and the Philippines). In India, the channel presents itself as zany, colorful, and light-hearted. For example, comedian Cyrus Barocha hosts a show called MTV Bakra that plays hidden camera pranks on unsuspecting victims. Programming in Taiwan, by contrast, is similar to that in the United States: edgy and in your face. Overall, MTV Mandarin's playlist contains about 80 percent local music, while MTV Philippines features predominantly international artists.

TOP 5 MOST DOMESTIC MUSIC MARKETS (IN PERCENT)

Country	Domestic	International Pop
Turkey	95.7	4.1
China	92.6	0.5
Indonesia	87.5	12.5
Venezuela	85.0	10.0
Japan	77.2	17.8

SOURCES: Anne-Marie Crawford, "MTV: Out of Its Teens," *Ad Age Global* 1, no. 9 (May 2001), pp. 25–26; Magz Osborne, "Second Chance in Japan," *Ad Age Global* 1, no. 9 (May 2001), pp. 26, 28; Claudia Penteado, "MTV Brazil Wins Success with Local Programming," *Ad Age Global* 1, no. 9 (May 2001), p. 29; Mimi Turner, "A Q&A with Bill Roedy," *Billboard* 112, no. 36 (September 2, 2000), pp. 48, 54; Owen Hughes, "MTV Asia's Five Branches," *Billboard* 112, no. 36 (September 2, 2000), pp. 48, 54; Sally Beatty and Carol Hymowitz, "How MTV Stays Tuned in to Teens," *The Wall Street Journal* (March 21, 2000), pp. B1, B4.

to develop the most effective approach. Market segmentation also provides input into corporate-level strategic planning. For example, in 1998 former Mattel CEO Jill Barad announced a goal of doubling the toy company's international sales over the next five years. Doing so will mean that the relative contribution of the U.S. market to overall sales must decline from its current level of 65 percent to 50 percent. It is the job of Mattel's marketing managers to identify which country or regional segments and which products are most likely to deliver the necessary sales growth.[6]

Global market segmentation can be based on one or more of the following variables: demographics (including national income and size of population), psychographics (values, attitudes, and lifestyles), behavioral characteristics, and benefits sought. It is also possible to cluster different national markets in terms of their environments—for example, the presence or absence of government regulation in a particular industry—to establish groupings.

---

[6] Lisa Bannon, "Mattel Plans to Double Sales Abroad," *The Wall Street Journal* (February 11, 1998), p. A3.

Demographic Segmentation

Demographic segmentation is based on measurable characteristics of populations such as income, population, age distribution, gender, education, and occupation. A number of global demographic trends—fewer married couples, smaller family size, changing roles of women, higher incomes and living standards, for example—have contributed to the emergence of global market segments. Here are several key demographic facts and trends from around the world:

- In the European Union, the number of consumers aged 16 and under is rapidly approaching the number of consumers aged 60-plus.
- Asia is home to 500 million consumers aged 16 and under.
- American's three main ethnic groups—African Americans, Hispanic Americans, and Asian Americans—represent a combined annual buying power of $1 trillion.
- 28.4 million foreign-born people live in the United States with a combined income of $233 billion.

Statistics such as these can provide valuable insights to marketers who are scanning the globe for opportunities.

Segmenting Global Markets by Income and Population

When a company charts a plan for global market expansion, it often finds that income is a valuable segmentation variable. After all, a market consists of those who are willing and *able* to buy. For cigarettes, soft drinks, photographic film, movie tickets, and other consumer products and services that have a very low unit cost, population is often a more valuable segmentation variable than income. Nevertheless, for the vast range of industrial and consumer products in international markets today, the single most valuable and important indicator of market potential is income. About 65 percent of world GNP is generated in the Triad; however, only 10 percent of the world's population is located in Triad countries. The concentration of wealth in a handful of industrialized countries has significant implications for global marketers. After segmenting in terms of a single demographic variable—income—a company can reach the most affluent markets by targeting fewer than twenty nations: the European Union, North America, and Japan. By doing so, however, the marketers are *not* reaching 90 percent of the world's population!

Ideally, GNP and other measures of national income converted to U.S. dollars should be calculated on the basis of purchasing power parities (i.e., what the currency will buy in the country of issue) or through direct comparisons of actual prices for a given product. This would provide an actual comparison of the standards of living in the countries of the world. Table 7-2 ranks the top ten countries in terms of 2000 per capita income followed by a ranking adjusted for purchasing power parity. While the U.S. ranks eighth in per capita income, its standard of living—as measured by what money can buy—is second only to Luxembourg's.[7] By most measures, the U.S. market is enormous: more than $8.2 trillion in 2000 national income, and a population of 275 million people, and per capita income of $29,953. Little wonder, then, that so many non-U.S. companies target and cater to American consumers and organizational buyers! A case in point is Mitsubishi Motors, which had begun redesigning its Montero Sport SUV with the goal of creating a "global vehicle" that could be sold worldwide with little adaptation. Now the design program has changed course;

---

[7] For a more detailed discussion, see Malcolm Gillis et. al., *Economics of Development* (New York: Norton, 1996), pp. 37–40.

Table 7-2

Per Capita Income, 2000

2000 PER CAPITA INCOME		2000 INCOME ADJUSTED FOR PURCHASING POWER	
1. Luxembourg	$38,587	1. Luxembourg	$37,708
2. Norway	$38,070	2. United States	$29,953
3. Singapore	$36,484	3. Singapore	$28,648
4. Switzerland	$36,479	4. Norway	$25,807
5. Kuwait	$35,242	5. Hong Kong	$24,602
6. Japan	$34,796	6. Switzerland	$24,222
7. Denmark	$33,894	7. Denmark	$23,555
8. United States	$29,953	8. Japan	$23,353
9. Hong Kong	$27,463	9. Belgium	$22,765
10. Austria	$25,854	10. Austria	$21,787

Source: Reprinted by permission of Warren Keegan Associates, Inc.

the new goal is to make the vehicle more "American" by providing more interior space and more horsepower. Hiroshi Yajima, a Mitsubishi executive in North America, attributes the change to the vibrancy and sheer size of the American auto market. "We wouldn't care if the vehicle didn't sell outside the U.S.," he said.[8]

Despite having comparable per capita incomes, other industrialized countries are nevertheless quite small in terms of *total* annual income. In Sweden, for example, per capita GNP is $24,487; however, Sweden's smaller population—8.9 million—means that annual national income is only about $220 billion. This helps explain why companies based in Sweden or other small countries must look beyond their borders for significant growth opportunities.

While Table 7-2 highlights differences between straightforward income statistics and standard of living in the world's most affluent nations, such differences can be even more pronounced in less-developed countries. A visit to a mud house in Tanzania will reveal many of the things that money can buy: an iron bed frame, a corrugated metal roof, beer and soft drinks, bicycles, shoes, photographs, radios, and even televisions. What Tanzania's per capita income of $222 does not reflect is the fact that instead of utility bills, Tanzanians have the local well and the sun. Instead of nursing homes, tradition and custom ensure that families will take care of the elderly at home. Instead of expensive doctors and hospitals, villagers may utilize the services of witch doctors and healers.

In industrialized countries, a significant portion of national income is the value of goods and services that would be free in a poor country. Thus, the standard of living in many low-income countries is often higher than income data might suggest. In low-income countries, the *actual* purchasing power of the local currency may be much higher than that implied by exchange values. For example, the per capita income average for China of $930 equals 7,719 Chinese Renminbi (8.3 Renminbi = US$1.00), but 7,719 Renminbi will buy much more in China than $930 will buy in the United States. Adjusted for purchasing power parity, per capita income in China is estimated to be $4,472; this amount is nearly five times higher than the unadjusted

---

[8] Norihiko Shirouzu, "Tailoring World's Cars to U.S. Tastes," *The Wall Street Journal* (January 1, 2001), p. B1.

Table 7-3

Top 10 Nations Ranked by GNP, 2000

COUNTRY	GNP (IN MILLIONS)
USA	8,285,358
Japan	4,427,104
Germany	2,127,086
France	1,446,515
U.K.	1,359,764
China	1,179,345
Italy	1,168,771
Brazil	850,852
Canada	602,158
Spain	544,944

Source: Reprinted by permission of Warren Keegan Associates, Inc.

Table 7-4

Top 10 Nations Ranked by GNP, 2010 Projections

COUNTRY	GNP (IN MILLIONS)
1. USA	11,763,698
2. Japan	5,137,835
3. Germany	2,722,849
4. China	2,319,949
5. France	1,851,661
6. U.K.	1,792,234
7. Italy	1,424,726
8. Brazil	1,188,665
9. Canada	833,131
10. Rep. of Korea	734,718

Source: Reprinted by permission of Warren Keegan Associates, Inc.

figure suggests. Similarly, calculated in terms of purchasing power, per capita income in Tanzania is approximately $575. Indeed, a visit to the capital city of Dar Es Salaam reveals that stores are stocked with televisions and CD players, and businessmen can be seen negotiating deals using their cellular phones.[9]

No one knows with certainty what the future will bring, but using 2000 GNP data as a baseline (Table 7-3) and extrapolating current economic growth trends to the year 2010 produces interesting results (Table 7-4). The United States, Japan, and Germany retain their rankings in the first three positions. China moves up to fourth place; Spain is no longer on the list. South Korea appears in the top ten for the first time. These extrapolation results suggest that China, with its combination of high real income growth and relatively low population growth, is a strong candidate to become a leading world economic power. Even if this forecast turns out to be overly optimistic in the face of the current economic slowdown, China is expected to fare better than other Asian countries.

Population

In 2000, the ten most populous countries in the world accounted for 52 percent of world income; the five most populous accounted for 35 percent (see Table 7-5). Although population is not as concentrated as income, there is, in terms of size of nations, a pattern of considerable concentration. The ten most populous countries in the world account for roughly 60 percent of the world's population today. The concentration of income in the high-income and large-population countries means that a company can be "global" by targeting buyers in ten or fewer countries. World population is now approximately 6.1 billion; at the present rate of growth it will reach 12 billion by the middle of the century. Simply put, global population will probably double during the lifetime of many students using this textbook.

As noted previously, for products whose price is low enough, population is a more important variable than income in determining market potential. Former

---

[9]   Robert S. Greenberger, "Africa Ascendant: New Leaders Replace Yesteryear's 'Big Men,' and Tanzania Benefits," *The Wall Street Journal* (December 10, 1996), pp. A1, A6.

Table 7-5
The Ten Most Populous Countries, 2000 and 2010 Projections

GLOBAL INCOME AND POPULATION	2000 POPULATION (THOUSANDS)	PERCENT OF WORLD POPULATION	PROJECTED POPULATION 2010	2000 GNP (MILLIONS)	PER CAPITA GNP	PERCENT OF WORLD GNP
WORLD TOTAL	6,134,466	100.00	7,203,265	30,251,491	—	100.0
1. China	1,268,121	20.67	1,428,781	889,882	723	3.2
2. India	1,015,287	16.55	1,225,550	430,096	424	1.3
3. USA	275,746	4.50	301,592	8,259,358	29,953	27.3
4. Indonesia	210,785	3.44	247,045	247,846	1,176	.8
5. Brazil	170,661	2.78	200,019	850,852	4,986	2.8
6. Russia	146,866	2.39	151,331	342,008	2,329	1.1
7. Pakistan	138,334	2.26	184,112	66,219	479	.2
8. Bangladesh	129,663	2.11	158,058	47,489	366	.2
9. Nigeria	128,454	2.09	170,963	38,416	299	.1
10. Japan	127,229	2.07	132,411	4,427,104	34,796	14.6

Source: Reprinted by permission of Warren Keegan Associates, Inc.

Kodak CEO George Fisher once commented, "Half the people in the world have yet to take their first picture. The opportunity is huge, and it's nothing fancy. We just have to sell yellow boxes of film."[10] Thus, China and India, with respective populations of 1.3 billion and 1 billion, represent attractive target markets. In a country like China, one segmentation approach would call for serving the existing mass market for inexpensive consumer products. Procter & Gamble, Unilever, Kao, Johnson & Johnson, and other packaged goods companies are targeting and developing the China market, lured in part by the possibility that as many as 100 million Chinese customers are affluent enough to spend, say, 14 cents for a single-use pouch of shampoo. GM's original strategy for entering China was based on its success in reaching the segment comprised of government and company officials who are entitled to a large sedan-style automobile. In 2001, GM planned to begin production of a compact family car aimed at China's middle class.

McDonald's global expansion illustrates the significance of both income and population on marketing activities. On the one hand, as noted in Case 1-1, McDonald's operates in more than 120 countries. What this figure conceals, however, is that McDonald's generated 87 percent of sales and 92 percent of operating income in 1997 in only 11 major markets: Australia, Brazil, Canada, England, France, Germany, Hong Kong, Japan, the Netherlands, Taiwan, and the United States. Seven of these countries appear in the top ten GNP ranking shown in Table 7-4; however, only two appear in the Table 7-5 population rankings. As former CEO Michael Quinlan noted in a recent McDonald's annual report, the restaurants in the company's approximately 100 non-major country markets contributed less than 20 percent to 1997 operating income. McDonald's is counting on an expanded presence in the most populous country markets to drive corporate growth in the twenty-first century.

---

10 Mark Maremont, "Kodak's New Focus," *Business Week* (January 30, 1995), p. 63.

Segmenting decisions can be complicated by the fact that national income figures, such as those cited for China and India, are averages. There are also large, fast-growing, high-income segments in both of these countries. An estimated 100 million Indians can be classified as "upper-middle-class," with average incomes of more than $1,400. Pinning down a demographic segment may require additional information; India's middle class has been estimated to range from 250 to 300 million people. However, if middle class is defined as "persons who own a refrigerator," the figure would be 30 million people. If television ownership were used as the benchmark, the middle class would be 100 to 125 million people.[11] The lesson is to guard from being blinded by averages; as Samli has suggested, do not *assume* homogeneity.

Age Segmentation

Age is another useful demographic variable in global marketing. One global segment based on demographics is **global teens**—young people between the ages of 12 and 19. Teens, by virtue of their shared interest in fashion, music, and a youthful lifestyle, exhibit consumption behavior that is remarkably consistent across borders. As Renzo Rosso, creator of the Diesel designer jeans brand, explains, "A group of teenagers randomly chosen from different parts of the world will share many of the same tastes."[12] Young consumers may not yet have conformed to cultural norms—indeed, they may be rebelling against them. This fact, combined with shared universal wants, needs, desires, and fantasies (for name brands, novelty, entertainment, trendy, and image-oriented products), make it possible to reach the global teen segment with a unified marketing program. This segment is attractive both in terms of its size (about 1.3 billion) and its multi-billion dollar purchasing power. Coca-Cola, Benetton, Swatch, and Sony are some of the companies pursuing the global teenage segment. The global telecommunications revolution is a critical driving force behind the emergence of this segment. Global media such as MTV and the Internet are perfect vehicles for reaching this segment. Satellites such as AsiaSatI are beaming Western programming and commercials to millions of viewers in China, India, and other countries.

Another global segment is the so-called **global elite:** older, more affluent consumers who are well traveled and have the money to spend on prestigious products with an image of exclusivity. This segment's needs and wants are spread over various product categories: durable goods (luxury automobiles such as Mercedes Benz), nondurables (upscale beverages such as Perrier mineral water or Chivas Regal scotch), and financial services (American Express Gold and Platinum cards). Technological change in telecommunications makes it easier to reach the global elite segment. Global telemarketing is a viable option today as AT&T International 800 services are available in more than 40 countries. Increased reliance on catalogue marketing by upscale retailers such as Harrods, Laura Ashley, and Ferragamo has also yielded impressive results.

Gender Segmentation

For obvious reasons, segmenting markets by gender is an approach that makes sense for many companies. Less obvious, however, is the need to ensure that opportunities

---

[11] John Bussey, "India's Market Reform Requires Perspective," *The Wall Street Journal* (May 8, 1994), p. A1. See also Miriam Jordan, "In India, Luxury is Within Reach of Many," *The Wall Street Journal* (October 17, 1995), p. A1.

[12] Alice Rawsthorn, "A Hipster on Jean Therapy," *Financial Times* (August 20, 1998), p. 8.

Table 7-6
Psychographic Profiles of Porsche's American Customers

CATEGORY	PERCENT OF ALL OWNERS	DESCRIPTION
Top Guns	27%	Driven and ambitious. Care about power and control. Expect to be noticed.
Elitists	24%	Old-money. A car—even an expensive one—is just a car, not an extension of one's personality.
Proud Patrons	23%	Ownership is what counts. A car is a trophy, a reward for working hard. Being noticed doesn't matter.
Bon Vivants	17%	Cosmopolitan jet setters and thrill seekers. Car heightens excitement.
Fantasists	9%	Car represents a form of escape. Don't care about impressing others; may even feel guilty about owning car.

Source: Alex Taylor III, "Porsche Slices Up Its Buyers," *Fortune* (January 16, 1995), p. 24.

for sharpening the focus on the needs and wants of one gender or the other do not go wasted. While some companies—fashion designers and cosmetics companies, for example—market primarily or exclusively to women, other companies offer different lines of products to both genders. For example, in 2000, Nike generated $1.4 billion in global sales of women's shoes and apparel, a figure representing 16 percent of total Nike sales. Nike executives believe its global women's business is poised for big growth. To make it happen, Nike is opening concept shops inside department stores and creating free-standing retail stores devoted exclusively to women.[13]

Psychographic Segmentation

Psychographic segmentation involves grouping people in terms of their attitudes, values, and lifestyles. Data are obtained from questionnaires that require respondents to indicate the extent to which they agree or disagree with a series of statements. Psychographics is primarily associated with SRI International, a market research organization whose original VALS and updated VALS 2 analyses of consumers are widely known. Finland's Nokia relies heavily on psychographic segmentation of mobile phone users; its most important segments are "poseurs," "trendsetters," "social contact seekers," and "highfliers." By carefully studying these segments and tailoring products to each, Nokia has captured 40 percent of the world's market for mobile communication devices.[14]

Porsche AG, the German sports car maker, turned to psychographics after experiencing a worldwide sales decline from 50,000 units in 1986 to about 14,000 in 1993. Its U.S. subsidiary, Porsche Cars North America, already had a clear demographic profile of its typical customer: a 40-plus-year-old male college graduate whose annual income exceeded $200,000. A psychographic study showed that, demographics aside, Porsche buyers could be divided into five distinct categories (see Table 7-6). Top Guns, for example, buy Porsches and expect to be noticed; for Proud Patrons and Fantasists, on the other hand, such conspicuous consumption is irrelevant. Porsche

---

[13] Paula Stepanowsky, "Nike Tones Up Its Marketing to Women with Concept Shops, New Apparel Lines," *The Wall Street Journal* (September 5, 2001), p. B19.

[14] John Micklethwait and Adrian Wooldridge, *Future Perfect: The Challenge and Hidden Promise of Globalization* (New York: Crown Business, 2000), p. 131.

With the explosion of cross-border communication such as Star TV and the Internet, and the increasing affordability of international travel, consumers are becoming more similar the world over.
—Sam Hill, Vice Chairman for Worldwide Strategic Planning and Business Development, D'Arcy Masius Benton & Bowles[16]

will use the profiles to develop advertising tailored to each type. Notes Richard Ford, Porsche vice president of sales and marketing, "We were selling to people whose profiles were diametrically opposed. You wouldn't want to tell an elitist how good he looks in the car or how fast he could go." The results were impressive; Porsche's U.S. sales improved nearly 50 percent after a new advertising campaign was launched.[15]

One early application of psychographics outside the United States focused on value orientations of consumers in the United Kingdom, France, and Germany. Although the study was limited in scope, the researcher concluded that "the underlying values structures in each country appeared to bear sufficient similarity to warrant a common overall communications strategy."[17] SRI International has recently conducted psychographic analyses of the Japanese market; broader-scope studies have been undertaken by several global advertising agencies, including Backer Spielvogel & Bates Worldwide (BSB), D'arcy Massius Benton & Bowles (DMBB), and Young & Rubicam (Y&R). The following analyses offer a detailed understanding of various segments, including the global teenager and global elite discussed previously.[18]

BSB's Global Scan

Visit the Web site
You can assess your own psychographic profile at the SRI Website: www.future.sri.com

Global Scan is a study that encompasses 18 countries, mostly located in the Triad. To identify attitudes that could help explain and predict purchase behavior for different product categories, the researchers studied consumer attitudes and values, as well as media viewership/readership, buying patterns, and product use. The survey attempts to identify both country-specific and global attitudinal attributes; sample statements are "The harder you push, the farther you get," and "I never have enough time or money."

Combining all the country data yielded a segmentation study known as TARGET SCAN, a description of five global psychographic segments that BSB claims represent 95 percent of the adult populations in the 18 countries surveyed (see Figure 7-1). BSB has labeled the segments Strivers, Achievers, Pressured, Adapters, and Traditionals.

Strivers (26 percent). This segment consists of young people with a median age of 31 who live hectic, on-the-go lives. Driven to achieve success, they are materialistic pleasure seekers for whom time and money are in short supply.

Achievers (22 percent). Older than the Strivers, the affluent, assertive Achievers, are upwardly mobile and already have attained a good measure of success. Achievers are status conscious consumers for whom quality is important.

Pressured (13 percent). The Pressured segment, largely comprised of women, cuts across age groups and is characterized by constant financial and family pressures. Life's problems overwhelm the members of this segment.

Adapters (18 percent). This segment is comprised of older people who are content with their lives and who manage to maintain their values while keeping open minds when faced with change.

[15] Alex Taylor III, "Porsche Slices Up Its Buyers," *Fortune* (January 16, 1995), p. 24.
[16] Sam Hill, "Super-Affluence and Star Gazers," *Financial Times* (September 8, 1997), p. 10.
[17] Alfred S. Boote, "Psychographic Segmentation in Europe," *Journal of Advertising Research* 22, no. 6 (December 1982–January 1983), p. 25.
[18] The following discussion is adapted from Rebecca Piirto, *Beyond Mind Games: The Marketing Power of Psychographics* (Ithaca, NY: American Demographics Books, 1991).

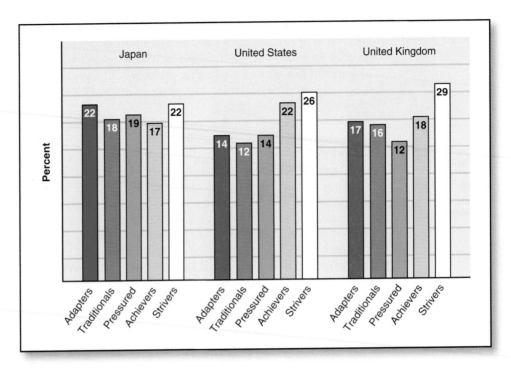

Figure 7-1
Global Scan

Traditionals (16 percent). This segment is "rooted to the past" and clings to their country's heritage and cultural values.

Global Scan is a helpful tool for identifying consumer similarities across national boundaries. For example, Strivers from Spain and France probably have more in common with each other in terms of attitudes and values than do, say, a Spanish Striver and a Spanish Traditional. Global Scan can also help highlight *differences* between segments in different countries. For example, in the United States, the 75 million baby boomers help swell the ranks of Strivers and Achievers to nearly half the population. In Germany, on the other hand, the Striver segment is older and comprises a smaller proportion of the population. Global Scan has also pinpointed important differences between Americans and Canadians, who are often considered to be part of the same geographic segment of North America.

Similarly, Global Scan revealed marked differences between the circumstances in which Strivers find themselves in different countries. In the United States, Strivers are chronically short of both time and money, while Japanese Strivers have ample monetary resources. These differences translate directly into different preferences: Whereas U.S. Strivers buy cars that are fun, stylish, and represent a good value, Japanese Strivers view cars as an extension of their homes and will accessorize them with lavish features—curtains and high-end stereo systems, for example. This implies that different advertising appeals would be necessary when targeting Strivers in the two countries.

DMBB's Euroconsumer Study

DMBB's research team focused on Europe and produced a 15-country study entitled "The Euroconsumer: Marketing Myth or Cultural Certainty?" The researchers identified four lifestyle groups: Successful Idealists, Affluent Materialists, Comfortable Belongers, and Disaffected Survivors. The first two groups represent the elite, the latter two, mainstream European consumers.

> *Successful Idealists* Comprising from 5 to 20 percent of the population, this segment consists of persons who have achieved professional and material success while maintaining commitment to abstract or socially responsible ideals.
>
> *Affluent Materialists* These status-conscious "up-and-comers"—many of whom are business professionals—use conspicuous consumption to communicate their success to others.
>
> *Comfortable Belongers* Comprising one-fourth to one-half of a country's population, this group, like Global Scan's Adapters and Traditionals, is conservative and most comfortable with the familiar. Belongers are content with the comfort of home, family, friends, and community.
>
> *Disaffected Survivors* Lacking power and affluence, this segment harbors little hope for upward mobility and tends to be either resentful or resigned. This segment is concentrated in high-crime urban inner-city-type neighborhoods. Despite Disaffecteds' lack of societal status, their attitudes nevertheless tend to affect the rest of society.

DMBB has also recently completed a psychographic profile of the Russian market. The study divides Russians into five categories, based on their outlook, behavior, and openness to Western products. The categories include *kuptsy*, Cossacks, students, business executives, and Russian Souls. Members of the largest group, the *kuptsy* (the label comes from the Russian word for "merchant"), theoretically prefer Russian products but look down on mass-produced goods of inferior quality. *Kuptsy* are most likely to admire automobiles and stereo equipment from countries with good reputations for engineering, such as Germany and Scandinavia. Nigel Clarke, the author of the study, notes that segmentation and targeting are appropriate in Russia, despite the fact that its broad consumer market is still in its infancy. "If you're dealing with a market as different as Russia is, even if you want to go 'broad,' it's best to think: 'Which group would go most for my brand? Where is my natural center of gravity?'"[19]

The study's marketing implications became more clear in 1996 as market share growth for many Western brands began to slow. As Sergei Platinin, director of a Russian company that markets fruit juices, noted, "People used to want only to buy things that looked foreign. Now they want Russian." In the world of fashion, expensive blue jeans from designer Valentin Yudashkin are supplanting Armani's as *the* jeans to be seen in. At the other end of the price spectrum, McDonald's has begun offering *pirozhki*—meat and cheese pies. The local Nestlé subsidiary has revived several brands of Russian chocolate candies. According to a survey conducted by Comcon 2, nearly two-thirds of upper-income Russians prefer to buy domestic chocolates, even though they can afford to buy imported brands.[20]

Y&R's Cross-Cultural Consumer Characterizations (4Cs)

4Cs is a 20-country psychographic segmentation study focusing on goals, motivations, and values that help to determine consumer choice. The research is based on the

---

[19] Stuart Elliot, "Figuring Out the Russian Consumer," *The New York Times* (April 1, 1992), pp. C1, C19.
[20] Betsy McKay, "In Russia, West No Longer Means Best; Consumers Shift to Home-Grown Goods," *The Wall Street Journal* (December 9, 1996), p. A9.

assumption that "there are underlying psychological processes involved in human behavior that are culture-free and so basic that they can be found all over the globe."[21]

In the 4Cs framework, seven different types are grouped into three overall categories: Constrained (Resigned Poor and Struggling Poor), Middle Majority (Mainstreamers, Aspirers, and Succeeders), and Innovators (Transitionals and Reformers). Each is classified in terms of *goals, motivation,* and *values* that dictate the choices they make as consumers. For example, Y&R's researchers assume that, in every country, there is a "Resigned Poor" segment for whom survival is the goal in life, motivation is nil (they have "given up"), and subsistence represents a basic value. At the other end of the spectrum are the Reformers, whose respective goals, motivations, and values are social betterment, social conscience, and social altruism. Figure 7-2 shows some of the attitudinal, work, lifestyle, and purchase behavior characteristics of the seven groups.

Combining the 4Cs data for a particular country with other data permits Y&R to predict lifestyle activities and product and category purchase behavior for the various segments. Yet, as noted in the discussion of Global Scan, marketers at global companies that are Y&R clients are cautioned not to assume they can develop one strategy or one commercial to be used to reach a particular segment across cultures. As a Y&R staffer notes, "As you get closer to the executional level, you need to be acutely sensitive to cultural differences. But at the origin, it's of enormous benefit to be able to think about people who share common values across cultures."

Behavior Segmentation

Behavior segmentation focuses on whether or not people buy and use a product, as well as how often, and how much they use or consume. Consumers can be categorized in terms of **usage rates**—for example, heavy, medium, light, and non-user. Consumers can also be segmented according to **user status:** potential users, non-users, ex-users, regulars, first-timers, and users of competitors' products. Campbell Soup Company has targeted China for the simple reason that the Chinese have the highest per capita consumption of soup in the world.[22] Similarly, tobacco companies are targeting China because the Chinese are heavy smokers.

For example, worldwide, only about 100 million women use tampons; the total market potential is estimated to be 1.7 billion women. In the mid-1990s, Tambrands Inc., marketers of Tampax brand tampons, approached market segmentation in terms of how resistant women are to using tampons. Cluster 1 (the United States, the United Kingdom, and Australia) is comprised of women who use tampons and believe themselves to be well informed about them. Tampon use in Cluster 2 (France, Israel, and South Africa) is limited to about 50 percent of women; some women in this cluster are concerned that tampon use may result in a loss of virginity. Advertising to women in Cluster 2 will focus on endorsements by gynecologists. Cluster 3, which includes big emerging markets such as Brazil, China, and Russia, presents the biggest marketing challenge. Tambrands must deal with two issues—virginity concerns and the fact that most women in the cluster have little or no experience using tampons. Despite the fact that advertising messages will vary by cluster, each ad will end with the slogan "Tampax. Women Know." Tambrands allocated $65 million for an advertising campaign targeted at the three clusters in 27 countries. One risk: The campaign's frank language would offend women. Commenting on

---

[21] Rebecca Piirto, *Beyond Mind Games: The Marketing Power of Psychographics* (Ithaca, NY: American Demographics Books, 1991), p. 161.

[22] Adam Heller, "A Recipe for Success?" *China Business Review* (July-August 1993), p. 30.

Resigned Poor			
ATTITUDES	WORK	LIFESTYLE	PURCHASE BEHAVIOR
Unhappy Distrustful	Labor Unskilled	Shut-in Television	Staples Price

Struggling Poor			
ATTITUDES	WORK	LIFESTYLE	PURCHASE BEHAVIOR
Unhappy Dissatisfied	Labor Craftsmen	Sports Television	Price Discount stores

Mainstreamers			
ATTITUDES	WORK	LIFESTYLE	PURCHASE BEHAVIOR
Happy Belong	Craftsmen Teaching	Family Gardening	Habit Brand loyal

Aspirers			
ATTITUDES	WORK	LIFESTYLE	PURCHASE BEHAVIOR
Unhappy Ambitious	Sales White collar	Trendy sports Fashion mags	Conspicuous consumption Credit

Succeeders			
ATTITUDES	WORK	LIFESTYLE	PURCHASE BEHAVIOR
Happy Industrious	Managerial Professional	Travel Dining out	Luxury Quality

Transitionals			
ATTITUDES	WORK	LIFESTYLE	PURCHASE BEHAVIOR
Rebellious Liberal	Student Health field	Arts/crafts Special int. mags	Impulse Unique products

Reformers			
ATTITUDES	WORK	LIFESTYLE	PURCHASE BEHAVIOR
Inner growth Improve world	Professional Entrepreneur	Reading Cultural events	Ecology Homemade/grown

Figure 7-2
Y&R's 4Cs

Tambrands' plans, Jeffrey Hill of Meridian Consulting Group commented, "The greatest challenge in the global expansion of tampons is to address the religious and cultural mores that suggest that vaginal insertion is fundamentally prohibited by culture."[23]

---

[23] Emily Nelson and Miriam Jordan, "Sensitive Export: Seeking New Markets for Tampons, P&G Faces Cultural Barriers," *The Wall Street Journal* (December 8, 2000), pp. A1, A8; Yumiko Ono, "Tambrands Ads Aim to Overcome Cultural and Religious Obstacles," *The Wall Street Journal* (March 17, 1997), p. B8. See also Dyan Machan, "Will the Chinese Use Tampons?" *Forbes* (January 16, 1995), pp. 86–87.

It may be a Single Market, but twenty-first century Europe still offers ample opportunities for market segmentation. One approach known as "3G" addresses issues pertaining to three distinct segments: youth aged 16 and under (Generation Y), adults aged 60 and over (the Golden Grays), and transnational corporations ("Globerations"). The following trends and traits associated with each have major implications for marketing strategy in the years 2005 and beyond.

Generation Y

- share few family activities
- display less reverence toward established authorities
- approach leisure time as "pay-per-play"
- maintain a heavy diet that is heavily weighted toward "convenience food"
- are tech-savvy
- are deluged with passive information

Golden Grays

- consider it important to mix fun and work
- are relatively affluent, meaning more out-of-home activities
- enjoy high-tech gaming
- expect home health-care devices and biotechnology to extend life expectancy
- are deluged with passive information

Globerations

- employees will be less inclined to leave their companies as nations gradually reduce the benefits associated with the "social safety net"
- knowledge workers will be challenged finding work-life balance
- customers will want build-to-order solutions
- online auctions will be a significant sales channel
- a few, powerful consumer-to-business buying groups will emerge

Given these trends, which industries will be the winners and which will be the losers? Likely losers in the leisure sector will include general interest consumer magazines and national newspapers; winners will include interactive services, audio books, and social sports such as golf and tennis. Business services losers will likely be newspaper publishers, grocery coupon distributors, and mass market retailers. Winning services offerings will likely be corporate concierges, personalized telecom networks, and domestic services. Marketers are particularly advised to take the Golden Grays seriously and market brands that provide happiness, convenience, and time savings.

SOURCE: Allyson L. Stewart-Allen, "EU's Future Consumers: Three Groups to Watch," *Marketing News* 35, no. 12 (June 4, 2001), pp. 9–10.

In 1993, before Tambrands had developed its cluster segmentation, the company launched a $20 million global advertising effort in North America, Eastern and Western Europe, Latin America, and the Pacific Rim. The campaign had two strategic purposes directly related to usage rates and user status. One ad was designed to show women new times to use tampons. It included advice from gynecologists that tampons can safely be worn overnight, a creative appeal based on research reports that two-thirds of tampon users don't use them at night. Beginning in 1997, this message strategy was largely limited to women in Cluster 1.

Marketers can benefit from attempting to understand the relationship between usage patterns and other segmentation variables. Diageo PLC, V&S Vin & Spirit AB, Seagram, and other marketers of distilled spirits know that Russians are heavy drinkers who consume a great deal of vodka. In fact, the word *vodka* is derived from the Russian word for "water," and Russians believe vodka originated in their country in the fourteenth century. Estimated 1996 vodka consumption in Russia was

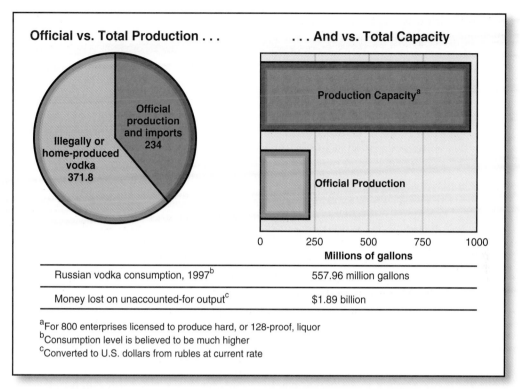

Official vs. Total Production . . .

Illegally or home-produced vodka 371.8

Official production and imports 234

. . . And vs. Total Capacity

Production Capacity[a]

Official Production

0   250   500   750   1000
Millions of gallons

Russian vodka consumption, 1997[b]	557.96 million gallons
Money lost on unaccounted-for output[c]	$1.89 billion

[a]For 800 enterprises licensed to produce hard, or 128-proof, liquor
[b]Consumption level is believed to be much higher
[c]Converted to U.S. dollars from rubles at current rate

Figure 7-3
Russia's Vodka Industry

250 million cases, compared with about 34 million cases in the United States; overall, vodka consumption outside of Russia is declining. However, as noted previously, Russian consumers have recently shown an increased preference for domestic brands. Production of homemade vodka, known as *samogon,* and illegal bootleg vodka surpasses official production by a ratio of 2 to 1 (see Figure 7-3), and the Russian government loses an estimated $1.9 billion in annual tax revenues. As a result of high duties, as well as the marketing goal of retaining a premium image, imports such as Smirnoff and Absolut are priced significantly higher than local brands. To date, imported vodka brands have only captured about 1 percent of the Russian market.

At a time when economic uncertainty is high and workers can go months without being paid, price is a significant factor for the average Russian. An entrepreneur named Vladimir Dovgan has prospered by launching several different brands of vodka priced between $5 and $10 per bottle. Dovgan's picture is featured on the label, and he also appears in print and television ads. Meanwhile, in March 1997, Diageo PLC began producing Smirnoff in St. Petersburg. Ironically, Smirnoff's heritage is truly Russian, although for decades it was produced only in the West. As a company executive noted, "This should make Smirnoff seem more Russian. We want Russians to realize that Smirnoff came to Russia to produce for Russians."[24] Even as marketers of distilled spirits adjust their strategies, market behavior is changing;

---

[24] Ernest Beck, "Absolut Frustration: Why Foreign Distillers Find It So Hard to Sell Vodka to the Russians," *The Wall Street Journal* (January 15, 1998), pp. A1, A9; Betsy McKay, "Vladimir Dovgan Is a Constant Presence in Capitalist Russia," *The Wall Street Journal* (March 20, 1998), pp. A1, A8.

young Russians are turning to beer, with demand up 25 percent in the five-year period between 1995–2000. Local brands are favored, as the weak ruble has priced imports out of the reach of the average consumer.[25]

Benefit Segmentation

Global benefit segmentation focuses on the numerator of the value equation—the B in $V = B/P$. This approach is based on marketers' superior understanding of the problem a product solves, the benefit it offers, or the issue it addresses, regardless of geography. Food marketers are finding success creating products that can help parents create nutritious family meals with a minimal investment of time. Campbell Soup is making significant inroads into Japan's $500 million soup market as time-pressed homemakers place a premium on convenience. Marketers of health and beauty aids also use benefit segmentation. Many toothpaste brands are straightforward cavity fighters, and as such they reach a very broad market. However, as consumers become more concerned about whitening, sensitive teeth, gum disease, and other oral care issues, marketers are developing new toothpaste brands suited to the different sets of perceived needs.

The European pet food market represents $30 billion in annual sales. Nestlé discovered that cat owners' attitudes toward feeding their pets are the same everywhere. In response, a pan-European campaign was created for Friskies Dry Cat Food. The appeal was that dry cat food better suits a cat's universally recognized independent nature. Likewise, many Europeans are concerned with improving the health and longevity of their pets. Accordingly, Procter & Gamble is marketing its Iams brand premium pet food as a way to improve pets' health.[26]

Ethnic Segmentation

In many countries, the population includes ethnic groups of significant size. In the United States, for example, there are three major ethnic segments: African Americans, Asian Americans, and Hispanic Americans. Each segment shows great diversity and can be further subdivided. For example, Asian Americans include Thais, Vietnamese, Japanese, and Chinese. America's Hispanic population includes Mexican Americans, Puerto-Rican Americans, Cuban Americans, and others. According to the U.S. Census Bureau, Hispanic Americans numbered 35 million in 2000 and comprised the fifth-largest Hispanic population in the world with $560 billion in annual buying power. As a group, Hispanic Americans are hard working and exhibit a strong family and religious orientation. In addition, consider the following statistics:

- Mexican households in California have after-tax income of $100 billion, half the total of all Mexican Americans.
- The number of Hispanic teens is projected to swell from 12 percent of the U.S. teen population to 18 percent in the next decade.

From a marketing point of view, these groups offer great opportunity. Companies in a variety of industry sectors, including food and beverages, consumer durables, and leisure and financial services are recognizing the need to include these

---

25 John Varoli, "Bored by Vodka, Russians Find More Style in Beer," *The New York Times* (December 19, 1999), sec. 3, p. 7.
26 Sarah Ellison and Emily Nelson, "Pet-Food Companies Compete to Be the Pick of the Litter," *The Wall Street Journal* (July 31, 2001), p. B11.

segments when preparing marketing programs for the United States. Consider Club Med, for example. Over the past decade, the Paris-based company has had difficulty generating a strong customer base in the United States. Traditionally, Club Med's U.S. advertising featured Caucasians; hoping to capture a broader demographic, the company rolled out a new print campaign that featured black and Asian children playing in the tropical surf.[27] Meanwhile, companies based in Mexico are zeroing in on opportunities to the north. Three Mexican retailers—Famso, Grupo Gigant SA, and Grupo Comercial Chedraui SA—have opened stores in the United States. As Famsa president Humberto Garza Valdez explained at the grand opening of a store in San Fernando, California, "We're not coming to the U.S. to face big companies like Circuit City or Best Buy. Our focus is the Hispanic market."[28]

In the two-year period 1999–2000, new-vehicle registrations by Hispanics in the United States grew 20 percent, twice the overall national growth rate. Honda, Toyota, and other Japanese automakers have been courting U.S. Hispanics for years and have built up a great deal of brand loyalty. Ford and GM are playing catch up, with mixed results; despite large increases in advertising targeting Hispanics, GM's market share is slipping.[29] Sales of Corona Extra beer in the United States have grown dramatically recently, thanks in part to savvy marketing to the Hispanic segment. In lower-income neighborhoods, imported premium beer brands represent "affordable luxuries." Although a six-pack of Corona typically costs at least a dollar more than Budweiser at a local bodega, it is usually cheaper than Heineken. Marketers must understand, though, that many Hispanic Americans live in two worlds; while they identify strongly with America, there is also a sense of pride associated with brands that connect to their heritage.[30]

GLOBAL TARGETING

As discussed previously, segmenting is the process by which marketers identify groups of consumers with similar wants and needs. **Targeting** is the act of evaluating and comparing the identified groups and then selecting one or more of them as the prospect(s) with the highest potential. A marketing mix is then devised that will provide the organization with the best return on sales while simultaneously creating the maximum amount of value to consumers.

Criteria for Targeting

After segmenting the market according to one or more of the variables described, it is necessary to create a product-market profile. The basic questions to be answered can be summarized as the nine W's:

1. Who buys our product?
2. Who does not buy our product?
3. What need or function does our product serve?

---

[27] Shelly Branch, "Club Med's New Ads to Push Family Fun," *The Wall Street Journal* (August 8, 1999), p. B9.

[28] Joel Millman, "Mexican Retailers Enter U.S. to Capture Latino Dollars," *The Wall Street Journal* (February 8, 2001), p. A18.

[29] Eduardo Porter, "Ford, Other Auto Makers Target Hispanic Community," *The Wall Street Journal* (November 9, 2000), p. B4.

[30] Suein L. Hwang, "Corona Ads Target Hispanics in Effort to Hop to Head of U.S. Beer Market," *The Wall Street Journal Europe* (November 21–22, 1997), p. 9; Michael Barone, "How Hispanics are Americanizing," *The Wall Street Journal* (February 6, 1998), p. A22.

4. What problem does our product solve?
5. What are customers currently buying to satisfy the need and/or solve the problem for which our product is targeted?
6. What price are they paying for the product they are currently buying?
7. When is our product purchased?
8. Where is our product purchased?
9. Why is our product purchased?

Any company must answer these critical questions if it is going to successfully target new market segments. Each answer provides an input into decisions concerning the four Ps. Remember, the general rule in marketing is that, if a company wants to penetrate an existing market, it must offer more value than competitors—better benefits, lower prices, or both. With this profile in hand, marketers then utilize three basic criteria for assessing opportunity in global target markets: current size of the segment and anticipated growth potential, competition, and compatibility with the company's overall objectives and the feasibility of successfully reaching a designated target.

Current Segment Size and Growth Potential

Is the market segment currently large enough to present a company with the opportunity to make a profit? If it is not large enough or profitable enough today, does it have high growth potential to make it attractive in terms of a company's long-term strategy? Indeed, one of the advantages of targeting a market segment globally is that, while the segment in a single-country market might be too small, even a narrow segment can be served profitably if the segment exists in several countries. The billion-plus members of the global MTV Generation constitute a huge market. Moreover, by virtue of its size and purchasing power, it is extremely attractive to consumer goods companies.

China represents an individual geographic market that offers attractive opportunities in many industries. Consider the growth opportunity in financial services, for example. There are currently only about 3 million credit cards in circulation, mostly used by businesses. Low product saturation levels are also found for personal computers; there is one PC for every 6,000 people. The ratio in the United States is one computer for every four people. The opportunity for automobile manufacturers is even greater. China has 1.2 million passenger cars—one car for every 20,000 Chinese. Only 60,000 of those cars are owned by private citizens.

The sports utility vehicle segment of the U.S. auto market was a textbook example of a growth segment from 1990 to 2000. During that time SUV sales tripled, growing from nearly one million units in 1990, reaching the two-million unit mark in 1996, and passing three million sold in 2000. Reacting to high demand for the Jeep Cherokee, Ford Explorer, and Chevy Blazer, manufacturers from outside the United States drew up plans for their own versions. At the low end, South Korea's Kia launched its $20,000 Sportage at the end of 1994; China is even exporting a revamped military vehicle to the United States that it intends to sell for $10,000. By 1997, 33 different vehicles classified as SUVs were available in the United States; popular models include the Honda CRV and Toyota RAV4. AutoPacific consultancy predicts that by 2006, 79 separate SUV models will be available as Toyota, Nissan, Rover, BMW, Mercedes, and other automakers target American buyers.[31] Even as growth slows in

---

[31] Joseph B. White, "Rollback: America's Love Affair with Sport Utilities Is Now Cooling Off," *The Wall Street Journal* (May 30, 2001), pp. A1, A8.

the United States, the SUV segment is growing in many other countries. Chrysler builds a right-seat drive Jeep Cherokee for the Japanese market. In the early 1990s, the strong yen enabled Chrysler to cut prices in Japan by 30 percent. In 1994, Chrysler sold 10,000 Cherokees priced at $36,000 in Japan, more than double the number sold the previous year; until the end of 1997, Chrysler's vehicles were distributed in Japan through Honda's dealer network.

Potential Competition

A market or market segment characterized by strong competition may be a segment to avoid. However, Kodak's position as the undisputed leader in the $2.4 billion U.S. color film market did not deter Fuji from launching a competitive offensive. In addition to offering traditional types of 35mm film at prices below Kodak's, Fuji quickly made inroads by introducing a number of new film products targeted at the "advanced amateur" segment that Kodak had neglected. Despite its early successes, after nearly two decades of effort, Fuji's U.S. market share has been only in the 10 to 12 percent range. Part of the problem is Kodak's distribution clout: Kodak is well entrenched in supermarket and drugstore chains, where Fuji must also jostle with other newcomers such as Konica and Polaroid. In addition, Kodak has agreements with dozens of U.S. amusement parks guaranteeing that only Kodak film will be sold on the premises. For these reasons, Fuji has shifted its attention from the U.S. market to Europe, where Kodak commands "only" 40 percent of the color film market. Fuji currently enjoys 25 percent of the European market, compared with 10 percent a decade ago. Meanwhile, Kodak has spent half a billion dollars in Japan, the world's second-largest market for photographic supplies; its market share there currently stands at about 10 percent.

Discussions with exporters, bankers, and other industry executives are extremely useful in appraising the level and quality of competition in the potential market. A country's commercial representatives abroad can also be valuable sources of competitive information. When contacting such a representative, it is important to provide as much specific information as possible. If a manufacturer simply says, "I make personal computers. Is there a market for them in your territory?", the representative cannot provide much helpful information. The manufacturer should provide information about the range of models available along with marketing literature detailing features and advantages. Then, the commercial representative should be able to provide a useful report comparing the company's product with those already available from established competitors.

Compatibility and Feasibility

If a global target market is judged to be large enough, and if strong competitors are either absent or not deemed to represent insurmountable obstacles, then the final consideration is whether a company can and should target that market. Managers must decide how well a company's product fits the market in question. To make this decision, a marketer must consider several criteria. First, does the product create value for target customers? Second, it is necessary to determine whether adaptation is required; if so, is this economically justifiable in terms of the expected sales volume? Third, import restrictions, high tariffs, or a strong home country currency may drive up the price of the product target market currency and effectively eliminate demand. In many cases, reaching global market segments requires considerable resources such as expenditures for distribution and travel by company personnel. Finally, and perhaps most importantly, the question is whether the pursuit of a

Table 7-7
Market Selection
Framework

MARKET	MARKET SIZE	COMPETITIVE ADVANTAGE		MARKET POTENTIAL	TERMS OF ACCESS	MARKET POTENTIAL
China (1.2 billion)	100	.07	=	7	.20	1.4
Russia (150 million)	50	.10	=	5	.60	3.0
Mexico (94 million)	20	.20	=	4	.90	3.6

particular segment is compatible with the company's overall goals and established sources of competitive advantage.

In the mid-1990s, French cosmetics giant L'Oreal proceeded with plans to roll out its Biotherm line in the United States despite the fact that Estee Lauder's Clinique line was firmly entrenched. L'Oreal had a $1 billion "war chest" at its disposal to help finance the effort. Chairman Lindsay Owen-Jones believed an expanded presence in the U.S. market—where the company ranked fourth in terms of market share—was critical if L'Oreal was to sustain double-digit growth. At the end of 1995, L'Oreal made an even bigger commitment to the U.S. market by announcing that it would acquire Maybelline for $508 million. The acquisition propelled L'Oreal from fourth place to second place in the U.S. cosmetics market.

Table 7-7 presents a market selection framework that incorporates some of the elements just discussed. Suppose an American company has identified China, Russia, and Mexico as potential target markets. The table shows the countries arranged in declining rank by market size. At first glance, China might appear to hold the greatest potential simply on the basis of size. However, the competitive advantage of our hypothetical firm is .07 in China, .10 in Russia, and .2 in Mexico. Multiplying the market size and competitive advantage index yields a market potential of 7 in China, 5 in Russia, and 4 in Mexico.

The next stage in the analysis requires an assessment of the various market access considerations. In Table 7-7 all these conditions or terms are reduced to an index number of terms of access, which is 0.2 for China, 0.6 for Russia and 0.9 Mexico. In other words, the "market access considerations" are more favorable in Mexico than in Russia, perhaps in this instance due to NAFTA. Multiplying the market potential by the terms of access index shows that Mexico, despite its small size, holds greater export potential than China or Russia. In this example, a company with limited resources would want to begin by targeting Mexico because it offers the highest market potential when a variety of criteria are considered.

SELECTING A TARGET MARKET STRATEGY

After evaluating the identified segments in terms of the three criteria presented, a decision is made whether to pursue a particular opportunity or not. If the decision is made to proceed, an appropriate targeting strategy must be developed. There are three basic categories of target marketing strategies: standardized marketing, concentrated marketing, and differentiated marketing.

Over the past decade, savvy export marketing has enabled Harley-Davidson to dramatically increase worldwide sales of its heavyweight motorcycles. Export sales increased from 3,000 motorcycles in 1983 to 15,000 units for the 1990 model year. By 1993, non-U.S. sales neared the $300 million mark, up from $115 million in 1989. From Australia to Germany to Mexico City, Harley enthusiasts are paying the equivalent of up to $25,000 to own an American-built classic. In many countries, dealers must put would-be buyers on a six-month waiting list because of high demand.

Harley's international success comes after years of neglecting overseas markets. Early on the company was basically involved in export selling, symbolized by its underdeveloped dealer network. Moreover, print advertising simply used word-for-word translations of the U.S. ads. By the late 1980s, after recruiting dealers in the important Japanese and European markets, company executives discovered a basic principle of global marketing. "As the saying goes, we needed to think global but act local," said Jerry G. Wilke, vice president for worldwide marketing. Harley began to adapt its international marketing, making it more responsive to local conditions.

In Japan, for example, Harley's rugged image and high quality helped make it the best-selling imported motorcycle. Still, Toshifumi Okui, president of Harley's Japanese division, was not satisfied. He worried that the tag line from the U.S. ads, "One steady constant in an increasingly screwed-up world," didn't connect with Japanese riders. Okui finally convinced Milwaukee to allow him to launch a Japan-only advertising campaign juxtaposing images from both Japan and the United States, such as American cyclists passing a rickshaw carrying a geisha. After learning that riders in Tokyo consider fashion and customized bikes to be essential, Harley opened two stores specializing in clothes and bike accessories.

In Europe, Harley discovered that an "evening out" means something different than it does in America. The company sponsored a rally in France, where beer and live rock music were available until midnight. Recalls Wilke, "People asked us why we were ending the rally just as the evening was starting. So I had to go persuade the band to keep playing and reopen the bar until 3 or 4 a.m." Still, rallies are less common in Europe than in the United States, so Harley encourages its dealers to hold open houses at their dealerships.

While biking through Europe, Wilke also learned that German bikers often travel at speeds exceeding 100 miles per hour. Now the company is investigating design changes to create a smoother ride at Autobahn speeds. Harley's German marketing effort may also begin focusing on accessories to increase rider protection.

Despite high levels of demand, the company intentionally limits production increases in order to uphold Harley's recent improvements in quality and to keep the product supply limited in relation to demand. Harley is still careful to make home-country customers a higher priority than those living abroad; thus, only 30 percent of its production goes outside the United States. The Harley shortage seems to suit company executives just fine. Notes Harley's James H. Patterson, "Enough motorcycles is too many motorcycles."

SOURCES: Kevin Kelly and Karen Lowry Miller, "The Rumble Heard Round the World: Harleys," *Business Week* (May 24, 1993), pp. 58, 60; Robert L. Rose, "Vrooming Back: After Nearly Stalling, Harley-Davidson Finds New Crowd of Riders," *The Wall Street Journal* (August 31, 1990), pp. A1, A6; John Holusha, "How Harley Outfoxed Japan with Exports," *New York Times* (August 12, 1990), p. F5; Robert C. Reid, "How Harley Beat Back the Japanese," *Fortune* (September 25, 1989), pp. 155+.

Standardized Global Marketing

Standardized global marketing is analogous to mass marketing in a single country. Strictly speaking, it involves creating the same marketing mix for a broad mass market of potential buyers. Standardized global marketing, also known as *undifferentiated target marketing,* is based on the premise that a mass market exists around the world. In addition, that mass market is served with a marketing mix of standardized elements. Product adaptation is minimized, and a strategy of intensive distribution ensures that the product is available in the maximum number of retail outlets. The appeal of standardized global marketing is clear: lower production costs. The same is true of standardized global communications.

Executives at Revlon International recently adopted a standardized strategy when they announced their intention of making Revlon a global name. President Paul Block declared, "All Revlon North American advertising for all products, whether they are cosmetics, skincare, haircare, or Almay, will now be used worldwide."[32] The global theme is keyed to a "Shake Your Body" campaign. Revlon's strategy calls for developing the huge consumer markets emerging in Central and Eastern Europe, including Hungary and the former Soviet republics.

Concentrated Global Marketing

The second global targeting strategy, concentrated target marketing, involves devising a marketing mix to reach a **niche**. A niche is simply a single segment of the global market. In cosmetics, the House of Lauder, Chanel, and other cosmetics marketers have used this approach successfully to target the upscale, prestige segment of the market. Similarly, Body Shop International PLC caters to consumers in many countries who wish to purchase "natural" beauty aids and cosmetics that have not been tested on animals. Concentrated targeting is also the strategy employed by the hidden champions of global marketing—companies unknown to most people that have succeeded by serving a niche market that exists in many countries. These companies define their markets narrowly and strive for global depth rather than national breadth. For example, Germany's Winterhalter is a hidden champion in the dishwasher market, but the company has never sold a dishwasher to a consumer, hospital, or school. Instead, it focuses exclusively on dishwashers and water conditioners for hotels and restaurants. As Jürgen Winterhalter noted recently, "The narrowing of our market definition was the most important strategic decision we ever made. It is the very foundation of our success in the past decade."[33]

Differentiated Global Marketing

The third target marketing strategy, **differentiated global marketing,** represents a more ambitious approach than concentrated target marketing. Also known as **multisegment targeting,** this approach entails targeting two or more distinct market segments with multiple marketing mix offerings. This strategy allows a company to achieve wider market coverage. For example, in the sport utility vehicle segment described previously, Land Rover offers a $68,000 Range Rover at the high end of the market. A scaled-down version, the Land Rover Discovery, competes directly with the Jeep Grand Cherokee and is available in two models priced from $33,350 to $37,450. Rover's newest vehicle, the Freelander, has been on sale in Europe for several years. Freelander was introduced in the U.S. market in December 2001 with prices starting at $25,000. Likewise, Stolichnaya produces three brands of Russian vodka, each targeted at a different market segment: low-priced Privet (the name means "greetings" in Russian), the premium "base" brand Stolichnaya, and superpremium Stolichnaya Gold.

In the cosmetics industry, Unilever NV and Cosmair Inc. pursue differentiated global marketing strategies by targeting both ends of the perfume market. Unilever targets the luxury market with Calvin Klein and Elizabeth Taylor's Passion; Wind

---

[32] Pat Sloan, "Revlon Eyes Global Image; Picks Y & R," *Advertising Age* (January 1, 1993), p. 1.
[33] Hermann Simon, *Hidden Champions: Lessons from 500 of the World's Best Unknown Companies* (Boston: Harvard Business School Press, 1996), p. 54.

Song and Brut are its mass-market brands. Cosmair sells Tresnor and Giorgio Armani Gio to the upper end of the market and Gloria Vanderbilt to the lower end. Mass marketer Procter & Gamble, known for its Old Spice and Incognito brands, also embarked upon this strategy with its 1991 acquisition of Revlon's EuroCos, marketer of Hugo Boss for men and Laura Biagiotti's Roma perfume. In the mid-1990s, P&G launched a new prestige fragrance, Venezia, in the United States and several European countries. Conversely, in 1997 Estee Lauder acquired Sassaby Inc., owner of the mass-market Jane brand. The move marked the first move by Lauder outside the prestige segment.[34]

POSITIONING

Visit the Web site
Learn more about Unilever's different brands at:
www.unilever.com

The term *positioning* is attributed to marketing gurus Al Ries and Jack Trout, who first introduced it in a 1969 article published in *Industrial Marketing* magazine. **Positioning** refers to the act of locating a brand in customers' minds over and against competitors in terms of attributes and benefits that the brand does and does not offer. Put differently, positioning is the process of developing strategies for "staking out turf" or "filling a slot" in the mind of target customers.[35] Positioning is frequently used in conjunction with the segmentation variables and targeting strategies discussed previously. For example, Unilever and other consumer goods companies often engage in differentiated target marketing, offering a full range of brands within a given product category. Unilever's 10 detergent brands include All, Wisk, Surf, and Persil; each is positioned slightly differently. In some instances, extensions of a popular brand can be positioned in different ways. For example, Procter & Gamble's Crest toothpaste is positioned as an all-around cavity fighter; Crest is also available in several other formulations, including tartar control formula and new Multicare Advanced Cleaning. Effective positioning differentiates each variety from the others.

In the decades since Ries and Trout first focused attention on the importance of the concept, marketers have utilized a number of general positioning strategies. These include positioning by attribute or benefit, quality and price, use or user, and competitor.[36] Recent research has identified three additional positioning strategies that are particularly useful in global marketing: global consumer culture positioning, local consumer culture positioning, and foreign consumer culture positioning.

Attribute or Benefit

A frequently used positioning strategy exploits a particular product attribute, benefit, or feature. Economy, reliability, and durability are frequently used attribute/benefit positions. Volvo automobiles are known for solid construction that offers safety in the event of a crash. By contrast, BMW is positioned as "the ultimate driving machine," a reference that signifies performance. In the ongoing credit card wars, Visa's advertising theme "It's Everywhere You Want to Be" draws attention to the benefit of worldwide merchant acceptance. In global marketing, it may be deemed important to communicate the fact that a brand is imported. This approach is known as *foreign consumer culture positioning* (FCCP).

---

[34] Tara Parker-Pope, "Estee Lauder Buys Jane Brand's Owner for Its First Venture into Mass Market," *The Wall Street Journal* (September 27, 1997), p. B8.

[35] Al Ries and Jack Trout, *Positioning: The Battle for Your Mind* (New York: Warner Books, 1982), p. 44.

[36] David A. Aaker and J. Gary Shansby, "Positioning Your Product," *Business Horizons* (May-June 1982), pp. 56–62.

Quality and Price

This strategy can be thought of in terms of a continuum from high fashion/quality and high price to good value (rather than "low quality") at a reasonable price. At the high end of the distilled spirits industry, marketers of imported vodkas such as Belvedere and Stolichnaya Gold have successfully positioned their brands as super premium entities selling for twice the price of premium ("ordinary") vodka. Ads for several export vodka brands emphasize their national origins, demonstrating how quality and price can also be reinforced by FCCP (see below). Marketers sometimes use the phrase "transformation advertising" to describe advertising that seeks to change the experience of buying and using a product—in other words, the product benefit—to justify a higher price/quality position. Presumably, buying and drinking Grey Goose (from France), Belvedere (Poland), Ketel One (the Netherlands), or Stolichnaya Gold (Russia) is a more gratifying consumption experience than that of buying and drinking a "bar brand" such as Popov (who knows where it is made?).

Use or User

Another positioning strategy represents how a product is used or associates the brand with a user or class of users. Marlboro's extraordinary success as a global brand is due in part to the product's association with cowboys—*the* archetypal symbol of freedom—and transformation advertising that targets urban smokers. As Clive Chajet, a corporate and brand identity expert, explains, "The cowboy is as enduring an icon as you can have. And the stronger your brand image, regardless of the environment in which you compete, the better off you are."[37] Smoking Marlboro is a way of getting in touch with a powerful urge to be free and independent. The message is reinforced in advertising that urges smokers to "join that rugged, independent cowboy in the Old West!" Of course, from the point of view of the health care community and anti-smoking activists around the world, Marlboro's advertising has worked all too well. In the United States and elsewhere, the Marlboro man is disappearing from the landscape as restrictions on tobacco advertising are tightened. As noted in the following paragraphs, some global brands are positioned as ones that are consumed throughout the world; buying and consuming the brand allows a person to feel that he or she is connected to a global cultural segment.

Competition

Implicit or explicit reference to competitors can provide the basis for an effective positioning strategy. For example, Body Shop International founder Anita Roddick achieved early success by emphasizing the difference between the principles pursued by "mainstream" cosmetics manufacturers and retailers and those of her company. The Body Shop brand stands for natural ingredients, no animal testing, and recyclable containers. Moreover, Roddick broke with the conventional industry approach of promising miracles. At Body Shop, women were given realistic expectations of what health and beauty aids can accomplish. Unfortunately, competitors such as Bath & Body Works quickly took notice and began mimicking both the Body Shop's positioning and its merchandising approach. After years of aggressive expansion, especially in the United States and Britain, the Body Shop brand remains well

---

[37] Stuart Elliott, "Uncle Sam is No Match for the Marlboro Man," *The New York Times* (August 27, 1995), sec. 3, p. 11.

To justify high prices, marketers of ultra premium vodka must differentiate their brands through packaging, distinctive flavors, or, as this ad for top-selling Belvedere illustrates, by positioning with respect to a country's heritage as a distiller. Competition in the category has increased dramatically in recent years; in 2001 alone, 42 new vodka brands were launched. Meanwhile, following years of explosive growth, the category is cooling as recession-pinched consumers trade down to lower-priced brands.

500 years ago, while others tried to turn lead into gold, Poland discovered a way to turn rye into vodka.

Following Old World traditions, Belvedere is handcrafted from 100% Polish rye and distilled 4 times for a creamy smoothness.

IMPORTED BY MILLENNIUM® IMPORT CO., MINNEAPOLIS, MINNESOTA U.S.A.
100% neutral spirits distilled from rye grain 40% ALC./VOL. (80 Proof) ©2000 Millennium® Import Co.

known but is not as distinctive as it was previously. Roddick resigned as the company's chief executive in 1998; by 2001, Mexico's Grupo Omnilife SA had begun discussions about acquiring the company.[38]

Global, Foreign, and Local Consumer Culture Positioning[39]

As noted in Chapter 4 and discussed briefly in this chapter, global consumer culture positioning is a strategy that can be used to target various segments associated with the emerging global consumer culture. **Global consumer culture positioning** (GCCP) is defined as a strategy that identifies the brand as a symbol of a particular global culture or segment. It has proven to be an effective strategy for communicating with global teens, cosmopolitan elites, globe-trotting laptop warriors who consider

---

[38] Sarah Ellison, "Body Shop Hopes for New Image with an Omnilife Deal," *The Wall Street Journal* (June 8, 2001), p. B4.

[39] The following discussion is adapted from Dana L. Alden, Jan-Benedict Steenkamp, and Rajeev Batra, "Brand Positioning through Advertising in Asia, North America, and Europe: The Role of Global Consumer Culture," *Journal of Marketing* 63, no. 1 (January 1999), pp. 75–87.

themselves members of a "transnational commerce culture," and other groups. For example, Sony's brightly colored "My First Sony" line is positioned as *the* electronics brand for youngsters around the globe with discerning parents. Philips's global corporate image campaign features people from all parts of the world with the theme "Let's make things better." Benetton uses the slogan "United Colors of Benetton" to position itself as a brand concerned with the unity of humankind. Heineken's strong brand equity around the globe can be attributed in good measure to a GCCP strategy that reinforces consumers' cosmopolitan self-image.

Certain categories of products lend themselves especially well to GCCP. High-tech and high-touch products are both associated with high levels of customer involvement and by a shared "language" among users.[40] *High-tech products* are sophisticated, technologically complex, and/or difficult to explain or understand. When shopping for them, consumers often have specialized needs or interests and rational buying motives. High-tech brands and products are frequently evaluated in terms of their performance against established objective standards. Portable MP3 players, cellular phones, personal computers, home theater audio/video components, luxury automobiles, and financial services are some of the high-tech product categories for which companies have established strong global positions. Buyers typically already possess—or wish to acquire—considerable technical information. Generally speaking, for example, computer buyers in all parts of the world are equally knowledgeable about Pentium microprocessors, thirty-gigabyte hard drives, and software RAM requirements. High-tech global consumer positioning also works well for special interest products associated with leisure or recreation. Fuji bicycles, Adidas sports equipment, and Canon cameras are examples of successful global special-interest products. Since most people who buy and use high-tech products "speak the same language" and share the same mindset, marketing communications should be informative and emphasize performance-related attributes and features to establish the desired GCCP.

By contrast, when shopping for *high-touch products*, consumers are generally energized by emotional motives rather than rational ones. Consumers may feel an emotional or spiritual connection with high-touch products, the performance of which is evaluated in subjective, aesthetic terms rather than objective, technical terms. Consumption of high-touch products may represent an act of personal indulgence, reflect the user's actual or ideal self-image, or reinforce interpersonal relationships between the user and family members or friends. High-touch products appeal to the senses more than the intellect; if a product comes with a detailed user's manual, it's probably high tech; it is probably not necessary to refer to an instruction manual before consuming a high-touch product. Luxury perfume, designer fashions, and fine champagne are all examples of high-touch products that lend themselves to GCCP. Some high-touch products are linked with the joy or pleasure found in "life's little moments." Ads that show friends chatting over a cup of coffee in a cafe or someone's kitchen put the product at the center of everyday life. As Nestlé has convincingly demonstrated with its Nescafé brand, this type of high-touch, emotional appeal is understood worldwide.

A brand's GCCP can be reinforced by the careful selection of the thematic, verbal, or visual components that are incorporated into advertising and other communications. For marketers seeking to establish a high-touch GCCP, leisure, romance, and materialism are three themes that cross borders well. By contrast, professionalism and experience are advertising themes that work well for high-tech products such as

---

[40] Teresa J. Domzal and Lynette Unger, "Emerging Positioning Strategies in Global Marketing," *Journal of Consumer Marketing* 4, no. 4 (Fall 1987), pp. 26–27.

THE WYNNEWOOD CHAMPAGNE FLUTE, LIKE ALL WATERFORD PATTERNS, WILL NEVER BE DISCONTINUED. FOR A BROCHURE, CALL 1-800-523-0009.

WATERFORD
WORTHY OF THE MOMENT
FOR OVER TWO CENTURIES.

global financial services. Several years ago, for example, Chase Manhattan bank launched a $75 million global advertising campaign geared to the theme "Profit from experience." According to Aubrey Hawes, a vice president and corporate director of marketing for the bank, Chase's business and private banking clients "span the globe and travel the globe. They can only know one Chase in their minds, so why should we try to confuse them?"[41] Presumably, Chase's target audience is sophisticated enough to appreciate the subtlety of the copywriter's craft—"profit" can be interpreted as either a noun ("monetary gain") or a verb ("reap an advantage").

In some instances, products may be positioned globally in a "bi-polar" fashion (i.e., as both high-tech and high-touch). This approach can be used when products satisfy buyers' rational criteria while evoking an emotional response. For example, audio-video components from Denmark's Bang & Olufsen, by virtue of their performance and elegant styling, are perceived as both high-tech ("advanced engineering and sonically superior") and high-touch ("modern design blends in nicely with the rest of the décor"). Nokia has become the world's leading cellular phone brand because the company combines state-of-the-art technical performance with a fashion

---

[41] Gary Levin, "Ads Going Global," *Advertising Age* (July 22, 1991), p. 42.

Writing in the Far Eastern Economic Review, *Charles Bickers praised Apple's Titanium G4 laptop for its "stunning" looks and noted that the laptop "oozes understated corporate power." Likewise, a reviewer for* eWeek *asserted that the G4's tough, sleek titanium shell "redefines how a notebook computer should appear and feel." High-touch products are designed to evoke these types of responses; the technical features of the Titanium G4 also satisfy users' performance needs.*

1" thick
5.3 pounds
DVD
5 hour battery
AirPort
15.2" mega-wide screen
Titanium
PowerBook G4.

Think different.

orientation that allows users to view their phones as extensions of themselves. Likewise, Apple Computer positions its products on the basis of both performance ("two G4 processors operating in parallel") and design (the unorthodox new iMac's flat-screen display mounted on a swiveling stainless-steel neck).

To the extent that English is the primary language of international business, mass media, and the Internet, one can make the case that English signifies modernism and a cosmopolitan outlook. Therefore, the use of English in advertising and labeling throughout the world is another way to achieve GCCP. Benetton's tag line "United Colors of Benetton" appears in English in all of the company's advertising. The implication is that fashion-minded consumers everywhere in the world shop at Benetton. Recall the Chapter 4 discussion of the use of English as a marketing tool in Japan. Even though a native English speaker would doubtless find the syntax to be muddled, it is the symbolism associated with the use of English that counts rather

Wine and beer brands from Australia's Foster's Group are available in more than 150 countries, but about three-fourths of the company's sales are in the Asia/Pacific region. In the United States, ads for Foster's lager play up the brand's Australian heritage and emphasize the sense of adventure associated with the country's exotic outback.

than specific meanings that the words might (or might not) convey. A third way to reinforce a GCCP is to use brand symbols that cannot be interpreted as associated with a specific country culture. Examples include Nestlé's "little nest" logo with an adult bird feeding its babies, the Nike swoosh, and the Mercedes-Benz star.

A second option is **foreign consumer culture positioning** (FCCP), which associates the brand's users, use occasions, or production origins with a foreign country or culture. Foster's Brewing Group's U.S. advertising proudly trumpets the brand's national origin; print ads feature the tag line "Foster's. Australian for beer" while TV and radio spots are keyed to the theme "How to speak Australian." Needless to say, these ads are not used in Australia itself. Advertising for Grupo Modelo's Corona Extra brand is identified more generally with Latin America. The "American-ness" of Levi jeans, Marlboro cigarettes, and Harley-Davidson motorcycles—sometimes conveyed with subtlety, sometimes not—enhances their appeal to cosmopolitans around the world and offers opportunities for FCCP. FCCP is sometimes used in automobile advertising; in the early 1990s, for example, Volkswagen ran an advertising campaign featuring a German word, "Fahrvergnügen," that was meant to signify both the cars' German origins and a European joy of driving. Sometimes, brand names suggest an FCCP even though a product is of local origin. For example, the name "Haägen-Dazs" was made up to imply Scandinavian origin even though the ice cream was launched by an American company. Conversely, a popular brand of chewing gum in Italy from an Italian manufacturer carries the brand name Brooklyn.

Marketers can also utilize **local consumer culture positioning** (LCCP), a strategy that associates the brand with local cultural meanings, reflects the local culture's norms, portrays the brand as consumed by local people in the national culture, or depicts the product as locally produced for local consumers. An LCCP approach can be seen in Budweiser's U.S. advertising; ads featuring the Clydesdale horses, for example, associate the brand with small-town American culture. Researchers studying television advertising in seven countries found that LCCP predominated, particularly in ads for food, personal nondurables, and household nondurables.

SUMMARY

The global environment must be analyzed before a company pursues expansion into new geographic markets. Through **global market segmentation,** a company can identify and group customers or countries according to common needs and wants. **Demographic segmentation** can be based on country income and population, age, ethnic heritage, or other variables. **Psychographic segmentation** groups people according to attitudes, values, and lifestyles. BSB's **Global Scan,** DMBB's **Euroconsumer Study,** and Young & Rubicam's **4Cs** are examples of proprietary psychographic segmentation studies prepared by advertising agencies for their global clients. **Behavioral characteristics** such as **user status** and **usage rate** can also be used as segmentation variables. Segmentation can also be based on the **benefits** buyers seek.

After marketers have identified segments, the next step is **targeting:** The identified groups are evaluated and compared, and one or more segments with the greatest potential is selected from them. The groups are evaluated on the basis of several factors, including segment size and growth potential, competition, and compatibility and feasibility. After evaluating the identified segments, marketers must decide on an appropriate targeting strategy. The three basic categories of global target marketing strategies are **standardized marketing, concentrated (niche) marketing,** and **differentiated (multisegment) marketing.**

Positioning a product or brand in the minds of targeted customers can be accomplished in various ways. **Attribute** or **benefit, quality** and **price, use** or **user,** and a company's **competition** can all serve as the basis for a strong positioning strategy. In global marketing **global consumer culture positioning** (GCCP), **foreign consumer culture positioning** (FCCP), and **local consumer culture positioning** (LCCP) are additional strategic options. ∎

DISCUSSION QUESTIONS

1. Identify the five basic segmentation strategies. Give an example of a company that has used each one.
2. Explain the difference between segmenting and targeting.

3. Compare and contrast standardized, concentrated, and differentiated global marketing. Illustrate each strategy with an example from a global company.

4. American Izuzu Motors recently introduced the AXIOM SUV in the United States with a base sticker price of $25,985. The base price for a Honda CRV is $18,750; prices for Toyota's RAV4 start at $16,365. Assess Isuzu's decision to target the U.S. market for sport utility vehicles.

5. What is positioning? Identify the different positioning strategies presented in the chapter and give examples of companies or products that illustrate each.

6. What is global consumer culture positioning (GCCP)? What other strategic positioning choices do global marketers have?

7. What is a high-touch product? Explain the difference between high-tech product positioning and high-touch product positioning. Can some products be positioned using both strategies? Explain.

SUGGESTED READINGS

Books

Piirto, Rebecca. *Beyond Mind Games: The Marketing Power of Psychographics*. Ithaca, New York: American Demographics Books, 1991.

Articles

Dubow, Joel S. "Occasion-Based vs. User-Based Benefit Segmentation: A Case Study." *Journal of Advertising Research* 32, no. 2 (March/April 1992), pp. 11–18.

Garland, Barbara C., and Marti J. Rhea. "American Consumers: Profile of an Import Preference Segment." *Akron Business and Economic Review* 19, no. 2 (1988), pp. 20–29.

Green, Paul E., and Abba M. Krieger. "Segmenting Markets with Conjoint Analysis." *Journal of Marketing* 55, no. 4 (October 1991), pp. 20–31.

Hassan, Salah S., and Lea Prevel Katsanis. "Identification of Global Consumer Segments: A Behavioral Framework." *Journal of International Consumer Marketing* 3, no. 2 (1991), pp. 11–28.

Hout, Thomas, Michael E. Porter, and Eileen Rudden. "How Global Companies Win Out." *Harvard Business Review* 60, no. 5 (September-October 1982), pp. 98–108.

Kumar, V., and Anish Pagpal. "Segmenting Global Markets: Look Before You Leap." *Marketing Research* 13, no. 1 (Spring 2001), pp. 8–13.

Morwitz, Vicki G., and David Schmittlein. "Using Segmentation to Improve Sales Forecasts Based on Purchase Intent: Which 'Intenders' Actually Buy?" *Journal of Marketing Research* 29, no. 4 (November 1992), pp. 391–405.

Murray, Janet Y., Masaaki Kotabe, and Albert R. Wildt. "Strategic and Financial Performance Implications of Global Sourcing Strategy: A Contingency Analysis," *Journal of International Business Studies* 26, no. 1 (First Quarter 1995), pp. 181–202.

Pawle, John. "Mining the International Consumer." *Journal of the Market Research Society* 41, no. 1 (1999), pp. 19–32.

Ter Hofstede, Frankel, Jan-Benedict E. M. Steenkamp, and Michel Wedel. "International Market Segmentation Based on Consumer-Product Relations." *Journal of Marketing Research* 36, no. 1 (1999), pp. 1–17.

C A S E S

Case 7-1   *HarperCollins—Is the "Global Book" a Reality?*

HarperCollins Publishers had a banner year in 1995, with revenues up 10 percent, to $1 billion, compared with 1994 (Table 1). The company's best-selling titles for adults included John Gray's *Men Are from Mars, Women Are from Venus* as well as a book by Newt Gingrich. Sales had increased in other categories as well, including audio books and children's books. The revenue growth provided evidence that a global strategy undertaken several years ago was paying off. In May 1990, the U.S. publisher Harper & Row merged with the British publisher William Collins & Sons. Both companies had come under the ownership of Rupert Murdoch's News Corporation, and HarperCollins Publishers instantly became the largest English-language publisher in an industry with $13 billion in worldwide sales. *The New York Times* once described Harper—which published John F. Kennedy's *Profiles in Courage*—as the embodiment of the American establishment publisher. Harper's strength was in trade books, which are hardcover and paperback books sold in bookstores. Collins, whose authors included Agatha

Table 1
Estimated Global Book Market, 1995 ($ billions)

Publisher	Sales
Bertelsmann (Germany)	$4,766
Warner Books (USA)	3,722
Simon & Schuster (USA)	2,171
Pearson (UK)	1,748
Reader's Digest (USA)	1,629
Random House (USA)	1,500
Groupe de la Cité	1,480
Planeta	1,364
Hachette Livre (France)	1,251
Reed Books (UK)	1,111
Harcourt Brace (USA)	900
HarperCollins (USA)	711
Putnam Publishing	381
Dorling Kindersley	220
Total	**22,954**

Source: Alice Rawsthorn, "World Book Market 'Faces Further Consolidation,'" *Financial Times* (October 2, 1996), p. 16.

Christie, was known in Britain for its strong commercial instincts, aggressive marketing, and diverse titles. One of its strengths was in mass-market books—standardized in format, less expensive than trade books, and sold on newsstands as well as in bookstores. The symbol of the new company is a blue and red water-and-fire symbol, combining the former corporate symbols of Harper (a torch) and Collins (a fountain).

The rationale for the merger was the increasingly global nature of the publishing industry as evidenced by the worldwide success of such books as Alex Haley's *Roots* and Umberto Eco's *The Name of the Rose*, as well as books by John Le Carré and Gore Vidal. A "global book" is one that achieves worldwide popularity and sales, much like recordings by opera singer Lucianno Pavarotti or pop star Madonna. A recent study by Euromonitor showed that two-thirds of the world's book market is outside the United States; as shown in the chart, the United States ranks fifth in per capita expenditures on books. According to some observers, the best approach for growth in this global publishing market is the "bigger is better" approach. Theoretically, larger companies—including those resulting from mergers—with higher sales volumes can enjoy economies of scale and reduce costs. Before the merger, George Craig had slashed overhead at Harper & Row by $20 million a year and boosted profits from $5.7 million in 1987 to $58 million in 1989. As the chief executive of HarperCollins, Craig moved quickly to exploit the advantages of global scale in the marketing (especially in distribution) of books.

Craig's actions are consistent with the point of view that publishing companies are actually in the entertainment business—just like major motion picture studios or record companies, which are also global in scope. In the film and music industries, fixed costs are high, and a few hit movies or recordings pay for a multitude of misses. Thus, the argument goes, a publishing company must be big enough and rich enough to have numerous projects in the production pipeline and to pay multimillion-dollar advances to popular authors whose books are usually hits. For example, Harper paid $1 million for the rights to E. L. Doctorow's *Billy Bathgate*. This side of the argument was recently summarized in the British magazine *The Economist*: "Only a diversified global publisher can grab all

World-class book buyers

The average American spent almost $97 on books last year — up from about $80 in 1991. The world's top book-buying countries[1] in spending per person (U.S. dollars):

Norway — $137
Germany — $122
Belgium — $117
Switzerland — $114
Austria — $101
USA — $97

1 – Includes all books distributed by retail, institutional, direct mail and mail order outlets in 51 countries.

Source: Euromonitor

By Anne R. Carey and Marcy E. Mullins, USA TODAY

the various hardback and paperback profits from its best-sellers around the world." Or, as William Shinker, head of the adult book division until 1994, put it, "Publishing for the world English market simply makes sense."

Some critics, however, believe that Craig's strategy—which also includes the introduction of a new line of mass-market paperbacks—will tarnish the image of the American half of the new company and thus backfire. But, according to Craig, Harper had grown "old fashioned, a bit dull, very bureaucratic, and it suffered from a lack of direction." Sonia Land, who quit as chief executive of Collins a few months before the merger, had this response to Craig's criticism: "By trying to create the true international publishing conglomerate, all George has done is destroy two great publishing traditions." In her view, both publishers—Harper, with its old-line, establishment American tradition, and Collins with its more commercial British one—would suffer as a result of the merger. Land's concern is that the HarperCollins name will not be a source of synergy in the global marketplace; it will stand for less, not more. Speaking of HarperCollins's new corporate symbol, Land says that someone should tell Craig that "fire and water do not mix." Land feels that, because it is the foundation on which the company's reputation was built, it is a mistake to change the venerable Collins name. Craig is said to have replied that "we are a world-wide publishing group. International branding is what we're all about."

The controversy over Craig's global ambitions for HarperCollins is perhaps most evident in the area of the children's books published by Harper Junior Books. Children's books represent a $1.5 billion growth segment in an otherwise stagnant industry; in the first half of 1989, sales of hardcover children's books were 15 percent ahead of 1988 sales, and sales of children's paperback books increased 51 percent in the same period. According to Harper Junior Books publisher Elizabeth Gordon, despite the fact that Collins has its own children's department, Craig was unfamiliar with the children's book market in the United States. Libraries and schools buy the titles first; only later do sales of children's books pick up in American bookstores. Moreover, as part of his global plan, Craig intended to co-publish children's books. Gordon disagreed: "American children want to read what they know," she said. "There are books that transcend national boundaries, such as *The Secret Garden*. But the majority tend to be set in the child's very particular world." Dissatisfied with the changes, Gordon resigned.

Many people in the publishing industry agree with Gordon. "The whole idea of global publishing like HarperCollins is crazy," says Roger Straus III of Farrar, Straus & Giroux. "A book is about as personal as deodorant. You can count on one hand the authors who can really be sold globally." Publishing consultant Charles Elbaum agrees: "You can't move ideas, techniques and technologies from another country and jam them down people's throats." His recommendation for Craig's globalization strategy: Establish semi-autonomous operating units and allow them the discretion to customize when necessary. ∎

1. Is trade book publishing a global industry? Why or why not?
2. Why does Ms. Land feel that Mr. Craig is "destroying two great publishing traditions?" Do you agree? Why? Why not?
3. Do you agree that there is a global segment for children's books?
4. What recommendations would you make to Mr. Craig?

SOURCES: John F. Baer, "Reinventing the Book Business," *Publisher's Weekly* (March 14, 1994), pp. 36–40; Roger Cohen, "Birth of a Global Book Giant," *The New York Times* (June 11, 1990), pp. D1, D10; "The Diseconomies of Scale," *The Economist* (April 7, 1990), pp. 25–28; Eden Ross Lipson, "The Little Industry That Could," *The New York Times Magazine* (December 3, 1989), pp. 20, 50, 52; Meg Cox, "Murdoch Puts Global Imprint on Books," *The Wall Street Journal* (May 4, 1990), pp. B1, B5.

Case 7-2   *The Global Cigarette Industry*

The Altria Group (formerly Philip Morris) produces one out of every six cigarettes in the world. The company's Marlboro man and distinctive red-and-black chevron are global advertising icons. Not surprisingly, the Altria Group has prospered by seeking out new markets and mobilizing its formidable marketing machine in an effort to win smokers over to its brand. Turkey provides a case study in the approach the Atria Group has perfected over the years. For years, the state tobacco monopoly had a virtual lock on the market. In 1984, however, foreign cigarettes were legalized; since that time, the Altria Group has captured one-quarter of the market. And what a market it is! An estimated 43 percent of Turkey's 63 million people smoke. Moreover, the market is especially attractive because cigarette consumption is *increasing* at an average annual rate of nearly 5 percent. However, to effectively tap that market, the Altria Group first had to lobby the Turkish government for the right to set its own prices and distribute its own products. The company succeeded in that effort, in part by promising to invest tens of millions of dollars in a state-of-the-art cigarette manufacturing facility. Engineers carefully crafted the tobacco blend to appeal to Turkish smokers; company representatives dressed like cowboys make deliveries to stores in brightly-painted vans. Thousands of stores were outfitted with racks and advertising displays.

In addition to Turkey, the Altria Group, Great Britain's B.A.T Industries PLC, and other tobacco companies are targeting smokers in China, South Korea, Thailand, India, Russia, and other industrializing countries. These are nations in which a combination of forces—relatively high economic growth, the public's acceptance of smoking as a fashionable activity, and the status assigned to Western cigarette brands—may interact. Moreover, because many women in these countries view smoking as a symbol of their improving status in society, the tobacco companies are aggressively targeting women. In 1996, nearly 600 billion cigarettes—including local brands—were sold in Eastern Europe and the former Soviet Union; total U.S. sales were 488 billion cigarettes. The Altria Group, whose Marlboro brand is smoked throughout the world, was the market leader in Eastern Europe with sales of 90 billion cigarettes. R.J. Reynolds Tobacco ranked second with 65 billion, and B.A.T sold 40 billion cigarettes. One reason for the success of Western brands is that "American-blend" cigarettes are milder than most domestic brands. Also, notes RJR's Andre Benoit, "There's a perception that locally-made products are of lower quality. One of the biggest challenges is destroying that myth." Currently, top brands such as Marlboro, Camel, Lucky Strike, and HB are imported; all three Western companies are investing in factories with the intention of boosting local production in the near future.

TOP FIVE CIGARETTE MARKETS, 1996

Country	Sales (billions of cigarettes)
China	1,791
USA	488
Japan	335
Russia	180
Indonesia	173

Cigarettes constitute a $28 billion market in Japan, the country widely believed to have the highest smoking rate in the world. Sixty percent of Japanese men smoke, and, overall, smokers comprise about 36 percent of the population. Cigarette advertising on television is permitted late at night. Japan also has half a million cigarette vending machines. Nevertheless, foreign cigarette sales still represent only 17 percent of the market. The reason is simple: Japan Tobacco Inc. is a government monopoly. Taxes make up 60 percent of the price of a pack of cigarettes; Japan Tobacco generates $15 billion in tax revenues each year. Thus, the government's attitude of tolerance stands in stark contrast to much of the industrialized world. Indeed, the warning on cigarette packs says only, "For the sake of health, don't smoke too much."

A great deal of the cigarette advertising in Asia—for both local and Western brands—targets women. The shift in focus of the global tobacco giants—both in terms of geography and gender—is alarming to many observers. Officials at the World Health Organization accuse the tobacco companies of exploiting increased prosperity in emerging economies by pushing an addictive product linked to serious health problems. Moreover, observers note that the Western invasion is forcing local cigarette companies to step up their promotional activities. For example, a cigarette company in the Philippines distributed wall calendars with a portrait of the Virgin Mary juxtaposed with logos of its brands. ■

DISCUSSION QUESTIONS

1. Summarize the different segmentation variables that tobacco companies such as the Altria Group use in their global marketing efforts.
2. Apart from segmentation considerations, identify additional factors that help explain why tobacco companies are focusing their marketing efforts on developing countries.
3. How should the tobacco industry respond to criticism of its marketing activities by the World Health Organization, anti-smoking activists, and other groups?

SOURCES: Suein L. Hwang, "Sucked In: How Philip Morris Got Turkey Hooked on American Tobacco," *The Wall Street Journal* (September 11, 1998), pp. A1, A8; Neela Banerjee, "Western Cigarettes Are Smoking in Russia," *The Wall Street Journal* (August 14, 1995), p. A8; Richard J. Barnet and John Cavanagh, *Global Dreams: Imperial Corporations and the New World Order* (New York: Simon & Schuster, 1994); Philip Shenon, "Asia's Having One Big Nicotine Fit," *The New York Times* (May 15 , 1994), sec. 4, p. 1; James Sterngold, "When Smoking Is a Patriotic Duty," *The New York Times* (October 17, 1993), sec. 3, pp. 1, 6; Peter Schmeisser, "Pushing Cigarettes Overseas," *The New York Times Magazine* (July 10, 1988).

Chapter 8

Exporting, Importing, and Sourcing

*E*xporting is a way of life for 3.2 million small and midsize companies in Germany. Known as the *Mittelstand*, these companies employ 20 million people and account for approximately 20 percent of Germany's DM900 billion in annual exports. For steelmaker J. N. Eberle, machine tool manufacturer Trumpf, J. Eberspächer, which makes auto exhaust systems, and many others, exports represent as much as 40 percent of sales. *Mittelstand* owner-managers target global niche markets and prosper by focusing on quality, innovation, and heavy investment in research and development. For example, the chief executive of G. W. Barth, a company that manufactures cocoa-bean roasting machines, invested nearly $2 million in infrared technology that reduced temperature variances. The company's global market share stands at 70 percent—a threefold increase in a 10-year period—as Ghirardelli Chocolate, Hershey Foods, and other companies have snapped up Barth's roasters. At ABM Baumüller, a $40 million manufacturer of motors and other components for cranes, a major investment in flexible manufacturing technology allows the company to tailor products to customer needs. New automated production equipment was installed—at a cost of $20 million—to allow changeover to different products in a matter of seconds. The story is repeated throughout Germany; as a result, in industry after industry, the *Mittelstand* are world-class exporters.[1]

The success of the *Mittelstand* serves as a reminder of the impact exporting can have on a country's economy. It also demonstrates the difference between **export selling** and **export marketing.** Export selling does not involve tailoring the product, the price, or the promotional material to suit the requirements of global markets. The only marketing mix element that differs is the "place,"—that is, the country where the

---

[1] Gail E. Schares and John Templeman, "Think Small: The Export Lessons to Be Learned from Germany's Midsize Companies," *Business Week* (November 4, 1994), pp. 58–60+.

German companies of all sizes actively export; one in four jobs in Germany is directly or indirectly tied to exports. For example, German manufacturers supply one-third of the world's textile machinery. ThyssenKrupp is one of the world's largest producers of carbon and stainless steel; the steel plant pictured here is located in Dulsburg. A great deal of information about German industry is available from a government-sponsored Web site at www.germany-info.org. Another informative site is maintained by the Federation of German Wholesale and Foreign Trade. The address is www.bga.de.

product is sold. This selling approach may work for some products or services; for unique products with little or no international competition, such an approach is possible. Similarly, companies new to exporting may initially experience success with selling. Even today, the managerial mind-set in many companies still favors export selling. But, as companies mature in the global marketplace or as new competitors enter the picture, export *marketing* becomes necessary.

Export marketing targets the customer in the context of the total market environment. The export marketer does not simply take the domestic product "as is" and sell it to international customers. To the export marketer, the product offered in the home market represents a starting point. It is modified as needed to meet the preferences of international target markets. *Mittelstand* companies such as ABM Baumüller exemplify this approach. Similarly, the export marketer sets prices to fit the marketing strategy and does not merely extend home-country pricing to the target market. Charges incurred in export preparation, transportation, and financing must be taken into account in determining prices. Finally, the export marketer also adjusts strategies and plans for communications and distribution to fit the market. In other words, effective communication about product features or uses to buyers in export markets may require creating brochures with different copy, photographs, or artwork. As the vice president of sales and marketing of one manufacturer noted, "We have to approach the international market with *marketing* literature as opposed to *sales* literature."

Export marketing is the integrated marketing of goods and services that are destined for customers in international markets. Export marketing requires:

1. An understanding of the target market environment
2. The use of marketing research and identification of market potential

3. Decisions concerning product design, pricing, distribution and channels, advertising, and communications—the marketing mix

After the research effort has zeroed in on potential markets, there is no substitute for a personal visit to size up the market firsthand and begin the development of an actual export marketing program. A market visit should do several things. First, it should confirm (or contradict) assumptions regarding market potential. A second major purpose is to gather the additional data necessary to reach the final go-no-go decision regarding an export marketing program. Certain kinds of information simply cannot be obtained from secondary sources. For example, an export manager or international marketing manager may have a list of potential distributors provided by the U.S. Department of Commerce. He or she may have corresponded with distributors on the list and formed some tentative idea of whether they meet the company's international criteria. It is difficult, however, to negotiate a suitable arrangement with international distributors without actually meeting face to face to allow each side of the contract to appraise the capabilities and character of the other party. A third reason for a visit to the export market is to develop a marketing plan in cooperation with the local agent or distributor. Agreement should be reached on necessary product modifications, pricing, advertising and promotion expenditures, and a distribution plan. If the plan calls for investment, agreement on the allocation of costs must also be reached.

One way to visit a potential market is through a **trade show** or a state- or federally-sponsored **trade mission.** Each year hundreds of trade fairs—usually organized around a product category or industry—are held in major markets. For example, Bauma 2001, a construction industry trade show held in Munich, Germany, attracted nearly 400,000 visitors from 43 countries. By attending trade shows and missions, company representatives can conduct market assessment, develop or expand markets, find distributors or agents, or locate potential end users. Perhaps most important, attending a trade show enables company representatives to learn a great deal about competitors' technology, pricing, and depth of market penetration. For example, exhibits often offer product literature with strategically useful technological information. Overall, company managers or sales personnel should be able to get a good general impression of competitors in the marketplace as they try to sell their own company's product.

ORGANIZATIONAL EXPORT ACTIVITIES

Exporting is becoming increasingly important as companies in all parts of the world step up their efforts to supply and service markets outside their national boundaries.[2] Research has shown that exporting is essentially a developmental process that can be divided into the following distinct stages:

1. The firm is unwilling to export; it will not even fill an unsolicited export order. This may be due to perceived lack of time ("too busy to fill the order"), or to apathy or ignorance.

---

2 This section relies heavily on Warren J. Bilkey, "Attempted Integration of the Literature on the Export Behavior of Firms," *Journal of International Business Studies* 8, no. 1 (1978), pp. 33–46. The stages are based on Rogers' adoption process. See Everett M. Rogers, *Diffusion of Innovations* (New York: Free Press, 1995).

2. The firm fills unsolicited export orders but does not pursue unsolicited orders. Such a firm is an export seller.
3. The firm explores the feasibility of exporting (this stage may bypass stage 2).
4. The firm exports to one or more markets on a trial basis.
5. The firm is an experienced exporter to one or more markets.
6. After this success, the firm pursues country- or region-focused marketing based on certain criteria (e.g., all countries where English is spoken or all countries where it is not necessary to transport by water).
7. The firm evaluates global market potential before screening for the "best" target markets to include in its marketing strategy and plan. *All* markets—domestic and international—are regarded as equally worthy of consideration.

The probability that a firm will advance from one stage to the next depends on different factors. Moving from Stage 2 to Stage 3 depends on management's attitude toward the attractiveness of exporting and their confidence in the firm's ability to compete internationally. However, *commitment* is the most important aspect of a company's international orientation. Before a firm can reach Stage 4, it must receive and respond to unsolicited export orders. The quality and dynamism of management are important factors that can lead to such orders. Success in Stage 4 can lead a firm to Stages 5 and 6. A company that reaches Stage 7 is a mature, geocentric enterprise that is relating global resources to global opportunity. To reach this stage requires management with vision and commitment.

One recent study noted that export procedural expertise and sufficient corporate resources are required for successful exporting. An interesting finding was that even the most experienced exporters express lack of confidence in their knowledge about shipping arrangements, payment procedures, and regulations. The study also showed that, although profitability is an important expected benefit of exporting, other advantages include increased flexibility and resiliency and improved ability to deal with sales fluctuations in the home market. Although research generally supports the proposition that the probability of being an exporter increases with firm size, it is less clear that export intensity—the ratio of export sales to total sales—is positively correlated with firm size. Table 8-1 lists some of the export-related problems that a company typically faces.[3]

NATIONAL POLICIES GOVERNING EXPORTS AND IMPORTS

It is hard to overstate the impact of exporting and importing on the world's national economies. In 1997, for example, total imports of goods and services by the United States passed the $1 trillion mark for the first time; in 2000, the combined figure was $1.4 trillion. China's pace-setting economic growth in the Asia-Pacific region is reflected by trends in both exports and imports. Since 1979, exports from China have grown significantly; they will grow at a faster rate now that China has joined the WTO. As shown in Table 8-2, $6.5 billion worth of Chinese textiles and apparel were exported to the United States in 2000. Historically, China protected its own producers by imposing double-digit import tariffs. These will gradually be reduced as China complies with WTO regulations. Needless to say, representatives of the textile and apparel industries in the United States are deeply concerned about the impact

---

[3] Masaaki Kotabe and Michael R. Czinkota, "State Government Promotion of Manufacturing Exports: A Gap Analysis," *Journal of International Business Studies* 23, no. 4 (Fourth Quarter 1992), pp. 637–658.

Table 8-1

Potential Export
Problems

Logistics	Servicing Exports
Arranging transportation	Providing parts availability
Transport rate determination	Providing repair service
Handling documentation	Providing technical advice
Obtaining financial information	Providing warehousing
Distribution coordination	
Packaging	**Sales Promotion**
Obtaining insurance	Advertising
	Sales effort
Legal Procedure	Marketing information
Government red tape	
Product liability	**Foreign Market Intelligence**
Licensing	Locating markets
Customs/duty	Trade restrictions
Contract	Competition overseas
Agent/Distributor Agreements	

Table 8-2

Top 15 Apparel and
Textile Exporting
Countries to the
United States, 2000
($ billions)

Mexico	$9.70
China	$6.52
Hong Kong	4.71
Canada	3.30
South Korea	3.01
Taiwan	2.75
India	2.74
Dominican Republic	2.45
Thailand	2.44
Indonesia	2.38
Honduras	2.32
Bangladesh	2.20
Philippines	2.20
Italy	2.10
Pakistan	1.83

Source: United States Department of Commerce.

increased trade with China will have on the sector. As this example suggests, national policies toward exports and imports can be summarized in one word: contradictory. For centuries, nations have combined two opposing policy attitudes toward the movement of goods across national boundaries. On the one hand, nations directly encourage exports; the flow of imports, on the other hand, is generally restricted.

Government Programs That Support Exports

To see the tremendous results that can come from a government-encouraged export strategy, consider Japan, Singapore, South Korea, and the so-called greater-China or

"China triangle" market, which includes Taiwan, Hong Kong, and the People's Republic of China. Japan totally recovered from the destruction of World War II and became an economic superpower as a direct result of export strategies devised by the Ministry for International Trade and Industry (MITI). The four tigers—Singapore, South Korea, Taiwan, and Hong Kong—learned from the Japanese experience and built strong export-based economies of their own. Although Asia's "economic bubble" burst in 1997 as a result of uncontrolled growth, Japan and the tigers are moving forward in the twenty-first century at a more moderate rate. China, an economy unto itself, has attracted increased foreign investment from DaimlerChrysler, Hewlett-Packard, GM, and other companies that are setting up production facilities to support local sales, as well as exports to world markets.

Any government concerned with trade deficits or economic development should focus on educating firms about the potential gains from exporting. This is true at the national, regional, and local government levels. Governments commonly use three activities to support export activities of national firms. First, *tax incentives* treat earnings from export activities preferentially either by applying a lower rate to earnings from these activities or by refunding taxes already paid on income associated with exporting. The tax benefits offered by export-conscious governments include varying degrees of tax exemption or tax deferral on export income, accelerated depreciation of export-related assets, and generous tax treatment of overseas market development activities. Naturally, in many cases, the actual treatment of export-related income is even more favorable than tax statutes would imply. Far Eastern, Latin American, and European trading nations have been particularly generous in providing these kinds of special aids to exporting companies. From 1985 until 2000, the major tax incentive under U.S. law was the foreign sales corporation (FSC), through which American exporters could obtain a 15 percent exclusion on earnings from international sales. However, in 2000, the World Trade Organization ruled that FSC tax credits constituted illegal subsidies. The FSC law will be replaced by a new regime exempting most income earned overseas from U.S. taxes. The new law is expected to cost the U.S. government $4.5 billion during the first ten years it is in effect.[4]

Governments also support export performance by providing outright *subsidies,* which are direct or indirect financial contributions that benefit producers. Export subsidies can severely distort trade patterns when less competitive but subsidized producers displace competitive producers in world markets. Subsidies of banana exports to the European Union were the subject of Case 3-2. Export subsidies to support agricultural trade will be reduced under the WTO. The third support area is *governmental assistance* to exporters. As noted in the chapter introduction, Germany's *Mittelstand* companies can avail themselves of a great deal of information concerning the location of markets and credit risks. Assistance may also be oriented toward export promotion. Government agencies at various levels often take the lead in setting up trade fairs and trade missions designed to promote sales to foreign customers.

Governmental Actions to Discourage Imports and Block Market Access

Measures such as tariffs, import controls, and a host of nontariff barriers are designed to limit the inward flow of goods. **Tariffs** can be thought of as the "three R's" of global business: rules, rate schedules (duties), and regulations of individual

---

[4] David Rogers, "U.S. is Set to Clear Export-Tax Regime," *The Wall Street Journal* (November 13, 2000), p. A2.

The Rest of the Story
Germany's *Mittelstand*

As noted in the chapter introduction, some of the *Mittelstand*'s success can be attributed to the customer focus and service orientation of company personnel. Another factor is Germany's export infrastructure. Diplomats, bankers, and other officials around the world are constantly on the lookout for opportunities; information about promising deals is conveyed back to Germany. Meanwhile, representatives from trade associations, export trading companies, and banks assist exporters with documentation and other issues. Some banks have special *Mittelstand* departments to provide export financing and assist companies in obtaining insurance.

The business environment both outside and inside Germany has presented difficult challenges to the *Mittelstand* in recent years. In response to the 1992–1993 recession in Europe, several countries—notably Great Britain, Italy, and Sweden—devalued their currencies. This move brought down prices on exports from those countries and, in turn, made Germany's exports less price competitive. Meanwhile, German unions have won wage hikes for workers, and the mark's strength put additional upward pressure on export prices. *Mittelstand* owners are taking steps to ensure their own survival, but a lack of organization has limited their political influence in Bonn.

Germany's banks have tightened loan terms, resulting in a credit crunch. Many companies are going public to raise capital, but venture capital can be hard to find. Professional managers are being hired to assist the owners. Some companies may even move production out of Germany. Melitta, for example, began assembling home coffeemakers in Portugal in 1995. For companies where money is tight, licensing production is an economical alternative.

Visit the Web site
www.it-mittelstand.de

Information technology represents another problem area for the *Mittelstand.* According to one recent study, only four percent of *Mittelstand* companies use the Internet, while two-thirds of Germany's large companies do. Dietmar Hopp, chief executive of Germany's largest software firm, says, "The *Mittelstand* is lagging behind. Opportunities to improve productivity are being missed. With globalization there is no difference now between the *Mittelstand* and big companies—the business processes are comparable. It is only a matter of time before foreign competitors use the Internet to strengthen their foothold in Germany. German companies should follow their example and build up their U.S. and Asian activities through electronic marketing and commerce."

SOURCES: Nigel Dudley, "Germany's Unloved Mittelstand," *Euromoney* (December 2000), pp. 38–42; "Mittelstand or Mittelfall?" *The Economist* (October 17, 1998), pp. 68–69; Graham Bowley, "Industry's Hidden Winners," *Financial Times Survey—World Economy and Finance* (December 12, 1997), p. 12; Bowley, "In the Information Technology Slow Lane," *Financial Times* (November 11, 1997), p. 14; Peter Marsh, "March of the Mittelstanders," *Financial Times* (May 19, 1997), p. 8; Matt Marshall, "Timid Lending Hits Germany's Exporters," *The Wall Street Journal* (November 21, 1995), p. A14; Karen Lowry Miller, "The *Mittelstand* Takes a Stand," *Business Week* (April 10, 1995), pp. 54–55; Gail E. Schares and John Templeman, "Think Small: The Export Lessons to Be Learned from Germany's Midsize Companies," *Business Week* (November 4, 1994), pp. 58–60+.

countries. **Duties** on individual products or services are listed in the schedule of rates (see Table 8-3 on page 300). As defined by one expert on global trade, duties are "taxes that punish individuals for making choices of which their governments disapprove."[5]

The **Harmonized Tariff System** (HTS) went into effect in January 1989 and has since been adopted by the majority of trading nations. Under this system, importers and exporters have to determine the correct classification number for a given product or service that will cross borders. With the Harmonized Tariff Schedule B, the export classification number for any exported item is the same as the import classification number. Also, exporters must include the Harmonized Tariff Schedule B number on their export documents to facilitate customs clearance. Accuracy—especially in the eyes of customs officials—is essential. The U.S. Census Bureau compiles trade

---

5   Edward L. Hudgins, "Mercosur Gets a 'Not Guilty' on Trade Diversion," *The Wall Street Journal* (March 21, 1997), p. A19.

statistics from the HTS system. In its quest for a more precise picture of U.S. trade flows, the Census Bureau is cracking down on exporters whose documentation is incorrect. Even so, any HTS with a value of less than $2,500 is not counted as a U.S. export. However, *all* imports, regardless of value, are counted.

As noted in earlier chapters, a major U.S. objective in the Uruguay round of GATT negotiations was to improve market access for U.S. companies with major U.S. trading partners. When the round ended in December 1993, the United States had secured reductions or total elimination of tariffs on 11 categories of U.S. goods exported to the EU, Japan, five of the EFTA nations (Austria, Switzerland, Sweden, Finland, and Norway), New Zealand, South Korea, Hong Kong, and Singapore. The categories affected included equipment for the construction, agricultural, medical, and scientific industry sectors, as well as steel, beer, brown distilled spirits, pharmaceuticals, paper, pulp and printed matter, furniture, and toys. In most instances, the tariffs were scheduled to be phased out over a five-year period.

For example, Weyerhaeuser and other exporters of paper products to Europe have been burdened with tariffs of 6 to 9 percent. Scandinavian paper companies, meanwhile, have enjoyed tariff-free access to the European market. Although elimination of tariffs means improved market access and new commercial opportunities, the paper industry is unhappy with the 10-year time frame for phasing out current duties. Exports of electronics products to the EU have also been subject to tariff barriers—14 percent for semiconductors and 4 percent for computer components. The Uruguay round resulted in cuts and elimination of tariffs on these items. Overall, the Commerce Department predicts that enhanced market access conditions could increase U.S. output by more than $1 trillion over the next decade.

In spite of the progress made in simplifying tariff procedures, administering a tariff is an enormous problem. People who work with imports and exports must familiarize themselves with the different classifications and use them accurately. Even a tariff schedule of several thousand items cannot clearly describe every product traded globally. The introduction of new products and new materials used in manufacturing processes creates new problems. Often, determining the duty rate on a particular article requires assessing how the item is used or determining its main component material. Two or more alternative classifications may have to be considered. A product's classification can make a substantial difference in the duty applied. For example, is GI Joe a doll or a toy soldier? If it is classified as a doll, the duty for import into the United States is lower. Similarly, the duty on dolls that represent "human figures" is negligible. The duty on "non-human figures" is much higher. It is rumored that the reason Darth Vader takes his helmet off in the third installment of the first "Star Wars" trilogy is to clarify his "human" origin as well as to qualify for a lower import duty!

A **nontariff trade barrier** (NTB) is any measure other than a tariff that is a deterrent or obstacle to the sale of products in a foreign market. Also known as *hidden trade barriers*, NTBs include quotas, discriminatory procurement policies, restrictive customs procedures, arbitrary monetary policies, and restrictive regulations. A **quota** is a government-imposed limit or restriction on the number of units or the total value of a particular product or product category that can be imported. The trade distortion caused by a quota is even more severe than that due to tariffs because once the quota has been reached, market price mechanisms are not allowed to operate. The phrase *state trade controls* refers to the practice of monopolizing trade in certain commodities. The Swedish government, for example, controls the import of all alcoholic beverages and tobacco products, and the French government controls all imports of coal.

The United States has more than 8,000 different tariff classifications, of which some 3,600 are restricted by quotas and other control mechanisms. For example,

Open to Discussion
Why Doesn't the United States Export More?

Many nations export up to 20 percent of their total production; the United States exports only about 10 percent. Businesses in smaller industrialized countries easily exhaust the potential of their home market and are forced to search internationally for expansion opportunities. Meanwhile, their U.S. counterparts appear to have fallen victim to one or more barriers to successful exporting. First, the limited ambition of many American business managers may result in complacency and a lack of export consciousness. A second barrier is lack of knowledge of market opportunities abroad or misperceptions about those markets. The perceived lack of necessary resources—managerial skill, time, financing, and productive capacity—are often cited as reasons for not pursuing export opportunities. Unrealistic fears are a fourth type of barrier to exporting. When weighing export expansion opportunities, managers may express concerns about operating difficulties, environmental differences, credit or other types of risks, and possible strains upon the company. A fifth type of barrier is management inertia—the simple inability of company personnel to overcome export myopia.

U.S. exports have historically been dominated by the large companies of the Fortune 500. As noted at the beginning of the chapter, small businesses in Germany are export powerhouses. Studies have shown that, in the United States, it is smaller-sized businesses rather than the Fortune 500 that are the major source of new jobs. Until recently, relatively few of these smaller companies were involved with exports. Dun & Bradstreet tracks U.S. exports in 70 industries; its figures now show that

the majority of companies exporting employ less than 100 people. Yet, the U.S. Small Business Administration estimates that there are tens of thousands of small companies that could export but do not. For many of these firms, exporting represents a major untapped market opportunity. To address this issue, in October 2001 the U.S. Commercial Service launched BuyUSA.com, a Web site that helps companies set up e-commerce operations to serve customers outside the United States.

Visit the Web site
BuyUSA.com

A quick look at the suggested readings at the end of this chapter highlights the fact that export activities at small- and medium-sized enterprises (SMEs) is a popular research topic. For example, one recent study of 114 companies in California questioned the effectiveness of standardized promotional messages in government pamphlets for motivating managers at SMEs to consider exporting. The researcher found that company personnel were more likely to be persuaded by arguments that stated exporting's benefits in microeconomic terms. Another recent study examined companies with previous export experience; the researchers focused on the relationship between management's intention to continue exporting and the extent to which management valued the learning gained from previous export activities. The researchers determined that, financial criteria aside, management at companies with export experience welcomed the opportunity to acquire new knowledge and new skills and to broaden organizational capabilities.

SOURCES: Tahi J. Gnepa, "Persuading Small Manufacturing Companies to Become Active Exporters: The Effect of Message Framing and Focus on Behavioral Intentions," *Journal of Global Marketing* 14, no. 4 (2001), pp. 49–66; William J. Burpitt and Dennis A. Rondinelli, "Small Firms' Motivations for Exporting: To Earn and Learn?" *Journal of Small Business Management* 38, no. 4 (October 2000), pp. 1–14.

---

there are machine tool agreements with Japan and Taiwan, 20 steel trade agreements, textile quotas for most Southeast Asian and developing countries, the U.S.-Japan Semiconductor Agreement, and Japanese "voluntary" restraints on the export of cars and TVs to the United States. The United States even has a "Memorandum of Understanding on Softwood Lumber" with Canada, its largest trading partner. The United States and the EU have a combined total of 250 quotas on imports of Chinese textiles.[6] The extent of these and other similar agreements on a worldwide basis has led some critics to argue that the United States engages in "managed" trade rather than free trade.

---

6   Joseph Kahn, "Dragon Flies: China Swiftly Becomes an Exporting Colossus, Straining Western Ties," *The Wall Street Journal* (November 13, 1995), p. A6.

A recent case involving Ukraine and the United States shows how politics and export-import issues are often intertwined. The United States is encouraging Ukraine's transition to a market economy and provides foreign aid totaling hundreds of millions of dollars each year. Yet, after Ukrainian imports of women's coats grew dramatically in the early 1990s, the Clinton administration imposed an import quota in November 1994. The stylish, well-made coats retailed in the United States at prices ranging from $89 to $139. (By 1994, only the Dominican Republic and Guatemala surpassed Ukraine in unit imports of wool coats to the United States; the Latin American countries are exempt from quotas under the Caribbean Basin Initiative.) The popularity of the Ukrainian goods provoked accusations of unfair trade from the American woolen industry and, in particular, from the coat-making industry that is centered in Maine. Wool coat imports were already subject to a 21.5 percent tariff. The quota, which was supported by Senator George Mitchell of Maine and the U.S. Commerce Department, limited Ukrainian imports in 1995 to 85,000 dozen coats, approximately the level of 1994 imports. Ukrainian producers had expected 1995 orders to double compared with 1994.[7]

Discriminatory procurement policies can take the form of government rules and administrative regulations specifying that local vendors or suppliers receive priority consideration. For example, the Buy American Act of 1933 stipulates that U.S. federal agencies must buy articles produced in the United States unless domestically produced goods are not available, the cost is unreasonable, or purchasing U.S. materials would be inconsistent with the public interest. Similarly, the Fly American Act stipulates that employees of the U.S. government must fly on domestic airlines whenever possible. Formal or informal company policies can also discriminate against foreign suppliers. In the automotive industry, the relatively low level of Japanese imports of U.S.-made auto parts is a contentious issue that centers on procurement policies.

Customs procedures are considered restrictive if they are administered in a way that makes compliance difficult and expensive. For example, the U.S. Department of Commerce might classify a product under a certain harmonized number; Canadian customs may disagree. The U.S. exporter may have to attend a hearing with Canadian customs officials to reach an agreement. Such delays cost time and money for both the importer and exporter.

Discriminatory exchange rate policies distort trade in much the same way as selective import duties and export subsidies. A country may require importers to place on deposit—at no interest—an amount equal to the value of imported goods. Such an action constitutes an **arbitrary monetary policy** that, in effect, raises the price of foreign goods by the cost of money for the term of the required deposit.

Finally, **restrictive administrative and technical regulations** can create barriers to trade. These may take the form of antidumping regulations, size regulations, and safety and health regulations. Some of these regulations are intended to keep out foreign goods; others are directed toward legitimate domestic objectives. For example, the safety and pollution regulations being developed in the United States for automobiles are motivated almost entirely by legitimate concerns about highway safety and pollution. However, an effect of these regulations has been to make it so expensive to comply with U.S. safety requirements that some automakers have withdrawn certain models from the market. Volkswagen, for example, was forced to stop selling diesel automobiles in the United States for several years.

---

[7] Jane Perlez, "In Ukraine, a Free-Market Lesson Learned Too Well," *The New York Times* (January 1, 1995), sec. 3, p. 5. See also James Dean, "Ukraine: Europe's Forgotten Economy," *Challenge* 43, no. 6 (November-December 2000), pp. 93–108.

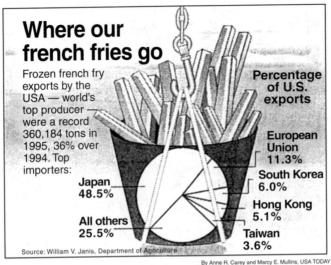

Where our french fries go

Frozen french fry exports by the USA — world's top producer — were a record 360,184 tons in 1995, 36% over 1994. Top importers:

Percentage of U.S. exports

Japan 48.5%

All others 25.5%

European Union 11.3%

South Korea 6.0%

Hong Kong 5.1%

Taiwan 3.6%

Source: William V. Janis, Department of Agriculture

By Anne R. Carey and Marcy E. Mullins, USA TODAY

Despite a GATT agreement concerning technical barriers to trade, Japan used technical standards unrelated to performance to bar U.S. forest products from its market. In May 1989, these restrictive technical regulations became part of the basis for listing Japan as guilty of unfair trade practices under Section 301 of the 1988 Trade Act.

As discussed in earlier chapters, there is a growing trend to remove all such restrictive trade barriers on a regional basis. The largest single effort was undertaken by the European Union in an effort to create a single market starting January 1, 1993. The intent is to have one standard for all of Europe for such things as automobile safety, drug testing and certification, and food and product quality controls, as well as the development of a single currency, the euro, to facilitate trade and commerce. Some observers believe that elimination of these intra-European barriers will result in the creation of a so-called Fortress Europe with new external barriers designed to keep out the foreign (e.g., Japanese) competition.

Visit the Web site
The U.S. Department of Commerce provides export support through its Market Access and Compliance Web site. Visit Mac online at: www.mac.doc.gov

TARIFF SYSTEMS

Tariff systems provide either a single rate of duty for each item applicable to all countries, or two or more rates applicable to different countries or groups of countries. Tariffs are usually grouped into two classifications.

The **single-column tariff** is the simplest type of tariff, a schedule of duties in which the rate applies to imports from all countries on the same basis. Under the **two-column tariff** (Table 8-3), column 1 includes "general" duties plus "special" duties indicating reduced rates determined by tariff negotiations with other countries. Rates agreed upon by "convention" are extended to all countries that qualify for **normal trade relations** (NTR; formerly most-favored nation or MFN) status within the framework of the WTO. Under the WTO, nations agree to apply their most favorable tariff or lowest tariff rate to all nations—subject to some exceptions—that are signatories to the WTO. Column 2 shows rates for countries that do not enjoy NTR status.

Beth Dorrell is an export coordinator with a multimillion dollar company that manufactures writing and marking inks. From its headquarters in Southern California, the company exports ink to more than 30 countries. Beth is responsible for all exports from the main manufacturing plant in Tennessee. Beth's background includes a BA degree in international management and French from a small liberal arts college in the Midwest.

During the summer after her sophomore year, Beth traveled in Europe and studied a number of corporations including Swarski Crystal, Club Med, and Moet Chandon. During the fall of her junior year, Beth attended a 10-week Import & Export Seminar led by a representative of the state economic development commission. Beth is convinced that the seminar gave her the upper hand during her job search. "In interviews, I was able to confidently answer questions about documentary credits and Incoterms. I have utilized and expanded upon that knowledge on a daily basis in my job," says Beth. "We have hundreds of different customers, each with different shipping terms and different payment terms. It is essential that I know the difference, and know the document requirements of each."

Beth's workday begins early. Because the company has offices on the west coast, manufacturing facilities on the east coast, and customers throughout the world, time zones are always an issue. Beth arrives at work early to take late night phone calls from Europe and Asia; she also must deal with any problems on the east coast that need to be solved that day. She also checks correspondence received overnight via fax and e-mail. This may consist of new order inquiries, requests for cost quotes or product availability, changes to existing orders, or payment advice from Poland, China, Taiwan, or Pakistan.

"Because the majority of our international customers are in Asia, I usually have the full work day to compose responses and/or proforma invoices for those customers. The exceptions are our customers in Mexico, Venezuela, and Argentina and other Latin American countries. I try to structure my day so that I can reply to those inquiries early in the day, thereby providing same-day service to those customers," Beth explains.

On any given day, a freight forwarder may call and inform Beth that freight did not arrive at the port in time to meet an expected ocean booking. Beth must then track down the shipment through the trucking company, establish a new booking, ensure that the freight is delivered, advise the customer of the delay and, if necessary, arrange to air freight a portion of the order. "One of the worst things that can happen," notes Beth, "is that a customer's plant has to stop production because we were late in delivering product. With so much of the world operating on just in time systems, one little slip can backlog multiple companies. If one of our suppliers is delayed in providing a raw material, then we are delayed in providing ink, our customer is delayed in providing pens, and *their* retail customer is delayed in putting product on the shelf. No one wants to put a Christmas product on the shelf in January, or a Back To School product on the shelf in October."

Another important part of Beth's job involves documents and banks. Company policy requires that orders over a certain established dollar amount move under a letter of credit. Before the shipment can leave the factory, Beth must ensure that the letter of credit has been received, that the details of the L/C are accurate, and that the company is capable of satisfying the date and document requirements. She must then check that every single detail of the L/C is abided by. Beth provides all the documents demanded of the company (invoice, packing lists, certificates of quality, etc.) under the L/C and double checks all of the documents that must be provided by other sources (e.g., bills of lading and certificates of insurance) and sends them all to the advising bank in the United States. Beth says, "I love the way L/Cs work—how they enable companies around the world to contract large business deals with little to no risk for either party. But I'll take a DP (documents against payment) over an L/C any day! The work involved in processing an L/C properly is extensive. It requires incredible attention to detail, and sometimes even that isn't enough. Every once in a while you simply cannot determine how the document examiner will interpret some phrasing."

Beth concludes, "Global marketing is amazing. A commodity raw material from Africa can be refined in Asia, then shipped to South America to be incorporated into a component of a final product that is produced in the Middle East and then sold around the world. The things we all use every day are truly products of the world."

Table 8-3
Sample Rates of
Duty for U.S.
Imports

	COLUMN 1	COLUMN 2
GENERAL	SPECIAL	NON-NTR
1.5%	Free (A, E, IL, J, MX) 0.4 % (CA)	30%

A, Generalized System of Preferences
E, Caribbean Basin Initiative (CBI) Preference
IL, Israel Free Trade Agreement (FTA) Preference
J, Andean Agreement Preference
MX, NAFTA Canada Preference
CA, NAFTA Mexico Preference

Table 8-4 shows a detailed entry from chapter 89 of the harmonized system pertaining to "Ships, Boats, and Floating Structures" (for explanatory purposes, each column has been identified with an alphabet letter). Column A contains the heading level numbers that uniquely identify each product. For example, the product entry for heading level 8903 is "yachts and other vessels for pleasure or sports; row boats and canoes." Subheading level 8903.10 identifies "inflatable"; 8903.91 designates "sailboats with or without auxiliary motor." These six-digit numbers are used by more than 100 countries that have signed on to the harmonized system. Entries can extend to as many as ten digits, with the last four used on a country-specific basis for

Table 8-4
Chapter 89 of the Harmonized System

A	B	C	D	E	F	G
8903		Yachts and other vessels for pleasure or sports; row boats and canoes				
8903.10.00		Inflatable		2.4%	Free (A,E,IL,J,MX)[a] 0.4% (CA)	
		Valued over $500				
	15	With attached rigid hull......No				
	45	Other.....................No				
	60	Other.....................No				
		Other:		1.5%	Free	
8903.91.00		Sailboats, with or without auxiliary motor			(A,E,IL,J,MX) 0.3% (CA)	

A, Generalized System of Preferences
E, Caribbean Basin Initiative (CBI) Preference
IL, Israel Free Trade Agreement (FTA) Preference
J, Andean Agreement Preference
MX, NAFTA Canada Preference
CA, NAFTA Mexico Preference

Table 8-5
Tariff Rates for
China, NTR vs.
Non-NTR

	NTR	Non-NTR
Gold jewelry, such as plated neckchains	6.5%	80%
Screws, lock washers, misc. iron/steel parts	5.8%	35%
Steel products	0–5%	66%
Rubber footwear	0	66%
Women's overcoats	19%	35%

Source: U.S. Customs Service.

Visit the Web site
The U.S. Federal gov-
ernment provides
Information on
the HTS at:
www.usitc.gov/
taffairs.htm
The database main-
tained by the
U.S. International Trade
Commission
can be accessed at:
205.197.120.17/scripts/
tariff.asp

each nation's individual tariff and data collection purposes. Taken together, E and F correspond to Column 1 as shown in Table 8-3, while G corresponds to Column 2.

The United States has given NTR status to some 180 countries around the world, so the name is really a misnomer. Only North Korea, Iran, Cuba, and Libya are excluded, showing that NTR is really a political tool more than an economic one. In the past, China had been threatened with the loss of NTR status because of alleged human rights violations. The landed prices of its products would rise by 60 to 100 percent or more, which would price Chinese products out of the market. The loss of NTR status would have a significant impact on its trade with the United States. The U.S. Congress recently granted China permanent NTR as a precursor to its joining the WTO. Table 8-5 illustrates what a loss of NTR status would have meant to China.

A **preferential tariff** is a reduced tariff rate applied to imports from certain countries. GATT prohibits the use of preferential tariffs, with three major exceptions. First are historical preference arrangements such as the British Commonwealth preferences and similar arrangements that existed before GATT. Second, preference schemes that are part of a formal economic integration treaty, such as free trade areas or common markets, are excluded. Third, industrial countries are permitted to grant preferential market access to companies based in less-developed countries.

The United States is now a signatory to the GATT customs valuation code. U.S. customs value law was amended in 1980 to conform to the GATT valuation standards. Under the code, the primary basis of customs valuation is "transaction value." As the name implies, *transaction value* is defined as the actual individual transaction price paid by the buyer to the seller of the goods being valued. In instances where the buyer and seller are related parties (e.g., when Honda's U.S. manufacturing subsidiaries purchase parts from Japan), customs authorities have the right to scrutinize the transfer price to make sure it is a fair reflection of market value. If there is no established transaction value for the good, alternative methods that are used to compute the customs value sometimes result in increased values and, consequently, increased duties. In the late 1980s, the U.S. Treasury Department began a major investigation into the transfer prices charged by the Japanese automakers to their U.S. subsidiaries. It charged that the Japanese paid virtually no U.S. income taxes because of their "losses" on the millions of cars they import into the United States each year.

During the Uruguay round of GATT negotiations, the United States successfully sought a number of amendments to the Agreement on Customs Valuations. Most important, the United States wanted clarification of the rights and obligations of importing and exporting countries in cases where fraud was suspected. Two overall categories of products were frequently targeted for investigation. The first included exports of textiles, cosmetics, and consumer durables; the second included entertainment software such as videotapes, audiotapes, and compact discs. Such amendments improve the ability of U.S. exporters to defend their interests if charged with fraudulent practices. The amendments were also designed to encourage nonsignatories—especially developing countries—to become parties to the agreement.

Customs Duties

Customs duties are divided into two categories. They may be calculated either as a percentage of the value of the goods (ad valorem duty), as a specific amount per unit (specific duty), or as a combination of both of these methods. Before World War II, specific duties were widely used and the tariffs of many countries, particularly those in Europe and Latin America, were extremely complex. Since the war, the trend has been toward the conversion to ad valorem duties—that is, duties expressed as a certain percentage of the value of the goods.

An **ad valorem duty** is expressed as a percentage of the value of goods. The definition of customs value varies from country to country. An exporter is well advised to secure information about the valuation practices applied to his or her product in the country of destination. The reason is simple: to be price competitive with local competitiors. In countries adhering to GATT conventions on customs valuation, the customs value is landed cost, insurance, and freight (CIF) amount at the port of importation. This cost should reflect the arm's-length price of the goods at the time the duty becomes payable.

A **specific duty** is expressed as a specific amount of currency per unit of weight, volume, length, or other units of measurement; for example, "50 cents U.S. per pound," "$1.00 U.S. per pair," or "25 cents U.S. per square yard." Specific duties are usually expressed in the currency of the importing country, but there are exceptions, particularly in countries that have experienced sustained inflation.

Both ad valorem and specific duties are occasionally set out in the custom tariff for a given product. Normally, the applicable rate is the one that yields the higher amount of duty, although there are cases where the lower is specified. These duties provide for specific, plus ad valorem, rates to be levied on the same articles. Compound or mixed duties provide for specific, plus ad valorem, rates to be levied on the same articles.

Other Duties and Import Charges

Dumping, which is the sale of merchandise in export markets at unfair prices, is discussed in detail in Chapter 12. To offset the impact of dumping and to penalize guilty companies, most countries have introduced legislation providing for the imposition of **antidumping duties** if injury is caused to domestic producers. Such duties take the form of special additional import charges equal to the dumping margin. Antidumping duties are almost invariably applied to products that are also manufactured or grown in the importing country. In the United States, antidumping duties are assessed after the Commerce Department finds a foreign company guilty of dumping and the International Trade Commission rules that the dumped products injured American companies.

Countervailing duties (CVDs) are additional duties levied to offset subsidies granted in the exporting country. In the United States, countervailing duty legislation and procedures are very similar to those pertaining to dumping. The Commerce Department and the International Trade Commission jointly administer both the countervailing duty and antidumping laws under provisions of the Trade and Tariff

Act of 1984. Subsidies and countervailing measures received a great deal of attention during the Uruguay GATT negotiations. In 2001, the ITC and Commerce Department imposed both countervailing and antidumping duties on Canadian lumber producers. The CVDs were intended to offset subsidies to Canadian sawmills in the form of low fees for cutting trees in forests owned by the Canadian government. The antidumping duties on imports of softwood lumber, flooring, and siding were in response to complaints by American producers that the Canadians were exporting lumber at prices below their production cost.

Several countries, including Sweden and some other members of the EU, apply a system of **variable import levies** to certain categories of imported agricultural products. If prices of imported products would undercut those of domestic products, the effect of these levies would be to raise the price of imported products to the domestic price level. **Temporary surcharges** have been introduced from time to time by certain countries, such as the United Kingdom and the United States, to provide additional protection for local industry and, in particular, in response to balance-of-payments deficits.

KEY EXPORT PARTICIPANTS

Anyone with responsibilities for exporting should be familiar with some of the people and organizations who can assist with various tasks. Some of these, including purchasing agents, export brokers, and export merchants, have no assignment of responsibility from the client. Others, including export management companies, manufacturers' export representatives, export distributors, and freight forwarders, are assigned responsibilities by the exporter.

Foreign purchasing agents are variously referred to as *buyer for export, export commission house,* or *export confirming house.* They operate on behalf of, and are remunerated by, an overseas customer. They generally seek out the manufacturer whose price and quality match the demands of a client in another country.

Foreign purchasing agents often represent governments, utilities, railroads, and other large users of materials abroad. Foreign purchasing agents do not offer the manufacturer stable volume except when long-term supply contracts are agreed upon. Purchases may be completed as domestic transactions with the purchasing agent handling all export packing and shipping details, or the agent may rely on the manufacturer to handle the shipping arrangements.

The **export broker** receives a fee for bringing together the seller and the overseas buyer. The fee is usually paid by the seller, but sometimes the buyer pays it. The broker takes no title to the goods and assumes no financial responsibility. A broker usually specializes in a specific commodity, such as grain or cotton, and is less frequently involved in the export of manufactured goods.

Export merchants are sometimes referred to as *jobbers.* They seek out needs in foreign markets and make purchases in world markets to fill these needs. Export merchants often handle staple, openly traded products, for which brand names or manufacturers' identifications are not important. **Export management company** (EMC) is the term used to designate an independent export firm that acts as the export department for more than one manufacturer. The EMC usually operates in the name of a manufacturer-client for export markets, but it may operate in its own name. It may act as an independent distributor, purchasing and reselling goods at an established price or profit margin, or as a commission representative, taking no title and bearing no financial risks in the sale. Combination export management firms often refer to themselves as **manufacturer's export representatives** whether they act as export distributors or as export commission representatives. An **export distributor** assumes financial risk. The firm usually has the exclusive right to sell a manufacturer's products in all or some markets outside the country of origin. The distributor pays for the goods and assumes all financial risks associated with the foreign sale. The firm ordinarily sells at manufacturer's list price abroad, receiving an agreed percentage of list price as remuneration. The distributor may operate in its own name or in the manufacturer's. It handles all shipping details. The export distributor usually represents several manufacturers and hence is a combination export manager.

The **export commission representative** assumes no financial risk and is sometimes termed an *agent*, although this term is generally avoided because of the legal connotations. The commission representative is assigned all or some foreign markets by the manufacturer. The manufacturer carries all accounts, although the representative often provides credit checks and arranges financing. The representative may operate in his or her own name or in the manufacturer's. Generally, the export commission representative handles several accounts and hence is a combination export management company. The **cooperative exporter,** sometimes called a *mother hen, piggyback exporter,* or *export vendor,* is an export organization of a manufacturing company retained by other independent manufacturers to sell their products in some or all foreign markets. Cooperative exporters usually operate as export distributors for other manufacturers, but in special cases they operate as export commission representatives. They are regarded as a form of export management company.

Freight forwarders are licensed specialists in traffic operations, customs clearance, and shipping tariffs and schedules; simply put, they can be thought of as travel agents for freight. They seek out the best routing and the best prices for transporting freight and assist exporters in determining and paying fees and insurance charges. Forwarders may also do export packing, when necessary. They usually handle freight from port of export to overseas port of import. They may also move inland freight

U.S. customs agents on the job in Texas. Beginning exporters can utilize the services of freight forwarders, export management companies, and other firms that specialize in moving goods across borders.

from factory to port of export and, through affiliates abroad, handle freight from port of import to customer. Freight forwarders also perform consolidation services for land, air, and ocean freight. Because they contract for large blocks of space on a ship or airplane, they can resell that space to various shippers at a rate lower than is generally available to individual shippers dealing directly with the export carrier.

A licensed forwarder receives brokerage or rebates from shipping companies for booked space. Some companies and manufacturers engage in freight forwarding or some phase of it on their own, but they may not, under law, receive brokerage from shipping lines.

ORGANIZING FOR EXPORTING IN THE MANUFACTURER'S COUNTRY

Home-country issues involve deciding whether to assign export responsibility inside the company or to work with an external organization specializing in a product or geographic area. Most companies handle export operations within their own in-house export organization. Depending on the company's size, responsibilities may be incorporated into an employee's domestic job description. Alternatively, these responsibilities may be handled as part of a separate division or organizational structure.

The possible arrangements for handling exports include the following:

1. As a part-time activity performed by domestic employees
2. Through an export partner affiliated with the domestic marketing structure that takes possession of the goods before they leave the country
3. Through an export department that is independent of the domestic marketing structure
4. Through an export department within an international division
5. For multidivisional companies, the previous arrangements can be adopted on a division-by-division basis

A company that assigns a sufficiently high priority to its export business will establish an in-house organization. It then faces the question of how to organize effectively. This depends on two things—the company's appraisal of the opportunities in export marketing and its strategy for allocating resources to markets on a global basis. It may be possible for a company to make export responsibility part of a domestic employee's job description. The advantage of this arrangement is obvious: It is a low-cost arrangement requiring no additional personnel. However, this approach can work under only two conditions: First, the domestic employee assigned to the task must be thoroughly competent in terms of product and customer knowledge. Second, that competence must be applicable to the target international market(s). The key issue underlying the second condition is the extent to which the target export market is different from the domestic market. If customer circumstances and characteristics are similar, the requirements for specialized regional knowledge are reduced.

The company that chooses not to perform its own marketing and promotion in-house has numerous external export service providers to choose from. As described previously, these include export trading companies (ETCs), export management companies (EMCs), export merchants, export brokers, combination export managers, manufacturers' export representatives or commission agents, and export distributors. However, because these terms and labels may be used inconsistently, the reader is urged to check and confirm the services performed by a particular independent export organization.

A typical export management company acts as the export department for several unrelated companies that lack export experience. EMCs perform a variety of services, including marketing research, channel selection, arrangement of financing and shipping, and documentation. According to one recent survey of U.S.-based EMCs, the most important activities for export success are marketing information gathering, communication with markets, setting prices, and ensuring parts availability. The same survey ranked export activities in terms of degree of difficulty; analyzing political risk, sales force management, setting pricing, and obtaining financial information were deemed most difficult to accomplish. One of the study's conclusions was that the U.S. government should do a better job of helping EMCs and their clients analyze the political risk associated with foreign markets.[8]

ORGANIZING FOR EXPORTING IN THE MARKET COUNTRY

In addition to deciding whether to rely on in-house or external export specialists in the home country, a company must also make arrangements to distribute the product in the target market country. There is one basic decision that every exporting organization faces: To what extent do we rely on direct market representation as opposed to representation by independent intermediaries?

There are two major advantages to direct representation in a market—control and communications. Direct market representation allows decisions concerning program development, resource allocation, or price changes to be implemented unilaterally. Moreover, when a product is not yet established in a market, special efforts are necessary to achieve sales. The advantage of direct representation is that these special efforts are ensured by the marketer's investment. With indirect or independent representation, such efforts and investment are often not forthcoming; in many cases, there is simply not enough incentive for independents to invest significant time and money in representing a product. The other great advantage to direct representation is that the possibilities for feedback and information from the market are much greater. This information can vastly improve export marketing decisions concerning product, price, communications, and distribution.

Direct representation does not mean that the exporter is selling directly to the consumer or customer. In most cases, direct representation involves selling to wholesalers or retailers. For example, the major automobile exporters in Germany and Japan rely upon direct representation in the U.S. market in the form of their distributing agencies, which are owned and controlled by the manufacturing organization. The distributing agencies sell products to franchised dealers.

In smaller markets, it is usually not feasible to establish direct representation because the low sales volume does not justify the cost. Even in larger markets, a small manufacturer usually lacks adequate sales volume to justify the cost of direct representation. Whenever sales volume is small, use of an independent distributor is an effective method of sales distribution. Finding "good" distributors can be the key to export success.

---

[8] Donald G. Howard, "The Role of Export Management Companies in Global Marketing," *Journal of Global Marketing* 8, no. 1 (1994), pp. 95–110.

Export Financing and Methods of Payment

The appropriate method of payment for a given international sale is a basic credit decision. A number of factors must be considered, including currency availability in the buyer's country, creditworthiness of the buyer, and the seller's relationship to the buyer. Finance managers at companies that have never exported often express concern regarding payment. Many CFOs with international experience know that there are generally fewer collections problems on international sales than on domestic sales, provided the proper financial instruments are used. The reason is simple: A letter of credit can be used to guarantee payment for a product.

The export sale begins when the exporter-seller and the importer-buyer agree to do business. The agreement is formalized when the terms of the deal are set down in a **proforma** invoice, contract, fax, or some other document. Among other things, the proforma spells out how much, and by what means, the exporter-seller wants to be paid.

Documentary Credit

Documentary credits (also known as letters of credit or L/Cs) are widely used as a payment method in international trade. A **letter of credit** is essentially a document stating that a bank has substituted its creditworthiness for that of the importer-buyer. Next to cash in advance, an L/C offers the exporter the best assurance of being paid. That assurance arises from the fact that the payment obligation under an L/C lies with the buyer's bank and not with the buyer. The international standard by which L/Cs are interpreted is ICC Publication No. 500 of the Uniform Customs and Practice for Documentary Credits, also known as UCP 500.

The importer-buyer's bank is the "issuing" bank; the importer-buyer is, in essence, asking the issuing bank to extend credit. The importer-buyer is thus considered the applicant. The issuing bank may require that the importer–buyer deposit funds in the bank or use some other method to secure a line of credit. After agreeing to extend the credit, the issuing bank requests that the exporter-seller's bank advise and/or confirm the L/C. (A bank "confirms" an L/C by adding its name to the document.) The seller's bank becomes the "advising" and/or "confirming" bank. Whether it is advised or confirmed, the L/C represents a guarantee that assures payment contingent on the exporter-seller's (the beneficiary in the transaction) complying with the terms set forth in the L/C.

The actual payment process is set in motion when the exporter-seller physically ships the goods and submits the necessary documents as requested in the L/C. These could include a transportation bill of lading (which may represent title to the product), a commercial invoice, a packing list, a certificate of origin, or insurance certificates. For most of the world, a commercial invoice and bill of lading represent the minimum documentation required for customs clearance. If the proforma invoice specifies a confirmed L/C as the method of payment, the exporter-seller receives payment at the time the correct shipping documents are presented to the confirming bank. The confirming bank, in turn, requests payment from the issuing bank. In the case of an irrevocable L/C, the exporter-seller receives payment only after the advising bank negotiates the documents and requests payment from the issuing bank in accordance with terms set forth in the L/C. Once the shipper sends the documents to the advising bank, the advising bank negotiates those documents and is referred to as the negotiating bank. Specifically, it takes each shipping document and closely

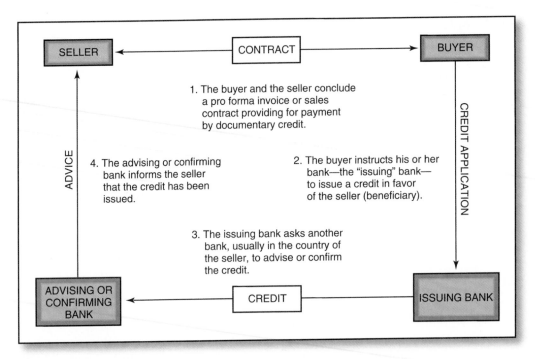

Figure 8-1
Flowchart of a Documentary Credit

compares it to the L/C. If there are no discrepancies, the negotiating or confirming bank transfers the money to the exporter/seller's account.

The fee for an irrevocable L/C—for example, "1/8 of 1 percent of the value of the credit, with an $80 minimum"—is lower than that for a confirmed L/C. The higher bank fees associated with confirmation can drive up the final cost of the sale; fees are also higher when the transaction involves a country with a high level of risk. Good communication between the exporter-seller and the advising or confirming bank regarding fees is important; the selling price indicated on the pro forma invoice should reflect these and other costs associated with exporting. The process described here is illustrated in Figures 8-1 and 8-2.

Documentary Collections (Sight or Time Drafts)

After an exporter and an importer have established a good working relationship, and the finance manager's level of confidence increases, it may be possible to move to a documentary collection or open-account method of payment. A documentary collection is a method of payment that uses a bill of exchange, also known as a *draft*. A **bill of exchange** is a negotiable instrument that is easily transferable from one party to another. In its simplest form, it is a written order from one party (the *drawer*) directing a second party (the *drawee*) to pay to the order of a third party (the *payee*). Drafts are distinctly different from L/Cs; a draft is a payment instrument that transfers all the risk of nonpayment onto the exporter-seller. Banks are involved as intermediaries but they do not bear financial risk. Because a draft is negotiable, however, a bank may be willing to buy the draft from the seller at a discount and thus assume the risk. Also, because bank fees for drafts are lower than those for L/Cs, drafts are frequently used when the monetary value of an export transaction is relatively low.

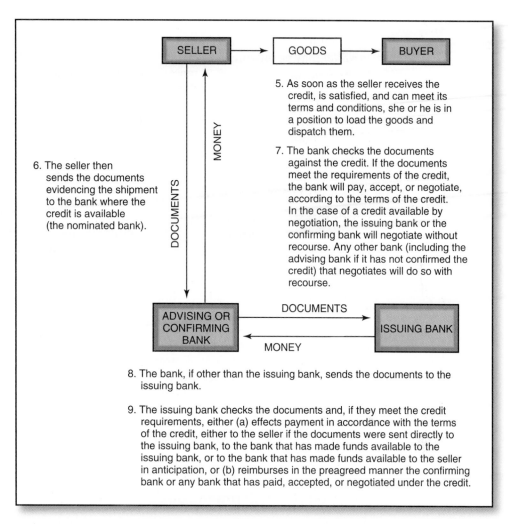

Figure 8-2
Flowchart of Documentary Credit Documents

With a documentary draft, the exporter delivers documents such as the bill of lading, the commercial invoice, a certificate of origin, and an insurance certificate to a bank in the exporter's country. The shipper or bank prepares a collection letter (draft) and sends it via courier to a correspondent bank in the importer/buyer's country. The draft is presented to the importer; payment takes place in accordance with the terms specified in the draft. In the case of a *sight draft* (also known as a D/P or *documents against draft*), the importer-buyer is required in principle to make payment when presented with both the draft and the shipping documents, even though the buyer may not have taken possession of the goods yet. *Time drafts* can take two forms. As the name implies, an *arrival draft* specifies that payment is due when the importer-buyer receives the goods; a *date draft* requires payment on a particular date, irrespective of whether the importer has the goods in hand.

Cash in Advance

A number of conditions may prompt the exporter to request cash payment—in whole or in part—in advance of shipment. Examples include times when credit risks abroad are high, when exchange restrictions within the country of destination may delay return of funds for an unreasonable period, or when, for any other reason, the exporter may be unwilling to sell on credit terms. Because of competition and restrictions against cash payment in many countries, the volume of business handled on a cash-in-advance basis is small. Cash in advance can also be used by a company that manufactures a unique product for which there are no substitutes available. For example, Compressor Control Corporation is a midwestern firm that manufactures special equipment for the oil industry. It can stipulate cash in advance because no other company offers a competing product.

Sales on Open Account

Goods that are sold on open account are paid for after delivery. Intracorporate sales to branches or subsidiaries of an exporter are frequently on open-account terms. Open-account terms also generally prevail in areas where exchange controls are minimal and exporters have had long-standing relations with good buyers in nearby or long-established markets. For example, Jimmy Fand is the owner of the Tile Connection in Tampa, Florida. He imports high-quality ceramic tile from Italy, Spain, Portugal, Colombia, Brazil, and other countries. Fand takes pride in the excellent credit rating that he has built up with his vendors. The manufacturers from whom he buys no longer require an L/C; Fand's philosophy is "pay in time," and he makes sure that his payables are sent electronically on the day they are due.

The main objection to open-account sales is the absence of a tangible obligation. Normally, if a time draft is drawn and then dishonored after acceptance, it can be used as a basis of legal action. By contrast, if an open-account transaction is dishonored, the legal procedure may be more complicated. Starting in 1995, the Export-Import Bank expanded insurance coverage on open-account transactions to limit the risk for exporters.

Sales on a Consignment Basis

A **free trade zone** (FTZ) is a geographic entity that may include a manufacturing facility and a warehouse. Goods sold on consignment are delivered by the exporter-consignor to the importer-consignee who then sells them. As in the case of sales on open account, no tangible obligation is created by consignment sales. In countries with free ports or free trade zones, consigned merchandise can be placed under bonded warehouse control in the name of a foreign bank. Sales can then be arranged by the selling agent and arrangements made to release partial lots out of the consigned stock against regular payment terms. The merchandise is not cleared through customs until after the sale has been completed. The import duty is not paid until the goods come out of the FTZ and are cleared through customs.

SOURCING

In global marketing, the issue of customer value is inextricably tied to the **sourcing decision.** If customers are nationalistic, they may put a positive value on the feature "made in the home country." Such preferences must be identified with market research and factored in to solve for V in the value equation $V = B/P$. Those global companies located outside the United States that have achieved the greatest success in the U.S. market have done so by convincing American customers that their products offer higher quality and superior value than competing products from U.S. companies.

Another key variable in the sourcing decision is the vision and values of company leadership. Some chief executives are obsessed with manufacturing in their home country. Such is the case with Nicolas Hayek. He is head of the Swatch Group, the company best known for its line of inexpensive Swatch watches. Hayek presided over the spectacular revitalization of the Swiss watch industry. The Swatch brand has become a pop culture phenomenon; however, the company targets several segments of the watch market. The Swatch Group's portfolio of brands includes Omega, Breguet, and Rado. In 1992, Swatch acquired Blancpain, a luxury mechanical watch company that produces 9,000 watches each year priced from $15,000 to $700,000. Hayek demonstrated that the fantasy and imagination of childhood and youth can be translated into breakthroughs that allow mass-market products to be manufactured in high-wage countries side-by-side with handcrafted luxury products. The Swatch story is a triumph of engineering, as well as a triumph of the imagination.

The sourcing decision highlights three roles for marketing in a global competitive strategy. The first relates to the configuration of marketing. Although many marketing activities must be performed in every country, advantage can be gained by concentrating some of the marketing activities in a single location. Service, for example, must be dispersed to every country. Training, however, might be at least partially concentrated in a single location for the world. A second role for marketing is the coordination of marketing activities across countries to leverage a company's know-how. This integration can take many forms, including the transfer of relevant experience across national boundaries in areas such as global account management, and the use of similar approaches or methods for marketing research, product positioning, or other marketing activities. A third critical role of marketing is its role in tapping opportunities for product development and R&D. The development of Canon's AE-l camera is a case in point. Research provided the information on market requirements that enabled Canon to develop a "world" product. Canon was able to develop a physically uniform product that required fewer parts, far less engineering, lower inventories, and longer production runs. Such advantages would have been lacking if Canon had developed separate camera models that were adapted to the unique conditions in each national market.

Public scrutiny of the sourcing issue has become more common in recent years for a variety of reasons. One is the authenticity of "Made in Country X" claims. In 1994, the U.S. Federal Trade Commission (FTC) charged athletic shoe manufacturer New Balance with misleading labeling. New Balance shoes incorporate a rubber outer sole that is made in China; the FTC charged that the company was not entitled to use the "Made in the USA" label. In 1996, the FTC set launched a review of the "Made in the USA" definition. Current rules require that nearly 100% of a product be made and assembled in the United States if it is to carry the label. A second sourcing issue that has made headlines involves sweatshop labor conditions in developing countries where factories turn out apparel, athletic equipment, and other products on contract for American companies.

Sourcing Decision Criteria

There are no simple rules to guide sourcing decisions. Indeed, the sourcing decision is one of the most complex and important decisions faced by a global company. Six factors must be taken into account in the sourcing decision:

1. Factor costs and conditions
2. Logistics (time required to fill orders, security and safety, and transportation costs)

3. Country infrastructure
4. Political risk
5. Market access (tariff and nontariff barriers to trade)
6. Exchange rate, availability, and convertibility of local money

Factor Costs and Conditions

Factor costs are land, labor, and capital costs (remember Economics 101!). Labor includes the cost of workers at every level: manufacturing and production, professional and technical, and management. Basic manufacturing direct labor costs today range from less than one dollar per hour in the typical LDC to $6 to $12 per hour in the typical developed country. In certain industries in the United States, direct labor costs in manufacturing exceed $20 per hour without benefits.

German hourly compensation costs for production workers in manufacturing are 160 percent of those in the United States while those in Mexico are only 15 percent of those in the United States. For Volkswagen, the wage differential between Mexico and Germany, combined with the strength of the mark in the 1990s, dictated a Mexican manufacturing facility that builds Golf and Jetta models destined for the United States. Do lower wage rates demand that a company relocate its manufacturing to the low-wage country? Hardly. During his tenure as chairman at VW, Ferdinand Piech improved his company's competitiveness by convincing unions to accept flexible work schedules. For example, during peak demand, employees work six-day weeks; when demand slows, factories produce cars only three days per week.

Moreover, wages are only one of the costs of production. Many other considerations enter into the sourcing decision, such as management's aspirations. For example, Swatch assembles all of the watches it sells, and it builds most of the components for the watches it assembles. It manufactures in Switzerland, a country with one of the world's highest wage rates. Hayek decided that he wanted to manufacture in Switzerland in spite of the fact that a secretary in Switzerland makes more money than a chief engineer in Thailand. He did this by making a commitment to drive wage costs down to less than 10 percent of total costs. At this level, wage rates are no longer a significant factor in competitiveness. As Hayek puts it, he does not care if his competitors' workers work for free! He will still win in a competitive marketplace because his value is so much greater.

The other factors of production are land, materials, and capital. The cost of these factors depends upon their availability and relative abundance. Often, the differences in factor costs will offset each other so that, on balance, companies have a level field in the competitive arena. For example, some countries have abundant land and Japan has abundant capital. These advantages partially offset each other. When this is the case, the critical factor is management, professional, and worker team effectiveness.

World factor costs that affect manufacturing can be divided into three tiers. The first tier consists of the industrialized countries, where factor costs are tending to equalize. The second tier consists of the industrializing countries—for example, Singapore and other Pacific Rim countries—that offer significant factor cost savings, as well as an increasingly developed infrastructure and political stability, making them extremely attractive manufacturing locations. The third tier includes Russia and other countries that have not yet become significant locations for manufacturing activity. Third-tier countries present the combination of lower factor costs (especially wages) offset by limited infrastructure development and greater political uncertainty.

The application of advanced computer controls and other new manufacturing technologies has reduced the proportion of labor relative to capital for many businesses. In formulating a sourcing strategy, company managers and executives should also recognize the declining importance of direct manufacturing labor as a percentage of total product cost. The most advanced global companies are no longer blindly chasing cheap labor manufacturing locations because direct labor cost may be a very small percentage of the total. As a result, it may not be worthwhile to incur the costs and risks of establishing a manufacturing activity in a distant location. For example, Greg Petsch, senior vice president of manufacturing at Compaq, had to decide whether to close plants in Houston and Scotland and contract out assembly work to the Far East. After determining that the human labor content in a PC is only about 15 minutes, he opted to run Compaq's existing Houston factory 24 hours a day. Another decision was whether to source motherboards from a vendor in Asia. Petsch calculated that Compaq could produce the boards—which account for 40 percent of the cost of a PC—for $25 less than suppliers in the Far East. Manufacturing in Houston also saved two weeks in shipping time, which translated into inventory savings.[9]

The experience of the Arrow Shirt Company also illustrates several issues relating to factor costs. During the 1980s, Arrow sourced 15 percent of its dress shirts from the Far East at a cost savings of $15 per dozen over U.S.-manufactured shirts. Arrow decided to phase out imports after spending $15 million to automate its U.S. plants. Productivity increased 25 percent, and Arrow is no longer at the mercy of a 12-month lead time between ordering and delivery; U.S.-sourced shirts can be ordered a mere three months in advance—a critical issue in the fashion industry. Interestingly, the Arrow experience illustrates how the decision to source at home rather than abroad does not automatically defuse the political issue of "exporting jobs": After automating, Arrow laid off 400 U.S. workers and closed four factories.[10]

Many companies have been chagrined to discover that today's cheap factor costs can disappear as the law of supply and demand drives up wages and land prices. Shirtmakers like Arrow began sourcing in Japan in the 1950s. As wages and real estate costs increased, production was shifted to Hong Kong, then to Taiwan, and Korea. During the 1970s and 1980s, production kept shifting to China, Indonesia, Thailand, Malaysia, Bangladesh, and Singapore. In recent years, shirt production has shifted from the Far East to Costa Rica, the Dominican Republic, Guatemala, Honduras, and Puerto Rico. In addition to low wages, these countries offer tax incentives under the 1983 Caribbean Basin Initiative agreement.[11]

Logistics

In general, the greater the distance between the product source and the target market, the greater the time delay for delivery and the higher the transportation cost. However, innovation and new transportation technologies are cutting both time and dollar costs. To facilitate global delivery, transportation companies such as CSX Corporation are forming alliances and becoming an important part of industry value systems. Manufacturers can take advantage of intermodal services that allow containers to be transferred between rail, boat, air, and truck carriers. Today, transportation expenses for U.S. exports and imports represent approximately 5 percent of total costs. In Europe, the advent of the single market means fewer border controls, which greatly speeds up delivery times and lowers costs.

---

[9] Doron P. Levin, "Compaq Storms the PC Heights from Its Factory Floor," *The New York Times* (November 4, 1994), sec. 3, p. 5.

[10] Cynthia Mitchell, "Coming Home: Some Firms Resume Manufacturing in U.S. After Foreign Fiascoes," *The Wall Street Journal* (October 14, 1986), p. 1.

[11] Peter C. T. Elsworth, "Can Colors and Stripes Rescue Shirt Makers from a Slump?" *The New York Times* (March 17, 1991), sec. 3, p. 5.

Memorex Telex provides an excellent illustration of how companies can reconfigure inbound logistics in the value chain to support an overseas sourcing strategy. Memorex, which manufactures computer peripherals in Raleigh, North Carolina, sources components in Asia. The company originally shipped by water from Taiwan, through the Panama Canal, and on to the Port of Norfolk. A short trip by truck to Raleigh completed the journey. In the late 1980s, Memorex switched to ship-and-train intermodal transport; using Long Beach as the port of entry cut ten days off the water route and saved $400 to $800 per container. In 1992, Memorex began using long-haul trucks instead of trains, resulting in additional savings of more than $1,000 per container.[12]

Country Infrastructure

In order to present an attractive setting for a manufacturing operation, it is important that the country's infrastructure be sufficiently developed to support a manufacturing operation. The required infrastructure will vary from company to company, but minimally, it will include power, transportation and roads, communications, service and component suppliers, a labor pool, civil order, and effective governance. In addition, a country must offer reliable access to foreign exchange for the purchase of necessary material and components from abroad as well as a physically secure setting where work can be done and product can be shipped to customers.

A country may have cheap labor, but does it have the necessary supporting services or infrastructure to support a manufacturing activity? Many countries offer these conditions, including Hong Kong, Taiwan, and Singapore. There are many other countries that do not, such as Lebanon, Uganda, and El Salvador. One of the challenges of doing business in the new Russian market is an infrastructure that is woefully inadequate to handle the increased volume of shipments. The Mexican government, anticipating much heavier trade volume because of NAFTA, has committed $14 billion for infrastructure improvements.

Political Risk

Political risk, or the risk of a change in government policy that would adversely impact a company's ability to operate effectively and profitably, is a deterrent to investment in local sourcing. Conversely, the lower the level of political risk, the less likely it is that an investor will avoid a country or market. The difficulty of assessing political risk is inversely proportional to a country's stage of economic development: All other things being equal, the less developed a country, the more difficult it is to predict political risk. The political risk of the Triad countries, for example, is quite limited as compared to that of a less developed pre-industrial country in Africa, Latin America, or Asia.

The recent rapid changes in Central and Eastern Europe and the dissolution of the Soviet Union have very clearly demonstrated the risks *and* opportunities resulting from political upheavals.

Market Access

A key factor in locating production facilities is market access. If a country or a region limits market access because of local content laws, balance-of-payments problems, or

---

[12] Gregory L. Miles, "Think Global, Go Intermodal," *International Business* (March 1993), pp. 61+.

any other reason, it may be necessary to establish a production facility within the country itself. The Japanese automobile companies invested in U.S. plant capacity because of concerns about market access. By producing cars in the United States, they have a source of supply that is not exposed to the threat of tariff or nontariff barriers. In the 1950s and 1960s, U.S. companies created production capacity abroad to ensure continued access to markets that had been established with supply exported from U.S. plants.

Market access figured heavily in Boeing's decision to produce airplane components in China. China ordered 100 airplanes valued at $4.5 billion; in return, Boeing is making investments and transferring engineering and manufacturing expertise.[13] Similarly, Motorola is building a chip plant in northeastern China. In 1994, NEC Corp. opened a semiconductor fabrication plant to supply China's consumer electronics industry. Some manufacturers have balked at China's demands; Daimler-Benz was awarded a contract to build the first independent auto plant in China after Chrysler refused to share patent rights for van production technology. Many observers warn that the technology transfer, currently so important to China's modernization, will lead to the emergence of strong Chinese competition in aviation, telecommunications, semiconductors, and a host of other industries. Bob Donovan, head of ABB's U.S. unit warns, "If someone's knocking off Mariah Carey CDs in China, that's unfortunate for Ms. Carey. But patents represent 230 years of accumulated knowledge and work. If lesser countries can make a 230-year leap and pay nothing, that will alter the course of industrial development in the world."[14]

Foreign Exchange Rates

In deciding where to locate a manufacturing activity, the cost of production supplied by a country source will be determined in part by the prevailing foreign exchange rate for the country's currency. Exchange rates are so volatile today that many companies pursue global sourcing strategies as a way of limiting exchange-related risk. At any point in time, what has been an attractive location for production may become much less attractive due to exchange rate fluctuation. For example, the exchange value of the U.S. dollar declined more than 50 percent vis-à-vis the Japanese yen between 1985 and the present. Of course, the flip side of this adjustment is that the yen appreciated more than 100 percent in the same period. The prudent company will incorporate exchange volatility into its planning assumptions and be prepared to prosper under a variety of exchange rate relationships.

The dramatic shifts in price levels of commodities and currencies are a major characteristic of the world economy today. Such volatility argues for a sourcing strategy that provides alternative country options for supplying markets. Thus, if the dollar, the yen, or the mark becomes seriously overvalued, a company with production capacity in other locations can achieve competitive advantage by shifting production among different sites. For example, in mid-1993, Bridgestone Corp. increased the production of European- and U.S.-made tires carrying the Bridgestone brand name in the face of a strong yen.

---

[13] Jeff Cole, Marcus W. Brauchli, and Craig S. Smith, "Orient Express: Boeing Flies into Flap over Technology Shift in Dealings with China," *The Wall Street Journal* (October 13, 1995), pp. A1, A11. See also Joseph Kahn, "Clipped Wings: McDonnell Douglas's High Hopes for China Never Really Soared," *The Wall Street Journal* (May 22, 1996), pp. A1, A10.
[14] James Cox, "Siphoning U.S. Companies' Knowledge," *USA Today* (February 16, 1996), pp. 1B, 2B.

SUMMARY

A company's first business dealings outside the home country often take the form of **exporting** or **importing.** Such companies should recognize the difference between **export marketing** and **export selling.** By attending **trade shows** and participating in **trade missions,** company personnel can learn a great deal about new markets. Governments use a variety of programs to support exports, including tax incentives, subsidies, and export assistance. Governments also discourage imports with a combination of **tariffs** and **nontariff barriers.** The latter include **quotas** and **discriminatory procurement policies.**

The **Harmonized Tariff System** has been adopted by most countries that are actively involved in export-import trade. **Two-column tariffs** include special rates such as those available to countries with **most favored nation status.** Customs duties can take the form of **ad valorem** or **specific duties.** Governments can also impose special types of duties. These include **antidumping duties** imposed on products whose prices government officials deem too low and **countervailing duties** to offset government subsidies.

Key participants in the export-import process include **foreign purchasing agents, export brokers, export merchants, export management companies, manufacturers' export representatives,** and **export distributors.**

A number of export-import payment methods are available. A basic payment instrument is the **letter of credit** that assures payment from the buyer's bank. Sales may also be made using a **bill of exchange, cash in advance, sales on open account,** or a **consignment** agreement.

Exporting and importing is directly related to a company's **sourcing strategy.** A number of factors determine whether a company makes or buys its products as well as *where* it makes or buys. A paramount consideration is **factor costs;** other issues include **logistics, country infrastructure, political risk,** ease of **market access,** and **foreign exchange rates.**

DISCUSSION QUESTIONS

1. What is the difference between export marketing and export selling?
2. Why is exporting from the United States dominated by large companies? What, if anything, could be done to increase exports from smaller companies?
3. Describe the stages a company typically goes through as it learns about exporting.
4. Governments often pursue policies that promote exports while limiting imports. What are some of those policies?
5. What are the various types of duties that export marketers should be aware of?
6. What is the difference between a letter of credit and other forms of export-import financing? Why do sellers often require letters of credit in international transactions?
7. What criteria should company management consider when making sourcing decisions?

SUGGESTED READINGS

Books

Branch, Alan E. *Elements of Export Marketing Management.* London: Chapman and Hall, 1990.

Gordon, John S. *Profitable Exporting: A Complete Guide to Marketing Your Products Abroad.* New York: Wiley, 1993.

Johnson, Thomas E. *Export /Import Procedure and Documentation.* New York: Anacom, 1991.

Masggiori, Herman J. *How to Make the World Your Market: The International Sales and Marketing Handbook.* Los Angeles: Burning Gate Press, 1992.

Pattison, Joseph E. *Acquiring the Future: America's Survival and Success in the Global Economy.* Homewood, IL: Dow-Jones-Irwin, 1990.

Raynauld, Andre. *Financing Exports to Developing Countries.* Paris, France: Development Centre of the

Organization for Economic Cooperation and Development, 1992.

Rommel, Gunter, Jurgen Kluge, Rolf-Dieter Kempis, Raimund Diederichs, and Felix Bruck, *Simplicity Wins: How Germany's Mid-sized Industrial Companies Succeed.* Boston: Harvard Business Review Press, 1995.

Rossen, Philip J., and Stan D. Reid, eds. *Managing Export Entry and Expansion.* New York: Praeger, 1987.

Schaffer, Matt. *Winning the Countertrade War: New Export Strategies for America.* New York: John Wiley & Sons, 1989.

U.S. Department of Commerce. *A Basic Guide to Exporting.* Washington, DC: U.S. Department of Commerce, 1992.

———. *Toward a National Export Strategy: U.S. Exports = U.S. Jobs: Reports to the United States Congress.* Washington, DC: Trade Promotion Coordinating Committee, 1993.

Venedikian, Harry M. *Export-Import Financing.* New York: Wiley, 1992.

Verzriu, Pompiliu. *Countertrade, Barter, and Offsets: New Strategies for Profit in International Trade.* New York: McGraw-Hill, 1985.

Articles

Bonaccorsi, Andrea. "On the Relationship Between Firm Size and Export Intensity." *Journal of International Business Studies* 23, no. 4 (Fourth Quarter 1992), pp. 605–636.

———. "What Do We Know About Exporting by Small Italian Exporting Firms?" *Journal of International Marketing* 1, no. 3 (1993), pp. 49–76.

Burpitt, William J., and Dennis A. Rondinelli. "Small Firms' Motivations for Exporting: To Earn and Learn?" *Journal of Small Business Management* 38, no. 4 (October 2000) pp. 1–14.

Carrier, Camille. "The Training and Development Needs of Owner-Managers of Small Businesses with Export Potential." *Journal of Small Business Mangement* 37, no. 4 (October 1999) pp. 30–41.

Cavusgil, S. Tamer, and V. H. Kirpalani. "Introducing Products into Export Markets: Success Factors." *Journal of Business Research* 27, no. 1 (May 1993), pp. 1–15.

———, Shaoming Zou, and G. M. Naidu. "Product and Promotion Adaptation in Export Ventures: An Empirical Investigation." *Journal of International Business Studies* 24, no. 3 (Third Quarter 1993), pp. 449–464.

Chan, T. S. "Emerging Trends in Export Channel Strategy: An Investigation of Hong Kong and Singaporean Firms." *European Journal of Marketing* 26, no. 3, pp. 18–26.

Davis, Edward W. "Global Outsourcing: Have U.S. Managers Thrown the Baby Out with the Bath Water?" *Business Horizons* 35, no. 4 (July-August 1992), pp. 58–65.

Dominguez, Luis V., and Carlos G. Gequeira. "Strategic Options for LDC Exports to Developed Countries." *International Marketing Review* 8, no. 5 (1991), pp. 27–43.

Gnepa, Tahi J. "Persuading Small Manufacturing Companies to Become Active Importers: The Effect of Message Framing and Focus on Behavioral Intentions." *Journal of Global Marketing* 14, no. 4 (2001) pp. 49–66.

Haigh, Robert W. "Thinking of Exporting? Export Management Companies Could Be the Answer." *Columbia Journal of World Business* 24 (Winter 1994), pp. 66–81.

Howard, Donald G. "The Role of Export Management Companies in Global Marketing." *Journal of Global Marketing* 8, no. 1 (1994), pp. 95–110.

Katsikeas, Constantine S. "Perceived Export Problems and Export Involvement: The Case of Greek Exporting Manufacturers." *Journal of Global Marketing* 7, no. 4 (1994), pp. 29–57.

———, and Nigel F. Piercy. "Long-Term Export Stimuli and Firm Characteristics in a European LDC." *Journal of International Marketing* 1, no. 3 (1993), pp. 23–48.

Koh, Anthony C., James Chow, and Sasithorn Smittivate. "The Practice of International Marketing Research by Thai Exporters." *Journal of Global Marketing* 7, no. 2 (1993), pp. 7–26.

Korth, Christopher M. "Managerial Barriers to U.S. Exports." *Business Horizons* 34, no. 2 (March/April 1991), pp. 18–26.

Kotabe, Masaaki. "Patterns and Technological Implications of Global Sourcing Strategies: A Study of European and Japanese Multinational Firms." *Journal of International Marketing* 1, no. 1 (1993), pp. 26–43.

———, and Michael R. Czinkota. "State Government Promotion of Manufacturing Exports: A Gap Analysis." *Journal of International Business Studies* 23, no. 4 (Fourth Quarter 1992), pp. 637–658.

———, and K. Scott Swan. "Offshore Sourcing: Reaction, Maturation, and Consolidation of U.S. Multinationals." *Journal of International Business Studies* 25, no. 1 (First Quarter 1994), pp. 115–140.

Leonidou, Leonidas C. "Empirical Research on Export Barriers: Review, Assessment, and Synthesis." *Journal of International Marketing* 3, no. 1 (1995), pp. 29–44.

Louter, Pieter J., Cok Ouwerkerk, and Ben A. Bakker. "An Inquiry into Successful Exporting." *European Journal of Marketing* 25, no. 6 (1991), pp. 7–23.

MacCormack, Alan David, Lawrence James Newman III, and Donald B. Rosenfield. "The New Dynamics of Global Manufacturing Site Locations." *Sloan Management Review* 35, no. 4 (Summer 1994), pp. 69–80.

Mahone, Charlie E. Jr. "Penetrating Export Markets: The Role of Firm Size." *Journal of Global Marketing* 7, no. 3 (1994), pp. 133–148.

Murphy, Paul R., James M. Daley, and Douglas R. Dalenberg. "Doing Business in Global Markets: Perspectives of International Freight Forwarders." *Journal of Global Marketing* 6, no. 4 (1993), pp. 53–68.

Namiki, Nobuaki. "A Taxonomic Analysis of Export Marketing Strategy: An Exploratory Study of U.S. Exporters of Electronics Products." *Journal of Global Marketing* 8, no. 1 (1994), pp. 27–50.

Parke, David. "US National Security Export Controls: Implications for Global Competitiveness of U.S. High-Tech Firms." *Strategic Management Journal* 13, no. 1 (January 1992), pp. 47–66.

Quinn, James Brian, and Frederick G. Hilmer. "Strategic Outsourcing." *Sloan Management Review* 35, no. 4 (Summer 1994), pp. 43–56.

Rao, C. P., M. Krishna Eerramilli, and Gopala K. Ganesh. "Impact of Domestic Recession on Export Marketing Behavior." *International Marketing Review* 7, no. 2 (1990), pp. 54–65.

Raven, Peter V., Jim M. McCullough, and Patriya S. Tansuhaj. "Environmental Influences and Decision-Making Uncertainty in Export Channels: Effects on Satisfaction and Performance." *Journal of International Marketing* 2, no. 3 (1994), pp. 37–60.

Reich, Michael R. "Why the Japanese Don't Export More Pharmaceuticals: Health Policy as Industrial Policy." *California Management Review* 32, no. 2 (Winter 1990), pp. 124–150.

Robock, Stefan H. "The Export Myopia of U.S. Multinationals: An Overlooked Opportunity for Creating U.S. Manufacturing Jobs." *Columbia Journal of World Business* 28, no. 2 (Summer 1993), pp. 24–32.

Rynning, Marjo-Riitta, and Otto Andersen. "Structural and Behavioral Predictors of Export Adoption: A Norwegian Study." *Journal of International Marketing* 2, no. 1 (1994), pp. 73–90.

Samiee, Saeed. "Strategic Considerations of the EC 1992 Plan for Small Exporters." *Business Horizons* 22, no. 2 (March-April 1990), pp. 48–52.

Seringhaus, F. H. Rolf. "A Comparison of Export Marketing Behavior of Canadian and Austrian High-Tech Firms." *Journal of International Marketing* 1, no. 4 (1993), pp. 49–70.

———. "Export Promotion in Developing Countries: Status and Prospects." *Journal of Global Marketing* 6, no. 4 (1993), pp. 7–32.

Simon, Hermann. "Lessons from Germany's Midsize Giants." *Harvard Business Review* (March-April 1992), pp. 115–123.

Singer, Thomas Owen, and Michael R. Czinkota. "Factors Associated with Effective Use of Export Assistance." *Journal of International Marketing* 2, no. 1 (1994), pp. 53–72.

Swamidass, Paul M. "Import Sourcing Dynamics: An Integrative Perspective." *Journal of International Business Studies* 24, no. 4 (Fourth Quarter 1993), pp. 671–692.

Taylor, William. "Message and Muscle: An Interview with Swatch Titan Nicolas Hayek." *Harvard Business Review* 71, no. 2 (March-April 1993), pp. 99–110.

Terpstra, Vern, and Chow-Ming Joseph Yu. "Export Trading Companies: An American Trade Failure?" *Journal of Global Marketing* 6, no. 3 (1992), pp. 29–54.

Venkatesan, Ravi. "Strategic Sourcing: To Make or Not To Make." *Harvard Business Review* 70, no. 6 (November-December 1992), pp. 98–107.

Wolff, James A., and Timothy L. Pett. "Internationalization of Small Firms: An Examination of Export Competitive Patterns, Firm Size, and Export Performance." *Journal of Small Business Management* 38, no. 2 (April 2000) pp. 34–47.

CASES

Case 8-1   *Concerns about Factory Safety and Worker Exploitation in Developing Countries*

In April 1997, President Bill Clinton announced the creation of a code of conduct aimed at combating sweatshops on a worldwide basis. Representatives from Phillips-Van Heusen (PVH), Nike, Reebok, Liz Claiborne, and six other manufacturers had served on a task force that spent eight months studying the sweatshop issue. The code established a minimum age of 14 for apparel workers and a maximum work week of 60 hours. Companies were required to pay the prevailing minimum wage in the country where the factory was located. Michael Posner, executive director of the Lawyers Committee for Human Rights, hailed the code as a breakthrough agreement. "It establishes a framework that provides consumers with confidence that companies are making good-faith efforts to address sweatshop practices," he said. Despite such optimism, the manufacturers and human rights advocates that were task force members disagreed on several issues. One concern was countries in which the official minimum wage was not a true "living wage" sufficient to support a family. Another issue was monitoring labor practices; the manufacturers wanted the right to select accounting firms, while activists and labor groups wanted nonprofit groups to perform the task of monitoring.

BACKGROUND TO THE CODE OF CONDUCT

In August 1995, federal agents raided a garment-manufacturing facility near Los Angeles. The agents discovered 60 people, all from Thailand, who worked as many as 22 hours per day for $1.60 an hour to repay expenses for travel to the United States. The U.S. Labor Department charged the six Thai nationals believed to be running the sweatshop operation with harboring illegal immigrants and smuggling immigrants. The Labor Department also alleged that May Department Stores, Sears, and other retailers were selling goods that originated in the Los Angeles factory. Under the Fair Labor Standards Act, the Labor Department was authorized to hold the various apparel manufacturers that bought goods from the sweatshop legally liable for $5 million in worker back pay.

A year later, the sweatshop issue stayed in the news thanks to Kathie Lee Gifford, best known to television viewers as host of a popular talk show and as a celebrity endorser who appeared in ads for Carnival Cruise Lines and Ultra Slim-Fast. Many Wal-Mart shoppers also asso-

ciated Kathie Lee's name with a line of moderately-priced apparel. Some items in the Kathie Lee clothing line were produced under contract in factories in Honduras and other developing countries. Labor rights activist Charles Kernaghan charged that working conditions in many of those factories fit the definition of "sweatshop": long hours, low wages, and abusive supervisors. Moreover, many employees in the factories were alleged to be minors. Kernaghan accused Kathie Lee and other endorsers of profiting from worker exploitation.

SWEATSHOPS IN THE SPOTLIGHT

The sweatshop bust in Los Angeles and the revelations surrounding Kathy Lee Gifford finally focused the public's attention on an issue that had been gathering momentum for years. Catastrophic industrial fires in several countries have resulted in extensive loss of life. In Dongguan, China, 80 workers died in a fire at a raincoat factory in 1991. In 1993, 84 people were killed in a handicrafts factory fire in the Chinese city of Shenzhen. The most deadly industrial fire in history broke out on May 10, 1993, in a four-story toy factory near Bangkok, Thailand. Nearly 200 workers—most of whom were women and teenage girls—died in the blaze. The factory was owned by Kader Industrial Toy Company, which supplies toys to well-known U.S. companies such as Fisher-Price, Toys 'R' Us, and Hasbro. One reason so many perished is that several emergency exit doors were locked.

Government support is just one reason that companies can rely on far-flung manufacturing; 900 million—about 15 percent—of the world's six billion people are unemployed. Thus, governments in many countries encourage foreign investment that will create jobs. Moreover, manufacturing companies account for nearly three-fourths of the dollar value of world trade. Improved communications technology allows company headquarters to closely monitor operations throughout the world. As John Cavanagh, a fellow at Washington's Institute for Policy Studies, explains, "Companies can coordinate production in plants scattered all over the world on a real-time, minute-to-minute basis."

Not surprisingly, many U.S. companies are scouring the globe for low-cost sources of labor. As wages have increased in South Korea, Taiwan, and Singapore, offshore assembly and manufacturing has moved to developing countries such as Indonesia, Thailand, India, Mexico, and China. For example, almost half of all the toys sold in the United States are produced in Asia; in 1992, Chinese factories turned out $3.3 billion worth of toys for the United States. The minimum wage in China is about 80 cents per day.

Disturbed by the trend, many U.S. observers had long characterized factories in developing countries as sweatshops where "semi-slave labor" was forced to work in inhumane, unsafe working conditions for very low wages. These critics suggest that profit-hungry American executives often turn a blind eye to working conditions outside the United States. For their part, executives and industry spokespersons point out that, in many cases, U.S. companies do not own the factories where goods are made. Labor movement representatives in the United States, concerned that U.S. companies are unwilling to support improved working conditions abroad, have even attempted to align with labor movements in developing countries.

Despite the terrible tragedies in Thailand and China, not everyone in the United States agrees with the view that workers in developing countries are being exploited. Although wages in some countries may seem low by U.S. standards, they are relatively high by Asian standards. Compared to an agriculture-based subsistence standard of living, these wages represent both an improvement and an important step forward in terms of economic development. As advocates of global production point out, wages in Japan, Taiwan, and South Korea were low in the years after World War II, but increased as those countries' economies developed. The first step toward a developed economy involved sweatshops. As economist Paul Krugman noted recently, "The overwhelming mainstream view among economists is that the growth of this kind of employment is tremendous good news for the world's poor." Krugman has adopted a pragmatic viewpoint on the child labor issue. Noting that some impoverished parents sell their children to syndicates who force them to work as beggars, Krugman says, "If that is the alternative, it is not so easy to say that children should not be working in factories."

Still, some experts predict that business executives are starting to realize that it is simply good business to be concerned with factory conditions. Notes Professor Elliot Schrage of Columbia University, "Many companies are being forced to examine their labor practices around the world by consumer pressure or fear of consumer backlash." Indeed, the U.S. government hoped that publicizing the names of retailers who bought from the Los Angeles manufacturers would encourage retailers to improve their social responsibility policies.

NIKE AND THE SNEAKER CONTROVERSY

The truth in Schrage's observation has been amply illustrated in the athletic shoe industry. Nike, Reebok, and other sneaker marketers source virtually 100 percent of their shoes in Asia, where contractors are responsible for the production of the shoes. For example, 80 million pairs of Nikes are manufactured each year in dozens of factories outside the United States. During the 1980s, most of Nike's manufacturing was located in South Korea and Taiwan. As workers there gained the right to organize and strike, wage rates increased. Nike responded by shifting production to China, Malaysia, Indonesia, and Thailand and leaving 20 closed factories in its wake. In Indonesia, where 50 factories make shoes for Nike, the nonunion workforce is made up mostly of young women paid wages starting at about $1.35 a day. In all, an estimated 300,000 young Asian women are employed by Nike subcontractors.

Nike's practice of following cheap labor around the globe made it the target of criticism from the ranks of workers and scholars alike. For example, *Solidarity* magazine, published by the United Auto Workers, once urged union members to send their "dirty, smelly, worn-out" running shoes to Nike as a way of protesting overseas production. John Cavanagh and others have written numerous articles criticizing Nike for profiting at the expense of low-wage workers. Cavanagh has pointed out that, although 2.5 million people enter the Indonesian job market each year, employment options are so limited that most people can only find work making athletic shoes. Low wages permit only subsistence living in shanties without electricity or plumbing and also result in malnutrition. Nike pays superstar Michael Jordan $20 million annually in endorsement fees, an amount that has been estimated to exceed the total annual wages for Indonesian workers who make the sneakers.

For several years, Nike executives responded to inquiries about working conditions in contract factories by noting that the company focuses on marketing and design rather than manufacturing. Still, the company was coming under increased pressure from both human rights groups and the general public to address the sweatshop issue. In 1997, Nike commissioned former U.N. ambassador Andrew Young to visit some of the Asian factories and report his findings. After spending 15 days personally inspecting working conditions, Young reported that he did not find abuse or mistreatment of workers. Critics took Nike to task for asking Young to focus only on working conditions and failing to investigate wage rates as well. However, in September 1997, Nike canceled contracts with four factories in Indonesia where pay was below minimum government

Doonesbury

BY GARRY TRUDEAU

levels. By 1998, the controversy began to affect Nike's bottom line. Nike's profits dropped as sneaker sales slumped. The sweatshop backlash was not the only cause, however; increasing numbers of consumers were turning to "brown shoes," snapping up casual wear from Hush Puppies, Timberland, and other makers.

Nike was not the only company caught up in the controversy. Allegations surfaced that a subcontractor for Adidas-Salomon AG employed Chinese political prisoners in labor camps near Shanghai to sew soccer balls that commemorated the 1998 World Cup. Adidas, like Nike, has adopted a code of conduct and closely monitors production to prevent such things from occurring. The allegations came as President Clinton was visiting China with an agenda that downplayed human rights issues. An estimated 230,000 Chinese are held in camps dedicated to "reeducation through labor." Soccer balls are hand sewn from 32 precut panels, a process that is so labor-intensive that the work is often done in rural "stitching centers" with the country's lowest labor costs. Adidas confirmed that the allegations were based in fact but that the prison labor had been utilized without the company's knowledge. Adidas announced that it would not source soccer balls in China until production was centralized in one location that excluded the possibility of using prison labor. ∎

Visit the Web site
Read Nike's Revised Code of Conduct and learn more about the company's labor practices at:
www.nikebiz.com
Global Exchange, a human rights group, offers information on efforts to combat sweatshops:
www.globalexchange.org

DISCUSSION QUESTIONS

1. Do you think toy company executives—in Japan, the United States, and elsewhere—should take steps to ensure the safety and welfare of factory workers in developing countries? Why or why not?
2. How have the low wages paid in developing country manufacturing operations affected the number of manufacturing jobs in the high-wage triad countries?
3. If higher wages in toy factories led to higher prices in the United States for toys, how would the toy industry be affected?
4. Should the subject of working conditions be included in international trade agreements?
5. Do you think companies are doing enough to act responsibly and ensure that human rights standards are upheld for workers both inside and outside their home countries?

SOURCES: Craig S. Smith and A. Craig Copetas, "For Adidas, China Could Prove Trouble," *The Wall Street Journal* (June 26, 1998), p. A13; Holman W. Jenkins Jr. "The Rise and Stumble of Nike," *The Wall Street Journal* (June 3, 1998), p. A19; Steven Greenhouse, "Accord to Battle Sweatshop Labor Faces Obstacles," *The New York Times* (April 13, 1997), pp. 1, 13; Allen R. Myerson, "In Principle, a Case for More 'Sweatshops,' " *The New York Times* (June 22, 1997), p. 5; Asra Q. Nomani, "Labor Department Asks $5 Million for Alleged Worker Enslavement," *The Wall Street Journal* (August 16, 1995), p. B4; Lori Ioannou, "Capitalizing on Global Surplus Labor," *International Business* (April, 1995),

Chapter 8   Exporting, Importing, and Sourcing

321

pp. 32–34+; G. Pascal Zachary, "Multinationals Can Aid Some Foreign Workers," *The Wall Street Journal* (April 24, 1995), p. A1; Bob Herbert, "Terror in Toyland," *The New York Times* (December 21, 1994), p. A27; "102 Dead in Thai Factory Fire; Higher Toll Seen," *The New York Times* (May 11, 1993), p. A3; "Thai Factory Fire's 200 Victims Were Locked Inside, Guards Say," *The New York Times* (May 12, 1993), p. A5; Jeffrey Ballinger, "The New Free-Trade Heel," *Harper's Magazine* (August, 1992), pp. 46–47; Geraldine E. Willigan, "High-Performance Marketing: An Interview with Nike's Phil Knight," *Harvard Business Review* (July-August 1992), pp. 91–101; Richard J. Barnet and John Cavanagh, "Just Undo It: Nike's Exploited Workers," *The New York Times* (February 13, 1994), sec. 3, p. 11.

Case 8-2   *Jimmy Fand: The Tile Connection*

Jimmy Fand has built his business from the ground up—literally. A high school dropout in his native Colombia, Fand traveled extensively as a youth and ended up in New York City. After completing his education and working as a teacher, Fand moved with his growing family to Tampa, Florida. Today, Fand is the owner of the Tile Connection, the largest importer of ceramic tile in the United States. As is the case with many other entrepreneurs, Fand's inspiration for starting a business was the result of simple observation. While shopping in Tampa for tile to install in his own home, Fand came to the conclusion that prices were too high and the selection was inadequate. Realizing that this situation represented a market opportunity, Fand set up his own distributorship in Florida and began importing tile.

Because Fand had earned a degree in geology, his expertise helped him as he searched the world for ceramic tile manufacturers that could satisfy his rigorous quality requirements. Fand understood that, to carve out a niche for himself in the local market, he had to offer products that were truly superior. Fand's three criteria for suppliers are quality, availability, and price. Important tile-producing countries include Italy, Spain, Portugal, Colombia, and Brazil. Tile is also manufactured in the United States, but Fand could not find the types of tile he was looking for, and U.S. producers could not maintain a consistent supply of the quantities he needed at a competitive price. Fand buys only from manufacturers that are reliable and capable of meeting his quality standards. For example, after assessing nearly 1,000 tile producers in Italy and Spain alone, Fand concluded that fewer than 100 factories were capable of meeting his standards.

Before starting the Tile Connection, Fand gained considerable experience and wisdom through his involvement in other business ventures. He knows that market research can give him an edge on competitors and endeavors to understand what styles of tile are likely to be popular with his customers. Fand has also learned that high overhead can be fatal to a business and that proper money management and strict financial controls are crucial. Fand takes pride in the excellent credit rating that he has built up with his vendors. When buying goods abroad, many small importers are required to open a letter of credit (L/C), which is a document stating that a bank has substituted its creditworthiness for that of the importer. The manufacturers from whom Fand buys no longer require L/Cs. Such trust does not come automatically in a business relationship; it must be earned. Fand's practice is to pay bills on time. "That, to me, is sacred," Fand says. "That money doesn't belong to us, it belongs to the suppliers who in turn need it to pay their employees." When paying, Fand makes sure that bank-to-bank transfers are carried out on the day bills are due.

Strict attention to financial considerations is not Fand's only concern. Because his business is international in scope, he has to pay particular attention to the logistics of transporting fragile tile from his far-flung network of suppliers. Fand takes advantage of containerization, a modern form of transportation technology with steel trailers measuring 20 feet, 40 feet, or longer. To minimize breakage and protect the tiles, Fand requires that his manufacturers ship the tiles on special tilt-resistant pallets with special corner beads. Once the pallets are loaded in containers, the containers are sealed and transferred via truck or rail to a port in the country of manufacture. The tiles then make the trip to Tampa by ocean-going freighter. After a local customs broker clears the containers for entry into the United States, they are shipped to the Tile Connection's warehouse. There, Fand inspects each container to make sure the seals have not been tampered with.

In Fand's view, it is easier than ever to conduct business abroad. He notes that the United States is surrounded by friendly nations and that other countries are only hours away by airplane or seconds away by telephone or fax machine. Still, many American business owners are reluctant to become importers or exporters. Some are held back by a lack of knowledge of market opportunities abroad, and others simply have misconceptions about those markets. Fand explains, "The more we look for international places to deal with, the more chances of success we can have. We can sell our products to those people as well as buy their products and distribute them as I do." Many U.S. business owners speak only English and believe this is an obstacle to doing business abroad. Fand points out that the U.S. Commerce Department, local Chambers of Commerce, and private organizations have qualified translators available to facilitate business relationships.

Despite the fact that such resources are readily available, Fand knows from experience that it takes a major investment of managerial time to succeed in any business, especially an international one. "Prospective importers should be cautious about who they deal with. Go to trade shows, meet manufacturers and agents that represent those manufacturers as well. You need to do a lot of homework in finding out the products you need to buy, and whether or not they are good products for your marketplace," Fand advises. Prospective importers must learn to identify and eliminate from consideration any factories that do not maintain quality controls. The other side of the equation for importers is understanding the needs of the local market and customers. Fand monitors the Florida market closely and attempts to stay ahead of competitors by anticipating the types and styles of tile that will be in demand.

Fand is proud of his business success, and he knows he has earned it himself through hard work. "I'm self-made," he says. "A lot of people are used to getting things for free, but only those who work hard for those things are able to appreciate them." But he also knows there are important things in life besides work. What does he value the most? He reflects, "The ability to be a human being. To think in terms of the needs of others. To create, to raise your family with very high standards, and to raise them with a high degree of education." ∎

DISCUSSION QUESTIONS

1. What are some of the nuts and bolts of exporting and importing discussed in Chapter 8 that are relevant to Jimmy Fand and the Tile Connection?
2. What must a small-business owner be willing to do to succeed in global business?

3. Describe Jimmy Fand's sense of social responsibility and what ethics means to him.

Chapter 9

Global Market Entry Strategies: Licensing, Investment, and Strategic Alliances

AT&T, America's largest telecommunications company, spent the 1990s trying to expand its presence outside the United States. The goal was to provide AT&T's corporate customers with communications services and networks in all parts of the world. Typically, AT&T formed partnerships with national telecommunications companies. For example, WorldPartners began in 1993 as an alliance of AT&T, Kokusai Denshin Daiwa (KDD) of Japan, and Telecom of Singapore. By 1998, WorldPartners comprised 10 companies, including Telecom New Zealand, Telestra (Australia), Hong Kong Telecom, and Unisource. Unisource, in turn, was itself a joint venture that originally included Sweden's Telia AB, Swiss Telecom PTT, and PTT Telecom Netherlands. In 1995, Telefonica de España became an equal equity partner in Unisource. Unisource and AT&T then agreed to form a 60–40 joint venture known as AT&T-Unisource Communications services to offer voice, data, and messaging services to businesses with European operations.

Despite these efforts, industry observers used words such as *indecisive* and *unfocused* when describing AT&T's approach to entering global markets. After joining AT&T in November 1997, new chairman C. Michael Armstrong quickly set about the task of bolstering AT&T's loose collection of alliances and joint ventures. Simply put, AT&T did not have ownership or control of the networks or their operating facilities and was therefore not in a position to guarantee the high level of service customers demand. Armstrong's response was an ambitious new 50–50 joint venture with British Telecommunications PLC (BT), Britain's largest telephone company. The new company would be an independently run operation with projected first-year revenues of $11 billion. Its main businesses would be voice and data services, wholesale transmission and capacity, and full service communications for global

Twenty years after a federal judge ordered the breakup of the Bell system, AT&T is being transformed once again. After spinning off AT&T Wireless in 2001, chief executive C. Michael Armstrong is set to implement a merger of AT&T Broadband with rival Comcast. The restructured AT&T will be focused on two markets: residential long distance and business services. These are difficult times for telecommunications companies: The industry is in turmoil as a result of the dot-com implosion and the worldwide economic slowdown.

companies. The deal was welcome news at BT, which had previously formed an alliance called Concert based on a 20 percent investment in MCI. However, BT executives had just watched their new strategy for globalization—a proposed merger with MCI—unravel at the last minute, thanks to a rival bid from WorldCom.

The saga of AT&T and BT in the global marketplace illustrates the fact that every firm, at various points in its history, faces a broad range of strategy alternatives. In many cases, executives fail to appreciate the range of alternatives open to them and therefore employ only one strategy—often to their grave disadvantage. The same executives also fail to consider the strategy alternatives open to their competitors and thereby set themselves up to be victims of the dreaded Titanic syndrome—the thud in the night that comes without warning and sinks the ship. AT&T's existence was not in question at the time, but there were clear signs that the company was adrift. In this instance, it took a management change plus the arrival on the scene of an attractive alliance partner to set the stage. The AT&T-BT alliance is intended to get the company back on course.

Some companies are making the decision to go global for the first time; other companies are seeking to expand their share of world markets. Companies in either situation face the same basic sourcing issues introduced in the previous chapter. Companies must also address issues of marketing and value chain management before deciding to enter or expand their share of global markets by means of licensing or some form of direct investment. The particular market entry strategy company executives choose will depend on their vision, attitude toward risk, how much investment capital is available, and how much control is sought.

Licensing can be defined as a contractual arrangement whereby one company (the licensor) makes an asset available to another company (the licensee) in exchange for royalties, license fees, or some other form of compensation.[1] The licensed asset may be a patent, trade secret, brand name and product formulation, or company name. Licensing is a global market entry and expansion strategy with considerable appeal. A company with advanced technology, know-how, or a strong brand image can use licensing agreements to supplement its bottom-line profitability with little initial investment. Licensing is also an ideal way to circumvent tariffs, quotas, or similar export barriers discussed in Chapter 8. Licensing can offer an attractive return on investment for the life of the agreement, provided that the necessary performance clauses are in the contract. The only cost is signing the agreement and policing its implementation.

Sanofi SA, a French pharmaceutical company, has pursued a licensing strategy with great success. Drug research is extremely expensive; although it ranks only 25th in the industry, Sanofi has dozens of drugs under development, with each program costing as much as $400 million. Sanofi's chief executive turns to rivals such as Bristol-Myers Squibb to help fund the research; licensees are then permitted to market the new drugs in return for royalties of up to 15 percent of total sales.[2] Licensing was also the cornerstone of Pilkington's market expansion strategy. In the 1950s, after seven years of research and an investment of $21 million, the British company developed a process innovation that dramatically lowered the cost of producing high-quality plate glass for the automotive and building industries. In addition to exporting its new "float glass" to dozens of countries, Pilkington licensed its technology to competitors and created a worldwide industry standard. As Richard D'Aveni has noted, this strategy "generated substantial income for Pilkington, helping to assure its continued technological leadership in the industry for decades."[3]

Trademarks can also be the basis for lucrative license deals, as demonstrated by organizations as diverse as Coca-Cola, Disney, the National Basketball Association, and Caterpillar Inc. Coca-Cola and Disney license trademarked names and logos to producers of clothing, toys, and watches for sale throughout the world. In Asia and the Pacific alone, sales of licensed Disney products doubled between 1988 and 1990 and doubled again by 1994. Similarly, there is burgeoning global demand for licensed products bearing the names of professional sports teams. For example, *The Wall Street Journal* recently reported that, between 1987 and 1997, annual sales of National Basketball Association merchandise outside the United States jumped from $10 million to $500 million. Yearly worldwide sales of licensed Caterpillar merchandise are running at $900 million as consumers make a fashion statement with boots, jeans, and handbags bearing the distinctive black-and-yellow Cat label. Stephen Palmer is the head of London-based Overland Ltd., which holds the world-wide license for Cat apparel. He notes, "Even if people here don't know the brand, they have a feeling that they know it. They have seen Caterpillar tractors from an early age. It's subliminal, and that's why it's working."[4]

---

1 Franklin R. Root, *Entry Strategies for International Markets* (New York: Lexington Books, 1994), p. 107.
2 Stephen D. Moore, "French Drug Maker Reaps Profits with Offbeat Strategy," *The Wall Street Journal* (November 14, 1996), p. B4.
3 Richard D'Aveni, *Hypercompetition: Managing the Dynamics of Strategic Maneuvering* (New York: The Free Press, 1994), pp. 59–60.
4 Stefan Fatsis, "European Basketball Sensations Get Dunked in U.S.," *The Wall Street Journal Europe* (November 10, 1997), p. 11; Cecilie Rohwedder and Joseph T. Hallinan, "In Europe, Hot New Fashion for Urban Hipsters Comes from Peoria," *The Wall Street Journal* (August 8, 2001), p. B1.

Licensing is associated with several disadvantages and opportunity costs. The principal disadvantage is that licensing can be a very limited form of participation. By allowing another party to license its technology or know-how, what a company doesn't know can put it at risk. Potential returns from marketing and manufacturing may be lost, and the licensor typically lacks control over the licensee's marketing program. The agreement may have a short life if the licensee develops its own know-how and capability to stay abreast of technology in the licensed product area. Even more distressing, licensees have a troublesome way of turning themselves into competitors or industry leaders. A case in point is Pilkington, which has seen its leadership position in the glass industry erode as Glaverbel, Saint-Gobain, PPG, and other competitors have achieved higher levels of production efficiency and lower costs.[5] Licensing also enables a company to "borrow"—leverage and exploit—another company's resources. In Japan, for example, Meiji Milk produced and marketed Lady Borden premium ice cream under a licensing agreement with Borden Inc. Meiji learned important skills in dairy product processing; as the expiration dates of the licensing contracts drew near, Meiji rolled out its own premium ice cream brands.[6] When Borden tried to market ice cream without Meiji's help, it had problems developing new sales channels.

Perhaps the most famous example of the opportunity costs associated with licensing dates back to the mid-1950s, when Sony cofounder Masaru Ibuka obtained a licensing agreement for the transistor from AT&T's Bell Laboratories. Ibuka dreamed of using transistors to make small, battery-powered radios. However, the Bell engineers with whom he spoke insisted that it was impossible to manufacture transistors that could handle the high frequencies required for a radio; they advised him to try making hearing aids. Undeterred, Ibuka presented the challenge to his Japanese engineers who spent many months improving high-frequency output. Sony was not the first company to unveil a transistor radio; a U.S.-built product, the Regency, featured transistors from Texas Instruments and a colorful plastic case. However, it was Sony's high quality, distinctive approach to styling and marketing savvy that ultimately translated into worldwide success.

Conversely, the *failure* to seize an opportunity to license can also lead to dire consequences. In the mid-1980s, Apple Computer chairman John Sculley decided against a broad licensing program for Apple's famed operating system (OS). Such a move would have allowed other computer manufacturers to produce Mac-compatible units. Meanwhile, Microsoft's growing world dominance in both OS and applications got a boost in 1985 from Windows, which featured a Mac-like graphic interface. Apple sued Microsoft for infringing on its intellectual property; however, attorneys for the software giant successfully argued in court that Apple had in fact shared crucial aspects of its OS without limiting Microsoft's right to adapt and improve it. Belatedly, Apple licensed its operating system, first to Power Computing Corp. in December 1994, then to IBM and Motorola. The Mac clones proved very popular at first; Power Computing shipped 170,000 Macintosh clones in 1996, and IBM sublicensed the operating system to a company in Taiwan that was to produce computers for Asia and Europe. Despite these actions, the global market share for machines running the Mac OS slipped below 5 percent. Apple's introduction of the new iMAC in 1998 helped reverse the company's fortunes; today, there are an estimated eight million Macintosh computers in use worldwide. However, Apple's failure to license its technology in the pre-Windows era arguably cost the company more than $370 billion.

---

[5] Charis Gresser, "A Real Test of Endurance," *Financial Times—Weekend* (November 1–2, 1997), p. 5.
[6] Yumiko Ono, "Borden's Breakup with Meiji Milk Shows How a Japanese Partnership Can Curdle," *The Wall Street Journal* (February 21, 1991), p. B1.

That amount represents the market capitalization of Microsoft, the company that won the operating systems war.

As the Borden and transistor stories make clear, companies may find that the upfront easy money obtained from licensing turns out to be a very expensive source of revenue. To prevent a licensor-competitor from gaining unilateral benefit, licensing agreements should provide for a cross-technology exchange between all parties. At the absolute minimum, any company that plans to remain in business must ensure that its license agreements include a provision for full cross-licensing (i.e., that the licensee shares its developments with the licensor). Overall, the licensing strategy must ensure ongoing competitive advantage. For example, license arrangements can create export market opportunities and open the door to low-risk manufacturing relationships. They can also speed diffusion of new products or technologies.

Special Licensing Arrangements

Contract manufacturing such as that discussed in Case 8-1 requires a global company—Nike, for example—to provide technical specifications to a subcontractor or local manufacturer. The subcontractor then oversees production. Such arrangements offer several advantages. The licensing firm can specialize in product design and marketing, while transferring responsibility for ownership of manufacturing facilities to contractors and subcontractors. Other advantages include limited commitment of financial and managerial resources and quick entry into target countries, especially when the target market is too small to justify significant investment.[7] One disadvantage, as already noted, is that companies may open themselves to public scrutiny and criticism if workers in contract factories are poorly paid or labor in inhumane circumstances.

Franchising is another variation of licensing strategy. A franchise is a contract between a parent company-franchisor and a franchisee that allows the franchisee to operate a business developed by the franchisor in return for a fee and adherence to franchise-wide policies and practices. Franchising has great appeal to local entrepreneurs anxious to learn and apply Western-style marketing techniques. The International Franchising Association's Global Marketing Group (GLOMAK) provides guidance to franchisors that want to expand globally. To Peter Holt, chair of GLOMAK, franchising represents a powerful format with which to develop a global brand; he notes that the technology is forcing companies to respond to international interests.[8] Franchising is a cornerstone of global growth in the fast-food industry. As discussed in Chapter 1, McDonald's global expansion is built on franchising; the company has a business system that can be replicated in multiple country markets and a well-known global brand name. International franchising is also used in the retailing industry. For example, there are more than 1,800 Body Shop stores around the world; 90 percent of the stores are operated by franchisees.

When companies do decide to license, they should sign agreements that anticipate more extensive market participation in the future. Insofar as is possible, a company should keep options and paths open for other forms of market participation. Many of these forms require investment and give the investing company more control than is possible with licensing.

---

7 Root, p. 138.
8 Ralph T. King, Jr., "Quiet Boom: U.S. Service Exports are Growing Rapidly, But Almost Unnoticed," *The Wall Street Journal* (April 21, 1993), p. A6.

After companies gain experience outside the home country via exporting or licensing, the time often comes when executives desire a more extensive form of participation. In particular, the desire to have partial or full ownership of operations outside the home country can drive the decision to invest. **Foreign direct investment** (FDI) figures reflect investment flows out of the home country as companies invest in or acquire plants, equipment, or other assets. Foreign direct investment allows companies to produce, sell, and compete locally in key markets. Examples of FDI abound: United Parcel Service (UPS) plans to invest more than $1 billion in Europe over five years, Ford Motor Company is building a $500 million factory in Thailand, South Korea's LG Electronics purchased a 58 percent stake in Zenith Electronics, and Coca-Cola has spent $600 million on bottling plants in Russia. Each of these represents foreign direct investment.

The final years of the twentieth century were a boom time for cross-border mergers and acquisitions. At the end of 2000, cumulative foreign investment by U.S. companies totaled $1.2 trillion. The top three target countries for U.S. investment were the United Kingdom, Canada, and the Netherlands. Investment in the United States by foreign companies also totaled $1.2 trillion; the United Kingdom, Japan, and the Netherlands were the top three sources of investment.[9] Investment in developing nations also grew rapidly in the 1990s. For example, as noted in Case 2-1, investment interest in Vietnam is increasing, especially in the automobile industry and other sectors critical to the country's economic development. Table 9-1 shows approved FDI for India. Central and Eastern Europe have also attracted a great deal of investment; Table 9-2 summarizes investment in the former Soviet Union. Daewoo Group's investment in the former Soviet bloc is shown in Table 9-3.

Table 9-1
Approved Foreign Direct Investment in India
(Cumulative 1991–96)

COUNTRY	AMOUNT (BILLIONS)
USA	$7.1
UK	1.5
Mauritius	1.3
Japan	1.2

Source: Jonathan Karp, "Japanese Companies Dash into India in Challenge to U.S. Firms' Dominance," *The Wall Street Journal* (March 13, 1997), p. A19.

Table 9-2
Foreign Direct Investment in Former Soviet Union
2000 and 2001 ($Millions)

COUNTRY	2000	2001*
Russia	$2,000	$2,500
Kazakhstan	1,150	1,810
Azerbaijan	500	1,000
Ukraine	594	800
Armenia	150	200
Turkmenistan	100	150
Georgia	101	124
Belarus	90	100
Uzbekistan	73	71
Kyrgyzstan	41	65
Moldova	100	60
Tajikistan	22	19

*projected

Source: Guy Chazan, "For Western Business, Uzbekistan Beckons," *The Wall Street Journal* (November 6, 2001), p. A20.

---

[9] Maria Borga and Raymond J. Mataloni Jr., "Direct Investment Positions for 2000: Country and Industry Detail," *Survey of Current Business* 81, no. 7 (July 2001), pp. 16–29.

The enthusiasm that followed the announcement of the alliance between the two telephone titans was tempered by the realization that similar alliances had posted disappointing results. For example, France Telecom, Deutsche Telekom, and Sprint created Global One to bring international telecommunications services to Volvo, Samsung, SmithKline Beecham, and other global businesses. As part of the deal, Sprint sold 10 percent of its stock to each of its French and German partners. One hurdle for the Brussels-based company has been to integrate the three partners' communication networks into a unified whole. Startup costs have been high, and the need to communicate in three different languages has created some friction among personnel. Early on, lengthy negotiations were required before agreement could be reached about the value each company brought to the venture. A former Global One executive noted, "There is no trust among the partners."

Despite the problems evident at Global One, many industry observers believed the AT&T-BT linkup made sense. Noted the *Financial Times:*

> There is strong industrial logic for a partnership which would result in a high quality, high capacity network with global reach which would give Concert access to the US and better coverage of the Asia Pacific region. AT&T

would have improved access to Europe and would be assured of better network quality.

The new alliance, according to a press release, gives both companies "a single vehicle to provide true end-to-end service for their customers." From the customer's point of view, that means buying "seamless," reliable service from a single corporate entity. Although most expected the new company to be a major force in the market, it was also clear that industry newcomers such as WorldCom and Colt Communications would initially enjoy cost advantages. Technology was an important reason: The upstarts had built state-of-the-art fiber optic networks using technology known as Internet protocol (IP). These were faster and more efficient than systems based on the circuit switching used by AT&T and BT. By joining forces, the two companies could reap economies of scale as they converted to IP. Meanwhile, as the new partners continued to lay the groundwork for their new company, AT&T announced that WorldPartners would be dismantled by the end of 1999. AT&T also indicated it would exercise its contractual right to withdraw from Unisource by July 2000. Unisource had already been weakened earlier in 1997 when Telefonica announced plans to ally itself with Concert.

SOURCES: Gautam Naik and Stephanie N. Mehta, "AT&T and BT to Form World-Wide Alliance," *The Wall Street Journal* (July 27, 1998), p. A3; Tracy Corrigan, "Deal with BT Completes Reformation of Once-Lagging AT&T," *Financial Times* (July 27, 1998), p. 15; Alan Cane, "The Real Thing," *Financial Times* (July 28, 1998), p. 13; Cane, "WorldPartners and Unisource to be Unraveled," *Financial Times* (July 27, 1998), p. 13.

Foreign investments may take the form of minority or majority shares in joint ventures, minority or majority equity stakes in another company, or, as in the case of Sandoz and Gerber, outright acquisition. A company may choose to use a combination of these entry strategies by acquiring one company, buying an equity stake in another, and operating a joint venture with a third. In recent years, for example, UPS has made more than 16 acquisitions in Europe and has also expanded its transportation hubs.

Joint Ventures

A joint venture with a local partner represents a more extensive form of participation in foreign markets than either exporting or licensing. Strictly speaking, a **joint venture** is an entry strategy for a single target country in which the partners share own-

Table 9-3
Daewoo Group Investment in Central/Eastern Europe

COUNTRY	AMOUNT (MILLIONS)
Poland	$1,540
Hungary	198
Romania	654
Czech Republic	200
Uzbekistan	1,860
Russia	195

Source: Matthew Brzezinski, "Daewoo Boldly Invades Old Soviet Bloc," *The Wall Street Journal* (May 7, 1997), p. A14.

ership of a newly-created business entity.[10] This strategy is attractive for several reasons. First and foremost is the sharing of risk. By pursuing a joint venture entry strategy, a company can limit its financial risk as well as its exposure to political uncertainty. Second, a company can use the joint venture experience to learn about a new market environment. If it succeeds in becoming an insider, it may later increase the level of commitment and exposure. Third, joint ventures allow partners to achieve synergy by combining different value chain strengths. One company might have in-depth knowledge of a local market, an extensive distribution system, or access to low-cost labor or raw materials. Such a company might link up with a foreign partner possessing well-known brands or cutting-edge technology, manufacturing know-how, or advanced process applications. A company that lacks sufficient capital resources might seek partners to jointly finance a project. Finally, a joint venture may be the only way to enter a country or region if government bid award practices routinely favor local companies, if import tariffs are high, or if laws prohibit foreign control but permit joint ventures.

Many companies have experienced difficulties when attempting to enter the Japanese market. Anheuser-Busch's experience in Japan illustrates both the interactions of the entry modes discussed so far, as well as the advantages and disadvantages of the joint venture approach. Access to distribution is critical to success in the Japanese market; Anheuser-Busch first entered by means of a licensing agreement with Suntory, the smallest of Japan's four top brewers. Although Budweiser had become Japan's top-selling imported beer within a decade, Bud's market share in the early 1990s was still less than 2 percent. Anheuser-Busch then created a joint venture with Kirin Brewery, the market leader. Anheuser-Busch's 90 percent stake in the venture entitled it to market and distribute beer produced in a Los Angeles brewery through Kirin's channels. Anheuser-Busch also had the option to use some of Kirin's brewing capacity to brew Bud locally. For its part, Kirin was well positioned to learn more about the global market for beer from the world's largest brewer. By the end of the decade, however, Bud's market share hadn't increased and the venture was losing money. On January 1, 2000, Anheuser-Busch dissolved the joint venture and eliminated most of the associated job positions in Japan; it reverted instead to a

---

[10] Root, p. 309.

Table 9-4
Market Entry and Expansion by Joint Venture

COMPANIES INVOLVED	PURPOSE OF JOINT VENTURE
GM (USA), Toyota (Japan)	NUMMI—a jointly operated plant in Freemont, California
GM (USA), Shanghai Automotive Industry (China)	50/50 joint venture to build assembly plant to produce 100,000 midsized sedans for Chinese market beginning in 1997 (total investment of $1 billion)
GM (USA), Hindustan Motors (India)	Joint venture to build up to 20,000 Opel Astras annually (GM's investment $100 million)
GM (USA), governments of Russia and Tatarstan	25/75 joint venture to assemble Blazers from imported parts and, by 1998, to built a full assembly line for 45,000 vehicles (total investment $250 million)
Ford (USA), Mazda (Japan)	Joint operation of a plant in Flat Rock, Michigan
Ford (USA), Mahindra Ltd. (Japan)	50/50 joint venture to build Ford Fiestas in Indian state of Tamil Nadu ($800 million)
Chrysler (USA), BMW (Germany)	50/50 joint venture to build a plant in South America to produce small-displacement 4-cylinder engines ($500 million)

Source: Compiled by authors.

licensing agreement with Kirin. The lesson for consumer products marketers considering market entry in Japan is clear. It may make more sense to give control to a local partner via a licensing agreement rather than making a major investment.[11]

Joint venture investment in the big emerging markets (BEMs) is growing rapidly. China is a case in point; for many companies, the price of market entry is the willingness to pursue a joint venture with a local partner. Procter & Gamble has several joint ventures in China. China Great Wall Computer Group is a joint-venture factory in which IBM is the majority partner with a 51 percent stake. In automotive joint ventures, the Chinese government limits foreign companies to minority stakes. Despite this, Japan's Isuzu Motors has been a joint-venture partner with Jiangling Motors for more than a decade. The venture produces 20,000 pickup trucks and one-ton trucks annually. As indicated in Table 9-4, in 1995 General Motors pledged $1.1 billion for a joint venture with Shanghai Automotive Industry to build Buicks for government and business use. GM was selected after giving high-level Chinese officials a tour of GM's operations in Brazil and agreeing to the government's conditions regarding technology transfer and investment capital.[12] In 1997, GM was chosen by the Chinese government as the sole Western partner in a joint venture in Guangzhou that will build smaller, less expensive cars for the general public. Other global carmakers competing with GM for the project were BMW, Mercedes-Benz, Honda Motor, and Hyundai Motor.

Although Russia is not currently considered a BEM, it represents a huge, barely tapped market for a number of industries. The number of joint ventures is increasing. For example, annual new car sales are expected to reach the 1 million mark by 2002. In 1997, GM became the first Western automaker to begin assembling vehicles in Russia. To avoid hefty tariffs that pushed the street price of an imported Blazer over

[11] Yumiko Ono, "Beer Venture of Anheuser, Kirin Goes Down Drain on Tepid Sales," *The Wall Street Journal* (November 3, 1999), p. A23.
[12] Keith Naughton, "How GM Got the Inside Track in China," *Business Week* (November 6, 1995), pp. 56–57.

Visit the Web site
(if you can read
Russian):
www.elaz.ru
www.vaz.ru

$65,000, GM invested in a 25–75 joint venture with the government of the autonomous Tatarstan republic. Elaz-GM assembled Blazer sport utility vehicles from imported components until the end of 2000. Young Russian professionals were expected to snap up the vehicles as long as the price was less than $30,000. However, after about 15,000 vehicles had been sold, market demand evaporated. At the end of 2001, GM terminated the joint venture.

GM has also launched a venture with AvtoVAZ, the largest carmaker in the former Soviet Union. AvtoVAZ is home to Russia's top technical design center and also has access to low-cost Russian titanium and other materials. GM originally intended to assemble a stripped-down, reengineered car based on its Opel model. However, market research revealed that a "Made in Russia" car would only be acceptable if it sported a very low sticker price; GM had anticipated a price of approximately $15,000. The same research pointed GM toward an opportunity to put the Chevrolet nameplate on a redesigned domestic model, the Niva. With GM's financial aid, the Chevrolet Niva will be launched in fall 2002.[13] In addition to GM, several other automakers are joining with Russian partners. BMW Group AG has already begun the local manufacture of its 5-series sedans; Renault SA is producing Megane and Clio Symbol models at a plant near Moscow. Fiat SpA and Ford also anticipate starting production at joint venture plants. Some other recent joint venture alliances are outlined in Table 9-4.

The disadvantages of joint venturing can be significant. Joint venture partners must share rewards as well as risks. The main disadvantage associated with joint ventures is that a company incurs very significant costs associated with control and coordination issues that arise when working with a partner. (However, in some instances, country-specific restrictions limit the share of capital help by foreign companies.)

A second disadvantage is the potential for conflict between partners. These often arise out of cultural differences, as was the case in a failed $130 million joint venture between Corning Glass and Vitro, Mexico's largest industrial manufacturer. The venture's Mexican managers sometimes viewed the Americans as too direct and aggressive; the Americans believed their partners took too much time to make important decisions.[14] Such conflicts can multiply when there are several partners in the venture. For example, James River's European joint venture, Jamont, was actually a consortium of 13 companies from 10 countries. Major problems included incompatible computer systems and varying measures of production efficiency; Jamont used committees to solve these and other problems as they arose. For example, agreement had to be reached on a standardized table napkin size; for some country markets, the norm was 30 by 30 centimeters; for others, 35 by 35 centimeters was preferred.[15] Conflict can also arise when a joint venture is a source of supply for third-country markets. Disagreements about third-country markets where partners face each other as actual or potential competitors can lead to "divorce." To avoid this, it is essential to work out a plan for approaching third-country markets as part of the venture agreement.

A third issue, also noted in the discussion of licensing, is that a dynamic joint venture partner can evolve into a stronger competitor. Many developing countries are very forthright in this regard. Yuan Sutai, a member of China's Ministry of Electronics Industry, told *The Wall Street Journal*, "The purpose of any joint venture,

---

[13] Gregory L. White, "Off Road: How the Chevy Name Landed on SUV Using Russian Technology," *The Wall Street Journal* (February 20, 2001), pp. A1, A8.

[14] Anthony DePalma, "It Takes More Than a Visa to Do Business in Mexico," *The New York Times* (June 26, 1994), sec. 3, p. 5.

[15] James Guyon, "A Joint-Venture Papermaker Casts Net Across Europe," *The Wall Street Journal* (December 7, 1992), p. B6.

or even a wholly-owned investment, is to allow Chinese companies to learn from foreign companies. We want them to bring their technology to the soil of the People's Republic of China."[16] GM and South Korea's Daewoo Group formed a joint venture in 1978 to produce cars for the Korean market. By the mid-1990s, GM had helped Daewoo improve its competitiveness as an auto producer, but Daewoo chairman Kim Woo-Choong terminated the venture because its provisions prevented the export of cars bearing the Daewoo name.[17]

As one global marketing expert warns, "In an alliance you have to learn skills of the partner, rather than just see it as a way to get a product to sell while avoiding a big investment." Yet, compared with U.S. and European firms, Japanese and Korean firms seem to excel in their ability to leverage new knowledge that comes out of a joint venture. For example, Toyota learned many new things from its partnership with GM—about U.S. supply and transportation and managing American workers—that have been subsequently applied at its Camry plant in Kentucky. However, some American managers involved in the venture complained that the manufacturing expertise they gained was not applied broadly throughout GM. To the extent that this complaint has validity, GM has missed opportunities to leverage new learning. Still, many companies have achieved great successes in joint ventures. Gillette, for example, has used this strategy to introduce its shaving products in the Middle East and Africa.

Investment via Ownership or Equity Stake

The most extensive form of participation in global markets is investment that results in majority or 100 percent ownership. This may be achieved by start-up of new operations, known as *greenfield operations* or *greenfield investment,* or by merger or acquisition of an existing enterprise. According to Thomson Financial Securities Data, worldwide merger and acquisition (M&A) deals worth nearly $3 trillion were struck in 2000. Significantly, about one-third of these were cross-border transactions. M&A activity in Europe and Latin America grew at a faster rate than in the United States. As one might expect after reading the vignette at the beginning of this chapter, the telecommunications industry was among the busiest for M&A worldwide. Ownership requires the greatest commitment of capital and managerial effort and offers the fullest means of participating in a market. Companies may move from licensing or joint venture strategies to ownership in order to achieve faster expansion in a market, greater control, or higher profits. In 1991, for example, Ralston Purina ended a 20-year joint venture with a Japanese company to start its own pet food subsidiary. Monsanto and Bayer AG, the German pharmaceutical company, are two other companies that have also recently disbanded partnerships in favor of wholly-owned subsidiaries in Japan.

If government restrictions prevent majority or 100 percent ownership by foreign companies, the investing company will have to settle for a minority equity stake. In Russia, for example, the government restricts foreign ownership in joint ventures to a 49 percent stake. A minority equity stake may also suit a company's business interests. For example, Samsung was content to purchase a 40 percent stake in computer maker AST. As Samsung manager Michael Yang noted, "We thought 100 percent would be very risky, because any time you have a switch of ownership, that creates a

---

[16] David P. Hamilton, "China, With Foreign Partners' Help, Becomes a Budding Technology Giant," *The Wall Street Journal* (December 7, 1995), p. A10.
[17] "Mr. Kim's Big Picture," *The Economist* (September 16, 1995), pp. 74–75.

Table 9-5
Investment in Equity Stake

INVESTING COMPANY (HOME COUNTRY)	INVESTMENT (SHARE, AMOUNT, DATE)
General Motors (USA)	Suzuki Motor Co. (Japan, 3.5% stake, in 1981; increased to 10%, in 1998; increased to 20%, in 2000)
	Fiat SpA auto unit (Italy, 20% stake, share swap, 2000)
	Saab Automobiles AB (Sweden, 50% stake, $500 million, 1990)
Volkswagen AG (Germany)	Skoda (Czech Republic, 31% stake, $6 billion, 1991; increased to 50.5%, in 1994; currently owns 70% stake)
Ford (USA)	Mazda Motor Corp. (Japan, 25% stake in 1979; increased to 33.4%, $408 million, 1996)
DaimlerChrysler (Germany/USA)	Mitsubishi Motors Corp. (Japan, 34% stake, 2000)
Renault SA (France)	Nissan Motors (Japan, 35% stake, $5 billion, 2000)
Proton (Malaysia)	Lotus Cars (Great Britain, 80% stake, $100 million, 1996)

lot of uncertainty among the employees."[18] In other instances, the investing company may start with a minority stake and then increase its share. In 1991, Volkswagen AG made its first investment in the Czech auto industry by purchasing a 31 percent share in Skoda. By 1995, Volkswagen had increased its equity stake to 70 percent. Similarly, Ford purchased a 25 percent stake in Mazda in 1979; in 1996, Ford spent another $408 million to raise its stake to 33.4 percent.

Large-scale direct expansion by means of establishing new facilities can be expensive and require a major commitment of managerial time and energy. However, political or other environmental factors sometimes dictate this approach. For example, Japan's Fuji Photo Film Company invested hundreds of millions of dollars in the United States after the U.S. government ruled that Fuji was guilty of dumping (i.e. selling photographic paper at substantially lower prices than in Japan). As an alternative to "greenfield" investment in new facilities, acquisition is an instantaneous—and sometimes, less expensive—approach to market entry or expansion. Although full ownership can yield the additional advantage of avoiding communication and conflict of interest problems that may arise with a joint venture or coproduction partner, acquisitions still present the demanding and challenging task of integrating the acquired company into the worldwide organization and coordinating activities.

Tables 9-5, 9-6, and 9-7 provide a sense of how companies in the automotive industry utilize a variety of market entry options discussed previously, including equity stakes, investments to establish new operations, and acquisition.

What is the driving force behind many of these acquisitions? It is globalization. In cases like Gerber, management realizes that the path to globalization cannot be undertaken independently. Management at Helene Curtis Industries came to a similar realization and agreed to be acquired by Unilever. Ronald J. Gidwitz, president and CEO, said, "It was very clear to us that Helene Curtis did not have the capacity to project itself in emerging markets around the world. As markets get larger, that forces the smaller players to take action."[19] Still, management's decision to invest

---

[18] Ross Kerber, "Chairman Predicts Samsung Deal Will Make AST a Giant," *The Los Angeles Times* (March 2, 1995), p. D1.
[19] Richard Gibson and Sara Calian, "Unilever to Buy Helene Curtis for $770 Million," *The Wall Street Journal* (February 19, 1996), p. A3.

Table 9-6

Investment to Establish New Operations

Investing Company (Home Country)	Investment (Location)
Mercedes-Benz AG (Germany)	$300 million auto assembly plant (South Carolina, USA)
Bayerische Motoren Werke AG (Germany)	$400 million auto assembly plant (South Carolina, USA, 1995)
Toyota (Japan)	$3.4 billion manufacturing plant producing Camry, Avalon, and minivan models (Kentucky, USA); $400 million engine plant (West Virginia, USA)

Table 9-7

Market Entry and Expansion by Acquisition

Acquiring Company	Target (Country, Date, Amount)
DaimlerBenz (Germany)	Merger with Chrysler Corporation (USA, 1998, $40 billion)
Volkswagen AG (Germany)	Sociedad Española de Automoviles de Turisme (SEAT, Spain, $600 million, purchase completed in 1990)
BMW (Germany)	Rover (UK, $1.2 billion, 1994)
Ford Motor Company (USA)	Jaguar (UK, $2.6 billion, 1989) Volvo car unit (Sweden, $6.5 billion, 1999)
Paccar (USA)	DAF Trucks (Netherlands, $543 million, 1996)

abroad sometimes clashes with investors' short-term profitability goals. Although this is an especially important issue for publicly held U.S. companies, there is an increasing trend toward foreign investment by U.S. companies. As noted previously, cumulative U.S. direct investment abroad exceeded $1 trillion in 1995.

Several of the advantages of joint ventures also apply to ownership, including access to markets and avoidance of tariff or quota barriers. Like joint ventures, ownership also permits important technology experience transfers and provides a company with access to new manufacturing techniques. For example, the Stanley Works, a tool maker with headquarters in New Britain, Connecticut, has acquired more than a dozen companies since 1986, among them Taiwan's National Hand Tool/Chiro company, a socket wrench manufacturer and developer of a "cold-forming" process that speeds up production and reduces waste. Stanley is now using that technology in the manufacture of other tools. Former chairman Richard H. Ayers presided over the acquisitions and envisioned such global cross-fertilization and "blended technology" as a key benefit of globalization.[20] In 1998, former GE executive John Trani succeeded Ayers as CEO; Trani brought considerable experience with international acquisitions, and his selection was widely viewed as evidence that Stanley intended to boost global sales even more.

---

[20] Louis Uchitelle, "The Stanley Works Goes Global," *The New York Times* (July 23, 1989), sec. 3, pp. 1, 10.

In 1989, the Ford Motor Company acquired Jaguar PLC of Coventry, England, for $2.6 billion. L. Lindsay Halstead, then chairman of Ford of Europe, said the acquisition fulfilled "a longtime strategic objective of entering the luxury car market in a significant way." Ford lacked a high-end luxury model for both the U.S. and European markets, and the company was betting it could leverage an exclusive nameplate by launching a new, less expensive line of Jaguars and selling it to more people. The challenge was to execute this strategy without diminishing Jaguar's reputation; as Daniel Jones, a professor at the University of Cardiff and an auto industry expert, noted, the Ford name is synonymous with "bread and butter" cars. Meanwhile, Ford's Japanese competitors, including Honda, Nissan, and Toyota, pursued a different strategy: They launched new nameplates and upgraded their dealer organizations. In the past decade, status- and quality-conscious car buyers have embraced Lexus, Infiniti, and other new luxury sedans that offer high performance and outstanding dealer organizations.

In 1988, its best sales year before the acquisition, Jaguar sold just under 50,000 cars worldwide. Ford set a production target of 150,000 cars by the end of the 1990s, two-thirds of which would be the lower-priced sporty sedan. Ford executives also expected Jaguar to show a positive cash flow by the end of 1992. Unfortunately, the Jaguar acquisition coincided with the global recession that hurt sales in Japan, Germany, and the United States. To make matters worse, a 10 percent luxury tax imposed in the United States scared off potential buyers. By 1991, Jaguar sales slipped to 25,676 cars. In the face of losses totaling $431 million in 1990 and 1991, Ford scaled back its original end-of-decade volume target to 100,000 cars.

Ford also confronted other challenges. Despite Jaguar's classy image and distinguished racing heritage, the cars were also legendary for their unreliability. Gears sometimes wouldn't shift, headlights wouldn't light, and the brakes sometimes caught fire. Part of the problem could be traced to manufacturing: In 1990, there were 2,500 defects per 100 cars produced. By 1992, that number had been reduced to 500 defects per 100 cars. Even so, in the closely-watched J. D. Power rankings, Jaguar's quality in 1992 was rated just a notch above that of the lowly Yugo. Ironically, die-hard Jaguar loyalists seemed to thrive on the misery associated with owning an unreliable car. In fact, Jaguar clubs in the United States bestowed Cat Bite awards on members with the best tales of woe.

Because Jaguar was arguably one of the world's worst auto-manufacturing operations, Ford invested heavily to update and upgrade Jaguar's plant facilities and improve productivity. As a benchmark, Ford's manufacturing experts knew that German luxury carmakers could build a vehicle in 80 hours; in Japan, the figure was 20 hours. If Jaguar were ever to achieve world-class status, Jaguar's assembly time of 110 hours per car had to be drastically reduced. Jaguar chief executive Sir Nicholas Scheele attacked the quality problem on a number of different fronts. For example, line employees made telephone calls to Jaguar owners who were experiencing problems with their vehicles.

In 1998, amid industry estimates that Ford's total investment had reached $6 billion, Jaguar unveiled its S-type sedan to widespread acclaim. One observer called it a "handsome car, instantly recognizable as a Jaguar, yet totally contemporary." In 2000, Jaguar sold 90,000 cars worldwide. In 2001, the long-awaited "baby Jaguar," the X-type, was launched. Company executives hope to capture a significant share of the entry-level luxury market dominated by the BMW 3-series and another newcomer, the Mercedes C-Class.

SOURCES: Danny Hakim, "Restoring the Heart of Ford," *The New York Times* (November 14, 2001), pp. C1, C6; Haig Simonian, "Jag's Faces for the Future," *Financial Times* (November 7–November 8, 1998), p. 12; Joann S. Lublin and Craig Forman, "Going Upscale: Ford Snares Jaguar, But $2.5 Billion is High Price for Prestige," *The Wall Street Journal* (November 3, 1989), pp. A1, A4; Steven Prokesch, "Jaguar Battle at a Turning Point," *The New York Times* (October 29, 1990), p. C1; Steven Prokesch, "Ford's Jaguar Bet: Payoff Isn't Close," *The New York Times* (April 21, 1992), p. C1; Robert Johnson, "Jaguar Owners Love Company and Sharing Their Horror Stories," *The Wall Street Journal* (September 28, 1993), p. A1.

The alternatives discussed here—licensing, joint ventures, minority or majority equity stake, and ownership—are, in fact, points along a continuum of alternative strategies for global market entry and expansion. The overall design of a company's global strategy may call for combinations of exporting-importing, licensing,

Jaguar's S-type represented the venerable automaker's bid to become a mainstream luxury nameplate and double its North American sales to 80,000 cars each year. In terms of styling, the $45,000 S-type recalls the classic Jaguar designs of the 1950s and 1960s. Worldwide, Jaguar executives hope to quadruple sales from 50,000 units to 200,000 within five years.

joint ventures, and ownership among different operating units. Avon Products uses both acquisition and joint ventures to enter developing markets. Similarly, Jamont, the European paper-products company discussed earlier, utilizes both joint ventures and acquisitions. A company's strategy preference may change over time. For example, Borden Inc. ended licensing and joint venture arrangements for branded food products in Japan and set up its own production, distribution, and marketing capabilities for dairy products. Meanwhile, in nonfood products, Borden has maintained joint venture relationships with Japanese partners in flexible packaging and foundry materials.

It can also be the case that competitors within a given industry pursue different strategies. For example, Cummins Engine and Caterpillar both face very high costs—in the $300 to $400 million range—for developing new diesel engines suited to new applications. However, the two companies vary in their strategic approaches to the world market for engines. Cummins management looks favorably on collaboration; also, the company's relatively modest $6 billion in annual revenues presents financial limitations. Thus, Cummins prefers joint ventures. Indeed, the biggest joint venture between an American company and the Soviet Union linked Cummins with the KamAZ truck company in Tatarstan. The joint venture allowed the Russians to implement new manufacturing technologies while providing Cummins with access to the Russian market. Cummins also has joint ventures in Japan, Finland, and Italy. Management at Caterpillar, by contrast, prefers the higher degree of control that comes with full ownership. The company has spent more than $2 billion in recent years on purchases of Germany's MaK, British enginemaker Perkins, and others. Management believes that it is often less expensive to buy existing firms than to develop new applications independently. Also, Caterpillar is concerned about safeguarding proprietary knowledge that is basic to manufacturing in its core construction equipment business.[21]

---

[21] Peter Marsh, "Engine Makers Take Different Routes," *Financial Times* (July 14, 1998), p. 11.

Gerber Products is the undisputed leader in the U.S. baby food market. Despite a 70 percent market share, Gerber faces a mature market and stagnant growth at home. Because 9 out of 10 of the world's births take place outside the United States, Gerber executives hoped to make international sales a greater part of the company's $1.17 billion in annual revenues. Overall, Gerber's international sales increased 150 percent between 1989 and 1993, from $86.5 million to $216.1 million.

Still, for two decades Gerber's globalization effort had been slowed by a combination of changing market conditions, management inconsistency, and decisions that didn't pay off. Gerber entered the Latin American market in the 1970s, but then closed down operations in Venezuela in the wake of government-imposed price controls. Management's focus on the U.S. market resulted in a series of diversifications into nonfood categories that were not successful. Meanwhile, management was not willing to sacrifice short-term quarterly earnings growth to finance an international effort. As Michael A. Cipollaro, Gerber's former president of international operations, remarked, "If you are going to sow in the international arena today to reap tomorrow, you couldn't have that [earnings] growth on a regular basis." In the 1980s, Gerber pursued a strategy of licensing the manufacture and distribution of its baby food products to other companies. In France, for example, Gerber selected CPC International as a licensee.

Unfortunately, Gerber couldn't force its licensees to make baby food a priority business. In France, for example, baby food represented a meager 2 percent of CPC's European revenues. When CPC closed down its French plant, Gerber had to find another manufacturing source. It bought a stake in a Polish factory, but production was held up for months while quality improvements were made. The delay ended up costing Gerber its market position in France.

Belatedly, Gerber discovered that strong competitors already dominated many markets around the globe. Heinz has about one-third of the $1.5 billion baby food market outside the United States; Gerber's share of the global market is 17 percent. Competitors with less global share than Gerber—including France's BSN Group (15 percent market share), and Switzerland's Nestlé SA (8 percent)—have been aggressively building brand loyalty. In France, for example, parents traveling with infants can get free baby food and diapers through Nestlé's system of roadside changing stations. Another barrier is that many European mothers think homemade baby food is healthier than food from a jar.

Meanwhile, Gerber's global efforts were interrupted by the resignations of several key executives. Cipollaro, the chief of international operations, left, as did the vice president for Europe and the international director of business development. Gerber's management team was forced to rethink its strategy. In May 1994, it agreed to be acquired by Sandoz AG, a $10.3 billion Swiss pharmaceutical and chemical company. As market analyst David Adelman noted, "It was very expensive for Gerber to build business internationally. This was one of the driving reasons why Gerber wanted to team up with a larger company."

Some industry analysts expressed doubts about the logic behind the acquisition. London broker Peter Smith said, "I'm sorry: Baby food and anticancer drugs don't really come together." Nevertheless, the deal gave Gerber immediate access to a global marketing and distribution network that is particularly strong in developing countries such as China and India. Sandoz, which faces expiring patents for some of its most profitable drugs, instantly assumed a strong position in the U.S. nutrition market.

SOURCES: Jennifer Reingold, "The Pope of Basel," *Financial World* (July 18, 1995), pp. 36–38; Margaret Studer, "Sandoz AG is Foraging for Additional Food Holdings," *The Wall Street Journal* (February 21, 1995), p. B4; Richard Gibson, "Growth Formula: Gerber Missed the Boat in Quest to Go Global, So It Turned to Sandoz," *The Wall Street Journal* (May 24, 1994), pp. A1, A7; Leah Rickard and Laurel Wentz, "Sandoz Opens World for Gerber," *Advertising Age* (May 30, 1994), p. 4; Margaret Studer and Ron Winslow, "Sandoz, Under Pressure, Looks to Gerber for Protection," *The Wall Street Journal* (May 25, 1994), p. B3.

In Chapter 8 and the first half of Chapter 9, we surveyed the range of options—exporting, licensing, joint ventures, and ownership—traditionally used by companies wishing either to enter global markets for the first time or to expand their activities beyond present levels. However, recent changes in the political, economic, sociocultural, and technological environments of the global firm have combined to change the relative importance of those strategies. Trade barriers have fallen, markets have globalized, consumer needs and wants have converged, product life cycles have shortened, and new communications technologies and trends have emerged. Although these developments provide unprecedented market opportunities, there are strong strategic implications for the global organization and new challenges for the global marketer. Such strategies will undoubtedly incorporate—or may even be structured around—a variety of collaborations. Once thought of only as joint ventures with the more dominant party reaping most of the benefits (or losses) of the partnership, cross-border alliances are taking on surprising new configurations and even more surprising players.

Why would any firm—global or otherwise—seek to collaborate with another firm, be it local or foreign? For example, despite its commanding 37 percent share of the global cellular handset market, Nokia recently announced that it would make the source code for its proprietary Series 60 software available to competing handset manufacturers such as Siemens AG. Why did Nokia's top executives decide to collaborate, thereby putting the company's competitive advantage with software development (and healthy profit margins) at risk? As noted, a "perfect storm" of converging environmental forces is rendering traditional competitive strategies obsolete. Today's competitive environment is characterized by unprecedented degrees of turbulence, dynamism, and unpredictability; global firms must respond and adapt quickly. To succeed in global markets, firms can no longer rely exclusively on the technological superiority or core competence that brought them past success. In the twenty-first century, firms must look toward new strategies that will enhance environmental responsiveness. In particular, they must pursue "entrepreneurial globalization" by developing flexible organizational capabilities, innovating continuously, and revising global strategies accordingly."[22] Moreover, to be successful in a world of alliances, managers will have to acquire new skills. In the second half of this chapter, we will focus on global strategic partnerships. In addition, we will examine the Japanese *keiretsu* and various other types of cooperation strategies that global firms are using today.

THE NATURE OF GLOBAL STRATEGIC PARTNERSHIPS

The terminology used to describe the new forms of cooperation strategies varies widely. The phrases **collaborative agreements, strategic alliances, strategic international alliances,** and **global strategic partnerships** (GSPs) are frequently used to refer to linkages between companies from different countries to jointly pursue a common goal. A broad spectrum of interfirm agreements, including joint ventures, can be covered by this terminology. However, the strategic alliances discussed here exhibit three characteristics (Figure 9-1).[23]

---

22 Michael A. Yoshino and U. Srinivasa Rangan, *Strategic Alliances: An Entrepreneurial Approach to Globalization* (Boston: Harvard Business School Press, 1995), p. 51.
23 Yoshino and Rangan, p. 5. For an alternative description see Riad Ajami and Dara Khambata, "Global Strategic Alliances: The New Transnationals," *Journal of Global Marketing* 5, no. 1/2, (1991), pp. 55–59.

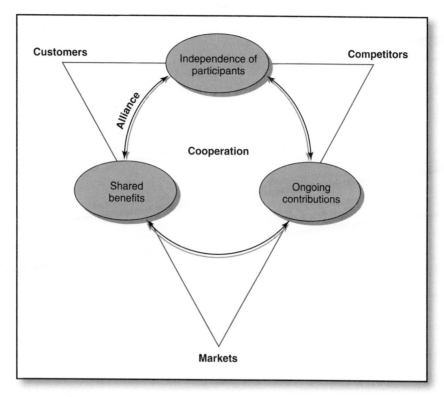

Figure 9-1
Three Characteristics of Strategic Alliances

1. The participants remain independent subsequent to the formation of the alliance.
2. The participants share the benefits of the alliance as well as control over the performance of assigned tasks.
3. The participants make ongoing contributions in technology, products, and other key strategic areas.

According to estimates, the number of strategic alliances has been growing at a rate of 20 to 30 percent since the mid-1980s. The upward trend for GSPs comes in part at the expense of traditional cross-border mergers and acquisitions. Since the mid-1990s, a key force driving partnership formation is the realization that globalization and the Internet will require new inter-corporate configurations. According to data compiled by Thomson Financial, 5,200 new strategic alliances were formed in 1996; that number had almost doubled by 2000.[24] Table 9-8 lists some of the GSPs that have been formed recently.

Roland Smith, chairman of British Aerospace, offers a straightforward reason why a firm would enter into a GSP: "A partnership is one of the quickest and cheapest ways to develop a global strategy."[25] Like traditional joint ventures, GSPs have some disadvantages. Partners share control over assigned tasks, a situation that creates management challenges. Also, there are potential risks associated with strengthening a competitor from another country.

[24] Matthew Schifrin, "Partner or Perish," *Forbes* (May 21, 2001), pp. 26–28.
[25] Main, p. 121.

Table 9-8

Examples of Global Strategic Partnerships

NAME OF ALLIANCE OR PRODUCT AND WEB ADDRESS	MAJOR PARTICIPANTS	PURPOSE OF ALLIANCE
Beverage Partners Worldwide	Coca-Cola and Nestlé	Offer new coffee, tea, and herbal beverage products in "rejuvenation" category
Star Alliance www.star-alliance.com	United Airlines, Air Canada, SAS, Lufthansa, Thai Airways International, and Varig Airlines	Create a global travel network by linking airlines and providing better service for international travelers
Advanced Photo System www.kodak.com/global/en/consumer	Kodak, Fuji Photo Film, Minolta Camera, Canon, and Nikon	Create a new photography system that will enable users to take better pictures

Despite these drawbacks, GSPs are attractive for several reasons. First, high product development costs in the face of resource constraints may force a company to seek partners; this was part of the rationale for Boeing's partnership with a Japanese consortium to develop a new jet aircraft, the 777. Second, the technology requirements of many contemporary products mean that an individual company may lack the skills, capital, or know-how to go it alone.[26] Third, partnerships may be the best means of securing access to national and regional markets. Fourth, partnerships provide important learning opportunities; in fact, one expert regards GSPs as a "race to learn." Professor Gary Hamel of the London Business School has observed that the partner that proves to be the fastest learner can ultimately dominate the relationship.[27]

As noted earlier, GSPs differ significantly from the market entry modes discussed in the first half of the chapter. Because licensing agreements do not call for continuous transfer of technology or skills among partners, such agreements are not strategic alliances.[28] Traditional joint ventures are basically alliances focusing on a single national market or a specific problem. The Chinese joint venture described previously between GM and Shanghai Automotive fits this description; the basic goal is to make cars for the Chinese market. A true global strategic partnership is different; it is distinguished by the following five attributes:[29]

1. Two or more companies develop a joint long-term strategy aimed at achieving world leadership by pursuing cost-leadership, differentiation, or a combination of the two.
2. The relationship is reciprocal. Each partner possesses specific strengths that it shares with the other; learning must take place on both sides.
3. The partners' vision and efforts are truly global, extending beyond home countries and the home regions to the rest of the world.

---

26 Kenichi Ohmae, "The Global Logic of Strategic Alliances," *Harvard Business Review* 67, no. 2 (March-April 1989), p. 145.
27 Main, p. 122.
28 Michael A. Yoshino and U. Srinivasa Rangan, *Strategic Alliances: An Entrepreneurial Approach to Globalization* (Boston: Harvard Business School Press, 1995), p. 6.
29 Howard V. Perlmutter and David A. Heenan, "Cooperate to Compete Globally," *Harvard Business Review* 64, no. 2 (March-April 1986), p. 137.

4. The relationship is organized along horizontal, not vertical, lines. Continual transfer of resources laterally between partners is required, with technology sharing and resource pooling representing norms.
5. When competing in markets excluded from the partnership, the participants retain their national and ideological identities.

Motorola's Iridium program embodied several prerequisites that experts believe are the hallmarks of good alliances (see Case 11-3). First, Motorola formed an alliance to exploit a unique strength, namely, its leadership in wireless communications. Second, the Iridium alliance partners all possessed unique strengths of their own. Third, it was unlikely that any of the partners had the ability or the desire to acquire Motorola's unique strength. Finally, rather than focusing on a particular market or product, Iridium was an alliance based upon skills, know-how, and technology.

SUCCESS FACTORS

Assuming that a proposed alliance meets these five prerequisites, it is necessary to consider six basic factors deemed to have significant impact on the success of GSPs: mission, strategy, governance, culture, organization, and management.[30]

1. *Mission.* Successful GSPs create win-win situations, where participants pursue objectives on the basis of mutual need or advantage.
2. *Strategy.* A company may establish separate GSPs with different partners; strategy must be thought out up front to avoid conflicts.
3. *Governance.* Discussion and consensus must be the norms. Partners must be viewed as equals.
4. *Culture.* Personal chemistry is important, as is the successful development of a shared set of values. The failure of a partnership between Great Britain's General Electric Company and Siemens AG was blamed in part on the fact that the former was run by finance-oriented executives, the latter by engineers.
5. *Organization.* Innovative structures and designs may be needed to offset the complexity of multicountry management.
6. *Management.* GSPs invariably involve a different type of decision making. Potentially divisive issues must be identified in advance and clear, unitary lines of authority established that will result in commitment by all partners.

Companies forming GSPs must keep these factors in mind. Moreover, successful collaborators will be guided by the following four principles. First, despite the fact that partners are pursuing mutual goals in some areas, partners must remember that they are competitors in others. Second, harmony is not the most important measure of success—some conflict is to be expected. Third, all employees, engineers, and managers must understand where cooperation ends and competitive compromise begins. Finally, as noted earlier, learning from partners is critically important.[31]

The issue of learning deserves special attention. As one team of researchers notes,

> The challenge is to share enough skills to create advantage vis-à-vis companies outside the alliance while preventing a wholesale transfer of core skills to the partner. This is a very thin line to walk. Companies must carefully select what skills and technologies they pass to their partners. They must

---

30 Perlmutter and Heenan, p. 137.
31 Gary Hamel, Yves L. Doz, and C. K. Prahalad, "Collaborate with Your Competitors—and Win." *Harvard Business Review* 67, no. 1 (January-February 1989), pp. 133–139.

develop safeguards against unintended, informal transfers of information. The goal is to limit the transparency of their operations.[32]

Alliances with Asian Competitors

Western companies may find themselves at a disadvantage in GSPs with an Asian competitor, especially if the latter's manufacturing skills are the attractive quality. Unfortunately for Western companies, manufacturing excellence represents a multifaceted competence that is not easily transferred. Non-Asian managers and engineers must also learn to be more receptive and attentive—they must overcome the "not-invented-here" syndrome and begin to think of themselves as students, not teachers. At the same time, they must learn to be less eager to show off proprietary lab and engineering successes. To limit transparency, some companies involved in GSPs establish a "collaboration section." Much like a corporate communications department, this department is designed to serve as a gatekeeper through which requests for access to people and information must be channeled. Such gatekeeping serves an important control function that guards against unintended transfers.

A 1991 report by McKinsey and Company shed additional light on the specific problems of alliances between Western and Japanese firms.[33] Often, problems between partners had less to do with objective levels of performance than with a feeling of mutual disillusionment and missed opportunity. The study identified four common problem areas in alliances gone wrong. The first problem was that each partner had a "different dream"; the Japanese partner saw itself emerging from the alliance as a leader in its business or entering new sectors and building a new basis for the future; the Western partner sought relatively quick and risk-free financial returns. Said one Japanese manager, "Our partner came in looking for a return. They got it. Now they complain that they didn't build a business. But that isn't what they set out to create."

A second area of concern is the balance between partners. Each must contribute to the alliance and each must depend on the other to a degree that justifies participation in the alliance. The most attractive partner in the short run is likely to be a company that is already established and competent in the business with the need to master, say, some new technological skills. The best long-term partner, however, is likely to be a less competent player or even one from outside the industry.

Another common cause of problems is "frictional loss," caused by differences in management philosophy, expectations, and approaches. All functions within the alliance may be affected, and performance is likely to suffer as a consequence. Speaking of his Japanese counterpart, a Western businessperson said, "Our partner just wanted to go ahead and invest without considering whether there would be a return or not." The Japanese partner stated that "the foreign partner took so long to decide on obvious points that we were always too slow." Such differences often lead to frustration and time-consuming debates that stifle decision making.

Last, the study found that short-term goals can result in the foreign partner limiting the number of people allocated to the joint venture. Those involved in the venture may perform only two- or three-year assignments. The result is "corporate amnesia," that is, little or no corporate memory is built up on how to compete in Japan. The original goals of the venture will be lost as each new group of managers takes their turn. When taken collectively, these four problems will almost ensure that the Japanese partner will be the only one in it for the long haul.

---

[32] Hamel, Doz, Prahalad, p. 136.
[33] Kevin K. Jones and Walter E. Schill, "Allying for Advantage," *The McKinsey Quarterly* no. 3, (1991), pp. 73–101.

CFM International, GE, and SNECMA: A Success Story

Commercial Fan Moteur (CFM) International, a partnership between GE's jet engine division and Snecma, a government-owned French aerospace company, is a frequently cited example of a successful GSP. GE was motivated, in part, by the desire to gain access to the European market so it could sell engines to Airbus Industrie; also, the $800 million in development costs was more than GE could risk on its own. While GE focused on system design and high-tech work, the French side handled fans, boosters, and other components. Today the company has more than 300 commercial and military customers worldwide including Boeing, Airbus, and the United States Air Force. In 2000, the partnership generated sales of $6.7 billion.

The alliance got off to a strong start because of the personal chemistry between two top executives, GE's Gerhard Neumann and the late General René & Ravaud of Snecma. The partnership thrives despite each side's differing views regarding governance, management, and organization. Brian Rowe, senior vice president of GE's engine group, has noted that the French like to bring in senior executives from outside the industry, whereas GE prefers to bring in experienced people from within the organization. Also, the French prefer to approach problem solving with copious amounts of data, and Americans may take a more intuitive approach.[34] Still, senior executives from both sides of the partnership have been delegated substantial responsibility.

AT&T and Olivetti: A Failure

In theory, the partnership in the mid-1980s between AT&T and Italy's Olivetti appeared to be a winner: The collective mission was to capture a major share of the global market for information processing and communications.[35] Olivetti had what appeared to be a strong presence in the European office equipment market; AT&T executives, having just presided over the divestiture of their company's regional telephone units, had set their sights on overseas growth with Europe as the starting point. AT&T promised its partner $260 million and access to microprocessor and telecommunications technology. The partnership called for AT&T to sell Olivetti's personal computers in the United States; Olivetti, in turn, would sell AT&T computers and switching equipment in Europe. Underpinning the alliance was the expectation that synergies would result from the pairing of companies from different industries: communications and computers.

Unfortunately, that vision was nothing more than a hope: There was no real strength in Olivetti in the computer market, and Olivetti had no experience or capability in communications equipment. Tensions ran high when sales did not reach expected levels. AT&T group executive Robert Kavner cited communication and cultural differences as important factors leading to the breakdown of the alliance. "I don't think we or Olivetti spent enough time understanding behavior patterns," Kavner said. "We knew the culture was different but we never really penetrated. We would get angry, and they would get upset."[36] In 1989, AT&T cashed in its Olivetti stake for a share in the parent company Compagnie Industriali Riunite SpA (CIR). In 1993, citing a decline in CIR's value, AT&T sold its remaining stake.

---

[34] Bernard Wysocki, "Global Reach: Cross Border Alliances Become Favorite Way to Crack New Markets," *The Wall Street Journal* (March 26, 1990), p. A12.
[35] Perlmutter and Heenan, p. 145.
[36] Wysocki, p. A12.

Boeing and Japan: A Controversy

In some circles, GSPs have been the target of criticism. Critics warn that employees of a company that becomes reliant on outside suppliers for critical components will lose expertise and experience erosion of their engineering skills. Such criticism is often directed at GSPs involving U.S. and Japanese firms. For example, a proposed alliance between Boeing and a Japanese consortium to build a new fuel-efficient airliner, the 7J7, generated a great deal of controversy. The project's $4 billion price tag was too high for Boeing to shoulder alone. The Japanese were to contribute between $1 billion and $2 billion; in return, they would get a chance to learn manufacturing and marketing techniques from Boeing. Although the 7J7 project was shelved in 1988, a new widebody aircraft, the 777, was developed with about 20 percent of the work subcontracted out to Mitsubishi, Fuji, and Kawasaki.[37]

Critics envision a scenario in which the Japanese use what they learn to build their own aircraft and compete directly with Boeing in the future—a disturbing thought since Boeing is a major exporter to world markets. One team of researchers has developed a framework outlining the stages that a company can go through as it becomes increasingly dependent on partnerships:[38]

Stage One: Outsourcing of assembly for inexpensive labor
Stage Two: Outsourcing of low-value components to reduce product price
Stage Three: Growing levels of value-added components move abroad
Stage Four: Manufacturing skills, designs, and functionally related technologies move abroad
Stage Five: Disciplines related to quality, precision-manufacturing, testing, and future avenues of product derivatives move abroad
Stage Six: Core skills surrounding components, miniaturization, and complex systems integration move abroad
Stage Seven: Competitor learns the entire spectrum of skills related to the underlying core competence

Yoshino and Rangan have described the interaction and evolution of the various market entry strategies in terms of cross-market dependencies (Figure 9-2).[39] Many firms start with an export-based approach as described in Chapter 8. For example, the striking success of Japanese firms in the automobile and consumer electronics industries can be traced back to an export drive. Nissan, Toyota, and Honda initially concentrated production in Japan, thereby achieving economies of scale. Eventually, an export-driven strategy gives way to an affiliate-based one. The various types of investment strategies described previously—equity stake, investment to establish new operations, acquisitions, and joint ventures—create operational interdependence within the firm. By operating in different markets, firms have the opportunity to transfer production from place to place, depending on exchange rates, resource costs, or other considerations. Although at some companies, foreign affiliates operate as autonomous fiefdoms (the prototypical multinational business with a polycentric orientation), other companies realize the benefits that operational flexibility can bring. The third and most complex stage in the evolution of a global strategy comes with management's realization that full integration and a network of shared knowl-

---

37 John Holusha, "Pushing the Envelope at Boeing," *The New York Times* (November 10, 1991), sec. 3, pp. 1, 6.
38 David Lei and John W. Slocum Jr., "Global Strategy, Competence-Building and Strategic Alliances," *California Management Review* 35, no. 1 (Fall 1992), pp. 81–97.
39 Michael A. Yoshino and U. Srinivasa Rangan, *Strategic Alliances: An Entrepreneurial Approach to Globalization* (Boston: Harvard Business School Press, 1995), pp. 56–59.

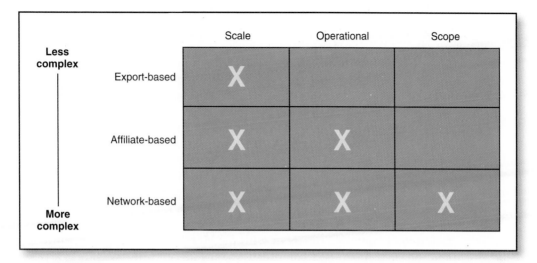

Figure 9-2
Evolution and Interaction of Entry Strategies

Source: Adapted from Michael A. Yoshino and U. Srinivasa Rangan, *Strategic Alliances: An Entrepreneurial Approach to Globalization* (Boston: Harvard Business School Press, 1995), p. 51.

edge from different country markets can greatly enhance the firm's overall competitive position. As implied by Figure 9-2, as company personnel opt to pursue increasingly complex strategies, they must simultaneously manage each new interdependency as well as preceding ones. The stages described here are reflected in the evolution of Taiwan's Acer Group as described in Case 1-2.

INTERNATIONAL PARTNERSHIPS IN DEVELOPING COUNTRIES

Central and Eastern Europe, Asia, India, and Mexico offer exciting opportunities for firms that seek to enter gigantic and largely untapped markets. An obvious strategic alternative for entering these markets is the strategic alliance. Like the early joint ventures between U.S. and Japanese firms, potential partners will trade market access for know-how. Other entry strategies are also possible, of course; in 1996, for example, Chrysler and BMW agreed to invest $500 million in a joint venture plant in Latin America capable of producing 400,000 small engines annually. While then-Chrysler chairman Robert Eaton was skeptical of strategic partnerships, he believed that limited forms of cooperation such as joint ventures make sense in some situations. Eaton said, "The majority of world vehicle sales are in vehicles with engines of less than 2.0 liters, outside of the United States. We have simply not been able to be competitive in those areas because of not having a smaller engine. In the international market, there's no question that in many cases such as this, the economies of scale suggest you really ought to have a partner."[40]

Assuming that risks can be minimized and problems overcome, joint ventures in the transition economies of Central and Eastern Europe could evolve at a more

---

[40] Angelo B. Henderson, "Chrysler and BMW Team Up to Build Small-Engine Plant in South America," *The Wall Street Journal* (October 2, 1996), p. A4.

accelerated pace than past joint ventures with Asian partners. A number of factors combine to make Russia an excellent location for an alliance: There is a well-educated workforce, and quality is very important to Russian consumers. However, several problems are frequently cited in connection with joint ventures in Russia; these include organized crime, supply shortages, and outdated regulatory and legal systems in a constant state of flux. Despite the risks, the number of joint ventures in Russia is growing, particularly in the services and manufacturing sectors. In the early-post Soviet era, most of the manufacturing ventures were limited to assembly work, but higher value-added activities such as component manufacture are now being performed.

A Central European market with interesting potential is Hungary. Hungary already has the most liberal financial and commercial system in the region. It has also provided investment incentives to Westerners, especially in high-tech industries. Like Russia, this former communist economy has its share of problems. Digital's recent joint venture agreement with the Hungarian Research Institute for Physics and the state-supervised computer systems design firm Szamalk is a case in point. Although the venture was formed so Digital would be able to sell and service its equipment in Hungary, the underlying importance of the venture was to stop the cloning of Digital's computers by Central European firms.

COOPERATIVE STRATEGIES IN JAPAN: *KEIRETSU*

Japan's *keiretsu* represent a special category of cooperative strategy. A *keiretsu* is an interbusiness alliance or enterprise group that, in the words of one observer, "resembles a fighting clan in which business families join together to vie for market share."[41] *Keiretsu* exist in a broad spectrum of markets, including the capital market, primary goods markets, and component parts markets.[42] *Keiretsu* relationships are often cemented by bank ownership of large blocks of stock and by cross-ownership of stock between a company and its buyers and nonfinancial suppliers. Further, *keiretsu* executives can legally sit on each other's boards, share information, and coordinate prices in closed-door meetings of "presidents' councils." Thus, *keiretsu* are essentially cartels that have the government's blessing. While not a market entry strategy per se, *keiretsu* played an integral role in the international success of Japanese companies as they sought new markets.

Some observers have disputed charges that *keiretsu* have an impact on market relationships in Japan and claim instead that the groups primarily serve a social function. Others acknowledge the past significance of preferential trading patterns associated with *keiretsu* but assert that the latter's influence is now weakening. Although it is beyond the scope of this chapter to address these issues in detail, there can be no doubt that, for companies competing with the Japanese or wishing to enter the Japanese market, a general understanding of *keiretsu* is crucial. Imagine, for example, what it would mean in the United States if an automaker (e.g., GM), an electrical products company (e.g., GE), a steelmaker (e.g., USX), and a computer firm (e.g., IBM) were interconnected, rather than separate, firms. Global competition in

---

[41] Robert L. Cutts, "Capitalism in Japan: Cartels and Keiretsu," *Harvard Business Review* 70, no. 4 (July-August 1992), p. 49.
[42] Michael L. Gerlach, "Twilight of the *Keiretsu*? A Critical Assessment," *Journal of Japanese Studies* 18, no. 1 (Winter 1992), p. 79.

the era of *keiretsu* means that competition exists not only among products, but between different systems of corporate governance and industrial organization.[43]

As the hypothetical example from the United States suggests, some of Japan's biggest and best-known companies are at the center of *keiretsu*. For example, several large companies with common ties to a bank are at the center of the Mitsui Group and Mitsubishi Group. These two, together with the Sumitomo, Fuyo, Sanwa, and DKB groups make up the "big six" *keiretsu* (in Japanese, *roku dai kigyo shudan* or six big industrial groups). The big six strive for a strong position in each major sector of the Japanese economy; because intra-group relationships often involve shared stock-holdings and trading relations, the big six are sometimes known as *horizontal keiretsu*.[44] Annual revenues in each group are in the hundreds of billions of dollars. In absolute terms, *keiretsu* constitute a small percentage of all Japanese companies. However, these alliances can effectively block foreign suppliers from entering the market and result in higher prices to Japanese consumers, while at the same time resulting in corporate stability, risk sharing, and long-term employment. The Mitsubishi Group's *keiretsu* structure is shown in detail in Figure 9-3.

In addition to the big six, several other *keiretsu* have formed, bringing new configurations to the basic forms described previously. *Vertical* (i.e., supply and distribution) *keiretsu* are hierarchical alliances between manufacturers and retailers. For example, Matsushita controls a chain of 25,000 National stores in Japan through which it sells its Panasonic, Technics, and Quasar brands. About half of Matsushita's domestic sales are generated through the National chain, 50 to 80 percent of whose inventory consists of Matsushita's brands. Japan's other major consumer electronics manufacturers, including Toshiba and Hitachi, have similar alliances. (Sony's chain of stores is much smaller and weaker by comparison.) All are fierce competitors in the Japanese market.[45]

Another type of manufacturing *keiretsu* consists of vertical hierarchical alliances between automakers and suppliers and component manufacturers. Intergroup operations and systems are closely integrated, with suppliers receiving long-term contracts. Toyota, for example, has a network of about 175 primary and 4,000 secondary suppliers. One supplier is Koito; Toyota owns about one-fifth of Koito's shares and buys about half of its production. The net result of this arrangement is that Toyota produces about 25 percent of the sales value of its cars, compared with 50 percent for GM. Manufacturing *keiretsu* show the gains that can result from an optimal balance of supplier and buyer power. Because Toyota buys a given component from several suppliers (some are in the *keiretsu*, some are independent), discipline is imposed down the network. Also, since Toyota's suppliers do not work exclusively for Toyota, they have an incentive to be flexible and adaptable.[46]

The *keiretsu* system ensured that high-quality parts were delivered on a just-in-time basis, a key factor in the high quality for which Japan's auto industry is well known. However, as U.S. and European automakers have closed the quality gap, larger Western parts makers are building economies of scale that enable them to operate at lower costs than small Japanese parts makers. Moreover, the stock holdings that Toyota, Nissan, and others have in their supplier network ties up capital

---

[43] Ronald J. Gilson and Mark J. Roe, "Understanding the Japanese Keiretsu: Overlaps Between Corporate Governance and Industrial Organization," *The Yale Law Journal* 102, no. 4 (January 1993), p. 883.

[44] Kenichi Miyashita and David Russell, *Keiretsu: Inside the Hidden Japanese Conglomerates* (New York: McGraw-Hill, 1996), p. 9.

[45] The importance of the chain stores is eroding due to increasing sales at mass merchandisers not under the manufacturers' control.

[46] "Japanology, Inc.-Survey," *The Economist* (March 6, 1993), p. 15.

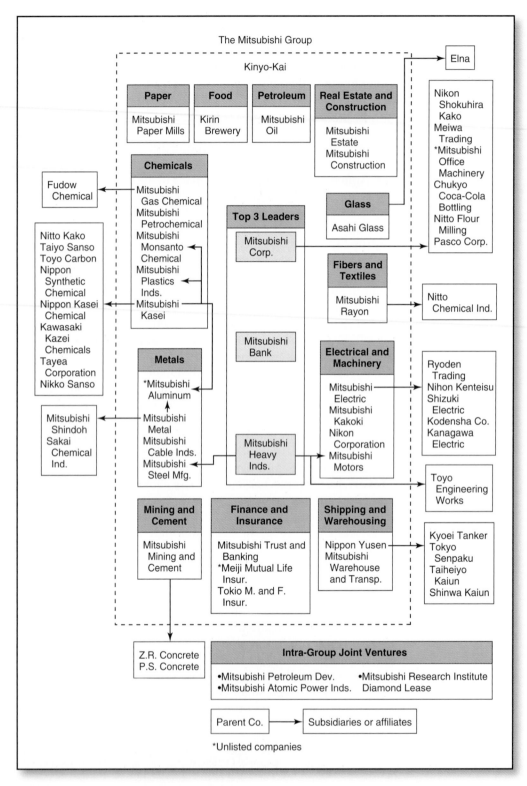

Figure 9-3
Mitsubishi Group's *Keiretsu* Structure

Source: Courtesy of the Mitsubishi Group, from Collins and Doorley, *Teaming Up for the 90s*
(Deloitte & Touche, 1991).

that could be used for product development and other purposes. At Nissan, for example, a new management team from France recently began divesting some of the company's 1,300 *keiretsu* investments.[47]

Some observers have questioned whether *keiretsu* violate antitrust laws. As many observers have noted, the Japanese government frequently puts the interests of producers ahead of the interests of consumers. In fact, the *keiretsu* were formed in the early 1950s as regroupings of four large conglomerates—*zaibatsu*—that dominated the Japanese economy until 1945. *Zaibatsu* were dissolved after the occupational forces introduced antitrust as part of the reconstruction. Today, Japan's Fair Trade Commission appears to favor harmony rather than pursuing anticompetitive behavior. As a result, the U.S. Federal Trade Commission has launched several investigations of price fixing, price discrimination, and exclusive supply arrangements. Hitachi, Canon, and other Japanese companies have also been accused of restricting the availability of high-tech products in the U.S. market. The Justice Department has considered prosecuting the U.S. subsidiaries of Japanese companies if the parent company is found guilty of unfair trade practices in the Japanese market.[48]

How *Keiretsu* Affect American Business: Two Examples

Clyde Prestowitz provides the following example to show how *keiretsu* relationships have a potential impact on U.S. businesses. In the early 1980s, Nissan was in the market for a supercomputer to use in car design. Two vendors under consideration were Cray, the worldwide leader in supercomputers at the time, and Hitachi, which had no functional product to offer. When it appeared that the purchase of a Cray computer was pending, Hitachi executives called for solidarity; both Nissan and Hitachi were members of the same big six *keiretsu,* the Fuyo group. Hitachi essentially mandated that Nissan show preference to Hitachi, a situation that rankled U.S. trade officials. Meanwhile, a coalition within Nissan was pushing for a Cray computer; ultimately, thanks to U.S. pressure on both Nissan and the Japanese government, the business went to Cray.

Prestowitz describes the Japanese attitude toward this type of business practice:[49]

> . . . It respects mutual obligation by providing a cushion against shocks. Today Nissan may buy a Hitachi computer. Tomorrow it may ask Hitachi to take some of its redundant workers. The slightly lesser performance it may get from the Hitachi computer is balanced against the broader considerations. Moreover, because the decision to buy Hitachi would be a favor, it would bind Hitachi closer and guarantee slavish service and future Hitachi loyalty to Nissan products. . . . This attitude of sticking together is what the Japanese mean by the long-term view; it is what enables them to withstand shocks and to survive over the long term.[50]

Because *keiretsu* relationships are crossing the Pacific and directly affecting the American market, U.S. companies have reason to be concerned with *keiretsu* outside the Japanese market as well. According to 1991 data compiled by Dodwell

---

[47] Norihiko Shirouzu, "U-Turn: A Revival at Nissan Shows There's Hope for Ailing Japan Inc.," *The Wall Street Journal* (November 16, 2000), pp. A1, A10.
[48] Rapoport, p. 84.
[49] For years, Prestowitz has argued that Japan's industry structure—*keiretsu* included—gives its companies unfair advantages. A more moderate view might be that any business decision must have an economic justification. Thus, a moderate would caution against overstating the effect of *keiretsu.*
[50] Clyde Prestowitz, *Trading Places: How We Are Giving Our Future to Japan and How to Reclaim It* (New York: Basic Books, 1989), pp. 299–300.

Marketing Consultants, in California alone *keiretsu* own more than half of the Japanese-affiliated manufacturing facilities. But the impact of *keiretsu* extends beyond the West Coast. Illinois-based Tenneco Automotive, a maker of shock absorbers and exhaust systems, does a great deal of worldwide business with the Toyota *keiretsu*. In 1990, however, Mazda dropped Tenneco as a supplier to its U.S. plant in Kentucky. Part of the business was shifted to Tokico Manufacturing, a Japanese transplant and a member of the Mazda *keiretsu*; a non-*keiretsu* Japanese company, KYB Industries, was also made a vendor. A Japanese auto executive explained the rationale behind the change: "First choice is a *keiretsu* company, second choice is a Japanese supplier, third is a local company."[51]

COOPERATIVE STRATEGIES IN SOUTH KOREA: *CHAEBOL*

South Korea has its own type of corporate alliance groups, known as *chaebol*. Like the Japanese *keiretsu*, *chaebol* are composed of dozens of companies, centered around a central bank or holding company, and dominated by a founding family. However, *chaebol* are a more recent phenomenon; in the early 1960s, Korea's military dictator granted government subsidies and export credits to a select group of companies. By the 1980s, Daewoo, Hyundai, LG, and Samsung had become leading producers of low-cost consumer electronics products. The *chaebol* were a driving force behind South Korea's economic miracle; GNP increased from $1.9 billion in 1960 to $238 billion in 1990. Since the economic crisis of 1997, however, South Korean president Kim Dae Jung has pressured *chaebol* leaders to initiate reform. Prior to the crisis, the *chaebol* had become bloated and heavily leveraged; recently, some progress has been made in improving corporate governance, changing corporate cultures, and reducing debt levels.[52]

COOPERATIVE STRATEGIES IN THE UNITED STATES: TARGETING THE DIGITAL FUTURE

Increasing numbers of U.S. companies are entering into alliances that resemble *keiretsu*. In fact, the phrase *digital keiretsu* is frequently used to describe alliances between companies in several industries—computers, communications, consumer electronics, and entertainment—that are undergoing transformation and convergence. These processes are the result of tremendous advances in the ability to transmit and manipulate vast quantities of audio, video, and data and the rapidly approaching era of an electronic "superhighway" in the United States composed of fiber optic cable and digital switching equipment.

One U.S. technology alliance, Sematech, is unique in that it is the direct result of government industrial policy. The U.S. government, concerned that key companies in the domestic semiconductor industry were having difficulty competing with Japan, agreed to subsidize a consortium of 14 technology companies beginning in 1987. Sematech was comprised of 700 employees, some permanent and some on loan from IBM, AT&T, Advanced Micro Devices, Intel, and other companies. The task facing the consortium was to save the U.S. chipmaking equipment industry, whose

---

[51] Carla Rappoport, "Why Japan Keeps on Winning," *Fortune* (July 15, 1991), p. 84.
[52] "The Chaebol Spurn Change," *The Economist* (July 27, 2000), pp. 59–60.

manufacturers were rapidly losing market share in the face of intense competition from Japan. Although initially plagued by attitudinal and cultural differences between different factions, Sematech eventually helped chipmakers try new approaches with their equipment vendors. By 1991, the Sematech initiative, along with other factors such as the economic downturn in Japan, reversed the market share slide of the semiconductor equipment industry.

Sematech's creation heralded a new era in cooperation among technology companies. As the company has expanded internationally, its membership roster has expanded to include Agere Systems, Conexant, Hewlett-Packard, Hynix, Infineon, Motorola, Philips, STMicroelectronics, and Taiwan Semiconductor. Companies in a variety of industries are pursuing similar types of alliances. For example, Lufthansa Cargo is developing a worldwide air-freight, parcel-express, and logistics network in partnership with Singapore Airlines, SAS, and Deutsche Post. The alliance will offer airport-to-airport, door-to-door, and business-to-business services; its creation was based on the reality that customers are no longer looking for pure transportation services. Rather, they are seeking innovative solutions to complex logistics requirements.[53] Likewise, Japan's Nikko Hotels International and the London-based Le Meridien Hotels & Resorts formed an alliance in 2000 in an effort to compete more effectively with such global hotel giants as Starwood and Marriott. Nikko has few hotels in Europe, and Le Meridien lacks a significant presence in Asia. The alliance represents an attractive strategic alternative to committing significant resources toward building new properties; the partners' sales teams will channel business to each other's hotel groups when appropriate.[54]

Beyond Strategic Alliances

The "relationship enterprise" is said to be the next stage of evolution of the strategic alliance. Groupings of firms in different industries and countries, they will be held together by common goals that encourage them to act almost as a single firm. Cyrus Freidheim, vice chairman of the Booz, Allen, & Hamilton consulting firm, recently outlined an alliance that, in his opinion, might be representative of an early relationship enterprise. He suggests that, within the next few decades, Boeing, British Airways, Siemens, TNT, and Snecma might jointly build several new airports in China. As part of the package, British Airways and TNT would be granted preferential routes and landing slots, the Chinese government would contract to buy all its aircraft from Boeing/Snecma, and Siemens would provide air traffic control systems for all ten airports.[55]

More than the simple strategic alliances we know today, relationship enterprises will be super-alliances among global giants, with revenues approaching $1 trillion. They would be able to draw on extensive cash resources, circumvent antitrust barriers, and, with home bases in all major markets, enjoy the political advantage of being a "local" firm almost anywhere. This type of alliance is not driven simply by technological change, but by the political necessity of having multiple home bases.

Another perspective on the future of cooperative strategies envisions the emergence of the "virtual corporation." As described in a recent *Business Week* cover story, the virtual corporation "will seem to be a single entity with vast capabilities but will really be the result of numerous collaborations assembled only when they're

---

[53] Michael A. Taverna, "Lufthansa Spearheads Alliances in Freight, Express and Logistics," *Aviation Week & Space Technology* (August 27, 2001), pp. 58–60.

[54] Christina Binkley, "Nikko Hotels and Le Meridien Expand Alliance into Japan," *Asian Wall Street Journal Weekly* (August 13–19, 2001), p. 15.

[55] "The Global Firm: R.I.P.," *The Economist* (February 6, 1993), p. 69.

needed."[56] On a global level, the virtual corporation could combine the twin competencies of cost effectiveness and responsiveness; thus, it could pursue the "think globally, act locally" philosophy with ease. This reflects the trend toward "mass customization." The same forces that are driving the formation of the digital *keiretsu*—high-speed communication networks, for example—are embodied in the virtual corporation. As noted by William Davidow and Michael Malone in their book *The Virtual Corporation,* "The success of a virtual corporation will depend on its ability to gather and integrate a massive flow of information throughout its organizational components and intelligently act upon that information."[57]

One of the hallmarks of the virtual corporation will be the production of "virtual products"—a product that practically exists before it is manufactured. As described by Davidow and Malone, the concept, design, and manufacture of virtual products are stored in the minds of cooperating teams, in computers, and in flexible production lines. Finland's Nokia, a $25 billion global company that is the world's leading mobile telephone manufacturer, opted for an experimental virtual approach when entering the U.S. market for high-end computer monitors in 1992. Nokia Display Products Inc. started with only seven employees who, in conjunction with several independent partners, were responsible for marketing, distributing, and servicing the monitors. Annual sales of $170 million in the early years exceeded expectations in Helsinki.[58] Among the company's latest product offerings is the Nokia Pro 800+, a flat-screen display that carries a price tag of $3,395.

Why has the virtual corporation suddenly burst onto the scene? Previously, firms lacked the technology to facilitate this type of data management. Today's distributed databases, networks, and open systems make possible the kinds of data flow required for the virtual corporation. In particular, these data flows permit "supply-chain management." Ford provides an interesting example of how technology is improving information flows among the farflung operations of a single company. Ford's $6 billion "world car"—known as the Mercury Mystique and Ford Contour in the United States, the Mondeo in Europe—was developed using an international communications network linking computer workstations of designers and engineers on three continents.[59]

MARKET EXPANSION STRATEGIES

Companies must decide whether to expand by seeking new markets in existing countries or, alternatively, seeking new country markets for already identified and served market segments.[60] These two dimensions in combination produce four strategic options, as shown in Table 9-9. Strategy 1 concentrates on a few segments in a few countries. This is typically a starting point for most companies. It matches company resources and market investment needs. Unless a company is large and endowed with ample resources, this strategy may be the only realistic way to begin.

---

[56] John Byrne, "The Virtual Corporation," *Business Week* (February 8, 1993), p. 103.

[57] William Davidow and Michael Malone, *The Virtual Corporation: Structuring and Revitalizing the Corporation for the 21st* Century (New York: HarperBusiness, 1993), p. 59.

[58] Ralph T. King, "The Company We Don't Keep," *The Wall Street Journal* (November 18, 1996), p. R22.

[59] Julie Edelson Halpert "One Car, Worldwide, with Strings Pulled from Michigan," *The New York Times* (August 29, 1993), sec. 3, p. 7.

[60] This section draws on I. Ayal and J. Zif, "Market Expansion Strategies in Multinational Marketing," *Journal of Marketing* 43 (Spring 1979), pp. 84–94; and "Competitive Market Choice Strategies in Multinational Marketing," *Columbia Journal of World Business* (Fall 1978), pp. 72–81.

Table 9-9
Market Expansion
Strategies

		MARKET	
		CONCENTRATION	DIVERSIFICATION
COUNTRY	Concentration	1. Narrow Focus	2. Country Focus
	Diversification	3. Country Diversification	4. Global Diversification

In Strategy 2, country concentration and segment diversification, a company serves many markets in a few countries. This strategy was implemented by many European companies that remained in Europe and sought growth by expanding into new markets. It is also the approach of the American companies that decide to diversify in the U.S. market as opposed to going international with existing products or creating new global products. According to the U.S. Department of Commerce, more than 80 percent of U.S. companies that export limit their sales to five or fewer markets. This means that the majority of U.S. companies are pursuing Strategies 1 or 2.

Strategy 3, country diversification and market segment concentration, is the classic global strategy whereby a company seeks out the world market for a product. The appeal of this strategy is that, by serving the world customer, a company can achieve a greater accumulated volume and lower costs than any competitor and therefore have an unassailable competitive advantage. This is the strategy of the well-managed business that serves a distinct need and customer category.

Strategy 4, country and segment diversification, is the corporate strategy of a global, multibusiness company such as Matsushita. *Overall*, Matsushita is multicountry in scope and its various business units and groups serve multiple segments. Thus, at the level of corporate strategy, Matsushita may be said to be pursuing Strategy 4. At the operating business level, however, managers of individual units must focus on the needs of the world customer in their particular global market. In Table 9-9, this is Strategy 3—country diversification and market segment concentration. An increasing number of companies all over the world are beginning to see the importance of market share not only in the home or domestic market but also in the world market. Success in overseas markets can boost a company's total volume and lower its cost position.

SUMMARY

Companies that wish to move beyond exporting and importing can avail themselves of a wide range of alternative market entry strategies. Each alternative has distinct advantages and disadvantages associated with it; the alternatives can be ranked on a continuum representing increasing levels of investment, commitment, and risk. **Licensing** can generate revenue flow with little new investment; it can be a good choice for a company that possesses advanced technology, a strong brand image, or valuable intellectual property. **Contract manufacturing** and **franchising** are two specialized forms of licensing that are widely used in global marketing.

A higher level of involvement outside the home country may involve **foreign direct investment.** This can take many forms. **Joint ventures** offer two or more companies the opportunity to share risk and combine value chain strengths. Companies considering joint ventures must plan carefully and communicate with partners to avoid "divorce." Foreign direct investment can also be used to establish company operations outside the home country through **greenfield investment,** acquisition of an minority or majority **equity stake** in a foreign business, or taking **ownership** of an existing business entity through merger or outright acquisition.

Cooperative alliances known as **global strategic partnerships** (GSPs) represent an important market entry strategy in the twenty-first century. GSPs are ambitious, reciprocal, cross-border alliances that may involve business partners in a number of different country markets. GSPs are particularly well suited to emerging markets in Central and Eastern Europe, Asia, and Latin America. Western businesspeople should also be aware of two special forms of cooperation found in Asia, namely Japan's *keiretsu* and South Korea's *chaebol.*

To assist managers in thinking through the various alternatives, market expansion strategies can be represented in matrix form: **country and market concentration, country concentration and market diversification, country diversification and market concentration,** and **country and market diversification.** The preferred expansion strategy will be a reflection of a company's stage of development (i.e., whether it is international, multinational, global, or transnational). The Stage 5 transnational combines the strengths of these three stages into an integrated network to leverage worldwide learning.

DISCUSSION QUESTIONS

1. What are the advantages and disadvantages of using licensing as a market entry tool? Give examples of companies from different countries that use licensing as a global marketing strategy.
2. The president of XYZ Manufacturing Company of Buffalo, New York, comes to you with a license offer from a company in Osaka. In return for sharing the company's patents and know-how, the Japanese company will pay a license fee of 5 percent of the ex-factory price of all products sold based on the U.S. company's license. The president wants your advice. What would you tell him?
3. What is foreign direct investment (FDI)? What forms can FDI take?
4. Do you agree with Ford's decision to acquire Jaguar? What was more valuable to Ford—the physical assets or the name?
5. What is meant by the phrase *global strategic partnership*? In what ways does this form of market entry strategy differ from more traditional forms such as joint ventures?
6. What are *keiretsu*? How does this form of industrial structure affect companies that compete with Japan or that are trying to enter the Japanese market?
7. Which strategic options for market entry or expansion would a small company be likely to pursue? A large company?

SUGGESTED READINGS

Books

Bleeke, Joel, and David Ernst. *Collaborating to Compete.* Somerset, New Jersey: John Wiley & Sons, 1991.

Cauley de la Sierra, Margaret. *Managing Global Alliances: Key Steps for Successful Collaboration.* Reading, MA: Addison-Wesley Publishing Company, 1995.

Contractor, Farok, and Peter Lorange. *Cooperative Strategies in International Business.* Cambridge, MA: Ballinger, 1987.

Davidow, William H., and Michael S. Malone. *The Virtual Corporation.* New York: HarperBusiness, 1993.

Doorley, Thomas L. III. *Teaming Up for the '90s: A Guide to International Joint Ventures and Strategic Alliances.* New York: Business One Irwin, 1991.

Doz, Yves L., and Gary Hamel. *Alliance Advantage: The Art of Creating Value Through Partnering.* Cambridge: Harvard Business School Press, 1998.

Gerlach, Michael L. *Alliance Capitalism: The Social Organization of Japanese Business.* Berkeley: University of California Press, 1992.

Harbison, John R., and Peter Pekar. *Smart Alliances: A Practical Guide to Repeatable Success.* San Francisco: Jossey-Bass, 1998.

James, Harvey S., and Murray L. Weidenbaum. *When Businesses Cross International Borders: Strategic Alliances and Their Alternatives*. Westport, Conn.: Praeger, 1993.

Lorange, Peter, and Johan Roose. *Strategic Alliances: Formation, Implementation and Evolution*. Cambridge, Mass.: Blackwell, 1992.

Miyashita Kenichi, and David Russell. *Keiretsu: Inside the Hidden Japanese Conglomerates*. New York: McGraw-Hill, 1996.

Oster, Sharon. *Modern Competitive Analysis*. New York: Oxford University Press, 1990.

Prestowitz, Clyde V. Jr. *Trading Places: How We Are Giving Our Future to Japan and How to Reclaim It*. New York: Basic Books, 1989.

Robert, Michel. *Strategy Pure and Simple: How Winning CEOs Outthink Their Competition*. New York: McGraw-Hill, 1993.

Root, Franklin R. *Entry Strategies for International Markets*. New York: Lexington Books, 1994.

Starr, Martin Kenneth. *Global Corporate Alliances and the Competitive Edge: Strategies and Tactics for Management*. New York: Quorum Books, 1991.

Yip, George S. *Total Global Strategy: Managing for Worldwide Competitive Advantage*. Englewood Cliffs, New Jersey: Prentice Hall, 1992.

Yoshino, Michael Y., and U. Srinivasa Rangan. *Strategic Alliances: An Entrepreneurial Approach to Globalization*. Boston: Harvard Business School Press, 1995.

Articles

Agarwal, Sanjeev. "Socio-Cultural Distance and the Choice of Joint Venture: A Contingency Perspective." *Journal of International Marketing* 2, no. 2 (1994), pp. 63–80.

———, and Sridhar N. Ramaswami. "Choice of Foreign Market Entry Mode: Impact of Ownership, Location and Internalization Factors." *Journal of International Business Studies* 23, no. 1 (First Quarter 1992), pp. 1–27.

Ali, Abbas J., and Robert C. Camp. "The Relevance of Firm Size and International Business Experience to Market Entry Strategies." *Journal of Global Marketing* 6, no. 4 (1993), pp. 91–112.

Atuahene-Gime, Kwaku. "International Licensing of Technology: An Empirical Study of the Differences between Licensee and Non-Licensee Firms." *Journal of International Marketing* 1, no. 2 (1993), pp. 71–88.

Beamish, Paul W. "The Characteristics of Joint Ventures in the People's Republic of China." *Journal of International Marketing* 1, no. 2 (1993), pp. 29–48.

Chang, Sea-Jin, and Philip M. Rosenzweig. "The Choice of Entry Mode in Foreign Direct Investment." *Strategic Management Journal* 22, no. 8 (August 2001), pp. 747–776.

Egelhoff, William G. "Great Strategy or Great Strategy Implementation—Two Ways of Competing in Global Markets." *Sloan Management Review* 34, no. 2 (Winter 1993), pp. 37–50.

Fey, Carl F., and Paul W. Beamish. "Strategies for Managing Russian International Joint Venture Conflict." *European Management Journal* 17, no. 1 (February 1999), pp. 99–106.

Hamel, Gary, and C. K. Prahalad. "Do You Really Have A Global Strategy?" *Harvard Business Review* 63, no. 4 (July-August 1985), pp. 139–148.

Hemphill, Thomas A. "Airline Marketing Alliances and U.S. Competition Policy: Does the Consumer Benefit?" *Business Horizons* 43, no. 2 (March-April 2000), pp. 17–24.

Hill, Charles W. L., Peter Hwang, and W. Chan Kim. "An Eclectic Theory of the Choice of International Entry Mode." *Strategic Management Journal* 11, no. 2 (March-April 1990), pp. 117–128.

Hwang, Peter, William P. Burgers, and W. Chan Kim. "Global Diversification Strategy and Corporate Profit Performance." *Strategic Management Journal* 10, no. 1 (January-February 1989), pp. 45–57.

Kim, W. Chan, and Peter Hwang. "Global Strategy and Multinationals' Entry Mode Choice." *Journal of International Business Studies* 23, no. 1 (1992), pp. 29–54.

Kotabe, Masaaki, Arvind Sahay, and Preet S. Aulakh, "Emerging Role of Technology Licensing in the Development of Global Product Strategy: Conceptual Framework and Research Propositions." *Journal of Marketing* 60, no. 1 (January 1996), pp. 73–88.

Lamming, Richard. "Japanese Supply Chain Relationships in Recession." *Long Range Planning* 33, no. 6 (December 2000), pp. 757–778.

Lin, Xiaohua, and Richard Germain. "Sustaining Satisfactory Joint Venture Relationships: The Role of Conflict Resolution Strategy." *Journal of International Business Studies* 29, no. 1 (1998), pp. 179–196.

Lorange, Peter, and Johan Roos. "Why Some Strategic Alliances Succeed and Others Fail." *Journal of Business Strategy* 12, no. 1 (January-February 1991), pp. 25–30.

Madhok, Anoop. "Revisiting Multinational Firms' Tolerance for Joint Ventures: A Trust-Based Approach." *Journal of International Business Studies* 26, no. 1 (1995), pp. 117–138.

McDougall, Patricia. "New Venture Strategies: An Empirical Identification of Eight 'Archetypes' of Competitive Strategies for Entry." *Strategic Management Journal* 11, no. 6 (October 1990), pp. 447–467.

Morrison, Allen J., and Kendall Roth. "A Taxonomy of Business-Level Strategies in Global Industries."

Strategic Management Journal 13, no. 6 (September 1992), pp. 399–417.

Nair, Ajit S., and Edwin R. Stafford. "Strategic Alliances in China: Negotiating the Barriers." *Long Range Planning* 31, no. 1 (February 1998), pp. 139–146.

Osland, Gregory E. "Successful Operating Strategies in the Performance of U.S.-China Joint Ventures." *Journal of International Marketing* 32, no. 4 (1994), pp. 53–78.

Reuer, Jeffrey. "The Dynamics and Effectiveness of International Joint Ventures." *European Management Journal* 16, no. 2 (April 1998), pp. 160–168.

Schill, Ronald L., and David N. McArthur. "Redefining the Strategic Competitive Unit: Towards a New Global Marketing Paradigm?" *International Marketing Review* 9, no. 3 (1992), pp. 5–24.

Schoemaker, Paul J. H. "How to Link Strategic Vision to Core Capabilities." *Sloan Management Review* 34, no. 1 (Fall 1992), pp. 67–81.

Shama, Avraham. "Entry strategies of U.S. Firms to the Newly Independent States, Baltic States, and Eastern European countries." *California Management Review* 37 (Spring 1995), pp. 90–109.

Steensma, H. Kevin, and Marjorie A. Lyles. "Explaining IJV Survival in a Transitional Economy Through Social Exchange and Knowledge-based Perspectives." *Strategic Management Journal* 21, no. 8 (August 2000), pp. 831–851.

Yavas, Ugur, Dogan Eroglu, and Sevgin Eroglu. "Sources and Management of Conflict: The Case of Saudi-U.S. Joint Ventures." *Journal of International Marketing* 2, no. 3 (1994), pp. 61–82.

CASES

Case 9-1 Federal Express Encounters Turbulence in the Global Package Express Business

Federal Express achieved extraordinary success in the 1970s with a pioneering approach to overnight letter and package distribution in the United States. After many successful years of serving customers with the pledge "When it absolutely, positively has to get there overnight," FedEx's growth in the United States slowed considerably. One problem was arch-competitor United Parcel Service, which started overnight package deliveries in 1982. In addition, the increasing popularity of fax machines began to erode demand for overnight letter delivery. Accordingly, founder Frederick Smith began to look abroad for new growth opportunities.

International delivery services had been part of Smith's strategic plan since the early 1980s. Between 1983 and 1990, FedEx made more than 20 international acquisitions, including courier services and trucking operations. Unfortunately, strong overseas rivals such as DHL Worldwide Express and Australia-based TNT were becoming entrenched in Europe at the same time. Another problem was foreign government regulations. For example, Japanese regulators took steps to protect local express companies. It took three years of negotiations before FedEx could get permission to make four flights a week from Memphis to Tokyo. Then, in May 1988, just days before service to Japan was to begin, FedEx was informed that no packages weighing more than 70 pounds could be flown into Tokyo, even if they were en route to other destinations. The result: FedEx lost more than a million dollars per month on the Tokyo route for a year.

In December 1988, Smith announced his intention to acquire Tiger International, the world's biggest air heavy-cargo company, which included the Flying Tiger Line. FedEx gained delivery routes in North and South America that it could service with its own airplanes plus Flying Tiger's fleet of long-range aircraft for use in the international heavy-freight industry. Tiger also provided FedEx with additional routes in Europe. Although the price tag was steep—$880 million—Smith believed that the acquisition was an important step toward his goal of making FedEx "the largest and best transportation company in the world." This statement said a lot about Smith's ambitions. In fact, *Business Week* magazine concluded that, of all the factors contributing to the success of FedEx, the most important might well be Smith's over-whelming desire to be number one. As Smith confidently proclaimed in 1988: "We consider our international business to be as important as our domestic business."

However, the Tiger acquisition brought with it a number of challenges. First, the move more than doubled FedEx's debt, to $2.1 billion. Second, Tiger's system was designed for slow-moving heavy freight—a sharp contrast to FedEx's high-speed network for handling small packages. A third problem: DHL and TNT seemed likely to follow FedEx's lead and make their own acquisitions to expand globally. Finally, and perhaps most important, FedEx stood to lose customers that had traditionally used Flying Tiger. Some of these customers, such as UPS and DHL World Airways, were actually FedEx's competitors in the overseas express delivery business. They relied on Tiger for shipping to countries where they had no airport landing rights.

A related issue concerned freight forwarders, companies with no airplanes or trucks that contract with customers to provide door-to-door delivery of shipments anywhere in the world. Freight forwarders booked space in planes and ships, took care of paperwork, hired trucks, and took care of all the red tape. In the United States, FedEx's door-to-door service put most domestic freight forwarders out of business. In the international markets served by Flying Tiger, however, cultural and political factors helped preserve the freight forwarding industry. Thus, FedEx had to reassure such customers that it would not encroach on their business, lest freight forwarders work with another carrier. Some industry observers expected passenger lines like Northwest and American Airlines to seek business from disgruntled freight forwarders.

Despite these hurdles, FedEx had gained the ability to operate in all 12 countries of the European Community and was thus well positioned to take advantage of reduced restrictions on surface transportation companies that were expected in 1992. The acquisition meant FedEx could seek additional growth overseas faster than if it tried to develop the foreign business on its own, especially in Asia.

Still, Federal had to change some parts of its formula to meet the needs of its new markets. For example, headquarters designated a 5 p.m. deadline for pickups on the European continent, even though it is customary in

Table 1

Carrier	U.S. Shipments (%)	U.S. Exports (%)	Logistics Services
FedEx	44	30.0	Logistics Division
UPS	27	10.0	UPS Worldwide Logistics
DHL	2	13.5	World Wide Express Logistics
Airborne Express	17	2.0	

Source: Adapted from data in Lisa Coleman, "Overnight Isn't Fast Enough," *Brandweek* (July 31, 1995), pp. 26–27.

Spain for employees to work until 8 p.m. Also, all of FedEx's brochures and shipping bills were available only in English, a situation that has only recently been addressed. In general, overnight delivery has not been nearly as popular in Europe as it has in the United States. One symbol of the European pace: FedEx became owner of a German-based barge business, and barges painted with FedEx's distinctive orange and purple colors could be seen floating down the Rhine carrying salad oil.

By 1992, it became clear that the European market was much harder to crack than Smith had thought. Losses from four years of operations totaled $1.2 billion, forcing a cost-cutting campaign. About 6,600 employees were fired, and FedEx operations in 100 cities across Europe were closed. Some of its delivery business between the United States and Europe was contracted out to other firms. Meanwhile, rivals UPS and DHL began picking up some of FedEx's former customers.

What went wrong? Besides the fierce competitive rivalry, Smith concedes he overestimated the size of the market, expecting daily shipment volume to approach the U.S. level of three million units. In anticipation of this growth, Smith set up an operations center in Brussels that duplicated the hub-and-spokes approach that had been at the heart of the company's U.S. success. Unfortunately, the volume of European express shipments leveled off at about 100,000 units per day. Many of the planes in FedEx's fleet flew their routes with partial loads. To address this problem, Smith began to de-

emphasize the heavy cargo business and focus on the more lucrative small package overnight business. Also, he replaced some of the company's older 747 cargo jets with smaller, more efficient aircraft; the resulting savings on the Hong Kong-Anchorage route alone could amount to $12 million.

Meanwhile, the nature of the express delivery business was changing. DHL had begun offering "same day" delivery in the late 1980s; FedEx launched a similar service in June 1995. The global opportunities for package delivery and related services were huge; in 1994, the United States accounted for only 5 percent of the market, or a total of 61 million of the 1.1 billion industry shipments. DHL's global strength could be inferred from the fact that only about 25 percent of its 95 million shipments were generated in the United States. DHL, FedEx, and UPS all stressed technology as ways to differentiate themselves from each other. All three companies offered PC software that allowed customers to track their packages from desktop computers. In March 1995, FedEx became the first of the three to have a home page on the World Wide Web from which customers could obtain information and order pickups. All three companies offered logistics support to companies seeking assistance with warehousing and mail-order distribution. FedEx Vice President Robert Miller noted, "Our industry has become central to how companies do business, and they are putting within our hands increasingly larger parts of their business." ∎

DISCUSSION QUESTIONS

1. Why did FedEx decide to "go global"? Do you agree with the decision?
2. Evaluate FedEx's European entry strategy. What mistakes did management make?
3. Formulate a new European entry strategy for FedEx.
4. What are the future prospects for FedEx, DHL, and UPS around the world?

SOURCES: Lisa Coleman, "Overnight Isn't Fast Enough," *Brandweek* (July 31, 1995), pp. 26–27; Donna Rosato, "FedEx Displays Ability to Deliver," *USA Today* (March 16, 1994), p. 3B; Chuck Hawkins, "FedEx: Europe Nearly Killed the

Messenger," *Fortune* (May 25, 1992), pp. 124, 126; Daniel Pearl, "Innocents Abroad: Federal Express Finds Its Pioneering Formula Falls Flat Overseas," *The Wall Street Journal* (April 15, 1991), p. A1; Dean Foust, "Mr. Smith Goes Global," *Business Week* (February 13, 1989), pp. 66–69, 72; Larry C. White, "Federal Express: Managing Ahead for 1992 Is Risky," *Business Month* (August 1989), pp. 32–34;

Rick Christie, "Federal Express Needs a Lift Overseas after Expansion," *The Wall Street Journal* (March 22, 1989), p. A9; Keith Bradsher, "A Fragile Air Freight Strategy," *The New York Times* (September 6, 1989), p. 29; Kathryn Graven, "Air Express Firms Battle for Turf in Japan," *The Wall Street Journal* (December 27, 1988), p. A8.

Case 9-2   Airlines Take to the Skies in Global Strategic Alliances

Since January 1, 1997, airline companies based in the European Union have been able to fly into more countries and offer lower ticket prices to passengers. The deregulation of air travel has resulted in sweeping changes for European carriers such as Lufthansa, British Airways, Alitalia, and KLM. Ownership of many airline companies is shifting from government to private hands as a wave of privatization sweeps across Europe. Also, the carriers are rushing to form strategic alliances as the pace of industry globalization increases. Simply put, the alliances allow one airline to book seats on flights operated by another airline if the two are alliance partners. The primary target market is business travelers who have to change planes and carriers while en route to a particular destination. Alliances have been formed between KLM and Northwest, Lufthansa and United, and British Air and USAir, and among Swissair, Delta, and Singapore Air. In theory, alliances should enable carriers to offer better customer service and lower fares. The alliances are designed to cut costs by reducing the number of aircraft in use, pooling maintenance staffs, and jointly purchasing fuel and other supplies. Some observers believe that within a few years, a handful of mega-carriers will dominate the scene; currently, more than 120 different airlines fly in Europe. Despite such predictions, however, a study conducted by the Boston Consulting Group indicated that only one-third of the intercontinental airline alliances that were operating in 1992 were still in place in 1995. Three of the biggest alliances are discussed here.

KLM/Northwest

The global strategic alliance between KLM Royal Dutch Airlines and U.S.-based Northwest Airlines is viewed by many as the most successful in financial terms. The origins of the alliance date back to 1989 when KLM purchased 20 percent of Northwest for $400 million. Today, combined annual revenues make the alliance partners

the third-largest carrier in the world behind American and United. Although only half the size of British Airways and Lufthansa, KLM is now Europe's fastest-growing carrier. KLM's visionary chairman Pieter Bouw succeeded in cutting costs without firing employees while increasing the percentage of seats filled on each flight. The Dutch government owns only about one-third of KLM; the company had a net profit of $298 million in 1994, a year in which government-owned Air France, Alitalia, and Iberia sustained huge losses. For its part, Northwest's $296 million profit in 1994 allowed it to surpass American Airlines in profitability. Meanwhile, the European Union has approved billions of dollars in government subsidies to Europe's state-run airlines, including $3.7 billion to Air France in 1994.

Thanks to a 1992 "open-sky" treaty between the United States and the Netherlands, airline companies from both countries have unrestricted rights to fly into each other's markets. The alliance was also granted exemption from U.S. antitrust laws, so the two carriers can set prices jointly. Thanks to the alliance, Northwest added seven U.S.-Amsterdam routes on KLM to its schedule. Dozens more KLM routes to Europe, Africa, and Asia are also available to Northwest. For example, Northwest flights are not allowed to land in Rome, but KLM can exercise its privileges as a European Union-based company to provide Northwest passengers with service to Rome.

KLM and Northwest also engage in "code sharing," whereby each alliance partner can add its two-letter airline identification code to flights operated by the other partner. This can have a significant impact on how international connecting flights are booked because computer reservation systems are programmed to give higher priority to flights bearing codes from two airlines as opposed to one. Therefore, when booking connections, travel agents are likely to show preference to alliance partners as opposed to an independent carrier flying the same route. Notes Michael E. Levine, a senior Northwest marketing executive, "We sit down and conspire, we set prices, we share routes—it's wonderful."

Despite the success the KLM/Northwest alliance has enjoyed to date, some industry observers believe a number of issues must still be addressed. One airline analyst noted that KLM-Northwest is not widely perceived by the general public as a common entity, something that could be changed with advertising or public relations. Service standards on the two carriers must be harmonized so that passengers are content to fly on either airline. Cultural and operating differences are evident; for example, first-class passengers on KLM receive complimentary Dutch gin in miniature china houses while Northwest passes out rock music CDs. The demeanor of Dutch cabin attendants has been described as "formal," and Northwest's American crews have been described as too "enthusiastic" for European tastes.

There are also objections to the KLM/Northwest alliance on a variety of different grounds. Some object to code sharing. David Schwarte, an attorney for American Airlines, believes the practice may violate antitrust regulations. In his view, code sharing "virtually ensures that the code sharing partner will not launch independent service to compete with the operating partner, and that the two will refrain from lowering fares against one another." Another issue is whether airline companies are rushing into alliances for the wrong reasons. Explains industry consultant Albert DeLauro, "They saw somebody else doing it and got worried about being left out in the cold. Or, they got into it as a hedge. You're seeing people taking shots in the dark."

Despite the financial success of the alliance, there were clear signs of turbulence at the executive level. Writing in *Fortune* magazine, journalist Shawn Tully called the alliance "a marriage from hell, an eye-gouging, rabbit-punching slugfest, with accusations flying like dinner plates." Gary Wilson and Al Checchi, the U.S. financiers who owned 44 percent of Northwest, became locked in a power struggle with KLM President Pieter Bouw. Wilson himself called the U.S.-Dutch relationship "dysfunctional." Bouw attributed the problems to "the European way versus the American way." On paper, the deal has been good for the European side, whose original $400 million investment was worth $1.6 billion by 1996. Wilson and Checchi did even better: Their original $40 million investment for a 44 percent share of Northwest swelled to $1 billion. Differing views of the gains from the deal contributed to the discord. In general, Europeans tend to be disdainful of wheeler-dealer finance types who emphasize cash flow and make a killing with OPM (other people's money). For their part, Wilson and Checchi viewed the Europeans as risk-

We knew the global alliance was a winner. Now it's official.

*Air Transport World's
1997 Airline of the Year
Northwest Airlines/
KLM Royal Dutch Airlines*

*Air Transport World's
1997 Regional Airline of the Year
Northwest Airlink
Mesaba Airlines*

Northwest and KLM Royal Dutch Airlines are pleased and proud to be the first commercial alliance ever awarded Airline of the Year by Air Transport World. And we also salute Northwest Airlink Mesaba Airlines which was awarded Regional Airline of the Year. Our global alliance provides you with a number of innovative services which have become the industry leading standard. Integrated schedules, reciprocal frequent flyer benefits, joint airport lounges and the space and comfort of World Business Class™. All while flying to over 400 destinations in 80 countries on 6 continents.
A victorious combination by any standard.

1-800-447-4747 / www.nwa.com

averse, slow-moving bureaucrats who were too conservative about matters such as debt. By mid-1997, Checchi had stepped down as chairman of Northwest to pursue a career in California politics. To defuse Northwest's concerns that it was trying to take control of the U.S. carrier, KLM was set to sell its stake in the company. As one analyst said, "This is the most efficient transatlantic alliance at the moment and there is enormous potential for more cost savings through further integration. Quitting would be a disaster for both companies."

British Airways-American

A proposed alliance between British Airways (BA) and American Airlines (AA) generated a great deal of comment and controversy following the deal's announcement in June 1996. The two companies had a history of antagonism, due in part to a long-running feud between Robert L. Crandall, chairman and CEO of American, and BA chairman Sir Colin Marshall. Crandall, in particular, had been an outspoken critic of alliances, calling them deceptive and anticompetitive. A strategic reversal as well as a new era of congeniality became evident after Robert Ayling was named chief executive at BA and Donald Carty became president at American. If approved, the alliance would allow American to ticket its customers to destinations beyond London such as Rome, Moscow, and New Delhi. British Airways would benefit in several ways; in addition to ranking number one in passenger traffic in the United States, American was very competitive in the lucrative business travel market and also was well established in Latin America.

However, the proposed alliance faced a number of regulatory hurdles. Because it would create the world's biggest aviation alliance, the deal had to be approved by the European Commission, the Department of Fair Trading (DTI) in the United Kingdom, and the U.S. Department of Transportation. In addition, the United Kingdom and the United States would have to sign an open-sky treaty before the alliance would be approved. BA had formed an earlier alliance in 1993 with USAir; when the new alliance as proposed, USAir immediately filed suit in U.S. district court. The matter was ultimately resolved when BA agreed to sell its stake in USAir.

The concessions demanded by Karel Van Miert, the EU's competition commissioner, presented a bigger obstacle to the alliance. In particular, the commissioner was adamant about the number of take-off and landing slots that the two carriers would have to give up at Heathrow. BA and AA already controlled 60 percent of the lucrative U.K.-U.S. traffic into and out of London's Heathrow Airport, with United Airlines and Virgin Atlantic accounting for the rest. In an effort to maintain competition on transatlantic routes, Van Miert wanted 353 weekly slots, and BA was willing to give up only 168. The issue was compounded by Van Miert's insistence that the slots be surrendered to rival carriers for free; the airlines wanted to sell them. The carriers would also be required to cut back service on some routes such as London to Dallas or Chicago and restrict frequent flyer awards.

During the two-plus years that the deal was subject to scrutiny on both sides of the Atlantic, the chief executives of both airlines—British Airways chairman Robert Ayling and Robert Crandall of American—spent a great deal of time lobbying the relevant authorities. Richard Branson, chairman of Virgin Atlantic Airways, was vehemently opposed to the alliance, which he branded "monopolistic" and "anti-competitive." He was also concerned that U.K. aviation negotiators would give in too easily to U.S. demands for more access to Heathrow. In Branson's view, open-skies treaties negotiated by the United States unfairly favor

U.S. carriers. For example, a "Fly America" provision in the treaties requires U.S. government employees and U.S. mail to fly on U.S. carriers. Also, foreign airlines are limited in their ability to engage in cabotage (i.e., transporting passengers from point to point within another country). Branson, who is legendary for his ability to generate publicity, went to great lengths to make his displeasure known. He wrote letters to members of Virgin Atlantic's frequent flyer club, took out full-page newspaper ads, and wrote editorials. Stating his case in the *Financial Times,* Branson wrote:

> It really is a ludicrous situation. When I open a Virgin Megastore in New York I am welcomed with open arms, just as Tower Records is in London. But try to operate an air service between New York and Boston, using U.S. aircraft and U.S. crews, and governments scream that I am mad!

Star Alliance

In May 1997, as negotiations concerning the BA/AA alliance moved slowly along, a new airline alliance was announced. The Star Alliance linked United Airlines, Air Canada, SAS, Lufthansa, and Thai Airways International. All five carriers, notably United and Lufthansa, had already been cooperating on a bilateral basis for several years. The alliance was expected to generate $42 billion in annual revenues; Brazil's Varig Airlines joined in October of that year. In its first year as part of the alliance, Lufthansa reported increased revenues of DM300 million. None of the partners acquired an equity stake in any of the others; generally, the alliance was evolving at a deliberate pace. As Chris Bowers, senior vice president at United, noted, "We're trying to make sure that we don't bite off more than we can chew." ∎

DISCUSSION QUESTIONS

1. Identify some of the immediate benefits for an American airline company forming an alliance with a European one.
2. How is the global strategic alliance between KLM and Northwest different from a traditional joint venture?
3. What are some of the internal issues that could yet emerge and threaten the relationship between KLM and Northwest in the future?
4. Who do you think benefits more from an airline alliance, the airlines themselves or the customers they serve?

SOURCES: Michael Skapinker, "Flights in Formation," *Financial Times* (January 10–11, 1998), p. 6; Emma Tucker and Michael Skapinker, "Stand-off in Airline Alliance Battle," *Financial Times* (September 23, 1997), p. 7; Barbara Smit, "KLM Shares Take Off on Sale Talk," *Financial Times* (July 4, 1997), p. 22; Richard Branson, "Open Skies for Everyone," *Financial Times* (December 4, 1996), p. 15; Skapinker, "Five Airlines Launch Global Alliance," *Financial Times* (May 15, 1997), p. 17; Shawn Tully, "The Alliance from Hell," *Fortune* (June 24, 1996), pp. 64–66+; Scott McCartney, "Airline Alliances to Alter Overseas Travel," *The Wall Street Journal* (June 11, 1996), pp. B1, B4; Stewart Toy, "Flying High: Why KLM's Global Strategy is Working," *Business Week* (February 27, 1995), pp. 90–91; Brian Coleman, "Among European Airlines, the Privatized Soar to the Top," *The Wall Street Journal* (July 21, 1995), p. B4; Susan Carey, "Flight Patterns: Cross-Border Linkups Bring Airlines Range But Uncertain Benefits," *The Wall Street Journal* (June 7, 1995), p. A1, A5; Joan M. Feldman, "Cross-border Airline Links: Naughty or Nice?" *Air Transport World,* (June 1994), pp. 173–176; John Tagliabue, "Swissair Plies the Unfriendly Skies of United Europe," *The New York Times* (September 18, 1994), sec. 3, p. 10.

10

Strategic Elements of Competitive Advantage

From its home base in Sweden, IKEA has become a $8 billion global furniture powerhouse. With 160 stores in 30 countries, the company's success reflects founder Ingvar Kamprad's "social ambition" of selling a wide range of stylish, functional home furnishings at prices so low that the majority of people can afford to buy them. The store exteriors are painted bright blue and yellow—Sweden's national colors. Shoppers view furniture on the main floor in scores of realistic settings arranged throughout the cavernous showrooms. In a departure from standard industry practice, IKEA's furniture bears names such as "Ivar" and "Sten" instead of model numbers. At IKEA, shopping is very much a self-service activity; after browsing and writing down the names of desired items, shoppers can pick up their furniture on the lower level. There they find flat cartons containing the furniture in kit form; one of the cornerstones of IKEA's strategy is having customers take their purchases home in their own vehicles and assemble the furniture themselves. The lower level of a typical IKEA store also contains a restaurant, a grocery store called the Swede Shop, a supervised play area for children, and a baby care room.

The essence of marketing strategy is successfully relating the strengths of an organization to its environment. As the horizons of marketers have expanded from domestic to regional and global, so too have the horizons of competitors. The reality in almost every industry today—including home furnishings—is global competition. This fact of life puts an organization under increasing pressure to master techniques for conducting industry analysis and competitor analysis, and understanding competitive advantage at both the industry and national levels. These topics are covered in detail in this chapter.

Global marketing experts cite IKEA as an illustration of several key strategic principles. IKEA exemplifies the concept of the flagship firm: The company has built a network of more than 2,000 suppliers in 50 countries. This arrangement has helped IKEA achieve and maintain a low-cost position in the global furniture industry. IKEA reaps further economies by minimizing transportation and delivery costs. Furniture is shipped to the stores in flat packaging; customers assemble the finished pieces themselves.

INDUSTRY ANALYSIS: FORCES INFLUENCING COMPETITION

A useful way of gaining insight into competitors is through industry analysis. As a working definition, an industry can be defined as a group of firms that produce products that are close substitutes for each other. In any industry, competition works to drive down the rate of return on invested capital toward the rate that would be earned in the economist's "perfectly competitive" industry. Rates of return that are greater than this so-called "competitive" rate will stimulate an inflow of capital either from new entrants or from existing competitors making additional investment. Rates of return below this "competitive" rate will result in withdrawal from the industry and a decline in the levels of activity and competition.

According to Michael E. Porter of Harvard University, a leading theorist of competitive strategy, there are five forces influencing competition in an industry (Figure 10-1): the threat of new entrants, the threat of substitute products or services, the bargaining power of buyers, the bargaining power of suppliers, and the competitive rivalry among current members of the industry. In industries such as soft drinks, pharmaceuticals, and cosmetics, the favorable nature of the five forces has resulted in attractive returns for competitors. However, pressure from any of the forces can limit profitability, as evidenced by the recent fortunes of some competitors in the personal computer and semiconductor industries. A discussion of each of the five forces follows.

Threat of New Entrants

New entrants to an industry bring new capacity, a desire to gain market share and position, and, very often, new approaches to serving customer needs. The decision to become a new entrant in an industry is often accompanied by a major commitment

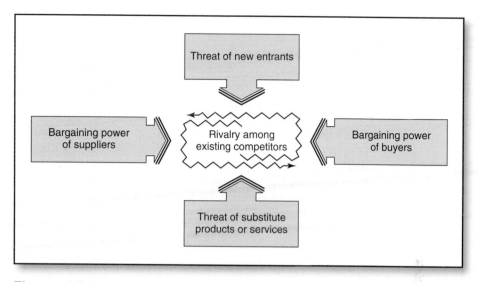

Figure 10-1
Forces Influencing Competition in an Industry

Source: Adapted with permission of The Free Press, a Division of Simon & Schuster, Inc., from COMPETITIVE STRATEGY: Techniques for Analyzing Industries and Competitors by Michael E. Porter. Copyright © 1980, 1988 by The Free Press.

of resources. New players mean prices will be pushed downward and margins squeezed, resulting in reduced industry profitability in the long run. Porter describes eight major sources of barriers to entry, the presence or absence of which determines the extent of threat of new industry entrants.[1]

The first barrier, **economies of scale,** refers to the decline in per-unit product costs as the absolute volume of production per period increases. Although the concept of scale economies is frequently associated with manufacturing, it is also applicable to R&D, general administration, marketing, and other business functions. Honda's efficiency at engine R&D, for example, results from the wide range of products it produces that feature gasoline-powered engines. When existing firms in an industry achieve significant economies of scale, it becomes difficult for potential new entrants to be competitive.

Product differentiation, the second major entry barrier, is the extent of a product's perceived uniqueness—in other words, whether or not it is a commodity. Differentiation can be achieved as a result of unique product attributes or effective marketing communications, or both. Product differentiation and brand loyalty "raise the bar" for would-be industry entrants who would be required to make substantial investments in R&D or advertising. For example, managers at Monsanto's G. D. Searle subsidiary achieved differentiation and erected a barrier in the artificial sweetener industry by insisting that the Nutrasweet name and brand mark—a red-and-white swirl—appear on diet soft drink cans.

A third entry barrier relates to **capital requirements.** Capital is required not only for manufacturing facilities (fixed capital) but also for financing R&D, advertising, field sales and service, customer credit, and inventories (working capital). The enormous capital requirements in such industries as pharmaceuticals, mainframe computers, chemicals, and mineral extraction present formidable entry barriers.

---

[1] Michael E. Porter, *Competitive Strategy* (New York: Free Press, 1980), pp. 7–33.

A fourth barrier to entry are the one-time **switching costs** caused by the need to change suppliers and products. These might include retraining, ancillary equipment costs, the cost of evaluating a new source, and so on. The perceived cost to customers of switching to a new competitor's product may present an insurmountable obstacle preventing industry newcomers from achieving success. For example, Microsoft's huge installed base of PC operating systems and applications presents a formidable entry barrier.

A fifth barrier to entry is access to **distribution channels.** If channels are full, or unavailable, the cost of entry is substantially increased because a new entrant must invest time and money to gain access to existing channels or to establish new channels. Some Western companies have encountered this barrier in Japan.

Government policy is frequently a major entry barrier. In some cases, the government will restrict competitive entry. This is true in a number of industries, especially those outside the United States, that have been designated as "national" industries by their respective governments. Japan's postwar industrialization strategy was based on a policy of reserving and protecting national industries in their development and growth phases. The result was a market that proved difficult for non-Japanese competitors to enter, an issue that was targeted by the Clinton administration. American business executives in a wide range of industries urged adoption of a government policy that would reduce some of these barriers and open the Japanese market to more U.S. companies.

Established firms may also enjoy **cost advantages independent of scale economies** that present barriers to entry. Access to raw materials, favorable locations, and government subsidies are several examples.

Finally, expected **competitor response** can be a major entry barrier. If new entrants expect existing competitors to respond strongly to entry, their expectations about the rewards of entry will certainly be affected. A potential competitor's belief that entry into an industry or market will be an unpleasant experience may serve as a strong deterrent. Bruce Henderson, former president of the Boston Consulting Group, used the term "brinkmanship" to describe a recommended approach for deterring competitive entry. Brinkmanship occurs when industry leaders convince potential competitors that any market entry effort will be countered with vigorous and unpleasant responses.

G. D. Searle used brinkmanship—especially price cuts—to deter competitors from entering the low-calorie artificial sweetener market as Nutrasweet's patents expired. At the end of 1989, Systse T. Kuipers, a marketing manager at Holland Sweetener Company, complained that "it is a bloody fight and everybody's losing money. [Nutrasweet managers] go for the last kilo even if they have to give the product away." In Kuipers's view, G. D. Searle's tactic of deep price cuts on Nutrasweet had "the sole intent of chasing competitors out of the marketplace."[2] In fact, several European producers abandoned the business, proof that G. D. Searle's policy of brinkmanship was an effective competitive response to the threat of new entrants.

In the two decades since Porter first described the five forces model, the digital revolution appears to have altered the entry barriers in many industries. First and foremost, technology has lowered the cost for new entrants. For example, Barnes & Noble watched an entrepreneurial upstart, Amazon.com, storm the barriers protecting traditional "brick and mortar" booksellers. Amazon.com founder Jeff Bezos identified and exploited a glaring inefficiency in book distribution: Bookstores ship unsold copies of books back to publishers to be shredded and turned into pulp.

---

2   Eben Shapiro, "Nutrasweet's Bitter Fight," *The New York Times* (November 19, 1989), p. C4.

Amazon's centralized operations and increasingly personalized online service enable customers to select from millions of different titles at discount prices and have them delivered to their homes within days. For a growing number of book-buying consumers, Amazon.com eclipses the value proposition of local bookstores that offer "only" a few thousand titles and gourmet coffee bars. Since Bezos founded Amazon.com in 1995, sales have grown to $3 billion and the company has expanded into new product lines such as CDs and videos. To date, the company has served tens of millions of customers in 160 countries. Barnes & Noble has responded by entering the online book market itself even as it continues to be profitable in its traditional bricks and mortar business. In the meantime, although Amazon.com has repositioned itself as an Internet superstore, its economic viability remains unclear.

Threat of Substitute Products

A second force influencing competition in an industry is the threat of substitute products. The availability of substitute products places limits on the prices market leaders can charge in an industry; high prices may induce buyers to switch to the substitute. Once again, the digital revolution is dramatically altering industry structures. In addition to lowering entry barriers, the digital era means that certain types of products can be converted to bits and distributed in pure digital form. For example, the development of the MP3 file format for music was accompanied by the increased popularity of peer-to-peer (p-to-p) file swapping among music fans. Napster and other online music services offer a substitute to consumers who are tired of paying $15 or more for a CD. Although a U.S. court severely curtailed Napster's activities, other services—including several outside the United States—have sprung up in its place. Bertelsmann, Sony, and the top players in the music industry were taken by surprise, and even now are struggling to develop a coherent response to the threat to their core businesses (see Case 15-1.)

Bargaining Power of Buyers

In Porter's model, "buyers" refers to manufacturers (e.g., GM) and retailers (e.g., Wal-Mart), rather than consumers. The ultimate aim of such buyers is to pay the lowest possible price to obtain the products or services that they require. Usually, therefore, if they can, buyers drive down profitability in the supplier industry. To accomplish this, the buyers have to gain leverage over their vendors. One way they can do this is to purchase in such large quantities that supplier firms are highly dependent on the buyers' business. Second, when the suppliers' products are viewed as commodities—that is, as standard or undifferentiated—buyers are likely to bargain hard for low prices, since many firms can meet their needs. Buyers will also bargain hard when the supplier industry's products or services represent a significant portion of the buying firm's costs. A fourth source of buyer power is the willingness and ability to achieve backward integration.

For example, because it purchases massive quantities of goods for resale, Wal-Mart is in a position to dictate terms to any vendor wishing to distribute its products at the retail giant's stores. This includes the recorded music industry; Wal-Mart accounts for approximately 10 percent of the market for CD sales. Wal-Mart refuses to stock CDs stickered with parental advisories for explicit lyrics or violent imagery. Artists who want their recordings available at Wal-Mart have the option of altering lyrics and song titles or deleting offending tracks. Likewise, artists are sometimes asked to change album cover art if Wal-Mart deems it offensive. Nina Crowley, executive director of the Massachusetts Music Industry Coalition, objects to such changes. "What really upsets us is that they're using their financial power to change

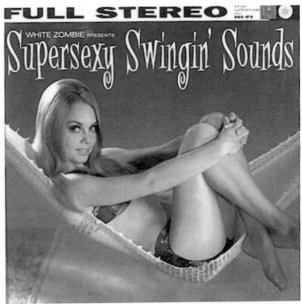

Wal-Mart has become one of the biggest sellers of recorded music in the United States. Much of the discounter's growth in this area has come at the expense of specialty music stores whose share of the market fell from 70 percent in 1990 to 44.5 percent in 1999. One way that Wal-Mart exercises its buying power is by refusing to stock recordings bearing "Parental Advisory" stickers; many artists release edited versions so that Wal-Mart will carry them. White Zombie leader Rob Zombie agreed to change the cover art of this 1996 release; the original cover is shown on the left. The airbrushed version on the right was deemed acceptable by Wal-Mart executives.

art," she said. A Wal-Mart spokesperson noted, "We do not quibble or argue with anyone's right to sing what they want, to print what they want, and say what they want. But we reserve the right to sell what we want."[3]

Bargaining Power of Suppliers

Supplier power in an industry is the converse of buyer power. If suppliers have enough leverage over industry firms, they can raise prices high enough to significantly influence the profitability of their organizational customers. Suppliers' ability to gain leverage over industry firms is determined by several factors. Suppliers will have the advantage if they are large and relatively few in number. Second, when the suppliers' products or services are important inputs to user firms, are highly differentiated, or carry switching costs, the suppliers will have considerable leverage over buyers. Suppliers will also enjoy bargaining power if their business is not threatened by alternative products. A fourth source of supplier power is the willingness and ability of suppliers to develop their own products and brand names if they are unable to get satisfactory terms from industry buyers. In the tech world, Microsoft and Intel are two excellent examples of companies with substantial supplier power. Since about 90 percent of the world's 500 million PCs use Microsoft's operating systems and Intel's microprocessors, the two companies enjoy a great deal of leverage relative to Dell, Compaq, and other computer manufacturers. In fact, it was precisely because Microsoft became so powerful that the U.S. government and the European Union launched separate antitrust investigations.

Rivalry among Competitors

Rivalry among firms refers to all the actions taken by firms in the industry to improve their positions and gain advantage over each other. Rivalry manifests itself

---

3   "Wal-Mart Rules Prompt Changes in Music," *Associated Press* (November 19, 1996).

in price competition, advertising battles, product positioning, and attempts at differentiation. To the extent that rivalry among firms forces companies to rationalize costs, it is a positive force. To the extent that it drives down prices, and therefore profitability, and creates instability in the industry, it is a negative factor. Several factors can create intense rivalry. Once an industry becomes mature, firms focus on market share and how it can be gained at the expense of others. Second, industries characterized by high fixed costs are always under pressure to keep production at full capacity to cover the fixed costs. Once the industry accumulates excess capacity, the drive to fill capacity will push prices—and profitability—down. A third factor affecting rivalry is lack of differentiation or an absence of switching costs, which encourages buyers to treat the products or services as commodities and shop for the best prices. Again, there is downward pressure on prices and profitability. Fourth, firms with high strategic stakes in achieving success in an industry generally are destabilizing because they may be willing to accept unreasonably low profit margins to establish themselves, hold position, or expand.

The personal computer industry is a case in point. For years, demand for PCs grew at an annual rate of 15 percent. Since the tech bubble burst in early 2000, however, firms have been dealing with a worldwide slowdown in demand. In 2001, industry experts expected growth to be under 6 percent. Dell Computer is aggressively cutting prices in a bid to boost share. With profit margins collapsing, competitors are struggling to adjust. The price war has claimed one victim already; in mid-2001, key rival Compaq agreed to be acquired by Hewlett-Packard. Dell is legendary for its lean operating philosophy; just 11.5 cents of every sales dollar go to overhead, compared with 16 cents at Gateway, 21 cents at Compaq and 22.5 cents at Hewlett-Packard. With a build-to-order strategy at the heart of its business model, Dell's sales staff maintains close ties with the company's customers. This gives Dell a great deal of flexibility when making pricing decisions.[4]

COMPETITIVE ADVANTAGE

Competitive advantage exists when there is a match between a firm's distinctive competencies and the factors critical for success within its industry. Any superior match between company competencies and customers needs permits the firm to outperform competitors. There are two basic ways to achieve competitive advantage. First, a firm can pursue a low-cost strategy that enables it to offer products at lower prices than competitors. Competitive advantage may also be gained by a strategy of differentiating products so that customers perceive unique benefits, often accompanied by a premium price. Note that both strategies have the same effect: They both contribute to the firm's overall value proposition. Michael E. Porter explored these issues in two landmark books, *Competitive Strategy* (1985) and *Competitive Advantage* (1990); the latter is widely considered to be one of the most influential management books in years.

The quality of a firm's strategy is ultimately decided by customer perception. Operating results such as sales and profits are measures that depend on the level of psychological value created for customers: The greater the perceived consumer value, the better the strategy. A firm may market a better mousetrap, but the ultimate success of the product depends on customers deciding for themselves whether or not

---

[4] Gary McWilliams, "Lean Machine: How Dell Fine-Tunes its PC Pricing to Gain Edge in a Slow Market," *The Wall Street Journal* (June 8, 2001), p. A1,

to buy it. Value is like beauty—it's in the eye of the beholder. In sum, competitive advantage is achieved by creating more value than is done by the competition, and value is defined by customer perception.

Two different models of competitive advantage have received considerable attention. The first offers "generic strategies," four routes or paths that organizations choose to offer superior value and achieve competitive advantage. According to the second model, generic strategies alone don't account for the astonishing success of many Japanese companies in recent years. The more recent model, based on the concept of "strategic intent," proposes four different sources of competitive advantage. Both models are discussed in following paragraphs.

Generic Strategies for Creating Competitive Advantage

In addition to the "five forces" model of industry competition, Michael Porter has developed a framework of so-called generic business strategies based on the two types or sources of competitive advantage mentioned previously: *low-cost* and *differentiation*. Figure 10-2 shows that the combination of these two sources with the scope of the target market served (narrow or broad) or product mix width (narrow or wide) yields four **generic strategies:** *cost leadership, product differentiation, cost focus,* and *focused differentiation.*

Generic strategies aiming at the achievement of competitive advantage or superior marketing strategy demand that the firm make choices. The choices concern the **type** of competitive advantage it seeks to attain (based on cost or differentiation) and the **market scope** or **product mix width** within which competitive advantage will be attained.[6] The nature of the choice between types of advantage and market scope is a gamble, and it is the nature of every gamble that it entails *risk*. By choosing a given generic strategy, a firm always risks making the wrong choice.

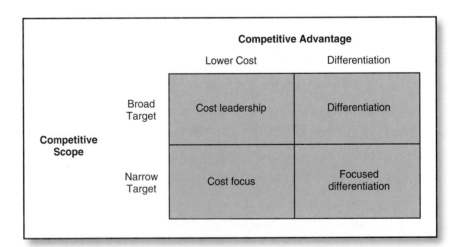

Figure 10-2
Generic Competitive Strategies

Source: Adapted with permission of The Free Press, a Division of Simon & Schuster, Inc., from THE COMPETITIVE ADVANTAGE OF NATIONS by Michael E. Porter. Copyright © 1990, 1998 by The Free Press.

---

5   Regina Fazio Maruca, "The Right Way to Go Global: An Interview with Whirlpool CEO David Whitwam," *Harvard Business Review* 72, no. 2 (March April 1994), p. 135.
6   Michael E. Porter, *Competitive Advantage: Creating and Sustaining Superior Performance* (New York: Free Press, 1985), p. 12.

Broad Market Strategies: Cost Leadership and Differentiation

Cost leadership advantage is based on a firm's position as the industry's low-cost producer, in broadly defined markets or across a wide mix of products. This strategy has become increasingly popular in recent years as a result of the popularization of the experience curve concept. In general, a firm that bases its competitive strategy on overall cost leadership must construct the most efficient facilities (in terms of scale or technology) and obtain the largest share of market so that its cost per unit is the lowest in the industry. These advantages, in turn, give the producer a substantial lead in terms of experience with building the product. Experience then leads to more refinements of the entire process of production, delivery, and service, which leads to further cost reductions.

Whatever its source, cost leadership advantage can be the basis for offering lower prices (and more value) to customers in the late, more-competitive stages of the product life cycle. In Japan, companies in a range of industries—35mm cameras, consumer electronics and entertainment equipment, motorcycles, and automobiles—have achieved cost leadership on a worldwide basis.

Cost leadership, however, is a sustainable source of competitive advantage only if barriers exist that prevent competitors from achieving the same low costs. In an era of increasing technological improvements in manufacturing, manufacturers constantly leapfrog over one another in pursuit of lower costs. At one time, for example, IBM enjoyed the low-cost advantage in the production of computer printers. Then the Japanese took the same technology and, after reducing production costs and improving product reliability, gained the low-cost advantage. IBM fought back with a highly automated printer plant in North Carolina, where the number of component parts was slashed by more than 50 percent and robots were used to snap many components into place. Despite these changes, IBM ultimately chose to exit the business; the plant was sold.

When a firm's product has an actual or perceived uniqueness in a broad market, it is said to have a **differentiation advantage.** This can be an extremely effective strategy for defending market position and obtaining above-average financial returns; unique products often command premium price. Examples of successful differentiation include Maytag in large home appliances, Caterpillar in construction equipment, and almost any successful branded consumer product. Maytag has been called "the Rolls-Royce of washers and dryers;" half the washers sold in the United States are priced at $399 or less, and Maytag does offer a model at that price point. However, the Maytag line also includes the Neptune, a high-tech, water-saving machine; the two Neptune models are priced at $999 and $1,399. IBM traditionally has differentiated itself with a strong sales/service organization and the security of the IBM standard in a world of rapid obsolescence. (Unfortunately for IBM, as customer preferences have shifted away from mainframes, IBM's differentiation advantage has eroded.) Among athletic shoe manufacturers, Nike stands out as the technological leader thanks to unique product features found in a wide array of shoes.

Narrow Target Strategies: Cost Focus and Focused Differentiation

The preceding discussion of cost leadership and differentiation considered only the impact on broad markets. By contrast, strategies to achieve a narrow focus advantage target a narrowly defined market/customer. This advantage is based on an ability to create more customer value for a narrowly targeted segment and results from a better understanding of customer needs and wants. A narrow-focus strategy can be combined with either cost- or differentiation-advantage strategies. In other words, while a *cost focus* means offering a narrow target market low prices, a firm pursuing *focused differentiation* will offer a narrow target market the perception of product uniqueness at a premium price.

The German *Mittelstand* companies discussed in Chapter 8 have been extremely successful pursuing **focused differentiation** strategies backed by a strong export effort. The world of "high-end" audio equipment offers another example of focused differentiation. A few hundred small companies design speakers, amplifiers, and related hi-fi gear that costs thousands of dollars per component. While audio components represent a $21 billion market worldwide, annual sales in the high-end segment are only about $1.1 billion. American companies such as Audio Research, Conrad-Johnson, Krell, Mark Levinson, Martin-Logan, and Thiel dominate the segment, which also includes hundreds of smaller enterprises with annual sales of less than $10 million. The state-of-the-art equipment these companies offer is distinguished by superior craftmanship and performance and is highly sought after by audiophiles in Asia (especially Japan and Hong Kong), and Europe. Industry growth in the United States is occuring as companies learn more about overseas customers and build relationships with distributors in other countries.[7]

The final strategy is **cost focus,** when a firm's lower cost position enables it to offer a narrow target market and lower prices than the competition. In the shipbuilding industry, for example, Polish and Chinese shipyards offer simple, standard vessel types at low prices that reflect low production costs.[8] IKEA, the Swedish furniture company described in the chapter introduction, has grown into a successful global company by combining both the focused differentiation and cost focus strategies. As George Bradley, president of Levitz Furniture in Boca Raton, Florida, noted, "[IKEA] has really made a splash. They're going to capture their niche in every city they go into." Of course, such a strategy can be risky. As Bradley explains, "Their market is finite because it is so narrow. If you don't want contemporary, knock-down furniture, it's not for you. So it takes a certain customer to buy it. And remember, fashions change."[9]

The issue of sustainability is central to this strategy concept. As noted, cost leadership is a sustainable source of competitive advantage only if barriers exist that prevent competitors from achieving the same low costs. Sustained differentiation depends on continued perceived value and the absence of imitation by competitors.[10] Several factors determine whether or not focus can be sustained as a source of competitive advantage. First, a cost focus is sustainable if a firm's competitors are defining their target markets more broadly. A focuser doesn't try to be all things to all people: Competitors may diminish their advantage by trying to satisfy the needs of a broader market segment—a strategy which, by definition, means a blunter focus. Second, a firm's differentiation focus advantage is only sustainable if competitors cannot define the segment even more narrowly. Also, focus can be sustained if competitors cannot overcome barriers that prevent imitation of the focus strategy, and if consumers in the target segment do not migrate to other segments that the focuser doesn't serve.

---

[7] Personal communication from Kerry Moyer, products division director, Consumer Electronics Association, Arlington, Virginia.

[8] Michael E. Porter, *The Competitive Advantage of Nations* (New York: Free Press, 1990), p. 39.

[9] Jeffrey A. Trachtenberg, "Home Economics: IKEA Furniture Chain Pleases With Its Prices, Not With Its Service," *The Wall Street Journal* (September 17, 1991), pp. A1, A5.

[10] Michael E. Porter, *Competitive Advantage: Creating and Sustaining Superior Performance* (New York: Free Press, 1985), p. 158.

The Rest of the Story
IKEA

IKEA's unconventional approach to the furniture business has enabled it to rack up impressive growth in a $30 billion industry in which overall sales have been flat. Sourcing furniture from a network of more than 2,300 suppliers in 70 countries helps the company maintain its low-cost, high quality position. During the 1990s, IKEA opened several stores in Central and Eastern Europe. Because consumers in those regions have relatively low purchasing power, the stores offer a smaller selection of goods; some furniture was designed specifically for the cramped living styles typical in former Soviet bloc countries. Throughout Europe, IKEA benefits from the perception that Sweden is the source of high-quality products and efficient service. The United Kingdom represents the fastest-growing market in Europe; although Britons initially viewed the company's less-is-more approach as cold and "too Scandinavian," they were eventually won over. IKEA currently has 10 stores in the UK and plans to open 20 more in the next decade.

"Ikea is anticonventional. It does what it shouldn't do. That's the overall theme for all Ikea ads: liberation from tradition."
—Allan Young, creative director, St. Luke's, London

Industry observers predict that North America will eventually be IKEA's largest market. The company opened its first U.S. store in Philadelphia in 1985; as of 2001, IKEA operated 15 stores in the United States and seven in Canada. Notes Jeff Young, chief operating officer of Lexington Furniture Industries, "IKEA is on the way to becoming the Wal-Mart Stores of the home-furnishing industry. If you're in this business, you'd better take a look." Some American customers, however, are irked to find popular items sometimes out of stock. Another problem is the long lines resulting from the company's no-frills approach. Complained one shopper, "Great idea, poor execution. The quality of much of what they sell is good, but the hassles make you question whether it's worth it."

Goran Carstedt, president of IKEA North America, responds to such criticism by referring to the company's mission. "If we offered more services, our prices would go up," he explains. "Our customers understand our philosophy, which calls for each of us to do a little in order to save a lot. They value our low prices. And almost all of them say they will come back again." To keep them coming back, IKEA spends between $40 million and $50 million on advertising to get its message across. While it is a common industry practice to rely heavily on newspaper and radio advertising, two-thirds of IKEA's North American advertising budget is allocated for TV. John Sitnik, an executive at IKEA U.S. Inc., says, "We distanced ourselves from the other furniture stores. We decided TV is something we can own."

SOURCES: Alan M. Rugman and Joseph R. D'Cruz, *Multinationals as Flagship Firms* (Oxford: Oxford University Press, 2000), Chap. 3; Ernest Beck, "IKEA Sees Quirkiness as Selling Point in UK," *The Wall Street Journal* (January 4, 2001), pp. A1, A5; Loretta Roach, "IKEA: Furnishing the World," *Discount Merchandiser* (October 1994), pp. 46, 48; "Furnishing the World," *The Economist* (November 19, 1994), pp. 79–80.

The Flagship Firm: The Business Network with Five Partners[11]

According to Professors Alan Rugman and Joseph D'Cruz, Porter's model is too simplistic given the complexity of today's global environment. Rugman and D'Cruz have developed an alternative framework based on business networks that they call the flagship model (Figure 10-3). The success of Japanese vertical *keiretsu* and Korean *chaebol*, Rugman and D'Cruz argue, is that they adopt strategies that are mutually reinforcing within a business system and foster a collective long-term outlook among the partners. Moreover, the authors note, "long-term competitiveness in global industries is less a matter of rivalry between firms and more a question of competition between business systems." A major difference between their model and Porter's is that Porter's is based on the notion of corporate individualism and individual business transactions. For example, as discussed previously, Microsoft's

---

[11] The following discussion is adapted from Alan M. Rugman and Joseph R. D'Cruz, *Multinationals as Flagship Firms* (Oxford: Oxford University Press, 2000).

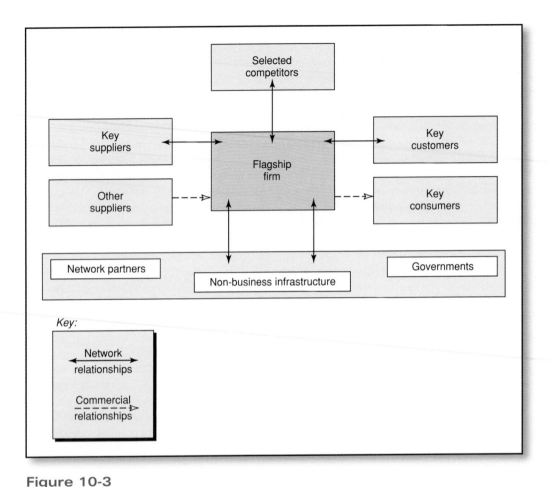

Figure 10-3
The Flagship Model

Source: Alan M. Rugman and Joseph R. D'Cruz, *Multinationals as Flagship Firms* (Oxford: Oxford University Press, 2000), p. 9.

tremendous supplier power allows it to dictate to, and even prosper at the expense of, the computer manufacturers it supplies with operating systems and applications. The flagship model is evident in the strategies of Ford, Volkswagen, and other global automakers; Sweden's Ikea and Italy's Benetton are additional examples.

As shown in Figure 10-3, the flagship firm is at the center of a collection of five partners; together, they form a business system that consists of two types of relationships. The flagship firm provides the leadership, vision, and resources to "lead the network in a successful global strategy." *Key suppliers* are those that perform some value-creating activities, such as manufacturing of critical components, better than the flagship. The double-headed arrows that penetrate the flagship and key suppliers in Figure 10-3 indicate that this is a network relationship, with a sharing of strategies, resources, and responsibility for the success of the network. Other suppliers are kept at "arm's length"; these traditional commercial relationships are depicted diagrammatically by arrows that stop at the border of the flagship. Likewise, the flagship has network relationships with *key customers* and more traditional, arm's length commercial relationships with *key consumers*. In the case of Volkswagen, for example, dealers are its key customers while individual car buyers are key consumers; similarly, Benetton's key customers are its retail outlets while the individual clothes shopper is the key consumer. *Key competitors* are companies with which the flagship develops alliances such as those described at the end of Chapter 9. The fifth partner is the *non-business infrastructure* (NBI), comprised of universities, governments, trade unions, and other entities that can supply the network with intangible inputs such as intellectual property and technology. In the flagship model, flagship firms often play a role in the development of a country's industrial policy.

Benetton's success in the global fashion industry illustrates the flagship model (for a discussion of Benetton's advertising, see Case 16-1). Benetton is the world's largest purchaser of wool, and its centralized buying enables the company to reap scale economies. The core activities of cutting and dyeing are retained in-house, and Benetton has made substantial investments in computer-assisted design and manufacturing. However, Benetton is linked to approximately 400 subcontractors that produce finished garments in exclusive supply relationships with the company. In turn, the subcontractors are linked to the 4,000 Benetton retail shops by a network of 80 agents who find investors, train managers, and assist with merchandising. As Rugman and D'Cruz note, "Benetton is organized to reward cooperation and relationship building and the company's structure has been created to capitalize on the benefits of long-term relationships."

Creating Competitive Advantage via Strategic Intent

An alternative framework for understanding competitive advantage focuses on competitiveness as a function of the pace at which a company implants new advantages deep within its organization. This framework identifies **strategic intent,** growing out of ambition and obsession with winning, as the means for achieving competitive advantage. Writing in the *Harvard Business Review,* Gary Hamel and C. K. Prahalad note:

> Few competitive advantages are long lasting. Keeping score of existing advantages is not the same as building new advantages. The essence of strategy lies in creating tomorrow's competitive advantages faster than competitors mimic the ones you possess today. An organization's capacity to improve existing skills and learn new ones is the most defensible competitive advantage of all.[12]

This approach is founded on the principles of W. E. Deming, who stressed that a company must commit itself to continuing improvement in order to be a winner in a competitive struggle. For years, Deming's message fell on deaf ears in the United States, while the Japanese heeded his message and benefited tremendously. Japan's most prestigious business award is named after him. Finally, however, U.S. manufacturers are starting to respond.

The significance of Hamel and Prahalad's framework becomes evident when comparing Caterpillar and Komatsu. As noted earlier, Caterpillar is a classic example of differentiation: The company became the largest manufacturer of earthmoving equipment in the world because it was fanatical about quality and service. Caterpillar's success as a global marketer has enabled it to achieve a 35 percent share of the worldwide market for earthmoving equipment—more than half of which represents sales to developing countries. The differentiation advantage was achieved

---

[12] Gary Hamel and C.K. Prahalad, "Strategic Intent," *Harvard Business Review* 67, no. 3 (May-June 1989), pp. 63–76. See also Hamel and Prahalad, "The Core Competence of the Corporation," *Harvard Business Review* 68, no. 3 (May-June 1990), pp. 79–93.

with product durability, global spare parts service (including guaranteed parts delivery anywhere in the world within 48 hours), and a strong network of loyal dealers.

Caterpillar faced a very challenging set of environmental forces during the past decade. Many of Caterpillar's plants were closed by a lengthy strike in the early 1980s; a worldwide recession at the same time caused a downturn in the construction industry. This hurt companies that were Caterpillar customers. In addition, the strong dollar gave a cost advantage to foreign rivals.

Compounding Caterpillar's problems was a new competitive threat from Japan. Komatsu was the world's number-two construction equipment company and had been competing with Caterpillar in the Japanese market for years. Komatsu's products were generally acknowledged to offer a lower level of quality. The rivalry took on a new dimension after Komatsu adopted the slogan "*Maru-c*," meaning "encircle Caterpillar." Emphasizing quality and taking advantage of low labor costs and the strong dollar, Komatsu surpassed Caterpillar as number one in earthmoving equipment in Japan and made serious inroads in the United States and other markets. Yet the company continued to develop new sources of competitive advantage even after it achieved world-class quality. For example, new product development cycles were shortened and manufacturing was rationalized. Caterpillar struggled to sustain its competitive advantage because many customers found that Komatsu's combination of quality, durability, and lower price created compelling value. Yet even as recession and a strong yen put new pressure on Komatsu, the company sought new opportunities by diversifying into machine tools and robots.[13]

The Komatsu/Caterpillar saga is just one example of how global competitive battles are shaped by more than the pursuit of generic strategies. Many firms have gained competitive advantage by *disadvantaging* rivals through "competitive innovation." Hamel and Prahalad define *competitive innovation* as "the art of containing competitive risks within manageable proportions" and identify four successful approaches utilized by Japanese competitors. These are: *building layers of advantage, searching for loose bricks, changing the rules of engagement,* and *collaborating.*

Layers of Advantage. A company faces less risk in competitive encounters if it has a wide portfolio of advantages. Successful companies steadily build such portfolios by establishing layers of advantage on top of one another. Komatsu is an excellent example of this approach. Another is the TV industry in Japan. By 1970, Japan was not only the world's largest producer of black-and-white TV sets but was also well on its way to becoming the leader in producing color sets. The main competitive advantage for such companies as Matsushita at that time was low labor costs.

Because they realized that their cost advantage could be temporary, the Japanese also added an additional layer of *quality and reliability* advantages by building plants large enough to serve world markets. Much of this output did not carry the manufacturer's brand name. For example, Matsushita Electric sold products to other companies such as RCA that marketed them under their own brand names. Matsushita was pursuing a simple idea: A product sold was a product sold, no matter whose label it carried.[14]

In order to build the next layer of advantage, the Japanese spent the 1970s investing heavily in marketing channels and Japanese brand names to gain recognition. This strategy added yet another layer of competitive advantage: the *global brand fran-*

---

[13] Robert L. Rose and Masayoshi Kanabayashi, "Komatsu Throttles Back on Construction Equipment," *The Wall Street Journal* (May 13, 1992), p. B4.

[14] James Lardner, *Fast Forward: Hollywood, The Japanese, and the VCR Wars* (New York: New American Library, 1987), p. 135.

chise—that is, a global customer base. By the late 1970s, channels and brand awareness were established well enough to support the introduction of new products that could benefit from global marketing—VCRs and photocopy machines, for example. Finally, many companies have invested in *regional manufacturing* so their products can be differentiated and better adapted to customer needs in individual markets.

The process of building layers illustrates how a company can move along the value chain to strengthen competitive advantage. The Japanese began with manufacturing (an upstream value activity) and moved on to marketing (a downstream value activity) and then back upstream to basic R&D. All of these sources of competitive advantage represent mutually reinforcing layers that are accumulated over time.

Loose Bricks.   A second approach takes advantage of the "loose bricks" left in the defensive walls of competitors whose attention is narrowly focused on a market segment or a geographic area to the exclusion of others. For example, Caterpillar's attention was focused elsewhere when Komatsu made its first entry into the Eastern Europe market. Similarly, Taiwan's Acer Inc. prospered by following founder Stan Shih's strategy of approaching the world computer market from the periphery. Shih's inspiration was the Asian board game Go, in which the winning player successfully surrounds opponents. Shih gained experience and built market share in countries overlooked by competitors such as IBM and Compaq. By the time Acer was ready to target the United States in earnest, it was already the number one PC brand in key countries in Latin America, Southeast Asia, and the Middle East.[15] Intel's loose brick was its narrow focus on complex microprocessors for personal computers. Even as it built its core business to a commanding 90 percent share of the market, markets for non-PC consumer electronics products were exploding. The new products, which include television desk-top boxes, digital cameras, and so-called smart cards, require chips that are far cheaper than those produced by Intel. Competitors such as NEC Corp and LSI Logic recognized the opportunity and beat Intel into an important new market.[16]

Changing the Rules.   A third approach involves changing the so-called "rules of engagement" and refusing to play by the rules set by industry leaders. For example, in the copier market, IBM and Kodak imitated the marketing strategies used by market leader Xerox. Meanwhile Canon, a Japanese challenger, wrote a new rulebook.

While Xerox built a wide range of copiers, Canon built standardized machines and components, reducing manufacturing costs. While Xerox employed a huge direct sales force, Canon chose to distribute through office-product dealers. Canon also designed serviceability, as well as reliability, into its products so that it could rely on dealers for service rather than incurring the expense required to create a national service network. Canon further decided to sell rather than lease its machines, freeing the company from the burden of financing the lease base. In another major departure, Canon targeted its copiers at secretaries and department managers rather than at the heads of corporate duplicating operations.[17]

Canon introduced the first full-color copiers and the first copiers with "connectivity"—the ability to print images from such sources as video camcorders and computers. The Canon example shows how an innovative marketing strategy—with

---

[15] Dan Shapiro, "Ronald McDonald, Meet Stan Shih," *Sales & Marketing Management* (November 1995), p. 86.
[16] Dean Takahashi, "Hand-Held Combat: How the Competition Got Ahead of Intel in Making Cheap Chips," *The Wall Street Journal* (February 12, 1998), pp. A1, A10.
[17] Gary Hamel and C.K. Prahalad, "Strategic Intent," *Harvard Business Review* 67, no. 3 (May-June 1989), p. 69.

fresh approaches to the product, pricing, distribution, and selling—can lead to overall competitive advantage in the marketplace. Canon is not invulnerable, however; in 1991 Tektronix, a *U.S.* company, leap-frogged past Canon in the color copier market by introducing a plain-paper color copier that offered sharper copies at a much lower price.[18]

Collaborating. A final source of competitive advantage is using know-how developed by other companies. Such *collaboration* may take the form of licensing agreements, joint ventures, or partnerships. History has shown that the Japanese have excelled at using the collaborating strategy to achieve industry leadership. As noted in Chapter 9, one of the legendary licensing agreements of modern business history is Sony's licensing of transistor technology from AT&T's Western Electric subsidiary in the 1950s for $25,000. This agreement gave Sony access to the transistor and allowed the company to become a world leader. Building on its initial successes in the manufacturing and marketing of portable radios, Sony has grown into a superb global marketer whose name is synonymous with a wide assortment of high-quality consumer electronics products.

More recent examples of Japanese collaboration are found in the aircraft industry. Today, Mitsubishi Heavy Industries Ltd. and other Japanese companies manufacture airplanes under license to U.S. firms and also work as subcontractors for aircraft parts and systems. Many observers fear that the future of the American aircraft industry may be jeopardized as the Japanese gain technological expertise. Various examples of "collaborative advantage" are discussed in the next section.[19]

GLOBAL COMPETITION AND NATIONAL COMPETITIVE ADVANTAGE[20]

An inevitable consequence of the expansion of global marketing activity is the growth of competition on a global basis. In industry after industry, global competition is a critical factor affecting success. As Yoshino and Rangan have explained, **global competition** occurs when a firm takes a global view of competition and sets about maximizing profits worldwide, rather than on a country-by-country basis. If, when expanding abroad, a company encounters the same rival in market after market, then it is engaged in global competition.[21] In some industries, global companies have virtually excluded all other companies from their markets. An example is the detergent industry, where three companies—Colgate, Unilever, and Procter & Gamble—dominate an increasing number of detergent markets in Latin America and

18 G. Pascal Zachary, "Color Printer Gives Tektronix Jump on Canon," *The Wall Street Journal* (June 14, 1991), p. B1.

19 Hamel and Prahalad have continued to refine and develop the concept of strategic intent since it was first introduced in their groundbreaking 1989 article. Recently the authors outlined five broad categories of resource leverage that managers can use to achieve their aspirations: Concentrating resources on strategic goals via convergence and focus; accumulating resources more efficiently via extracting and borrowing; complementing one resource with another by blending and balancing; and conserving resources by recycling, co-opting, and shielding. Gary Hamel and C.K. Prahalad, "Strategy as Stretch and Leverage," *Harvard Business Review* (March-April 1993), pp. 75–84.

20 This section draws heavily on Chapter 3, "Determinants of National Competitive Advantage," and Chapter 4, "The Dynamics of National Advantage," in Porter 1990. For an extended country analysis based on Porter's framework, see Michael Enright, Antonio Francés, and Edith Scott Assavedra, *Venezuela: The Challenge of Competitiveness* (New York: St. Martins Press, 1996).

21 Michael Y. Yoshino and U. Srinivasa Rangan, *Strategic Alliances: An Entrepreneurial Approach to Globalization* (Boston: Harvard Business School Press, 1995), p. 56.

the Pacific Rim. Many companies can make a quality detergent, but brand-name muscle and the skills required for quality packaging overwhelm local competition in market after market.[22]

The automobile industry has also become fiercely competitive on a global basis. Part of the reason for the initial success of foreign automakers in the United States was the reluctance—or inability—of U.S. manufacturers to design and manufacture high quality, inexpensive small cars. The resistance of U.S. manufacturers was based on the economics of car production: the bigger the car, the higher the list price. Under this formula, small cars meant smaller unit profits. Therefore, U.S. manufacturers resisted the increasing preference in the U.S. market for smaller cars—a classic case of ethnocentrism and management myopia. European and Japanese manufacturers' product lines have always included cars smaller than those made in the U.S. In Europe and Japan, market conditions were much different than in the Unites States: less space, high taxes on engine displacement and fuel, and greater market interest in functional design and engineering innovations. First Volkswagen, then Japanese automakers such as Nissan and Toyota discovered a growing demand for their cars in the U.S. market. It is noteworthy that many significant innovations and technical advances—including radial tires, anti-lock brakes, and fuel injection—also came from Europe and Japan. Airbags are a notable exception.

The effect of global competition has been highly beneficial to consumers around the world. In the two examples cited—detergents and automobiles—consumers have benefited. In Central America, detergent prices have fallen as a result of global competition. In the United States, foreign companies have provided consumers with the automobile products, performance, and price characteristics they wanted. If smaller, lower-priced imported cars had not been available, it is unlikely that Detroit manufacturers would have provided a comparable product as quickly. What is true for automobiles in the United States is true for every product class around the world. Global competition expands the range of products and increases the likelihood that consumers will get what they want.

The downside of global competition is its impact on the producers of goods and services. Global competition creates value for consumers, but it also has the potential to destroy jobs and profits. When a company offers consumers in other countries a better product at a lower price, this company takes customers away from domestic suppliers. Unless the domestic supplier can create new values and find new customers, the jobs and livelihoods of the domestic supplier's employees are threatened.

This section addresses the following issue: Why is a particular nation a good home base for specific industries? Why, for example, is the United States the home base for the leading competitors in PCs, software, credit cards, and movies? Why is Germany the home of so many world leaders in printing presses, chemicals, and luxury cars? Why are so many leading pharmaceutical, chocolate/confectionery, and trading companies located in Switzerland? Why are the world leaders in consumer electronics home based in Japan?

Harvard professor Michael E. Porter addressed these issues in his landmark 1990 book *The Competitive Advantage of Nations.* Many observers hailed the book as a groundbreaking guide for shaping national policies on competitiveness. According to Porter, the presence or absence of particular attributes in individual countries influences industry development, not just the ability of individual firms to create core competences and competitive advantage.[23] Porter describes these attributes—

---

[22] See Joseph Kahn, "Cleaning Up: P&G Viewed China as a National Market and Is Conquering It," *The Wall Street Journal* (September 12, 1995), pp. A1, A6.

[23] Michael E. Porter, *The Competitive Advantage of Nations* (New York: Free Press, 1990).

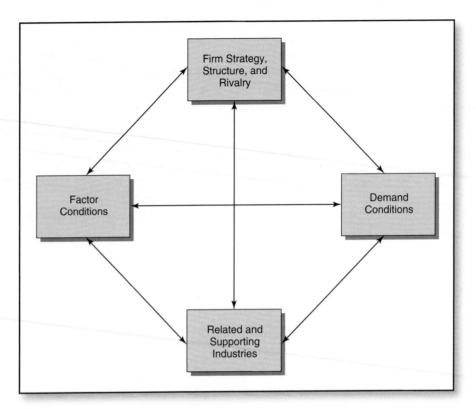

Figure 10-4
Determinants of National Advantage

Source: Adapted with permission of The Free Press, a Division of Simon & Schuster, Inc., from THE COMPETITIVE ADVANTAGE OF NATIONS by Michael E. Porter. Copyright © 1990, 1998 by The Free Press.

factor conditions, demand conditions, related and supporting industries, and firm strategy, structure, and rivalry—in terms of a national "diamond" (Figure 10-4). The diamond shapes the environment in which firms compete.

Factor Conditions

The phrase *factor conditions* refers to a country's endowment with resources. Factor resources may have been created or inherited, and may be divided into five categories: human, physical, knowledge, capital, and infrastructure.

Human Resources.   The quantity of workers available, the skills possessed by these workers, the wage levels, and the overall work ethic of the workforce together constitute a nation's human resource factor. Countries with a plentiful supply of low-wage workers have an obvious advantage in the production of labor-intensive products. On the other hand, such countries may be at a *disadvantage* when it comes to the production of sophisticated products requiring highly skilled workers capable of working without extensive supervision.

Physical Resources.   The availability, quantity, quality, and cost of land, water, minerals, and other natural resources determine a country's physical resources. A country's size and location are also included in this category, since proximity to markets and sources of supply, as well as transportation costs, are strategic considerations. These factors are obviously important advantages or disadvantages to industries dependent on natural resources.

Knowledge Resources. The availability within a nation of a significant population having scientific, technical, and market-related knowledge means that the nation is endowed with knowledge resources. The presence of this factor is usually a function of the number of research facilities and universities—both government and private—operating in the country. This factor is important to success in sophisticated products and services, and to doing business in sophisticated markets. This factor relates directly to Germany's leadership in chemicals; for some 150 years, Germany has been home to top university chemistry programs, advanced scientific journals, and apprenticeship programs.

Capital Resources. Countries vary in the availability, amount, cost, and types of capital available to the country's industries. The nation's savings rate, interest rates, tax laws, and government deficit all affect the availability of this factor. The advantage enjoyed by industries in countries with low capital costs versus those located in nations with relatively high capital costs is sometimes decisive. Firms paying high capital costs are frequently unable to stay in a market where the competition comes from a nation with low capital costs. The firms with the low cost of capital can keep their prices low and force the firms paying high costs to either accept low returns on investment or leave the industry.

Infrastructure Resources. Infrastructure includes a nation's banking system, healthcare system, transportation system, communications system, as well as the availability and cost of using these systems. More sophisticated industries are more dependent on advanced infrastructures for success.

Competitive advantage accrues to a nation's industry if the mix of factors available to the industry is such that it facilitates pursuit of a generic strategy: low-cost production or the production of a highly differentiated product or service. Competitive advantage may also be created indirectly by nations that have selective factor *disadvantages*. For example, the absence of suitable labor may force firms to develop forms of mechanization that give the nation's firms an advantage. High transportation costs may motivate firms to develop new materials that are less expensive to transport.

Demand Conditions

The nature of home demand conditions for the firm's or industry's products and services is important because it determines the rate and nature of improvement and innovation by the firms in the nation. These are the factors that either train firms for world-class competition or that fail to adequately prepare them to compete in the global marketplace. Three characteristics of home demand are particularly important to creation of competitive advantage: the composition of home demand, the size and pattern of growth of home demand, rapid home market growth, and the means by which a nation's home demand pulls the nation's products and services into foreign markets.

Composition of Home Demand. It is this that determines how firms perceive, interpret, and respond to buyer needs. Competitive advantage can be achieved when the home demand sets the quality standard and gives local firms a better picture of buyer needs at an earlier time than is available to foreign rivals. This advantage is enhanced when home buyers pressure the nation's firms to innovate quickly and frequently. The basis for advantage is the fact that the nation's firms can stay ahead of the market when firms are more sensitive to and more responsive to home demand, and when that demand, in turn, reflects or anticipates world demand.

Size and Pattern of Growth of Home Demand. These are important only if the composition of the home demand is sophisticated and anticipates foreign demand. Large home markets offer opportunities to achieve economies of scale and learning while dealing with familiar, comfortable markets. There is less apprehension about investing in large scale production facilities and expensive R&D programs when the home market is sufficient to absorb the increased capacity. If the home demand accurately reflects or anticipates foreign demand, and if the firms do not become content with serving the home market, the existence of large-scale facilities and programs will be an advantage in global competition.

Rapid home market growth is another incentive to invest in and adopt new technologies faster, and to build large, efficient facilities. The best example of this is in Japan, where rapid home market growth provided the incentive for Japanese firms to invest heavily in modern automated facilities. *Early home demand*, especially if it anticipates international demand, gives local firms the advantage of getting established in an industry sooner than foreign rivals. Equally important is *early market saturation*, which puts pressure on a company to expand into international markets and innovate. Market saturation is especially important if it coincides with rapid growth in foreign markets.

Means by Which a Nation's Products and Services Are Pushed or Pulled into Foreign Countries. The issue here is whether a nation's people and businesses go abroad and then demand the nation's products and services in those second countries. For example, when the U.S. auto companies set up operations in foreign countries, the auto parts industry followed. The same is true for the Japanese auto industry. Similarly, when overseas demand for the services of U.S. engineering firms skyrocketed after World War II, those firms in turn established demand for U.S. heavy construction equipment. This provided an impetus for Caterpillar to establish foreign operations.

A related issue is that of a nation's people going abroad for training, pleasure, business, or research. After returning home, they are likely to demand the products and services with which they became familiar while abroad. Similar effects can result from professional, scientific, and political relationships between nations. Those involved in the relationships begin to demand the products and services of the recognized leaders.

It is the interplay of demand conditions that produces competitive advantage. Of special importance are those conditions that lead to initial and continuing incentives to invest and innovate, and to continuing competition in increasingly sophisticated markets.

Related and Supporting Industries

A nation has an advantage when it is home to internationally competitive industries in fields that are related to, or in direct support of, other industries. Internationally competitive supplier industries provide inputs to downstream industries. The latter, in turn, are likely to be internationally competitive in terms of price and quality and thus gain competitive advantage from this situation. Downstream industries will have easier access to these inputs and the technology that produced them, and to the managerial and organizational structures that have made them competitive. Access is a function of proximity both in terms of physical distance and cultural similarity. It is not the inputs in themselves that give advantage. It is the *contact* and *coordination* with the suppliers—the opportunity to structure the value chain so that linkages with suppliers are optimized. These opportunities may not be available to foreign firms.

Similar advantages accrue when there are internationally competitive, related industries in a nation. Opportunities are available for coordinating and sharing value chain activities. A clear example of this are the opportunities for sharing between computer hardware manufacturers and software developers. Related industries also create "pull through" opportunities as described previously. For example, non-U.S. sales of PCs from Compaq, Dell, IBM, and others have bolstered demand for software from Microsoft and other U.S. companies. Porter notes that the development of the Swiss pharmaceuticals industry can be attributed in part to Switzerland's large synthetic dye industry; the discovery of the therapeutic effects of dyes in turn led to the development of pharmaceutical companies.[24]

Firm Strategy, Structure, and Rivalry

Differences in management styles, organizational skills, and strategic perspectives create advantages and disadvantages for firms competing in different types of industries, as do differences in the intensity of domestic rivalry. In Germany, for example, company structure and management style tends to be hierarchical. Managers tend to come from technical backgrounds and to be most successful when dealing with industries that demand highly disciplined structures, like chemicals and precision machinery. Italian firms, on the other hand, tend to look like, and be run like, small family businesses that stress customized over standardized products, niche markets, and substantial flexibility in meeting market demands.

Capital markets and attitudes toward investments are important components of the national environments. For example, U.S. laws prohibit banks from taking an equity stake in companies to which they extend loans. This drives a short-term focus on quarterly and annual gains and losses. This focus is carried into equity markets where low profits produce low share prices and the threat of a takeover. As a result, U.S. firms tend to do well in new-growth industries and other rapidly expanding markets. They do not do well in more mature industries where return on investment is lower and patient searching for innovations is required. Many other countries have an opposite orientation. Banks are allowed to take equity stakes in the customer companies to which they loan, which therefore take a long-term view and are less concerned about short-term results.

Perhaps the most powerful influence on competitive advantage comes from domestic rivalry. Domestic rivalry keeps an industry dynamic and creates continual pressure to improve and innovate. Local rivalry forces firms to develop new products, improve existing ones, lower costs and prices, develop new technologies, and improve quality and service. Rivalry with foreign firms lacks this intensity. Domestic rivals have to fight each other not just for market share, but also for employee talent, R&D breakthroughs, and prestige in the home market. Eventually, strong domestic rivalry will push firms to seek international markets to support expansions in scale and R&D investments—as Japan amply demonstrates. The absence of significant domestic rivalry will create complacency in the home firms and eventually cause them to become noncompetitive in the world markets.

It is not the number of domestic rivals that is important, rather, it is the intensity of the competition and the quality of the competitors that make the difference. It is also important that there be a fairly high rate of new business formations to create new competitors and safeguard against the older companies becoming comfortable with their market positions and products and services. As noted earlier in the discussion

---

[24] Michael E. Porter, *The Competitive Advantage of Nations* (New York: Free Press, 1990), p. 324.

of the forces shaping industry competition, new entrants bring new perspectives and new methods. They frequently define and serve new market segments that established companies have failed to recognize.

There are two final external variables to consider in the evaluation of national competitive advantage—chance and government.

Chance

Chance events play a role in shaping the competitive environment. Chance events are occurrences that are beyond the control of firms, industries, and usually governments. Included in this category are such things as wars and their aftermaths, major technological breakthroughs, sudden dramatic shifts in factor or input cost, like an oil crisis, dramatic swings in exchange rates, and so on.

Chance events are important because they create major discontinuities in technologies that allow nations and firms that were not competitive to leapfrog over old competitors and become competitive, even leaders, in the changed industry. For example, the development of microelectronics allowed many Japanese firms to overtake U. S. and German firms in industries that had been based on electromechanical technologies—areas traditionally dominated by the Americans and Germans.

From a systemic perspective, the role of chance events lies in the fact that they alter conditions in the diamond shown previously in Figure 10-4. The nation with the most favorable "diamond," however, will be the one most likely to take advantage of these events and convert them into competitive advantage. For example, Canadian researchers were the first to isolate insulin, but they could not convert this breakthrough into an internationally competitive product. Firms in the United States and Denmark were able to do that because of their respective national "diamonds."

Government

Although it is often argued that government is a major determinant of national competitive advantage, the fact is that government is not a determinant, but rather an influence on determinants. Government influences determinants by virtue of its role as a buyer of products and services, and by its role as a maker of policies on labor, education, capital formation, natural resources, and product standards. It also influences determinants by its role as a regulator of commerce, for example, by telling banks and telephone companies what they can and cannot do.

By reinforcing determinants in industries where a nation has competitive advantage, government improves the competitive position of the nation's firms. Governments devise legal systems that influence competitive advantage by means of tariffs and nontariff barriers and laws requiring local content and labor. In the United States, for example, the dollar's decline over the past decade has been due in part to a deliberate policy to enhance U.S. export flows and stem imports. In other words, government can improve or lessen competitive advantage, but it cannot create it.

The System of Determinants of National Competitive Advantage

It is important to view the determinants of national competitive advantage as an interactive system where activity in any one of the four points of the diamond impacts on all the others and vice versa. This interplay between the determinants is depicted in Figures 10-5 and 10-6. The interaction of all the forces is presented in Figure 10-7.

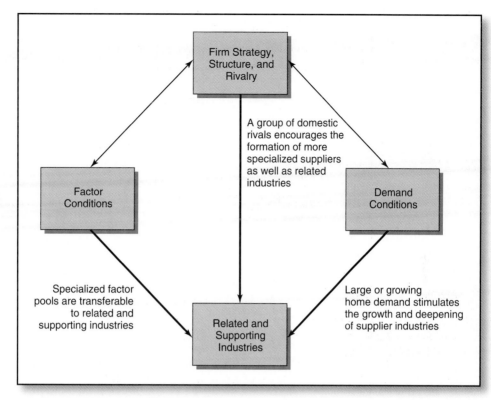

Figure 10-5
Influences on the Development of Related and Supporting Industries

Source: Adapted with permission of The Free Press, a Division of Simon & Schuster, Inc., from THE COMPETITIVE ADVANTAGE OF NATIONS by Michael E. Porter. Copyright © 1990, 1998 by The Free Press.

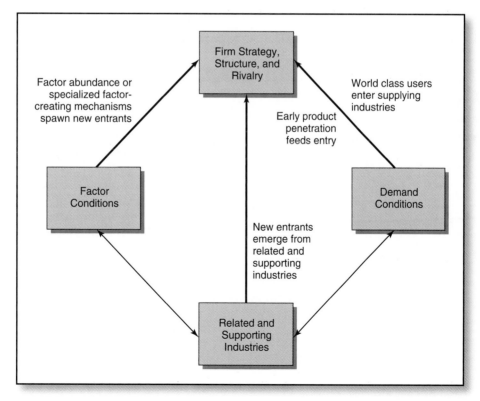

Figure 10-6
Influences on Domestic Rivalry

Source: Adapted with permission of The Free Press, a Division of Simon & Schuster, Inc., from THE COMPETITIVE ADVANTAGE OF NATIONS by Michael E. Porter. Copyright © 1990, 1998 by The Free Press.

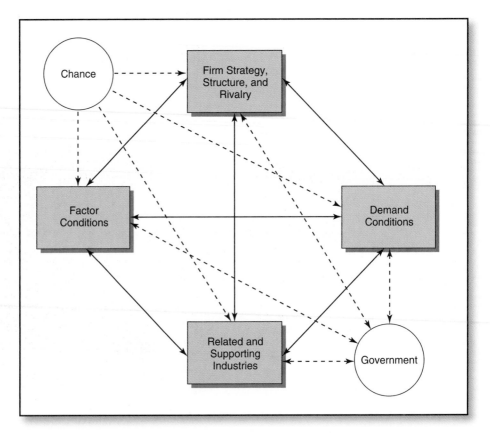

Figure 10-7
The Complete System

Source: Adapted with permission of The Free Press, a Division of Simon & Schuster, Inc., from THE COM-
PETITIVE ADVANTAGE OF NATIONS by Michael E. Porter. Copyright © 1990, 1998 by The Free Press.

CURRENT ISSUES IN COMPETITIVE ADVANTAGE

Porter's work on national competitive advantage has stimulated a great deal of further research. The Geneva-based World Economic Forum issues an annual report
ranking countries in terms of their competitiveness. A recent study by Morgan
Stanley used the Porter framework to identify 238 companies with a sustainable
competitive advantage worldwide. "National advantage" was then assessed by analyzing how many of these companies were headquartered in a particular country.
The United States ranked first, with 125 companies identified as world leaders (see
Table 10-1). Among the world's automakers, Morgan Stanley's analysts considered
only BMW, Toyota, and Honda to have worldwide competitive advantage.[25]

In a recent book, Dartmouth College professor Richard D'Aveni suggests that the
Porter strategy frameworks fail to adequately address the dynamics of competition
in the 1990s.[26] D'Aveni takes a different approach. He notes that, in today's business

---

[25] Tony Jackson, "Global Competitiveness Observed from an Unfamiliar Angle," *Financial Times*
(November 21, 1996), p. 18.

[26] Richard D'Aveni, *Hypercompetition: Managing the Dynamics of Strategic Maneuvering* (New York: Free
Press, 1994).

Table 10-1
Location of
Companies with
Global Competitive
Advantage

Country	Number of Companies
1. USA	125
2. UK	21
3. Japan	19
4. France	12
5. Germany	10
6. Netherlands	7
7. Canada	6
8. Switzerland	6
9. Sweden	3
10. Finland	3

environment, market stability is undermined by short product life cycles, short product design cycles, new technologies, and globalization. The result is an escalation and acceleration of competitive forces. In light of these changes, D'Aveni believes the goal of strategy has shifted from sustaining to disrupting advantages. The limitation of the Porter models, D'Aveni argues, is that they are static; that is, they provide a snapshot of competition at a given point in time. Acknowledging that Hamel and Prahalad broke new ground in recognizing that few advantages are sustainable, D'Aveni aims to build upon their work in order to shape "a truly dynamic approach to the creation and destruction of traditional advantages." D'Aveni uses the term *hypercompetition* to describe a dynamic competitive world in which no action or advantage can be sustained for long. In such a world, D'Aveni argues, "everything changes" because of the dynamic maneuvering and strategic interactions by hypercompetitive firms such as Microsoft and Gillette.

According to D'Aveni's model, competition unfolds in a series of dynamic strategic interactions in four arenas: cost-quality, timing and know-how, entry barriers, and deep pockets. Each of these arenas is "continuously destroyed and recreated by the dynamic maneuvering of hypercompetitive firms." According to D'Aveni, the only source of a truly sustainable competitive advantage is a company's ability to manage its dynamic strategic interactions with competitors by means of frequent movements and countermovements that maintain a relative position of strength in each of the four arenas.

Competition in the first arena, cost-quality, occurs via seven dynamic strategic interactions: price wars, quality and price positioning, "the middle path," "cover all niches," outflanking and niching, the move towards an ultimate value marketplace, and escaping from the ultimate value marketplace by restarting the cycle. D'Aveni cites the global watch industry as an example of hypercompetitive behavior in the cost-quality arena. In the 1970s, the center of the industry shifted from Switzerland to Japan as the Japanese created high quality quartz watches that could be sold cheaply. In the early 1980s, the merger of two Swiss companies into Suisse Microelectronique et d'Horlogerie SA (SMH, now the Swatch Group) was followed by a highly automated manufacturing innovation that allowed a quartz movement to be integrated into a stylish plastic case. As a result of this innovation and a strong marketing effort in support of the Swatch brand, the center of the watch industry shifted back to Switzerland. The watch industry continues to be highly segmented, with prestige brands competing on reputation and exclusivity; as with many other luxury goods, higher prices are associated with higher perceived quality. In the low-cost segment, brands compete on price and value.

The second arena for hypercompetition is based on organizational advantages derived from timing and know-how. As described by D'Aveni, a firm that has the skills to be a "first mover" and arrive first in a market has achieved a *timing advantage*. A *know-how advantage* is the technological knowledge—or other knowledge of a new method of doing business—that allows the firm to create an entirely new product or market (D'Aveni 1994, 71). D'Aveni identifies six dynamic strategic interactions that drive competition in this arena: capturing first mover advantages; imitation and improvement by followers; creating impediments to imitation; overcoming the impediments; transformation or leapfrogging; and downstream vertical integration. As the consumer electronics industry has globalized, Sony and its competitors have exhibited hypercompetitive behavior in this second arena. Sony has an enviable history of first-mover achievements based on its know-how in audio technology: first pocket-sized transistor radio, first consumer VCR, first portable personal stereo, and first compact disc player. While each of these innovations literally created an entirely new market, Sony has fallen victim to the risks associated with being a first mover. The second dynamic strategic interaction—imitation and improvement by followers—can be seen in the successful efforts of JVC and Matsushita to enter the home VCR market a few months after Sony's Betamax launch. VHS technology offered longer recording times and now, two decades later, is the dominant consumer format worldwide. In the 1990s, Sony found technological leaps harder to achieve, as evidenced by the slow market acceptance of its MiniDisc digital recording/playback units. Sony has also shown a willingness to be a follower; the company only entered the video game industry in 1994, but its 64-bit Playstation outsold a competitive product from Sega. After Sony launched the Playstation 2 in 2000, Sega halted production of its Dreamcast game player; the company will now concentrate on developing game software.

After years of moves and countermoves between Sony and its imitators, Sony progressed to downstream vertical integration with the 1988 purchase of CBS Records for $2 billion and then, later, the purchase of Columbia Pictures. The acquisitions, which represent the sixth dynamic strategic interaction, were intended to complement Sony's core "hardware" businesses (e.g., TVs, VCRs, and hi-fi equipment) with "software" (e.g., videocassettes and CDs). However, Matsushita quickly imitated Sony by paying $6 billion for MCA Inc. Neither Sony nor Matsushita has proved successful at managing the acquisitions. Sony took a $2.7 billion pre-tax write-off in 1995 for losses relating to its motion picture group; Matsushita sold 80 percent of its MCA stake to Seagram. Meanwhile, Sony has faced a more fundamental challenge: personal computers are dramatically changing the consumer electronics industry. Digital storage devices may soon render Sony's core competencies in analog audio technology obsolete. Sony executives must develop new know-how resources if the company is to continue to lead in the information age.

Industries in which barriers to entry have been built up comprise the third arena in which hypercompetitive behavior is exhibited. As described earlier in the chapter, these barriers include economies of scale, product differentiation, capital investments, switching costs, access to distribution channels, cost advantages other than scale, and government policies. D'Aveni describes how aggressive competitors erode these traditional entry barriers via eight strategic interactions. For example, a cornerstone of Dell's global success in the PC industry is a direct-sales approach that bypasses dealers and other distribution channels. Similarly, in the long distance industry, ring-back services based in the United States and elsewhere enable persons making long-distance calls from Europe to sidestep exorbitant rates charged by government-owned PTTs.

The first dynamic strategic interaction comes as a company builds a geographic "stronghold" by creating and reinforcing barriers. After securing a market—especially the home-country market—competitors begin to seek markets outside the stronghold. Thus, the second dynamic strategic interaction takes place when companies target the product market strongholds of competitors in other countries. Honda's geographic expansion outside Japan with motorcycles and automobiles—a series of forays utilizing guerrilla tactics—is a case in point. The third dynamic strategic interaction comes when incumbents make short-term counterresponses to the guerrilla attacks. Strong incumbents may try to turn back the invader with price wars, factory investment, or product introductions, or they may adopt a "wait and see" attitude before responding. In the case of both Harley-Davidson and the Detroit-based U.S. auto industry, management originally underestimated and rationalized away the full potential of the threat from Honda and other Japanese companies. Realizing that their company was a weak incumbent, Harley-Davidson management had little choice but to appeal for government protection. The resulting "breathing room" allowed Harley to put its house in order. Similarly, the U.S. government heeded Detroit's pleas for relief and imposed tariffs and quotas on Japanese auto imports. This gave the Big Three time to develop higher quality, fuel-efficient models to offer U.S. consumers.

The fourth dynamic strategic interaction occurs when the incumbent realizes it must respond fully to the invader by making strategic responses to create new hurdles. U.S. automakers, for example, waged a public relations campaign urging U.S. citizens to "Buy American." The fifth dynamic strategic interaction takes place when competitors react to these new hurdles. In an effort to circumvent import quotas as well as co-opt the "Buy American" campaign, the Japanese automakers built plants in the United States. The sixth dynamic strategic interaction consists of long-run counterresponses to the attack via defensive moves or offensive moves. GM's 1990 introduction of Saturn is a good illustration of a well formulated and executed defensive move. As the first decade of the twenty-first century gets underway, GM is launching another defensive move; in an effort to defend its Cadillac nameplate from Lexus, Acura, and Infiniti, GM is developing a global strategy for Cadillac. Competition in the third arena continues to escalate; in the seventh dynamic strategic interaction, competition between the incumbent and entrant is exported to the entrant's home turf. President Clinton's threat of trade sanctions against Japanese automakers in 1995 was intended to send a message that Japan needed to open its auto market. In 1997, GM intensified its assault on Japan with the introduction of Saturn. The eighth and final dynamic strategic interaction in this arena consists of an unstable standoff between the competitors. Over time the stronghold erodes as entry barriers are overcome, leading competitors to the fourth arena.

As the preceding discussion shows, the irony and paradox of the hypercompetition framework is that, in order to achieve a sustainable advantage, companies must seek a series of *unsustainable* advantages! D'Aveni is in agreement with Peter Drucker, who has long counseled that the role of marketing is innovation and the creation of new markets. Innovation begins with abandonment of the old and obsolete. In Drucker's words, "Innovative organizations spend neither time nor resources on defending yesterday. Systematic abandonment of yesterday alone can transfer the resources . . . for work on the new."

D'Aveni urges managers to reconsider and reevaluate the use of what he believes are old strategic tools and maxims. He warns of the dangers of commitment to a given strategy or course of action. The flexible, unpredictable player may have an advantage over the inflexible, committed opponent. D'Aveni notes that, in hypercompetition, pursuit of generic strategies results in short-term advantage at best. The winning companies are the ones that successfully move up the ladder of escalating competition, not the ones that lock into a fixed position. D'Aveni is also critical of the five forces model. The best entry barrier, he argues, is maintaining the initiative, not mounting a defensive attempt to exclude new entrants.

Other researchers have challenged Porter's thesis that a firm's home-base country is the main source of core competencies and innovation. For example, Professor Alan Rugman argues that the success of companies based in small economies such as Canada and New Zealand stems from the "diamonds" found in a particular set or combination of home and related countries. For example, a company based in a European Union nation may rely on the national "diamond" of one of the 14 other EU members. Similarly, one impact of NAFTA on Canadian firms is to make the U.S. "diamond" relevant to competency creation. Rugman argues that, in such cases, the distinction between the home nation and the host nation becomes blurred. He proposes that Canadian managers must look to a "double diamond" and assess the attributes of both Canada and the United States when formulating corporate strategy.[27] In other words, he argues that, for smaller countries, the nation is not the relevant unit of analysis in formulating strategy. Rather, corporate strategists must look beyond the nation to the region or to sets of closely-linked countries. Other critics have argued that Porter generalized inappropriately from the American experience, while confusing industry-level competition with trade at the national level. In the *Journal of Management Studies,* Howard Davies and Paul Ellis assert that nations can, in fact, achieve sustained prosperity without becoming innovation-driven; the authors also note the absence of strong diamonds in the home bases of many internationally successful industries.[28]

As for Michael Porter himself, his views on corporate strategy and competitive advantage evolved throughout the 1990s. In a recent interview, he emphasized the difference between operational efficiency and strategy. The former, in Porter's view, concerns improvement via time-based competition or total quality management; the latter entails "making choices." Porter explains, "'Choice' arises from doing things differently from the rival. And strategy is about trade-offs, where you decide to do this and not that. Strategy is the deliberate choice not to respond to some customers, or choosing which customer needs you are going to respond to." Porter is not convinced of the validity of competitive advantage models based on core competency or hypercompetitive industries. As for core competencies, Porter notes:

> Any individual thing that a company does can usually be imitated. The whole notion that you should rest your success on a few core competencies is an idea that invites destructive competition. Successful companies don't compete that way. They fit together the things they do in a way that is very hard to replicate. [Competitors] have to match everything, or they've basically matched nothing.

On the subject of hypercompetition, Porter says:

> I don't think we're moving towards a hypercompetitive world in which there are no tradeoffs. We're probably moving in the other direction. There are more customer segments than ever before, more technological options, more distribution channels. That ought to create lots of opportunities for unique positions.[29]

27 Alan M. Rugman and Lain Verbeke, "Foreign Subsidiaries and Multinational Strategic Management: An Extension and Correction of Porter's Single Diamond Framework," *Management International Review* 3, no. 2 (1993), pp. 71–84.
28 Howard Davies and Paul Ellis, "Porter's Competitive Advantage of Nations: Time for the Final Judgment?" *Journal of Management Studies* 37 no. 8 (December 2000), pp. 1189–1213.
29 Tony Jackson, "Why Being Different Pays," *Financial Times* (June 23, 1997), p. 14.

SUMMARY

In this chapter we focus on factors that help industries and countries achieve **competitive advantage.** According to Porter's **five forces model,** industry competition is a function of the threat of new entrants, the threat of substitutes, the bargaining power of suppliers and buyers, and rivalry among existing competitors. Porter's **generic strategies** model can be used by managers to conceptualize possible sources of competitive advantage. A company can pursue broad market strategies of **low cost** and **differentiation** or the more targeted approaches of **cost focus** and **focused differentiation.** Rugman and D'Cruz have developed a framework known as the **five partners model** to explain how networked business systems have achieved success in global industries. Hamel and Prahalad have proposed an alternative framework for pursuing competitive advantage, growing out of a firm's **strategic intent** and use of competitive innovation. A firm can build **layers of advantage,** search for **loose bricks** in a competitor's defensive walls, **change the rules of engagement,** or **collaborate with competitors** and utilize their technology and know-how.

Today, many companies are discovering that industry competition is changing from a purely domestic to a global phenomenon. Thus, competitive analysis must also be carried out on a global scale. Global marketers must also have an understanding of national sources of competitive advantage. Porter has described four determinants of **national advantage. Factor conditions** include human, physical, knowledge, capital, and infrastructure resources. **Demand conditions** include the composition, size, and growth pattern of home demand. The rate of home market growth and the means by which a nation's products are pulled into foreign markets also affect demand conditions. The final two determinants are the presence of related and supporting industries and the nature of firm strategy, structure, and rivalry. Porter notes that chance and government also influence a nation's competitive advantage. Porter's work has been the catalyst for promising new research into strategy issues, including D'Aveni's work on **hypercompetition** and Rugman's recent **double-diamond framework** for national competitive advantage.

DISCUSSION QUESTIONS

1. How can a company measure its competitive advantage? How does a firm know if it is gaining or losing competitive advantage?
2. Outline Porter's five forces model of industry competition. How are the various barriers to entry relevant to global marketing?
3. How does the five partners, or flagship model, developed by Rugman and D'Aveni differ from Porter's five forces model?
4. Give an example of a company that illustrates each of the four generic strategies that can lead to competitive advantage: overall cost leadership, cost focus, differentiation, and differentiation focus.
5. Briefly describe Hamel and Prahalad's framework for competitive advantage.
6. How can a nation achieve competitive advantage?
7. According to current research on competitive advantage, what are some of the shortcomings of Porter's models?
8. What is the connection, if any, between *national* competitive advantage and *company* competitive advantage? Discuss and explain.

SUGGESTED READINGS

Books

Abegglen, James C., and George Stalk Jr. *Kaisha: The Japanese Corporation.* New York: Basic Books, 1985.

D'Aveni, Richard. *Hypercompetition: Managing the Dynamics of Strategic Maneuvering.* New York: Free Press, 1994.

Day, George S. *Market Driven Strategy: Processes for Creating Value.* New York: Free Press, 1990.

Hamel, Gary, and C. K. Prahalad. *Competing for the Future.* Boston: Harvard Business School Press, 1994.

Micklethwait, John. *The Witch Doctors: Making Sense of the Management Gurus.* New York: Times, 1996.

Ohmae, Kenichi. *Triad Power.* New York: Free Press, 1985.

Pattison, Joseph E. *Acquiring the Future: America's Survival and Success in the Global Economy.* Homewood, IL: Dow Jones-Irwin, 1990.

Porter, Michael E. *Competitive Advantage: Creating and Sustaining Superior Performance.* New York: Free Press, 1985.

―――. *Competition in Global Industries.* Boston: Harvard Business School Press, 1986.

―――. *The Competitive Advantage of Nations.* New York: Free Press, 1990.

―――. *Competitive Strategy.* New York: Free Press, 1980.

Rugman, Alan M., and Joseph R. D'Cruz. *Multinationals as Flagship Firms.* Oxford: Oxford University Press, 2000.

Slywotzky, Adrian J. *Value Migration: How to Think Several Moves Ahead of the Competition.* Boston: Harvard Business School Press, 1996.

Womack, James P., Daniel T. Jones, and Daniel Roos. *The Machine That Changed the World.* New York: HarperCollins, 1990.

Yip, George S. *Total Global Strategy: Managing for Worldwide Competitive Advantage.* Englewood Cliffs, NJ: Prentice Hall, 1995.

Articles

Bartmess, Andrew, and Keith Cerny. "Building Competitive Advantage Through a Global Network of Capabilities." *California Management Review* 35, no. 2 (Winter 1993), pp. 78–103.

Chadee, Doren, and Rajiv Kumar. "Sustaining the International Competitive Advantage of Asian Firms: A Conceptual Framework and Research Propositions." *Asia-Pacific Journal of Management* 18, no. 4 (December 2001) pp. 461–480.

Cravens, David W., H. Kirk Downey, and Paul Lauritano. "Global Competition in the Commercial Aircraft Industry: Positioning for Advantage by the Triad Nations," *Columbia Journal of World Business* 26, no. 4 (Winter 1992), pp. 46–58.

Davies, Howard, and Paul Ellis. "Porter's Competitive Advantage of Nations: Time for the Final Judgment?" *Journal of Management Studies* 37 no. 8 (December 2000), pp. 1189–1213.

Egelhoff, William G. "Great Strategy or Great Strategy Implementation—Two Ways of Competing in Global Markets." *Sloan Management Review* 34, no. 2 (Winter 1993), pp. 37–50.

Ghosal, Sumantra, and D. Eleanor Westney. "Organizing Competitor Analysis Systems." *Strategic Management Journal* 12, no. 1 (January 1991), pp. 17–31.

Hamel, Gary, and C. K. Prahalad. "Strategic Intent." *Harvard Business Review* 67, no. 3 (May-June 1989), pp. 63–76.

―――. "The Core Competence of the Corporation." *Harvard Business Review* 68, no. 3 (May-June 1990), pp. 79–93.

―――. "Strategy as Stretch and Leverage." *Harvard Business Review* 71, no. 2 (March-April 1993), pp. 75–85.

Henzler, Herbert A. "The New Era of Eurocapitalism." *Harvard Business Review* 70, no. 4 (July-August 1992), pp. 57–68.

Li, Jiatao, and Stephen Guisinger. "How Well Do Foreign Firms Compete in the United States?" *Business Horizons* 34, no. 6 (November-December 1991), pp. 49–53.

Mascarenhas, Briance. "Order of Entry and Performance in International Markets." *Strategic Management Journal* 13, no. 7 (October 1992), pp. 499–510.

Morrison, Allen J., and Kendall Roth. "A Taxonomy of Business-Level Strategies in Global Industries." *Strategic Management Journal* 13, no. 6 (September 1992), pp. 399–417.

Peters, Tom. "Rethinking Scale." *California Management Review* 35, no. 1 (Fall 1992), pp. 7–29.

Robert, Michel M. "Attack Competitors by Changing the Game Rules." *Journal of Business Strategy* 12, no. 5 (September-October 1991), pp. 53–56.

Rugman, Alan M., and Alain Verbeke. "Foreign Subsidiaries and Multinational Strategic Management: An Extension and Correction of Porter's Single Diamond Framework." *Management International Review* 33, no. 2 (Special Issue 1993/2), pp. 71–84.

―――. "Subsidiary-Specific Advantages in Multinational Enterprises." *Strategic Management Journal* 22, no. 3 (March 2001), pp. 237–250.

Schill, Ronald L., and David N. McArthur. "Redefining the Strategic Competitive Unit: Towards a New Global Marketing Paradigm?" *International Marketing Review* 9, no. 3, pp. 5–24.

Schoemaker, Paul J. H. "How to Link Strategic Vision to Core Capabilities." *Sloan Management Review* 34, no. 1 (Fall 1992), pp. 67–81.

Spannos, Yiannis E., and Spyros Lioukas. "An Examination into the Causal Logic of Rent Generation: Contrasting Porter's Competitive Strategy Framework and the Resource-based Perspective." *Strategic Management Journal* 22, no. 10 (October 2001), pp. 907–934.

Williams, Jeffrey R. "How Sustainable is Your Competitive Advantage?" *California Management Review* 34, no. 3 (Spring 1992), pp. 29–51.

CASE

Case 10-1   The Photo Wars: Fuji vs. Kodak

Eastman Kodak, headquartered in Rochester, New York, has long been synonymous with amateur and professional photography in the United States and around the world. Ranked 155th in the 2002 *Fortune* 500, Kodak has enjoyed decades of undisputed leadership in the silver-halide chemical processes that formed the basis of the photography industry. Taken together, film and photofinishing represent a $15 billion worldwide market. Sales of Kodak film—packaged in familiar yellow boxes—and easy-to-use "point and shoot" Kodak cameras contributed to the company's domination of photography throughout the twentieth century. Profits from camera sales were modest; profits on film were spectacular.

In recent years, Kodak has faced serious challenges to its leadership position. The company's long-entrenched conservative corporate culture, bureaucratic organizational structure, and go-slow approach to innovation resulted in sluggish, ill-fated reactions to changes in the photography market. The company that has been a particular headache for Kodak is Japan's Fuji Photo Film Co. Fuji launched an ambitious attack on the market leader by offering film products that many believed offered better color at lower prices. Kodak's share of the U.S. color-negative film market—in which it once enjoyed a near monopoly—slipped to 82 percent by the mid-1980s.

Fuji proved adept at innovating by launching new products and targeting new segments. In 1982, it was the first to launch color print film with a speed of 400, which made it the world's fastest film ("faster"—or "higher speed"—film gives superior results under low-light or fast-action conditions). Kodak's fast color film was not introduced until months later. In 1984, Fuji introduced 1600-speed color film; Kodak was not able to match it until 1990. Kodak and Fuji have both introduced new film products targeted at "advanced amateurs"—a new segment midway between the traditional segments of consumer and professional. Fuji also recently introduced a new professional slide film, Velvia, that offers super-saturated colors; although Kodak quickly responded with a competitive product, Velvia has gained wider acceptance.

Fuji's innovations eventually enabled it to achieve more than a 10 percent penetration of the U.S. market during the 1980s. Moreover, Fuji scored another important competitive victory when it beat out Kodak for the honor of official photographic sponsor of the 1984 Olympics. Kodak, apparently convinced of its own

invulnerability, offered the Olympic committee $1 million dollars plus free film; Fuji bid $7 million, was awarded the sponsorship, and achieved high visibility at the event with its green blimps. Since that time, Fuji's annual sales volume has grown at rates exceeding 20 percent—outpacing growth in the overall market. Chastened by one missed opportunity, Kodak successfully bid $10 million for a sponsorship position at the 1988 Olympics in Seoul, Korea.

Fuji has demonstrated superiority in operations as well as marketing. Sales per employee at Fuji totaled $380,000 in 1988, compared to Kodak's per-employee sales figure of only $140,000. Fuji also adopted a more innovative approach to distribution: Although Kodak, for example, kept warehouses stocked to overflowing with most of its products, Fuji used overnight air shipments to cut inventory costs and delivery times. Fuji also artfully infiltrated Kodak's home turf; it managed to obtain technology licenses from Kodak's patent attorneys, who failed to inform Kodak executives of their actions. According to the manager who first uncovered and then reported this fact, Kodak executives were unresponsive.

Kodak management has not been content to sit back and idly watch as Fuji encroached on its home turf; it has retaliated. Yet, Kodak has had mixed success in launching a counterattack in Fuji's home market, the world's second largest photographic market. Each year, amateur Japanese photographers buy 300 million rolls of film. Even though Kodak has invested half a billion dollars in the Japanese market during the past several years, headquarters had a tendency to turn a deaf ear to employee suggestions. Specifically, employees based in Japan urged Kodak to behave more like a Japanese corporation and less like a foreign-based one. For example, Kodak supplied the Japanese market film in boxes with English printing on them until 1985. Kodak also waited until the mid-1980s to open offices in Japan. When Kodak did open for business in Japan, it imposed its U.S. work policies and procedures; for example, it did not offer its Japanese employees a housing allowance—a common practice among Japanese firms. This approach resulted in high employee turnover and slow acceptance of Kodak in the Japanese market, where consumers show high awareness of the companies behind the brand names.

Although dollar sales of all Kodak products in Japan have increased to $1.3 billion, sales of color print film have been below expectations. Kodak has only a 7 percent share of the Japanese market—about equivalent to Fuji's share in the United States. Nevertheless, Kodak has been successful with two disposable camera products: one with a wide-angle lens, the other, a disposable underwater model. The Japanese like to take group pictures—on the golf course, for example—and the wide-angle disposable gets everyone in the picture better than a conventional camera. Meanwhile, the underwater disposable has proven to be a big hit with Japanese youth, who are fond of snorkeling. Still, Kodak's disposable cameras have to compete with Fuji's—which reached the market a year earlier and were promoted as "film with lens."

Back in the United States, after a slow start, sales of cardboard "single-use" or "one-time" cameras from both companies have also taken off. Thanks to a name change—Kodak's "Fling" was rechristened "Funsaver"—and a recycling program, the cameras overcame objections from environmentalists; today Kodak and Fuji command about 80 percent of the market. In 1991, Americans bought 15 million one-time cameras, which accounted for all the growth in film sales. Sales passed the 50 million mark by the mid-1990s. Touted as "the perfect second camera" and ranging in price from $4 to $13, the cameras appeal to vacationers, tourists, and parents who buy them for children to use. In addition to the underwater and wide-angle models, the cameras also are available in flash and telephoto models.

Kodak's final line of defense in the domestic market may well be its distribution clout. Kodak products are well entrenched in supermarket and drugstore chains, where Fuji must jostle with other newcomers such as Konica and Polaroid for shelf space. In addition, Kodak has agreements with 40 of America's largest amusement parks guaranteeing that only Kodak film will be sold on the premises. Kodak is the exclusive supplier to the Air Force Exchange Service (AFES), which stocks film at PX stores on military bases. These are some of the reasons Fuji has shifted its attention from the United States to Europe, where Kodak has a 40 percent share of the film market and Germany's Agfa has about 20 percent. Fuji currently has about a 25 percent share of the European market, compared with 10 percent a decade ago.

The distribution issue was at the center of a trade dispute between Kodak and Fuji that erupted in 1995. George Fisher, Kodak's new CEO, decided to turn up the pressure on Japan. Kodak charged Fuji with unfairly dominating the Japanese photography market and requested that the U.S. government intervene. Fuji responded with similar charges about Kodak's behavior in the United States. One of Kodak's concerns is the fact that Fuji is closely linked with the four biggest film distributors in Japan and holds equity stakes in two of them. Kodak alleges that this arrangement allows Fuji to dissuade distributors from handling other brands of film. Fuji says its Japanese distributors are not prevented from dealing with other suppliers; moreover, it says Kodak's Japanese problems are self-inflicted, the result of poor strategy execution such as concentrating the marketing effort on large cities. Fuji claims that *Kodak* is the film industry's unfair competitor that binds U.S. stores with exclusive arrangements by paying them fees and rebates. A Kodak spokesperson replied to these allegations by noting, "We offer incentives, but retailers are free to carry other brands if they wish. These relationships are completely voluntary."

The dispute was ultimately brought before the World Trade Organization. Back at home, CEO Fisher moved forward with his strategy to launch a new family of digital products. In 1996, after years of development, the Advanced Photo System (APS) was introduced. The APS line of cameras and film—both of which are incompatible with the traditional 35mm format—incorporate digital technology that allow snapshots taken by amateur shutterbugs to be enhanced in the photofinishing lab. APS had been developed by a strategic partnership consisting of Kodak, Minolta Camera, Canon, Nikon, and, ironically, Fuji Photo Film. As a retired Kodak executive recalled, "It was a real challenge to get our people to view Fuji as an ally while simultaneously viewing them as a samurai on the street." In the United States, the launch was supported by Kodak's $100 million trade and consumer ad campaign that proclaimed, "The dawn of a new era in photography is here!" Each company's APS system carried a different brand name: Kodak Advantix, Minolta Vectis, and Nikon Nuvis. Unfortunately, production problems were so serious that, at an industry trade show in Las Vegas in February of 1996, key retailers were warned that supplies would be short on the planned April 22 in-store date. French retailers had to discard 10,000 copies of a catalog featuring the system because no product was available.

Meanwhile, Fuji launched a fresh, multifront assault on Kodak's American stronghold. First, in July 1996, Fuji announced the purchase of six regional photofinishing labs from Wal-Mart. Fuji also won a 10-year contract as sole provider of photofinishing services for Wal-Mart. Then, in May 1997, Fuji officials announced that they would invest $200 million and produce 35mm color film at the company's South Carolina production facility. As a Fuji spokesperson explained, "To win against the competition, we must be closer to the customer, to make products that meet market needs." Industry observers noted that the move would enable Fuji both to sidestep tariffs of 3.7 percent on film imports and to pursue more flexible pricing policies in the huge U.S. market without risking charges of dumping. During the first six months of 1997, even before the new plant came on line, Fuji cut its film prices with a resulting 28 percent increase in shipments. One industry analyst predicted that Fuji's gains in the U.S. market would push it past Kodak in terms of world market share by 1999. ■

DISCUSSION QUESTIONS

1. Evaluate Kodak's competitive strategy and give the company a grade for its strategy during the 1980s. Explain the basis of your grade.
2. Which company, in your view, has the greatest competitive advantage, Fuji or Kodak? Explain your choice.
3. What must Kodak do to dominate the photography business in the twenty-first century the way it did in the twentieth century? What must Fuji do to prevent this?
4. What is your assessment of the trade dispute? Do you think Kodak or Fuji engages in anticompetitive acts?
5. Why did Kodak pursue a strategic alliance to develop the Advantix system?

SOURCES: Michiyo Nakamoto, "Fujifilm in New Push to Boost Exposure in U.S." *Financial Times* (May 13, 1997), p. 8; Wendy Bounds, "Camera System is Developed but Not Delivered," *The Wall Street Journal* (Aug. 7, 1996), pp. B1, B6; Wendy Bounds, "Film Exposures: Fuji, Accused by Kodak of Hogging Markets, Spits Back: 'You Too'," *The Wall Street Journal* (July 31, 1995), pp. A1, A4; Joan E. Rigdon, "For Cardboard Cameras, Sales Picture Enlarges and Seems Brighter than Ever," *The Wall Street Journal* (February 11, 1992), p. B1; Clare Ansberry and Masayoshi Kanabayashi, "Kodak Remains Out of Focus in Japan When It Comes to Key Color Film Market," *The Wall Street Journal* (December 7, 1990), p. B1; Ansberry, "New Kodak and Fuji Films Target Advanced Amateurs," *The Wall Street Journal* (March 17, 1989), p. B1; Ansberry and Carol Hymowitz, "Last Chance: Kodak Chief is Trying, for the Fourth Time, to Trim Firm's Costs," *The Wall Street Journal* (September 19, 1989), pp. A1, A24; Gale Eisenstodt and Amy Feldman, "Sharply Focused," *Forbes* (December 24, 1990), pp. 50, 53; Alex Taylor III, "Kodak Scrambles to Refocus," *Fortune* (March 3, 1986), pp. 34–36+; "Now for Kodak," *Economist* (July 30, 1988), pp. 67–68.

Chapter **11**

Product and Brand Decisions

*E*xecutives at Boeing Company, the world's largest manufacturer of commercial aircraft, have plenty of experience making "bet the company" type of product decisions. In the 1950s, when the company was best known for military aircraft such as the B-52 bomber, Boeing single-handedly created the commercial market for jet aircraft with the introduction of the 707. In the mid-1960s, Boeing gambled that the world's airlines would be enthusiastic about a new wide-body aircraft. The gamble paid off handsomely: Since its first passenger flight in 1970, the Boeing 747 jumbo jet has generated more than $130 billion in sales. In 2001, Boeing made headlines again when it announced plans for a revolutionary new delta-wing aircraft called the Sonic Cruiser. The new jet would carry between 100 and 300 passengers and fly just below the speed of sound (Mach 1) with a range of up to 10,000 miles. On the same day it announced the Sonic Cruiser, Boeing cancelled development of the 747X, a larger, updated version of the venerable jumbo jet. The strategic decision to proceed with the Sonic Cruiser was based in part on Boeing's belief that air travelers are keenly interested in saving time, especially on long routes; the Sonic Cruiser would cut travel time by one hour for each 3,000 miles flown. Boeing also predicts that airline deregulation in Europe and Asia will result in increased industry competition, a situation that will result in more direct flights between cities that bypass the congestion of major regional hubs. The stakes are high: The world's airlines are expected to spend $1.5 trillion on new aircraft during the next two decades.

Products are arguably the most crucial element of a company's marketing program. Product decisions are integral to the company's value proposition; in addition, every aspect of the enterprise, including pricing, communication, and distribution policies, must fit the product. A firm's customers and competitors are determined by the products it

A visitor to the Aviation Expo in Beijing looks at a model of Boeing's proposed new Sonic Cruiser passenger jet. Although China is home to 16 of the world's 25 most populous cities, the level of annual trips per capita in China is currently among the lowest in the world: only .05, compared with 3 in the United States. However, China's air transport needs are expected to grow dramatically; Boeing executives estimate that China will spend about $140 billion over the next twenty years to buy 1,700 new regional and long-haul aircraft.

offers. In many purchase situations, customers seek out particular brands, not just products. The challenge facing a company with global horizons is to develop product and brand policies and strategies that are sensitive to market needs, competition, and company ambitions and resources on a global scale. Effective global marketing entails finding a balance between the payoff from extensively adapting products and brands to local market preferences and the benefits that come from concentrating company resources on relatively standardized global products and brands.

This chapter examines the major dimensions of global product and brand decisions. First is a review of basic product and brand concepts, followed by a discussion of local, international, and global products and brands. Product design criteria are identified, and attitudes toward foreign products are explored. The next section outlines strategic alternatives available to global marketers. Finally, new product issues in global marketing are discussed.

BASIC PRODUCT CONCEPTS

A **product** is a good, service, or idea with tangible and/or intangible attributes that collectively create value for a buyer or user. A product's *tangible* attributes can be assessed in physical terms such as weight, dimensions, or materials used. Suppose, for example, a particular cellular phone model measures 1.5 by 5.5 inches, weighs 5.5 ounces, employs long-life, quick-charging lithium-ion batteries, and comes equipped with a display screen and a GSM (global system for mobile communications) chip. These tangible, physical features translate into benefits that enhance the convenience of making or receiving telephone calls or pages. Accessories such as

Visit the Web site
www.boeing.com

hands-free kits and designer faceplates enhance the value offering by enabling users to customize their handsets and make them extensions of their personalities. *Intangible* product attributes, including status associated with product ownership, a manufacturer's service commitment, and a brand's overall reputation or mystique, are also important. When shopping for a cellular phone, for example, many people want "the best": They want a phone loaded with features (tangible product elements), as well as one that makes a status statement (intangible product elements).

Product Types

A frequently used framework for classifying products distinguishes between consumer and industrial goods. For example, Kodak offers products and services to both amateur and professional photographers worldwide. Consumer and industrial goods, in turn, can be further classified on the basis of criteria such as buyer orientation. Buyer orientation is a composite measure of the amount of effort a customer expends, the level of risk associated with a purchase, and buyer involvement in the purchase. The buyer orientation framework includes such categories as convenience, preference, shopping, and specialty goods. Although film is often a low-involvement purchase, many film buyers in the United States show a strong preference for Kodak film, and significant numbers of Japanese photographers prefer Fuji. Products can also be categorized in terms of their life span (durable, nondurable, and disposable). Kodak and other companies market both single-use (disposable) cameras as well as more expensive units that are meant to last for many years. As these examples from the photo industry suggest, traditional product classification frameworks are fully applicable to global marketing.

Brands

A **brand** is a complex bundle of images and experiences in the customer's mind. A brand represents a promise by a particular company about a particular product; it is a sort of quality certification. Brands also enable customers to better organize their marketplace experience by helping them seek out and zero in on particular products. An important brand function is to differentiate a particular company's offering from all others. Customers integrate all their experiences of observing, using, or consuming a product with everything they hear and read about it. Information about products and brands comes from a variety of sources and cues, including advertising, publicity, sales personnel, and packaging. Perceptions of service after the sale, price, and distribution are also taken into account (Figure 11-1). The sum of impressions is a **brand image,** a single—but often complex—mental image about both the product itself and the company that markets it. Another important brand concept is **brand equity,** which represents the added value that accrues to a product as a result of a company's prior investments in the marketing of the brand. Brand equity can also be thought of as an asset representing the value created by the relationship between the brand and customers over time. The stronger the relationship, the greater the equity. For example, the value of global megabrands such as Coca-Cola and Marlboro has been estimated to run in the tens of *billions* of dollars.[1]

Warren Buffett, the legendary American investor who heads Berkshire Hathaway, asserts that the global power of brands such as Coca-Cola and Gillette permits the companies that own them to set up a protective moat around their economic castles. Buffett explains, "The average company, by contrast, does battle daily

---

[1] For a complete discussion of brand equity, see Kevin Lane Keller, *Strategic Brand Management* (Upper Saddle River, NJ: Prentice Hall, 1998), chapter 2.

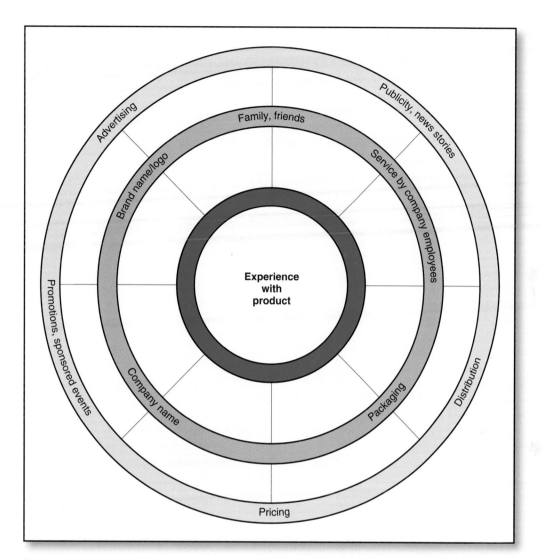

Figure 11-1
Components of a Brand Image

without any such means of protection."[2] That protection often yields added profit, since the owners of powerful brand names can typically command higher prices for their products than can owners of lesser brands. In other words, the strongest global brands have tremendous brand equity.

As noted, the essence of a brand exists in the mind; as such, brands are intangible. However, companies develop logos, distinctive packaging, and other communication devices to provide visual representations of their brands. A **logo** can take a variety of forms, starting with the brand name itself. For example, the Coca-Cola brand is expressed in part by a *word mark* consisting of the words "Coke" and "Coca-Cola" written in a distinctive white script. The "wave" that appears on red Coke cans and bottle labels is an example of a *non-word mark logo,*

2   John Willman, "Labels That Say It All," *Financial Times—Weekend Money* (October 25–26, 1997), p. 1.

The Rest of the Story
Boeing's Big Bet

Boeing's announcement came as a shock to the entire global aerospace industry, including archrival Airbus. Airbus, which until 2000 was a consortium of five European companies, had spent ten years planning a double-decker, super jumbo craft, the A380. The new jet, which will be put into service in 2006, will cost as much as $12 billion to develop. Airbus executives believe *their* new aircraft is the one that will revolutionize air travel in the twenty-first century. After assessing strategic opportunities, Airbus arrived at a different conclusion than Boeing. While agreeing that the business will become more fragmented as deregulation spreads around the world, they predict large increases in passenger traffic but a limited amount of new airport construction. The conclusion: The airlines will need a new super jumbo to carry more passengers while reducing the number of flights between key hubs.

Airbus executives also dismissed Boeing's announcement as a public relations tactic to divert the public's attention from its decision not to compete head-to-head with the A380. Moreover, some industry observers questioned whether Boeing could build a faster airplane for which the total cost of operation would be feasible. One issue was whether current aerospace technology, including supercomputers for design and new composite materials containing graphite, could be employed effectively. Roy V. Harris, a former assistant director of research at NASA, asked,

"Can they do it? I can't say that for sure right now. I think it will be a challenge." Airbus conceded that it, too, had considered building a faster aircraft but, as one executive said, "We have seen no great change in the laws of economics and physics that have given us any hope." John Leahy, the top sales executive for Airbus, is skeptical as well. "If there is such a thing as a free lunch, I am sure we are all interested," he said

For now, Boeing executives stand by their decision. Alan Mulally, the top executive at Boeing's commercial airplane division, said, "People don't need bigger airplanes. The only reason the airlines were asking for a 747X was so that they would have something to compare to the A380. They don't want either." However, Boeing has backpedaled in the past, canceling new product development programs such as a proposed fuel-efficient model 7J7 and the 747X. Mulally defends that record, saying that Boeing is a nimble, customer-driven company. "What a neat thing it is to look at your customers and the market and make your investments accordingly. The fact that Boeing is listening and flexible is a great thing," he said. One competitor predicted that Boeing would ultimately cancel the Sonic Cruiser program and offer airlines a scaled down version of its 777 instead.

"What if you could differentiate service in a new way: faster, higher, a smoother ride, above the weather?"
—Alan Mulally, Boeing executive

SOURCES: J. Lynn Lunsford, "Lean Times: With Airbus on Its Tail, Boeing Is Rethinking How It Builds Planes," *The Wall Street Journal* (September 5, 2001), pp. A1, A16; Alan Levin, "Boeing's Sonic Cruiser: Gambling on Speed," *USA Today* (June 18, 2001), pp. 1A, 2A; Laurence Zuckerman, "Boeing Plays an Aerial Wild Card," *The New York Times* (June 17, 2001), sec. 3, pp. 1, 11; Daniel Michaels, "New Approach: Airbus Revamp Brings Sense to Consortium, Fuels Boeing Rivalry," *The Wall Street Journal* (April 3, 2001), pp. A1, A8; Jeff Cole, "Wing Commander: At Boeing, an Old Hand Provides New Tricks in Battle with Airbus," *The Wall Street Journal* (January 10, 2001), pp. A1, A12.

"It is the intangible value that comes from the name 'Picasso' that creates the value. Don't think for a minute that if you had a fake Van Gogh on the wall you'd enjoy it just as much. And a Sara Lee cake without the Sara Lee brand name doesn't taste as good." —Bryan Lee, CEO, Sara Lee Corp[3]

sometimes known as a *brand symbol*. Non-word marks such as the Nike swoosh, the three-pronged Mercedes star, and McDonald's golden arches have the great advantage of transcending language and are therefore especially valuable to global marketers. To protect the substantial investment of time and money required to build and sustain brands, companies register brand names, logos, and other brand elements as trademarks or service marks. As discussed in Chapter 5, safeguarding trademarks and other forms of intellectual property is a key issue in global marketing.

---

[3]   Lucy Kellaway, "The Art of Brand Promotion," *Financial Times* (July 3, 1998), p. 9.

Local Products and Brands

A local product or brand is one that has achieved success in a single national market. Sometimes a global company creates local products and brands in an effort to cater to the needs and preferences of particular country markets. For example, Coca-Cola has developed several branded drink products for sale only in Japan, including a noncarbonated, ginseng-flavored beverage, a blended tea known as Sokenbicha, and Lactia-brand fermented milk drink. In Poland, B.A.T Industries recognized that consumption of local cigarette brands was much higher than that of premium-priced global brands such as Marlboro. In the mid-1990s, B.A.T introduced a new brand, Jan Sobieski, named for a Polish king. Thanks to high-quality packaging and a price that was 30 percent less than global brands, Jan Sobieski quickly captured 8 percent of total cigarette sales in Poland. Similarly, the rosters of the giant global record companies frequently include artists whose popularity is limited to a single country. For example, BMG International releases recordings by local stars such as B'z (Japan), Bronco (Mexico), and Joaquin Sabina (Spain). Artists such as these may sell one million CDs or cassettes in their home markets while remaining virtually unknown elsewhere.

Local products and brands also represent the lifeblood of domestic companies. Entrenched local products and brands can represent significant competitive hurdles to global companies entering new country markets. In developing countries, global brands are sometimes perceived as overpowering local ones. Growing national pride can result in a social backlash that favors local products and brands. In China, a local TV set manufacturer, Changhong Electric Appliances, has built its share of the

In April 1996, Kodak, Minolta, and several other companies launched a new camera and film format known as the Advanced Photo System (APS). With about $1.2 billion in camera sales and $2.7 billion in film sales each year, the United States is the world's number one photo market. However, the point-and-shoot camera category has been mature for years. One reason is demographic: Americans in their 30s are the most avid shutterbugs, but that segment of the U.S. population is shrinking. Meanwhile, increasing numbers of baby boomers are turning 50, an age at which picture taking begins to decline dramatically. The camera manufacturers developed the new 24mm APS format in an effort to breathe new life into camera sales. APS-format cameras are small, light, and convenient to carry; they also allow the photographer to take three different sizes of pictures on the same roll of film. Even as expensive new filmless digital cameras from Kodak and other companies slowly gain market acceptance, Kodak is hoping that APS will drive sales of film and photofinishing services for years to come.

As noted in Case 10-1, APS got off to a slow start. During the summer of 1996, Paul Gordon, director of U.S. marketing for Konica Corporation, declared, "This has to be the worst product launch in the history of the photographic industry." Despite spending $500 million on the launch of its Advantix brand camera, Kodak's initial advertising campaign failed to adequately explain the benefits of the new system over traditional 35mm photography. Kodak was hesitant to portray the 35mm format in a negative (no pun intended) light because that traditional format was the company's cash cow. Meanwhile, manufacturing problems resulted in camera shortages at Wal-Mart and other key retail outlets. The story was the same in Europe and Japan. Third, a classic chicken-and-egg situation materialized: Retailers were reluctant to spend $200,000 for one-hour APS photofinishing equipment until the system caught on with consumers, but consumers were reluctant to buy APS cameras until one-hour processing was available.

Anxious to protect its investment in the fledgling APS format, Kodak assembled a "tiger team" headed by Larry Morgan, worldwide marketing director for film products. Armed with an additional $100 million in marketing funds, Morgan rolled out ads that hammered home the advantages of APS over 35mm photography. Cooperative advertising support with retailers was also boosted. In addition, Kodak and other manufacturers began offering retail sales representatives spiffs—cash or gifts—for each camera sold. Meanwhile, Wal-Mart dramatically increased the number of retail outlets offering one-hour APS processing. Kodak and Fuji also introduced devices that allowed images from APS film cartridges to be scanned into home computers. By the end of 1997, there was evidence that APS was gaining market acceptance: The new format accounted for an estimated 30 percent of camera sales and 8 percent of film sales in the United States. Unit sales gains in Europe were also impressive.

At the Photo Marketing Trade show in February 1998, a total of 20 new APS camera models were unveiled. Kodak introduced a new $50 camera that Wal-Mart targeted for special promotion and display support. Many of the new models represented a new generation of miniature cameras. Not much bigger than a credit card, these ranged from such high-end products as Canon's $300 Elph to a key-ring model from Kalimar that sells for $4.95. Canon was the innovator, thanks to a designer who challenged company engineers to make a camera the size of a pack of cigarettes. The name Elph was chosen to convey the message about small size; the distinctive *ph* spelling was intended to draw a connection between the cameras and the word *photography*. Because the cameras are so small, they are more convenient to take along in a pocket or purse. Some industry observers note that the tiny cameras are popular with travelers who want to avoid the stereotype of the camera-toting tourist. Canon's Elph has been selling at the rate of about 20,000 units per month.

SOURCES: Geoffrey Smith, "Can George Fisher Fix Kodak?" *Business Week* (October 20, 1997), pp. 116–120+; Laura Johannes, "For New Film, a Brighter Picture," *The Wall Street Journal* (May 5, 1998), pp. B1, B7; Emily Nelson, "Camera Makers Focus on Tiny and Cute," *The Wall Street Journal* (March 14, 1997), pp. B1, B2.

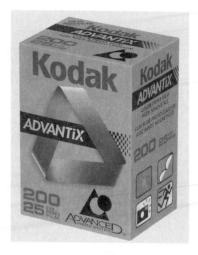

Canon's compact Elph, shown on the left, is one of several new camera models that use the Advanced Photo System (APS). APS-format film, such as Kodak's Advantix brand (right), helps eliminate flawed photos and permits great flexibility in print size. Kodak officials hope that Advantix and other new products will enable the company to reaffirm its leading role in the photo industry.

Chinese market from 6 percent to more than 22 percent by cutting prices and using patriotic advertising themes such as "Let Changhong hold the great flag of revitalizing our national industries." White-goods maker Haier Group has also successfully fought off foreign competition and now accounts for 40 percent of China's refrigerator sales. In addition, Haier enjoys a 30 percent share of both the washing machine and air conditioner markets. The aspirations of the company's president, Zhang Ruimin, can be glimpsed from slogans stenciled on office walls: "Haier–Tomorrow's Global Brand Name," and "Never Say 'No' to the Market."[4]

International Products and Brands

International or regional products are offered in several markets in a particular region. For example, there are a number of "Euro products" and "Euro brands" that are offered in Europe but not the rest of the world. Similarly, the two-seat Smart car developed by DaimlerChrysler is currently offered for sale in Europe only (see Case 11-3). The experience of General Motors with its Corsa model in the early 1990s provides a case study in how an international product or brand can be taken global. The Opel Corsa was a new model originally introduced in Europe. GM then decided to build different versions of the Corsa in China, Mexico, and Brazil. As David Herman, chairman of Adam Opel AG, noted, "The original concept was not that we planned to sell this car from the tip of Tierra del Fuego to the outer regions of Siberia. But we see its possibilities are limitless." GM calls the Corsa its "accidental world car."[5] One might describe GM's actions as "think internationally, act globally."

Global Products and Brands

The globalization of industry is putting pressure on companies to develop global products and to leverage brand equity on a worldwide basis. A **global product** meets the wants and needs of a global market. A true global product is offered in all world regions, including the Triad and countries at every stage of development. A **global brand** has the same name and a similar image and positioning throughout the world.

---

4   John Ridding, "China's Own Brands Get Their Acts Together," *Financial Times* (December 30, 1996), p. 6; Kathy Chen, "Global Cooling: Would America Buy a Refrigerator Labeled 'Made in Quingdao'?" *The Wall Street Journal* (September 17, 1997), pp. A1, A14.
5   Diana Kurylko, "The Accidental World Car," *Automotive News* (June 27, 1994), p. 4.

Some companies are well established as global brands. For example, when Nestlé asserts that it "Makes the very best," the quality promise is understood and accepted globally. The same is true for Gillette ("The best a man can get"), BMW ("The ultimate driving machine"), GE ("We bring good things to life"), Harley-Davidson ("An American legend,") and many other global companies. Former Gillette CEO Alfred Zeien explained his company's approach as follows:

> A multinational has operations in different countries. A global company views the world as a single country. We know Argentina and France are different, but we treat them the same. We sell them the same products, we use the same production methods, we have the same corporate policies. We even use the same advertising—in a different language, of course.[6]

As this quote implies, companies such as Gillette enjoy several benefits and advantages that derive from creating global products and utilizing global branding. These include economies of scale associated with creating a single ad campaign for the world and the advantages of executing a single brand strategy. All global companies are trying to increase the visibility of their brands, especially in the key U.S. market. Examples include Philips with its "Let's make things better" global image advertising and Siemens' recent "Be inspired" campaign.

Note that a global brand is not the same thing as a global product. For example, personal stereos are a category of global product; Sony is a global brand. Many companies, including Sony, make personal stereos. However, Sony created the category more than 20 years ago when it introduced the Walkman in Japan. The history of the Walkman illustrates the fact that global brands must be created by marketers. Initially, Sony's personal stereo was to be marketed under three brand names. In their book *Breakthroughs!*, Ranganath Nayak and John Ketteringham describe how the global brand as we know it today came into being when famed Sony Chairman Akio Morita realized that global consumers were one step ahead of his marketing staffers:

> At an international sales meeting in Tokyo, Morita introduced the Walkman to Sony representatives from America, Europe, and Australia. Within two months, the Walkman was introduced in the United States under the name "Soundabout"; two months later, it was on sale in the United Kingdom as "Stowaway." Sony in Japan had consented to the name changes because their English-speaking marketing groups had told them the name "Walkman" sounded funny in English. Nevertheless, with tourists importing the Walkman from Japan and spreading the original name faster than any advertising could have done, Walkman became the name most people used when they asked for the product in a store. Thus, *Sony managers found themselves losing sales because they had three different names for the same item.* Morita settled the issue at Sony's United States sales convention in May 1980 by declaring that, funny or not, Walkman was the name everybody had to use.[7]

The Sony Walkman is an excellent example of **combination** or **tiered branding,** whereby a corporate name (Sony) is combined with a product brand name

6   Victoria Griffith, "As Close as a Group Can Get to Global" *Financial Times* (April 7, 1998), p. 21.
7   P. Ranganath Nayak and John M. Ketteringham. *Breakthroughs! How Leadership and Drive Create Commercial Innovations that Sweep the World* (San Diego, California: Pfeiffer & Company, 1994), pp. 128–129.

(Walkman). By using tiered branding, marketers can leverage a company's reputation while developing a distinctive identity for a line of products. A tiered brand approach can be a powerful tool for introducing new products. Although Sony markets a number of local products, the company also has a stellar track record as a global corporate brand, a creator of global products, and a marketer of global brands. For example, using the Walkman brand name as a point of departure, Sony created the Discman portable CD player and the Watchman portable TV. Sony's recent global product-brand offerings include the Minidisc digital music recording-playback system, a full line of DVD players, and a new Super Audio Compact Disc (SACD) music system.

Cobranding is a variation on tiered branding in which two or more *different* company or product brands are featured prominently on product packaging or in advertising. Properly implemented, cobranding (or *dual branding,* as it is sometimes called) can engender customer loyalty and allow companies to achieve synergy. However, cobranding can also confuse consumers and dilute brand equity. The approach works most effectively when the products involved complement each other. Credit card companies were the pioneers, and today it is possible to use cards to earn frequent flyer miles and discounts on automobiles. Another well-known example of cobranding is the Intel Inside campaign promoting both the Intel Corporation and its Pentium-brand processors in conjunction with advertising for various brands of personal computers. BellSouth International has successfully utilized a wireless cobranding strategy to penetrate the telecommunications market in Latin America; today, BellSouth is the largest provider of cellular services in the region.

Companies can also leverage strong brands by creating **brand extensions.** This strategy entails using an established brand name as an umbrella when entering new businesses or developing new product lines that represent new categories to the company. British entrepreneur Richard Branson is an acknowledged master of this approach: The Virgin brand has been attached to a wide range of businesses and

Richard Branson has built a business empire by extending the Virgin brand name to a variety of products, including Virgin vodka and Virgin cola.

Table 11-1
The Virgin Group

- Virgin Entertainment
  Virgin Megastores and
  MGM Cinemas
- Virgin Trading
  Virgin Cola and Virgin Vodka
- Virgin Radio
- Virgin Media Group
  Virgin Publishing, Virgin Television,
  Virgin Net
- Virgin Hotels

- Voyager Investments
  Virgin Bride
- Virgin Travel Group
  Virgin Atlantic Airways, Virgin Holidays
- Virgin Direct Personal Financial Services
- Virgin Rail Group
- V2 Records
- Victory Corporation
  Cosmetics and Clothing
- Virgin Express

products. Virgin is a global brand, and the company's businesses include an airline, a railroad franchise, retail stores, movie theaters, financial services, and soft drinks. Some of these businesses are global, and some are local. For example, Virgin Megastores are found in many parts of the world, while the operating scope of Virgin Rail Group is limited to the UK. The brand has been built on Branson's shrewd ability to exploit weaknesses in competitors' customer service skills, as well as a flair for self-promotion. Branson's business philosophy is that brands are built around reputation, quality, innovation, and price rather than image.[8] Although Branson is intent on establishing Virgin as *the* British brand of the new millennium, some industry observers wonder if the brand has been spread too thin (Table 11-1).

Visit the Web site
To learn more about
the Virgin Group,
go online to:
www.virgin.com

Global Brand Development

Table 11-2 shows global brands ranked in terms of their economic value at the beginning of the twenty-first century as determined by analysts at the Interbrand consultancy and Citigroup. To be included in the rankings, the brand had to generate at least 20 percent of sales outside the home country (brands owned by privately held companies such as Mars are not included). Not surprisingly, Coca-Cola tops the list. However, one of the telling findings of the rankings is that strong brand management is now being practiced by companies in a wide range of industries, not just by consumer-packaged goods marketers.[9]

Developing a global brand is not always an appropriate goal. As David Aacker and Erich Joachimsthaler noted recently in the *Harvard Business Review,* managers who seek to build global brands must first consider whether such a move fits well with their company or their markets. First, managers must realistically assess whether anticipated scale economies will actually materialize. Second, they must recognize the difficulty of building a successful global brand team. Finally, managers must be alert to instances in which a single brand cannot be imposed on all markets successfully. Aacker and Joachimsthaler recommend that companies place a priority on creating strong brands in *all* markets through **global brand leadership:**

> Global brand leadership means using organizational structures, processes, and cultures to allocate brand-building resources globally, to create global synergies, and to develop a global brand strategy that coordinates and leverages country brand strategies.[10]

---

8   Alison Smith, "A Genius for Publicity," *Financial Times* (August 4, 1997), p. 9.
9   Gerry Khermouch, " The Best Global Brands," *Business Week* (August 6, 2001), pp. 50+.
10   David Aacker and Erich Joachimsthaler, "The Lure of Global Branding," *Harvard Business Review* 77, no. 6 (November-December 1999), pp. 137–144.

Table 11-2
The World's Most
Valuable Brands

RANK	VALUE (BILLIONS)
1. Coca-Cola	69.9
2. Microsoft	65.1
3. IBM	52.8
4. GE	42.4
5. Nokia	35.0
6. Intel	34.7
7. Disney	32.6
8. Ford	30.1
9. McDonald's	25.3
10. AT&T	22.8
11. Marlboro	22.0
12. Mercedes	21.7
13. Citibank	19.0
14. Toyota	18.5
15. Hewlett-Packard	17.9
16. Cisco Systems	17.2
17. American Express	16.9
18. Gillette	15.3
19. Merrill Lynch	15.0
20. Sony	15.0
21. Honda	14.6
22. BMW	13.9
23. Nescafé	13.2
24. Compaq	12.3
25. Oracle	12.2

Source: Adapted from "The 100 Top Brands,"
Business Week (August 8, 2001), pp. 60–61.

The following eight guidelines can assist marketing managers in their efforts to establish global brand leadership:

- Create a compelling value proposition for customers in every market entered, beginning with the home country market. A global brand begins with this foundation of value.
- Before taking a brand across borders, think about all elements of brand identity and select names, marks, and symbols that have the potential for globalization. Give special attention to the Triad and BEMs.
- Companies with an established national brand should thoroughly research the alternatives of extending it versus adopting a new brand identity globally. For example, AT&T changed its name from American Telephone & Telegraph, and Bavarian Motor Works (Bayerische Motoren Weke AG) adopted the acronym BMW as its global brand.
- Develop a company-wide communication system to share and leverage knowledge and information about marketing programs and customers in different countries.
- Develop a consistent planning process across markets and products. Make a process template available to all managers in all markets.

From big to small to flat to thin, you can't escape the power of Zenith Digital.

- Assign specific responsibility for managing branding issues to ensure that local brand managers accept global best practices. This can take a variety of forms, ranging from a business management team or a brand champion (led by senior executives) to a global brand manager or brand management team (let by middle managers).
- Execute brand-building strategies that leverage global strengths and respond to relevant local differences.
- When in doubt, harmonize, unravel confusion, and eliminate complexity. For example, a consumer packaged-goods marketer with 25 bar soap brands should ask whether five would work just as well in the markets served.[11]

11 Warren J. Keegan, "Global Brands: Issues and Strategies," Center for Global Business Strategy, Pace University, Working Paper Series, 2002.

In the world of agricultural marketing, different brand names are typically developed for different regions and country markets. For example, Syngenta launched a selective herbicide product using the brand name Discover in the United States; the same product was known as Horizon in Canada. However, when American Cyanamid (now a unit of BASF Corp.) created a new global herbicide-tolerant crop production system in the late 1990s, management wanted a single global brand name. As Kaye Iftner, director of global strategic marketing communications, explains, "The world is getting smaller and smaller. And just because you call a product 'X' in Brazil and 'Y' in Argentina doesn't mean the farmer doesn't know they're the same product."

To develop the new brand, Iftner engaged the services of Landor Associates, a New York-based brand consultancy. According to Bruce Steinberg, marketing director at Landor, the first task was to convince managers at Cyanamid of the importance of branding.

Steinberg says, "The time has come for this marketplace to get on the branding bandwagon, not only to get name recognition, but to foster understanding."

Iftner and her staff generated 600 possible names. The list was then trimmed to 30 names that were carefully tested for linguistic appropriateness. Steinberg notes that one of the challenges was to develop a brand identity that, both verbally and visually, communicated compatibility between the seeds and herbicides. Finally, "Clearfield" was tested against one other name with six crops in seven countries. Clearfield made the strongest showing. Steinberg explains, "Farmers around the world 'got it' immediately. It was unmistakable." Iftner was convinced. "Testing showed the Clearfield name and logo to be meaningful, credible, appropriate, memorable, and likable," she says. In May 1999, Cyanamid launched a global marketing campaign that included radio, TV, print ads, and direct mail.

SOURCE: Adapted from Erika Rasmusson, "Growing a Global Brand," *Sales & Marketing Management* (August 1999), p. 17.

Mars Inc. confronted the global brand issue with its chocolate-covered caramel bar that sold under a variety of national brand names such as Snickers in the United States and Marathon in the United Kingdom. Management decided to transform the candy bar—already a global product—into a global brand. This decision entailed some risk, such as the possibility that consumers in the United Kingdom would associate the name Snickers with knickers, the British slang for a woman's undergarment. Mars also changed the name of its successful European chocolate biscuit from Raider to Twix, the same name used in the United States. In both instances, a single brand name gives Mars the opportunity to leverage all of its product communications across national boundaries. Managers were forced to think globally about the positioning of Snickers and Twix, something that they were not obliged to do when the candy products were marketed under different national brand names. The marketing team rose to the challenge; as Lord Saatchi described it:

> Mars decided there was a rich commercial prize at stake in ownership of a single human need: hunger satisfaction. From Hong Kong to Lima, people would know that Snickers was "a meal in a bar." Owning that emotion would not give them 100 percent of the global confectionery market but it would be enough. Its appeal would be wide enough to make Snickers the number one confectionery brand in the world, which it is today.[12]

Coke is arguably the quintessential global product and global brand. Coke relies on similar positioning and marketing in all countries; it projects a global image of fun, good times, and enjoyment. The product itself may vary to suit local

---

[12] Lord Saatchi, "Battle for Survival Favours the Simplest," *Financial Times* (January 5, 1998), p. 19.

tastes; for example, Coke increased the sweetness of its beverages in the Middle East where customers prefer a sweeter drink. Also, prices may vary to suit local competitive conditions, and the channels of distribution may differ. Since the mid-1990s, Coke's advertising theme has been "Always Coca-Cola." Each new "always" campaign includes more than a dozen TV commercials with different story lines designed to appeal to audiences in different parts of the world. However, the basic, underlying strategic principles that guide the management of the brand are the same worldwide. Only an ideologue would insist that a "global product" cannot be adapted to meet local preferences; certainly, no company building a global brand needs to limit itself to absolute uniformity of marketing mix elements. The issue is not exact uniformity but rather: Are we offering *essentially* the same product? As discussed in the next few chapters, other elements of the marketing mix—for example, price, communications appeal and media strategy, and distribution channels—may also vary. At Avon Products, global brands generate $725 million in annual sales and account for approximately 25 percent of personal care product revenues. Avon's global fragrances include Far Away and Rare Gold. Even as it has created new global perfume brands, Avon has consolidated some of its national brands in an effort to improve quality and cut costs. Avon has found that uniform ingredients and packaging for global brands result in gross profit margins that are 4 percent higher than those of its regional and national brands. In 1998, Avon launched the Women of Earth fragrance brand with the promise that it "captures a feminine spirit that transcends geographic and cultural boundaries." The Women of Earth brand was launched simultaneously on six continents through Avon's network of 2 million sales representatives.

Avon's new Women of Earth global brand is used on a variety of products, including perfume and body lotion.

Local versus Global Products and Brands: A Needs-Based Approach

Coca-Cola, McDonald's, Singapore Airlines, Mercedes-Benz, and Sony are a few of the companies that have transformed local products and brands into global ones. The essence of marketing is finding needs and filling them. Maslow's hierarchy of needs, a staple of sociology and psychology courses, provides a useful framework for understanding how and why local products and brands can be extended beyond home country borders. Maslow hypothesized that people's desires can be arranged into a hierarchy of five needs.[13] As an individual fulfills needs at each level, he or she progresses to higher levels (Figure 11-2). At the most basic level of human existence, physiological and safety needs must be met. People need food, clothing, and shelter, and a product that meets these basic needs has potential for globalization. However, the basic human need to consume food and liquids is not the same thing as wanting or preferring a Big Mac or a Coke. Before the Coca-Cola Company and McDonald's conquered the world, they built their brands and business systems at home. Because their products fulfilled basic human needs, and because both companies are masterful marketers, they were able to cross geographic boundaries and build global brand franchises. At the same time, Coca-Cola and McDonald's have learned from experience that some food and drink preferences

Figure 11-2
Maslow's Hierarchy of Needs

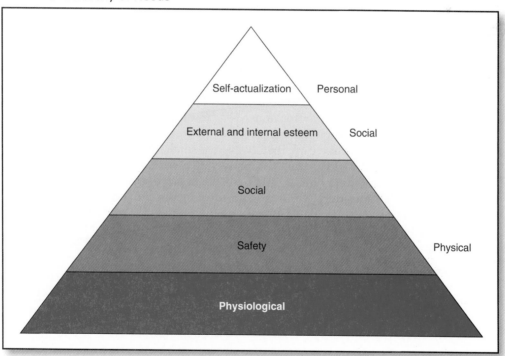

---

[13] A. H. Maslow, "A Theory of Human Motivation," in *Readings in Managerial Psychology*, Harold J. Levitt and Louis R. Pondy, eds. (Chicago: University of Chicago Press, 1964), pp. 6–24.

remain deeply embedded in culture. Responding to those differences has meant creating local products and brands for particular country markets. Sony has prospered for a similar reason. Audio and video entertainment products fulfill important social functions. Throughout its history, Sony's corporate vision has called for developing new products such as the transistor radio and the Walkman personal stereo that fulfill the need for entertainment.

Mid-level needs in the hierarchy include self-respect, self-esteem, and the esteem of others. These social needs can create a powerful internal motivation driving demand for status-oriented products, irrespective of a country's stage of development. Gillette's Alfred Zeien understood this. Marketers in Gillette's Parker Pen subsidiary are confident that consumers in Malaysia and Singapore shopping for an upscale gift will buy the same Parker pen as Americans shopping at Neiman Marcus. "We are not going to come out with a special product for Malaysia," Zeien has said.[14] In Asia today, young women are taking up smoking as a status symbol—and showing a preference for Western brands such as Marlboro. However, as noted earlier, smokers' needs and wants may be tempered by economic circumstances. Recognizing this, companies such as B.A.T create local brands that allow individuals to indulge their desire or need to smoke at a price they can afford to pay.

Luxury goods marketers are especially skilled at catering to esteem needs on a global basis. Rolex, Louis Vuitton, and Dom Perignon are just a few of the global brands that consumers buy in an effort to satisfy esteem needs. Some consumers flaunt their wealth by buying expensive products and brands that others will notice. Such behavior is referred to as *conspicuous consumption* or *luxury badging*. Any company with a premium product or brand that has proven itself in a local market by fulfilling esteem needs should consider devising a strategy for taking the product global.

Products can fulfill different needs in different countries. Consider the refrigerator as used in industrialized, high-income countries. The *primary function* of the refrigerator in these countries is related to basic needs as fulfilled in that society. These include storing frozen foods for extended periods, keeping milk, meat, and other perishable foods fresh between car trips to the supermarket, and making ice cubes. In lower-income countries, by contrast, frozen foods are not widely available. Homemakers shop for food daily rather than weekly. Because of lower incomes, people are reluctant to pay for unnecessary features such as icemakers. These are luxuries that require high-income levels to support. The functions of the refrigerator in a lower-income country are merely to store small quantities of perishable food for one day and to store leftovers for slightly longer periods. Because the needs fulfilled by the refrigerator are limited in these countries as compared with advanced countries, a much smaller refrigerator is quite adequate. In some developing countries, refrigerators have an important *secondary purpose* related to higher-order needs: They fulfill a need for prestige. In these countries, there is demand for the largest model available, which is prominently displayed in the living room rather than hidden in the kitchen.

Hellmut Schütte has proposed a modified hierarchy to explain the needs and wants of Asian consumers (Figure 11-3).[15] While the two lower-level needs are the same as in the traditional hierarchy, the three highest levels emphasize the intricacy and importance of social needs. *Affiliation needs* in Asia are satisfied when an individ-

14 Louis Uchitelle, "Gillette's World View: One Blade Fits All," *The New York Times* (January 3, 1994), p. C3.
15 Hellmut Schütte, "Asian Culture and the Global Consumer," *Financial Times–Mastering Marketing* (September 21, 1998), p. 2.

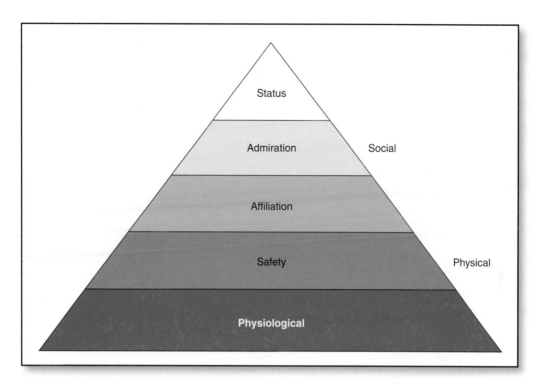

Figure 11-3
Maslow's Hierarchy: The Asian Equivalent
Source: Reprinted by permission of New York University Press

ual has been accepted by a group. Conformity with group norms becomes a key force driving consumer behavior. For example, when Tamagotchis and other brands of electronic pets were the "in" toy in Japan, every teenager who wanted to fit in bought one (or more). Knowing this, managers at Japanese companies develop local products specifically designed to appeal to teens. The next level is *admiration,* a higher-level need that can be satisfied through acts that command respect within a group. At the top of the Asian hierarchy is *status,* the esteem of society as a whole. In part, attainment of high status is character driven. However, the quest for status also leads to luxury badging. Support for Schütte's contention that status is the highest-ranking need in the Asian hierarchy can be seen in the geographic breakdown of the $35 billion global luxury goods market. Fully 20 percent of industry sales are generated in Japan alone, with another 22 percent of sales occurring in the rest of the Asia-Pacific region. Nearly half of all sales revenues of Italy's Gucci Group are generated in Asia.

"COUNTRY OF ORIGIN" AS BRAND ELEMENT

One of the facts of life in global marketing is that perceptions about and attitudes toward particular countries often extend to products and brands known to originate in those countries. These perceptions become part of a brand's image and contribute to brand equity. This is particularly true for automobiles, electronics, fashion, beer, recorded music, and certain other product categories. These perceptions and attitudes can be positive or negative. On the positive side, as one marketing expert has pointed out, " 'German' is synonymous with quality engineering, 'Italian' is synonymous with style, and 'French' is synonymous with chic."[16] Within a given country, consumers are likely to differ in terms of both the importance they ascribe to a product's country of origin and their perceptions of different countries. A recent Gallop poll showed that, among Americans, people 61 years of age or older were most likely to determine a product's origin before buying (Table 11-3).

The manufacturing reputation of a particular country can change over time. Studies conducted during the 1970s and 1980s indicated that the "made in the USA" image lost ground to the "made in Japan" image. Today, however, U.S. brands are finding renewed acceptance globally. Examples include Jeep Cherokee sports utility vehicles, Lands' End clothing, and Budweiser beer, all of which are being successfully marketed with strong "USA" themes. Korea's image has improved greatly in recent years, thanks to the reputations of global companies such as Hyundai, Daewoo, and Samsung. Industry observers expect other Asian corporate megabrands to emerge in the coming years.

Finland is home to Nokia, which rose in stature from a local brand to a global brand in little more than a decade. However, as brand strategy expert Simon Anholt points out, other Finnish companies need to move quickly to capitalize on Nokia's success if Finland is to become a valuable nation-brand. For example, Raisio Oy has developed Benecol brand margarine that has been proven to lower cholesterol levels. If large numbers of health-conscious consumers around the world embrace so-called nutraceutical products, Raisio and Benecol may become well-known brands and further raise Finland's profile on the global scene. Anholt also notes that some countries are "launch brands" in the sense that they lack centuries of tradition and foreign interaction upon which to build their reputations:

> For a country like Slovenia to enhance its image abroad is a very different matter than for Scotland or China. Slovenia needs to be launched: Consumers around the world first must be taught where it is, what it makes, what it has to offer, and what it stands for. This in itself represents a powerful opportunity: The chance to build a modern country brand, untainted by centuries of possibly negative associations.[17]

Country stereotyping can present a disadvantage to a competitor in a given market. One study investigated the relationship between a product's country of origin

Table 11-3

Influence of Country of Manufacture on Consumer Purchase Decisions

AGE	PERCENTAGE
18–30	19%
31–45	35%
46–60	29%
61+	50%

Source: Gallop poll conducted for the International Mass Retail Association.

---

16 Dana Milbank, "Made in America Becomes a Boast in Europe," *The Wall Street Journal* (January 19, 1994), p. B1.
17 Simon Anholt, "The Nation as Brand," *Across the Board* 37, no. 10 (November-December 2000), pp. 22–27.

and American consumer perceptions of risk. Specifically, the study compared perceptions of two product categories—microwave ovens and blue jeans—produced in the United States, Mexico, and Taiwan. Overall, the study found a significant consumer bias in favor of U.S.-made microwaves and jeans. However, the study also showed no difference in perceived risk between microwave ovens in terms of "made in the USA" and "made in Taiwan." By contrast, respondents indicated a higher perceived risk for jeans manufactured in Taiwan compared with those from the United States. Comparison of the two product categories for the United States and Mexico showed a negative country-of-origin bias for Mexican-made products. Finally, the survey indicated a significantly higher perceived risk for a Mexican microwave oven than for one made in Taiwan; there was no significant difference between Mexico and Taiwan in terms of perceived risk for jeans.[18] Since this study was completed, the "made in Mexico" image has gained enormous ground as local companies and global manufacturers have established world-class manufacturing plants in Mexico to supply world demand. For example, General Motors, Volkswagen, DaimlerChrysler, Nissan, Ford, and other global automakers have established Mexican operations that produce nearly two million vehicles per year, three-fourths of which are exported.[19]

"Consider labels such as 'Made in Brazil' and 'Made in Thailand.' Someday they may be symbols of high quality and value, but today many consumers expect products from those countries to be inferior."
—Christopher A. Bartlett and Sumantra Ghoshal[20]

If a country's manufacturers produce high-quality products that are nonetheless *perceived* as being of lower quality than similar goods from other countries, there are two alternatives. One is to disguise the foreign origin of the product. Package, label, and product design can minimize evidence of foreign derivation. A brand policy of using local names will contribute to a domestic identity. The other alternative is to continue the foreign identification of the product and attempt to change buyer attitudes toward the product. Over time, as consumers experience higher quality, the perception will change and adjust. It is a fact of life that perceptions of quality often lag behind reality.

In some product categories, foreign products have a substantial advantage over their domestic counterparts simply because of their "foreign-ness." Global marketers have an opportunity to capitalize on the situation by charging premium prices. The import segment of the beer industry is a case in point. In one study of American attitudes about beer, subjects who were asked to indicate taste preference for beer in a blind test indicated a preference for domestic beers over imports. The same subjects were then asked to indicate preference ratings for beers in an open test with labels attached. In this test, the subjects preferred imported beer. Increasing numbers of Americans are developing a taste for imported beers; 2000 import sales added up to about 20 million barrels, an increase of 12.3 percent over 1999. In 1997, thanks to a brilliant marketing campaign, Corona Extra surpassed Heineken as the best-selling imported beer in America. With distribution in 150 countries, Corona is a textbook example of a local brand that has been built into a global powerhouse. Meanwhile, America's best-known beer brands are finding acceptance abroad as well. In the United Kingdom, for example, many pubs stock Budweiser and Michelob. Craft brew brands such as Pete's Wicked are also widely available.

---

[18] Jerome Witt and C. P. Rao, "The Impact of Global Sourcing on Consumers: Country-of-Origin Effects on Perceived Risk," *Journal of Global Marketing* 6, no. 3 (1992), pp. 105–128.

[19] Elliot Blair Smith, "Early PT Cruiser Took a Bruisin'," *USA Today* (August 8, 2001), pp. 1B, 2B; see also Joel Millman, "Trade Wins: The World's New Tiger on the Export Scene Isn't Asian; It's Mexico," *The Wall Street Journal* (May 9, 2000), pp. A1, A10.

[20] Christopher A. Bartlett and Sumantra Ghoshal, "Going Global: Lessons from Late Movers," *Harvard Business Review* 78, no. 2 (March-April 2000), p. 133.

Extend, Adapt, and Create: Strategic Alternatives in Global Marketing

To capitalize on opportunities outside the home country, company managers must devise and implement appropriate marketing programs. Depending on organizational objectives and market needs, a particular program may consist of extension strategies, adaptation strategies, or a combination of the two. A company that has developed a successful local product or brand can implement an **extension strategy,** which calls for offering that product virtually unchanged (i.e., "extending" it) in markets outside the home country. A second option is an **adaptation strategy;** this involves changing elements of design, function, or packaging in response to needs or conditions in particular country markets. These product strategies can be used in conjunction with extension or adaptation communication strategies. A third strategic option, **product invention,** entails developing new products "from the ground up" with the world market in mind.

The decision to extend, adapt, or create is contingent on a number of factors relating to company-specific objectives as well as the sociocultural, economic, and political environments described in earlier chapters. In some instances, the key to meeting market share or unit sales objectives is making product design changes in response to local market conditions. However, the benefits of achieving such objectives must be weighed against the cost of changing a product's design and testing it in the market. Also, despite the evidence cited in earlier chapters that tastes and preferences are converging around the globe, significant differences do still exist in terms of what customers want and need. Marketers who ignore such differences and pursue extension strategies for the sake of economy or expediency do so at their own peril.

Laws and regulations in different countries frequently lead to obligatory product design adaptations. This may be seen most clearly in Europe, where one impetus for the creation of the single market was the desire to dismantle regulatory and legal barriers that prevented pan-European sales of standardized products. These were particularly prevalent in the areas of technical standards and health and safety standards. In the food industry, for example, there were 200 legal and regulatory barriers to cross-border trade within the EU in ten food categories. Among these were prohibitions or taxes on products with certain ingredients and different packaging and labeling laws. Experts predict that the removal of such barriers will reduce the need to adapt product designs and will result in the creation of standardized "Euro-products."[21] Many safety standards that remain on the books have not been harmonized, a situation that can create problems for foreign companies. Dormont Manufacturing, appropriately based in Export, Pennsylvania, makes hoses that hook up to deep-fat fryers and similar appliances used in the food industry. Dormont's gas hose is made of stainless-steel helical tubing with no covering. British industry requirements call for galvanized metal annular tubing and a rubber covering; Italian regulations specify stainless steel annual tubing with no covering. The cost of complying with these regulations effectively shuts Dormont out of the European market.[22]

Apart from regulatory issues, other technical requirements or standards can mandate adaptation. Consider the voltage and cycle requirements for electrical appliances. Electrical systems in different parts of the world range from 50 to 230 volts

---

21 John Quelch, Robert Buzzell, and Eric Salama, *The Marketing Challenge of Europe 1992* (Reading, MA: Addison-Wesley, 1991), p. 71.
22 Timothy Aeppel, "Europe's 'Unity' Undoes a U.S. Exporter," *The Wall Street Journal* (April 1, 1996), p. B1.

and from 50 to 60 cycles. This means that the design of any product powered by electricity must be compatible with the power system in the country of use. Manufacturers of televisions and video equipment find that the world is a very incompatible place for reasons besides those related to electricity. Three different TV broadcast and video systems are found in the world today: the U.S. NTSC system and the European SECAM and PAL systems. Companies that are aiming for the global market design products that comply with these technical requirements. For example, Remington shavers have built-in power converters that allow users to recharge their razors virtually anywhere. All that is required for foreign use is the proper plug adapter. Similarly, manufacturers of cellular phones create models that can be quickly adapted to wireless standards in different parts of the world. In the United States, the standard communication frequency is 1900 MHz. Outside the United States, 1800 MHz and 800 MHz frequencies are widely used. Nokia's 6100 series of cell phones is designed with interchangeable sleeves that control phone operations.

The extension/adaptation/creation decision is one of the most fundamental issues in global marketing. While it pertains to all elements of the marketing mix, extension/adaptation is of particular importance in product and communications decisions. As a framework for guiding product and communications decisions, the extend/adapt issue can be represented in matrix form. Figure 11-4 shows how a company can select from four strategic alternatives to expand from its local base into other geographic markets. It is possible to identify extension strategies being employed by international, global, and transnational companies. The critical difference is one of execution and mind-set. In an international company, for example, the extension strategy reflects an ethnocentric orientation and the *assumption* that all markets are alike. A global company such as Gillette does not fall victim to such assumptions; the company's geocentric orientation allows it to thoroughly understand its markets and consciously take advantage of similarities in world markets. Likewise, a multinational company utilizes the adaptation strategy because of its

Figure 11-4
Global Product Planning: Strategic Alternatives

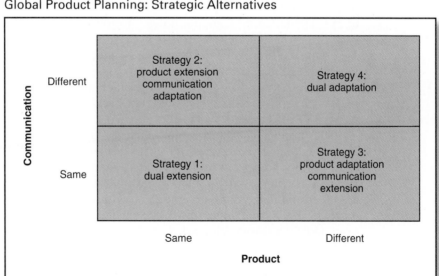

polycentric orientation and the assumption that all markets are different. By contrast, the geocentric orientation of managers and executives in a global company has sensitized them to actual, rather than assumed, differences between markets.

Strategy 1: Product–Communication Extension (Dual Extension)

Many companies employ **product–communication extension** as a strategy for pursuing opportunities outside the home market. Under the right conditions, this is the easiest product marketing strategy; it can be the most profitable one as well. Companies pursuing this strategy sell the same product with virtually no adaptation, using the same advertising and promotional appeals used domestically, in two or more country markets or segments.

As a general guideline, it should be noted that extension/standardization strategies can be utilized more frequently with industrial (business-to-business) products than with consumer products. Industrial products tend not to be as rooted in culture as consumer goods. Manufacturers of industrial products should be especially alert to extension possibilities. For example, Henkel KgaA's Loctite Corp. subsidiary manufactures industrial adhesives and sealants that are sold in more than 80 countries. Loctite's double-digit sales and earnings growth over the past several years can be partially attributed to top management's recognition that the products it had developed for the U.S. market could be sold without adaptation virtually anywhere.

Some marketers have learned the hard way that the dual extension approach does not work in every market. When Campbell Soup tried to sell its tomato soup in the United Kingdom, it discovered, after substantial losses, that the English prefer a more bitter taste than Americans. Campbell learned its lesson and subsequently succeeded in Japan by creating corn pottage and other flavors specifically for the Japanese markets. In 2000, H.J. Heinz Company launched a new green ketchup in an easy-to-grasp squeeze bottle. The target market was American children who account for about 50 percent of ketchup consumption in the United States. The question now facing Heinz's marketing staff is whether EZ Squirt can be extended to other markets. In Canada, for example, research suggests that kids will embrace both the new bottle and the green ketchup inside. However, since parents will be making the actual purchase, it is important to win them over as well. As Susan Yorke, a manager at H.J. Heinz Co. of Canada, notes, "Coloured ketchup is definitely polarizing because you have your loyal users who have grown up with ketchup and can't imagine doing anything to it—certainly not a different color." Will an extension strategy work with EZ Squirt? Yorke is optimistic. "We have a skilled marketing team . . . If we do launch these products, like every other launch, it's because we think it's going to be successful," she said.[23] Meanwhile, back in the United States, Heinz launched *purple* EZ Squirt in 2001.

The product–communication extension strategy has an enormous appeal to global companies because of the cost savings associated with this approach. The most obvious sources of savings are design and manufacturing economies of scale, inventory savings, and elimination of duplicate product R&D costs. Also important are the substantial economies associated with standardization of marketing communications. For a company with worldwide operations, the cost of preparing separate print and TV ads for each market can be enormous. Although these cost savings are

---

[23] Heidi Staseson, "Not So Easy Being Green at Heinz," *Marketing Magazine* 105, no. 30 (July 31, 2000), p. 6.

important, they should not distract executives from the more important objective of maximum profit performance, which may require the use of an adaptation or invention strategy. As we have seen, product extension, in spite of its immediate cost savings, may in fact result in market failure.

Strategy 2: Product Extension–Communication Adaptation

When taking a product beyond the home-country market, management sometimes discovers that consumer perceptions about "quality" and "value" are different from those in the home country. It may also turn out that a product fills a different need, appeals to a different segment, or serves a different function. Whatever the reason, market success may be achieved by extending the product while adapting the marketing communications program. The appeal of the **product extension–communication adaptation** strategy is its relatively low cost of implementation. Because the physical product is unchanged, expenditures for R&D, manufacturing setup, and inventory are avoided. The biggest costs associated with this approach are in researching the market and revising advertising, sales promotion, point-of-sale material, and other communication elements as appropriate.

For example, before executives at Ben & Jerry's Homemade launched their ice cream in the United Kingdom, the company conducted extensive research to determine whether the package design effectively communicated the brand's "super premium" position. It was determined that British consumers perceived the colors differently than U.S. consumers. The package design was changed, and Ben & Jerry's was launched successfully in the U.K. market. The British-made Mini Cooper automobile has also enjoyed success in Japan. The boxy little car has a "retro" appeal among affluent young Japanese. Volkswagen's Rover Group, the car's manufacturer, ships about 8,000 vehicles to Japan each year, a figure that accounts for about half of the total production. To maintain consumer interest, Rover creates special promotional campaigns expressly for Japan, including limited edition cars such as a Paul Smith designer vehicle.[24] However, the Mini's basic design has not been changed for more than 40 years.

In some cases a particular country or regional environment will allow local managers a greater degree of creativity and risk taking when approaching the communication task. As a result, managers "push the envelope" in an effort to stand out amid the message clutter. For example, Europeans exhibit a higher tolerance for sexual innuendo in advertising than do Americans. A 1997 billboard campaign in Europe for VF Corporation's Lee brand boot-cut jeans showed a naked man lying on his stomach with a woman's stiletto-heeled foot poised over his buttocks. Although the visual left little to the imagination, the copy drove home the point by commanding, "Put the boot in." A London newspaper described the campaign as "one of the most provocative of the year"; it is safe to say that such billboards will never appear in America. Recently, European ad bureaus have responded to government complaints by clamping down on "porno-chic" ads. In particular, French authorities have objected to the portrayal of women in ads from Emanuel Ungaro, Christian Dior, and Benetton Group. Groups such as France's Truth in Advertising Bureau and Italy's Advertising Self-Regulation Bureau ask member agencies to voluntarily withdraw offending ads; most agencies comply.[25]

---

[24] Lisa Shuchman, "Quirky U.K. Mini Has Hot Year in Japan," *The Wall Street Journal* (October 30, 1998), p. A17.

[25] Allesandra Galloni, "Clampdown on 'Porno-chic' Ads Is Pushed by French Authorities," *The Wall Street Journal* (October 25, 2001), p. B4.

In some instances, the product extension–communication adaptation strategy—either by design or by accident—can result in **product transformation.** The same physical product ends up serving a different function or use than that for which it was originally designed or created. Perrier is a classic example of product transformation in the food and beverage industry. Mineral water had long been advertised and consumed in Europe as a staple with healthful qualities. Perrier became a success in America only after it was marketed as *the* chic beverage to order in restaurants and bars instead of a cocktail. By the early 1990s, Perrier Group of America shifted to a dual extension strategy by bringing U.S. advertising more in line with the parent company's European approach.

Strategy 3: Product Adaptation–Communication Extension

A third approach to global product planning is to extend, without change, the basic home-market communications strategy while adapting the product to local use or preference conditions. Exxon adheres to this third strategy option, which is known as **product adaptation–communication extension.** Exxon adapts its gasoline formulations to meet the weather conditions prevailing in different markets without changing the basic communications appeal, "Put a Tiger in Your Tank." There are many other examples of products that have been adjusted to perform the same function around the globe under different environmental conditions. Hon Industries of Muscatine, Iowa, markets value-priced office furniture throughout the United States and Canada. When executives began to explore the possibility of exporting to Japan, they realized that they would have to scale down the size of their designs to accommodate the smaller Japanese physique. Similarly, soap and detergent manufacturers have adjusted their product formulations to meet local water and washing equipment conditions with no change in their basic communications approach. Household appliances have been scaled to sizes appropriate to different use environments, and clothing has been adapted to meet fashion criteria.

Strategy 4: Product–Communication Adaptation (Dual Adaptation)

Sometimes, when comparing a new geographic market to the home market, marketers discover that environmental conditions or consumer preferences differ; the same may be true of the function a product serves or consumer receptivity to advertising appeals. In essence, this is a combination of the market conditions associated with Strategies 2 and 3. In such a situation, a company will utilize the **product–communication adaptation** strategy. Historically, this approach has been associated with the decentralized structure of the multinational corporation. Unilever's experience with fabric softener in Europe exemplifies the classic multinational road to adaptation. For years, the product was sold in ten countries under seven different brand names, with different bottles and marketing strategies. Unilever's decentralized structure meant that product and marketing decisions were left to country managers. They chose names that had local-language appeal and selected package designs to fit local tastes. Today, rival Procter & Gamble is introducing competitive products with a pan-European strategy of standardized products with single names, suggesting that the European market is more similar than Unilever assumed. In response, Unilever's European brand managers are attempting to move gradually toward standardization.[26]

---

[26] E. S. Browning, "In Pursuit of the Elusive Euroconsumer," *The Wall Street Journal* (April 23, 1992), p. B2.

American computer manufacturers have discovered that Germans view computers as commodities. Germans will not pay extra for a well-known brand, and, because of their price sensitivity, it is difficult to convince them of the need for feature upgrades. As a result, despite the fact that its chairman was German, Compaq did not do well in Germany against local brands and no-name computers. Compaq has revised its product offering in Germany and its entire marketing mix to compete more effectively in the German computer market.

It is important to understand that these strategic options are not mutually exclusive. Sometimes, a company will draw upon all four of these strategies simultaneously when marketing a given product in different parts of the world. For example, H.J. Heinz utilizes a mix of strategies in its ketchup marketing. While a dual-extension strategy works in England, spicier, hotter formulations are also popular in central Europe and Sweden. Recent ads in France featured a cowboy lassoing a bottle of ketchup and thus reminded consumers of the product's American heritage. Swedish ads conveyed a more cosmopolitan message; by promoting Heinz as "the taste of the big world" and featuring well-known landmarks such as the Eiffel Tower, the ads disguised the product's origins.[27]

Strategy 5: Product Invention

Extension and adaptation strategies are effective approaches to many but not all global market opportunities. For example, they do not respond to markets where there is a need but not the purchasing power to buy either the existing or adapted product. This latter situation applies to the emerging markets of the world, which are home to roughly three-quarters of the world's population. When potential customers have limited purchasing power, a company may need to develop an entirely new product designed to address the market opportunity at a price point that is within the reach of the potential customer. The converse is also true: Companies in low-income countries that have achieved local success may have to go beyond mere adaptation by "raising the bar" and bringing product designs up to world-class standards if they are to succeed in high-income countries. **Invention** is a demanding but potentially rewarding product strategy for reaching mass markets in less developed countries as well as important market segments in industrialized countries.

Two entrepreneurs working independently recognized that millions of people around the globe need low-cost eyeglasses. Robert J. Morrison, an American optometrist, created Instant Eyeglasses. These glasses utilize conventional lenses, can be assembled in minutes, and sell for about $20 per pair. Joshua Silva, a physics professor at Oxford University, took a more high-tech approach—glasses with transparent membrane lenses filled with clear silicone fluid. Using two manual adjusters, users can increase or decrease the power of the lenses by regulating the amount of fluid in them. Professor Silva hopes to sell the glasses in developing countries for about $10 per pair.[28] Another example of the invention strategy is the South African company that licensed the British patent for a hand-cranked, battery-powered radio. The radio was designed by an English inventor responding to the need for radios in low-income countries. Consumers in these countries do not have electricity in their

---

[27] Gabriella Stern, "Heinz Aims to Export Taste for Ketchup," *The Wall Street Journal* (November 20, 1992), pp. B1, B9.

[28] Amy Borrus, "Eyeglasses for the Masses," *Business Week* (November 20, 1995), pp. 104–105; Gautam Naik, "Inventor's Adjustable Glasses Could Spark Global Correction," *The Wall Street Journal* (October 14, 1998), pp. B1, B4.

homes, and they cannot afford the cost of replacement batteries. His invention is an obvious solution: a hand-cranked radio. It is ideal for the needs of low-income people in emerging markets. Users simply crank the radio, and it will play on the charge generated by a short cranking session for almost an hour.

Sometimes manufacturers in developing countries that intend to go global also utilize the product invention strategy. For example, Thermax, an Indian company, had achieved great success in its domestic market with small industrial boilers. Engineers developed a new design for the Indian market that significantly reduced the size of the individual boiler unit. However, the new design was not likely to succeed outside India. In India, where labor costs are low, relatively elaborate installation requirements are not an issue. The situation is different in higher-wage countries where industrial customers demand sophisticated integrated systems that can be installed quickly. The managing director at Thermax instructed his engineers to design for the world market. The gamble paid off: Today, Thermax is one of the world's largest producers of small boilers.[29]

Colgate pursued the product invention strategy in developing Total, a new toothpaste brand whose formulation, imagery, and ultimate consumer appeal were designed from the ground up to readily cross national boundaries. The product was tested in six countries, each of which had a different cultural profile: the Philippines, Australia, Colombia, Greece, Portugal, and the United Kingdom. Total is now available in 100 countries and generates $150 million in revenues. According to John Steel, senior vice president for global business development at Colgate, Total's success results from the application of a fundamental marketing principle: Consumers are the ones who make or break brands. "There ain't no consumers at 300 Park Avenue," he says, referring to company headquarters. Steel explains, "You get a lot more benefit and you can do a lot more with a global brand than you can a local brand. You can bring the best advertising talent from the world on to a problem. You can bring the best research brains, the best leverage of your organization onto something that is truly global. Then all your R&D pays off, the huge packaging costs pay off, the advertising pays off, and you can leverage the organization all at once."[30]

The winners in global competition are the companies that can develop products offering the most benefits, which in turn create the greatest value for buyers anywhere in the world. In some instances, value is not defined in terms of performance, but rather in terms of customer perception. The latter is as important for an expensive perfume or champagne as it is for an inexpensive soft drink. Product quality is essential—indeed, it is frequently a given—but it is also necessary to support the product quality with imaginative, value-creating advertising and marketing communications. Most industry experts believe that a global appeal and a global advertising campaign are more effective in creating the perception of value than a series of separate national campaigns. For example, Global One was created to offer telephone service to global companies around the world. A $10 million advertising campaign in 14 countries utilized the same creative approach translated into 14 languages. As Russ Ryan, director of corporate communications for Global One, explained, "When you're trying to set up a global company with an ad budget that's not huge, it's better to strive for continuity with ads that appear the same in all markets to create a bigger impression."[31]

[29] Bartlett and Ghoshal, p. 137.
[30] Pam Weisz, "Border Crossings: Brands Unify Image to Counter Cult of Culture," *Brandweek* (October 31, 1994), p. 24.
[31] Rebecca A. Fannin, "Global One Kicks Off Ads in 14 Countries," *Advertising Age* (October 14, 1996), p. 54.

How to Choose a Strategy

Most companies seek product–communication strategies that optimize company profits over the long term. Which strategy for global markets best achieves this goal? There is no general answer to this question. For starters, the considerations noted before must be addressed. In addition, it is worth noting that managers run the risk of committing two types of errors regarding product and communication decisions. One error is to fall victim to the "not invented here" (NIH) syndrome, *ignoring* decisions made by subsidiary or affiliate managers. Managers who behave in this way are essentially abandoning any effort to leverage product–communication policies outside the home-country market. The other error has been to *impose* policies upon all affiliate companies on the assumption that what is right for customers in the home market must also be right for customers everywhere.

German carmaker Volkswagen AG learned the consequences of this latter error; VW saw its position in the U.S. import market erode from leader to also-ran over the course of two decades. By the early 1970s, Volkswagen was manufacturing cars in Pennsylvania for the American market; a product extension strategy enabled the company to sell more cars in the United States than all other foreign automakers combined. By the early 1990s, however, VW commanded a scant 0.5 percent share of the U.S. auto market. By clinging to the assumption that vehicles designed for European tastes would continue to be embraced by American car buyers seduced by more stylish Japanese imports, Volkswagen fell victim to its own ethnocentricity. (Negative publicity about engines leaking oil and exploding didn't help either.) Volkswagen was offering a German-designed car built to American quality standards while competing with Japanese cars that incorporated much higher standards of quality. After becoming CEO in 1993, Ferdinand Piëch engineered a brilliant turnaround; the enthusiastic response of American car buyers to the new Beetle and updated Passat and Jetta models have boosted U.S. market share to 2.5 percent. Buoyed by a 14 percent increase in U.S. sales, VW's $1.8 billion profit in 2000 was double the previous year's figure.[32]

Companies differ in terms of both their willingness and capability to identify and produce profitable product adaptations. Unfortunately, in companies where an ethnocentric mindset predominates, executives and managers are oblivious to the issues presented here. One new-product expert has described three stages that a company must go through as follows:

1. *Cave dweller.* The primary motivation behind launching new products internationally is to dispose of excess production or to better utilize plant capacity.
2. *Naive nationalist.* The company recognizes growth opportunities outside the domestic market. It realizes that cultures and markets differ from country to country and, as a result, sees product adaptation as the only possible alternative.
3. *Globally sensitive.* The company views regions or the entire world as the competitive marketplace. New product opportunities are evaluated across countries, with some standardization planned as well as some differentiation to accommodate cultural variances. New product planning processes and control systems are reasonably standardized.[33]

---

[32] Christine Tierney, "Volkswagen," *Business Week* (July 23, 2001), pp. 60–65+.
[33] Thomas D. Kuczmarski, *Managing New Products: The Power of Innovation* (Upper Saddle River, NJ: Prentice Hall, 1992), p. 254.

To sum up, the choice of product–communication strategy in global marketing is a function of three key factors: (1) the product itself, defined in terms of the function or need it serves; (2) the market, defined in terms of the conditions under which the product is used, the preferences of potential customers, and the ability to buy the products in question; and (3) the adaptation and manufacture costs to the company considering these product–communication approaches. Only after analysis of the product-market fit and of company capabilities and costs can executives choose the most profitable strategy.

NEW PRODUCTS IN GLOBAL MARKETING

The matrix shown in Figure 11-4 provides a framework for assessing whether extension or adaptation strategies can be effective. However, the four strategic options described in the matrix do not necessarily represent the best possible responses to global market opportunities. To win in global competition, marketers, designers, and engineers must think outside the box and create innovative new products that offer superior value worldwide. In today's dynamic, competitive market environment, many companies realize that continuous development and introduction of new products are keys to survival and growth. That is the point of Strategy 5, product invention. Similarly, marketers should look for opportunities to create global advertising campaigns to support the new product or brand.

Gary Reiner, a new product specialist with the Boston Consulting Group, has identified global companies that excel at new product development, including Honda, Compaq, Motorola, Canon, Boeing, Merck, Microsoft, Intel, and Toyota. One common characteristic: They are global companies that pursue opportunities in global markets where competition is fierce, thus ensuring that new products will be world class. Other characteristics noted by Reiner are:

1. They focus on one or only a few businesses.
2. Senior management is actively involved in defining and improving the product development process.
3. They have the ability to recruit and retain the best and the brightest people in their fields.
4. They understand that speed in bringing new products to market reinforces product quality.[34]

Identifying New Product Ideas

What is a new product? A product's newness can be assessed in the context of its relation to those who buy or use it. Newness may also be organizational, as when a company acquires an already existing product with which it has no previous experience. Finally, an existing product that is not new to a company may be new to a particular market. The starting point for an effective worldwide new product program is an information system that seeks new product ideas from all potentially useful sources and channels these ideas to relevant screening and decision centers within the organization. Ideas can come from many sources, including customers, suppliers,

---

[34] Gary Reiner, "Lessons from the World's Best Product Developers," *The Wall Street Journal* (April 4, 1990), p. A12.

competitors, company salespeople, distributors and agents, subsidiary executives, headquarters executives, documentary sources (e.g., information service reports and publications), and, finally, actual firsthand observation of the market environment.

The product may be an entirely new invention or innovation that requires a relatively large amount of learning on the part of users. When such products are successful, they create new markets and new consumption patterns that literally represent a break with the past; they are sometimes called **discontinuous innovations.**[35] For example, the VCR's revolutionary impact can be explained by the concept of time shifting: The device's initial appeal was that it freed TV viewers from the tyranny of network programming schedules. For the first time, it was possible to record television programming for viewing at a later time. The VCR's market growth and acceptance was also driven by the video rental industry, which sprang up to serve the needs of VCR owners. Likewise, the personal computer revolution that began two decades ago has resulted in the democratization of technology. When they were first introduced, PCs were a discontinuous innovation that dramatically transformed the way users live and work.

An intermediate category of newness is less disruptive and requires less learning on the part of consumers; such products are called **dynamically continuous innovations.** Products that embody this level of innovation share certain features with earlier generations while incorporating new features that offer added value such as a substantial improvement in performance or greater convenience. Personal stereos such as Sony's Walkman provide music on the go, something that people had grown accustomed to since the transistor radio was introduced in the 1950s; the innovation was a miniaturized cassette playback system. The advent of the Compact Disc provided an improved music listening experience but didn't require significant behavioral changes. Similarly, the Sensor, SensorExcel, and MACH3 shaving systems represent Gillette's ongoing efforts to bring new technology to bear on wet shaving, an activity that is performed today pretty much as it has been for decades. Such products cause relatively smaller disruptions of previously existing consumption patterns.

Most new products fall into a third category, **continuous innovation.** Such products are typically "new and improved" versions of existing ones and require less R&D expenditure to develop than dynamically continuous innovations. Continuous innovations cause minimal disruption of existing consumption patterns and require the least amount of learning on the part of buyers. As noted previously, newness can be evaluated relative to a buyer or user. When a current PC user seeking an upgrade buys a new model with a faster processor or more memory, the PC can be viewed as a continuous innovation. However, to a first-time user, the same computer represents a discontinuous innovation. Consumer packaged goods companies and food marketers rely heavily on continuous innovation when rolling out new products. These often take the form of **line extensions** such as new sizes, flavors, and low-fat versions. The three degrees of product newness can be represented in terms of a continuum as shown in Figure 11-5.

New Product Development

A major driver for the development of global products is the cost of product R&D. As competition intensifies, companies discover they can reduce the cost of R&D for a product by developing a global product design. Often the goal is to create a single

---

[35] The terminology and framework described here are adapted from Thomas Robertson, "The Process of Innovation and the Diffusion of Innovation," *Journal of Marketing* 31, no. 1 (January 1967), pp. 14–19.

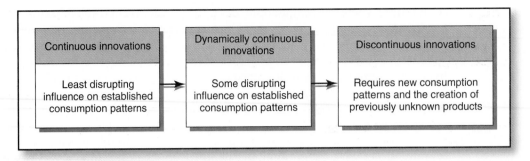

Figure 11-5
New Product Continuum

platform, or core product design element or component, that can be quickly and cheaply adapted to various country markets. As Christopher Sinclair noted during his tenure as president and CEO of PepsiCo Foods and Beverages International, "What you really want to do is look at the four or five platforms that can allow you to cut across countries, become a scale operator, and do the things that global marketers do."[36] Even products like automobiles, which must meet national safety and pollution standards, are now designed with global markets in mind. With a global product platform, companies can offer an adaptation of a global design as needed instead of unique designs for individual countries or geographic regions. The new Ford Focus, launched in Europe at the end of 1998 and in the United States in 1999, represented the company's first major new vehicle since the much-vaunted Ford 2000 reorganization. Focus is being marketed in Europe and the United States with a minimum of adaptation. The chief program engineer on the Focus project was from Great Britain, the chief technical officer was German, an Irishwoman managed the project, and an Anglo-Australian was chief designer. Under Ford 2000, about $1,000 per vehicle was cut out of the development cost.[37] The Focus platform will be used on the next generation of Mazda 323 and Volvo S40 and V40 models.

A standardized platform was also a paramount consideration when GM set about the task of redesigning its minivan. GM's globally-minded board directed the design team to create a vehicle that would be popular in both the United States and Europe. Because roads in Europe are typically narrower and fuel is more expensive, the European engineers lobbied for a vehicle that was smaller than the typical minivan. In the end, interior designers were able to provide ample interior space in a slightly smaller body. By using lightweight metals such as magnesium for some components, vehicle weight was minimized, with a corresponding improvement in fuel economy. In the United States, the new minivans are marketed as the Chevrolet Venture, Pontiac Transport, and Oldsmobile Silhouette. The Opel Sentra version will be exported to Germany; the right-hand-drive Vauxhall Sintra is destined for the British market.[38]

Other design-related costs—whether incurred by the manufacturer or the end user—must also be considered. *Durability* and *quality* are important product characteristics that must be appropriate for the proposed market. The durability and quality of home appliances, for example, must be suited to the availability of service

[36] "Fritos 'Round the World," *Brandweek* (March 27, 1995), pp. 32, 35.
[37] Robert L. Simison, "Ford Hopes Its New Focus Will Be a Global Bestseller," *The Wall Street Journal* (October 8, 1998), p. B10.
[38] Rebecca Blumenstein, "While Going Global, GM Slips at Home," *The Wall Street Journal* (January 8, 1997), pp. B1, B4.

within a market. In lower-income markets, appliances are more likely to be repairable—indeed, a repairable appliance is a quality appliance in these markets. Conversely, in advanced countries, where the cost of labor makes it prohibitively expensive to repair appliances that cost under $40, appliances are designed without the additional "quality" that would allow a technician to take the appliance apart and repair it. Because the availability of small-appliance repair in advanced countries is either nonexistent or prohibitively expensive, building repairability into appliances adds little of value for the consumer. However, an attempt to sell the high-income product in a low-income market may result in failure; it may be perceived as a *lower*-quality product because of its lack of repairability.

In the United States and Europe, car buyers do not wish to incur high service bills. The new Ford Focus was designed to be less expensive to maintain and repair. For example, engine removal takes only about 1.5 hours, about half the time required to remove the engine in the discontinued Escort. In addition, body panels are bolted together rather than welded, and the rear signal lights are mounted higher so they are less likely to be broken in minor parking lot mishaps.

The actual cost of producing the product will create a cost floor. Japanese companies have traditionally approached cost issues in a way that results in substantial savings. Western companies are beginning to adopt some of these money-saving ideas. As shown in Figure 11-6, the Japanese begin with market research and product characteristics. Up to this point, the processes are parallel in the United States and Japan. At the next step, the processes diverge. In Japan, the planned selling price minus the desired profit is calculated, resulting in a target cost figure. Only at this point are design, engineering, and supplier pricing issues dealt with; extensive consultation between all value chain members is used to meet the target. Once the necessary negotiations and trade-offs have been settled, manufacturing begins, followed by continuous cost reduction. In the U.S. process, cost is typically determined after design, engineering, and marketing decisions have been made in sequential fashion; if the cost is too high, the process cycles back to square one—the design stage.[39]

The International New Product Department

As noted previously, a high volume of information flow is required to scan adequately for new product opportunities, and considerable effort is subsequently required to screen these opportunities to identify candidates for product development. The best organizational design for addressing these requirements is a new product department. Managers in such a department engage in several activities. First, they ensure that all relevant information sources are continuously tapped for new product ideas. Second, they screen these ideas to identify candidates for investigation. Third, they investigate and analyze selected new product ideas. Finally, they ensure that the organization commits resources to the most likely new product candidates and is continuously involved in an orderly program of new product introduction and development on a worldwide basis.

With the enormous number of possible new products, most companies establish screening grids in order to focus on those ideas that are most appropriate for investigation. The following questions are relevant to this task:

1. How big is the market for this product at various prices?
2. What are the likely competitive moves in response to our activity with this product?

---

[39] Michel Robert, *Strategy Pure and Simple: How Winning CEOs Outthink Their Competition* (New York: McGraw-Hill, 1993), pp. 114–115.

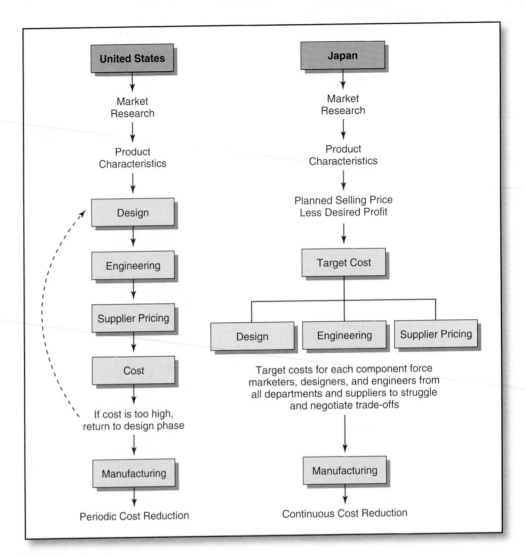

Figure 11-6
How the Japanese Keep Costs Low

3. Can we market the product through our existing structure? If not, what changes will be required, and what costs will be incurred to make the changes?
4. Given estimates of potential demand for this product at specified prices with estimated levels of competition, can we source the product at a cost that will yield an adequate profit?
5. Does this product fit our strategic development plan? (a) Is the product consistent with our overall goals and objectives? (b) Is the product consistent with our available resources? (c) Is the product consistent with our management structure? (d) Does the product have adequate global potential?

For example, the corporate development team at Virgin evaluates more than a dozen proposals each day from outside the company, as well as proposals from Virgin staff members. The team is headed by Brad Rosser, who is director of corporate management. When assessing new product ideas, Rosser and his team look for synergy with existing Virgin products, pricing, marketing opportunities, risk versus return on investment, and whether the idea "uses or abuses" the Virgin brand. Recent ventures that have been given the green light are Virgin Jeans, a denim clothing store chain; Virgin Bride, a wedding consulting service; and Virgin Net, an Internet service provider.[40]

Testing New Products

The major lesson of new product introduction outside the home market has been that whenever a product interacts with human, mechanical, or chemical elements, there is the potential for a surprising and unexpected incompatibility. Because virtually *every* product matches this description, it is important to test a product under actual market conditions before proceeding with full-scale introduction. A test does not necessarily involve a full-scale test-marketing effort. It may be simply observing the actual use of the product in the target market.

Failure to assess actual use conditions can lead to big surprises, as Unilever learned when it rolled out a new detergent brand in Europe without sufficient testing. Unilever spent $150 million to develop the new detergent, which was formulated with a stain-fighting manganese complex molecule intended to clean fabrics faster at lower temperatures than competing products such as Procter & Gamble's Ariel. Backed by a $300 million marketing budget, the detergent was launched in April 1994 as Persil Power, Omo Power, and other brand names. After a restructuring, Unilever had cut the time required to roll out new products in Europe from three years to 16 months. In this particular instance, the increased efficiency combined with corporate enthusiasm for the new formula resulted in a marketing debacle. Consumers discovered that some clothing items were damaged after being washed with Power. P&G was quick to capitalize on the situation; P&G ran newspaper ads denouncing Power and commissioned lab tests to verify that the damage did, in fact, occur. Unilever chairman Sir Michael Perry called the Power fiasco, "the greatest marketing setback we've seen." Unilever reformulated Power, but it was too late to save the brand. The company lost the opportunity to gain share against P&G in Europe.[41]

THE INTERNATIONAL PRODUCT TRADE CYCLE MODEL

The **international product trade cycle model** describes the relationship between the product life cycle (PLC), trade, and investment. The model accurately describes the way sequential international market development affected trade patterns and the location of production in textiles, consumer electronics, and other industries from 1950 to the mid-1970s. Simply stated, high-income, mass-consumption countries such as Japan and the United States were initially exporters but ultimately became importers. A second tier of advanced countries initially imported and, in time, exported the product. Later in time, a third tier of low-income countries initiated manufacturing operations and then exhibited the same shift from importing to exporting. These shifts corresponded to the introduction,

---

[40] Elena Bowes, "Virgin Flies in Face of Conventions," *Ad Age International* (January 1997), p. i4.
[41] Laurel Wentz, "Unilever's Power Failure a Wasteful Use of Haste," *Advertising Age* (May 6, 1995), p. 42.

growth, and maturity stages of the product life cycle: The high-income countries were exporters during the introduction phase, the middle-income countries were exporters during the growth phase, and the low-income countries were exporters during the mature phase.

The history of the VCR illustrates several aspects of the model. Starting in the mid-1970s, Sony, JVC, and other Japanese companies produced VCRs for the domestic consumer market and for export. Customers in the United States and Europe who bought Beta- and VHS-format VCRs were buying Japanese-made goods, even if they carried local brand names such as RCA and Zenith. Exports grew to a steady stream as the VCR entered the growth phase of the PLC. South Korean companies such as Goldstar and Samsung were quick to note the opportunity. In short order, they initiated production to take advantage of lower labor and factor costs; production outside Japan marked the beginning of Phase 2 of the trade cycle. During the growth phase of the PLC, exports from both Japan and South Korea supplied the United States and other high-income markets. In the mid-1980s, VCRs matured as design, technology, and demand stabilized. In Phase 3, production sources in low-income countries displaced production sources in high-income countries. By the early 1990s, for example, American consumers could buy South Korean-built VCRs for $99. South Korea and other lower-income countries reached high production volumes based on domestic and export markets and, thanks to lower factor costs, achieved the status of low-cost producers. By 1996, Japan's imports of VCRs surpassed exports for the first time. The cycle was complete, and companies in Japan that once had a monopoly in VCR production found themselves facing stiff foreign competition in their key markets. Their best hope was to create new products and launch the cycle again and again (Figure 11-7). This is exactly what Sony and other Japanese companies have done with products such as portable personal stereos, video camcorders, DVD players, and high-definition television sets.

The international product trade cycle is an empirical record of trade patterns. It reflects the behavior of many U.S. and European firms in consumer electronics and other industries. The firms have abandoned the investment and effort necessary to maintain world-class production facilities in their home country because they faced the challenge of high wages and other costs. In the United States, for example, many executives faced with quality and cost problems at home made the strategic choice to shift production to lower-cost countries or to give up market share to low-cost producers in other countries. Unfortunately, such an approach may have put the focus of strategy on the wrong dimension. The companies that shifted production to low-wage countries did, indeed, gain a one-time advantage. All other things being equal, they lowered their labor costs. However, a company that focuses too obsessively on getting costs down by moving production to low-income countries may, in the long run, trail its competitors in innovation, product features, manufacturing processes, and quality.

The product trade cycle model represents a potential trap for global marketers: Company executives in high-income countries sometimes act as if the shifting cycle of consumption, trade, and investment is inevitable. Under this assumption, companies in advanced countries are forced to constantly discover and introduce new products because lower-wage competitors have an unassailable advantage in mature, established products. Two comments are in order, however. First, *the cycle is inevitable only if the product does not change.* Innovations in existing products and manufacturing processes enable companies in high-income countries to thrive and prosper in global industries. Innovators can, in effect, make an end run around the international trade cycle. Innovative global companies do not leave an opening for competitors with low-income country production sources. Rather, innovators make

Figure 11-7
International
Product Trade
Cycle

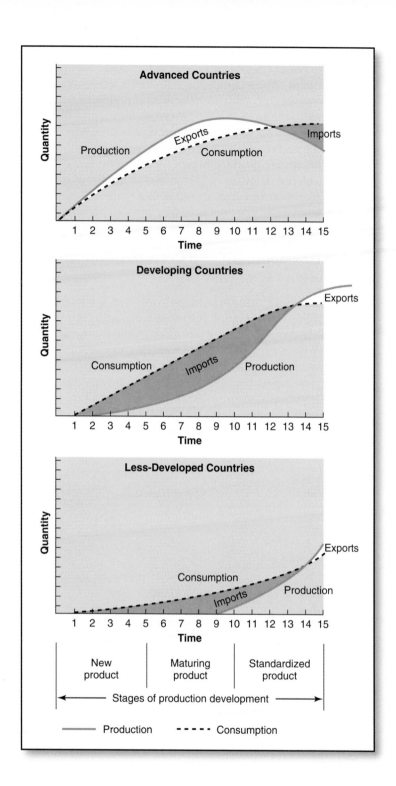

the strategic choice to keep manufacturing facilities close to home-country customers, the better to give those customers what they want. Second, firms in high-wage countries *can* be competitive if production processes are more efficient than those in low-wage countries. The key is constant investment in process-related research and development, employee training, and other productivity-enhancing programs. A second strategic alternative is focusing on a luxury segment where unique value and creativity, not low cost, are the key elements of value. For example, Steinway pianos are used by 99 percent of the world's concert pianists. The company does not discount its prices or pay artists to use the instruments, despite the fact that Steinway pianos are manufactured in the United States and Germany. Pianists buy Steinway instruments not because they are inexpensive; they buy them because they are the best. Each Steinway instrument is a craft-produced work of art.

Market Development and Consumption in the Twenty-First Century

The international trade cycle model reflected a *trickle-down* or *waterfall* pattern of market development (Figure 11-8).

As the twenty-first century begins, global marketers need strategies based on a different pattern of market development and consumption. Product development costs continue to mount. In addition, many products, especially those with digital technology, become obsolete very quickly. One strategy is to develop a product and introduce it virtually simultaneously in world markets (a *shower* instead of a trickle). Gillette used this approach for the global launch of its MACH3 razor in 1998. Gillette spent $750 million over a six-year period to develop the new three-bladed successor

Figure 11-8
International Product Trade Cycle—Trickle Down/Waterfall Pattern

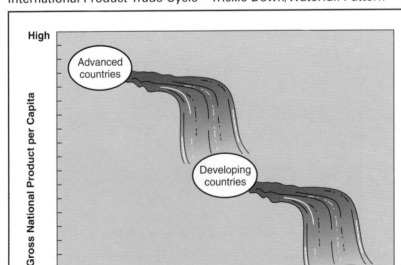

Panasonic, Sony, and other consumer electronics companies are enjoying strong worldwide demand for DVD players.

to the Sensor; the first-year marketing budget was $300 million. Company plans called for marketing the MACH3 in 100 countries by 1999.[42] Similarly, in 1996, Panasonic, Toshiba, Matsushita, Sony, and other consumer electronics companies launched the digital video disc (DVD) as a product that they envisioned would be the successor to the VCR. Worldwide sales of DVD hardware quickly passed the billion-dollar level. As the MACH3 and DVD examples show, managerial assumptions about the nature of world markets influence the planning process and market approach chosen. Strategies based on the waterfall view reflect the assumption that markets develop sequentially over time. Strategies based on the shower approach acknowledge that, in a global village, market opportunities frequently emerge simultaneously on a regional or global basis.

SUMMARY

The product is the most important element of a marketing program. Global marketers face the challenge of formulating coherent product and brand strategies on a worldwide basis. A **product** can be viewed as a collection of tangible and intangible attributes that collectively provide benefits to a buyer or user. A **brand** is a complex bundle of images and experiences in the mind of the customer. Products and brands can be classified as local, international, and global. A **global product**

---

[42] Mark Maremont, "How Gillette Brought Its MACH3 to Market," *The Wall Street Journal* (April 15, 1998), pp. B1, B8.

meets the wants and needs of a global market. A **global brand** has the same name and a similar image and positioning throughout the world. Many global companies have leveraged favorable **brand images** and high **brand equity** by employing **combination (tiered) branding, cobranding,** and **brand extension** strategies. **Maslow's hierarchy** is a needs-based framework that offers a way of understanding opportunities to develop local and global products in different parts of the world. An understanding of **product saturation levels** and **country-of-origin** effects can guide marketers in search of opportunities around the world.

Product and communications strategies can be viewed within a framework of **extend, adapt,** or **create.** Five strategic alternatives are open to companies pursuing geographic expansion: **product–communication extension; product extension–communication adaptation; product adaptation–communication extension; product–communication adaptation;** and **product invention.** The strategic alternative(s) that a particular company chooses will depend on the product and the need it serves, customer preferences and purchasing power, and the costs of adaptation versus standardization. Global competition has put pressure on companies to excel at developing standardized product **platforms** that can serve as a foundation for cost-efficient adaptation. New products can be classified as **discontinuous, dynamically continuous** or **continuous innovations.** A successful product launch requires an understanding of how markets develop: sequentially over time or simultaneously. Today, many new products are launched in multiple national markets as product development cycles shorten and product development costs soar.

DISCUSSION QUESTIONS

1. What is the difference between a product and a brand?
2. How do local, international, and global products differ? Cite examples.
3. What are some of the elements that make up a brand? Are these elements tangible or intangible?
4. What criteria should global marketers consider when making product design decisions?
5. How can buyer attitudes about a product's country of origin affect marketing strategy?
6. Identify several global brands. What are some of the reasons for the global success of the brands you chose?
7. Briefly describe various combinations of product–communication strategies available to global marketers. When is it appropriate to use each?
8. Is Kodak's Advantix photo system a continuous innovation, a dynamically continuous innovation, or a discontinuous innovation? Explain your reasoning.

SUGGESTED READINGS

Books

Aacker, David. *Building Strong Brands.* New York: Free Press, 1996.

Kuczmarski, Thomas D. *Managing New Products; The Power of Innovation.* Englewood Cliffs, New Jersey: Prentice-Hall, Inc., 1992.

Macrae, Chris. *World Class Brands.* Reading, Mass.: Addison-Wesley, 1991.

Nayak, P. Ranganath, and John M. Ketteringham. *Breakthroughs! How Leadership and Drive Create Commercial Innovations that Sweep the World.* San Diego, California: Pfeiffer & Company, 1994.

Temporal, Paul. *Branding in Asia: The Creation, Development, and Management of Asian Brands for the Global Market.* New York: John Wiley & Sons, 2000.

Wheelwright, Steven C., and Kim B. Clark. *Revolutionizing Product Development: Quantum Leaps in Speed, Efficiency, and Quality.* New York: The Free Press, 1992.

Articles

Aacker, David A., and Erich Joachimsthaler. "The Lure of Global Branding." *Harvard Business Review* 77, no. 6 (November-December 1999), pp. 137–144.

Alden, Dana L., Jan-Benedict Steenkamp, and Rajeev Batra. "Brand Positioning through Advertising in Asia, North America, and Europe: The Role of Global Consumer Culture." *Journal of Marketing* 63, no. 1 (January 1999), pp. 75–87.

Carpano, Claudio, and James J. Chrisman. "Performance Implications of International Product Strategies and the Integration of Marketing Activities." *Journal of International Marketing* 3, no. 1 (1995), pp. 9–28.

Chao, Paul. "Partitioning Country of Origin Effects: Consumer Evaluations of a Hybrid Product." *Journal of International Business Studies* 24, no. 2 (Second Quarter 1993), pp. 291–306.

Cordell, Victor V. "Effects of Consumer Preferences for Foreign Sourced Products." *Journal of International Business Studies* 23, no. 2 (Second Quarter 1992), pp. 251–270.

Du Preez, Johann P., Adamantios Diamantopoulos, and Bodo B. Schlegelmilch. "Product Standardization and Attribute Saliency: A Three-Product Empirical Comparison." *Journal of International Marketing* 2, no. 1 (1994), pp. 7–28.

Elliott, Gregory R., and Ross C. Cameron. "Consumer Perception of Product Quality and the Country-of-Origin Effect." *Journal of International Marketing* 2, no. 2 (1994), pp. 49–62.

Ewing, Michael, Julie Napoli, and Leyland Pitt. "Managing Southeast Asian Brands in the Global Economy." *Business Horizons* 44, no. 3 (May-June 2001), pp. 52–58.

Hamilton, Kate. "Project Galore: Qualitative Research and Leveraging Scotland's Brand Equity." *Journal of Advertising Research* 40, no. 1-2 (January-April 2000), pp. 107–111.

Hill, John S., and William L. James. "Product and Promotion Transfers in Consumer Goods Multinationals." *International Marketing Review* 8, no. 2, pp. 6–17.

———, and Up Kwon. "Product Mixes in U.S. Multinationals: An Empirical Study." *Journal of Global Marketing* 6, no. 3 (1992), pp. 55–73.

Joachimsthaler, Erich, and David A. Aacker, "Building Brands Without Mass Media," *Harvard Business Review* (January-February 1997), pp. 39+.

———, Ilkka A. Ronkainen, and Michael R. Czinkota. "Negative Country-of-Origin Effects: The Case of the New Russia." *Journal of International Business Studies* 25, no. 1 (First Quarter 1994), pp. 157–176.

Kim, W. Chan, and Renee Maugorgne. "Value Innovation: The Strategic Logic of High Growth." *Harvard Business Review* 75, 1 (January-February 1997), pp. 102–115.

Lint, Onno, and Enrico Pennings. "An Option Approach to the New Product Development Process: A Case Study at Philips Electronics." *R&D Management* 31, no. 2 (April 2001), pp. 163–172.

Moskowitz, Howard R., and Samuel Rabino. "Sensory Segmentation: An Organizing Principle for International Product Concept Generation." *Journal of Global Marketing* 8, no. 1 (1994), pp. 73–94.

Ogbuehi, Alphonso O., and Ralph A. Bellas Jr. "Decentralized R&D for Global Product Development: Strategic Implications for the Multinational Corporation." *International Marketing Review* 9, no. 5, pp. 60–70.

Prasad, V. Kanti, and G. M. Naidu. "Perspectives and Preparedness Regarding ISO-9000 International Quality Standards." *Journal of International Marketing* 2, no. 2 (1994), pp. 81–98.

Roth, Martin S. "The Effects of Culture and Socioeconomics on the Performance of Global Brand Image Strategies." *Journal of Marketing Research* 32 (May 1995), pp. 163–175.

Roth, Martin S., and Jean B. Romeo. "Matching Product Category and Country Image Perceptions: A Framework for Managing Country-of-Origin Effects." *Journal of International Business Studies* 23, no. 3 (Third Quarter 1992), pp. 477–498.

Samiee, Saeed. "Customer Evaluation of Products in a Global Market." *Journal of International Business Studies* 25, no. 3 (Third Quarter 1994), pp. 579–604.

Tse, David K., and Gerald Gorn. "An Experiment on the Salience of Country-of-Origin in the Era of Global Brands." *Journal of International Marketing* 1, no. 1 (1993), pp. 57–76.

———, and Wei-na Lee. "Removing Negative Country Images: Effects of Decomposition, Branding, and Product Experience." *Journal of International Marketing* 1, no. 4 (1993), pp. 25–48.

Ulgado, Francis M., and Moonku Lee. "Consumer Evaluations of Bi-National Products in the Global Market." *Journal of International Marketing* 1, no. 3 (1993), pp. 5–22.

Washburn, Judith H., Brian D. Till, and Randi Priluck. "Co-Branding: Brand Equity and Trial Effects." *Journal of Consumer Marketing* 17, no. 7 (2000), pp. 591–604.

Witt, Jerome, and C. P. Rao. "The Impact of Global Sourcing on Consumers: Country-of-Origin Effects on Perceived Risk." *Journal of Global Marketing* 6, no. 3 (1992), pp. 105–128.

Zhang, Shi, and Bernd H. Schmitt. "Creating Local Brands in Multilingual International Markets." *Journal of Marketing Research* 38, no. 3 (August 2001), pp. 313–325.

CASES

Case 11-1 Smart Cards

Smart is the operative word among many product developers these days. For example, *smart card* is the name of an advanced form of pocket- and purse-sized cards that may soon usher in a new era of cashless electronic commerce. Although they resemble familiar ATM cards, each smart card is equipped with a computer chip instead of a black magnetic strip. Basic designs equipped with memory chips function simply as stored value cards that are loaded with money over the phone or at a cash machine. The cards can then be used to make purchases and pay for telephone calls. More sophisticated smart cards containing actual microprocessors are capable of carrying several different currencies—French francs, Deutsche marks, and British pounds, for example—in different electronic "pockets."

The high-tech cards can also be loaded with the user's identification, medical histories, and other personal information. Smart cards can provide retailers with a mechanism for tracking individual purchase behavior at the point of sale and using the information for store loyalty programs. Moreover, a new generation of digital mobile telephones has a swipe slot that can be used to transfer data to a smart card. "Contactless" smart cards contain miniature antennas that allow the cards to communicate with a remote transmitter or receiver. The Java programming language devised by Sun Microsystems allows quick adaptation of smart card technology to a multitude of applications. According to Kevin Loosemore, managing director of UK-based De La Rue Card Systems, the capabilities built into the new cards have been made possible by quantum leaps in the computing power built into a single tiny chip. "As we go into the new millennium we will be able to put the same computer capability on a smart card as we can on a PC today," he said.

Smart cards containing a chip from Motorola were first developed by France's Machines Bull more than 20 years ago to provide French consumers with an alternative to carrying loose change. Card reader terminals in shops provide an online connection between the card and the user's bank. Retailers benefit from the smart cards' added convenience and security. Today, more than 23 million smart cards are in circulation in France, where they are a popular substitute for ATM cards and credit cards. France is also home to smart card manufacturer Gemplus, which produces approximately 40 percent of the smart cards in use today.

Smart cards are catching on in other countries as well. As of mid-1998, an estimated 2.3 billion cards were in circulation. Most of them were simple memory-type cards. Some experts expect 30 percent annual growth in the number of cards issued, with more than four billion cards in use by 2002. In the United Kingdom, a major push is on to replace or upgrade some 530,000 shop terminals and 23,000 ATM machines. Fifty percent annual growth is forecast for the Asia-Pacific region. In Singapore, for example, smart card holders are entitled to free parking at the popular Takashimaya shopping mall. Contactless smart cards sold by the Hong Kong Transit Authority allow commuters to quickly enter metro stations without having to manually swipe their pass at a turnstile. According to Andy Agnew, an analyst with the Cap Gemini consulting firm, the willingness of Asians to try the new cards stems in part from the absence of an established infrastructure; there is little resistance because there are few entrenched habits to be changed. Similarly, consumers in South Africa and other developing countries have yet to join the banking culture. Plus, Agnew noted recently, "In places such as Singapore, they're seen to be very interested in the take-up of technology."

Consumer response has been less enthusiastic in the United States, where traditional magnetic-strip cards are widely used. During the summer Olympics in Atlanta, Visa International distributed about two million Visa cash cards. They were accepted by MARTA, Atlanta's mass transit system, as well as about 1,500 retail locations. Surveying consumer response to the cards, researcher Bruce Brittain observed the chicken-and-egg problem: Consumers won't use smart cards unless more merchants accept them, but merchants won't make the necessary investments in terminals if customers don't ask to use the cards. Brittain commented, "The convenience of *not* carrying cash is a hard sell to most people. Cash doesn't seem that inconvenient."

During 1997 and 1998, another pilot program was undertaken in New York's Upper West Side by Visa, MasterCard, Citibank, and Chase Manhattan Bank. However, only about 10 percent of the stored value cards issued were actually used during the 6-month trial. The trial's sponsors pointed to a variety of reasons for the poor results. Carole Lockie of Visa International said, "We are asking merchants to do something new and different. We have barriers with these merchants, many of

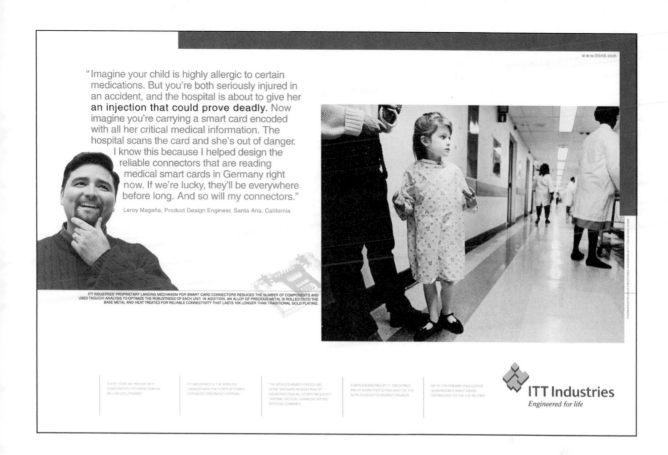

whom have never used a terminal of any kind before." MasterCard's Richard Phillimore noted, "We need to find the right merchant sectors. The heartland for stored value is really self-service, fast food and mass transit—anywhere which needs exact change or has turnstiles."

Such lukewarm results support the widespread view it will be several years before smart cards become popular in the United States. Nevertheless, the race is on as key players vie with each other to establish the first global infrastructure for electronic commerce. In 1996, MasterCard bought a 51 percent stake in British smart card manufacturer Mondex International. Visa International and American Express joined an alliance of investors in a Belgian company, Proton, that has 30 million cards in circulation plus 200,000 terminals in 15 countries. The goal of the new venture, known as Proton World International (PWI), is to further develop standards and technology to expand the ways smart cards can be used. Peter Godfrey, president of American Express Europe, noted, "As a market leader in payment instruments and a global organization, it's very important that we have the technology that allows us to move to the future."

"The combination of the convenience of a small plastic card coupled with an on-board microprocessor and memory has produced a product with an almost unlimited variety of potential applications."
—Datamonitor

Ultimately, the rivalry between competing technological formats will have to be resolved. Doubts remain, moreover, about broad-based consumer acceptance of the cards. Some industry observers point out that losing a fully-loaded smart card would be like losing a wallet. Also, the current smart card technology makes transaction times longer than those for traditional magnetic-strip cards. As for the future of smart cards, a senior analyst at a technology marketing research firm said, "The business case for consumers is shaky. The technology exists to be able to buy goods over the Internet using electronic cash. I don't think the issue is technology. The issue is partly marketing and partly cultural acceptance." ■

Visit the Web site
To learn more about smart cards, visit Gemplus at:
www.gemplus.com

1. Who stands to benefit most from smart cards: banks, retailers, or consumers? Explain.
2. Why might consumers and merchants in developing countries be more receptive to using smart cards than consumers and merchants in the United States?
3. What are some applications of smart cards that would entice you to use them?

SOURCES: Paul Beckett, "Glitches Trip Up Real-Life Test of Plastic Cash," *The Wall Street Journal* (October 8, 1998), pp. B1, B10; Michael Dempsey, "Asia Warms to Smartcards," *Financial Times Survey—Information Technology* (July 1, 1998), p. 10; Christopher Brown-Humes, "Where the Smart Money Is Headed," *Financial Times* (July 11/12, 1998), p. 7; Paul Taylor, "A Winning Hand for Smartcards," *Financial Times* (March 4, 1998), p. 21; Martin du Bois and Douglas Lanvin, "American Express, Visa Form Smart-Card Unit," *The Wall Street Journal* (July 30, 1998), p. 6; Mark Vernon, "Still a Long Way to Go," *Financial Times Survey — Information Technology* (April 1, 1998), p. X; John Authers, "Smart Cards Fail to Impress American Shoppers," *Financial Times* (March 30, 1998), p. 4; George Graham, "MasterCard Pins its Hopes on Mondex," *Financial Times* (November 19, 1996), p. 6; Douglas Lavin, "French Smart Card Proves a Bright Idea," *The Wall Street Journal* (April 22, 1996), p. A14; Christine Dugas, "Rival Card Networks Join in Pilot Program," *USA Today* (April 11, 1996), pp. 1B, 2B; Nikhil Deogun, "The Smart Money Is on 'Smart Cards,' But Electronic Cash Seems Dumb to Some," *The Wall Street Journal* (August 5, 1998), p. B1; Amy Cortese, "The Ultimate Plastic," *Business Week* (May 19, 1997), pp. 119, 122.

Case 11-2 *The Smart Car*

In 1991, Nicolas Hayek, chairman of Swatch, announced an agreement with Volkswagen to develop a battery-powered "Swatch car." At the time, Hayek said his goal was to build "an ecologically inoffensive, high-quality city car for two people" that would sell for about $6,400. The Swatchmobile concept was based on Hayek's conviction that consumers become emotionally attached to cars just as they do to watches. Like the Swatch, the Swatchmobile (officially named "Smart") was designed to be affordable, durable, and stylish. Early on, Hayek noted that safety would be another key selling point, declaring, "This car will have the crash security of a Mercedes." Composite exterior panels mounted on a cage-like body frame would allow owners to change colors by switching panels. Further, Hayek envisioned a car that emitted almost no pollutants, thanks to its electric engine. The car would also be capable of gasoline-powered operation, using a highly efficient, miniaturized engine capable of achieving speeds of 80 miles per hour. Hayek predicted that worldwide sales would reach one million units, with the United States accounting for about half the market.

Some observers attributed the hoopla surrounding the Swatchmobile concept to Hayek's charismatic personality. His automotive vision was dismissed as being overly optimistic; less ambitious attempts at extending the Swatch brand name to new categories, including a brightly colored unisex clothing line, had flopped. Other products such as Swatch telephones, pagers, and sun-glasses also met with lukewarm consumer acceptance. The Swatchmobile represented Hayek's attempt to pioneer a completely new market segment. Industry observers warned, moreover, that the Swatch name could be hurt if the Smart were plagued by recall or safety problems.

In 1993, the alliance with Volkswagen was dissolved; Hayek claimed it was because of disagreement on the concept of the car (Volkswagen officials said low profit projections were the problem). In the spring of 1994, Hayek announced that he had lined up a new joint venture partner. The Mercedes-Benz unit of Daimler-Benz AG would invest 750 million Deutsche marks in a new factory in Hambach-Saargemuend, France. In November 1998, after several months of production delays and repeated cost overruns, Hayek sold Swatch's remaining 19 percent stake in the venture, officially known as Micro Compact Car GmBH (MCC), to Mercedes. A spokesman indicated that Mercedes' refusal to pursue the hybrid gasoline/battery engine was the reason Swatch withdrew from the project.

The decision by Mercedes executives to take full control of the venture was consistent with its strategy for leveraging its engineering skills and broadening the company's appeal beyond the luxury segment of the automobile market. As Mercedes chairman Helmut Werner said, "With the new car, Mercedes wants to combine ecology, emotion, and intellect." Approximately 80 percent of the Smart's parts are components and

then passed by conveyer into the main hall. There VDO, another German company, installs the instrument panel. At this point, modules and parts manufactured by Krupp-Hoesch, Bosch, Dynamit Nobel, and Ymos are delivered for assembly by MCC employees. To encourage integration of MCC employees and system partners and to underscore the need for quality, both groups share a common dining room overlooking the main assembly hall.

The Smart City Coupé officially went on sale in Europe in October 1998. Sales got off to a slow start amid concerns about the vehicle's stability. That problem was solved with a sophisticated electronic package that monitors wheel slippage. Late-night TV comedians gave the odd-looking car no respect and referred to it as "a motorized ski boot" and "a backpack on wheels." During the first quarter of 1999, the 150 Smart dealers in 19 countries in continental Europe sold a total of 8,400 cars, an average of 56 cars each. The sales picture was brightest in the United Kingdom, where a London dealer sold 160 vehicles between the Smart launch in October 1998 and May 1999. The brisk sales pace in Britain was especially noteworthy because MCC was only building left-hand drive models (the UK is the only country in Europe in which right-hand drive cars are the norm). Industry observers noted that Brits' affection for the Austin Mini, a tiny vehicle that first appeared in the 1960s, appeared to have been extended to the Smart. MCC reduced its annual sales target from 130,000 to 100,000. Robert Easton, joint chairman of DaimlerChrysler, went on record as being skeptical of the vehicle's future. In an interview with *Automotive News*, he said, "It's possible we'll conclude that it's a good idea but one whose time simply hasn't come."

In 2000, the Smart exceeded its revised sales target, and interest in the vehicle was growing. Wolf-Garten GmbH & Company, a German gardening equipment company, announced plans to convert the Smart to a lawn mower suitable for use on golf courses. A convertible and diesel-engine edition have been added to the product line. In 2001, executives at DaimlerChrysler announced plans to research the U.S. market to determine prospects for the Smart. The announcement came as Americans were facing steep increases in gasoline prices. ∎

Visit the Web site
www.smart.com

modules engineered by and sourced from outside suppliers and subcontractors known as "system partners." The decision to locate the assembly plant in France disappointed German labor unions, but Mercedes executives expected to save 500 marks per car. The reason: French workers are on the job 275 days per year, while German workers average only 242 days; also, overall labor costs are 40 percent lower in France than in Germany.

MCC claims that at Smart Ville, as the factory is known, only 7.5 hours are required to complete a vehicle. This is 25 percent less time than required by the world's best automakers. The first three hours of the process are performed by systems partners. A Canadian company, Magna International, starts by welding the structural components, which are then painted by Eisenmann, a German company. Both operations are performed outside the central assembly hall; the body is

DISCUSSION QUESTIONS

1. In 1998, Daimler-Benz acquired Chrysler; the new company is called DaimlerChrysler. Does the Smart project still make sense for DaimlerChrysler?
2. Assess the U.S. market potential for the Smart. Do you think the car will be introduced in the United States? Why or why not?
3. Identify other target markets where you would introduce this car. What sequence of countries would you recommend for the introduction?

SOURCES: Will Pinkston and Scott Miller, "DaimlerChrysler Steers Toward 'Smart' Debut in U.S.," *The Wall Street Journal* (August 20, 2001), pp. B1, B4; Scott Miller, "Daimler May Roll Out Its Tiny Car Here," *The Wall Street Journal* (June 9, 2001), p. B1; Scott Miller, "DaimlerChrysler's Smart Car May Have a New Use," *The Wall Street Journal* (February 15, 2001), pp. B1, B4; Haig Simonian, "Carmakers' Smart Move," *Financial Times* (July 1, 1997), p. 12; William Taylor, "Message and Muscle: An Interview with Swatch Titan Nicolas Hayek," *Harvard Business Review* (March-April 1993), pp. 99–110; Kevin Helliker, "Swiss Movement: Can Wristwatch Whiz Switch Swatch Cachet to an Automobile?" *The Wall Street Journal* (March 4, 1994), pp. A1, A3; Ferdinand Protzman, "Off the Wrist, Onto the Road: A Swatch of Wheels," *The New York Times* (March 4, 1994), p. C1.

Case 11-3 *Iridium LLC*

Executives at Motorola had high expectations for Iridium. The company spent more than a decade developing the ambitious new business, at the heart of which would be a network of 66 powerful satellites orbiting the earth from a distance of 420 nautical miles. Iridium LLC would offer global personal communications services to supplement ground-based wire and cellular telephone services. If it succeeded, Iridium would be an historic first: A business that was truly global from its first day of operation. Iridium's first customers were expected to include globetrotting business executives who need to send and receive voice messages and data and who want a single telephone number that will work anywhere on the planet. In addition, the business concept was based on the fact that 90 percent of the world's population lacks access to telephones. Iridium could bring wireless telephone service to rural areas in South America, India, and Africa. With a price tag of $5.9 billion, Iridium was too expensive for Motorola to undertake on its own. Iridium's global reach also required cooperation and participation from 200 different governments because, in many countries, governments own the telephone systems and broadcast spectrum rights and rely on them for revenues. Motorola executives projected that Iridium would attract five million users by the year 2002. Each subscriber was expected to contribute $1,000 per year in net revenues to Iridium.

To realize the Iridium vision, Motorola kept a 25 percent stake in the venture and partnered with companies in several different nations. Each partner brought a specific strength to the project. Lockheed, for example, built the satellites at a cost of $13 million each; other equipment subcontractors included Raytheon, Martin Marietta, and Siemens AG. Some partners were responsible for connecting calls in specific geographic regions; for example, Vebacom GmbH, a subsidiary of Germany's Veba AG, agreed to provide service in northern and western Europe. Other participants included Krunichev Enterprise, a Russian rocket manufacturer, and Great Wall Industry Corporation, which is affiliated with the Chinese army.

All the participants were betting that the varying technology standards of conventional cellular telephone systems would provide the key to Iridium's success. For example, cellular phone standards are different in Europe and the United States, so a European businessperson's cell phone unit is rendered inoperable across the Atlantic in the United States. Moreover, callers using cellular systems need to know the geographic location of the party they wish to reach. Iridium's early customers would pay approximately $3,000 for new telephones. Usage fees for satellite telephone calls were set in a range from $1.75 to $7.00 per minute.

Industry observers noted that Iridium would have to overcome several major hurdles if it were to succeed. For one thing, Iridium was just one of several telephone and data systems in development. Competitors included Globalstar, a satellite system one-third owned by Loral, the U.S. defense contractor. Globalstar's partners included Vodafone of Great Britain, France Telecom, and Deutsche Aerospace. Another competitor, Odyssey, was a satellite venture created by TRW with Teleglobe, a Canadian firm, as a major partner. Hughes Electronics was also designing less expensive regional satellite networks that might be dedicated to specific geographic regions such as Asia and Africa.

Motorola also faced the daunting task of achieving process improvements in satellite assembly. Satellites, or "birds" as they were known to industry insiders, typically cost $150 to $200 million apiece and require two years to build. To create the initial supply of birds, plus improved versions in the future, Motorola had to reduce the assembly time to about five days. Some employees viewed the deadlines with skepticism; to prove that the impossible could in fact be achieved, Iridium management used the Rolling Stones "Voodoo Lounge" tour as a case study in logistics. On the Stones' worldwide tour, three 747 jets hauled 600 tons of equipment from city to city, where crews had to set up and tear down the stage in a matter of days. The Iridium team got the message; before long, Motorola had reduced the cost to produce each bird by 80 percent.

Another problem was that the high risks associated with a venture such as Iridium initially limited interest from outside investors. In the fall of 1995, Iridium was forced to withdraw a $300 million offering of high-yield "junk" bonds after investors demanded a return of approximately 25 percent. As Ira Brodsky, a consultant at Datacomm Research, commented, "There's an issue of high-stakes projects here." Brodsky predicted that Iridium could cost as much as $6 billion. "Can they really make that back?" he asks. Stuart Lipoff, a consultant with Arthur D. Little, expressed similar concerns. "The biggest single issue is, can they sell it? There is no good head count of international businessmen who need this." For their part, Iridium executives reasoned that some 40 million people travel from the United States each year. Even if a small percentage of them became Iridium users, the service would be a success. Investors appeared to agree; they pumped $315 million in equity into the company. By summer 1996, Iridium secured a $750 million

line of credit. The 62 banks participating in the deal were encouraged by the fact that Motorola guaranteed the loan. In the spring of 1997, management announced plans to go public by issuing 10 million shares of stock. At the time, Iridium was spending about $100 million each month.

Also early in 1997, Iridium management announced a number of strategic changes. The company was now aiming to sign up three million businesspeople such as contractors, people employed in the oil and gas industries, maritime workers, and employees of heavy construction firms such as Schlumberger and Bechtel. Such professional travelers, it was hoped, would account for about two-thirds of Iridium's revenues. As Iridium vice chairman and chief executive Dr. Edward Staiano said, "The guy who's going to pay for this system is the guy who doesn't look at his phone bill." This change de-emphasized the opportunity in emerging markets with undeveloped telephone systems. The move also could be interpreted as tacit recognition that lower-cost competitors such as Globalstar would be strong competitors in rural markets. Also, land-based digital cellular technology had improved dramatically during the 1990s, and the number of subscribers around the world had grown as well. It was decided that Iridium's satellites would not necessarily transmit conversations on every call made using the system. Rather, the satellites would be used primarily for caller identification, call routing, and billing. A new pocket-sized phone would connect callers with existing land-based digital cellular networks that would carry the actual voice communications.

This new approach, it was hoped, would provide increased revenues and sidestep the problem of poor reception between satellites and telephones used inside buildings or on city streets surrounded by tall buildings. Because nearly a dozen different cellular standards are in use around the world, Iridium phones would have

removable cards to make them compatible with any cellular system. In locations where no cellular network was available, the conversation would be transmitted via satellite. As CEO Staiano said, "Our pitch is, 'Where cellular is available, use cellular. Where it isn't, use satellite.' " The pricing plan was changed as well, with customers charged $50 per month plus usage fees. Voice communications would be charged at a rate of $1.75 per minute for satellite links plus point-to-point fees between land-based transmitters.

Even as management was overhauling its strategy and business plan, problems arose with the satellites. The first launch, planned for January 1997, was delayed after questions arose concerning the Delta II rocket's reliability. By August, 16 satellites had been successfully launched into orbit on three different rockets. In January 1998, Iridium announced that the U.S. Department of Defense had agreed to use Iridium for military communications. In July, however, there was more bad news. Two satellites failed in orbit, bringing to seven the number of satellites that had to be replaced. Software was also creating problems; the decision to link up with ground-based cellular meant that millions of lines of computer code had to be revised. Iridium executives remained optimistic that the new service would be launched on schedule. In the end, the 1998 startup was delayed only five weeks beyond the September 23 target date; voice services began on November 1, with paging services available November 15. A $140 million global print advertising campaign created by Ammirati Puris Lintas was launched in June. ∎

DISCUSSION QUESTIONS

1. What was the marketing challenge facing Iridium's management team?
2. Is the concept behind Iridium well suited to today's business environment? Explain.
3. Do you think Iridium will be a success? Why or why not?

SOURCES: Quentin Hardy, "Motorola Loses Two More Satellites; Iridium Stock Drops 14% on the News," *The Wall Street Journal* (July 24, 1998), p. B6; Hardy, "Iridium Gets U.S. as First Big Customer of Wireless Communications System," *The Wall Street Journal* (January 26, 1998), p. B6; Sally Beatty, "Iridium Hopes to Ring Up Global Sales," *The Wall Street Journal* (June 22, 1998), p. B8; Hardy, "Iridium Creates New Plan for Global Cellular Service," *The Wall Street Journal* (August 18, 1997), p. B4; Hardy, " Satellite-Phone Pioneer Iridium Prepares to Go Public," *The Wall Street Journal* (March 18, 1997), p. B4; Hardy, "Iridium Phone Project Maps an Upscale Orbit," *The Wall Street Journal* (January 10, 1997), p. B2; Hardy, "Higher Calling: How a Wife's Question Led Motorola to Chase Global Cell-Phone Plan," *The Wall Street Journal* (August 26, 1996), p. B6; Hardy, "Iridium Gets $750 Million Credit Line, Helped by Guarantee from Motorola," *The Wall Street Journal* (December 16, 1996), pp. A1, A10; Jeff Cole, "Star Wars: In New Space Race, Companies are Seeking Dollars from Heaven," *The Wall Street Journal* (October 10, 1995), pp. A1, A12; Harlan S. Byrne, "Far Out," *Barron's* (June 19, 1995), pp. 31–35; Joe Flowers, "Iridium, Parts I and II," *Wired* (Fall 1993); Quentin Hardy, "Iridium Pulls $300 Million Bond Offer; Analysts Cite Concerns About Projects," *The Wall Street Journal* (September 22, 1995), p. B5; Nancy Hass, "Preemptive Strike," *Financial World,* (September 14, 1993), pp. 36–39; Rob Frieden, "Satellite-based Personal Communications Services," *Telecommunications* (December 1993), pp. 25–28.

Chapter 12

Pricing Decisions

When Reebok, the world's number two athletic shoe company, decided to enter India in 1995, it faced several basic marketing challenges. For one thing, Reebok was creating a market from scratch. Upscale sports shoes were virtually unknown, and the most expensive sneakers available at the time cost 1,000 rupees (about $23). Reebok officials also had to select a market entry mode. The decision was made to subcontract with four local suppliers, one of which became a joint venture partner. Only a limited number of distribution options were available. Bata, a Canadian company with global operations, was the sole shoe retailer with national coverage. American-style sports stores were unknown in India. To reinforce Reebok's high-tech brand image, company officials decided to establish their own retail infrastructure. There were two other crucial pieces of the puzzle: product and price. Should Reebok create a line of mass-market shoes specifically for India and priced at Rs 1,000? The alternative was to offer the same designs sold in other parts of the world and price them at Rs 2,500 ($58), a figure that represented the equivalent of a month's salary for a junior civil servant.

In any country, two basic factors determine the boundaries within which market prices should be set. The first is product cost, which establishes a *price floor,* or minimum price. Although pricing a product below the cost boundary is certainly possible, few firms can afford to do this for long. Second, prices for comparable substitute products create a *price ceiling,* or upper boundary. In many instances, international competition puts pressure on the pricing policies and related cost structures of domestic companies. Generally speaking, international trade results in lower prices for goods. Lower prices, in turn, help keep a country's rate of inflation in check. Between the lower and upper boundary for every product there is an *optimum price,* which is a function

445

of the demand for the product as determined by the willingness and ability of customers to buy. As Reebok's experience in India illustrates, a basic issue in global marketing is establishing a pricing policy.

BASIC PRICING CONCEPTS

In a true global market, the *law of one price* would prevail: All customers in the market could get the best product available for the best price. As Lowell Bryan and his collaborators note in *Race for the World*, a global market exists for certain products such as integrated circuits, crude oil, and commercial aircraft: A Boeing 777 costs the same worldwide. By contrast, beer, compact discs, and many other products that are available around the world are actually being offered in markets that are national rather than global in nature. That is, these are markets where national competition reflects differences in factors such as costs, regulation, and the intensity of the rivalry among industry members.[1] The beer market is extremely fragmented; as shown in Table 12-1, even though Budweiser is the leading global brand, it commands less than 4 percent of the total market. The nature of the beer market explains why, for example, a six-pack of Heineken varies in price by as much as 50 percent (adjusted for purchasing power parity, transportation, and other transaction costs) depending on where it is sold. In Japan, for example, the price is a function of the competition between Heineken, other imports, and five national producers—Kirin, Asahi, Sapporo, Suntory, and Orion—that collectively command 60 percent of the market.

Because of these differences in national markets, the global manager must develop pricing systems and pricing policies that address price floors, price ceilings, and optimum prices in each of the national markets in which his or her company operates. A firm's pricing system and policies must also be consistent with other

Table 12-1
Top 10 Global Beer Brands, 1999

BRAND	BREWER	MARKET SHARE %
1. Budweiser	Anheuser-Busch	3.6
2. Bud Light	Anheuser-Busch	2.6
3. Asahi Super Dry	Asahi Breweries	1.8
4. Skol	Ambev	1.8
5. Corona Extra	Grupo Modelo	1.7
6. Heineken	Heineken	1.6
7. Brahman Chopp	Ambev	1.5
8. Miller Lite	Miller Brewing (Philip Morris)	1.4
9. Coors Light	Coors Brewing	1.4
10. Polar	Cerveceria Polar	1.1

Source: © 2001 The Economist Newspaper Group, Inc. Reprinted with permission. Further reproduction prohibited. www.economist.com

---

[1] Lowell Bryan, *Race for the World: Strategies to Build a Great Global Firm* (Boston: Harvard Business School Press, 1999), pp. 40–41.

uniquely global opportunities and constraints. For example, companies that are active in the 12 nations of the euro zone will have to adjust to the new cross-border transparency of prices. Similarly, the Internet has made price information for many products available around the globe. Companies must carefully consider how customers in one country or region will react if they discover they are paying significantly higher prices for the same product as customers in other parts of the world.

There is another important internal organizational consideration besides cost. Within the typical corporation, there are many interest groups and, frequently, conflicting price objectives. Divisional vice presidents, regional executives, and country managers are each concerned about profitability at their respective organizational levels. Similarly, the director of global marketing seeks competitive prices in world markets. The controller and financial vice president are concerned about profits. The manufacturing vice president seeks long production runs for maximum manufacturing efficiency. The tax manager is concerned about compliance with government transfer pricing legislation. Finally, company counsel is concerned about the antitrust implications of global pricing practices. Ultimately, price generally reflects the goals set by members of the sales staff, product managers, corporate division chiefs, and/or the company's chief executive.

GLOBAL PRICING OBJECTIVES AND STRATEGIES

Whether dealing with a single home-country market or multiple country markets, marketing managers must develop pricing objectives as well as strategies for achieving those objectives. The overall goal may be to contribute to an internal performance measure such as unit sales, market share, or return on investment. However, a number of pricing issues are unique to global marketing. The pricing strategy for a particular product may vary from country to country; a product may be positioned as a low-priced, mass-market product in some countries and a premium-priced, niche product in others. Pricing objectives may also vary depending on a product's life cycle stage and the country-specific competitive situation. In making global pricing decisions, it is also necessary to factor in external considerations such as the added cost associated with shipping goods long distances across national boundaries. The issue of global pricing can also be fully integrated in the product design process, an approach widely used by Japanese companies.

Market Skimming and Financial Objectives

Price can be used as a strategic variable to achieve specific financial goals, including return on investment, profit, and rapid recovery of product development costs. When financial criteria such as profit and maintenance of margins are the objectives, the product must be part of a superior value proposition for buyers; price is integral to the total positioning strategy. The **market skimming** pricing strategy is often part of a deliberate attempt to reach a market segment that is willing to pay a premium price for a particular brand or for a specialized or unique product. Companies that seek competitive advantage by pursuing differentiation strategies or positioning their products in the premium segment frequently use market skimming. LVMH and other luxury goods marketers that target the global elite market segment use skimming strategies. For years, Mercedes-Benz utilized a skimming strategy; however, this created an opportunity for Toyota to introduce its luxury Lexus line and undercut Mercedes.

The skimming pricing strategy is also appropriate in the introductory phase of the product life cycle when both production capacity and competition are limited. By setting a deliberately high price, demand is limited to innovators and early adopters who are willing and able to pay the price. When the product enters the growth stage of the life cycle and competition increases, manufacturers start to cut prices. This strategy has been used consistently in the consumer electronics industry; for example, when Sony introduced the first consumer VCRs in the 1970s, the retail price exceeded $1,000. The same was true when compact disc players were launched in the early 1980s. Within a few years, prices for these products dropped well below $500. This pattern was evident in the fall of 1998, when HDTV sets went on sale in the United States with prices starting at about $7,000. This price both maximizes revenue on limited volume and matches demand to available supply. Already, prices for HDTV sets are dropping significantly as more prime-time programming is broadcast in the new format and consumers become more familiar with HDTV and its advantages.

Penetration Pricing and Non-Financial Objectives

Some companies are pursuing non-financial objectives with their pricing strategy. Price can be used as a competitive weapon to gain or maintain market position. Market share or other sales-based objectives are frequently set by companies that enjoy cost-leadership positions in their industry. A **penetration pricing** strategy calls for setting price levels that are low enough to quickly build market share. Many companies that use this type of pricing are located in the Pacific Rim. Scale-efficient plants and low-cost labor allow these companies to blitz the market.

When Sony was developing the Walkman in 1979, initial plans called for a retail price of ¥50,000 ($249) to achieve breakeven. However, it was felt that a price of ¥35,000 ($170) was necessary to attract the all-important youth market segment. After the engineering team conceded that they could trim costs to achieve breakeven volume at a price of ¥40,000, Chairman Akio Morita pushed them further and insisted on a retail price of ¥33,000 ($165) to commemorate Sony's 33rd anniversary. At that price, even if the initial production run of 60,000 units sold out, the company would lose $35 per unit. The marketing department was convinced the product would fail: Who would want a tape recorder that couldn't record? Even Yasuo Kuroki, the project manager, hedged his bets: He ordered enough parts for 60,000 units but had only 30,000 actually produced. Although sales were slow immediately following the Walkman's launch in July 1979, they exploded in late summer. The rest, as the saying goes, is history.[2] Sony has used penetration strategies with numerous other product introductions. When the portable CD player was in development in the mid-1980s, the cost per unit at initial sales volumes was estimated to exceed $600. Because this was a no-go price in the United States and other target markets, Chairman Morita instructed management to price the unit in the $300 range to achieve penetration. Because Sony was a global marketer, the sales volume it expected to achieve in these markets led to scale economies and lower costs.

It is not unusual for a company to change its objectives as a product proceeds through its life cycle and as competitive conditions change. For example, with supplies tight during the 1996 Christmas season, Nintendo maintained a price of $299 for its new Nintendo 64 video game players. A few months later, Nintendo lowered the price to $150 to aggressively compete with Sony PlayStation and Sega Genesis. In

---

2 P. Ranganath Nayak and John M. Ketteringham, *Breakthroughs! How Leadership and Drive Create Commercial Innovations That Sweep the World* (San Diego, CA: Pfeiffer, 1994), pp. 124–127.

2000, Sony rolled out its next-generation game console, the PlayStation 2, for $299; competing systems from Microsoft (Xbox) and Nintendo (GameCube) were launched several months later. By March 2001, Sony had reached its goal of shipping 10 million units worldwide. As of mid-2002, Sony had shipped more than 10 million units to the United States alone; according to industry estimates, one out of three American households owns a PlayStation. In an effort to further increase its customer base, in May 2002 Sony lowered PlayStation 2's price to $199. The price of the original PlayStation, which at this point was $99, was dropped to $49.

Fuji has used penetration pricing very aggressively in its bid to gain market share against Kodak in the United States. Thus far, Kodak has declined to follow suit and engage in a price war because every 1 percent cut in Kodak film prices results in a 1 percent drop in earnings per share. Fuji had record sales of $22 billion in 1996 and near-record profits; the company has a net cash position of about $4.5 billion and access to low-cost loans. By contrast, Kodak is burdened with more than $1 billion in short- and long-term debt. In addition to facing write-offs of approximately $1 billion, the rate of interest Kodak pays is approximately 7 percent.[3]

It should be noted that a first-time exporter is unlikely to use penetration pricing. The reason is simple: Penetration pricing often means that the product may be sold at a loss for a certain length of time. Unlike Sony, many companies that are new to exporting cannot absorb such losses. Nor are they likely to have the marketing system in place (including transportation, distribution, and sales organizations) that allows global companies like Sony to make effective use of a penetration strategy. Many companies, especially those in the food industry, launch new products that are not innovative enough to qualify for patent protection. When this occurs, penetration pricing is recommended as a means of achieving market saturation before the product is copied by competitors.

Calculating Prices: Cost-Plus Pricing and Price Escalation

The following is a list of eight basic considerations for persons whose responsibility includes setting prices outside the home country.[4]

1. Does the price reflect the product's quality?
2. Is the price competitive given local market conditions?
3. Should the firm pursue market penetration, market skimming, or some other pricing objective?
4. What type of discount (trade, cash, quantity) and allowance (advertising, trade-off) should the firm offer its international customers?
5. Should prices differ with market segment?
6. What pricing options are available if the firm's costs increase or decrease? Is demand in the international market elastic or inelastic?
7. Are the firm's prices likely to be viewed by the host-country government as reasonable or exploitative?
8. Do the foreign country's dumping laws pose a problem?

Companies frequently use a method known as cost-plus pricing when selling goods outside their home-country markets. **Cost-plus pricing** is based on an analysis of internal (e.g., materials, labor, testing) and external costs. As a starting point, firms

---

3   Edward W. Desmond, "What's Ailing Kodak? Fuji," *Fortune* (October 27, 1997), pp. 185+; see also Geoffrey Smith, "Can George Fisher Fix Kodak?" *Business Week* (October 20, 1997), p. 124.
4   Adapted from "Price, Quotations, and Terms of Sale Are Key to Successful Exporting," *Business America* (October 4, 1993), p. 12.

The Rest of the Story
Pricing Reeboks in India

In the end, Reebok decided to offer Indian consumers about 60 models chosen from the company's global offerings. The decision was based in part on a desire to sustain Reebok's brand image of high quality. Management realized that the decision would limit the size of the market. Despite estimates that India's "middle class" was comprised of 300 million people, the number who could afford premium-priced products was estimated to be about 30 million. Reebok's least expensive shoes were priced at about Rs 2,000 per pair; for about the same amount of money, a farmer could buy a dairy cow or a homeowner could buy a new refrigerator. Nevertheless, customer response was very favorable, especially among middle-class youths. As Muktesh Pant, Reebok's regional manager, noted, "For Rs 2,000 to Rs 3,000, people feel they can really make a statement. It's cheaper than buying a new watch, for instance, if you want to make a splash at a party. And though our higher-priced shoes put us in competition with things like refrigerators and cows, the upside is that we're now being treated as a prestigious brand."

Reebok was also pleased to discover that demand was strong outside of key metropolitan markets such as Delhi, Mumbai, and Chennai. The cost of living is lower in small towns, so consumers have more disposable income to spend. In addition, inhabitants of rural areas have had less opportunity to travel abroad and therefore have not had the opportunity to shop for trendy brands elsewhere. Reebok now has about 100 branded franchise stores that sell about 300,000 pairs of athletic shoes in India each year. The company exports twice that number of Indian-made shoes to Europe and the United States. As Pant observed, "At first we were embarrassed about our pricing. But it has ended up serving us well."

Visit the Web site
www.reebok.com
www.bata.com

SOURCE: Mark Nicholson, "Where a Pair of Trainers Costs as Much as a Cow," *Financial Times* (August 19, 1998), p. 10.

that comply with Western cost accounting principles typically use the *full absorption cost method*; this defines per-unit product cost as the sum of all past or current direct and indirect manufacturing and overhead costs. However, when goods cross national borders, additional costs and expenses such as transportation, duties, and insurance are incurred. If the manufacturer is responsible for them, they too must be included. By adding the desired profit margin to the cost-plus figure, managers can arrive at a final selling price. It is important to note that, in China and some other developing countries, many manufacturing enterprises are state run and state subsidized. This makes it very difficult to calculate accurate cost figures and opens a country's exporters to charges that they are selling products for less than the "true" cost of producing them.

Companies using *rigid cost-plus pricing* set prices without regard to the eight considerations listed previously. They make no adjustments to reflect market conditions outside the home country. The obvious advantage of rigid cost-based pricing is its simplicity: Assuming that both internal and external cost figures are readily available, it is relatively easy to arrive at a quote. The disadvantage is that this approach ignores demand and competitive conditions in target markets; the risk is that prices will either be set too high or too low. If the rigid cost-based approach results in market success, it is only by chance. A major U.S. appliance manufacturer introduced its line of household appliances in Germany and, using U.S. sourcing, set price by simply marking up every item in its line by 28.5 percent. The result of this pricing method was a line that contained a mixture of underpriced and overpriced products. The overpriced products did not sell because better values were offered by local companies. The underpriced products sold very well, but they would have yielded greater profit at higher prices. What was needed was product-line pricing, which took lower-than-normal margins in some products and higher margins in others to maximize the profitability of the full line. Rigid cost-plus pricing is attractive to inexperienced exporters, who are frequently less concerned with financial goals than with issues such as assessing market potential. Such exporters are typically responding to global market opportunities in a reactive manner, not proactively seeking them.

An alternative method, *flexible cost-plus pricing,* is used to ensure that prices are competitive in the context of the particular market environment. This approach is frequently used by experienced exporters and global marketers. They realize that the rigid cost-plus approach can result in severe **price escalation,** with the unintended result that exports are priced at levels above what customers can pay. Managers who utilize flexible cost-plus pricing are acknowledging the importance of the eight criteria listed earlier. Flexible cost-plus sometimes incorporates the *estimated future cost method* to establish the future cost for all component elements. For example, the automobile industry uses palladium in catalytic converters. Because the market price of heavy metals is volatile and varies with supply and demand, component manufacturers might use the estimated future cost method to ensure that the selling price they set enables them to cover their costs.

Terms of the Sale

Every commercial transaction is based on a contract of sale, and the trade terms in that contract specify the exact point at which the ownership of merchandise is transferred from the seller to the buyer and which party in the transaction pays which costs. The following activities must be performed when goods cross international boundaries:

1. Obtaining an export license if required (in the United States, nonstrategic goods are exported under a general license that requires no specific permit)
2. Obtaining a currency permit if required
3. Packing the goods for export
4. Transporting the goods to the place of departure (this would normally involve transport by truck or rail to a seaport or airport)
5. Preparing a land bill of lading
6. Completing necessary customs export papers
7. Preparing customs or consular invoices as required by the country of destination
8. Arranging for ocean freight and preparation
9. Obtaining marine insurance and certificate of the policy

Who is responsible for carrying out these steps? It depends on the terms of the sale. The internationally accepted terms of trade are known as **Incoterms.** Two Incoterms apply to all modes of transportation. If a contract specifies **ex-works,** the seller places goods at the disposal of the buyer at the time specified in the contract. The buyer takes delivery at the premises of the seller and bears all risks and expenses from that point on. If, instead, the contract specifies **delivered duty paid,** the seller has agreed to deliver the goods to the buyer at the place he or she names in the country of import, with all costs, including duties, paid. Under this contract, the seller is also responsible for obtaining the import license if one is required.

Several Incoterms apply to sea and inland waterway transportation only. Some contracts call for the seller to place goods alongside, or available to, the vessel or other mode of transportation and pay all charges up to that point. This is known as **F.A.S. (free alongside ship) named port of destination.** The seller's legal responsibility ends once a clean wharfage receipt has been obtained. With **F.O.B. (free on board),** the responsibility and liability of the seller do not end until the goods have actually been placed aboard a ship. Terms should preferably be "F.O.B. ship (name port)." The term F.O.B. is frequently misused in international sales. F.O.B. means "goods must be loaded on board, *and* buyer pays freight." Because freight charges generally include loading the goods, in essence, a double payment is made; the buyer pays twice! Similar to F.O.B is **C.I.F. (cost, insurance, freight) named port of destination.** Under this contract, like the F.O.B. contract, the risk of loss or damage to goods is transferred to the buyer once the goods have passed the ship's rail. But the seller has to pay the expense of transportation for the goods up to the port of destination, including the expense of insurance. If the terms of the sale are **C.F.R. (cost and freight),** the seller is not responsible for risk or loss at any point outside the factory.

Table 12-2 is a typical example of the kind of **price escalation** that can occur when some of these costs are added to the per-unit cost of the product itself. In this example, a Kansas City-based distributor of agricultural equipment is shipping a load of farm implements to Yokohama, Japan, through the port of Oakland. A shipment of product that costs ex-works $30,000 in Kansas City ends up with a total retail price in excess of $50,000 in Yokohama. A line-by-line analysis of this shipment shows how price escalation occurs. First, there is the total shipping charge of $5,453.07, which is 18 percent of the ex-works Kansas City price. The principal component of this shipping charge is a combination of land and ocean freight totaling $5,267.80. A currency adjustment factor (CAF) is assessed to protect the seller from possible losses from disadvantageous shifts in the dollar-yen exchange rate. This figure will vary depending on the perceived volatility of exchange rates.

All import charges are assessed against the landed price of the shipment (C.I.F. value). Note that there is no line item for duty in this example; no duties are charged on agricultural equipment sent to Japan.[5] Duties may be charged in other countries.

Table 12-2
Price Escalation: A 20-foot Container of Agricultural Equipment Shipped from Kansas City to Yokohama[*]

ITEM			PERCENTAGE OF EX-WORKS PRICE
Ex-Works Kansas City		$30,000.00	100%
Container Freight Charges from K.C. to Seattle	$1,475.00		
Terminal handling fee	350.00		
Ocean freight for 20-ft. container	2,280.00		
Currency Adjustment Factor (CAF) (51% of ocean freight)	1,162.80		
Insurance (110% of C.I.F. value)	35.27		
Forwarding fee	150.00		
Total shipping charges	5,453.07		18
Total C.I.F. Yokohama value		35,453.07	
V.A.T. (3% of C.I.F. value)		1,063.69	3
		36,516.76	
Distributor markup (10%)		3,651.67	12
		40,168.43	
Dealer markup (25%)		10,042.10	33
Total retail price		$50,210.53	166%

[*]This was loaded at the manufacturer's door, shipped by stack train to Seattle, and then transferred via ocean freight to Yokohama. Total transit time from factory door to foreign port is about 28 days.

---

[5] Since the Uruguay Round of GATT negotiations, Japan has lowered or eliminated duties on thousands of categories of imports. Japan's average duty rate as of 1997 was 9.4%; approximately 60 percent of tariff lines (including most industrial products) were rated 5% or lower.

Table 12-3
An American-Built
Jeep Goes to
Japan

Item	Amount of Escalation	Total
Ex-works price	0	$19,100
Exchange rate adj.	$1,333	$20,433
Shipping	$ 200	$20,633
Customs fees	$ 682	$21,315
Distributor margin	$1,569	$22,884
Inspection, accessories	$1,100	$23,984
Added options, prep	$1,925	$25,909
Final sticker price	$5,463	$31,372

Source: Sheryl WoDunn, "An Uphill Journey to Japan: How the Price of a Jeep Climbs 64% after Leaving the Factory," *The New York Times,* May 16, 1995, p. D1.

A nominal distributor markup of 10 percent ($3,652) actually represents 12 percent of the C.I.F. Yokohama price because it is a markup not only on the ex-works price but on freight and V.A.T. as well. (It is assumed here that the distributor's markup includes the cost of transportation from the port to Yokohama.) Finally, a dealer markup of 25 percent adds up to $10,042 (33 percent) of the C.I.F. Yokohama price. Like distributor markups, dealer markup is based on the total landed cost.

The net effect of this add-on accumulating process is a total retail price in Yokohama of $50,210, or 166 percent of the ex-works Kansas City price. This is price escalation. The example provided here is by no means an extreme case. Indeed, longer distribution channels or channels that require a higher operating margin—as are typically found in export marketing—can contribute to price escalation. Because of the layered distribution system in Japan, the markups in Tokyo could easily result in a price that is 200 percent of the C.I.F. value. An example of price escalation for a single product is shown in Table 12-3. An American Jeep with a sticker price of $19,100 ends up costing the equivalent of $31,000—a 164 percent increase—by the time it reaches a dealer in Japan.

These examples of cost-plus pricing show an approach that a beginning exporter might use to determine the C.I.F. price. This approach could also be used for differentiated products such as the Jeep Cherokee for which buyers are willing to pay a premium. However, as noted earlier, experienced global marketers are likely to take a more flexible approach and view price as a strategic variable that can help achieve marketing and business objectives.

ENVIRONMENTAL INFLUENCES ON PRICING DECISIONS

Global marketers must deal with a number of environmental considerations when making pricing decisions. Among them are currency fluctuations, inflation, government controls and subsidies, and competitive behavior. Some of these factors work in conjunction with others; for example, inflation may be accompanied by government controls. Each is discussed in detail in the following paragraphs.

Currency Fluctuations

In global marketing, the task of setting prices is complicated by fluctuating exchange rates. Currency fluctuations can create significant problems and opportunities for the classic international company that exports from the home country. Management faces different decision situations, depending on whether currencies in key markets have strengthened or weakened relative to the home-country currency. A weakening of the home-country currency swings exchange rates in a favorable direction: Overseas earnings can result in windfall revenues when translated into the home-country currency. It is a different situation when a company's home currency strengthens; this is an unfavorable turn of events for the typical exporter because overseas revenues are reduced when translated into the home-country currency. Today's business environment is characterized by "roller coaster"-style swings in currency values; they may move in a favorable direction for several quarters and then abruptly reverse.

For the transnational corporation, however, it is not simply a matter of home-country currency value relative to the value of currencies in key markets. Honda Motor is a case in point; the company is heavily dependent on the North American market, which accounts for more than half its operating income. Although some Japanese automakers serve foreign markets primarily by exporting from Japan, about three-fourths of the cars Honda sells in America are produced in the United States. In late 2000, the dollar had fallen to ¥108 to $1 compared with ¥113 to $1 the previous year; the unfavorable shift had a direct negative impact on corporate profits. The situation was even more complicated in Europe; Honda serves the entire European market from a single plant in the United Kingdom. The pound's recent strength relative to the euro has resulted in a significant decline in Honda's European sales. At the same time, the euro has weakened relative to the British pound as well. So, not only have currency fluctuations negatively affected sales on the continent, but the revenue that Honda realizes from those sales is reduced as well![6]

Needless to say, currency fluctuations can have an impact on prices as well as other elements of the marketing mix. Table 12-4 provides several guidelines. In some instances, slight upward price adjustments due to the strengthening of a country's currency have little effect on export performance, especially if demand is relatively inelastic. The first two strategies in the right-hand column of Table 12-4 call for focusing attention on competitive issues besides price as well as productivity and cost reduction efforts. Companies in the strong-currency country can also choose to absorb the cost of maintaining international market prices at previous levels—at least for a while. Companies using the rigid cost-plus pricing method described earlier may be forced to change to the flexible approach. The use of the flexible cost-plus method to reduce prices in response to unfavorable currency swings is an example of a **market holding** strategy and is adopted by companies that do not want to lose market share. If, by contrast, large price increases are deemed unavoidable, managers may find their products can no longer compete.

In the three years immediately after the euro zone was established, the euro declined in value more than 25 percent relative to the dollar. This situation forced American companies, in particular small exporters, to choose from among the options associated with strong currencies listed in Table 12-4. The strategy chosen varies according to a company's particular circumstances. For example, Vermeer Manufacturing of Pella, Iowa, with annual sales of $650 million, prices its products in

---

6 Todd Zaun, "Honda Takes Currency Hit in Europe," *The Wall Street Journal* (March 28, 2001), p. A16.

Table 12-4
Global Pricing
Strategies

WHEN DOMESTIC CURRENCY IS WEAK	WHEN DOMESTIC CURRENCY IS STRONG
1. Stress price benefits.	1. Engage in nonprice competition by improving quality, delivery, and after-sale service.
2. Expand product line and add more costly features.	2. Improve productivity and engage in cost reduction.
3. Shift sourcing to domestic market.	3. Shift sourcing outside home country.
4. Exploit market opportunities in all markets.	4. Give priority to exports to countries with stronger currencies.
5. Use full-costing approach, but employ marginal-cost pricing to penetrate new or competitive markets.	5. Trim profit margins and use marginal-cost pricing.
6. Speed repatriation of foreign-earned income and collections.	6. Keep the foreign-earned income in host country; slow down collections.
7. Minimize expenditures in local or host-country currency.	7. Maximize expenditures in local or host-country currency.
8. Buy advertising, insurance, transportation, and other services in the domestic market.	8. Buy needed services abroad and pay for them in local currencies.
9. Bill foreign customers in their own currency.	9. Bill foreign customers in the domestic currency.

Source: Columbia Journal of World Business, 31, no. 4, S. Tamer Cavusgil, "Pricing for Global Markets," p. 69. Copyright © 1996, with permission of Elsevir Science.

euros for the European market. As 2000 came to an end, Vermeer had been forced to raise its European prices four times since the euro's introduction. Its subsidiary in the Netherlands pays employees in euros and also buys materials locally, illustrating Strategies number 7 and 8. By contrast, Stern Pinball of Melrose Park, Illinois, prices its machines in dollars in export markets. Company president Gary Stern is utilizing the first strategy in Table 12-4: To offset price increases in Europe, the company is developing new features such as pinball machines that "speak" several European languages. It has also produced new products such as a soccer game themed to European interests as well as an Austin Powers game targeted at the United Kingdom. As Stern commented recently, "If I were bright enough to know which way the euro was going, I sure wouldn't be making pinball machines. I'd be trading currency."[7]

Consider an example based on the currency crisis in Asia in 1997 and 1998. The Thai baht, Indonesian rupiah, South Korean won, and other Asian currencies fell dramatically. The economic turmoil in the affected countries depressed domestic demand for many manufactured goods; at the same time, the prices for Asian goods in export markets fell dramatically. The left-hand column of Table 12-4 shows strategies to use when the domestic currency is weak. One approach is **marginal-cost pricing** to penetrate new markets. Marginal-cost pricing entails setting the selling price equal to the variable (incremental) costs of producing one additional unit of output.

---

[7] Christopher Cooper, "Euro's Drop Is Hardest for the Smallest," *The Wall Street Journal* (October 2, 2000), p. A21.

This approach makes sense for a manufacturer with excess capacity in a weak-currency country if the manufacturer has already achieved sales levels sufficient to cover fixed costs. With fixed costs covered, the manufacturer can price the product aggressively for export in a bid to penetrate new markets. A word of caution is in order, however; companies that utilize marginal-cost pricing may be vulnerable to charges of dumping. According to Table 12-4, what else should Samsung, Hyundai, Daewoo, and other manufacturers do?

If U.S.-based companies marketing internationally had maintained their price levels in the early to mid-1980s, when the dollar appreciated against most other currencies, currency translations tied to the strong dollar would have automatically increased the price of many products. From the middle to late 1980s, as the dollar weakened against world currencies, the situation was reversed. Companies based in Japan, Germany, France, and elsewhere attempted to hold the line on U.S. prices. Needless to say, adjusting prices to fit the competitive situation may mean lower profit margins. When Max Imgruth, head of Charles Jourdan USA, vetoed double-digit price increases for the company's shoes in 1992, he noted, "The American consumer is not going to swallow those price increases." Speaking of his company, he lamented, "We're taking a tremendous hit. We're living on air and inspiration." Jourdan was forced to pull its menswear line from the U.S. market and concentrate on women's fashions.[8]

By early 1993, as the yen's strength brought it close to parity (¥100 equals $1), management at Nikon, Sharp, and other Japanese companies felt compelled to raise prices. As noted in the right-hand column of Table 12-4, a strong domestic currency may also force a company to consider offshore manufacturing or licensing agreements, rather than exporting, to maintain market share. When a company has a manufacturing presence in multiple key markets, it can avoid price escalation due to high home-country manufacturing costs or unfavorable exchange rates. Global and transnational companies simply shift production from one country to another as business conditions dictate. For example, Acura, Honda's luxury division, made its market entry in the United States by exporting from Japan. However, when the yen strengthened to ¥90 to $1 in the mid-1990s, Acura shifted production of the popular TL model to Marysville, Ohio, to avoid having to raise dollar prices. By 1999, because of improved manufacturing efficiencies and the fact that the yen had weakened to about ¥120 to $1, Acura was able to offer American car buyers a dramatically improved new model for substantially less money. The 1999 base model TL carried a U.S. sticker price of $28,405, which was $2,730 less than the base TL model in 1998. Fully loaded, the 1999 TL cost $5,180 less than the 1998 version.[9] Because Honda is a transnational corporation, it is in an extremely advantageous position: It can choose options from either column of Table 12-4 in response to favorable or unfavorable shifts in the currency values.

If a country's currency weakens relative to a trading partner's currency, a producer in a weak-currency country can choose to cut export prices to increase market share or leave prices alone for healthier profit margins. The experience of the Campbell Soup Company in Japan illustrates that currency fluctuations can create pricing opportunities for low-priced products as well. In 1985, when the yen-dollar exchange rate was

---

8   Joan E. Rigdon and Valerie Reitman, "Pricing Paradox: Consumers Still Find Imported Bargains Despite Weak Dollar," *The Wall Street Journal* (October 7, 1992), p. A1. See also Reitman, "Currency Waves: Global Money Trends Rattle Shop Windows in Heartland America," *The Wall Street Journal* (November 26, 1993), pp. A1, A8.

9   James R. Healey, "Acura TL: What a Difference a Year Makes," *USA Today* (November 13, 1998), p. 12D.

Table 12-5
Automobile Price
Differences in
the EU (pre-Euro)

SMALL SEGMENT		MEDIUM SEGMENT		LARGE SEGMENT	
Opel Corsa	24.0%	VW Golf	43.5%	BMW 318I	12.0%
Ford Fiesta	44.7%	Opel Astra	26.0%	Audi A4	13.0%
Renault Clio	33.8%	Ford Escort/Orion	33.8%	Ford Mondeo	58.5%
Peugeot 106	21.1%	Renault Mégane	27.9%	Opel Vectra	18.2%
VW Polo	36.7%	Peugeot 306	46.2%	VW Passat	36.4%

Source: European Commission.

¥240 to $1, a can of Campbell's soup sold in Japan for ¥220, which was the equivalent of $.91 (220/240 = 0.91). By 1987, the exchange rate was ¥142 to $1, reflecting a weaker dollar (one that bought fewer yen) and a stronger yen (fewer yen could buy $1). If Campbell had not adjusted its prices in Japan, it would have enjoyed windfall revenues: The can of soup priced at ¥220 would translate into $1.69—an increase of 85 percent (220/142 = 1.69). Campbell adopted a proactive approach and *lowered* the yen price of a can of soup to ¥185, but even with the lower price, the stronger yen *still* translated that yen price into $1.30 per can (185/142 = 1.30), versus 91¢ at the old exchange rate. Campbell opted to use price as a strategic variable to increase sales volume; the company also reinvested the extra profit by increasing its sales staff and offering deals to retailers in an effort to gain wider distribution.[10]

As noted earlier, price discrepancies across the euro zone are expected to be reduced because manufacturers will no longer be able to use currency fluctuations to justify the discrepancies. Another driving force behind price convergence is **price transparency,** which means that buyers will be able to comparison shop easily because goods will be priced in euros as opposed to marks, francs, or lira. In 1998, a European Commission report showed automobile price differences in the EU. For example, as shown in Table 12-5, prices for a medium-sized Volkswagen Golf are as much as 43 percent higher depending on the country of purchase. In the large-size category, prices for a Ford Mondeo can vary by more than 50 percent. Not surprisingly, these differences encourage cross-border shopping, a phenomenon that is expected to decline in the next few years.

Some automobile price differences in Europe are due to different standards for safety equipment and different tax levels. For example, Denmark has a high consumption tax and also taxes luxury goods heavily. Taxes are also high in Finland, Ireland, Portugal, and the Netherlands. Volkswagen has already begun to harmonize its wholesale prices for vehicles distributed in Europe.

"The car industry is going to be hurt. There will be greater price transparency. Prices are higher in northern Europe and once consumers there get wind of this there will be a move down in prices towards the southern countries."[11]
—Marcie Krempel
AT Kearney

Inflationary Environment

Inflation, or a persistent upward change in price levels, is a worldwide phenomenon. Inflation requires periodic price adjustments. These adjustments are necessitated by rising costs that must be covered by increased selling prices. An essential requirement for pricing in an inflationary environment is the maintenance of operating profit margins. Regardless of cost accounting practices, if a company maintains its margins, it has effectively protected itself from the effects of inflation. To keep up with inflation in Peru in

---

[10] Damon Darlin, "Trade Strategies: Most U.S. Firms Seek Extra Profits in Japan, at the Expense of Sales," *The Wall Street Journal* (May 15, 1987), p. A1.
[11] Graham Bowley, "On the Road to Price Convergence," *Financial Times* (November 12, 1998), p. 29.

the late 1980s, for example, Procter & Gamble resorted to biweekly increases in detergent prices of 20 to 30 percent.[12] Such actions, in turn, require retailers of all types to become more technologically adept. In Brazil, where inflation was running at 2,000 percent annually, retailers sometimes changed prices several times each day. Shelf pricing, rather than individual unit pricing, became the norm throughout the retailing sector nearly 15 years before Wal-Mart arrived in the region. Because their warehouses contained goods that had been bought at different prices, local retailers were forced to invest in sophisticated computer and communications systems to help them keep pace with the volatile financial environment. They utilized sophisticated inventory management software to help them maintain financial control. As Wal-Mart came to Brazil in the mid-1990s, it discovered that local competitors had the technological infrastructure that allowed them to match its aggressive pricing policies.[13]

Low inflation presents pricing challenges of a different type. With inflation in the United States in the low single digits in the late 1990s and strong demand forcing factories to run at or near capacity, companies should be able to raise prices. However, the domestic economic situation is not the only consideration. In the mid-1990s, excess manufacturing capacity in many industries, high rates of unemployment in many European countries, and the lingering recession in Asia make it difficult for companies to increase prices. As John Ballard, CEO of a California-based engineering firm, noted, "We thought about price increases. But our research of competitors and what the market would bear told us it was not worth pursuing." By the end of the decade, globalization, the Internet, and a new cost-consciousness among buyers were also significant constraining factors.[14]

Government Controls, Subsidies, and Regulations

Governmental policies and regulations that affect pricing decisions include dumping legislation, resale price maintenance legislation, price ceilings, and general reviews of price levels. If government action limits the freedom of management to adjust prices, the maintenance of margins is definitely compromised. Under certain conditions, government action is a real threat to the profitability of a subsidiary operation. In a country that is undergoing severe financial difficulties and is in the midst of a financial crisis (e.g., a foreign exchange shortage caused in part by runaway inflation), government officials are under pressure to take some type of action. This has been true in Brazil for many years. In some cases, governments take expedient steps such as selective or broad price controls.

When *selective controls* are imposed, foreign companies are more vulnerable to control than local businesses, particularly if the outsiders lack the political influence over government decisions that local managers have. For example, Procter & Gamble encountered strict price controls in Venezuela in the late 1980s. Despite increases in the cost of raw materials, P&G was only granted about 50 percent of the price increases it requested; even then, months passed before permission to raise prices was forthcoming. As a result, by 1988, detergent prices in Venezuela were less than what they were in the United States.[15]

[12] Alecia Swasy, "Foreign Formula: Procter & Gamble Fixes Aim on Tough Market: The Latin Americans," *The Wall Street Journal* (June 15, 1990), p. A1.
[13] Pete Hisey, "Wal-Mart's Global Vision," *Retail Merchandiser* 41, no. 4 (April 2001), pp. 21–49.
[14] Lucinda Harper and Fred R. Bleakley, "Like Old Times: An Era of Low Inflation Changes the Calculus for Buyers and Sellers," *The Wall Street Journal* (January 14, 1994), p. A1. See also Jacob M. Schlesinger and Yochi J. Dreazen, "Counting the Cost: Firms Start to Raise Prices, Stirring Fear in Inflation Fighters," *The Wall Street Journal* (May 16, 2000), pp. A1, A8.
[15] Alecia Swasy, "Foreign Formula: Procter & Gamble Fixes Aim on Tough Market: The Latin Americans," *The Wall Street Journal* (June 15, 1990), p. A7.

Government control can also take the form of prior cash deposit requirements imposed on importers. As discussed in Chapter 8, this is a requirement that a company has to tie up funds in the form of a non-interest-bearing deposit for a specified period of time if it wishes to import products. Such requirements clearly create an incentive for a company to minimize the price of the imported product; lower prices mean smaller deposits. Other government requirements that affect the pricing decision are profit transfer rules that restrict the conditions under which profits can be transferred out of a country. Under such rules, a high transfer price paid for imported goods by an affiliated company can be interpreted as a device for transferring profits out of a country.

Government subsidies can also force a company to make strategic use of sourcing to be price competitive. In Europe, government subsidies to the agricultural sector make it difficult for U.S. distributors of processed food to compete on price. In the United States some, but not all, agricultural sectors are subsidized. For example, U.S. poultry producers and processors are not subsidized; although Tyson has a significant export business with Russia, subsidies make U.S. poultry prices noncompetitive in some country markets. One midwestern chicken processor with European customers sourced its product in France for resale in the Netherlands. By doing so, the company took advantage of lower costs derived from subsidies and eliminated price escalation due to tariffs and duties.

Government regulations can affect prices in other ways. In Germany, for example, price competition was historically severely restricted in a number of industries. This was particularly true in the service sector. The German government's recent moves toward deregulation have improved the climate for market entry by foreign firms in a range of industries, including insurance, telecommunications, and air travel. Deregulation is also giving German companies their first experience with price competition in the domestic market. In some instances, deregulation represents a *quid pro quo* that will allow German companies wider access to other country markets. For example, the United States and Germany recently completed an open-skies agreement that will allow Lufthansa to fly more routes within the United States. At the same time, the German air market has been opened to competition. As a result, air travel costs between German cities have fallen significantly. Change is slowly coming to the retail sector as well. The Internet and globalization have forced policy makers to repeal two archaic laws. The first, the *Rabattgesetz* or Discount Law, limited discounts on products to 3 percent of the list price. The second, the *Zugabeverordnung* or Free Gift Act, banned companies from giving away free merchandise such as shopping bags.[16]

Competitive Behavior

Pricing decisions are constrained not only by cost and the nature of demand but also by competitive action. If competitors do not adjust their prices in response to rising costs, management—even if acutely aware of the effect of rising costs on operating margins—will be severely constrained in its ability to adjust prices accordingly. Conversely, if competitors are manufacturing or sourcing in a lower-cost country, it may be necessary to cut prices to stay competitive.

In the United States, Levi Strauss & Company is under price pressure from several directions. First, Levi faces stiff competition from the Wrangler and Lee brands marketed by VF Corporation. A pair of Wrangler jeans retails for about $20 at Penney's and other department stores, compared with about $30 for a pair of Levi 501s. Second, Levi's two primary retail customers, J.C. Penney and Sears, are aggressively marketing their

---

[16] Greg Steinmetz, "Mark Down: German Consumers Are Seeing Prices Cut in Deregulation Push," *The Wall Street Journal* (August 15, 1997), pp. A1, A4; David Wessel, "German Shoppers Get Coupons," *The Wall Street Journal* (April 5, 2001), p. A1.

own private label brands. Finally, designer jeans from Calvin Klein, Polo, and Diesel are enjoying renewed popularity. An exclusive new jeans brand, Seven, retails for more than $100 per pair. Outside the United States, thanks to the heritage of the Levi brand and less competition, Levi jeans command premium prices—$80 or more for one pair of 501s. To support the prestige image, Levis are sold in boutiques. Not surprisingly, Levi's non-U.S. sales represent about one-third of revenues but more than 50 percent of profits. In an attempt to apply its global experience and enhance the brand in the United States, Levi has opened a number of Original Levi's Stores in select American cities. Despite such efforts, Levi rang up only $4.26 billion in sales in 2001 compared with $7.1 billion in 1996. In 2002, officials announced plans to close six plants and move most of the company's U.S. production offshore in an effort to cut costs.[17]

Using Sourcing as a Strategic Pricing Tool

The global marketer has several options for addressing the problem of price escalation or the environmental factors described in the last section. The choices are dictated in part by product and market competition. Marketers of domestically manufactured finished products may be forced to switch to offshore sourcing of certain components to keep costs and prices competitive. In particular, the Far East and South America are emerging as attractive low-cost sources of production. For example, U.S. bicycle manufacturers such as Huffy are relying more heavily on production sources in China and Taiwan.

Another option is a thorough audit of the distribution structure in the target markets. A rationalization of the distribution structure can substantially reduce the total markups required to achieve distribution in international markets. Rationalization may include selecting new intermediaries, assigning new responsibilities to old intermediaries, or establishing direct marketing operations. For example, Toys 'Я' Us has invaded the Japanese toy market because it bypassed layers of distribution and adopted a warehouse style of selling similar to its U.S. approach. Toys 'Я' Us has been viewed as a test case of the ability of Western retailers—discounters in particular—to change the rules of distribution.

GLOBAL PRICING: THREE POLICY ALTERNATIVES

What pricing policy should a global company pursue? Viewed broadly, there are three alternative positions a company can take on worldwide pricing.

Extension or Ethnocentric

The first can be called an *extension* or *ethnocentric* pricing policy. An extension pricing policy calls for the per-unit price of an item to be the same no matter where in the world the buyer is located. In such instances, the importer must absorb freight and import duties. The extension approach has the advantage of extreme simplicity because no information on competitive or market conditions is required for implementation. The disadvantage of the ethnocentric approach is that it does not respond to the competitive and market conditions of each national market and, therefore, does not maximize the company's profits in each national market or globally. When toymaker Mattel adapted U.S. products for overseas markets, for example, little consideration was given to price

---

[17] Nina Munk, "The Levi Straddle," *Forbes* (January 17, 1994), pp. 44–45. See also Leslie Kaufman, "Levi Strauss to Close 6 U.S. Plants and Lay Off 3,300," *The New York Times* (April 9, 2002), p. C2.

levels that resulted when U.S. prices were converted to local currency prices. As a result, Holiday Barbie and some other toys were overpriced in global markets.[18]

Similarly, Mercedes-Benz executives have only recently moved beyond an ethnocentric approach to pricing. As sales chief Dieter Zietsche noted recently, "We used to say that *we* know what the customer wants, and he will have to pay for it . . . we didn't realize the world had changed."[19] Mercedes got its wake-up call when Lexus began offering "Mercedes quality" for $20,000 less. Since coming on board in 1993, Mercedes CEO Helmut Werner has boosted employee productivity, increased the number of low-cost outside suppliers, and invested in production facilities in the United States and Spain in an effort to move toward more customer- and competition-oriented pricing. *Advertising Age* hailed management's new attitude for transforming Mercedes from "a staid and smug purveyor into an aggressive, market-driven company that will go bumper-to-bumper with its luxury car rivals—even on price."[20]

Adaptation or Polycentric

The second pricing policy can be termed *adaptation* or *polycentric*. This policy permits subsidiary or affiliate managers or independent distributors to establish whatever price they feel is most desirable in their circumstances. There is no requirement that prices be coordinated from one country to the next. One recent study of European industrial exporters found that companies utilizing independent distributors were the most likely to utilize polycentric pricing. Such an approach is sensitive to local market conditions, but opportunities for product arbitrage are created when disparities in local market prices exceed the transportation and duty costs separating markets. Enterprising individuals can engage in arbitrage by locating and purchasing goods in the lower-price country market and then transporting them for sale in markets where higher prices prevail. Such activities, known as gray marketing or parallel importing, are discussed in more detail later in the chapter. There is also the problem that, with a polycentric approach, valuable knowledge and experience within the corporate system concerning effective pricing strategies are not brought to bear on each local pricing decision. Because the distributors or local managers are free to price in the way they see fit, they may not be fully informed about company experience when they set prices.

Geocentric

The third approach, *geocentric pricing*, is more dynamic and proactive than the other two. A company using geocentric pricing neither fixes a single price worldwide, nor allows subsidiaries or local distributors to make independent pricing decisions. Instead, the geocentric approach represents an intermediate course of action. Geocentric pricing is based on the realization that unique local market factors should be recognized in arriving at pricing decisions. These factors include local costs, income levels, competition, and the local marketing strategy. Price fit must also be integrated with other elements of the marketing program. For example, when a "pull" strategy calls for using mass media advertising and intensive distribution, the price selected must be appropriate given the costs of advertising and the choice of distribution channels. The geocentric approach recognizes that price coordination from headquarters is necessary in dealing with international accounts and product arbitrage. The geocentric approach also consciously and systematically seeks to ensure that accumulated national pricing experience is leveraged and applied wherever relevant.

---

[18] Lisa Bannon, "Mattel Plans to Double Sales Abroad," *The Wall Street Journal* (February 11, 1998), pp. A3, A11.
[19] Alex Taylor III, "Speed! Power! Status!" *Fortune* (June 10, 1996), pp. 46–58.
[20] Raymond Serafin, "Mercedes-Benz of the '90s Includes Price in Its Pitch," *Advertising Age* (November 1, 1993), p. 1.

Local costs plus a return on invested capital and personnel fix the price floor for the long term. In the short term, however, headquarters might decide to set a market penetration objective and price at less than the cost-plus return figure by using export sourcing to establish a market. This was the case described earlier with the Sony Walkman launch. Another short-term objective might be to arrive at an estimate of the market potential at a price that would be profitable given local sourcing and a certain scale of output. Instead of immediately investing in local manufacture, a decision might be made to supply the target market initially from existing higher-cost external supply sources. If the price and product are accepted by the market, the company can then build a local manufacturing facility to further develop the identified market opportunity in a profitable way. If the market opportunity does not materialize, the company can experiment with the product at other prices because it is not committed to a fixed sales volume by existing local manufacturing facilities.

For consumer products, local income levels are critical in the pricing decision. If the product is normally priced well above full manufacturing costs, the global marketer should consider accepting reduced margins and price below prevailing levels in low-income markets. *The important point here is that in global marketing there is no such thing as a "normal" margin.* Of the three methods described, only the geocentric approach lends itself to global competitive strategy. A global competitor will take into account global markets and global competitors in establishing prices. Prices will support global strategy objectives rather than the objective of maximizing performance in a single country. Table 12-6 lists some comments by European exporters that provide insights into the real-world process of setting prices.

Table 12-6
How Managers Calculate Export Prices for Industrial Products

STATEMENT BY MANAGEMENT	IMPLICATION/INTERPRETATION
"We have the competitors' price list on our desk. I may speak frankly—who does not? We know exactly what our competitors charge for certain products, and we calculate accordingly."	When calculating prices for foreign markets, managers benchmark competitors' prices.
"An interesting way of evaluating whether a product will fit requirements of the market has emerged. You give some machines to an auction house and set a very low price limit. Your products are then auctioned off. That way, you get a feel for the right price level as well as the potential demand for the product. It is a very easy and cost-effective method."	As a practical matter, some companies use innovative, trial and error approaches to determine price elasticity.
"At trade shows, we go directly to our customers and try to find out what prices we can charge. We scan our price limits sensitively. This is how we get to a price list in the end."	Some companies take a methodical approach to determining price elasticity.
"We differentiate simply because there are some countries where we can get a better price. Then there are countries where we can't."	Rationale for differentiating prices using either polycentric or geocentric approach.
"I decided not to listen to people who advise me to differentiate prices. Wherever we are active, we want to have the image and the reputation of calculating our prices correctly and honestly."	Rationale for using standardized pricing.

Source: Adapted from Barbara Stöttinger, "Strategic Export Pricing: A Long and Winding Road," *Journal of International Marketing* 9, no. 1 (2001), pp. 40–63.

GRAY MARKET GOODS

Gray market goods are trademarked products that are exported from one country to another where they are sold by unauthorized persons or organizations. Consider the following illustration:

> Suppose that a golf equipment manufacturer sells a golf club to its domestic distributors for $200; it sells the same club to its Thailand distributor for $100. The lower price may be due to differences in overseas demand or ability to pay. Or, the price difference may reflect the need to compensate the foreign distributor for advertising and marketing the club. The golf club, however, never makes it to Thailand. Instead, the Thailand distributor resells the club to a gray marketer in the United States for $150. The gray marketer can then undercut the prices charged by domestic distributors who paid $200 for the club. The manufacturer is forced to lower the domestic price or risk losing sales to gray marketers, driving down the manufacturer's profit margins. Additionally, gray marketers make liberal use of manufacturer's trademarks and often fail to provide warranties and other services that consumers expect from the manufacturer and its authorized distributors.[21]

This practice, known as **parallel importing,** typically flourishes when a product is in short supply, when producers employ skimming strategies in certain markets, or when the goods are subject to substantial markups. This has happened with French champagne sold in the United States; it is also true of the European market for pharmaceuticals, where prices vary widely from country to country. In the United Kingdom and the Netherlands, for example, parallel imports account for as much as 10 percent of the sales of some pharmaceutical brands.

Sometimes, gray marketers bring a product produced in one country—French champagne, for example—into a second country market in competition with authorized importers. The gray marketers sell at prices that undercut those set by the legitimate importers. In another type of gray marketing, a company manufactures a product in the home-country market as well as in foreign markets. In this case, products manufactured abroad by the company's foreign affiliate for sales abroad are sometimes sold by a foreign distributor to gray marketers. The latter then bring the products into the producing company's home-country market, where they compete with domestically produced goods. For example, in the mid-1980s, Caterpillar's U.S. dealers found themselves competing with gray market construction equipment manufactured in Europe. The strong dollar had provided gray marketers with an opportunity to bring Caterpillar equipment into the United States at lower prices than domestically produced equipment. Even though the gray market goods carry the same trademarks as the domestically produced ones, they may differ in quality, ingredients, or some other way. Manufacturers may not honor warranties on some types of gray market imports such as cameras and consumer electronics equipment.[22]

As these examples show, the marketing opportunity that presents itself requires gray market goods to be priced lower than goods sold by authorized distributors or domestically produced goods. Clearly, buyers gain from lower prices and increased

---

[21] Adapted from Perry J. Viscounty, Jeff C. Risher, and Collin G. Smyser, "Cyber Gray Market is Manufacturers' Headache," *The National Law Journal* (August 20, 2001), p. C3.
[22] James E. Inman, "Gray Marketing of Imported Trademarked Goods: Tariffs and Trademark Issues," *American Business Law Journal* (May 1993), pp. 59–116; Paul Lansing and Joseph Gabriella, "Clarifying Gray Market Gray Areas," *American Business Law Journal* (September 1993), pp. 313–337.

choice. In the United Kingdom alone, for example, total annual retail sales of gray market goods are estimated to be as high as $1.6 billion. A recent case in Europe resulted in a ruling that strengthened the rights of brand owners. Silhouette, an Austrian manufacturer of upscale sunglasses, sued the Hartlauer discount chain after the latter obtained thousands of pairs of sunglasses that Silhouette had intended for sale in Eastern Europe. The European Court of Justice found in favor of Silhouette. In clarifying a 1989 directive, the court ruled that stores cannot import branded goods from outside the EU and then sell them at discounted prices without permission of the brand owner. The *Financial Times* denounced the ruling as "bad for consumers, bad for competition, and bad for European economies."[23]

In the United States, gray market goods are subject to a 60-year-old law, the Tariff Act of 1930. Section 526 of the act expressly forbids importation of goods of foreign manufacture without the permission of the trademark owner. There are, however, several exceptions spelled out in the act; the U.S. Customs Service, which implements the regulation, and the court system have considerable leeway in decisions regarding gray market goods. For example, in 1988, the U.S. Supreme Court ruled that trademarked goods of foreign manufacture such as champagne could legally be imported and sold by gray marketers. In many instances, however, the court's interpretation of the law differs from that of the Customs Service.

Because of problems associated with regulating gray markets, one legal expert has argued that, in the name of free markets and free trade, the U.S. Congress should repeal Section 526. In its place, a new law should require gray market goods to bear labels clearly explaining any differences between them and goods that come through

To combat the gray market for Swiss watches, TAG Heuer runs print ads during the holiday shopping season urging consumers to buy its famous sports watch only from authorized dealers.

23 Peggy Hollinger and Neil Buckley, "Grey Market Ruling Delights Brand Owners," *Financial Times* (July 17, 1998), p. 8.

authorized channels. Other experts believe that, instead of changing the laws, companies should develop proactive strategic responses to gray markets. One such strategy would be improved market segmentation and product differentiation to make gray market products less attractive; another would be to aggressively identify and terminate distributors that are involved in selling to gray marketers. Even as the debate over legal recourse continues, the Internet is emerging as a powerful new tool that allows would-be gray marketers to both access pricing information and reach customers.[24]

DUMPING

Dumping is an important global pricing strategy issue. GATT's 1979 antidumping code defined **dumping** as the sale of an imported product at a price lower than that normally charged in a domestic market or country of origin. In addition, many countries have their own policies and procedures for protecting national companies from dumping. For example, China has retaliated against years of Western antidumping rules by introducing rules of its own. China's State Council passed the Antidumping and Anti-subsidy Regulations in March 1997. The regulations are designed to counter the effects of dumping or export subsidization that result in injury to an established Chinese industry or that substantially impede the establishment of a comparable Chinese industry. The Ministry of Foreign Trade and Economic Cooperation and the State Economic and Trade Commission have responsibility for antidumping matters.[25]

The U.S. Congress has defined *dumping* as an unfair trade practice that results in "injury, destruction, or prevention of the establishment of American industry." Under this definition, dumping occurs when imports sold in the U.S. market are priced either at levels that represent less than the cost of production plus an 8 percent profit margin or at levels below those prevailing in the producing country. The U.S. Commerce Department is responsible for determining whether products are being sold in the United States at below-market prices; the International Trade Commission (ITC) then determines whether the dumping has resulted in injury to U.S. firms.

In Europe, antidumping policy is administered by the European Commission; a simple majority vote by the Council of Ministers is required before duties can be imposed on dumped goods. Six-month provisional duties can be imposed; more stringent measures include definitive, five-year duties. Low-cost imports from Asia have been the subject of dumping disputes in Europe. Another issue concerns $650 million in annual imports of unbleached cotton from China, Egypt, India, Indonesia, Pakistan, and Turkey. A dispute pitted an alliance of textile importers and wholesalers against Eurocoton, which represents textile weavers in France, Italy, and other EU countries. Eurocoton supports the duties as a means of protecting jobs from low-priced imports; the job issue is particularly sensitive in France. British textile importer Broome & Wellington maintains, however, that imposing duties would drive up prices and cost even more jobs in the textile finishing and garment industries.[26] The issue is likely to remain contentious for some time to come.

---

[24] Viscounty, p. C3.
[25] Lester Ross and Susan Ning, "Modern Protectionism: China's Own Antidumping Regulations," *China Business Review* (May-June 2000), pp. 30–33.
[26] Neil Buckley, "Commission Faces Fight on Cotton 'Dumping'," *Financial Times* (December 2, 1997), p. 5; Emma Tucker, "French Fury at Threat to Cotton Duties," *Financial Times* (May 19, 1997), p. 3.

Dumping was a major issue in the Uruguay round of GATT negotiations. Many countries took issue with the U.S. system of antidumping laws, in part because, historically, the Commerce Department almost always ruled in favor of the U.S. company that filed the complaint. For their part, U.S. negotiators were concerned that U.S. exporters were often targeted in antidumping investigations in countries with few formal rules for due process. The U.S. side sought to improve the ability of U.S. companies to defend their interests and understand the basis for rulings.

The result of the GATT negotiations was an agreement on interpretation of Article VI. From the U.S. point of view, one of the most significant changes between the Agreement and the 1979 code is the addition of a "standard of review" that will make it harder for GATT panels to dispute U.S. antidumping determinations. There are also a number of procedural and methodological changes. In some instances, these have the effect of bringing GATT regulations more in line with U.S. law. For example, in calculating "fair price" for a given product, any sales of the product at below-cost prices in the exporting country are not included in the calculations; inclusion of such sales would have the effect of exerting downward pressure on the fair price. The agreement also brought GATT standards in line with U.S. standards by prohibiting governments from penalizing differences between home market and export market prices of less than 2 percent.

"It hurts us and America's high technology base when we lose the largest single sale for the next several years, The Washington Post, *to a foreign producer that has quoted prices at substantially below its cost of production."* —Statement issued by Rockwell International Corp.

As noted, the last few years have seen an increased incidence of antidumping investigation and penalties. These have originated primarily in the United States but also in the EU, Canada, and Australia. Many of the dumping cases in the United States involve manufactured goods from Asia. Most of the U.S. cases involve a single or narrowly defined group of products and are initiated by U.S. companies that claim to be materially damaged by the low-priced imports. In some cases, like tungsten from China and nitrocellulose from Yugoslavia, the company bringing action is the sole U.S. producer. In 1996, the U.S. Department of Commerce issued a preliminary ruling that importers of large German and Japanese printing presses into the United States had engaged in dumping. Rockwell Graphic Systems filed an antidumping petition after *The Washington Post* bought presses from Mitsubishi Heavy Industries. Investigators from both Commerce and the International Trade Commission (ITC) reported that they had found evidence of injury to the U.S. producer, and antidumping duties ranging from 17.17 percent to 58.14 percent were put into effect.

In 1998, in the wake of the global financial crisis, 12 U.S. steel producers filed dumping complaints against producers of hot-rolled steel in Japan, Russia, and Brazil. Paul Wilhelm, president of U.S. Steel Group, declared, "We are in a crisis. I know what it costs to make a ton of steel, and these imports are clearly being dumped and subsidized." Although the U.S. steel producers believed they had a strong case, the steel industry has a reputation for using trade laws as a competitive tool. Steel makers routinely file complaints of unfair trade with the ITC; over the past two decades, the industry has been the instigator of 45 percent of all complaints filed.[27]

For positive proof that dumping has occurred in the United States, both price discrimination and injury must be demonstrated. **Price discrimination** is the practice of setting different prices when selling the same quantity of "like-quality" goods to different buyers. The existence of either one without the other is an insufficient condition to constitute dumping. Companies concerned with running afoul of

---

[27] Chris Adams, "Paper Victories: U.S. Steelmakers Win Even When They Lose an Unfair-Trade Case," *The Wall Street Journal* (March 27, 1998), pp. A1, A8; Nancy Dunne and Edward Alden, "Canadian, US Steel Makers Launch Anti-Dumping Cases," *Financial Times* (October 1, 1998), p. 7.

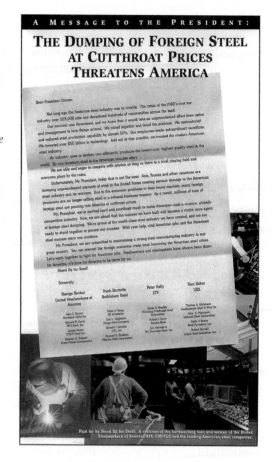

Representatives of the U.S. steel industry sponsored this 1998 ad to urge President Clinton to get tough on low-price steel that was sold in the United States by producers in Western Europe, Asia, and Russia. In 2001, the International Trade Commission launched an investigation to determine whether steel imports were hurting American steel producers. Based on the ITC's recommendation, in March 2002 President George W. Bush imposed sweeping tariffs of up to 30 percent on a wide range of steel imports for a three-year period. The European Union responded by drawing up a list of U.S. product imports that would be taxed in retaliation for the president's action.

antidumping legislation have developed a number of approaches for avoiding the dumping laws. One approach is to differentiate the product sold from that in the home market so it does not represent "like quality." An example of this is an auto accessory that one company packaged with a wrench and an instruction book, thereby changing the "accessory" to a "tool." The duty rate in the export market happened to be lower on tools, and the company also acquired immunity from antidumping laws because the package was not comparable to competing goods in the target market. Another approach is to make nonprice competitive adjustments in arrangements with affiliates and distributors. For example, credit can be extended and essentially have the same effect as a price reduction.

TRANSFER PRICING

Transfer pricing refers to the pricing of goods, services, and intangible property bought and sold by operating units or divisions of a company doing business with an affiliate in another jurisdiction. In other words, transfer pricing concerns *intracorporate exchanges*—transactions between buyers and sellers that have the same corporate parent. For example, Toyota subsidiaries sell to, and buy from, each other. The same is true of other companies operating globally. For any company expanding and creating decentralized operations, profit center considerations at the subsidiary or affiliate level take on increased importance. When a company extends its operations across national boundaries, transfer pricing takes on new dimensions and complications.

According to analyst Joseph Quinlan, about 25 percent of U.S. exports represent shipments by American companies to their foreign affiliates and subsidiaries. Similarly, intracompany shipments by non-U.S. companies to U.S. units represent one-fourth of U.S. merchandise shipments.

In determining transfer prices to subsidiaries, global companies must address a number of issues, including taxes, duties and tariffs, country profit transfer rules, conflicting objectives of joint venture partners, and government regulations. Not surprisingly, tax authorities such as the Internal Revenue Service in the United States, Inland Revenue in the United Kingdom, and Japan's National Tax Administration Agency take a keen interest in transfer pricing policies. One unidentified company recently paid a fine of $1.6 billion to Inland Revenue to settle a transfer-pricing suit. Transfer pricing is expected to be a corporate key issue in Europe after the advent of the Euro makes it easier for tax authorities to audit transfer pricing policies.[28]

There are three major alternative approaches to transfer pricing. The approach used will vary with the nature of the firm, products, markets, and historical circumstances of each case. **Cost-based transfer pricing** can take the same forms as the cost-based pricing methods discussed earlier in the chapter, including full cost and estimated future cost. The way costs are defined may have an impact on tariffs and duties of sales to affiliates and subsidiaries by global companies. A **market-based transfer price** is derived from the price required to be competitive in the international market. In other words, it represents an approximation of an arm's-length transaction. The constraint on this price is cost. Today's global companies have many outsourcing options available to them. This puts additional pressure on intracorporate supply groups to control and cut costs in an effort to compete with outside vendors. In some instances, no market exists for a particular product; how, then, can one arrive at a market-based price? A third alternative is to allow the organization's affiliates to determine **negotiated transfer prices** among themselves. Table 12-7 summarizes the results of recent studies comparing transfer pricing methods by country. As shown in the table, market-based and cost-based transfer pricing are the two preferred methods in the United States, Canada, Japan, and the United Kingdom.

Tax Regulations and Transfer Prices

Because the global corporation conducts business in a world characterized by different corporate tax rates, there is an incentive to maximize system income in countries

Table 12-7
Transfer Pricing Methods Used in Selected Countries

METHODS	UNITED STATES	CANADA	JAPAN	UNITED KINGDOM
1. Market-based	46%	37%	37%	31%
2. Cost-based	41%	33%	41%	38%
3. Negotiated	13%	26%	22%	20%
4. Other	0%	4%	0%	11%
	100%	100%	100%	100%

Source: Adapted from Charles T. Horngren, George Foster, and Srikant M. Datar, *Cost Accounting: A Managerial Emphasis* (Upper Saddle River, NJ: Prentice Hall, 2000), p. 802.

---

[28] Jim Kelly, "Time to Tackle the Most Taxing Issue," *Financial Times* (September 24, 1998), p. 25.

with the lowest tax rates and to minimize income in high-tax countries. Governments, naturally, are well aware of this situation. In recent years, many governments have tried to maximize national tax revenues by examining company returns and mandating reallocation of income and expenses.

Sales of Tangible and Intangible Property

Section 482 of the U.S. Treasury regulations deals with controlled intracompany transfers of raw materials and finished and intermediate goods, as well as intangibles such as charges for the use of manufacturing technology. The general rule that applies to sales of tangible property is known as the "arm's-length" formula, defined as the price that would have been charged in independent transactions between unrelated parties under similar circumstances. The complete text of Section 482 appears in the appendix to this chapter.

Competitive Pricing

Because Section 482 places so much emphasis on arm's-length price, a manager at a U.S. company who examines the regulations might wonder whether the spirit of these regulations permits pricing decisions to be made with regard to market and competitive factors. Clearly, if only the arm's-length standard is applied, a company may not be able to respond to the competitive factors that exist in every market, domestic and global. Fortunately, the regulations provide an opening for the company that seeks to be price-competitive or to aggressively price U.S.-sourced products in its international operations. Many interpret the regulations to mean that it is proper for a company to reduce prices and increase marketing expenditures through a controlled affiliate to gain market share, even when it would not do so in an arm's-length transaction with an independent distributor. This is because market position represents, in effect, an investment and an asset. A company would invest in such an asset only if it controlled the reseller—that is, if the reseller is a subsidiary. The regulations may also be interpreted as permitting a company to lower its transfer price for the purpose of entering a new market or meeting competition in an existing market either by instituting price reductions or by increasing marketing efforts in the target markets. Companies must have and use this latitude in making price decisions if they are to achieve significant success in international markets with U.S.-sourced goods.

Importance of Section 482 Regulations

Whatever the pricing rationale, executives and managers involved in international pricing policy decisions familiarize themselves with the Section 482 regulations. The pricing rationale must conform with the intention of these regulations. In an effort to develop more workable transfer pricing rules, the IRS issued temporary regulations on January 13, 1993, calling for "contemporaneous documentation" that supports transfer price decisions. Such documentation will require participation of management and marketing personnel in transfer pricing decisions, as opposed to the tax department. Companies should be prepared to demonstrate that their pricing methods are the result of informed choice, not oversight.

Treasury regulations and IRS enforcement policies often seem perplexingly inscrutable. However, there is ample evidence that the government simply seeks to prevent tax avoidance and to ensure fair distribution of income from the operations of companies doing business internationally. Still, the government does not always succeed in its efforts to enforce Section 482 by reallocating income. In a recent court decision, Merck sued the U.S. government on the grounds that the IRS's allocation of 7 percent of the income from a wholly owned subsidiary to the parent company was "arbitrary, capricious, and unreasonable." The IRS had argued that Merck artificially shifted income to the subsidiary by sharing costs associated with R&D, marketing facilities, and management personnel. The court agreed with Merck and ordered the IRS to issue a tax refund.

As the Merck case demonstrates, even companies that make a conscientious effort to comply with the regulations, and that document this effort, may find themselves in tax court. Should a tax auditor raise questions, executives should be able to make a strong case for their decisions. Fortunately, consulting services are available to help managers deal with the arcane world of transfer pricing. It is not unusual for large global companies to invest hundreds of thousands of dollars and hire international accounting firms to review transfer pricing policies. For companies with tighter budgets, Worldwide Transfer Pricing Institute in Schaumburg, Illinois, offers a package of software, documentation, and training.

Joint Ventures

Joint ventures present an incentive to set transfer prices at higher levels than would be used in sales to wholly owned affiliates because a company's share of the joint venture earnings is less than 100 percent. Any profits that occur in the joint venture must be shared. The increasing frequency of tax authority audits is an important reason for working out an agreement that will also be acceptable to the tax authorities. The tax authorities' criterion of "arm's-length" prices is probably most appropriate for the majority of joint ventures.

To avoid potential conflict, companies with joint ventures should work out pricing agreements in advance that are acceptable to both sides. The following are several considerations for joint venture pricing.[29]

1. The way in which transfer prices will be adjusted in response to exchange-rate changes.
2. Expected reductions in manufacturing costs arising from learning curve improvements and the way these will be reflected in transfer prices.
3. Shifts in the sourcing of products or components from parents to alternative sources.
4. The effects of competition on volume and overall margins.

COUNTERTRADE

In recent years, many exporters have been forced to finance international transactions by taking full or partial payment in some form other than money.[30] A number of alternative finance methods, known as *countertrade,* are widely used. In a **countertrade** transaction, a sale results in product flowing in one direction to a buyer; a separate stream of products and services, often flowing in the opposite direction, is also created. Countertrade generally involves a seller from the West and a buyer in a

---

[29] Thomas L. Dooley III and Timothy Collins, *Teaming Up for the '90s: A Guide to International Joint Ventures and Strategic Alliances* (Homewood, IL: BusinessOne-Irwin, 1991), pp. 212–213.

[30] Many of the examples in the following section are adapted from Matt Schaffer, *Winning the Countertrade War: New Export Strategies for America* (New York: John Wiley & Sons, 1989).

Open to Discussion
Is Competitiveness a Dangerous Obsession?

Massachusetts Institute of Technology economist Paul Krugman wants every student of international trade to reflect carefully on the following proposition:

> Today, America is part of a truly global economy. To maintain our standard of living, America must learn to compete in an ever tougher world marketplace. That's why high productivity and product quality have become essential. We can only be competitive in the new global economy if we forge a new partnership between government and business.

To many, this proposition will sound reasonable. In style and substance, it echoes assertions made in the 1990s by such well-known figures as economist Lester Thurow, presidential advisor Ira Magaziner, and U.S. Secretary of Labor Robert Reich. Krugman, however, says that the proposition is "baloney." In his words, it represents "the rhetoric of competitiveness," in which the United States is likened to a large corporation like GM. According to the rhetoric of competitiveness, America—like GM—is suffering because of global competition, and the nation's standard of living has stagnated as a result.

In numerous articles and a recent book, Krugman offers a painstaking analysis of what he believes to be a mistakenly held proposition. In sorting out the salient issues, Krugman's reasoning flies in the face of positions held by Thurow, Magaziner, Reich, and others; Krugman calls these individuals "strategic traders" and "policy entrepreneurs." Surprisingly, Krugman's critiques are not based on partisan politics; he himself is a liberal. His complaint is that fundamental economic concepts—especially comparative advantage—are being misinterpreted, misapplied, or ignored altogether in the name of public policy.

First, Krugman disputes the assertion that America is "part of a truly global economy." The reason: Approximately 90 percent of the goods and services produced in the United States are for domestic consumption; only 10 percent are destined for world markets. Indeed, 70 percent of the U.S. economy is based on services, and services are less likely than manufactured products to be marketed abroad. Thus, despite all the talk about "global integration," the "global economy" is not as interconnected as people might think.

Next, Krugman attacks the notion that America itself "competes in the global marketplace." Krugman

argues that Japan, the United States, and other nations of the world are not in competition with each other in the sense that, say, Coca-Cola and PepsiCo or Reebok and Nike are. Few Coca-Cola employees buy Pepsi products, and vice versa. Thus a company is not like a nation: No company sells 90 percent of its output to its own employees. In the "cola wars," PepsiCo can only win by taking customers away from Coca-Cola. The same cannot be said of nations, Krugman asserts. The world's major industrial nations can be successful without each other because they are not just competitors; trading partners also represent export markets and sources of imports. In other words, every potential problem also presents opportunities, and those opportunities may outweigh the problems.

Third, Krugman objects to linking the issue of higher U.S. productivity with international trade. Contrary to the message coming out of Washington, the fact that productivity improvement rates in other nations exceed those in the United States does not make the United States less competitive or lessen Americans' standard of living. Krugman asserts quite simply that America needs to be productive to produce more. That may sound tautologous, but it is a plain and simple economic truth that would be valid even if the United States did not engage in international trade. In his writings, Krugman reviews the basics of comparative advantage to demonstrate that, in fact, no special problems are created for a country that is less productive than its trading partners.

Finally, Krugman argues that the issues related to the "rhetoric of competitiveness" are not simply academic ones. If the strategic traders' "rhetoric of competitiveness" message is heeded, the results could have far-reaching, undesirable consequences. First, it could lead to wasteful government spending in a misguided effort to enhance competitiveness. In the interest of competitiveness, government support might be directed at manufacturing. Yet it is the service sector, which is not a major part of international trade, where productivity is lagging. Second, it could lead to protectionism and trade wars. Finally, it could lead to poor public policy decisions in a variety of areas—health care, for example—that are unrelated to trade.

SOURCES: Paul Krugman, "A Country Is Not a Company," *Harvard Business Review* 74, no. 1 (January-February 1996), pp. 40–44+; Paul Krugman, "Competitiveness: A Dangerous Obsession," *Foreign Affairs* (March-April 1994), pp. 28–44; Paul Krugman, "Competitiveness: Does It Matter?" *Fortune* (March 7, 1994), pp. 109+; Krugman, *Peddling Prosperity: Economic Sense and Nonsense in the Age of Diminished Expectations* (New York: W. W. Norton & Co., 1994).

developing country; for example, the countries in the former Soviet bloc have historically relied heavily on countertrade. This approach, which reached a peak in popularity in the mid-1980s, is now used in some 100 countries. Within the former Soviet Union, countertrade has flourished in the 1990s, following the collapse of the central planning system.

As one expert notes, countertrade flourishes when hard currency is scarce. Exchange controls may prevent a company from expatriating earnings; the company may be forced to spend money in-country for products that are then exported and sold in third-country markets. Historically, the single most important driving force behind the proliferation of countertrade was the decreasing ability of developing countries to finance imports through bank loans. This trend resulted in debt-ridden governments pushing for self-financed deals.[31] According to Pompiliu Verzariu of the U.S. Commerce Department:

> In the 1990s, countertrade pressures abated in many parts of the world, notably Latin America, as a result of debt reduction induced by the Brady plan initiative, lower international interest rates, policies that liberalized trade regimes, and the emergence of economic blocs such as NAFTA and Mercosur, which integrate regional trade based on free-market principles.[32]

Today, several conditions affect the probability that importing nations will demand countertrade. First is the priority attached to the Western import. The higher the priority, the less likely it is that countertrade will be required. The second condition is the value of the transaction; the higher the value, the greater the likelihood that countertrade will be involved. Third, the availability of products from other suppliers can also be a factor. If a company is the sole supplier of a differentiated product, it can demand monetary payment. However, if competitors are willing to deal on a countertrade basis, a company may have little choice but to agree or risk losing the sale altogether. Overall, the advantages to nonmarket and developing economies are access to Western marketing expertise and technology in the short term, and creation of hard currency export markets in the long term. The U.S. government officially opposes government-mandated countertrade, which represents the type of bilateral trade agreement that violates the free trading system established by GATT.

Two categories of countertrade are discussed here. Barter falls into one category; the mixed forms of countertrade, including counterpurchase, offset, compensation trading, and cooperation agreements belong in a separate category. They incorporate a real distinction from barter because money or credit is involved in the transaction.

Barter

The term **barter** describes the least complex and oldest form of bilateral, nonmonetized countertrade. Simple barter is a direct exchange of goods or services between two parties. Although no money is involved, both partners construct an approximate shadow price for products flowing in each direction. One contract formalizes simple barter transactions, which are generally for less than one year to avoid problems in price fluctuations. However, for some transactions, the exchange may span months or years, with contract provisions allowing adjustments in the exchange ratio to handle fluctuations in world prices.

Companies sometimes seek outside help from barter specialists. For example, New York-based Atwood Richards engages in barter in all parts of the world.

---

[31] Pompiliu Verzariu, "Trends and Developments in International Countertrade," *Business America* (November 2, 1992), p. 2.
[32] Janet Aschkenasy, "Give and Take," *International Business* (September 1996), p. 11.

Visit the Web site
Atwood Richards' Web site contains several concise case studies describing how some of the world's best-known global companies use barter.
www.atwoodrichards. com

Generally, however, distribution is direct between trading partners, with no middleman included. For example, General Electric sold a turbine generator to Romania in the late 1970s; for payment, GE Trading Company accepted $150 million in chemicals, metals, nails, and other products, which it then sold on the world market. One of the highest-profile companies involved in barter deals is PepsiCo, which has done business in the Soviet and post-Soviet market for more than 20 years. In the Soviet era, PepsiCo bartered soft-drink syrup concentrate for Stolichnaya vodka, which was, in turn, exported to the United States by the PepsiCo Wines & Spirits subsidiary and marketed by M. Henri Wines. In the post-Soviet market economy in the Commonwealth of Independent States, barter is no longer required. Today, Stolichnaya is imported into the United States and marketed by Carillon Importers, a unit of Diageo PLC.

Counterpurchase

This form of countertrade, also termed *parallel trading* or *parallel barter,* is distinguished from other forms in that each delivery in an exchange is paid for in cash. For example, Rockwell International sold a printing press to Zimbabwe for $8 million. The deal went through, however, only after Rockwell agreed to purchase $8 million in ferrochrome and nickel from Zimbabwe, which it subsequently sold on the world market.

The Rockwell-Zimbabwe deal illustrates several aspects of counterpurchase. Generally, products offered by the foreign principal are not related to the Western firm's exports and thus cannot be used directly by the firm. In most counterpurchase transactions, two separate contracts are signed. In one, the supplier agrees to sell products for a cash settlement (the original sales contract); in the other, the supplier agrees to purchase and market unrelated products from the buyer (a separate, parallel contract). The dollar value of the counterpurchase generally represents a set percentage—and sometimes the full value—of the products sold to the foreign principal. When the Western supplier sells these goods, the trading cycle is complete.

Offset

Offset is a reciprocal arrangement whereby the government in the importing country seeks to recover large sums of hard currency spent on expensive purchases such as military aircraft or telecommunications systems. In effect, the government is saying, "If you want us to spend government money on your exports, you must import products from our country." Offset arrangements may also involve cooperation in manufacturing, some form of technology transfer, placing subcontracts locally, or arranging local assembly or manufacturing equal to a certain percentage of the contract value.[33] In one recent deal involving offsets, Lockheed Martin Corp. sold F-16 fighters to the United Arab Emirates for $6.4 billion. In return, Lockheed agreed to invest $160 million in the petroleum-related UAE Offsets Group.[34]

Offset may be distinguished from counterpurchase because the latter is characterized by smaller deals over shorter periods of time.[35] Another major distinction between offset and other forms of countertrade is that the agreement is not contractual

---

[33] The commitment to local assembly or manufacturing under the supplier's specifications is commonly termed a *coproduction agreement,* which is tied to the offset but does not, in itself, represent a type of countertrade.

[34] Daniel Pearl, "Arms Dealers Get Creative with 'Offsets,' " *The Wall Street Journal* (April 20, 2000), p. A18.

[35] Patricia Daily and S. M. Ghazanfar, "Countertrade: Help or Hindrance to Less-Developed Countries?" *Journal of Social, Political, and Economic Studies* 18, no. 1 (Spring 1993), p. 65.

but reflects a memorandum of understanding that sets out the dollar value of products to be offset and the time period for completing the transaction. In addition, there is no penalty on the supplier for nonperformance. Typically, requests range from 20 to 50 percent of the value of the supplier's product. Some highly competitive sales have required offsets exceeding 100 percent of the valuation of the original sale.

Offsets have become a controversial facet of today's trade environment. To win sales in important markets such as China, global companies are facing demands for offsets even when transactions do not involve military procurement. For example, the Chinese government requires Boeing to spend 20 to 30 percent of the purchase price of each aircraft on purchases of Chinese goods. As Boeing executive Dean Thornton explained recently:

> "Offset" is a bad word, and it's against GATT and a whole bunch of other stuff, but it's a fact of life. It used to be twenty years ago in places like Canada or the UK, it was totally explicit, down to the decimal point. "You will buy 20 percent offset of your value." Or 21 percent or whatever. It still is that way in military stuff. Commercially, it's not legal so it becomes less explicit.[36]

Compensation Trading

This form of countertrade, also called *buyback*, involves two separate and parallel contracts. In one contract, the supplier agrees to build a plant or provide plant equipment, patents or licenses, or technical, managerial, or distribution expertise for a hard currency down payment at the time of delivery. In the other contract, the supplier company agrees to take payment in the form of the plant's output equal to its investment (minus interest) for a period of as many as 20 years.

Essentially, the success of compensation trading rests on the willingness of each firm to be both a buyer and a seller. The People's Republic of China has used compensation trading extensively. Egypt also used this approach to develop an aluminum plant. A Swiss company, Aluswiss, built the plant and also exports alumina (an oxide of aluminum found in bauxite and clay) to Egypt. Aluswiss takes back a percentage of the finished aluminum produced at the plant as partial payment for building the plant. As this example shows, compensation differs from counterpurchase in that the technology or capital supplied is related to the output produced.[37] In counterpurchase, as noted before, the goods taken by the supplier typically cannot be used directly in its business activities.

Cooperation Agreements

Sometimes industrial-country firms doing business with nonmarket economies are reluctant to pursue countertrade deals that link selling and buying. When this is the case, cooperation agreements may be worked out between two different industrial-country companies. What distinguishes these arrangements from other types of countertrade is the specialization of each industrialized-country firm for either buying or selling, but not both. Each of the three forms of cooperation agreements represents an increasingly complex accommodation to the needs of trading partners. They

---

36 William Greider, *One World, Ready or Not: The Manic Logic of Global Capitalism* (Upper Saddle River, NJ: Simon & Schuster, 1997), p. 130.
37 Patricia Daily and S. M. Ghazanfar, "Countertrade: Help or Hindrance to Less-Developed Countries?" *Journal of Social, Political, and Economic Studies* 18, no. 1 (Spring 1993), p. 66.

include cooperation and simple barter (triangular deals); cooperation and counterpurchase; and cooperation, counterpurchase, and credit by a bank. As an example of cooperation and simple barter, the parties to the transaction might be two unrelated Western firms, with a U.S. firm specialized as a seller and a Western European firm as a buyer, and an Eastern European foreign trade organization (FTO). The U.S. firm may perform the selling function by delivering goods to the FTO. In payment for the goods, the FTO might deliver raw materials to the Western European firm, which acts as the buyer. The Western European firm then pays the U.S. firm an amount equivalent to the value of goods originally sent to the FTO. The advantage to the U.S. firm offering goods is in removing the obligation to buy; the Western European firm receives the raw materials with a considerable reduction in transport costs. Problems associated with these arrangements include finding two industrial-country firms with the appropriate supply-demand fit and the flexibility to handle time delays in receipt of payment or in delivery of goods.

Hybrid Countertrade Arrangements

Hybrid forms of countertrade are becoming more prevalent in trading arrangements. For example, the investment performance contract in Third World markets is an additional condition of offset arrangements. Countries such as Brazil, Mexico, and even Canada now make official approval of investment proposals contingent on commitments by the investors to export. As a second example, "project accompaniment" typifies an arrangement in which a Western supplier is encouraged to buy a greater volume, wider range of products, or both, compared with the countertrade commitment. Project accompaniment has surfaced as a condition to the exchange of industrial goods by the West for oil from Middle Eastern producers.

Switch Trading

Also called *triangular trade* and *swap*, **switch trading** is a mechanism that can be applied to barter or countertrade. In this arrangement, a professional switch trader, switch trading house, or bank steps into a simple barter or other countertrade arrangement when one of the parties is not willing to accept all the goods received in a transaction. The switching mechanism provides a "secondary market" for countertraded or bartered goods and reduces the inflexibility inherent in barter and countertrade. Fees charged by switch traders range from 5 percent of market value for commodities to 30 percent for high-technology items. Switch traders develop their own networks of firms and personal contacts and are generally headquartered in Vienna, Amsterdam, Hamburg, and London. If a party anticipates that the products received in a barter or countertrade deal will be sold eventually at a discount by the switch trader, the common practice is to price the original products higher, build in "special charges" for port storage or consulting, or require shipment by the national carrier.

The advantages of switching are that: (1) its multilateral character offers a greater degree of economic efficiency in pricing and in increasing trade; (2) discounted prices can open new markets more rapidly; and (3) Western firms can shed the responsibilities of marketing goods received in countertrade. Disadvantages include: (1) disruptions of producers' established markets when switch dealers offer their products at a discount to such markets; (2) products that may be in oversupply or difficult to sell on the world market; (3) the foreign principal's assessment of the Western firm as uncommitted to a long-term trade relationship, particularly if the foreigner's established markets are threatened by discounted products; and (4) the complex and cumbersome nature of switching transactions. Switch trading's complexity is rooted in the mechanics of the transaction; typically, the switch trader sells a commodity for "soft" (i.e., nonconvertible) currency, uses the soft currency to purchase another commodity, and repeats the process until he or she can purchase a commodity that can be sold for hard currency.

SUMMARY

Pricing decisions are a critical element of the marketing mix that must reflect costs, competitive factors, and customer perceptions regarding value of the product. Pricing strategies include **market skimming, market penetration,** and **market holding.** Novice exporters frequently use **cost-plus pricing.** International terms of a sale such as **ex-works, F.A.S., F.O.B.,** and **C.I.F.** are known as **Incoterms** and specify which party to a transaction is responsible for covering various costs. These and other costs lead to **price escalation,** the accumulation of costs that occurs when products are shipped from one country to another. Expectations regarding currency fluctuations, inflation, government controls, and the competitive situation must also be factored into pricing decisions. Global companies can maintain competitive prices in world markets by shifting production sources as business condi-

tions change. Overall, a company's pricing policies can be categorized as **ethnocentric, polycentric,** or **geocentric.**

Several additional pricing issues are related to global marketing. The issue of **gray market goods** arises because price variations between different countries lead to **parallel imports. Dumping** is another contentious issue that can result in strained relations between trading partners. **Transfer pricing** is an issue because of the sheer monetary volume of intra-corporate sales and because country governments are anxious to generate as much tax revenue as possible. Various forms of **countertrade** play an important role in today's global environment. **Barter, counterpurchase, offset, compensation trading, cooperation agreements,** and **switch trading** are the main countertrade options.

DISCUSSION QUESTIONS

1. What are the basic factors that affect price in any market? What considerations enter into the pricing decision?
2. Define the various types of pricing strategies and objectives available to global marketers.
3. Identify some of the environmental constraints on global pricing decisions.
4. Why do price differences in world markets often lead to gray marketing?
5. What is dumping? Why was dumping such an important issue during the Uruguay Round of GATT negotiations?
6. What is a transfer price? Why is it an important issue for companies with foreign affiliates? Why did transfer pricing in Europe take on increased importance in 1999?

7. What is the difference between ethnocentric, polycentric, and geocentric pricing strategies? Which one would you recommend to a company that has global market aspirations?
8. If you were responsible for marketing CAT scanners worldwide (average price, $1,200,000), and your country of manufacture was experiencing a strong and appreciating currency against almost all other currencies, what options are available to you to maintain your competitive advantage in world markets?
9. Compare and contrast the different forms of countertrade.

SUGGESTED READINGS

Books

Abadallah, Wagdy M. *International Transfer Pricing Policies: Decision Making Guidelines for Multinational Companies.* New York: Quorum Books, 1989.

Lowell, Cym, Marianne Burge, and Peter Brige. *U.S. International Transfer Pricing.* 2nd ed. Boston: Warren, Gorham & Lamont, 1998.

Nagle, Thomas T., and Reed Holden. *The Strategy and Tactics of Pricing: A Guide to Profitable Decision Making.* 3rd ed. Upper Saddle River, New Jersey: Prentice Hall, 2002.

Schaffer, Matt. *Winning the Countertrade War: New Export Strategies for America.* New York: John Wiley & Sons, 1989.

Verzariu, Pompiliu. *Countertrade, Barter, and Offsets: New Strategies for Profit in International Trade.* New York: McGraw-Hill, 1985.

Articles

Assmus, Gert, and Carsten Wiese. "How to Address the Gray Market Threat Using Price Coordination." *Sloan Management Review* 36 (Spring 1995), pp. 31–41.

Bateman, Connie Rae, Neil C. Herndon Jr., and John P. Fraedrich. "The Transfer Pricing Decision Process for Multinational Corporations." *International Journal of Commerce and Management* 7, nos. 3 & 4 (1997), pp. 18–38.

Bernstein, Jerry, and David Macias. "Engineering New-Product Success—The New-Product Pricing Process at Emerson." *Industrial Marketing Management* 31, no. 1 (January 2002), pp. 51–61.

Cannon, Hugh M., and Fred W. Morgan. "A Strategic Pricing Framework." *Journal of Business and Industrial Marketing* 6, nos. 3, 4 (Summer-Fall 1991); pp. 59–70.

Cavusgil S. Tamer. "Pricing for Global Markets." *Columbia Journal of World Business* 31, no. 4 (Winter 1996), pp. 66–78.

Choi, Chong Ju, Soo Hee Lee, and Jai Boem Kim. "A Note on Countertrade: Contractual Uncertainty and Transaction Governance in Emerging Economies." *Journal of International Business Studies* 30, no. 1 (1999) pp. 189–201.

Cohen, Stephen S., and John Zysman. "Countertrade, Offsets, Barter and Buyouts." *California Management Review* 28, no. 2 (1986), pp. 41–55.

Faulds, David J., Orlen Grunewald, and Denise Johnson. "A Cross National Investigation of the Relationship Between the Price and Quality of Consumer Products: 1970–1990." *Journal of Global Marketing* 8, no. 1 (1994), pp. 7–26.

Kostecki, Michel M. "Marketing Strategies Between Dumping and Anti-Dumping Action." *European Journal of Marketing* 25, no. 12 (1992), pp. 7–19.

Lancioni, Richard, and John Gattorna. "Strategic Value Pricing: Its Role In International Business." *International Journal of Physical Distribution and Logistics* 22, no. 6 (1992), pp. 24–27.

Lasagni, Andrea. "Does Country-targeted Anti-dumping Policy by the EU Create Trade Diversion?" *Journal of World Trade* 34, no. 4 (August 2000), p. 137.

Lindsay, Brink. "The U.S. Antidumping Law: Rhetoric Versus Reality." *Journal of World Trade* 34, no. 1 (February 2000), pp. 1–38.

Marn, Michael V., and Robert L. Rosiello. "Managing Price, Gaining Profit." *Harvard Business Review* 70, no. 5 (September-October 1992), pp. 84–94.

Mehafdi, Messaoud. "The Ethics of International Transfer Pricing." *Journal of Business Ethics* 28, no. 4 (December 2000), pp. 365–381.

Michael, James. "A Supplemental Distribution Channel?: The Case of U.S. Parallel Export Channels." *Multinational Business Review* 6, no. 1 (Spring 1998), pp. 24–35.

Paun, Dorothy A., Larry D. Compeau, and Shruv Grewal. "A Model of the Influence of Marketing Objectives on Pricing Strategies in International Countertrade." *Journal of Public Policy & Marketing* 16 (Spring 1997), pp. 69–82.

Prince, Melvin, and Mark Davies. "Seeing Red Over International Gray Markets." *Business Horizons* 43, no. 2 (March-April 2000), pp. 71–74.

Qureshi, Asif H. "Drafting Anti-Dumping Legislation: Issues and Tips." *Journal of World Trade* 34, no. 6 (December 2000), pp. 19–32.

Samli, A. Coskun, and Laurence Jacobs. "Pricing Practices of American Multinational Firms: Standardization vs. Localization Dichotomy." *Journal of Global Marketing* 8, no. 2 (1994), pp. 51–74.

Seifert, Bruce, and John Ford. "Are Exporting Firms Modifying Their Product, Pricing and Promotion Policies?" *International Marketing Review* 6, no. 6 (1989), pp. 53–68.

Shoham, Aviv, and Dorothy A. Paun. "A Study of International Modes of Entry and Orientation Strategies Used in Countertrade Transactions." *Journal of Global Marketing* 11, no. 3 (1998), pp. 5–19.

Simon, Hermann. "Pricing Opportunities—And How to Exploit Them." *Sloan Management Review* 33, no. 2 (Winter 1992), pp. 55–65.

———, and Eckhard Kucher. "The European Pricing Time Bomb: And How to Cope With It." *European Management Journal* 10, no. 2 (June 1992), pp. 136–145.

Sinclair, Stuart. "A Guide to Global Pricing." *Journal of Business Strategy* 14, no. 3 (May-June 1993), pp. 16–19.

Stöttinger, Barbara. "Strategic Export Pricing: A Long and Winding Road." *Journal of International Marketing* 9, no. 1 (2001), pp. 40–63.

CASES

Case 12-1   Pricing AIDS Drugs in Emerging Markets

For years, the war against AIDS has been heavily dependent on drugs developed and produced by global pharmaceutical companies such as Merck & Co., Bristol-Myers Squibb Company, and GlaxoSmithKline PLC. The most effective treatment against the deadly virus is a "cocktail" consisting of several different drugs, and the per-person cost of a one-year supply can run as high as $10,000 (see Table 1). Such prices are far beyond the means of AIDS victims in low-income nations; in Africa alone, an estimated 25 million people are infected with HIV, the virus that causes AIDS. At the end of the 1990s, AIDS patients in countries such as Uganda were paying approximately $6 per day for a drug cocktail such as Glaxo's Combivir.

In May 2000, following discussions with representatives of the United Nations AIDS Program, Merck and four other major pharmaceutical companies announced an agreement to cut drug prices in developing countries by as much as 85 to 90 percent compared with prices in the United States. For example, Merck set a discounted price of $1,044 for its Crixivan protease inhibitor. Although many in the world community welcomed the announcement, it was clear that even these prices were still beyond the reach of many AIDS victims. Employers, governments, the World Bank, and other donor organizations would be required to provide subsidies if the drugs were to be truly affordable.

The announcement also highlighted the fact that pricing is only one element in the fight against the spread of AIDS. To be effective, AIDS drugs have to be taken in strict daily regimens. A patient's condition can worsen if the regimen is not followed faithfully; in addition, there are concerns in the medical community about the development of new drug-resistant strains of the disease. Thus, related issues include the need for improving the public health infrastructure in countries such as Uganda with an emphasis on drug distribution, counseling, AIDS education, HIV testing, and prevention.

The proposed price cuts also entailed potential risks to Glaxo and other industry leaders. The companies treat the costs associated with drug manufacturing as trade secrets. According to some estimates, profit margins are as high as 90 percent once research and development costs have been recovered. By cutting prices in developing countries, the companies were opening themselves to pressure to cut prices in developed countries as well. Also, there was a risk that the cheaper drugs would fall into the hands of black marketers who would then re-export them to developed countries and undercut established prices. Merck representatives planned to negotiate with government officials from each nation and seek assurance that the drugs would stay off the black market before actually implementing the price cuts.

There was one other critical factor in the decision to cut prices—the threat from manufacturers of low-priced generic AIDS drugs. Several manufacturers in India, Brazil, and Thailand had already created "generic" versions of Zerit, 3TC, Crixivan, and other name-brand drugs. Production of these "copycat" versions was possible because India currently does not recognize international patent laws. In February 2001, less than one year after the initiative with USAIDS was announced, Yusuf K. Hamied, the president of India's Cipla Ltd., stunned the world community by announcing that he was prepared

Table 1
Per Patient Per Year Price of Aids Drugs

DRUG/COMPANY	U.S. PRICE	CIPLA	HETERO	PROPOSED PRICE IN AFRICA
Zerit (Bristol-Myers)	$3,589	$70	$47	$252
3TC (Glaxo)	3,271	190	98	232
Crixivan (Merck)	6,016	NA	2,300	600
Combivir (Glaxo)	7,093	635	293	730
Stocrin (Merck)	4,730	NA	1,179	500
Viramune (Boehringer)	3,508	340	202	483

to offer a year's supply of three AIDS drugs to governments in sub-Saharan Africa for $600 per patient. That price was about 40 percent below the prices offered by GlaxoSmithKline and others. He also asserted that he would make the three-drug cocktail available to a private organization, Doctors without Borders, for $350 per year. Another Indian manufacturer, Hetero Drugs Ltd., quickly followed suit and set a price of $347 per year.

The announcements were hailed by AIDS activists, even though there were two complications. First, the Indian companies would somehow have to circumvent laws in various African nations that protect the patent holders of drugs that had been copied. In South Africa, for example, the government filed a lawsuit against the Western pharmaceutical companies in an effort to secure distribution. Second, Cipla and other generic producers had to obtain approval from local regulatory agencies before their drugs could be made available. Meanwhile, activists continued to pressure the big drug companies for reductions beyond those originally announced as well as price cuts on drugs not covered in the UNAIDS agreement. For example, the University of Minnesota holds the patent on Ziagen, which is produced by GlaxoSmithKline but had not been among the discounted drugs. Student activists at the university have been urging administrators to consider asking Glaxo to add Ziagen to the list of AIDS drugs that will be discounted.

Several of the drug companies that had announced price cuts in 2000 responded quickly to the announcements from India. Less than a month after Cipla's announcement, a Merck spokesperson indicated that the company would slash prices in Africa by an additional 40 to 55 percent. The new price for Crixivan was set at $600; another Merck drug, Stocrin, was priced at $500 per year per patient. Thus, a Crixivan/Stocrin cocktail would cost about $1,100, compared with about $11,000 in the United States; at the discounted prices, Merck indicated it was generating zero profit. Merck also indicated that it would make the discounted drugs available to other low-income nations besides those in Africa. Bristol-Myers Squibb and GlaxoSmithKline also announced plans for a new round of price cuts.

Despite the moves, the global pharmaceutical giants appeared to be losing a public relations war in which AIDS activists portrayed them as both secretive and as withholding needed drugs from millions who need them. At the 1998 world AIDS conference in Geneva, UN officials announced a pilot program to reduce AIDS drug prices in low-income countries. However, Merck elected not to participate in the program; executives argued that issues pertaining to infrastructure and health-service networks had to be addressed first. AIDS activists responded by dismantling Merck's booth at the conference. Merck and other Western companies remained concerned that, if a broader base of public opinion turned against them, the ongoing controversy might ultimately undermine their international patents. ∎

DISCUSSION QUESTIONS

1. Given the discount prices that Merck and the other global drug companies are making available in Africa and other developing countries, are they charging too much for AIDS drugs in the United States? Should they be required to disclose their cost structures?

2. Do you think intellectual property laws in countries such as South Africa should be changed to allow generic producers such as Cipla access to the market?

3. What should Merck, Glaxo, and other pharmaceutical manufacturers do to improve their image with the general public?

SOURCES: Michael Waldholz, "Into Africa: Makers of AIDS Drugs Agree to Slash Prices for Developing World" (May 11, 2000), pp. A1, A12; Daniel Pearl and Alix Freedman, "The Catalyst: Behind Cipla's Offer of Cheap AIDS Drugs: Potent Mix of Motives" (March 12, 2001), pp. A1, A8; Mark Schoofs and Michael Waldholz, "New Regimen: AIDS-Drug Price War Breaks Out in Africa, Goaded by Generics," *The Wall Street Journal* (March 7, 2001), pp. A1, A14; Rachel Zimmerman and Michael Waldholz, "Abbott to Cut African AIDS-Drug Prices," *The Wall Street Journal* (March 27, 2001), pp. A3, A8.

Case 12-2   LVMH and Luxury Goods Marketing

Do you know anyone who spends $1,700 on a suit plus $600 for a matching handbag? When it comes to champagne and perfume, do your friends spend $100 or more for a single bottle? Welcome to the rarefied world of luxury goods marketing. In this world, affluent consumers eagerly seek out luxury brands such as Armani, Christian Dior, Gucci, Louis Vuitton, Prada, and Versace. They are willing and able to pay high prices for top-quality merchandise from fashion houses whose names are synonymous with status, good taste, and prestige. In France, *haute couture* traditionally meant that one outfit was meticulously crafted for members of the aristocracy, "old money" socialites, or celebrities. Today, however, the concept and meaning of *haute couture* are being transformed.

Although the *couture* image of the supermodel strutting down the catwalk is still a mainstay of the fashion world, some of the world's best-known fashion houses are redefining the notion of luxury by catering to the needs of a more diverse, *nouveau riche* clientele. Whereas in years past, fashion houses produced only clothing, today numerous licensing deals are generating more

cash than the clothing itself. Countless items bearing the names of venerable *couture* houses are now available worldwide. Thanks to the stock market boom of the 1990s and rising prosperity levels in developing nations, a new class of affluent consumers has begun to develop a taste for luxury branded products, ranging from Gucci sunglasses to Dior pantyhose. In fact, apparel goods constitute less than 20 percent of total sales volume by Hermés. As Lord Thurso, chief executive of a luxury health spa in Great Britain, noted, "The trick is not to sell real luxury to very rich people. It's to sell a *perception* of luxury to aspiring people."

One fashion house that is changing with the times is LVMH Moët Hennessy Louis Vuitton SA, the largest marketer of luxury products and brands in the world. Chairman Bernard Arnault presides over a diverse empire of products and brands, sales of which totaled more than $10 billion in 2001. Arnault, whom some refer to as "the pope of high fashion," recently summed up the luxury business as follows: "We are here to sell dreams. When you see a couture show on TV around the world, you dream.

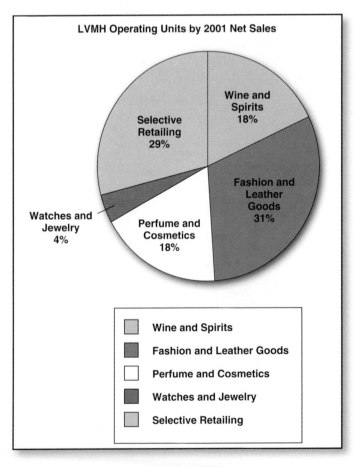

Taïga leather. For men.

Available exclusively in Louis Vuitton shops and select department stores. 1.800.458.4135.

LOUIS VUITTON

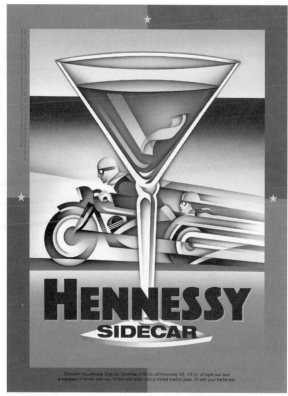

HENNESSY
SIDECAR

Discover the ultimate Sidecar. Combine 1 1/2 oz. of Hennessy VS, 1/2 oz. of triple sec and a squeeze of lemon over ice. Shake and strain into a chilled martini glass. Or ask your bartender.

When you enter a Dior boutique and buy your lipstick, you buy something affordable, but it has the dream in it." Sales of luggage and leather fashion goods, including the 100-year-old Louis Vuitton brand, account for 30 percent of revenues. The company's specialty group includes Duty Free Shoppers (DFS) and Sephora. DFS operates stores in international airports around the world; Sephora is a French-based chain specialty store that focuses on luxury products and brands. Sales of luggage and leather fashion goods, including the 100-year old Louis Vuitton brand, account for 25 percent of revenues. Driven by such well-known brands as Christian Dior, Givenchy, and Kenzo, perfumes and body products generate nearly 20 percent of revenues. LVMH has two separate drinks units. Champagne and wine include such prestigious brands as Dom Perignon, Moët & Chandon, and Veuve Clicquot.

Despite the high expenses associated with operating elegant stores and purchasing advertising space in upscale magazines, the premium retail prices that luxury goods command translate into handsome profits. In 2000, the Louis Vuitton brand alone accounted for 80 percent of LVMH's $1.37 billion operating profit. Not surprisingly, unscrupulous operators have taken note of the high margins associated with Vuitton handbags, gun cases, and luggage displaying the distinctive beige-on-brown latticework LV monogram. Louis Vuitton SA spends $10 million annu-

ally battling counterfeiters in Turkey, Thailand, China, Morocco, South Korea, and Italy. Some of the money is spent on lobbyists who represent the company's interests in meetings with foreign government officials. Yves Carcelle, chairman of Louis Vuitton SA, recently explained, "Almost every month, we get a government somewhere in the world to destroy canvas, or finished products."

Another problem is a flourishing gray market. Givenchy and Christian Dior's Dune fragrance are just two of the luxury perfume brands that are sometimes diverted from authorized channels for sale at mass-market retail outlets. LVMH and other luxury goods marketers recently found a new way to combat gray market imports into the United States. In March 1995, the U.S. Supreme Court let stand an appeals court ruling prohibiting a discount drugstore chain from selling Givenchy perfume without permission. Parfums Givenchy USA had claimed that its distinctive packaging should be protected under U.S. copyright law. The ruling means that Costco, Wal-Mart, and other discounters will no longer be able to sell some imported fragrances without authorization.

Asia—particularly Japan—represents important markets for companies such as LVMH. The financial turmoil that began in July 1997 and the subsequent currency devaluations and weakening of the yen have translated into lower demand for luxury goods. Because price perceptions

Table 1

Gray Market Prices for Designer Perfumes

FRAGRANCE/ DESIGNER	AUTHORIZED DISTRIBUTOR/PRICE	UNAUTHORIZED DISCOUNT DISTRIBUTOR/PRICE
Dune (Christian Dior) 3.4 oz spray	Saks Fifth Avenue New York City $60.00	Wal-Mart Bedford Park, Ill $49.94
Shalimar (Guerlain) 1.7 oz spray	Saks Fifth Avenue New York City $49.00	Wal-Mart Bedford Park, Ill. $37.76
Trésor (Lancome) 3.4 oz spray	Macy's New York City $68.00	Drug Emporium Decatur, GA $64.60
Jil Sander (Lancaster Group) 1.7 oz spray	Neiman Marcus White Plains, NY $50.00	Drug Emporium Decatur, GA $40.50

Source: Faye Rice, "Closeout Sale on Gray Goods," *Fortune* (April 3, 1995), p. 18.

are a critical component of luxury goods' appeal, LMVH executives are making a number of adjustments in response to changing business conditions. For example, Patrick Choel, president of the perfume and cosmetics division, has raised wholesale prices in individual Asian markets. The goal is to discourage discount retailers from stocking up with designer products and then selling them to down-market consumers. Also, expenditures on perfume and cosmetics advertising have been reduced to maintain profitability in the face of a possible sales decline. Yves Carcelle, Vuitton chairman is also making adjustments. He has canceled plans for a new store in Indonesia; group managers have raised prices to counteract the effect of currency devaluations. Because the DFS chain depends on Japanese tourists in Asia and Hawaii for 75 percent of sales, Louis Vuitton managers also work with tour operators to predict the flow of Japanese tourists. When tourism is at a peak, price increases from 10 to 22 percent help maximize profits on merchandise sales.

Arnault was confident that the Asian crisis would not severely affect his company's performance in the long term. As Arnault explained in the spring of 1998, "One has to distinguish between Japan, where most of our business is, and the rest of Asia. Japan is in a growth slump, but it isn't going to have the same difficulties as Korea or Indonesia. And our business in Japan is doing very well." Because the Louis Vuitton unit controls its own distribution, management has even been able to take advantage of the crisis by renegotiating store leases in key Asian cities. In some instances, the company has secured longer lease terms plus reductions in rates by as

much as a third. Arnault's optimism was well founded; with interest rates at record lows and a gloomy outlook for the stock market, Japanese consumers have few other spending options these days. In 2001, executives actually raised prices at Louis Vuitton's 45 Japanese stores.

"One friend of mine has 10 Louis Vuitton bags. In Japan, it's a status symbol. It's very important to have European luxury goods." —a 39-year-old flight attendant based in Tokyo

The United States is also a key market for LVMH. One particular marketing program focused on increasing awareness of Hennessy cognac. Thanks to a revival of "cocktail culture" in the United States, sales of hard spirits are up. To promote awareness and consumption among a younger demographic, Hennessy marketing managers recruit twentysomethings to go to upscale bars in major metropolitan markets and order drinks such as the "Hennessy martini" and "Hennessy sidecar" made with cognac. If a bartender doesn't know how to create a particular drink, the Hennessy agent helpfully explains the recipe while attracting the attention of other patrons. Hennessy also picks up the tab when their "secret agents" buy rounds of cognac-based drinks for everyone at the bar. The promotion is designed to increase awareness with young adults and to communicate that cognac can be enjoyed by people other than "old fogies." Chairman Pierre Letzelter is leveraging the company's U.S. success by sending "drink kits" containing swizzle sticks and highball glasses to distributors in Asia.

Such marketing tactics are a world away from the old days, when the companies that today make up LVMH were family-run enterprises focused more on prestige than on profit. They sold mainly to a small, very rich clientele. Even as he broadens the company's consumer base, Arnault has taken a number of steps to raise the level of professionalism of LVMH's management team. In 1997, Arnault implemented a corporate restructuring that groups the company's subsidiaries into divisions. Previously, the heads of individual subsidiaries reported directly to Arnault; now, division heads meet with him to discuss strategy. Notes Arnault, "It's much more efficient, because it allows us to put into practice all the synergies between the different brands in a coordinated way."

Changing times can also be seen in Arnault's choice of American designer Marc Jacobs to create the first-ever Louis Vuitton ready-to-wear line. The line is priced quite high, and to preserve its exclusivity, it is currently available only through Louis Vuitton boutiques. There will be no markdowns on unsold merchandise. Any stocks that remain at the end of the season will be destroyed. Jacobs's first collection included a plain white cotton poplin raincoat that prompted one observer to ask, "Is this luxury?" Ironically, the signature LV is hard to spot on many pieces in the collection, such as a white-on-white patent leather bag.

In the late 1990s, Arnault sensed that cosmetics-buying habits were changing in key markets. He opened Sephora stores in New York, Chicago, and San Francisco in conjunction with a new Web site, Sephora.com. Today, there are more than 70 Sephora stores in the United States; plans call for expanding into Japan and Latin America as well. Customers who visit Sephora USA stores are encouraged to wander freely and sample products on an open floor without waiting for sales clerks to assist them. However, high start-up and promotion costs have reduced the financial contribution that Sephora makes to LVMH, and some analysts have asked when Sephora will be profitable.

Profitability is also an issue with another of Arnault's acquisitions, Donna Karan International Inc. In 2001, Arnault paid more than $600 million for the company and its trademarks. Arnault had tried without success to acquire Giorgio Armani; Donna Karan is LVMH's first American designer label. As Arnault noted, "What appealed to us is the fact that it is one of the best-known brand names in the world." After the deal was completed, however, company executives were surprised to learn that some items from the DKNY line could be found in discount stores such as TJ Maxx. Arnault appointed Giuseppe Brusone, a former managing director of Armani, as Donna Karan's chief executive and instructed him to reshape the company. Brusone intends to improve quality, close company-owned outlet stores, and reduce shipments to department stores to keep the clothes from being marked down. He also intends to shift manufacturing out of New York; the move will both cut costs and lend the line the added prestige associated with garments that are "made in Italy."

All of these actions are designed to keep LVMH—and Arnault himself—at the forefront of the luxury goods business and one step ahead of an ever-changing business environment. Arnault is widely admired for his business instincts and acumen. However, some in the industry view his bold moves as emblematic of all that is wrong with luxury at the dawn of the new millennium. An executive at a competitor noted disapprovingly, "They run this thing like Procter & Gamble." ∎

Visit the Web site
www.lvmh.com
www.sephora.com

DISCUSSION QUESTIONS

1. Bernard Arnault has built LVMH into a luxury goods empire by making numerous acquisitions. What strategy is evident here?
2. How do LVMH executives adjust prices in response to changing economic conditions?
3. Do you think the high retail prices charged for luxury goods are worth paying?
4. How will luxury goods marketers be affected by the slowdown in tourism that followed the terror attacks of September 11, 2001?

SOURCES: Teri Agins and Deborah Ball, "Changing Outfits: Did LVMH Commit a Fashion Faux Pas Buying Donna Karan?" *The Wall Street Journal* (March 21, 2002), pp. A1, A8; Deborah Ball, "Despite Downturn, Japanese Are Still Having Fits for Luxury Goods," *The Wall Street Journal* (April 24, 2001), pp. B1, B4; Bonnie Tsui, "Eye of the Beholder: Sephora's Finances," *Advertising Age* (March 19, 2001), p. 20; Lucia van der Post, "Life's Brittle Luxuries," *Financial Times* (July 18/19, 1998), p. I. Gail Edmondson, "LVMH: Life Isn't All Champagne and Caviar," *Business Week* (November 10, 1997), pp. 108+; Jennifer Steinhauer, "The King of Posh," *The New York Times* (August 17, 1997), sec. 3, pp. 1, 10–11; David Owen, "A Captain Used to Storms," *Financial Times* (June 21/22, 1997); Holly Brubach, "And Luxury for All," *The New York Times Magazine* (July 12, 1998), pp. 24–29+; Amy Barrett, "LVMH's Chairman Remains Calm Despite Turbulence," *The Wall Street Journal* (March 16, 1998), p. B4; Amy Barrett, "Gucci's Big Makeover is Turning Heads," *The Wall Street Journal* (August 26, 1997), p. 12; Stewart Toy, "100 Years of Louis Vuitton," *Cigar Aficionado* (Autumn 1996), pp. 378–379+.

APPENDIX

Section 482 of the Internal Revenue Code

In any case of two or more organizations, trades, or businesses (whether or not incorporated, whether or not organized in the United States, and whether or not affiliated) owned or controlled directly or indirectly by the same interests, the Secretary may distribute, apportion, or allocate gross income, deductions, credits, or allowances between or among such organizations, trades, or businesses, if he determines that such distribution, apportionment, or allocation is necessary in order to prevent evasion of taxes or clearly to reflect the income of any of such organizations, trades, or businesses. In the case of any transfer (or license) of intangible property (within the meaning of section 936(h)(3)(B)), the income with respect to such transfer or license shall be commensurate with the income attributable to the intangible.

SOURCE: *Internal Revenue Code* (New York: The Research Institute of America, 1987), p. 695.

Chapter 13

Global Marketing Channels and Physical Distribution

*H*ypermarkets are giant stores as big as four or more football fields. Part supermarket, part department store, they feature a wide array of product categories—groceries, toys, furniture, fast food, and financial services—all under one roof. Hypermarkets have flourished in Europe for more than three decades. France's Carrefour SA opened the first hypermarket in 1962; with help from the French government, zoning laws ensured that competing stores would be kept from the vicinity. By 1973, the hypermarket concept had been introduced in Spain; today, Carrefour operates 9,000 stores in 27 countries. It is the world's second largest retailer. Most of the European stores were well established before competing retailing concepts such as shopping malls and discount stores made the Atlantic crossing from America. Now the hypermarket concept is being transplanted around the globe. Carrefour has established a strong presence in Asia; in December 2000, it became the first foreign retailer to open a hypermarket in Japan.

Hypermarkets comprise just one of the many elements that make up distribution channels around the globe. The American Marketing Association defines **channel of distribution** as "an organized network of agencies and institutions which, in combination, perform all the activities required to link producers with users to accomplish the marketing task."[1] **Distribution** is the physical flow of goods through channels; as suggested by the definition, channels are made up of a coordinated group of individuals or firms that perform functions that add utility to a product or service. As noted in previous chapters, new global consumer market segments are emerging around the globe. Hypermarket operators are both responding to and fueling this trend;

---

[1] Peter D. Bennett, *Dictionary of Marketing Terms* (Chicago: American Marketing Association, 1988), p. 29.

Customers enter a Carrefour hypermarket in Toulouse, a city in southwestern France. In August 1999, Carrefour and food retailer Promodès announced a merger that created Europe's largest retail chain. The action represents a European counteroffensive against U.S. based Wal-Mart stores, which ranks as the world's #1 retailer.

when Western retailers set up shop in developing countries such as Poland and Indonesia, they provide customers with access to more products and lower prices than ever before. As Tadeusz Donocki, undersecretary of state at Poland's economics ministry, noted recently, "It's a way of bringing dreams closer to people, dreams which before they saw only in films."[2] In developed countries, the arrival of innovators such as Wal-Mart often serves as the catalyst for wrenching changes in long-established distribution traditions (see Case 13-1).

The appearance of hypermarkets around the world adds greater diversity to distribution channels, which already represent the most highly differentiated aspects of national marketing systems. On the opposite end of the spectrum from hypermarkets, for example, are small stores in Latin America called *pulperías*. The diversity of channels and the wide range of possible distribution strategies and market entry options can present challenges to managers responsible for designing global marketing programs. Smaller companies are often blocked by their inability to establish effective channel arrangements. In larger companies that operate via country subsidiaries, channel strategy is the element of the marketing mix that headquarters understands the least. It is important for managers responsible for world marketing programs to understand the nature of international distribution channels. Channels and physical distribution are crucial aspects of the total marketing program; without them, a great product at the right price and effective communications mean very little.

---

2   Stefan Wagstyl, "Eastern Europe Takes a Shine to Hypermarket Shopping," *Financial Times* (January 20, 1999), p. 2.

CHANNEL OBJECTIVES

Marketing channels exist to create utility for customers. The major categories of channel utility are *place* (the availability of a product or service in a location that is convenient to a potential customer), *time* (the availability of a product or service when desired by a customer), *form* (the availability of the product processed, prepared, in proper condition and/or ready to use), and *information* (the availability of answers to questions and general communication about useful product features and benefits). Since these utilities can be a basic source of competitive advantage and comprise an important element of the firm's overall value proposition, choosing a channel strategy is one of the key policy decisions management must make. For example, the Coca-Cola Company's leadership position in world markets is based in part on its ability to put Coke "within an arm's reach of desire"—in other words, to create place utility.

The starting point in selecting the most effective channel arrangement is a clear focus of the company's marketing effort on a target market and an assessment of the way(s) in which distribution can contribute to the firm's overall value proposition. Who are the target customers, and where are they located? What are their information requirements? What are their preferences for service? How sensitive are they to price? Customer preference must be carefully determined because there is as much danger to the success of a marketing program from creating too much utility as there is from creating too little. Moreover, each market must be analyzed to determine the cost of providing channel services. What is appropriate in one country may not be effective in another. Even marketers concerned with a single-country program can study channel arrangements in different parts of the world for valuable information and insight into possible new channel strategies and tactics. For example, retailers from Europe and Asia studied self-service discount retailing in the United States and then introduced the self-service concept in their own countries. Similarly, governments and business executives from many parts of the world have examined Japanese trading companies to learn from their success. Wal-Mart's formula has been closely studied and copied by competitors in the markets it has entered.

DISTRIBUTION CHANNELS: TERMINOLOGY AND STRUCTURE

As defined previously, distribution channels are systems that link manufacturers to customers. Although channels for consumer products and industrial products are similar, there are also some distinct differences. Consumer channels are designed to put products in the hands of people for their own use; as participants in a process known as business-to-business marketing (b-to-b or B2B), industrial channels deliver products to manufacturers or other types of organizations that use them as inputs in the production process or in day-to-day operations. Distributors play important roles in both consumer and industrial channels; a **distributor** is a wholesale intermediary that typically carries product lines or brands on a selective basis. An **agent** is an intermediary who negotiates transactions between two or more parties but does not take title to the goods being purchased or sold.

Consumer Products and Services

Figure 13-1 summarizes six channel structure alternatives for consumer products. The characteristics of both buyers and products have an important influence on

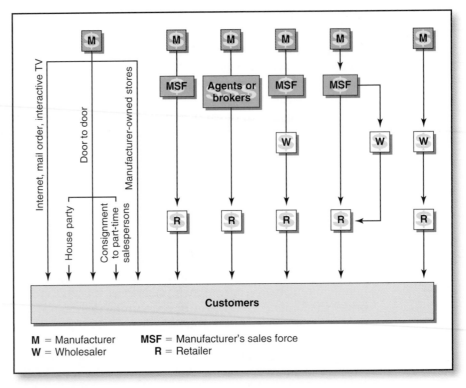

Figure 13-1
Marketing Channel Alternatives: Consumer Products

channel design. The first alternative is to market directly to buyers via the Internet, mail order, various types of door-to-door selling, or manufacturer-owned retail outlets. The other options utilize retailers and various combinations of sales forces, agents/brokers, and wholesalers. The number of individual buyers and their geographic distribution, income, shopping habits, and reaction to different selling methods frequently vary from country to country and may require different channel approaches. Product characteristics such as degree of standardization, perishability, bulk, service requirements, and unit price have an impact as well. Generally speaking, channels tend to be longer (require more intermediaries) as the number of customers to be served increases and the price per unit decreases. Bulky products usually require channel arrangements that minimize the shipping distances and the number of times products change hands before they reach the ultimate customer.

The Internet and related forms of new media are dramatically altering the distribution landscape. eBay pioneered a form of online commerce known as peer-to-peer (p-to-p) marketing; the Internet's potential was quickly recognized by traditional merchants. Now, eBay is assisting large companies such as Disney and IBM set up online "storefronts" to sell items for fixed prices in addition to conducting business-to-consumer (b-to-c) auctions. "As we evolved from auction-style bidding to adding Buy It Now last year, the logical next step for us was to give sellers a place to showcase their listings," said Bill Cobb, eBay's senior vice president for global marketing.[3]

---

3   Nick Wingfield, "Ebay Allows Sellers to Set Up Storefronts Online in Bid to Expand Beyond Auctions," *The Wall Street Journal* (June 12, 2001), p. B8.

Some observers predict that interactive television (ITV) will also become a viable direct distribution channel in the coming years as more households are wired with the necessary two-way technology. Time-pressed consumers in many countries are increasingly attracted to the time and place utility created by the Internet and similar communication technologies.

Low cost, mass-market nondurables products and certain services can be sold door-to-door via a direct sales force. Door-to-door selling is a form of distribution that is mature in the United States; however, it is growing in popularity elsewhere. For example, by the mid-1990s, AIG had 5,000 agents selling insurance policies door-to-door in China. This innovative channel strategy was so successful that domestic Chinese companies such as People's Insurance and Ping An Insurance copied it. Noted one local insurance executive, "We have to adjust ourselves to the rising competition."[4] However, in April 1998, the State Council imposed a blanket ban on all types of direct selling. Although the ban was aimed most directly at illegal pyramid schemes, Mary Kay, Tupperware, Avon, and Amway have been forced to adapt their business models. In the United States, for example, Mary Kay sales representatives are independent entrepreneurs who buy products from the company and then resell them. By contrast, to comply with the new government regulations, members of Mary Kay's Chinese sales force act as agents selling on behalf of the company.[5]

In Japan, the biggest barrier facing U.S. auto manufacturers isn't high tariffs; rather, it's the fact that half the cars that are sold each year are sold door-to-door. Toyota and its Japanese competitors maintain showrooms, but they also employ more than 100,000 car salespeople. Unlike their American counterparts, many Japanese car buyers never visit dealerships. In fact, the close, long-term relationships between auto salespersons and the Japanese people can be thought of as a consumer version of the *keiretsu* system discussed in Chapter 9. Japanese car buyers expect numerous face-to-face meetings with a sales representative, during which trust is established. The relationship continues after the deal is closed; sales reps send cards and continually seek to ensure the buyer's satisfaction. American rivals such as Ford, meanwhile, try to generate showroom traffic. Nobumasa Ogura manages a Ford dealership in Tokyo. "We need to come up with some ideas to sell more cars without door-to-door sales, but the reality is that we haven't come up with any," he said recently."[6]

Another direct selling alternative is the *manufacturer-owned store* or *independent franchise store*. One of the first successful U.S.-based international companies, Singer, established a worldwide chain of company-owned and -operated outlets to sell and service sewing machines. More recently, the Walt Disney Company has revamped its chain of retail outlets that offer apparel, videos, toys, and other merchandise featuring the company's trademarked characters. The company will spend $300 million to establish 600 new stores around the world. The stores are designed to boost annual merchandise sales beyond the current level of $13 billion.[7] As noted in Chapter 9, Japanese consumer electronics companies integrate stores into their distribution groups. Nike, Levi Strauss, well-known fashion design houses, and other companies

---

[4] Craig Smith, "AIG Reshapes China's Insurance Industry," *The Wall Street Journal* (February 9, 1996), p. A8.

[5] Ricky Y. K. Chan, "At the Crossroads of Distribution Reform: China's Recent Ban on Direct Selling," *Business Horizons* 42, no. 5 (September-October 1999), pp. 41–46. See also Virginia A. Hulme, "Mary Kay in China: More Than Makeup," *China Business Review* 28, no. 1 (January-February 2001), pp. 42–46.

[6] Valerie Reitman, "Toyota Calling: In Japan's Car Market, Big Three Face Rivals Who Go Door-to-Door," *The Wall Street Journal* (September 28, 1994), pp. A1, A6.

[7] Bruce Orwall, "Disney's Magic Transformation," *The Wall Street Journal* (October 4, 2000), pp. B1, B4.

Amway and Avon are two companies that have succeeded in extending their direct sales systems outside the United States. Amway currently has operations in 42 countries; in 1997, foreign markets accounted for about three-fourths of the company's $6.8 billion in revenues. Amway's foreign prices tend to be relatively high because all products are exported from the company's Michigan headquarters. In the Philippines, for example, most Amway products are subject to a 30 percent import charge; a 150-milliliter tube of Glister toothpaste sells for $6.54 versus $1.50 for a comparable tube of Colgate.

Avon has successfully used door-to-door sales in dozens of countries identified by company executives as having weak retail infrastructures. Also, it recognized that low discretionary income levels translate into modest expenditures on cosmetics and toiletries. Thus, the role of the sales force is to communicate the benefits of cosmetics and build demand. In such countries as Hungary, the Czech Republic, and Russia, in-home direct selling is the perfect channel strategy. In fact, Avon became the first company permitted to sell door-to-door in China. Since 1990, Avon has operated a joint venture with Guangzhou Cosmetics Factory in the province of Old Canton. However, when Chinese consumers proved to be annoyed by the door-to-door

sales approach, Avon moved quickly to set up branch stores that were more compatible with Chinese shopping behavior. Meanwhile, in the United States, Avon has been forced to update its marketing program to keep pace with a changing marketing environment. Company officials are implementing an e-commerce strategy; in addition, Avon has opened its own beauty centers in malls and also plans to distribute its products through the J.C. Penney retail chain. Analysts forecast that store sales could generate $300 million in retail revenues by 2004. In 2000, Avon also launched its first global advertising campaign.

Avon has recruited several thousand distributors in India, but its efforts to date have been surpassed by Sweden's Oriflame International. Oriflame's cosmetics are available throughout India, thanks to the company's success at recruiting nearly 100,000 sales representatives. The scale and scope of Oriflame's effort make it the most ambitious direct sales effort ever launched in India. Traditionally, India has had a bias against direct selling since it was associated with salesmen hawking goods of dubious quality. However, Avon and Oriflame have succeeded in part by targeting Indian women who are active socially and in part because India has a tradition of "kitty" parties where women sell each other saris and jewelry.

SOURCES: Emily Nelson and Ann Zimmerman, "Avon Goes Store to Store," *The Wall Street Journal* (September 18, 2000), pp. B1, B4; Erin White, "Ding-Dong, Avon Calling (on the Web, Not Your Door)," *The Wall Street Journal* (December 28, 1999), p. A1; Sumit Sharma, "Sell It Yourself: Direct Sales Help Makeup Brand Storm across India," *The Asian Wall Street Journal* (April 28, 1997), p. 10; Emily Nelson and Ann Zimmerman, "Avon Goes Store to Store," *The Wall Street Journal* (September 18, 2000), pp. B1, B4; Erin White, "Ding-Dong, Avon Calling (on the Web, Not Your Door)," *The Wall Street Journal* (December 28, 1999), p. B4; Yumiko Ono, "On a Mission: Amway Grows Abroad, Sending 'Ambassadors' to Spread the Word," *The Wall Street Journal* (May 14, 1997), pp. A1, A6.

with strong brands sometimes establish one or a few flagship retail stores as products showcases or as a means of obtaining marketing intelligence. Such channels supplement, rather than replace, distribution through independent retail stores.

Other channel structure alternatives for consumer products include various combinations of a manufacturer's sales force and wholesalers calling on independent retail outlets, which in turn sell to customers (retailing is discussed in detail later in the chapter). For mass-market consumer products such as ice-cream novelties, cigarettes, and light bulbs that are bought by millions of consumers, a channel that links the manufacturer to distributors and retailers is generally required to achieve market coverage. A channel structure that appears to have more intermediaries than necessary may actually reflect rational adjustment to costs and preferences in a market; it may also present an opportunity to the innovative marketer to pursue competitive advantage by introducing more effective channel arrangements. A cor-

The most successful new market entry in Avon's history is Russia. In 1997, Avon Russia's sales doubled, reaching $56 million. The 44,000 Russian sales representatives promote Avon cosmetics in factories, beauty parlors, and, occasionally, in the homes of friends. Avon has aggressively recruited highly qualified women from the ranks of doctors and engineers, offering them the opportunity to achieve financial independence despite Russia's highly unstable economic environment.

nerstone of Wal-Mart's phenomenal growth in the United States was its ability to achieve significant economies by buying huge volumes of goods directly from manufacturers. However, individual country customs vary. For example, Toys 'R' Us faced considerable opposition from Japanese toy manufacturers that refused to engage in direct selling after the U.S. company opened its first stores in Japan.

Perishable products impose special form utility demands on channel members who must ensure that the merchandise is in satisfactory condition at the time of customer purchase. In developed countries, distribution of perishable food products is handled by a company's own sales force or by independent channel members; in either case, stock is checked by the distributor organization to ensure that it is fresh. In less developed countries, public marketplaces are important channels; they provide a convenient way for producers of vegetables, bread, and other food products to sell their goods directly. Sometimes, a relatively simple channel innovation in a developing country can significantly increase a company's overall value proposition. In the early 1990s, for example, the Moscow Bread Company (MBC) needed to improve its distribution system in the Russian capital. For Russians, bread is truly the staff of life, with consumers queuing up daily to buy fresh loaves at numerous shops and kiosks. Unfortunately, MBC's staff was burdened by excessive paperwork that resulted in the delivery of stale bread. Andersen Consulting found that as much as one-third of the bread the company produced was wasted. In developed countries, about 95 percent of food is sold packaged; the figure is much lower in the former Soviet Union. Whether a consumer bought bread at an open air market or in an enclosed store, it was displayed unwrapped. Therefore, it was imperative for the bread to get from MBC's ovens to the stores in the shortest possible time. Barring an improvement in delivery time, the bread's shelf life had to be extended. The consulting team devised a simple solution—plastic bags to keep the bread fresh. Russian consumers responded favorably to the change; not only did the bags guarantee freshness and extend the shelf life of the bread by 600 percent, but also the bags themselves created utility. In a country where such extras are virtually unknown, the bags constituted a reusable "gift."[8]

Piggyback marketing is another channel innovation that has grown in popularity. In this arrangement, one manufacturer obtains product distribution by utilizing another company's distribution channels. Both parties can benefit: The active distribution partner makes fuller use of its distribution system capacity and thereby increases the total revenue generated by the channel members. The manufacturer using the piggyback arrangement does so at a cost that is much lower than that required for any direct arrangement. Successful piggyback marketing requires that the combined product lines be complementary. They must appeal to the same customer, and they must not compete with each other. If these requirements are met, the piggyback arrangement can be a very effective way of fully utilizing a global channel system to the advantage of both parties.

A case in point is Avon Products, which has a network of direct sales representatives in more than 100 countries. Dozens of companies have taken advantage of the opportunity to piggyback with Avon. Several of Mattel's toy lines are being marketed in China by 85,000 Avon reps; in 1997, Mattel reaped more than $30 million in revenues from sales of Barbie dolls and cosmetics, Hot Wheel toys, and Sesame Street characters. As Andrea Jung, president of global marketing at Avon, explained, "We knew we had a great thing in our hands. Our powerful distribution channel combined with their powerful brand is a huge opportunity." In Australia, New Zealand, Brazil, Canada, and France, Avon reps offer *Reader's Digest* subscriptions along with Avon's health and beauty products. The agreement is reciprocal; Avon's direct response offers "ride along" in Reader's Digest product shipments and targeted mailings. In emerging markets, Avon offers a second catalog featuring products from Timex, Duracell, Time-Life, and others. The products are sold on consignment; piggyback products already account for 15 percent of sales in some emerging markets.[9]

Industrial Products

Figure 13-2 summarizes marketing channel alternatives for the industrial- or business-products company. As is true with consumer channels, product and customer characteristics have an impact on channel structure. Three basic elements are involved: the manufacturer's sales force, distributors or agents, and wholesalers. A manufacturer can reach customers with its own sales force, a sales force that calls on wholesalers who sell to customers, or a combination of these two arrangements. A manufacturer can sell directly to wholesalers without using a sales force, and wholesalers, in turn, can supply customers. Finally, a distributor or agent can call on wholesalers or customers for the manufacturer. For vendors serving a relatively small customer base, a shorter channel design with relatively few (or no) intermediaries may be possible. For example, if there are only ten customers for an industrial product in each national market, these ten customers must be directly contacted by either the manufacturer or an agent.

Channel innovation can be an essential element of a successful marketing strategy. Dell's rise to a leading position in the global PC industry was based on Michael

---

8   "Case Study: Moscow Bread Company," Andersen Consulting, 1993.
9   Tara Parker-Pope and Lisa Bannon, "Avon's New Calling: Sell Barbie in China," *The Wall Street Journal* (May 1, 1997), pp. B1, B5; Clarence Murphy, "Scents and Sensibility," *The Economist* (July 13, 1996), p. 57.

The Rest of the Story
Hypermarkets

In the United States, retailing channels are quite diverse. In addition to long-entrenched shopping malls and discount stores, wholesale clubs such as Pace and Sam's offer rock-bottom prices, and Toys 'R' Us, Circuit City, and other "category killers" offer tremendous depth in particular product categories. In February 1988, Carrefour ("Crossroads" in French) opened its first U.S. hypermarket, a gigantic store in Philadelphia with 330,000 square feet of floor space. Carrefour soon built a second American unit, but then shut down both stores in October 1993. The problem? Many shoppers simply found the stores too big and too overwhelming. Also, although the product assortment was very broad, there was little depth in some product categories. For many products, only one brand or one flavor was available.

The stores' outsized physical scale also changed the economics of profitable operation. For example, consultants for Kmart noted that its hypermarket near Atlanta could only succeed if it attracted four times as many shoppers as a regular discount department store and if the average transaction equaled $43—double the average for discount stores. Meanwhile, costs associated with running the huge stores translated into gross margins of around 8 percent—half the margin of the typical discount store. Finally, Americans just didn't take to mixing food and nonfood purchases in one location. As retail consultant Kurt Barnard noted, "One-stop shopping did not take hold easily. Working parents don't have time for their kids, let alone a shopping expedition that takes hours."

Despite problems in the United States, hypermarkets are thriving elsewhere. There are several reasons for this. First, in countries where shoppers must visit many smaller stores or markets to complete their shopping, the mega-store concept is viewed as a welcome innovation, even though many customers feel loyalty to traditional family-owned stores. Also, hypermarket operators offer free parking in spacious lots, a lure to shoppers in countries where parking spaces are in short supply. A third reason is demographic: As more women enter the workforce, they have less time to shop. While U.S. shoppers can choose from many discount stores and supermarkets, consumers in other countries find that hypermarkets are the only convenient alternative to shopping store-to-store.

Venezuela's first hypermarket, Tiendas Exilo, opened in May 2001. A French/Venezuelan/Colombian partnership opened the store despite Venezuela's relatively small population of 24 million people and an economy mired in recession. The partners reasoned that the soaring cost of living would motivate cconsumers to go bargain hunting.

Carrefour is still fine-tuning its global strategy. In November 1999, it acquired French rival Promodes; valued at $13.6 billion, the deal was the world's largest retail acquisition. In their quest to build a global brand, Carrefour executives changed the names of hundreds of Promodes' Pryca and Continent stores in Spain and France to Carrefour. Confused by the changes, shoppers are going elsewhere. Meanwhile a competitor, the Netherlands-based supermarket operator Royal Ahold NV, is retaining local store names as it expands around the globe. As the company's chief executive said, "Everything the customer sees, we localize. Everything they don't see, we globalize."

"In the future, we will have local companies or global companies but not much in between. Globalization will lead those who are not in the first team, or who are national retailers, to make alliances."
—Daniel Bernard, Chairman Carrefour

SOURCES: Sarah Ellison, "Carrefour and Ahold Find Shoppers Like to Think Local," *The Wall Street Journal* (August 31, 2001), p. A5; Peggy Hollinger, "Carrefour's Revolutionary," *Financial Times* (December 4, 1998), p. 14; Laurie Underwood, "Consumers at a Crossroad," *Free China Review* (February 2, 1995), pp. 66–67; Laurie M. Grossman, "Hypermarkets: A Sure-Fire Hit Bombs," *The Wall Street Journal* (June 25, 1992), p. B1.

Dell's decision to bypass conventional channels by selling direct and by building computers to customers' specifications. Dell began life as a b-to-b marketer; its business model proved so successful that the company then began marketing direct to the home PC market. Consider Boeing aircraft, for example; given the price, physical size, and complexity of a jet airliner, it is easy to understand why Boeing utilizes its own sales force. Other products sold in this way include mainframe computers and

Figure 13-2
Marketing Channel
Alternatives:
Industrial Products

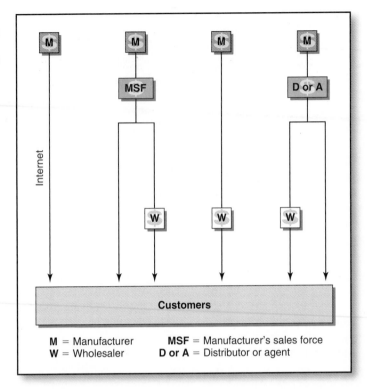

M = Manufacturer   MSF = Manufacturer's sales force
W = Wholesaler   D or A = Distributor or agent

large photocopy systems; these are expensive, complicated products that require both explanation and applications analysis focused on the customer's needs. A company-trained salesperson, sales engineer, or sales team is well suited for the task of creating information utility for computer buyers.

Before deciding which structure to use and which wholesalers and agents to select, managers must study each country individually. In general, the larger the market, the more feasible it is for a manufacturer to use its own sales force. Kyocera Corporation of Kyoto, Japan, has successfully used its own sales force to achieve leadership in the billion-dollar global market for ceramic microchip covers. Company founder Kazuo Inamori went to great lengths to make sure the spiritual drive of Kyocera's unique corporate culture extended to all parts of the company, including the sales force. Kyocera successfully entered the U.S. market by custom-tailoring ceramic chip housings to each customer's needs. Kyocera also became legendary for its service among California's Silicon Valley chipmakers. Breaking with the norm in the electronics industry of using independent distributors, Kyocera relied on a salaried sales force. Early on, Kyocera earned a reputation for answering customer questions overnight, while domestic suppliers often took weeks to respond. Employees worked around the clock to satisfy customer requests for samples. Another hallmark: No company is too small for Kyocera to serve. Jerry Crowley of Gazelle Microcircuits in Santa Clara reported, for example, that Kyocera salespeople began calling on him when he had only 11 employees. Gazelle has been buying custom chip packages from Kyocera ever since. Today, Kyocera has sales forces in the United States, Europe, and Japan that place unwavering emphasis on quality and customer service.

Dell rings up $30 billion in direct sales of made-to-order PC systems. The company experienced phenomenal growth thanks in part to sales generated through the company's Web site. Now founder Michael Dell is moving beyond business-to-business marketing by targeting consumers. He also hopes to achieve success in Asia using the same direct-sales approach that has been effective in more than 100 countries.

Reprinted by permission of Dell Computer Corporation.

ESTABLISHING CHANNELS AND WORKING WITH CHANNEL INTERMEDIARIES

A global company expanding across national boundaries must utilize existing distribution channels or build its own. Channel obstacles are often encountered when a company enters a competitive market where brands and supply relationships are already established. If management chooses *direct involvement*, the company establishes its own sales force or operates its own retail stores. As described earlier, Kyocera used this approach; Kodak adopted the direct approach in Japan, where Kodak Japan is a company-owned distributor. The other option is *indirect involvement*, which entails utilizing independent agents, distributors, and/or wholesalers. Channel strategy in a global marketing program must fit the company's competitive position and overall marketing objectives in each national market. Direct involvement in distribution in a new market can entail considerable expense. Sales representatives and sales management must be hired and trained. The sales organization will inevitably be a heavy loser in its early stage of operation in a new market because it will not have sufficient volume to cover its overhead costs. Therefore, any company contemplating establishing its own sales force should be prepared to underwrite losses for this sales force for a reasonable period of time. As noted previously, whichever strategy a company uses, the process of shaping international channels to fit overall company objectives is constrained by customer and product characteristics.

Channel decisions are important because of the number and nature of relationships that must be managed. Channel decisions typically involve long-term legal commitments and obligations to various intermediaries. Such commitments are often extremely expensive to terminate or change. Even if there is no legal obligation, commitments must be backed by good faith and feelings of mutual obligation. In short, the selection of distributors and agents in a target market is critically important. A good agent or distributor can make the difference between zero performance and performance that is much better than expected.

Companies entering emerging markets for the first time must exercise particular care in choosing a channel intermediary. Typically, a local distributor is required because the market entrant lacks knowledge of local business practices and needs a partner with links to potential customers. In addition, newcomers to a particular market generally want to limit their risk and financial exposure. Although initial results may be satisfactory, with time the local distributor comes to be perceived as performing poorly. This is when managers from the global company often intervene and attempt to take control from the local distributor. Harvard professor David Arnold offers seven specific guidelines to help prevent such problems from arising.[10]

- *Select distributors. Don't let them select you.* A company may link up with a distributor by default after being approached by representatives at a trade fair. In fact, such eager candidates may already be serving a company's competitors. Their objective may be to maintain control over the product category in a given market. A proactive market entrant can identify potential distributors by requesting a list from the U.S. Department of Commerce or its equivalent in other countries. The local chamber of commerce or trade association in a country can provide similar information.
- *Look for distributors capable of developing markets, rather than those with a few good customer contacts.* A distributor with good contacts may appear to be the "obvious" choice in terms of generating quick sales and revenues. However, a better choice is often a partner willing both to make the investment necessary to achieve success and draw upon the marketing experience of the global company. Such a partner may, in fact, have no prior experience with a particular product category. In this case, the distributor may devote more effort and assign the new partner a higher priority simply because taking on the product line does not represent the status quo.
- *Treat local distributors as long-term partners, not temporary market-entry vehicles.* A contractual agreement that provides strong financial incentives for customer acquisition, new product sales, or other forms of business development is a signal to the distributor that the market entrant is taking a long-term perspective. Such development can be done with the input of managers from the global company.
- *Support market entry by committing money, managers, and proven marketing ideas.* In addition to providing sales personnel and technical support, management should consider demonstrating its commitment early on by investing in a

---

[10] The following discussion is adapted from David Arnold, "Seven Rules of International Distribution," *Harvard Business Review* 78, no. 6 (November-December 2000), pp. 131–137.

minority equity stake in an independent distributor. The risks associated with such investment should be no greater than risks associated with independent distribution systems in the manufacturer's home country. The earlier such a commitment is made, the better the relationship that is likely to develop.

- *From the start, maintain control over marketing strategy.* To exploit the full potential of global marketing channels, the manufacturer should provide solid leadership for marketing in terms of which products the distributor should sell and how to position them. Again, it is necessary to have employees on site or to have country or regional managers monitor the distributor's performance. As one manager noted, "We used to give far too much autonomy to distributors, thinking that they knew their markets. But our value proposition is a tough one to execute, and time and again we saw distributors cut prices to compensate for failing to target the right customers or to sufficiently train salespeople." This is not to say that the intermediary should not be allowed to adapt the distribution strategy to suit local conditions. The point is for the manufacturer to take the lead.

- *Make sure distributors provide you with detailed market and financial performance data.* Distributor organizations are often a company's best source—maybe the only source—of market information. The contract between a manufacturer and distributor should include specific language to the effect that local market information and financial data will be transferred back to the manufacturer. One sign that a successful manufacturer/distributor relationship can be established is the latter's willingness to provide such information.

- *Build links among national distributors at the earliest opportunity.* A manufacturer should attempt to establish links between its networks of national distributors. This can be accomplished by setting up a regional corporate office or by establishing a distributor council. At any point in time, a company may have some excellent agents and distributors, others that are satisfactory, and a third group that is unsatisfactory. By creating opportunities for distributors to communicate, ideas for new product designs based on individual market results can be leveraged, and overall distributor performance can be improved.

When devising a channel strategy, it is necessary to be realistic about the motives of the typical channel intermediary. On the one hand, it is the intermediary's responsibility to implement an important element of a company's marketing strategy. Left to their own devices, however, middlemen may seek to maximize their own profit rather than the manufacturer's. Middlemen sometimes engage in **cherry picking,** the practice of taking orders only from manufacturers with established demand for products and brands. Cherry picking can also take the form of selecting only a few choice items from a vendor's product lines. This is a rational course of action for the middleman, but it can present a serious obstacle to a manufacturer who is attempting to break into a market with a new product. The cherry picker is not interested in developing a market for a new product, which is a problem for the expanding international company. As noted previously, a manufacturer should provide leadership and invest resources to build the relationship with a desired distributor. A manufacturer with a new product or a product with a limited market share may find it more desirable to set up some arrangement for bypassing the cherry-picking channel member. In some cases, a manufacturer must incur the costs of direct involvement by setting up its own distribution organization to obtain a share of the market. When the company sales finally reach critical mass, management may decide to shift from direct involvement to a more cost-effective independent intermediary. The move does not mean that intermediaries are "better" than direct distribution. Such a move

A Matter of Culture
Channels in Less-Developed Countries

One of the conspicuous features of retail channels in less-developed countries is the remarkable number of people engaged in selling very small quantities of merchandise. In Ethiopia and other East African countries, for example, an open window in the side of a building is likely to be a *souk,* a small walk-up store whose proprietor sells everything from toilet paper and playing cards to rice and eggs. To maximize sales, *souks* are strategically interspersed throughout neighborhood areas. The proprietors know what customers want and need. For example, early in the day they may sell incense and a paper cone with enough coffee for the morning coffee ceremony. In the evening, cigarettes and gum may be in demand, especially if the *souk* is located near a neighborhood nightclub. If a *souk* is closed, it is often possible to rouse the proprietor by knocking on the window, because the store also serves as the proprietor's domicile. Some *souk* owners even provide curb service and bring items to a customer waiting in a car.

By comparison, government department stores in East Africa are less likely to display such a service orientation. Government stores may be stocked with mass quantities of items that are slow to sell. For example, the shelves may hold row after row of tinned tomatoes, even though fresh tomatoes are readily available year around in the market. Customers must go through several steps before actually taking possession of their purchases—determining what goods are available, making a purchase decision, moving to another area to pay, and finally, taking possession of the goods. This usually involves a substantial number of papers, seals, and stamps, as well as interaction

with two or three clerks. Clerk jobs are highly prized in countries where jobs are scarce; compared to the *souk* proprietor, who is willing to work from dawn to dusk, the government employee works from 9:00 a.m. to 5:00 p.m. with two hours off for lunch.

In Costa Rica, the privately owned *pulpería* is similar to the Western-style general store that was popular in the first part of the twentieth century. Customers enter the store, tell clerks what items are desired, and the clerks fetch the items—which may range from chicken feed to thumb tacks. A typical *pulpería* stocks staples such as sugar and flour in 50-kilo bags, which the proprietor resells in smaller portions. Most *pulperías* have a refrigeration unit so they can sell ice cream novelties; in areas where there is no electricity, the *pulpería* owner will use a generator to provide power for the refrigerator. *Pulperías* are serviced by a fleet of private wholesalers; on any given day, the soft drink truck, the candy truck, or the staples truck may make deliveries. The *pulpería* serves as a central gathering place for the neighborhood and generally has a public telephone from which patrons can make calls for a fee. This attracts many people to the store in communities where there are few, if any, telephones.

Both the *souk* and the *pulpería* typically offer an informal system of credit. People who patronize these shops usually live in the neighborhood and are known to the proprietor. Often, the proprietor will extend credit if he or she knows that a customer has suffered a setback such as loss of a job or a death in the family. Informally, the proprietors of private retail shops fulfill the role of a lender, especially for people who do not have access to credit through regular financial institutions.

SOURCE: Private communication from Brian Larson of CARE Niger.

is simply a response by a manufacturer to cost considerations and the newly acquired attractiveness of the company's product to independent distributors.

An alternative method of dealing with the cherry-picking problem does not require setting up an expensive direct sales force. Rather, a company may decide to rely on a distributor's own sales force by subsidizing the cost of the sales representatives the distributor has assigned to the company's products. This approach has the advantage of holding down costs by tying selling in with the distributor's existing sales management team and physical distribution system. With this approach it is possible to place managed direct selling support and distribution support behind a product at the expense of only one salesperson per selling area. The distributor's incentive for cooperating in this kind of arrangement is that he or she obtains a "free" sales representative for a new product with the potential to be a profitable addition to his or her line. This cooperative arrangement is ideally suited to getting a new export-sourced product into distribution in a market. A company may also decide to provide special incentives to independent channel agents; however, this approach can be expensive. The company might offer outright payments—either direct cash bonuses or contest awards—tied to sales performance. In competitive markets with sufficiently high prices, incentives could take the form of gross margin guarantees.

GLOBAL RETAILING

Global retailing is any retailing activity that crosses national boundaries. Since the mid-1970s, there has been growing interest among successful retailers in expanding globally. However, this not a new phenomenon. For centuries, entrepreneurial merchants have ventured abroad both to obtain merchandise and ideas and to establish retail operations. During the nineteenth and early twentieth centuries, British, French, Dutch, Belgian, and German trading companies established retailing organizations in Africa and Asia. International trading and retail store operation were two of the economic pillars of the colonial system of that era. In the twentieth century, Dutch retailer C&A expanded across Europe, and Woolworth crossed the Atlantic from the United States to the United Kingdom. Today's global retailing scene is characterized by great variety (the top 25 companies are listed in Table 13-1). Before proceeding to a detailed discussion of global retailing issues, we will briefly survey some of the different forms retailing can take. Retail stores can be divided into categories according to the amount of square feet of floor space, the level of service offered, width and depth of product offerings, or other criteria.

Department stores literally have several departments under one roof, each representing a distinct merchandise line and staffed with a limited number of salespeople. Departments in a typical store might include men's, women's, children's, beauty aids, housewares, and toys. Examples from around the world include Marks & Spencer, Macy's, Bay, Auchan, and Mitsukoshi.

Specialty retailers offer less variety than department stores. They are more narrowly focused and feature a relatively narrow merchandise mix aimed at a particular target market. Specialty stores offer a great deal of merchandise depth (e.g., many styles, colors, and sizes), high levels of service from knowledgeable staff persons, and a marketing premise that is both clear and appealing to consumers. Laura Ashley, Body Shop, Victoria's Secret, Gap, Starbucks, and the Disney Store are examples.

Supermarkets are departmentalized, single-story retail establishments that offer a variety of food (e.g., produce, baked goods, meats) and nonfood items (e.g., paper products, health and beauty aids), mostly on a self-service basis. Tesco, Sainsbury, Safeway, A&P, and Sparr are some examples; on average, supermarkets have between 50,000 and 60,000 square feet of floor space. A comparison of food distribution in countries at different stages of development illustrates how channels reflect and respond to underlying market conditions in a country. In the United States, several factors combine to make the supermarket or the self-service one-stop food store the basic food-retailing unit: high incomes, large-capacity refrigerator-freezer units, high levels of automobile ownership, and high reliance on frozen and convenience foods. Many shoppers want to purchase a week's worth of groceries in one trip to the store. They have the money, ample storage space in the refrigerator, and the hauling capacity of the car to move this large quantity of food from the store to the home. The supermarket, because it is efficient, can fill the food shoppers' needs at lower prices than butcher shops and other traditional full-service food stores. Additionally,

Table 13-1
Top 25 Global Retailers (1999 sales; $ millions)

RANK	COMPANY	COUNTRY	FORMATS	SALES
1	Wal-Mart Stores	USA	Discount store, Wholesale club	$156,250
2	Carrefour (incl. Promodes)	France	Hypermarket	55,302
3	Metro	Germany	Diversified	46,633
4	Kroger	USA	Supermarket	45,352
5	Home Depot	USA	Home improvement	38,434
6	Albertson's	USA	Supermarket	37,478
7	Sears Roebuck	USA	Department store/General merchandise	36,728
8	Rewe Gruppe	Germany	Diversified	36,561
9	Kmart	USA	Discount store/Specialty	35,925
10	Ahold	Netherlands	Supermarket/Hypermarket	35,775
11	ITM Entreprises (incl. Spar)	France	Diversified	35,218
12	Target	USA	Discount/Department store	33,212
13	Edeka Gruppe (incl. AVA)	Germany	Diversified	31,788
14	Aldi Gruppe	Germany	Food/Discount	31,570
15	J.C. Penney	USA	Department store/Drug store	31,391
16	Tesco	UK	Supermarket/Hypermarket	30,401
17	Tengelmann Gruppe	Germany	Diversified	29,501
18	Safeway	USA	Supermarket	28,860
19	Costco	USA	Food/General merchandise	26,976
20	Sainsbury	UK	Supermarket, Hypermarket, DIY	25,835
21	Leclerc	France	Diversified	23,532
22	Auchan	France	Hypermarket/Diversified	23,449
23	Otto Versand	Germany	Mail order	22,066
24	Daiei	Japan	Food/General merchandise	19,391
25	CVS	USA	Drug store	18,098

Source: Reprinted by permission from *Chain Store Age* (November 1997), Copyright Lebhar-Friedman, Inc. 425 Park Ave, NY, NY 10022

supermarkets can offer more variety and a greater selection of merchandise than can smaller food stores, a fact that appeals to affluent consumers.[11]

In other parts of the world the supermarket revolution came many years later. France, Belgium, Spain, Brazil, and Colombia are some of the countries in which supermarket retailing quickly took hold as large, modern, highly efficient stores were built. In Italy, by contrast, legislation limiting the opening of large supermarkets has been a restraining force; as a result, large format stores grew in popularity more gradually. Asia is the next frontier for the grocery business; as Laurent Zeller, managing director of a French market research firm, commented, "When I got to Asia in 1996, retailers here were still very traditional compared to, say, South America, where hypermarkets had been growing for ten years." Although Wal-Mart is generating headlines as it moves around the globe, American retailers lag behind

---

[11] For an excellent account of the history of supermarket retailing in the United States, see David B. Sicilia, "Supermarket Sweep," *Audacity* (Spring 1997), pp. 10–19.

the Europeans in moving outside their home countries. One reason is the sheer size of the domestic U.S. market.[12]

Convenience stores offer some of the same products as supermarkets, but the merchandise mix is limited to high-turnover convenience products. In terms of square footage, these are the smallest stores of the various retail categories discussed here. Prices for some products may be 15 to 20 percent higher than supermarket prices. As the name implies, these stores are located in high-traffic locations and offer expanded hours to accommodate commuters, students, and other highly mobile consumers. Some convenience store chains are regional (e.g., Casey's, Kum & Go, Tom Thumb, Love's); others, such as 7-Eleven, have operations in several countries.

Discount stores can be divided into several categories. The most general characteristic that they have in common is the emphasis on low prices. *Full-line discounters* typically offer a wide range of merchandise, including non-food items and nonperishable food, in a limited-service format. In Canada, for example, Hudson Bay's Zellers is the largest discount-store chain. French discounter Tati is going global; in addition to opening a store on New York's Fifth Avenue, Tati currently has stores in Lebanon, Turkey, Germany, Belgium, Switzerland, and the Cote d'Ivoire.

Wal-Mart is the reigning king of the full-line discounters, with many stores covering 120,000 square feet (or more) of floor space; food accounts for about a third of floor space and sales. Wal-Mart stores typically offer middle-class customers a folksy atmosphere and value-priced brands. Wal-Mart doesn't stock Levi's blue jeans, for example, but they do carry the Rustler and Wrangler brands. Wal-Mart also features the company's Sam's Club private label in a number of categories.

Wal-Mart is also a leader in the **warehouse club** segment of discount retailing; consumers "join" the club to take advantage of low prices on products displayed in their shipping boxes in a "no frills" atmosphere. Wal-Mart has taken its Sam's Club stores into Mexico and Brazil.

Hypermarkets, which were discussed in the chapter introduction, are a hybrid retailing format combining the discounter, supermarket, and warehouse club approaches under a single roof. Size-wise, hypermarkets are huge, covering 200,000 to 300,000 square feet.

Supercenters offer a wide range of aggressively priced grocery items plus general merchandise in a space that occupies about half the size of a hypermarket. Supercenters are an important aspect of Wal-Mart's growth strategy, both at home and abroad. Wal-Mart opened its first supercenter in 1988; today, it operates more than 450 supercenters, including 12 stores in Mexico and units in Argentina and Brazil. Some prices at Wal-Mart's supercenters in Brazil are as much as 15 percent lower than competitors', and some observers wonder if the company has taken the discount approach too far. Company officials insist that profit margins are in the 20 to 22 percent range.[13]

Category killers is the label many in the retailing industry use when talking about stores such as Toys 'R' Us, Home Depot, and IKEA. The name refers to the fact that such stores specialize in a particular product category such as toys or furniture and offer a vast selection at low prices. In short, these stores represent retailing's "900-pound gorillas" that essentially demolish smaller, more traditional competitors

---

[12] Michael Flagg, "In Asia, Going to the Grocery Increasingly Means Heading for a European Retail Chain," *The Wall Street Journal* (April 24, 2001), p. A21.

[13] Matt Moffett and Jonathan Friedland, "Wal-Mart Won't Discount Its Prospects in Brazil, Though Its Losses Pile Up," *The Wall Street Journal* (June 4, 1996), p. A15; Wendy Zellner, "Wal-Mart Spoken Here," *Business Week* (June 23, 1997), pp. 138–139+.

and prompt department stores to scale down merchandise sections that are in direct competition (see Case 13-1).

Outlet stores are retail operations that allow companies with well-known consumer brands to dispose of excess inventory, out-of-date merchandise, or factory seconds. To attract large numbers of shoppers, outlet stores are often grouped together in **outlet malls.** The United States is home to 320 outlet malls such as the giant Woodbury Common mall in Central Valley, New York. Now, the concept is catching on in Europe and Asia as well. The acceptance reflects changing attitudes among consumers and retailers; in both Asia and Europe, brand-conscious consumers are eager to save money.

Currently, a number of environmental factors have combined to push retailers out of their home markets in search of opportunities around the globe. Saturation of the home country market, recession or other economic factors, strict regulation on store development, and high operating costs are some of the factors that prompt management to look abroad for growth opportunities. Wal-Mart is a case in point; its international expansion in the mid-1990s coincided with disappointing financial results in its home market (see Case 13-1).

Even as the domestic retailing environment grows more challenging for many companies, an ongoing environmental scanning effort is likely to turn up markets in other parts of the world that are underdeveloped or where competition is weak. In addition, high rates of economic growth, a growing middle class, a high proportion of young people in the population, and less stringent regulation combine to make some country markets very attractive.[14] Laura Ashley, Body Shop, Disney Stores, and other specialty retailers are being lured to Japan by developers who need established names to fill space in large, suburban, American-style shopping malls.[15] Such malls are being developed as some local and national restrictions on retail development are being eased and as consumers tire of the aggravations associated with shopping in congested urban areas.

However, the large number of unsuccessful cross-border retailing initiatives suggests that anyone contemplating a move into global retailing should do so with a great deal of caution. Among those that have scaled back expansion plans in the face of disappointment are France's Galeries Lafayette and Shanghai-based Yaohan Group. Galeries Lafayette opened a New York store on fashionable Fifth Avenue; however, the merchandise mix suffered in comparison with offerings at posh competitors such as Henri Bendel and Bonwit Teller. Yaohan has more than 400 stores in 13 countries, including the United States and China. However, Chinese expansion plans are on hold as consumers have reacted indifferently to the 10-story megastore in Shanghai. As one Chinese consumer remarked, "It's just so-so. I'm not really impressed."[16] Speaking of global opportunities for U.S.-based retailers, one industry analyst noted, "It's awfully hard to operate across the water. It's one thing to open up in Mexico and Canada, but the distribution hassles are just too big when it comes to exporting an entire store concept overseas."[17]

---

[14] Ross Davies and Megan Finney, "Retailers Rush to Capture New Markets," *Financial Times—Mastering Global Business,* Part VII, 1998, pp. 2–4.

[15] Norihiko Shirouzu, "Japanese Mall Mogul Dreams of American Stores," *The Wall Street Journal* (July 30, 1997), pp. B1, B10; Shirouzu, "Jusco Bets That U.S.-Style Retail Malls Will Revolutionize Shopping in Japan," *The Wall Street Journal* (April 21, 1997), p. A8.

[16] Norihiko Shirouzu and Fara Waner, "Asian Retailing Titan Hits a Great Wall," *The Wall Street Journal* (January 17, 1997), p. A10.

[17] Neil King Jr., "Kmart's Czech Invasion Lurches Along," *The Wall Street Journal* (June 8, 1993), p. A11.

The critical question for the would-be global retailer is, "What advantages do we have relative to local competition?" The answer will often be, "Nothing," when competition, local laws governing retailing practice, distribution patterns, or other factors are taken into account. However, a company may possess competencies that can be the basis for competitive advantage in a particular retail market. A retailer has several things to offer consumers. Some are readily perceived by customers, such as selection, price, and the overall manner in which the goods are offered in the store setting. The last includes such things as store location, parking facilities, in-store atmosphere, and customer service. Competencies can also be found in less visible value chain activities such as distribution, logistics, and information technology.

For example, contrary to Japan's service-oriented reputation, Japanese retailers traditionally offered few extra services to their clientele. There were no special orders, no returns, and stock was chosen not according to consumer demand but, rather, according to purchasing preferences of the stores. Typically, a store would buy limited quantities from each of its favorite manufacturers and then, when the goods sold out, consumers had no recourse. Instead of trying to capitalize on the huge market, many retailers simply turn a deaf ear to customer needs. From the retailers' point of view, this came out fine in the end, however; most of their stock eventually sold as buyers were forced to purchase what was left over. They had no other choice. As Gap, Eddie Bauer, and other American retailers have entered Japan with liberal return policies, a willingness to take special orders, and a policy of replenishing stock, many Japanese consumers have switched loyalties. Also, thanks to economies of scale and modern distribution methods unknown to some Japanese department store operators, the American companies offer a greater variety of goods at lower prices. While upscale foreign competition has hurt Japanese department store operators, Japan's depressed economy is another factor. Traditional retailers are also being squeezed from below as recession-pressed consumers flock to discounters such as the ¥100 Shop chain.

JC Penney is expanding retailing operations internationally for a number of reasons cited here. After touring several countries, Penney executives realized that retailers outside the United States often lack marketing sophistication when grouping and displaying products and locating aisles to optimize customer traffic. For example, a team visiting retailers in Istanbul in the early 1990s noted that one store featured lingerie next to plumbing equipment. As CEO William R. Howell noted at the time, Penney's advantage in such instances was its ability to develop an environment that invites the customer to shop. Although it struggled in Indonesia, the Philippines, and Chile, Penney has met with great success in Brazil. In 1999, the American retailer purchased a controlling stake in Renner, a regional chain with 21 stores. Crucially, Penney maintained the local name and local management team. Meanwhile, Renner, benefiting from Penney's expertise in logistics, distribution, and branding, has become Brazil's fastest-growing chain, with a total of 49 stores.[18]

A matrix-based scheme for classifying global retailers is shown in Figure 13-3.[19] One axis represents private or own-label focus versus a manufacturer brands focus. The other axis differentiates between retailers specializing in relatively few product categories and retailers that offer a wide product assortment. IKEA, in quadrant A, is

---

[18] Miriam Jordan, "Penney Blends Two Business Cultures," *The Wall Street Journal* (April 5, 2001), p. A15.
[19] The discussion in this section is adapted from Jacques Horovitz and Nirmalya Kumar, "Strategies for Retail Globalization," *Financial Times—Mastering Global Business*, part VII, 1998, pp. 4–8.

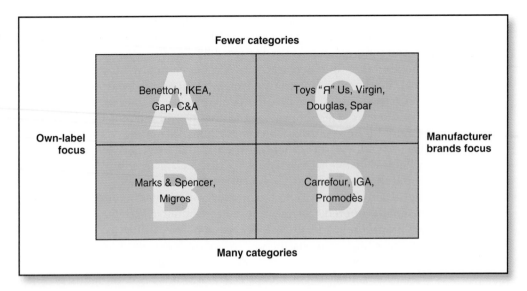

Figure 13-3
Global Retailing Categories

Source: Adapted from Jacques Horovitz and Nirmalya Kumar, "Strategies for Retail Globalization," *Financial Times—Mastering Global Business*, part VII, 1998, p. 4.

a good example of a global retailer with a niche focus (assemble-yourself furniture for the home) as well as an own-label focus (IKEA sells its own brand). IKEA and other retailers in quadrant A typically use extensive advertising and product innovation to build a strong brand image.

In quadrant B, the private-label focus is retained, but many more product categories are offered. This is the strategy of Marks & Spencer (M&S), the British-based department store company whose St. Michael private label is found on a broad range of clothing, food, home furnishings, jewelry, and other items. Private label retailers that attempt to expand internationally face a double-edged challenge: They must attract customers to both the store and the branded merchandise. M&S has succeeded by virtue of an entrepreneurial management style that has evolved over the last 100-plus years. M&S opened its first store outside the United Kingdom in 1974; it currently operates in 32 countries. In 1997, then-chairman Sir Richard Greenbury announced an ambitious plan to put M&S "well on its way to establishing a global business." It was his belief that consumer tastes are globalizing, at least with respect to fashion apparel. Food is a different story; because tastes are more localized, M&S executives anticipate that the proportion of revenues from food sales will be lower than they are in Great Britain.[20] The difficulty of today's retailing environment is underscored by Marks & Spencer's recent financial woes. The company's profits and share price plunged in the late 1990s amid a sales slump and infighting between top executives; Sir Richard left the company in 1998. A turnaround is underway, with a new human resources strategy as an important element.

Retailers in the upper right quadrant offer many well-known brands in a relatively tightly defined merchandise range. Here, for example, we find Toys 'R' Us,

[20] Rufus Olins, "M&S Sets Out Its Stall for World Domination," *The Sunday Times* (November 9, 1997), p. 6. See also Andrew Davidson, "The Andrew Davidson Interview: Sir Richard Greenbury," *Management Today* (November 2001), pp. 62–67; and Judi Bevan, *The Rise and Fall of Marks & Spencer* (London: Profile Books, 2001).

which specializes in toys and includes branded products from Mattel, Nintendo, and other marketers. Additional examples include such category killers as Blockbuster Video and Virgin Stores. As noted earlier, this type of store tends to quickly dominate smaller established retailers by out-merchandizing local competition and offering customers superior value by virtue of extensive inventories and low prices. Typically, the low prices are the result of buyer power and sourcing advantages that local retailers lack. The retailing environment in which Richard Branson built the Virgin Megastore chain illustrates once again the type of success that can be achieved through an entrepreneurial management style:

> It required little retailing expertise to see that the sleepy business practices of traditional record shops provided a tremendous opportunity. To rival the tiny neighborhood record shops, with their eclectic collections of records, a new kind of record store was coming into being. It was big; it was well-lit, and records were arranged clearly in alphabetical order by artist; it covered most tastes in pop music comprehensively; and it turned over its stock much faster than the smaller record retailer. . . It was the musical equivalent of a supermarket.[21]

Visit the Web site
www.marks-and-spencer.com
www.carrefour.com
www.virgin.com

Starting with one Megastore location on London's Oxford Street in 1975, Branson's Virgin Retail empire now extends throughout Europe, North America, Japan, Hong Kong, and Taiwan.

Carrefour, Promodès, Wal-Mart, and other retailers in the fourth quadrant offer the same type of merchandise available from established local retailers. What the newcomers bring to a market, however, is competence in distribution or some other value chain element. To date, Wal-Mart's international division has established more than 1,000 stores outside the United States; it is already the biggest retailer in Mexico and Canada. Other store locations include Argentina, Brazil, China, and Germany. International revenues for the fiscal year ended January 31, 2001, totaled $37.7 billion, compared with only $7.5 billion four years previously.

Richard Branson, founder and chairman of the Virgin Group, at the opening of a Megastore in New York's Time Square. The $15 million facility occupies 75,000 square feet of space on three levels and features more than one thousand music listening stations. The charismatic Branson is so closely associated with his company that, in the minds of many observers, the man is the brand.

---

[21] Tim Jackson, *Virgin King: Inside Richard Branson's Business Empire* (London: HarperCollins, 1995), p. 277.

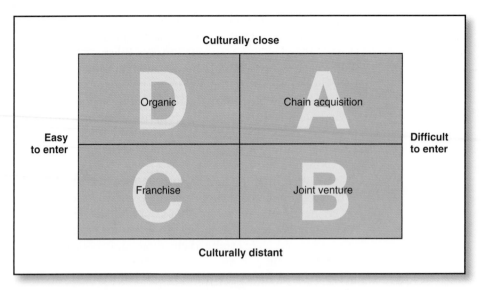

Figure 13-4
Global Retailing Market Entry Strategy Framework

Source: Adapted from Jacques Horovitz and Nirmalya Kumar, "Strategies for Retail Globalization," *Financial Times—Mastering Global Business,* part VII, 1998, p. 5.

Four market entry expansion strategies are available to retailers that wish to cross borders. As shown in Figure 13-4, these strategies can be captured conceptually by a matrix that differentiates between (1) markets that are easy to enter versus those that are difficult to enter and (2) culturally close markets versus culturally distant ones. The upper half of the matrix encompasses quadrants A and D and represents markets in which shopping patterns and retail structures are similar to those in the home country. In the lower half of the matrix, quadrants C and B represent markets that are significantly different from the home country market in terms of one or more cultural characteristics. The right side of the matrix, in quadrants A and B, represents markets that are difficult to enter because of the presence of strong competitors, location restrictions, excessively high rent or real estate costs, or other factors. In quadrants C and D, any barriers that exist are relatively easy to overcome. The four entry strategies indicated by the matrix are organic, franchise, chain acquisition, and joint venture.

Organic growth occurs when a company uses its own resources to start a store from scratch or to acquire existing retail facilities from others. In 1997, for example, Marks & Spencer announced plans to expand from one store to four in Germany via the purchase of three stores operated by Cramer and Meerman. When Richard Branson set up the first Virgin Megastore in Paris, he did so by investing millions of pounds in a spectacular retail space on the Champs-Elysées. From the perspective of M&S and Virgin, the retail environments of Germany and France are both culturally close and easy to enter. Of course, the success of this strategy hinges on the availability of company resources to sustain the high cost of the initial investment.

Franchising, shown in quadrant C of Figure 13-4, is the appropriate entry strategy when barriers to entry are low yet the market is culturally distant in terms of consumer behavior or retailing structures. As defined in Chapter 9, franchising is a contractual relationship between two companies. The parent company-franchisor authorizes a franchisee to operate a business developed by the franchisor in return for a fee and adherence to franchise-wide policies and practices. The key to a successful franchise operation is the ability to transfer company know-how to new markets. Benetton, IKEA, and other focused, private-label retailers often use franchising as a market-entry strategy in combination with wholly owned stores that represent organic growth. IKEA has more than 100 company-owned stores across Europe and the United States; its stores in the Middle East and Hong Kong are franchise operations.

In global retailing, **acquisition** is a market-entry strategy that entails purchasing multiple existing outlets in a foreign country. This strategy can provide the buyer with quick growth as well as access to existing brand suppliers, distributors, and customers. Marks & Spencer, for example, had no plans for organic growth in the United States; rather, it acquired the upscale private-label American retailer Brooks Brothers in 1988 for $750 million. Executives at Brooks Brothers spent most of 1990 trying to expand the brand's customer base, and recent results have been promising. With hindsight, however, it is clear that M&S paid too much for the acquisition. As noted previously, M&S is currently in the midst of its own financial retrenchment; at the end of 2001, it was announced that Brooks Brothers would be sold to Retail Brand Alliance, a private holding company.

Joint ventures, the final entry strategy, have been examined in detail in an earlier chapter. With regard to global retailing, a joint-venture strategy is advisable when culturally distant, difficult-to-enter markets are targeted. Many Western retailers are using joint ventures to enter China, Japan, and other Asian countries. The ownership split can be adjusted in proportion to perceived entry difficulty and previous experience. Virgin Group's retail expansion in Asia provides a case study in the appropriateness of the joint-venture approach. In Japan, commercial landlords typically require millions in up-front payments before they will lease retail space. Accordingly, in 1992, Virgin established a joint venture called Virgin Megastores Japan with Marui, a local retailer with a good track record of catering to the preferences of young people. The first megastore was set up in the basement of an existing Marui department store in Japan's Shinjuku district. That and subsequent stores have been wildly successful; Virgin has duplicated the joint-venture approach elsewhere in Asia, including Hong Kong, Taiwan, and South Korea. In each location, Virgin establishes a joint venture with a leading industrial group.[22]

Of course, achieving retailing success outside the home country market is not simply a matter of consulting a matrix and choosing the recommended entry strategy. Management must also be alert to the possibility that the merchandise mix, sourcing strategy, distribution, or other format elements will have to be adapted. Management at Crate & Barrel, for example, is hesitant to open stores in Japan. Part of the reason is research indicating that at least half the company's product line would have to be modified to accommodate local preferences. Another issue is the company's ability to transfer its expertise to new country markets.

INNOVATION IN INTERNATIONAL RETAILING

As noted at the beginning of this chapter, distribution channels around the world are highly differentiated. On the surface, it appears this differentiation can be explained only in terms of culture and the income level that exists in the market. However, the

---

[22] Tim Jackson, *Virgin King: Inside Richard Branson's Business Empire* (London: HarperCollins, 1995), pp. 289–291.

British retailers have had a very difficult time in the United States because they often fail to appreciate that the United States is a very different retailing environment. What works in the United Kingdom, in spite of the common language and the apparent similarity in consumer tastes, will not automatically work in the United States. In the United Kingdom, retailers typically locate their stores on "high streets," which are roughly equivalent to downtown in the United States. However, America is the land of the mall; there are no "high streets" in most American cities. Site selection is critically important for retailing success, and the British have often done a poor job in this key area.

Other problems include breaking through to get the consumer's attention. Because U.S. consumers are brand loyal, overcoming their resistance to change requires huge marketing budgets, and the British are accustomed to skimping in this area. Product line policy and pricing are also areas of difference where many British retailers have tripped up. British retailers don't offer the variety that U.S. consumers expect, and they don't rely nearly as much on price discounting. In the United States, fresh product assortments and aggressive pricing drive retailing. Anita Roddick got her Body Shop off to a good start in the United States and

then watched as Limited jumped into the category with Bath & Body Works, a division it launched in 1992. Bath & Body Works captured Body Shop's market by constantly changing products, entering as many malls as possible, and by keeping prices lower. Meanwhile, Body Shop did not even have a formal marketing department. Today, Bath & Body Works dominates the category that Body Shop created.

All of the differences identified here are clear to successful American retailers. They are not always clear to successful British retailers. The reason for this is the self-reference criterion (SRC). As described in Chapter 4, this is the practice of seeing what one knows and remembers from previous experience instead of what is actually true. Instead of seeing the reality of the U.S. market, many British retailers have seen (dimly) a copy of the British market. The companies that have avoided this trap are the exceptions to the rule. Richard Branson, the entrepreneurial leader of Virgin, has built the Virgin brand in the United States the American way—by adding more and more products and by being noisy and loud about the brand. The more traditional British approach is "if we provide a quality product, the customer will come to us and love us forever."

SOURCES: Ernest Beck, "Marks & Spencer to Focus on Key Brands," *The Wall Street Journal* (July 15, 1999), p. B1; Jennifer Steinhauer, "The British Are Coming, and Going," *The New York Times* (September 22, 1998), pp. C1, C4.

incidence and rate of retail innovation can be explained in terms of the following four observations:

1. Innovation takes place only in the most highly developed systems. In general, channel agents in less-developed systems will adapt developments already tried and tested in more highly developed systems.
2. The ability of a system to successfully adapt innovations is directly related to its level of economic development. Certain minimum levels of economic development are necessary to support anything beyond the most simple retailing methods.
3. Even when the economic environment is conducive to change, the process of adaptation may be either hindered or helped by local demographic factors, geographic factors, social mores, government action, and competitive pressures.
4. The process of adaptation can be greatly accelerated by the actions of aggressive individual firms.

Self-service is a major twentieth century channel innovation. It provides an excellent illustration of the four points just outlined. Self-service retailing, which allows customers to handle and select merchandise themselves in a store with minimal assistance from sales personnel, originated in the United States. The spread of self-service to other countries supports the tendency of an economic system to support innovations only after a certain level of economic development has been achieved. Self-service was first introduced internationally into the most highly developed countries. It has spread to the countries at middle and lower stages of development but serves very small segments of the total market in these countries.

If a country market has reached a stage of economic development that will support a channel innovation, it is clear that the action of well-managed firms can contribute considerably to the diffusion of the channel innovation. The rapid growth of Benetton and McDonald's is a testament to the skill and competence of these firms as well as to the appeal of their product. In some instances, retail innovations are improved, refined, and expanded outside the home country. For example, 7-Eleven stores in Japan are half the size of U.S. stores and carry one-third the inventory, yet they ring up twice as much in sales. They boast a fourth-generation point-of-sale (POS) information system that is more sophisticated than the system used in the United States. Another Japanese 7-Eleven innovation is an in-store catalog, *Shop America,* that allows Japanese shoppers to order imported luxury products from companies like Tiffany's and Cartier. The Japanese successes came even as Southland Corporation, the U.S.-based parent company, slipped into financial difficulty. Commenting on the comparison between the Japanese and American sides of the business, retailing analyst Takayuki Suzuki noted, "Their [U.S. management's] merchandising has been really backwards, and the gap between us is rather large. The biggest reason is that they kept their old style and did not improve their methods and adapt to consumers' changing tastes. They became really rigid."[23] Eventually 7-Eleven Japan acquired the U.S.-based parent company; with 7,300 stores, it is now Japan's largest retailer.

Japanese shoppers can pay their household bills at their neighborhood 7-Eleven. Recent merchandising innovations include Shop America, a catalog service specializing in imported luxury goods such as Rolex watches.

23 James Sterngold, "New Japanese Lesson: Running a 7-11," *The New York Times* (May 9, 1991), p. C7. See also Bethan Hutton, "Japan's 7-Eleven Sets Store by Computer Links," *Financial Times* (March 17, 1998), p. 26.

Physical Distribution and Logistics Management

The value chain and value system are conceptual tools that provide a framework integrating various organizational activities, including physical distribution of goods (Figure 13-5). Physical distribution and outbound logistics are the means by which products are made available to customers when and where they want them. The most important distribution activities are order processing, warehousing, inventory management, and transportation.

Order Processing

Activities relating to order processing provide information inputs that are critical in fulfilling a customer's order. Order processing includes order entry, in which the order is actually entered into a company's information system; order handling, which involves locating, assembling, and moving products into distribution; and order delivery, the process by which products are made available to the customer.

Warehousing

Warehouses are used to store goods until they are sold; another type of facility, the **distribution center** is designed to efficiently receive goods from suppliers and then

Figure 13-5
Distribution Functions in the Value Chain

- Purchasing
- **Inbound Logistics**
- R&D
- Assembly & Manufacturing
- **Outbound Logistics**
- Marketing
    - Information and Research
    - Target Market Selection
    - Product Policy and Strategy
    - Pricing Policy and Strategy
    - **Distribution Policy and Strategy**
    - Communications Policy and Strategy
        - Messages, Appeals
        - Media Strategy and Plan
        - Advertising Plan
        - Promotion Plan
        - Personal Selling
        - Direct Marketing Plan
            - Direct Mail
            - Telemarketing
- Installation and Testing Service
- Margin

Table 13-2
Comparison of
Major International
Transportation
Modes

	HIGHEST/ LONGEST			LOWEST/ SHORTEST
Cost	Air	Truck	Rail	Water
Time/ Capability	Water	Rail	Truck	Air
Reliability/ Accessibility	Truck	Rail	Air	Water
Ease of Tracing	Truck Air		Rail Water	

fill orders for individual stores or customers. Distribution centers represent such an automated, high-tech business today that many companies outsource this function. Federal Express, Airborne, and other shipping specialists leverage their hub systems by serving as distribution centers for a variety of companies.

Inventory Management

Proper inventory management ensures that a company neither runs out of manufacturing components or finished goods nor incurs the expense and risk of carrying excessive stocks of these items. Another issue is balancing order-processing costs against inventory-carrying costs. The more often a product is ordered, the higher the order-processing costs associated with unloading, stocking, and related activities. The less frequently a product is ordered, the higher the inventory-carrying costs, since more product must be kept in inventory to cover the longer period between orders.

Transportation

Finally, transportation decisions concern method or mode a company should utilize when moving products through domestic and global channels. The most important modes for the products discussed in this book are rail, truck, air, and water. Each of these modes has its advantages and disadvantages, as summarized in Table 13-2. However, a particular mode may be unavailable in some countries because of an underdeveloped infrastructure or geographic barriers. A fifth mode, pipeline, is highly specialized and used by companies transporting energy-related resources such as oil and natural gas.

Rail is the most heavily used mode in the United States, accounting for nearly 40 percent of all cargo moved. Railroads provide very cost-effective means for moving large quantities of merchandise long distances. Rail's capability is second only to water in terms of the variety of products that can be transported. However, trains are less reliable than trucks. Poor track maintenance leads to derailments, and bottlenecks on heavily traveled lines can create delays.

Trucks are an excellent mode for both long-haul, transcontinental transport and local delivery of goods. In nations with well-developed highway systems, truck freight provides the highest level of accessibility of any mode. Thanks to modern

Pepper . . . and Salt

THE WALL STREET JOURNAL

"That sounds expensive. Is there any way you could ship it without handling it?"

information technology, truck shipments are also easily traced. In the United States alone, the trucking industry generates $50 billion in annual revenues. Thanks to government deregulation and a business trend toward focusing on core competencies, companies such as General Motors, Hewlett Packard, and PPG Industries are turning to truck companies for assistance. Ryder Systems, Roadway Services, and Schneider National are analyzing, designing, and managing supply chains for these and many other companies.[24]

There are two main types of water transportation. *Inland water transportation* is an extremely low-cost mode generally used to move agricultural commodities, petroleum, fertilizers, and other goods that, by their nature, lend themselves to bulk shipping via barge. However, inland water transportation can be slow and subject to weather-related delays. Virtually any product can be shipped via *ocean transportation*. The world's deep-water ports can receive a variety of types of ocean-going vessels, such as container vessels, bulk and break-bulk vessels, and ro-ro (roll-on, roll-off) vessels. Although sailing times are not competitive with air transportation, it is generally more cost effective to ship large quantities of merchandise via ocean than by air.

Air is the fastest transport mode and the carrier of choice for perishable exports such as flowers or fresh fish, but it is also the most expensive. The size and the

---

[24] Jon Bigness, "Driving Force: In Today's Economy, There is Big Money to be Made in Logistics," *The Wall Street Journal* (September 6, 1995), pp. A1, A9.

A crane operator sits more than 100 feet above the pier as he works the controls of a monster crane and moves a 40-foot container from ship to shore at the Port of Tacoma.

weight of an item may determine that it is more cost effective to ship via air than ocean. For example, medical devices are typically small and lightweight, so companies such as Med-Tec in Orange City, Iowa, and Minnesota-based Medtronic, ship the majority of their exports via air. If a shipment is time sensitive, such as emergency parts replacement, air is also the logical mode.

Channel strategy involves an analysis of each shipping mode to determine which mode, or combination of modes, will be both effective and efficient in a given situation. An aspect of transportation technology that has revolutionized global trade is containerization, a concept that was first utilized in the United States starting in the mid-1950s. **Containerization** refers to the practice of loading ocean-going freight into steel boxes measuring 20 feet, 40 feet, or longer. Containerization offers many advantages, including flexibility in the product that can be shipped via container, as well as flexibility in shipping modes. **Intermodal transportation** of goods is a combination of land and water shipping from producer to customer.[25] The growing importance of intermodal transportation can be seen in that in the United States alone railroads handle more than $150 billion in seaport goods. That figure is more than double the 1980 total. Unfortunately, lack of investment in America's rail infrastructure has resulted in delays at seaports. As Bernard LaLonde, a professor of transportation and logistics, noted recently, "It's the Achilles' heel of global distribution. The ships keep getting bigger and faster. Trade keeps growing. But we don't have the rail links we need."[26]

Use of a particular mode of transportation may be dictated by a particular market situation, by the company's overall strategy, or by conditions at the port of

---

[25] For an excellent case study of the evolution of intermodal technology in the United States, see Jon R. Katzenback and Douglas K. Smith, *The Wisdom of Teams: Creating the High-Performance Organization* (New York: HarperBusiness, 1994), chapter 2.

[26] Daniel Machalaba, "Cargo Hold: As U.S. Seaports Get Busier, Weak Point is a Surprise: Railroads," *The Wall Street Journal* (September 19, 1996), p. A1.

importation. For example, every November, winemakers from France's Beaujolais region participate in a promotion celebrating the release of the current vintage. While wine destined for European markets may travel by rail or truck, U.S.-bound wine is shipped via air freight. Normally, owing to weight and bulk considerations, French wine makes the transatlantic journey by water. Similarly, Acer Group ships motherboards and other high-tech components from Taiwan via air freight to ensure that the latest technology is incorporated into its computers. Every Christmas, supplies of the season's hottest-selling toys and electronics products are shipped via air from factories in Asia to ensure just-in-time delivery by Santa Claus. Sony's PlayStation 2 is a case in point; in October 2000, the company shipped the first 500,000 PS2 units by air to stores around the world. Likewise, in 2002, in the face of high demand for the new flat-screen iMac, Apple Computer shipped about half its Asian production by air. An estimated $1 billion is added to U.S. shipping costs each year because companies are forced to compensate for railway delays by keeping more components or parts in inventory or by shipping via air.

Logistics Management

The term **logistics management** describes the integration of activities necessary to ensure the efficient flow of raw materials, in-process inventory, and finished goods from producers to customers. For example, 3M has developed great expertise in logistics management. The company does an excellent job of managing the physical distribution aspects of the value chain to support global market exports. Outbound logistics, for example, represent just one aspect of the company's overall global strategic plan to support burgeoning exports to Europe. In St. Paul, 3M's international distribution center receives more than 5,000 orders per week. In 1985, export orders took 11 days to get through the center. By 1990, only 5.5 days were required; shipping mistakes were cut 71 percent, despite the fact that volume was up 89 percent. In Europe, meanwhile, 3M set up a distribution center in Breda, Netherlands, to receive containers from Norfolk, Virginia, and other ports. Logistics managers convinced 3M to spend as much as $1 million per year for additional trucks to provide daily delivery service to each of 3M's 19 European subsidiaries. The outlay was approved after the managers demonstrated that savings could be achieved—due to lower inventories and faster deliveries—even if trucks were not filled to capacity.[27]

Laura Ashley, the global retailer of traditional English-style clothing for women, recently reconfigured its supply chain. The company has more than 500 company-owned retail stores around the world, supplying them with goods manufactured in 15 different countries. In the past, Laura Ashley's suppliers all sent goods to the company's distribution center in Wales. This meant that blouses manufactured in Hong Kong were first sent to Wales; blouses bound for the company's Tokyo store then had to be sent back to the Far East. Not surprisingly, this was not an effective arrangement; Laura Ashley stores were typically sold out of 20 percent of goods even though the company's warehouses were full. To cut costs and improve its inventory management, Laura Ashley has subcontracted physical distribution to Federal Express's Business Logistics Service. FedEx's information system is tied in with the retail stores; when a Laura Ashley buyer orders blouses from Hong Kong, FedEx arranges shipment from the manufacturer directly to the stores.[28] Unfortunately, top-notch

[27] Robert L. Rose, "Success Abroad: 3M, by Tiptoeing Into Foreign Markets, Became a Big Exporter," *The Wall Street Journal* (March 29, 1991), p. A10.
[28] Stephanie Strom, "Logistics Steps onto Retail Battlefield," *The New York Times* (November 3, 1993), pp. D1, D2.

Each year, wine and spirits worth more than $1 billion are exported from France, Germany, Italy, and other European countries to all parts of the world. Have you ever wondered how a case of wine finds its way from, say, France to your local liquor store? In fact, after leaving the winery, the wine may pass through the hands of brokers, freight forwarders, shipping agents, export agents, shippers, importers, wholesalers, and distributors before it finishes its journey at your local retailer.

In France, the structure of the wine industry is quite complex. An intermediary called a **négociant** plays an important role that varies according to region. Négociants sometimes act as brokers and have standing contracts to buy specified quantities of finished wine on behalf of various U.S. **importers.** The *négociant* also functions somewhat like a banker, paying the producer as much as 25 percent in advance of delivery. *Négociants* may also buy grapes from growers to make their own wine, blending and bottling them under their own labels. Wine may be bottled and packed in cases by the producer or by the *négociant.*

Wine destined for France or other European markets travels by truck. If the wine is to be exported to the U.S. or Japan, a **freight forwarder** or **shipping agent** sends a truck to the winery to pick up the wine. For the largest producers, the simplest type of consolidation takes place at the winery itself; a truck carrying a 20- or 40-foot shipping container is backed up to the door of the winery and loaded there for the ocean voyage. For smaller producers, the wines are picked up and then delivered to a warehouse. There, the shipping agent consolidates various deliveries before filling a container for the shipping line of the importer's choosing.

Shipping dates and rates will vary depending on the availability of containers. In general, a 20-foot container can hold 800 cases of wine; a single 40-foot container can take up to 1,300 cases. The weight of the wine is a consideration when determining how many cases to ship in a given container. Not only do wine bottles vary in size (750 ml bottles are the most common, with 12 bottles in a case), but there is likely to be a difference in weight between two cases of different types of wine. For example, heavier bottles are required for champagne and other sparkling wines since the contents are under pressure; bottles of fine Bordeaux are packaged in wooden crates that weigh more than ordinary cardboard cartons.

Shipping wine is a challenging venture because of the perishable nature of the product. Proper storage and transportation are vital; light, heat, and temperature fluctuations are wine's worst enemy. Ideally, wine should be kept at a constant temperature near 55 degrees. To prevent improper shipping from ruining a shipment, temperature-controlled containers (known as "reefers") are often used, even though they add about $3 per case to the cost of the shipment. To further protect the wine, some importers avoid shipping during the hot summer months. Because ownership of the wine is transferred to the importer at the moment the wine leaves the French storage warehouse, it is important to insure the shipment. Wine shipments can even be insured against possible losses due to war and terrorism. The best importers arrange for proper warehouse storage even before taking title to the wines.

The transatlantic trip for U.S.-bound wine takes a week or more. The port of entry depends on the location of the importer or **wholesaler/distributor.** The port of New York is used when wines are destined for the East Coast. Wine bound for the nation's midsection often enters through Baltimore or Norfolk, Virginia. Ships going to a western destination may chart a course through the Gulf of Mexico on their way to Houston; wines bound for the port of San Francisco pass through the Panama Canal. Once the wine enters the United States, it must clear U.S. customs. Customs agents and the importer or wholesaler make sure the shipment meets all government regulations and that paperwork is properly prepared. The Bureau of Alcohol, Tobacco, and Firearms is the U.S. government agency with jurisdiction over wines and spirits.

After it has cleared customs, the wine is shipped to the wholesaler's warehouse. Again, the importance of temperature-controlled shipping comes into play. If the wholesaler is too busy to pick up the container immediately, it may sit on the dock for a week or more in warm weather; without refrigeration, the wine—and the importer's investment—might be lost. If the distributor is located in Chicago, the wine often enters the country in Baltimore and completes the next leg of the trip via rail. Sometimes, trucks will bring a shipment of wine to the Midwest from the East Coast and return full of meat to make the trip cost effective. After the wine has been unloaded at the warehouse, the distributor's sales staff arranges for the cases of wine to be delivered by truck or van to individual retailers.

logistics alone are no guarantee of market success. Although Laura Ashley's global brand image remains strong, the company has floundered during the 1990s. An ambitious expansion effort in the U.S. market resulted in too many new stores being built in poor locations. Other U.S. marketing missteps included an ill-advised emphasis on home furnishings at the expense of the company's popular clothing. In 1997, Laura Ashley's woes cost American Ann Iverson her position as chief executive after only two years on the job.[29]

Case Example: Japan

Japan's distribution system has bedeviled many a foreign company. For example, several layers of small wholesalers play an important role in food distribution. Attempts to bypass these apparently unnecessary units in the channel have failed because the cost to a manufacturer of providing their service (frequent small deliveries to small grocery outlets) is greater than the margin they require. Typically, foreign marketers in Japan have made two mistakes when making distribution decisions. The first is their assumption that distribution problems can be solved the same way they would be in the West, that is, by going as directly as possible to the customer and thus cutting out the middleman. In Japan, because of the very fragmented nature of retailing, it is simply not cost effective to go direct. The second mistake often made is in treating the Japanese market at arm's length by selling to a trading company. The trading company may sell in low volumes to a very limited segment of the market, such as the luxury segment, with the result that there is usually limited interest on the part of the trading company. The experience is likely to be disappointing to all parties involved.

GE's recent experiences in Japan show how an entrepreneurial insider can go against the grain of conventional wisdom and rewrite the rules. In 1991, GE established a partnership with Toshiba; the latter was responsible for moving GE appliances through Japan's distribution system. The marketing strategy called for selling GE refrigerators as high-priced luxury goods using selective distribution through low-volume specialty stores. Akitoshi Kojima, the managing director of the Kojima Co., a chain of 162 discount stores, recognized that inefficient outbound logistics were driving up the costs of refrigerators handled by the GE-Toshiba venture. Refrigerators were shipped to a warehouse in Long Beach, California, where they were packed in ocean-going containers with other appliances bound for Kawasaki. Once in port, the refrigerators had to be separated from the other appliances, after which they were handled by several trucking companies and passed through several different warehouses before being delivered to stores in volumes as low as one unit. Working directly with GE and bypassing the GE-Toshiba venture, Mr. Kojima arranged to have containers exclusively loaded with refrigerators. After the containers arrive in Kawasaki, Kojima Company's own truck fleet picks up the refrigerators and delivers them directly to the chain's stores. The list price of a refrigerator handled by GE-Toshiba is $2,400; the identical model sells for $800 at Kojima's stores.[30]

As this example shows, successful distribution in Japan (or any other market) means understanding the realities of the marketplace. In Japan, this means first and foremost adaptation to (or, as in the Kojima example, leapfrogging over) the reality of fragmented distribution. Second, successful distribution requires research into the market itself, including customer needs and competitive products. Then a company

---

[29] Matthew Lynn, "Laura Ashley Wakes Up to Nightmare," *The Sunday Times* (November 23, 1997), p. 8.
[30] Norihiko Shirouzu, "Flouting 'Rules' Sells GE Fridges in Japan," *The Wall Street Journal* (October 31, 1995), pp. B1, B2.

must develop an overall marketing strategy that: (1) positions the product vis-á-vis market segment identified according to need, price, and other issues; (2) positions the product against competitors; and (3) lays out a marketing plan—including a distribution plan—for achieving volume and share-of-market objectives.

Shimaguchi and Rosenberg identified several considerations for any company formulating and implementing a Japanese distribution strategy. The first called for finding a Japanese partner such as an import agent to help navigate the unfamiliar waters. Import agents range in size from small local distributors to the giant *sogo-sosha* (general trading companies). The authors also advised companies to pursue a strategy of offering better quality, lower price, or a distinctive positioning as a foreign product. Foreigners are advised to prepare for a long-term effort and modest returns; nothing happens quickly in Japanese distribution, and patience is required. Finally, the authors advised cultivating personal relationships in distribution. Loyalty and trust are important.[31]

While these considerations are still relevant today, some recent studies have described ways to bypass the Japanese distribution quagmire by pursuing alternative distribution channels. For example, foreign companies may wish to follow the example of Toys 'R' Us and establish their own retail stores in Japan. Toys 'R' Us attempted to circumvent the multilayered wholesale system by buying direct from manufacturers. A second approach is to use direct marketing techniques. While telemarketing is relatively new and has proven more successful with business-to-business rather than consumer marketing, mail order in Japan has been experiencing 17 percent annual growth. L.L. Bean sells a substantial amount of merchandise in Japan despite the fact that it has never published a Japanese catalog. Door-to-door selling is a third alternative channel strategy in Japan that has been successfully pursued by Amway. Amway has established its own system of independent distributors; most of the 150-plus products sold are imported from the United States. Finally, a company may wish to explore creative ways of piggybacking with other successful companies. For example, Shop America successfully launched a specialty catalog business by piggybacking with Japan's 7-Eleven convenience stores.

SUMMARY

A **channel of distribution** is the network of agencies and institutions that links producers with users. Channel decisions are difficult to manage globally because of the variation in channel structures from country to country. Marketing channels can create place, time, form, and information utility for buyers. The characteristics of customers, products, middlemen, and environment all affect channel design and strategy.

Consumer channels may be relatively direct, utilizing direct mail or door-to-door selling, as well as manufacturer-owned stores. A combination of manufacturers' sales force, agents-brokers, and wholesalers may also be used. **Piggyback marketing** is a distribution innovation in which one manufacturer gains distribution in a particular country market by "riding along" with the products of another manufacturer. Channels for industrial products are less varied, with manufacturers' sales force, wholesalers, and dealers or agents utilized.

Retail distribution takes many different forms, including **department stores, specialty retailers, supermarkets, convenience stores, discount stores, warehouse clubs, hypermarkets, supercenters,** and **category killers. Global retailing** is a growing trend as successful retailers expand around the world in support of growth objectives. Selection, price, store location, and customer service are a few of the competencies that can be used strategically to enter a new market. It is possible to classify retailers

---

[31] Mitsuaki Shimaguchi and Larry R. Rosenberg, "Demystifying Japanese Distribution," *Columbia Journal of World Business* (Spring 1979), pp. 38–41.

in a matrix that distinguishes companies offering few product categories with an own-label focus; many categories-own-label focus; few categories-manufacturer-brand focus; and many categories-manufacturer-brand focus. Global retail expansion can be achieved via organic growth, franchising, chain acquisition, and joint venture.

Transportation and physical distribution issues are critically important in global marketing because of the geographical distances involved in sourcing products and serving customers in different parts of the world. Important activities include **order processing, warehousing,** and **inventory management.** To cut costs and improve efficiency, many companies are reconfiguring their supply chains by outsourcing some or all of these activities. Four transportation modes—**air, truck, water,** and **rail**—are widely used in global distribution. Distributing products around the globe is made easier by **containerization** and **intermodal transportation.** Individual country markets such as Japan can present unique distribution challenges.

DISCUSSION QUESTIONS

1. In what ways can channel intermediaries create utility for buyers?
2. What factors influence the channel structures and strategies available to global marketers?
3. What is *cherry picking?* What approaches can be used to deal with this problem?
4. Compare and contrast the typical channel structures for consumer products and industrial products.
5. Identify the different forms of retailing, and cite an example of each form. Identify retailers from as many different countries as you can.
6. Identify the four retail market expansion strategies discussed in the text. What factors determine the appropriate mode?
7. Briefly discuss the global issues associated with physical distribution and transportation logistics. Cite one example of a company that is making efficiency improvements in its channel or physical distribution arrangements.
8. What special distribution challenges exist in Japan? What is the best way for a non-Japanese company to deal with these challenges?

BUILD YOUR GLOBAL MARKETING SKILLS

Each December, *Chain Store Age* magazine publishes its survey of the world's largest retailers. The top-ranked companies for 2000 were shown in Table 13-1. Browse through the list and choose any company that interests you. Compare its 2000 ranking with the most recent ranking (which you can find either by referring to the print version of *Chain Store Age* or by visiting www.chainstoreage.com).

How have the industry rankings changed? Consult additional sources (e.g., magazine articles, annual reports, the company's Web site) to enhance your understanding of the factors and forces that contributed to the company's move up or down in the rankings. What do the current rankings tell you about changes in global retailing?

SUGGESTED READINGS

Books

Bauer, P. T. *West African Trade.* Cambridge: Cambridge University Press, 1954.

Coughlin, Anne, Erin Anderson, Louis Stern, and Adel L. El-Ansary. *Marketing Channels.* 6th ed. Englewood Cliffs, N.J.: Prentice-Hall, 2001.

Czinkota, Michael R. *The Japanese Distribution System.* Homewood, Ill.: Irwin, 1994.

————. *Gucci on the Ginsa.* Tokyo and New York: Kodansha International, 1989.

Articles

Allen, Randy L. "The Why and How of Global Retailing." *Business Quarterly* 57, no. 4 (Summer 1993), pp. 117–122.

Arnold David. "Seven Rules of International Distribution." *Harvard Business Review* 78, no. 6 (November-December 2000), pp. 131–137.

Berry, Leonard. "The Old Pillars of New Retailing: Fundamental Ways of Creating Customer Value." *Harvard Business Review* 7, no. 4 (April-June 2001), pp. 131–137.

Camuffo, Arnold, Pietro Romano, and Andrea Vinelli. "Back to the Future: Benetton Transforms Its Global Network." *Sloan Management Review* 43, no. 1 (Fall 2001), pp. 46–52.

Gentry, Julie R., Janjaap Semeijn, and David B. Vellenga. "The Future of Road Haulage in the New European Union—1995 and Beyond." *The Logistics and Transportation Review* 31, no. 2 (1995), pp. 145–160.

Goldman, Arich. "The Transfer of Retail Formats into Developing Economies: The Example of China." *Journal of Retailing,* 77 no. 2 (Summer 2001), pp. 221–242.

Hill, John S., Richard R. Still, and Unal O. Boya. "Managing the Multinational Sales Force." *International Marketing Review* 8, no. 1 (1991), pp. 19–31.

Kaitaki, Jack G. "Don't Crack the Japanese Distribution System—Just Circumvent It." *Columbia Journal of World Business* 28, no. 2 (Summer 1993), pp. 34–45.

Kunitomo, Ryuichi. "Seven-Eleven is Revolutionizing Grocery Distribution in Japan." *Long Range Planning* 30, no. 7 (December 1997), pp. 877–889.

Luk, Sherriff T. K., Lorna Fullgrabe, and Stephen C. Y. Li. "Managing Direct Selling Activities in China: A Cultural Explanation." *Journal of Business Research* 45, no. 3 (July 1999), pp. 257–266.

Merrilees, Bill, and Dale Miller. "Direct Selling in the West and East: The Relative Roles of Product and Relationship (*Guanxi*) Drivers." *Journal of Business Research* 45, no. 3 (July 1999), pp. 267–273.

Raguraman, K., and Claire Chan. "The Development of Sea-Air Intermodal Transportation: An Assessment of Global Trends." *The Logistics and Transportation Review* 30, no. 4 (December 1994), pp. 379–396.

Rosenbloom, Bert. "Motivating Your International Channel Partners." *Business Horizons* 33, no. 2 (March-April 1990), pp. 53–57.

Sachdev, Harash J., Daniel C. Bello, and Bruce K. Pilling. "Control Mechanisms Within Export Channels of Distribution." *Journal of Global Marketing* 8, no. 2 (1994), pp. 31–50.

Samiee, Saeed. "Retailing and Channel Considerations in Developing Countries: A Review and Research Propositions." *Journal of Business Research* 27, no. 2 (June 1993), pp. 103–129.

Vida, Irena, James Reardon, and Ann Fairhurst. "Determinants of International Retail Involvement: The Case of Large U.S. Retail Chains." *Journal of International Marketing* 8, no. 4 (2000), pp. 37–60.

Weigand, Robert E. "Parallel Import Channels—Options for Preserving Territorial Integrity." *Columbia Journal of World Business* 26, no. 1 (Spring 1991), pp. 53–60.

CASE

Case 13-1   Wal-Mart's Global Expansion

Wal-Mart, the discount retail giant whose very name strikes fear in the hearts of many small-town retailers in the United States, is going global. The company utilizes a variety of different retail formats, including discount stores, supercenters that feature a full line of groceries and general merchandise, and Sam's Club, a warehouse operation offering goods in unbroken bulk packages. As Wal-Mart extends its reach around the globe, observers are using words such as "assault" and "invasion" to describe what it's like for a nation that the company has in its sights. As the chief executive of one supplier noted, "Wal-Mart is going to change the retailing landscape internationally exactly the same way it's done domestically." Some industry observers expect that, within a few years, four or five giant firms will dominate the world's retail scene. Retail consultant Daniel O'Connor summed up the situation this way: "We're really moving to

boundaryless retailing." Needless to say, Wal-Mart executives intend to put their company in first place.

North America

Wal-Mart's first foray outside the United States was in Mexico in 1991. Although Wal-Mart executives had no previous foreign experience, they recognized that there were substantial income and cultural differences in Mexico. Accordingly, the American retail giant established a 50-50 joint venture with Cifra SA, Mexico's largest retailer. Despite having a partner, the company made a number of blunders. Among them were poorly translated signs and a merchandise assortment that included inappropriate items such as ice skates, leaf blowers, and riding lawn mowers. To make matters worse, Wal-Mart's vaunted information system would

Table 1
Wal-Mart International Division, Revenues

	1997	1998	1999	2000	2001*
Revenue (millions)	$7,517	$12,247	$22,728	$33,644	$37,739
Operating Margin	3.5%	4.5%	3.6%	3.4%	3.5%

*estimate

Table 2
Wal-Mart Stores by Country

	NO. OF STORES	% OF TOTAL	AVG. STORE SIZE
Mexico	483	26%	40,827
Canada	169	26%	115,150
UK	240	25%	78,438
Germany	95	12%	97,841
Argentina	11	3%	203,715
Brazil	18	3%	123,125
Puerto Rico	15	2%	116,573
China	8	1%	101,524
Korea	6	1%	104,121
Total	1,045	100%	

automatically re-stock merchandise that local managers had tried to close out. The Mexican stores sold American-style packaged meat and vegetables, which many shoppers preferred to purchase from small neighborhood stores. Also, most Mexican suppliers shipped directly to stores rather than to retailer warehouses and distribution centers. Thus, Wal-Mart lacked the control that translates into low prices in the United States. As Sam Dunn, director of administration for Wal-Mart de Mexico, commented, "The key to this market is distribution. The retailer who solves that will dominate."

One sign of Wal-Mart's long-term commitment to Mexico was its decision in mid-1997 to convert its joint venture shares into Cifra common stock and purchase enough additional shares to have a controlling stake in the company; the new enterprise is called Wal-Mart de Mexico S.A. de C.V. (Walmex). Meanwhile, Wal-Mart turned its sights further south. In 1995, the company teamed up with Lojas Americanas SA and opened five stores in Brazil; operating without a partner in Argentina, Wal-Mart opened four stores. By 2000, the company was operating 12 Supercenters and eight Sam's Clubs in Brazil and 11 Supercenters in Argentina. The stores offer a staggering variety, with a typical mix of approximately 50,000 different products.

In 1994, Wal-Mart entered Canada by acquiring the 122-store Woolco chain. The market appeared very attractive, because a high percentage of the Canadian population lives within 100 miles of the border. In addition to a high familiarity with Wal-Mart, Canadians also speak English and have a monetary system that is similar to the American one. The small size of existing Woolco stores resulted in disappointing sales; Wal-Mart responded by moving to new locations or expanding units. Much early sales growth came at the expense of existing department stores. Future growth may be hampered by the relatively small Canadian population and a trend towards cross border shopping to escape high value-added taxes. Also, management at Zeller's, Wal-Mart's main competitor in Canada, has responded by renovating stores and expanding beyond its traditional discount formula.

South America

The retailing environment in South America is very competitive, in part because Carrefour had arrived first. The French company inked distribution deals with manufacturers of leading local brands; this is a key advantage, because well-known consumer packaged-goods brands such as Tide detergent are not widely accepted in South America. Moreover, Carrefour played hardball,

undercutting Wal-Mart's prices on key items such as cooking oil, rice, and shampoo. Some observer's noted that Carrefour's French heritage undoubtedly gave it the upper hand in presenting fresh fish, meat, and produce. Local retailers were strong as well; faced with rampant inflation in the late 1980s, they had invested in sophisticated cash registers and an inventory control system to help them make frequent—even daily—price adjustments.

"You have to be culturally sensitive in the selection of merchandise in order to succeed in emerging markets, or in any foreign market. Carrefour is very good at making adjustments in local markets, and is very good at developing local management. I think that's the major lesson that the world's largest retailer can learn from the second largest retailer."
—Ira Kalish, director, Global Retail Intelligence, PricewaterhouseCoopers Los Angeles

Despite these competitive challenges, Wal-Mart quickly adapted to the unfamiliar environment. It hired local managers, who in turn helped develop the right product assortment and merchandising approaches. For example, the Wal-Mart Supercenters in Argentina initially kept fresh seafood in glass display cases. However, South Americans typically want to examine prospective food purchases up close and even touch them; Wal-Mart made the appropriate changes. Wal-Mart quickly discovered that, in South America, the entire family shops together; it turned out that Wal-Mart's aisles were not wide enough to accommodate such groups. Shoppers also were information deprived; Wal-Mart responded with clinics and in-store demonstrations such as weekly makeovers in the cosmetics departments. Wal-Mart also had to adjust the approach of its Sam's Club warehouse stores. Small business operators were expected to account for a significant amount of purchases at Sam's Club. However, even these buyers were unable to afford the bulk packs that are mainstays of Wal-Mart's wholesale club format. Sam's managers were forced to break down bulk quantities into smaller packs and even sell individual items.

Europe

Market entry in Europe came in 1997 with the purchase of 21 hypermarkets from Wertkauf GmbH. The following year Wal-Mart acquired 74 additional hypermarkets from Spar Handels AG. The early going was difficult; the two acquired companies were merged under a centralized headquarters, a major remodeling program affecting most of the stores was launched, and distribution was centralized. In addition, the company's aggressive pricing resulted in a price war among Germany's retailers who had already been through traumatic changes related to the reunification with East Germany in 1990. Wal-Mart's losses in Germany for 1999 were estimated to run as high as $200 million. However, with the transition largely in place, in 2000, company officials announced plans to open 50 more stores in Germany and to double its share of the hypermarket sector to 20 percent by 2003.

In 1999, Wal-Mart shocked the European retailing world by offering more than $10 billion for Britain's third-largest supermarket chain, Asda Group PLC. It was the largest cash offer ever made for a UK business. Industry observers noted that Asda had spent years studying such fundamental elements of the Wal-Mart approach as everyday low pricing and an "anti-management" management culture that, for example, calls for having a greeter at the front of the store and stresses the importance of calling store personnel "colleagues." As Asda chairman Archie Norman said, "The culture and attitude of Wal-Mart is one that we aspired to."

"In order to be big globally we have to be big in Europe."
—Jay Fitzsimmons,
Wal-Mart Senior Vice President

Asia

Wal-Mart is also targeting Asia. With China due to join the World Trade Organization, Wal-Mart executives intend to capitalize on the economic expansion that will follow. Wal-Mart's earliest foray into China, a joint venture launched in 1996 with Thailand's Charoen Pokphand Group, was terminated after 18 months due to management differences. Although Beijing restricts the operations of foreign retailers, Wal-Mart executives have made a point of building relationships with government officials. In addition, Wal-Mart exports approximately $4 billion worth of goods from China each year. Joe Hatfield, Wal-Mart's chief in Asia, spent a great deal of time checking in local shops to better understand the type of merchandise the typical Chinese consumer wants to buy. Through trial-and-error, Wal-Mart has learned what type of merchandise sells and what doesn't. By the end of 2000, Wal-Mart had 10 stores in China. However, it still lags behind France's Carrefour SA, which has opened more than 20 small-scale discount stores in 14 Chinese cities.

Wherever Wal-Mart goes, competitors are forced to adjust to the new retail climate. In China, Dutch retailer Royal Ahold NV and Hong Kong supermarket chain Park 'N Shop have scaled back. In the face of Wal-Mart's voracious appetite for acquisitions, Metro AG, Germany's number one retailer, bought the Allfauf and Kriegbaum hypermarket chains. New slogans that closely resemble Wal-Mart's such as "ehrliche Niedrigpreise" ("honestly low prices") greet shoppers at Metro's Real hypermarkets, and the stores open earlier in the day. Still, the size and scale of Wal-Mart's operation give it tremendous buying power. For example, Wal-Mart buys 20 percent of all the Pampers brand disposable diapers produced by Procter & Gamble. In Mexico, Francisco Martínez, CFO of rival Comercial Mexicana SA, noted, "I buy 20,000 plastic toys, and Wal-Mart buys 20 million. Who do you think gets them cheaper?"

DISCUSSION QUESTIONS

1. Which of the market entry strategy options identified in Figure 13-4 has Wal-Mart utilized in its global expansion?
2. What are the keys to Wal-Mart's success in the United States? Will those factors help the company as it expands around the globe?
3. How do the ways in which Wal-Mart creates utility for buyers vary in different parts of the world?
4. If you were a small, independent retailer threatened by Wal-Mart, what would you do?

SOURCES: David Luhnow, "Crossover Success: How Nafta Helped Wal-Mart Reshape the Mexican Market," *The Wall Street Journal* (August 31, 2001), pp. A1, A2; William Boston, "Wal-Mart Girds for Major German Expansion," *The Wall Street Journal* (July 20, 2000), pp. A21, A22; Peter Wonacott, "Wal-Mart Finds Market Footing in China," *The Wall Street Journal* (July 17, 2000), p. A31; Ernest Beck and Emily Nelson, "Differences of Style: As Wal-Mart Invades Europe, Rivals Rush to Match Its Formula," *The Wall Street Journal* (October 6, 1999), pp. A1, A6; Elizabeth Robinson, "Mutual Admiration Society Bonds Together," *Financial Times* (June 15, 1999), p. 30; John Schmid, "In Germany, Wal-Mart Touches Off a Price War," *International Herald Tribune* (November 11, 1998), pp. 1, 10; Jonathan Friedland and Louise Lee, "Foreign Aisles: The Wal-Mart Way Sometimes Gets Lost in Translation Overseas," *The Wall Street Journal* (October 8, 1997), pp. A1, A12; Wendy Zellner, "Wal-Mart Spoken Here," *Business Week* (June 23, 1997), pp. 138–139+; Bob Ortega, "Tough Sale: Wal-Mart is Slowed By Problems of Price and Culture in Mexico," *The Wall Street Journal* (July 28, 1994), pp. A1, A5.

Chapter *14*

Global Marketing Communications Decisions I: Advertising and Public Relations

*I*n the summer of 2000, Jacques Nasser, president and CEO of Ford Motor Company, and Yoichiro Kaizaki, chief executive of Bridgestone Corporation, faced the biggest crisis of their professional careers. For several months, evidence had been accumulating that 88 deaths in the United States, 47 deaths in Venezuela, and hundreds of injuries suffered by occupants of Ford Explorer SUVs and light trucks could be attributed to the failure of the Firestone tires with which the vehicles had been equipped. The tires had been manufactured by the Japanese company's Bridgestone/Firestone unit; as an inquiry by the U.S. National Highway Traffic Safety Administration (NHTSA) broadened, 6.5 million Firestone tires were recalled. When news stories surfaced about tire failures in 1998 in the Middle East, critics began asking why Ford and Firestone had waited to take action. With media coverage of the problem intensifying, Nasser sought to reassure jittery customers that they could replace the suspect tires at no charge. The headline in full-page print ads proclaimed "Your Safety is Our Top Priority." Nasser also appeared in TV ads broadcast on national television.

Clearly, advertising, publicity, and other forms of communication are critical tools in the global auto wars. Marketing communications—the promotion *P* of the marketing mix—refers to all forms of communication used by organizations to inform, remind, explain, persuade, and influence the attitudes and buying behavior of customers and others. The primary purpose of marketing communications is to tell customers about the benefits and values that a company, product, or service offers. The elements of the promotion mix are advertising, public relations, personal selling, and sales promotion. All of these elements can be utilized in global marketing, either alone or in varying combinations. The environment in which marketing communications programs and strategies are implemented also varies from country to country. The

Bridgestone/Firestone faced more than 300 lawsuits in the United States stemming from injuries resulting from tire separation. At a news conference in November 2001, Mississippi Attorney General Mike Moore announces a $530,000 settlement with Bridgestone/Firestone over defective tires; the tires had been recalled one year earlier. The award is part of a $41.5 million nationwide settlement.

challenge of effectively communicating across borders is one reason Nike, Nestlé, Microsoft, and other companies are embracing a concept known as *integrated marketing communications* (IMC). Adherents of an IMC approach explicitly recognize that the various elements of a company's communication strategy must be carefully coordinated.[1] This chapter examines advertising and public relations from the perspective of the global marketer. The next chapter is devoted to the remaining elements of the promotion mix: sales promotion and personal selling.

GLOBAL ADVERTISING

Advertising may be defined as any sponsored, paid message that is communicated in a nonpersonal way. Some advertising messages are designed to communicate with persons in a single country or market area. Regional or pan-regional advertising is created for audiences across several country markets such as Europe or Latin America. **Global advertising** may be defined as messages whose art, copy, headlines, photographs, tag lines, and other elements have been developed expressly for their worldwide suitability. In Chapter 11, we noted that a global company may simultaneously offer local, international, and global products and brands to buyers in different parts of the

---

1   Thomas R. Duncan and Stephen E. Everett, "Client Perception of Integrated Marketing Communications," *Journal of Advertising Research* (May-June 1993), pp. 119–122; see also Stephen J. Gould, Dawn B. Lerman, and Andreas F. Green, "Agency Perceptions and Practices on Global IMC." *Journal of Advertising Research* 39, no. 1 (January-February 1999), pp. 7–20.

world. The same is true with advertising: A global company may utilize single-country advertising in addition to campaigns that are regional and global in scope.

In Japan, for example, PepsiCo has achieved great success with a local campaign featuring Pepsiman, a superhero action figure. Prior to 1996, the ads shown in Japan were the same global spots used throughout the rest of the world. However, in Japan's $24 billion soft drink market, Pepsi trailed far behind Coca-Cola; Pepsi had a mere 3 percent market share compared with Coke's 30 percent share. The Pepsiman character was designed by local Japanese talent, but Industrial Light & Magic, the special-effects house owned by *Star Wars* creator George Lucas, was hired to give the TV spots a U.S.-style high-tech edge. By breaking with its usual strategy of running global ads and increasing the ad budget by 50 percent over 1995, Pepsi's 1996 sales in Japan rose by 14 percent. The campaign was so successful that Pepsi officials plan to introduce it in South Korea, Hong Kong, and elsewhere.[2]

A global company that has the ability to successfully transform a domestic campaign into a worldwide one, or to create a new global campaign from the ground up, possesses a critical advantage. The creative process will force a company to determine whether there is a global market for its product. The first company to find a global market for any product is always at an advantage over competitors that make the same discovery later. *The search for a global advertising campaign can be the cornerstone of the search for a coherent global strategy.* Such a search should bring together everyone involved with the product to share information and leverage their experiences. Global campaigns attest to management's conviction that unified themes not only spur short-term sales but also help to build long-term product and brand identities and offer significant savings in production costs. Regional trading centers such as Europe are experiencing an influx of standardized global brands as companies align themselves, buy up other companies, and get their pricing policies and production plans organized for a united region. From a marketing point of view, there is a great deal of activity going on that will make brands truly pan-European in a very short period of time. This phenomenon is accelerating the growth of global advertising.

"Today, pan-European campaigns account for up to 40 percent of what we do. Five years ago it might have been half that amount."[3]
—Fernan Montera, chairman of European operations, Young & Rubicam

The potential for effective global advertising also increases as companies recognize and embrace new concepts such as "product cultures." An example is the globalization of beer culture, which can be seen in the popularity of German-style beer halls in Japan and Irish-style pubs in the United States. Similarly, the globalization of coffee culture has created market opportunities for companies such as Starbucks. Companies also realize that some market segments can be defined on the basis of global demography—youth culture, for example—rather than ethnic or national culture. Athletic shoes and other clothing products, for instance, can be targeted to a worldwide segment of 18- to 25-year-old males. William Roedy, president of MTV Networks International, sees clear implications of such product cultures for advertising. MTV is just one of the media vehicles that enable people virtually anywhere to see how the rest of the world lives and to learn about products that are popular in other cultures. Many human wants and desires are very similar if presented within recognizable experience situations. People everywhere want value, quality, and the latest technology made available and affordable; everyone everywhere wants to be loved and respected, and we all get hungry.[4]

Because advertising is often designed to add psychological value to a product or brand, it plays a more important communications role in marketing consumer

2   John Herskovitz, "Pepsiman Comes Calling Again," *Advertising Age International* (January 11, 1999), p. 9.
3   Alison Smith, "Border Crossings," *Financial Times* (May 7, 1998), p. 22.
4   Dean M. Peebles, "Executive Insights: Don't Write Off Global Advertising," *International Marketing Review* 6, no. 1 (1989), pp. 73–78.

The Rest of the Story
Ford and Bridgestone/Firestone Recall

At headquarters, a 500-person crisis team was assembled to investigate the problem and respond to customer inquiries. Nasser communicated with dealers on a weekly basis using the company's interactive Fordstar communication network. Nasser also tried to address employee concerns about the recall's possible negative impact on their jobs and compensation.

In Japan, the corporate response was more muted. Bridgestone's Mr. Kaizaki had a reputation as a combative, non-conformist, tough-minded cost cutter who was fully up to the task of restructuring an old-line Japanese company like Bridgestone. However, the tire crisis raised the question of whether he had the public relations skills required to address concerns while trying to determine the cause of the problem. Initially, he put president Masatoshi Ono in charge of dealing with the press. However, Mr. Ono was perceived as tentative and unforthcoming. After Mr. Ono failed to get Bridgestone's message across in testimony to a U.S. Congressional committee, Mr. Kaizaki took the lead. At a press conference, Mr. Kaizaki defended Firestone and offered assurances that Firestone was not to blame. In particular, he denied reports that Bridgestone had withheld pertinent information from U.S. investigators. He also acknowledged the possibility that quality assurance standards in the U.S. plants might not be on a par with those in Japan.

SOURCES: David Barboza, "Bridgestone/Firestone to Close Tire Plant at Center of Huge Recall," *The New York Times* (June 28, 2001), pp. C1, C14; Joann Muller, "Ford vs. Firestone: A Corporate Whodunit," *Business Week* (June 11, 2001), pp. 46–47; Robert L. Simison, "Behind the Wheel: For Ford CEO Nasser, Damage Control in the New 'Job One,' " *The Wall Street Journal* (September 11, 2000), pp. A1, A8; Todd Zaun, "Pushing Back: Bridgestone Boss Has Toughness, but is That What Crisis Demands," *The Wall Street Journal* (September 12, 2000), pp. A1, A18.

products than in marketing industrial products. Frequently purchased, low-cost products generally require heavy advertising support to remind consumers about the product. Not surprisingly, consumer products companies top the list of big global advertising spenders. Procter & Gamble, the Altria Group (formerly Philip Morris), and Unilever are just a few of the companies with significant advertising expenditures outside the home-country markets. *Advertising Age*'s ranking of global marketers in terms of advertising expenditures outside the United States is shown in Table 14-1. The top 100 advertisers spent a total of $41.24 billion in 1999 in 73 countries; in addition, the top 100 spent $27.34 billion on U.S. advertising. A close examination of Table 14-1 provides clues to the extent of a company's globalization efforts. For example, packaged-goods giants P&G and Unilever spend significant amounts in all major world regions. Japan's Kao, however, has only a limited presence in Europe and no presence at all in Latin America. Similarly, the table shows that the geographic scope of France's Renault is largely limited to Europe.

Global advertising also offers companies economies of scale in advertising as well as improved access to distribution channels. Where shelf space is at a premium, as with food products, a company has to convince retailers to carry its products rather than those of competitors. A global brand supported by global advertising may be very attractive because, from the retailer's standpoint, a global brand is less likely to languish on the shelves. Landor Associates, a company specializing in brand identity and design, recently determined that Coke has the number one brand-awareness and esteem position in the United States, number two in Japan, and number six in Europe. However, standardization is not always required or even advised. Nestlé's Nescafé coffee is marketed as a global brand, even though advertising messages and product formulation vary to suit cultural differences.

Table 14-1
Top 25 Global Marketers, 1999 ($ millions)

COMPANY	NON-U.S. AD SPENDING	U.S. AD SPENDING	WORLDWIDE AD SPENDING	ASIA AD SPENDING*	EUROPE AD SPENDING	LATIN AMERICA
1. Unilever	$3,110	$588	$3,698	$839	$1,785	$419
2. Procter & Gamble	2,988	1,704	4,693	527	1,805	550
3. Nestlé SA	1,580	329	1,909	342	1,023	197
4. Coca-Cola Co.	1,178	355	1,533	283	519	334
5. Ford Motor Co.	1,150	1,272	2,422	126	825	142
6. General Motors Corp.	1,148	2,960	4,108	110	723	214
7. L'Oreal	1,120	450	1,570	36	1,003	51
8. Volkswagen AG	1,009	372	1,381	23	796	163
9. Toyota Motor Corp.	1,007	718	1,725	607	320	24
10. PSA Peugeot-Citroen	906	NA	906	16	840	47
11. Sony Corp.	886	590	1,477	387	398	71
12. Mars Inc.	841	298	1,139	69	732	31
13. Renault SA	809	NA	809	1	766	41
14. Philip Morris Cos.	767	1,358	2,125	92	567	75
15. Henkel Group	728	19	747	14	714	0
16. Nissan Motor Co.	657	527	1,184	346	227	52
17. McDonald's Corp.	649	633	1,282	186	376	51
18. Fiat	649	3	651	13	572	63
19. Danone Group	642	49	691	68	543	31
20. Ferrero	603	27	630	3	584	15
21. Colgate-Palmolive	591	134	725	117	230	234
22. Deutsche Telekom	578	5	583	0	578	0
23. DaimlerChrysler	556	1,533	2,090	50	363	96
24. Reckitt Benckiser	543	211	597.1	83	417	27
25. Johnson & Johnson	486	899	965.3	151	208	103

*Asia includes Australia and New Zealand.

Source: AdAge Global (November 2000), p. 38.

Global Advertising Content: The "Extension" versus "Adaptation" Debate

Communication experts generally agree that the overall requirements of effective communication and persuasion are fixed and do not vary from country to country. The same thing is true of the components of the communication process: The marketer's-sender's message must be encoded, conveyed via the appropriate channel(s), and decoded by the customer-receiver. Communication takes place only when meaning is transferred. Four major difficulties can compromise an organization's attempt to communicate with customers in any location:

1. The message may not get through to the intended recipient. This problem may be the result of an advertiser's lack of knowledge about appropriate media for reaching certain types of audiences. For example, the effectiveness of television

In February 1993, a group of investors headed by Robert Louis-Dreyfus, former CEO of Saatchi & Saatchi Advertising, bought a controlling interest in Adidas AG. Adidas markets sports shoes, athletic clothing, and equipment in 160 countries. The German company has an illustrious history dating back many decades; in fact, Jesse Owens was wearing Adidas track shoes when he won four gold medals at the 1936 Olympic games. Such public triumphs helped make Adidas the world leader in the sports shoe market; by successfully leveraging its heritage, the company generated revenues of $5.4 billion in 2001. This financial performance represents a sweet victory for the new owners.

Years of financial controversy and changing ownership had diverted management's attention from the market and gradually eroded the company's fortunes. In Germany, Adidas's share of sports shoe sales declined from 60 percent to 40 percent from the early 1980s to the early 1990s, including a 10-point slide in a two-year period. Sneaker sales doubled in Europe between 1985 and 1995, and Nike and Reebok's share of the market jumped to 50 percent from 5 percent despite very high import duties. The Americans' success is due in part to big spending on advertising. Nike and Reebok each spend nearly $100 million annually to promote their shoes in Europe; Adidas's ad spending in Europe was considerably less. The popularity of American sneakers got an extra boost thanks to the high visibility of the American Dream Team at the 1992 Olympics; NBA stars endorse both Reebok and Nike.

The American athletic shoe companies are skilled global marketers. In 2001, Nike rang up $9.5 billion in worldwide sales, while Reebok's sales totaled $2.9 billion. Reebok is the market leader in France, Spain, and England, and Nike is number one in many other European countries. Although advertising tag lines such as "Just Do It" and "Planet Reebok" are presented in English, other parts of the message are adapted to reflect cultural differences. In France, for example, violence in ads is unacceptable, so Reebok replaced boxing scenes with images of women running on a beach. Also, European participation in sports is lower than in America; accordingly, Europeans are less likely to visit sporting goods stores. In France, Reebok shoes are now sold in nearly 1,000 traditional shoe stores.

Even in the face of such tough and growing competition, Adidas still enjoys high brand loyalty among older Europeans. The company recruits young people and pays them to wear Adidas shoes in public; they are also paid to work at sporting goods stores and promote Adidas products in other ways. Adidas also updated its image among younger European consumers by creating a new sport called Streetball. Ads airing on MTV Europe feature players outfitted in the company's new Streetball apparel line. Unlike its American rivals, Adidas does not utilize a global ad campaign. For example, a 1995 campaign that ran outside the U.S. featured Emil Zatopke, a Czechoslovakian Olympic runner.

The company does, however, maintain a single advertising agency—London-based Leagas Delany—for all its global markets. Bruce Haines, the agency's chief executive, notes, "Adidas is structured by geographic territories and sports-based business units. We're anxious to make sure there's one hand writing, one signature whatever the work, whatever the sport." In a move that indicated optimism about Adidas's future, in 1995 Dreyfus's group raised its stake to full ownership. In 1997, Dreyfus acquired Salomon, a French company. The move created Adidas-Salomon, the second largest sports equipment company in the world after Nike.

SOURCES: Dagmar Mussey, "Adidas Strides on its Own Path," *Advertising Age* (February 13, 1995), p. 6; Kevin Goldman, "Adidas Tries to Fill its Rivals' Big Shoes," *The Wall Street Journal* (March 17, 1994), p. B5; Joseph Pereira, "Off and Running: Pushing U.S. Style, Nike and Reebok Sell Sneakers to Europe," *The Wall Street Journal* (July 22, 1993), pp. A1, A8; Stephen Barr, "Adidas on the Rebound," *CFO* (September 1991), pp. 48–56; Igor Reichlin, "Where Nike and Reebok Have Plenty of Running Room," *Business Week* (March 11, 1991), pp. 56–60.

as a medium for reaching mass audiences will vary proportionately with the extent to which television viewing occurs within a country.

2. The message may reach the target audience but may not be understood or may even be misunderstood. This can be the result of an inadequate understanding of the target audience's level of sophistication or improper encoding.

3. The message may reach the target audience and may be understood but still may not induce the recipient to take the action desired by the sender. This could result from a lack of cultural knowledge about a target audience.
4. The effectiveness of the message can be impaired by *noise*. Noise in this case is an external influence such as competitive advertising, other sales personnel, and confusion at the receiving end. These factors can detract from the ultimate effectiveness of the communication.

The key question for global marketers is whether the *specific* advertising message and media strategy must be changed from region to region or country to country because of environmental requirements. Proponents of the "one world, one voice" approach to global advertising believe that the era of the global village is fast approaching and that tastes and preferences are converging worldwide. According to the standardization argument, because people everywhere want the same products for the same reasons, companies can achieve great economies of scale by unifying advertising around the globe. Advertisers who follow the localized approach are skeptical of the global village argument. Rather, they assert that consumers still differ from country to country and must be reached by advertising tailored to their respective countries. Proponents of localization point out that most blunders occur because advertisers have failed to understand—and adapt to—foreign cultures. Nick Brien, managing director of Leo Burnett, explains the situation this way:

> As the potency of traditional media declines on a daily basis, brand building locally becomes more costly and international brand building becomes more cost effective. The challenge for advertisers and agencies is finding ads which work in different countries and cultures. At the same time as this global tendency, there is a growing local tendency. It's becoming increasingly important to understand the requirements of both.[5]

During the 1950s, the widespread opinion of advertising professionals was that effective international advertising required assigning responsibility for campaign preparation to a local agency. In the early 1960s, this idea of local delegation was repeatedly challenged. For example, Eric Elinder, head of a Swedish advertising agency, wrote: "Why should three artists in three different countries sit drawing the same electric iron and three copywriters write about what, after all, is largely the same copy for the same iron?"[6] Elinder argued that consumer differences between countries were diminishing and that he would more effectively serve a client's interest by putting top specialists to work devising a strong international campaign. The campaign would then be presented with insignificant modifications that mainly entailed translating the copy into language well suited for a particular country.

As the decade of the 1980s began, Pierre Liotard-Vogt, former CEO of Nestlé, expressed similar views in an interview with *Advertising Age*.

Advertising Age: Are food tastes and preferences different in each of the countries in which you do business?

Liotard-Vogt: The two countries where we are selling perhaps the most instant coffee are England and Japan. Before the war they didn't drink coffee in those countries, and I heard people say that it wasn't any use to try to sell instant coffee to the English because they drink only tea and still less to the Japanese because they drink green tea and they're not interested in anything else.

5 Meg Carter, "Think Globally, Act Locally," *Financial Times* (June 30, 1997), p. 12.
6 Eric Elinder, "International Advertisers Must Devise Universal Ads, Dump Separate National Ones, Swedish Ad Man Avers," *Advertising Age* (November 27, 1961), p. 91.

When I was very young, I lived in England and at that time, if you spoke to an Englishman about eating spaghetti or pizza or anything like that, he would just look at you and think that the stuff was perhaps food for Italians. Now on the corner of every road in London you find pizzerias and spaghetti houses.

So I do not believe [preconceptions] about "national tastes." They are "habits," and they're not the same. If you bring the public a different food, even if it is unknown initially, when they get used to it, they will enjoy it too.

To a certain extent we know that in the north they like a coffee milder and a bit acid and less roasted; in the south, they like it very dark. So I can't say that taste differences don't exist. But to believe that those tastes are set and can't be changed is a mistake.[7]

The "standardized versus localized" debate picked up tremendous momentum after the 1983 publication, noted in earlier chapters, of Professor Ted Levitt's *Harvard Business Review* article, "The Globalization of Markets." Recently, some industry observers have detected a trend toward the increased use of localized advertising, sometimes known as **pattern advertising,** on a panregional or global basis. This is analogous to the concept of global product platforms discussed in Chapter 11. Representing a middle ground between 100 percent standardization and 100 percent adaptation, a pattern strategy calls for developing a basic communication platform or concept for which copy, artwork, or other elements can be adapted as required by individual country markets. For example, ads in a 1997 European print campaign for Boeing shared basic design elements, but the copy and the visual elements were localized on a country-by-country basis.

Ali Kanso surveyed two different groups of advertising managers—those taking localized approaches to overseas advertising and those taking standardized approaches. One finding was that managers who are attuned to cultural issues tended to prefer the localized approach, whereas managers less sensitive to cultural issues preferred a standardized approach.[8] Bruce Steinberg, ad sales director for MTV Europe, has discovered that the people responsible for executing global campaigns locally can exhibit strong resistance to a global campaign. Steinberg reported that he sometimes had to visit as many as 20 marketing directors from the same company to get approval for a pan-European MTV ad.[9]

As Kanso correctly notes, the debate over advertising approaches will probably continue for years to come. Localized and standardized advertising both have their place and both will continue to be used. Kanso's conclusion: What is needed for successful international advertising is a global commitment to local vision. In the final analysis, the decision of whether to use a global or localized campaign depends on recognition by managers of the trade-offs involved. On the one hand, a global campaign will result in the substantial benefits of cost savings, increased control, and the potential creative leverage of a global appeal. On the other hand, localized campaigns focus on the most important attributes of a product or brand in each nation or culture. The question of *when* to use each approach depends on the product involved and a company's objectives in a particular market.

7   "A Conversation with Nestlé's Pierre Liotard-Vogt," *Advertising Age* (June 30, 1980), p. 31.
8   Ali Kanso, "International Advertising Strategies: Global Commitment to Local Vision," *Journal of Advertising Research* 32, no. 1 (January-February 1992), pp. 10–14.
9   Ken Wells, "Selling to the World: Global Ad Campaigns, after Many Missteps, Finally Pay Dividends," *The Wall Street Journal* (August 27, 1992), p. A1.

Ogilvy & Mather Worldwide created this corporate image campaign for Boeing in 1997. The ads, which appeared in European print media such as the London Times, Le Figaro, *and* Der Spiegel, *communicate the point that Boeing relies extensively on European expertise in avionics. A textbook example of pattern advertising, the ads feature similar layouts (i.e., the dominant visual element is a photo in the upper half of the page; caption copy is reversed and superimposed on a black background in the lower half; a photo of an airplane is inset) whereas the copy and photos are localized for individual country markets.*

McDonald's advertising has enjoyed a surge of popularity in Japan during the past several years. One explanation is that McDonald's is utilizing its global approach that invites consumers to associate the restaurant with family members interacting in various situations. Starting in 1996, McDonald's campaign in Japan depicted various aspects of fatherhood. For example, one spot showed a father and son bicycling home with burgers and fries; another showed a father driving a van full of boisterous kids to McDonald's for milkshakes. The ads came at a time when many Japanese "salarymen" are reassessing the balance between work and family life. Although part of McDonald's global campaign, the spots have local elements as well: Japanese actors are used, and local musicians composed music reminiscent of Japanese prime time TV shows.[10]

Localized ads are less likely to be required for industrial products or for technology-oriented products sold to either consumers or business customers. For example, South Dakota-based Gateway recently commissioned Yankelovich Partners to conduct a survey of technology buying behavior in the United States, Great Britain,

---

[10] Yumko Ono, "Japan Warms to McDonald's Doting Dad Ads," *The Wall Street Journal* (May 8, 1997), pp. B1, B12.

Generally speaking, Japanese companies prefer a localized approach to advertising. For example, Nissan officials perceive a great deal of variation in consumer tastes and values across the company's markets. As a Nissan spokesman said recently, "The marketing and advertising decisions are made by the individual markets." This attitude explains why it is unlikely that the recent campaign for Nissan created by TBWA Chiat/Day for the United States will be used in other markets. Keyed to the slogan "Life is a journey. Enjoy the ride," the campaign was designed to increase brand awareness among American car buyers. Bob Thomas, president and CEO of Nissan Motor Corporation USA, budgeted a record $200 million for the campaign; Thomas instructed the agency "to create advertising that everybody would be talking about." Recalling the origins of the campaign, Lee Clow, creative director at TBWA Chiat/Day, told *The New York Times*, "People don't really like car advertising. It's all the same; it's all sheet metal, features, and usually some kind of deal at the end. We're changing the rules of how car advertising can be done."

Each ad in the TV campaign features a cameo by a Japanese-American actor modeled on Yutaka Katayama, Nissan's U.S. executive in the company's early export days. In "Toys," one of the campaign's most memorable spots, stop-motion animation is set against Van Halen's version of "You Really Got Me." In the 60-second spot, a GI Joe-like doll drives a 300ZX to pick up a Barbie look-alike, much to the dismay of a third, preppy figure. Production costs for the "Toys" spot alone totaled $1 million, twice as much as Nissan usually spends on a commercial. Both ads received popular and critical acclaim; unfortunately, however, Nissan's U.S. sales actually fell. As marketing consultant Jack Trout said, "They're not doing very well, but they're being talked about. There's something wrong: They've spent too much time and effort and money trying to entertain people, and they're not really showing their cars effectively."

Responding to complaints from dealers that the ads were not building showroom traffic, hard sell regional ads without Mr. K were created. Tom Patten, president of TBWA Chiat/Day, explained, "We wanted to spend more time on the critical element of motivating people to get out of their chairs on a Saturday afternoon and go to a dealer. In doing that, we don't see a need to utilize Mr. K. He's not relevant at this level." By 1998, however, the brand image ads were gone. A new campaign prominently features new models such as a four-door Frontier pickup truck. In one ad, a fisherman hooks a submarine, which he then lands with the help of his truck. Nissan dealers in the United States applaud the new approach. As one said, "Enough with the esoteric marketing concepts."

SOURCES: Robert L. Simison, "Nissan's Crisis Was Made in the U.S.A.," *The Wall Street Journal* (November 25, 1998), pp. B1, B4; Yumiko Ono, "McCann Finds Global a Tough Sell in Japan," *The Wall Street Journal* (June 19, 1997), p. B12; Sally Goll Beatty, "Mixed Message: Nissan's Ad Campaign was a Hit Everywhere but in the Showrooms," *The Wall Street Journal* (April 8, 1997), pp. A1, A14.

France, Australia, and Japan. As Luanne Flikkema, director of global research at Gateway, reported:

> We found that cultural differences had essentially no effect on the attitudes, motivators, and needs involved in purchasing technology. A first-time PC buyer in Japan was more similar to a first-time buyer in France than to a repeat buyer in Japan. An "Enthusiast" buyer was an Enthusiast buyer around the world. Were there any subtle regional differences? Of course. Did they make any appreciable difference in the purchase process? No.[11]

The brochures shown here for Fisher Controls International illustrate the same point. The product represented a breakthrough in valve technology with broad-

---

[11] Luanne Flikkema, "Global Marketing's Myth: Differences Don't Matter," *Marketing News* (July 20, 1998), p. 4.

Advertisements and other promotional materials for many industrial goods can often be standardized to a very significant degree. However, as illustrated by these brochures from Fisher Controls International, such materials should be translated into the appropriate language for individual country markets. Less evident but equally important, the dimensions of the brochures are in compliance with the International Standards Organization (ISO). This means that the brochures are printed so that they fit in a standard business-sized envelope for each country.

Eighteen-year-olds in Paris have more in common with 18-year-olds in New York than with their own parents. They buy the same products, go to the same movies, listen to the same music, sip the same colas. Global advertising merely works on that premise.[12]
—William Roedy, President, MTV Networks International

based applications that had worldwide sales potential. After soliciting input from affiliates in Asia, Europe, and South America, Thomas C. Porter & Associates, Fisher's advertising agency, created a single brochure that was translated into seven different languages.

By contrast, Teresa Hinrichs, senior manager for marketing communications, advertising, and brand management at Pioneer Hi-Bred International, noted recently that some of the company's advertising executions are becoming increasingly localized. While Pioneer's message is the same in different parts of the world, Hinrichs and her staff believe that some messages lend themselves to straight translation, while others need to be created in a way that is suited to the people, marketplace, and style of the particular country or region. Of the ads shown on page 534, the left is for the United States, and the ad on the right was created for Québec.

---

[12] Ken Wells, "Selling to the World: Global Ad Campaigns, after Many Missteps, Finally Pay Dividends," *The Wall Street Journal* (August 27, 1992), p. A1.

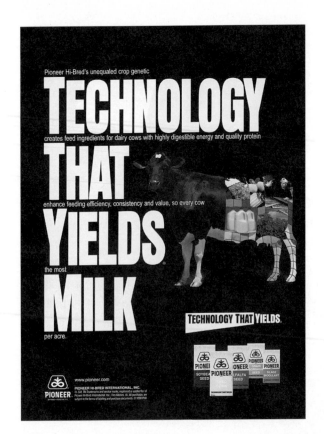

These ads for Pioneer Hi-Bred International exhibit localization that goes beyond translation of copy. The layouts, visual elements, and copy are different; elements common to the two ads are the trapezoid-shaped logo and the slogan "Technology That Yields."

ADVERTISING AGENCIES: ORGANIZATIONS AND BRANDS

Advertising is a fast-paced business, and the ad agency world is fluid and dynamic. New agencies are formed, existing agencies are dismantled, and cross-border investment, spin-offs, joint ventures, mergers, and acquisitions are a fact of life. There is also a great deal of mobility in the industry as executives and top talent move from one agency to another. The 20 largest global advertising organizations ranked by 1997 gross income are shown in Table 14-2. The key to understanding the table is the word *organizations*; each firm identified in Table 14-2 is an umbrella corporation that includes one or more "core" advertising agencies, as well as units specializing in direct marketing, marketing services, public relations, or research. As shown in Figure 14-1, the family tree of Omnicom Group is quite complex. The group includes several large agencies, including BBDO Worldwide, DDB Needham Worldwide, and TBWA International. Each of those agency "brands," in turn, includes a variety of firms. Individual agencies (agency "brands") are ranked in Table 14-3 by 1997 worldwide income. Most of the agency brands identified in Table 14-3 are **full-service agencies:** In addition to creating advertising, they provide other services, such as market research and media buying. A few offer more specialized services; Rapp Collins Worldwide, for example, is devoted to direct marketing. The agencies listed in Table 14-3 are not equally

Table 14-2
Top 20 Global
Advertising
Organizations

Organization and Headquarters Location	Gross Income 2000 (Millions)
1. WPP Group (London)	$7,971.0
2. Omnicom Group (New York)	6,986.2
3. Interpublic Group of Cos. (New York)	6,595.9
4. Dentsu (Tokyo)	3,089.0
5. Havas Advertising (Levallois-Perret)	2,757.3
6. Publicis Group (Paris)	2,479.1
7. Bcom3 Group (Chicago)	2,215.9
8. Grey Global Group (New York)	1,863.2
9. True North Communications (Chicago)	1,539.1
10. Cordiant Communications Group (London)	1,254.8
11. Hakuhodo (Tokyo)	1,008.7
12. Asatsu-DK (Tokyo)	431.4
13. Carlson Marketing Group (Minneapolis)	390.2
14. TMP Worldwide (New York)	332.1
15. Digitas (Boston)	288.2
16. Aspen Marketing Group (Los Angeles)	256.2
17. Tokyu Agency (Tokyo)	235.4
18. Ha-Lo Industries (Niles, Illinois)	233.1
19. Daiko Advertising (Tokyo/Osaka)	226.0
20. Incepta Group (London)	217.5

Source: "World's Top Ad Organizations," *Advertising Age* (April 23, 2001), p. s18.

global; Dentsu, for example, derives approximately 85 percent of its revenue from the home market. The need for a broader scope was one reason that Dentsu executives acquired a stake in Leo Burnett at the end of 1998.

Selecting an Advertising Agency

Companies can create ads in-house, use an outside agency, or combine both strategies. For example, Chanel, Benetton, and Diesel rely on in-house marketing and advertising staffs for creative work; Coca-Cola has its own agency, Edge Creative, but also uses the services of outside agencies such as Leo Burnett. When one or more outside agencies are used, they can serve product accounts on a multicountry or even global basis. It is possible to select a local agency in each national market or an agency with both domestic and overseas offices. Like Coca-Cola, Levi Strauss, and Polaroid also use local agencies. Today, however, there is a growing tendency for Western clients to designate global agencies for product accounts to support the integration of the marketing and advertising functions; Japan-based companies are less inclined to use this approach. For example, in 1995, Colgate-Palmolive consolidated its $500 million in global billings with Young & Rubicam. Similarly, Bayer AG consolidated most of its $300 million consumer products advertising with BBDO Worldwide; Bayer had previously relied on 50 agencies around the globe. Agencies are aware of this trend and are themselves pursuing international acquisitions and joint ventures to extend their geographic reach and their ability to serve clients on a global account basis. In an effort to remain competitive, many small independent

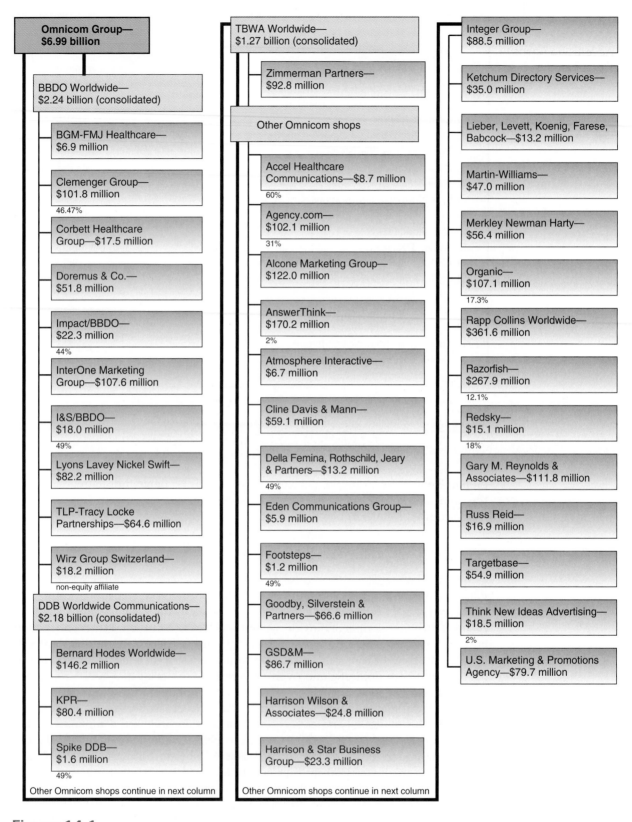

Figure 14-1
Omnicom Group Corporate Structure

Source: Adapted from "Advertising Organization Family Trees," *Advertising Age* (April 23, 2001).

Table 14-3

Top 10 Global Advertising Agency Brands

AGENCY	GROSS INCOME (MILLIONS)
1. Dentsu (Tokyo)	$2,432.0
2. McCann-Erickson Worldwide (New York)	1,824.9
3. BBDO Worldwide (New York)	1,534.0
4. J. Walter Thompson Co. (New York)	1,489.1
5. Euro RSCG Worldwide (New York)	1,430.1
6. Grey Worldwide (New York)	1,369.8
7. DDB Needham Worldwide (New York)	1,176.8
8. Ogilvy & Mather Worldwide (New York)	1,109.4
9. Publicis Worldwide (Paris)	1,040.9
10. Leo Burnett Co. (Chicago)	1,029.3

Source: "World's Top 10 Agency Brands," *Advertising Age* (April 23, 2001), p. s10.

agencies in Europe, Asia, and the United States belong to the Transworld Advertising Agency Network. TAAN allows member agencies to tap into worldwide resources that would not otherwise be available to them.

In selecting an advertising agency, the following issues should be considered:

Company organization. Companies that are decentralized may want to leave the choice to the local subsidiary.

National responsiveness. Is the global agency familiar with local culture and buying habits in a particular country, or should a local selection be made?

Area coverage. Does the candidate agency cover all relevant markets?

Buyer perception. What kind of brand awareness does the company want to project? If the product needs a strong local identification, it would be best to select a national agency.

Despite an unmistakable trend toward using global agencies to support global marketing efforts, companies with geocentric orientations will adapt to the global market requirements and select the best agency or agencies accordingly. For example, Colgate recently acquired the Kolynos line of oral care products in Latin America; McCann-Erickson Worldwide is responsible for that account, even though Young & Rubicam has the bulk of Colgate's business elsewhere. Western agencies still find markets such as South Korea and Japan very complex; similarly, Japanese and Korean agencies find it just as difficult to establish local agency presence in Western markets. Not surprisingly, as the Saturn unit of General Motors prepared for its 1997 entry into the Japanese market, it hired the Tokyo-based Dai-Ichi Kikaku as its agency.

As noted later in the chapter, advertising professionals face escalating pressure to achieve new heights of creativity. Some critics of advertising complain that agencies sometimes try to create advertising that will win awards and generate acclaim and prestige rather than advertising that serves clients' needs. The search for fresh answers to market challenges has prompted some client companies to look outside the advertising industry for input and ideas. For example, Coca-Cola utilizes the services of Creative Artists Agency, a legendary Hollywood talent agency. Client companies are also turning to companies such as the Boston Consulting Group for new strategic approaches and ideas for breathing new life into existing brands.

Certain consumer products lend themselves to advertising extension. If a product appeals to the same need around the world, there is a possibility of extending the appeal to that need. The list of products "going global," once confined to a score of consumer and luxury goods, is growing. Global advertising is partly responsible for increased worldwide sales of disposable diapers, diamond watches, shampoos, and athletic shoes. Some longtime global advertisers are benefiting from fresh campaigns. Jeans marketer Levi Strauss racked up record sales in Europe in 1991 on the strength of a campaign extended unchanged to Europeans, Latin Americans, and Australians. The basic issue is whether there is, in fact, a global market for the product. If the market is global, appeals can be standardized and extended. Soft drinks, Scotch whiskey, Swiss watches, and designer clothing are examples of product categories whose markets are truly global. For example, Seagrams recently ran a global campaign keyed to the theme line, "There will always be a Chivas Regal." The campaign featured a series of universal images and was translated into 15 languages. Managers in each of 34 countries were authorized to choose individual ads from the campaign that they deemed appropriate for their markets.

In 1991, Seagrams launched a global billboard campaign to enhance the universal appeal for Chivas. The theory: The rich all over will sip the brand, no matter where they made their fortune.

Gillette took a standardized "one product, one brand name, one strategy" global approach when it introduced the Sensor razor in 1990. The campaign slogan was "Gillette. The best a man can get," an appeal that was expected to cross boundaries with ease. Peter Hoffman, marketing vice president of the North Atlantic Shaving Group, noted in a press release: "We are blessed with a product category where we're able to market shaving systems across multinational boundaries as if they were one country. Gillette Sensor is the trigger for a total Gillette megabrand strategy which will revolutionize the entire shaving market." In the Japanese market, Gillette's standardized advertising campaign differs strikingly from that of arch-rival Schick. Prior to the Sensor launch, Gillette custom-made advertising for the Japanese market; now, the phrase "The best a man can get" is translated into Japanese; otherwise, the ads shown in Japan are the same as in the United States and the rest of the world. Schick, meanwhile, uses Japanese actors in its ads.

CREATING GLOBAL ADVERTISING

As suggested earlier in the discussion of the extension versus standardization debate, the *message* is at the heart of advertising. The particular message and the way it is presented will depend on the advertiser's objective. Is the ad designed to inform, entertain, remind, or persuade? Moreover, in a world characterized by information overload, ads must break through the clutter, grab the audience's attention, and linger in their minds. This requires developing an original and effective **creative strategy,** which is simply a statement or concept of what a particular message or campaign will say. Advertising agencies can be thought of as "idea factories"; in industry parlance, the Holy Grail in creative strategy development is something known as the **big idea.** Legendary ad man John O'Toole defined the *big idea* as "that flash of insight that synthesizes the purpose of the strategy, joins the product benefit with consumer desire in a fresh, involving way, brings the subject to life, and makes the reader or audience stop, look, and listen.[13] In his book about Subaru of America, Randall Rothenberg describes the big idea in the following way:

> The Big Idea is easier to illustrate than define, and easier to illustrate by what it is not than by what it is. It is not a "position" (although the

---

[13] John O'Toole, *The Trouble With Advertising* (New York: Random House, 1985), p. 131.

CHINA

In 1994, the Chinese government banned tobacco advertising from television and radio; the ban also extended to newspaper, magazine, and cinema ads. With a population of 1.2 billion people, including one-third of the world's smokers, China is considered to be a massive potential market for cigarette manufacturers at a time when Western markets are shrinking. The ban was part of China's first law of advertisements. The World Health Organization has asked Chinese leaders to launch antismoking campaigns and impose tougher controls on cigarette smuggling and higher taxes on domestic cigarette producers.

CENTRAL EUROPE

Tobacco companies face the prospect of tougher marketing regulations as countries in Central Europe work to meet requirements for entry into the EU. In the Czech Republic, the Association of Advertising Agencies (ARA) is battling a proposal to ban all cigarette advertising, effective from April 2001. Jiri Mikes, vice president of ARA, said his organization was not completely opposed to changes in the law, but questioned the government's implementation date since the EU's deadline for meeting tobacco advertising restrictions was not until 2006. In Lithuania, authorities began to enforce the country's three-year-old tobacco advertising ban on May 1, 2000; some newspapers printed blank pages in protest. Jurga Karmanoviene, media director for Saatchi & Saatchi Lithuania, interprets the enforcement as evidence that the government is sending a signal that it is beginning to meet EU requirements. Similar developments are occurring in Poland, Hungary, Bulgaria, and Romania.

AUSTRALIA

In June 1994, the Philip Morris Company initiated legal action to overturn the Australian government's ban on cigarette advertising, contending that it in-fringed on the company's freedom of speech. Under legislation passed in 1992, tobacco advertising and sponsorship in Australia was phased out and banned entirely in 1996, except for international events such as Formula One racing. Philip Morris attempted to have the Commonwealth Tobacco Advertising Prohibition Act declared invalid on the grounds that the act went beyond preventing cigarette advertising and imposed a wide array of restrictions that infringe on basic rights. According to a company executive, "The Philip Morris Australian subsidiary says the anti-tobacco laws breach the Australian Constitution's implied guarantee of freedom of communication, breaches the states and is beyond the powers of the federal Government."

EUROPEAN UNION

A Union-wide tobacco ad ban proposal was introduced in mid-1991 with the aim of fulfilling single-market rules of the Maastricht Treaty. The directive would have prohibited tobacco advertising on billboards as of July 2001; newspaper and magazine advertising was slated to end by 2002, with sports sponsorship banned by 2003 (such "world level" sports as Formula One racing were excluded until 2006). Not surprisingly, the proposed ban was opposed by tobacco companies and advertising associations. The European Commission justified the directive on the grounds that various countries had or were considering restrictions on tobacco advertising and that there was a need for common rules on cross-border trade. Prior to the directive's implementation date, however, the German government took the issue to the European Court of Justice. The Germans argued that the directive was illegal because tobacco advertising is a health issue; thus, the directive could only be adopted if the member states agreed unanimously. The EU's advocate general concurred with the German government. On October 5, 2000, the court ruled that the directive prohibiting tobacco ads should be annulled.

For RJ Reynolds International, Philip Morris International, B.A.T, and other tobacco marketers, the receding threat of a pan-European ban on tobacco ads comes as welcome news. The industry spends between $600 million and $1 billion on advertising in the EU annually. An EU ban would have hurt them most in the countries where they compete with entrenched state tobacco monopolies, namely, France, Italy, and Spain.

SOURCES: Joyce-Ann Gatsoulis, "EU Aspirants Shake Up Tobacco Marketing Scene," *Advertising Age International* (July 2000), p. 15; Tony Koenderman and Paul Meller, "EU Topples Tobacco Ad Rules," *Advertising Age* (October 9, 2000), pp. 4, 97; Juliana Koranteng, "EU Ad Ban on Tobacco Under File as Illegal," *Advertising Age* (July 10, 2000), pp. 4, 49; "Australia's Ad Ban Is Fought," *The New York Times* (June 7, 1994), p. 19; Marcus Brauchli, "China Passes Law in Move to Prohibit Ads for Tobacco," *The Wall Street Journal* (October 31, 1994), p. B10; Lili Cui, "Mass Media Boycott Tobacco Ads," *Beijing Review* (June 6, 1994), p. 8; "Tobacco Adverts: Fuming," *The Economist* (February 5, 1994), pp. 60–61.

place a product occupies in the consumer's mind may be a part of it). It is not an "execution" (although the writing or graphic style of an ad certainly contributes to it). It is not a slogan (although a tag line may encapsulate it).

The Big Idea is the bridge between an advertising strategy, temporal and worldly, and an image, powerful and lasting. The theory of the Big Idea assumes that average consumers are at best bored and more likely irrational when it comes to deciding what to buy.[14]

Some of the world's most memorable advertising campaigns have achieved success because they originate from an idea that is so "big" that the campaign can run for many years. Such a campaign is said to have *legs*. The print campaign for Absolut vodka is a perfect example of both a big idea and legs: Over the course of fifteen years, Absolut's agency has created more than 500 two-word puns on the brand name linked with pictoral renderings of the distinctive bottle shape.

The **advertising appeal** is the communications approach that relates to the motives of the target audience. For example, ads based on a *rational approach* depend on logic and speak to the audience's intellect. Ads using an *emotional approach* tug at the heartstrings of the intended audience. In other words, some ads use a knowledge-based appeal whereas others appeal to feelings. The **selling proposition** is the promise or claim that captures the reason for buying the product or the benefit that ownership confers. Because products are frequently at different stages in their life cycle in various national markets, and because of cultural, social, and economic differences that exist in those markets, the most effective appeal or selling proposition for a product may vary from market to market.

Effective global advertising may also require developing different presentations of the product's appeal or selling proposition. The way an appeal or proposition is presented is called the **creative execution.** In other words, there can be differences between *what* one says and *how* one says it. Many execution alternatives are available including straight sell, scientific evidence, demonstration, comparison, testimonial, slice of life, animation, fantasy, and dramatization. The responsibility for deciding on the appeal, the selling proposition, and the appropriate execution lies with *creatives*, a term that applies to art directors and copywriters.

Art Directors and Art Direction

The visual presentation of an advertisement—the "body language"—is a matter of **art direction.** An *art director* is an advertising professional who has the general responsibility for the overall look of an ad. In addition, the art director chooses graphics, pictures, type styles, and other visual elements that appear in an ad. Some forms of visual presentation are universally understood. Revlon, for example, has used a French producer to develop television commercials in English and Spanish for use in international markets. These commercials are filmed in Parisian settings but communicate the universal appeals and specific benefits of Revlon products. By producing its ads in France, Revlon obtains effective television commercials at a much lower cost than it would have paid for commercials produced in the United States. PepsiCo has used four basic commercials to communicate its advertising themes. The basic setting of young people having fun at a party or on a beach has been adapted to reflect the general physical environment and racial characteristics of North America, South America, Europe, Africa, and Asia. The music in these commercials has also

---

[14] Randall Rothenberg, *Where the Suckers Moon* (New York: Vintage Books, 1995), pp. 112–113.

been adapted to suit regional tastes, ranging from rock 'n' roll in North America to bossa nova in Latin America to high life in Africa.

The global advertiser must make sure that visual executions are not inappropriately extended into markets. Benetton recently encountered a problem with its United Colors of Benetton campaign. The campaign appeared in 77 countries, primarily in print and on billboards. The art direction focused on striking, provocative interracial juxtapositions—a white hand and a black hand handcuffed together, for example. Another version of the campaign, depicting a black woman nursing a white baby, won advertising awards in France and Italy. However, because the image evoked the history of slavery in America, that particular creative execution was not used in the U.S. market (see Case 14-1).

Copy

The words that are the spoken or written communication elements in advertisements are known as **copy.** Copywriters are language specialists who develop the headlines, subheads, and body copy used in print advertising and the scripts containing the words that are delivered by spokespeople, actors, or hired voice talents in broadcast ads. As a general rule, copy should be relatively short and avoid slang or idioms. Languages vary in terms of the number of words required to convey a given message; thus the increased use of pictures and illustrations. European and Japanese advertisements are often purely visual, conveying a specific message and invoking the company name.[15] Low literacy rates in many countries seriously compromise the use of print as a communications device and require greater creativity in the use of audio-oriented media.

It is important to recognize overlap in the use of languages in many areas of the world (e.g., the European Union, Latin America, and North America). Capitalizing on this, global advertisers can realize economies of scale by producing advertising copy with the same language and message for these markets. Of course, the success of this approach will depend in part on avoiding unintended ambiguity in the ad copy. Then again, in some situations, ad copy must be translated into the local language. Translating copy has been the subject of great debate in advertising circles. Advertising slogans often present the most difficult translation problems. The challenge of encoding and decoding slogans and tag lines in different national and cultural contexts can lead to unintentional errors. For example, the Asian version of Pepsi's "Come alive" copy line was rendered as a call to bring ancestors back from the grave.

Advertising executives may elect to prepare new copy for a foreign market in the language of the target country, or to translate the original copy into the target language. A third option is to leave some (or all) copy elements in the original (home-country) language. In choosing from these alternatives, the advertiser must consider whether a translated message can be received and comprehended by the intended foreign audience. Anyone with a knowledge of two or more languages realizes that the ability to think in another language facilitates accurate communication. To be confident that a message will be understood correctly after it is received, one must understand the connotations of words, phrases, and sentence structures, as well as their translated meaning.

The same principle applies to advertising—perhaps to an even greater degree. A copywriter who can think in the target language and understands the consumers in

---

[15] Vern Terpstra and Ravi Sarathy, *International Marketing* (Orlando, FL: The Dryden Press, 1991), p. 465.

In a recent speech, Martin Sorrell, CEO of the WPP Group, warned of changes in the business environment that have enormous implications for the advertising industry. Quoting business gurus such as Harvard professor John Kao and management author-philosopher Charles Handy, Sorrell suggested that the information age is already giving way to the creative age, an era that will require not just creativity, but *actionable* creativity. The problem, in Sorrell's view, is twofold: client companies aren't yet asking for "actionable creativity," and few advertising agencies are prepared to offer it. Sorrell noted:

We must first recognize ourselves, and then convey to others, that creativity is not simply about communications. . . I believe that, over the last 30 years and in most parts of the world, agencies have become more, rather than less, specialized in the forms of creativity they offer. By "more specialized," I mean more narrowly focused and therefore more limited.

There was once a time when client companies would welcome an agency's thoughts on just about all aspects of their business: diversification, brand strategy, investment, internal training, presentation—as well as advertising and promotion. For a wide variety of reasons, all that has changed: certainly in the US and the UK. Increasingly, clients expect only creativity in their communications from their agencies—and, increasingly, that's all that agencies are organized to provide.

Sorrell continued by cautioning that in today's world, it is not enough for creativity to be the exclusive domain of agency creatives:

In a business world that is going to put a higher and higher value on integrated creativity, we are in danger of losing what should be our overwhelming advantage—by allowing something called "creativity" to be confined to the creative compound. What we sell are pearls. Whether we are designers or planners or writers or art directors or corporate strategists, our raw material is knowledge. We turn that knowledge into ideas, insights, and objects that have a material, quantifiable value to our clients. They are all pearls: of wisdom, of beauty, of desire, of wonder.

Sorrell concluded his remarks by noting that advertising agencies will have to develop new organizational forms, structures, and processes to remain competitive in the twenty-first century. In particular, he suggests that agency personnel have much to learn from their "creative cousins"—those who work in the theater, the arts, and electronic publishing and design.

---

the target country will be able to create the most effective appeals, organize the ideas, and craft the specific language, especially if colloquialisms, idioms, or humor are involved. For example, in southern China, McDonald's is careful not to advertise prices with multiple occurrences of the number 4. The reason is simple: In Cantonese, the pronunciation of the word *four* is similar to that of the word *death*.[16] In its efforts to develop a global brand image, Citicorp discovered that translations of its slogan "Citi never sleeps" conveyed the meaning that Citibank had a sleeping disorder such as insomnia. Company executives decided to retain the slogan but use English throughout the world.[17]

Cultural Considerations

Knowledge of cultural diversity, especially the symbolism associated with cultural traits, is essential for creating advertising. Local country managers can share important information, such as when to use caution in advertising creativity. Use of colors and man-woman relationships can often be stumbling blocks. For example, in Japan, intimate scenes between men and women are considered to be in bad taste; they are

---

[16] Jeanne Whalen, "McDonald's Cooks Worldwide Growth," *Advertising Age International* (July-August 1995), p. I4.
[17] Stephen E. Frank, "Citicorp's Big Account Is at Stake as it Seeks a Global Brand Name," *The Wall Street Journal* (January 9, 1997), p. B6.

outlawed in Saudi Arabia. Veteran adman John O'Toole offers the following insights to global advertisers:

> Transplanted American creative people always want to photograph European men kissing women's hands. But they seldom know that the nose must never touch the hand or that this rite is reserved solely for married women. And how do you know that the woman in the photograph is married? By the ring on her left hand, of course. Well, in Spain, Denmark, Holland, and Germany, Catholic women wear the wedding ring on the right hand.
>
> When photographing a couple entering a restaurant or theater, you show the woman preceding the man, correct? No. Not in Germany and France. And this would be laughable in Japan. Having someone in a commercial hold up his hand with the back of it to you, the viewer, and the fingers moving toward him should communicate "come here." In Italy it means "good-bye."[18]

Tamotsu Kishii identified seven characteristics that distinguish Japanese from American creative strategy:

1. Indirect rather than direct forms of expression are preferred in the messages. This avoidance of directness in expression is pervasive in all types of communication among the Japanese, including their advertising. Many television ads do not mention what is desirable about the brand in use and let the audience judge for themselves.
2. There is often little relationship between ad content and the advertised product.
3. Only brief dialogue or narration is used in television commercials, with minimal explanatory content. In the Japanese culture, the more one talks, the less others will perceive him or her trustworthy or self-confident. A 30-second advertisement for young menswear shows five models in varying and seasonal attire, ending with a brief statement from the narrator: "Our life is a fashion show!"
4. Humor is used to create a bond of mutual feelings. Rather than slapstick, humorous dramatizations involve family members, neighbors, and office colleagues.
5. Famous celebrities appear as close acquaintances or everyday people.
6. Priority is placed on company trust rather than product quality. Japanese tend to believe that if the firm is large and has a good image, the quality of its products should also be outstanding.
7. The product name is impressed on the viewer with short, 15-second commercials.[19]

Green, Cunningham, and Cunningham conducted a cross-cultural study to determine the extent to which consumers of different nationalities use the same criteria to evaluate soft drinks and toothpaste. Their subjects were college students

---

[18] John O'Toole, *The Trouble With Advertising* (New York: Random House, 1985), pp. 209–210.
[19] C. Anthony di Benedetto, Mariko Tamate, and Rajan Chandran, "Developing Creative Advertising Strategy for the Japanese Marketplace," *Journal of Advertising Research* (January-February 1992), pp. 39–48. A number of recent studies have been devoted to comparing ad content in different parts of the world, including Mary C. Gilly, "Sex Roles in Advertising: A Comparison of Television Advertisements in Australia, Mexico, and the United States," *Journal of Marketing* (April 1988), pp. 75–85; Marc G. Weinberger and Harlan E. Spotts, "A Situation View of Information Content in TV Advertising in the U.S. and U.K.," *Journal of Advertising* 53 (January 1989), pp. 89–94.

from the United States, France, India, and Brazil. Compared to France and India, the U.S. respondents placed more emphasis on the subjective, as opposed to functional, product attributes. The Brazilian respondents appeared even more concerned with the subjective attributes than the Americans were. The authors concluded that advertising messages should not use the same appeal for these countries if the advertiser is concerned with communicating the most important attributes of its product in each market.[20]

Ads that strike viewers in some countries as humorous or irritating may not necessarily be perceived that way by viewers in other countries. American ads make frequent use of spokespeople and direct product comparisons; they use logical arguments to try to appeal to the reason of audiences. Japanese advertising is more image oriented and appeals to audience sentiment. In Japan, what is most important frequently is not what is stated explicitly but, rather, what is implied. Nike's U.S. advertising is legendary for its irreverent, "in your face" style and relies heavily on celebrity sports endorsers such as Michael Jordan. In other parts of the world, where soccer is the top sport, some Nike ads are considered to be in poor taste and its pitchmen have less relevance. Nike has responded by adjusting its approach; notes Geoffrey Frost, director of global advertising, "We have to root ourselves in the passions of other countries. It's part of our growing up."[21] Some American companies have canceled television ads created for the Latin American market portraying racial stereotypes that were offensive to persons of color. Nabisco, Goodyear, and other companies are also being more careful about the shows during which they buy airtime; some very popular Latin American programs feature content that exploits class, race, and ethnic differences.[22]

There are also widely varying standards for use of sexually explicit or provocative imagery. Partial nudity and same-sex couples are frequently seen in ads in Latin America and Europe. In the U.S. market, advertisers are constrained by network television decency standards and the threat of boycotts by conservative consumer activists. Some industry observers note a paradoxical situation in which the programs shown on American TV are frequently racy, but the ads that air during those shows are not. As Marcio Moreira, worldwide chief creative officer at the McCann-Erickson agency, noted recently, "Americans want titillation in entertainment but when it comes to advertising they stop being viewers and become consumers and critics."[23] However, it is certainly not the case that anything goes outside the United States. Women in Monterrey, Mexico recently complained about billboards for the Playtex unit of Sara Lee Corporation that featured supermodel Eva Herzegova wearing a Wonderbra. The campaign was created by a local agency, Perez Munoz Publicidad. Playtex responded by covering up the model on the billboards in some Mexican cities. Similarly, British citizens complained to the Advertising Standards Authority in London about a billboard campaign showing a model in repose clad only in Glossies brand underwear. The copy declared, "Who said a woman can't get pleasure from something soft."[24]

---

[20] Robert T. Green, William H. Cunningham, and Isabella C. M. Cunningham, "The Effectiveness of Standardized Global Advertising," *Journal of Advertising* (Summer 1975), pp. 25–30.

[21] Roger Thurow, "Shtick Ball: In Global Drive, Nike Finds its Brash Ways Don't Always Pay Off," *The Wall Street Journal* (May 5, 1997), p. A10.

[22] Leon E. Wynter, "Global Marketers Learn to Say 'No' to Bad Ads," *The Wall Street Journal* (April 1, 1998), p. B1.

[23] Melanie Wells and Dottie Enrico, "U.S. Admakers Cover It Up; Others Don't Give a Fig Leaf," *USA Today* (June 27, 1997), pp. B1, B2.

[24] Juliana Koranteng and Richard Bruner, "Sexy Bras Drawing Protests," *Ad Age International* (July 1996), p. i6.

Food is the product category most likely to exhibit cultural sensitivity. Thus, marketers of food and food products must be alert to the need to localize their advertising. A good example of this is the recent effort by H. J. Heinz Company to develop the overseas market for ketchup. Heinz's strategy called for adapting both the product and advertising to target country tastes.[25] In Greece, for example, ads show ketchup pouring over pasta, eggs, and cuts of meat. In Japan, they instruct Japanese homemakers on using ketchup as an ingredient in Western-style food such as omelettes, sausages, and pasta. Barry Tilley, London-based general manager of Heinz's Western Hemisphere trading division, says Heinz uses focus groups to determine what foreign consumers want in the way of taste and image. Americans like a sweet ketchup, but Europeans prefer a spicier, more piquant variety. Significantly, Heinz's foreign marketing efforts are most successful when the company quickly adapts to local cultural preferences. In Sweden, the made-in-America theme is so muted in Heinz's ads that "Swedes don't realize Heinz is American. They think it is German because of the name," says Tilley. In contrast to this, American themes still work well in Germany. Kraft and Heinz are trying to outdo each other with ads featuring strong American images. In Heinz's latest TV ad, American football players in a restaurant become very angry when the 12 steaks they ordered arrive without ketchup. The ad ends happily, of course, with plenty of Heinz ketchup to go around.[26]

"Everybody likes to think that there is some mystique about China, but the Chinese consumer actually behaves much like any other. The key to getting it right is the advertising strategy, not the execution of the advertising."[27]
—Soames Hines, former managing director, J. Walter Thompson, Shanghai

GLOBAL MEDIA DECISIONS

The next issue facing advertisers is which medium or media to use when communicating with target audiences. Traditionally, the agency that creates advertising also makes decisions about media placement. The alternatives can be broadly categorized as print media, electronic media, and other. Print media range in form from local daily and weekly newspapers to magazines and business publications with national, regional, or international audiences. Electronic media include broadcast television, cable television, radio, and the Internet. Additionally, advertisers may utilize various forms of outdoor, transit, and direct mail advertising. Media availability can vary from country to country. Some companies use virtually the entire spectrum of available media; Coca-Cola is a good example. Other companies prefer to utilize one or two media categories. Benetton, for example, relied exclusively on print and outdoor media for many years. The same was true of the Swatch Group's advertising for Swatch watches. However, faced with increasing competition with Timex in the U.S. fashion watch market, Swatch rolled out a new line of metal watches in 1995. Simultaneously, Swatch began using television advertising for the first time in conjunction with its sponsorship of the 1996 Olympics. As Denise Benou, vice president of marketing at Swatch, noted, "People know our brand, but they don't have as clear an awareness of what Swatch is today. We needed to show that we don't have limited appeal."[28]

[25] Gary Levin, "Ads Going Global," *Advertising Age* (July 22, 1991), pp. 4, 42.
[26] Gabriella Stern, "Heinz Aims to Export Taste for Ketchup," *The Wall Street Journal* (November 20, 1992), p. B1.
[27] James Harding, "Consumer Revolution," *Financial Times* (July 14, 1997), p. 10.
[28] Fara Warner, "Timex, Swatch Get Set for Battle with Expensive Ad Campaigns," *The Wall Street Journal* (May 31, 1995), p. B8.

Media Vehicles and Expenditures

As shown in Table 14-4, more money is spent on advertising in the United States than anywhere else in the world. In fact, expenditures in the United States are four times greater than in the second-ranked country, which is Japan. As one might expect, the largest per capita advertising expenditures occur in highly developed countries. The lowest per capita expenditures were in the less-developed countries. Television is the number one medium in seven of the nine nations included in Table 14-4; newspapers are the leading medium in Germany and Japan, with television ranked second. In Germany, outlays for newspaper advertising surpass those for television by a ratio of two to one. By contrast, in Brazil, expenditures on television advertising are nearly three times higher than those for newspapers. The availability of media and the conditions affecting media buys vary greatly around the world. In Mexico, an advertiser that can pay for a full-page ad may get the front page, while in India, paper shortages may require booking an ad six months in advance. In some countries, especially those where the electronic media are government-owned, television and radio stations can broadcast only a restricted number of advertising messages. In Saudi Arabia, no commercial television advertising was allowed prior to May 1986; currently, ad content and visual presentation are restricted. In such countries, the proportion of advertising funds allocated to print is extremely high. In April 1995, Russia's national Channel 1 banned all commercial advertising; the ban was subsequently lifted.

The United States and Japan lead the world in television advertising with combined expenditures in 2000 of $67 billion. In real terms, television spending in the European Union increased by 78 percent between 1990 and 2000, compared with 26 percent for newspapers and 11 percent for magazines during the same period. This trend is likely to continue as digital broadcasting gains acceptance in Europe. Television is also important in the Latin American market. Of the ten countries where more than 50 percent of measured media expenditures are allocated to television, most are located in Central or South America or the Caribbean. In Brazil, for example, television accounts for 60 percent of advertising spending. As ownership of television sets increases in other areas of the world such as Southeast Asia, television advertising will become more important as a communication vehicle. Figure 14-2 shows recent figures for advertising in the European Union.

Table 14-4
Top 10 Countries for Ad Expenditures

COUNTRY	PROJECTED TOTAL AD SPENDING 2000 ($ BILLIONS)
United States	$134.3
Japan	33.2
Germany	21.6
United Kingdom	15.8
France	11.1
Italy	8.3
Brazil	6.9
Spain	5.4
Canada	5.3

Sources: Zenith Media, *The Economist.*

Figure 14-2
Total EU Ad
Expenditures 1996

*Source: International
Journal of Advertising,*
February 1998.

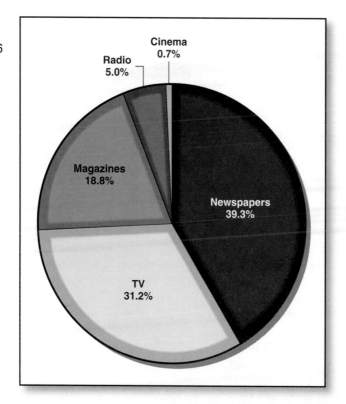

Worldwide, radio continues to be a less important advertising medium than print and television. As a proportion of total measured media advertising expenditures, radio trailed considerably behind print, television, and direct advertising. However, in countries where advertising budgets are limited, radio's enormous reach can provide a cost-effective means of communicating with a large consumer market. Also, radio can be effective in countries where literacy rates are low.

As countries add mass transportation systems and build and improve their highway infrastructures, advertisers are utilizing more indoor and outdoor posters and billboards to reach the buying public. Spending on outdoor and transit advertising in Japan is much higher than in other countries. Transit advertising was recently introduced in Russia, where drab streetcars and buses have been emblazoned with the bright colors of Western brands.

Media Decisions

Although markets are becoming increasingly similar in industrial countries, the availability of television, newspapers, and other forms of electronic and print media varies around the world. This fact of life has a direct impact on media decisions. For example, circulation figures of newspapers on a per capita basis cover a wide range. In Japan, where readership is high, there is one newspaper in circulation for every two people. There are approximately 65 million newspapers in daily circulation in the United States, a per capita ratio of approximately one to four. The ratio is one paper to approximately 20 people in Latin America, and one to 200 persons in Nigeria and Sweden.

Within a particular industry, media strategies can differ greatly. As indicated in this exhibit, New Balance is the only major athletic shoe marketer to allocate most of its budget toward print advertising. Why do you think that is the case?

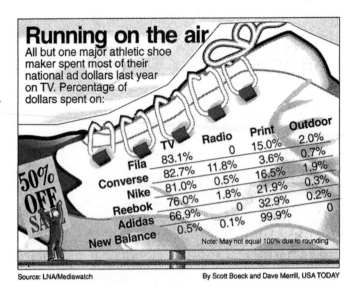

Running on the air
All but one major athletic shoe maker spent most of their national ad dollars last year on TV. Percentage of dollars spent on:

	TV	Radio	Print	Outdoor
Fila	83.1%	0	15.0%	2.0%
Converse	82.7%	11.8%	3.6%	0.7%
Nike	81.0%	0.5%	16.5%	1.9%
Reebok	76.0%	1.8%	21.9%	0.3%
Adidas	66.9%	0	32.9%	0.2%
New Balance	0.5%	0.1%	99.9%	0

Note: May not equal 100% due to rounding

Source: LNA/Mediawatch   By Scott Boeck and Dave Merrill, USA TODAY

Even when media availability is high, its use as an advertising vehicle may be limited. For example, in Europe, television advertising either does not exist or is very limited in Denmark, Sweden, and Norway. The time allowed for advertising each day varies from 12 minutes in Finland to 80 in Italy, with 12 minutes per hour per channel allowed in France and 20 in Switzerland, Germany, and Austria. Regulations concerning content of commercials vary, and there are waiting periods of up to two years in several countries before an advertiser can obtain broadcast time. In Germany, advertising time slots are reserved and paid for one year in advance.

In Saudi Arabia, where all advertising is subject to censorship, regulations prohibit a long list of subject matter, including the following:

Advertisements of horoscope or fortune-telling books, publications, or magazines are prohibited.

Advertisements that frighten or disturb children are to be avoided.

Use of preludes to advertisements that appear to indicate a news item or official statement are to be avoided.

Use of comparative advertising claims is prohibited.

Noncensored films cannot be advertised.

Women may only appear in those commercials that relate to family affairs, and their appearance must be in a decent manner that ensures their feminine dignity.

Female children under six years of age may appear in commercials, provided that their roles are limited to a childhoodlike activity.

Women should wear a long, suitable dress, which fully covers the body except face and palms. Sweat suits or similar garments are not allowed.[29]

---

[29] National Trade Data Bank: The Export Connection, USDOC, *International Trade Administration*, Market Research Reports (October 2, 1992). See also Mushtag Luqmani, Ugur Yavas, and Zahir Quraeshi, "Advertising in Saudi Arabia: Content and Regulation," *International Marketing Review* 6, no. 1 (1989), pp. 59–72.

PUBLIC RELATIONS AND PUBLICITY

A company's **public relations (PR)** effort should foster goodwill and understanding among constituents both inside and outside the company. One of the tasks of the PR practitioner is to generate favorable **publicity.** By definition, publicity is communication about a company or product for which the company does not pay. (In the PR world, publicity is sometimes referred to as "earned media," and advertising and promotions are known as "unearned media.") PR personnel also play a key role in responding to unflattering media reports or controversies that arise because of company activities in different parts of the globe. In such instances, PR's job is to make sure that the company responds promptly and gets its side of the story told. The basic tools of public relations include news releases, newsletters, media kits, press conferences, tours of plants and other company facilities, articles in trade or professional journals, company publications and brochures, TV and radio talk show appearances by company personnel, special events, and home pages on the Internet. In addition to the examples discussed in the following pages, Table 14-5 summarizes several recent instances of global publicity involving well-known firms.

As noted earlier, a company exerts complete control over the content of its advertising and pays for message placement in the media. However, the media typically receive many more press releases and other public relations materials than they can use. Generally speaking, a company has little control over when, or if, a news story runs. Nor can the company directly control the spin, slant, or tone of the story. To compensate for this lack of control, many companies utilize **corporate advertising** which, despite the name, is generally considered part of the PR function. As with "regular" advertising, corporate advertising is created and paid for by a company or organization identified in the ad. However, unlike regular advertising, the objective of corporate advertising is not to generate demand by informing, persuading, entertaining, or reminding customers. In the context of integrated marketing communications, corporate advertising is often used to call attention to the company's other communications efforts.

Table 14-5
Negative Publicity Affecting Global Marketers

COMPANY OR BRAND (HOME COUNTRY)	NATURE OF PUBLICITY
Ford Motor Company (USA) and **Bridgestone/ Firestone** (Japan/USA)	A rash of tire failures on Ford vehicles prompted a recall in 2000 of several tire models. Ultimately, Ford severed its decades-old relationship with Firestone.
Coca-Cola (USA)	In June 1999, hundreds of people in Belgium and France reported feeling ill after drinking Coke. The company responded by making the largest product recall in its history.
Nike (USA)	Since the mid-1990s, Nike has been responding to the criticism that its subcontractors operate factories in which sweatshop conditions prevail. Filmmaker Michael Moore featured an interview with Nike CEO Phil Knight in the anti-globalization documentary "The Big One."
McDonald's (USA)	Concerns about mad cow disease in Europe, a bitter legal battle in Great Britain, and media reports about beef-tainted fries have all presented public relations challenges to the fast-food giant.

Image advertising is designed to enhance the public's perception of a company, create goodwill, or announce a major change such as a merger or acquisition. The Boeing ads that appear earlier in this chapter were part of a European print campaign launched in 1997 to enhance Boeing's image by raising awareness of the number of jobs the company created locally. Following the merger of Daimler and Chrysler in the fall of 1998, a series of full-page print ads announced the formation of the new company. Global companies frequently utilize image advertising in an effort to present themselves as good corporate citizens in foreign countries. As noted previously, Boeing recently ran a series of print ads in Europe to increase awareness of its role as an employer in the region.

Other examples of image advertising by global companies include Nokia's purchase of full-page newspaper ads to congratulate Florida for winning the 1997 Sugar Bowl (which Nokia sponsored). The ads also mentioned the Nokia Sweepstakes, which featured a million-dollar prize if a contestant could throw a football through an inflated cellular phone at a distance of about ten yards. Similarly, Japan's Fuji Photo Film asked its advertising agency, Angotti, Thomas, and Hedge, to develop an image campaign for the United States. At the time, Fuji was embroiled in a trade dispute with Kodak. Fuji had also invested more than $1 billion in U.S. production facilities and had won a long-term photofinishing contract with Wal-Mart. The campaign was designed to appeal both to Wal-Mart and to the giant retailer's customers. As a Wal-Mart spokesman told *The Wall Street Journal,* "We've long said we buy American when we can. The more people understand how American Fuji is, the better."[30]

In **advocacy advertising,** a company presents its point of view on a particular issue. A recent example of advocacy advertising is the full-page newspaper ad sponsored by Virgin Airlines, in which company founder Richard Branson attacked a proposed alliance between British Airways and American Airlines. Similarly, in 1995, Japanese car marketers hired Hill & Knowlton to create a public relations campaign designed to convince President Clinton that his plan to impose 100 percent tariffs on 13 luxury cars was ill-advised and could even cost him California's 54 electoral votes in the 1996 election. Nissan and other companies also sent position papers and information packets to dealers and the media. Interviews with representatives from auto dealers were carried by both print and electronic media.

Senior executives at some companies relish the opportunity to generate publicity. For example, Benetton's striking print and outdoor ad campaigns keyed to the "United Colors of Benetton" generated both controversy and wide media attention. Richard Branson, the flamboyant founder of the Virgin Group, is a one-man publicity machine. His personal exploits as a hot-air balloon pilot have earned him and his company a great deal of free ink. The company does employ traditional media advertising; however, as Will Whitehorn, Virgin's corporate affairs director, recently noted, "PR is the heart of the company. If we do things badly, it will reflect badly on the image of the brand more than most other companies." At Virgin, Whitehorn notes, "advertising is a subset of PR, not the other way around."[31]

These examples notwithstanding, most global companies attempt to create an overall balance of promotion mix elements. PepsiCo made good use of integrated marketing communications when it undertook an ambitious global program to revamp the packaging of its flagship cola. To raise awareness of its new blue can, Pepsi spent $500 million on advertising and public relations; to generate publicity, Pepsi leased a Concorde jet and painted it in the new blue color. Pepsi also garnered

[30] Wendy Bounds, "Fuji Considers National Campaign to Develop All-American Image," *The Wall Street Journal* (October 1, 1996), p. B8.
[31] Elena Bowes, "Virgin Flies in Face of Conventions," *Ad Age International* (January 1997), p. i4.

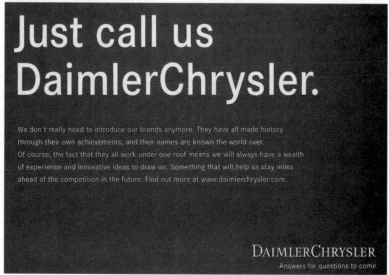

How do you make a $10 billion global food company even more appetizing to investors?

Serve it up as two hungry new companies.

CPC International has become Bestfoods and Corn Products International.

BESTFOODS
Satisfying a Global Appetite

$8.5 billion in revenue; thriving operations in over 60 countries and sales in 110; a roster of some of the world's best-loved brands; a seasoned international management team; a track record of growing profits. Credentials any company would prize. With two powerhouse global brands, *Knorr* and *Hellmann's*, and more than 90 years of experience in international markets, the new Bestfoods continues a tradition of satisfying a global appetite—for high-quality foods and for profitable global expansion. You'll find Bestfoods products in kitchens all over the world. And you'll find our stock listed under **BFO** on the New York Stock Exchange.

Visit us at www.bestfoods.com

CornProducts
INTERNATIONAL

$1.5 billion in revenue and alliances generating another $1 billion in unconsolidated sales; an organization spanning 21 countries; more than 90 years of international experience; products for a host of industries, including pharmaceutical, soft drink, paper and corrugating. As one of the world's largest corn refiners and the world leader in dextrose and corn starch, Corn Products International is a newcomer on Wall Street, but no neophyte in business. Focused operations, experienced management and great competitive spirit position newly independent Corn Products International to grow. Our NYSE ticker symbol is **CPO**.

© 1998 Bestfoods

All of these products contain essential ingredients derived from corn.

free ink by spending $5 million to film an ad with two Russian cosmonauts holding a giant replica of the new can while orbiting the earth in the Mir space station. As Massimo d'Amore, PepsiCo's head of international marketing, told reporters, "Space is the ultimate frontier of global marketing. The cola wars have been fought all over the place, and it's time to take them to space."[32]

IBM spent about $5 million to stage a rematch of a 1996 chess game between a computer called Deep Blue and Garry Kaparov. The match, which took place in New York City, was hailed as one of the best publicity stunts in recent years. To build visibility and interest, IBM purchased full-page newspaper ads, sent out numerous press releases, established an Internet site, and purchased bus posters in Manhattan. The effort was a textbook study in integrated marketing communications; the match was widely covered by the world media. As Peter Harleman of Landor Associates, a

---

[32] Melanie Wells, "Pepsi, Coke Go into Orbit," *USA Today* (May 22, 1996), p. 1B.

corporate-identity firm, told *The Wall Street Journal*, "Money almost can't buy the advertising [IBM] is getting out of this." John Lister, of the Lister Butler brand identity consulting firm, agreed. "They're doing a tremendous job of leveraging the brand in this. Not only do they have the IBM name attached to virtually every news report about, but they even branded their computer the corporate color, blue." Industry experts estimate that the match generated about $100 million in favorable earned media. IBM's Internet site provided live coverage and generated a million visits during a single match, a number which is believed to be a record for the World Wide Web. The publicity was especially gratifying to IBM officials because problems with its much-ballyhooed information system at the 1996 Olympics resulted in a great deal of negative news coverage.[33]

Sometimes publicity is generated when a company simply goes about the business of global marketing activities. As noted in Case 8-1, Nike and other marketers have received a great deal of negative publicity regarding alleged sweatshop conditions in factories run by subcontractors. To date, Nike's public relations team has not done an effective job of counteracting the criticism by effectively communicating the positive economic impact Nike has had on the nations where its sneakers are manufactured.

Any company that is increasing its activities outside the home country can utilize PR personnel as boundary spanners between the company and employees, unions, stockholders, customers, the media, financial analysts, governments, and suppliers. Many companies have their own in-house PR staff. Companies may also choose to engage the services of an outside PR firm. During the past few years, some of the large advertising holding companies discussed previously have acquired PR agencies. For example, Omnicom Group bought Fleishman-Hillard, WPP Group acquired Canada's Hill & Knowlton, and Interpublic Group bought Golin/Harris International. Other PR firms, including the London-based Shandwick PLC, Edelman Public Relations Worldwide, and Canada's Hill & Knowlton, are independent. Several independent PR firms in the United Kingdom, Germany, Italy, Spain, Austria, and the Netherlands have joined together in a network known as Globalink. The purpose of the network is to provide members with various forms of assistance such as press contacts, event planning, literature design, and suggestions for tailoring global campaigns to local needs in a particular country or region.[34]

The Growing Role of Public Relations in Global Marketing Communications

Public relations professionals with international responsibility must go beyond media relations and serve as more than a company mouthpiece; they are called upon to simultaneously build consensus and understanding, create trust and harmony, articulate and influence public opinion, anticipate conflicts, and resolve disputes.[35] As companies become more involved in global marketing and the globalization of industries continues, company management must recognize the value of international public relations. One recent study found that, internationally, PR expenditures are growing an average of 20 percent annually. Fueled by soaring foreign investment,

---

[33] Bart Ziegler, "Checkmate! Deep Blue is IBM Publicity Coup," *The Wall Street Journal* (May 9, 1997), p. B1.

[34] Joe Mullich, "European Firms Seek Alliances for Global PR," *Business Marketing* 79 (August 1994), pp. 4, 31.

[35] Karl Nessman, "Public Relations in Europe: A Comparison with the United States," *Public Relations Journal* 21, no. 2 (Summer 1995), p. 154.

industry privatization, and a boom in initial public offerings (IPOs), PR expenditures in India are reported to be growing by 200 percent annually.

The number of international PR associations is growing as well. The new Austrian Public Relations Association is a case in point; many European PR trade associations are part of the Confédération Européenne des Relations Publiques and the International Public Relations Association. Another factor fueling the growth of international PR is increased governmental relations between countries. Governments, organizations, and societies are dealing with broad-based issues of mutual concern such as the environment and world peace. Finally, the technology-driven communication revolution that has ushered in the information age makes public relations a profession with truly global reach. Faxes, satellites, high-speed modems, and the Internet allow PR professionals to be in contact with media virtually anywhere in the world.

In spite of these technological advances, PR professionals must still build good personal working relationships with journalists and other media representatives, as well as with leaders of other primary constituencies. Therefore, strong interpersonal skills are needed. One of the most basic concepts of the practice of public relations is to know the audience. For the global PR practitioner, this means knowing the audiences in both the home country and the host country or countries. Specific skills needed include the ability to communicate in the language of the host country and familiarity with local customs. Obviously, a PR professional who is unable to speak the language of the host country will be unable to communicate directly with a huge portion of an essential audience. Likewise, the PR professional working outside the home country must be sensitive to nonverbal communication issues in order to maintain good working relationships with host-country nationals. Commenting on the complexity of the international PR professional's job, one expert notes that, in general, audiences are "increasingly more unfamiliar and more hostile, as well as more organized and powerful . . . more demanding, more skeptical and more diverse." International PR practitioners can play an important role as "bridges over the shrinking chasm of the global village."[36]

How Public Relations Practices Differ around the World

Public relations practices in specific countries can be affected by cultural traditions, social and political contexts, and economic environments. As noted earlier in the chapter, the mass media and the written word are important vehicles for information dissemination in many industrialized countries. In developing countries, however, the best way to communicate might be through the gongman, the town crier, the market square, or the chief's courts. In Ghana, dance, songs, and storytelling are important communication channels. In India, where half of the population cannot read, writing press releases will not be the most effective way to communicate.[37] In Turkey, the practice of PR is thriving in spite of that country's reputation for harsh treatment of political prisoners. Although the Turkish government still asserts absolute control as it has for generations, corporate PR and journalism are allowed to flourish so that Turkish organizations can compete globally.

Even in industrialized countries, there are some important differences between PR practices. In the United States, much of the news in a small, local newspaper is

---

[36] Larissa A. Grunig, "Strategic Public Relations Constituencies on a Global Scale," *Public Relations Review* 18, no. 2 (Summer 1992), pp. 127–136.

[37] Carl Botan, "International Public Relations: Critique and Reformulation," *Public Relations Review* 18, no. 2 (Summer 1992), pp. 150–151.

placed by means of the hometown news release. In Canada, on the other hand, large metropolitan population centers have combined with Canadian economic and climatic conditions to thwart the emergence of a local press. The dearth of small newspapers means that the practice of sending out hometown news releases is almost nonexistent.[38] In the United States, PR is increasingly viewed as a separate management function. In Europe, that perspective has not been widely accepted; PR professionals are viewed as part of the marketing function rather than as distinct and separate specialists in a company. In Europe, fewer colleges and universities offer courses and degree programs in public relations than in the United States. Also, European coursework in PR is more theoretical; in the United States, PR programs are often part of mass communication or journalism schools and there is more emphasis on practical job skills.

A company that is ethnocentric in its approach to PR will extend home-country PR activities into host countries. The rationale behind this approach is that people everywhere are motivated and persuaded in much the same manner. Obviously, this approach does not take cultural considerations into account. A company adopting a polycentric approach to PR gives the host-country practitioner more leeway to incorporate local customs and practices into the PR effort. Although such an approach has the advantage of local responsiveness, the lack of global communication and coordination can lead to a PR disaster.[39]

The ultimate test of an organization's understanding of the power and importance of public relations occurs during a time of environmental turbulence, especially a potential or actual crisis. When disaster strikes, a company or industry often finds itself thrust into the spotlight. A company's swift and effective handling of communications during such times can have significant implications. The best response is to be forthright and direct, reassure the public, and provide the media with accurate information.

China's ongoing trade-related friction with the United States highlights the need for a better public relations effort on the part of the Chinese Foreign Ministry. Some sources of this friction have been discussed in earlier chapters, such as estimates that Chinese counterfeiting of copyrighted material alone costs U.S. companies $800 million annually or that 98 percent of the computer software used in China is pirated. Such revelations reflect poorly on China. Hong Kong businessman Barry C. Cheung notes, "China lacks skills in public relations generally and crisis management specifically, and that hurts them."[40] Part of the problem stems from the unwillingness of China's Communist leaders to publicly explain their views on these issues, to admit failure, and to accept advice from the West.

SUMMARY

Marketing communications—the promotion P of the marketing mix—includes advertising, public relations, sales promotion, and personal selling. **Global advertising** consists of the same advertising appeals, messages, artwork, and copy in campaigns around the world. The effort required to create a global campaign forces a

---

[38] Melvin L. Sharpe, "The Impact of Social and Cultural Conditioning on Global Public Relations," *Public Relations Review* 18, no. 2 (Summer 1992), pp. 103–107.

[39] Carl Botan, "International Public Relations: Critique and Reformulation," *Public Relations Review* 18, no. 2 (Summer 1992), p. 155.

[40] Marcus W. Brauchli, "A Change of Face: China Has Surly Image, but Part of the Reason Is Bad Public Relations," *The Wall Street Journal* (June 16, 1996), p. A1.

company to determine whether or not a global market exists for its product. The trade-off between standardized and adapted advertising is often accomplished by means of **pattern advertising,** which can be used to create localized global advertising. Many advertising agencies are part of larger **advertising organizations.** Advertisers may place a single global agency in charge of worldwide advertising; it is also possible to use one or more agencies on a regional or local basis.

The starting point in ad development is the **creative strategy,** a statement of what the message will say. The people who create ads often seek a **big idea** that can serve as the basis for memorable, effective messages. The **advertising appeal** is the communication approach—rational or emotional—that best relates to buyer motives. The **selling proposition** is the promise that captures the reason for buying the product. The **creative execution** is the way an appeal or proposition is presented. **Art direction** and **copy** must be created with cultural considerations in mind. Perceptions of humor, male-female relationships, and sexual imagery vary in different parts of the world. Media availability varies considerably from country to country. When selecting media, marketers are sometimes as constrained by laws and regulations as by literacy rates.

A company utilizes **public relations (PR)** to foster goodwill and understanding among constituents both inside and outside the company. In particular, the PR department attempts to generate favorable **publicity** about the company and its products and brands. The PR department must also manage corporate communications when responding to negative publicity. The most important PR tools are press releases, media kits, interviews, and tours. Many global companies make use of various types of **corporate advertising,** including **image advertising** and **advocacy advertising.** Public relations is also responsible for providing accurate, timely information, especially in the event of a crisis.

DISCUSSION QUESTIONS

1. In what ways can global brands and global advertising campaigns benefit a company?
2. How does the "standardized versus localized" debate apply to advertising?
3. Worldwide advertising expenditures by Philip Morris Companies in 1999 totaled $2.1 billion compared with 1995 spending of $3.4 billion. What is the explanation for the decline?
4. What is the difference between an advertising appeal and creative execution?
5. When creating advertising for world markets, what are some of the issues that art directors and copywriters should take into account?
6. How do the media options available to advertisers vary in different parts of the world? What can advertisers do to cope with media limitations in certain countries?
7. How does public relations differ from advertising? Why is PR especially important for global companies?
8. What are some of the ways public relations practices vary in different parts of the world?

BUILD YOUR GLOBAL MARKETING SKILLS

Each spring, *Advertising Age* magazine publishes its survey of the top 50 global advertising organizations. The top-ranked companies for 2000 were shown in Tables 14-2 and 14-3. Browse through either table and choose any agency organization or brand that interests you. Compare its 1999 ranking with the most recent ranking (which you can find either by referring to the print version of *Advertising Age* or by visiting www.adage.com). How have the industry rankings changed? Consult additional sources (e.g., magazine articles, the company's Web site) to enhance your understanding of the factors and forces that contributed to the company's move up or down in the rankings. Has the agency been acquired by a large organization? Has it gained or lost an important account?

SUGGESTED READINGS

Books

Anholt, Simon. *Another One Bites the Grass: Making Sense of International Advertising.* New York: John Wiley & Sons, 2000.

Mooij, Marieke K. De. *Advertising Worldwide: Concepts, Theories, and Practice of International, Multinational and Global Advertising*, 2nd ed. Upper Saddle River, NJ: Prentice Hall, 1994.

Mueller, Barbara. *International Advertising: Communicating Across Cultures.* Belmont, CA: Wadsworth Publishing Company, 1995.

Articles

Alden, Dana L., Wayne D. Hoyer, and Chol Lee. "Identifying Global and Culture-Specific Dimensions of Humor in Advertising: A Multinational Analysis." *Journal of Marketing* 57, no. 2 (April 1993), pp. 64–75.

Andrews, J. Craig, Srinivas Durvasula, and Richard G. Netemeyer. "Testing the Cross-National Applicability of U.S. and Russian Advertising." *Journal of Advertising* 23, no. 1 (March 1994), pp. 71–82.

Banerjee, Anish. "Transnational Advertising Development and Management: An Account Planning Approach and Process Framework." *International Journal of Advertising* 13, no. 2 (1994), pp. 95–124.

Botan, Carl. "International Public Relations: Critique and Reformulation." *Public Relations Review* 18, no. 2 (Summer 1992), pp. 149–159.

Bovet, Susan Fry. "Building An International Team." *Public Relations Journal* (August-September 1994), pp. 26–28+.

Covellon, Marie-Cecile, and Laurette Dube. "Standardization Versus Cultural Adaptation in Food Advertising, Insights from a Two-Culture Market." *International Journal of Advertising* 19, no. 4 (2000), pp. 429–447.

Duncan, Thomas R., and Stephen E. Everett. "Client Perception of Integrated Marketing Communications." *Journal of Advertising Research* (May-June 1993), pp. 119–122.

Epley, Joe S. "Public Relations in the Global Village: An American Perspective." *Public Relations Review* 18, no. 2 (Summer 1992), pp. 109–116.

Gould, Stephen J., Dawn B. Lerman, and Andreas F. Green. "Agency Perceptions and Practices on Global IMC." *Journal of Advertising Research* 39, no. 1 (January-February 1999), pp. 7–20.

Grunig, Larissa A. "Strategic Public Relations Constituencies on a Global Scale." *Public Relations Review* 18, no. 2 (Summer 1992), pp. 127–136.

Hanni, David A., John K. Rynas Jr., and Ivan R. Vernon, "Coordinating International Advertising—The Goodyear Case Revisited for Latin America," *Journal of International Marketing* 3, no. 2 (1995), pp. 83–98.

Harris, Greg. "International Advertising Standardization: What Do the Multinationals Actually Standardize?" *Journal of International Marketing* 2, no. 4 (1994), pp. 13–30.

Hiebert, Ray E. "Advertising and Public Relations in Transition from Communism: The Case of Hungary, 1989–1994." *Public Relations Review* 20, no. 4 (Winter 1994), pp. 357–372.

Hill, John S., and Alan T. Shao. "Agency Participants in Multicountry Advertising: A Preliminary Examination of Affiliate Characteristics and Environments." *Journal of International Marketing* 2, no. 2 (1994), pp. 29–48.

Johansson, Johny K. "The Sense of 'Nonsense': Japanese TV Advertising." *Journal of Advertising* 23, no. 1 (March 1994), pp. 17–26.

Josephs, Ray, and Juanita W. Josephs. "Public Relations, the U.K. Way." *Public Relations Journal* (April 1994), pp. 14–18.

Kruckeberg, Dean. "A Global Perspective on Public Relations Ethics: The Middle East." *Public Relations Review* 22, no. 2 (Summer 1996), pp. 181–189.

Leslie, D. A. "Global Scan: The Globalization of Advertising Agencies, Concepts, and Campaigns." *Economic Geography* 71, no. 4 (October 1995), pp. 402–426.

Lohtia, Ritu, Wesley J. Johnston, and Linda Aab. "Creating an Effective Print Advertisement for the China Market: Analysis and Advice." *Journal of Global Marketing* 8, no. 2 (1994), pp. 7–30.

Luqmani, Mushtag, Ugur Yavas, and Zahir Quraeshi. "Advertising in Saudi Arabia: Content and Regulation." *International Marketing Review* 6, no. 1 (1989), pp. 59–72.

Mueller, Barbara. "Standardization vs. Specialization: An Examination of Westernization in Japanese Advertising." *Journal of Advertising Research* 32 (January-February 1992), pp. 15–24.

Na, Woonbong, and Roger Marshall. "A Cross-Cultural Assessment of the Advertising Agency Selection Process: An Empirical Test in Korea and New Zealand." *International Journal of Advertising* 20, no. 1 (2001) pp. 49–66.

Nessmann, Karl. "Public Relations in Europe: A Comparison with the United States." *Public Relations Journal* 21, no. 2 (Summer 1995), pp. 151–160.

Newsom, Doug, and Bob Carrell. "Professional Public Relations in India: Need Outstrips Supply." *Public Relations Journal* 20, no. 2 (Summer 1994), pp. 183–188.

Onkvisit, Sak, and John J. Shaw. "Standardized International Advertising: Some Research Issues and Implications." *Journal of Advertising Research* 39, no. 6 (November-December 1999), pp. 19–24.

Parameswaran, Ravi, and R. Mohan Pisharodi. "Facets of Country of Origin Image: An Empirical Assessment." *Journal of Advertising* 23, no. 1 (March 1994), pp. 43–56.

Roth, Martin S. "Depth Versus Breadth Strategies for Global Brand Image Management." *Journal of Advertising* 21, no. 2 (June 1992).

Sharpe, Melvin L. "The Impact of Social and Cultural Conditioning on Global Public Relations." *Public Relations Review* 18, no. 2 (Summer 1992), pp. 103–107.

Sirisagul, Kanya. "Global Advertising Practices: A Comparative Study." *Journal of Global Marketing* 14, no. 3 (2000), pp. 77–97.

Tansey, Richard, and Michael R. Hyman. "Dependency Theory and the Effects of Advertising by Foreign-Based Multinational Corporations in Latin America." *Journal of Advertising* 23, no. 1 (March 1994), pp. 27–42.

Taylor, Charles R., R. Dale Wilson, and Gordon E. Miracle. "The Effect of Brand Differentiating Messages on the Effectiveness of Korean Advertising." *Journal of International Marketing* 2, no. 4 (1994), pp. 31–52.

Wells, Ludmilla Gricenko. "Western Concepts, Russian Perspectives: Meanings of Advertising in the Former Soviet Union." *Journal of Advertising* 23, no. 1 (March 1994), pp. 83–95.

Zandpour, Fred. "Global Reach and Local Touch: Achieving Cultural Fitness in TV Advertising." *Journal of Advertising Research* 34, no. 5 (September/October 1994), pp. 35–63.

———, and Katrin R. Harich. "Think and Feel Country Clusters: A New Approach to International Advertising Standardization." *International Journal of Advertising* 15, no. 4 (1996), pp. 325–344.

Zavrl, Frani, and Dejan Vercic. "Performing Public Relations in Central and Eastern Europe." *International Public Relations Journal* 18, no. 2 (1995), pp. 21–23.

Zhou, Nan, and Russell W. Belk. "China's Advertising and the Export Marketing Curve: The First Decade." *Journal of Advertising Research* 33, no. 6 (November-December 1993), pp. 50–66.

CASE

Case 14-1   Benetton Group S.p.A.: Raising Consciousness and Controversy with Global Advertising

Benetton Group S.p.A., the Italy-based global clothing retailer, exhibits something of a dual personality. Academics have hailed the company's information technology expertise (see Chapter 6); Benetton has also been cited as a textbook example of a flagship global firm that excels at building relationships (see Chapter 10). Moreover, the company continues to innovate in the area of upstream value chain activities: A recent article in *Sloan Management Review* explains how Benetton is rethinking its global supplier and distributor network.[41] By contrast, the company has gained a great deal of publicity—much of it negative—for an advertising strategy that, over the course of nearly two decades, has emphasized social issues rather than the company's products.

Worldwide sales of Benetton's brightly-colored knitware and contemporary clothing doubled between 1988 and 1993 to 2.75 trillion lire ($1.63 billion). In 1993 alone, sales were up about 10 percent, and net income increased by 13 percent. The strong showing in 1993 was due in part to the devaluation of the Italian lira, which enabled Benetton to cut prices for its clothing around the world. By contrast, 1994 results were discouraging. Sales were flat at $1.69 billion, operating profits fell 5 percent, to $245 million, and margins narrowed to 13.9 percent, down from 14.7 percent during 1991 to 1993. The sales slump was surprising in view of the fact that Benetton had opened stores in China, Eastern Europe, and India and extended the brand into new categories, such as footwear and cosmetics.

Some industry observers believed that Benetton's wounds were due in part to a backlash from Benetton's highly controversial global advertising campaigns, now several years old, keyed to the theme "The United Colors of Benetton." Various executions of the ads, in magazines and on posters and billboards, featured provocative, even shocking photos designed to focus public attention on social and political issues such as the environment, terrorism, racial issues, and sexually transmitted diseases. The creative concept of the ads reflected the views

of Oliviero Toscani, creative director and chief photographer for Benetton. "I have found out that advertising is the richest and most powerful medium existing today. Therefore, I feel responsible to do more than say, 'Our sweater is pretty,'" he told *The New York Times*. Noted Victorio Rava, worldwide advertising manager, "We believe our advertising needs to shock, otherwise people will not remember it."

One of the first ads to stir controversy depicted a white hand and a black hand joined by handcuffs; another showed an angelic white child embracing a black child whose hair was unmistakably styled to resemble the horns of a devil. An ad with a picture of a black woman nursing a white baby appeared in 77 countries; while banned in the United States and the United Kingdom, the ad won awards in France and Italy. In fall 1991, several U.S. magazine publishers refused to carry some of the ads; one depicted a nun kissing a priest. A picture of a newborn baby covered with a bloody placenta was also rejected. According to Benetton's Rava, "We didn't envision a political idea when we started this "Colors" strategy five years ago, but now, with racist problems becoming more important in every country it has become political on its own."

With its next series of ads, Benetton used images associated with sexuality. As Peter Fressola, director of communications, explained the message strategy, "We're saying there are two important issues to be addressed, and they are overpopulation and sexually transmitted diseases such as AIDS. I think it is time to take the gloves off and put on the rubbers and address these issues." In an interview with *Advertising Age,* Toscani explained, "Everybody uses emotion to sell a product. The difference here is we are not selling a product. We want to show, in this case, human realities that we are aware of." The ads broke new ground for the images they presented: A man dying of AIDS surrounded by his family; a montage of multicolored condoms; a group of people with the initials *HIV* stamped on their arms; test tubes filled with blood labeled with the names of world leaders.

In France, the HIV ad caused a great deal of controversy. One man who was dying of AIDS ran an ad with a picture of his own face above a headline that read, "during the agony, the sales continue." In the United States,

---

[41] Arnald Canuffo, Pietro Romano, and Andrea Vinelli, "Back to the Future: Benetton Transforms Its Global Network," *Sloan Management Review* 43, no. 1 (Fall 2001), pp. 46–52.

2001 International Year of Volunteers

UNITED COLORS
OF BENETTON.

UN
Volunteers

Name: William "Weazrock" Huezo
Nationality: Salvadorian
Volunteer working against
gang violence

For more information:
COLORS
www.colorsmagazine.com

where the number of Benetton stores had been slowly dwindling, the ads were poorly received by many customers and Benetton retailers. The manager of a Benetton store in Biloxi, Mississippi, received telephone calls from people who said they refused to shop at stores selling products from a "sick" company. In Florida, one franchisee closed a dozen Benetton locations, noting, "It is not our function as retailers to raise the consciousness of people. I've had long, hard fights with Italy over the advertising." In an effort to help mollify its American licensees, Benetton began providing them with local ads featuring clothing instead of social issues. At the national level, however, Benetton continued the controversial ads. When asked about the possible negative impact of customer boycotts, Luciano Benetton, president of the company's U.S. division, said, "It's silly to change direction because someone in the market thinks it's not right. We are sincere, and we are consistent in pursuing it this way."

Simon Anholt, an industry consultant and author of a book about international advertising, has asserted that the campaign's critics were missing the point. For one thing, notes Anholt, the goal of much youth-oriented advertising is to make a brand famous rather than to sell a product; Benetton's advertising has certainly accomplished this goal. A second point is that there is not meant to be a rational link between the message and the product per se; the target audience for the Benetton brand neither looks for nor desires such a link. Instead, Anholt believes, young people often wish to identify with a mindset or a philosophy; the marketer's task in such instances is to

link the philosophy to the company's brand. Finally, Anholt suggests that the Benetton campaign may well have been designed to shock the *parents* of Benetton's target consumers; according to this view, young people are often attracted to the "hot" brands or "cool" styles that an older demographic may find offensive.

In the spring of 1994, Toscani pushed the envelope even further. A new $15 million ad campaign that ran in 25 countries featured a picture of the bloody uniform of a Croatian soldier who had died in the Yugoslavian civil war. Although Benetton executives had come to expect criticism, they were unprepared for the latest reaction. The company was accused of exploiting the war for the sake of profit. In France, many of the offending posters were pulled down or covered with grafitti reading "boycott Benetton" and "this is blood for money." The French minister for humanitarian affairs even made a public announcement discouraging people from buying Benetton sweaters; he called for his fellow citizens to "pull [the sweaters] off people who are going to wear them." In some parts of Germany and Switzerland, the company's products were banned. Some media reports in Europe questioned the authenticity of the uniform and alleged it did not belong to the fallen soldier named in the ad. The Vatican newspaper charged Benetton with "advertising terrorism."

Luciano Benetton acknowledged that, "This is not what a corporate communications campaign should do. It should create interest." Still, he vowed the company would continue "to search for new facts and new emotions" to include in its ads. Indeed, when the Sarajevo daily newspaper *Oslo bodhenie* (Liberation) requested posters of the ad to put up around the city, Benetton supplied 10,000 copies.

Benetton occasionally put controversy aside and ran more mainstream ads. In 1995, the Chiat/Day agency created a television campaign that featured models posing and dancing against a white background while a voiceover presented the models' thoughts. In mid-1997, a new print campaign featured individual closeup portraits of young people from around the world juxtaposed with photos of Benetton apparel on the facing page. Benetton also teamed up with the United Nations for a campaign keyed to the International Year of Volunteers 2001. In 1998, aiming to boost sales and reach a broader market in the United States, Benetton reached an accord with retailer Sears, Roebuck and Co. A new, lower-priced clothing line, Benetton USA, was created especially for Sears.

By 1999, however, Toscani was championing a new cause: prisoners on death row in the United States. Once again, a number of critics took the company to task. Bob Garfield, the highly-regarded ad reviewer for *Advertising Age* magazine, awarded the campaign zero stars on a one-to four-star rating system. Garfield had dismissed some of Benetton's previous ads as "banal expressions of moral outrage over war, racism, and disease." Although Garfield acknowledged that the issue of capital punishment was worth exploring, he asserted that "no brand has the right to increase its sales on the backs, on the misery, on the fates of condemned men and women. . . ."

"Spare us all the consciousness raising, please. There is nothing a sportswear company can add to the discussion."
—Bob Garfield
Advertising Age ad critic

In 2000, the state of Missouri filed a lawsuit against Benetton alleging that the company had misrepresented itself when requesting the interviews with death-row inmates. A week after the suit was filed, Sears cancelled its agreement with Benetton. (The lawsuit was settled after Benetton officials agreed to apologize to several Missouri families whose relatives were murder victims.) In May 2000, three months after the launch of the "We, On Death Row" campaign, Oliviero Toscani resigned from Benetton. In an interview with *Ad Age Global* in 2001, Toscani defended his body of work. "Most good ads are forgotten after six months, but who still remembers the Benetton ad with the priest kissing the nun? Ten years later and people remember! That's immortality!" he said. He also noted that Benetton's sales in 2000 were 20 times greater than they had been at the beginning of his career with the company.

Still, in 2000, U.S. sales accounted for just 11 percent of the Benetton's $1.8 billion in revenues, and the number of stores in the United States had dwindled to 150. In 2001, Benetton launched a new $10 million campaign in the United States that sidestepped social issues. The new ads, which some observers viewed as similar to ads for Gap, featured lively multiethnic models dancing in the company's knitwear. Benetton also announced plans to open new megastores in key U.S. cities such as New York and Atlanta. ∎

DISCUSSION QUESTIONS

1. Do you believe Benetton is sincere in its efforts to promote social causes through its advertising?
2. Compare and contrast the controversy over the "We, On Death Row" advertising campaign with the controversies generated by the earlier campaigns of the 1990s. Do you think Americans would respond differently than, say, Europeans? Why?
3. There is a saying in the marketing world that "there is no such thing as bad publicity." Does that apply in the Benetton case?
4. Assess Benetton's efforts to boost sales in the United States. What recommendations would you make to management?

SOURCES: Simon Anholt, *Another One Bites the Grass: Making Sense of International Advertising* (New York: John Wiley & Sons, 2000), pp. 138–139; Leigh Gallagher, "About Face," *Forbes* (March 19, 2001), pp. 178–180; Jerry Della Famina, "Benetton Ad Models are Dressed to Kill Sales," *The Wall Street Journal* (March 20, 2000), p. A35; Bob Garfield, "The Colors of Exploitation: Benetton on Death Row," *Advertising Age* (January 10, 2000), p. 45; John Rossant, "The Faded Colors of Benetton," *Business Week* (April 10, 1995), pp. 87, 90; Peter Gumbel, "Benetton is Stung by Backlash Over Ad," *The Wall Street Journal* (March 4, 1994), p. A8; Gary Levin, "Benetton Ad Lays Bare the Bloody Toll of War," *Advertising Age* (February 21, 1994); Dennis Rodkin, "How Colorful Can Ads Get?" *Mother Jones* (January 1990), p. 52; Stuart Elliott, "Benetton Stirs More Controversy," *The New York Times* (July 23, 1991), p. 19; Gary Levin, "Benetton Brouhaha," *Advertising Age* (February 17, 1992), p. 62; Teri Agins, "Shrinkage of Stores and Customers in U.S., Causes Italy's Benetton to Alter Its Tactics," *The Wall Street Journal* (June 24, 1992), pp. B1, B10.

Chapter 15

Global Marketing Communications Decisions II: Sales Promotion, Personal Selling, Special Forms of Marketing Communication, New Media

*A*merica Online, or AOL as it is known, is the world's largest Internet service provider. One measure of the company's strength can be seen in its recent $156 billion merger with media giant TimeWarner. In the United States, nearly 20 million subscribers pay monthly fees of approximately $25 for unlimited use of the service. The company is known for its easy-to-use technology; AOL's signature greeting, "You've got mail," has become a cultural icon in the United States. The TimeWarner acquisition greatly increased the amount of media content available to subscribers. AOL was one of the stars of the tech boom in the 1990s; its subscription base grew rapidly as the company utilized an aggressive direct mail campaign to distribute its software via free computer disc and CD-ROM. Typically, AOL also offers new subscribers a free trial period (as much as 1000 hours). The company quickly surpassed established online companies such as Prodigy; AOL eventually acquired the well-known CompuServe. To maintain its fast-paced growth, AOL executives are looking to new markets in Europe, Latin America, and Asia. Currently, AOL and CompuServe have about 4.5 million subscribers. However, leadership status has eluded AOL outside its home country: The company ranks 10th in Japan and 4th in Brazil. A key question for AOL is whether the marketing strategy that built the business at home will work abroad.

Sales promotion has been an important marketing tool for AOL, both in the United States and abroad. When developing integrated marketing communications solutions and strategies, global companies and advertising agencies are giving sales promotion an increasingly prominent role; at the end of the 1990s, worldwide expenditures on sales promotion were growing at double-digit rates. Direct marketing, event sponsorship, and specialized forms of marketing communication such as infomercials and the Internet are also growing in importance. Of course, personal selling remains an important promotional tool as well. Taken together, the mar-

AOL grew its subscriber base by distributing software for free on CD-ROMs. In the twenty-first century, AOL TIme Warner's business model calls for creating a "community" of subscribers who will buy items from across all sectors of the company. Company officials hope to achieve synergies with cross promotions that lower the cost of acquiring new subscribers. Of the $5 billion that AOL Time Warner spent on advertising in 2001, $468 million was allocated to ads across its media portfolio.

keting mix elements discussed in this chapter and Chapter 14 can be used to create highly effective integrated campaigns that support global brands.

SALES PROMOTION

Sales promotion refers to any paid consumer or trade communication program of limited duration that adds tangible value to a product or brand. In a *price promotion,* tangible value may take the form of a price reduction, coupon, or mail-in refund. *Nonprice promotions* may take the form of free samples, premiums, "buy one, get one free" offers, sweepstakes, and contests. **Consumer sales promotions** may be designed to make consumers aware of a new product, to stimulate nonusers to sample an existing product, or to increase overall consumer demand. **Trade sales promotions** are designed to increase product availability in distribution channels. An example is Coca-Cola's recent offer of 200 to 600 gallons of soft drink syrup to McDonald's franchisees in the United Kingdom who agree to serve only Coca-Cola beverages. The goal of the promotion was to push rival Cadbury Schweppes out of fast-food outlets. At many companies, expenditures for sales promotion activities have surpassed expenditures for media advertising. At any level of expenditure, however, sales promotion is only one of several marketing communication tools. Sales promotion plans and programs should be integrated and coordinated with those for advertising, public relations, and personal selling.

Worldwide, the increasing popularity of sales promotion as a marketing communication tool can be explained in terms of several strengths and advantages. Besides providing a tangible incentive to buyers, sales promotions can also reduce the perceived risk buyers may associate with purchasing the product. From the point of view of the sponsoring company, sales promotion provides accountability; the manager in charge of the promotion can immediately track the results of the promotion. Overall, promotional spending is increasing at many companies as they shift advertising allocations away from traditional print and broadcast advertising.

In addition, sweepstakes, rebates, and other forms of promotion require consumers to fill out a form and return it to the company, which can then build up information in its database for use when communicating with customers in the future. For example, Clicquot, a unit of LVMH Moët Hennessy Louis Vuitton, markets Hine

This consumer trade promotion was targeted at the global elite: affluent cosmopolitans who gladly pay $50 or more for a premium cognac that can be savored after a fine meal or with an expensive cigar. Entrants who successfully completed the crossword puzzle received a Hine cigar ashtray and matches; Hine added each entrant's name and address to its database for use in subsequent direct mail promotions.

The Hine Cognac Crossword

ACROSS

1 Granted to Hine by QEII
11 Interjection
13 Large city in NW France
14 _ _ _ _ _ Y: stuck-up
15 *Hine ___ & Delicate Fine Champagne Cognac*
17 Heroin (slang)
18 Year Hine was founded (Rom. num.)
20 Law (Lat.)
22 Unit of measure (abbr.)
24 Hine Cognacs are known for ___ & finesse
27 Sparkling: _ _ U S S E _ _ (Fr.)
30 ___ Bois: a Cognac appellation
31 Male diminuitive (It.)
33 Small dogs
34 Chances
35 ___ *Family Reserve Grande Champagne Cognac*
36 Long-time president of Syria
39 Flew too close to the sun: _ _ A R U S
40 Tennessee Valley Authority (abbr.)
42 Attached to bit
43 NYC cultural institution
44 Connect
45 Preposition
46 Every
47 House founder Thomas ___
49 Bernard & Jacques Hine are ___ generation Hines
51 Of the Christian era
53 Perform
54 Standard Wire Gauge (abbr.)
56 Wildebeest
57 Lees are made from these cells
59 Same
62 Eight (comb. form)
63 Small country
65 ___ Champagne: second best Cognac appellation
67 Pot-still for making Cognac
68 Byzantine governor

DOWN

1 Royal College of Surgeons (abbr.)
2 Barrels for aging Cognac
3 Final
4 Evaporates during aging
5 Backward social work degree?
6 From certain South American mountains
7 Man-eating bird of Arabian legend
8 Boxer
9 Another name for Attila
10 *Hine ___ Grande Champagne Cognac*
11 Canton of Switzerland
12 Pronoun
16 Exclamation
19 % alcohol in Cognac (Rom. num.)
21 Yes (Sp.)
23 Cut out
24 Do: past tense
25 Classic Cognac accompaniment
26 Bernard and Jacques Hine are ___
28 Yes (Fr.)
29 Cognac grape
30 Mist
32 Boston's favorite apparel
37 Six (It.)
38 *Hine ___ Très Rare Fine Champagne Cognac*
40 Two times
41 Hine is known for its ___ Cognacs
43 First state alphabetically (abbr.)
46 In the year of the Hegira
47 Make it while the sun shines
48 Cognac is 300 miles ___ of Paris (abbr.)
50 Optimum shape glass for enjoying Cognac
52 Invented Cognac
54 Knife
55 They "bring good things to life"
56 One who goes
58 Total
60 As much as you please (Lat. abbr.)
61 Chewed
64 Third not of scale
66 Half of British good-bye

cognac and other fine wines and spirits. In an effort to build the company's in-house mailing list, managers offered cognac drinkers a prize for filling out the Hine Cognac crossword puzzle. Clicquot rented a list with the addresses of persons who had attended cigar "smoker" events in major cities.

A global company can sometimes leverage experience gained in one country market and use it in another market. For example, PepsiCo experienced great success

NEWS RELEASE

For release: Immediately

Contact: Christine Deussen
Desirée Charles

THE HINE COGNAC CROSSWORD
Another Assemblage

Cognac Hine invites Cognac and crossword lovers to complete *The Hine Cognac Crossword* to win a Hine cigar ashtray and matches. Hine Cognacs are complex blends, or *assemblages*, of dozens of *eaux-de-vie*, each element dependent on the others; crossword puzzles, while not as complex, similarly hinge on dozens of interdependent words completing the assemblage. Certainly both invite relaxation—so why not pour a Hine, light a cigar and enjoy *The Hine Cognac Crossword*?

The House of Hine Cognac, located in Jarnac, France, was founded in 1763 and made famous by Thomas Hine, an expatriate Briton, who established the Hine style of complex, long-aged Cognacs with enduring elegance and finesse. Today, sixth-generation descendants of Thomas Hine, cousins Jacques and Bernard Hine, blend Hine Cognacs following his tradition. The House of Hine uses grapes from only the finest *appellations* in Cognac, *Grande* and *Petite Champagne*, and ages all its Cognacs in small French oak barrels. Distillation is strictly controlled at all stages, and all blends are aged far beyond the legally required minimums. Hine is honored to hold the royal warrant as suppliers of Cognac to Queen Elizabeth II.

To give puzzle solvers a jump start:
- **Hine Rare & Delicate Fine Champagne Cognac** is aged an average of 8-10 years and blended exclusively from Cognacs of *Grande* and *Petite Champagne*. *Rare & Delicate* is especially characterized by a bouquet of fruit and floral aromas.

- **Hine Antique Très Rare Fine Champagne Cognac** is aged an average of 20-25 years, and blended only from Cognacs of *Grande* and *Petite Champagne*. *Antique's* abundant fruitiness is tempered by *rancio*, and hints of flowers, honey, leather, vine and vanilla.

- **Hine Triomphe Grande Champagne Cognac** is aged an average of 40-50 years and made only of Cognacs from the premier *Grande Champagne* district. *Triomphe* is loved for its elegant nose, rich palate and complex spicy flavors.

Please send the completed puzzle and your full address including telephone number to *The Hine Cognac Crossword*, Clicquot, Inc., 717 Fifth Avenue - 20th floor, New York, NY, 10022, tel. 212/ 888-7575. Answers are available from the same address. Void where prohibited; limit one prize per person while supplies last.

# # #

· CLICQUOT, INC. ·

6/96

717 Fifth Avenue, New York, New York 10022
(212) 888-7575 Fax (212) 888-7554

in Latin America with its Numeromania contest. When soft drink sales stalled in Poland during the summer of 1996, Pepsi rolled out Numeromania there; lured by the promise of big cash prizes, many economically-squeezed Poles rushed out to buy Pepsi so they could enter the contest.[1] International managers can learn about American-style promotion strategies and tactics by attending seminars such as those offered by the Promotional Marketing Association of America (PMAA). Sometimes adaptation to country-specific conditions is required; for example, TV ads in France cannot have movie tie-ins. Ads must be designed to focus on the promotion rather than the movie. Such regulations would have an impact on Disney, for example.

As with other aspects of marketing communication, a key issue is whether promotion efforts should be directed by headquarters or left to local country managers. The authors of one recent study noted that Nestlé and other large companies that once had a polycentric approach to consumer and trade sales promotion have redesigned their efforts. Kashani and Quelch identify four factors that contribute to more headquarters involvement in the sales promotion effort: cost, complexity, global branding, and transnational trade. First, as sales promotions command ever-larger budget allocations, headquarters naturally takes a greater interest. Also, the formulation, implementation, and follow-up of a promotion program may require skills that local managers lack. Third, the increasing importance of global brands justifies headquarters involvement to maintain consistency from country to country and ensure that successful local promotion programs are leveraged in other markets. Finally, as mergers and acquisitions lead to increased concentration in the retail industry and as the industry globalizes, retailers will seek coordinated promotional programs from their suppliers.[2]

The implementation of sales promotion by global firms will continue to be a national organization activity. The reason is simple: Local managers in the market know the specific local situation. In countries with low levels of economic development, low incomes limit the range of promotional tools available. In such countries, free samples and demonstrations are more likely to be used than coupons or on-pack premiums. Market maturity can also be different from country to country; consumer sampling and coupons are appropriate in growing markets, but mature markets might require trade allowances or loyalty programs. Local perceptions of a particular promotional tool or program can vary. Japanese consumers, for example, are reluctant to use coupons at the checkout counter. A particular premium can be seen as a waste of money. A fourth factor is local regulations, which may rule out use of a particular promotion in certain countries, trade structure, and special situations. Several company-specific examples of sales promotion programs are shown in Table 15-1.

Sampling

Sampling is a sales promotion technique that provides consumers with the opportunity to try a product or service at no cost. Traditionally, sampling often took the form of an individual portion of consumer packaged goods such as breakfast cereal, shampoo, or detergent distributed through the mail, door to door, or at a retail location. Today, many companies utilize *event marketing* to take advantage of concerts, sports events, or special events such as food and beverage festivals attended by large numbers of people. In the information age, sampling may also consist of a week's free viewing of a cable TV channel or a no-cost trial subscription to an online computer service.

---

[1] Roderick Oram, "Brand Experiences," *Financial Times* (October 30, 1996), FT Survey, p. III.
[2] Kamran Kashani and John A. Quelch, "Can Sales Promotion Go Global?" *Business Horizons* 33, no. 3 (May-June 1990), pp. 37–43.

The Rest of the Story
AOL Goes Global

By the middle of 2001, American Online Latin America surpassed the 1-million subscriber milestone. Market entry in Brazil had come at the end of 1998 via a joint venture with Miami-based Cisnero Group. Brazil had been identified as the best opportunity because it is home to half the Internet users in Latin America. However, the early going was inauspicious, to say the least. Following its practice in other countries, AOL distributed free CD-ROMs loaded with software in shopping malls and video stores. However, due to a manufacturing error, several hundred of the disks contained music rather than computer software. There was also a problem with the disks that weren't faulty; as the software loaded, it updated a user's Web browser and changed the appearance of home pages. The problems were reported in local newspapers and represented a minor public relations crisis for AOL.

Some observers also took exception to AOL's advertising claims that it was the "biggest" ISP. In fact, that distinction belonged to a local company, Universo Online SA (UOL), that claimed to have 500,000 sub-scribers at the time of the AOL launch. AOL executives maintained that the claim was accurate because it referred to the company's global position. Another problem was the fact that a local Brazilian company had registered the domain name aol.com.br. The two sides are trying to resolve the issue in court. Another issue was a significant currency devaluation in Brazil. Despite these problems, AOL launched services in Mexico, Argentina, and Puerto Rico.

AOL Latin America President Charles Herington is upbeat about his company's prospects in the region. Although industry observers have questioned when the company will break even, Herington maintains that the company's strategy is on track. One indicator is the fact that recently subscriber revenue has grown at a faster rate than subscriber growth. In short, this means that once the promotional trial period ends, users are converting to paying subscribers. "We've been successful at growing our membership faster than anybody else, but at the same time we have grown our revenue even more aggressively. Sometimes this message gets lost," Herington said.

SOURCES: Pamela Druckerman and Nick Wingfield, "Lost in Translation: AOL's Big Assault on Latin America Hits Snags in Brazil," *The Wall Street Journal* (July 11, 2000), pp. A1, A16; Matt Pottinger, "AOL to Unveil China Venture of $200 Million," *The Wall Street Journal* (June 4, 2001), p. A19; Druckerman, "Brazil is Test Case for Free Web Access," *The Wall Street Journal* (February 7, 2000), p. A28.

Table 15-1
Local Sales Promotions by Global Marketers

COMPANY AND COUNTRY MARKET FOR PROMOTION	PROMOTION
Seagram Spirits and Wine Group/global	Online charity auction in fall 2001 to celebrate 200th anniversary of Chivas Regal scotch
Toyota Motor Manufacturing/USA	Sweepstakes offering all-expense paid trip for two to Kentucky Derby, spring 1997
Toyota Motor Corp./Japan	Half-price lottery will give 100 winners a cash incentive on purchase of GM Cavalier model that Toyota sells in Japan, May 1997
Guinness Import Company/USA	"Voyage to the Titanic" sweepstakes
Porsche	Distributed floppy disks with "World Time Zone," a screensaver utility for PCs; disk also contained a multimedia presentation about the new Boxter

Compared with other forms of marketing communication, sampling is more likely to result in actual trial of the product. This can be especially important if consumers may be skeptical about claims made in advertising or other channels. In China, for example, shoppers are reluctant to buy full-sized packages of imported consumer products that they haven't tried—especially because the price may be several times higher than the price of local brands. Procter & Gamble achieved great success in China by distributing millions of free samples of its shampoo and detergent products; after the no-risk trial, many consumers became adopters. By 1996, a survey conducted in three large cities indicated that Procter & Gamble's three shampoo brands commanded a 57 percent market share.[3]

Couponing

A **coupon** is a printed certificate that entitles the bearer to a price reduction or some other special consideration for purchasing a particular product or service. Coupons are frequently delivered with newspapers, either on a regular page or in a printed ride-along vehicle known as a *free-standing insert* (FSI). Coupons can both reward loyal users and stimulate product trial by nonusers. The United States is by far the world leader in terms of the number of coupons issued. In 1997, 276 billion coupons were distributed in the United States; consumers redeemed about 1.7 percent with an average value of 64 cents. In the European Union, couponing is widely used in the UK and Belgium. Couponing is not as widely used in Asia where saving face is important; although Asian consumers have a reputation for thriftiness, some are reluctant to use coupons because doing so might bring shame upon them or their families. According to Joseph Potacki, who teaches a "Basics of Promotion" seminar for the PMAA, couponing is the aspect of the promotion mix for which the practices in the United States differ the most from those in other countries. In the United States, couponing accounts for 70 percent of consumer promotion spending. Elsewhere, the percentage is much lower. According to Potacki, "It is far less—or

Coupon clippers

Of 276 billion product coupons issued last year, shoppers redeemed 4.8 billion (1.7%) worth an average 64 cents each. Households by income that clip coupons:

Less than $15,000	79%
$15,000-$24,999	91%
$25,000-$49,000	78%
$50,000 or more	83%

Source: NCH NuWorld 1998 Consumer Behavior Study, America Coupon Council

By Cindy Hall and Quin Tian, USA TODAY

---

[3] Joseph Kahn, "Cleaning Up: P&G Viewed China as a National Market and Is Conquering It," *The Wall Street Journal* (September 12, 1995), pp. A1, A6.

nonexistent—in most other countries simply because the cultures don't accept couponing." Potacki notes that one reason couponing is gaining importance in countries such as the United Kingdom is because retailers are learning more about its advantages.[4]

Sales Promotions: Issues and Problems

As noted earlier in the chapter, companies must take extreme care when formulating and executing sales promotions. In some emerging markets, sales promotion efforts can raise eyebrows if companies appear to be exploiting regulatory loopholes and lack of consumer resistance to intrusion. For example, consumer packaged-goods companies have experimented with sampling in Central and Eastern Europe. Representatives from Kellogg visited elementary schools in Prague and passed out free boxes of Rice Krispies. The representatives had presented a letter from the Czech Ministry of Education to the school's principal, who, in turn, mistakenly interpreted the letter as government endorsement of the sampling program.[5]

Sales promotion in Europe is highly regulated. Sales promotions are popular in Scandinavia because of restrictions on broadcast advertising, but promotions in the Nordic countries are themselves subject to regulations. If such regulations are relaxed as the single market develops in Europe and regulations are harmonized, companies may be able to roll out pan-European promotions.

A recent study examined coupon usage and attitudes toward both coupons and sweepstakes in Taiwan, Thailand, and Malaysia. The study has particular relevance to global companies that are targeting these and other developing nations in Asia where consumers have relatively little experience with coupons. The study utilized Hofstede's social values framework as a guide. All three countries in the studies are collectivist, and the researchers found that an individual's positive attitude toward coupons and coupon usage was influenced by positive attitudes of family members and society as a whole. However, the three nations show some differences in value orientation. For example, Malaysia has a higher power distance and lower uncertainty avoidance than the others. For Malaysians, the fear of public embarrassment was a constraint on coupon usage. In all three countries, media consumption habits were also a factor; persons who were not regular readers of magazines or newspapers were less likely to be aware that coupons were available. Consumers in Taiwan and Thailand look more favorably upon coupons than sweepstakes. The impact of religion surprised the researchers. In Malaysia, where the population is primarily Muslim, the researchers assumed that consumers would avoid sweepstakes promotions. Sweepstakes can be compared to gambling, which is frowned on by Islam. However, Malaysians showed a preference for sweepstakes over coupons. In Taiwan, where Buddhism, Confucianism, and Taoism are all practiced, religion appeared to have little impact on attitudes toward promotions. One implication for marketing in developing countries is that, despite cultural differences, increased availability of promotions will result in higher levels of consumer utilization.[6]

---

[4]   Leslie Ryan, "Sales Promotion: Made in America," *Brandweek* (July 31, 1995), p. 28.
[5]   Ann Marsh, "From Toothpaste to Cereal, Czechs Face Promo Free-for-All," *Advertising Age International* (July 18, 1994), p. I23.
[6]   Lenard C. Huff and Dana L. Alden, "An Investigation of Consumer Response to Sales Promotions in Developing Markets: A Three Country Analysis," *Journal of Advertising Research* 38, no. 3 (May-June 1998), pp. 47–57.

Promotions are enjoying increased popularity among consumer-products companies, especially those targeting younger audiences. In recent years, for example, Allied Domecq, the U.K.-based company that markets Ballantine Scotch and other spirits, has sponsored concert events in Paris, Moscow, and several other European cities. Dubbed "Urban High," the event gives the under-35 crowd a chance to "bump into Ballantine's" and associate the brand with fun experiences as they listen to music by top groups such as The Prodigy and watch world-champion skateboarders in action. However, Allied Domecq is careful not to lose its credibility by overcommercializing the events. Likewise, The Prodigy and other performers are not asked to endorse any products. As Paul Morrison of event-marketing firm KLP comments, "Ballantine's have the good sense not to ask [the band members] to hold a bottle of whisky and do a thumbs-up."

Some attempts at promotion, however, have to be scaled back or revamped. In 1998, for example, Carlsberg, the Danish brewer, paid millions of dollars for the privilege of sponsoring the Commonwealth Games in Malaysia. The company distributed promotional items such as beer mugs and coasters, and also painted city buses in the company's trademark bright yellow and green. Unfortunately, the Malay-language press objected to such blatant attempts to promote beer in a country where the population is predominantly Moslem.

A 1992 promotion sponsored by Maytag Corporation's Hoover European Appliance Group was a smashing success that turned into a financial and public relations fiasco. Over a period of several months, Hoover offered free round-trip airline tickets to the United States and Europe to purchasers of vacuum cleaners or other Hoover appliances. The promotion was designed to take advantage of low-cost, space available tickets; executives hoped that the cost of the tickets would be offset by commissions paid to Hoover when customers rented cars or booked hotel rooms. Finally, it was expected that a percentage of customers who bought appliances would fail to meet certain eligibility requirements and thus be denied free tickets.

In the United Kingdom, the word *Hoover* is both a brand name and a verb (as in "Hoover the carpet"). The number of people who actually qualified for the free tickets—more than 200,000 in all—exceeded company forecasts, and the number of car rentals and hotel bookings was lower than expected. Hoover was swamped by the volume of inquiries; many customers were angered by long delays in responses to their requests for the tickets. The bottom line was that Hoover had failed to budget enough for the promotion, forcing Maytag CEO Leonard Hadley to take pretax charges of $72.6 million. In an effort to honor its commitment to Hoover customers, Maytag bought several thousand seats on various airlines. "The Hoover name in the United Kingdom is valuable, and this investment in our customer base there is essential to our future," Hadley said.

Hadley fired the president and director of marketing services at Hoover Europe and the vice president of marketing at Hoover UK. Fallout from the promotion became an ongoing PR nightmare, as headlines in the London *Daily Mail* trumpeted "Hoover fiasco: Bosses sacked" and "How dumb can you get?" Meanwhile, complaints from angry Europeans poured into Maytag's Newton, Iowa, headquarters. A Hoover Holiday Pressure Group was rumored to have thousands of members; three people even traveled to Newton in an unsuccessful attempt to meet with CEO Hadley.

By May 1995, Hadley had had enough: He decided to sell Hoover Europe to Italy's Candy for $170 million. Hadley has since refocused Maytag on the North American market, with excellent results.

SOURCES: John Willman, "'Molecular Marketing' at an Urban High," *Financial Times* (October 13, 1997), p. 17; Sheila McNulty, "A Campaign Too Far for Carlsberg," *Financial Times* (August 11, 1998), p. 8; Carl Quintanilla, "So, Who's Dull? Maytag's Top Officer, Expected to Do Little, Surprises His Board," *The Wall Street Journal* (June 23, 1998), pp. A1, A8; Rick Jost, "Maytag Wrings Out after Flopped Hoover Promotion," *The Des Moines Register* (April 5, 1993), p. 3B; Jost, "Mail Flying in from Britons Upset by Maytag Promotion," *The Des Moines Register* (July 11, 1994), p. B3.

Personal selling is person-to-person communication between a company representative and a prospective buyer. The seller's communication effort is focused on informing and persuading the prospect, with the short-term goal of making a sale and with a longer-term goal of building a relationship with that buyer. The salesperson's job is to correctly understand the buyer's needs, match those needs to the company's product(s), and then persuade the customer to buy. Because selling provides a two-way communication channel, it is especially important in marketing industrial products that may be expensive and technologically complex. Sales personnel can often provide headquarters with important customer feedback that can be utilized in design and engineering decisions.

Effective personal selling in a salesperson's home country requires building a relationship with the customer; global marketing presents additional challenges because the buyer and seller may come from different national or cultural backgrounds. Despite such challenges, it is difficult to overstate the importance of a face-to-face, personal selling effort for industrial products in global markets. In 1993, a Malaysian developer, YTL Corp., sought bids on a $700 million contract for power-generation turbines. Siemens of Germany and General Electric were among the bidders. Datuk Francis Yeoh, managing director of YTL, requested meetings with top executives from both companies. "I wanted to look them in the eye to see if we can do business," Yeoh said. Siemens complied with the request, GE did not send an executive, and Siemens was awarded the contract.[7]

Personal selling is also a popular marketing communication tool in countries with various restrictions on advertising. As noted in Chapter 14, it is very difficult to obtain permission to present product comparisons in any type of advertising in Japan. In such an environment, selling is the best way to provide hard-hitting, side-by-side comparisons of competing products. Personal selling is also used frequently in countries where low wage rates allow large local sales forces to be hired. For example, Home Box Office built its core of subscribers in Hungary by selling door-to-door. In fact, the cost effectiveness of personal selling in certain parts of the world has been a key driver behind the decision at many U.S.-based firms to begin marketing products and services overseas. A company is more likely to test a new territory or product if the entry price is relatively low. For example, some high-tech firms have utilized lower-cost sales personnel in Latin America to introduce new product features to their customers. Only if the response is favorable do the firms commit major resources to a U.S. rollout.

The challenge to companies that wish to pursue low-cost personal selling overseas, however, is to establish and maintain acceptable quality among members of the sales team. The old saying, "You get what you pay for" has come to haunt more than one company that has undertaken global expansion. When MCI Communications first entered Latin America several decades ago, it was attracted in part by the prospect of achieving inexpensive market penetration for its large multinational client companies. Management's initial enthusiasm quickly gave way to an alarming realization that the quality of support in this part of the world was not on a level with what MCI's major accounts were used to in the United States. As a result, there was a period when both MCI and its competition chose the costlier sales approach of using

---

[7] Marcus W. Brauchili, "Looking East: Asia, on the Ascent, Is Learning to Say No to 'Arrogant' West," *The Wall Street Journal* (April 13, 1994), pp. A1, A8.

U.S.-based personnel to provide remote, but higher quality, support to the Latin American sites of their respective global customer bases. However, MCI's upper management ultimately decided to invest more to create in-country sales and service teams whose output more closely mirrored that of their U.S. counterparts.

The risks inherent in establishing a personal selling structure overseas remain today. The crucial issue is not whether in-country sales and marketing people can provide more benefit than a remote force. Today, it's a given that, in the vast majority of scenarios, they can. The issue is whether the country team should consist of in-country nationals or expatriates from the headquarters country of the parent company. It should be noted that many of the environmental issues and challenges identified in earlier chapters often surface as a company completes the initial stages of implementing a personal selling strategy. These include:

- *Political risks.* Unstable or corrupt governments can completely change the rules for the sales team. Establishing new operations in a foreign country is especially tricky if a coup is imminent or if a dictator demands certain "considerations" (which has been the case in many developing countries). For example, Colombia offers great market potential and its government projects an image of openness. However, many companies have found the unspoken rules of the Cabal to be inordinately burdensome. In a country ruled by a dictatorship, the target audience and accompanying message of the sales effort tend to be far narrower and more restricted since government planners mandate how business will be conducted. Firms selling in Hong Kong were concerned that China would impose its will and dramatically alter the selling environment after the transfer of power in 1997. In response to such concerns, British Telecom brought many members of its Hong Kong sales staff back to London prior to the changeover. However, to the great relief of Hong Kong's business community, Chinese officials ultimately recognized that a policy of minimal intervention would be the wisest approach.
- *Regulatory hurdles.* Many countries set up quotas, tariffs, and capricious rules that affect entering foreign sales forces. In part, governments consider such actions to be an easy source of revenue, but, even more importantly, policy makers want to ensure that sales teams from local firms retain a competitive edge in terms of what they can offer and at what price. For example, a number of U.S. firms have encountered difficulty selling in Canada due to tariffs imposed on any revenues generated there.
- *Currency fluctuations.* There have been many instances where a company's sales effort has been derailed not by ineffectiveness or lack of market opportunity, but by fluctuating currency values. In the mid-1980s, for example, Caterpillar's global market share declined when the dollar's strength allowed Komatsu to woo U.S. customers away. Then, while Caterpillar's management team was preoccupied with domestic issues, competitors chipped away at the firm's position in global markets.
- *Market unknowns.* When a company enters a new region of the world, its selling strategy may unravel because of a lack of knowledge of market conditions, the accepted way of doing business, or the positioning of its in-country competitors. When a game plan is finally crafted to counter the obstacles, it is sometimes too late for the company to succeed. However, if management devotes an inordinate amount of time conducting market research prior to entry, it may discover that its window of opportunity has been lost to a fast moving competitor that did not fall victim to the "analysis paralysis" syndrome. Thus, it is difficult to make generalizations about the optimal time to enter a new country.

If all of these challenges can be overcome, or at least minimized, the personal selling endeavor can be implemented with the aid of a tool known as the Strategic/Consultative Selling Model.

The Strategic/Consultative Selling Model

Figure 15-1 shows the Strategic/Consultative Selling Model, which has gained wide acceptance in the United States. The model consists of five interdependent steps, each with three prescriptions that can serve as a checklist for sales personnel.[8] Many U.S. companies have begun developing global markets and have established face-to-face sales teams either directly, using their own personnel, or indirectly, through contracted sales agents. As a result, the Strategic/Consultative Selling Model is increasingly utilized on a worldwide basis. The key to ensuring that the model produces the desired outcome—building quality partnerships with customers—is to have it implemented and followed on a consistent basis. This is far more difficult to achieve with international sales teams than it is with U.S.-based units that are much more accessible to corporate headquarters.

First, a sales representative must develop a **personal selling philosophy**. This requires a commitment to the marketing concept and a willingness to adopt the role of problem solver or partner in helping customers. A sales professional must also be secure in the belief that selling is a valuable activity. The second step is to develop a **relationship strategy,** which is a game plan for establishing and maintaining high-quality relationships with prospects and customers. The relationship strategy provides a blueprint for creating the rapport and mutual trust that will serve as the basis of a lasting partnership. This step connects sales personnel directly to the concept of *relationship marketing,* an approach that stresses the importance of developing long-term partnerships with customers. Relationship marketing has been embraced by many U.S.-based companies that apply the concept when selling in the American market; it is equally relevant—and perhaps even more so—to any company hoping to achieve success in global marketing.

In developing personal and relationship strategies on an international level, the representative is wise to take a step back and understand how these strategies will likely fit in the foreign environment. For example, an aggressive "I'll do whatever it takes to get your business" is the exact worst approach in some cultures, even though in many large U.S. cities it would be viewed as a standard, even preferred, practice. This is why it is prudent for a company's sales management and rep teams to invest the time and energy necessary to learn about the global market in which they will be selling. In many countries, people have only a rudimentary understanding of sales techniques; acceptance of those techniques may be low as well. A sophisticated sales campaign that excels in the United States may never hit the mark in other countries. In-country experts such as consultants or agents can be excellent sources of real world intelligence that can help a rep create an effective international relationship strategy. Such people are especially helpful if the sales force will include many expatriates who will not have resident nationals as colleagues to whom they can turn for advice. Sales representatives must understand that patience and a willingness to assimilate host-country norms and customs are important attributes in developing relationships built on respect.

---

[8] This discussion of the Strategic/Consultative Selling Model is adapted from Gerald L. Manning and Barry L. Reece, *Selling Today: Building Quality Partnerships* (Upper Saddle River, NJ: Prentice Hall, 1998), chapter 1. The authors are also indebted to Larry Sirhall, a marketing consultant based in Bend, Oregon.

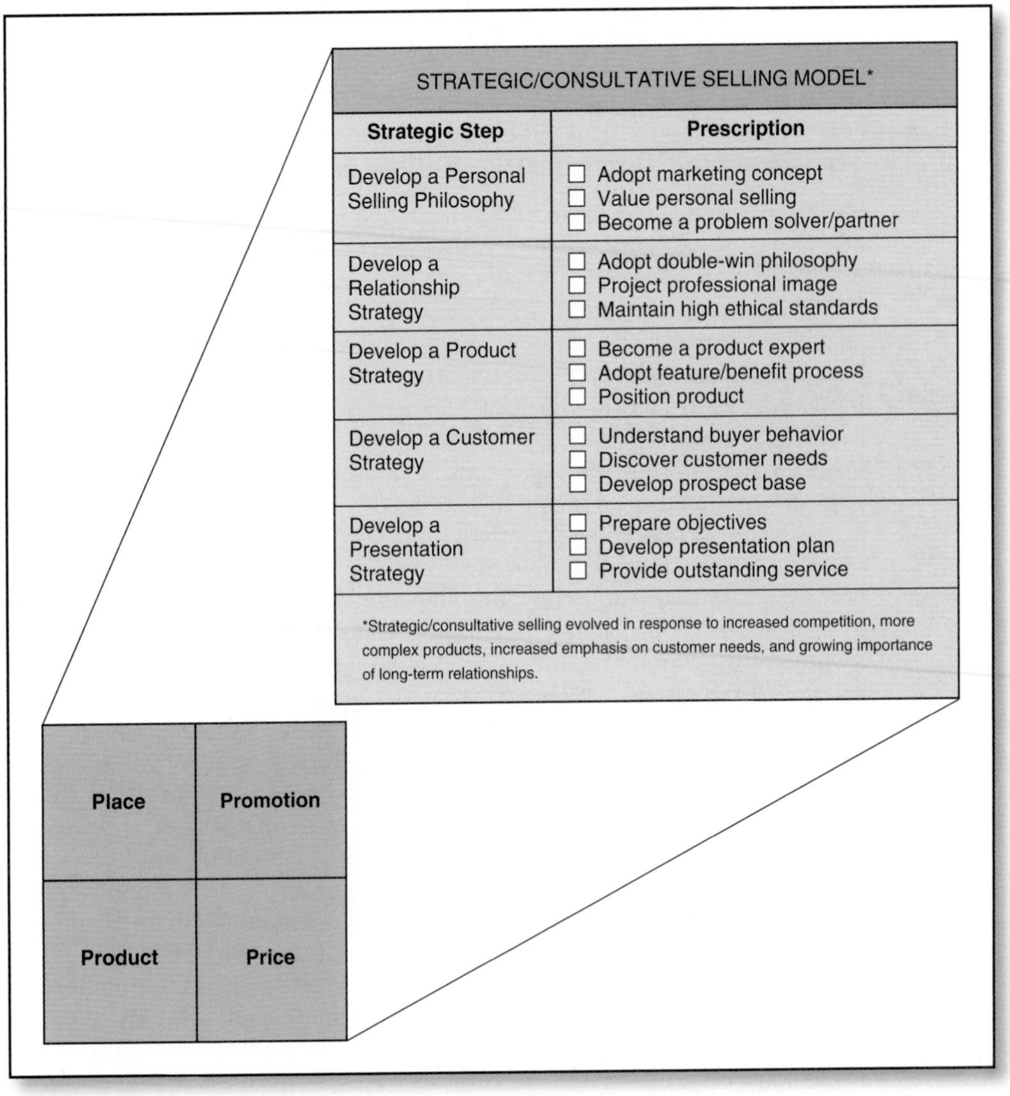

STRATEGIC/CONSULTATIVE SELLING MODEL*	
Strategic Step	**Prescription**
Develop a Personal Selling Philosophy	☐ Adopt marketing concept ☐ Value personal selling ☐ Become a problem solver/partner
Develop a Relationship Strategy	☐ Adopt double-win philosophy ☐ Project professional image ☐ Maintain high ethical standards
Develop a Product Strategy	☐ Become a product expert ☐ Adopt feature/benefit process ☐ Position product
Develop a Customer Strategy	☐ Understand buyer behavior ☐ Discover customer needs ☐ Develop prospect base
Develop a Presentation Strategy	☐ Prepare objectives ☐ Develop presentation plan ☐ Provide outstanding service

*Strategic/consultative selling evolved in response to increased competition, more complex products, increased emphasis on customer needs, and growing importance of long-term relationships.

Place	Promotion
Product	**Price**

Figure 15-1
The Strategic/Consultative Selling Model

Source: SELLING TODAY 7/E by Manning/Reece, © Reprinted by permission of Pearson Education, Inc., Upper Saddle River, NJ

The third step, developing a **product strategy,** results in a plan that can assist the sales representative in selecting and positioning products that will satisfy customer needs. A sales professional must be an expert who possesses not only a deep understanding of the features and attributes of each product he or she represents but also an understanding of competitive offerings. That understanding is then used to position the product and communicate benefits that are relevant to the customer's wants and needs. As with the selling philosophy and relationship strategy, this step must include comprehension of the target market's characteristics and the fact that prevailing needs and wants may mandate products that are different than those offered in the home country. Until recently, most American companies engaged in interna-

Figure 15-2
Building a High-Quality Sales Partnership

Source: SELLING TODAY 7/E by Manning/Reece, © Reprinted by permission of Pearson Education, Inc., Upper Saddle River, NJ

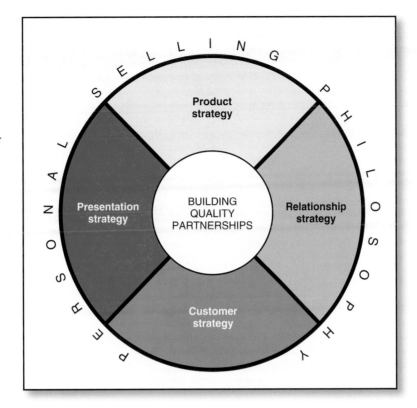

tional selling have offered products rather than services. For example, John Deere did a marvelous job of increasing its global market share by supplying high quality but relatively mundane farming equipment to countries where agriculture remains a mainstay of local economies. However, complex services such as management consulting have been difficult to market in many parts of the world. Even today, it is rare to find a consumer services company that flourishes on a worldwide basis.

Next comes a **customer strategy,** a plan that ensures that the sales professional will be maximally responsive to customer needs. Doing so requires a general understanding of consumer behavior; in addition, the salesperson must collect and analyze as much information as possible about the needs of each customer or prospect. The customer strategy step also includes building a prospect base, consisting of current customers as well as potential customers (or leads). A qualified lead is someone whose probability of wanting to buy the product is high. Many sales organizations diminish their own productivity by chasing after too many nonqualified leads. This issue can be extremely challenging for an international sales unit because customer cues or "buying signs" may not coincide with those that have been proven in the sales rep's home country.

The final step, the actual face-to-face selling situation, requires a **presentation strategy.** This consists of setting objectives for each sales call and establishing a presentation plan to meet those objectives. The presentation strategy must be based on the sales representative's commitment to provide outstanding service to customers. As shown in Figure 15-2, when these five strategies are integrated with an appropriate personal selling philosophy, the result is a high-quality partnership.

Figure 15-3
The Six-Step
Presentation Plan

Source: SELLING
TODAY 7/E by
Manning/Reece, ©
Reprinted by permis-
sion of Pearson
Education, Inc., Upper
Saddle River, NJ

THE SIX-STEP PRESENTATION PLAN*	
Step One: Approach	☐ Review strategic/consultative selling model ☐ Initiate customer contact
Step Two: Presentation	☐ Determine prospect needs ☐ Select product or service ☐ Initiate sales presentation
Step Three: Demonstration	☐ Decide what to demonstrate ☐ Select selling tools ☐ Initiate demonstration
Step Four: Negotiation	☐ Anticipate sales resistance ☐ Plan negotiating methods ☐ Initiate double-win negotiations
Step Five: Close	☐ Plan appropriate closing methods ☐ Recognize closing clues ☐ Initiate closing methods
Step Six: Servicing the Sale	☐ Suggestion selling ☐ Follow through ☐ Follow-up calls

*Service, retail, wholesale, and manufacturer selling.

The **presentation plan** that is at the heart of the presentation strategy is typically divided into six stages: approach, presentation, demonstration, negotiation, closing, and follow-up (Figure 15-3). The relative importance of each stage can vary by country or region. As mentioned several times already, the global salesperson must understand cultural norms and proper protocol, from proper exchange of business cards to the volume of one's voice during a discussion to the level of eye contact made with the decision maker. In some countries, the approach is drawn out, as the buyer gets to know or takes the measure of the salesperson on a personal level with no mention of the pending deal. In such instances, the presentation comes only after rapport has been firmly established. In some regions of Latin America and Asia, rapport development may take weeks, even months. The customer may place more importance on what occurs *following* work than on what is accomplished during the formal work hours of 8 a.m. to 5 p.m.

In the six-step presentation plan, the first step, *approach,* is the sales representative's initial contact with the customer or prospect. The most crucial element of this step is to completely understand the decision-making process and the roles of each participant, such as decision maker, influencer, ally, or blocker. In some societies, it is difficult to identify the highest-ranking individual based on observable behavior in group meetings. This crucial bit of strategic information often is uncovered only after the rep has spent considerable time developing rapport and getting to know the overall customer organization from various perspectives and in various contexts.

In the *presentation* step, the prospect's needs are assessed and matched to the company's products. To communicate effectively with a foreign audience, the style and message of the presentation must be carefully thought out. In the United States, the presentation is typically designed to sell and persuade, whereas the intent of the international version should be to educate and inform. High-pressure tactics rarely succeed in global selling, despite the fact that they are natural components of many American sales pitches. The message is equally critical because what may be regarded as fully acceptable in U.S. discussions may either offend or confuse the overseas sales audience. A humorous example of this occurred during a session between representatives from Adolph Coors Company and a foreign prospect. The first slide in the presentation contained a translation of Coors's slogan "Turn It Loose," but within seconds of this slide being shown, the audience began to chuckle. As translated, the slogan described diarrhea—obviously something that the presenter had no desire to convey to this group!

Next comes the *sales demonstration*, during which the salesperson has the opportunity to tailor the communication effort to the customer and alternately tell and show how the product can meet the customer's needs. This step represents one of selling's important advantages as a promotional tool. The prospect's senses become involved, and he or she can actually see the product in action, touch it, taste it, or hear it, as the case may be.

During the presentation, the prospect may express concerns or objections about the product itself, the price, or some other aspect of the sale. Dealing with objections in an international setting is a learned art. In some cases, this is simply part of the sales ritual and the customer expects the representative to be prepared for a lively debate on the pros and cons of the product in question. In some instances, it is taboo to initiate an open discussion where any form of disagreement is apparent; such conversations are to be handled in a one-to-one situation or in a small group with a few key individuals present. A common theme in sales training is the concept of **active listening;** naturally, in global sales, verbal and nonverbal communication barriers of the type discussed in Chapter 4 present special challenges. When objections are successfully overcome, serious negotiations can begin.

Negotiation is required to ensure that both the customer and the salesperson come away from the presentation as winners. Experienced American sales reps know that persistence during the negotiation stage is one tactic often needed to win an order in the United States. However, American-style persistence inferring tenacity or arm-twisting can be considered rude and offensive by some foreign customers. This can end the negotiations quickly. Or, in the worst case, such behavior can be taken as a display of self-perceived American superiority, which then must be countered aggressively or brought to an immediate end. Inappropriate application of American-style negotiation tactics has plagued some U.S. sales reps attempting to assertively close deals with Canadian companies. Conversely, in other countries, persistence often means endurance, a willingness to patiently invest months or years before the effort results in an actual sale. For example, a company wishing to enter the Japanese market must be prepared for negotiations to take from 3 to 10 years.

Having completed the negotiation step, the sales representative is able to move on to the *close* and thus asks for the order. Attitudes toward the degree of bluntness that is acceptable in making this request vary among countries. In Latin America, a bold closing statement is respected, whereas in Asia, it is something that must be done with more deference toward the decision maker. As with objection handling and negotiation, the close is a selling skill that comes with both knowledge and experience in global business and sales.

The final step is the *follow up*. A successful sale does not end when the order is written; to ensure customer satisfaction with the purchase, an implementation process (which may include delivery and installation) must be outlined and a customer service program established. Implementation can be complicated because of logistical and transportation issues as well as potential problems with the in-country resources to handle all the necessary steps. Transportation alternatives were discussed in Chapter 13. Decisions regarding resources for implementation and after-sale service are similar to decisions about the personal selling structure described in following paragraphs. There are cost benefits to using in-country nationals for implementation, but quality control is more difficult to guarantee. Establishing expatriates for the primary function of implementation is costly and normally cannot be justified until international operations are more mature and profitable. But sending an implementation team to the host country creates a variety of expense and regulatory concerns. Even when implementation has been adequately addressed, the requirement for solid customer service raises all of the same questions again: in-country nationals, expatriates, or third-country nationals?

Sales Force Nationality

As noted previously, a basic issue for companies that sell globally is the composition of the sales force in terms of nationality. It is possible to utilize expatriate salespersons, hire host-country nationals, or utilize third-country sales personnel. The staffing decision is contingent on several factors, including management's orientation, the technological sophistication of the product, and the stage of economic development exhibited by the target country. These are summarized in Table 15-2. Not surprisingly, a company with an ethnocentric orientation is likely to prefer expatriates and adopt a standardized approach without regard to technology or the level of economic development in the target country. Polycentric companies selling in developed countries should opt for expatriates to sell technologically sophisticated products; a host-country sales force can be used when technological sophistication is lower. In less-developed countries, host-country nationals should be used for products in which technology is a factor; host-country agents should be used for low-tech products. The widest diversity of sales force nationality is found in a company in which a regiocentric orientation prevails. Except in the case of high-tech products in developed countries, third-country nationals are likely to be used in all situations.

Table 15-2
Contingency Factors in Selecting Sales Force Nationality

TECHNOLOGY LEVEL	MANAGEMENT ORIENTATION					
	ETHNOCENTRIC		POLYCENTRIC		REGIOCENTRIC	
	DEVELOPED	LESS DEVELOPED	DEVELOPED	LESS DEVELOPED	DEVELOPED	LESS DEVELOPED
High	Expatriates	Expatriates	Expatriates	Host-country nationals	Expatriates	Third-country nationals
Low	Expatriates	Expatriates	Host-country nationals	Host-country nationals (agents)	Third-country nationals	Third-country nationals (agents)

Source: Industrial Marketing Management, 24, March, Earl D. Honeycutt & John B. Ford, *Guidelines for Managing an International Sales Force*, p. 139, Copyright © 1995, with permission of Elsevir Science.

Table 15-3
Advantages and
Disadvantages of
Different Sales
Types

CATEGORY	ADVANTAGES	DISADVANTAGES
Expatriates	Superior product knowledge Demonstrated commitment to high customer service standards Train for promotion Greater HQ control	Highest cost High turnover Cost for language and cross-cultural training
Host country	Economical Superior market knowledge Language skills Superior cultural knowledge Implement actions sooner	Needs product training May be held in low esteem Language skills may not be important Difficult to ensure loyalty
Third country	Cultural sensitivity Language skills Economical Allows regional sales coverage	Face identity problems Blocked promotions Income gaps Needs product or company training Loyalty not assured

Source: Adapted from Earl D. Honeycutt Jr. and John B. Ford, "Guidelines for Managing an International Sales Force," *Industrial Marketing Management* 24 (March 1995), p. 138.

In addition to the factors just cited, management must also weigh the advantages and disadvantages of each nationality type (Table 15-3). First, because they come from the home country, expatriates often possess a high level of product knowledge and are likely to be thoroughly versed in their company's commitment to after-sales service. They come with corporate philosophies and culture well engrained. Also, they are better able to institute the acceptable practices and follow the policies of the home office and, generally, there is less potential for control or loyalty issues to arise. Finally, a foreign assignment can also provide employees with valuable experience that can enhance promotion prospects. There are also several disadvantages to utilizing expatriates. If the headquarters mindset is *too* firmly ingrained, the expat may have a difficult time understanding the foreign environment and assimilating into it. This can eventually lead to significant losses; the sales effort may be poorly received in the market, or homesickness can lead to a costly reversal of the relocation process. Indeed, maintaining expat sales personnel is very expensive; the average annual cost to U.S. companies of posting employees and their families overseas exceeds $250,000. In addition to paying expat salaries, companies must pay moving expenses, cost-of-living adjustments, and host-country taxes. Despite the high investment, many expats fail to complete their assignments due to inadequate training and orientation prior to the cross-border transfer. In addition, studies have shown that one-quarter of U.S. expats leave their companies within a year of returning home.

An alternative is to build a sales force with host-country personnel. Locals offer several advantages, including intimate knowledge of the market and business environment, language skills, and superior knowledge of local culture. The last consideration can be especially important in Asia and Latin America. In addition, because in-country personnel are already in place in the target country, there is no need for expensive relocations. However, host-country nationals may possess work habits or selling styles that do not mesh with those of the parent company. Furthermore, the firms' corporate sales executives tend to have less control over an operation that is dominated by host-country nationals. Headquarters executives may also experience difficulty cultivating loyalty, and host-country nationals are likely to need hefty doses of training and education regarding both the company and its products.

A third option is to hire persons who are not natives of either the headquarters country or the host country; such persons are known as *third-country nationals*. For example, a U.S.-based company might hire someone from Thailand to represent it in China. This option has many advantages in common with the host-country national approach. In addition, if conflict, diplomatic tension, or some other form of disagreement has driven a wedge between the home country and the target sales country, a sales representative from a third country may be perceived as sufficiently neutral or "arm's-length" to enable the company to continue its sales effort. However, there are several disadvantages of the third-country option. For one thing, sales prospects may wonder why they have been approached by someone who is neither a local national nor a native of the headquarters country. Third-country nations may lack motivation if they are compensated less generously than expats or host-country sales personnel; also, they may find themselves passed over for promotions as coveted assignments go to others.

After much trial and error in creating sales forces, most companies today attempt to establish a hybrid sales force comprised of a balanced mix of expatriates and in-country nationals. The operative word for this approach is *balanced*, as there always remains the potential for conflict between the two groups. It is also the most expensive proposition in terms of up-front costs because, both relocation of expats and extensive training of in-country nationals are required. But the short term costs are usually deemed necessary in order to do business and conduct personal selling overseas.

After considering the options shown in Table 15-3, management may question the appropriateness of trying to create personal selling units made up of their own people. A fourth option is to utilize the services of **sales agents**. Agents work under contract rather than as full-time employees. In the United States, companies have used sales agents for many years, often with mixed results. From a global perspective, it often makes a great deal of sense to set up one or more agent entities to at least gain entry to a selected country or region. In some cases, because of the remoteness of the area or the lack of revenue opportunity (beyond servicing satellite operations of customers headquartered elsewhere), agents are retained on a fairly permanent level. To this day, the majority of U.S., Asian, and European companies with an Africa-based sales presence maintain agent groups to represent their interests.

Agents are much less expensive than full-time employees and possess the same advantage of understanding the market as a team of in-country nationals. Subsequently, if a certain degree of success is achieved, the role of agents can be diminished in favor of employee-based teams. Conversely, if the market does not prove to be financially viable, it is much less costly to pull out from an agent-oriented territory. However, the challenge of control that was discussed earlier is even greater due to the fact that agents frequently have other sources of income available to them. Thus, a company may find itself in a relatively weak bargaining position when coming to terms with agents. Additionally, because there are other job opportunities for agents (especially with the growing trend of firms in the same industry concurrently targeting the same overseas markets), the question of loyalty is significant. A company that employs foreign sales agents has to determine just what to provide in terms of product and strategic training because of the very real possibility that a competitor will lure those agents away with more attractive compensation packages. Agents have even used their remote locations as a shield to avoid detection as they accept assignments from competing firms, offering customers the best deal among the several options they represent. Situations such as this mean that companies must create some type of monitoring system within agent territories, either through an in-country manager or regular visits from the home office sales department.

Other international personal selling approaches that fall somewhere between sales agents and full-time employee teams include:

- *Exclusive license arrangements* where a firm will pay commissions to an in-country company's sales force to conduct personal selling on its behalf. For example, when Canada's regulatory agency prevented U.S. telephone companies from entering the market on their own, AT&T, MCI, Sprint, and other firms crafted a series of exclusive license arrangements with Canadian telephone companies.
- *Contract manufacturing or production* with a degree of personal selling made available through warehouses or showrooms that are open to potential customers. Sears has employed this technique in various overseas markets, with emphasis placed on the manufacturing and production but with the understanding that opportunities for some sales results do exist.
- *Management-only agreements* through which a corporation will manage a foreign sales force in a mode that is similar to franchising. Hilton Hotels has these types of agreements all over the world; not only for hotel operations but also for personal selling efforts aimed at securing conventions, business meetings, and large group events.
- *Joint ventures* with an in-country (or regional) partner. Since many countries place restrictions on foreign ownership within their borders, partnerships can serve as the best way for a company to obtain both a personal sales capability as well as an existing base of customers.

SPECIAL FORMS OF MARKETING COMMUNICATIONS: DIRECT MARKETING, EVENT SPONSORSHIP, AND PRODUCT PLACEMENT

The Direct Marketing Association defines **direct marketing** as an interactive marketing system that produces measurable results and uses one or more media to start or complete a sale. As the name implies, direct marketing involves an exchange with individuals whose names and addresses are known to the company. Companies use direct mail, telemarketing, television, print, and other media to generate responses and build databases filled with purchase histories and other information about customers. By contrast, mass marketing efforts are typically aimed at broad segments of consumers with certain demographic, psychographic, or behavioral characteristics in common. Other differences between direct marketing and "regular" marketing are shown in Table 15-4.

Worldwide, the popularity of direct marketing has been steadily increasing in recent years. One reason is the availability of credit cards—widespread in some countries, growing in others—as a convenient payment mechanism for direct response purchases. (In fact, Visa, American Express, and MasterCard generate enormous revenues by sending direct mail offers to their cardholders.) Another reason is societal: Whether in Japan, Germany, or the United States, dual-income families have

Table 15-4
Comparison of
Direct Marketing
and Mass
Marketing

DIRECT MARKETING	MASS MARKETING
Marketer adds value (creates place utility) by arranging for delivery of product to customer's door.	Product benefits do not typically include delivery to customer's door.
Marketer controls the product all the way through to delivery.	Marketer typically loses control as product is turned over to distribution channel intermediaries.
Direct response advertising is used to generate an immediate inquiry or order.	Advertising is used for cumulative effect over time to build image, awareness, loyalty, and benefit recall. Purchase action is deferred.
Repetition is used within the ad.	Repetition is used over a period of time.
Customer perceives higher risk since product is bought unseen. Recourse may be viewed as distant or inconvenient.	Customer perceives less risk due to direct contact with product. Recourse is viewed as less distant.

Source: Adapted from Direct Marketing Association.

money to spend but less time to shop outside the home. Technological advances have made it easier for companies to reach customers directly. Cable and satellite television allow advertisers to reach very specific audiences on a global basis. As noted in Chapter 7, MTV reaches 340 million households worldwide and attracts a young viewership. A company wishing to reach business people can buy time on CNN, Fox News Network, or CNBC.

Direct marketing's popularity in Europe increased sharply during the 1990s. The European Commission expects investment in direct marketing to surpass expenditures for traditional advertising in the near future. One reason is that direct marketing programs can be readily made to conform to the "think global, act local" philosophy. Notes Tony Coad, managing director of a London-based direct marketing and database company, "Given the linguistic, cultural, and regional diversity of Europe, the celebrated idea of a Euro-consumer is Euro-baloney. Direct marketing's strength lies in addressing these differences and adapting to each consumer."[9] Obstacles still remain, however, including the European Commission's concerns about data protection and privacy, high postal rates in some countries, and the relatively limited development of the mailing list industry. Rainer Hengst of Deutsche Post offers the following guidelines for U.S.-based direct marketers that wish to go global:[10]

- The world is full of people who are not Americans. Be sure not to treat them like they are.
- Like politics, all marketing is local. Just because your direct mail campaign worked in Texas, do not assume it will work in Toronto.
- While there may be a European Union, there is no such thing as a "European."
- Pick your target, focus on one country, and do your homework.

---

9   Bruce Crumley, "European Market Continues to Soar," *Advertising Age* (February 21, 1994), p. 22.
10 Rainer Hengst, "Plotting Your Global Strategy," *Direct Marketing* 63, no. 4 (August 2000), pp. 52–57.

- You'll have a hard time finding customers in Paris, France, if your return address is Paris, Texas. Customers need to be able to return products locally, or at least believe there are services available in their country.

Direct Mail

Direct mail uses the postal service as a vehicle for delivering an offer to prospects targeted by the marketer. Direct mail is the primary marketing tool for retail specialists such as L.L. Bean and Lands' End; it is also popular with banks, insurance companies, and other financial services providers. Direct marketing is now often referred to as "customer relationship marketing" because each response allows the company to add information to its database. That information, in turn, allows marketers to refine the offer and generate more precisely targeted lists. In the United States, there is a well-developed mailing list industry. A company can rent a list to target virtually any type of buyer; naturally, the more selective and specialized the list, the more expensive it is. The availability of good lists and the sheer size of the market are important factors in explaining why Americans receive more direct mail than anyone else (Table 15-5). However, on a per capita basis, German consumers are world-leader mail-order shoppers, buying more than $500 each in merchandise annually. Americans rank second, with annual per capita spending of $379 (Table 15-6).

Compared with the United States, list availability in Europe and Japan is much more limited. The lists that are available may be lower in quality and contain more errors and duplications than lists from the United States. Despite such problems, direct mail is growing in popularity in some parts of the world. In Europe, for example, regulators are concerned about the extent that children are exposed to—or even targeted by—traditional cigarette advertising. Faced with the threat of increased restriction on its advertising practices, the tobacco industry is making a strategy shift toward direct mail. As David Robottom, development director at the Direct Marketing Association, noted, "Many of the promotions on cigarette packets are about collected data. [The tobacco companies] are working very hard at building up loyalty." Table 15-7 lists direct mail volume for selected European countries.

Following the economic crisis in Asia, a number of companies in that region have turned to direct mail in an effort to use their advertising budgets more effectively.

Table 15-5
Pieces of Direct
Mail Received
per Capita

United States	350+
Switzerland	107
Germany	68
France	65
Norway	53
Denmark	50
Finland	46
England	40
Ireland	20

Source: Deutsche Post.

Table 15-6
Per Capita Mail
Order Sales

Country	Per Capita Sales
Germany	$528
United States	379
Switzerland	333
United Kingdom	280
France	231
Denmark	227
Norway	219
Finland	212

Source: Deutsche Post.

Table 15-7
Addressed
European Direct
Mail Volume
(millions of items)

	1996	1997	1998	1999	2000
Belgium	1,095	1,122	1,117	1,091	—
Denmark	241	270	292	235	237
Finland	267	305	310	315	—
France	3,703	3,769	3,990	4,252	—
Germany	6,605	6,834	6,048	6,398	—
Ireland	80	87	90	101	—
Netherlands	1,225	1,272	1,379	1,449	532
Norway	327	332	337	377	374
Poland	80	160	170	—	—
Portugal	138	164	176	189	196
Spain	—	728	789	790	796
Sweden	588	—	—	—	—
Switzerland	761	1,461	1,502	1,300	1,535
UK	3,173	3,588	4,014	4,345	4,664

Source: Direct Mail Information Service.

Historically, the Asian direct marketing sector has lagged behind its counterparts in the United States and Europe. Grey Global Group established a Kuala Lumpur office of Grey Direct Interactive in 1997; OgilvyOne Worldwide is the Malaysian subsidiary of Ogilvy & Mather Group specializing in direct marketing. Companies in the banking and telecommunications sectors have been to the forefront of direct marketing initiatives in Asia, using their extensive databases to target individual consumers by mail or Internet. In 2000, Nestlé launched a successful direct mail campaign in Malaysia that offered cat owners free samples of Friskies brand cat food, coupons for discounts on purchases of Friskies, and the opportunity to join the Friskies Cat Club. Nestlé expanded its existing database of 450,000 names by placing newspaper ads offering coupons to readers who wrote to the company, distributing questionnaires in conjunction with in-store sampling, and by hosting contests on its Web site. The 20 percent response rate to the Friskies mailing was well above the single-digit rates typical of direct mail campaigns in the United States. As Leong Ming Chee, marketing and communications director for Nestlé Products, noted, "You can spend 100,000 ringgit ($26,320) on TV ads for a product like this and have no idea how many viewers have cats and so how much of it goes to waste. This way, you can target those exact consumers directly."[11]

A recent campaign by Mercedes-Benz shows the role that direct mail can play in a coordinated communications program. Prior to the launch of the new American-built All Activity Vehicle (AAV), the company targeted 135,000 prospective buyers with a mailing designed to build traffic at dealerships. An initial mailing consisted of a detailed questionnaire covering topics that ranged from the appropriate number of cupholders to safety. After the questionnaires were analyzed, respondents received a second mailing customized according to their earlier responses. For example, prospects interested in safety received information about airbags. Because production of the vehicle had not yet begun, Mercedes managers were able to make some minor changes in accordance with respondent preferences, such as placing the spare tire inside the vehicle and offering a roof rack as standard equipment. As the launch date approached, potential customers were able to reserve an AAV by mail and specify the color and options that they wanted.[12]

Visit the Web site
Located in the United Kingdom, the Direct Mail Information Service compiles statistics on direct mail in Europe. To review current statistics, log on to: www.dmis.co.uk

Catalogs

Worldwide, mail order represents a $196 billion market. Catalogs have a long and illustrious history as a direct marketing tool in both Europe and the United States. (One of the authors lives in a home that was ordered in kit form from the 1910 Sears catalog.) The European catalog market flourished after World War II as consumers sought convenience, bargain prices, and access to a wider range of goods. U.S.-based catalog marketers include Lands' End, L.L. Bean, The Sharper Image, and Victoria's Secret; in Europe, Great Universal Stores, Littlewoods, Freemans, and Otto Versand Group (which includes Spiegel and Eddie Bauer) are well-known catalog companies. Catalogs are widely recognized as an important part of an integrated marketing communications program, and many companies use catalogs in tandem with traditional retail distribution. The U. S. mail order market generates $90 billion in annual revenues; U.S. companies are the world's leading catalog marketers, accounting for 50 percent of global catalog sales. European companies rank second, with a 40 percent share. As shown in Table 15-8, Germany accounts for 50 percent of European catalog sales; 1996 revenues from catalog sales totaled $37.8 billion.

Historically, catalogers in the United States benefited from the ability to ship goods from one coast to the other, crossing multiple state boundaries with relatively few regulatory hurdles. By contrast, prior to the advent of the single market, catalog sales in Europe were hindered by the fact that mail order products passing through customs at national borders were subject to value-added taxes (VAT). Because VAT drove up prices of goods that crossed borders, a particular catalog tended to be targeted at intracountry buyers. In other words, Germans bought from German catalogs, French consumers bought from French catalogs, and so on. Market-entry strategies were also affected by the customs regulations; catalogers grew by acquiring existing companies in various countries. For example, Otto Versand Group has 36 mail order operations in 16 European countries.

Today, the single market means that mail order goods can move freely throughout the EU without incurring VAT charges. Also, since January 1993, VAT exemptions have been extended to goods bound to the European Free Trade Area countries

---

[11] Cris Prystay, "In Malaysia, Advertisers Adopt Direct Mail to Keep Sales Purring," *Asian Wall Street Journal* (March 26–April 1, 2001), p. 12.
[12] Joshua Levine, "Give Me One of Those," *Forbes* (June 3, 1996), p. 134.

Table 15-8
Catalog Sales
in Europe

Country	Share of European Catalog Sales (%)
Germany	50
France	16
UK	14
Other*	20

*"OTHER" 20%	
Sweden	15%
Italy	14%
Switzerland	14%
Austria	12%
Netherlands	12%
Belgium	8%
Denmark	7%
Spain	7%
Finland	6%
Norway	5%

Source: Reprinted by permission of Hoke Communications, Inc.

(Norway, Iceland, Switzerland, and Liechtenstein). Some predict robust growth in Europe's mail order business, thanks to the increased size of the potential catalog market and the VAT-free environment. The single market is also attracting American catalogue retailers, who will be faced with higher costs for paper, printing, and shipping as well as the familiar issue of whether to adapt their offerings to local tastes. Stephen Miles, director of international development, Lands' End, said recently, "The most difficult thing is to know in which areas to be local. We're proud that we're an American sportswear company, but that doesn't mean your average German consumer wants to pick up the phone and speak English to someone."[13]

In Japan, the domestic catalog industry is well developed. Leading catalog companies include Cecile, with $1 billion in annual sales of women's apparel and lingerie; Kukutake Publishing, which sells educational materials; and Shaddy, a general merchandise company. As noted in Chapter 13, Japan's fragmented distribution system represents a formidable obstacle to market entry by outsiders. An increasing number of companies use direct marketing to circumvent the distribution bottleneck. Annual revenues for all forms of consumer and business direct response advertising in Japan passed the $1 trillion mark in the mid-1990s; they declined to $525 billion in 2000 as Japan's economic difficulties continued. Direct mail (including catalogs) accounted for about $175 billion in 2000 direct response sales. Success can be achieved using different strategies. For example, Patagonia dramatically increased sales after publishing a Japanese-language catalog, whereas L.L. Bean offers a Japanese-language insert in its traditional catalog.

---

[13] Cacilie Rohwedder, "U.S. Mail-Order Firms Shake Up Europe," *The Wall Street Journal* (January 6, 1998), p. A15.

Even as they continue to develop the Japanese market, Western catalogers are now turning their attention to other Asian countries. In Hong Kong and Singapore, efficient postal services, highly educated populations, wide use of credit cards, and high per capita income are attracting the attention of catalog marketers. Notes Michael Grasee, the former director of international business development at Lands' End, "We see our customer in Asia as pretty much the same customer we have everywhere. It's the time-starved, traveling, hardworking executive."[14] Catalogers are also targeting Asia's developing countries. Otto Versand Group, with 2001 revenues of $15.6 billion and about 9 percent of global mail order sales, is planning to enter China, Korea, and Taiwan. Because these countries have few local mail order companies for acquisition, executives at Otto Versand have mapped out an entry strategy based on acquiring a majority stake in joint ventures with local retailers.[15]

Infomercials and Teleshopping

Infomercials are a form of paid television programming in which a particular product is demonstrated, explained, and offered for sale to viewers who call a toll-free number shown on the screen. Thomas Burke, president of Saatchi & Saatchi's infomercial division, calls infomercials "the most powerful form of advertising ever created." Home shopping channels such as QVC, the Home Shopping Network (HSN), and ValueVision take the infomercial concept one step further; the programming is *exclusively* dedicated to product demonstration and selling. Worldwide, home shopping is a multi-billion dollar industry. The leading home shopping channels are also leveraging the Internet; in 2001, HSN generated $2 billion in sales through television and the company's www.HSN.com Web site. Industry observers expect the popularity of home shopping will increase over the next few years as interactive television (ITV or t-commerce) technology finds its way into more households. ITV has a greater presence in Europe than in the United States; in the United Kingdom alone, an estimated 60 percent of households will have access to ITV by 2003.[16]

The cost of producing a single infomercial can reach $3 million; advertisers then pay as much as $500,000 for time slots on U.S. cable and satellite systems and local TV channels. Because infomercials are typically 30 minutes in length and often feature studio audiences and celebrity announcers, many viewers believe they are watching regular talk show-type programming. Although originally associated with personal care, fitness, and household products such as those from legendary direct-response pitchman Ron Popeil, infomercials have gone up-market in recent years. For example, Philips Electronics produced a groundbreaking infomercial during the launch of its CD-i multiplayer in the early 1990s. Unfortunately, Philips's execution of the infomercial was flawed—callers were given the name of a local dealer but not given a chance to order CD-i directly—and CD-i ultimately failed. By contrast, Lexus generated more than 40,000 telephone inquiries after launching its used-car program with an infomercial; 2 percent of those who responded ultimately purchased a Lexus automobile. Mainstream advertisers have also discovered the power of teleshopping; for example, Saks Fifth Avenue rang up $1 million in sales after its private-label apparel was featured on QVC.

As these figures indicate, infomercials and home shopping television are important marketing communications channels for global marketers. Both formats have proven

---

14 James Cox, "Catalogers Expand in Asia," *USA Today* (October 18, 1996), p. 4B.
15 Dagmar Mussey, "Otto Expands Family-Owned Catalog Empire," *Advertising Age International* (September 1996), p. i4.
16 "Europe Wants Its ITV," *Chain Store Age* 77, no. 7 (July 2001), pp. 76–78.

viable outside the United States. E4L (formerly National Media Corp.) produces infomercials that are shown in more than 200 million homes worldwide. As Mark Hershorn, the company's former president and CEO, told *Advertising Age International:*

> "We're realizing very significant opportunities in the global marketplace. Our goal isn't to be an infomercial company, but a global marketer that goes direct to the consumer through the TV. Infomercials represent a powerful marketing vehicle that is not limited by geographic borders. U.S. manufacturers are in a fierce competition to create brands and infomercials that can create shelf space for products in consumers' homes on a global basis. Down the road, we'll be able to put a product simultaneously into the homes of 300 to 500 million people around the globe. Now *that's* powerful."[17]

E4L relies heavily on alliances with TV stations in individual country markets. For many of the products the company offers, "not available in stores" is a powerful selling point. However, advertisers whose products are also available through traditional channels can use infomercials and home shopping television to identify prospective buyers, to support advertising campaigns in other media, and to help educate consumers by offering them a complete product demonstration.

In Asia, infomercials generate several hundred million dollars in annual sales. Costs for a late-night time slot range from $100,000 in Japan to $20,000 in Singapore. Infomercials are also playing a part in the development of China's market sector. The government has given its blessing by allowing China Central Television, the state-run channel, to air infomercials and give Chinese consumers access to Western goods. Despite low per capita incomes, Chinese consumers are thought to achieve a savings rate as high as 40 percent because housing and health care are provided by the state. China Shop-A-Vision is in the vanguard, signing up 20,000 "TV shopping members" in its first year of airing infomercials. As these and other pioneers in Chinese direct-response television have learned, however, many obstacles remain, including the limited number of private telephones, low penetration of credit cards, high product prices due to import tariffs, and problems with delivery logistics in crowded cities such as Shanghai.[18]

While home shopping giants QVC and Home Shopping Network are staying out of China for now, QVC's agreement with Rupert Murdoch's British Sky Broadcasting (BSkyB) satellite company enables it to reach England, Ireland, and parts of the European continent. Similarly, Mexico's Grupo Televisa beams QVC into Mexico and South America. A number of local and regional teleshopping channels have sprung up in Europe. Germany's HOT (Home Order Television) is a joint venture with Quelle Schickedanz, a mail order company. Sweden's TV-Shop is available in 15 European countries and racked up $100 million in sales in 1995. Europeans are likely to be more discriminating than the average American teleshopping customer. As QVC executive Francis Edwards explained, "European customers respond in different ways, though the basic premise and concept is the same. The type of jewelry is different. German consumers wouldn't buy 14-karat gold. They go for a higher karat. We can sell wine in Germany, but not in the U.S."[19]

---

[17] Kim Cleland, "Infomercial Audience Crosses over Cultures," *Advertising Age International* (January 15, 1996), p. i8.

[18] Jon Hilsenrath, "In China, a Taste of Buy-Me TV," *The New York Times* (November 17, 1996), sec. 3, pp. 1, 11.

[19] Michelle Pentz, "Teleshopping Gets a Tryout in Europe but Faces Cultural and Legal Barriers," *The Wall Street Journal* (September 9, 1996), p. A8.

Sponsorship

Sponsorship is an increasingly popular form of marketing communications whereby a company pays a fee to have its name associated with a particular event, team or athletic association, or sports facility. An Olympic sponsorship can help a company reach a global audience; sponsors are also drawn to events that reach national or regional audiences, such as professional team sports, car racing, hot air balloon competitions, rodeos, and music concerts. Sony recently became an official U.S. sponsor of the National Basketball Association with the signing of a $10 million per year deal. One part of the deal calls for recordings by musicians on the Sony Music label—Aerosmith, Pearl Jam, and Mariah Carey, for example—to get priority consideration for air time during games. Hoping to achieve higher levels of brand awareness in the United States, Nokia sponsors the Sugar Bowl; Ericsson paid to have its name emblazoned on the new stadium where the Carolina Panthers football team plays. In 1997, Fila and Adidas engaged in a bidding war for sponsorship rights to the New York Yankees baseball team. Adidas eventually won a 10-year deal with a total value of $100 million; although that deal sets a record for sponsorship of an American sport, it is dwarfed by Nike's $200 million deal to sponsor the Brazilian national soccer team.

Sponsorship can be an effective component of an integrated marketing communications program. It can be used in countries where regulations limit the extent to which a company can use advertising or other forms of marketing communication. In China, for example, where tobacco advertising is prohibited, B.A.T and Philip Morris spend tens of millions of dollars sponsoring events such as a Hong Kong-Beijing car rally and China's national soccer tournament. Sponsorship is also popular in the United Kingdom, where Benson & Hedges paid £4 million for a five-year contract to sponsor cricket matches, and Rothman's spends £15 million annually to

Shang.   Tang.   Yuan.   Ring.

Until April 30, your Nokia phone gets you a free guest ticket of equal or lesser value when you buy a ticket to *China: 5000 Years* at the Solomon R. Guggenheim Museum and Guggenheim Museum SoHo. And visit the museum store to see the Nokia 252 Art Edition wireless masterpiece. **NOKIA** CONNECTING PEOPLE

Nokia is a registered trademark of Nokia Corporation.

Many global companies use fine arts sponsorships to enhance their image with upscale customers. This ad from Finland's Nokia appeared in conjunction with the company's sponsorship of exhibits at the two Guggenheim Museum locations in New York City. As noted in the text, Nokia also sponsors events with more general appeal such as the annual Sugar Bowl football game. Reprinted by permission of Nokia.

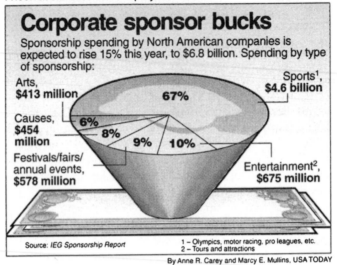

USA SNAPSHOTS®
A look at statistics that shape your finances

Corporate sponsor bucks
Sponsorship spending by North American companies is expected to rise 15% this year, to $6.8 billion. Spending by type of sponsorship:

Arts, $413 million

Sports[1], $4.6 billion

67%

Causes, $454 million

6%

8%

9%   10%

Festivals/fairs/ annual events, $578 million

Entertainment[2], $675 million

Source: *IEG Sponsorship Report*

1 – Olympics, motor racing, pro leagues, etc.
2 – Tours and attractions

By Anne R. Carey and Marcy E. Mullins, USA TODAY

sponsor a Formula One racing team. However, the announcement in May 1997, by Britain's newly elected Labour government that it intends to ban sports sponsorships by tobacco companies casts some doubt on the future of this type of arrangement.

Product Placement in Motion Pictures and Television Shows

In 1996, when BMW introduced a sporty new convertible, the Z3, it wanted to make a major global splash. BMW garnered extensive publicity by placing the Z3 in a lavish new James Bond film, *Goldeneye*. In the film, 007 is given a Z3 in place of his Aston-Martin; the car also figured prominently in movie previews and print ads. BMW dealers were provided with "BMW 007 kits" that allowed prospective buyers to learn more about both the movie and the car before either was available. As *Advertising Age* observed, "BMW has shaken, not just stirred, the auto industry with unprecedented media exposure and awareness for the Z3 and BMW in the U.S." *Tomorrow Never Dies*, the follow up to "Goldeneye," featured global brand promotional tie-ins worth an estimated $100 million. Ericsson, Heineken, Omega, Brioni, and Visa International all placed products in the new film. Actor Pierce Brosnan also appeared as Agent 007 in specially filmed television commercials.[20]

New Media and E-Commerce

As the Internet has developed into a crucial global communication tool, decision makers in many organizations are realizing that they must include new media in their communications planning. Many companies purchase banner ads on popular Web browsers such as AOL or Yahoo!; typically, the ads are linked to the company's home page or product- or brand-related sites. Although creative possibilities are limited with banner ads and click-through rates are typically low, the number of companies that use the Web as a medium for global advertising is expected to increase

---

[20] Jon Rappoport, "BMW Z3," *Advertising Age* (June 24, 1996), p. S37; Bruce Orwall, "James Bond Gets a New License to Sell Everything from Credit to Watches," *The Wall Street Journal* (June 12, 1997), p. B10.

Table 15-9
Interactive
Agencies

Agency/HQ Location	Clients	Selected Office Locations
iXL (Atlanta)	GE, VirginAtlantic, Chase Manhattan, Stern	Japan, U.K., Canada, Brazil
IconMedialab (Stockholm, Brussels)	VW, gifts.com	Denmark, Finland, France, Germany, U.S., Hong Kong
Pixelpark (Berlin)	Lufthansa, Credit Suisse, Bertelsmann	Austria, France, Germany, Switzerland, U.K., U.S.
AKQA (London)	Energizer, BMW	New Zealand, U.K.

Source: Adapted from "Interactive 100," *Advertising Age* (June 19, 2000), pp. s46–s54.

dramatically over the next few years. Some companies are devising innovative new ways to harness the power of the Internet. For example, Unilever PLC has begun digitizing its vast library of television commercials. Computer users can download the full-frame, full-motion videos for products such as Salon Selectives shampoo and watch them at any time. Although some industry observers are skeptical, Unilever's interactive marketing staff believes that the Web may represent an important new, low-cost channel for showing ads.[21] McDonald's is also putting digitized versions of its ads on the Web, but for a different purpose. The fast-food giant has established an online digital commercial archive, www.mcdcommercials.com, that allows McDonald's ad agencies anywhere in the world to review a library of 15,000 TV commercials. The agency can then request pre-existing footage to incorporate into new ads.[22]

The decision to use the Web must be accompanied by the commitment of significant monetary and human resources. Increased traffic and higher user expectations are driving up costs, and organizations should make every effort to design Web sites that are visually stimulating, entertaining, and informative. The Global Web 100 lists global companies that use the Net; it can be accessed at www.metamoney.com. There are separate Web 100 listings for the 100 largest U.S. corporations that have established Web sites, as well as the top 100 non-U.S. companies (listings include major subsidiaries). As a quick review of this site confirms, virtually every company mentioned in this text is on the Net.

Web sites can be developed in-house, or an outside firm can be engaged. During the past few years, a new breed of interactive advertising agency has emerged to help companies globalize their Internet offerings. Planet Leap Global Communications helps Apple Computer, Nike, and other clients address issues such as multiple languages, cultural differences, and data privacy. For example, a German language Web site requires more than double the capacity of an English language site because the German copy takes more space.[23] Agencies specializing in interactive media can also advise clients on local or regional laws that prohibit sales promotion tools such as sweepstakes. Table 15-9 lists additional interactive agencies working for clients on a global basis.

Web sites can be classified by purpose: *promotion sites* promote goods or services, *content sites* provide news and entertainment and support a company's public

---

[21] Vanessa O'Connell, "Unilever to Run Some TV Spots, Digitized, Online," *The Wall Street Journal* (March 2, 2001), pp. B1, B5.
[22] Kata MacArthur, "Fast Food Meets the Internet," *Advertising Age* (June 19, 2000), p. 28.
[23] Patricia Riedman, "Think Globally, Act Globally," *Advertising Age* (June 19, 2000), p. s48.

Table 15-10
Projected
Worldwide B-to-C
Revenues, by
Region, 2000–2004
(billions)

REGION	2000	2001	2002	2003	2004
North America	$47.5	$74.4	$110.6	$135.2	$197.9
Europe	$8.1	$16.5	$37.1	$81.8	$183.5
Asia	$3.2	$8.3	$15.6	$26.4	$38.0
Latin America	$0.7	$1.8	$3.3	$5.5	$8.1
Africa/Middle East	$0.2	$0.3	$0.6	$1.1	$1.6
World	$59.7	$101.1	$167.2	$250.0	$428.1

Source: eGlobal Report, e-Marketer, 2001.

"Shopping on the Internet is no different than traditional sales channels. It's all about trusting the brand and having a strong relationship with one's customers."[24]
—Ron Fry
Internet Business Manager, Lands' End

relations efforts, and *transaction sites* are cyberspace retail operations by means of which customers can purchase goods and services. Transaction sites must be capable of handling orders in different languages and payment in different currencies. The Internet can be used as an advertising channel, as a public relations tool, as a means for running a contest or sales promotion, and as support for the personal selling effort.

Internet use by individuals is highest in the United States; more than 100 million Americans aged 14 and up are active Internet users. Several factors contribute to this high usage rate, including the presence of a high quality telecommunications infrastructure. Moreover, at least one computer is present in more than 60 percent of U.S. households. According to projections from eMarketer, global online business-to-consumer (b-to-c) sales revenues will reach $428 billion by 2004, up from $100 billion in 2001. About three-fourths of 2001 revenue was generated in North America; that figure is expected to drop to 50 percent as online sales in Europe increase over the next few years (see Table 15-10).

The increased importance of the Internet in global marketing can also be seen in the number and variety of alliances that advertisers are establishing with Web sites. For example, Unilever PLC sponsors the Microsoft Network (MSN) and MSN WomenCentral in the United States, France, Germany, and the United Kingdom. This type of sponsorship generally means banner ads and links to other brand-related sites are featured prominently.[25] The trend towards consolidation among media companies allows advertisers to efficiently achieve greater reach across media platforms. For example, Toyota Motors advertised its 2002 Camry on AOL Time Warner's various media properties. One of Toyota's objectives was to reposition Camry from a brand associated with older women to a brand that appeals to younger men. In fall 2001, Toyota sponsored a special issue of *Time* titled "Music Goes Global"; part of AOL's "Music Goes Global" Web site was dedicated to the Camry. Also, Toyota sponsored some music programming on CNN and TNT, which are also part of the AOL Time Warner family.[26]

Quelch and Klein have developed a matrix to categorize the different types of Web sites in terms of content and audience focus (Figure 15-4). In Quadrant 1, the focus is on providing information and service to domestic customers. Quadrant 2 companies are more transaction-oriented but still with a domestic focus. Companies

---

[24] Christopher Price, "Fashion Suits the Internet Shopper," *Financial Times* (June 24, 1998), p. 23.
[25] Sarah Ellison, "Unilever, Microsoft in European Net Deal," *The Wall Street Journal* (February 2, 2000), p. B8.
[26] Julia Angwin, "AOL Lands Toyota for Multimedia Pact," *The Wall Street Journal* (August 28, 2001), p. B7.

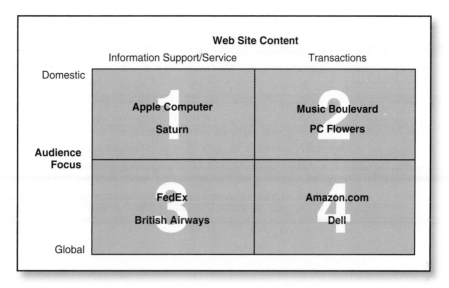

Web Site Content

	Information Support/Service	Transactions

Domestic

Audience Focus

1 Apple Computer Saturn	**2** Music Boulevard PC Flowers
3 FedEx British Airways	**4** Amazon.com Dell

Global

Figure 15-4
Categories of Web Sites

Source: Reprinted from 'The Internet and International Marketing' by John A. Quelch and Lisa R. Klein, MIT Sloan Management Review, 37, no. 3 (Spring 1996), p. 65 by permission of publisher. Copyright © 1996 by Massachusetts Institute of Technology. All rights reserved.

in both Quadrants 1 and 2 do attract international traffic, but the focus is still domestic. In Quadrant 3, the audience focus is global. Companies such as Federal Express and British Airways are already global in scope, and the Internet constitutes a powerful, cost-effective communication tool. In Quadrant 4, companies seek transactions with customers on a worldwide basis.

Amazon.com is perhaps the most successful example of the global audience-transaction business model. Online book shoppers can chose from more than 2.5 million titles; many titles carry discounted prices. After assessing a number of potential products in terms of their suitability for online sales, company founder Jeffrey Bezos settled on books for two reasons. First, there are too many titles for any one "brick-and-mortar" store to carry. The second reason is related to industry structure: The publishing industry is highly fragmented, with 4,200 publishers in the United States alone. That means that no single publisher has a high degree of supplier power. Bezos's instincts proved sound: Sales exploded after Amazon.com's Web site became operational in mid-1995. Within a year, orders were coming in from 66 countries.[27]

As indicated in Table 14-1, Procter & Gamble ranks number one in advertising outside the United States. Because women are the heaviest purchasers and users of P&G products, it is not surprising that P&G has ambitious plans for the Net. P&G has registered a number of Internet domains based on brand names, including www.covergirl.com, www.oldspice.com, and www.sunnyd.com. P&G has also registered nearly 100 other generic domains that relate to its various product lines, including cakemix.com, laundry.com, and nails.com. Although it is possible that these domains will not ultimately be developed into Web sites, P&G's actions sent a signal to others in the industry that it is striving for a first mover advantage on the Net. George Rosenbaum, CEO of the Chicago-based Leo Shapiro & Associates market research firm, commented, "P&G's commitment means that all major competitors

---

[27] G. Bruce Knecht, "Reading the Market: How Wall Street Whiz Found a Niche Selling Books on the Internet," *The Wall Street Journal* (May 16, 1996), pp. A1, A12.

will also have to play seriously. This is going to raise the tempo of advertising on the Internet."[28] P&G Far East Inc., the company's operation in Japan, is using the Web to build its portfolio of brands in the region. The company has launched shufufufu.com, Japan's first women's community Web site. The Web address combines *shufu* ("housewife") and *fu-fu-fu* (the sound of a woman's laughter); the P&G logo has been de-emphasized. The site's success can be attributed in part to the popularity of Harumi Kurihara, who writes a weekly essay on the site and provides tips on cooking, homemaking, and personal care.[29]

Benetton's Web site (www.benetton.com) provides a good example of the Internet's potential as a public relations tool. One would be hard pressed to think of a company whose advertising has generated more controversy than Benetton. As noted in the Chapter 14 case, Italy-based Benetton markets brightly colored knitwear and contemporary clothing throughout the world at its own stores. For many years Benetton's advertising was created in-house by creative director and chief photographer, Oliviero Toscani. Annual sales are $19 billion; Benetton spends 4 percent of sales on advertising, less than most retailers. Until 1994, Benetton relied almost exclusively on print ads and out-of-home media such as billboards. For years, every campaign has been keyed to the theme "the united colors of Benetton." The art direction has consistently "pushed the envelope" in terms of race relations, sexuality, AIDS, religion, and other issues. A "what we say" link allows visitors to view the entire gallery of Benetton ads dating back more than 10 years.

The fact that the Internet is a relatively new and rapidly evolving medium means that surprises are inevitable. For example, Volvo was one of the first automakers with a Web site keyed toward product information and advertising. Unfortunately, rather than attracting potential new car buyers, the Volvo site was swamped with hits from current Volvo owners wanting to swap complaints about their vehicles. Volvo responded by shutting down the site. Likewise, Richard Branson's Virgin Atlantic Airways earned the dubious distinction of being the first Internet advertiser to be fined by the U.S. Department of Transportation for allegedly posting false advertising on its Web site.

SUMMARY

Sales promotion is any paid, short-term communication program that adds tangible value to a product or brand. **Consumer sales promotions** are targeted at ultimate consumers; **trade sales promotions** are used in business-to-business marketing. **Sampling** gives people a chance to try a product or service at no cost. A **coupon** is a certificate that entitles the bearer to a price reduction or other consideration when purchasing a product or service.

Personal selling is face-to-face communication between a prospective buyer and a company representative. The **strategic/consultative selling model** that is widely used in the United States is also being utilized worldwide. The model's five strategic steps call for developing a **personal selling philosophy**, a **relationship strategy**, a **product strategy**, a **customer strategy**, and a **presentation strategy**. The six steps in the presentation plan are: **approach, presentation, demonstration, negotiation, close**, and **servicing the sale**. Successful global selling may require adaptation of one or more steps in the presentation plan. An additional consideration in global selling is the composition of the sales force, which may include expatriates,

---

[28] Raju Narisetti, "P&G Steps Up Ad Cyber-Surfing: Tide Could Have a Major Effect," *The Wall Street Journal* (April 18, 1997), p. B10.
[29] Campbell Gray, "P&G Recruits Asia's 'Martha Stewart' H. Kurihara on Procter & Gamble Far East Web Site," *Ad Age Global* (June 2001), p. 14.

host-country natives, third-country natives, or sales agents.

Several others forms of communication can be used in global marketing. These include **direct marketing**, a measurable system that uses one or more media to start or complete a sale. **Direct mail, catalogs, infomercials**, and **teleshopping** are some of the direct marketing tools that have been suc-cessfully used on a global basis. Global marketers frequently try to place their products in block-buster movies that will reach global audiences. The **Internet** is also becoming a vital communication tool that can be used to disseminate information about a particular company, to provide customer service or marketing and sales support, and for actual sales transactions.

DISCUSSION QUESTIONS

1. Briefly review how the main tools of sales pro-motion (e.g., sampling and couponing) can be used in global markets. What issues and prob-lems can arise in different country markets?

2. What potential environmental challenges must be taken into account by a company that uses personal selling as a promotional tool outside the home country?

3. Identify the six steps in the strategic/consultative selling model and six-step presentation plan outlined in Chapter 15. Do these steps have global applicability, or are they only used for selling in the home-country market? What spe-cial challenges face a sales representative out-side his or her home country?

4. How does management's orientation (e.g., eth-nocentric, polycentric, or regiocentric) correlate with decisions about sales force nationality? What other factors affect sales force composition?

5. What role does direct marketing have in a global company's promotion mix? Name three compa-nies that have successfully used direct mail or other forms of direct-response advertising.

6. Why are infomercials, sponsorship, and prod-uct placement growing in importance for global marketers?

7. Briefly discuss e-commerce trends as they per-tain to global marketing. Identify three global companies that have integrated the Internet into their marketing communications.

SUGGESTED READINGS

Articles

Honeycutt, Earl D. Jr., and John B. Ford. "Guidelines for Managing an International Sales Force." *Industrial Marketing Management* 24 (March 1995), pp. 135–144.

Huff, Lenard C., and Dana L. Alden. "An Investigation of Consumer Response to Sales Promotions in Developing Markets: A Three Country Analysis." *Journal of Advertising Research* 38, no. 3 (May/June 1998), pp. 47–57.

Kashani, Kamran, and John A. Quelch, "Can Sales Promotion Go Global?" *Business Horizons* (May/June 1990), pp. 37–43.

McGuinness, Dalton Mike Brennan, and Philip Gendall. "The Effect of Product Sampling and Couponing on Purchase Behavior: Some Empirical Evidence." *International Journal of Advertising* 14, no. 3 (1995), pp. 219–230.

Mehta, Raj, Rajdeep Grewal, and Eugene Sivadas. "International Direct Marketing on the Internet: Do Internet Users Form a Global Segment?" *Journal of Direct Marketing* 10 (Winter 1996), pp. 45–58.

Quelch, John A., and Lisa R. Klein. "The Internet and International Marketing." *Sloan Management Review* 37, no 3 (Spring 1996), pp. 60–75.

Samiee, Saeed. "The Internet and International Marketing: Is There a Fit?" *Journal of Interactive Marketing* 12, no. 4 (Autumn 1998), pp. 5–21.

Samli, A. Coskun, Gregory P. Wirth, and James R. Wills, Jr. "High-Tech Firms Must Get More Out of Their International Sales Efforts." *Industrial Marketing Management* 23 (October 1994), pp. 333–342.

Taylor, Charles R., George K. Franke, and Michael L. Maynard. "Attitudes Toward Direct Marketing and Its Regulation: A Comparison of the United States and Japan." *Journal of Public Policy & Marketing* 19, no. 2 (Fall 2000), pp. 228–237.

CASE

Case 15-1   Napster and the Global Music Industry

While the online revolution has affected many industries, perhaps none was more directly impacted than the recorded music industry. Most PCs include a drive that can play CDs, and a new generation of software allows users to "rip" tunes by copying them from CDs and converting them into compressed digital music files in a format known as MP3. Moreover, the advent of recordable CDs enables individuals to "burn" CDs with their favorite songs. In 1999, Shawn Fanning, an American college dropout, developed a Web site called Napster that allowed individuals to swap songs for free. Other sites, including MP3.com and gnutella.com, offered similar services. Tens of millions of music fans—college students in particular—flocked to Napster; in February 2001 alone, an estimated 2.75 billion songs were downloaded from the site. It was not unusual for individuals to have hundreds of downloaded songs residing in the hard drives of their PCs. The songs could also be transferred into portable MP3 players to provide music on the go. In short, Napster appeared to offer an attractive alternative to paying $15 for a CD that contained one or two hit songs out of a total of 10 to 15 tracks.

Annual worldwide sales of recorded music are about $40 billion. The industry is dominated by five global players: Sony (Japan), Bertelsmann (Germany), AOL TimeWarner (United States), EMI (Great Britain), and Vivendi Universal (France). The popularity of Napster and similar services caught the industry by surprise; company executives, trade groups such as the Recording Industry Association of America (RIAA), and many recording artists denounced Napster for infringing on the copyrights of songwriters and recording artists. More broadly, Napster and other sites threatened the foundations of a business model that hadn't changed significantly for decades. Record companies discovered new artists, signed them to contracts, provided career guidance, paid the expenses associated with recording albums and creating videos, and then distributed the finished recordings through retail stores, mail-order clubs, and other outlets. Unknown to the general public was the fact that record companies lose money on most releases. The companies rely on million-selling releases by superstars such as 'NSync, U2, and Britney Spears to subsidize money-losing projects by less successful artists.

Many observers believe that online distribution will play an increasingly important role in the industry. One study suggests that revenues from online music could reach $1.5 billion by 2004. Despite such projections, a fundamental question facing the majors was: How much are people willing to pay for access to online music? Another challenge was devising a mechanism that would allow artists to be paid for downloaded songs. The latter issue was especially interesting to the National Music Publishers' Association, a trade group that controls the publishing rights to most songs in the United States. The association collects 7.5 cents for every individual song on a compact disc; a portion of that amount is then distributed to the song's publisher and the songwriter. The association is pushing the record labels for a better deal for songs distributed online; their argument is based in part on the fact that the labels will have lower expenses. A Copyright Arbitration Royalty Panel was established to conduct hearings on the issue.

The artist's community itself was divided on the issue of free Napster-style file swapping. Some artists noted that they were disenchanted by restrictive radio playlists that tend to ignore artists on independent labels. They also expressed disdain for record company executives (or "suits" as they were sometimes called) who didn't appreciate the music. Such artists viewed the Internet as a way of building an audience without the support or backing of a major label. Other artists shared a less charitable view, believing that unauthorized file swapping was theft. Members of Metallica, in particular, lashed out against Napster.

The major labels responded to Napster on several different fronts. First, in December 1999, they filed suit in U.S. court in an effort to shut Napster down. An initial court ruling found that Napster violated copyright laws, and on Wednesday, July 26, 2000, district judge Marilyn Hall Patel ordered Napster shut down. Napster immediately filed an appeal; on February 12, 2001, the Ninth Circuit court of appeals upheld the lower court's ruling. In March, to comply with a preliminary injunction, the company installed a filter that blocked approximately 1 million copyrighted titles from being downloaded. Hank Barry, Napster's chief executive, offered to pay the record labels $1 billion over a five-year period. Napster proposed a basic subscription service costing between $2.95 per month and $4.95 per month that would entitle a user to a fixed number of downloads. The record companies rejected that proposal.

Even as the Napster case was under review, executives from the major labels were under increased pressure from the U.S. Congress to make online music available legally, and to do so quickly. In a series of hearings, Congressional leaders made it clear that if the record companies couldn't create acceptable licensing arrangements on Internet music distribution, Congress would make such licensing compulsory. The record companies began setting up alliances that would allow them to establish online music subscription services. AOL TimeWarner, Bertelsmann AG, and EMI Group formed a venture called MusicNet, in conjunction with Seattle-based RealNetworks. RealNetworks had become a key player in online entertainment with its RealPlayer software that allows PC users to listen to radio stations that use streaming audio technology to broadcast over the Internet. MusicNet will tap into AOL's 29 million subscribers. Vivendi and Sony teamed up to form Duet, a subscription service available through Yahoo! In May 2001, Vivendi also acquired MP3.com for $372 million. Bertelsmann, meanwhile, angered some of its competitors by striking an agreement with Napster to provide a "secure membership-based service." As Thomas Middelhoff, Bertelsmann's chief executive, noted, "Now the show begins. We have to evolve Napster and make it the best service available to people who love music."

A number of issues confronted the companies. Different technologies such as Windows Media Player, Macintosh iTunes, and Realplayer, were available for digitizing music, and several were incompatible with the others. Also, to the dismay of some consumers, however, the pay-for-play services incorporate a technology that obliterates downloaded music files if a user cancels his or her subscription. Moreover, downloaded songs can't be transferred to portable MP3 players or burned into CDs. Industry analysts also noted that consumers would not be satisfied if a subscription service gave them access to catalog offerings of only a few record labels. Another issue was ease of use: Some existing sites that offered songs encrypted with copy-prevention code were prone to crashing.

Viacom's MTV was jockeying for position as well. Its MTV.com Web site attracted about six million visitors each month. The cable giant took an equity stake in RioPort, a technology company that had signed licensing deals with the major labels. RioPort's business model was different in that the company proposed a "pay-per-download" approach instead of subscriptions. Music files could be downloaded into portable players, and the system was capable of handling most available digital formats. Executives at several of the major labels dismissed the pay-per-download approach. Meanwhile, a number of new file-sharing networks were appearing on the scene, including Aimster, LimeWire, and KaZaA. ∎

DISCUSSION QUESTIONS

1. Do you agree with the court's decision to shut down Napster?
2. Which approach to online distribution do you favor, subscription or pay-per-download?

3. What recommendations would you make to an executive at one of the five major labels?

SOURCES: Martin Peers and William Boston, "Sour Note: Plugging into the Web is a Jarring Experience for the Music Industry," *The Wall Street Journal* (April 12, 2001), pp. A1, A10; Devin Leonard, "The Music Men are Out of Tune," *Fortune* (June 11, 2001), pp. 144–146+; Don Clark, "Napster Offers Annual Fees to CD Labels," *The Wall Street Journal* (February 21, 2001), p. B6; Anna Wilde Mathews, "The Flip Side: Royalty Fight Threatens Record Industry's Plans to Deliver Songs Online," *The Wall Street Journal* (May 1, 2001), pp. A1, A8; Lee Gomes, "Napster Ruling May Be Just the Overture," *The Wall Street Journal* (July 28, 2000), pp. B1, B4; Ted Bridis, "Online Music: Is It Time to Rewind or Fast Forward?" *The Wall Street Journal* (April 14, 2001), p. B3; Gomes, "Bertelsmann, Napster Agree on Service," *The Wall Street Journal* (November 1, 2000), pp. A3, A8.

Chapter 16

Leading, Organizing, and Controlling the Global Marketing Effort

*R*upert Murdoch has been described as a media visionary. Murdoch is chairman and CEO of the News Corporation, a global power-house that produces and distributes news and entertainment around the world. Murdoch's empire includes important print media compa-nies such as HarperCollins Publishers and London's *Herald & Weekly Times.* The Fox Film Entertainment group produces movies, TV shows, and animated features that can be shown on the Fox TV net-work. Murdoch purchased 12 TV stations in the United States that now serve as network affiliates and carry Fox-produced program-ming; in 1994, he startled the broadcast world by bidding $1.6 billion for the rights to NFL broadcasts that had previously belonged to CBS. Outside the United States, Murdoch's company has stakes in several satellite systems, including British Sky Broadcasting in the United Kingdom and Hong Kong-based Star TV, which services Asia. Murdoch's biographer describes him as "an extraordinarily energetic person." Jessica Reif, a media analyst with Merrill Lynch, says of Murdoch, "He has an uncanny ability to see the world in different ways."

This final chapter focuses on the integration of each element of the marketing mix into a total plan that addresses opportunities and threats in the global marketing environment. Rupert Murdoch illus-trates the critical role of leadership in a global firm. Leaders must be capable of articulating a coherent global vision and strategy that inte-grates local responsiveness, global efficiency, and leverage. The leader is also the architect of an organization design that is appropri-ate for the company's strategy. The leader must also ensure that appropriate control mechanisms are in place so that, in a world in which industries and markets are rapidly globalizing, organizational goals can be achieved.

Global marketing demands exceptional leadership. As we have said throughout this book, the hallmark of a global company is the capacity to formulate and implement global strategies that leverage worldwide learning, respond fully to local needs and wants, and draw on the talent and energy of every member of the organization. This heroic task requires global vision and sensitivity to local needs. Overall, the leader's challenge is to direct the efforts and creativity of everyone in the company toward a global effort that best utilizes organizational resources to exploit global opportunities. As Hewlett-Packard CEO Carly Fiorina said recently in a commencement address at the Massachusetts Institute of Technology:

> Leadership is not about hierarchy or title or status: It is about having influence and mastering change. Leadership is not about bragging rights or battles or even the accumulation of wealth; it's about connecting and engaging at multiple levels. It's about challenging minds and capturing hearts. Leadership in this new era is about empowering others to decide for themselves. Leadership is about empowering others to reach their full potential. Leaders can no longer view strategy and execution as abstract concepts, but must realize that both elements are ultimately about people.[1]

An important leadership task is articulating beliefs, values, policies, and the intended geographic scope of a company's activities. Using the mission statement or similar document as a reference and guide, members of each operating unit must address their immediate responsibilities and at the same time cooperate with functional, product, and country experts in different locations. For example, while Percy Barnevik was chairman of ABB, the basic tool for coordinating local operations with global strategies was a 55-page manual written by the chairman himself. Referring to "the bible," as the document is known internally, Barnevik recently noted, "If you can make this work real well, then you get a competitive edge out of the organization which is very, very difficult to copy."[2]

At Levi Strauss, an aspirations statement that reflects the vision of chairman and CEO Robert Haas is clearly posted in every company facility. The statement spells out Levi's values-based formula for achieving profit and making the world a better place; it addresses issues ranging from workforce diversity and employee empowerment to honest communication and ethical management practices. In 1993, Levi cancelled operations in China because of the Chinese government's record of human rights violations. As David Schmidt, Levi's vice president for corporate marketing, noted at the time, "There are wonderful commercial opportunities in China. But when ethical issues collide with commercial appeal, we try to ensure ethics as the trump card. For us, ethical issues precede all others."[3] In 1998, Levi resumed manufacturing in China; management noted that Chinese suppliers are now able to comply with its criteria for fair treatment of workers. Levi has also applied its ethics code in other parts of the world. About half of the apparel sold by the company is manufactured in plants located in low-wage countries such as Bangladesh, Indonesia, and

---

[1]   Carleton "Carly" S. Fiorina, Commencement Address, Massachusetts Institute of Technology, Cambridge, MA, June 2, 2000.

[2]   Janet Guyon, "ABB Fuses Units with One Set of Values," *The Wall Street Journal* (October 2, 1996), p. A9.

[3]   Michale Janofsky, "Levi Strauss: American Symbol with a Cause," *The New York Times* (January 3, 1994), p. C4. See also Russell Mitchell, "Managing by Values: Is Levi Strauss' Approach Visionary—or Flaky?" *Business Week* (August 1, 1994), pp. 46–52; William Beaver, "Levi's Is Leaving China," *Business Horizons* 38, no. 2 (March-April 1995), pp. 35–40.

Malaysia. Levi is strict about enforcing International Labor Organization standards that prohibit hiring children below the age of 14. However, company personnel are also sensitive to the economic issues that lead to ILO violations. In one instance, Levi executives learned that some underage factory employees in Bangladesh were the sole breadwinners in small families. Instead of firing the children, Levi arranged to pay their wages while they returned to school. Levi's intent was to hire the youths back after they turn 14.

As the ABB and Levi Strauss examples show, the leader's global vision must be codified and clarified for all organizational members. However, it is one thing to spell out the vision, and another thing entirely to secure commitment to it throughout the organization. As we noted in Chapter 1, global marketing entails engaging in significant business activities outside the home country. This means exposure to different languages and cultures. In addition, global marketing involves skillful application of specific concepts, considerations, and strategies. Such endeavors may represent substantial change, especially in U.S. companies with a long tradition of domestic focus. When the "go global" initiative is greeted with skepticism, the CEO must be a change agent who prepares and motivates employees. Whirlpool CEO David Whitwam recently described his own efforts in this regard in the early 1990s:

> When we announced the Philips acquisition, I traveled to every location in the company, talked with our people, explained why it was so important. Most opposed the move. They thought, "We're spending a billion dollars on a company that has been losing money for 10 years? We're going to take resources we could use right here and ship them across the Atlantic because we think this is becoming a 'global' industry? What the hell does that mean?"[4]

Jack Welch encountered similar resistance at GE. "The lower you are in the organization, the less clear it is that globalization is a great idea," he said. As Paolo Fresco, a former GE vice chairman who is now chairman of Fiat S.P.A., explained:

> To certain people, globalization is a threat without rewards. You look at the engineer for X-ray in Milwaukee and there is no upside on this one for him. He runs the risk of losing his job, he runs the risk of losing authority—he might find his boss is a guy who does not even know how to speak his language.[5]

In addition to "selling" their visions, top management at both Whirlpool and GE face the formidable task of building a cadre of globally-oriented managers. Similar challenges are facing corporate leaders in other parts of the world. For example, Uichiro Niwa, president of Itochu Corp., is taking steps to ensure that more of the trading company's $115 billion in annual transactions are conducted online.[6] He is also radically changing the way he communicates with employees. He is relying more on e-mail, a practice that until recently was virtually unknown in Japan. He also convenes face-to-face meetings and conferences with employees to solicit suggestions and to hear complaints. This too represents a dramatic change in the way Japanese companies are being led; traditionally, low-level employees were expected to accept the edicts of top management without questioning them.

---

4   William C. Taylor and Alan M. Webber, *Going Global: Four Entrepreneurs Map the New World Marketplace* (New York: Penguin Books USA, 1996), p. 12.
5   Noel M. Tichy and Stratford Sherman, *Control Your Destiny or Someone Else Will* (New York: HarperBusiness, 1994), p. 227.
6   Robert Guth, "Facing a Web Revolution, a Mighty Japanese Trader Reinvents Itself," *The Wall Street Journal* (March 27, 2000), p B1.

Top Management Nationality

Many globally minded companies realize that the best person for a top management job or board position is not necessarily someone born in the home country. Speaking of U.S. companies, Christopher Bartlett of the Harvard Business School has noted:

> Companies are realizing that they have a portfolio of human resources worldwide, that their brightest technical person might come from Germany, or their best financial manager from England. They are starting to tap their worldwide human resources. And as they do, it will not be surprising to see non-Americans rise to the top.[7]

The ability to speak foreign languages is one difference between managers born and raised in the United States and those born and raised elsewhere. For example, according to one recent report, 20,000 Japanese businesspeople who are fluent in English are working in the United States, but only 200 American businesspersons doing business in Japan can speak Japanese.[8] Roberto Goizueta, the Cuban-born CEO of Coca-Cola who died in 1997, spoke English, Spanish, and Portuguese; Ford's former chief executive, Alexander Trotman, was born in England and speaks English, French, and German. Sigismundus W. W. Lubensen, the former president and CEO of Quaker Chemical Corporation, is a good example of today's cosmopolitan executive. Born in the Netherlands and educated in Rotterdam as well as New York, Lubensen, who speaks Dutch, English, French, and German, says, "I was lucky to be born in a place where if you drove for an hour in any direction, you were in a different country, speaking a different language. It made me very comfortable traveling in different cultures."[9] Additional examples of corporate leaders who are not native to the headquarters country are shown in Table 16-1.

Generally speaking, Japanese companies have been reluctant to place non-Japanese nationals in top positions. For years, only Sony, Mazda, and Mitsubishi had foreigners on their boards. In March 1999, however, after Renault SA bought a 36.8 percent stake in Nissan Motor, the French company installed a Brazilian, Carlos Ghosn, as president. An outsider, Ghosn was required to move aggressively to cut costs and make drastic changes in Nissan's structure. He also introduced two new words into Nissan's lexicon: speed and commitment. Ghosn's turnaround effort was so successful that his life story and exploits have been celebrated in Big Comic Story, a comic that is popular with Japan's salarymen.[10]

Leadership and Core Competence

Core competence, a concept developed by global strategy experts C. K. Prahalad and Gary Hamel, was introduced in Chapter 10. In the 1980s, many business executives were assessed on their ability to reorganize their corporations. In the 1990s, Prahalad and Hamel believe executives have been judged on their ability to identify, nurture, and exploit the core competencies that make growth possible. Core competence must provide potential access to a wide variety of markets, make a significant contribution to the perceived customer benefits of the end product, and be difficult for competitors

---

7   Kerry Peckter, "The Foreigners Are Coming," *International Business* (September 1993), p. 53.
8   Charlene Marmer Solomon, "Success Abroad Depends on More Than Job Skills," *Personnel Journal* (April 1994), p. 52.
9   Peckter, p. 58.
10 Norihiko Shirouzu, "U-Turn: A Revival at Nissan Shows There's Hope for Ailing Japan Inc.," *The Wall Street Journal* (November 16, 2000), pp. A1, A10. See also Todd Zaun, "Look! Up in the Sky! It's Nissan's Chief Executive!" *The Wall Street Journal* (December 27, 2001), p. B1.

Table 16-1
Who's in Charge?

COMPANY (HEADQUARTERS COUNTRY)	EXECUTIVE NATIONALITY	POSITION
Nissan Motor (Japan)	Carlos Ghosn (Brazil)	President and CEO
Pearson PLC (Great Britain)	Marjorie Scardino (USA)	Chief executive
Ford Motor Company (USA)	Jacques Nasser (Egypt)[a]	Chief executive
Goodyear Tire and Rubber (USA)	Samir Gibara (Egypt)	Chairman, president, and CEO
Pharmacia Corporation (USA)	Fred Hassan (Pakistan)	Chairman, president, and CEO
Atlas Copco AB (Sweden)	Giulio Mazzalupi (Italy)[b]	President and CEO

[a]Resigned in 2001.
[b]Retired in 2002.

to imitate. Few companies are likely to build world leadership in more than five or six fundamental competencies. In the long run, an organization will derive its global competitiveness from its ability to bring high-quality, low-cost products to market faster than its competitors. To do this, an organization must be viewed as a portfolio of competencies rather than a portfolio of businesses. Many companies have the technical resources to build competencies, but key executives lack the vision to do so. The concept of distinctive competencies challenges executives to rethink the concept of the corporation itself. It also requires redefining the task of management as building both competencies and the administrative means for assembling resources spread across multiple businesses.[11]

ORGANIZATION

The goal in organizing for global marketing is to find a structure that enables the company to respond to relevant market environment differences while ensuring the diffusion of corporate knowledge and experience from national markets throughout the entire corporate system. The pull between the value of centralized knowledge and coordination and the need for individualized response to the local situation creates a constant tension in the global marketing organization. A key issue in global organization is how to achieve balance between autonomy and integration. Subsidiaries need autonomy to adapt to their local environment, but the business as a whole needs integration to implement global strategy.[12]

When management at a domestic company decides to pursue international expansion, the issue of how to organize arises immediately. Who should be responsible for this expansion? Should product divisions operate directly, or should an international division be established? Should individual country subsidiaries report directly to the company president, or should a special corporate officer be appointed to take full-time responsibility for international activities? After the decision of how to organize initial international operations has been reached, a growing company is

---

[11] C. K. Prahalad and Gary Hamel, "The Core Competence of the Corporation," *Harvard Business Review* 68, no. 3 (May-June 1990), pp. 79–86.
[12] George S. Yip, *Total Global Strategy* (Upper Saddle River, NJ: Prentice Hall, 1992), p. 179.

faced with a number of reappraisal points during the development of its international business activities. Should a company abandon its international division, and, if so, what alternative structure should be adopted? Should an area or regional headquarters be formed? What should be the relationship of staff executives at corporate, regional, and subsidiary offices? Specifically, how should the marketing function be organized? To what extent should regional and corporate marketing executives become involved in subsidiary marketing management?

Even companies with years of experience competing around the globe find it necessary to adjust their organizational designs in response to environmental change. It is perhaps not surprising that, during his tenure at Quaker Chemical, Sigismundus Lubensen favored a global approach to organizational design over a domestic/international approach. He advised Peter A. Benoliel, his predecessor CEO, to have units in Holland, France, Italy, Spain, and England report to a regional vice president in Europe. "I saw that it would not be a big deal to put all of the European units under one common denominator," Lubensen recalled.[13]

As markets globalize and as Japan opens its own market to more competition from overseas, more Japanese companies are likely to break from traditional organization patterns. Many of the Japanese companies discussed in this text qualify as global or transnational companies because they serve world markets, source globally, or do both. Typically, however, knowledge is created at headquarters in Japan and then transferred to other country units. For example, Canon enjoys a high reputation for world-class, innovative imaging products such as bubble-jet printers and laser printers. In recent years, Canon has shifted more control to subsidiaries, hired more non-Japanese staff and management personnel, and assimilated more innovations that were not developed in Japan. In 1996, R&D responsibility for software was shifted from Tokyo to the United States, responsibility for telecommunication products to France, and computer language translation to Great Britain. As Canon President Fujio Mitarai explained in a recent interview, "The Tokyo headquarters cannot know everything. Its job should be to provide low-cost capital, to move top management between regions, and come up with investment initiatives. Beyond that, the local subsidiaries must assume total responsibility for management. We are not there yet, but we are moving step by step in that direction." Toru Takahashi, director of R&D, shares this view. "We used to think that we should keep research and development in Japan, but that has changed," he said. Despite these changes, Canon's board of directors includes only Japanese nationals.[14]

There is no single correct organizational structure for global marketing. Even within a particular industry, worldwide companies have developed very different strategic and organizational responses to changes in their environments.[15] Still, it is possible to make some generalizations. Leading-edge global competitors share one key organizational design characteristic: Their corporate structure is flat and simple, rather than tall and complex. The message is clear: The world is complicated enough, so there is no need to add to the confusion with a complex internal structuring. Simple structures increase the speed and clarity of communication and allow the concentration of organizational energy and valuable resources on learning, rather than on controlling, monitoring, and reporting.[16] According to David Whitwam,

---

[13] Peckter, p. 58.
[14] William Dawkins, "Time to Pull back the Screen," *Financial Times* (November 18, 1996), p. 12.
[15] Christopher Bartlett and Sumantra Ghoshal, *Managing Across Borders: The Transnational Solution* (Boston: Harvard Business School Press, 1989), p. 3.
[16] Vladimir Pucik, "Globalization and Human Resource Management," in V. Pucik, N. Tichy, and C. Barnett (eds.), *Globalizing Management: Creating and Leading the Competitive Organization* (New York: J. Wiley & Sons, 1992), p. 70.

CEO of Whirlpool, "You must create an organization whose people are adept at exchanging ideas, processes, and systems across borders, people who are absolutely free of the 'not-invented-here' syndrome, people who are constantly working together to identify the best global opportunities and the biggest global problems facing the organization."[17]

A geographically dispersed company cannot limit its knowledge to product, function, and the home territory. Company personnel must acquire knowledge of the complex set of social, political, economic, and institutional arrangements that exist within each international market. Many companies start with ad hoc arrangements such as having all foreign subsidiaries report to a designated vice president or to the president. Eventually, such companies establish an international division to manage their geographically dispersed new businesses. It is clear, however, that the international division in the multiproduct company is an unstable organizational arrangement. As a company grows, this initial organizational structure frequently gives way to various alternative structures.

In the fast-changing competitive global environment of the twenty-first century, corporations will have to find new, more creative ways to organize. New forms of flexibility, efficiency, and responsiveness are required to meet the demands of globalizing markets. The need to be cost effective, to be customer-driven, to deliver the best quality, and to deliver that quality quickly are some of today's global realities. Recently, several authors have described new organization designs that represent responses to the competitive environment of the late twentieth century. These designs acknowledge the need to find more responsive and flexible structures, to flatten the organization, and to employ teams. There is the recognition of the need to develop networks, to develop stronger relationships among participants, and to exploit technology. These designs also reflect an evolution in approaches to organizational effectiveness. At the turn of the century, Frederick Taylor claimed that all managers had to see the world the same way. Then came the contingency theorists who said that effective organizations design themselves to match their conditions. These two basic theories are reflected in today's popular management writings. As Henry Mintzberg has observed, "To Michael Porter, effectiveness resides in strategy, while to Tom Peters it is the operations that count—executing any strategy with excellence."[18]

Kenichi Ohmae has written extensively on the implications of globalization on organization design. He recommends a type of "global superstructure" at the highest level that provides a view of the world as a single unit. The staff of this unit are responsible for ensuring that work is performed in the best location and coordinating efficient movement of information and products across borders. Below this level, Ohmae envisions organizational units assigned to regions "governed by economies of service and economies of scale in information." In Ohmae's view of the world, there are 30 regions with populations ranging from 5 million to 20 million people. For example, China would be viewed as several distinct regions; the same is true of the United States. The first task of the CEO in such an organization is to become oriented to the single unit that is the borderless business sphere, much as an astronaut might view the earth from space. Then, zooming in, the CEO attempts to identify differences. As Ohmae explains,

---

[17] Regina Fazio Maruca, "The Right Way to Go Global: An Interview with Whirlpool CEO David Whitwam," *Harvard Business Review* 72, no. 2 (March-April 1994), pp. 134–145.

[18] Henry Mintzberg, "The Effective Organization: Forces and Forms," *Sloan Management Review* 32, no. 2 (Winter 1991), pp. 54–55.

It takes more than one person to run News Corporation's far-flung empire. Murdoch exerts control by keeping things simple and delegating authority to a small inner circle of close associates who are known inside the company as "clones." "You can't build a strong corporation with a lot of committees and a board that has to be consulted at every turn. You have to make your own decisions," he says. He expects newcomers to hit the ground running. "He gives you great freedom, but he lets you know from the beginning that you have no safety net under you," says one manager. Executives at News Corporation's various units know that, at any moment, they are likely to receive a telephone call that begins, "Murdoch here. How're things at your shop?" A former Fox TV executive recalls, "The atmosphere is sort of like a monarchy. Everybody works for the king, and nothing else matters."

The Wall Street Journal has called Murdoch's approach "micromanagement on a global scale." Murdoch is viewed as an autocratic leader who often relies on his own intuition for major decisions. He tends to focus on the News Corporation's various businesses one at a time, immersing himself in the most minute details. "If you're going to get into a business, you should get as close to it as possible, even run it yourself for a period," Murdoch says. Murdoch also has a propensity for making quick decisions. "I like to be able to move fast," he explains. "Sometimes it leads to making mistakes, but other times it leads to getting an opportunity before other people see it." Frank Barlow, a director at competitor Pearson PLC, says, "Most corporations are much more analytical about making acquisitions, while Rupert is instinctive."

"Rupert Murdoch has established the norm for the worldwide, vertically-integrated strategy."
—John Malone

Not surprisingly, Murdoch's style of leadership has invited criticism. He has been known to use his newspapers as public outlets for his own views and opinions. Sometimes he rushes into deals that don't work out; in other instances, industry observers say, he pays too much for his acquisitions. In 1995, he shocked the broadcast industry by paying $565 million for the rights to broadcast major league baseball through 1999 (meanwhile, News Corporation took a $350 million writeoff in 1995 for losses on its NFL broadcasts). The move reflects Murdoch's goal of transforming News Corporation into a global sports programming leader; other sports investments include $375 million to start a rugby team in Australia and $400 million for broadcast rights to professional soccer games in Great Britain. Murdoch recently launched a 24-hour news channel to compete head-to-head with CNN and plans to start up a direct-broadcast satellite television service in the United States.

SOURCES: Kevin Maney, "Media Firms Shift to Gain Product Control," *USA Today* (September 14, 1995), p. 2B; Meg Cox, "One-Man Show: How Do You Tame a Global Company? Murdoch Does It Alone," *The Wall Street Journal* (February 14, 1994), pp. A1, A6; Richard W. Stevenson, "Networking, Globally and Relentlessly," *The New York Times* (May 29, 1994), sec. 3, pp. 1, 3; Albert Scardino, "How Murdoch Makes It Work," *The New York Times* (August 14, 1988), sec. 3, pp. 1, 5.

A CEO has to look at the entire global economy and then put the company's resources where they will capture the biggest market share of the most attractive regions. Perhaps as you draw closer from outer space you see a region around the Pacific Northwest, near Puget Sound, that is vibrant and prosperous. Then you recognize the region stretching from New York to Boston that is still doing awful. You might see a booming concentration of computer companies and software publishers around Denver, and similar concentrations around Dallas-Fort Worth. Along the coast of California and in parts of New England you will see regions that are strong centers for health care and biotechnology. As a CEO, that's where you put your resources and shift your emphasis.[19]

[19] William C. Taylor and Alan M. Webber, *Going Global: Four Entrepreneurs Map the New World Marketplace* (New York: Penguin, 1996), pp. 48–58.

We believe that successful companies, the real global winners, must have both good strategies and good execution.

Patterns of International Organizational Development

Organizations vary in terms of the size and potential of targeted global markets and local management competence in different country markets. Conflicting pressures may arise from the need for product and technical knowledge; functional expertise in marketing, finance, and operations; and area and country knowledge. Because the constellation of pressures that shape organizations is never exactly the same, no two organizations pass through organizational stages in exactly the same way, nor do they arrive at precisely the same organizational pattern. Nevertheless, some general patterns hold.

A company engaging in limited export activities often has a small in-house export department as a separate functional area. Most domestically oriented companies undertake initial foreign expansion by means of foreign sales offices or subsidiaries that report directly to the company president or other designated company officer. This person carries out his or her responsibilities without assistance from a headquarters staff group. This is a typical initial arrangement for companies getting started in international marketing operations.

International Division Structure. As a company's international business grows, the complexity of coordinating and directing this activity extends beyond the scope of a single person. Pressure is created to assemble a staff that will take responsibility for coordination and direction of the growing international activities of the organization. Eventually, this pressure leads to the creation of the international division, as illustrated in Figure 16-1. The executive in charge of the international division typically has a direct reporting relationship to corporate staff and thus ranks at the same level as the executives in charge of finance, marketing, operations, and other functional areas. Wal-Mart and Levi Strauss are two companies whose structures include international divisions.

Four factors contribute to the establishment of an international division. First, top management's commitment to global operations has increased enough to justify an organizational unit headed by a senior manager. Second, the complexity of international operations requires a single organizational unit whose management has sufficient authority to make its own determination on important issues such as which market entry strategy to employ. Third, an international division is frequently formed when the firm has recognized the need for internal specialists to deal with the special demands of global operations. A fourth contributing factor is management's recognition of the importance of proactively scanning the global horizon for opportunities and competitive threats rather than simply responding to situations as they arise.

Regional Management Centers. When business is conducted in a single region that is characterized by similarities in economic, social, geographical, and political conditions, there is both justification and need for a management center. Thus, another stage of organizational evolution is the emergence of an area or regional headquarters as a management layer between the country organization and the international division headquarters. The increasing importance of the European Union as a regional market has prompted a number of companies to change their organizational structures by setting up regional headquarters there. Quaker Oats recently established its European headquarters in Brussels; Electrolux, the Swedish

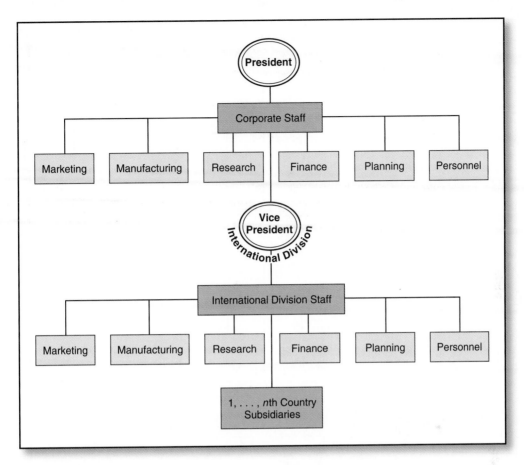

Figure 16-1
Functional Corporate Structure, Domestic Corporate Staff Orientation, International Division

home appliance company, has also regionalized its European operations.[20] A regional center typically coordinates decisions on pricing, sourcing, and other matters. Executives at the regional center also participate in the planning and control of each country's operations with an eye toward applying company knowledge on a regional basis and optimally utilizing corporate resources on a regional basis. This organizational design is illustrated in Figure 16-2.

Regional management can offer a company several advantages. First, many regional managers agree that an on-the-scene regional management unit makes sense where there is a real need for coordinated, pan-regional decision making. Coordinated regional planning and control are becoming necessary as the national subsidiary continues to lose its relevance as an independent operating unit. Regional management can probably achieve the best balance of geographical, product, and functional considerations required to implement corporate objectives effectively. By shifting operations and decision making to the region, the company is better able to maintain an insider advantage.[21]

---

[20] "... And Other Ways to Peel the Onion," *The Economist* (January 7, 1995), pp. 52–53.
[21] Allen J. Morrison, David A. Ricks, and Kendall Roth, "Globalization versus Regionalization: Which Way for the Multinational?" *Organizational Dynamics* (Winter 1991), pp. 17–29.

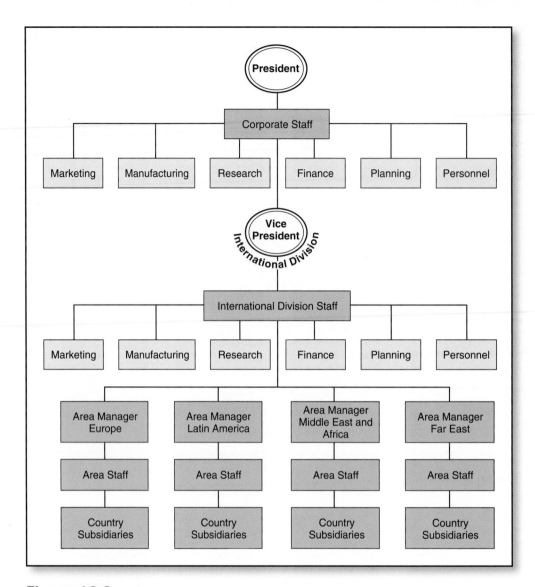

Figure 16-2
Functional Corporate Structure, Domestic Corporate Staff Orientation, International Division, Area Divisions

A major disadvantage of a regional center is its cost. The cost of a two-person office could exceed $600,000 per year. The scale of regional management must be in line with the scale of operations in a region. A regional headquarters is inappropriate if the size of the operations it manages is inadequate to cover the costs of the additional layer of management. The basic issue with regard to the regional headquarters is "Does it contribute enough to organizational effectiveness to justify its cost and the complexity of another layer of management?"

Geographical and Product Division Structures.   As a company becomes more global, management frequently faces the dilemma of whether to organize by geography or by product lines. The geographical structure involves the assignment of operational responsibility for geographic areas of the world to line managers. The corporate headquarters retains responsibility for worldwide planning and control,

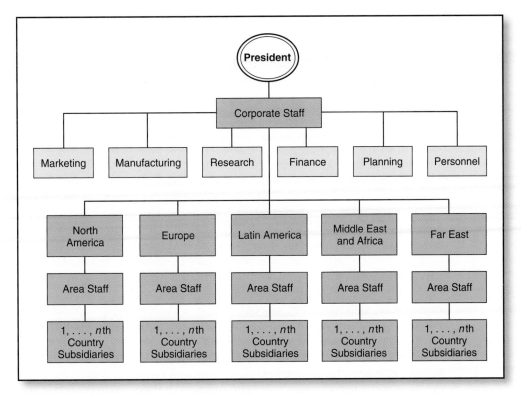

Figure 16-3
Geographic Corporate Structure, World Corporate Staff Orientation, Area Divisions Worldwide

and each area of the world—including the "home" or base market—is organizationally equal. For the company with French origins, France is simply another geographic market under this organizational arrangement. This structure is most common in companies with closely related product lines that are sold in similar end-use markets around the world. For example, the major international oil companies utilize the geographical structure, which is illustrated in Figure 16-3. McDonald's organizational design integrates the international division and geographical structures. McDonald's U.S. is organized into five geographical operating divisions, and McDonald's International has four.

When an organization assigns regional or worldwide product responsibility to its product divisions, manufacturing standardization can result in significant economies. For example, Whirlpool recently reorganized its European operations, switching from a geographic or country orientation to one based on product lines. One potential disadvantage of the product approach is that local input from individual country managers may be ignored with the result that products will not be sufficiently tailored to local markets. The essence of the Ford 2000 reorganization initiated in 1995 was to integrate North American and European operations. Over a three-year period, the company saved $5 billion in development costs. However, by 2000, Ford's European market share had slipped nearly 5 percent. In a shift back toward the geographic model, Ford's then-CEO Jacques Nasser returned to regional executives some of the authority they had lost.[22]

---

[22] Joann S. Lublin, "Division Problem: Place vs. Product: It's Tough to Choose a Management Model," *The Wall Street Journal* (June 27, 2001), pp. A1, A4.

The challenges associated with devising the structure that is best suited to improving global sales can be seen in Procter & Gamble's ambitious Organization 2005 plan. Initiated by CEO Durk Jager in 1999, this reorganization entailed replacing separate country organizations with five global business units for key product categories such as paper products and feminine hygiene. A number of executives were reassigned; in Europe alone, 1,000 staff members were transferred to Geneva. Many managers, upset about the transfers and news that P&G intended to cut 15,000 jobs worldwide, quit the company; the resulting upheaval cost CEO Jager his job. To appease middle managers, new CEO A.G. Lafley is restoring some of the previous geographic focus.[23]

The Matrix Design. In the fully developed large-scale global company, product or business, function, area, and customer know-how are simultaneously focused on the organization's worldwide marketing objectives. This type of total competence is a **matrix organization.** Management's task in the matrix organization is to achieve an organizational balance that brings together different perspectives and skills to accomplish the organization's objectives. In 1998, both Gillette and Ericsson announced plans to reorganize into matrix organizations. Ericsson's matrix will be focused on three customer segments: network operators, private consumers, and commercial enterprises.[24] Gillette's new structure will separate product-line management from geographical sales and marketing responsibility.[25] Likewise, Boeing has reorganized its commercial transport design and manufacturing engineers into a matrix organization built around five platform or aircraft model-specific groups. Previously, Boeing was organized along functional lines; the new design is expected to lower costs and quicken updates and problem solving. It will also unite essential design, engineering, and manufacturing processes between Boeing's commercial transport factories and component plants, enhancing product consistency.[26] Why are executives at these and other companies implementing matrix designs? The matrix form of organization is well suited to global companies because it can be used to establish a multiple-command structure that gives equal emphasis to functional and geographical departments.

Professor John Hunt of the London Business School suggests four considerations regarding the matrix organizational design. First, the matrix is appropriate when the market is demanding and dynamic. Second, employees must accept higher levels of ambiguity and understand that policy manuals cannot cover every eventuality. Third, in country markets where the command-and-control model persists, it is best to overlay matrices on only small portions of the workforce. Finally, management must be able to clearly state what each axis of the matrix can and cannot do. However, this must be accomplished without creating a bureaucracy.[27]

Having established that the matrix is appropriate, management can expect the matrix to integrate four basic competencies on a worldwide basis:

1. *Geographic knowledge.* An understanding of the basic economic, social, cultural, political, and governmental market and competitive dimensions of a country is essential. The country subsidiary is the major structural device employed today to enable the corporation to acquire geographical knowledge.

---

[23] Emily Nelson, "Rallying the Troops at P&G: New CEO Laffley Aims to End Upheaval by Revamping Program of Globalization," *The Wall Street Journal* (August 31, 2000), pp. B1, B4.

[24] "Ericsson to Simplify Business Structure," *Financial Times* (September 29, 1998), p. 21.

[25] Mark Maremont, "Gillette to Shut 14 of its Plants, Lay Off 4,700," *The Wall Street Journal* (September 29, 1998), pp. A3, A15.

[26] Paul Proctor, "Boeing Shifts to 'Platform Teams,' " *Aviation Week & Space Technology* (May 17, 1999), pp. 63–64.

[27] John W. Hunt, "Is Matrix Management a Recipe for Chaos?" *Financial Times* (January 12, 1998), p. 10.

2. *Product knowledge and know-how.* Product managers with a worldwide responsibility can achieve this level of competence on a global basis. Another way of achieving global product competence is simply to duplicate product management organizations in domestic and international divisions, achieving high competence in both organizational units.

3. *Functional competence in such fields as finance, production, and, especially, marketing.* Corporate functional staff with worldwide responsibility contributes toward the development of functional competence on a global basis. In a handful of companies, the appointment of country subsidiary functional managers is reviewed by the corporate functional manager who is responsible for the development of her functional activity in the organization on a global basis.

4. *A knowledge of the customer or industry and its needs.* Certain large and very sophisticated global companies have staff with a responsibility for serving industries on a global basis to assist the line managers in the country organizations in their efforts to penetrate specific customer markets.

Under this arrangement, instead of designating national organizations or product divisions as profit centers, both are responsible for profitability—the national organization for country profits and the product divisions for national and worldwide product profitability. Figure 16-4 illustrates the matrix organization. This organization chart starts with a bottom section that represents a single-country responsibility level, moves to representing the area or international level, and finally moves to representing global responsibility from the product divisions to the corporate staff, to the chief executive at the top of the structure.

At Whirlpool, North American operations are organized in matrix form. CEO David Whitwam expects to extend this structure into Europe and other regional markets. Whirlpool managers from traditional functions such as operations, marketing, and finance also work in teams devoted to specific products, such as dishwashers or ovens. To encourage interdependence and integration, the cross-functional teams are headed by "brand czars" such as the brand chief for Whirlpool or Kenmore. As Whitwam explains, "The Whirlpool-brand czar still worries about the Whirlpool name. But he also worries about all the refrigerator brands that we make because he heads that product team. It takes a different mind-set."[28]

Some companies are moving away from the matrix in response to changing competitive conditions. For nearly a decade, ABB was a matrix organized along regional lines. Local business units—factories that make motors or power generators, for example—reported both to a country manager and to a business area manager who set strategy for the whole world. This structure allowed ABB to execute global strategies while still thriving in local markets. However, in 1998, new chairman Göran Lindahl dissolved the matrix. As the chairman explained in a press release, "This is an aggressive move aimed at greater speed and efficiency by further focusing and flattening the organization. This step is possible now thanks to our strong, decentralized presence in all local and global markets around the world." In January 2001, Lindahl stepped down and his successor, Jorgen Centerman, revamped the organizational structure yet again. The new design will focus on industries and large corporate customers; Centerman wants to ensure that all of ABB's products are designed to the same systems standards.[29]

---

[28] William C. Taylor and Alan M. Webber, *Going Global: Four Entrepreneurs Map the New World Marketplace* (New York: Penguin USA, 1996), p. 25.

[29] David Woodruff, "New ABB Chairman Unveils Overhaul, Reacting to Rival GE," *The Wall Street Journal* (January 12, 2001), p. A16.

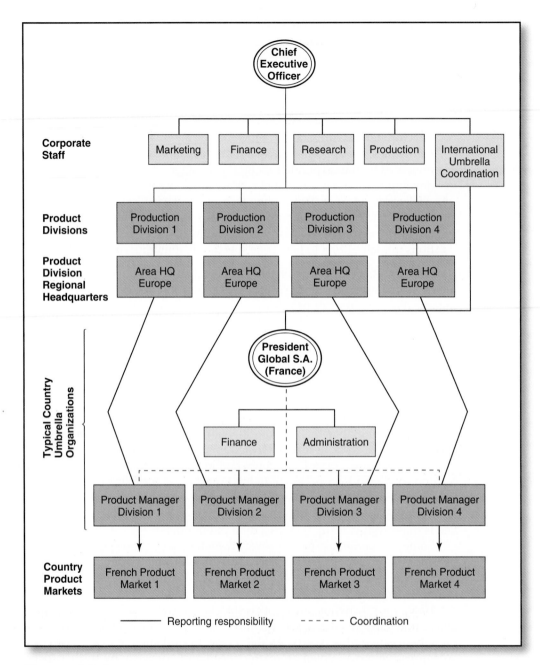

Figure 16-4
The Matrix Structure

The key to successful matrix management is ensuring that managers are able to resolve conflicts and achieve integration of organization programs and plans. The mere adoption of a matrix design or structure does not create a matrix organization. The matrix organization requires a fundamental change in management behavior, organizational culture, and technical systems. In a matrix, influence is based on technical competence and interpersonal sensitivity, not on formal authority. In a matrix culture, managers recognize the absolute need to resolve issues and choices at the lowest possible level and do not rely on higher authority.

The increasing need for responsiveness to local markets has prompted many companies to transfer global headquarters of key business units outside the home country. Hyundai Electronics has transferred its personal computer headquarters from South Korea to California, and Hewlett-Packard moved its desktop PC headquarters from the United States to France. Germany's Siemens has moved its nuclear medicine products division to the United States. Du Pont has also transferred several units out of the United States; headquarters for the company's electronics unit is now in Japan, and its Lycra and agricultural products businesses are now based in Switzerland. In 1995, RJR Nabisco consolidated its international tobacco business by merging two regional offices in Geneva, Switzerland, and eliminating duplicate jobs in Winston-Salem, North Carolina.

Such organizational changes can result in cost savings by eliminating duplication and also bring managers closer to important markets. Notes Jack Malloy, a senior vice president with Du Pont, "The name of the game is to get close to the customer and to understand the customer." At the same time, employees have the opportunity to gain a much-needed global perspective on their industry and line of business. Electronic communications technology helps

executives cut down on travel and maintain control. For example, Philip J. Chauveau heads up AT&T's corded telephone business from an office near the French Riviera. He makes a weekly conference call from France to Thailand and the United States to review sales figures with senior managers.

Sometimes headquarters transfers don't work as planned and must be reversed. Cadbury Schweppes moved its beverage business headquarters from London to the United States in 1987 but moved it back to London in 1991. The original shift reflected the axiom "structure follows strategy." John Carson, the current president of Cadbury Beverages North America, recalled that the goal was to create "a strategic, coherent approach to the business and be in the backyard of where the big guys are." Cadbury had acquired stakes in Canada Dry and Dr Pepper/7-Up, aiming to become the world's leading non-cola producer with a strong presence in the $47 billion U.S. soft-drink market. However, the growth objectives of James P. Schadt, president of the U.S. division at the time, may have conflicted with those of corporate headquarters. A Cadbury official noted that the return to London "allows our chief executive to have his top managers around him" and cuts down on the amount of international travel.

SOURCES: ". . . And Other Ways to Peel the Onion," *The Economist* (January 7, 1995), pp. 52–53; "RJR Moving International Tobacco Unit to Europe," *The New York Times* (October 14, 1995), p. A35; Joann S. Lublin, "Firms Ship Unit Headquarters Abroad," *The Wall Street Journal* (December 9, 1992), pp. B1, B8; Judith Valente, "Cadbury Hopes Dr Pepper Will Satisfy Its Sweet Tooth," *The Wall Street Journal* (November 26, 1993), p. B3.

In the twenty-first century, an important task of top management is to eliminate a one-dimensional approach to decisions and encourage the development of multiple management perspectives and an organization that will sense and respond to a complex and fast-changing world. By thinking in terms of changing behavior rather than changing structural design, company management can free itself from the limitations of the structural chart and focus instead on achieving the best possible results with available resources.

LEAN PRODUCTION: ORGANIZING THE JAPANESE WAY

In the automobile industry, a comparison of early craft production processes, mass production, and modern "lean" production provides an interesting case study of the

Table 16-2

Craft versus Mass Production, 1913 versus 1914

Minutes of Effort to Assemble	Late Craft Production, Fall 1913	Mass Production, Spring 1914	Percent Reduction in Effort
Engine	594	226	62
Magneto	20	5	75
Axle	150	26.5	83
Major Components into a Complete Vehicle	750	93	88

Source: James P. Womack, Daniel T. Jones, and Daniel Roos, *The Machine That Changed the World: The Story of Lean Production* (New York: Harper Collins, 1990), p. 29.

Table 16-3

GM Framingham Assembly Plant versus Toyota Takaoka Assembly Plant, 1986

	GM Framingham	Toyota Takaoka
Gross assembly hours per car	40.7	18.0
Adjusted assembly hours per car	31	16
Assembly defects per 100 cars	130	45
Assembly space per car (sq. ft.)	8.1	4.8
Average inventories of parts	2 weeks	2 hours

Source: James P. Womack, Daniel T. Jones, and Daniel Roos, *The Machine That Changed the World: The Story of Lean Production* (New York: Harper Collins, 1990), p. 81.

effectiveness of new organizational structures in the twentieth century.[30] Table 16-2 provides dramatic evidence of the productivity differences between craft and mass producers in the first part of the twentieth century. The mass producers gained their substantial advantage by changing their value chain in such a way that each worker was able to do far more work each day than the craft producers. The innovation that made this possible was the moving assembly line, which required the originators to conceptualize the production process in a totally new way. The assembly line also required a new approach to organizing people, production machinery, and supplies. By rearranging their value chain activities, the mass producers were able to achieve reductions in effort ranging from 62 percent to 88 percent over the craft producers. These productivity improvements provided an obvious competitive advantage.

The advantage of the mass producers lasted until the Japanese auto companies further revised the value chain and created **lean production,** thereby gaining for themselves the kinds of dramatic competitive advantages that mass producers had previously gained over craft producers. Table 16-3 displays the productivity differences between a mass production operation (GM Framingham) and a lean production operation (Toyota Takaoka).

The Toyota production system, as the company's manufacturing methods are known, achieves efficiencies of about 50 percent over typical mass production systems.

---

[30] This section is adapted from the following sources: James P. Womack, Daniel T. Jones, and Daniel Roos, *The Machine That Changed the World: The Story of Lean Production* (New York: HarperCollins, 1990); Ranganath Nayak and John M. Ketteringham, *Breakthroughs!* (San Diego, CA: Pfeiffer, 1994), Chapter 9; and Michael Williams, "Back to the Past: Some Plants Tear Out Long Assembly Lines, Switch to Craft Work," *The Wall Street Journal* (October 24, 1994), pp. A1, A4.

Even with the reduced assembly time, the lean producer's car has two-thirds fewer defects than the mass producer. The lean producer is also using about 40 percent less factory space and maintaining only a fraction of the inventory stored by the mass producer. Again, the competitive advantages are obvious. Whether the strategy is based on differentiation or low cost, the lean producer has the advantage.

To achieve these gains, the lean producer made changes to operations within the auto companies themselves, to operations within supplier firms and the interfaces between assemblers and suppliers, and to the interfaces with distributors and dealers. Individual firms' value chains were modified, and interfaces between firms were optimized to create an extremely effective and efficient value system.

Assembler Value Chains.   Employee ability is emphasized in a lean production environment. Before being hired, people seeking jobs with Toyota participate in the Day of Work, a 12-hour assessment test to determine who has the right mix of physical dexterity, team attitudes, and problem-solving ability. Once hired, workers receive considerable training to enable them to perform any job in their section of the assembly line or area of the plant, and they are assigned to teams in which all members must be able to perform the functions of all other team members. Workers are also empowered to make suggestions and to take actions aimed at improving quality and productivity. Quality control is achieved through *kaizen*, a devotion to continuous improvement that ensures that every flaw is isolated, examined in detail to determine the ultimate cause, and then corrected. Mechanization—and particularly flexible mechanization—is increased within the lean production firm. Toyota's new Sienna minivan, for example, is produced on the same assembly line in Georgetown, Kentucky, as the company's Camry models. The Sienna and Camry share the same basic chassis and 50 percent of their parts. There are 300 different stations on the assembly line, and Sienna models require different parts at only 26 stations. Toyota expects to build one Sienna for every three Camrys that come off the assembly line.[31]

In contrast to the lean producers, the U.S. mass producers maintained operations that had greater direct labor content, less mechanization, and much less flexible mechanization. They also divided their employees into a large number of discrete specialties with no overlap. Employee initiative and teamwork were not encouraged. Quality control was expressed as an acceptable number of defects per vehicle. The advantages enjoyed by the lean producers can be seen in Table 16-4.

Even when the comparisons are based on industry averages, the Japanese lean producers continue to enjoy substantial productivity and quality advantages. Again, these advantages put the lean producers in a better position to exploit low cost or differentiation strategies. They are getting better productivity out of their workers and machines, and they are making better use of their factory floor space. The relatively small size of the repair area reflects the higher quality of their products. The "suggestions per employee" section of Table 16-4 provides some insight into why lean producers outperform mass producers. They invest a great deal more in the training of their workers. They rotate all workers through all jobs for which their teams are responsible. They encourage all workers to make suggestions, and they act on those suggestions. These changes to the value chain translate into major improvements in the value of their products.

---

[31]   Micheline Maynard, "Camry Assembly Line Delivers New Minivan," *USA Today* (August 11, 1997), p. 3B.

Table 16-4

Selected
Assembly Plant
Characteristics,
Volume Producers

	Japanese in Japan	Japanese in North America	Americans in North America	All Europe
Productivity (hours/vehicle)	16.8	21.2	25.1	36.2
Defects/100 vehicles	60.0	65.0	82.3	97
Suggestions/employee	61.1	1.4	.4	.4
Painting automation (% of direct steps)	54.6	40.7	33.6	38.2

Source: Adapted from James P. Womack, Daniel T. Jones, and Daniel Roos, *The Machine That Changed the World: The Story of Lean Production* (New York: Harper Collins, 1990), p. 92.

It should come as no surprise that many of the world's automakers are studying lean production methods and introducing them in both existing and new plants throughout the world. In 1999, for example, GM announced plans to spend nearly $500 million to overhaul its Adam Opel plant in Germany. Pressure for change came from several sources, including increasing intense rivalry in Europe's car market, worldwide overcapacity, and a realization that European car prices are likely to fall after the introduction of the euro. GM hopes to transform the plant into a state-of-the-art lean production facility with a 40 percent workforce reduction by 2005. As GM Europe President Michael J. Burns said, "Pricing is more difficult today . . . You have to work on product costs, structural costs . . . everything."[32]

Downstream Value Chains. The differences between lean producers and U.S. mass producers in the way they deal with their respective dealers, distributors, and customers are as dramatic as the differences in the way they deal with their suppliers. U.S. mass producers follow the basic industry model and maintain an "arm's-length" relationship with dealers that is often characterized by a lack of cooperation and even open hostility. There is often no sharing of information because there is no incentive to do so. The manufacturer is often trying to force on the dealer models the dealer knows will not sell. The dealer, in turn, is often trying to pressure the customer into buying models he or she does not want. All parties are trying to keep information about what they really want from the others. This does little to ensure that the industry is responsive to market needs.

The problem starts with the market research, which is often in error. It is compounded by lack of feedback from dealers regarding real customer desires. It continues to worsen when the product planning divisions make changes to the models without consulting the marketing divisions or the dealers. This process invariably results in production of models that are unpopular and almost impossible to sell. The manufacturer uses incentives and other schemes to persuade the dealers to accept the unpopular models, such as making a dealer accept one unpopular model for every five hot-selling models it orders. The dealer then has the problem of persuading customers to buy the unpopular models.

Within the mass assembler's value chain, the linkage between the marketing elements and the product planners is broken. The external linkage between the sales divisions and the dealers is also broken. The production process portion of the

---

[32] Joseph B. White, "GM Plans to Invest $445 Million, Cut Staff," *The Wall Street Journal* (May 27, 1999), p. A23.

value chain is also broken in that it relies on the production of thousands of unsold models that then sit on dealer lots, at enormous cost, while the dealer works to find customers.

Within the dealerships, there are even more problems. The relationship between the salesperson and the customer is based on sparring and trying to outsmart each other on price. When the salesperson gets the upper hand, the customer gets stung. It is very much like the relationship between the dealer and the manufacturer. Each is withholding information from the other in the hope of outsmarting the other. Too often, salespeople do not investigate customers' real needs and try to find the best product to satisfy those needs. Rather, they provide only as much information as is needed to close the deal. Once the deal is closed, the salesperson has virtually no further contact with the customer. There is no attempt to optimize the linkage between dealers and manufacturers or the linkage between dealers and customers.

The contrast with the lean producer is again striking. In Japan, the dealer's employees are true product specialists. They know their products and deal with all aspects of the product, including financing, service, maintenance, insurance, registration and inspection, and delivery. A customer deals with one person in the dealership, and that person takes care of everything from the initial contact through eventual trade-in and replacement and all the problems in between. Dealer representatives are included on the manufacturer's product development teams and provide continuous input regarding customer desires. The linkages between dealers, marketing divisions, and product development teams are totally optimized.

The stress caused by large inventories of finished cars is also absent. A car is not built until there is a customer order for it. Each dealer has only a stock of models for the customer to look at. Once the customer has decided on the car he or she wants, the order is sent to the factory and in a matter of a couple of weeks the car is delivered, by the salesperson, to the customer's house.

Once a Japanese dealership gets a customer, it is absolutely determined to hang on to that customer for life. It is also determined to acquire all of the customer's family members as customers. A joke among the Japanese says that the only way to escape from the salesperson who sold a person a car is to leave the country. Japanese dealers maintain extensive databases on actual and potential customers. These databases deal with demographic data and preference data. Customers are encouraged to help keep the information in the database current, and they cooperate in this. This elaborate store of data becomes an integral part of the market research effort and helps ensure that products match customer desires. The fact that there are no inventories of unpopular models because every car is custom-ordered for each customer and the fact that the dealer has elaborate data on the needs and desires of its customers change the whole nature of the interaction between the customer and the dealer. The customer literally builds the car she or he wants and can afford. There is no need to try to outsmart each other.

The differences between U.S. mass producers and the Japanese lean producers reflect their fundamental differences in business objectives. The U.S. producers focus on short-term income and return on investment. Today's sale is a discrete event that is not connected to upstream activities in the value chain and has no value in tomorrow's activities. Efforts are made to reduce the cost of the sales activities. The Japanese see the process in terms of the long-term perspective. There are two major goals of the sales process. The first is to maximize the income stream from each customer over time. The second is to use the linkage with the production processes to reduce production and inventory costs and to maximize quality and therefore differentiation.

Global marketing presents formidable problems to managers responsible for marketing control. Each national market is different from every other market. Distance and differences in language, custom, and practice create communications problems. As noted earlier in the chapter, in larger companies, the size of operations and number of country subsidiaries often result in the creation of an intermediate headquarters. This adds an organizational level to the control system. This section reviews global marketing control practices, compares these practices with domestic marketing control, and identifies the major factors that influence the design of a global control system.

In the managerial literature, **control** is defined as the process by which managers ensure that resources are used effectively and efficiently in the accomplishment of organizational objectives. Control activities are directed toward marketing programs and other programs and projects initiated by the planning process. Data measures and evaluations generated by the control process are also a major input to the planning process. Thus, planning and control are intertwined and interdependent. The planning process can be divided into two related phases. *Strategic* planning is the selection of product and market opportunities and the commitment of human and financial resources to achieve these objectives. *Operational* planning is the process in which strategic product or market objectives and resource commitments to these objectives are translated into specific projects and programs. The relationship of strategic planning, operational planning, and control is illustrated in Figure 16-5.

For companies with global operations, marketing control presents additional challenges. The rate of environmental change in a global company is a dimension of each of the national markets in which it operates. In Chapters 2 through 6 of this book, we examined these environments; each is changing at a different rate and each exhibits unique characteristics. The multiplicity of national environments challenges the global marketing control system with much greater environmental diversity and, therefore, greater complexity in its control. Finally, global marketing can create special communications problems associated with the great distance between markets and headquarters and the differences among managers in languages, customs, and practices.

When company management decides that it wants to develop a global strategy, control of subsidiary operations must be shifted from the subsidiary to the headquarters. The subsidiary will continue to provide vital input into the strategic planning process; even so, such a shift in the organization's balance of power may result in strong resistance to change. In many companies, a tradition of subsidiary autonomy and self-sufficiency limits the influence of headquarters. To overcome such limits, headquarters must facilitate the shift in the perception of self-interest from subsidiary autonomy to global business performance. The conflicts that inevitably arise should be anticipated to the extent possible and the appropriate interventions made. In addition, headquarters can use both formal and informal approaches to maintain control.

Formal Control Methods

Planning and budgeting are two basic tools of formal marketing control. Planning is determining desired sales and profit objectives and projected market-

Figure 16-5
Relationships of
Strategic Control
and Planning

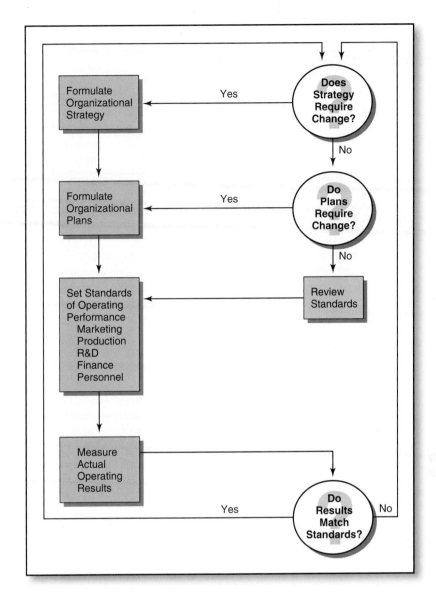

ing program expenditures in unit and money terms. The formal document in which these objectives and expenditures are expressed is a budget. How is the budget established? In practice, many companies rely on two standards—last year's actual performance and some kind of industry average or historical norm. For global companies, a better approach is for headquarters to develop an estimate of the kind of growth that would be desirable and attainable in each national market. This estimate can be based on company studies of national and industry growth patterns.

Control consists of measuring actual sales and expenditures. In the case of no variance (or a favorable variance) between actual and budget, no action is usually taken. An unfavorable variance—lower unit sales than planned, for example—acts as a red flag that attracts the attention of line and staff executives at regional and international headquarters. They will investigate and attempt to determine the cause of the unfavorable variance and what might be done to improve performance.

Larger companies may have sufficient business volume to justify staff product specialists at corporate headquarters who follow the performance of products worldwide. Global marketing product managers have staff responsibility for their product(s) from introduction to termination. Because markets are at different stages of development, a company's products may be at different stages of the product life cycle in different geographical areas. A major responsibility of staff specialists is to ensure that lessons learned in world markets are applied to the management of products worldwide. The task of the global marketing product manager is to try to avoid making the same mistake twice and to capitalize on what the company has learned in world markets—in short, to ensure that all learning is applied wherever relevant. This includes transfers from markets that are at similar stages of development, as well as transfers across stages of development.

Smaller companies focus on key products in key markets. Key products are those that are important to the company's sales, profit objectives, and competitive position. They are frequently new products that require close attention in their introductory stage in a market. If any budget variances develop with a key product, headquarters intervenes directly to learn about the nature of the problem and to assist local management in dealing with the problem.

Another principal measure of marketing performance is share of market, which compares company performance with that of other competitors in the market. Companies that do not obtain this measure, even if it is an estimate, are flying blind. In larger markets, data are reported for subsidiaries and, where significant sales are involved, on a product-by-product basis. Share-of-market data in larger markets are often obtained from independent market audit groups. In smaller markets, share-of-market data are often not available because the market is not large enough to justify the development of an independent commercial marketing audit service. In smaller markets, it is possible for a country manager or agent to hide a deteriorating market position or share of market behind absolute gains in sales and earnings.

INFLUENCES ON MARKETING BUDGETS

In preparing a budget or plan, the following factors are important:

Market Potential.　How large is the potential market for the product being planned? In every domestic market, management must address this question in formulating a product plan. A company that introduces a product in more than one national market must answer this question for each market.

Competition.　A marketing plan or budget must be prepared in light of the competitive level in the market. The more entrenched the competition, the more difficult it is to achieve market share and the more likely it is that a competitive reaction will meet any move that promises significant success in the target market. Competitive moves are particularly important as a variable in international market planning because many companies are moving from strong competitive positions in their base markets to foreign markets where they have a minor position and must compete against entrenched companies. Domestic market standards and expectations of marketing performance are based on experience in markets where the company has a major position. These standards and expectations are simply not relevant to a market where the company is in a minor position and trying to break into the market.

Impact of Substitute Products. One of the sources of competition for a product in a market is availability of substitute products. As a product is moved into markets at different stages of development, improbable substitute products often emerge. For example, in Colombia a major source of competition for manufactured boxes and other packaging products is woven bags and wood boxes made in the handicraft sector of the economy. Marketing officials of global companies in the packaging industry report that the garage-based small business producing a handmade product is very difficult competition because of costs of materials and labor in Colombia.

Process. The manner in which performance targets are communicated to subsidiary management is as important as the way in which they are derived. One of the most sophisticated methods used today is the *indicative planning method.* Headquarters estimates of regional potential are disaggregated and communicated to subsidiary management as *guidance.* The subsidiaries are in no way bound by guidance. They are expected to produce their own plan by taking into account the headquarters guidance that is based on global data and their own data from the market, including a detailed review of customers, competitors, and other relevant market developments. This method produces excellent results because it combines a global perspective and estimate with specific country marketing plans that are by the country management teams themselves.

Headquarters, in providing guidance, does not need to understand a market in depth. For example, the headquarters of a manufacturer of electrical products does not need to know how to sell electric motors to a French consumer. What headquarters can do is gather data on the expected expansion in generating capacity in France and use experience tables drawn from world studies that indicate what each megawatt of additional generating capacity will mean in terms of the growth in demand in France for electrical motors. The estimate of total market potential, together with information on the competitiveness of the French subsidiary, can be the basis for guidance in terms of expected sales and earnings in France. The guidance may not be accepted by the French subsidiary. If the indicative planning method is used properly, the subsidiary educates the headquarters if its guidance is unrealistic. When headquarters does its job well, it will select an attainable but ambitious target. If subsidiary personnel doubt they can achieve the headquarters goal, discussion and headquarters involvement in the planning process will lead to either a plan that will achieve the guidance objective or a revision of the guidance by headquarters.

Informal Control Methods

In addition to budgeting, informal control methods, especially the transfer of people from one market to another, play an important role. When people are transferred, they take with them their experience in previous markets, which normally includes some standards for marketing performance. Investigation of a new market that has lower standards than a previous market leads to revised standards or to the discovery of a reason for the difference. Another valuable informal control device is face-to-face contact between subsidiary staff and headquarters staff, as well as contact among subsidiary staff. These contacts provide the opportunity for an exchange of information and judgments that can be valuable input into the planning and control process. Annual meetings that bring together staff from throughout a region of the world often result in informal inputs to the process of setting standards.

THE GLOBAL MARKETING AUDIT

A **global marketing audit** can be defined as a comprehensive, systematic examination of the marketing environment and company objectives, strategies, programs, policies, and activities. The audit can be companywide in scope, or it can encompass a particular line of business or organizational subunit. The objective of periodic audits is to identify existing and potential problems and opportunities in a company's marketing performance and to recommend a plan of action for improving that performance. In other words, the global marketing audit is a tool for evaluating and improving a company's (or business unit's) global marketing operations.

A full marketing audit has two basic characteristics. First, it is formal and systematic. Random questions may result in useful insights, but this is not a marketing audit. The effectiveness of an audit normally increases to the extent that it involves a sequence of orderly diagnostic steps. Second, a marketing audit should be conducted periodically. Most companies in trouble are well on their way to disaster before the trouble is fully apparent. An audit can reveal such troubles while there is still time to deal with them. The audit may be broad, or it may be a narrowly focused assessment. A full marketing audit is comprehensive. It reviews the company's marketing environment, competition, objectives, strategies, organization, systems, procedures, and practices in every area of the marketing mix, including product, pricing, distribution, communications, customer service, and research strategy and policy.

There are two types of audit: independent and internal. An independent marketing audit is conducted by someone who is free from the influence of the organization being audited. The independent audit may or may not be objective: It is quite possible for company management to influence the consultant or professional firm. The company that wants a truly independent audit should understand the importance of objectivity. A potential limitation of an independent marketing audit is the auditor's lack of understanding of the industry. In many industries, there is no substitute for experience: An industry outsider may simply not see the subtle clues that an industry veteran would easily recognize. Then again, the independent auditor may see obvious indicators that the veteran may be unable to see.

An internal audit or self-audit may be quite valuable because it is conducted by marketers who understand the industry. However, it may lack the objectivity of an independent audit. Because the two types of audits have complementary strengths and limitations, both should be conducted periodically for the same scope and time period so that the results may be compared. The comparison may lead to insights on how to strengthen the performance of the marketing team.

Setting Objectives and Scope of the Audit

The first step of an audit is a meeting between company executives and the auditor to agree on objectives, coverage, depth, data sources, report format, and time period for the audit.

Gathering Data. One of the major tasks in conducting an audit is data collection. A detailed plan of interviews, secondary research, review of internal documents, and the like is required. This effort usually involves an auditing team. A basic rule in data collection is not to rely solely on the opinion of people being audited for data. In auditing a sales organization, it is absolutely essential to talk to field sales personnel as well as to sales management, and, of course, no audit is complete without direct contact with customers and suppliers.

Creative auditing techniques should be encouraged and explored by the auditing team. For example, if an auditor wants to determine whether top executives are really in touch with the organization and all of its activities, the auditor should speak with mailroom personnel and find out if chief executives have ever visited the facility. If they have never been there, it speaks volumes about the management style and the degree of hands-on management in the organization. Similarly, if an organization has developed an elaborate marketing incentive program that is purported to generate results with customers, an audit should involve customer contact to find out if, indeed, the program is actually having any impact.

Preparing and Presenting the Report. The next step after data collection and analysis is the preparation and presentation of the audit report. This presentation should restate the objectives and scope of the audit, present the main findings, and list major recommendations, conclusions, and topics for further study and investigation.

Components of the Marketing Audit. There are six major components of a full global marketing audit:

1. The marketing environment audit
2. The marketing strategy audit
3. The marketing organization audit
4. The marketing systems audit
5. The marketing productivity audit
6. The marketing function audit

The marketing audit presents a number of potential problems and pitfalls. Setting objectives can be a pitfall if, indeed, the objectives fail to anticipate major problems or contingencies. The auditor must have the authority to revise objectives and priorities during the course of the audit itself. Similarly, new data sources may appear during the audit, and the auditor should be open to such sources. The approach of the auditor should be simultaneously systematic, following a predetermined outline, and perceptive and open to new directions and sources that appear in the course of the audit investigation.

Report Presentation. One of the biggest problems in marketing auditing is that the executive who commissions the audit may have unrealistically high expectations about what the audit will do for the company. An audit is valuable even if it does not identify major new directions or offer cure-alls. All concerned must recognize that improvements at the margin make the difference between success and mediocrity. Experienced marketers don't look for dramatic revolutionary findings or cure-alls; rather, they know that incremental improvements can lead to success in global marketing. Global marketers, even more than their domestic counterparts, need marketing audits to assess far-flung efforts in highly diverse environments. The global marketing audit should be at the top of the list of programs for strategic excellence and implementation excellence for the winning global company.

CONCLUSION

This is an exciting time to prepare for a career in global marketing. Until very recently, one sure way to put your career at risk in many companies (especially U.S. companies) was to go overseas. There was nothing wrong with being overseas per se, but management did not always recognize the value of global experience and turned to executives who were close at hand for promotions.

Today, global experience counts. We are in a global market with global competition, and those with global experience have a definite advantage. Top U.S. executives with international experience include Samir F. Gibara, president and CEO of Goodyear Tire & Rubber; Michael Hawley, president and COO of Gillette; Lucio A. Noto, chairman and CEO of Mobil; and Raymond G. Viault, vice chairman of General Mills.[33]

How do you establish a career in global marketing? There are two broad paths:

1. Get directly into a job outside your home country or into a multicountry headquarters job in a global company.
2. Get company experience in an industry that prepares you for promotion to a job with multicountry responsibility or to an assignment outside your home country.

For many, the second choice is better than the first. There is no substitute for solid industry experience, and your best opportunity to get it may be in your home country. You speak the language, understand the culture, and are trained in business and marketing. You are ready to learn. An option is to get this basic experience in another country. The advantage of this move is that you will learn a new culture and language and broaden your international experience while you learn about a company and industry. Good luck!

SUMMARY

To respond to the opportunities and threats in the global marketing environment, organizational **leaders** must develop a global vision and strategy. Leaders must also be able to communicate that vision throughout the organization and build global competencies. Global companies are increasingly realizing that the "right" person for top jobs is not necessarily a home-country national.

In **organizing** for the global marketing effort, the goal is to create a structure that enables the company to respond to significant differences in international market environments and to extend valuable corporate knowledge. Alternatives include an **international division structure, regional management centers, geographical struc-** ture, **regional** or **worldwide product division structure,** and the **matrix** design. Whichever form of organization is chosen, balance between autonomy and integration must be established. Many companies are adopting the organizational principle of **lean production** that was pioneered by Japanese automakers.

The differences between global marketing **control** practices and purely domestic control must be recognized. Appropriate adjustments should be made to the way in which global planning and control practices are formulated and implemented. The **global marketing audit** can be an effective tool for improving global marketing performance.

---

[33] Joann S. Lublin, "An Overseas Stint Can Be a Ticket to the Top," *The Wall Street Journal* (January 29, 1996), p. B1.

DISCUSSION QUESTIONS

1. Are top executives of global companies likely to be home-country nationals?
2. In a company involved in global marketing, which activities should be centralized at headquarters and which should be delegated to national or regional subsidiaries?
3. Identify some of the factors that lead to the establishment of an international division as an organization increases its global business activities.
4. "A matrix structure integrates four competencies on a worldwide scale." Explain.
5. In the automobile industry, how does "lean production" differ from the traditional assembly line approach?
6. In preparing a marketing budget or plan, what factors should managers should take into account?

SUGGESTED READINGS

Books

Abrahams, Jeffrey. *The Mission Statement Book.* Berkeley, Calif.: Ten Speed Press, 1995.

Bartlett, Christopher A., and Sumantra Ghoshal. *Managing Across Borders: The Transnational Solution.* Boston: Harvard Business School Press, 1989.

Davidow, William H., and Michael S. Malone. *The Virtual Corporation.* New York: Harper Business, 1993.

Gerlach, Michael L. *Alliance Capitalism: The Social Organization of Japanese Business.* Berkeley and Los Angeles: University of California Press, 1992.

Going Global: Succeeding in World Markets. Boston: Harvard Business School Press, 1991.

Hammer, Michael, and James Champy. *Reengineering the Corporation.* New York: Harper Collins Publishers, 1993.

Katzenbach, Jon R., and Douglas K. Smith. *The Wisdom of Teams: Creating the High Performance Organization.* Boston: Harvard Business School Press, 1993.

Nakatani, Iwao. *The Japanese Firm in Transition.* Tokyo: Asian Productivity Organization, 1988.

Robock, Stefan H., and Kenneth Simmonds. *International Business and Multinational Enterprises.* Homewood, Ill.: Irwin, 1989.

Snyder, Neil. *Vision, Values, and Courage.* New York: Free Press, 1995.

Stopford, John M., and Louis T. Wells. *Managing the Multinational Enterprise.* New York: Basic Books, 1972.

Tuller, Lawrence W. *Going Global: New Opportunities for Growing Companies to Compete in World Markets.* Homewood, Ill.: Business One Irwin, 1991.

Yip, George S. *Total Global Strategy.* Upper Saddle River, N.J.: Prentice Hall, 1992.

Articles

Asakawa, Kazuhiro. "Evolving Headquarters-Subsidiary Dynamics in International R&D. The Case of Japanese Multinationals." *R&D Management* 31 no. 1 (January 2001), pp. 1–14.

Beaver, William. "Levi's Is Leaving China." *Business Horizons* 38, no. 2 (March-April 1995), pp. 35–40.

Birkinshaw, Julian. "Encouraging Entrepreneurial Activity in Multinational Corporations." *Business Horizons* 38, no. 3 (May-June 1995), pp. 32–38.

———, and Neil Hood. "Unleash Innovation in Foreign Subsidiaries." *Harvard Business Review* 79 no. 3 (March 2001), pp. 131–137.

Cohen, Susan G. "Designing Effective Self-Managing Work Teams." *CEO Publication—University of Southern California,* pp. G93–G99.

Gupta, Anil, and Vijay Govindarayam. "Managing Global Expansion: A Conceptual Framework." *Business Horizons* 43, no. 2 (March-April 2000), pp. 45–54.

Halal, William E. "Global Strategic Management in a New World Order." *Business Horizons* 36, no. 6 (November-December 1993).

Hankinson, Philippa, and Graham Hankinson. "The Roles of Organizational Structure in Successful Global Brand Management: A Case Study of the Pierre Smirnoff Company." *The Journal of Brand Management* 6, no. 1 (1998), pp. 29–43.

Harzing, Anne-Wil. "Of Bears, Bumble Bees and Spiders: The Role of Expatriates in Controlling Foreign Subsidiaries." *Journal of World Business* 36, no. 4 (Winter 2001), pp. 366–379.

Hax, Arnoldo C. "Building the Firm of the Future." *Sloan Management Review* 30, no. 3 (Spring 1989), pp. 75–82.

Hewett, Kelly, and William O. Bearden. "Dependence, Trust, and Relational Behavior on the Part of Foreign Subsidiary Marketing Operations: Implications for Managing Global Marketing Operations." *Journal of Marketing* 65 no. 4 (October 2001), pp. 51–66.

Katzenbach, Jon R., and Douglas K. Smith. "The Discipline of Teams." *Harvard Business Review* 71, no. 2 (March-April 1993).

Krugman, Paul. "Competitiveness: A Dangerous Obsession." *Foreign Affairs* 73, no. 2 (March-April 1994), pp. 28–44.

Kuniyasu, Sakai. "The Feudal World of Japanese Manufacturing." *Harvard Business Review* 68, no. 6 (November-December 1990), pp. 38–49.

Maruca, Regina Fazio. "The Right Way to Go Global: An Interview with Whirlpool CEO David Whitwam." *Harvard Business Review* 72, no. 2 (March-April 1994), pp. 134–145.

Mintzberg, Henry. "The Effective Organization: Forces and Forms." *Sloan Management Review* (Winter 1991).

Morrison, Allen J., David A. Ricks, and Kendall Roth. "Globalization Versus Regionalization: Which Way for the Multinational?" *Organizational Dynamics* (Winter 1991), pp. 17–29.

O'Reilly, Anthony J. F. "Leading a Global Strategic Charge." *Journal of Business Strategy* 12, no. 4 (July-August 1991), pp. 10–13.

Prahalad, C. K., and Gary Hamel. "The Core Competence of the Corporation." *Harvard Business Review* 68, no. 3 (May-June 1990), pp. 79–93.

Schill, Ronald L., and David N. McArthur. "Redefining the Strategic Competitive Unit: Towards a New Global Marketing Paradigm?" *International Marketing Review* 9, no. 3, pp. 5–24.

Taggart, James H. "Strategy and Control in the Multinational Corporation: Too Many Recipes?" *Long Range Planning* 31, no. 4 (August 1998), pp. 571–585.

Thurow, Lester. "Who Owns the Twenty-First Century?" *Sloan Management Review* 33, no. 3 (Spring 1992), pp. 5–17.

CASES

Case 16-1 Volkswagen AG: The Second Time's the Charm for Would-Be Global Automaker

Volkswagen AG enjoys the distinction of being the number-one carmaker in Europe and the fourth largest in the world. The compact Golf is the best-selling car in Europe, where VW commands a 17 percent market share. Initial European demand for a new midsize model, the Passat, was so strong that there was an eight-month waiting list. The company can boast that its giant Wolfsburg plant is home to the most automated production line in the world, capable of completing 80 percent of a car's assembly by machine. VW ranks as the second-largest company in the new Germany; only DaimlerChrysler is bigger. Outside Europe, Volkswagen has also achieved considerable success. In Mexico, for example, the company's share of the passenger car market is 40 percent. Volkswagen is also the number one Western auto manufacturer in China, where it commands 55 percent of the market.

Despite its stature in the global auto industry, VW's financial performance has been erratic in recent years. In 1992, vehicle sales reached an all-time high of 3.5 million units. In 1993, VW was in the red due to a DM 1.84 billion loss at its Sociedad Española de Automoviles de Turisme (SEAT) unit in Spain. In 1994, net income rebounded to DM 150 million on sales of DM 80 billion. As these results suggest, VW faced enormous challenges as the twentieth century came to a close. The company has been forced to confront the fact that its costs are out of control. Much of the huge Wolfsburg assembly plant, parts of which date back to 1938, is woefully inefficient in comparison to lean-production facilities operated by competitors like Toyota and Nissan. VW's German plants must run at 90 percent of production capacity for the company to break even; European rivals can break even at production levels of 70 percent. Meanwhile, Japanese production capacity in Europe is approaching one million vehicles. The advent of the single market brought an end to trade barriers and quotas; as a result, competition in Europe is heating up.

VW has also been plagued by headaches as plans to source cars in lower-wage countries such as Portugal and Mexico have gone awry. Despite efforts to train Mexican workers to be quality conscious, manufacturing problems with new Jetta and Golf models made in Puebla, Mexico, caused a severe shortage of vehicles in North America during the 1993 model year. The situation only worsened Volkswagen's fortunes in the United States, where the company was clinging to a market share of barely 1 percent.

These and other problems can be traced in part to former chairman Carl Hahn's attempts to implement his vision of VW as Europe's first global automaker. In fact, management guru Peter Drucker credits Volkswagen for developing the first truly global strategy more than 30 years ago. By 1970, the Beetle was a mature product in Europe; sales were still moderately strong in the United States, and booming in Brazil. Drucker describes what happened next:

> The chief executive officer of Volkswagen proposed switching the German plants entirely to the new model, the successor to the Beetle, which the German plants would also supply to the United States market. But the continuing demand for Beetles in the United States would be satisfied out of Brazil, which would then given Volkswagen do Brasil the needed capability to enlarge its plants and to maintain for another ten years the Beetle's leadership in the growing Brazilian market. To assure the American customers of the "German quality" that was one of the Beetle's main attractions, the critical parts such as engines and transmissions for all cars sold in North America would, however, still be made in Germany. The finished car for the North American market would be assembled in the United States.[34]

Unfortunately, this visionary strategy failed. One problem was resistance on the part of German unions. A second problem was confusion among American dealers about a car that was equally "made in Germany," "made in Brazil," and "made in the USA." Two decades later, as described in an interview with *Harvard Business Review*, Hahn's strategic plan for the 1990s and beyond called for a decentralized structure of four autonomous divisions. In pursuit of this vision, Hahn invested tens of billions of dollars in Czechoslovakia's Skoda autoworks and SEAT in Spain. The Volkswagen, Audi, Skoda, and SEAT units each would have its own chief executive. As a whole, the company would be capable of turning out more than four million cars annually in low-cost plants located close to buyers. The company's R&D center, however,

---

[34] Peter F. Drucker, *Innovation and Entrepreneurship: Practice and Principles* (New York: Harper & Row, 1985), p. 87.

would continue to be in Germany. Highly automated plants in Germany would provide components such as transmissions, engines, and axles to assembly operations in other parts of the world.

In Spain, VW hoped to take advantage of labor rates 50 percent lower than in West Germany and roughly on par with those paid by Japanese companies with factories in Britain. Because labor makes up a larger share of production costs for subcompacts than for larger models, and because annual demand in Spain amounts to 500,000 cars, Spain was an attractive location for small-car production. Besides serving the domestic market, VW hoped to use Spain as a production source that would allow it to cut prices and boost margins in Europe. Between 1986 and 1990, VW paid the Spanish government a total of $600 million in exchange for 100 percent ownership of SEAT. The company increased Spanish production from 350,000 to 500,000 vehicles; the popular Golf model represents about one-quarter of the output. VW invested $1.9 billion in a new plant in Martorell capable of producing 300,000 cars each year.

Similar reasoning was behind VW's 1991 purchase of a 31 percent stake in Skoda from the Czechoslovak government. Located northeast of Prague in the city of Mlada Boleslav, the Skoda works enjoyed distinction as the most efficient plant in the former Soviet bloc. However, product quality was low, and the plant was a major source of pollution. With an eye to doubling production to 450,000 cars, VW pledged to invest $5 billion by the end of the decade. VW's presence has also persuaded TRW, Rockwell International, and other parts suppliers interested in serving Skoda and other automakers in Central and Eastern Europe, to establish operations in the Czech Republic. However, to maintain their low-cost position and ensure quality control, VW and Skoda executives are hoping to go a step beyond the Japanese-style "lean production" system that emphasizes just-in-time delivery from nearby suppliers. Several different suppliers, including the American company Johnson Controls and Pelzer, a carpet maker based in Germany, will manufacture components such as seats, instrument panels, and rear axles *inside* the plant itself. As Skoda CFO Volkhard Kohler explained in 1994, "We have to organize better than in the Western world and use supplier integration. Wages will increase, so we have to find other ways of being cost-effective. Supplier integration is part of the new thinking and what we do here can be a model for the West." Professor Daniel Jones of the Cardiff University Business School supports the effort. "It's physically integrated, but in terms of management and performance each runs his own show. It makes a lot of sense because you have the direct integra-tion of people making the parts and the people putting them in the car," he said in an interview.

Hahn also earmarked $3 billion for a project in which he took a keen personal interest: investment in the former East Germany, where he was born. On October 3, 1990, German reunification added 16 million people to Volkswagen's home-country market virtually overnight. Under communism, the citizens of East Germany had a choice of basically one car: the notoriously low-quality Trabant. Hahn's strategy for a reunited Germany included building a new $1.9 billion factory that would employ 6,500 workers and produce a quarter of a million Golf and Polo models each year. The investment was justified in part by forecasts that East Germans would buy 750,000 cars each year; VW aimed to capture a third of the market, equal to its share in West Germany.

Unfortunately, Hahn's vision did not anticipate a global recession. First quarter 1993 sales in Germany were off by 25 percent; across Europe, sales declined by 17 percent. Needless to say, Hahn's multibillion-dollar investments weren't paying off. In January 1993, Hahn was succeeded as chairman by Ferdinand Piech, head of VW's Audi AG subsidiary and grandson of Ferdinand Porsche, designer of the legendary cars that bear his name, as well as the Volkswagen Beetle. Piech, who has been described as "steely eyed and intense," immediately declared a state of crisis in the company and began taking drastic actions; cost cutting topped the list. Piech planned to trim VW's worldwide employment of about 274,000, starting with 20,000 jobs in 1993. Despite sales increases in the Spanish market, SEAT was such a money loser that VW was forced to lay off several thousand workers. Spain's rigid labor laws make layoffs so costly that Piech was forced to ask the Spanish government for a subsidy of more than 30 billion pesetas ($230 million) to pay for the restructuring.

Meanwhile, the new chairman was facing a different kind of challenge. With great fanfare, VW announced in March 1993 that it had succeeded in luring a new production chief away from General Motors. José Ignacio Lopéz de Arriortúa was expected to play a major role in cost cutting at VW, but he arrived amid accusations of industrial espionage. Specifically, GM alleged that López and several colleagues had left with secret information on product development and other sensitive issues. The controversy did not stop López from doing what he had been hired to do. He broke long-term contracts with many of VW's suppliers and put new contracts up for bid; as a result, a higher percentage of components are now sourced outside Germany. At VW's new General Pachecho plant in Buenos Aires, López subcontracted various aspects of production to a dozen outside companies. VW workers build a few crucial parts such as the

What color do you dream in?

©1998 Volkswagen. 1-800-DRIVE-VW or www.vw.com

Drivers wanted. VW

chassis and power train; suppliers are responsible for various other tasks such as assembling instrument panels. López anticipated a 50 percent reduction in costs. In the end, the espionage controversy cost López his job, and CEO Piech settled the civil case by agreeing to pay GM $100 million and buy $1 billion in GM parts.

Even though his tenure at VW was brief and stormy, the positive aspects of the López legacy are likely to endure. Maryann Kellar, author of a book about VW, calls the Czech and Argentine experiment "something that has been talked about for years as the next great productivity and cost enhancement move by the industry." The strong leadership effort by VW's top executives is one reason why many observers remain bullish on the company, despite overall slow growth in the European auto market. Piech pledged to slash the number of auto platforms VW offers in its various nameplates from 16 to 4 by 1998. In 1996, Skoda rolled out the Octavia, the first new car developed by the Czech plant during the Volkswagen era and the first to use a VW chassis platform. Piech also won concessions from IG Metall, the German autoworkers union. The union agreed to 2.5 per-

cent annual pay raises and a pledge of job security. In addition, the work day for many assembly line workers has been reduced to five hours and 46 minutes—in essence, a four-day week. The union also agreed that paid hourly breaks would be cut to 2.5 minutes from 5 minutes. CFO Bruno Adelt estimated that all the agreed-upon changes would boost productivity 4 to 5 percent.

Even as VW expands production in emerging markets and introduces production efficiencies, it is devising a strategy for a comeback in the United States. Mexican production of a new version of the legendary Beetle began in 1997 with a U.S. launch in 1998. As board member Jen Neumann said, "The Beetle is the core of the VW soul. If we put it back in people's minds, they'll think of our products more." Like its predecessor, the new Beetle has curved body panels and running boards. However, it is a front-wheel-drive model with more headroom and legroom. Marketing managers priced the new model at about $15,000, 10 percent higher than the company's entry-level Golf. This strategy de-emphasizes appeal to college-age, first-time buyers and targets a broad group of consumers who are looking for more than cheap transportation. ■

DISCUSSION QUESTIONS

1. Evaluate Volkswagen's goal of becoming Europe's first global automaker. What is the rationale behind the strategy?
2. What is the biggest challenge currently facing Volkswagen management?

3. In 2002, VW launched a new super luxury model, the $85,000 Phaeton. Assess its prospects for success.

SOURCES: Gabriella Stern, "VW's U.S. Comeback Rides on Restyled Beetle," *The Wall Street Journal* (May 6, 1997), pp. B1, B2; Haig Simonian, "Alliances Forged in the Factories," *Financial Times* (November 4, 1996), p. 10; David Woodruff, "VW is Back—But for How Long?" *Business Week* (March 4, 1996), pp. 66–67; Jonathan Friedland, "VW Puts Suppliers on Production Line," *The Wall Street Journal* (February 15, 1996), p. A11; James Bennet, "Eurocars: On the Road Again," *The New York Times* (August 20, 1995), sec. 3, p. 1; Jane Perlez, "Skoda Gives Its Suppliers a Place in the Auto Plant," *The New York Times* (November 19, 1994), pp. 41, 52; Richard W. Stevenson, "In a Czech Plant, VW Shows How to Succeed in the East," *The New York Times* (November 19, 1994), pp. D1, D6; Steven Greenhouse, "Carl Hahn's East European Homecoming," *The New York Times* (September 23, 1990), sec. 3, pp. 1, 6; Bernard Avishai, "A European Platform for Global Competition: An Interview with VW's Carl Hahn," *Harvard Business Review* 69, no. 4 (July-August 1991), pp. 103–113; Ferdinand Protzman, "New Leadership for Volkswagen," *The New York Times* (March 30, 1992), pp. C1, C2; Timothy Aeppel, "VW Chief Declares a Crisis and Prescribes Bold Action," *The Wall Street Journal* (April 1, 1993), p. B3; Peter Drucker, *Innovation and Entrepreneurship: Practice and Principles* (New York: Harper & Row, 1985).

Case 16-2   Kazuo Inamori: Spiritual Leadership at Kyocera Corp.

With headquarters in Kyoto, Japan, Kyocera Corp. is a $10.2 billion company that built its global reputation by developing and manufacturing products and product components containing high-tech synthetic ceramics. Although Kyocera (the name is short for Kyoto Ceramics) is unknown to most people, the company has for many years been *the* world leader in the production and sales of ceramic housings for computer microchips. Like many other Japanese companies, Kyocera's original competitive advantage stemmed from its ability to make high-quality products faster and cheaper than competitors. The housings serve as a ceramic "cocoon" to protect the fragile chips during transit.

In other ways, however, Kyocera breaks the mold usually associated with Japan Inc. The company is one of only a handful of companies in Japan with foreign directors on its board. Its San Diego-based subsidiary is mostly run by Americans. Rather than recruit graduates of prestigious schools, Kyocera prefers to hire its employees from second-tier technical schools. Company founder Kazuo Inamori and chairman emeritus believes his employees work harder because they are grateful to be given a chance to work for a top company. And while most Japanese companies strive for consensus and adherence to company norms, Inamori encourages creativity and independence within Kyocera.

In Kyocera's early days, Inamori often spent a great deal of time on the plant floor, personally overseeing the kilns and the mixing of raw materials. It was precisely this approach that helped it win its first crucial contract with Texas Instruments. Making chip packages is both an art and a science; they must be baked for 18 hours at temperatures as high as 1,600 degrees Celsius. Recalls Inamori, "We got the contract because we were so good at mixing and baking, because the top people in the company were in front of the kilns all the time, and they could control the variances and keep the quality consistent, which is very hard in ceramics." Inamori earned the nickname "Mr. A.M." because he stayed at work until 3 or 4 in the morning.

Despite this close attention to production details, as Inamori explains in his recently published autobiography, the secret to Kyocera's growth is not its grasp of technology. Rather, it is the "spiritual energy of the workers." In an interview with *Business Japan,* Inamori said, "I feel that the strength of an enterprise is determined by the number of workers who really understand the spiritual qualities which enable a business to succeed. That is why I always endeavor to get my thoughts across to them. My time is often taken up in that connection rather than in dealing with technological problems concerning ceramic manufacture."

Inamori exhorts his employees to ever-higher levels of performance with Inamorisms, such as "When a company is no longer on the offensive, that company is already beginning to go downhill." Part of Inamori's directness and driven nature may be explained by the fact that, as a young man, his goal was to become a kamikaze pilot (the term used to describe Japanese volunteers who flew suicide attacks) during World War II. However, because the war ended before he could fulfill his dream, he dedicated his life to staging offensive maneuvers in marketing, rather than in the military. Inamori believes that when a company is first founded, the employees have a burning drive for work and military-style discipline. When such organizations grow in size, however, top management's attention shifts away from the maintenance of worker energy. According to Inamori, the spiritual drive that was present when Kyocera was founded has not waned. This fact distinguishes Kyocera from most other organizations—Japanese, American, or otherwise.

Inamori implemented that spiritual drive by striving for efficiency. He insists that all employees work at holding down costs and engage in high-quality work. For example, instead of following the electronics industry norm of using distributors for its products, Kyocera relies on a salaried sales force. The result: Kyocera spends 12 to 13 percent of revenues on general, administrative, and sales expenses compared to the 20 percent that is normal for other companies. There has never been a layoff at Kyocera's U.S. plant in San Diego; in return, the company enjoys high employee loyalty. These are just a few of the reasons why Kyocera is such a tough competitor.

Kyocera's early opportunities were tied to the fledgling semiconductor industry in the United States; ceramic components play a significant role in high-technology products because they are heat-resistant and do not conduct electricity. The road to Kyocera's domination of the chip package market began in the mid-1960s, when it bid successfully against a West German firm for a Texas Instruments contract to build ceramic insulating rods for silicon transistors. Soon thereafter, Fairchild Semiconductor (the forerunner to Intel) drafted technically demanding designs for housings to protect the chips it manufactured. However, Fairchild was unable to find any U.S. company willing to build the housings for a reasonable price, even though Coors Electronic Packaging was the world leader in ceramic semiconductor package manufacturing at the time. Fairchild turned to Kyocera, which was anxious to expand into electronic applications for its ceramic business. Asa Jonishi, Kyocera's first U.S. salesman, worked hard for the account; not only was Kyocera willing to take on the Fairchild project for a low price but also it delivered its first order against a seemingly impossible deadline of three months.

Kyocera's success in the U.S. market can also be attributed to its willingness to customize tailor chip housings to each customer's needs. Among California's Silicon Valley chipmakers, Kyocera has become legendary for its service. Kyocera backs up its $100 million-per-year R&D expenditures with sales forces in both the United States—50 direct salespeople at 12 direct sales offices—and Japan that pay heed to Inamori's unwavering emphasis on quality and customer service. Early on, Kyocera earned a reputation for answering customer questions overnight, whereas U.S. suppliers often took weeks to respond. Employees would work around the clock to satisfy customer requests for samples.

Today, Kyocera is targeting new applications for ceramics, including replacements for human body parts, automobile engines, and knives. Soaring demand for portable communications devices has translated into strong sales of the miniature electronic parts that are Kyocera's specialty. Despite its past successes, however, Kyocera faces new challenges in the future. Plastic packaging has replaced ceramics for some types of integrated circuits; by the late 1990s, for example, Intel was substituting cheaper resins in its microprocessor packaging. Kyocera's engineers responded by developing heat-resistant plastic packages and plastic/ceramic hybrids. Kyocera has diversified; acquisitions include Elco Corporation, a U.S. manufacturer of electrical connectors, Japanese camera maker Yashica Corporation, and Mita Industrial, a photocopier producer. Kyocera's environmentally-friendly laser printers are particularly popular in Germany. Kyocera has also gotten out of unattractive business segments such as PCs and fax machines. Kyocera lost a bet big on the now-bankrupt Iridium satellite-telephone venture (see Case 11-3). Kyocera was a handset supplier and also handled sales in Japan and other Asian countries. However, Kyocera started marketing a regular cellular phone in 2001; company executives hope to challenge Nokia and other leading suppliers. ∎

DISCUSSION QUESTIONS

1. What factors have helped Kyocera succeed in serving organizational markets?
2. How is Kyocera different from the "typical" Japanese company?

3. How important is Inamori's spiritual drive to Kyocera's success? What will happen to the company's culture now that Inamori has retired?

SOURCES: Benjamin Fulford, "Kyocera's Pay Dirt," *Forbes* (September 20, 1999) pp. 113–114; Kazuo Inamori, *A Passion for Success: Practical, Inspiration, and Spiritual Insight from Japan's Leading Entrepreneur* (New York: McGraw-Hill, 1995); George Taninecz, "Kazuo Inamori: 'Respect the Divine and Love People,' " *Industry Week* (June 5, 1995), pp. 47–51; "Kyocera's Secrets: Flexibility, Spirituality and Teamwork," *Business Japan* (January 1987), pp. 31–32; Gene Bylinsky, "The Hottest High-Tech Company in Japan," *Fortune* (January 1, 1990), pp. 83–84+; "Cult of Personality," *Business Month* (August 1990), pp. 42–44; David Halberstam, "Coming In from the Cold War," *The Washington Monthly* (January-February 1991), pp. 32–34; Jacob M. Schlesinger, "Kyocera Plays an Ambivalent Role in U.S. Weaponry," *The Wall Street Journal* (February 5, 1991), p. A15; Jonathan Friedland, "Samurai Sorcerer," *Far Eastern Economic Review* (June 3, 1993), pp. 60–65.

GLOSSARY

The chapter number follows the definition in parenthesis.

acquisition. A market-entry strategy that entails purchasing multiple existing outlets in a foreign country. (13)

ad valorem duty. A duty that is expressed as a percentage of the value of goods. (8)

adaptation strategy. A strategy that involves changing elements of design, function, or packaging in response to needs or conditions in particular country markets. (11)

adopter categories. The categories of buyers in the adoption process developed by Everett Rogers at different stages of the "adoption" or product life cycle. The buyer or adopter categories are: innovators, early majority, late majority, and laggards. These buyer categories correspond to the introduction, growth, maturity, and decline stages of the product life cycle. (4)

adoption process. A model developed by Everett Rogers that describes the "adoption" or purchase decision process. The stages consist of awareness, interest, evaluation, trial, and adoption. (4)

advertising appeal. The communications approach that relates to the motives of the target audience. (14)

advocacy advertising. A form of corporate advertising in which a company presents its point of view on a particular issue. (14)

aesthetics. A shared sense within a culture of what is beautiful as opposed to ugly and what represents good taste as opposed to tastelessness. (4)

agent. An intermediary who negotiates transactions between two or more parties but does not take title to the goods being purchased or sold. (13)

antidumping duties. Duties imposed on products whose prices government officials deem too low. (8)

arbitrary monetary policy. Policy that, in effect, raises the price of foreign goods by the cost of money for the term of the required deposit. (8)

art direction. The visual presentation of an advertisement. (14)

attitude. A learned tendency to respond in a consistent way to a given object or entity. (4)

balance of payments. The record of all economic transactions between the residents of a country and the rest of the world. (2)

barter. The least complex and oldest form of bilateral, non-monetized countertrade consisting of a direct exchange of goods or services between two parties. (12)

belief. An organized pattern or knowledge that an individual holds to be true about the world. (4)

big emerging markets (BEMs). Countries that have experienced rapid economic growth and represent significant marketing opportunities. (2)

big idea. A concept that can serve as the basis for a memorable, effective message. (14)

bill of exchange. A written order from one party directing a second party to pay to the order of a third party. (8)

brand. A representation of a promise by a particular company about a particular product; a complex bundle of images and experiences in the customer's mind. (11)

brand equity. The reflection of the brand's value to a company as an intangible asset. (11)

brand extensions. A strategy that uses an established brand name as an umbrella when entering new businesses or developing new product lines that represent new categories to the company. (11)

brand image. A single, but often complex, mental image about both the physical product and the company that markets it. (11)

call option. The right to buy a specified number of foreign currency units at a fixed price, up to the option's expiration date. (2)

capital account. A record of all long-term direct investment, portfolio investment, and other short- and long-term capital flows. (2)

capital requirements. Costs that can be seen as fixed capital, as in manufacturing facilities, or working capital, as in financing R&D, advertising, field sales and service, customer credit, and inventories. (10)

cartel. A group of separate companies that collectively set prices, control output, or take other actions to maximize profits. (5)

category killers. Stores that specialize in a particular product category and offer a vast selection at low prices. (13)

centrally-planned capitalism. An economic system characterized by command resource allocation and private resource ownership. (2)

centrally-planned socialism. An economic system characterized by market resource allocation and state resource ownership. (2)

CFR (cost and freight). A contract in which the seller is not responsible for risk or loss at any point outside the factory. (12)

chaebol. A type of corporate alliance group composed of dozens of companies, centered around a central bank or holding company and dominated by a founding family. (9)

channel of distribution. An organized network of agencies and institutions that, in combination, perform all the activities required to link producers with users to accomplish the marketing task. (13)

cherry picking. The practice of taking orders only from manufacturers with established demand for products and brands. (13)

CIF (cost, insurance, freight) named port of destination. A contract similar to the FOB contract, in which the risk of loss or damage to goods is transferred to the buyer once the goods have passed the ship's rail. (12)

cobranding. A variation on tiered branding in which two or more different company or product brands are featured prominently on product packaging or in advertising. (11)

collaborating with competitors. A source of competitive advantage in which the know-how developed by other companies is used. (10)

combination umbrella. A strategy in which a corporate name is combined with a product brand name; also called tiered branding. (11)

common-law country. A country in which the legal system relies on past judicial decisions, or cases, to resolve disputes. (5)

common market. A group of countries with economic cooperation that eliminates internal barriers to trade, establishes common external barriers, and allows free movement of factors of production. (3)

comparability. The degree to which research results from different countries can be used to make valid comparisons. (6)

compensation trading (buyback). A countertrade deal typically involving sale of plant equipment or technology licensing in which the seller or licensor agrees to take payment in the form of the products produced using the equipment or technology for a specified number of years. (12)

competitive advantage. The situation when there is a match between a firm's distinctive competencies and the factors critical for success within its industry. (1)

concentrated global marketing. A strategy that calls for devising a marketing mix to reach a single segment of the global market. (7)

consumer panels. A method of research often used by organizations such as Nielsen Media Research to track television viewership. (6)

consumer sales promotions. Promotion designed to make consumers aware of a new product, to stim-ulate nonusers to sample an existing product, or to increase overall consumer demand. (15)

containerization. The practice of loading ocean-going freight into steel boxes 20 or 40 feet long, or longer; it offers flexibility in the product that can be shipped via container, as well as flexibility in shipping modes. (13)

continuous innovation. A product that is "new and improved" but requires little R&D expenditures to develop and causes minimal disruption of existing consumption patterns and requires the least amount of learning on the part of buyers. (11)

contract manufacturing. An arrangement in which a global company provides technical specifications to a subcontractor or local manufacturer. (9)

control. The process by which managers ensure that resources are used effectively and efficiently in the accomplishment of organizational objectives. (16)

convenience stores. A form of retail distribution that offers some of the same products as supermarkets, but the merchandise mix is limited to high turnover convenience products. (13)

cooperative exporter. An export organization of a manufacturing company retained by other independent manufacturers to sell their products in some or all foreign markets. (8)

copy. The words that are the spoken or written communication elements in advertisements. (14)

copyright. The establishment of ownership of a written, recorded, performed, or filmed creative work. (5)

corporate advertising. A PR tool used to call attention to the company's other communications efforts; it is not used to generate demand. (14)

cost leadership advantage. A broad market strategy based on a firm's position as the industry's low-cost producer. (10)

cost-plus price. The price that results from adding the additional costs and expenses not directly related to the manufacturing cost to the full-cost price. (12)

counterfeiting. The unauthorized copying and production of a product. (5)

counterpurchase. A monetized countertrade deal in which the seller agrees to purchase products of equivalent value that it must then sell in order to realize revenue from the original deal. (12)

countertrade. An export transaction in which a sale results in product flowing in one direction to a buyer, and a separate stream of products and services, often flowing in the opposite direction. (12)

countervailing duties (CVDs). Additional duties levied to offset subsidies granted in the exporting country. (8)

coupon. A printed certificate that entitles the bearer to a price reduction or some other special consideration for purchasing a particular product or service. (15)

creative execution. The way that an advertising appeal or proposition is presented. (14)

creative strategy. A statement or concept of what a particular advertising message or campaign will say. (14)

culture. Ways of living, built up by a group of human beings, that are transmitted from one generation to another. (4)

current account. A record of all recurring trade in merchandise and services, private gifts, and public aid transactions between countries. (2)

customer strategy. A plan that ensures that the sales professional will be maximally responsive to customer needs. (15)

customs procedures. Procedures that are considered restrictive if they are administered in a way that makes compliance difficult and expensive. (8)

customs union. A group of countries with economic cooperation that eliminates internal barriers to trade and establishes common external tariffs (CET). (3)

data warehouses. Databases used to support management decision making. (6)

delivered duty paid. A type of contract in which the seller has agreed to deliver the goods to the buyer at the place he or she names in the country of import, with all costs, including duties, paid. (12)

demand conditions. Conditions that determine the rate and nature of improvement and innovations by the firms in the nation. (10)

demographic segmentation. Segmentation based on measurable characteristics of populations, such as income, population, age distribution, gender, education, and occupation. (7)

department stores. A form of retail distribution in which there are several departments under one roof, each representing a distinct merchandise line and staffed with a limited number of salespeople. (13)

devaluation. The decline in value of a currency relative to other currencies. (2)

developed countries. Countries that can be assigned to the high-income category. (2)

developing countries. Countries that can be assigned to the upper-middle-income category. (2)

differentiated global marketing. A strategy that calls for targeting two or more distinct market segments with multiple marketing mix offerings. (7)

differentiation advantage. A product's actual or perceived uniqueness in a broad market. (10)

direct marketing. An interactive marketing system that produces measurable results and uses one or more media to start or complete a sale. (15)

discontinuous innovation. A new product that, upon its success, creates new markets and new consumption patterns. (11)

discount stores. A form of retail distribution that has an emphasis on low prices. (13)

discriminatory exchange rate policies. Policies that distort trade in much the same way as selective import duties and export subsidies. (8)

discriminatory procurement policies. Policies that can take the form of government rules and administrative regulations, as well as formal or informal company policies that discriminate against foreign suppliers. (8)

distribution. The physical flow of goods through channels. (13)

distribution center. A facility designed to efficiently receive goods from suppliers and then fill orders for individual stores or customers. (13)

distribution channels. A barrier to entry into an industry created by the need to create and establish new channels. (10)

distributor. A wholesale intermediary that typically carries product lines or brands on a selective basis. (13)

dumping. The sale of a product in an export market at a price lower than that normally charged in the domestic market or country of origin. (8)

duties. Rate schedule; can sometimes be thought of as a tax that punishes individuals for making choices of which their government disapprove. (8)

dynamically continuous innovation. An intermediate category of newness that is less disruptive and requires less learning on the part of consumers. (11)

economic exposure. The degree to which exchange rates affect a company's market value as measured by its stock price. (2)

economic freedom. An index based on a number of key economic variables, including trade policy, taxation policy, government consumption of economic output, monetary policy, capital flows and foreign investment, banking policy, wage and price controls, property rights, regulations, and the black market. (2)

economic union. A group of countries with economic cooperation that eliminates internal tariff barriers, establishes common external barriers, allows the free flow of factors of production, and coordinates and harmonizes economic and social policy within the union. (3)

economies of scale. The decline in per-unit product costs as the absolute volume of production per period increases. (10)

efficient consumer response (ECR). A technique used by retailers in an effort to work more closely with vendors on stock replenishment. (6)

electronic data interchange (EDI). A system that allows a company's business units to submit orders, issue invoices, and conduct business electronically with other company units as well as outside companies. (6)

electronic point of sale (EPOS). Purchase data gathered by checkout scanners that help retailers identify patterns about what products are selling and how consumer preferences vary with geography. (6)

emic. Country market analysis using the local system of meaning and values. (6)

environmental sensitivity. The extent to which products must be adapted to the culture-specific needs of different national markets. (4)

ethnocentric orientation. The view that one's home country is superior to the rest of the world. (1)

ethnocentric pricing. A policy that calls for the per unit price of an item to be the same, no matter where in the world the buyer is located. (12)

etic. Country market analysis from an outside perspective. (6)

euro. The single European currency. (3)

euro zone. Austria, Belgium, Finland, Ireland, the Netherlands, France, Germany, Greece, Italy, Luxembourg, Portugal, and Spain. (3)

Euroconsumer Study. A study by DMBB in which four lifestyle groups are identified: Successful Idealists, Affluent Materialists, Comfortable Belongers, and Disaffected Survivors. (7)

expanded Triad. The dominant economic centers of the world: the Pacific region, North America, and Europe. (2)

export broker. A broker who receives a fee for bringing together the seller and the overseas buyer. (8)

export commission representative. Representative assigned to all or some foreign markets by the manufacturer. (8)

export management company (EMC). Term used to designate an independent export firm that acts as the export department for more than one manufacturer. (8)

export marketing. Exporting using the product offered in the home market as a starting point and modifying it as needed to meet the preferences of international target markets. (8)

export merchants. Merchants who seek out needs in foreign markets and make purchases in world markets to fill these needs. (8)

export selling. Exporting without tailoring the product, the price, or the promotional material to suit individual country requirements. (8)

extension strategy. Marketing a standardized product using a standardized communications approach in multiple markets. (11)

ex-works. A type of contract in which the seller places goods at the disposal of the buyer at the time specified in the contract. (12)

factor conditions. A country's endowment with resources. (10)

focus. The concentration of attention on a core business or competence. (1)

focus group. A group interview led by a trained moderator, who facilitates discussion of a product concept, advertisement, social trend, or other topic at a specially equipped research facility. (6)

focused differentiation. A strategy in which a product has an actual or perceived uniqueness in a focused market. (10)

foreign consumer culture positioning. A positioning strategy that associates a brand with the country or culture of origin. (7)

Foreign Corrupt Practices Act (FCPA). A law that makes it illegal for U.S. corporations to bribe an official of a foreign government or political party to obtain or retain business. (5)

foreign direct investment. Figures that reflect investment flows out of the home country as companies invest in or acquire plants, equipment, or other assets. (9)

foreign purchasing agents. Purchasing agents who operate on behalf of, and are renumerated by, an overseas customer. (8)

forward market. A mechanism for buying and selling currencies at a preset price for future delivery. (2)

4Cs. A 20-country psychographic segmentation study by Y&R that focuses on goals, motivations, and values that help to determine consumer choice. (7)

franchising. A contract between a parent company–franchisor and franchisee that allow the franchisee to operate a business developed by the franchisor in return for a fee and adherence to franchise-wide policies and practices. (9)

free alongside ship (FAS) named port of destination. A contract that calls for the seller to place goods alongside, or available to, the vessel or other mode of transportation and pay all charges up to that point. (12)

free on board (FOB). A contract in which the responsibility and liability of the seller do not end until the goods have actually been placed aboard a ship. (12)

free trade area (FTA). A group of countries with economic cooperation that abolishes all internal barriers to trade but allows member countries to maintain independent trade policies vis-à-vis other countries. (3)

freight forwarders. Specialists in traffic operations, customs clearance, and shipping tariffs and schedules. (8)

full-service agencies. Agencies that provide services in addition to creating advertising, such as market research and media buying. (14)

generic strategies. Michael Porter's model of four routes to competitive advantage, including cost leadership, product differentiation, cost focus, and focused differentiation. (10)

geocentric orientation. The view that the entire world is a potential market; the company seeks to develop integrated world market strategies. (1)

geocentric pricing. A policy in which a company neither fixes a single price worldwide nor remains aloof from subsidiary pricing decisions, but instead strikes an intermediate position. (12)

geographical structure. A pattern of organization in which the operational responsibility for a geographical area of the world is assigned to line managers; the corporate headquarters retains responsibility for worldwide planning and control. (16)

global advertising. Designing an ad for multiple country markets using the same advertising appeals, messages, art, copy, photographs, stories, and video segments. (14)

global brand. A brand that has the same name and a similar image and positioning throughout the world. (11)

global brand leadership. The use or organizational structures, processes, and cultures to allocate brand-building resources globally, to create global synergies, and to develop a global brand strategy that coordinates and leverages country brand strategies. (11)

global competition. A success strategy in which a firm takes a global view of competition and sets about maximizing profits worldwide, rather than on a country-by-country basis. (10)

global consumer culture positioning. A positioning strategy that identifies a brand as a symbol of a global culture or segment. (7)

global elite. Older, more affluent consumers who are well traveled and have money to spend on prestigious products with an image of exclusivity. (7)

global industry. An industry in which competitive advantage can be achieved by integrating and leveraging operations on a worldwide scale. (1)

global market segmentation. The process of identifying specific segments of potential customers with homogeneous attributes who are likely to exhibit similar buying behavior. (7)

global marketing. The process of focusing an organization's resources on global market opportunities and threats. (1)

global marketing audit. A comprehensive, systematic examination of the marketing environment and company objectives, strategies, programs, policies, and activities. (16)

global marketing research. The project-specific gathering of data on a global scale. (6)

global product. A product that meets the wants and needs of a global market. (11)

global retailing. Any retailing activity that crosses national boundaries. (13)

Global Scan. A study by BSB that identifies attitudes that could explain and predict purchase behavior for different product categories. (7)

global strategic partnerships (GSP). Ambitious, reciprocal, cross-border alliances that may involve business partners in a number of different country markets. (9)

global teens. Persons aged 13–19 whose purchase behavior is shaped by shared interests in fashion, music, and youth lifestyle issues. (7)

government policy. A barrier to entry into an industry created by the policies instituted by the government. (10)

gray market goods. Trademarked products that are exported from one country to another, where they are sold by unauthorized persons or organizations. (12)

greenfield investment. Investment that results in 100 percent ownership achieved by the start-up of new operations. (9)

Group of Seven (G7). A group of seven high-income countries: the United States, Japan, Germany, France, Britain, Canada, Italy. (2)

Harmonized Tariff System (HTS). A system in which importers and exporters have to determine the correct classification number for a given product or service that will cross borders. (8)

high-context culture. A culture in which messages and knowledge are more implicit and in which less information is contained in the verbal part of a message and more information resides in the context of communication. (4)

high-income country. A country with per capita GNP above $9,655. (2)

hypercompetition. A dynamic competitive world in which no action or advantage can be sustained for long. (10)

hypermarkets. A hybrid retailing format that combines the discounter, supermarket, and warehouse club approaches under a single roof; hypermarkets are huge in size. (13)

image advertising. A form of corporate advertising designed to enhance the public's perception of a company, create goodwill, or announce a major change. (14)

incipient market. A market that will emerge if a particular economic, political, or socio-cultural trend continues. (6)

Incoterms. Internationally accepted terms of trade. (12)

infomercial. A form of paid television programming in which a particular product is demonstrated, explained, and offered for sale to viewers who call a toll-free number shown on the screen. (15)

information overload. Overload that occurs when executives and other company personnel cannot effectively assimilate all the information available to them. (6)

intermodal transportation. A combination of land and water shipping from producer to customer. (13)

international division structure. A pattern of organization in which the executive in charge of the international division has a direct reporting relationship to corporate staff. (16)

international product trade cycle model. A model that describes the relationship between the product life cycle, trade, and investment. (11)

intranet. An electronic system that allows authorized company personnel or outsiders to share information electronically in a secure fashion while reducing the amount of paper generated. (6)

invention. A demanding but potentially rewarding product strategy for reaching mass markets in less developed countries. (11)

inventory management. A distribution activity that ensures that a company neither runs out of manufacturing components or finished goods nor incurs the expense and risk of carrying excessive stocks of these items. (13)

joint venture. A market entry strategy in which partners share ownership of a commercial entity. (9)

keiretsu. An interbusiness alliance or enterprise group that resembles a fighting clan in which business families join together to vie for market share. (9)

latent market. An undiscovered market segment in which demand for a product would materialize if an appropriate product were offered. (6)

layers of advantage. A strategy for creating competitive advantage by building a wide portfolio of advantages. (10)

leader. Someone whose job is to direct the efforts and creativity of everyone in the company toward a global effort that best utilizes organizational resources to exploit global opportunities. (16)

lean production. An extremely effective and efficient production system. (16)

legal environment. Laws, courts, attorneys, legal customs, and practices. (5)

less-developed countries (LDCs). Countries that can be assigned to the lower-income and lower-middle-income categories. (2)

letter of credit. A payment method in export/import in which a bank substitutes its creditworthiness for that of the buyer. (8)

leverage. Some type of advantage that a company enjoys by having experience in more than one country. (1)

licensing. A contractual arrangement whereby one company (the licenser) makes an asset available to another company (the licensee) in exchange for royalties or some other form of compensation. (5)

line extension. A variation of an existing product such as a new flavor or new design. (11)

local consumer culture positioning. A positioning strategy that identifies a brand with a company's home country or culture. (7)

localized (adaptation) approach. A strategy that is responsive to country or regional differences. (1)

logistics management. The integration of activities necessary to ensure the efficient flow of raw materials, in-process inventory, and finished goods from producers to customers. (13)

loose bricks. A strategy for creating competitive advantage by taking advantage of a competitor whose attention is narrowly focused on a market segment or geographic area to the exclusion of others. (10)

low-context culture. A culture in which messages and knowledge are more explicit and words carry most of the information in communication. (4)

low-income country. A country with per capita GNP of $785 or less. (2)

lower-middle-income country. A country with GNP per capita between $786 and $3,125. (2)

Maastricht Treaty. The 1991 treaty that set the stage for the transition from the European monetary system to an economic and monetary union. (3)

management information system (MIS). A system that provides managers and other decision makers with a continuous flow of information about company operations. (6)

manufacturers' export representatives. Combination export management firms. (8)

maquiladora. A program that allows manufacturing, assembly, or processing plants to import materials, components, and equipment duty-free; in return they use Mexican labor. (2)

marginal-cost pricing. A pricing strategy that sets the selling price equal to the variable costs of producing one additional unit of output. (12)

market. People or organizations with needs and wants and both the ability and willingness to buy. (2)

market capitalism. An economic system characterized by market allocation of resources and private resource ownership. (2)

market holding. A pricing strategy adopted by companies that want to maintain their share of the market by adjusting prices as demanded by competitive or economic considerations. (12)

market penetration. A pricing strategy that calls for setting price levels that are low enough to quickly build market share. (12)

market skimming. A pricing strategy that is often part of a deliberate attempt to reach a market segment that is willing to pay a premium price for a particular brand or for a specialized or unique product. (12)

market socialism. An economic system characterized by limited market resource allocation within an overall environment of state ownership. (2)

marketing mix. Product, price, place, and promotion—the four Ps. (1)

marketing research. The project-specific, systematic gathering of data in the search scanning mode. (6)

Maslow's hierarchy. A needs-based framework that offers a way of understanding opportunities to develop local and global products in different parts of the world. (11)

matrix organization. A pattern of organization in which management's task is to achieve an organizational balance that brings together different perspectives and skills to accomplish the organization's objectives. (16)

mixed allocation system. A system containing elements of both market and command allocation systems. (2)

most favored nation status (MFN). A privileged trading status in which a GATT signatory nation agrees to apply its favorable tariff or lowest tariff rate to all nations that are also signatories to GATT. (8)

multisegment targeting. A marketing strategy that entails targeting two or more distinct market segments with multiple marketing mix offerings. (7)

newly industrializing economies (NIEs). Upper-middle-income countries that achieve the highest rates of economic growth. (2)

niche. A single segment of the global market. (7)

nontariff barriers (NTBs). Control that can range from "buy local" campaigns to bureaucratic obstacles that make it difficult for companies to gain access to some individual country and regional markets. (1)

normal trade relations (NTR). A trading stratus under WTO rules that entitles a country to low tariff rates. (8)

North American Free Trade Agreement (NAFTA). A free trade area encompassing Canada, Mexico, and the United States. (3)

observation. A data collection method in which one or more trained observers watch and record the behavior of actual or prospective buyers. (6)

offset. A countertrade deal in which a government recoups hard-currency expenditures by requiring some form of cooperation by the seller, such as importing products or transferring technology. (12)

order processing. The distribution activity that provides information inputs that are critical in fulfilling a customer's order. (13)

organic growth. An entry strategy in which a company uses its own resources to start a store from scratch or to acquire existing retail facilities from others. (13)

Organization for Economic Cooperation and Development (OECD). An institution of 29 high-income countries that believes in market-allocation economic systems and pluralistic democracy. (2)

organizing. The goal of creating a structure that enables the company to respond to significant differences in international market environments and to extend valuable corporate knowledge. (16)

parallel importing. The practice of gray marketers selling at prices that undercut those set by the legitimate importers. (12)

patent. A formal legal document that gives an inventor the exclusive right to make, use, and sell an invention for a specified period of time. (5)

pattern advertising. Global advertising based on a single communication platform or concept to which minimal adaptation of copy, artwork, or other elements can be made as required by individual country markets. (14)

penetration pricing policy. A pricing strategy of setting price levels that are low enough to quickly build market share. (12)

personal interviews. A survey method that allows researchers to ask why and then explore answers. (6)

personal selling. Person-to-person communication between a company representative and a prospective buyer. (15)

personal selling philosophy. A sales representative's philosophy that requires a commitment to the marketing concept and a willingness to adopt the role of problem solver or partner in helping customers. (15)

piggyback marketing. An arrangement whereby one manufacturer obtains distribution of products through another's distribution channels. (13)

platform. A core product design element or component that can be quickly and cheaply adapted to various country markets. (11)

political environment. The set of governmental institutions, political parties, and organizations that are the expression of the people in the nations of the world. (5)

political risk. The risk of a change in political environment or government policy that would adversely affect a company's ability to operate effectively and profitably. (5)

polycentric orientation. The view that each country in which a company does business is unique. (1)

polycentric pricing. A policy that permits subsidiary or affiliate managers to establish whatever price they feel is most desirable in their circumstances. (12)

positioning. The act of locating a brand in customers' minds over and against other products in terms of product attributes and benefits that the brand does and does not offer. (7)

preferential tariff. A reduced tariff rate applied to imports from certain countries. (8)

preferential trading agreements. Agreements among countries that can be conceptualized on a continuum of increasing economic integration. (3)

presentation strategy. Setting objectives for each sales call and establishing a presentation plan to meet those objectives. (15)

price discrimination. The practice of setting different prices when selling the same quantity of like-quality goods to different buyers. (12)

price escalation. The increase in a product's price as transportation, duty, and distributor margins are added to the factory price. (12)

price transparency. Euro-denominated prices for goods and services that enable consumers and organizational buyers to comparison shop across Europe. (12)

primary data. Data gathered through original research pertaining to the particular problem, decision, or issue under study. (6)

product. A collection of physical, psychological, service, and symbolic attributes that collectively yield satisfaction or benefits to a buyer or user. (11)

product adaptation–communication extension strategy. A strategy of extending, without change, the basic home-market communications strategy while adapting the product to local use or preference conditions. (11)

product-communication adaptation. A dual-adaptation strategy that uses a combination of marketing. (11)

product-communication extension. A strategy for pursuing opportunities outside the home market. (11)

product differentiation. A product's perceived uniqueness that can serve as a barrier to entry in an industry. (10)

product extension–communications adaptation strategy. The strategy of marketing an identical product by adapting the marketing communications program. (11)

product invention. In global marketing, developing new products with the world market in mind. (11)

product saturation level. The percentage of potential buyers or households who own a particular product. (2)

product strategy. A plan that can assist the sales representative in selecting and positioning products that will satisfy customer needs. (15)

product transformation. The result when the same physical product ends up serving a different function or use than that for which it was originally designed or created. (11)

psychographic segmentation. The process of grouping people in terms of their attitudes, values, and lifestyles. (7)

public relations. The effort to foster goodwill and understanding among constituents both inside and outside the company. (14)

publicity. Communication about a company or product for which the company does not pay. (14)

purchasing power parity (PPP). A concept that permits adjustment of national income measurements in various countries to reflect what a unit of each country's currency can actually buy. (2)

put option. The right to sell a specified number of foreign currency units at a fixed price, up to the option's expiration date. (2)

quota. Government-imposed limit or restriction on the number of units or the total value of a particular product or product category that can be imported. (8)

reactivity. The tendency of research subjects to behave differently because they are being studied. (6)

regiocentric orientation. The view that each region in which a company does business is unique; the company seeks to develop an integrated regional strategy. (1)

regional management center. A pattern of organization in which there is an area or regional headquarters as a management layer between the country organization and the international division headquarters. (16)

regional or worldwide product division structure. A pattern of organization in which the international responsibility is shifted from a corporate international division to the product division international departments, which in turn shift to total divisional organization. (16)

regulatory environment. Agencies, both governmental and nongovernmental, that enforce laws or set guidelines for conducting business. (5)

relationship strategy. A game plan for establishing and maintaining high-quality relationships with prospects and customers. (15)

restrictive administrative and technical regulations. Regulations that can create barriers to trade; it may take the form of antidumping, size, or safety and health regulations. (8)

rules of engagement. A strategy for creating competitive advantage that involves breaking these rules and refusing to play by the rules set by industry leaders. (10)

sales agents. Agents who work under contract rather than as full-time employees. (15)

sales promotion. Any paid consumer or trade communication program of limited duration that adds tangible value to a product or brand. (15)

sampling. A sales promotion technique that provides consumers with the opportunity to try a product or service at no cost. (15)

search. The scanning mode characterized by formal information gathering activity. (6)

secondary data. Existing data in personal files, libraries, and databases. (6)

self-reference criterion (SRC). The unconscious reference to one's own cultural values. (4)

selling proposition. The promise or claim that captures the reason for buying the product or the benefit that ownership confers. (14)

single-column tariff. A schedule of duties in which the rate applies to imports from all countries on the same basis; the simplest type of tariff. (8)

sourcing decision. A company's strategy of whether a company makes or buys its products as well as where it makes or buys. (8)

specialty retailers. A form of retail distribution that is narrowly focused and features a relatively narrow merchandise mix aimed at a particular target market. (13)

specific duty. A duty expressed as a specific amount of currency per unit of weight, volume, length, or other unit of measurement. (8)

sponsorship. A form of marketing communications in which a company pays a fee to have its name associated with a particular event, team or athletic association, or sports facility. (15)

standardized (extension) approach. A strategy that calls for creating the same marketing mix for a broad mass market of potential buyers around the world. (1)

strategic intent. Hamel and Prahalad's model for achieving competitive advantage by means of ambition and obsession with winning. (10)

subgroups. Smaller groups of people with their own shared subset of attitudes, beliefs, and values. (4)

supercenters. A form of retail distribution that offers a wide range of aggressively priced grocery items plus general merchandise in a space that occupies about half the size of a hypermarket. (13)

supermarkets. Departmentalized, single-story retail establishments that offer a variety of food and nonfood items. (13)

surveillance. The scanning mode in which a marketer engages in informal information gathering. (6)

survey research. Research that utilizes questionnaires designed to elicit either quantitative data, qualitative data, or both. (6)

switch trading. A transaction in which a professional switch trader, switch trading house, or bank steps into a simple barter arrangement or other countertrade arrangement in which one of the parties is not willing to accept all the goods received in the transaction. (12)

switching costs. A barrier to entry into an industry created by the need to change suppliers and products. (10)

targeting. The process of evaluating market segments and focusing marketing efforts on a country, region, or group of people. (7)

tariffs. The rules, rate schedules (duties), and regulations of individual countries. (8)

temporary surcharge. Surcharges introduced from time to time to provide additional protection for local industry and, in particular, in response to balance-of-payments deficits. (8)

tiered branding. A strategy in which a corporate name is combined with a product brand name; also called combination umbrella. (11)

trade deficit. A negative current account balance. (2)

trade mission. A state-sponsored or federally sponsored show organized around a product, a group of products, or an activity at which company personnel can learn a great deal about new markets. (8)

trade sales promotion. Promotion designed to increase product availability in distribution channels. (15)

trade show. A show organized around a product, a group of products, or an activity at which company personnel can learn a great deal about new markets. (8)

trade surplus. A positive current account balance. (2)

trademark. A distinctive mark, motto, device, or emblem that a manufacturer affixes to a particular product or package to distinguish it from goods produced by other manufacturers. (5)

transfer pricing. The pricing of goods, services, and intangible property bought and sold by operating units or divisions of a company doing business with an affiliate in another jurisdiction. (12)

transportation. The distribution activity that involves deciding which method a company should utilize when moving products through domestic and global channels; the most important modes are rail, truck, air, and water. (13)

Triad. The three regions of Japan, Western Europe, and the United States, which represented the dominant economic centers of the world. (2)

two-column tariff. General duties plus special duties indicating reduced rates determined by tariff negotiations with other countries. (8)

upper-middle-income country. A country with GNP per capita between $3,126 and $9,655. (2)

usage rate. A behavior segmentation variable that categorizes consumers as heavy, medium, light, or nonusers of a product. (7)

user status. A behavior segmentation variable that categorizes consumers into categories such as potential users, nonusers, ex-users, regular users, first-timer users, and users of competitors' products. (7)

value. An enduring belief or feeling that a specific mode of conduct is personally or socially preferable to another mode of conduct. (4)

value chain. Organizational activities that create value, including product design, manufacture, marketing, and after-sales service. (1)

value equation. $V = B/P$, where V = Value, B = Benefits, and P = Price. (1)

variable import levies. A system of levies applied to certain categories of imported agricultural products. (8)

warehouse club. A segment of discount retailing in which consumers join the club to take advantage of low prices on products displayed in their shipping boxes in a "no frills" atmosphere. (13)

World Trade Organization (WTO). The successor to the General Agreement on Tariffs and Trade. (3)

CREDITS

AUTHOR/NAME INDEX

Tung, Rosalie L., 166
Turner, Mimi, 254
Turner, Richard, 168
Tyler, Christian, 143n
Tyler, Gus, 125

U

Uchitelle, Louis, 336n, 414n
Ulgado, Francis M., 437
Underwood, Laurie, 493
Unger, Lynette, 278n
Up Kwon, 437
Urquhart, John, 169
Usunier, Jean-Claud G., 166

V

Vagts, Detlev, 196n, 208
Valdez, Humberto Garza, 269
Valente, Judith, 237n, 613
Vallianatos, Mark A., 188
Van den Bulte, Christophe, 3n
Van Halen, 148
Van Miert, Karel, 363
Varoli, John, 268n
Vellenga, David B., 519
Venedikian, Harry M., 317
Venkatesan, Ravi, 318
Verbeke, Alain, 392n, 394
Vercic, Dejan, 558
Verity, John W., 220n
Vermeulen, Karla, 191n
Vernon, Ivan R., 557
Vernon, Mark, 440
Vernon, Raymond, 209
Verzariu, Pompiliu, 317, 472, 477
Viault, Raymond G., 624
Vida, Irena, 519
Vidal, Gore, 284
Villalonga, Juan, 133
Vinelli, Andrea, 519, 559n
Viscounty, Perry J., 463n
Vlasic, Bill, 250
Vogel, David, 209
Vogel, Thomas T., Jr., 202n, 216
Voitovich, Sergei A., 209

W

Wagstyl, Stefan, 83, 486n
Waldholz, Michael, 479
Warner, Fara, 138n, 140n, 502n, 545n
Wasilewski, Nikolai, 247
Waterschoot, Walter van, 3n
Watson, Alexander, 214
Watson, Brian, 78
Watson, James L., 30

Webber, Alan M., 8, 9n, 26n, 30, 600n,
    605n, 611n
Wedel, Michel, 283
Wei-na Lee, 437
Weidenbaum, Murray L., 357
Weigand, Robert E., 519
Weinberg, Marc G., 543n
Weinberg, Steven M., 210
Weiner, Elizabeth, 211
Weiss, Nelio, 194
Welch, Jack, 13, 18, 600
Wells, Ken, 530, 533n
Wells, Louis T., 625
Wells, Ludmilla Gricenko, 558
Wells, Melanie, 544n, 552n
Wendt, Henry, 30
Wentz, Laurel, 339, 431n
Werner, Helmut, 440, 461
Werther, William B., Jr., 166
Wessel, David, 66n, 459n
West, Cynthia D., 31
Westney, D. Eleanor, 394
Whalen, Jeanne, 542n
Wheelwright, Steven C., 436
While, Gregory, 236n
White, Erin, 490
White, Gregory L., 333n
White, Joseph B., 270n, 616n
White, Larry C., 361
Whitehorn, Will, 550
Whitwam, David, 8, 25, 248–250, 372,
    600, 603, 611
Wiese, Carsten, 477
Wildt, Albert R., 283
Wilhelm, Paul, 466
Wilke, Jerry G., 273
Wilke, John R., 192n, 193n
Williams, Frances, 190n
Williams, Jeffrey R., 394
Williams, Michael, 129, 614n
Williamson, Marlene, 36
Willigan, Geraldine E., 322
Willman, John, 87n, 140n, 155, 401n, 570
Wills, James R., 595
Wilson, Gary, 362
Wilson, R. Dale, 558
Wind, Yoram, 43
Winestock, Geoff, 36
Wingfield, Nick, 488n, 567
Winslow, Ron, 339
Winterhalter, Jürgen, 274
Wirth, Gregory P., 595
Witt, Jerome, 417n, 437
WoDunn, Sheryl, 453
Wogland, James, 218
Wolf, Julie, 216
Wolf, Martin, 93n, 104
Wolfe, William G., 247
Womack, James P., 394, 614, 616
Won, Grace, 199n

Wonacott, Peter, 225n, 522
Woo, Junda, 211
Woodruff, David, 250, 611n, 629
Woodside, Arch G., 136n
Wooldridge, Adrian, 5, 30, 260n
Wooton, Ian, 125
Worthley, Reginald, 137n, 166
Wu, Friedrich, 125
Wynter, Leon E., 544n
Wynyard, Robin, 165
Wysocki, Bernard, 345n

Y

Yajima, Hiroshi, 256
Yan, Rick, 77
Yang, Michael, 334
Yavas, Ugur, 187n, 358, 548n, 557
Yeats, Alexander, 104
Yeltsin, Boris, 176, 187
Yeo Cheow Tong, 110
Yeoh, Datuk Francis, 571
Yergin, Daniel, 25, 30, 54, 177n
Yip, George S., 357, 394, 602n, 625
Yoder, Stephen Kreider, 353n
Yorke, Susan, 420
Yoshino, Michael, 20n, 340n, 342n, 346,
    347, 357, 380
Young, Allan, 375
Young, Andrew, 320
Young, Jeffrey R., 51, 375
Yu, Chow-Ming Joseph, 318
Yudashkin, Valentin, 263

Z

Zachary, G. Pascal, 237n, 322, 353n, 380n
Zander, Udo, 31
Zandpour, Fred, 558
Zatopke, Emil, 528
Zaun, Todd, 454n, 526, 601n
Zavrl, Frani, 558
Zbar, Jeffery D., 235n, 237n
Zeien, Alfred, 406, 414
Zeller, Laurent, 500
Zellner, Wendy, 501n, 522
Zhang Ruimin, 405
Zhou, Nan, 558
Zhu Rongji, 60
Ziegler, Bart, 553n
Zietsche, Dieter, 461
Zif, J., 354n
Zimmerman, Ann, 490
Zimmerman, Rachel, 479
Zoellick, Robert, 90
Zuccaro, Bruno, 226
Zuckerman, Laurence, 402
Zysman, John, 477

SUBJECT/ORGANIZATION INDEX

D

D/P, 309
Dabhol Power Company, 111
Dacia, 27
Daewoo, 66, 78, 329, 331, 334, 352, 416
DAF Trucks, 336
Dai-Ichi Kikaku, 537
Daiei, 500
Daihatsu Auto, 143
Daiko Advertising, 535
Daimler-Benz Aerospace AG (Dasa), 87, 88
Daimler-Benz AG, 12, 87, 88, 135, 136, 315, 336, 440, 550
DaimlerChrysler, 11, 15, 64, 293, 335, 405, 417, 441, 527, 551
Danone Group, 527
D'arcy Massius Benton & Bowles (DMBB), 261–263
Data analysis, 238–240
Data collection, 232–238, 244–245
Data warehouse, 220
Date draft, 309
DDB Needham Worldwide, 534, 537
De Beers, 62
De La Rue Card Systems, 438
Delivered duty paid, 451
Dell Computer, 370, 371, 385, 390, 492, 493, 495
Delta Air Lines, 361
Demand conditions, 383–384
Demand pattern analysis, 238
Demographic segmentation, 255
Dentsu, 535, 537
Department stores, 499
Deutsche Aerospace, 442
Deutsche Telekom, 330, 527
Devaluation, 85
Developed countries, 66–68
Developing countries, 61–64
DHL Worldwide Express, 359–360
Diageo PLC, 7, 16, 132, 219, 266, 267, 473
Dietary preferences, 138–141, 155
Differentiated global marketing, 274
Differentiation, 43, 46, 373
Diffusion of Innovations (Rogers), 155
Diffusion theory, 155–159
Digital, 348
Digital *keiretsu*, 352–354
Digitas, 535
Direct mail, 583–585
Direct marketing, 581–583
Direct Marketing Association, 583
Direct perception, 225
Direct selling, 489
Disaffected survivors, 263
Discontinuous innovations, 427
Discount stores, 501
Discovery, 202
Discriminatory exchange rate policies, 297
Discriminatory procurement policies, 297
Disney. *See* Walt Disney Company
Disney Stores, 499, 502
Disneyland Paris, 167–168
Displacing time, 239

Dispute settlement, 201–204
Distribution, 485
Distribution center, 510
Distribution channels, 368. *See* Channels of distribution
Distributor, 487
Divisibility, 157
DKB Group, 349
Doctors without Borders, 479
Documentary collection, 308–309
Documentary credits, 307–308
Documentary draft, 309
Documents against draft, 309
Dom Perignon, 414
Domestic companies, 17
Domestic rivalry, 385
Donna Karan International Inc., 481
Door-to-door selling, 489, 490
Dorling Kindersley, 284
Dormont Manufacturing, 418
Double diamond framework, 392
Downstream industries, 384
Downstream value chains, 616–617
Dr. Martens, 2
Dr Pepper/7-Up, 16, 613
Draft, 308–309
Dreyer's Grand Ice Cream, 139
Du Pont, 111, 172, 613
Dual adaptation, 422–423
Dual branding, 407
Dual extension, 420
Dumping, 302, 465–467
Dun & Bradstreet, 296
Dunkin' Donuts, 16, 72, 85
Duties, 302
Duty Free Shoppers (DFS), 481
Dynamically continuous innovations, 427
Dynamit Nobel, 441

E

Early adopters, 157
Early home demand, 384
Early majority, 157
Early market saturation, 384
Earned media, 549
Earnings stripping, 182
East African Cooperation, 121–122
"East Asian Miracle, The," 110
Eastman Kodak, 87, 189, 395–397
eBay, 50, 488
Economic Community of West African States (ECOWAS), 120–121, 122
Economic exposure, 86–88
Economic freedom, 55, 56
Economic growth, 24
Economic nationalism, 184
Economic systems, 51–55
Economic trends, 24–25
Economic union, 94, 96
Economies of scale, 26, 367
Economist, The, 62, 176
ECOWAS, 120–121, 122
ECR, 220
ECU, 112
Edea Gruppe, 500
Edelman Public Relations Worldwide, 553

EDI, 219
EDS, 26
EEA, 113–114
Efficient consumer response (ECR), 220
EFTA, 113–114
Eisenmann, 441
Electrolux, 7, 8, 62, 248, 606
Electronic data interchange (EDI), 219
Electronic point of sale (EPOS), 220
Electronic scanning, 237
Eli Lilly and Company, 18
Elitists, 260
Emanuel Ungaro, 421
EMC, 14, 303
EMI Group PLC, 148, 195, 596–597
Emic analysis, 243
EMS, 112
Endesa, 202
Energizer, 591
Engel's law, 239
English language, 143, 144, 280
Enron Corporation, 111
Entry barriers, 367–368
Entry strategies. *See* Market entry strategies
Environmental sensitivity, 159, 160
EPOS, 220
EPRG framework, 15, 17
Ericsson, 14, 589, 590, 610
Estee Lauder, 275
Estimated future cost method, 451
Estimation by analogy, 239
Ethnic segmentation, 268–269
Ethnocentric approach to pricing, 460–461
Ethnocentric international company, 17
Ethnocentric orientation, 15–18
Ethyl Corporation, 183
Etic analysis, 243
EU. *See* European Union (EU)
Euro, 112, 454
Euro Disney, 154, 167–168
Euro products, 405
Euro RSCG Worldwide, 537
Euro zone, 113
Euroconsumer study, 262–263
European Central Bank, 82
European Currency Unit (ECU), 112
European Economic Area (EEA), 113–114
European Free Trade Association (EFTA), 113–114
European Monetary System (EMS), 112
European Monetary Union (EMU), 81–83
European Patent Convention, 192
European Union (EU), 111–114
  advertising, 548
  bananas, 129–131
  catalog sales, 586
  direct marketing, 582
  dumping, 465
  EFTA/EEA, 113–114
  EMU, 81–83
  euro, 112
  Fortress Europe, as, 298
  legal dimensions, 205–207
  mailing list industry, 583
  marketing issues, 114

Meridian Consulting Group, 265
Merrill Lynch, 244, 409, 598
Metro AG, 136, 500
Mexico
    foreign exchange restrictions, 162
    privatization, 174
    trade secrets, 197
MGM/UA, 196
Micro Compact Car GmBH (MCC),
    440–441
Microsoft, 14, 75, 192, 196, 368, 370, 375,
    389, 409, 426, 524
Microsoft Network (MSN), 592
MicroStrategy, 220
Midas Muffler, 207
Miller Brewing, 193, 446
Millward Brown International, 228
Ministry of International Trade and
    Industry (MITI), 233, 293
Minolta Camera, 342, 404
Minute Maid, 7
MIS, 218
MIT, 51
Mitsubishi, 15, 111, 255, 256, 335, 346,
    349, 601
Mitsubishi Heavy Industries Ltd.,
    380, 466
Mitsui Group, 15, 349
Mitsukoshi, 499
Mittelstand, 220–221, 288–289, 293, 294
MMT, 183
MNC, 19n
MNE, 19n
Mobil, 78, 175, 624
Moet Chandon, 299
Mondex International, 439
Monitoring, 222
Monsanto, 172, 180, 181, 334, 367
Morphology, 142
Morris, 49
Moscow Bread Company (MBC), 491
Mother hen, 304
Motion Picture Export Association of
    America, 211
Motorola, 47, 60, 315, 327, 343, 426, 438,
    442, 443
MTV, 23, 148, 251, 253, 254, 259, 525, 530,
    533, 597
Multilateral Agreement on Investment
    (MAI), 188
Multinational company, 18
Multinational corporations
    (MNC), 19n
Multinational enterprises (MNE), 19n
Multisegment targeting, 274
Music, 137–138, 148
Myopia, 27

N

Nabisco, 544
NAFTA, 96–98
Naive nationalist, 425
Napoleonic Code, 186, 187
Napster, 50, 369, 596
Nation-states, 174
National Basketball Association,
    326, 589

National competitive advantage,
    380–388
National controls, 28, 184
National Hand Tool/Chiro, 336
National Media Corp., 588
National Trade Data Base
    (NTDB), 232
Nationalization, 182
NEC Corp., 315, 379
Negative publicity, 549
Négociant, 515
Negotiated transfer prices, 468
Negotiation, 577
Neiman Marcus, 414
Nescafé, 409
Nestlé SA, 6, 7, 87, 132, 172, 180, 222,
    263, 268, 278, 281, 339, 342, 524, 526,
    527, 565, 584
New Balance, 311, 548
New entrants, 366–369
New product continuum, 428
New product development, 426–431
New York Convention, 202
Newly industrializing economies
    (NIEs), 62, 107
News Corporation, 284, 598, 605
NFO Worldwide, 228
Niche, 274
Nickelodeon, 251
Nielsen Marketing Research, 230, 235
NIEs, 62
Nike, 57, 61, 63, 219, 260, 281, 319, 320,
    321, 328, 489, 524, 528, 544, 549, 553,
    589, 591
Nikon, 342, 456
Nintendo, 448, 505
Nippon Life Insurance, 15
Nippon Paper Industries, 193
Nippon Telegraph & Telephone (NTT),
    13–15
Nissan Motor Co., 4, 17, 24, 27, 49, 138,
    230, 270, 335, 337, 346, 349, 351,
    381, 417, 527, 532, 550, 601, 602
Nissho Iwai, 15
Noise, 529
Nokia, 14, 143, 260, 279, 354, 409, 416,
    419, 550, 589
Non-tariff barriers (NTBs), 28
Non-word mark logo, 401
Nonmaterial culture, 134
Nonprice promotions, 563
Nonprobability sample, 238
Nontariff trade barrier (NTB), 295
Nonverbal communication, 142, 144
Normal trade relations (NTR),
    298, 301
Nortel Networks, 14
Northern Telecom, 25
Northwest Airlines, 361–362
Novartis, 16, 24, 172
NTB, 295
NTBs, 28
NTDB, 232
NTR, 298, 301
NTT, 13, 14
NTT DoCoMo, 14
Nutrasweet, 368

O

Observation, 235–236
Ocean transportation, 512
OECD, 67–68
Offset, 473–474
Ogilvy & Mather Group, 78, 531,
    537, 584
OgilvyOne Worldwide, 584
OIEC, 116
Olivetti, 345
Olympic sponsorship, 589
Omega, 590
Omnicom Group, 534, 535, 553
One world, one voice approach to
    advertising, 529
One World, Ready or Not (Greider), 13
Open-account sales, 310
Open-ended questions, 234
Operating exposure, 87
Operational planning, 618
Optimum price, 445
Options, 89
Oracle, 14, 409
Order processing, 510
Orderly political transfer, 177
ORG-MARG, 217, 227
Organic growth, 506
Organization for Economic Cooperation
    and Development (OECD), 67–68
Organization for International Economic
    Cooperation (OIEC), 116
Organizational culture, 27–28
Organizational design, 602–613
Organizational export activities, 290–291
Organized intelligence, 244–245
Oriflame International, 490
Orion, 446
Otis Elevator, 78, 214
Otto Versand Group, 500, 585, 587
Outlet malls, 502
Outlet stores, 502
Overland Ltd., 326
Overseas Private Investment
    Corporation (OPIC), 179–180
Overview of book, 28
Ovum Limited, 227

P

Paccar, 336
Pace, 493
Panasonic, 435
Parallel barter, 473
Parallel importing, 463
Parallel trading, 473
Parallel translations, 235
Paramount, 196
Paris Convention, 191
Paris Union, 191
Parker Pen, 9, 27–28, 414
Patagonia, 586
Patent, 189–192
Patent Cooperation Treaty (PCT), 192
Pattern advertising, 530
PCT, 192
PDI, 149, 152
Peace Corps, 163